A Dictionary

Eighteenth-Century
World History

A Dictionary of

Eighteenth-Century
World History

Edited by

Jeremy Black and Roy Porter

First published 1994

Blackwell Publishers
108 Cowley Road
Oxford OX4 1JF
UK

238 Main Street
Cambridge, Massachusetts 02142
USA

British Library Cataloguing in Publication Data

A CIP catalogue record for this book is available from the British Library.

Library of Congress Cataloging-in-Publication Data

A Dictionary of eighteenth-century world history / edited by Jeremy
  Black and Roy Porter.
       p. cm.
    Includes bibliographical references (p.   ).
    ISBN 0–631–18068–0 (acid-free paper)
    1. History, Modern—18th century—Dictionaries. I. Black,
Jeremy. II. Porter, Roy.
    D286.D53 1994
    909.7′03—dc20   94–9472
                                                                    CIP

Commissioning editor: Alyn Shipton

Desk editor: Alison Cowan/Sarah McNamee

Production controller: Pam Park/John Keston-Hole

Picture researcher: Ginny Stroud-Lewis

Typeset in 10 on 12 pt Sabon
by Graphicraft Typesetters Ltd., Hong Kong
Printed in Great Britain by Hartnoll Ltd., Bodmin, Cornwall

This book is printed on acid-free paper

To

Bill Doyle, Nigel Ramsay and Mark Stocker

Contents

Contributors

Jeremy Adler
Queen Mary and Westfield College,
University of London

D. D. Aldridge
University of Newcastle upon Tyne

M. S. Anderson
London

Jonathan Andrews
Wellcome Unit for the History of Medicine,
University of Glasgow

Jeffrey Barnouw
University of Texas at Austin

M. L. Benjamin
London

J. A. Bennett
Whipple Museum of the History of Science,
Cambridge

Maxine Berg
University of Warwick

Ann Bermingham
University of California

Jeremy Black
University of Durham

Peter Borsay
University of Wales, Lampeter

Jeremy Boulton
University of Newcastle upon Tyne

Huw Bowen
University of Leicester

James Bowen
University of New England

D. A. Brading
University of Cambridge

Laurence Brockliss
Magdalen College, Oxford

Michael Broers
University of Leeds

James G. Buickerood
Delaware

Peter Burke
Emmanuel College, Cambridge

Sandra Cavallo
University of Exeter

John Childs
University of Leeds

Stuart Clark
University College of Swansea

Harold J. Cook
*University of Wisconsin-
Madison*
Maurice Crosland
University of Kent
Patrick Curry
London
Anne Darlington
La Manouba
J. W. Dauben
City University of New York
John Morgan Dederer
Connecticut
John W. Derry
*University of Newcastle upon
Tyne*
Michael Dillon
University of Durham
G. M. Ditchfield
University of Kent
Mary J. Dobson
*Wellcome Unit for the History
of Medicine,
Oxford*
Michael Duffy
University of Exeter
Hugh Dunthorne
University College of Swansea
R. J. W. Evans
*Brasenose College,
Oxford*
Patricia Fara
*Darwin College,
Cambridge*
John Feather
Loughborough University
Mary E. Fissell
The Johns Hopkins University
Tore Frängsmyr
Uppsala University
Robert I. Frost
*King's College,
University of London*

John Gascoigne
University of New South Wales
Johanna Geyer-Kordesch
*Wellcome Unit for the History
of Medicine,
University of Glasgow*
Sheridan Gilley
University of Durham
Mark Goldie
*Churchill College,
Cambridge*
David Goodman
Open University
Jeremy Gregory
*University of Northumbria at
Newcastle*
Basil Guy
University of California
G. B. Hagelberg
Canterbury
Tony Hayter
Blandford Forum
David Hempton
*Queen's University,
Belfast*
Lindsey Hughes
*School of Slavonic and Eastern
European Studies,
London*
Michael Hughes[†]

Marylla Hunt
London
Michael Hunter
*Birkbeck College,
London*
Colin Jones
Stanford University
Marc Jordan
London
H. Kamen
*Higher Council for Scientific
Research,
Barcelona*

Gerry Kearns
University of Wisconsin-Madison

Margaret Kinnell
Loughborough University

David Knight
University of Durham

Thomas W. Laqueur
University of California

Robin Law
University of Stirling

Christopher Lawrence
Wellcome Unit for the History of Medicine,
London

Philip Lawson
University of Alberta

Bruce P. Lenman
University of St. Andrew's

Andrew Louth
Goldsmith's College,
University of London

J. T. Lukowski
University of Birmingham

Francis McKee
Wellcome Unit for the History of Medicine,
University of Glasgow

Angus McLaren
University of Victoria

David Mackay
Victoria University of Wellington

Christine MacLeod
University of Bristol

Hilary Marland
Erasmus University,
Rotterdam

Hayden Mason
University of Bristol

Rudi Matthee
University of Delaware

Kenneth Maxwell
Council for Foreign Relations,
New York

G. E. Mingay
University of Kent at Canterbury

John Mullan
Fitzwilliam College,
Cambridge

Ian Netton
University of Exeter

Michael Neve
Wellcome Institute for the
History of Medicine,
London

Charles C. Noel
Madrid

David Nokes
King's College,
London

Clarissa Campbell Orr
Anglia Polytechnic University,
Cambridge Campus

Ronald Paulson
The Johns Hopkins University

Iain Pears
Christ Church,
University of Oxford

Nicholas Phillipson
University of Edinburgh

Stuart Piggott
University of Oxford

Jeremy D. Popkin
University of Kentucky

Dorothy Porter
Birkbeck College,
University of London

Roy Porter
Wellcome Institute for the
History of Medicine,
London

Wilfred Prest
University of Adelaide

Stephen Pumfrey
University of Lancaster

Donald J. Ratcliffe
University of Durham
Mario Relich
Open University
Graham Richards
Staffordshire University
Ruth Richardson
Institute of Historical Research,
University of London
Marie Mulvey Roberts
University of the West of
England,
Bristol
N. A. M. Rodger
National Maritime Museum
Pat Rogers
University of South Florida
Karl A. Roider Jr
Louisiana State University
Daniel Rosenberg
University of California,
Berkeley
Thomas J. Schaeper
St. Bonaventure University
J. A. Sharpe
University of York
J. H. Shennan
University of Lancaster
Phillip R. Sloan
University of Notre Dame
Charles Saumarez Smith
National Portrait Gallery,
London
Nigel Smith
Keble College, Oxford

Virginia Smith
London
Christine Stevenson
University of Reading
Mikuláš Teich
Robinson College,
Cambridge
Sylvana Tomaselli
Cambridge
David Trotter
University College London
Randolph Trumbach
Baruch College,
City University of New York
James Walvin
University of York
Fritz Weber
University of Vienna
Joachim Whaley
Gonville and Caius College,
Cambridge
Philip K. Wilson
Yale University School of
Medicine
Robert Wokler
University of Manchester
Philip Woodfine
University of Huddersfield
Jan Woudstra

John P. Wright
University of Windsor
Nuala Zahedieh
University of Edinburgh

Acknowledgements

An enormous amount of administrative work in connection with commissioning and processing contributions was handled with customary efficiency and grace by Frieda Houser, while Caroline Overy has worked like a Trojan in checking the text and completing references. Our deepest thanks to both. Alison Cowan at Blackwell Publishers was of great assistance. And thanks not least to our contributors themselves, for agreeing to take on what must often have seemed like thankless tasks, and carrying them out with despatch and cheer.

Introduction

There is little need to justify a work documenting the history of the eighteenth century. Although off-putting appellations like '*ancien régime*' and 'age of reason' still circulate, by any standards a century that saw the French Revolution and the origins of the industrial revolution must be regarded as of great importance in its own right and of immense significance for the future. And it is not only those events that render it important. The eighteenth century saw a spectacular extension of European empires – for the first time, colonial territories really did span the globe; a new continent (Australasia) was, in effect, discovered by the West, the Pacific was opened up to the European consciousness and much of India was subdued. Europe was exported to the ends of the earth, but at the same time the habits and customs, the art and religion, of Africa and Oceania, the wise Oriental and the noble savage, were all introduced into the West, bringing a new relativism reflected in the Enlightenment.

Alongside the expansion of Europe there was a remarkable turnabout: the loss of a major colonial territory, which inaugurated the most astonishing event of the modern world, the declaration of independence of the United States of America. Even as economic and cultural hegemony continued to grow, European political domination was thereby challenged, not least because the revolutionary epoch at the end of the eighteenth century saw the wars of liberation in much of Spanish America, leaving most of the Americas independent of European powers. By 1815 the world map of imperial and commercial power was highly complex. The United States of America was arguably the first major power founded on the basis of an intellectual creed, the Enlightenment. Events in the 1980s and 1990s, the apparent triumph of liberal, free-market, capitalist democracy over Communism,

have reminded us just how deeply indebted our own regimes remain
to the thinkers of the eighteenth century, to Locke and Rousseau,
Adam Smith and Thomas Jefferson, with all their ambiguities and
begged questions. The *Vindication of the Rights of Woman* (1792), by
Mary Wollstonecraft, affords yet a further example of the 'modernity'
of the century covered by this volume.

Yet such formulations also risk Whiggery and anachronism. Important and diverse historiographical currents rightly insist that it is
at our own peril that we see the eighteenth century through a late-
twentieth-century telescope. Much in the pre-Napoleonic world remained deeply traditional: nations without kings, aristocracies and
established churches looked both eccentric and, to many, obsolescent;
and terms like *la longue durée*, pioneered by the Braudelian *Annales*
school correctly draw attention to the way in which the eighteenth-
century rural economy that predominated in Europe resembled more
that of 400 years earlier than that of 100 years later – which is
reflected in the population figures. Most of Europe in 1800 was still
trapped in an agrarian and biological *ancien régime*, dominated by
peasants and characterized by low yields, low productivity, low
prosperity and low life expectations. It says much of contemporary
expectations that Malthus's *Essay on Population* (1798) should still
have entertained such a profound fear that any significant rise in
population could be neither absorbed nor put to good economic use,
but would rather spell socio-economic disaster: so small seemed the
prospects of any real and lasting economic improvement. For that
matter, the eighteenth century socio-economic foundations still rested
on slavery – serfdom was in place in much of trans-Elbian Europe and
plantation slavery mushroomed in the provinces. The revolutionary
attempts to free the European masses in the name of liberty, fraternity
and equality found their echo in slave risings and helped to spark
emancipation movements. Thus the close of the eighteenth century
saw the most extraordinary paradoxes: an age of industrial revolution
(the unbinding of Prometheus), dependent on chattel slavery, an age of
the proclamation of 'universal liberty' and the rights of man which, in
reality, left the vast majority of the peoples even of advanced nations
condemned by the new laws of political economy to the Ricardian
iron laws of subsistence.

It is a century that defies monocular analysis; and the age depicted
in the following thousand or so entries will often appear contradictory,
opening with the Sun King in his prime, and closing with the eclipse
of a Napoleon whose ambitions, superficially at least, resembled his
glorious predecessor's, but whose career proved very different in its
consequences. Developments were uneven, not least because the advance
of one nation, or one economic sector, necessarily meant the decline

of another. Neither the editors nor the contributors have seen it as the function of this volume to provide an overall interpretation of the eighteenth century. Yet alongside the intention to present material – an obvious function in a work of reference – we have also aimed for interpretation, albeit in respect of individual themes, people, events and regions. Contributors have been asked, wherever possible, to set material within current interpretative frameworks, but also to avoid the citation of a mass of scholarship or academic debate. No party line emerges, however: in a work such as this, that would be both impossible and deeply undesirable.

The organization of the entries is broadly consistent. The first sentence is generally definitional except where this is considered unnecessary; cross-references are in small capitals, with the letter under which the entry is alphabetized a large capital. Readers will note, or will discover by following up cross-references, that entries are organized in thematic clusters. Longer articles cover bigger subjects and themes (for example, France, Russia) with some breadth, and briefer articles feed into and lead off from these. We have hoped by this means to present a wider view without losing easy access to specific information. Readers wishing to pursue topics further will find general bibliographies at the end of most articles and suggestions for further reading at the back of the book.

Further nuts-and-bolts information is available in a chronology, dynastic charts and a selection of maps. There are limits to which it is practical to publish extensive statistics in a work like this: such figures are often doubtful for the eighteenth century, or at least need careful interpretation.

We recognize that most students and general readers who consult this book, for some essential date or development will be concerned with mainstream European affairs: politics, wars, dynasties, the *philosophes*. This reflects deeply ingrained priorities – and not necessarily narrow or unreasonable ones at that – and we have striven hard to cater to the needs of such users. But we have also tried, within strict space constraints, to go beyond that, by giving a fair amount of attention to world affairs – not just to colonialism but to the internal histories of Africa, China and other great empires. And we have given a generous allotment to the life of the mind, to art, literature, music, ideas – to Mozart, Kant and Goya, to the Enlightenment and the novel, believing that the eighteenth century saw the rise of the Fourth Estate and the March of Mind. And we have given attention to the basics of living (the family, elementary economic facts), and also to less tangible aspects of the attitudes and outlooks of the time. The browsing reader will, we hope, find much to catch his or her interest.

A few final words of explanation. This is a volume on the eighteenth century. It is a somewhat 'long' eighteenth century, which begins around the time of the wars of the 1690s and ends with the defeat of Napoleon. Such an extension allows some thematic unity. It is also a volume of world history, but one in which the European powers are displayed stage centre. This is no unthinking act of scholarly ethnocentrism. It is because Europe was, indeed, coming to dominate the rest of the world, militarily, economically, politically and culturally as never before, while other powers (in the Indian subcontinent, for instance, or the empires of Islam) were waning and coming under European influence.

JEREMY BLACK and ROY PORTER

A

Aboukir Bay, Battle of (1 August 1798) After a long hunt in the Mediterranean Rear-Admiral Horatio NELSON, with a fleet of fourteen battleships, came up against the French fleet under Admiral Brueys (1753–98) of thirteen ships, including the 120 gun *L'Orient*, lying at anchor in a bay of the Nile delta east of Alexandria. Nelson had been too late to prevent the landing in Egypt of the French army under Napoleon BONAPARTE but in the night battle that followed, Brueys's fleet was overwhelmed, and the French soldiers, though successful on land, were cut off from their European base. This was the first of Nelson's victories of annihilation. By breaking through the enemy line by way of a gap which the French admiral had neglected to close, and attacking from both sides, he captured or destroyed eleven of the thirteen battleships and two of four frigates. This success re-established British command of the Mediterranean, which had been lost in the dark days of 1796–7, enabled Sicily to be protected and Turkey encouraged, and set the pattern for the next decade of increasing deadlock between an unbeatable land power and a consistently successful naval power.

Oliver Warner, *The Battle of the Nile* (London: Batsford, 1960).

TONY HAYTER

absolutism More often known as despotism in the eighteenth century, absolutism was a form of strong individual rule seen as resembling the Asiatic despotism of the Ottoman Empire and China. Its converse was either limited rule by a monarch confined by laws and consultative assemblies, or republicanism, which was confined to smaller powers. Limited monarchy on the English model enjoyed support from

European intellectuals, especially following Montesquieu's *L'Esprit des lois*. However, absolutism also enjoyed the support and encouragement of Enlightenment writers, because of the potential for decisive action which strong monarchy enjoyed. Enlightened rulers could introduce substantial reforms, especially in a small state, as was demonstrated by Charles, king of Naples and Sicily, later CHARLES III of Spain, and Grand Duke Leopold in Tuscany, later Emperor LEOPOLD II. Absolutism, however, had two great limitations: it was always constrained in practice by the apparatus of government and ADMINISTRATION; and if the central figure lacked the qualities of a strong leader then absolutism became weak factionalism.

Even in the Chinese autocracy, the image of Oriental despotism belied the way in which the emperor's power was eroded by the bureaucracy. Centralized power was a vital device for governing such a huge country, as it was in Russia, and by the 1730s the earlier Manchu traditions of collective leadership had given way to autocratic rule. As power in China became increasingly centralized, however, the would-be despot was engulfed in a sea of paperwork and consultation. Bureaucrats could frustrate most imperial initiatives, and the execution of policies at a distance had to be entrusted to provincial governors, who in turn depended on co-operation from local elites. The same problems beset even the most energetic of European absolutists, Frederick the Great of Prussia (*see* FREDERICK II). Like the Chinese, he set up a system of checks and secret reports on his bureaucrats and ministers, and insisted on the utmost streamlining of paperwork coming to the centre. He had a working routine of unremitting dedication to business, and spent two months each year on tours of inspection; yet he was still the captive of the systems of administration needed to enforce his policies and ideas. Like other absolutists, he was most free to make a mark in such personal spheres of action as diplomacy and war, and most constrained in the attempt to enforce novel or unpopular domestic policies.

Reforms often went against the beliefs of the mass of the people, and could be unenforceable, as JOSEPH II found in the 1790 Belgian Catholic backlash against his liberalization plans. LOUIS XV of France found himself in the toils of his administrators, and the growing body of the magistracy, the *parlementaires*. The centralization introduced in Russia by PETER I led also to bureaucratic power and noble vested interests, limiting the autocrat; and reflected the problem of entrusting power to an individual, and the failure to create effective government agencies. The senate created by Peter in 1711 became after his death in 1725 a paper-bound administrative body. Control during regencies passed to a supreme privy council, one source of the plotting and instability which so often surrounded the imperial throne. From 1725 to the accession of CATHERINE II in 1762, the weakness of absolutism in unsuitable hands was manifest, as it was in Austria under MARIA THERESA from 1740 to 1780 and in France under Louis XV, who would spend weeks in hunting and entertainments, hindering the normal processes of government and diplomacy. Even in such hands, however, absolutism was capable of revival. Louis in 1766 fought back against the encroachment of the regional oligarchies controlling the *parlements* and reasserted his primacy in the state, under God, and his role as the fount of the kingdom's laws. He began to rebuild the nation's finances, entered the third Family Compact with Spain, and arguably could have secured the monarchy's prestige if he had enjoyed greater military success abroad. Even in France, the mystique of absolutism, its potential for success and energy, was by no means finished. Absolutism rested on strong traditional beliefs, and offered what many people wanted: ideas of justice, divine sanction and glory. Absolute rulers depended on the complicity of their peoples, and on an obedience that was not blind or automatic, even for Russians prostrating themselves in the mud as the sovereign's coach went by.

See also ENLIGHTENED ABSOLUTISM, MONARCHY.

H. L. Kahn, *Monarchy in the Emperor's Eyes: Image and Reality in the Ch'ien-lung Reign* (Cambridge, Mass.: Harvard University Press, 1971).
A. Lentin (ed.), *Enlightened Absolutism (1760–1790)* (Newcastle upon Tyne: Avero, 1985).
H. M. Scott (ed.), *Enlightened Absolutism: Reform and Reformers in Later Eighteenth-Century Europe* (London: Macmillan, 1990).

PHILIP WOODFINE

Académie des Sciences The Paris Académie des Sciences was founded in 1666. Unlike the Royal Society, the Académie was a government agency whose members were crown appointees and *pensionnaires*, expected to assist the government in developing state power. As permanent membership was granted only to the most innovative and productive of French scientists, the Académie formed an exclusive, professional club. The Académie also exercised a controlling influence over the wider French scientific community. By setting an annual prize competition, vetting research and publishing selected papers by non-members in its *Mémoires*, the Académie was able to direct and validate the work of France's aspiring experimental philosophers. Until the 1730s it used this influence to search for a defence of Cartesian vortex theory. Thereafter it was captured by Newtonians, a number of whom made significant contributions to the mathematical consolidation of the theory of universal gravitation. By 1789, however, the Académie had many enemies. As its membership was fixed and the French scientific community had expanded over the century, many ambitious scientists were excluded. To most French revolutionaries the Académie was a privileged corporation which had no place in an egalitarian society. The Académie was closed in August 1793.

See also SCIENTIFIC SOCIETIES.

Roger Hahn, *The Anatomy of a Scientific Institution: The Paris Academy of Sciences 1666–1803* (Berkeley, Calif.: University of California Press, 1971).

LAURENCE BROCKLISS

Académie Française   The Cardinal Richelieu (1585–1642), on hearing of the secret meetings of a group of literary men, persuaded them to form themselves into an official body. These men included Valentin Conrart (1603–75), a grammarian at whose house the meetings were conducted; Jean Chapelain (1595–1674), a poet who conceived of the idea of the Académie's dictionary; Antoine Godeau (1605–72); and Jean Ogier de Gombauld (1570–1666). Members of the Académie frequented the Hôtel de Rambouillet, the home of Catherine de Vivonne, marquise de Rambouillet (1588–1665), whose *salon*, with its emphasis on controlled and delicate speech, was the embodiment of the spirit of the Académie.

The Académie received its letters of patent in 1635, which were registered by the *parlement* in 1637. In 1672 the Académie moved to the Louvre. Its purpose was to preserve the French language and to encourage its use in a form devoid of coarseness or innovation. As the eighteenth century unfolded, however, the philosophical party turned it into a more adventurous institution and it became the forum of some very important debate, especially after 1754, when the historiographer and contributor to the *Encyclopédie* Charles Pinot Duclos (1704–72) became its permanent secretary. D'Alembert, who had been elected to the Académie that year, succeeded him in 1772. Suppressed in 1793 by the National Convention, the Académie was reinstated by Napoleon in 1803.

Lucien Brunel, *Les Philosophes et l'Académie Française au dix-huitième siècle* (Paris: Hachette, 1884).

SYLVANA TOMASELLI

academies of art   The eighteenth century saw a rapid growth in the number and the influence of art academies. Fundamental to this was the international hegemony of French culture and the prestige of one of its most important institutions, the Académie Royale de Peinture et de Sculpture (founded 1648). This was both an instrument of the centralizing statecraft of the reign of Louis XIV, and a means by which artists were able to free themselves from the restrictive embrace and the lowly status of the craft guilds. The Académie Royale sought to formalize all aspects of artistic activity from training to exhibiting, and to provide a platform from which artists might deal on more equal terms with their patrons. Its precepts were based on the idea that the practice of art should be principally an intellectual and only secondarily a manual activity. Central to the academic doctrines that held sway throughout the eighteenth century was training based on the intensive study of the canonical sculptures of classical antiquity, drawing of the nude human (generally male) body, and respect for selected Old Masters, chief among them Raphael and the Carracci. This was supplemented by the study of anatomy, perspective, geometry and so on. The application of paint or the carving of marble was learned in the traditional way in a master's studio. Equally important to the academic idea was a hierarchy of genres of subject-matter that placed history painting at its pinnacle and relegated portraiture, landscape and still-life (the means by which most eighteenth-century painters earned their living) to the bottom (*see* PAINTING).

In the first half of the century court-sponsored academies based on the French model were established at Berlin (1701), Vienna (1704), St Petersburg (1724) and Madrid (1744). After around 1750 the spread of Enlightenment ideas led to the foundation of numerous art academies in the French provinces, the Netherlands, Italy and the German states. Many of these were little more than private drawing-schools, but among those of substance were the ones at Venice (1756), Dresden (1762) and Brussels (1769). The ROYAL ACADEMY in London, the culmination of thirty years of efforts by British artists to improve their status, training and exhibiting opportunities, received its royal charter in 1768. It was, and remains, a private institution. The *Discourses* of its first President, Sir Joshua Reynolds, were one of the most complete and accessible articulations of the academic idea.

N. Pevsner, *Academies of Art Past and Present* (Cambridge: Cambridge University Press, 1940; repr. 1973).

MARC JORDAN

academies of science *see* SCIENTIFIC SOCIETIES.

Adam, Robert (1728–1792)   Scottish architect. Like his brothers John (1721–92) and James (1734–94), he trained in the Edinburgh office of his father William (1688–1748), who was Scotland's leading architect. He had a particularly fruitful Grand Tour (1754–8), most of which he spent studying Roman imperial architecture: PIRANESI was a major influence on him. Back in England, he made his name replanning and decorating country houses, many of which had been built at the height of PALLADIANISM. The 'Adam style' became synonymous with a particularly graceful and unemotional recombination, in the best English tradition, of antique and Italian Renaissance influences in furniture and interior decoration for town and country mansions like Kedleston Hall in Derby (from 1759) and Home House (1773–7) in London. He recovered from the ruinous Adelphi Terrace (London) speculation (1768–72) to pursue a surprising strain of GOTHIC REVIVAL in such mock fortresses as Culzean Castle, Ayrshire (1777–90). Other work at the end of his career – for example the Edinburgh Bridewell (1791), whose plan reflected his correspondence with Jeremy Bentham – confirms his talent as an institutional architect.

Arthur T. Bolton, *The Architecture of Robert and James Adam, 1758–94*, 2 vols (London: Country Life, 1922).

CHRISTINE STEVENSON

Adams, John Quincy (1767–1848)   Sixth president of the United States (1825–8) and famous diarist. He gained early public notice as the eldest son of John Adams (1735–1826), the second president of the United States. He served as secretary on missions to Russia and Britain before becoming minister to the Netherlands (1794–6) and Prussia (1797–1801). Elected to the senate as a Massachusetts Federalist in 1802, he was compelled to resign in 1808 after supporting President Jefferson's embargo policy. His reward was promotion at Republican hands: minister to Russia (1809–14), chairman of the delegation that negotiated peace with Britain in 1814 and minister to Britain (1815–17). As James Monroe's (1758–1831) secretary of state from 1817 to 1825, he acquired Florida from Spain in 1819 and helped formulate the Monroe Doctrine in 1823. After an indecisive election in 1824, he was elected president by the House of Representatives in controversial circumstances. As president he pressed forward a national programme of internal improvements, but alienated many special interests and was defeated by Andrew Jackson (1767–1845) in 1828. He then served as congressman from 1831 until his death, becoming known as 'Old Man Eloquent' for defending the right to present antislavery petitions.

S. F. Bemis, *John Quincy Adams and the Foundations of American Foreign Policy* (New York: Knopf, 1949).

DONALD J. RATCLIFFE

Addington, Henry, first viscount Sidmouth (1757–1844)   English politician. After serving as speaker of the House of Commons, he succeeded Pitt as premier in 1801. He was a man of robust common sense who appealed to many of the country gentlemen in the Commons. His premiership was overshadowed by the failure of the Amiens settlement, but he was a capable finance minister, whose administration of the income tax was expeditious. Resumption of war with France eventually compelled him to resign as premier, but he later served in a succession of ministries, most significantly as home secretary from 1812 to 1821. Conservative in outlook, he was not without sympathy for the common people, though he disapproved of attempts to exploit distress for political ends. As home secretary he was responsible for the maintenance of public order, a difficult task before the existence of a police force. Compelled to rely on the local magistracy and on information supplied by spies and informers, he was no alarmist: had his advice been followed by the Manchester magistrates in 1819 there would have been no Peterloo affair. To the end of his career he remained opposed to Catholic emancipation and parliamentary reform.

P. Ziegler, *Addington* (London: Collins, 1965).

JOHN W. DERRY

Addison, Joseph (1672–1719) English poet, essayist and statesman. He was educated at Oxford, travelled on the Continent between 1699 and 1703, became under-secretary of state in 1706, secretary to the marquis of Wharton (1648–1714) when he was lord-lieutenant of Ireland (1708–10), and member of parliament for Malmesbury from 1709 until his death. He defended the Whigs in the *Whig Examiner* (1710), contributed to Richard STEELE's (1672–1729) *Tatler* (1709–11) and with him produced *The Spectator* (1711–12). Their essays were extremely influential throughout the century and on both sides of the Channel, being instrumental in the reformation of manners by providing ordinary men and women with a guide to a life of virtue within modern commercial society. They also established a genre which was frequently imitated. (*See* MAGAZINES.) His tragedy *Cato* (1713) was extremely well received, unlike his comedy *The Drummer*. He wrote for Steele's *Guardian* and revived *The Spectator* in 1714. Boswell remarked that Addison's style came increasingly to be compared with that of Johnson, adding: 'let us not ungratefully undervalue that beautiful style, which has pleasingly conveyed to us much instruction and entertainment. Though comparatively weak, opposed to Johnson's Herculean vigour, let us not call it positively feeble.'

Peter Gay, 'The Spectator as Actor: Addison in Perspective', *Encounter*, 39/6 (Dec. 1967), 27–32.

SYLVANA TOMASELLI

administration Traditional patterns of government organization experienced accelerated change in the eighteenth century. States generally became more interventionist and energetic in the collection and use of their resources. Government ordinances had usually been negative and proscriptive, a trend continued in reforms such as those of Joseph II in Austria-Hungary, with sumptuary legislation governing in minute detail the clothing which the various ranks of his subjects could wear. However, alongside this restrictive interference went a newer emphasis on the positive restructuring of civil society. Frederick II of Prussia attempted, in his codification of the laws begun in 1749 and in numerous orders, to reshape the behaviour and attitudes of the people, towards religious toleration, illegitimacy, property rights and a host of other subjects. Catherine II's Police Ordinance of April 1782 was similarly an attempt to change the way that society worked, rather than to enforce old, usually religious, prescriptions. If governments were to become more efficient and more interventionist, a class of administrators was indispensable, and officialdom accordingly grew. This was not yet a bureaucracy on the nineteenth-century model, but an expanding class of officials drawn largely from the older privileged classes. They shared a code of civic duty on the classical Roman model, and their interconnections were cemented by the quest for patronage and advancement.

The size of countries placed great burdens on this growing administrative body, not least in the vast distances to be covered and poor communications, but also in terms of population. England by 1800 had a population of roughly 9 million, and France some 27 million, while Japan had 30 million and Russia around 40 million: for the centre efficiently to administer such a population, spread over such an area, was a task beyond the powers of government. The whole population of Europe was then under 190 million, however, while that of China was some 300 million. Not surprisingly, eighteenth-century China had the most advanced administration in the world, its highly organized examination system linked to sophisticated evaluation of its thousands of personnel. Its immense paperwork and record-keeping made the Chinese system truly bureaucratic, yet personal influence and privilege were still present, even essential. The boundaries of administrative bodies were left deliberately vague and overlapping, to provide mutual checks, and the towns and countryside were in the hands of local social leaders. In the central imperial bureaucracy the educated and privileged Lower Yangtze elites were dominant, providing stability and continuity in office.

Such a pattern was characteristic of Europe also, and since the established elites usually controlled officialdom, the administrations tended to reinforce and preserve existing hierarchies. (*See* ARISTOCRACY, NOBILITY.) Typically, the distinction between judicial and administrative functions was blurred in the localities, and purely administrative officials were more likely to exist at the centre. In Russia local officials, like the overburdened British justices of the peace, were both judges and administrators. (*See* ADMINISTRATION OF JUSTICE.) Even tax-collection could be contracted out by the state, like the British land tax, farmed out in each county to landowners or merchants willing to gather in the revenues and – tardily, so as to gather interest on the large sums involved – remit them to the centre. The French developed bureaucracies to perform a similar role, and were the European specialists in efficient TAX FARMING: in Prussia the French-run *régie* was the main agency of revenue-raising, with a staff at its height of 2,000. The essentials of a bureaucracy were emerging, however imperfectly, beginning with information-gathering and the development of standardized rules for collection and recording. From the 1690s in Prussia there were standard forms for tax-collection, while in Russia Peter I ordered all documents to be kept in book form, for easy reference, rather than in scrolls, with each document stitched to the one before it, and kept in a huge roll. Latin was being displaced by the vernacular as the language of administration, a process that was already advanced in Britain and Germany by the 1730s. Officials could think in terms of a career structure with, increasingly, the expectation of a pension at the end of their service. As states formalized and enhanced their administrative control, so they had increasingly to devote resources to supporting the administration itself.

C. H. Church, *Revolution and Red Tape: The French Ministerial Bureaucracy, 1770–1850* (Oxford: Clarendon, 1981).

S. Naquin and E. S. Rawski, *Chinese Society in the Eighteenth Century* (New Haven, Conn.: Yale University Press, 1987).

M. Raeff, *The Well Ordered Police State: Social and Institutional Change through the Law in the Germanies and Russia, 1600–1800* (New Haven, Conn.: Yale University Press, 1983).

PHILIP WOODFINE

Adolf Fredrik (1710–1771) King of Sweden (1751–71). Born into the ducal house of Holstein-Gottorp, he was a nephew by marriage, through his uncle Duke Fredrik IV, of Charles XII. In 1727 he became prince bishop of Lübeck, and in 1739 administrator of the Holstein-Gottorp duchy. After Sweden's defeat by Russia in 1743, Tsarina Elizabeth made it a condition of the peace that Adolf Fredrik, uncle of her favoured heir, Charles Peter of Holstein-Gottorp (1728–62), should be the heir of the childless Fredrik I of Sweden. In 1744 he married the brilliant Louisa Ulrika of Prussia (1720–82), sister of Frederick II. Their eldest son (born 1746), was the future GUSTAV III. In contrast to his wife, Adolf Fredrik was a nonentity, but he took the unusual step of visiting Finland soon after his succession, showed a keen and informed interest in the navy and, when strongly prompted, asserted the dignity of the impossibly hobbled Swedish crown. In 1756 the royal couple were especially humiliated through a failed *coup* to recover some power for the crown. He died at a time when the degradation of Swedish public life was becoming acknowledged by all contending parties.

L. V. A. Stavenow, *Frihetstiden* (Stockholm, 1922).

D. D. ALDRIDGE

aesthetics The term 'aesthetics' was coined (from Greek *aisthesis* – sense perception, feeling) by Alexander Gottlieb Baumgarten in the conclusion of his 1735 thesis, translated as *Reflections on Poetry*, as the name for a new science which was to refine sensuous ('confused') representation and knowledge, as logic did rational thought, based on 'clear and distinct ideas'. He began his *Aesthetica* (1750) by equating it with 'the theory of the liberal arts, epistemology of less-than-rational knowing [*gnoseologia inferior*] and art of thinking beautifully'. This discipline would absorb the functions traditionally assumed by rhetoric and poetics, but its focus was as much social perception and conduct as art and literature. Thus, while the core of Baumgarten's idea of aesthetics was an extension of Leibniz's subtle conception of sensation in terms of 'con-fusion', it drew on many 'aesthetic' currents of the preceding age associated with such terms as *gusto* or *goût*, *finesse, délicatesse, sentiment,* and *je ne sais quoi,* which bore only a marginal resemblance to things now considered aesthetic. The emphasis on intuitive, affective modes of knowing complemented and compensated for rationalist privileging of the distinct and the calculable.

After Baumgarten, theories concerning art and natural beauty, along with the sublime, picturesque, grotesque and so on increasingly assumed central importance in aesthetics and by the end of the eighteenth century the field roughly had its now familiar scope. But with Immanuel Kant and Friedrich Schiller the term 'aesthetic' still often functioned as the adjective corresponding to sensation and feeling (*Empfindung* or *Gefühl*), and it is not clear that they saw their arguments – which remain important to today's aesthetics – as falling under a discipline of that name.

What distinguished the aesthetics of the eighteenth century from most earlier writing on art and beauty was the emphasis on feeling (*see* SENTIMENT). Both perception and passion were seen to include appreciation, in the sense of enjoyment and assessment. This tendency was reinforced by theories of the SUBLIME, brought into neoclassicism by the translation of Longinus' *On the Sublime* by Nicolas Boileau. In England John Dennis (1657–1734) held that poetry pleases by exciting 'enthusiastic passion' whose cause we cannot comprehend, which ultimately refines and reforms the mind. (See his *Advancement and Reformation of Modern Poetry* (1701) and *The Grounds of Criticism in Poetry* (1704).)

One of the most influential writers of the century on aesthetic questions was the third earl of Shaftesbury, for whom sensitivity to order and beauty, innate in humans but needing nurture, was indistinguishable from what he dubbed 'the moral sense'. TASTE implied not only finely attuned discrimination beyond the control of reflection but also relish verging on enthusiasm. Aesthetic disinterestedness was really participation in the order and prosperity of the whole, a counterweight to self-interest. Joseph Addison developed his own idea of the sublime in several issues of *The Spectator* from 1712 devoted to 'Pleasures of the Imagination'. Like Dennis, he believed that it arises when the mind is filled with an object too great for its capacity. Expressly following Shaftesbury, but owing as much to Addison, Francis Hutcheson developed the analogy between innate senses of the morally good and the beautiful in *Inquiry concerning Beauty, Order, Harmony, and Design* (1725). Edmund Burke in *A Philosophical Enquiry into the Origin of our Ideas of the Sublime and Beautiful* (1757) held that feelings of beauty are rooted in passions 'of society' (like Shaftesbury), but the sublime in the stronger passions of self-preservation and fear.

The abbé Jean-Baptiste Dubos (1670–1742) put forward a theory in *Reflexions critiques sur la poésie et la peinture* (Critical Reflections on Poetry and Painting, 1719) which based aesthetic pleasure in the universal human need to be affected, even violently moved, in order to avoid lassitude. Judgements of works of art are grounded in the feelings they evoke, and reason enters only to justify these *décisions du sentiment*. But feeling and taste are influenced by culture and climate, so that far from allowing the anarchy of individual fancy, Dubos introduced historical and social dimensions to the study of SENSIBILITY. Montesquieu in his 1754 'Essay on Taste' for the *Encyclopédie* defined taste as 'that which attaches us to an object by means of sentiment'. Taste is 'the prompt and exquisite application of rules we have no knowledge of'. Denis Diderot developed a similar conception of sensibility or taste as the distillatiion of 'an infinity of delicate observations' or minute experiments (*petites expériences, essais*) which we have forgotten but which have cumulatively formed our capacity to be readily yet deeply moved and thus to judge. Thus we have what they call taste, instinct, tact. The legacy of Leibniz's conception of sensation, the core of the original 'aesthetics', makes itself felt again.

JEFFREY BARNOUW

Africa The different regions of Africa have to be considered separately, since their historical experience in the eighteenth century was very diverse.

North Africa

From Egypt west to modern Algeria north Africa had been conquered by the Ottoman Empire in the sixteenth century. EGYPT in the eighteenth century was still formally ruled by a viceroy (or pasha) appointed by the Ottoman sultan, but in practice effective power was exercised by the commanders of the locally based garrison of janissaries, or Turkish slave soldiers, who were in turn split into factions which competed for predominance. The divisions of the janissaries, in turn, allowed the mamluks, another military group of servile origin whose origins pre-dated the Turkish conquest, to recover much of their influence, especially after their successful intervention in a major civil war (the 'Great Sedition') in 1711. The power and prestige of both Ottomans and mamluks in Egypt was, however, decisively smashed by the invasion of Egypt by French forces under Napoleon Bonaparte in 1798; although the French occupation was only brief (being withdrawn in 1801), it irremediably shattered the old political system in Egypt, and also (together with earlier Ottoman defeats at the hands of Russia), by demonstrating the overwhelming military superiority of Europe, initiated a period of crisis for Muslim societies obliged to come to terms with the decisive shift of the balance of power against them.

In north Africa west of Egypt, called the Maghrib ('the west') in Arabic but more generally 'Barbary' by the Europeans, the three provinces (or regencies) of Tripoli, Tunis and Algiers were likewise Ottoman possessions in name, but Ottoman authority here was even more nominal. In Tripoli, the office of viceroy or pasha in 1711 was usurped by a Turkish cavalry commander called Ahmad Qaramanli, and then remained hereditary in the Qaramanli family until the Ottoman reconquest of Tripoli in 1835. In Tunis the office of pasha had already been superseded in effective power by the military office of bey, which in 1705 was secured by another Ottoman cavalry commander called Husain b. 'Ali (*d* 1740), who likewise made it the hereditary possession of his family, which was to survive as the ruling dynasty until the proclamation of the Tunisian Republic in 1957. In Algiers the elected head of the Turkish military commanders, the dey, assumed the pashalik in 1711. Morocco, west of Algeria, remained an independent kingdom outside Ottoman rule, but underwent a similar (albeit more temporary) take-over by a military group. Mawlay Isma'il (1672–1727) had strengthened the central authority of the monarchy, creating an army of black slaves imported from the south (called 'abid), but his death was followed by thirty years of disputed successions and civil wars among rival claimants to the throne, which the 'abid were able to exploit to make themselves the effective rulers of the country. The states of the Maghrib, and especially the regencies of Algiers and Tripoli, remained notorious in this period for serving as bases for Muslim pirates (called 'corsairs' by Europeans) who preyed on Christian shipping in the Mediterranean and Atlantic. As the power of the Christian states grew, this was eventually to provoke punitive counter-action, beginning with the intervention of the US navy in Tripoli in 1803. (*See* BARBARY STATES.)

East Africa

The power of the Christian kingdom of Ethiopia (Abyssinia) was in decline, after the assassination of the emperor Iyasu (Jesus) I in 1706. In the second half of the eighteenth century the central authority of the monarchy collapsed altogether. The period from 1769 onwards is known in Ethiopian history as the 'era of the princes', when the emperors were no more than puppets and effective power lay rather with the hereditary provincial governors, who fought one another for pre-eminence. This period of anarchy was to come to an end only with the reunification of Ethiopia by the emperor Tewodros (Theodore) (1818–68) in 1855.

Further south, the east African coast as far south as modern Tanzania was subject to the sultans of Oman in Arabia, who had liberated the Swahili city-states of the area from the Portuguese, taking the leading port of Mombasa (in modern Kenya) from them in 1698; although the Portuguese were able to reoccupy Mombasa in 1728–9, this revival proved ephemeral, and Portuguese rule was restricted to the area of Mozambique in the extreme south. Omani authority was at first merely nominal, the various Swahili towns being effectively independent. During the eighteenth century, however, the growth of trade, including the export of slaves to the French sugar-producing colonies of Ile de France and Bourbon (modern Mauritius and Réunion) in the Indian Ocean as well as to the Muslim world, heightened Omani interest in the area, while at the same time the accession of the Busai'idi dynasty in Oman in 1741 gave it a more effective leadership. The principal port of Mombasa took the opportunity of this change of dynasty in Oman to assert its independence, and continued to defy Omani authority until 1837. The Busa'idi emirs therefore occupied the island of Zanzibar, off the coast of Tanzania, which became the principal base of Omani authority in east Africa. The foundations were thus laid for the emergence of Zanzibar, under a dynasty of Omani origin, as a great commercial empire in the nineteenth century.

West and West-Central Africa

The major factor in the eighteenth-century history of this region was the growth of the transatlantic SLAVE TRADE, primarily to supply labour for the sugar plantations of Brazil and the Caribbean colonies. Although slaves were also exported from northern and eastern Africa, to the Muslim world, the transatlantic trade was much greater in its scale and impact. During the whole of the eighteenth century, it is thought that over 6 million slaves were taken from Africa for export over the Atlantic, rather more than half of total exports over the entire period of the trade between the sixteenth and nineteenth centuries. Although other commodities were also purchased from Africa, including gold, ivory and dye-woods, slaves were by now of overwhelming importance. Even the section of the west African coast known as the Gold Coast (modern Ghana) now became primarily a supplier of slaves rather than of gold; but the main centres of the slave trade were the 'Slave Coast', immediately east of the Gold Coast, where the principal slaving port was Whydah (in the modern Republic of Benin), and Angola in west-central Africa. The volume of slave exports across the Atlantic grew for most of the eighteenth century, reaching its highest level probably in the 1780s. From the 1790s, however, the volume of the slave trade began to decline, although it was to remain at a high level until the mid nineteenth century (and the decline in transatlantic exports was offset by the increase in exports from east Africa to supply markets in and around the Indian Ocean, so that slave exports from Africa as a whole probably continued to rise, reaching a peak in the 1820s or 1830s). The decline in the transatlantic trade was initially due to the disruption of shipping by the European wars of 1792–1815, but this was soon supplemented by the effects of legal abolition, the first European nation to ban the trade being revolutionary France in 1794 (although Napoleon re-legalized it in 1802), followed by Denmark in 1803 and Britain and the USA in 1808.

The effects of the slave trade on the African societies involved are a matter of controversy. The export of so many slaves must, first, have had a significant demographic impact. Africa is today the least densely populated of the major continents, and this has often been held to reflect the impact of slave exports; but most recent scholarship suggests that the drain of population through the slave trade was probably not sufficient to cause actual depopulation, but merely inhibited population growth. The slave trade also depended on violence, since the principal source of the slaves exported was capture in war. The growth of slave exports from west Africa coincided with the emergence of new military states, of which the most notable were Asante (Ashanti) behind the Gold Coast and Dahomey on the Slave Coast, which conquered Whydah in 1727. Asante and Dahomey were highly militarized societies, whose armies used imported European firearms, and which celebrated their military successes by the public sacrifice of a portion of their captives. The relationship between this militarism and the slave trade was already a subject of debate in the eighteenth century; opponents of the slave trade argued that the militarization of African societies was a consequence of the overseas demand for war captives, while anti-abolitionists insisted that it reflected indigenous cultural traits which were independent of and older than the slave trade; modern scholarship has also been divided on this issue, although the general weight of detailed research tends to support the suggestion that Asante and Dahomian militarism derived from, or at least was substantially reinforced by, their involvement in the slave trade.

The European nations involved in the slave trade maintained various fortified trading posts along the west African coast: the French held the islands of Gorée and St Louis in modern Senegal (although the latter was briefly taken by the British in 1758–79); the British had Fort James on the Gambia River; the British, Dutch and Danes all had forts on the Gold Coast; and the British, French and Portuguese had forts at Whydah, the principal centre of the slave trade. In addition, the Portuguese still held their colony at Luanda in Angola, although this was much reduced in territorial scale from the sixteenth and seventeenth centuries. A colony of a different sort was established in 1787, when Freetown in Sierra Leone was founded for the resettlement of free blacks from Britain, Canada and the West Indies.

For most of the eighteenth century, Europeans made little attempt to penetrate into the interior of Africa, although they held these possessions on the coast. By the end of the century, however, interest in opening up the African interior was growing, as seen in the establishment of the Association for Promoting the Discovery of the Interior Parts of Africa (more commonly known as the African Association) in Britain in 1788, which funded the explorations of Mungo Park in West Africa in 1795–6. This movement for EXPLORATION was not solely motivated by scientific curiosity, but also reflected interest in the commercial potential of the African market, and more particularly the desire to promote alternative forms of trade to that in slaves. Interest was especially concentrated in exploration of the great inland river systems, such as the River Niger (the object of Park's expedition), which were thought to offer the best prospects of opening up commercial communication with the interior. During the period of the slave trade, Protestant nations such as Britain (unlike the Catholic Portuguese) had shown little interest in converting Africans to Christianity. But by the end of the eighteenth century, in close connection with the campaign against the slave trade, British interest in the evangelization of Africa was also growing, reflected in the foundation of the London Missionary Society (which undertook missionary work mainly in South Africa) in 1792 and the Church Missionary Society (which worked mainly in west and east Africa) in 1799 (see MISSIONARIES).

Although the West African societies most directly involved in the Atlantic slave trade (such as Asante and Dahomey) were generally still pagan, much of the interior of West Africa was already Muslim. Muslim west Africa was profoundly affected in this period by a series of re- vivalist movements, which sought to purify the practice of local Islam by suppressing surviving pagan practices and enforcing more rigorous observance of the shariah, or system of Islamic law. Although these may have drawn some inspiration from contemporary revivalist move- ments in the heartlands of Islam, such as the Wahhabiyya in Arabia, they seem to have owed more to local traditions of Islamic scholar- ship, which had been debating the problems of applying Islamic law in the west African context long before the eighteenth century. Propa- ganda for Islamic reform was pursued by a series of leaders, of whom the most widely influential was Sidi al-Mukhtar al-Kunti (1729–1811), chief of the Kunta Arabs in southern Sahara (in modern Mali), who propagated the Qadiriyya brotherhood. Although many revivalist leaders, including al-Kunti, pursued their reform project purely by peaceful propaganda, in several cases reformers ended up by resorting to violence, declaring holy wars (jihads) against existing rulers in the cause of Islam. Such Muslim revolutions occurred, for example, in the states of Futa Jallon (in modern Guinea) in 1725 and Futa Toro (in Senegal) in 1776. By the end of the eighteenth century, the most celebrated of the west African revivalist leaders, 'Uthman b. Fudi (Usuman dan Fodio) (1754–1817), was already preaching reform in Hausaland (northern Nigeria), laying the foundation for the successful jihad which he launched there in 1804, and which created an extensive and powerful new Muslim state, the Sokoto Caliphate.

South Africa
South Africa was distinguished from the rest of the continent by the presence of significant numbers of European settlers, and the conse- quent extension of European occupation over considerable areas of the interior. The settlement at CAPE TOWN had originally been estab- lished by the Dutch in 1652, as a victualling station for ships going to the East Indies; but in 1795, during the course of the French Revolu- tionary war, it was occupied by the British and (apart from a brief restoration to the Dutch in 1803–6) remained in British hands there- after. The settlement developed as a racially stratified society, the European settlers employing both indigenous Khoi ('Hottentots') as dependent labourers and slaves imported from the East Indies and

from elsewhere in Africa. The European population grew steadily during the eighteenth century, through both immigration and natural increase, from around 1,000 in the 1690s to about 16,000 by the end of the eighteenth century. It also began to develop a distinct colonial identity, the designation of 'Afrikaner' (or 'Africans') being already used in the eighteenth century (although not common until the nineteenth century). The settlers also grew increasingly resentful of the control of the Cape government. The first attempt to establish autonomous settlers' republics in frontier areas occurred in 1795, shortly before the British take-over. With the expansion of European settlement into the interior, clashes with the indigenous population who had to be dispossessed of their land became increasingly frequent and bitter. The Khoi of the Cape area had been unable to offer effective resistance, but by the 1770s the frontier of European settlement had reached the Great Fish River, where it met the distinct Xhosa people, the most southerly of the Bantu (or Kaffir) peoples; more technologically advanced and more populous than the Khoi, the Bantu presented a much more formidable barrier to the expansion of European settlement, and in 1779 began the series of Kaffir Wars against the Xhosa which was to last until the 1850s.

See also BLACKS.

Richard Gray (ed.), *The Cambridge History of Africa*, vol. 4: *From c.1600 to c.1790* (Cambridge: Cambridge University Press, 1975).

ROBIN LAW

agriculture, European By far the largest sector of the eighteenth-century European economy, agriculture generally employed well over a half of the occupied population. If, in addition to farmers and farmworkers, ancillary craftsmen are taken into account and others who drew all or part of their income from agriculture, then the proportion would be even greater.

Agriculture was concerned primarily with production of food for the human population; but substantial areas of land were devoted to pasture for the breeding of horses used in both rural and urban haulage and transport, and for the cultivation of grains for animal fodder. Further acreages were used for producing raw materials for industrial use, such as flax and plants used in making vegetable dyes. Wool, hides and tallow were by-products of animal husbandry, while some crops were grown for medicinal purposes and use in country crafts. Areas of poor soils were reserved for woods and rabbit warrens. Some woodlands were cultivated on a commercial basis to provide timber for house- and boat-building, for making charcoal and a large variety of useful wooden objects.

Because of variations in climate, relief and soils, and also in transport conditions and access to markets, agriculture was marked by regional specialization. In the drier areas of northern Europe grain predominated, while wetter districts were generally devoted to pasture for livestock. Much of the farming was mixed in character, with grain production dependent in large degree on the supply of manure from the livestock. In southern Europe large areas were given over to vines and olives, with the poorer soils supporting sheep and goats. Access to major towns determined the location of market-gardens, orchards, dairies, and barley and hops grown for brewing and distilling. Regional specialization made for a large internal and international trade in agricultural produce, including the export of wines from France and Portugal, and of grain from the Baltic.

Although small-scale peasant farming survived over large areas of Europe, there was generally little 'subsistence farming' as such. Quite small acreages produced a marketable surplus, and cultivators were usually involved in some cash transactions. As the eighteenth century advanced there was often a tendency for farms to grow in size, due not so much to economies of scale, for little machinery was in use, but rather because of a thinning out of less-efficient cultivators, whose land was taken over by the more successful.

With the growth of urban centres, the market exercised an increasing influence on agricultural specialization and scale of production. Major cities drew on supplies of food and raw materials from considerable distances, and exerted a demand for improvement of roads, inland navigation and coastal shipping. As farming became more market-orientated, a major impulse was given to technical improvements. Farmers tried to become more efficient to take advantage of expanding markets and profitable prices, as well as to survive periods of low prices and poor seasons. Enlightened landowners and farmers experimented systematically with rotations and manures, replaced traditional breeds of livestock by new ones, and sought improved implements. They joined agricultural societies, attended shows, read the farming press and exchanged information by personal contacts and correspondence. Improvements in arable farming concerned attempts to improve yields, and by introducing temporary grass leys and fodder crops to carry more livestock, and hence increase supplies of manure. In livestock experimental breeders sought to produce animals that would fatten more quickly and produce a more profitable carcass.

Progress was made, though it was regionally uneven, and some fundamental problems remained, especially effective treatment of blights and pests, and of diseases in livestock, as well as adequate drainage of wet soils. Powered machinery was little used before the end of the century, and over large parts of Europe the OPEN-FIELD SYSTEM remained

an obstacle to more rational use of the land. Everywhere, poorly educated farmers and conservative workers persisted with outdated methods. Nevertheless, the eighteenth century witnessed the spread of a
variety of important new ideas and reform of farming structure and
organization, which provided a sound base for subsequent more far-
reaching advances. (*See also* ENCLOSURES.)

G. E. Mingay (ed.), *The Agrarian History of England and Wales*, vol. 6: *1750–
1850* (Cambridge: Cambridge University Press, 1989).
Joan Thirsk (ed.), *The Agrarian History of England and Wales*, vol. 5: *1640–
1750* (Cambridge: Cambridge University Press, 1984).

G. E. MINGAY

aides   One of the major indirect taxes of the absolute monarchy in
France, the *aides* originated as the feudal aids a vassal owed his suze-
rain, but from the fourteenth century developed as a state tax. By the
eighteenth century they included the *gros*, imposed on wine, beer and
cider; the *droit réglé*, also on beverages; the *annuel*, a tax on tavern-
keepers; the *droits rétablis* on meat as well as drinks; and the *trop bu*,
a tax on wine and other beverages over and above a fixed level for
personal consumption. They were criticized in the Enlightenment, attacked in the 1789 *cahiers* and the Constituent Assembly, and abolished in 1790. Like other indirect taxes, their imposition on circulation
and sale seemed an affront to economic freedom, while their policing
interfered with production. Geographical, social and institutional exemptions and privileges in their imposition were legion, and favoured
those most able to pay. Their collection formed part of the contract
of the FARMERS GENERAL, who usually, however, subcontracted the task.
In 1780, Necker removed it from the remit of the Farmers General,
placing it under direct state administration. In 1789 this highly unpopular tax brought the royal treasury about 50 million livres.

COLIN JONES

Aix-la-Chapelle, Treaty of (18 October 1748)   This brought the WAR
OF THE AUSTRIAN SUCCESSION to an end. In preliminary form it was signed
between France and the Maritime Powers on 30 April 1748 and formally on 18 October, when the signatories also included Austria, Prussia
and Spain. While there was a return to the undertakings of the Treaty
of Utrecht, there was also a general recognition of the PRAGMATIC
SANCTION and of Prussian retention of Silesia. This loss was accepted
by Maria Theresa only under pressure from Britain, and, reinforced by
her disgust at the failure of the Dutch to defend the Austrian Netherlands, now returned to her by France, the empress was disposed towards improved relations with France, for which a basis had been laid

during negotiations over Lorraine ten years before. With French aid, Kaunitz planned a resumption of war with Prussia, however militarily secure Frederick II might now seem to be. The makings of the DIPLOMATIC REVOLUTION were hence already present; but the peace had not touched on Anglo-French commercial issues, and all parties realized that future conflict was most likely to occur in this area. Spain was now territorially satisfied in northern Italy, but Britain's negotiated surrender of the ASIENTO removed only one contentious issue in Anglo-Spanish relations.

A. de Broglie, *La Paix d'Aix la Chapelle 1748* (Paris: C. Lévy, 1891).

D. D. ALDRIDGE

Alembert, Jean le Rond d' (1717–1783) French mathematician and philosopher. A foundling of aristocratic birth, d'Alembert was born in Paris and educated at a Jansenist college. After early devoting himself to law and medicine he resolved in his twenties to pursue mathematics, for which he had a precocious talent. In 1741 he was admitted a member of the Académie des Sciences. His first major work was the *Traité de Dynamique* (Treatise on Dynamics, 1743), distinguished for its contributions to the understanding of the problems of the equilibrium and motion of fluids. An exponent of calculus, he applied it in novel ways to many problems in mechanics and geophysics.

D'Alembert is best known today for his collaboration from 1747 with Diderot on the *Encyclopédie*, writing in 1754 perhaps the best-known entry, the 'Discours Preliminaire' (Preliminary Discourse). It mapped out an influential cognitive plan of the various disciplines, espoused a largely Baconian, empiricist epistemology and eloquently championed belief in the progress of knowledge and the role of knowledge in guaranteeing general human advancement. Though a radical himself (he wrote a work supporting the suppression of the Jesuits), he became in later years estranged from Diderot, repelled by his atheistic materialism and anxious over public criticism. He resigned from the *Encyclopédie* in 1758.

D'Alembert was courted by Frederick the Great and Catherine the Great, who wanted him to lead their respective scientific academies. He remained in France, however, forming a deep emotional attachment to Mademoiselle de Lespinasse (*d* 1776). In 1772 he became secretary to the Académie des Sciences. In his later years he was a leading figure in Parisian intellectual society.

T. Hankins, *Jean D'Alembert: Science and the Enlightenment* (Oxford: Clarendon, 1970).

ROY PORTER

Alexander I (1777–1825)   Emperor of Russia (1801–25).   The eldest son of emperor Paul and Maria Fedorovna, he was raised by his grandmother Catherine II, becoming emperor on 12 March 1801, following the assassination of Paul, whose deposition, if not murder, he approved. Historians sometimes divide Alexander's reign into 'liberal' and 'reactionary' halves. The first saw ministries reorganized and universities founded, but promise of political reform (M. Speranskii's draft constitution, 1809) and abolition of serfdom (law on free agriculturalists, 1803) was unfulfilled. There were territorial gains: Georgia (1801), Finland (1809), Bessarabia (1812), Azerbaijan (1813). Victory over Napoleon in 1812–14 brought Alexander's troops to Paris, but 'reaction' set in with the HOLY ALLIANCE (1815). Victory abroad was not to be followed by reform at home. The latter years, dominated by A. Arakcheev, saw tighter censorship and military colonies, but also the emancipation of the Baltic serfs (1816–19). After 1819 Alexander virtually abandoned government, adding substance to rumours that his death on 19 November 1825 was faked in order to allow him to retire as Fedor Kuzmich. His marriage to Louise of Baden (1793) was childless.

Alan Palmer, *Alexander I: Tsar of War and Peace* (London: Weidenfeld & Nicolson, 1974).

LINDSEY HUGHES

Alexis [Aleksei Petrovich] (1690–1718)   Tsarevich. The eldest son of PETER I of Russia, he was born to Peter's first wife, Evdokia. On returning from Europe in 1698 Peter banished Evdokia to a convent, whereupon she and Alexis became a rallying point for conservative opposition. Alexis was a disappointment to his father; he was educated but idle and ailing, and disliked military affairs. After the birth in 1715 of sons to Alexis's wife, Princess Charlotte of Wolfenbüttel, and to Peter's wife, Catherine, Peter threatened to disinherit Alexis, who agreed that he was unfit to rule. Forced to choose between entering a monastery and going to war, in October 1716 Alexis fled with his mistress Avfrosinia to Vienna. He returned to Russia in February 1718 on promise of forgiveness, but was excluded from the succession and interrogated under torture to reveal accomplices in an alleged treason plot. There was no plot, but widespread opposition to Peter, of which Alexis was a symbol rather than an active instigator, was revealed. Senate passed the death penalty on 24 June 1718, but on the 26th Alexis died, officially of apoplexy. Foul play is suspected.

Robert K. Massie, *Peter the Great* (London: Gollancz, 1981), chs 51–4.

LINDSEY HUGHES

Algarotti, Francesco (1712–1764)   Italian poet, art and music critic, dandy and man of letters. The son of a wealthy merchant, he became the darling of the European aristocracy. In 1733 he captured the attention of Émilie du Châtelet when he stayed with her and Voltaire to write *Il Neutonianismo per le dame* (Newtonianism for Ladies, 1739), which was translated into English by Elizabeth Carter. Leaving France for London, he became the paramour of Lady Mary Wortley Montagu who was ready to sacrifice her reputation and move to Italy with him. But Algarotti fled with Lord Baltimore to Russia, a trip recorded in his *Viaggi in Russia* (1760).

During his travels, Algarotti enchanted Prince Frederick of Prussia, and when Frederick assumed the throne in 1740, they became lovers and constant companions. A row forced Algarotti to reside with Augustus III of Saxony, in whose service he purchased work for the Dresden art gallery. But Frederick enticed him back in 1747 by conferring on him the title of count and an Order of Merit. Weary of being an itinerant courtier, Algarotti returned to Italy for good in 1752. His *Saggio sopra la pittura* and *Essay on Opera* appeared in 1763.

Vernon Lee, *Studies of the Eighteenth Century in Italy*, second edn (London: T. Fisher Unwin, 1907).

M. L. BENJAMIN

Algiers *see* BARBARY STATES.

America, Spanish   The eighteenth century was an epoch for Spanish America in which population grew rapidly, the export trades gathered new momentum and hitherto remote frontier provinces acquired the institutions of central government. Under the Habsburgs Spain's American empire had been based on the conscripted labour and tributes of the Indian peasantry of the Andean highlands and Meso-America, thus building on foundations laid down by the Inca and Aztec states. But under the Bourbon dynasty the mines and haciendas of northern Mexico, the plantations of CUBA and VENEZUELA, the goldfields of New Granada, the copper mines and wheat-fields of CHILE and the estancias of ARGENTINA all relied on new forms of labour recruitment, varying from African slaves to mestizos, free mulattos and poor Spaniards. By 1800 Spanish America had an estimated population of 14.5 million, and where 60 per cent of the inhabitants of MEXICO and PERU were counted as Indians the majority of the population of Chile and Argentina were of mixed or Spanish origin. Although silver-mining still constituted the most dynamic industry in the empire, its workers were now paid a wage rather than being coerced by state draft. In Cuba, Venezuela and New Granada tropical agriculture and gold production were sustained by importation of slaves from Africa.

The economic and demographic expansion was matched by new institutions when, in 1739, a viceroy was installed in Bogatá to govern New Granada and, in 1776, a vast new viceroyalty was established at Buenos Aires and a captain-general at Caracas. All these new centres of government attracted resources and were to emerge as capitals of their countries once independence came. During the 1780s most provinces were divided into intendancies which acted to focus regional identity. It was during the reign of Charles III that administrative innovation and economic expansion were most apparent as both transatlantic trade and crown revenue dramatically increased after the Free Trade Decree of 1778 which abolished the old convoy system in favour of a free flow of shipping between the chief ports of Spain and America.

Where Charles III and his ministers erred was in the expulsion of the Jesuits in 1767, for the Spanish American elite was alienated by this harsh measure. Indeed it was a Peruvian Jesuit in exile, Juan Viscardo Guzman, who issued the first call for independence. The very success of the Bourbon reforms, together with the growth in population and a deepening of patriotic sentiment, rendered the Spanish American elite increasingly impatient with imperial rule, an impatience that was exacerbated by their exclusion from high office in church and state. In 1808–10, encouraged by the example of the American and French Revolutions, they took advantage of Napoleon's invasion of Spain to seize power and proclaim independence, Buenos Aires and Caracas soon emerging as the most radical leaders of this movement.

See also SOUTH AND CENTRAL AMERICAN INDIANS.

Bethell, Leslie (ed.), *The Cambridge History of Latin America*, vols 1 and 2 (Cambridge: Cambridge University Press, 1984).

D. A. BRADING

American War of Independence (1775–1783) America's War of Independence, also known as the American Revolutionary War, began as a revolt against what Britain's thirteen North American Atlantic seaboard colonies perceived as England's oppressive policies; when it ended, a new nation existed – the United States of America. Long-brewing animosities between Britain and its colonies unified normally contentious American colonists following the Seven Years War (in America, the French and Indian War, 1754–63). By 1775 mutual intransigence and increasing turmoil had created a highly volatile situation; it exploded in April when British soldiers killed several militiamen at Lexington, Massachusetts. Armed citizens rose in popular rebellion, drove the British into Boston, and laid siege to it. Insurrection quickly spread throughout the colonies.

Governance and leadership devolved upon colonial representatives meeting in Philadelphia as the Continental Congress. Even as Congress fruitlessly petitioned George III, it established an army and named George WASHINGTON its commander. Without a recognized legitimate government, funds or a military force which could be called an army by even the loosest eighteenth-century definition, the Americans pitted themselves against a true superpower. Initial success soon gave way to wartime reality, and shortly after the Americans declared their independence (4 July 1776), the loss of New York forced Washington to rethink his strategy. He would protract the war: whenever opportunity presented itself, he would attack (the Battles of Trenton, Princeton, Germantown and Monmouth), but he would never risk his army's survival.

British strategy should have aggressively focused on destroying organized American resistance; instead, under Lord George Germain and less than dynamic commanders (Generals Howe, Clinton, Burgoyne and Cornwallis, and Admirals Parker, Howe, Rodney and Hood) British forces were badly misused in a series of uncoordinated campaigns. Fighting a European-style war on the vast expanse of North America where control of cities and seaports meant little, British troops, loyal Americans and German mercenaries won nearly every battle they fought; but once the British army left an area, it immediately reverted to rebel control. This was especially true in the American South where Nathanael Greene combined regulars and guerrillas in a highly innovative operational strategy. Moreover, by not destroying Washington's army early on the British let American amateurs become veterans and brought European (that is, French and Spanish) intervention closer.

Following the American victory at Saratoga in 1777 in which a British army surrendered, France signed a treaty of alliance (1778) with America. Spain soon did likewise, and a localized colonial rebellion turned into a world-wide war with fighting at Gibraltar, the West Indies, India and even the Philippines. Eager to restore a balance of power, other European powers joined in an Armed Neutrality, leaving Britain without a continental ally. Supporting armies around the globe, plus guarding home waters, stretched even British naval might thin. Off the Virginia Capes in September 1781, France achieved temporary tactical naval superiority. Washington's combined Franco-American army rapidly advanced and captured another British army at YORKTOWN. The war continued until 1783, but for all intents and purposes, American independence was ensured.

D. Higginbotham, *The American War of Independence* (Bloomington, Ind.: Indiana University Press, 1971).
Piers Mackesy, *The War for America* (Cambridge, Mass.: Harvard University Press, 1965).

JOHN MORGAN DEDERER

Amsterdam   For Amsterdam, the eighteenth century was a period of economic and cultural decline, especially compared to its golden age in the seventeenth century. Although it retained its position as the financial heart of Europe, with the Amsterdam Exchange Bank (1609) and DUTCH EAST INDIA COMPANY, the city's trade was in decline. It had a population of around 200,000 by 1796, and was the chief manufacturing city of an industrially weak country, with important shipbuilding, brewing, cotton, tobacco, sugar-refining, book-printing and diamond industries. Protestant and Jewish refugees, attracted by the city's religious tolerance, made important contributions to commerce, especially the manufacture of luxury products. Most of Amsterdam's fine churches and civic buildings, and great works of art and literature, date from the seventeenth century or earlier, and extensive building programmes that had been started in a more prosperous era largely came to a standstill in the eighteenth century. In 1787 Amsterdam was occupied by the Prussians. The French, welcomed as liberators by Amsterdam's 'patriots', who supported the French Revolution, entered the city in 1795. In 1806 Napoleon proclaimed the Netherlands a kingdom with Amsterdam as its capital, but in 1810 the country was incorporated into the French empire, and independence was not gained until 1813.

See also UNITED PROVINCES.

H. Brugmans, *Geschiedenis van Amsterdam* (History of Amsterdam), vol. 4: *1697–1795*, second edn (Utrecht: Het Spectrum, 1973).
P. Burke, *Venice and Amsterdam: A Study of Seventeenth-Century Elites* (London: Temple Smith, 1974).

HILARY MARLAND

analysis, mathematical   A method typical of the Enlightenment, analysis, or resolution into simple components, was understood by contemporary mathematicians to mean the reduction of mathematical problems to equations. It thus included algebra but also the powerful new techniques of calculus, independently developed, and then bitterly contested early in the century by Isaac Newton and Gottfried Leibniz.

Classical problems involved the analysis of curved and vibratory motions, which allowed spectacular progress to be make in MECHANICS. Consequently analysis received the most extensive development, culminating in the *Mécanique Analytique* (Analytical Mechanics, 1788) of JOSEPH LOUIS LAGRANGE. Lagrange and others even felt that they had taken mathematics to the limit.

The success of mathematical analysis confirmed for many *philosophes* that it represented the exclusively true, even natural, way of reasoning, to which Newtonian physics already did, and other fields would, conform. The abbé de Condillac concluded from his version of empiricism that thought and language were algebraic in form. Such excesses contributed to a turn away from mathematics later in the century. *See also* MATHEMATICS.

I. Grattan-Guinness, *The Development of the Foundations of Mathematical Analysis from Euler to Riemann* (Cambridge, Mass.: Harvard University Press, 1970).

STEPHEN PUMFREY

anatomy The study of anatomy in the eighteenth century reflected the Enlightenment curiosity and faith in progress surrounding the medical sciences. Progress in the identification and explanation of DISEASE, depended heavily on anatomical studies, especially dissection. Anatomy made possible the new science of pathology. Clinical observations at the patient's bedside and post-mortem dissection became closely correlated. Padua, Bologna and Leiden were leading centres in the development of the study of anatomy. Influential figures included Giovanni Battista Morgagni of Padua (1682–1771); the Dutchman BOERHAAVE; the French clinician Joseph Lieutaud (1703–80); Albrecht von Haller (1708–77), a Swiss pupil of Boerhaave; and Britain's William Hunter (1718–83). The subject flourished at Europe's leading universities and private anatomy schools. As part of a broader interest in natural phenomena, anatomy was closely linked to the study of physiology, BIOLOGY and NATURAL HISTORY, finding expression in museums of natural history and in sumptuously illustrated anatomical atlases. Dissections on the bodies of convicted murderers and the unclaimed poor attracted large audiences, although towards the end of the century body-snatching brought revulsion and popular protest against the medical profession. While progress made in anatomy was significant in modernizing the medical sciences, without the therapeutic tools to treat disease, it represented little in the way of progress for the eighteenth-century patient.

L. S. King, *The Medical World of the Eighteenth Century* (New York: Robert E. Krieger, 1958).

HILARY MARLAND

ancients and moderns The ancients versus moderns debate, or 'the battle of the books', was the late-seventeenth-century intelligentsia's evaluation of its status in respect of its intellectual and artistic heritage. In the Renaissance it had been argued that the thought and literature of the Greeks and Romans could not be surpassed: what had been first must be best. The task of humanism was to preserve, purify and emulate that birthright. (*See* CULT OF ANTIQUITY.) In their turn, the thinkers of the early Enlightenment had to assess their own standing not just in respect of antiquity but also in regard to the Renaissance. By 1700 there was a powerful sense of transformation in certain fields of human endeavour – in technology (printing), in exploration (the discovery of America) and in science. With this went a new sense of historical change. Modernity could no longer simply be assimilated to antiquity. Change was apparent. What was debatable was whether such change was progress or deterioration.

In the ensuing debate, some championed the ancients. William Temple's (1628–99) *Essay upon the Ancient and Modern Learning* (1690) maintained the superiority of Greek philosophy and science. But the savants increasingly argued, with William Wotton's (1666–1727) *Reflections upon Ancient and Modern Learning* (1694), that, in the sciences at least, the moderns had surpassed the ancients. Enthusiasts for modernity were fired by Francis Bacon's (1561–1626) conviction that the methods of natural science would launch a comprehensive 'advancement of learning', not just in the natural sciences but in all fields of human learning. There was far less agreement whether Graeco-Roman achievements in poetry, rhetoric, drama, moral philosophy and the visual arts had been surpassed. One strand of Enlightenment aesthetics maintained that, because the arts were necessarily culture-bound, the moderns should not emulate the ancients but should pioneer distinctive art forms of their own, for example prose fiction.

R. F. Jones, *Ancients and Moderns: A Study of the Background of the Battle of the Books* (St Louis: Washington University Press, 1936).
Joseph Levine, *The Battle of the Books: History and Literature in the Augustan Age* (Ithaca NY: Cornell University Press, 1991).

ROY PORTER

Anglicanism   The period between the Toleration Act of 1689 and the inception of the Oxford Movement in 1833 has traditionally been castigated as the bleakest era in the history of the Church of England. Deprived of the spiritual and intellectual integrity of the Nonjurors, the Church of England has been seen as staffed by politically acquiescent bishops and by clergy who had little sense of their pastoral responsibilities. Historical attention has thus been more directed to those groups, such as the Methodists and evangelicals, who seemed to stand outside the Anglican establishment. Recent research has modified many of these assumptions. A number of outstanding bishops, such as Edmund Gibson (1669–1748) and Thomas Secker (1693–1768), have been shown to stand against the government when the interests of the church were at stake, and the pastoral mission of the parish clergy has been reassessed. High Church sentiments continued, especially in the writings of George Horne (1730–92) and William Jones

(1726–1800). Within Anglicanism it is possible to detect opposing intellectual tendencies, though these are by no means as clearly defined as the church parties which developed in the nineteenth century. Counter to the High Church spirit existed a 'latitudinarian' tradition, whose main exponents included Samuel Clarke (1675–1729) and Benjamin Hoadly (1676–1761).

J. C. D. Clark, *English Society, 1688–1832: Ideology, Social Structure and Political Practice during the Ancien Regime* (Cambridge: Cambridge University Press, 1985).
N. Sykes, *Church and State in England in the Eighteenth Century* (Cambridge: Cambridge University Press, 1934).

JEREMY GREGORY

Anna (1693–1740)   Empress of Russia (1730–40). She was born to Ivan V (1666–96), who was co-tsar with PETER I, and Praskovia Saltykova. In 1710 she married Duke Friedrich Wilhelm of Courland (*d* 1711). When PETER II died in January 1730, the Supreme Privy Council, headed by the Dolgorukiis and Golitsyns, invited Anna to rule and to sign a list of conditions limiting the sovereign's power, but opponents of oligarchy persuaded her to repudiate the document. She responded by abolishing the council, and ruled as an autocrat. Historians have dubbed her reign a reign of terror. It was dominated by Germans, notably Ernst Bühren (1690–1772), and the Secret Investigations Chancellery, but revisionists see continuity and progress, for example in provincial administration, and economic and foreign affairs. The cabinet replaced the supreme privy council. Poland was subordinated during the War of the Polish Succession (1733–5), and Azov regained in the Russo-Turkish War (1735–9). The nobility obtained reductions in state service (1736), repeal of the Entail Law (1731), creation of the elite Cadet Academy (1731) and concessions on serf-owning. Anna designated as her successor the infant Ivan, son of her niece Anna of Brunswick.

Mina Curtiss, *A Forgotten Empress: Anna Ivanovna and her Era* (New York: Ungar, 1974).

LINDSEY HUGHES

Anne (1665–1714)   Queen of Great Britain and Ireland (1702–14). She was the second daughter of James, duke of York and later James II (1633–1701), and his first wife, Anne Hyde (1637–71). Like her elder sister Mary II (1662–94), Anne was brought up in the Protestant faith. In 1683 she married Prince George of Denmark (1653–1708), a colourless but conjugally dependable husband. He fathered seventeen children only one of whom survived infancy. The couple's closest associates were John and Sarah Churchill (*see* MARLBOROUGH), but an intimate friendship with Sarah ended in the years after Anne's accession. She was temperamentally unfitted to moderate the political factionalism which marked her reign, but stood her ground in her preferences and aversions, and could never be underestimated. She held to the Hanoverian succession established by the Act of Settlement (1701) against the dynastic right of her Catholic half-brother James Francis Edward Stuart; yet her instinctive Toryism, if not statesmanship, made her resist all moves to give the house of Hanover a high-profile representation in England (during her reign). Under Anne, the parliaments of England and Scotland were united in 1707.

E. R. Gregg, *Queen Anne* (London: Routledge & Kegan Paul, 1982).

D. D. ALDRIDGE

Anson, George (1697–1762) English naval commander. An ambitious, conscientious and unemotional man, he acquired administrative control of the British Royal Navy by a combination of patronage and success in naval warfare. He started as a teenage midshipman, and for nearly thirty years his career was one of solid but undistinguished active service at home and overseas. He then led a small, poorly equipped squadron on a five-year voyage around the world, returning an immensely rich national hero after capturing and looting a Spanish ship in 1743. The account of his journey became a best-seller, and he was promoted and later made a peer after victory in a sea battle against the French in 1747. The following year, he gained further wealth and influence by marrying Elizabeth Yorke, the lord chancellor's daughter, and in 1751 his role as acting head of the Admiralty was officially ratified, a post he held intermittently until his death. Although strongly criticized for a humiliating British defeat in the Mediterranean in 1756, he was respected for effecting major reforms in naval techniques, codes of warfare, Admiralty and dockyard administration and ship construction.

P. Brock, 'Anson and his Importance as a Naval Reformer', *Naval Review*, 17 (1929), 497–528.

PATRICIA FARA

anthropology The science of man, or of mankind, embracing human physiology and psychology, has its roots in ancient Greek philosophy, and especially in Aristotle (384–322 BC). The idea of the NOBLE SAVAGE and interest in primitivism also have pedigrees reaching far into the past. Thus the eighteenth century did not witness the rise of an entirely novel discipline or even a new approach to a very old subject. Moreover, the word 'anthropology' (*anthropologie*) was used mostly in the sense in which 'anthropomorphism' is understood today, that is, to refer to the tendency to attribute human properties and passions to God. 'Anthropology' was also used to refer to the study of anatomy, and was used in the titles of several eighteenth-century treatises on the subject.

Having said this, the science of man flourished during the Enlightenment, in particular what has become known as 'philosophical anthropology', that is, the study of the nature of man and of the relation between human physiology and psychology. In this area, the work of men such as Maupertius, Condillac, Diderot, David Hume, Herder and Kant was of considerable importance. They attempted, in their different ways, to place the science of man on a sound empirical basis and hence to pursue the goals of their seventeenth-century predecessors, especially John Locke. Important though this was in itself, they achieved a great deal more than furthering knowledge about the nature of man and woman abstracted from their cultural setting, for the Enlightenment continued to cultivate an age-old European interest in the Other and married this interest to a historical analysis of its own culture. The various peoples of the world were increasingly seen as belonging to different stages of what was a single civilization, while observations of their respective modes of living were increasingly conceived as enhancing understanding of human nature: to know the mores and beliefs of American Indians was to learn about man and woman in general. It was also seen as providing an insight into the lives of the Europeans either in, or shortly after, the stage of human history referred to as 'the state of nature'.

Understanding human nature involved not only the recording and classifying of the manners of all nations, but also examining those animals which seemed closest to the human species (*see* WILD MEN), the study of languages, and other comparative analyses, not least that of MYTH. The science of man was an ambitious enterprise in the eighteenth century. Many of its aspirations were embodied in the Buffon's great *Histoire Naturelle*.

Sylvana Tomaselli, 'Reflections on the History of the Science of Woman', *History of Science*, 29 (1991), 185–205.
Robert Wokler, 'Perfectible Apes in Decadent Cultures: Rousseau's Anthropology Revisited', in 'Rousseau for our Time', *Daedalus*, 107 (3) (summer 1978), 107–34.
Robert Wokler, 'Anthropology and Conjectural History in the Enlightenment', in Christopher Fox, Roy Porter and Robert Wokler (eds), *Inventing Human Science* (Berkeley, Calif.: University of California Press, 1994).

SYLVANA TOMASELLI

anticlericalism While it did not necessarily imply hostility to religion itself, anticlericalism involved antipathy towards its professional votaries, their supposed wealth and their influence over the population via education and the rites of passage. It should be distinguished from the policies of rulers of national states who, while sometimes seeking to limit the independence of their clergy, none the less sustained (and were sustained by) an established church. Because of the close links between monarchy and church throughout Europe, many historians have identified anticlericalism with republicanism. This had not invariably been so: Voltaire in the *Henriade* (1722) combined monarchism with anticlericalism, depicting monks as fanatical regicides. But later the connection was generally valid: anticlericalism permeated the French Enlightenment and informed many of the more radical articles in the *Encyclopédie*. When intellectual anticlericalism joined certain popular grievances against the privileges of the clergy in the early years of the French Revolution, the Gallican Church suffered heavily (*see* GALLICANISM). Anticlericalism never reached such extremes elsewhere, but, with hindsight, it may be regarded as an important component of nineteenth-century European liberalism.

William Doyle, *The Old European Order, 1660–1800* (Oxford: Oxford University Press, 1978), chs 7–9, 14–15.

G. M. DITCHFIELD

antiquity, cult of   The veneration of antiquity, understood as the literature, arts and culture of the Graeco-Roman world, formed the basis of the earliest humanism and the Renaissance in early modern Europe. Arising from this, classical ideals were set as models for emulation, notably in architecture and the visual arts, while literature and abstract thought were infused with the philosophical systems of Greece and Rome: new historical perspectives were thus opened up, replacing the medieval world-picture. Classical manuscripts were collected and printed and the principles of textual criticism established. The study of Greek and Latin was thus entrenched as the essential of polite learning in schools and universities through the eighteenth and into the last century. From 1763 to 1768 Winckelmann established similarly revered canons of art criticism.

Two views arose in the seventeenth century, the pessimistic attitude of the ancients, for whom classical antiquity could be emulated but not outdone, as against the optimistic and soon successful moderns who, supported by the Baconian scientific tradition and a belief in the perfectibility of man, used antiquity as a basis on which to build a self-conscious Enlightenment. (*See* ANCIENTS AND MODERNS.)

A. Momigliano, *Studies in Historiography* (London, 1956), pp. 1–39.

STUART PIGGOTT

archaeology   The discipline of interpreting the past from the evidence of material culture rather than from documents was a nineteenth-century phenomenon which replaced early antiquarianism. Digging for antiquities and works of art began at HERCULANEUM (1736) and POMPEII (1748). Greek vases looted from Etruscan tombs were collected and prized; Egyptian antiquities were dug for from the time of Napoleon's expedition (1798), and Mesopotamian antiquities from the 1840s. Chance finds in England and Scandinavia were attributed to prehistory. Excavation was never separate from treasure-hunting and plundering.

In France the students of antiquity from de Peiresc (1580–1637) to de Caylus (1692–1765) were despised as 'les Érudits' by *philosophes* like Diderot, d'Alembert and the *Encyclopédie* Enlightenment circle of the eighteenth century. The Society of Dilettanti, founded in 1732, sponsored the publication of Stuart and Revett from 1762 on Greek architecture.

Modern archaeology began in association with geology in the mid nineteenth century, and there was controlled excavation by the end of the century.

G. Daniel, *A Short History of Archaeology* (London: Thames & Hudson, 1981).

STUART PIGGOTT

architecture   Seventeenth-century Roman BAROQUE architecture continued to challenge both its admirers and detractors into the eighteenth century. Some Britons thought that the Italians had lost their way, and the world's categorical revolt against the baroque in fact began with PALLADIANISM, which advocated a return to the rationalism of the Italian Renaissance. Palladianism anticipated neoclassicism, not least in this respect: amid the ferment of impulses from archaeology, picturesque aesthetics and nationalism operating on architecture by 1800, the classicism of sixteenth-century Italy was still the most important single influence on its style.

Elsewhere after 1700, French classicism quietly continued on its influential course. The authority of *le bon goût* was respected everywhere except in Britain, but no one could resist the stylish extrapolation of the Roman baroque that was the ROCOCO, largely a style of interior design. Many duchies and kingdoms in central and northern Europe got their own editions of Versailles. Catholic central Europe, which in some ways had moved straight from the Gothic into the baroque, saw the latter's final flowering in palace-monasteries sensational for the intensity and complexity of their planning and ornament.

Around 1750, such strong regional flavours became diluted: NEO-CLASSICISM was the first universal style. Cosmopolitanism was encouraged by developments in architectural education and practice; by increasingly sophisticated theoretical (and thus easily transported) constructions of architecture's place in society; and by the art's increasing implication in wider developments that embraced the entire urbanizing Western world.

The French Académie Royale d'Architecture was founded in 1672. The example was followed by European regents concerned that lengthy, expensive and prestigious building enterprises should be conducted by good citizens, and not visiting foreigners. Training often included study abroad, and the promise of a civil service job back at home. French, German and Scandinavian departments managing civil construction gained more authority around 1800, when their functions extended to the identification of a style which offended neither national aspiration nor universal classical principle, and which was flexible enough to be applied to a wide variety of building types. British architects, who had neither academy nor ministry, also embarked on Grand Tours that allowed them to survey the exemplars, and to meet potential clients in relatively informal circumstances. Student architects of many nations became friends in Paris and Rome.

The notion of architecture as a cultural sign became more emphatic, and gained ramifications. The traditional formulation, that architecture reflects the moral and political conditions of its society, widened to influence the investigation of non-Western and non-classical architecture: that of the Iroquois and the Chinese, the ancient Jews and the Egyptians. One corollary was the investment of architecture with the possibility of change, and decline; another was that architecture could shape society in turn. The eighteenth century's version of this idea, which had arrived to stay, culminated with Claude Nicolas Ledoux (1736–1806), whose L'Architecture considérée sous le rapport de l'art, des mœurs et de la législation (Architecture in the Light of Art, Custom and Legislation) of 1804 was also an interesting example of another increasingly typical phenomenon, the architect's publication of his own work.

A proliferation of building types accompanied the development of such important social institutions as the public library and museum, the municipal theatre – the great size of some theatres, like Milan's La Scala (1776–8), in turn demanded changes in acting and singing styles – and national debts: it was realized in the 1760s that Britain's would be permanent, and the expansion of the Bank of England building then began.

Purpose-built structures also became indispensable to reform projects, notably within penology and hospital medicine. Language more explicitly functionalist than neoclassical bowed to reason, and architects began to appeal to 'nature' in response to increasingly detailed briefs, and in defence of their prerogatives against lay reformers like John Howard (1726–90), who evaluated prisons and hospitals by their quantifiable effects and criticized 'ornament', which did not strictly answer need. The perfect building was conceivable, or so scientists claimed during discussions about the replacement of the Hôtel-Dieu hospital in Paris after 1772: the 'pavilion' ward-plan was the solution to a universal hygienic problem, and as such could be applied any-where. Although sixty years passed before this began to happen, the conclusion marks one of the most decisive breaks with architectural convention in a century that saw so many.

See also TOWN PLANNING.

Joseph Rykwert, *The First Moderns: The Architects of the Eighteenth Century* (Cambridge, Mass.: MIT, 1980).
John Summerson, *The Architecture of the Eighteenth Century* (London: Thames & Hudson, 1986).

CHRISTINE STEVENSON

Argenson, René Louis de Voyer marquis d' (1694–1757)   French states-man. He was one of the most interesting political and literary figures of the reign of Louis XV. The son of Louis XIV's great police minister, he was a sexual libertine turned state servant: he was intendant of Hainaut and Cambrésis (1721–5), then served as minister of foreign affairs from 1744 to 1747 when France was engaged in the War of the Austrian Succession. Underestimating Frederick II of Prussia and un-dermined by court intrigue, his foreign policy strategy was a failure, and on his dismissal he returned to literary pursuits which had long interested him. He was patron of the Club de l'Entresol, an informal literary coterie attended by *philosophes* including Voltaire, who read in manuscript d'Argenson's *Considérations sur le gouvernement de la France* (Considerations on the Government of France, 1764), which like all his writings was published posthumously. His *Journal et mémoires* (Journal and Memoirs), an important source for the politi-cal history of the reign of Louis XV, was not published until the nineteenth century. In his writings he showed himself a daring radical and egalitarian thinker and an acerbic critic of social injustice, who was temperamentally more of a *philosophe* than a politician.

COLIN JONES

Argentina   In the early eighteenth century Argentina (Río de la Plata) was one of Spain's poorest colonies, but by 1810 it had become one of its most flourishing. This transformation was promoted by the fa-mous Bourbon reforms ordered by Madrid (1776–1800) and by the growing opportunities for trade and agriculture, especially cattle-raising, grasped by Buenos Aires' increasingly dominant mercantile and ranching elites. The establishment of the viceroyalty of Río de la Plata (present-day Argentina, Uruguay, Paraguay and Bolivia) in 1776 and the Free Trade Decree (1778) were milestones of military, administrative and economic reform ecouraging rapid commercial expansion. Other reforms promoted the slave trade and transferred the efficient and exploitive Jesuit missions of Guaraní Indians to secular hands. By 1810 Río de la Plata was a sophisticated, prosperous colony with two universities and a lively press. Spanish and creole elites dominated Indian, mestizo, black and mulatto labour in an economy ever more closely tied to Britain and subjected to British interests. In 1810, partly to protect those ties, merchant leaders and intellectuals rebelled against Spanish authority and in 1816 declared independence.

See also SPANISH AMERICA.

T. Halperin Donghi, *Politics, Economics, and Society in Argentina in the Revolutionary Period* (Cambridge: Cambridge University Press, 1975).

CHARLES C. NOEL

Arianism The term 'Arianism' derives from a fourth-century 'heresy' which held that Christ occupied a subordinate, but important, position in a fundamentally hierarchical view of the Trinity. Although it is often regarded – and sometimes was – a staging post for those moving from orthodoxy to Socinianism (an outright denial of Christ's divinity and hence the atonement), Arianism is an intellectual tradition in its own right. It staged a revival in the British Isles in the first half of the eighteenth century, largely through the influence of the Dissenting academies and the Scottish universities. Alleged Arian infiltration of Presbyterianism in the south-west of England led directly to the Salter's Hall conference in London in 1719.

Unorthodox views of the Trinity in the eighteenth century naturally created problems of ecclesiastical discipline and were often associated with a more rational and potentially radical view of Christianity and its relation to the state. Although Arianism served as a counterpoise to more extreme deistic positions in the early part of the century, it underpinned the natural RIGHTS theories of Richard Price and others in the age of the American and French Revolutions.

M. R. Watts, *The Dissenters from the Reformation to the French Revolution* (Oxford: Clarendon, 1978).

DAVID HEMPTON

aristocracy The NOBILITY in action as a ruling or predominant group was known as the aristocracy; impoverished nobles, lacking influence or connections, were only marginal members of the aristocracy.

Aristocratic power rested on owning land, but not only large agricultural estates (*see* LANDOWNERSHIP): urban aristocracies as in Italy could be powerful, and maintained their caste exclusiveness successfully over the eighteenth century (*see* URBAN PATRICIAN FAMILIES). In Milan the ancient nobility which had clear political hegemony kept strictly aloof from trade and other inferior professions. Some sixty of the oldest and wealthiest families, with extensive connections, exercised power as an elite within the region's aristocracy. The eighteenth century did not see the rise of the bourgeoisie and the end of feudalism. Instead, the aristocracy proved highly resilient in their hold on both power and wealth, and very adaptable in responding to new economic opportunities. Political gains made by merchants or industrialists at the expense of landowners were comparatively small. It was rare to see a successfully entrenched aristocracy ousted, as happened with the change of monarchy in Spain after 1700. During the Spanish Succession war the new Bourbon regime faced repeated disloyalty from the Castilian aristocracy who had controlled the country under the Habsburgs. They were therefore purged from high office, and a more streamlined government system on the French model imposed.

In most countries the aristocracy proved to have a firm grip on their wealth and privileges (*see* PRIVILEGE). Theirs was a world in which the norm was monarchical government, which depended in turn on the noble elite for every kind of military and administrative support (*see* ADMINISTRATION). In eastern Europe particularly, the strength of the aristocracy was the major constraint on centralization and reform. To rule large and economically backward countries involved securing the allegiance of provincial nobles and maintaining their privileges, a constraint evident also in contemporary China. The Manchu nobles who took over Han China in the mid seventeenth century were careful to woo the former Han aristocratic elite. By the early eighteenth century the Manchu Ch'ing dynasty gained the support of the cultivated and powerful lower Yangtze aristocracy, cultivating them by promoting traditional Chinese government ideals, by imperial visits and special privileges. To counteract the centrifugal influence of such powerful hereditary groups, princes of the imperial blood were placed in key bureaucratic positions. There as in Russia, however, the main way of securing aristocratic service was giving generous privileges and powers, and espousing the ideals of the noble group.

Self-perpetuating noble hierarchies tended to block the rise of new groups, and to guard against undue dilution of the caste by new wealth. In Italy nobles usually took up office at the highest state level as officials and magistrates, handing on their offices on death or retirement to members of their family. Town administrations were everywhere controlled by small, wealthy and powerful noble oligarchies. In

France the old noble families (of the 'sword' as opposed to the 'robe') opposed the entry into military service of the newer robe nobility. Wedded to military greatness as a means of preserving their status and power, they formed a pressure group close to the monarchy urging an aggressive foreign policy and continued military spending, cloaked in the persuasive language of glory and prestige. (*See* NOBLESSE D'ÉPÉE, NOBLESSE DE ROBE.) In Britain the peerage dominated parliament, the armed forces and regional life throughout the century, while their economic power grew as many large estates added mineral and industrial wealth to traditional rents. The British aristocracy made up perhaps 0.7 per cent of the population, a little lower than the roughly 1 per cent of France, a figure common in western Europe. Elsewhere the figure could be much higher, 8 to 9 per cent. In Sweden, Hungary and Poland this numerous aristocracy influenced and weakened the structures of politics, yet in Tuscany and Spain effective government could be introduced despite such sizeable vested interests. In an edict of 1773 Charles III of Spain ordered the poorest group of nobles by birth, the hidalgos, to work, and though the leading nobility still flourished within the Spanish state by the end of the century, the aristocracy shrank to around 4 per cent of the population.

Nowhere was the aristocracy simply a homogeneous class, as great variations in wealth and property were common. In Russia the usual measure of wealth was the ownership of serfs, the degree of which varied greatly among the 50,000 or so aristocrats in the mid eighteenth century. In 1762 1 per cent of landowners owned more than a thousand 'souls', while 82 per cent of the nobles owned fewer than 100 serfs. In a sense, all nobles themselves were enserfed to the state after the changes introduced by Peter the Great and codified in the 1722 Table of Ranks. Service to the state was rigidly enforced as the basis of the privileges of the aristocracy, and noble children spent a closely regulated life of training and state duties. After a 1762 decree of Peter III, nobles were no longer strictly bound to serve. Most continued to do so, since the patronage of the autocracy was essential to their wealth and power, but the change introduced a freer atmosphere of independence and of cultural growth. French-speaking Russian aristocrats became more like their counterparts in western Europe, sharing their literature and concerns, even though their economy and social organization were more basic. Land brought in lesser returns in eastern Europe than in the more advanced and specialized agricultural economies of the west. Everywhere, though, the basis of the aristocratic life was the wealth – however relative – that came from land, with its associated advantages of seigneurial jurisdiction (*see* SEIGNEURIALISM), exemptions from taxation and privileged access to government places and rewards. The aristocracies of Europe maintained and developed those advantages, and the political power that accompanied them.

J. M. Black, *Eighteenth Century Europe 1700–1789* (London: Macmillan, 1990).

J. Cannon, *Aristocratic Century: The Peerage of Eighteenth Century England* (Cambridge: Cambridge University Press, 1984).

G. Chaussinand-Nogaret, *The French Nobility in the Eighteenth Century* (Cambridge: Cambridge University Press, 1985).

PHILIP WOODFINE

Arkwright, Sir **Richard** (1732–1792)   English industrialist, inventor of the water frame for spinning cotton. The son of a Preston (Lancashire) tailor, he became a barber. In 1769 he patented the water frame, in which mechanically driven rollers rotating at differential speeds drew out cotton fibres and a flyer inserted twist into the yarn. Partners in the hosiery trade financed his first mills at Nottingham and Cromford, Derbyshire; a second patent in 1775 covered preparatory machinery. His prosecution of unauthorized users prompted a counter-action in 1785, in which his title to the inventions was disputed and his patents revoked – hurting his pride more than his pocket.

An archetypal entrepreneur, he pioneered the factory system, devising an orderly flow of processes through the mill, and paternalistically moulding his workforce through discipline tempered by incentives. With unremitting attention to business, he accumulated great wealth from interests in a dozen spinning-mills in northern England and Scotland, and diversified into government stock and land. A Derbyshire mansion (Willersley Castle), a fashionable London house, a knighthood in 1786 and the office of high sheriff of Derbyshire in 1787 showed that the Arkwrights had arrived.

R. S. Fitton, *The Arkwrights: Spinners of Fortune* (Manchester: Manchester University Press, 1989).

CHRISTINE MACLEOD

Armed Neutrality   The term 'Armed Neutrality' was used to describe a state of readiness for war, and of thinly disguised enmity to Britain, on the part of several European states. The hostility of the Baltic powers to Britain's naval policy first showed itself during the SEVEN YEARS WAR. During the AMERICAN WAR OF INDEPENDENCE Catherine II of Russia was able to organize a league of neutral states, all of whom had become irritated by Britain's over-assertive notion of its rights on the high seas. The Dutch, the chief partners of Russia, suffered for their policy and lost one of their trading stations in Ceylon when peace was signed in 1783. Russian resentment at Britain's insistence on the right

of searching neutral vessels at sea broke out again in the third Armed
Neutrality of 1800, between Russia, Denmark, Sweden and Prussia,
which attempted to close the Baltic to Britain. It came at a dangerous
time for Britain at war with revolutionary France, but the death of the
Anglophobe Paul 1 (1754–1801) of Russia in March 1801 and Nelson's victory at Copenhagen in April, which destroyed the Danish
fleet, brought to an end the last Armed Neutrality.

D. B. Horn, *Great Britain and Europe in the Eighteenth Century* (Oxford:
   Clarendon, 1967).

TONY HAYTER

armies The major international weapon and deterrent of the period,
armies, with their massed forces and simple, even crude, weaponry
were the main arbiter of most diplomatic disputes. As such, they were
central to the operation of the great powers of the eighteenth century,
France, Austria, Prussia, Russia and Great Britain. Powerful regular
armies went hand in hand with the development of more centralized
states, with improved tax-gathering powers, in China as in Europe.
Under the Manchu Ch'ing dynasty, the 'banner armies' of the Chinese
feudal lords were brought increasingly under central control, and stationed in Peking and other strategic points, along with an imperial
'Army of the Green Standard' deployed as a policing force. In self-
contained China the army was largely directed at controlling domestic
instability, whereas in Europe armies mainly served foreign policies.
When in the late seventeenth century the dominant European power,
France, increased the size of its armed forces to around 200,000, other
powers had little option but to follow suit, and large armies became
the norm for the countries that were in the 'big league' or, like Prussia,
intended to be so. Armies were essential also to the security, and
sometimes the economy, of lesser powers, which raised mercenary
forces. Some 10 per cent of the men of HESSE-KASSEL usually served in
the army, almost always for foreign hire. Great states regularly made
up their strength with mercenary regiments, even when in practice
some hired soldiers such as the hapless press-ganged forces of
WÜRTTEMBERG proved reluctant and inefficient. Foreign soldiers usually
made up around 10 per cent of the French army in peacetime, a figure
that doubled during wars, while Britain often deployed armies in
Continental warfare, under half of which were made up of British units.
   Some technological changes had taken place by the early eighteenth
century, including the shift from pike formations to the bayonet, but
the main change was a limited standardization in weapons, clothing
and drills. The basic infantry weapon was the flintlock musket, and the
infantry formed the majority of most armies. Armies used single-shot

muskets with a cumbersome reloading drill, and formed up in massed ranks, making no attempt to use cover or to fire at selected targets. Throughout the eighteenth century most battles involved encounters at close range, to maximize the efficiency of smooth-bored barrels often ovalled by the zealous use of the ramrod, and accuracy limited by the flight of the projectiles, roughly cast lead spheres. The training of infantrymen stressed not marksmanship but the drill and discipline needed to come to close quarters and stay there amid the smoke and chaos. In such armies three things were really important: numbers, training and morale.

Numbers varied greatly between times of peace and war, although sizeable wars were so frequent that only thirty-four years of the century were without one, and the longest period of European peace lasted only twelve years. Army sizes were reduced quickly after wars, as regiments were expensive to keep up and supply, so much so that even during wars there was little campaigning in the winter months. Forage for horses, and bread and meat for troops, were critical limitations to the size of an army, and the distances that it could travel. There were practical limits too to the numbers that could be deployed in the field, even after the watershed of the Seven Years War, which saw general improvements in drill and tactics, and a shift to greater use of ARTILLERY. Marshal Saxe led into battle around 120,000 troops at Laffeldt (1747) against the allied army of around 90,000, yet large numbers on both sides were ineffectively or little used. Frederick the Great never commanded more men in the field than the 65,000 he had at Prague (1757), when he almost completely lost control of their movements. Around 50,000 was seen by most commanders as the largest practicable field army. Even so, national armies were sizeable. Austria-Hungary had around 100,000 in the first half of the eighteenth century, rising to 200,000 in the second half. This was mirrored by the rival Prussians, whose army rose from some 80,000 when Frederick the Great began his reign in 1740 to around 190,000 by the time of his death in 1786. French forces rose from 250,000 in 1710 to 330,000 during the Seven Years War, falling again to 156,000 by 1789. Russia's army size was very similar to that of France up to the 1760s, but continued to rise to around 500,000 by 1789. Under Potemkin's reforms it improved as well as grew, gaining sensible dress and hair regulations and comfortable clothing, and also taking a smaller percentage of national expenditure: around 28 per cent in 1796 compared with 46 per cent in 1763. The usual size of the British army was under 80,000, reaching 100,000 only during the American War of Independence, as Britain relied much more on naval power, while the Spanish army varied between around 30,000 and 50,000, augmented also by a distinct improvement in naval power and efficiency.

Life, and life expectation, in the army was so poor that unforced volunteering could never fill all the necessary places, and various kinds of compulsion were used. The best method of raising armies in the century was the cantonal system, which originated in Sweden, was brought to perfection in Prussia, and later adopted in Austria-Hungary, Italy and the Netherlands, with a similar system of recruit levies in Russia. Each canton provided its quota of recruits who received two years of military training, serving thereafter each year only during the campaigning season. For the rest of the year, the soldiers could support themselves in their normal work. Morale and *esprit de corps* were higher under this essentially territorial system, regiments consisting largely of men from the same areas. None the less, desertion rates were always high and throughout the century life in every army was harsh, uncomfortable and demanding.

See also BARRACKS, WARFARE.

M. S. Anderson, *War and Society in Europe of the Old Régime, 1618–1789* (Leicester: Leicester University Press, 1988).

J. M. Black, *A Military Revolution? Military Change and European Society 1550–1800* (London: Macmillan, 1990).

J. Childs, *Armies and Warfare in Europe 1648–1789* (Manchester: Manchester University Press, 1982).

PHILIP WOODFINE

art academies *see* academies of art.

artillery There were two types of artillery – siege and field. The former, heavy cannon and mortars, demolished fortifications and travelled in a separate train while the latter, light cannon and howitzers, were employed in battle. Cannon fired solid shot, grape and canister while mortars and howitzers fired explosive shells. In 1759 the Prussians introduced horse artillery for increased mobility on the battlefield. All armies adopted these 'galloper guns' and most distributed two or three very light pieces to each battalion to serve as infantry guns. Artillery underwent some technical improvements during the eighteenth century: chambered breeches reduced barrel weight; the Holtzmann elevating wedge (1747) was copied all over Europe; and caisson limbers were introduced in Prussia in 1742. J. B. Vaquette de Gribeauval standardized and lightened the French artillery, and similar work was carried out in Austria by Prince Joseph Liechtenstein (1696–1772) and in Russia by Peter Shuvalov (1710–62). In battle, the field guns engaged in counter-battery fire before supporting infantry attacks or covering weak points in the line, although Frederick the Great used mass artillery fire against the Austrian infantry at Leuthen in 1757.

Concentrated mass artillery fire against opposing infantry and cavalry on the Napoleonic model was advocated by Jacques Guibert.

See also ARMIES, WARFARE.

I. V. Hogg, *A History of Artillery* (London: Hamlyn, 1974).

JOHN CHILDS

artisans Eighteenth-century manufactures, throughout Europe, were characterized by small-scale plant depending on personal labour power possessed of traditional craft skills. Before the emergence of the factory system in the industrial revolution, artisans thus comprised the backbone of the workforce in manufacturing, in town and country alike: tailors, cobblers, leather-workers, joiners and carpenters, metalworkers, coopers and so forth. An artisan had typically undergone a lengthy training, often a formal apprenticeship. He would in time become a journeyman, hoping to turn into a master in his own right, employing a handful of artisans and apprentices. Artisans were noted for a fierce sense of trade loyalty and personal independence. Often autodidacts with a high degree of literacy, they were commonly politically radical, and were often involved in protests and riots, defending their craft rights or demonstrating against unpopular governments – as for example in the Wilkite Riots in London in the 1760s. Artisans constituted the so-called 'aristocracy of labour' so prominent in nineteenth-century trade union movements, though the development of machine technology gradually undermined the industrial muscle power of skilled artisans in many occupations, sometimes leading to Luddite resistance.

See also DOMESTIC INDUSTRY, FACTORIES.

G. A. Williams, *Artisans and Sans-culottes: Popular Movements in France and Britain during the French Revolution* (London: Edward Arnold, 1968).

ROY PORTER

Asiento The Asiento de Negros was the exclusive concession to export slaves to the Spanish colonies in the New World (*see* SLAVE TRADE): in theory, since the 1494 Treaty of Tordesillas, it had been a Spanish monopoly. The Asiento company alone was allowed to trade directly with Spanish possessions without first being registered and taxed at Seville. From 1701 to 1703 this concession was held by France. The Asiento Treaty of 1713, which was part of the TREATY OF UTRECHT, gave the Asiento to the British SOUTH SEA COMPANY. Unprecedentedly, the Treaty allowed the company to send one (in practice refillable) 500 ton ship each year to the annual fairs at which the bulk of colonial trade was supposed to be transacted. Trading levels, though, were never high enough to justify the speculation that caused the 1720

South Sea Bubble. So much contraband trade went on from the British Caribbean and American colonies that it was not profitable for Spain to hold regular fairs: only seven were held from 1713 to 1739. The Asiento and annual ship concession focused attention, however, on the illicit trade to the Spanish Indies, and caused clashes and inflamed relations, leading to the outbreak of actual Anglo-Spanish war in 1739.

G. J. Walker, *Spanish Politics and Imperial Trade, 1700–1789* (London: Macmillan, 1979).

PHILIP WOODFINE

assemblies Public assemblies in eighteenth-century Europe can be broadly defined under four categories, although they are all overlapping: the public assembly, such as the village meeting; the official, representative assembly, such as the English parliament, the French provincial estates and the provincial diets of central Europe; the corporate assembly, such as the French *parlements*, the various assemblies of notables summoned by rulers at unfixed intervals and the meetings of trade guilds; and, finally, the unofficial popular gatherings – riots, protests, festivals – which played a crucial, if angular, role in public life. The eighteenth century saw fundamental developments in the nature of every type of assembly, but these developments were neither even nor uniform. One of the keys to these otherwise diffuse changes is the way in which the assemblies saw themselves altered in the course of the century.

The local public assembly, usually based on the parish meeting, depended on the existence of a landholding peasantry and a relatively well-developed sense of village community. It had virtually disappeared from those parts of eastern Europe dominated by serfdom and also from England, where most rural labourers were landless. In much of France, northern Italy and Spain, however, these assemblies retained important powers over the use and distribution of communal lands and the revenues they yielded. In some places, such as the fishing villages of Puglia, they embraced most of the community; in others they were gradually restricted to the members of municipal councils, as in Provence and Catalonia. If a general trend can be detected, it is usually of these assemblies becoming more elitist and bourgeois in character as the century progressed. The major exception is New England, where the village meeting increased its collectivist character. In the United Provinces there were similar assemblies in an urban context; one aspect of the Patriot revolt of 1787–8 was an attempt to reinforce their popular character.

The official, most overtly 'political' assemblies in this period were the diets and estates. They had disappeared from several important

European states before the eighteenth century – notably Prussia, the Savoyard states and Russia – but where they existed they grew in power. England was unique in having such a body, the parliament, which represented the whole country. Elsewhere, estates and diets represented only their own provinces, which meant that rulers had to deal with them individually. Within their territorial limits, these bodies were usually very powerful, as attested to by the failure of many active rulers to curtail their privileges and jurisdictions. This is particularly clear in the resistance of the Habsburg provinces to Joseph II in the 1780s and the Dutch Patriot revolt of 1787–8; the most striking examples of this are the steady rise of parliamentary authority over the crown in England, and the successful revolt of the British North American colonies. Most derived their power from their permanent, regular meetings; the exception that proves the rule is the French ESTATES GENERAL, which represented the whole realm but was not called between 1614 and 1789. The membership of some of these bodies was determined by regular elections, usually based on archaic, un-uniform franchises as in England and its American colonies. Between 1689 and 1716, England had elections every three years, which produced a lively, volatile political culture which was curbed by the Septennial Act of 1716. Usually, the composition of diets and estates reflected the corporate nature of society, their membership divided into nobles, commons and the ex officio representatives of guilds and towns; even the English parliament reflected this, with its division into Lords and Commons. In this respect their character is very similar to corporate assemblies, the crucial difference being that these bodies' main function was to bring different corporation – 'orders' – together.

'Corporate' assemblies are distinguished from diets and estates by their exclusiveness; they represented only one group, a trade in the case of guilds or a profession in the case of the French PARLEMENTS, bodies of lawyers and magistrates which also had such wide administrative powers that they duplicated the role of provincial estates. Their very nature necessitated permanent, regular meetings and, even more than the diets and estates, this is where they derived their power. The guilds wielded great influence in the life of commercial towns, particularly in the Rhineland and the Netherlands. The French parlements met more frequently than the estates and covered the whole of the kingdom, whereas by the eighteenth century estates no longer existed for every French province; they proved the most consistent and effective source of opposition to the growth of central authority. The parlements in France and the guilds in the smaller German states were the real centres of collective political life in the eighteenth century and it is significant that centralizing rulers, culminating in the French Revolutionary legislators, sought to abolish them.

In the course of the eighteenth century many representative bodies at provincial level moved beyond their role as defenders of traditional, local privileges to assert claims to represent 'PUBLIC OPINION' as a whole. This was clearest in the case of the French *parlements*, which as the century progressed, shifted their perception of their role from one of interpreting royal will to public opinion to that of representing public opinion to the crown; at times they also claimed a right to act together, beyond their provincial jurisdictions. There was often a contradiction at work within eighteenth-century assemblies, even when united in opposition to rulers, in that they sought to defend particular, local or corporate interests but often had to present a united front to do so. The clearest example of this is the difficult relations among the thirteen American colonial assemblies in co-ordinating resistance to Britain; the Dutch provinces in 1787–8 provide a similar case. In western Europe, 'public opinion' was placing more emphasis on the role of regularly elected assemblies at a national level by the 1780s, as witnessed by the repeated calls for a summoning of the Estates General in France followed by the creation of an elected National Assembly by the Constitution of 1790, and the growth of the parliamentary reform movement in Britain, with its desire to increase the importance of parliament, as well as to reform it. In central and southern Europe, and in North America until the mid nineteenth century, the emphasis remained on the defence of provincial rights.

Popular assemblies also played a role in eighteenth-century public life, particularly through the grain riot, which was almost a ritual in its forms and execution (*see* GRAIN RIOTS). Other forms of popular assemblies revolved around festivals and, in Catholic Europe, religious processions which often overlapped with corporate assemblies such as guilds and confraternities. It was a mark of cultural and political change that most such gatherings came to be disapproved of by all sources of authority by the close of the century, although popular, violent demonstrations acquired a specifically political content and acceptability at the height of the French Revolution in Paris.

K. M. Baker, 'Representation', in K. M. Baker (ed.), *The French Revolution and the Creation of Modern Political Culture*, vol. 1: *The Political Culture of the Old Regime* (Oxford: Pergamon, 1989), pp. 469–91.

J. Brewer, *Party Ideology and Popular Politics at the Accession of George III* (London: Cambridge University Press, 1976).

G. Rudé, *The Crowd in History: A Study of Popular Disturbances in England and France, 1730–1848* (New York, 1964).

G. S. Wood, *The Creation of the American Republic, 1776–1787* (Chapel Hill, NC: University of North Carolina Press, 1969).

MICHAEL BROERS

Assembly of Notables   The Assembly of Notables, an informally structured consultative body whose membership was designated by the monarch, had last been convoked in France in 1626. Its convocation on 22 February 1787 by Controller-General Calonne, who hoped it would prove more amenable to financial innovation than the PARLEMENT OF PARIS, the state's customary constitutional watchdog, was a sign of the state's desperate financial plight. All three estates of the realm were represented, although only two of the 144 members did not enjoy personal nobility. The Notables rejected Calonne's proposal for a unitary land tax, and brought about his downfall. They were dissolved by his successor, Loménie de Brienne, on 25 May 1787. Necker convoked a second Assembly on 6 November 1788 to seek advice on the composition of the ESTATES GENERAL which had been called for the spring of 1789. The Notables were again unconciliatory, urging the maintenance of procedural forms that favoured the nobility and clergy, and Necker dissolved them on 12 December 1788. Their unwillingness to co-operate marked growing noble intransigence against major constitutional reform in the run-up to the Estates General in May 1789.

Jean Egret, *The French Pre-Revolution, 1787–8* (Chicago: University of Chicago Press, 1977).

COLIN JONES

assignats   Initially a government bond secured ('assigned') on the lands of the French church which were nationalized on 2 November 1789, the *assignat* became a paper currency whose aim of producing economic and financial stability was to prove woefully over-optimistic. Initially, nationalized land up to 400 million livres was placed on the market, and *assignats* up to that value issued: creditors would be paid in interest-bearing *assignats* which could be used to purchase land. From 1790, the *assignat* was declared legal currency, and the tendency for governments to issue them without monitoring their redemption helped depreciate their market value, encourage the hoarding of specie and fuel inflation. The regulatory economic policies of the Terror checked the downward spiral of *assignat* values but the pressure of political uncertainty, economic instability and foreign war proved a death blow to monetary confidence, which was further shaken by the post-Thermidorian dismantling of the Terror. On 19 February 1796 the assignat was formally abolished and, after a further brief flirtation with paper (the *mandats territoriaux*), the Directory in 1797 returned definitively to a metallic currency.

Florin Aftalion, *The French Revolution: An Economic Interpretation* (Cambridge: Cambridge University Press, 1990).

COLIN JONES

astrology In a process beginning in the mid- to late seventeenth century, astrology was banished from polite and educated culture throughout Europe. The attack was led by *philosophes*, natural philosophers and literati, taking over from the church. As a result, throughout the eighteenth century astrology almost disappeared from mention in printed sources. This invisibility, however, is not synonymous with absence. It continued to survive throughout the century as a vigorous part of plebeian cultural beliefs, albeit in a simplified form, dominated by the moon and other visible celestial phenomena. If anything, the pressure from social superiors cemented these beliefs in place, as they were disseminated through continuing and increasing sales of annual popular almanacs. Pockets of the more sophisticated and individualized 'judicial' astrology flourished too, especially in the English counties of Rutland, Leicestershire and Lincolnshire. One such practitioner was William Stukeley (1687–1765). There were even some signs of a recrudescence in the 1790s, with the work, many times reprinted, of Ebenezer Sibly (1751–99). The tradition of high or cosmological astrology, however, was largely appropriated and absorbed by natural philosophers, particularly in Newtonian cometography and epidemiology. In France (and in English translations) astronomers and historians of astronomy mounted strenuous attempts to expunge from their science any remaining traces of divination or astral MAGIC.

P. Curry, *Prophecy and Power: Astrology in Early Modern England* (Cambridge: Polity, 1989).

PATRICK CURRY

astronomy Professionals and amateurs pursued distinct types of astronomy in the eighteenth century, and both branches flourished. The success of the professionals is evidenced by a great increase in the number of official observatories, equipped with fixed instruments for making accurate angular measurements. These measurements were employed in the refinement of Newtonian planetary theory and in the construction of star catalogues, ephemerides and navigational tables. This kind of astronomy was not concerned with the nature of the stars or the structure of the universe, and not particularly interested in the physical character of the sun, moon and planets. Amateur interest, on the other hand, was in observation and speculation, rather than in measurement, and the typical instrument was not a divided arc with a refractor for a telescopic sight, but a relatively large-aperture reflector. It is not surprising that when a radical charge of direction for astronomy was initiated, the challenge came from an amateur, William Herschel, whose discovery of Uranus in 1781, using a home-made reflector, gave him the standing to pursue a different kind of astronomy – his quest for 'the construction of the heavens' – in an influential way.

A. Pannekoek, *A History of Astronomy* (New York: Dover, 1989).

J. A. BENNETT

atheism 'Atheism' may be defined as the belief that the universe had originated and perpetuated itself without divine assistance; in it the only valid moral and other standards were therefore human ones. The possibility of such beliefs had been familiar since classical antiquity, and they were widely attacked in early modern Europe. Until the mid eighteenth century, atheism was more often imputed by controversialists to their opponents than professed by known individuals, although some of those against whom such accusations were made had certainly moved so far towards a naturalistic view of the world that, at the very least, they prepared the way for developments that followed: these would include writers like the English freethinker John Toland. The first professed atheists were to be found in Enlightenment France, notably Jean Meslier (1664–1729) in the first half of the eighteenth century (whose manuscript *Testament* has been published this century), and the *philosophes* d'Holbach and Andre Naigeon (1738–1810) in the second half of the century. In particular, d'Holbach's *Le Système de la nature* openly attacked religion as irrational and dysfunctional, advocating in its place a progressive, enlightened MATERIALISM.

Alan C. Kors, *Atheism in France 1650–1729*, 2 vols (Princeton, NJ: Princeton University Press, (1990 and forthcoming).

MICHAEL HUNTER

atomic theory Leibniz could not bring himself to believe in a world composed of identical atoms, but in the eighteenth century most natural philosophers accepted with NEWTON the probability 'that God in the Beginning form'd Matter in solid, massy, hard, impenetrable Particles . . . so very hard as never to wear or break in pieces'. Newton and his disciples further believed that there were 'powers' or forces associated with the atoms, attractive at long range (gravity) and repulsive at short range, preventing the particles from actually touching. All atoms were made of the same stuff, inert brute matter; stable arrangements of them composed the metals; and differences of density indicated more or less atoms in unit volume. The actual atoms were often believed to be very minute, mere points from which forces emanated. Newtonians hoped for a quantified chemistry based on the study of these forces, but it was not to be. In his *Traité élémentaire de chimie* Lavoisier wrote: 'it is extremely probable we know nothing at all' about 'those simple and indivisible atoms of which matter is composed'. He saw atomism as an untestable metaphysical doctrine, not a scientific theory, and based chemistry on elements and weights instead.

See also MATERIALISM, RELATIONSHIP BETWEEN MIND AND BODY.

A. Thackray, *Atoms and Powers: An Essay on Newtonian Matter-Theory and the Development of Chemistry* (Cambridge, Mass.: Harvard University Press, 1970).

DAVID KNIGHT

Augustanism   The adjective 'Augustan' began to be used from the 1750s to refer to the the the ruling culture of England, and particularly its literature, in the first decades of the eighteenth century (the earliest important example is in Oliver Goldsmith's 'Account of the Augustan Age in England' of 1759). In modern, literary critical, use, earlier writers such as Dryden and later ones such as Johnson also came to be called 'Augustan'; the word now designated neoclassical literary practice and conservative political values. Originally, it was often celebratory or nostalgic, and it is just this idealizing use of the word that has troubled historians. It drew a parallel between England in the early eighteenth century and Rome in the reign of the emperor Augustus, when Virgil, Ovid and Horace were writing (*see* CULT OF ANTIQUITY). The writers most often called 'Augustan' were those (like Pope and Swift) who frequently looked to such classical precedents. The tendency of these writers, however, was to use classical analogies in increasingly incongruous and parodic ways (Pope himself finding in Augustan Rome a model of corruption). For this reason, and because 'Augustanism' too easily implies a shared and confident world-picture, the word has fallen from grace and is rarely used with any precision or emphasis.

H. D. Weinbrot, *Augustus Caesar in 'Augustan' England* (Princeton, NJ: Princeton University Press, 1978).

JOHN MULLAN

Augustus II (1670–1733)   Elector of Saxony, as Frederick Augustus I; king of Poland (1697–1706, 1710–33). He succeeded to the electorate of Saxony in 1694. In 1697 he secured the election to the Polish throne by a combination of heavy bribery and military action – and by conversion to Catholicism, an act much resented in his strongly Lutheran electorate. By acquiring Poland, he hoped to rival the Austrian Habsburgs and outdistance Brandenburg. In Saxony and, to a far greater degree, Poland, his absolutist plans provoked resistance, compounded by his wretchedly unsuccessful participation in the Great Northern War, in alliance with Russia and Denmark. In 1704 the Swedes declared him deposed in favour of their candidate, Stanislas

LESZCZYŃSKI, an act which Augustus had to accept by the Treaty of Altranstädt in September 1706, after Charles XII invaded Saxony. Only the Russian victory at Poltava in 1709 permitted his restoration the following year. After 1721 he concentrated on building up internal Polish support for the succession of his son, but was as far as ever from his goal when he died.

J. T. Lukowski, *Liberty's Folly: The Polish-Lithuanian Commonwealth in the Eighteenth Century* (London: Routledge, 1991).

J. T. LUKOWSKI

Augustus III (1696–1763) Elector of Saxony, as Frederick Augustus II (1733–63); king of Poland (1733–63). He converted from Lutheranism to Catholicism in Rome, in 1712. He was groomed by his father, AUGUSTUS II, for the Polish throne, but only Russian military support in 1733 allowed him to make good his claim against his rival, Stanislas LESZCZYŃSKI. Following Frederick the Great's attack on Silesia in 1740, he hoped to share in a partition of the Austrian Habsburg patrimony on the basis of his wife's claim (he had married Maria Josefa (1699–1757), daughter of Joseph I, in 1719). Disillusioned by Frederick's treatment of Saxony, he adhered to Austria and Russia from 1745, partly in the hope of securing their support for the succession of one of his own sons in Poland. He visited Poland as little as possible, although the Prussian occupation of Saxony from 1756 to 1763 obliged him to take up residence in Warsaw. He and his chief minister, Heinrich Brühl (1700–63), were content to manœuvre among the Polish factions rather than to pursue real political reform.

J. T. Lukowski, *Liberty's Folly: The Polish-Lithuanian Commonwealth in the Eighteenth Century* (London: Routledge, 1991).

J. T. LUKOWSKI

Austerlitz, Battle of (2 December 1805) At Austerlitz Napoleon BONAPARTE's *Grande Armée* of 73,000 men defeated the 85,000 of Francis I of Austria and Alexander I of Russia. Napoleon employed his favourite tactical conception, the enemy deceived into splitting its armies and concentrating its attack on the part of the French line chosen by him. French troops and artillery then attacked and destroyed one wing of the enemy before concentrating all their force on the remainder. In the autumn of 1805 he had carried his armies from the Rhine to Munich, and then swept on to Vienna, dangerously overextended. He pressed north to Brünn, then withdrew, the pursuing Austro-Russian armies occupying the heights of Pratzen south-west of Austerlitz on 1 December. Napoleon concentrated the bulk of his forces on his own left wing, and created an extended right wing, apparently weak though in fact reinforced by force-marched relief divisions. At dawn on 2 December he was attacked by 45,000 men on his weak flank, and 13,000 on his stronger left. At 9 a.m. the surprise was unleashed, and Soult stormed the Pratzen heights to break the enemy forces in two. French casualties were 8,000 to the enemy's 27,000.

J. R. Elting, *Swords around a Throne: Napoleon's Grande Armée* (New York: Free Press, 1988).

PHILIP WOODFINE

Australia   As a geographical entity Australia did not exist in the minds of either eighteenth-century Europeans or Aborigines. Until the explorer Mathew Flinders coined the term in 1814, those parts which were known to Europeans were called New Holland and Van Dieman's Land, reflecting the role of the Dutch in its exploration during the seventeenth century. The Aborigines who had settled the continent at least 40,000 years earlier were predominantly hunter-gatherers rather than cultivators, and Europeans took a rather Lockean view of their economy, determining that Australia was *terra nullius* – a land without sovereignty – and therefore available for occupation.

Although Dampier (1652–1715) visited the western shore in 1700, there was no further European contact with Australia before COOK. His traverse of the eastern coast in 1770 and the later visit to Van Dieman's Land were necessary preliminaries to the 1786 decision to establish a penal colony at Botany Bay. The eventual site at Sydney Cove established a British foothold on the continent, and its own defensive and penal necessities gradually led to an expansion of the presence to other parts of Australia.

C. M. H. Clark, *A History of Australia*, vol. 1 (Melbourne: Melbourne University Press, 1979).

DAVID MACKAY

Austrian Succession, War of the   War long seemed likely over the succession to the Austrian imperial throne. Under the constitution of the Empire only males could inherit, and Emperor Charles VI had no son. The Habsburgs traditionally inherited the imperial dignity, conferred on them by the nine electors, who were rulers of smaller German states. From 1713 onwards Charles tried to persuade these electors and the interested great powers to agree to the PRAGMATIC SANCTION, by which the undivided inheritance of Austria and Hungary, the southern Netherlands (Belgium) and territories in Italy would pass to his eldest daughter, Maria Theresa. Since Bourbon France and Spain were active rivals of the Habsburgs, it was likely that one of them would take up the cause of some rival claimant to the empire, the chief of these being Augustus of Saxony and Charles Albert of Bavaria. Strangely, when Charles VI died on 20 October 1740 no immediate action took place. Spain had been at war with Austria's ally Britain for a year, and France had sent a fleet to the Caribbean to counter a British naval expedition there. A Franco-British war seemed likely, and Fleury's ministry, while risking war to prevent British expansion overseas, was in no hurry to stage a confrontation on the Continent.

The war was begun unexpectedly by Frederick II, who on 31 May 1740 inherited the Prussian throne and with it a formidable army machine. On 16 December 1740 he invaded the rich Austrian province of Silesia, and early the next spring beat the Austrians at MOLLWITZ. In June 1741 Frederick allied with France in the Treaty of Breslau, receiving French recognition of his Silesian gains in exchange for supporting the imperial candidature of Charles Albert. Maria Theresa was supported only cautiously by her British and Dutch allies even when Charles Albert was crowned Emperor Charles VII in February 1742. In the Treaty of Breslau the young queen abandoned Silesia to Frederick, who promptly deserted his French ally. A British-sponsored army, with George II at its head, defeated the French at Dettingen in June 1743, and gradually Maria Theresa regained control of the empire. Frederick, alarmed, re-entered the war in August 1744, and gained renewed confirmation of Silesia in the Treaty of Dresden (December 1745). By then Charles VII had died, and the focus of war was no longer on the succession but on the BALANCE OF POWER. From 1744 to 1746 the French, menaced by British navy successes, attempted to neutralize Britain by sponsoring a Jacobite invasion, and in 1745–6 they conquered most of the Austrian Netherlands. In 1747–8 they launched successful attacks into the United Provinces, weakening Britain's position. The TREATY OF AIX-LA-CHAPELLE, concluded on 18 October 1748, largely restored the pre-war territorial situation of the participants, but some power shifts had occurred. The Pragmatic Sanction was secured, with Maria Theresa's husband, Francis of Lorraine, elected Emperor Francis I; and, as Frederick II described it, Wittelsbach Bavaria remained on the bench of the electorates while Brandenburg Prussia stepped forward to join the great powers.

J. M. Black, *The Rise of the European Powers 1679–1793* (London: Edward Arnold, 1990).

PHILIP WOODFINE

Austro-Turkish wars The Austro-Turkish wars dominated the military and political history of south-eastern Europe from 1526 to 1791. From the outset the issues were both territorial and cultural: which of the two great empires – the Habsburg or the Ottoman – would rule the lands between Vienna and Constantinople and which of the world's great religions – Islam or Roman Catholicism – would hold that area as well. These wars represented a clash of two great states and two great cultures.

The struggle began in 1526 when, following the death of the childless Louis II of Hungary in battle against the Turks, the Habsburg dynasty laid claim to his inheritance, thus entering into direct competition with the Turks over the rule of Hungary. In the wars that followed, the Turks held the upper hand at first, but in the seventeenth century the advantage swung to the Austrians. The decisive event occurred in 1683 when a Turkish host was routed before Vienna. In the war that followed (1683–99) the allied forces inflicted many defeats on the Ottomans, finally forcing them to conclude a peace (TREATY OF CARLOWITZ) which gave to the house of Habsburg possession of most of the kingdoms of Hungary and Transylvania.

The eighteenth-century Austro-Turkish wars featured a progressively weaker Ottoman Empire doing battle with an increasingly stronger Austria. During the century the sultan's government became less able to corral provincial warlords and rebels or to arrest the financial and administrative rot spreading through the army and bureaucracy. At the same time, the Habsburg monarchy was enjoying a strengthening that was making it a modern political and military power.

There were three wars in the eighteenth century. In the first (1716–18) the Austrians, responding to an attack by Turkey on Venice, succeeded in adding the final portion of the Hungarian crown and the mighty fortress of Belgrade and its environs to the Habsburg possessions (TREATY OF PASSAROWITZ). In the second (1737–9) the Austrians joined the war as allies of Russia in hopes of exploiting Russia for purposes elsewhere but, to everyone's surprise, lost the war and the citadel of Belgrade (Treaty of Belgrade). In the final war (1788–91) the Austrians again went into combat as allies of the Russians and, although they conquered Belgrade again, agreed to a treaty based on the status quo *ante bellum* (Treaty of Sistova).

These wars of the eighteenth century had a different character from the wars of the previous centuries. In the earlier wars the issues had been control of territory and the clash of faiths. In the eighteenth century the Austrians were far more concerned with geopolitical issues than they were with acquiring Balkan land or forcing back Islam. In fact, in these wars the Austrian officials frequently expressed the wish not to annex more Balkan property because it was of marginal economic value and inhabited by unreliable Orthodox Christians. The last war marked the end of the great Austro-Turkish struggles; indeed, the two empires would be allies at their joint demise in the First World War.

See also HABSBURG EMPIRE, OTTOMAN EMPIRE.

KARL A. ROIDER JR

aviation Flight was the century's most exciting technological achievement. On 20 November 1783 the scientist Pilâtre de Rozier (1757–85) and the marquis d'Arlandes (1742–1809) flew 5 miles over Paris in a hot-air balloon and, to universal amazement, landed safely. The invention belonged to the brothers Joseph (1740–1810) and Etienne (1745–99) Montgolfier, papermakers from Lyons. Although their experiments, begun in 1782, were inspired by Henry Cavendish's discovery of hydrogen, a gas lighter than air, they unwittingly exploited instead the expansive property of heated air. Contemporaneous experiments with hydrogen, which offered a safer alternative to their open fire-basket, prevailed when the generation of hydrogen was improved.

Daring aeronauts competed for firsts and distance records, travelling at unprecedented speeds and attracting huge crowds, whose impatience often provoked rash ascents. In 1785 Jean Pierre Blanchard (1753–1809) and his patron, John Jeffries (1744–1819), crossed the English Channel, casting off even clothing to remain airborne. Astonishingly, considering the new skills required, it was nineteen months before the first fatality – de Rozier. In 1794 the French revolutionary government established the Aérostation Corps: its reconnaissance combined with its terror helped win the Battle of Fleurus.

L. T. C. Rolt, *The Aeronauts: A History of Ballooning, 1783–1903* (London: Longman, 1966).

CHRISTINE MACLEOD

B

━━━━◆━━━━

Babeuf, François Noël [Gracchus] (1760–1797)   French precursor of communist ideas. He served as a modest feudal clerk in Picardy prior to the French Revolution. After 1789 he won a reputation as a radical pamphleteer and agitator. He deplored the rightward lurch of the Convention after the fall of Robespierre, notably in his newspaper, called from October 1794 *Tribun du peuple* (Tribune of the People). After the failure of various agitational projects, he began to organize an insurrectionary committee, the 'Conspiracy of the Equals', comprising left-wing members of the Convention and other militants. Babeuf and the 'Equals' were arrested in May 1796 before their planned *coup* took place and arraigned for treason before the high court at Vendôme. Sentenced to death, Babeuf attempted to commit suicide in his cell, before being executed. His 'Conspiracy of Equals' was less effective in affecting the course of the Revolution than in the intellectual legacy it bequeathed nineteenth-century Europe of a proto-Leninist party organization, together with a set of communistic ideas about collective agrarian production and distribution.

R. Barry Rose, *Gracchus Babeuf: The First Revolutionary Communist* (London: Edward Arnold, 1978).

COLIN JONES

Bach, Carl Philipp Emanuel (1714–1788)   German composer. The second son of Johann Sebastian Bach, he introduced the symphonic form to chamber music, and in this influenced Haydn. His piano music pointed forward to Mozart and Beethoven. His *Versuch über die wahre Art das Clavier zu spielen* (Essay on the True Art of Playing Keyboard Instruments) is an important treatise on musical performance in the eighteenth century.

Hans-Gunter Ottenberg, *Carl Philipp Emanuel Bach* (Oxford: Oxford University Press, 1987).
Christoph Wolff, *The New Grove Bach Family* (London: Macmillan, 1983).

FRITZ WEBER

Bach, Johann Christian (1735–1782)   German composer, called 'the English Bach'. The youngest of Johann Sebastian Bach's sons, he had the greatest reputation of them. After studying music with his elder brother Carl Philipp Emanuel Bach, he moved to Italy where he lived from 1754 to 1762. He converted to Roman Catholicism and became organist at Milan Cathedral in 1760, composing mainly church music and some operas. In 1762 he went to London and became a composer to the *King's Theatre*. His main success, however, derived from writing and promoting symphonic music. Although he was well accepted by London society, he suffered from financial difficulties in the late 1770s. He had a nervous breakdown in 1781, and died in such penury that his funeral had to be paid for by the queen.

He wrote thirteen operas, around fifty symphonies, thirty-five keyboard concertos and a great deal of chamber music. His style combined the charming melodies of Neapolitan *opera* with the new *crescendo* technique of the *Mannheim School*, and in many respects anticipated *Haydn* and *Mozart*.

C. Wolff, *The New Grove Bach Family* (London: Macmillan, 1983).

FRITZ WEBER

Bach, Johann Sebastian (1685–1750)   German composer, considered the greatest baroque musician. He was born into an old Protestant family of musicians, who had been of no more than local prominence, and in a sense this was also true of Johann Sebastian among his European contemporaries. After the early death of his father, Johann Ambrosius Bach (1645–95), a town musician at Eisenach, he was looked after by his eldest brother, Johann Christoph Bach (1671–1721), who was an organist. From him Johann Sebastian received his fundamental musical education, and then aspired to a similar career. He became an organist in various cities and in 1708 accepted his first substantial post as organist and court musician at Weimar. There he composed mainly keyboard and organ music, including the famous Toccata and Fugue in D minor.

In 1717 he quit this post to become music director to Prince Leopold of Cöthen. He spent a fruitful time there, composing chamber music (including the solo suites and sonatas for cello and violin, the first book of *The Well-tempered Clavier*, and orchestral works like the six 'Brandenburg' Concertos.

In 1723 he was appointed cantor at St Thomas's Church in Leipzig, but only after Telemann and other well-known musicians had turned down the post. As cantor Bach had to teach music and to provide music for his church community, performances as well as compositions. But he also continued composing keyboard music: the second book of *The Well-Tempered Clavier* (1742), the *Clavier-Übungen* (Keyboard Exercises; 4 vols, 1731–43), which included the Italian Concerto and the Goldberg Variations. Here he also composed the *St Matthew Passion* (1729) (the *St John Passion* had been completed in Cöthen), the B minor Mass and the *Musical Offering* (both 1747). His last work, the ample *Art of Fugue*, a masterpiece of counterpoint, remained unfinished. Towards the end of his life he became blind. He died a well-respected man.

Only half of his *œuvre* has survived: two of four or five passions, 192 of more than 300 church cantatas, three oratorios, numerous choral pieces and other organ works, a few orchestral works and much chamber and keyboard music. Contemporary knowledge of his works remained restricted, because he had no access to the great publishing-houses. His work was rediscovered only in the early nineteenth century, when a performance of the *St Matthew Passion* in 1829, conducted by Felix Mendelssohn-Bartholdy (1809–47), inaugurated the Bach renaissance.

D. Arnold, *Bach* (Oxford: Oxford University Press, 1984).
C. Wolff, *The New Grove Bach Family* (London: Macmillan, 1983).

FRITZ WEBER

Baconianism   Francis Bacon (1561–1626), the English statesman-philosopher, headed the eighteenth century's list of new and heroic philosophers. Writers celebrated, selectively, his rejection of traditional philosophical systems, his separation of science and religion, his call for new sciences based on EMPIRICISM and, above all, his humanistic belief in PROGRESS, which was signified primarily by the improvement of the material conditions of life through the scientific control of nature.

In the seventeenth century Baconianism was largely confined to Britain, notably as the official methodology of the Royal Society. Then, led by Voltaire, Continental thinkers attempting to account for the achievements of Locke and Newton explained them in terms of a Baconian tradition, a notion which they subsequently elaborated. Especially in France, Bacon's ideas were refashioned to fight new and different battles, being called on in the struggles of Cartesians against Aristotelian system-builders, and in attempts to dismiss Christianity rather than merely demarcate it from science. Whereas UTILITARIANISM had been for Bacon a divine duty, it became for the French a secular goal. Such Baconianism was particularly evident in the *Encyclopédie*, where Bacon himself was presented as the inaugurator of progressive philosophy. His divisions of knowledge (subtly secularized) were the organizing principles of the *Encyclopédie*, and its incitement to progress through technology was quintessentially Baconian.

See also SCIENTIFIC REVOLUTION.

A. Rupert Hall, *The Revolution in Science 1500–1750*, third edn (Harlow: Longman, 1983).

STEPHEN PUMFREY

Baden A medium-sized territory in the south-west of Germany with a population of around 255,000, Baden was ruled by margraves from the house of Zähringen. In the sixteenth century it was divided into two, Baden-Baden and Baden-Durlach. Both became Protestant in the Reformation but the former reverted to Catholicism. They were reunited in 1771 when the Baden-Baden line died out. Baden-Durlach, with its capital at Karlsruhe after 1724, was the larger and more advanced of the two. In the eighteenth century it became an important centre of enlightened absolutism. Margrave CHARLES FREDERICK, who was seen as a model enlightened ruler, introduced substantial reforms and tried to implement the policies of the physiocrats. He was also a leader of the Third Germany movement, which sought to protect the constitution of Germany against attempts by Joseph II to subvert it. Baden was substantially enlarged during the territorial reorganization of Germany after the French Revolution, growing to a population of over 1 million by 1810. Further major reforms were introduced which made it one of the most liberal states in nineteenth-century Germany.

H. Liebel, *Enlightened Bureaucracy versus Enlightened Despotism in Baden 1750–1792* (Philadelphia: American Philosophical Society, 1965).

MICHAEL HUGHES

Bailly, Jean Sylvain (1736–1793) French astronomer. He succeeded his father as keeper of the king's paintings at the Louvre in 1768 but astronomy was his vocation. After training under Clairaut and Nicolas de Lacaille (1713–62), he commenced his own research in 1759 and in 1760 built an observatory at the Louvre where he investigated Jupiter's satellites. Once elected to the Académie des Sciences, he turned to trying to solve the inequalities in the motions of Jupiter's satellites, generating sufficient interest in the problem for the Académie to set the problem as a prize contest for 1766. It was won by Lagrange (1736–1813). Outshone in astronomical prowess and failing to climb the bureaucratic ladder of the Académie, Bailly turned to composing a four-volume history of astronomy (1775–82). Thereafter, his reputation rested on his reports for Académie commissions; in 1784 he penned a damning attack on mesmerism, and between 1786 and 1788 he produced three reports calling for reform of the hospital Hôtel-Dieu. These reports thrust Bailly into public life, and in 1789 he was proclaimed the first mayor of Paris. However, he lost favour with his advocacy of revolutionary containment, and in 1793 was tried and guillotined.

George Armstrong Kelly, *Victims, Authority and Terror* (Chapel Hill, NC: University of North Carolina Press, 1982).

M. L. BENJAMIN

balance of power In the eighteenth century it was believed that no state or combination of states should become so powerful as to threaten the independence or essential interests of other members of the European state system. Concepts of equilibrium achieved by a balance of opposing forces in the natural world, strengthened by Newtonian astronomy and mechanics, helped to popularize such ideas in international relations. Most analysts, however, agreed that a political equilibrium of this kind would not arise naturally and must be produced by conscious human effort. In the first half of the century the balance of power was still frequently thought of as one in which France and the Austrian Habsburgs headed opposing groups of states. In the second half of the century the rising power of Prussia, and still more Russia, complicated the situation and meant that east European issues played a larger role in balance of power calculations. It also became increasingly common to claim that, to be effective, a European balance must be complemented by one between the colonial and naval strengths of the major west European states.
See also POWER.

M. S. Anderson, 'Eighteenth-Century Theories of the Balance of Power', in Ragnhild Hatton and M. S. Anderson (eds), *Studies in Diplomatic History* (London: Longman, 1970), pp. 183–98.

M. S. ANDERSON

Balkans The Balkans are defined by Jelavich as that area which now comprises the modern states of Albania, Bulgaria, GREECE, Romania and the former Yugoslavia. By the beginning of the eighteenth century this area had long been under the control of the OTTOMAN EMPIRE. As the long decline of the empire continued into the eighteenth century, the Balkan peoples often shared to the full, directly or indirectly, in the political vicissitudes of the empire. The Balkan lands ceased to be the easy golden highway which led towards further future Ottoman conquest and expansion in Europe, and became more an area of intensive dispute between the Ottomans and the great powers like Austria and

Russia. The ravages of war and the consequent destruction of cities and villages in the Balkans are an eloquent witness to the increasing decline of Ottoman power in the Balkans.

The social consequences of the Ottoman decline were bad enough but the political consequences for the Ottomans were even worse. The latter are mirrored in the various treaties they concluded: by the Treaty of Carlowitz (1699), between the Ottoman Empire and Austria, Venice and Poland, the Ottomans lost to Austria parts of Hungary, Transylvania, Croatia and Slavonia. By the Treaty of Passarowitz (1718) northern Serbia, which included Belgrade, was gained by Austria, although the Ottomans later recovered northern Serbia in the 1739 Treaty of Belgrade. A roughly thirty-year period of peace ensued in Ottoman–European relations, but in 1768 the Ottomans declared war on Russia. The Treaty of Kuchuk-Kainardji which followed, in 1774, was a complete disaster for the Ottomans since, in effect, Russia overtook the Ottomans as the major power in the Black Sea area. Indeed, by the end of the eighteenth century it was Russia which had become the main European force in the Near East and threat to the continued supremacy of the Ottoman Empire.

The Ottoman Empire exercised a general administrative control over the Balkan regions. However, the villages with their own organizations often had a greater or lesser degree of independence, with their elders or leaders acting as mediators in affairs between the Ottoman government and the local village. In terms of religion, the eighteenth-century Balkans were a tangled and complex web of Catholics, Orthodox Christians and Muslims. Each of these groups could be said to have had a political as well as a spiritual dimension in Balkan history. For example, the Muslims of Albania, by virtue of their faith, enjoyed considerable privileges in both Albania and the rest of the Ottoman Empire. The Orthodox Christian Church might support the Ottoman regime or, as happened sometimes in Serbia or Montenegro, vigorously oppose it. Eighteenth-century Balkan history exhibits a fabric of war, decline and disintegration which often matched what was happening at or from the heart of the empire in ISTANBUL.

Barbara Jelavich, *History of the Balkans*, vol. 1: *Eighteenth and Nineteenth Centuries* (Cambridge: Cambridge University Press, repr. 1990).

IAN NETTON

ballet   Eighteenth-century ballet originated in France, where Jean-Baptiste Lully (1632–87) incorporated the *ballet de cour* (a very formal ballet danced by the court) into opera. From 1672, with the establishment of a ballet school attached to the Académie Royale de Musique in Paris, dancers began to be professionally trained.

Ballet as part of the opera, however, lacked dramatic spirit. The ballerina Marie-Anne Camargo (1710–70) shortened her skirts to just above the ankles so that her more lively footwork could be seen. This paved the way for Jean-Georges Noverre's (1727–1810) *ballet d'action*, which sought to introduce dramatic expression into dance. However, the choreographer Gaspero Angiolini (1731–1803) claimed that such reforms had been the work of his own master Franz Hilverding (1710–68). Gluck had composed the ballet music to *Don Juan* (1761) for Angiolini, who depicted the plot by pure pantomimical action. Jean Dauberval (1742–1816) and Charles Didelot (1767–1837) took the style of their teacher Noverre further, while in Italy Salvatore Viganò (1769–1821) combined elements of mime-dance and *ballet d'action*. Viganò collaborated with Beethoven on the ballet *Die Geschöpfe des Prometheus* (The Creatures of Prometheus, 1801).

By the end of the century ballet had stripped off the birthmarks of its courtly origin, developed gymnastic virtuosity and established itself as a genre in its own right.

J. Knight, *Ballet and its Music* (Clifton, NJ: Schott & Co, 1973).

FRITZ WEBER

Baltic The political significance of the Baltic in the sixteenth and seventeenth centuries had derived from its near-monopoly of important raw materials vital to the European economy: cheap grain to feed the growing European population, Swedish copper and iron, and timber, pitch, tar and hemp to supply the growing merchant and battle fleets of the new colonial powers. The eighteenth century saw important changes in the Baltic economy: the region was devastated first by the great famine of 1696–7 and then by the Great Northern War. There were also new challenges, as powers outside the Baltic, particularly Great Britain, sought to develop its colonies and Norway as alternative sources of such Baltic staples as timber, pitch and tar. The return of peace to the region in 1721, however, encouraged population growth, while the high quality of Baltic products and Britain's loss of its American colonies in 1783 ensured that the Baltic economies remained largely buoyant, although patterns of prosperity shifted: the seventeenth-century dominance of the Dutch as carriers was ended, and increased competition from Russia through St Petersburg, Estonia and Livonia affected the economies of Sweden, Denmark (where agriculture stagnated in the 1730s) and especially Poland-Lithuania, where Danzig never recovered its seventeenth-century dominance.

The greatest changes in the region during the eighteenth century were political. The struggle for control of the Baltic Sea (*Dominium Maris Baltici*) which had been waged since the mid sixteenth century reached its climax in the GREAT NORTHERN WAR. The eclipse of Sweden and the triumph of Russia in 1721 set the pattern for the rest of the century. Denmark and Sweden became minor powers, with Denmark pursuing a policy of neutrality as far as possible, and Sweden playing little more than a supporting role as foreign powers interfered increasingly in its chaotic internal politics after the revolution of 1719–20. The most dramatic transformation came on the Baltic's southern shore. The political decline of Poland-Lithuania during the Great Northern War led first to Russian domination of Polish politics and then, when Poland showed signs of revival after 1764, to the Partitions of Poland-Lithuania (1772, 1793 and 1795), which confirmed the hegemony of Russia over the eastern Baltic and finally established Prussia, through the acquisition of Danzig and the Vistula delta, as the dominant power in the south.

The extensive Continental interests of both Prussia and Russia underlined the relative decline in the political significance of the Baltic within the European system in the eighteenth century. Nevertheless, the region's continuing economic importance was demonstrated during the Revolutionary and Napoleonic wars. The attempt by Britain to enforce its blockade of France led to war with Denmark, which ultimately saw Denmark lose NORWAY to Sweden (1814). Sweden, which finally drew closer to the anti-French forces, received Norway in compensation for losing Finland to Russia (1809).

See DENMARK, LIVONIA, POLAND, SWEDEN.

P. Jeanin, *L'Europe du nord-ouest et du nord aux XVIIe et XVIIIe siècles* (Paris: Nouvelle Clio, 1969).

D. Kirby, *Northern Europe in the Early Modern Period: The Baltic World 1492–1792* (London: Longman, 1990).

ROBERT I. FROST

banks and banking Private money-handling and exchange is as old as capitalism, but modern public banks may be said to date from the foundation of the Bank of Venice (1584) and of the Amsterdamsche Wisselbank, or exchange bank (1609), later called the Bank of Amsterdam. Their basis was simple: the bank was open to all for the deposit of money or bullion, which could then be freely withdrawn. Similar banks were established at Middelburg, Rotterdam and, most importantly, Hamburg. The Bank of England was founded in 1694 as a device for securing a government loan of £1,200,000. The successful flotation of the Bank institutionalized the national debt. British ministries were thereby routinely able to spend beyond their annual taxation income, so long as they regularly paid the interest on capital invested and thereby gave investors confidence in their commitment to payment. Despite occasional alarms, deficit finance proved highly successful, and much of Britain's imperial expansion was financed not out of taxation but by borrowing.

By Acts of 1694 and 1697, the Bank of England was granted a virtual monopoly as a central joint-stock bank; but a multitude of lesser country banks developed in the provinces. Their role in securing credit and facilitating money transfers proved vital to the mobilization of capital in an age of rapid industrialization. The first French national bank, known as the Banque Génerale, was established in 1716 by John LAW, the author of the Mississippi Scheme (1717). Law's bank, from 1718 called the Banque Royale, crashed in 1720. As a result of this experience, French banking remained weak throughout the century, contributing greatly to the shaky state of French public finance.

Eric Kerridge, *Trade and Banking in Early Modern England* (Manchester: Manchester University Press, 1988).

L. S. Pressnell, *Country Banking in the Industrial Revolution* (Oxford: Clarendon, 1956).

ROY PORTER

Banks, Sir **Joseph** (1743–1820)   English botanist. Like Francis Bacon, his importance lies not in his own scientific contributions – which were few and slight – but rather in his ability to publicize the possibilities of science when linked with sympathetic patrons, particularly government. Banks received little systematic scientific training at Harrow (1752–6), Eton (1756–60) and Christ Church, Oxford (1760–3) where he was educated in a manner fitting his social status as the heir to a considerable landed estate. However, his youthful interest in natural history was given a disciplined and systematic form by his work as a scientific observer on board a naval expedition to Newfoundland and Labrador in 1766 and, still more, by his famous *Endeavour* voyage with Cook (1768–71), which began an illustrious tradition of combining British naval and scientific exploration. Banks's ability to promote science at the highest levels of government – including further voyages of discovery – owed much to his friendship with George III, an early manifestation of which was his appointment as virtual director of the Royal Gardens at Kew in 1773. His election as president of the Royal Society in 1778 (a post he held until his death) further strengthened his *de facto* role as the scientific adviser to government and his ability to integrate scientific concerns into the expanding apparatus of the British state and its imperial dependencies.

H. C. Carter, *Sir Joseph Banks 1743–1820: A Biography* (London: British Museum of Natural History, 1988).

JOHN GASCOIGNE

Barbary states The north African states of Morocco, Algiers and Tunis were significant to the outside world largely through the activity of corsairs based in their ports in preying on shipping in the Mediterranean. All suffered markedly from political instability, *coups d'état* and personal and factional rivalries. In Morocco the ferocious but energetic Mulay Ismail (1672–1727) and the more moderate Sidi Mohammed (1757–90) were able to impose a considerable degree of order; but at other times conflict and upheaval were very destructive. Algiers, ruled by often short-lived deys who had frequently little real power, was much less flourishing than in the past; the city's population of perhaps 30,000 at the end of the eighteenth century was probably about a third of that 100 years earlier. Corsair activity there declined markedly and only about a sixth of present-day Algeria was under any real control by the deys. In Tunis, ruled from 1705 by a hereditary dynasty of beys, piracy had always been less important than in Algiers. It was captured by Algerian forces in 1756 and for some time afterwards forced to pay a tribute to Algiers.

Ch.-André Julien, *Histoire de l'Afrique du Nord*, vol. 2 (Paris: Payot, 1952).

M. S. ANDERSON

baroque The predominant style of architecture, sculpture and painting in Europe between the 1630s and the 1730s, the baroque was developed in Rome by such artists as Gianlorenzo Bernini (1598–1680) and Pietro da Cortona (1596–1669). This overtly emotional and dramatic style was quickly adopted in those countries subject to the Counter-Reformation – Spain, Flanders, Austria, Hungary, Bohemia and the Catholic German states. Its formal characteristics are usually defined in antithesis to those of CLASSICISM. Where classical style is linear, the baroque is pictorial; where classical style is planar, the baroque is constructed in depth; where classicism employs closed forms, the baroque uses open ones; where classicism emphasizes the clear distinction of its component elements, the baroque emphasizes the indivisibility of its parts. Nowhere is the unitary character of the baroque more evident than in the complex interweaving of architecture, sculpture and painting in the religious works of Bernini and his followers. Outside Italy, particularly in France, the grandeur and pomp of the baroque were adapted to the secular purpose of the glorification of absolute monarchy. The palace of Versailles, a triumphant *Gesamtkunstwerk* in praise of Louis XIV, provided a model for similar monuments across Europe, including Hampton Court in Protestant and parliamentary England.

Although the baroque style continued to be used for religious art and architecture well into the eighteenth century, particularly in Italy and central Europe, the more intimate, delicate and refined French ROCOCO style began to be preferred from the 1720s for secular domestic art. By the 1750s changing political and intellectual attitudes in western Europe, together with the excavation of such classical sites as Herculaneum (1738) and Pompeii (1748), led to the gradual rejection of what came to be seen as an irrational and decadent style in favour of NEOCLASSICISM, with its formal clarity and democratic associations.

J. R. Martin, *Baroque* (London: Allen Lane, 1977).

MARC JORDAN

barracks Throughout the eighteenth century most soldiers were billeted on the civilian population, though towards the end of the period barrack accommodation became more common. In Britain a distrust of standing armies made quartering the norm, except for some border garrisons. In Austria-Hungary the military were segregated in barracks, often wretched temporary buildings, though in Hungary troops were normally billeted. In France towns had to quarter soldiers in exchange for inadequate taxation rebates. Under the Prussian canton system troops lived at home for ten months of the year, and for two months were billeted on others: only from the mid-1770s could Frederick the Great afford to build barracks in the main cities and fortresses. Everywhere, billeting was costly and caused friction: Russian troops in the Ukraine and Poland were particularly notorious for debauchery and assault. The French military engineer Vauban designed barracks to improve *esprit de corps* and morale, functional blocks which none the less brought troops together in uniform, tolerable conditions. First built in frontier garrisons, they were later adopted inland, erected at the expense of towns which found it cheaper than the old exploitative system of quartering.

See ARMIES.

J. C. Childs, *Armies and Warfare in Europe 1648–1789* (Manchester: Manchester University Press, 1982).

PHILIP WOODFINE

Bastille The Bastille was a late-fourteenth-century fortress on the eastern side of Paris which from the time of Richelieu served as a state prison. Its capture by Parisian insurgents on 14 July 1789 constituted the archetypal revolutionary act by which the people in arms triumphed over despotism. Even though conditions within the prison were relatively comfortable, and it housed only seven prisoners when it was stormed, the Enlightenment critique of LETTRES DE CACHET (sensationalist literature highlighting appalling prison conditions) and the frequent utilization of the prison against the book trade had made the Bastille synonymous with the abuse of power. In fact, the reason for the attack for 14 July was pragmatic rather then symbolic. Louis XVI was drawing up troops around the city in what looked like a projected *coup* to dissolve the National Assembly and reimpose authoritarian rule. The Bastille had to be neutralized as a military threat, and its gunpowder reserves seized for the armed defence of Paris. In the event, the capture of the Bastille obliged the king to withdraw his troops and accept the new constitutional settlement.

Jacques Godechot, *The Taking of the Bastille, 14 July 1789* (London: Faber, 1970).

COLIN JONES

Batavian Republic   The Batavian Republic was the name given to the UNITED PROVINCES in 1795 following French occupation. The French invasion of Belgium in 1792 threatened Dutch commercial and political influence, and the Dutch declared war on France in February 1793. The state was invaded in 1794–5 and, following military set-backs, the stadtholder William V fled to England, allowing the French to dictate terms in the Treaty of The Hague in 1795. The Dutch were forced to pay a subsidy, to fund a French garrison force and to accept the status of French satellite state as the 'Batavian Republic'. A convention was established in 1796 to work out a constitution for this new 'sister republic', but the troubled state of French politics spilled over into Dutch internal affairs and produced political instability even once a constitution was agreed in 1798. Invasion by an Anglo-Russian force in 1799 also posed a problem, and though this was forced out, Bonaparte, as new first consul, worked to make the state more docile. He changed the republic into a 'Batavian Commonwealth' in 1801, and this lasted down to 1806 when he put his brother Louis on the throne of a new kingdom of Holland.

COLIN JONES

Baumgarten, Alexander Gottlieb (1714–1762)   German founder of modern AESTHETICS. From 1740 until his death he was professor of philosophy at Frankfurt an der Oder. A follower of Wolff and Leibniz, he developed his theory in *Meditations on Poetry* (1735), and expanded it in his *Metaphysica* (1739; seventh edition, 1779) and his *Aesthetica* (2 volumes, 1750–8). Coining the term 'aesthetics', he placed the discipline beside logic as a 'science of cognition'. Logic dealt with reason, aesthetics treated the senses and their world, notably art. Unlike logic, aesthetics concerned 'clear and confused' (that is, heterogeneous) ideas: these were manifested to the senses by art, and provided a richer, more intuitive path to knowledge than 'abstraction', 'quickening the whole man'. This relativized the 'tyranny' of reason and revalued subjectivity, art and, in particular, poetry, which through beauty represented the 'harmony of the world'. Attacked by Gottsched, defended by Mendelssohn, Baumgarten's aesthetics subsequently played a key role in German philosophy from Kant and Schiller to Hegel and beyond.

G. E. Gilbert and H. Kuhn, *A History of Esthetics*, second rev. ed (London: Thames & Hudson, 1956), pp. 289–320.

JEREMY ADLER

Bavaria The electorate of Bavaria in south Germany was the most important second-rank German state after Austria and Prussia. It enjoyed the substantial advantage of a compact territory, declared indivisible in 1506, and was one of the earliest German states to acquire a centralized bureaucratic administration. In the sixteenth century its Wittelsbach rulers (*see* WITTELSBACHS) imposed absolutist government, enforcing strict Catholicism, emasculating the parliamentary estates and reducing the nobility to obedience. In the Thirty Years War it won more territory and the electoral title. Bavarian power was further enhanced when members of the ruling house were elected to a number of archbishoprics and bishoprics. In the eighteenth century it was the ambition of the Bavarian rulers to acquire more territory and to be elected Holy Roman Emperor. They pursued these aims by policies of opposition to the Austrian Habsburgs and alliance with France, often with disastrous consequences. Bavaria lacked the resources to be a great power, even in Germany. Between 1704 and 1714 it was occupied by Austrian forces and in 1706 the elector was placed under the ban of the Empire. French protection secured his reinstatement in 1714 but his lands had been devastated. Although after the extinction of the male Habsburg line the elector Charles Albert eventually won the imperial title in 1742, it was an empty victory. He was being used by France and Prussia, his country was again occupied by Austrian forces and, on his premature death in 1745, another Habsburg became emperor. Throughout the eighteenth century Bavaria was the object of exchange plans, under which the Wittelsbachs were to acquire the Netherlands or Lorraine and to recreate the kingdom of Burgundy in return for ceding the Bavarian lands to Austria. These plans, which would have had major consequences for Germany, came to nothing.

Bavaria remained a bastion of rigid Catholic orthodoxy until the reign of MAXIMILIAN JOSEPH – who, under the influence of the Enlightenment, opened his country to new ideas and carried out important administrative and legal reforms. Their impact was, however, limited and there was a sharp reaction against innovation in the later years of the elector Charles Theodore. Bavaria was briefly a centre of the Masonic ILLUMINATI movement, founded by Adam Weishaupt (1748–1830), which planned to put men of advanced ideas into positions of power in German states to hasten the implementation of enlightened policies. This was banned in 1784 and an official campaign was launched to root out all Illuminati. Bavaria was only superficially touched by the Enlightenment and remained characterized by a backward education system and an over-large bureaucracy and clergy. It was enlarged in the territorial reorganizations of Germany during the French revolutionary and Napoleonic period and became a kingdom in 1806. Important administrative and legal reforms were carried out by the chief minister Maximilian Joseph von Montgelas (1759–1838).

M. Spindler (ed.), *Handbuch der bayerischen Geschichte*, second edn, 4 vols (Munich: Beck, 1967–75).

MICHAEL HUGHES

Bavarian Succession, War of the   Joseph II's plan for Austrian recovery after its mid-century defeats envisaged the acquisition of neighbouring BAVARIA, and in January 1778 Austrian troops occupied Lower Bavaria on the death of Elector Maximilian Joseph without direct heir. Although accepted by the elector's designated successor in return for Austrian favours, this was opposed by Frederick the Great as a threat to the German balance of power and hence to Prussia. When Austria's ally France, intent on drawing advantage from the American Revolution, refused support, Frederick invaded northern Bohemia in July. However, since he was unwilling to take risks, the campaign stalemated in minor skirmishing, called by the Prussians 'the Potato War' from their efforts to find sustainance in such a barren area. Eventually a way out was found in the mediation of France and Russia. Austria gave up its larger claims but was awarded the Innviertal, which connected the Tyrol to Austria; Frederick withdrew from Bohemia but secured acceptance of his long-standing claim to Anspach and Bayreuth. Joseph's drive for a greater Austria had received a major setback, while Russia secured a claim to intervene in German affairs as guarantor of the Treaty of Teschen (May 1779).

MICHAEL DUFFY

Bayle, Pierre (1647–1706)   French Protestant philosopher. His youth was dominated by religious controversy. Reared as a Calvinist in France, he converted to Catholicism only to return to his own faith and eventually become professor of philosophy at Sedan under the mentorship of the Calvinist theologian Pierre Jurieu (1637–1713). In 1687 Bayle moved to Rotterdam where he published his first book, *Lettre sur la* *comète* (Letter on the Comet), in which he attacked intolerance and the current standards of philosophical and historical scholarship. The death of his brothers and father in France during the persecution of the HUGUENOTS deepened his commitment to the struggle for the right to free thought and the abolition of intolerance. Between 1684 and 1687 he published a monthly journal, *Nouvelles de la République des Lettres* (News of the Republic of Letters), reviewing books and establishing himself as one of Europe's pre-eminent FREETHINKERS.

In 1697 Bayle published his most influential work, the *Dictionnaire historique et critique* (Historical and Critical Dictionary). The *Dictionary* lists famous historical figures alphabetically and each entry is peppered with footnotes attacking previous scholarship and subverting any attempt to find rational truth. Although he may have been a fideist, it is more likely that Bayle was a pyrrhonist philosopher, basing his advocacy of tolerance on the argument that final certainties are unobtainable. The *Dictionary*'s scholarship and precision subsequently inspired Enlightenment encyclopaedists such as Diderot while Bayle's ambiguities provided one of the role models for eighteenth-century dialectical thought.

FRANCIS MCKEE

Beaumarchais, Pierre-Augustin Caron de (1732–1799)   French playwright. The son of a Parisian clock-maker, he took on the title of Beaumarchais from a small estate belonging to his first wife. He was apprenticed to his father and received little formal education. In 1753 he invented a new escapement for watches. In 1755 he became a minor court official and shortly after began to teach the harp to the royal princesses. Under the protection of the financier Joseph Pâris-Duverney (1684–1770), he entered the world of business and speculation and soon bought the sinecure of lieutenant-general of the hunt in the bailiwick and captaincy of the preserves of the Louvre. His life was marked by a series of adventures, romantic affairs, political intrigues and litigations.

His plays included *Eugénie* (1767), *Les Deux Amis, ou Le Négociant de Lyon* (The Two Friends, or The Negotiator from Lyons, 1770), and *L'Autre Tartuffe, ou La Mère coupable* (The Other Tartuffe, or The Guilty Mother, 1792). He also wrote an opera, *Tavare* (1787). The two comedies for which he is justly famous, *Le Barbier de Séville* (The Barber of Seville, 1775) and *Le Mariage de Figaro* (The Marriage of Figaro, 1784) are rich in social commentary and put into practice Diderot's theories about acting.

Frédéric Grendel, *Beaumarchais: The Man who was Figaro*, trans. Roger Greaves (London: Macdonald & Jane's, 1977).

SYLVANA TOMASELLI

Beccaria, Cesare marchese de (1738–1794) Italian moral and legal philosopher, political economist and reformer. Influenced by the leading *philosophes*, he was in his turn to be hailed by them when, at the age of 26, he published *Dei delitti e delle pene* (On Crimes and Punishments, 1764). Building on the notion that the true aim of society is 'the greatest happiness divided amongst the greatest number', he argued that the general interest resided in the diminution of crimes and that this consideration alone, rather than any notion of retribution, ought to govern the LAW. He combined utilitarian concerns with a theory of justice based on the doctrine of the social contract (differing in this respect from Jeremy Bentham, whom he influenced) to decry the practice of torture and capital punishment. He argued for the need for an intelligible and fixed legal code which would ascribe a specific and proportionate punishment to each offence, thereby putting an end to the arbitrariness of individual magistrates. Beccaria's book was phenomenally successful.

In 1768 a chair of political economy was created for him. He left a set of lectures on the subject, *Elementi di economia pubblica* (1804).

Marcello Maestro, *Cesare Beccaria and the Origins of Penal Reform* (Philadelphia: Temple University, 1973).

SYLVANA TOMASELLI

Beethoven, Ludwig van (1770–1827) German composer. Only his early work was written in the eighteenth century. This is of more than just biographical significance: with Beethoven a new age of music began. His music demanded unlimited attention from the listener, presenting an unprecedented challenge to an audience that was used to regarding art as an accessory to other activities.

He came from a Flemish family of musicians who settled in Bonn. His grandfather was a kapellmeister and his father a tenor singer. He himself was admitted to the court orchestra at the age of 11. Of his early compositions, a cantata on the death of the Austrian emperor Joseph II (1790) stands out, parts of which he later used for the final act of his opera *Fidelio*. In 1792 he moved to Vienna, primarily to take lessons from HAYDN. During the first years in Vienna he made his name mainly from performing as a piano virtuoso. His compositions were innovative in style, for example the String Quartets Op. 18 and the *Pathétique* Sonata.

Before 1800 Beethoven already knew that he was going deaf. The *Heiligenstadt Testament* (1802) is a stirring document of his deep personal crisis, which he overcame by means of music. Rebellion against fate can be heard in the Third Symphony (1803–4), with its powerful initial chord beats and stamping dissonant chords of the first movement. This symphony, which he called the *Eroica*, is also the work of a political radical: Beethoven had originally dedicated it to Napoleon Bonaparte, but erased the dedication when the latter proclaimed himself emperor. The formal achievements of the symphony, in particular the intensive thematic development within the sonata form of the first movement, influenced not only the structure of the next symphonies, but Beethoven's whole work, even the opera *Fidelio* (1805). From the Second Symphony onwards the Minuet was replaced by the Scherzo. There was even more formal freedom in the middle string quartets (Op. 59, 74 and 95) and the sonatas of this period (the *Kreutzer Sonata* for violin and piano, originally dedicated to the mulatto virtuoso George A. P. Bridgetower (1779–1840), and many of the piano sonatas such as the *Waldstein*, *Les Adieux* and *Appassionata*). The Seventh and Eighth Symphonies were written in 1811–12, and *Fidelio* was ultimately revised in 1814. By this time Beethoven was a well-respected composer with a reasonable income, from a group of wealthy Viennese patrons. However, his deafness proceeded rapidly, and he started to withdraw from public life. From 1819 he communicated with visitors only by means of his conversation books. He sketched a lot of music, but completed only a few works: the Piano Sonatas Op. 101 and 106 (*Hammerklavier*) and Op. 109 to 111 (1816–22), which broke new ground in their formal conception, the *Missa solemnis* (completed 1823), and the Ninth Symphony (1824), with its choral final movement and, in a change to the 'classical' order, a Scherzo second movement. Beethoven's last works, the String Quartets Op 130 to 133 and 135, point forward far into the future. The last quartet was completed in the autumn of 1826. When he died in March 1827, his funeral was attended by thousands of people.

Whereas Mozart had no direct successor, Beethoven was a strong influence on the next generation. He became the model of the independent artist, who composed from an inner necessity. He left behind him a far smaller number of works than either Haydn or Mozart: only nine symphonies, sixteen string quartets, five piano concertos, one violin and one triple concerto, one opera, thirty-two piano sonatas and some chamber music. His works were not variations on an established basic form. Every piece had a unique character, and a new, hitherto unknown, logical coherence; every detail was determined by the overall conception of the work. In that respect, too, his music set new standards for the future.

B. Cooper (ed.), *The Beethoven Compendium: A Guide to Beethoven's Life and Music* (London: Thames & Hudson, 1991).

J. Kerman and A. Tyson, *The New Grove Beethoven* (London: Macmillan, 1983).

M. Solomon, *Beethoven* (New York: Schirmer, 1977).

FRITZ WEBER

beggars Viewed as a social problem throughout the early modern period, begging seemed especially threatening in the eighteenth century as population growth spawned larger numbers of the indigent. Most states had devised means of treatment for beggars which involved some measure of confinement. Italian states had introduced 'hospitals' to imprison beggars from the late sixteenth century, and many Dutch and German cities followed suit in the seventeenth century. The English Poor Laws increasingly incorporated workhouses, while in France newly founded *hôpitaux généraux* (general hospitals) from the 1650s confined beggars, who were viewed as idle, ungodly, morally reprehensible and economically parasitic. The French state stepped up its policing operations over the eighteenth century – in 1724 the state mounted police rounded up beggars and deposited them in the 'general hospitals' while from 1767 state-run *dépôts de mendicité* were established. The French example reflected a growing involvement by central government in other states at about the same time. Yet this was accompanied by policies to provide work-schemes for the poor which would render begging less necessary for their livelihoods.

See also POVERTY AND POOR RELIEF, WORKHOUSE.

C. Lis and H. Soly, *Poverty and Capitalism in Pre-industrial Europe* (Brighton: Harvester, 1979).

COLIN JONES

Benedict XIV [Prospero Lorenzo Lambertini] (1675–1758) Pope (1740–58). Born in Bologna, he rose through the ranks of the church hierarchy, being consistorial advocate (1701), promoter of the faith (1708), assessor of the Congregation of Peter (1712), secretary of the Congregation of the Council (1718), archbishop of Ancona (1727), cardinal (1728), archbishop of Bologna (1731), and was elected pope in 1740, after a six-month conclave. He was interested in learning and intellectual developments, participating in the Italian CATHOLIC ENLIGHTENMENT which sought to purify and reform many aspects of church life. He wrote the standard history of diocesan synods, and the classic treatise on canonization, *De Servorum Dei Beatificatione et Beatorum Canonizatione* (1734–8), encouraged Winckelmann to establish the Vatican Museum of Antiquities, as well as showing interest in scientific matters, removing the ban of Copernicanism during his modernization of the work of the Index. He was an able administrator and sought to strengthen the pastoral role of his bishops, reducing the number of feast days, removing some legends from the Breviary and reviving the Mandatum – the custom of washing the feet of the poor on Maundy Thursday. He issued bulls concerning the suppression of pagan practices admitted into Christianity, especially by the Jesuits in

China, usury, mixed marriages and Jansenism. His debt to the Catholic Enlightenment was also shown in his conciliatory attitude not only to Catholic rulers, whom he allowed more control over church appointments within their own territories, but also to Protestant sovereigns.

Emilia Morelli, 'Benedetto XIV, Uomo et Pontifice', in *Tre Profili* (Rome: 1955), pp. 3–45.

JEREMY GREGORY

Bengal In the eighteenth century Bengal and the provinces of Bihar and Orissa formed a single political entity within the loose imperial structure of the MUGHAL EMPIRE. Although the three areas possessed very different cultures, traditions and economies, they had been brought together under the control of one nawab or governor, and that arrangement continued after the British secured control over the region in the 1760s.

Bengal itself was a very fertile region, well irrigated by the River Ganges and its ever-changing channels, and European observers often commented on the rich nature of the province. Even so, flood and famine often devastated the region, none more so than in 1769–70 when it was estimated that between a third and a fifth of a population of some 20 to 30 million people perished. In more stable times the region's agriculture was based on wheat, sugar, rice, betel nut, opium and tobacco, while in the west a significant proportion of the population were engaged in the production of silk and cotton goods.

European trading companies had been active in the region for more than a hundred years, but their ambitions had been restricted to the cultivation of commerce. However, the accession of Nawab Siraj-ud-daula in 1756 saw a concerted attempt made to restrict the scope of British activity, and this ultimately led to the BATTLE OF PLASSEY and the 'revolution' of 1757. The British now became the main power-brokers in the region, a fact that was recognized by the Mughal emperor in 1765 when he bestowed the office of Diwan upon the East India Company. This gave the Company the right to collect the territorial revenues of Bengal, Bihar and Orissa, and from this point on trade was subordinated to the need to transfer the revenue surplus from the region to London. Much of the revenue was absorbed by the Company's military and civil expenses, but the surplus, confidently but incorrectly expected to be several million pounds a year, was invested in commercial goods to be sold in London.

At first the British were content to supervise the existing revenue collection procedures, but diminishing returns meant that by the early 1770s a more active involvement was necessary. Company men replaced native officials at all levels of the collection process, and administrative control of Bengal was moved to CALCUTTA from the nawab's seat at Murshidabad. Yet these reforms, masterminded by Warren HASTINGS, did not have the desired effect and in 1793 the arrangement known as the Permanent Settlement was introduced. Landholders, or zemindars, now paid revenue to the company at a fixed rate in perpetuity, and provided that the sums were paid on time the land was regarded as their personal property. These changes drew the Company further into the administrative realm, and by the end of the century the British had taken responsibility for policing the region, administering justice and providing education on a small scale.

See also ENGLISH EAST INDIA COMPANY.

P. J. Marshall, *Bengal: The British Bridgehead: Eastern India 1740–1828* (Cambridge: Cambridge University Press, 1988).

HUW BOWEN

Bentham, Jeremy (1748–1832) English philosopher, jurist and reformer. The son and grandson of attorneys, he was called to the Bar in 1772. Although he never really practised it, the law remained the focal point of his concerns. In 1776 he published *Fragment on Government*, a critique of Sir William Blackstone's *Commentaries on the Laws of England*. Bentham argued for the need for the systematic codification of the law. He rejected the natural law tradition and ridiculed such notions as that of an original contract. Rather than being a system for securing promise-keeping, the law ought in his view to be based on the principle of utility. This principle received further exposition in the *Introduction to the Principles of Morals and Legislation* (1789). The springs of action, in his view, are the pursuit of pleasure and the avoidance of pain and this principle alone provides the true foundation for a theory of morals. Ensuring the greatest happiness for the greatest number of people was the only legitimate aim of government.

In 1785 Bentham visited Russia where he conceived of the idea of a penitentiary, the 'Panopticon', which ensured the total surveillance of prisoners. Although it was never built, Bentham had a considerable influence on penal reform, especially through his denial of criminal incorrigibility and his insistence on the feasibility and need for rehabilitation.

Bentham wrote on every conceivable topic, including gout, grammar, education, usury and embalmment, combining quintessential Enlightenment views with a reformist zeal typical of nineteenth-century philosophical radicalism. His name is principally associated with the doctrine of UTILITARIANISM and penal reform.

Ross Harrison, *Bentham* (London: Routledge & Kegan Paul, 1973).

SYLVANA TOMASELLI

Berkeley, George (1685–1753)   Bishop of Cloyne, friend of Jonathan Swift, philosopher, missionary and political pamphleteer. He is best known for his idealist contribution to British EMPIRICISM. Scornful of the ideas of deist freethinkers, like John Toland, who attributed activity to matter, Berkeley launched his attack on materialism. In his *Treatise concerning the Principles of Human Knowledge* (1710) he denied the existence of matter, claiming that it was only an idea. His doctrine 'esse est percipi' established that only ideas and spirits have ontological reality.

The South Sea crisis, which Berkeley blamed on irreligion, inspired his short-lived career as a missionary. His plan was to convert the natives of Bermuda to Christianity. But it was Newport, Boston, that he set sail for in 1728, once his quest for funds had elicited a promise of £20,000 from Walpole. No funds arrived and an embittered Berkeley returned to London in 1731 to pen further attacks on Newton's materialist disciples. After moving to Cloyne as bishop in 1734, he wrote the *Querist* (1735–7), but found fame with *Siris* (1744), in which he promoted tar-water as a panacea.

A. C. Grayling, *Berkeley: The Central Arguments* (London: Duckworth, 1986).

M. L. BENJAMIN

Berlin   The capital of the electorate of Brandenburg-Prussia/kingdom of PRUSSIA, Berlin owed its rise to its position as the residence of the Hohenzollerns rather than to natural factors. Its major development began during the reign of the Great Elector, Frederick-William I (1640–88), who built a number of new suburbs and attracted new people, most famously 5,000 Huguenot refugees from France, who made the city a manufacturing centre. It experienced substantial population growth in the eighteenth century, becoming a major commercial, manufacturing, cultural and administrative centre. It was also a large garrison town. Frederick I undertook substantial building work to make the city a fitting residence for his new royal house. His queen, Sophie Charlotte, in promoting cultural and scientific activities, transformed Berlin into a major artistic and intellectual centre. The first German Academy of Sciences was established there in 1711. A state bank was established in 1772 and the Seehandlung, a large state trading company, in 1772. By the last quarter of the eighteenth century it was second in size only to Vienna among German cities and was increasingly seen as the cultural capital of Protestant Germany.

750 Years Berlin: Information (Berlin: Presse- und Informationsamt des Landes Berlin, 1987).

MICHAEL HUGHES

Bernoulli, Daniel (1700–1782)   Swiss mathematician. The Groningen-born son of mathematician Jean Bernoulli (1667–1748), he was to outstrip his father's achievements, although for most of his professional life he held university posts in medicine. His *Exercitationes mathematicae* (1724) won him an invitation to St Petersburg, where he worked on oscillations and probability until he returned to Basle (where he had earlier studied) in 1733 to take up a chair in anatomy and botany.

Alongside Euler – with whom he developed close professional links – he dominated research into the dynamics of rigid bodies and the mechanics of flexible bodies. While he extended Leibniz's principle of *vis viva* for a system of mobile, mutually attracting mass points, his fame rests on his *Hydrodynamica* (1738), a comprehensive and far-reaching work on hydraulics. Bernoulli's pervasive interest in forces also guided his medical efforts and he wrote on muscular contraction, breathing and the heart as a pump. A genuine polymath, he submitted ten prize-winning essays to the Académie des Sciences, including one for best anchor design and one for improvements in compass construction. His appointment as professor of physics in 1750 was long overdue.

M. L. BENJAMIN

Bernoulli, Jakob [Jacques] (1654–1705)   Born in Basle to a merchant family of Dutch extraction, he studied mathematics and astronomy against his father's will. After becoming a tutor in Geneva, he began keeping a scientific diary, but this fascinating record of scientific life was abandoned when he went to France in 1679 (where he befriended Malebranche), and thence to England. On his return he published his *Dissertatio de gravitate aetheris* (1683), a treatise accounting for natural phenomena by collisions of ether particles.

In 1682, inspired by John Wallis (1616–1703) and Isaac Barrow (1630–77), he turned to the work for which he is best known, theories of exponential series. In 1685 he commenced medical studies under order of his father, but two years later became professor of mathematics at Basle, a post which he held until his death and to which his antagonistic brother Jean (1667–1748) succeeded. Though he solved the 'isoperimetric problem', his most original work was his *Ars conjectandi* (The Art of Conjecturing, 1713), an eclectic book containing his criticism of Huygens, his theory of combinations and his PROBABILITY theory – including his analysis of profit expectations in various games.

M. L. BENJAMIN

Bible   One of the most widely circulated books of the eighteenth century was the Holy Bible. The most popular translation was the Authorized Version which was without a serious rival among English-speaking

Protestants. Among Catholics the Vulgate remained the standard, but over seventy vernacular versions were in existence by the end of the century. The printing, distribution and readership of Bibles naturally varied from country to country, but circulation was particularly high in England, Scotland, Holland and those areas of Europe most influenced by Pietism. Conversely, the limited development of the printing trade in northern Europe produced a different pattern in Scandinavia. Although Bibles were widely distributed in the American colonies, the first indigenous printing of a European-language Bible occurred only in 1743 and the first English Bibles, for reasons of copyright, were not printed until after the Declaration of Independence.

Among the most significant developments of the century were the more widespread distribution of Bibles as both an expression of charity and a convenient tool of popular education, and the increased production of cheaper and smaller-scale versions. Bibles thus became more affordable, but Bible ownership and Bible-reading were still proportionately more common among the upper and middle classes. Although there was a plebeian Bible readership its size and level of understanding is relatively unknown.

See also EDUCATION, SUNDAY SCHOOLS.

S. L. Greenslade (ed.), *The Cambridge History of the Bible: The West from the Reformation to the Present Day* (Cambridge: Cambridge University Press, 1976).

DAVID HEMPTON

Bihar *see* BENGAL.

biology The term 'Biology' was not coined until 1800, but experimental studies of life (that is life science) were central to many natural philosophers' investigations during the Enlightenment. Chief among these were studies of reproductive generation in plants and animals (EMBRYOLOGY); qualifying the aliments and quantifying the air necessary to sustain animal life; explaining vital internal functions of the 'animal oeconomy' including digestion, respiration, and secretion (VITALISM); and identifying factors which internally regulated the animal oeconomy (for example soul versus nervous system). Information about living systems obtained from animal experimentation, dissection and vivisection was extrapolated to account for similar situations in humans.

In addition to determining the internal constitutions of living beings, influences of the external environment were also studied (nature versus nurture). Comparisons were made between healthy and disease-promoting environments, and studies were conducted to determine effects of the excess or deprivation of particular gases, foods, medicines and poisons. Investigators also compared structure–function relationships between different species and racially diverse groups. Overall, life science studies fostered speculation and experimentation in fields which later developed as physiology, anthropology, ethnography, ethology, ergonomics, evolution, agriculture and psychology.

T. S. Hall, *Ideas of Life and Matter: Studies in the History of General Physiology, 600 B.C.–A.D. 1900* (Chicago: University of Chicago Press, 1969).

PHILIP K. WILSON

Black, Joseph (1728–1799) Scottish chemist. The Scottish Enlightenment's best-known chemist, he was initiated into the field as William Cullen's (1710–90) assistant. His MD thesis was the basis for his classic paper on 'fixed air' (carbon dioxide), published in the *Essays and Observations* (1756) of the Edinburgh Philosophical Society. According to Black, when alkalis are heated an acidic air trapped within them which neutralizes their causticity is released. The paper ensured Black's appointment as professor of chemistry at Glasgow at the age of 28. In 1766 he succeeded Cullen at Edinburgh.

Black devoted himself to teaching and lecturing, but found time to run a small medical practice and to continue experimental work with fixed air. In 1760 he began investigating heat; he conceived of latent heat and calculated the amount of heat absorbed when various liquids vaporized, then, alongside James WATT, he calculated the specific heats of various substances. While he taught Lavoisier's new chemistry, he always believed in phlogiston. His friends included Adam Smith and James Hutton (1726–97) with whom he founded the Oyster Club, and the most illustrious of his pupils were John Robison (1739–1805) and Thomas Charles Hope (1766–1844).

A. D. C. Simpson (ed.), *Joseph Black 1728–1799: A Commemorative Symposium* (Edinburgh: Royal Scottish Museum, 1982).

M. L. BENJAMIN

blacks In the eighteenth century the word 'Negro' was applied to the many diverse peoples who lived in Africa south of the Sahara or who originated from there. The word in both its plural and singular forms had racist overtones then as now. Johnson's *Dictionary*, for instance, defined 'negro' as 'a blackamoor', which in turn was defined as 'a man by nature of a black complexion'. While the definition was not necessarily racist, it did emphasize the physical characteristic of skin colour rather than the cultural and geographical attributes which words like 'European' and 'Asian' imply.

As Africans, however, 'Negroes' in the eighteenth century had a rich history, in which the slave trade and European colonial penetration, as well as Arab influence and overlordship in east Africa, were only part of a much larger picture. There were many independent 'Negro' cultures that came to fruition during the period. In west Africa empires were forged by the Yorubas in Oyo and Benin, and by the Asante in what is now Ghana (and other areas); the Hausas founded feudal Islamic city-states in what is now northern Nigeria. In the early 1800s, Uthman dan Fodio (1754–1817), a Fulani, led a revolt which reorganized Hausaland along Islamic reformist lines, which also influenced political developments in the Sudan and elsewhere. In contrast to the various monarchical empires, the Ibos in what is now southern Nigeria lived in autonomous and democratically ruled villages. A freed slave named Equiano (c.1745–c.1801) vividly described the Ibo society from which he was kidnapped as a child in his autobiography *The Interesting Narrative of the Life of Olaudah Equiano, or Gustavus Vassa the African* (1789).

Another important 'Negro' people, the Bantu, were dominant in southern Africa. Among them, the Zulus, under the political and military leadership of Shaka the Great, held sway in the early nineteenth century. With British backing, freed slaves settled in Sierra Leone in 1787; and freed slaves from America settled in Liberia in 1821. Both settlements became forerunners of modern African nation states. The oldest 'Negro' state in Africa, the ancient Christian state of Ethiopia experienced great political upheavals in what was known as the 'era of the princes'.

'Negroes' in Africa during the eighteenth century present a complex picture. Equiano should have the last word: 'in regard to complexion, ideas of beauty are wholly relative. I remember while in Africa to have seen three negro children who were tawny, and another quite white, who were universally regarded by myself and the natives in general, as far as related to their complexions, as deformed'.

See also AFRICA, SLAVERY, SLAVE TRADE.

Basil Davidson, *Africa in History*, rev. edn (London: Granada, 1974).
Olaudah Equiano, *Equiano's Travels*, abridged and ed. Paul Edwards (Oxford: Heinemann, 1967).
Joseph E. Harris, *Africans and their History* (New York: New American Library, 1972).

MARIO RELICH

Blackstone, Sir **William** (1723–1780) English jurist. Called to the Bar in 1746, he became the first Vinerian professor of English law at Oxford in 1758. He was member of parliament for Hindon, in Wiltshire, and became solicitor-general to the queen in 1763. In 1765–9 he published his four-volume work *Commentaries on the Laws of England*. Based on the lectures he had been giving at Oxford since

1753, it consisted in a systematic statement of English law and was an instant success. The work, a formidable achievement by any standard, endeavoured to show the law as an ordered and rational body of knowledge and hence also as a worthy subject of general study. Although Blackstone appealed to the NATURAL LAW tradition, he sought to combine this approach with a historical account of English law. This led to some inconsistencies as well as a notable silence on the question of the validity of civil laws which defied the laws of nature. Joseph Priestley was among those who attacked Blackstone's account of the Toleration Act in 1769, while Jeremy Bentham's *Fragment on Government* took exception to nearly every aspect of the *Commentaries*.

David Lieberman, *The Province of Legislation Determined: Legal Theory in Eighteenth-Century Britain* (Cambridge: Cambridge University Press, 1989).

SYLVANA TOMASELLI

Blake, William (1757–1827)   English poet and artist. He started out as a book-engraver and innovated a method for printing and illustrating his own poems. *Songs of Innocence* (1789) represented his first attempt to merge image and text. For Blake, art, the imagination and spirituality were inseparable. This synthesis evolved into a cosmic mythology which he used in *The Book of Thel* (1789) and developed further in *The Four Zoas* (1797–1804), *Jerusalem* (1804–20) and *Milton* (1804–8). In 1794 the *Songs of Experience* appeared which included the lyric 'London', a spirited protest against social injustice. Resisting the mind-forged manacles of religion and state, Blake produced several revolutionary prophetic books, *The French Revolution* (1791), *America* (1793) and *Europe* (1794). His belief in the apocalypse was fuelled by SWEDENBORG, the founder of the Church of the New Jerusalem, who had inspired the poet's aphoristic *Marriage of Heaven and Hell* (1790–3). Because of his genius, mysticism and eccentric lifestyle, Blake was thought by some to have been insane, including Wordsworth who remarked that 'there is something in the madness of this man which interests me more than the sanity of Lord Byron and Walter Scott'. Blake's radical philosophy, rejection of materialism, reaction against orthodox Christianity and ability to convey his personal mythology, unique visionary and imaginative power through his painting and poetry has had a profound influence on psychoanalysts, Marxists, revolutionaries and freethinkers.

Northrop Frye, *Fearful Symmetry* (Princeton, NJ: Princeton University Press, 1947).

MARIE MULVEY ROBERTS

Blenheim, Battle of (13 August 1704)   In the summer of 1704 the duke of MARLBOROUGH cut loose from his base in the low countries and led a multinational army (Dutch, Germans and Danes, with less than 10,000 British) southwards to the Danube. His intention was to bring to battle the forces of France and Bavaria, which were menacing Vienna. On 13 August they were surprised by his early morning attack at Blenheim. Prince EUGENE's Austrian troops advanced against the Bavarians on one wing, while on the French right wing the village of Blenheim on the Danube was fiercely attacked. As both French wings became more and more heavily engaged and called for reinforcements, the centre, already too weak, collapsed in the late afternoon under Marlborough's combined infantry and cavalry assault. The French marshal Tallard (1652–1728) fell into the hands of the allies, having lost 18,000 men killed and wounded, and 13,000 prisoners. The army of Marlborough and Eugene suffered 12,000 casualties. The threat to Vienna had been averted, the alliance of Britain, the Habsburg Empire and the Netherlands was strengthened, and Marlborough was regarded as the most successful general of his time.

David Green, *Blenheim* (London: Collins, 1974).

TONY HAYTER

Bodmer, Johann Jakob (1698–1783)   Swiss critic. He collaborated closely with Johann Jakob Breitinger (1701–76) to extend the frontiers of literature. This entailed a feud with GOTTSCHED, in which they opposed the latter's rationalist concept of poetry and took the part of the imagination. They put forward their views jointly in works like the journal *Discourse der Mahlern* (The Discourses of the Painters, 1721–3), which emulated *The Spectator*, and in converging publications like Bodmer's *Von dem Wunderbaren in der Poesie* (Critical Dissertation on the Marvellous in Poetry, 1740) and Breitinger's *Critische Dichtkunst* (Critical Poetics, 1740). Against rationalist objections, they defended Milton's bold invention, HALLER's alleged obscurity, and KLOPSTOCK's imagination. If their understanding of the 'marvellous' was somewhat limited (Breitinger called it 'hidden plausibility'), their views, allied with those of Baumgarten and others, contributed to the revival of German letters.

F. Radant, *From Baroque to Storm and Stress* (London: Croom Helm, 1977), pp. 50–4.

JEREMY ADLER

Boerhaave, Hermann (1668–1738)   Dutch physician and natural philosopher. Internationally renowned as the head of the Leiden University medical faculty, he exerted a wide-ranging and long-lasting influence on the teaching and practice of natural philosophy and medicine throughout Europe. Changing to scientific studies after a religious education, Boerhaave was a popular and likeable man with extensive scholarly interests. He started lecturing on medicine at Leiden in 1701, and subsequently acquired several senior institutional posts, including chairs in botany, medicine and chemistry. He catalogued and dramatically expanded Leiden's botanical garden. Under his reorganizing initiative, Leiden rapidly gained prestige to become Europe's foremost medical centre, emulated by other universities and attracting hundreds of foreign students to study his creative, comprehensive systematization of old and new medical knowledge, and to pursue his revived Hippocratic practice of bedside clinical observation. Opposing the animistic organicism of many contemporaries, he favoured a mechanistic, corpuscular approach, stressing the need for methodical observation and quantitative analyses. Abroad, Boerhaave's medical and chemical texts, based on his lectures, became standard works of reference, and his followers played a key role in disseminating the Newtonian experimental approach to natural philosophy.

G. Lindeboom, *Herman Boerhaave* (London: Methuen, 1968).

PATRICIA FARA

Bohemia The Patent of Toleration and the Abolition of Serfdom proclaimed by Joseph II in 1781 were tangible expressions of the Enlightenment adapted to the reforming needs of Austrian absolutism. What is less appreciated is the Bohemian connection of the celebrated Josephinian measures. They represent partial, albeit significant, solutions to some of the contradictions inherent in a situation where the government and much of the nobility attached great importance to developments in industry, agriculture and trade in Bohemia, but hoped to achieve them without seriously undermining the existing feudal social order. From the interaction of political, social, economic and intellectual factors the idea grew that the sciences and education could have an active role to play in this process. This led to the formation of the Royal Bohemian Society of Sciences (*c.*1774), to the survey of natural wealth of Bohemia and to the introduction of 'industrial schooling'. Last but not least was the emergence of the study of Czech history and language, and the awakening of modern Czech national consciousness, as its product and consequence.

Mikuláš Teich, 'Bohemia: From Darkness into Light', in Roy Porter and Mikuláš Teich (eds), *The Enlightenment in National Context* (Cambridge: Cambridge University Press, 1981), pp. 141–63.

MIKULÁŠ TEICH

Boileau [Boileau Despréaux], **Nicolas** (1636–1711)   French poet and critic. Emerging in the early 1660s with Juvenalian satires on the *mœurs* of Paris, sycophantic poets and certain figures of authority, he became the leading critic and theorist of his era and the representative of neoclassicism for the eighteenth century. He translated (or adapted) Horace's *Art of Poetry* and Longinus' *On the Sublime* (published together in 1674). To many commentators this reflects a paradoxical ambivalence. Can an emphasis on rules, 'good sense', reason, probability (*vraisemblance*) and decorum (*les bienséances*) be consistent with a celebration of inspiration and exaltation in which poet and audience are taken out of themselves? For Boileau there was no antagonism: imitation of nature and of great poets was the basis of the Longinian sublime, rapture had need of method, and in writing and judging poetry good sense or reason worked as a subtly intuitive, inexplicable taste, a *je ne sais quoi*. His own satires were marked by exuberant play, alternately vehement and reflexive, and were a model for Dryden and Pope. His influence, as a critic, on La Fontaine, Molière and Racine has been exaggerated, but his negative reputation as a rule-bound pedant, prevalent since the romantic attack on neoclassicism, is undeserved.

G. Pocock, *Boileau and the Nature of Neo-classicism* (Cambridge: Cambridge University Press, 1980).

JEFFREY BARNOUW

Bolingbroke, Henry St John, first viscount (1678–1751)   Tory author and politician. He entered the Commons in 1701 and went to the Lords in 1712. From 1704 to 1708 he was secretary at war, allying with Robert Harley (1661–1724), and was his colleague and rival in the ministry of 1710–14. His great achievement was the Treaty of Utrecht (1713). However, it cost him Hanover's support, and he inclined towards a Stuart restoration. After Queen Anne's death he fled to France, and was briefly the Pretender's secretary of state.

Pardoned in 1723, but refused his Lords seat, he led a literary onslaught on the prime minister Walpole. With Pulteney, Swift, Pope and Gay in their newspaper *The Craftsman*, he lambasted the corrupt 'Robinocracy', demanding frequent elections and limits on placemen and standing armies. Although Walpole's Excise Bill (1733) was defeated, he was not dislodged, and after 1734 Bolingbroke went into retirement. His *Remarks on the History of England* (1730–1) and *Dissertation upon Parties* (1733–4) grew out of *Craftsman* essays. Together with *The Idea of a Patriot King* (1738), they argued for an end to party divisions to revitalize England's liberties. The *Letters on the Study of History* (1735) coined the phrase 'history is philosophy teaching by examples'. Bolingbroke's libertinism, deism and Whig view of history made him an odd sort of Tory.

H. T. Dickinson, *Bolingbroke* (London, 1970).

MARK GOLDIE

Simón Bolívar (1783–1830)   South American revolutionary, liberator of Venezuela, Colombia, Ecuador, Peru and Bolivia from Spanish rule. He was born into a rich creole family in Caracas. Having a mulatto heiress as one ancestor did not prevent him from living an elegant aristocratic existence. Orphaned as a boy and widowed as an adolescent, Bolívar was strongly educated in eighteenth-century enlightened thought and in the revolutionary heritage of 1789. In 1805 he vowed to dedicate himself to the liberation of SPANISH AMERICA and to his own glory. Thus, with the help of other radicals, he persuaded the Venezuelan elite to declare independence (5 July 1811) and embarked on a series of military campaigns which eventually liberated the northern half of Spanish South America. Bolívar was fortunate to lead many skilled officers, like Antonio José Sucre (1795–1830), who achieved many outstanding successes. His own greatness lay in his military skills, his energy and determination, his ability to inspire others by his example and his numerous writings, and his enlightened vision of a just, peace-loving, well-governed and well-educated Hispanic America. But by 1830 he had achieved only liberation, partly because of personal weaknesses. He died in political exile, poor and disillusioned.

G. Masur, *Simon Bolivar* (Albuquerque, NM: University of New Mexico, 1969).

CHARLES C. NOEL

Bonaparte Jerome (1784–1860)   King of Westphalia (1807–13), youngest brother of Napoleon BONAPARTE. Too young to play any part in his brother's rise to power, he spent the first years of the Consulate living in the Tuilieries, with Napoleon. At 16 he was made captain of a frigate patrolling the West Indies and, while in port in America, met and married an American, Betty Patterson, in 1803, without Napoleon's permission. This led to Jerome's estrangement from Napoleon, which ended in 1805 when he allowed his marriage to be annulled. Soon afterwards he was made a lieutanant-general and an admiral. Jerome's adult career began in 1807; that year saw his marriage to a daughter of the king of Württemberg and his creation as the king of Westphalia, following the Treaty of Tilsit between Napoleon and Alexander I of Russia. Westphalia was carved out of Hesse-Kassel, Hanover and Prussian territories between the Rhine and the Elbe, but its integrity was compromised by extensive land grants to Napoleonic nobles inside it and territorial losses to areas annexed directly to France. It was intended as a model kingdom, but many of Jerome's French-style reforms were frustrated, such as his attempts to abolish feudalism thoroughly. He served in the Russian campaign of 1812, but his tactics were bitterly criticized by Napoleon. He remained loyal throughout 1813–14, staying in Westphalia as long as possible, where he proved an able administrator in a crisis, although previously his personal conduct had been marked by loose living and high spending. Jerome rallied to Napoleon in 1815, retiring to Rome after Waterloo where he remained aloof from politics, denouncing his nephew Louis Napoleon's attempted coup in 1836. He played little part in the life of the Second Empire, despite living until 1860.

O. Connelly, *Napoleon's Satellite Kingdoms* (New York: Scholarly Resources, 1965–9).

S. J. Woolf, *Napoleon and the Integration of Europe* (London: Routledge, 1991).

MICHAEL BROERS

Bonaparte, Joseph (1768–1844)   King of Naples (1806–8) and Spain (1808–12), elder brother of Napoleon BONAPARTE. In 1779, when Napoleon was sent to military college, Joseph entered the seminary at Autun, but left it in 1784 to pursue a military career. During the revolutionary period, he held a number of posts in Corsican local government, being elected deputy for Liamone in 1797. He displayed considerable ability as a diplomat in the first years of the Consulate, most notably in the negotiations of the Treaties of Luneville (1801) and Amiens (1802). Despite his associations with opposition circles during the Consulate, he became king of the Two Sicilies in February 1806, following the occupation of its mainland possessions by French troops. Aided by able French ministers, notably Salicetti (1757–1809) and Roederer (1754–1835), he carried out sweeping reforms in the face of serious banditry and social disorder; these included the abolition of feudalism and enduring administrative and legal reforms which were continued by his successor, Murat. In 1808 he became king of Spain, where his reforming ideas were less successful, and the country was never really under his control. In 1810 much of northern Spain was put under direct French rule and by July 1812 Wellington had driven him from Madrid. His attempts at generalship ended in the defeat of Vittoria in June 1813 and he was soon removed to Paris, in disgrace, by Napoleon. Throughout 1813–14, he lobbied actively for a peace settlement; his conduct in 1814 was defeatist and it was due to him that Marie Louise (1791–1847) left Paris at a crucial point, destroying hopes of a Bonapartist regency. Exiled to Switzerland in

1814, he rallied to Napoleon in the Hundred Days, escaping to the United States after Waterloo, where he spent most of the rest of his life as a successful landowner and patron of the arts.

O. Connelly, *The Gentle Bonaparte: Napoleon's Elder Brother* (New York, 1968).

O. Connelly, *Napoleon's Satellite Kingdoms* (New York: Scholarly Resources, 1965-9).

G. H. Lovett, *Napoleon and the Birth of Modern Spain*, 2 vols (New York, 1965).

S. J. Woolf, *Napoleon and the Integration of Europe* (London: Routledge, 1991).

MICHAEL BROERS

Bonaparte, Josephine (1763–1814)   French empress, wife of Napoleon BONAPARTE. Born into an aristocratic creole family on the Caribbean island of Martinique, she was first married to the vicomte de Beauharnais, by whom she had two children, Eugene (Napoleon's viceroy in the kingdom of Italy) and Hortense (wife of Napoleon's younger brother Louis, king of Holland, and the mother of the future Napoleon III). De Beauharnais was a liberal noble who supported the Revolution and served as a general; disgraced and arrested, he was executed in 1794 and Josephine was spared execution only by the fall of Robespierre. She then briefly became the mistress of the director Barras, who discarded her, but introduced her to Napoleon Bonaparte, who married her in March 1796. Two days later he left to assume command of the army of Italy. Josephine was unfaithful to him between 1796 and 1798, but the marriage survived to see her crowned empress in December 1804. Her failure to produce an heir led Napoleon to consider divorce as early as 1807, particularly because he had illegitimate sons by Maria Walewska and Eleonore Denuelle, proving Josephine to be barren. The issue was compounded in 1807 by the death of Napoleon Charles, then the only son of Louis Bonaparte and Hortense, and thus the only heir in the Bonaparte family. After several attempts to marry Russian princesses, Napoleon divorced Josephine to marry Marie Louise, daughter of the Austrian emperor, in 1810. After the divorce, Josephine lived quietly at Marmottan and Napoleon continued to pay her extensive debts, which had always been a strain on their married life. She died in May 1814, after a short illness, having recently played hostess to Tsar Alexander I.

A. Castelot, *Josephine* (Paris, 1964).

MICHAEL BROERS

Bonaparte, Louis (1778–1846)   King of Holland (1806–10), younger brother of Napoleon BONAPARTE, father of Napoleon III (1808–73). His early career shadowed that of his famous elder brother more closely than those of Joseph or Lucien. He went to military school, entering the artillery in 1794, as did Napoleon and Joseph, then served on Napoleon's staff at the army of the interior and on the first Italian campaign of 1796, and followed him to Egypt in 1798. He married Hortense de Beauharnais (1783–1837), Josephine's daughter, in 1802, at Napoleon's instigation. Despite the birth of several children, among them Louis Napoleon (the future Napoleon III) in 1808, the marriage was never a happy one, and the couple formally separated in 1809, with Napoleon's grudging agreement.

Louis was highly trusted by Napoleon during the first years of the empire, and was offered the throne of Spain in 1808 before Joseph. He refused it, but accepted that of Holland in 1806. He proved an energetic, reforming and overly independent ruler, openly identifying with his subjects, rather than with the empire. He co-ordinated a series of major, enduring legal, financial and administrative reforms while opposing Napoleon's attempts to conscript the Dutch into the imperial armies. All this, together with his inability to enforce the Continental System, infuriated Napoleon. He refused to exchange the throne of Holland for Spain and was then forced to abdicate in 1810, although he contemplated armed resistance for a time. He spent the years 1811–13 in exile in Bohemia, rallied to Napoleon during the Hundred Days and spent the latter part of his life largely in Rome.

O. Connelly, *Napoleon's Satellite Kingdoms* (New York: Scholarly Resources, 1965–9).

S. Schama, *Patriots and Liberators* (New York: Collins, 1977), part 3.

MICHAEL BROERS

Bonaparte, Lucien (1775–1840)   Third son of Carlo (1746–85) and Letizia (1750–1836) Buonaparte, after Joseph and Napoleon. He was the only one of Napoleon BONAPARTE's brothers with any claim to a career not wholly dependent on him, and is also regarded as the most independent and rebellious member of the Bonaparte family. He played a crucial role in the *coup* of 18 Brumaire when, as president of the Council of 500 he kept his presence of mind to steer the seizure of power through the assembly when Napoleon temporarily lost his nerve. Although this was his most famous act, his most important contribution was as Napoleon's first minister of the interior (1800–2): he virtually laid the foundations of the regime through his key role in the choice of the first prefects, who were to form the backbone of the administration. His first wife, Christine Boyer, died in 1801 and he met his second, Alexandrine de Bleschamp, while he was ambassador to Madrid, in 1802. Napoleon recalled him from Spain, dissatisfied with the treaty Lucien had negotiated and angered at the marriage. Lucien intrigued with the opposition from 1802 to 1804. Although he was created prince of Canino by the pope, he refused to play an active part in politics, despite many attempts (the last in 1807) by Napoleon to reintegrate him, or to divorce his wife. In 1809 he attempted to emigrate to America but was captured by the British. He spent several years in Worcestershire, rallied to Napoleon in the Hundred Days and lived most of his later life in exile in Rome.

F. Markham, *Napoleon* (London: Weidenfeld & Nicolson, 1963).
G. Martineau, *Madame Mère* (London: John Murray, 1981).
J. Tulard, *Napoleon: Le mythe du sauveur* (Paris: Fayard, 1977).

MICHAEL BROERS

Bonaparte, Napoleon [Napoleon I] (1769–1821)   First consul and *de facto* ruler of France (1799–1804), emperor (1804–14, 1815). He was born into a family of minor nobility in Ajaccio, Corsica. His father, Carlo (1746–85), had been a supporter of the rebel leader Paoli (1725–1807), but then changed sides in the struggle against the French, and sent Napoleon to the royal military college at Brienne, from 1779 to 1784. This was followed by a year at the military college in Paris and a commission in the artillery at Valence. His early career was marked by steady progress rather than brilliance, but the events of the FRENCH REVOLUTION accelerated his advancement, as with many of his fellow officers, although its volatile politics also created certain dangers. In the period 1789–95 he was to experience both. He spent most of 1789–92 in Corsica, where his family allied itself to the radical faction in the island, now led by Paoli. Its defeat in the local power struggles led to the entire family's flight to Toulon. Regarded by the Montagnards as politically reliable, Napoleon served with distinction in the siege of Toulon, where he was promoted to brigadier-general. He was imprisoned briefly, in August 1794, following the fall of the Montagnards, and on his release went to Paris, where he spent the following year lobbying unsuccessfully for a posting. It was during this period that he came to the attention of the influential director Barras, who employed him to crush the attempted royalist rising of Vendemiaire, an action which brought him the command of the army of the interior. In 1796 he married Barras's ex-mistress, Josephine de Beauharnais (*see* Josephine BONAPARTE), and was appointed commander of the army of Italy.

Napoleon led the army of Italy to a series of stunning victories over the Austro-Russian armies, begining in the spring of 1796 and by February 1797 he had driven them out of the whole peninsula. During this period he conducted his own foreign policy, virtually independent of the Directory, the most important aspect of which was the creation of a satellite republic, the Cisalpine, based on Lombardy, which many viewed as his personal fief. The first Italian campaign established Napoleon as one of the foremost military and political figures in Europe, and he soon extended his influence into French domestic politics when he carried out the purge of Fructidor for the Directory, through his subordinate Augereau. It was also during this time that Napoleon established close relations with many of his ablest generals, such as Berthier (1753–1815) and Massena (1758–1817), and with the men of the army of Italy. These men were the core of the army he took across the Mediterranean in an attempt to seize Egypt, in 1798. Although initially successful on land, the expedition was cut off from France when the British sank the French fleet off Akabar in July 1798 (*see* BATTLE OF ABOUKIR BAY). Napoleon virtually abandoned his army, returning to France to plunge into politics. The army of Egypt also contained a scientific expedition, among whose most notable achievements was the discovery of the Rossetta Stone.

By 1799, the Directory was faced by discontent from both Left and Right, together with a series of military reverses which included the entire loss of Italy to the allies. A group of politicians within the government invited Napoleon to lead a purge, the coup of 18 Brumaire, which set up a new constitution centred on a stronger executive led by Napoleon as first consul with two leading politicians, Lebrun and Sieyès, as second and third consuls. Their authority quickly faded, as Napoleon consolidated his position in power.

He reconquered Italy in the second Italian campaign (1800–1), reestablishing the Cisalpine (later Italian) Republic, with himself as president. A series of treaties with the allies, culminating in that of Amiens in 1802, established the only comprehensive period of peace in Europe between 1792 and 1815. It was in this period that Napoleon consolidiated his grip on France and carried out his most important domestic reforms, chiefly the establishment of the prefectorial system, the negotiation of the Concordat with Rome and the systematic compilation of the legal reforms of the revolutionary period, the CODE NAPOLÉON. The power of the executive increased in this period; Napoleon became first consul for life in 1802, and was made hereditary emperor in 1804.

When hostilies resumed in 1803, a series of stunning military victories established French hegemony in central as well as western Europe. Abandoning a plan to invade England in August 1805, he marched his army into central Europe where he defeated the Austrians at Ulm on 20 October 1805, and comprehensively defeated an Austro-Russian force at AUSTERLITZ on 1 December 1805. Austria sued for peace and at the Treaty of Pressburg in 1806 the Holy Roman Empire was dissolved and a series of French satellite states created in western and central Germany. In October 1806 Napoleon crushed the Prussians in the Battles of JENA and Aurestaedt; Prussia was forced into an alliance with France and its territories between the Elbe and the Rhine were brought under French control. Napoleon was unable to match these successes at sea, against the British, and he never recovered from the destruction of his fleet at TRAFALGAR in October 1805.

Napoleon invaded Spain in 1808, but failed to consolidate his grip on the country, thereby allowing the British to intervene on land. The 1809 Wagram campaign against Austria was an unqualified victory, following which Napoleon divorced Josephine and married Marie Louise, daughter of Francis I. In 1811 a much-desired heir was born, the king of Rome.

From November 1806 onwards, Napoleon tried to defeat Britain through economic warfare, the Continental System, which never succeeded. In his attempts to enforce the blockade, he annexed the North Sea coast as far as Hamburg, which entailed the deposition of his brother Louis whom he had made king of Holland in 1806, and in 1809 he occupied the Papal States, which led to his excommunication. This policy also led to increasingly bad relations with the Baltic states, which culminated in Napoleon's invasion of Russia in 1812. After some initial successes, including the capture of Moscow, Napoleon's army was almost annihilated in a disastrous defeat, which was followed by a series of allied victories in central Europe. By the spring of 1814, Napoleon was fighting in France again. When Talleyrand and Fouche (1763–1829), his chief collaborators, turned against him, Napoleon abdicated on 11 April 1814. The allies restored Louis XVIII to the French throne and quickly dismembered Napoleon's empire at the Congress of Vienna. He was exiled to Elba, but escaped to France on 1 March 1815 and re-established his rule within a few weeks. Louis XVIII fled to Brussels where an allied army under Wellington was assembled. This force defeated Napoleon at WATERLOO on 18 June 1815. This episode, 'the Hundred Days', ended with a second abdication and Napoleon's exile to the remote island of St Helena. Here his health quickly deteriorated and he died on 5 May 1821, but not before he had written his influential memoirs.

L. Bergeron, *France under Napoleon* (Princeton: Princeton University Press, 1981).
G. Ellis, *The Napoleonic Empire* (London: Macmillan, 1991).
J. Tulard, *Napoleon, le mythe du sauveur* (Paris: Fayard, 1977).
S. J. Woolf, *Napoleon and the Integration of Europe* (London: Routledge, 1991).

MICHAEL BROERS

Bonnet, Charles (1720–1793) Swiss naturalist and philosopher. Blindness later made him dependent on assistants but theoretical creativity compensated for visual handicap and he stimulated the work of many correspondents. His discovery of the parthenogenesis of the aphid led to work on regeneration, summarized in his magisterial *Traité d'insectologie* (Treatise on Entomology, 1746). In plant physiology his concept of palingenesis has been held to prefigure a viable germ theory. His observations were conducted in the framework of an optimistic Christian natural philosophy indebted to Leibniz. His popular apologetics *Contemplation de la Nature* (The Contemplation of Nature, 1764) attracted widespread esteem. His belief in the CHAIN OF BEING precluded transmutation of species, but Bonnet saw all creation as progressing to higher life forms in a God-directed process of perfectibility. Bodily resurrection he saw as analogous to metamorphoses in the life-cycle, based on the soul's inherent growth potential. In embryological controversies he adhered to a form of preformationism.

Jacques Marx, *Charles Bonnet contre les lumières 1738–1850* (Oxford: Voltaire Foundation, 1976).

CLARISSA CAMPBELL ORR

bookselling *see* PUBLISHING.

Bordeu, Théophile de (1722–1776) French physician and thinker closely linked with the *philosophes*. Born into a medical family from the Béarn in south-western France, he trained in the Montpellier medical faculty before making his fortune in Paris. He combined scholarly with worldly ambition, and became a corresponding member of the Académie des Sciences as well as securing lucrative posts as intendant and inspector of mineral water spas in Aquitaine. Patronized by the circle of Madame du Barry, Louis XV's last mistress, he became one of the most sought-after physicians attendant on the court, successfully fighting off petty jealousies of rival Parisian physicians. The death of Louis XV in 1774 and the disgrace of Madame du Barry ended his hopes of reaching the post of first physician, and tragically he died shortly afterwards. Bordeu was a collaborator of the *philosophes*, contributing to the *Encyclopédie* and maintaining friendships with Diderot and d'Alembert. He appears in Diderot's *Rêve de d'Alembert*. A renowned practitioner, he was also a pioneer of hydrotherapy, while his work on secretions of the glands marks him out as an early precursor of endocrinology.

Marthe Fletcher (ed.), *Théophile de Bordeu: Correspondance*, 4 vols (Montpellier: CNRS, 1973).

COLIN JONES

Boscovich, Roger Joseph (1711–1787) Croatian Jesuit mathematician and natural philosopher. He had many interests, but is most famous today for his non-Newtonian analysis of force, space and matter, which is said to have influenced nineteenth-century formulations of field theory. Religiously trained in Italy from an early age, he became a professor of mathematics at Rome in 1740, where he wrote educational texts and carried out various engineering commissions and archaeological investigations. Between 1759 and 1763 he travelled to Paris and then throughout Europe, where he was celebrated in scientific, ecclesiastical and diplomatic circles. He spent the following ten years in Italy studying astronomy and applied mathematics, and went to Paris after the papal suppression of the Jesuits, returning to Italy in 1782. He published many books on a wide range of topics, and designed astronomical, optical and geodesic instruments, focusing on error reduction. Adopting a novel theoretical approach to mathematics, mechanics and natural philosophy, he postulated that matter consists of point centres of dynamic interaction, linked by forces alternately repulsive and attractive with distance.

Lancelot Whyte (ed.), *Roger Joseph Boscovich* (London: Allen & Unwin, 1961).

PATRICIA FARA

Bossuet, Jacques Bénigne (1627–1704)   French bishop, orator, historian and theorist of absolutism. From a legal family, and trained by the Jesuits, he made his mark as a preacher. His funeral orations were the apogee of French classical oratory. Briefly bishop of Condom (1670), he resigned to become the dauphin's tutor (1670–81) and was thereafter bishop of Meaux. Authoritarian yet conciliatory, he voiced the characteristic Catholicism of the age of Louis XIV. He approved the Revocation of the Edict of Nantes (1685), which led to the persecution of Protestant Huguenots.

Bossuet shared the Jansenists' puritanism. His distaste for the excrescences in Catholic religiosity resulted in his sober *Exposition de la doctrine catholique* (Exposition of Catholic Doctrine, 1671). No friend of papal power, he drafted the Gallican Four Articles (1682) which asserted French autonomy and the general council's superiority over the pope (*see* GALLICANISM). He fought Richard Simon's (1638–1712) innovations in scriptural scholarship, and François Fenelon's dalliance with Madame Guyon's (1648–1717) mysticism. His *Discours sur l'histoire universelle* (Discourse on Universal History, 1681) unfolded the workings of divine providence; it is held up as a pre-Enlightenment redoubt in contrast to Voltaire. *Politique tirée de l'écriture sainte* (Politics Drawn from Scripture, 1679) drew on Stoic, Augustinian and Hobbesian pessimism, asserting the necessity of absolute monarchical sovereignty.

Patrick Riley (ed.), *Bossuet: Politics Drawn from the Very Words of Holy Scripture* (Cambridge: Cambridge University Press, 1991).

MARK GOLDIE

Boston Tea Party (16 December 1773)   This catalytic event arose from the dispute between Britain and its American colonies over parliamentary taxation. The import of tea was first taxed in 1767, and the duty maintained in 1770 when the other Townshend Duties were repealed. As tea was highly popular, American opposition leaders struggled to maintain the boycott on this symbol of British taxation. Then the ministry decided to allow the East India Company to export tea to the colonies on special terms, provoking efforts in every colony to prevent the tea from being received. In Boston the local committee of correspondence feared that the authorities would seize the tea and force its sale, and so about sixty men, many roughly disguised as Indians, boarded three ships, broke open 340 chests and dumped the tea in the harbour.

The North ministry decided that the colony must be punished. By large majorities, parliament passed measures closing Boston as a port, unilaterally rescinding the Massachusetts charter of 1691 and imposing martial law. This assault on colonial self-government duly prompted the calling of the Continental Congress and initiated the course of events leading to independence.

B. W. Labaree, *The Boston Tea Party* (New York: Oxford University Press, 1964).

DONALD J. RATCLIFFE

Boswell, James (1740–1795)   Scottish writer. Despite Boswell's complex inheritance – in background, education and professional life – none of it explains his great contribution to literature. He came from an ancient Lowlands family; his father was a traditional Presbyterian and Whig as well as a senior judge of the Court of Session. Boswell studied at Edinburgh and Glasgow and then at the University of Utrecht, and made a lengthy Grand Tour involving contact with Voltaire and Rousseau. He attended classes by Adam Smith, planned a biography of Lord Kames (1696–1782) and interviewed Hume on his deathbed. He worked at the Bar in Edinburgh and in London, neither with great success. He became an apostle of Corsican liberty and a friend of Pasquale de Paoli (1725–1807). Yet his imperishable legacy derives not from these dealings with progressive and enlightened circles, but from his intimacy with Samuel JOHNSON between 1763 and 1784, and the detailed, anecdotal, warm, comic and arguably 'unenlightened' *Life of Johnson* (1791). As with Boswell's frank and self-revealing journals (discovered and published in the twentieth century), the *Life* develops a new art of biography while flouting many of the new values of the age. A mode of personal and confessional discourse was opened up by a man with feudal dreams, who could never fully cope with the real life demands of Hanoverian Britain.

F. Brady, *James Boswell: The Later Years 1769–1795* (London: Heinemann, 1984).
F. A. Pottle, *James Boswell: The Earlier Years 1740–1769* (London: Heinemann, 1966)

PAT ROGERS

Boucher, François (1703–1770)   French painter. He dominated French painting in the middle years of the century, until his colourful, elegant genre pictures drew the wrath of serious-minded advocates of neoclassicism such as Diderot. He won the protection of Madame de Pompadour early in his career and became a constant companion to her after his return from a period in Italy in 1731. In addition to painting in all styles, he was also director of the Gobelins tapestry factory, produced designs for the Sèvres porcelain works and was made official painter to the king. Stylistically he owed much to Watteau, Rembrandt and Tiepolo, and warned young artists against over-reverence for more orthodox inspirations like Michelangelo and Raphael.

Boucher's paintings are concerned with the emotional and the individual and, although he produced history paintings, he rarely attempted the grand moral themes that became the hallmark of later painters like David. The almost theatrical organization of his works made him vulnerable to changing tastes. After his death, his work was savagely criticized for artificiality, so much so that it fell out of favour for more than a century.

A. Laing (ed.), *François Boucher* (New York: Metropolitan Museum of Art, 1986).

IAIN PEARS

Bougainville, Louis-Antoine de (1729–1811)   French circumnavigator. He first served in Canada (1756) and was aide-de-camp to the marquis de Montcalm (1712–59) at the Battle of Quebec. Sent to establish a French colony in the Falkland Islands, he went around the world between 1766 and 1769. He visited many Pacific islands, including TAHITI in 1768, which he named 'Nouvelle Cythère'. His titillating *Voyage autour du monde* (Description of a Voyage around the World, 1771) captured not a few Enlightenment imaginations. In particular, his description of Tahiti as a paradisiacal place of easy sexual mores prompted Diderot to write a review of the work, which had some anticolonial implications, and subsequently, a *Supplèment au voyage de Bougainville* in 1772, a dialogue between a wise Tahitian and a Catholic priest on board Bougainville's ship, which put into question European sexual practices; the work was subtitled 'Dialogue between A and B on the Disadvantages of Attaching Moral Considerations to certain Physical Actions that do not Call for them'. Bougainville was made *chef d'escadre* during the American War of Independence, field-marshal in 1780, and a senator and count of the empire under Napoleon.

Bernard Smith, *European Vision and the South Pacific, 1768–1850* (Oxford: Clarendon, 1960).

SYLVANA TOMASELLI

Boulainvilliers, Henri, comte de (1658–1722) French historian, proponent of the *thèse nobiliaire*. He and the abbé Dubos (1670–1742) took opposite sides in a historical debate of great political import. Boulainvilliers argued that the Franks (the ancestors, as he saw it, of the French nobility) had conquered Gaul, enslaved the Gallo-Roman population (from which, in his view, the body of the people were descended) and elected one of their own as king, while Dubos held that the Franks had entered France as allies of the Romans and that, when he took possession of France, Clovis had retained Roman institutions. The implication of the latter view was that serfdom in France had been a relic of Roman serfdom and, more importantly, that the absolute authority with which French monarchs were invested was that of the Caesars. Boulainvilliers, on the other hand, sought to base the privileges of the aristocracy on the French monarchy having originally been elective. Montesquieu claimed that Boulainvilliers's system amounted to a conspiracy against the *tiers état*, and that Dubos's was one against the nobility. He himself urged a middle course. Boulainvilliers was the author of *État de la France* (1727), *Histoire de l'ancien gouvernement de France* (1727) and *Essai sur la noblesse de France* (1732).

Nannerl O. Keohane, *Philosophy and the State in France: The Renaissance to the Enlightenment* (Princeton, NJ: Princeton University Press, 1980).

SYLVANA TOMASELLI

Boulanger, Nicolas-Antoine (1722–1759) French engineer, geologist and historian. A road engineer by profession, he retired in 1758 and devoted himself to the study of geology and, subsequently, to the origins of myths and religions. One of the *philosophes*, he was highly thought of by Diderot, and contributed the entries 'Corvée', 'Déluge', 'Guèbres' (Parsees), 'Langue hébraïque' and 'Oeconomy politique' (republished as 'Gouvernement' in 1766) to the *Encyclopédie*. Boulanger wrote *Antiquité dévoilée* (1766) which seems to have been the continuation of a manuscript entitled *Anecdotes physiques de l'histoire de la terre*, and which has been compared to Vico's historical writings. Another posthumously published work, *Recherches sur l'origine du despotisme oriental* (1761), originally written as the last chapter of the *Antiquité*, was a politically daring work, to which Diderot added an anonymous letter by way of preface which attacked both state and church. Following on from Montesquieu's discussion of the subject, Boulanger's study of despotism examined its historical and religious origins and ended, as he insisted, at the point at which Montesquieu began. It acquired an international reputation and was translated into English by John Wilkes in 1764.

John Hampton, *Nicolas-Antoine Boulanger et la Science de son Temps* (Geneva: E. Droz, 1955).

SYLVANA TOMASELLI

Boulton, Matthew (1728–1809)   Leading English entrepreneur. Born and educated in Birmingham, at 17 he entered his father's buckle-making business. In 1762 with a new partner, John Fothergill, he diversified production and built a factory at Soho – one of the first in the Birmingham area. Boulton's ormolu and silver decorative wares enjoyed royal patronage, but mass production of small metalwares (mainly for export) was his forte: neither, however, proved profitable. The STEAM ENGINE rescued Boulton's fortune. Recognizing its potential value, he seized the opportunity in 1773 to acquire a two-third share in James Watt's patent and masterminded its extension in 1800. Boulton remained the driving force behind its commercial exploitation and successful litigation.

Boulton long campaigned for reform of the copper currency, and in 1790 patented improved machinery with which he minted copper for British and foreign governments and made commemorative medals. He planned the new Royal Mint and supplied minting machinery to Russia, Spain and Denmark. A stalwart of the Lunar Society, he was elected to the Royal Society in 1785. He served as high sheriff of Staffordshire in 1795 and died a wealthy man, his estate worth £150,000.

H. W. Dickinson, *Matthew Boulton* (Cambridge: Cambridge University Press, 1937).

CHRISTINE MACLEOD

bourgeoisie   Though one of the slipperiest of terms, 'bourgeoisie' – usually denoting non-noble townsmen engaged in capitalist production and exchange – remains an indispensable category to the eighteenth-century historian. Rigid attempts to project back into the eighteenth century a term profoundly influenced by Marxist social analysis are unsatisfactory, not least because Marx himself used the term in a number of competing ways: (1) at times, he viewed the bourgeoisie as the entrepreneurial class of capitalists in a mature capitalist economy; but (2) in his historical writings he widened the term to cover most middle-class groupings including the liberal professions; while (3) he also used the term to denote the values of a society in which the bourgeoisie formed the ruling class, values which might even be espoused (as a result of 'false consciousness') by non-bourgeois groups.

Meaning (1) has to be used with care in the largely pre- or proto-industrial societies of the eighteenth century, characterized by corporative hierarchies of status rather than by economic function. The entrepreneurial class was a composite one, including many nobles: most owners of mines and metallurgical works in France were noblemen, while the wealthier nobles were also heavily engaged in agricultural improvement, financial dealing and large-scale shipping. Conversely many bourgeois entrepreneurs accepted ennoblement over the century, or else retired from active economic life when they had made their fortune by purchasing land and aping the mores of the NOBILITY.

Meanings (2) and (3) are more acceptable. To the non-noble capitalist entrepreneurs can be added high state officials and wealthy commoners; plus, at a middling level, small-scale merchants and industrialists along with members of the PROFESSIONS (law, medicine, the church, the armed forces); plus, at a lower level, the 'petite bourgeoisie' of shopkeepers, artisans and petty clerks. All were emphatically urban. The strength of these groups varied enormously across Europe. In England and the Netherlands, they had achieved a good measure of social esteem and political power, while in eastern Europe and Russia, in contrast, they were small in size and extremely limited in influence. France was somewhere in between these two extremes, certainly at the beginning of the century. The expansion of the commercial and urban economy over the century had the effect of increasing the wealth and social ambitions of the bourgeoisie. The growth of the market also extended into the services, and the liberal professions were by 1789 showing an acute sensititvity to making their fortune in the market. They had an impact on culture too. Aristocratic court culture was increasingly subverted by cultural forms which were less closed and more orientated on civic virtue rather than caste honour. The 'public sphere' established in newspapers, literature, drama and material culture was pre-eminently a bourgeois construct.

J. Habermas, *The Structural Transformation of the Public Sphere*, trans. Thomas Burger (Cambridge, Mass.: MIT Press, 1989).

C. Jones, 'Bourgeois Revolution Revivified: 1789 and Social Change', in C. Lucas (ed.), *Rewriting the French Revolution* (Oxford: Oxford University Press, 1991), pp. 66–118.

COLIN JONES

Brandes, Ernst (1758–1810) German conservative political writer. After legal studies at Göttingen he entered the Hanoverian civil service. On a visit to Britain in 1784–5 he met Edmund Burke. He emerged as a leading conservative publicist and opponent of enlightened ideas. He criticized the rise of secret societies and the increasingly political tone of many German periodicals in the late eighteenth century, which he regarded as subversive. Among his commentaries on the contemporary situation was *Betrachtungen über den Zeitgeist in Deutschland in den letzten drei Decennien des vorigen Jahrhunderts* (Reflections on the Spirit of the Times in Germany in the Last Three Decades of the Previous Century, 1808). He was respected as a serious thinker even by his opponents.

J. Garber (ed.), *Kritik der Revolution: Theorien des deutschen Frühkonservatismus 1790 bis 1810*, vol. 1 (Kronberg: 1976).

MICHAEL HUGHES

Brazil This enormous Portuguese colony was in important exporter of sugar, tobacco and hides: these were supplemented from the 1760s by cotton and from the 1790s by coffee. A series of gold discoveries, beginning with that in the Minas Gerais province in 1693–5, added appreciably to the colony's importance and Europe's stock of precious metals, since much of the Brazilian gold imported to Portugal flowed out at once, especially to Great Britain, in payment for imports of manufactured goods. These discoveries also meant a considerable movement of population within Brazil, from a narrow settled area along the coast to the gold-producing parts of the interior. The discovery of diamonds in the Rio de Frio area in the 1720s had similar effects, though gold and diamond production fell fairly rapidly from the later 1750s. This was counterbalanced, however, by renewed agricultural growth in the main coastal areas around Bahia, Pernambuco and Rio de Janeiro from the 1780s or earlier, though the immense Amazon basin remained very thinly populated and undeveloped.

Heavy duties on trade with PORTUGAL, and government efforts to control it strictly, led to much smuggling and fraud; and the attempts of POMBAL, the autocratic Portuguese chief minister (1750–77), to develop the colony's commercial life by the creation of privileged and monopolistic trading companies had only moderate success. It seems likely that Brazil, in spite of its great potentialities, never made a very large contribution to the finances of the government in Lisbon; while by the 1780s there were a few faint signs of political discontent and desire for independence. The colony, whose boundary with Spanish America was fixed for the first time, after much friction, by a treaty signed in 1750 and confirmed in 1777, was governed by a viceroy with the seat of government until 1763 in Bahia and after that in Rio de Janeiro; but distance and extremely poor communications meant that his effective control over the captaincies into which Brazil was divided was often slight. Immigration from Portugal was considerable (about 400,000 during the century from a total Portuguese population of only about 2 million); and there was at times considerable bad feeling and even violence between such immigrants and those born in Brazil. White immigration, however (mainly from northern Portugal and the Azores), was far outweighed by the influx of slaves from Africa (perhaps 2 million, mainly from Guinea and Angola). There was also extensive slave-raiding directed against the indigenous population, although the Jesuits, who were influential until their expulsion by Pombal in 1759, made considerable efforts to protect the native tribes. The colony's economic life depended totally on African, and to a lesser extent Amerindian, slaves; and people of mixed race made up a uniquely high proportion of the population.

L. Bethell (ed.), *The Cambridge History of Latin America*, vol. 2: *Colonial Latin America* (Cambridge: Cambridge University Press, 1984).
C. R. Boxer, *The Golden Age of Brazil, 1695–1750: Growing Pains of a Colonial Society* (Berkeley, Calif.: University of California Press, 1962).

M. S. ANDERSON

Breitinger, Johann Jakob *see* BODMER, JOHANN JAKOB.

Brienne, Etienne Charles de Loménie de (1727–1794) Louis XVI's principal minister (May 1787 to August 1788), the last great reforming minister of the *ancien régime* monarchy. A careerist cleric, archbishop of Toulouse (though reputedly an atheist) from 1763, he was a highly competent administrator in the Turgot mould, playing a major role in the estates of Languedoc. Vehemently critical of Calonne's reforms in the Assembly of Notables in 1787, he adopted similar policies of tax reform and economy when he was himself projected into the role of principal minister. In 1788 he had himself appointed archbishop of Sens, and introduced the 'May Edicts' which set out to crush the political pretensions of the *parlement* of Paris. The edicts succeeded only in causing the judicial, military and ecclesiastical elites of the French state to close ranks against him, and, following court intrigues he had stirred up through his policies of retrenchment, he was compelled to resign. Brienne flirted with the possibility of a career in the Revolution, but failed to convince. He died under house arrest during the Terror.

COLIN JONES

Brissot (de Warville), Jacques Pierre (1754–1793)   French Revolutionary politician. He was one of the leaders of the Girondin faction in the French Legislative Assembly and National Convention. The son of a caterer from Chartres, he was typical of a generation of brilliant young intellectuals who tried and failed to make their fortunes as writers in pre-revolutionary Paris. Matters improved in 1788 when he formed the emancipationist Société des Amis des Noirs (Society of Friends of the Blacks), which brought him into contact with the philanthropic wing of the upper bourgeoisie and nobility. From 1789 he became well known for his journalism (notably in his popular *Patriote français* (French Patriot). In 1791 Paris elected him to the Legislative Assembly, where he became notorious for advocating war against Austria, buttressed by groupings of friends and supporters, including contacts from the Amis des Noirs and deputies from the department of the Gironde. After the overthrow of Louis XVI, however, the group of GIRONDINS (or Brissotins) was overtaken on the left and viewed as dangerously moderate. Brissot and fellow Girondins were expelled from the Convention in the *journées* of 31 May and 2 June 1793. He was tried by the Revolutionary Tribunal, which had him guillotined.

COLIN JONES

Brown, 'Capability' [Lancelot] (1716–1783)   English landscape gardener and architect. His nickname derives from his habit of referring to the 'capabilities' of the properties on which he was consulted.

Brown worked as gardener at Kirkhole and Kiddington before becoming clerk of works at Stowe. In 1749 he set up in private practice and became the most sought after landscape gardener of the period, working on over 200 English commissions, such as Croome Court, Corsham, Warwick Castle and Burghley. In addition, in 1764 he was appointed royal gardener at Hampton Court. Letters refer to designs for parks in Ireland, France and Germany.

He also developed a considerable skill in architecture, with work on country houses, greenhouses (orangeries), garden buildings and bridges. He was assisted by Henry Holland (1746–1806) in his architectural work, while after 1764 Samuel Lapidge and John Spyers worked closely with him on landscape commissions.

A 'Brownian' park laid out in accordance with his principles characteristically contained a serpentine lake, clumps and specimen trees set in grassland, a circumferential side often in association with tree belts, and grassland extending up to the house, uninterrupted by fences.

Dorothy Stroud, *Capability Brown* (London: Faber, 1975).

MARYLLA HUNT and JAN WOUDSTRA

Brunswick [Braunschweig] A small north German duchy ruled by one line of the house of Welf, Brunswick had a population of about 160,000 in 1750. Although its dukes tried to maintain their independence in European and German politics, they were overshadowed by their more powerful cousins in HANOVER, with whom they were frequently at loggerheads. Duke Antony Ulrich (1685–1714) was a colourful figure, a gifted writer and musician and a great builder. He became a convert to Catholicism and allied with France at the outbreak of the War of the Spanish Succession. He was preparing to invade Hanover but was stopped by a pre-emptive strike. From the 1730s Brunswick cultivated close links with Prussia, with which it allied in the Seven Years War. Several members of the ruling family rose high in Prussian military service. The dukes tried to install absolute government and to maintain a substantial army. The parliamentary estates were not convened between 1682 and 1768, when threatened bankruptcy forced the ruler to recall them. Charles I (1735–80) was a reforming ruler and is counted among the lesser enlightened absolutists. Charles William Ferdinand (1780–1806), a Prussian field marshal, commanded the allied army fighting against revolutionary France.

H. Grundmann (ed.), *Gebhardt Handbuch der deutschen Geschichte*, vol. 2, ninth edn (Stuttgart: 1970).

MICHAEL HUGHES

Buffon, Georges Louis Leclerc, comte de (1707–1788) French natural historian. With Linnaeus, he was one of the two leading natural historians of the century. He was the superintendent of the King's Garden in Paris (1739–88) and when he was appointed to the directorship he conceived the plan of a comprehensive 'natural history' to rival the works of Linnaeus. His *Histoire naturelle* (1749–66, with supplements to 1789) considered the history of the earth, anthropology and the natural history of the quadrupeds (mammals). To this were added the *Histoire naturelle des oiseaux* (1770–83) and the *Histoire naturelle des minéraux* (1783–8). His understudy Bernard de Lacépède (1756–1825) completed the natural histories of the serpents, fishes and whales (1788–1804), and the subsequent natural histories of specific groups of organisms, by workers at the Paris Muséum National d'Histoire Naturelle published between 1790 and 1840, continued aspects of Buffon's original vision.

Assessments of Buffon's importance have varied. His significance as a leading philosophical thinker and creative natural philosopher has been emphasized in recent studies.

O. Fellows and S. Milliken, *Buffon* (New York: Twayne, 1972).
J. Gayon et al. (eds), *Buffon 88* (Paris: Vrin, 1992).
Jacques Roger, *Buffon: un Philosophe au Jardin du Roi* (Paris: Fayard, 1989).

PHILLIP R. SLOAN

Burke, Edmund (1729–1797)   Irish philosopher and statesman. Born in Dublin, the son of a Protestant attorney and a Catholic mother, he studied at Trinity College, Dublin, before moving to London to read for the Bar. In 1756 he published *A Vindication of Natural Society* and what proved a philosophically interesting treatise, *On the Sublime and the Beautiful*. In 1765 he became private secretary to the marquess of Rockingham (1730–82), first lord of the Treasury. The following year, he became the member of parliament for Wendover. In 1769 he published two pamphlets, *Observations on a Late Publication Intituled 'The Present State of the Nation'* and in 1770 *Thoughts on the Cause of Present Discontents*. He attacked the government's American policy in his speeches 'On American Taxation' (1774) and 'Conciliation with the Colonies' (1775). From 1774 to 1780 he represented Bristol, and from 1780 to 1794 Malton. His defence of Ireland's commercial rights and his endeavours to impeach Warren Hastings for his conduct of the administration of India made him many enemies. Burke was also an advocate of Catholic emancipation in Ireland. *Reflections on the Revolution in France* (1790), his most famous work, was occasioned by the enthusiastic and, in his view, highly irresponsible English response to the early stages of the French Revolution. It provoked numerous replies, including Thomas Paine's *The Rights of Man* and Mary Wollstonecraft's *A Vindication of the Rights of Men*.

J. G. A. Pocock, *Virtue, Commerce, and History: Essays on Political Thought and History, Chiefly in the Eighteenth Century* (Cambridge: Cambridge University Press, 1985).

SYLVANA TOMASELLI

Burlamaqui, Jean-Jacques (1694–1748)   Swiss political philosopher, jurist and statesman. Professor of law at the Academy of Geneva, he was influenced by Jean Barbeyrac (1674–1744), the translator of Hugo Grotius (1582–1645) and Samuel Puffendorf (1632–94) and contributed to the natural law tradition. His *Principes du droit naturel* (Principles of Natural Law, 1747) and *Principes du droit politique* (Principles of Political Law, 1751) were important works in the second half of the century. Many of the *Encyclopédie* articles on jurisprudence, not least those penned by Diderot, owe much to his writings, though the latter rejected Burlamaqui's theocentric approach to natural law. It is probably through Burlamaqui's books that many eighteenth-century political thinkers became acquainted with the thought of Grotius and Puffendorf. He was cited only once by Rousseau, and it has been argued that he did not make a significant mark on his fellow countryman. Closer to Montesquieu, Burlamaqui emphasized the need for a balance of power and considered various forms of government. He thought reason the only means through which man could reach happiness and recognized the right of resistance in the face of tyranny. His influence on Alexander Hamilton (1757–1804) and American political thought, more generally, has been the subject of several studies.

Bernard Gagnebin, *Burlamaqui et le droit naturel* (Geneva: Editions de la Frégate, 1945).

SYLVANA TOMASELLI

Burney, Fanny [Frances] (1752–1840)   English writer. Brought up in the circle of London literary life which included Johnson, Burke and the Blue Stocking Circle, she came to public attention with her first novel, *Evelina* (1778), and continued her success with *Cecilia* (1782). Her writing was then interrupted at the insistence of her father, Dr Charles Burney, and, in spite of her lack of interest in dress, she become second keeper of the robes to Queen Charlotte in 1786. The intellectual starvation and tedium of the court routine for the next five years eventually affected her health. After her resignation, she met a French refugee, General d'Arblay, whom she married in 1793. To supplement her meagre court pension, she returned to writing and produced a verse drama *Edwy and Elgiva* which had such a disastrous reception at Drury Lane in 1795 that the audience 'only laughed when it was impossible to avoid it'. Returning to novel-writing, she produced *Camilla* (1796) and then *The Wanderer* (1814), written during a period of personal unhappiness while in France, which focused on women's suffering. Conscious of the impropriety of being a woman writer, Burney in her letters and journals provides a rare insight into the struggle between public and private selves.

Judy Simons, *Fanny Burney* (London: Macmillan, 1987).

MARIE MULVEY ROBERTS

Burns, Robert (1759–1796)   Scottish poet. Born near Alloway in Ayrshire to a cotter's family, he combined farming with writing poetry. He led a life of dissipation, and was castigated as a degenerate, but eventually married Jean Armour in 1788 and became an excise officer the following year. A radical who had initially supported the French Revolution, he expressed his subsequent disillusionment and opposition to France by joining the Dumfries Volunteers in 1795. He died a year later of heart disease. His birthday on 25 January is celebrated throughout the world as Burns Night.

Henry Mackenzie's description of him as 'a Heaven-taught plough-man' is misleading, since he could as easily write within the conventions of eighteenth-century English verse as in his native Scots dialect. While working on a farm at Mossgiel with his brother, he wrote 'To a Mouse', 'Holy Willie's Prayer' and 'The Cotter's Saturday Night', which were later included in *Poems, Chiefly in the Scottish Dialect* (1786), the volume that brought him literary acclaim and established his importance as a dialect poet. Burns was a talented song-writer and excelled in folk ballads like 'Tam O'Shanter' and lyrics such as 'Auld Lang Syne' and 'Ye Banks and Braes'. He was also renowned as a humorist and celebrated as a love poet for verses like 'O my luve's like a red, red rose'. An opponent of the kirk, he produced satires against religion and embraced some of the anticlericalism of the Enlightenment. As a clubbable man, Burns was committed to the values of fraternity and brotherly love. He was a member of the Bachelors club and the Freemasons who had helped him meet the publishing costs of the Kilmarnock edition. The tradition persists that in 1787 Burns was elected the first poet laureate at Canongate Kilwinning Lodge in Edinburgh.

David Daiches, *Robert Burns*, rev. edn (London: Deutsch, 1966).

MARIE MULVEY ROBERTS

Bute, John Stuart, third earl of (1713–1792)　a Scottish representative peer. After a twenty-year absence, he re-entered parliament in 1761 as secretary of the Northern Department. A year later he was first lord of the Treasury (effectively prime minister). He resigned in 1763 and never again held office. The rest of his life was spent in comparative obscurity. His career is the record of a royal favourite's sudden rise to, and brief hold on, ministerial power.

His significance lies in his winning the favour, and subsequently the trust, of Frederick, prince of Wales (1707–51) and his wife, Princess Augusta (1719–72), in 1747. After Frederick's death in 1751, the widowed princess increasingly looked to him for help, and in 1756, on the future GEORGE III's majority, he was appointed his groom of the stole. Although he was widely despised, especially by GEORGE II, Bute was now free to exercise his influence on the king's grandson and heir, who was lacking in self-confidence. Not without self-knowledge, Bute knew he was no match for politicians, and that he had to rely on the cynical astuteness of others to effect royal policy. Later on, George III deplored the example of Bute, and recognized his mentor's mediocrity.

J. L. McKelvey, *George III and Lord Bute: The Leicester House Years* (Durham, NC: University of North Carolina Press, 1973).

D. D. ALDRIDGE

Butler, Joseph (1692–1752)   Anglican theologian and philosopher. The son of a Presbyterian linen-draper, he was educated at a dissenting academy, became an Anglican and went to Oriel College, Oxford, where he found patronage through his friendship with Edward Talbot, son of the bishop of Chester. He was preacher at the Rolls Chapel from 1718, later publishing some of his sermons. In 1725 he was appointed to the living of Stanhope, became clerk of the closet, and in 1738 became bishop of Bristol. In 1750 he became bishop of Durham. His *Fifteen Sermons Preached at Rolls Chapel* (1729) maintained that true morality consisted in living in accordance with the principles of self-love, benevolence and conscience. In this he argued against those such as Thomas Hobbes (1588–1679) who believed that actions should lie in the natural passions and instincts. The *Analogy of Religion* (1736) was a rebuttal to the deist challenge in which he tried to establish the conformity of natural and revealed religion, emphasizing the importance of revelation and conscience, and proposed that 'probability is the very guide of life'. His *Charge* (1750) to the clergy of Durham was a trenchant statement of the need for externals in religious worship. His writings were much admired by the leaders of the Oxford Movement.

J. H. Bernard (ed.), *The Works of Bishop Butler* (London, 1900).
E. C. Mossman, *Bishop Butler and the Age of Reason* (New York, 1936).

JEREMY GREGORY

Buxar, Battle of (23 October 1764)   This battle paved the way for the extension of British control over north-east India. Trade disputes had brought the ENGLISH EAST INDIA COMPANY into conflict with the nawab of BENGAL, Mir Kasim, and fighting broke out in July 1763. The nawab was immediately forced out of Bihar, but he returned the following year supported by the wazir of Awadh and the Mughal emperor. At Buxar they confronted Company troops led by Hector Munro, and superior British firepower led to a rout of Mir Kasim's 50,000 strong army after a two-hour engagement. The British, now recognizing the logic of a situation that had existed since the Battle of Plassey in 1757, acknowledged that they could not coexist with a nawab who sought independence of action. Thus the Treaty of Allahabad (August 1765) saw the British formally integrated into the Mughal Empire as *diwans* (revenue collectors) of Bengal, Bihar and Orissa. It did not require great perception to see that the British were now the rulers of Bengal, although the new nawab, Najm-ud-daula, continued to exercise judicial and policing functions.

A. M. Khan, *The Transition in Bengal, 1756–1775: A Study of Saiyid Muhammed Reza Khan* (Cambridge: Cambridge University Press, 1969).

HUW BOWEN

Byng, John (1704–1757)　English naval commander. He owed much of his advance in the navy to the prestige of his father George, viscount Torrington (1663–1733). Vice-admiral of the Red in 1756 he was then appointed to the Mediterranean by the powerfully influential first lord, George ANSON. The government was receiving intelligence of French designs on Minorca and Gibraltar in possible alliance with Spain, though Anson himself critically underestimated the immediacy of the threat to Minorca despite imprudent seizures of French merchantmen in the Atlantic and fears of French invasion of Britain (hostilities formally opened only in June 1756). Concern for home-waters defence meant that Byng's preparations at Portsmouth were seriously hampered, and he subsequently found no back-up at Gibraltar. Off Minorca on 20 May (Fort St Philip had already been under siege since Easter by 15,000 French) Byng fought an indecisive action with a numerically equivalent but better-found French squadron, which was able to bear away. Fort St Philip fell on 29 June. Byng's signals in a snagged line of battle had been only partially complied with by subordinates, but he was dismissed from his command on the basis of a French report which reached London before Byng's own account of his proceedings. On 27 January 1757 he was sentenced to death for 'error of judgement' by court martial in Portsmouth, and was shot on 12 March. Despite a strong recommendation for mercy, political tensions were such that George II felt constrained to withhold pardon.

D. Pope, *At Twelve Mr Byng was Shot* (London: Weidenfeld & Nicolson, 1962).

D. D. ALDRIDGE

Byron, George Gordon, sixth baron (1788–1824)　British romantic poet. He rose to literary fame with *Childe Harold's Pilgrimage* in 1812. He was an advocate of liberal causes in the House of Lords, but it was his libertinism rather than his liberalism that caught the public imagination. His scandalous love affairs, alleged homosexuality and incestuous relationship with his half-sister Augusta provoked Annabella Milbanke, whom he had married in 1815, to arrange a legal separation. In 1816 he left for Geneva where he met up with Percy and Mary Shelley and wrote *The Prisoner of Chillon* (1816). Moving on to Venice, where he completed the Faustian *Manfred* (1817), he began *Beppo* (1818), which was denounced by critics as 'a gaudy riot, fit for the fingers of eunuchs, and the ears of courtesans'. This mock-heroic romance paved the way for his epic *Don Juan* (1819–24), which attacked the cruelty and shame of war, but was condemned by *Blackwood's* as a 'filthy and impious poem'. He died of a fever in Greece, where he had gone to join the fight for freedom from Ottoman control. Byron has become a byword for the romantic hero, but his greatest contribution is in having articulated through his poetry the language of liberty.

See also ROMANTICISM.

Michael Foot, *The Politics of Paradise: A Vindication of Byron* (London: Collins, 1988).

MARIE MULVEY ROBERTS

C

Cagliostro, Count **Alessandro di** [Balsamo, Giuseppe] (1743–1795) Italian charlatan. At the monastery of Caltagirone he acquired some knowledge of chemistry and medicine from the apothecary monks, and in 1769 he began travelling through Europe, selling his services as a physician and wonder-worker. He was involved in the Diamond Necklace Affair (1783–4), in which Cardinal Rohan (1734–1803) was duped. He was arrested in Rome in 1789 and condemned to death for freemasonry by the Inquisition. The sentence was commuted to life imprisonment in the fortress of San Leone, near Urbino. He inspired Alexandre Dumas's (1802–70) *Mémoires d'un médecin: Joseph Balsamo* (Memoirs of a Doctor, 1846–8).

Raymond Silva, *Joseph Balsamo alias Cagliostro* (Geneva: Éditions Ariston, 1975).

SYLVANA TOMASELLI

cahiers of 1789   *Cahiers de doléances* were 'books of grievances' which voters were enjoined to draw up at each stage of the electoral process to the ESTATES GENERAL in May 1789 and in which they were to state their wishes and demands. At the final stage of the process, a digest of these demands was to be drawn up in a general *cahier* which elected representatives were to take to Versailles and present to the monarch. The general *cahiers* of many noble and ecclesiastical assemblies show a commitment to enlightened liberal values also espoused in the general *cahiers* of the THIRD ESTATE. The sources of the *cahiers* of the latter still exist in the form of tens of thousands of 'preliminary' *cahiers*, drawn up by villages, towns, guilds, professional bodies and the like. The demands of peasants and urban consumers show marked hostility to state taxation, feudal and seigneurial dues and urban economic exploitation, and reflect the distress caused by the high price of bread at the time the *cahiers* were composed. The drawing up of the *cahiers* proved an essential ingredient in the politicization of the urban and rural masses in 1789.

COLIN JONES

Calas, Jean (1698–1762) French Huguenot merchant. He was tortured, broken on the wheel and then strangled by the executioner after having been convicted of murdering his son Marc-Antoine, because (so the charge ran) the latter had converted to Catholicism. The case, which proved to be the most famous miscarriage of justice of the century and one of the most publicized instances of RELIGIOUS PERSECUTION in France, moved Voltaire not only to seek to clear Calas's name, but to take a greater interest in criminal legislation. In truth Calas's son had committed suicide and, as this was a punishable crime, his father had simply sought to disguise the fact by making it seem an assassination. Voltaire wrote a number of pamphets about the trial and succeeded in March 1763 in having all the documents pertaining to the affair re-examined. In 1765 the verdict was quashed and Calas's innocence established by the Conseil d'État. The family received an indemnity.

David D. Bien, *The Calas Affair: Persecution, Toleration, and Heresy in Eighteenth-Century Toulouse* (Princeton, NJ: Princeton University Press, 1960).

SYLVANA TOMASELLI

Calcutta The factory settlement of Calcutta was established in BENGAL by the ENGLISH EAST INDIA COMPANY on the eastern bank of the River Hughli alongside three existing villages in 1686. The site, well served by water communications, was developed during the 1690s, the centrepiece being Fort William, which was built under the supervision of Job Charnock. During the eighteenth century Calcutta's role and status changed in accordance with military, political and economic developments in Bengal. Population growth was quite remarkable – from 17,000 in 1706 to 120,000 in 1760 – reflecting the city's importance as a major centre for Asian seaborne trade. However, development was haphazard, and the outskirts of the city remained no more than a series of shanty settlements.

The city became the capital of Bengal after the British displaced the nawab as effective ruler of the province in the 1760s. This was confirmed in 1772 when a reform of revenue collection heralded a transfer of the nawab's administrative offices from Murshidabad. The following year Fort William formally became the focal point of all British operations in India. There is much justification in the claim that by the end of the century Calcutta had become the second city of the British Empire.

S. N. Mukherjee, *Calcutta: Myths and History* (Calcutta: Subarnarekha, 1977).
HUW BOWEN

calendars Eighteenth-century Europe was in a process of transition between the older Julian calendar ('Old Style') and the Gregorian calendar which was fixed in 1582. Sweden changed its arrangements only in 1744, Britain in 1752 (at which stage eleven days in September had to be 'lost'), parts of Germany in 1776 and Switzerland in 1812, while Russia had to await 1918. In the French Revolution there was a move to replace the Gregorian calendar with a revolutionary calendar. On 5 October 1793 the Convention decreed that the establishment of the republic on 21 September 1792 had inaugurated a new era in human history, while on 24 November a new, revolutionary nomenclature was decreed. The year was to start at the autumn equinox, with twelve months of thirty days, each of which was given a name redolent of the natural world ('Nivôse' ('snowy') for late December/January, for example); each month was divided into three ten-day weeks, or *décadis*; and each day had its association with a saint replaced by commemoration of a natural phenomenon or hero from antiquity. The system proved difficult to enforce, especially in clerical areas, and was abandoned by Napoleon from 1 January 1806.
COLIN JONES

California Spanish explorers claimed California early in the sixteenth century, but settlement did not begin until the late eighteenth century. Fearful of Russian settlers from Alaska encroaching on modern northern California and of Hudson's Bay Company fur-traders setting up posts there, the Spanish viceroy of Mexico dispatched two expeditions in 1769. Under the Franciscan friar Junipero Serra (1713–84) and others of his order, a series of twenty-one missions was established from 1769 to 1823, beginning with San Diego. The objective of the missionaries was bold. After establishing a mission, the friars would Christianize the local Indians (*see* NORTH AMERICAN INDIANS), train them to be farmers and then, after ten years, return the land to them, leaving Spain with a new, well-organized colony. In some missions, however, the Indians were reduced to living in brutal peonage, but for the most part, the system worked well. Utilizing Indian labour, the friars irrigated large ranches, tanned hides, made wine and exchanged these products for manufactured goods brought around Cape Horn by ambitious American traders. California became part of independent Mexico in 1821 and an American territory as a result of the Mexican–American War (1846–8).

Kevin Starr, *Inventing the Dream* (New York: Oxford University Press, 1985).

JOHN MORGAN DEDERER

Calonne, Charles Alexandre de (1734–1802)   French statesman. He was a junior member of Louis XV's council in 1765 when, by supporting the crown in its dispute against the *parlement* of Brittany, he made long-lasting enemies among the judicial elite. An enlightened intendant at Metz (1766), then Lille (1778), his links with Marie Antoinette and the king's brother, the comte d'Artois (1757–1836), led to his being appointed controller-general in 1783. Despite some disreputable financial dealing, he stimulated economic growth, but his reforms ran up against impending state bankruptcy in 1786. He prepared a package of financial reforms, including a unitary land tax, and in order to circumvent the opposition of the *Parlements*, persuaded Louis XVI to convoke a hand-picked ASSEMBLY OF NOTABLES, to give the reforms the appearance of public assent. The Notables, meeting from February 1787, thwarted his plans and engineered his dismissal. Retiring to Britain in disgrace in April 1788, he approached d'Artois in 1789, returning to the Continent to become virtual prime minister to the *émigré* cause down to the overthrow of the king in August 1792 (see ÉMIGRÉS).

Robert Lacour-Gayet, *Calonne: financier, réformateur, contre-révolutionnaire, 1734–1802* (Paris: Hachette, 1963).

COLIN JONES

Calvinism in Europe   Calvinism remained one of the most powerful elements of Protestant Christianity in eighteenth-century Europe. In Brandenburg-Prussia (where Calvinistic monarchs ruled a mainly Lutheran population), the United Provinces, Geneva and Scotland Calvinists held political power. Such associations with the state encouraged allegations that the purity of Calvinistic doctrine was being eroded by secular priorities and the corruptions of patronage. Calvinistic regimes were challenged not only by traditional opponents (such as Dutch Remonstrants) but by secessions of their stricter adherents (such as the Erskinites in Scotland). In France, England and the Habsburg territories, Calvinistic minorities were perceived as a declining threat to authority, and improved their legal status if not their numbers. Theologically, Calvinism was attacked by deists for its emphasis on revealed religion and by Arminians for its apparent assumption of a cruel and implacable God. But with its predestinarian rigour somewhat tempered, Calvinism contributed significantly to the great religious revival in Germany, England, Wales and North America. However, the most important intellectual reassertion of Calvinism in the century came not from Europe but from the New Englander Jonathan Edwards (1703–58).

See also CAMISARDS, HUGUENOTS.

G. R. Cragg, *The Church and the Age of Reason, 1648–1789* (Harmondsworth: Penguin, 1960).

G. M. DITCHFIELD

Cambrai, Congress of   The Congress of Cambrai met in April 1724 in an attempt to tidy up a number of pieces of outstanding diplomatic business in the aftermath of Louis XIV's wars, notably Spain's wish to be compensated for the loss of its Italian domination in the TREATY OF UTRECHT. By October when it broke up, the congress had heightened mutual suspicion and worsened the temper of international relations. Spain had become disenchanted with Britain, which refused to budge over the cession of Gibraltar, and which did not give ample guarantees about a Spanish Bourbon succession in Tuscany and Parma. Spain consequently moved closer to Austria, whose relations with the maritime powers had been worsened in the congress by Dutch protests about Austria's newly formed Ostend Company. Spain and Austria went on to sign the Treaty of Vienna (1725), while Britain, Hanover, France and Prussia formed a counterpoise, the Alliance of Hanover, thus dividing Europe into armed camps down to 1731. The failure of the congress was regrettable since it might have become the basis of a system of international peace-keeping meetings similar to the Congress System in the nineteenth century.

COLIN JONES

cameralism   The name 'cameralism' is given to the seventeenth-century science of political management as practised by bureaucrats and advocated by political advisers in the German-speaking world, but it has also been used in other contexts, notably in eighteenth-century Russia. In the eighteenth century cameralism became an academic discipline as university chairs in the subject were established at Halle and Frankfurt an der Oder in 1727. Some of its greatest exponents during the Enlightenment included J. H. G. von JUSTI, the author of *Grundriss einer guten Regierung* (Outline of a Good Government, 1759), and the Austrian professor of *Polizeiwissenschaft* Josef von SONNENFELS. Both men linked the well-being of a state to the common good and, like mercantilists throughout Europe, argued that the size and happiness of the population of a nation were of vital importance to its ruler. Contrary to what might have been supposed, given their interest in state-building, their association with absolutism and their recognition of the importance of the state in managing the economy and reforming society, cameralists are said to have been generally very receptive to the ideas of Scottish political economy and to Adam Smith's *Wealth of Nations* in particular.

James J. Sheeman, *German History 1770–1866* (Oxford: Clarendon, 1989).
Keith Tribe, *Governing Economy: The Reformation of German Economic Discourse, 1750–1840* (Cambridge: Cambridge University Press, 1988).

SYLVANA TOMASELLI

Camisards French Calvinists from the Cévennes region in the southern Massif Central rebelled against the French state's persecution of Protestants following the REVOCATION OF THE EDICT OF NANTES in 1685. This area received Draconian treatment from the intendant of Languedoc, Lamoignon de Basville (1648–1724), who organized brutal military sorties (the so-called *dragonnades*) against recalcitrant Protestants in the 1680s. The assassination of the religious missionary the abbé de Chayla (*c*.1650–1702) in 1702 triggered off a revolt. The rebels, whose wearing of a traditional overshirt (or *camisa*) as uniform gave them their name, were drawn mainly from local artisans and peasants. They were fortunate in their leaders, notably Jean Cavalier (*c*.1689–1740), who was able to utilize the mountainous terrain to frustrate attempts at repression. The struggle was fought with singular fierceness, involving atrocities on both sides. Marshal de Villars (1653–1734), using clemency as well as force, brought the insurrection under control in 1704, although it rumbled on until 1710. Overall, the Camisards forced the government to accept a degree of *de facto* religious TOLERATION, and laid the basis for the clandestine reorganization of Calvinist communities after Louis XIV's death in 1715.

See also CALVINISM IN EUROPE.

Philippe Joutard, *Les Camisards* (Paris: Gallimard, 1976).

COLIN JONES

Campomanes, Count **Pedro Rodríguez de** (1723–1803) Spanish statesman. In 1762 he became *fiscal* (chief legal officer) of the Council of Castile and helped CHARLES III to introduce policies aimed at reforming basic elements of Spanish society. His programme was expressed in several memoranda, notably one on *The Right of Mortmain* (1765), designed to limit acquisition of property by the church; and he became identified with a liberal policy of free trade with America and in the peninsula. Plans were interrupted by the outbreak of riots in Madrid (1766) and popular risings throughout Spain which forced the king to sack his minister Esquilache. Under the new chief minister, Aranda, Campomanes prepared a prosecution of the Jesuits, who were considered to be the instigators of the riots; they were expelled by decree in 1767 from both Spain and America. In 1774 he encouraged the spread of Economic Societies of Friends of the Country, a group which played a key role in bringing the elite into the reform programme. In 1783 he was appointed head of the Council of Castile but was relieved of the post in 1791. He was an accomplished scholar, historian and practical intellectual, and his writings represent the most advanced thinking of the Enlightenment in Spain.

Laura Rodríguez Díaz, *Reforma e Ilustración en la España del siglo XVIII* (Madrid: 1975).

HENRY KAMEN

Canada   The history of Canada in the eighteenth century divides neatly in two. Until 1760 it was a colony that belonged to France. Early settlement had taken place in the colony, called New France, from the 1540s onwards, but growth was slow and haphazard. Not until the reign of Louis XIV, and a large injection of state funds, did the colony enjoy significant development. By 1760 the French government possessed a stable, devoutly Catholic society of some 70,000 souls. The mainstays of the economy were farming and the beaver-pelt trade of the interior which serviced and profited from the fashion for furs in Europe. The people of New France were popularly known as 'habitants', being characterized as fierce fighters, independent traders and well able to deal with the territorial ambitions of the British American colonies to the south.

This world came to an end in 1763 when the French gave up Canada to the British crown. The colony itself had been conquered through force of British arms in the Seven Years War, and after the TREATY OF PARIS was ruled from London. The next dozen years or so proved traumatic for both the conquerors and the conquered. British policy-makers had no experience of constructing legislation for so large a body of French Catholics, and had to make considerable adjustments to their own constitutional assumptions to accommodate this new territory. The legislative result appeared in 1774 with the passage of the Quebec Act which tolerated Catholicism in the colony and recognized French civil law in its courts. The Act represented a remarkable revision of the Protestant exclusionism practised by the British government since 1688, and offered a stark contrast to Irish policy-making. Indeed it could be said that Quebec policy pointed the way forward for toleration in politico-religious matters in Britain itself.

After the passage of the Quebec Act, Canada was convulsed by the outbreak of the American Revolution. The rebel Americans invaded Canada in 1775 and expected support from the habitants against their new 'oppressors'. Yet the invasion failed because existing British rule appeared more attractive than vague promises from American republicans to the French Catholic population. After the war ended in 1783, however, the nature of Canadian society changed with the influx of expelled loyalists from the American republic (*see* UNITED EMPIRE LOYALISTS). These new Canadians secured a division of the colony into Upper (Anglo-Protestant) and Lower (French-Canadian) Canada by a Constitution Act of 1791. They also influenced the anti-American foreign policy that culminated in the War of 1812 and several military successes for Canadian forces against the republic. By 1820 the colony had begun to feel the strain of certain constitutional and racial tensions which gave rise to armed rebellion the following decade: tensions that still plague the nation today.

W. J. Eccles, *Essays on New France* (Toronto: Oxford University Press, 1987).
P. Lawson, *The Imperial Challenge: Quebec and Britain in the Age of the American Revolution* (Montreal: McGill-Queen's University Press, 1989).

PHILIP LAWSON

Canaletto [Giovanni Antonio Canal] (1697–1768)   Italian painter and etcher. He was the son of a Venetian painter of theatrical scenery and followed that trade until a journey to Rome around 1719 aroused his interest in topographical painting. At first, influenced by the *capricci* of Marco Ricci (1676–1729), he painted architectural fanatasies. But from 1725, perhaps inspired by the work of Luca Carlevaris (1665–1731), he devoted himself almost entirely to realistic view-painting. His views of Venice, supplied mainly as souvenirs to English Grand Tourists, made him the most celebrated topographical painter of the eighteenth century (*see* GRAND TOUR).

His early manner, with its rich contrasts of light and shade and its free brushwork is superbly represented by the *Stonemason's Yard* (London, National Gallery). After about 1730 this gave way to a brighter, harder style that may have conformed more closely to his patrons' desire for memories of Venice on a sunny day. The British consul in Venice, Joseph Smith (1682–1770), with whom he had an informal business partnership, helped to make the 1730s Canaletto's most productive decade. As a result the quality of his work sometimes suffered. Although many of his paintings were destined for export, some of the best found their way into Smith's hands. They are now in the British Royal Collection, George III having bought Smith's pictures in 1765. In the 1740s the War of the Austrian Succession drastically reduced Canaletto's market. He found time to produce a sensitive set of etchings of imaginary views of Venice and the mainland, but by 1746 he was in London in search of work. He remained in England until 1755 and painted some of his most attractive pictures, including two masterpieces – the views of London from the terrace of Richmond House (*c.*1747; Goodwood House, Sussex) – which amply disprove the contention that Canaletto was unable to paint the light of northern Europe.

His output after his return to Venice was relatively small and his style became very mannered. He was, nevertheless, still capable of painting interesting *capricci.* His influence was formative on the development of topographical painting in England and through his nephew Bernardo Bellotto (1721–80) his style was carried as far afield as Warsaw. Many of his best works are still in British collections and he remains one of the most popular of eighteenth-century artists.

J. G. Links, *Canaletto* (Oxford: Phaidon, 1982; new edn, 1994).

MARC JORDAN

canals   These were an important extension of water transport: they joined navigable rivers into regional and national networks, extended the hinterlands of ports served by coastal and ocean shipping, and bypassed unsuitable stretches of river or coast, thereby shortening routes. The most spectacular examples are the Languedoc Canal (1692) between the Atlantic and the Mediterranean, and the Eider Canal (1784) between the Baltic and the North Sea. Water transport was most appropriate for bulky and non-perishable freight where the value-to-volume ratio was low: it was much cheaper than overland transport but slower. COAL-mining was the major stimulus to canal-building in England, where construction began relatively late but proceeded rapidly after 1760: 2,000 miles were built by 1800, privately financed through the issue of shares, mostly to local people. The technology of summit-canals, which traversed differences in level through pound-locks, had been developed in the Netherlands and Italy between the fourteenth and sixteenth centuries. Techniques of tunnelling, embanking, cutting and bridge-building were the engineering legacy that canals bequeathed to the railways, which often replaced them in the nineteenth century.

Charles Singer et al. (eds), *A History of Technology*, vols 3 and 4 (Oxford: Clarendon, 1957–8).

CHRISTINE MACLEOD

Cape Town   Founded in 1652 by the Dutch East India Company as a victualling station midway between Amsterdam and the East Indies, Cape Town developed as a colony from the 1680s when, contrary to their policy elsewhere, the company's directors began sending out Dutch,

Huguenot and later German settlers to strengthen the region's farming. The 1695 population of about 350 free-burghers (the name given to white settlers who were not employees of the company) rose to between 11,000 and 12,000 by 1780, of whom 3,000 lived in Cape Town itself and the remainder (known as Boers, from the Dutch word for 'peasant') in the expanding agricultural hinterland to the north and east. Here they occasionally clashed with indigenous bushmen and Hottentots and, from the 1770s, with the more energetic Bantu. In parallel to the growing number of Europeans at the Cape – and essential to their farming economy – there was the expanding slave population, imported from east Africa and the Indies and rising by 1780 to nearly 10,000. Miscegenation between whites and Asians or Africans produced the numerous so-called 'coloured' peoples of South Africa; while the later eighteenth century saw Afrikaans emerge as a spoken language, through interaction between the free-burghers' Dutch and the various languages of their slaves.

Occupied by Britain in 1795–1802 and again from 1806, Cape Colony was formally transferred to the British crown in 1814.

See also AFRICA.

C. R. Boxer, *The Dutch Seaborne Empire 1600–1800* (London: Hutchinson, 1965).

HUGH DUNTHORNE

capital cities In 1800 the three largest capitals were Edo (Tokyo), Peking (Beijing) and LONDON, each with around 1 million inhabitants. Peking had long been a huge city; Edo had almost reached the million mark by 1716, doubling its population since the great fire of 1657; London possessed 500,000 souls in 1700, and expanded most rapidly in the second half of the eighteenth century. Capitals could come and go. ST PETERSBURG (Leningrad), with a population of 300,000 by the 1780s, was founded only in 1702; and Shahjahanabad (Old Delhi), established in 1639 as the capital of the Mughal Empire in India, had 400,000 inhabitants in the early eighteenth century, and yet no more than 70,000 by 1800 after the collapse of the empire in 1739. Most capitals were dominated by a resident monarch, who strove to ensure that the city's physical fabric and form mirrored the authority and hierarchy of the state. Reality may not always have reflected this ideal, and in pluralist, multi-focused and relatively unplanned London, there existed a capital at odds with the patriarchal/absolutist model.

See also TOWNS AND CITIES.

S. P. Blake, *Shahjahanabad: The Sovereign City in Mughal India, 1639–1739* (Cambridge: Cambridge University Press, 1991).

PETER BORSAY

capitalism The term 'capitalism' is generally used to describe the economic system dominant in the Western world since the collapse of feudalism, involving private ownership of the means of production by capitalists who employ free but capital-less workers (proletarians) who sell their labour services to employers. Private profit is the goal within a competitive market system. The eighteenth century, a time when capitalism matured globally, saw the theory of capitalism put on to a formal and permanent footing.

This entailed several developments. For one thing, analysts increasingly insisted that the realm of production and exchange must be treated as an autonomous, self-contained natural system, to be comprehended in terms of the regular working of natural forces ('iron laws'). This necessitated abandoning the residues of medieval Catholic moralistic regulation regarding the 'just price' or scruples over interest rates. By analogy with Newtonian mechanics and hydraulics, it was now claimed by capitalist apologists such as John Locke and David Hume that wages and prices would find their own level in a natural economic system whose basic laws were the equilibriation of supply and demand and whose psychology was buying cheap and selling dear. Attempts to impose extraneous ethics and artificial norms would prove counter-productive, introducing into the system inefficiencies and opportunities for corruption and private manœuvring. The same strictures applied, it was argued, to 'mercantilist' policies whereby governments sought to control or stimulate the economy, typically for nationalistic purposes (*see* MERCANTILISM). Above all, Adam Smith in his *Inquiry into the Nature and Causes of the Wealth of Nations* contended that the protectionist and paternalist strategies commonly known as Colbertism or *Cameralwissenschaft* merely played into the hands of wily merchants and monopolists, adept at working the system (*see* CAMERALISM). Only fair and free competition would ensure true stimulus to efficient production, would align the interests of producer and consumer, individual and state, as if, so said Smith, by the action of a hidden (providential) hand. The duty of the ruler was thus to maintain the market.

The programmes of economic liberals won accolades; they seemed truly 'scientific', in line with Newtonian mechanics and the laws of mathematics; they also spoke to the outlooks and prejudices of Enlightened minds convinced that the remnants of feudal regulation and centralized paternalism were clogs on enterprise and the development of an 'opportunity society'. But the appeal of capitalism went beyond the merely economic: many scholars have argued that it was inseparable from profound moral and religious commitments. It has classically been argued, by Max Weber in *The Protestant Ethic and the Spirit of Capitalism*, which first appeared in 1904, that capitalism was more than an economic system: it was a frame of mind. Weber argued that the espousal of a capitalist ethos helped solve key dilemmas experienced by Protestants. As a way of coping with anxieties about salvation, Calvinists (Weber contended) developed a new type of worldly asceticism. A regime of disciplined labour, frugality, sobriety and efficiency in one's calling would be the best token of one's piety and moral worth. In the world of commerce and industry, Protestantism taught that accumulated wealth should not be dissipated but should be ploughed back into the business, to produce more wealth. By this hypothesis, Weber attempted to explain the strange mixture of rationality and irrationality integral to the dynamics of capitalism, while also showing how and why modern capitalism had developed earliest and further in the Protestant states.

European economies were undoubtedly moving in a more capitalist direction in the eighteenth century, not least thanks to the abolition of feudal relations within the Austrian Empire, and politicians took notice of the theories of the political economists. In Britain, William Pitt the younger became an advocate of the LAISSEZ-FAIRE policies recommended by Smith. In France the writings of Quesnay, Turgot and other physiocrats contended that all wealth arises naturally from the soil, from which it followed that agricultural capitalism should be freed of its fetters – which meant above all the deregulation of the GRAIN TRADE. In his role as minister to the crown, Turgot was able to implement some of these policies, though with deeply ambiguous results. The systematic adoption of *laissez-faire* and free-trade policies by governments was, however, largely the work of the future. In many ways, even in England, protectionism remained strong during the eighteenth century.

The Wealth of Nations became, nevertheless, the bible of modern capitalism. To Smith's followers, it seemed a clarion call for tearing down bureaucracy and letting market forces ensure the survival of the economically fittest. Especially after the French Revolution and the Napoleonic wars further undermined the vestiges of feudalism, the policies of the classical economists were increasingly implemented, above all FREE TRADE and the abolition of market regulation and apprenticeship laws. Capitalism brought with it a new liberal, individualist view of society, in which the individual was seen as prior to, and the reason for, the state.

Nevertheless, as economic liberals might have predicted, the progress of capitalism largely took place surreptitiously, within the very fabric of the economy, independent of government action. In England the heyday of commercial capital led to the reign of industrial capital, thanks in part to the development of new industrial TECHNOLOGY in TEXTILES – the flying shuttle, the water frame and the steam engine applied to the needs of factories thanks to the resourcefulness of James Watt. Notably in Britain, there was sufficient cheap capital available for the funding of industrial experiments, not least because businesses typically needed rather little fixed capital, and most circulating capital could be provided for via flexible credit arrangements. The opportunities provided by free-market capitalism, especially in Britain, gave incentives for technological change, risk-taking innovations and innovative entrepreneurship like that practised by Richard Arkwright. Capitalism provided new ways of multiplying existing wealth and putting it to productive use. On a global scale, it was arguably the freedom offered to individual capitalists in the increasingly liberal economic atmosphere of post-1660 Europe that explains the continued economic dynamism of the West in contrast to the relatively stagnant rich economies of the Eastern empires, notably China.

Maxine Berg, Pat Hudson and Michael Sonenscher (eds), *Manufacture in Town and County before the Factory* (Cambridge: Cambridge University Press, 1983).
W. Letwin, *The Origins of Scientific Economics* (London: Methuen, 1963).
C. B. MacPherson, *The Political Theory of Possessive Individualism: Hobbes to Locke* (Oxford: Oxford University Press, 1962).
Erich Roll, *A History of Economic Thought* (London: Faber, 1938).

ROY PORTER

capital punishment   During the eighteenth century most penal codes included capital punishment, although the methods by which it was inflicted, the offences for which it was prescribed and the frequency with which it was inflicted varied enormously between different cultures. Thus English observers felt that such Continental practices as breaking on the wheel were inhumane, while many Continental observers commented adversely on the frequency with which hangings were carried out in England (indeed, the English ambassador to China, Lord Macartney, commented in 1794 that Chinese penal practice was less dependent on capital punishment than was the English). Most penal codes had severer forms of capital punishment for what were considered especially heinous crimes: hence Robert François Damiens (1715–57), who attempted to assassinate Louis XV of France, suffered a terrible punishment which culminated in his being pulled apart by horses. Among the Ashanti (where the preferred method of execution was decapitation) those convicted of adultery with one of the king's wives suffered the '*atopere* dance of death'.

Towards the end of the century, as part of a wider shift in attitudes to PUNISHMENT, many European states moved towards a more restricted employment of the death penalty.

J. A. SHARPE

Caribbean Europe's richest overseas possessions were located in the Caribbean. On its south-western shores Cartagena and Porto Bello were the ports of the treasure ships of the Spanish empire, but increasingly the West Indian islands were the major producers of its wealth. The sugar they produced was by far Europe's biggest overseas commodity import; coffee and cotton assumed increasing importance; and cocoa, ginger and indigo were also produced. The TRADE of the British West Indies regularly exceeded that of Britain's other American colonies and in the 1780s the trade of the French colony of Saint-Domingue alone exceeded that of the entire United States. This wealth was the hub of the Atlantic trading system. It was responsible for over a fifth of total British and two-fifths of total French trade, and, while these were the main beneficiaries, Spain, Holland, Denmark and Sweden all had colonies there too. As the major centre of European overseas investment, these colonies and their trade were fiercely contested in wartime (and early on by pirates at all times) and as the main basis of the African SLAVE TRADE, they became no less fiercely debated in peacetime.

M. Duffy, *Soldiers, Sugar and Seapower* (Oxford: Oxford University Press, 1987).

MICHAEL DUFFY

Carlowitz, Treaty of (1699) The Treaty of Carlowitz (Sremski Karlovci) ended the great Austro-Turkish war of 1683–99, which represented the turning-point in the Habsburg–Ottoman struggles that had begun in 1526 and would continue to 1791. It began with the Turkish siege of Vienna, which led to a series of defeats for the Turks, ending in 1690 with their being driven far back into the Balkans. At that point they won a respite as Vienna turned its attention to another war with Louis XIV's France.

In the 1690s the Turks cautiously retook some of their lost lands, but in 1697 the weaker Austrian forces they faced were placed under the command of the greatest Austrian military hero, Prince Eugene of Savoy. Eugene added genius to the command and enthusiasm to the ranks, and in one great battle at Zenta in 1697 destroyed the Turkish field army, inflicting 30,000 deaths among the Turks while losing 300 Austrians.

The Treaty of Carlowitz gave to the Habsburgs most of Hungary and all of Transylvania and effectively recognized the military ascendancy of Austria in the Balkans. From then on the Ottoman Empire was firmly set on the road of decline.

See also AUSTRO-TURKISH WARS.

KARL A. ROIDER JR

carnivals The traditional festivities associated with carnival (eating, drinking, copulation and violence on an unusually massive scale, often combined with the wearing of fancy dress or, at any rate, masks) continued to take place in the towns and villages of Europe, especially in Mediterranean regions. What was new in this period was the spread of these festivities outside Europe (especially to Latin America and the Caribbean) and their increasing commercialization in major cities, notably in Venice, where the influx of foreign visitors was considerable (30,000 was a figure frequently quoted at the time). Carnival (not just a day but the whole period from Boxing Day to Shrove Tuesday) was the season when the Venetian theatres and opera-houses (open to anyone who could afford a ticket) made most of their money. Sideshows such as acrobatics, fist-fights and gambling became increasingly important at the expense of the traditional ritual, the public execution of twelve pigs and a bull on the Piazzetta of San Marco, which was finally abolished in 1797.

P. Burke, 'The Carnival of Venice', in *Historical Anthropology of Early Modern Italy* (Cambridge: Cambridge University Press, 1987), ch. 13.

PETER BURKE

Carnot, Lazare (1753–1823) French revolutionary and engineer. He trained at the Corps of Engineers under Gaspard Monge. While an army engineer in the 1770s he began entering prize competitions: in 1780 an essay on friction in machines which he submitted for an Académie des Sciences competition lost to Coulomb's entry. When Carnot published this in extended form in 1783, it attracted little attention; but when he revised it in 1803 during a glittering army career, he won acclaim for his observation of the principle of continuity in the transmission of power and his analysis of the balance between work done on and by a system (which influenced his son Sadi's thermodynamic cycle).

Though Carnot wanted a civilian life in science, military duties continued to beckon him: in 1791 he was elected deputy to the Legislative Assembly, and he fought for the republicans once the monarchy was overthrown in 1792. In 1793 he served on the emergency Committee for Public Safety. He was removed from government in 1797 when a leftist coup seized power. While Carnot served Napoleon in various offices he cultivated an interest in infinitesimal geometry. He fled to Magdeburg when the monarchy was restored.

Marcel Reinhard, *Le Grand Carnot*, 2 vols (Paris: 1952).

M. L. BENJAMIN

Caroline of Ansbach (1683–1737) Consort of GEORGE II, she married George in 1705 after dismissing an eminent Catholic suitor, the future emperor Charles VI. While her education was neglected in childhood, and she never learned to spell or punctuate, she was benignly influenced by two cultured relatives, Sophia Charlotte of Brandenburg (1668–1705) and the electress Sophia of Hanover. She had an ear for languages and was widely read, with an engaging penchant for controversial discussion. She would have adorned any court, and this was freely acknowledged by her husband, who was also sensible of an intelligence much superior to his. Of the seven surviving children born to them between 1707 and 1724, the most noteworthy, were Frederick, the future prince of Wales, whom his parents did not see between the ages of 7 and 21 since he was trained in Hanover at George I's behest, and William, duke of Cumberland. In her championship of inoculation against smallpox Caroline was strikingly enlightened, and was so acknowledged by the young Voltaire in 1728. Her ultimate political importance lies in her seconding Robert Walpole's ministerial services, after she had overcome her initial dislike of him.

R. L. Arkell, *Caroline of Ansbach* (Oxford: Oxford University Press, 1939).

D. D. ALDRIDGE

Carteret, Philip (1733–1796)   English navigator. Born in Jersey, he joined the navy at the age of 14. From 1751 his career was linked with John Byron (1723–86) and he was first lieutenant on the *Tamar* on a voyage around the world. Immediately on his return in 1766, he was appointed to the decrepit *Swallow* which accompanied Samuel Wallis (1728–95) on a voyage to the Pacific. Separated from Wallis off the Strait of Magellan in April 1767, he continued a search for the SOUTHERN CONTINENT. During his perilous crossing of the Pacific he touched at Juan Fernandez, discovered Pitcairn Island, later the ultimate resort of the *Bounty* mutineers, and the Southern Tuamotus including Mururoa. Driven north because of the frailty of his ship, he passed through the Solomons before returning to Spithead via Sulawesi, Batavia and the Cape of Good Hope. Although this circumnavigation did not produce many new discoveries, it was an epic of navigation, revealing the determination and courage of the commander. His later career was marked by Admiralty neglect but he eventually rose to the rank of rear admiral before his retirement in 1794.

Helen Wallis (ed.), *Carteret's Voyage round the World 1766–1769* (Cambridge: Hakluyt Society, 1965).

DAVID MACKAY

Cartesianism   The term 'Cartesianism' was applied to the philosophy of René DESCARTES and his disciples. It was characterized by a distinctive method and by its metaphysical and physical principles. The central aim of Descartes's physics was to explain the origin and operation of the universe through mechanical principles alone. Descartes made major contributions to the realization of this goal in his work in geometry and optics and in his formulation of the principle of inertia. After a long struggle, Cartesian physics became generally accepted in France by the beginning of the eighteenth century. However, by the 1730s it was seriously challenged by Newtonianism, both in its claim that all motion is caused by impulse and in its rejection of absolute space. Other Cartesian principles were debated throughout the eighteenth century, for example that all life is based on purely mechanical principles and that the soul of man is simply a thinking substance. The Cartesian methodology, based on the belief in the autonomy of the knowing subject and that human life can be improved by applying the principles of the MECHANICAL PHILOSOPHY to achieve control of nature, was to prevail among Enlightenment thinkers.

P. Schouls, *Descartes and the Enlightenment* (Kingston, Ont.: McGill-Queen's University Press, 1989).

JOHN P. WRIGHT

Cartouche, Louis Dominique (1693–1721) French criminal and sometime bohemian. He signed up for the army when drunk but soon left it and rekindled his early talent for theft. At 24 he became chief of a group of bandits specializing in burglary. He was captured in 1721 and sentenced to death. His life story became the subject of several plays.

M. L. BENJAMIN

Cartwright, Edmund (1743–1823) Anglican clergyman, poet and prolific inventor. Born into the minor Nottinghamshire gentry and educated at Wakefield Grammar School and Oxford University, he became rector of Goadby Marwood (Leicestershire) in 1779. A conversation about the demand for weavers generated by the mechanization of cotton-spinning turned Cartwright's life into an improbable new direction – to invent the power loom (patented 1784–8). He established a spinning and weaving factory at Doncaster (Yorkshire), but technical difficulties and weavers' hostility restricted the loom's immediate diffusion. Deeply in debt, he assigned the business to his brothers Charles and John (the radical MP). A parliamentary grant of £10,000 in 1808 provided partial compensation. Subsequent inventions included a prototype woolcombing machine, a steam engine and a plough; he assisted Robert Fulton (1765–1815) in developing steamboats. Appointed superintendent of the duke of Bedford's experimental farm at Woburn (Bedfordshire) in 1801, Cartwright doubled as domestic chaplain, and published sonnets and agricultural treatises. His versatile ingenuity was recognized by fellowships of both the Royal Society and the Royal Society of Literature in 1821.

K. G. Ponting, *A Memoir of Edmund Cartwright* (Bath: Adams & Dart, 1971).

CHRISTINE MACLEOD

Casanova de Seingalt [Giacomo Girolamo] (1725–1798) Italian adventurer, noted for his memoirs of his amorous intrigues. Born in Venice, he studied law at the University of Padua from which he obtained a doctorate in 1742. He travelled to the Middle East and throughout Europe, sometimes in search of adventure, mostly in quest for employment, but frequently also because he was either being expelled from a particular city or country (for example Warsaw, Vienna, France; he was thrown out of nine different capitals at least eleven times between 1759 and 1771), or pre-empting such expulsions or even arrest. He was not always successful in avoiding the latter.

Casanova was no doubt a man of learning and of many talents, who exhibited more than a passing interest in the philosophical issues of his day, but his gift resided in his ability to recount an extraordinary succession of sexual encounters with an eye to psychological and social truth. Settled at long last in 1785, when he became attached to the court of the count of Waldstein in the capacity of librarian, he began his *Mémoires* (written in French) in 1789. By 1792 he had reached the point at which they end (1772). He continued to revise them to the end of his life.

Giacomo Casanova, *The Memoirs of Jacques Casanova de Seingalt*, 8 vols (New York: G. P. Putnam's Sons, 1894).

SYLVANA TOMASELLI

Castlereagh, Robert Stewart, Viscount, second marquis of Londonderry (1769–1822) British statesman. A powerful defender of the Irish connection with Britain while advocating necessary reforms in Ireland, he was active in the suppression of the Irish rebellion in 1798 and prominent in carrying the Act of Union in Dublin. Thwarted over Catholic emancipation, he remained committed to it to the end of his life. As war secretary he improved recruitment to the British army and prepared and dispatched an expeditionary force to assist the Spaniards and Portuguese to resist the French in 1808. As foreign secretary from 1812 to 1822 he built up and sustained the coalition which defeated Napoleon and represented Britain at the Congress of Vienna where he worked hard to mitigate the horrors of the slave trade. He hoped to maintain European peace through a system of congresses but differences with the Holy Alliance over the principle of intervention led to the failure of the congress system as Castlereagh had envisaged it.

Carrying a heavy workload as leader of the House of Commons in addition to the foreign secretaryship, Castlereagh suffered a mental breakdown and committed suicide in August 1822.

J. W. Derry, *Castlereagh* (London: Allen Lane, 1976).

JOHN W. DERRY

Catherine I (1684–1727) Empress of Russia (1725–7). Her origins are obscure. She was probably born Martha Skavronskaia of Lithuanian peasant stock, then raised by a Lutheran pastor in Marienberg in Swedish Livonia. In 1702 Russian troops invaded and Martha entered the service of Field Marshal Boris Sheremetev, then of PETER I's favourite Alexander Menshikov. In 1703 she met Peter and became his mistress. They were secretly married in 1707 (publicly in 1712), when she was received into the Orthodox Church with the name Catherine (Ekaterina). The first of twelve children was born in 1704; only two survived beyond infancy. Catherine's coronation as empress-consort in May 1724 in recognition of her services (for example accompanying Peter on campaign) strengthened her claim to the throne after Peter's death on 28 January 1725. However, the illiterate and ailing Catherine had little aptitude for government, which was managed by Menshikov and the new six-man Supreme Privy Council (created 1726). Foreign policy was conducted by A. I. Osterman, who in 1726 signed an alliance with Austria. Catherine died on 6 May 1727 and was succeeded by PETER II, her designated heir.

Phillip Longworth, *The Three Empresses: Catherine I, Anne and Elizabeth of Russia* (New York: Constable, 1972).

LINDSEY HUGHES

Catherine II [Catherine the Great] (1729–1796) Empress of Russia (1762–96). Born Sophia Augusta Fredericka, in Stettin (Szczecin) to Prince Christian August of Anhalt-Zerbst and Joanna Elizabeth of Holstein-Gottorp, she married the future PETER III of Russia, in 1745, converting to Orthodoxy under the name Catherine (Ekaterina Alekseevna). Life at empress Elizabeth's court proved difficult and Catherine spent much time imbibing works of the Enlightenment, both French and German, and dabbling in court intrigues. Peter proved equally unsatisfactory as husband (Catherine's first child, Paul, born in 1754, was allegedly fathered by Sergei Saltykov) and sovereign. Catherine overthrew him on 28 June 1762 with the support of Guards regiments.

Her political philosophy was set out in her *Instruction* of 1767, which owed much to Montesquieu and the jurist Beccaria: Russia was a European state in need of absolute but enlightened rule. It was addressed to the LEGISLATIVE COMMISSION (1767–8), which awarded Catherine the titles 'Great' and 'All-wise Mother of the Fatherland'. The commission's deliberations and turns of events (for example the havoc wreaked by the Pugachev revolt) inspired legislation aimed at regulating society for the general good in the spirit of cameralism, for example the Provincial Statute (1775), Police Ordinance (1782), Charters to the Nobility and the Towns (1785) (a parallel charter to state peasants remained unpublished). The National Schools Statute (1786) established free schooling in major towns.

Foreign policy brought Catherine both glory and condemnation. A Black Sea coastline and the Crimea (annexed in 1783), together with rights of navigation and intervention, were acquired through wars with Turkey (1768–74, 1787–92), and most of Ukraine and present-day Lithuania and Belorussia added by the Partitions of Poland. More ambitious designs on Constantinople – the 'Greek Project' – foundered. The last years were overshadowed by the French Revolution, abhorrence of which determined intervention in Poland and banishment of the writer Alexander Radishchev, whose *Journey from St Petersburg to Moscow* (1790) condemned autocracy and serfdom.

Catherine was a workaholic who penned much of her own legislation as well as fictional and journalistic writings. She corresponded with Voltaire and Grimm and entertained Diderot. She patronized classical architecture, town-planning projects and painting. Her private life has aroused prurient interest. There were twelve lovers, who grew increasingly young as Catherine aged. Grigori POTEMKIN, favourite from 1774 to 1776, remained her adviser and possibly husband until his death in 1791. Traditionally Catherine was regarded as a vain 'hypocrite' who sought applause by providing the veneer of reform without the substance. Western historians have revised this view, in line with redefinitions of enlightened absolutism, pointing to the beginnings of civil rights, albeit for the upper echelons of society, in a climate of toleration under 'monarchy without despotism'. Since the 1980s works by and about Catherine have been published in Russia for the first time since the Revolution.

John T. Alexander, *Catherine the Great: Life and Legend* (New York: Oxford University Press, 1989).
Isabel de Madariaga, *Russia in the Age of Catherine the Great* (London: Weidenfeld & Nicolson, 1981).

LINDSEY HUGHES

Catholic Emancipation Reform sentiment and the particular problems of governing IRELAND combined to put Catholic Emancipation on the political agenda in the late eighteenth century, though George III was opposed to a relaxation of the disabilities by which Catholics were denied the vote, public office and election to parliament. Rising Catholic wealth and divisions among the Protestants were crucial, and the enormous expansion in the recruitment of Catholics during the war with France (1793–1815) had a significant bearing on the process of politicization. Irish Catholics were granted the vote in 1793. Reform in Britain became a crucial issue in 1828. The election of the Catholic Daniel O'Connell (1775–1847) for County Clare in 1828, and the probability that he would be the first of many, led the Tory government to decide to alter the law, despite the opposition of George IV and an appreciable number of Tory members opposed to any change. They were supported by an extensive petitioning and pamphleteering campaign which reflected lower-class anti-Catholicism. The Act of April 1829 repealed Catholic civil disabilities, though Jesuits were still banned from England and Catholics were still barred from the lord chancellorship, the lord-lieutenancy of Ireland and the universities. This has been seen as crucial to the collapse of the ideological underpinnings of the English *ancien régime*. The Catholic question became the Irish question.

T. Bartlett, *The Fall and Rise of the Irish Nation: The Catholic Question 1690–1830* (Dublin: 1992).
L. Colley, *Britons: Forging the Nation 1707–1837* (New Haven, Conn.: Yale University Press, 1992).

JEREMY BLACK

Catholic Enlightenment   The notion that the ENLIGHTENMENT was anti-Catholic is widely held, but does not survive critical examination. The Enlightenment was far from uniform, a tendency rather than a movement. Enlightenment thinkers believed it necessary to use REASON, uninhibited by authority and tradition, in order to appreciate man, society and the universe and thus to improve human circumstances. However, a striking feature of the writings of most Enlightenment figures was their ability to reconcile their theoretically universalist and subversive notions of reason with the particular circumstances of their countries and positions and with the suppositions of traditional authorities. The prerogatives, pretensions and personnel of the churches were criticized by many. The clergy could be seen as the intellectual heart of a conspiracy dedicated to limiting human progress. The Middle Ages, generally condemned as sunk in ignorance due to the dominance of the church, were held to substantiate this view. However, much of the criticism of clerics and of ecclesiastical practices and pretensions should be placed in the perspective of vigorous debates among believers about these matters. If Enlightenment figures attacked the Jesuits, so did the Jansenists. Reason was believed to support the established procedures of Christianity, not least in opposition to the claims of religious enthusiasts. By treating reason as a divine gift and the universe as a divine creation, they established a framework in which observation need not be viewed as hostile to faith. Far from being compromises between tradition and religion, these views reflected the attempts of pious men in a religious society to comprehend the achievements and possibilities of scientific discoveries. Some radical thinkers adopted materialist and psychological notions that left little role for divine action. It was also possible to advance ethical views that owed little directly to Christianity. Rousseau's rejection of the idea of original sin in the name of original goodness challenged the notion of divine grace. However, such challenges to Christian teaching, as opposed to Christian teachers, were few. (*See* NATURAL RELIGION.)

Catholic Enlightenment also entailed reform of the church. There was a widespread aspiration for what was regarded as rational progress through practical religious and social action. It was argued that traditional and contentious delimitations of secular and ecclesiastical authority could be discarded in favour of a more sympathetic symbiosis of church and state. This led to improvements in clerical standards, the foundation of new bishoprics, the limitation of clerical fiscal privileges, judicial immunities and control over education, moves against monastic orders, seen as illogical and a waste of resources, and against popular pilgrimages and cults, seen as superstitious, the limitation of papal authority and the suppression of the Jesuits in 1773. Such 'reforms' reflect the ambivalence of the Enlightenment. They did not command general support and often reflected a priori assumptions as much as reason. Dissatisfaction, however, reflected the importance of religion, the churches and the clergy. Few believed that they could or should be dispensed with.

See also CATHOLICISM.

W. J. Callahan and D. Higgs (eds), *Church and Society in Catholic Europe of the Eighteenth Century* (Cambridge: Cambridge University Press, 1979).

JEREMY BLACK

Catholicism   The role of the Catholic Church in the eighteenth century has received a bad press, not only from contemporary critics, but also from supporters of ultramontane Catholicism in the nineteenth century who believed that their eighteenth-century forebears had severely weakened the position of the church. Within Europe, Catholicism faced several set-backs during the eighteenth century which seemed to indicate that its startling successes in the seventeenth century in pushing back the advances of the Protestant Reformation were at an end. The first major indications of changing Catholic fortunes were the Protestant revolts of 1713–14 and 1732 within the Habsburg lands, and in England the failure of the Jacobite challenges of 1715 and 1745 which ended hopes of returning England to the Catholic fold. This meant that the religious divisions in Europe were finally confirmed, with the northern and north-western areas of Europe remaining almost solidly Protestant. Likewise, in political terms, the increasingly marginal role of the PAPACY in international relations, especially during the Wars of the Spanish (1701–14) and Polish (1733–5) Successions, the failure of Clement XI to persuade Catholic powers to unite to defeat the Turks in 1714 and the outcry by leading Catholic secular powers against the Jesuits, which led to the suppression of the order in 1773, and hostility towards the monastic orders, suggested that the great bastions of international Catholicism, which had been so fundamental to the strength of Catholicism in the century after the Council of Trent (1545–63), were fundamentally emasculated. A number of rulers in France and the Empire became increasingly suspicious of the interference of these various agents of Rome within their own territories.

Nevertheless, these developments must be set against pastoral and devotional advances which would suggest that the spiritual role of the church was, if anything, on the increase. If international Catholicism was weakened this was largely because of the development of 'state catholicism' by which certain Catholic rulers sought to bolster the position and influence of the church within their lands. Joseph II of Austria and the marquês de Pombal in Portugal were the prime exponents of a policy to create an autonomous church free from papal interference, and such attempts received support from German archbishops. A number of splendid baroque churches in Austria and south Germany built in this period testify to the devotional support such policies could give. The creation in France during the 1790s of the Constitutional Church was the logical outcome of these centrifugal tendencies.

Closely related to this phenomenon was the development of what has been called the CATHOLIC ENLIGHTENMENT. Traditional historiographical interpretations have suggested that the relationship between Catholicism and the Enlightenment was one of necessary conflict, but recent research has shown how far certain sections of the church shared Enlightenment ideals of clearing away the superstitious beliefs of the past. Catholic reform, especially in Spain, Austria and Italy involved attempts at church reorganization and the improvement of the education and pastoral training of the clergy. Joseph II, for example, suppressed MONASTERIES, the object of criticism from both Enlightenment and reformist clerical circles, to found seminaries, fund bishoprics and create new parishes. Evidence of Catholic Enlightenment can also be found among English Catholics. Here the Catholic community was suspicious of foreign, papal Catholicism and through the writings of Joseph Berington (1746–1827) and John Lingard (1771–1851) developed liberal and tolerant attitudes which ran counter to official positions, acknowledging religious pluralism. The English community also showed an awareness of the need to develop devotional piety. Richard Challoner (1691–1781), especially in his *Garden of the Soul* (1740) was concerned to buttress lay piety.

Within Catholic theology the major dispute was between the JESUITS and the JANSENISTS which in many ways was a continuation of a more fundamental tension between Thomist and Augustinian tendencies within Catholic thought and practice.

It has been customary to view the position of Catholicism in the eighteenth century largely through the eyes of Enlightenment thinkers, and this has led historians to dwell on the corrupt nature of the church as an institution and to conclude that its role in society was increasingly anachronistic and oppressive. Against such evidence we need to consider those sections of the church which were aiming at reform and we ought to give due weight to the ways in which the most reviled aspects of the church, such as the monasteries, could play a vital part within local communites, not only as centres of spirituality, but also of CHARITY and care. Such agencies of the church played a more considerable role within the local communities than later nineteenth-century detractors maintained.

See also ANTICLERICALISM, CHRISTIANITY.

J. Derek Baker and Bernard W. Bickers, *A Short History of the Catholic Church* (Tunbridge Wells, 1983).

W. J. Callahan and D. Higgs (eds), *Church and Society in Catholic Europe of the Eighteenth Century* (Cambridge: Cambridge University Press, 1979).

J. Delumeau, *Le Catholicisme entre Luther et Voltaire* (Paris: Nouvelle Clio, 1971), English translation, London 1978).

JEREMY GREGORY

Cavendish, Henry (1731–1810)   English natural philosopher. Wealthy, reclusive and internationally renowned, he was particularly famous for investigating heat and water. In 1766 he gave a demonstration of the existence of hydrogen, and also studied the properties of 'fixed air' (carbon dioxide). In geophysics, his main studies related to attempts to determine the density of the earth. In this his results remained unsurpassed for accuracy for over a century. He published relatively little of his wide-ranging and proficient work.

Russell MacCormmach, 'Henry Cavendish: A Study of Rational Empiricism in Eighteenth-Century Natural Philosophy', *Isis*, 60 (1969), 293–306.

PATRICIA FARA

cemeteries *see* DEATH.

censorship   Laws intended to prevent the publication or distribution
of unauthorized materials were very much a fact of eighteenth-century
life in most European countries other than Britain, where censorship
of printed materials lapsed in 1695. By 1700 civil authorities had
generally assumed this function, formerly shared with the church. The
French system, elaborated in the 1680s and maintained until 1789,
was a model: authors and publishers were required to submit manuscripts to the office of the director-general of the book trade, who sent
them to specialists for reports. Publishers might be forced to emend
the manuscript or forbidden to publish it altogether.

The effectiveness of eighteenth-century censorship varied widely, depending on the country and the moment. In many countries works
officially prohibited were quietly allowed to circulate. Authors in
countries with restrictions avoided the system by sending their manuscripts abroad for publication. Enlightenment thinkers regularly denounced censorship, and even the officials responsible for administering
it had sometimes lost faith in the practice. The French revolutionaries
abolished censorship, but, by demonstrating the danger of political
upheaval, the revolutionary period had the paradoxical effect of reviving
it, both in Jacobin France and elsewhere, at the very end of the century.
See also PUBLISHING.

JEREMY D. POPKIN

Ceylon   By 1700 the Dutch had settled the northern coastal plains of
Ceylon (modern-day Sri Lanka), but they had not managed to subordinate the mountainous interior of the island which remained under
the control of the king of Kandy. The SPICE TRADE was of considerable
importance, as was the strategic location of Trincomalee, a port town
which possessed the only reliable harbour on the west side of the Bay
of Bengal. The British coveted Ceylon as a counterweight to French-
held MAURITIUS, and as a base from which the east coast of India could
be threatened in time of war. While the Dutch remained neutral, the
problem was not acute, but when they were in league with the French
the British became vulnerable to seaborne attacks. Negotiations with
the king of Kandy in 1762 and 1782 failed to secure an alternative
port for the British, and this led to the seizure of Trincomalee in 1796
when the Dutch were once more allied with the French. Two years
later Ceylon was declared to be a crown colony, and British possession
was confirmed by the Vienna Settlement of 1814–15. By 1818 control
had been established over the whole of the island.

L. A. Mills, *Ceylon under British Rule, 1795–1932* (Oxford: Oxford University Press, new impression, 1964).

HUW BOWEN

Chain of Being The idea that everything from inorganic to organic nature, to man and the celestial world, was arranged in a graded hierarchy or 'chain of being', was not new, but it enjoyed fresh currency in the Enlightenment, following LEIBNIZ. As part of his philosophical optimism he believed that God's 'plenitude' was manifested by the graduated diversity of His handiwork. Others, such as Charles Bonnet, propounded their own interpretations. The idea stimulated research to look for the presupposed gaps and study the complex detail of the chain, whose existence the microscope helped substantiate. The chain could also be construed as emerging through time, entailing extinction and/or the perfectibility of species, but not their evolution. These issues were to prove controversial early in the next century. Pope's *Essay on Man* (1732–4) counselled ironic acceptance of man's limitations as a 'mixed' creature, straddling the terrestrial and celestial, but the 'temporalized' interpretation of the chain, pointing towards romanticism, underlined man's Protean striving. Lovejoy's study remains a classic, but Michel Foucault's historiography has since radically transformed the history of all ordering systems.

Arthur O. Lovejoy, *The Great Chain of Being* (Cambridge, Mass.: Harvard University Press, 1936).

CLARISSA CAMPBELL ORR

charity Since the Middle Ages, religiously inspired private charity had been a major stimulant behind the establishment of poor-relief institutions and arrangements. Post-Tridentine Catholicism had encouraged the formation of a 'baroque piety' in which copious testamentary giving for charitable purposes took a major place in a panoply of religious gestures associated with death (funeral ceremonial, masses, religious donations). In the late eighteenth century such voluntary charity was subjected to a rigorous and sometimes unjust critique. Even in Catholic countries like France, *philosophes* and physiocrats attacked it for being motivated by a concern for the donor's spiritual welfare rather than the temporal circumstances of the recipient: charity was accused of spawning poverty by indiscriminate giving which encouraged idleness and vice, and of failing to address a problem of poverty whose dimensions were growing under the pressure of demographic growth and social change. Seemingly linked to the growth of religious indifference and 'dechristianized' behaviour, this critique affected patterns of giving: as 'baroque piety' faded, the number and real value of testamentary charitable acts received by poor-relief institutions fell, often drastically.

As far as it is possible to judge, however, the charitable impulse remained strong. In certain areas it took the form of more selective giving: in France and the Low Countries, charity boards specializing

in home relief and small, clinically orientated hospitals received do-
nors' favour, while the big 'general hospitals' (*hôpitaux généraux*)
established in the seventeenth century saw their charitable income
dwindling. Such institutions were increasingly viewed as uneconomic,
socially parasitic and engendering disease, in contrast to methods of
relief which did not take the needy so completely off the labour market
and which were more successful in targeting the 'deserving poor'. As
before, manual almsgiving to beggars and undesirables was frowned
on – in Catholic as in Protestant regions not endowed with ecclesi-
astically dominated charitable institutions. A religious impulse was
often visible in the philanthropy evident in Protestant states too, even
though the actual structure of poor relief there had since the sixteenth
and seventeenth centuries assumed a more secular form. The voluntary
hospital movement in England, for example, was founded on charitable
subscriptions behind which a religious, often Dissenter, inspiration
was visible: yet the twenty-six such hospitals established by 1775 lay
outside the aegis of the church. The subscription method of charitable
fund-raising was increasingly copied in Europe by the late eighteenth
century, and witnessed the involvement of the wider social groups in
the running of poor-relief establishments. Changes in charity were
thus often as responsive to changes in the social elite as in the measurable dimensions of the problem of poverty.

See also PHILANTHROPY, POVERTY AND POOR RELIEF.

M. Vovelle, *Piété baroque et déchristianisation en Provence au XVIIIe siècle*
(Paris: Plon, 1973).
S. Cavallo, 'The Motivations of Benefactors: An Overview of Approaches to
the Study of Charity', in Jonathan Barry and Colin Jones (eds), *Medicine
and Charity before the Welfare State* (London: Routledge, 1991).

COLIN JONES

Charles II (1661–1700)   King of Spain (1665–1700). He suffered all
his life from precarious health. His marriages, to Marie Louise of
Orléans (*d* 1689) and then to Mariana of Neuburg, who outlived him,
produced no heir, making the succession the major issue of his reign.
The early years of his rule were a regency under his mother Mariana
of Austria, when factional rivalries dominated court politics. The subsequent emergence of his half-brother Don Juan of Austria as chief
minister (1677–9) inaugurated a promising period of reforms but was
cut short by Don Juan's untimely death. The reign was one of positive
advances in many areas of economy, demography and culture, but the
dominant reality was the collapse of Spanish power in Europe as a
result of the aggressions of Louis XIV. Peace treaties of 1684 and
1697 resulted in substantial territorial gains for France. Pressure from
the European powers obliged Louis to agree to secret partition treaties

of the Spanish empire in the event of Charles II dying without an heir, but Spanish opposition to these predatory agreements influenced Charles to leave a testament in which the entire crown was left to Louis's grandson the duke of Anjou, who became king in 1700 as Philip V.

Henry Kamen, *Spain in the Later Seventeenth Century 1665–1700* (London: Longman, 1980).

HENRY KAMEN

Charles III (1716–1788) King of Spain (1759–88). The younger son of Philip V and Elizabeth Farnese of Parma (1692–1766), he became duke of Parma and Piacenza in 1731, king of Naples and Sicily in 1734 and then succeeded his brother Ferdinand VI as king of Spain. The one capable ruler of a dynasty by then haunted by melancholia verging on madness, Charles preserved his sanity by hunting every day. An autocrat who figured among the generation of enlightened despots, he promoted a circle of ministers dedicated to the twin aims of the economic revival of Spain and its vast American empire, and the strengthening of royal power. The flow of revenue, especially from America, increased, and both the army and navy were enlarged. Industry was encouraged and transatlantic trade greatly expanded. A staunch advocate of the Bourbon FAMILY COMPACT with France, Charles plunged Spain into war against Great Britain in 1762–3 and in 1779–83, thereby reasserting Spain's status as a power of the second order. Despite his personal piety, Charles expelled the JESUITS in 1767, pressurized the papacy for the suppression of the Society in 1773 and promoted bishops of an Erastian, Jansenizing temper.

J. Lynch, *Bourbon Spain 1700–1808* (Oxford: Blackwell, 1989).

D. A. BRADING

Charles VI (1685–1740) Holy Roman Emperor (1711–40). The younger son of Leopold I, he succeeded in 1711 to the Austrian lands on the death without male heir of his brother Joseph I. He was subsequently elected Emperor. Earlier he had been a candidate for the Spanish throne and his brief experience as king of Spain had a lasting influence on him. He had an elevated view of his own position and continued his brother's policy of reasserting imperial influence in Germany. At the beginning of his reign Austria's gains from the Spanish and Turkish empires made it a European great power but the foundations of its power were weak and its international position declined in his later years. He was initially very interested in schemes for the economic development of Austria but later neglected internal reform. His failure to produce a male heir and the threatened division of the Habsburg Empire led him in April 1713 to promulgate the

PRAGMATIC SANCTION, which sought to ensure the undivided inheritance of his lands for his elder daughter, Maria Theresa. This was the first legal codification of an indivisible Austrian state.

M. Hughes, *Law and Politics in Eighteenth-Century Germany* (Woodbridge: 1988).

MICHAEL HUGHES

Charles VII [Charles Albert] (1697–1745) Elector of Bavaria (1726–45), Holy Roman Emperor (1742–5). In 1726 he inherited a state still suffering the effects of the disastrous War of the Spanish Succession. An amiable and high-minded man, he was an ineffective ruler, always subject to severe depression, which sapped his energy and resolution. He had an elevated idea of the importance of his Wittelsbach house, expressed in far-reaching ambitions and lavish spending on display. Instead of undertaking urgently needed internal reforms, he revived his father's policy of alliance with the French in the hope of gaining part of the Austrian lands if the male Habsburg line died out. In the 1730s he pursued an aggressive anti-Austrian policy in Germany. In 1742 he achieved the long-held ambition of his house, the title of Holy Roman Emperor – in his words 'the highest peak of human splendour' – but it was an empty triumph. He was a shadow emperor, used as a catspaw by Prussia and France. On the very day of his coronation his capital, Munich, was occupied by Austrian troops and he was forced to spend much of his reign, without lands or resources, in Frankfurt. He died suddenly in January 1745.

P. C. Hartmann, *Karl Albrecht – Karl VII* (Regensburg: 1985).

MICHAEL HUGHES

Charles XII (1682–1718) King of Sweden (1697–1718). He succeeded his father, Charles XI (1655–97), and was invested with the limitless powers the latter had wielded. The Great Northern War, which dominated his reign, was begun by Denmark in the spring of 1700 in the Holstein dominions of his brother-in-law, but this phase was ended by prompt Anglo-Dutch action. However, Sweden's war in defence of its empire in eastern Europe, against Saxony-Poland and Russia, proved more difficult: it demanded from Charles and his commanders exceptional military skills and sustained covert diplomacy from a 'Chancery in the Field'. Defeated by Peter at the BATTLE OF POLTAVA in 1709, Charles spent five and a half years in exile in Ottoman dominions before returning to continue the struggle from Stralsund. After a year's siege, the fall of this fortress, and of Wismar in April 1716, at length delivered Germany from the seventy-year Swedish presence. Returned to Sweden, Charles was able to exploit the fissile character of the anti-

Swedish front, and Peter's increasing desire to end the war. At the age of 36 Charles was killed by a Danish sniper when he was besieging the Fredriksten fortress in south Norway. He was unmarried and died intestate. The war was to continue for another three years.

R. M. Hatton, *Charles XII of Sweden* (London: Weidenfeld & Nicolson, 1968).

D. D. ALDRIDGE

Charles Albert *see* CHARLES VII.

Charles Emanuel III (1701–1773)   King of Sardinia (1730–73). He succeeded his father, Victor Amadeus II, on the latter's abdication. The first two years were marked by bitter conflict with his father, but the hallmark of his reign was the continuation and consolidation of the centralized, absolutist system of government that was his father's legacy. He continued the ruthless inquiry into noble titles and taxation that had been instituted by his father, the *Perequazione*, together with the latter's policy of keeping the older noble families outside the administration, in favour of the rising service nobility. His reign witnessed the WAR OF THE AUSTRIAN SUCCESSION, during which much of the country suffered in the fighting, and Savoy was occupied. By the TREATY OF AIX-LA-CHAPELLE he lost no territory, and instead made gains from Lombardy. The long period of peace after 1748 allowed him to concentrate on internal reform.

The grip of the central government tightened as, for example, in 1762 when local assemblies of householders were abolished. His regime was conservative, marked by strict censorship and rigid Catholic orthodoxy; the recodification of the legal constitutions in 1770 did not reflect the enlightened influences evident in other Italian states at this time and are characterized by their harsh penalties for criminal offences. Perhaps the most important legacy of his reign was the consolidation of a powerful administrative elite, composed of closely knit families which survived, first, the attempts by the new king, Victor Amadeus III, to replace them, and then the French Revolution, to re-emerge in the nineteenth century.

S. J. Woolf, *A History of Italy, 1700–1860* (London: Methuen, 1979).

MICHAEL BROERS

Charles Eugene (1728–1793)   Duke of Württemberg. He was a would-be enlightened despot the extent of whose grandiosity was matched only by the pettiness of his achievements. An ardent Francophile, he set about imitating the dazzling artistic trappings of Louis XIV's France: besides modelling the ducal palace and its interiors on Versailles, and constructing a number of sumptuous rural pleasure retreats, he also commissioned the largest opera-house in Europe (at Ludwigsburg). He corresponded with Voltaire, but also borrowed a great deal of money from him. His government had to take into account the solidly entrenched parliament (*Landsrat*) of Württemberg, which represented urban interests and on which the jurist J. J. Möser (1701–85) was a trenchant critic. The parliament was unable to prevent Charles Eugene imprisoning Möser without trial from 1759 to 1764 but it did limit some of his initiatives, including a poll-tax project in 1764 aimed at restoring the state's finances after the Seven Years War.

James A. Vann, *The Making of a State: Württemberg 1593–1793* (Ithaca, NY: Cornell University Press, 1984).

COLIN JONES

Charles Frederick (1728–1811)   Margrave, later duke of Baden. He was a typical enlightened despot, whose commitment to the welfare of his subjects was uninhibited by concern for their opinions: he aimed 'to make them, whether they like it or not, into free, opulent and law-abiding citizens' (*see* ENLIGHTENED ABSOLUTISM). His correspondence with Voltaire, Goethe and Linnaeus and personal consultations with physiocrats like Mirabeau and Dupont de Nemours underscored his Francophilic and enlightened credentials. He abolished torture in 1767 and serfdom in 1783, and fostered physiocratic agrarian plans (notably after the great famine of 1770–1), industrial initiatives (including the first cuckoo-clock factories in the Black Forest), ambitious educational projects and humanitarian schemes. His adherence to religious toleration made his succession in Catholic Baden-Baden on the death of his cousin in 1771 unproblematic. He worked hard to remain on good terms with the French after 1789, and won the title of elector by agreeing to surrender territory on the left bank of the Rhine in 1803. Napoleon made him grand duke in 1806 when he joined the Confederation of the Rhine. One of his last reforms was the introduction of the CODE NAPOLÉON to his state.

COLIN JONES

Charles Theodore (1724–1799)   Elector of the Palatinate and Bavaria (1742–99). A member of a minor branch of the Wittelsbach family, he eventually inherited two electorates when the Palatinate and Bavarian lines died out in 1742 and 1777. He was a strange mixture of the traditional and the modern, of obscurantism and Enlightenment. A devout Roman Catholic, he also devoted considerable effort to the internal reform of the PALATINATE and to the promotion of cultural and artistic activities. When he inherited BAVARIA he was obliged to move to Munich. He was never at home there and was regarded by the

Bavarians as an outsider. His desire to be rid of Bavaria led him in 1784 to agree to Joseph II's plans to exchange Bavaria for the Austrian Netherlands but this came to nothing. At first he continued the opening of Bavaria to enlightened ideas, initiated by his predecessor, Maximilian III, but in the 1780s his reforming zeal declined and after 1789 he moved to a policy of severe repression to prevent French revolutionary ideas spreading into his state. The biological exhaustion of the Wittelsbachs continued under Charles Theodore, who died childless.

K. O. von Aretin, *Bayerns Weg zum souveränen Staat 1714–1818* (Munich: 1976).

MICHAEL HUGHES

chartered trading companies During the eighteenth century a great deal of European trade with the wider world was conducted by chartered trading companies. These companies, which were granted monopoly commercial rights in specific geographical areas by their national sovereign authorities, reached the zenith of their power and influence in mid-century, but then the tide of economic thought began to turn against them and by 1800 they were regarded in many quarters as being inefficient and anachronistic. Nevertheless, it was partly through their activities that Europe increased its range of contacts with both the known and the recently discovered world. The English HUDSON'S BAY COMPANY was, for example, required by charter to search for the north-west passage, while the French Compagnie de la Mer du Sud established links with distant lands along the Pacific coast of South America during the early years of the century. These pioneering activities were hazardous and often unprofitable undertakings, and consequently many of the companies did not survive for long.

In many cases, chartered companies became the vehicles for European overseas imperial expansion, and this was particularly the case in the East. Trading posts and warehouses were established, and from there it was often only a short step to the establishment of formal control over the indigenous population. Fierce commercial competition and the need for trading privileges led to the deployment of military force in support of local rulers, and companies often found themselves drawn into the tangled web of regional politics. In India, for example, the disintegration of the MUGHAL EMPIRE brought the DUTCH, ENGLISH AND FRENCH EAST INDIA COMPANIES into direct conflict with one another as they supported rival interest groups, and consequently they rapidly became the dominant military and political agents in the area. By the 1760s the British had overcome their competitors, and had established control over much of north-east India. From then on, the

East India Company subordinated its commercial role to that of its new functions as administrator and revenue collector. Yet its ill-defined semi-official position as British representative troubled many in London, and from 1773 onwards increasing state control was exerted over the Company and a gradual transfer of responsibility took place.

Most of the companies were funded by investment capital raised in the European money markets, and in theory they were private organizations answerable only to their shareholders. However, the need periodically to renew chartered rights meant that the companies were dependent on the goodwill and favour of their governments, and this served to remind them of the need to work in the national interest. Companies such as the English East India Company and the SOUTH SEA COMPANY also found themselves indebted to the crown for the deployment of troops and ships in their support when they were engaged in conflict with European rivals. Although nominally under the control of small elected executive bodies, the companies developed sophisticated management and administrative structures which allowed them to embrace a wide range of functions and activities. In this sense the companies represent a key stage in the development of European business organization, as well as having a central role in the story of European overseas expansion.

See also COLONIZATION, IMPERIALISM.

J. H. Parry, *Trade and Dominion: The European Overseas Empires in the Eighteenth Century* (London: Weidenfield & Nicolson, 1971).

HUW BOWEN

Chateaubriand, François-René, vicomte de (1768–1848) French writer and statesman. Born of a Breton family in St Malo, he went to Paris in 1788 and travelled to North America in 1791. It was a trip he was to describe in *Voyage en Amérique* (Travels in America, 1827). Returning in 1792, he joined the army of the ÉMIGRÉS, and escaped to England in 1793, where he supported himself by teaching and translating. There he wrote *Les Natchez* (The Natchez), a long prose epic published in 1726, and *Essai historique, politique et moral sur les révolutions anciennes et modernes* (An Historical, Political and Moral Essay on Revolutions Ancient and Modern, 1797). He returned to France in 1800 and began to court fame in 1801 with a short tale, *Atala*, and in 1802 with *Le Génie du christianisme* (The Genius of Christianity), begun during his exile in London. He was appointed to the embassy at Rome by Napoleon, under whom he refused to hold office after 1804. Between 1806 and 1807 he travelled. He was elected to the Académie Française in 1811. Under Louis XVIII he was made a minister and was French ambassador to London from 1822 to 1824.

Mémoires d'outre-tombe (Memoirs from beyond the Grave; partly published in 1849–50) is held to be one of the greatest French auto-biographies.

George D. Painter, *Chateaubriand: A Biography*, vol. 1: *1768–93: The Longed-For Tempests* (London: Chatto & Windus, 1977).

SYLVANA TOMASELLI

Châtelet-Lomont, Gabrielle Émilie, marquise du (1706–1749)   French natural philosopher. Her talent for combining natural philosophy with the heady social whirl of the *ancien régime* led her long-term lover Voltaire to nickname her 'Mme Newton Pompom du Châtelet'. The marquise, along with her mathematics teachers Maupertuis and Clairaut, was among the first *philosophes* to adopt Newtonian ideas. She had translated Bernard de Mandeville's *Fable of the Bees* (1714), written a critique of Genesis and an 'Essai sur l'optique' (Essay on Optics) before she collaborated with Voltaire – a refugee in her chateau at Cirey – co-writing the *Eléménts de la philosophie de Newton* (Elements of the Philosophy of Newton, 1738). However, disputing the blind Newtonianism of Voltaire's essay on fire submitted for an Académie des Sciences competition, she secretly submitted her own essay. Neither won. Her conversion to Leibnizian philosophy, under the tutelage of Samuel König, culminated with the publication of her *Institutions du physiques* (Institutions of Physics, 1740). In 1745 she began a translation of Newton's *Principia* (published in 1759). Her ever-loyal husband of twenty-four years tolerated her exchanging Voltaire for the younger Saint-Lambert, but despaired when she died at the age of 42, after bearing Saint-Lambert's child.

Esther Ehrman, *Mme du Châtelet* (Leamington Spa: Berg, 1986).

M. L. BENJAMIN

Chatham, first earl of *see* PITT, WILLIAM, THE ELDER.

chemistry   In the eighteenth century chemistry made significant advances in many countries of western Europe. Around 1700 it flourished mostly in association with pharmacy, as in Nicolas Lemery's (1645–1715) famous *Cours de chymie* (Course of Chemistry, 1675). Robert Boyle (1627–91) had criticized the Aristotelian theory of matter as composed of four elements but the idea lived on, notably in the teaching of the Leiden professor BOERHAAVE. Although Boyle had favoured a corpuscular theory of matter, a more influential idea was that of affinity, which some compared to gravitational attraction.

STAHL used the idea of an inflammable principle called PHLOGISTON to explain combustion. The phlogiston theory, of which there were several forms, was very influential. Its challenge by LAVOISIER was to bring about a revolution in chemistry. The key to this new approach was an understanding of the gaseous state. It was Joseph BLACK who distinguished 'fixed air' (carbon dioxide) from atmospheric air and thus contributed to the appreciation that there were many distinct types of matter existing as gases. Further important work on gases was carried out by CAVENDISH and PRIESTLEY.

Lavoisier was able to build on the work of these British chemists to demonstrate the crucial role of oxygen gas in combustion. By the careful use of the balance he was able to show that, far from anything (phlogiston) being given off in combustion, there was something (oxygen) taken in from the surrounding air. Lavoisier introduced a new theory of chemical composition showing, for example, that water was a compound of the two gases hydrogen and oxygen, and that atmospheric air was a mixture of nitrogen and oxygen. Together with several colleagues, he introduced a new systematic nomenclature for chemistry in 1787. He also wrote a textbook, *Traité élémentaire de chimie* (1789), in which he included a table of thirty-three supposedly simple substances, most of which were to be accepted and became the building-blocks of the new chemistry. He refused, however, to accept atoms, thus leaving an important further step to Dalton (1766–1844). Lavoisier transformed chemistry from a branch of natural history to a physical science. Eighteenth-century chemistry clearly exemplified the Enlightenment idea of progress and in many ways the subject was seen around 1800 as the model science.

F. L. Holmes, *Eighteenth-Century Chemistry as an Investigative Enterprise* (Berkeley, Calif.: University of California Press, 1989).

MAURICE CROSLAND

Cheselden, William (1688–1752) English surgeon. As surgeon to London's St Thomas's, Westminster, St George's and Chelsea Hospitals, he gained renown for his speed and efficacy at 'cutting' for bladder stones. He was also acclaimed for his anatomical instruction, cataract 'couching' and committee work for incorporating surgeons, investigating quackery and designing Fulham Bridge.

Z. Cope, *William Cheselden 1688–1752* (Edinburgh: E. & S. Livingstone, 1953).

PHILIP K. WILSON

Chesterfield, Philip Dormer Stanhope, fourth earl of (1694–1773) English statesman and man of letters. He made his career in politics and diplomacy, but was also known as a patron of literature and of authors. He is remembered for *Letters to his Son*: a collection of the almost daily correspondence he conducted with his natural son,

Philip Stanhope. Designed to educate him in the ways of the world, these were published by his son's widow in 1774. Chesterfield's political career began in earnest after he succeeded to the peerage in 1726. He was ambassador at The Hague from 1728 to 1732, but on his return he was dismissed by Walpole from his post as lord steward for opposing the Excise Bill of 1733. He remained in parliamentary opposition until 1744, when he joined the Pelham ministry. Thereafter he was lord-lieutenant of Ireland, a secretary of state for the affairs of northern Europe and, sometimes self-consciously, a man of letters. His most lasting action as a politician was introducing to Britain the Gregorian, to replace the Julian, Calendar in 1751. After claiming – but failing – to support the writing of Johnson's *Dictionary*, he attracted the disdain of its author in a famous letter, fixing him for posterity as the typical patron: condescending and self-important.

S. M. Brewer, *Design for a Gentleman* (London: 1963).

JOHN MULLAN

children   In Britain, much of Europe and North America during this period attitudes towards children perceptibly shifted towards a greater concern for children's emotional as well as physical needs. An important influence for social change was the English philosopher John LOCKE, who expressed a new pragmatism in both rearing and teaching children. His educational writings were widely read and respected by parents and teachers throughout the eighteenth century; *Some Thoughts concerning Education* (1693) appeared in at least twenty-one English editions and also in Dutch, French, Swedish, German and Italian. Locke's view was that children's minds were a blank sheet upon which the tutor or parent should imprint ideas and knowledge through a carefully judged rational upbringing. Affection was also important.

An alternative vision of the child as a creature of nature was proposed by Jean Jacques ROUSSEAU, the celebrated political philosopher and novelist whose views were similarly significant. Contrary to Locke, he argued in *Émile* (1762) that children should be drawn into learning through experience. Despite their different approaches to children's educational needs, these two writers exemplified a new social attitude towards children as sensitive individuals. They also furthered an intense interest in schooling.

In Britain, with increasing numbers and kinds of schools, including the growth in Sunday and charity schools, even many of the poorest had access to some basic EDUCATION (*see* SUNDAY SCHOOLS). The various small private schools and academies, and middle-class parents seeking to educate and also now to amuse children, provided a ready market for entrepreneurs in exploiting the new child-centredness in society. Children were to be entertained, as well as instructed.

John Newbery (1713–67) was the first publisher to produce English children's books on a large scale. His *Little Pretty Pocket-Book* (1744) was sold 'with a ball or pincushion' and appeared as one of the earliest examples of pure literary entertainment for children, although priced at the better-off child. Many of his educational books, based on Locke's ideas, sold well to schools and tutors. Throughout the British Isles, printers began issuing small chap-books and by 1800 a diverse children's book trade had developed to serve the new market. There were also toy-shops for children: in *Gulliver's Travels* (1726) 'a London toyshop for the furniture of a baby house' is mentioned. There grew a flourishing toy trade with dolls, jigsaws, games, puzzles – even miniature tea-sets – being produced for children.

By the late eighteenth century, when BLAKE was writing *Songs of Innocence* (1789) and a romantic view of childhood emerged, children in the privileged classes were enjoying enhanced opportunities at school and at play. However, while concepts of childhood had changed, social inequality, hardship and punitive legal codes remained to blight poorer children, including those who now had some rudimentary teaching.

J. H. Plumb, 'The New World of Children in Eighteenth-Century England', *Past and Present*, 67 (1975), 64–95.
L. A. Pollock, *Forgotten Children: Parent–Child Relations from 1500 to 1900* (Cambridge: Cambridge University Press, 1983).

MARGARET KINNELL

Chile Throughout the eighteenth century Chile, a Spanish colony since the sixteenth century, remained an agrarian society in which economic and political life were dominated by a few hundred rich families of land- and mine-owners. Centred on the fertile central valley between the Andes and the Pacific, this enterprising agro-industrial creole elite exploited poor white, Indian and mestizo labour in a system of peonage tenantry. They raised livestock, grain and orchard crops and mined gold, all for export to Peru and increasingly overseas via Buenos Aires and Chilean ports. Reforms imposed by Madrid, mainly from 1778, encouraged trade but without ending Chile's dependence on the export of cheap primary goods. Other reforms, especially under the captain-general and governor, Ambrosio O'Higgins (1788–96) brought more vigorous government and improved communications, while the expensive almost permanent military campaigns against the Araucanian Indians continued. Creole leaders, threatened by some reforms, either rebelled (1776) or, more successfully, undermined reform through corruption and manipulation of patronage. Thus, by 1800, rich Chileans largely determined their own political fate. Revolution against Spanish rule (1810–18) formalized political independence, but helped open the economy to full-scale British commercial and financial domination.

See also SPANISH AMERICA.

J. A. Barbier, *Reform and Politics in Bourbon Chile 1755–1796* (Ottawa: University of Ottawa, 1980).

CHARLES C. NOEL

China After 1683 China enjoyed more than a century of prosperity under a succession of very able rulers. The last years of the otherwise glorious reign of the K'ang-hsi Emperor (1662–1722) were darkened by the uprising of minority peoples in Tibet (1705–17), Sinkiang (1718) and Formosa (1721), which did not otherwise affect domestic tranquility. Since the emperor's accession he had striven to bring peace to the empire, partly with the support of the neo-Confucianists and patronage of scholarship. He had founded the College of Inscriptions and ordered many compilations. Among the books published in part to demonstrate Manchu commitment were the *Complete T'ang Poetry* (1707), a repertory of works on painting (1708), a thesaurus of literary phrases (1711), the *K'ang-hsi Dictionary* (1716), and an encyclopaedia in some 5,000 volumes (published in 1726). Private scholars were active, notably the bibliographer Chu I-tsun (1629–1709) and the mathematician Mei Wen-ting (1633–1721). This was also the most brilliant period of the imperial kilns at Ching-te-chen, where techniques of composite monochrome glazing over colours, of application of blue underglaze in powder form and of decorative overglaze in *famille verte* enamels were perfected. The minor arts also flourished, with the establishment of a hierarchy of twenty-eight kinds of artisans.

Despite theological controversy with other missionary orders of the Roman Catholic Church, the JESUITS continued to enjoy toleration and favour in exchange for scientific services. Fr Fontaney cured the emperor of fever with quinine and Fr Régis supervised the first maps of the empire to be based on astronomical observation and triangulation (1708–18). Their preferential status was jeopardized, however, by the (in)famous quarrel over Chinese rites that, in China, merely accentuated the conflict between imperial and papal authority.

With the advent of the Yung-cheng Emperor (1723–35) the matter was settled in 1724 with the recision of the 1692 Edict of Toleration, followed by outright persecution. Although some Jesuits were allowed to remain at or near the court in Peking, many were exiled – either to Macao or to Europe. A final edict in 1784 removed those remaining in the capital, despite a gift to the emperor of a series of extraordinary engravings, *Les Conquêtes de l'Empereur de la Chine* (1767–74), whose subject was drawn from military expeditions to Sinkiang. Such operations led to the establishment of a military council (1732) which gradually usurped the executive functions of government.

The reign of the Ch'ien-lung Emperor (1736–95) saw China increase remarkably in population and wealth, allowing Peking to attempt once more to control the Buddhists of Tibet (1747–51, 1755–99) and the Muslims of central Asia (1755–9). In this last campaign smallpox decimated the native tribes and allowed the empire to absorb the region at last. In 1765–9 an attempted invasion of Burma was thwarted, although Chinese suzerainty was recognized. Nepal was likewise invaded in 1792 because of an attack on the Panchen Lama. The Gurkhas were defeated and recognized imperial authority, while the lama was taken to Urga (Mongolia) and forcibly enthroned (as the Dalai Lama had been at Lhasa in 1705). But these operations were in peripheral areas and posed no major threat to the dynasty.

None the less, a major economic crisis loomed. The area available for agriculture, which had been extended by the introduction of new crops (maize, sweet potato and tobacco), was now almost completely occupied. The only vacant area suitable for Chinese-style farming was in Manchuria; but that province had been preserved as a Manchu homeland and Chinese settlement banned. Meanwhile the population trebled, from 100 million to 300 million, between 1650 and 1800. The people had to be fed by even more intensive cultivation of a limited area, so that by the end of the eighteenth century population pressures were beginning to generate widespread hardship.

These problems placed a great strain on the financial administration. Foreign commerce was a factor here. After 1757 China's export trade in tea, silk, porcelain and handcrafts was limited to Canton and Kyakhta. The exports were paid for in silver, the standard medium of exchange, but late in the eighteenth century the foreign powers began to sell opium to China to pay for their imports, and a drain of silver began which had serious effects on the Chinese economy, further impoverishing state finances and preparing the way for the Opium Wars of the nineteenth century.

The quality of government began to decline too. The administration did not keep pace with the vast increase of population, and the bureaucracy was grossly understaffed, as more powers were delegated to the local gentry. In the late eighteenth century corruption became rife, affecting both the civil administration, especially under the venal Ho Shen (1750–99), and the military, whose demoralization and lack of supplies were revealed by insurrection, especially in the Chinese heartland (for example Shantung in 1776, Kansu in 1781 and Hunan and Kweichow in 1795). From this time also date uprisings inspired by secret societies: the Eight Trigrams in Shantung (1774–88); the White Lotus in Szechuan (1795–1804); the Heavenly Peace in Hopeh and

Hunan (1795–1814), all presaging the T'ai-p'ing rebellion of 1850–63, and put down with great cruelty the better to 'save face' by maintaining the semblance of internal security.

Nevertheless, cultural activity continued to enjoy inspired imperial patronage. In literature, a critical edition of the twenty-four standard histories was issued (1739–46), followed in 1772–81 by the *Complete Library of the Four Treasures*, so extensive that only seven copies were distributed. (The emperor used this enterprise to delete from Chinese literature all derogatory references to the Manchu; more than 2,000 works were thus condemned in 1774–82. Two fraudulent works were also compiled to prove that the dynasty was descended from the Juchen Chin.) Textual criticism developed, with able scholars contributing no little to its heyday. Among these were Lu Wen-ch'ao (1717–95), Chiang Sheng (1721–99) and Tuan Yü-ts'ai (1735–1815). Pi Yüan (1730–97) compiled a supplement to the general history of Ssu-Ma Ch'ien (*c*.145–87 BC), helping to refine neo-Confucianist thought. In the decorative arts the imperial kilns developed, between 1736 and 1749, the elaborate palette of the *famille rose*, where ferric oxide red is replaced by carmine derived from gold.

By 1800 effective control within the government was declining, while economic pressures that could be resisted only by large-scale technological innovation and reorganization mounted. Neither was likely to be forthcoming. The Ch'ien-lung Emperor abdicated in 1795 (*d* 1799) and was succeeded by the Chia-ch'ing Emperor (1796–1820) who had to face new challenges from almost every direction.

Nigel Cameron, *Barbarians and Mandarins* (Chicago, Ill: University of Chicago Press, 1970).

Albert Feuerwerker, *State and Society in 18th-c. China* (Ann Arbor, Mich: University of Michigan Press, 1976).

Harold L. Kahn, *Monarchy in the Emperor's Eyes* (Cambridge, Mass: Harvard University Press, 1971).

Philip A. Kuhn, *Soulstealers: the Chinese Sorcery Scare of 1768* (Cambridge, Mass: Harvard University Press, 1990).

D. G. Lion, and J-C. Moreau-Goba, *Chinese Art* (NY: Rizzoli, 1980).

Joseph Needham, *Science and Civilization in China*, 5 vols. (Cambridge: Cambridge University Press, 1954–85).

BASIL GUY

Chippendale, Thomas (1718–1779) English furniture designer. He was born in Otley in Yorkshire, the son of a local joiner. After marrying in 1748, he took a house first in Conduit Street off Long Acre and subsequently in Northumberland Court off the Strand. It is likely that he was taught to draw by Matthew Darly, a prolific artist, draughtsman and printmaker, who is first recorded as a print-seller in 1749, when he lived in Duke's Court, St Martin's Lane. Darly took over the lease of Chippendale's house in Northumberland Court and collaborated with him in the preparation of plates for *The Gentleman and Cabinet-Maker's Director*, first published in 1754.

It was one of the most lavish folio volumes ever devoted to furniture. As its subtitle indicates, it was 'a large collection of the most Elegant and Useful Designs of Household Furniture in the Gothic, Chinese and Modern Taste'; and it applied some of the principles employed in architectural publications to the design of furniture. It demonstrates the full range of furniture which was available at the time, from the bookcase to the tea-caddy, from a girandole to a clothespress. Moreover, it shows the stylistic diversity which was thought to be admissible, including ribband-back chairs next to Chinese, without any thought or worry about which was better.

As a result of the commercial success of the *Director*, Chippendale was able to go into partnership with James Rannie and open up a shop in St Martin's Lane, described as 'The Cabinet and Upholstery Warehouse'. It consisted of three houses fronting on to the street with an entrance leading through to a yard, round which there were a variety of sheds and workshops. The outbuildings housed journeymen cabinetmakers and upholsterers, with special rooms for veneering and drying deals. From these premises, Chippendale was able to supply the nobility and gentry with a colossal range of fashionable goods, including curtains, carpets, wallpapers, loose covers and even coffins, either made on the premises or subcontracted to workshops nearby. As he stated in an advertisement for the *Director*, 'All Commissions for Household Furniture, or Drawings thereof, sent to the Cabinet and Upholstery Warehouse, at the Chair in St. Martin's Lane, will be most punctually observed, and executed in the genteelest Taste, and on the most reasonable Terms.'

Christopher Gilbert, *The Life and Work of Thomas Chippendale*, 2 vols (London, 1978).

CHARLES SAUMAREZ SMITH

Choiseul, Étienne François, duc de (1719–1785) French politician, one of Louis XV's most outstanding ministers. As the comte de Stainville, a career soldier, in 1752 he won the protection of the king's mistress, Madame de Pompadour. Partly through her help, he was appointed ambassador in Rome (1754), then Vienna (1757), receiving his dukedom in 1758, then serving as minister of foreign affairs (1758–61), army minister (1761–6) and navy minister (1766–70). Achieving the effective role of first minister just as France was enduring humiliation at the hands of Britain in the Seven Years War, he signed the FAMILY

COMPACT in 1761, diplomatically uniting the Bourbons of France and Spain and limiting damage to France's position in the final peace. He then devoted himself whole-heartedly to preparing for revenge on Britain, instituting major military reforms and dramatically increasing the number of warships. He also helped negotiate the acquisition of Lorraine (1766) and Corsica (1768). Accommodating to the *philosophes* and friendly with the *parlements*, in 1764 he supported the expulsion of the Jesuits called for by both groups. He was preparing for war against Britain in 1770 when court intrigue led to his dismissal.

COLIN JONES

Christian V (1646–1699) King of Denmark (1670–99). The son of Frederik III (1609–70) and Sophia Amalia of Brunswick, he was the first Danish king to ascend the throne as an absolute monarch after the constitutional changes of 1660–5. Christian was conscientious if not gifted, but he did what he could to consolidate the system established by his father. He attempted to create a new high nobility based on large estates by creating the titles of count and baron, reviving Christian I's Order of the Elephant and introducing an elaborate Table of Ranks. His massive codification of the Danish Law (1683) extended and further defined his father's version (1665), and his Land Register of 1688 definitively established the basis of royal taxation. His reforms were not always successful and the new tax exemptions he introduced helped to undermine royal finances. His foreign policy was anti-Swedish, but French diplomacy deprived him of the rewards of Denmark's involvement in the Scanian War (1675–9), which reversed the tide of military defeats at the hands of Sweden. He was an enthusiastic proponent of an anti-Swedish league in the late 1690s.

S. Oakley, *The Story of Denmark* (London, 1982).

ROBERT I. FROST

Christian VII (1749–1808) King of Denmark (1766–1808). The son of Frederik V and Louise of Great Britain (1724–51), he was the heir to a monarchy which for a century had been endowed with almost unlimited power. However, while he was undoubtedly intelligent, he early on betrayed signs of schizophrenia. On succeeding in 1766 he married Princess Caroline Matilda of Great Britain (1751–75) and a son was born. This child (the future Frederik VI 1768–1839) seemed unlikely to survive, but the skills of the Halle-born physician J. F. STRUENSEE pulled him through and were also, initially, applied to improving relations between the royal couple. Within a year, however, Struensee had become the queen's lover, and from this perilous position he began to assume plenary power in government, exercising the unbalanced Christian's prerogatives and so committing the capital crime of lese-majesty. Early in 1772 Struensee was arrested and the queen expelled from the realm, which was then ruled by a reactionary Regency Council in Christian VII's name until 1784. That April the 16-year-old crown prince took over the government, and through advisers of high calibre introduced far-reaching reforms for the Danish peasantry. Perhaps for this reason above all Christian's reign is notable, but after 1772 he himself could play no part in it.

W. P. Reddaway, 'Christian VII', *English Historical Review*, 31 (1916), 59–84.

D. D. ALDRIDGE

Christianity   During the later seventeenth and eighteenth centuries, the Christian tradition, which was based on the belief in Christ as a divine saviour and in revealed evidence, was strained by the development of natural and rational theology. Their proponents found evidence for the existence and attributes of God and his purpose in the structure and beauty of the natural world. Although in many cases such positions were adopted to buttress Christian truths, they also led to potential attacks on Christianity through deism and Unitarianism. The rise of rational theology was connected with the growth of the new science in the seventeenth century where natural theolgians such as Robert Boyle (1627–91) and John Ray (1627–1705) showed a desire to stress the essential harmony between Christianity and science. Ray in his influential *The Wisdom of God Manifested in the Works of the Creation* (1678) freed himself from the old antithesis between the natural and supernatural which had formally led Christians to deprecate nature. Ray's delight in the physical universe was an insistence on the essential unity of natural and revealed, proceeding from the integrated nature of the divine purpose. Such theological positions developed especially in England in reaction to what were perceived to have been the excesses of the enthusiasts who had caused so much trouble in the mid-century and sought to understand theology in terms of REASON. The term 'reason' itself meant different things to different writers: for the Cambridge Platonists, notably Henry More (1614–87), reason was divinely implanted within us, whereas for John Locke and his followers reason was a process of deduction from information. Locke's *The Reasonableness of Christianity* (1695) was not so much an attempt to deny the importance of revealed religion as an attempt to indicate that the two worlds of reason and revelation were inseparable, For him revelation was natural religion enlarged. By the 'reasonableness of Christianity' Locke meant the Scripture can reasonably be shown to have come from God and that even revelation confirmed the essential reasonableness of Christianity. Christian dogmas were few, simple and intelligible to all.

While these developments did not necessarily result in an attack on Christan doctrines, the notion that God had so ordered the world that it abided by strict laws encouraged the spread of DEISM. Indeed, it has been suggested that most of the theologians of the period were in reality semi-deist, concentrating as they did on proving the existence of God, and thereby downplaying the role of Christ. But this kind of view misjudges the context of such writing. To the natural theologians, the threat was atheism. Deistical principles held a belief in a creator, but denied the need for the Christian God who intervened in his world and thus challenged traditional Christian evidences such as miracles and prophecies. John TOLAND's *Christianity Not Mysterious* (1696) was an influential deist manifesto, arguing for the need to rid theology of supernatural accretions. Matthew Tindal's (1657–1733) *Christianity as Old as the Creation* (1730) maintained that true religion was formed at the creation; there was thus no need for later revelation. Bishop BUTLER's *Analogy of Religion* (1736) was the most powerful Anglican attack on these positions, and he was widely believed to have been responsible for quashing the deists' case by arguing that both nature and revelation are baffling sources of evidence. By the mid-century English rationalism had spread to the Continent. Already Bendict SPINOZA had denied that Christianity was a revealed religion. LEIBNIZ attempted to promote Christian unity and to reconcile Christianity with scientific deductions in an idealistic system of theodicy, which was satirized by Voltaire (1694–1778) in *Candide* (1759).

A related threat to orthodox Christianity was the spread of UNITARIANISM which rejected the doctrine of the Trinity and denied the divinity of Christ. In the early eighteenth century Isaac Newton, William Whiston (1667–1752) and the Anglican cleric Samuel Clarke (1675–1729) were suspected of Unitarianism. Clarke's highly controversial *Scripture-Doctrine of the Trinity* (1712) asserted that no text in the Bible supported the doctrine. By the mid-century Unitarianism had more proponents. Joseph Priestley defended Unitarian principles in his *Appeal to the Serious and Candid Professors of Christianity* (1770) and in 1774 Theophilus Lindsey (1723–1808) broke from the Church of England to form his own Unitarian congregation. Penal acts against Unitarians continued in force until 1813.

Such developments had consequences for the ways in which biblical criticism was undertaken. Instead of what were perceived to be the contorted explanations of the events and mysteries of the Old Testament, critics favoured a much more literal undersanding of the biblical narratives. The French Oratorian Richard Simon (1638–1712) was influential in bringing historical and textual criticism to the Bible, and was expelled from his order. His findings were later used by deists and sceptics in their attacks on the Scriptures.

In reaction to these developments there existed a counter-stress on revealed religion, and what is often called the religion of the heart, forsaking reason and natural evidence for feeling and emotion (*see* ENTHUSIASM). William Law (1686–1761) and John Wesley were particularly influential in this respect. Most of the theologians associated with the religion of the heart argued that the revelation given to man in the Bible had to be matched by an internal revelation. In Germany this attitude was encapsulated in PIETISM and the group associated with the MORAVIAN Bretheren. Similar trends can be found in the writings of Emmanuel SWEDENBORG who became conscious in 1743–5 of a direct contact with the angels and the spiritual world. In works such as *The True Christian Religion* (1771) he formulated his conception of the New Church, which was supposed to be compatible with existing institutions. At the end of the century F. D. E. Schleirermacher (1763–1834), sometimes called 'the father of modern theology', wrote, under the influence of German Romanticism, his *Religion: Speeches to its Cultured Despisers* (1779). Stressing the need for a living faith, he defined religion as a 'sense and taste for the infinite'.

Yet it would be wrong to suggest that there was a necessary opposition between these two impulses to reason and revelation in the period. Many of the theologians were able to combine rational evidence with feeling, such as the French preacher Bishop Bossuet. It is a measure of the all-pervasive willingness to connect theology and nature that even those clerics who attacked Newton's theology and his views of the Bible did so not by rejecting his premise of the link between nature and theology, but his interpretation. John Hutchinson (1674–1737) produced an alternative synthesis of science and theology, arguing that the three persons of the Trinity corresponded to the fire, light and air in the world. It is easy to condemn what has often been considered the formalism and emotional aridity of Christianity in the eighteenth century, but at its best faith and reason, revelation and natural religion, head and heart were welded into a distinctive piety.

See also NATURAL RELIGION.

J. Dillenberger, *Protestant Thought and Natural Science* (London, 1961).
C. E. Raven, *Natural Religion and Christian Theology* (Cambridge, 1953).
John Redwood, *Reason, Ridicule and Religion: The Age of Enlightenment in England 1660–1750* (Cambridge, Mass., 1976).

JEREMY GREGORY

Church of England *see* ANGLICANISM.

cities *see* CAPITAL CITIES; TOWNS AND CITIES.

citizenship The term 'citizen' was preferred to 'subject', especially after the American and French Revolutions. It was used in the eighteenth century to denote the bearers of RIGHTS and duties, either under specific constitutions or, more generally, within a variety of political discourses. The word was powerfully evocative even before the Revolutions. It called to mind the much idealized democracies of the ancient world whose predominant spirit was, as Montesquieu emphasized, that of civic VIRTUE. This was a world of equality among equals, and one in which the interests of individual citizens and that of their native city were in perfect harmony. Such was the world that Rousseau sought to invoke by styling himself 'citoyen de Genève'.

As the century progressed citizenship became part of the aspirations of increasing numbers of people, not least women. The language of citizenship was woven into feminist discourse, as the rhetoric of Mary Wollstonecraft illustrates. 'The being who discharges the duties of its station is independent,' she wrote, 'and, speaking of women at large, their first duty is to themselves as rational creatures, and next, in point of importance, as citizens, is that, which includes so many, of a mother.' Wollstonecraft supposed that 'society will some time or other be so constituted, that man must necessarily fulfil the duties of a citizen, or be despised, and that while he was employed in any of the departments of civil life, his wife, also an active citizen, should be equally intent to manage her family, educate her children, and assist her neighbours'. For a woman to discharge these civil or motherly duties, Wollstonecraft argued, she required the protection of civil laws in such a way as to be fully independent of her husband: 'The conclusion which I wish to draw, is obvious; make women rational creatures, and free citizens, and they will quickly become good wives, and mothers; that is – if men do not neglect the duties of husbands and fathers.'

Simon Schama, *Citizens: A Chronicle of the French Revolution* (London: Penguin, 1989).
Judith N. Shklar, *Men and Citizens: A Study of Rousseau's Social Theory* (Cambridge: Cambridge University Press, 1965).
The Works of Mary Wollstonecraft, ed. Janet Todd and Marilyn Butler, vol. 5: *A Vindication of the Rights of Woman* (London: William Pickering, 1989).

SYLVANA TOMASELLI

Civil Constitution of the Clergy (12 July 1790) In France clerics had played an important role in the political changes of the late 1780s. The *prélats politiques* of the Brienne ministry (1787–8) portrayed themselves as supporters of generally beneficial reforms. The last General Assembly, that of 1788, supported the call for the summoning of the Estates General. Religion was not a central issue in the CAHIERS: only 10 per cent called for the abolition of the tithe, 4 per cent for that of the regular clergy and 2 per cent for the sale of all church land. Many of the bishops held liberal political views and were prepared to co-operate in the National Assembly's work of constitutional reform. However, though the breakdown of the relationship between those who sought both reform in the church and to make traditional teaching and practices relevant to a new age, and the secular reformers was not inevitable, the belief that clerical views must be subordinated to those of government was well developed before it occurred. The Civil Constitution was a nationalization of the church which removed the governmental role of the papacy. The clergy were put on a salary scale, the ecclesiastical map rationalized, residence requirements were enacted and all clerics were to be elected by the laity. Episcopal powers were to be exercised in conjunction with an advisory council. Clerical protests led the Assembly on 27 November 1790 to impose an oath on the clergy to support the new order, with dismissal as the penalty for refusal. The nationalization of the church was readily apparent.

See also CLERGY.

J. McManners, *The French Revolution and the Church* (London, 1969).
T. Tackett, *Religion, Revolution and Regional Culture in Eighteenth-Century France: The Ecclesiastical Oath of 1791* (Princeton, NJ: Princeton University Press, 1986).

JEREMY BLACK

civilization   Rousseau was a key figure in the eighteenth-century endeavour to trace the nature and development of civilization and CIVIL SOCIETY, particularly in his influential *Discours sur les sciences et les arts* (A Discourse on the Sciences and the Arts, 1750) and *Discours sur l'origine et les fondements de l'inégalité* (A Discourse on the Origins and Foundation of the Inequality among Mankind, 1755). In his critique of the impact of civilization he described the true cost of PROGRESS: man forfeited the happy condition he had enjoyed in the state of nature when he embarked on an irreversible course towards modernity, which led to alienation from himself, from nature and from other men. The sense of loss was echoed by Diderot and nearly all the thinkers of the Scottish Enlightenment. Where they differed, by and large, was in their appreciation of the benefits, no less than the demerits, of the march of history.

Kant in his *Idee zu einer allgemeinen Geschichte in Weltbürgerlicher Absicht* (Idea for a Universal History with a Cosmopolitan Purpose, 1784) sympathized with 'Rousseau's preference for the state of savagery' and argued: 'We are *cultivated* to a high degree by art and science. We are *civilised* to the point of excess in all kinds of social courtesies and proprieties. But we are still a long way from the point where we could consider ourselves *morally* mature. For while the idea of morality is indeed present in culture, an application of this idea which only extends to the semblances of morality, as in love of honour and outward propriety, amounts merely to civilisation.'

R. L. Meek, *Social Science and the Ignoble Savage* (Cambridge: Cambridge University Press, 1976).

Jean Starobinski, 'Le Mot civilisation', *Le Temps de La Réflexion*, 4 (1983), 13–51.

Sylvana Tomaselli, 'The Enlightenment Debate on Women', *History Workshop Journal*, 20 (autumn 1985), 101–24.

SYLVANA TOMASELLI

civil society The term 'civil society' was much in use in the eighteenth century, partly as a result of the methodology of the seventeenth-century school of Natural Law. The nature and history of civil society received a great deal of attention from a wide variety of thinkers, among them Vico, Giannone, Rousseau, Adam Smith and Herder.

In his *Essay on the History of Civil Society* (1767) the great Scottish Enlightenment thinker Adam Ferguson studied the process of social evolution which had led to the rise of commerce and manufactures and its accompaniments, liberty and the rule of law on the one hand, and the demise of true citizenship and civic virtue on the other. The work traced the evolution of the species from 'rudeness to civilization'. 'Civil society', for Ferguson, could mean a variety of things, including CIVILIZATION, a 'polished' as opposed to a savage, primitive or rude society, or the state of society ruled by law and government as opposed to 'the state of nature' as described by natural rights theorists.

'Man is, by nature, the member of a community,' Ferguson wrote, 'and when considered in this capacity, the individual appears to be no longer made for himself. He must forgo his happiness and his freedom, where these interfere with the good of SOCIETY. He is only part of a whole; and praise we think due to his virtue, is but a branch of that more general commendation we bestow on the member of a body, on the part of a fabric or engine, for being well fitted to occupy its place, and to produce its effect.' But he added that 'it is likewise true, that the HAPPINESS of individuals is the great end of civil society: for in what sense can a public enjoy any good, if its members, considered apart, be unhappy'. The interests of society and of individuals were easily reconciled, according to him, and it was in 'conducting the affairs of civil society, that mankind find the exercise of their best talents, as well as the object of their best affections'. Ferguson rejected the idea of civil society as formed by contract and disposed of the notion of the state of nature crucial to natural rights theorists' explanations of the nature of society.

Similarly, Hegel conceived of civil society as the domain of contracts, and not as the result of one. In his description of the modern state, civil society is constituted by men considered as creatures with needs and desires. Unlike the family or the state, it is not a unity. In civil society, men think and act purely as individuals and not as members of an affective (the family) or rational (the state) whole. It is as rights-bearing individuals that men enter into economic relations with one another. Civil society is that realm in which men are but agents in an economic market. Though Hegel went on to develop the idea of civil society and make his imprint on it, it is one of the areas of his thought which most clearly belongs to the Enlightenment and, more especially, to the Scottish Enlightenment.

Adam Ferguson, *An Essay on the History of Civil Society 1767*, ed. Duncan Forbes (Edinburgh: Edinburgh University Press, 1966).

SYLVANA TOMASELLI

Clairaut, Alexis Claude (1713–1765)   French mathematician. He made his mathematical debut at the Académie des Sciences at the age of 12. A passionate Newtonian, he taught Madame du Châtelet and nurtured her translation of the *Principia*. After he returned from Lapland with Maupertuis he turned to celestial mechanics, developed theories of the moon and comets and wrote major histories of geometry and algebra.

M. L. BENJAMIN

Clarkson, Thomas (1760–1846)   English campaigner against slavery, alongside William Wilberforce. In 1786 he published *An Essay on the Slavery and Commerce of the Human Species, particularly the African*, a translation of the prize-winning Latin essay he had submitted to Cambridge University in 1785. Through his publisher, James Phillips, he met the Clapham Sect, with whom he formed a committee for the suppression of the slave trade (*see* EVANGELICALISM). He toured Britain collecting information for the group whose successful lobbying of parliament sparked a debate on the slave trade in 1788 which resulted in the improvement in conditions of transport of slaves. In 1789 he went to Paris and attempted to convince the French to abolish the slave trade, winning support from Lafayette and Mirabeau. He resumed his proselytizing travels at home, but in 1794 his health gave way and he was obliged to retire for nine years. In 1807, two years after he resumed campaigning, the Abolition Bill met with royal approval. He was appointed vice-president of the Anti-Slavery Society in 1823, but it was not until 1833 that the Emancipation Act freed nearly a million slaves.

Ellen Gibson Wilson, *Thomas Clarkson: A Biography* (London: Macmillan, 1989).

M. L. BENJAMIN

classicism   The deliberate imitation of the works of antiquity was an attitude attributed to the ancients, whose quarrel with the moderns had enlivened academic debate in late-seventeenth-century France and Italy, but evolved in the eighteenth century into more of an accommodation. The ancients regarded antique forms as absolute and canonical; the moderns were prepared to modify those forms and to develop them in accordance with the principles of reason and nature. To the extent that nature remained the criterion of simplicity and regularity in both the literary and the visual arts, the moderns won. But the tenets of classicism, or NEOCLASSICISM, nevertheless continued to exert a wide influence; at least until their supersession by romanticism.

See ANCIENTS AND MODERNS, CULT OF ANTIQUITY.

Hugh Honour, *Neo-classicism* (Harmondsworth: Penguin, 1968).

DAVID TROTTER

classification   A scheme or arrangement of entities according to particular groups or classes is known as classification, or taxonomy. The dividing of members of the animal world according to similarities or differences of 'natural' form or archetype has been disputed since Aristotle. Enlightenment classifications centred around 'artificial' or assigned hierarchies within the great CHAIN OF BEING. LINNAEUS, a proponent of artificial classification, organized a scheme whereby each living component in the natural history world was distinguishable by select external and internal characteristics. Each plant and animal was identified by a broad genus and particular species name. Hierarchical levels between different genera were subdivided according to family, class and order.

Similar artificial classifications were constructed for diseases (for example by F. B. de Sauvages (1706–67)), anomalies (for example by C. F. Wolff (1734–94)) and knowledge (by the encyclopaedists). Several non-Linnaean classification schemes were introduced later in the century. Buffon, Kant and Girtanner (1760–1800), for example, distinguished themselves from Linnaean emulators by arranging hierarchies of relationships between animals based solely on similarity and difference. This line of reasoning greatly influenced pre-Darwinian thought about genealogical descent.

Michel Foucault, *The Order of Things: An Archaeology of the Human Sciences* (London: Tavistock, 1970).
A. O. Lovejoy, *The Great Chain of Being* (Cambridge, Mass.: Harvard University Press, 1936).

PHILIP K. WILSON

Clement XI [Giovanni Francesco Albani] (1649–1721) Pope (1700–21). Born in Urbino and educated at the academy in Rome that was supported by Queen Christina of Sweden (?1626–89), he entered the curial service in 1677, held governorships in the Papal States, was secretary of briefs in 1687 and became cardinal in 1690. In 1700 he was elected pope with the backing of the *zelanti* faction, who wanted a pastoral rather than a political pope. His political naivety was soon evident. He unsuccessfully challenged the elector Frederick II of Brandenburg's assumption of the title of king of Prussia in 1701, and in the War of the Spanish Succession he attempted a policy of neutrality but was obliged in 1701 to recognize Philip V of Spain whom he forsook in 1709 in favour of Archduke Charles. In the 1713 Treaty of Utrecht papal intervention was ignored, and when the Turks declared war on Venice in 1714 he failed to organize a Christian alliance against them. His reign was decisive in the repression of JANSENISM. He condemned Quesnel's (1634–1719) *Reflexions morales* (Moral Reflections) in 1708 and in 1713 issued the bull UNIGENITUS DEI FILIUS, which condemned 101 allegedly Jansenist propositions. He was interested in the church's missionary work to India, the Philippines and China. He had to decide in the dispute between the Dominicans and Jesuits over the use of pagan beliefs in spreading Christianity. The JESUITS accommodated them, but Clement found against them. In 1708 he declared the feast of the Blessed Virgin Mary obligatory throughout the church.

JEREMY GREGORY

Clement XII [Lorenzo Corsini] (1652–1740) Pope (1730–40). From a noble Florentine family, he entered the curial service in 1685 after renouncing his inheritance, and was made titular archbishop of Nicomedia in 1690 and cardinal in 1706. After a heated conclave he was elected pope in 1730 and imprisoned Cardinal Niccolo Coscia who had led the corruption in the curia during the reign of Benedict XIII (1649–1730). He suffered from gout and was largely bedridden, as well as blind from 1732. Not surprisingly, his reign saw the continuation of the decline of the power of the papacy in international disputes. During the War of the Polish Succession the Papal States were overrun by Spanish armies. In 1738 he proclaimed against Freemasonry and in 1737 canonized Vincent de Paul, the seventeenth-century opponent of Jansenism. He also tried unsuccessfully to rescue the papal finances by reviving state lotteries.

JEREMY GREGORY

Clement XIII [Carlo della Torre Rezzonico] (1693–1769) Pope (1758–69). He was educated by the Jesuits, became cardinal in 1737 and bishop of Padua in 1743, where he took the pastoral reforms of Bishop

Charles Borremeo (1538–84) as his model in improving the standards of his clergy. His reign was dominated by the Jesuit issue. In 1759 the marquês de Pombal expelled the JESUITS from Portugal, and in 1761 they were expelled from France. Clement tried to defend the Society in 1765, but to no avail, and Jesuits were expelled from Spain, Naples and Sicily in 1767 and from Parma in 1768. His reign ended with the French occupation of the papal enclaves of Avignon and Venaissin and a formal request from the Bourbon powers in 1769 for the dissolution of the order. He denounced Febronianism, a strategy devised by Bishop J. N. von Hontheim (1701–90) to limit the power of the papacy in the Empire, and placed several of the major texts of the Enlightenment on the INDEX notably Helvétius's *De l'Ésprit* and the *Encylopédie* in 1759, and Rousseau's *Émile* in 1763. His reign can be seen as a last-ditch attempt by the papacy to withstand the modernizing forces of nationalism and Enlightenment, as demonstrated in his controversial bull 'In Coena Domini' (At the Lord's Supper), which denounced the Bourbon powers, and in his order that all the nude statues and paintings in Rome be covered up.

JEREMY GREGORY

Clement XIV [Giovanni Vincenzo Antonio Ganganelli] (1705–1774) Pope (1769–74). The son of a surgeon from Rimini, he joined the Franciscans and dedicated his *Diatriba theologica* (Theoligical Diatribe, 1743) to Ignatius Loyola, the founder of the Jesuits. When he was created cardinal in 1759 he began to distance himself from the JESUITS. It was rumoured that he was elected pope in 1769 only after agreeing to the suppression of the order. He was able to establish better relations with Portugal by making the brother of the marquês de Pombal a cardinal, accepting all Pombal's ecclesiastical appointments and omitting to read the controversial bull 'In Coena Domini' (At the Lord's Supper). Although he engaged in delaying tactics in 1773, the brief 'Dominus ac Redemptor noster' (Our Lord and Redeemer) formally dissolved the order. Being forced to dissolve an order whose main purpose was to serve the interests of the Holy See was widely seen as the most telling instance of the weakness of the PAPACY in this period. Clement was similarly unable to stop the first partition of Poland. He received some support in England for his cordial relationship with members of the Hanoverian royal household, forsaking the traditional papal support for the exiled Catholic Stuarts.

JEREMY GREGORY

clergy The clergy fulfilled a wide range of duties, especially at the parish level, where they were responsible not only for the performance of church services, but also for much rudimentary education and for the distribution of poor relief. This period saw the continuation of the process of clerical professionalization in both Protestant and Catholic churches which had been such a feature of the previous era. Concern was shown by church hierarchies all over Europe to improve the education, training and pastoral commitments of the parish clergy. In Catholic countries seminaries were founded for this purpose and by the mid-century the results of this were being seen in the parishes. It has been suggested that the creation of an educated clergy helped to distance clergy from their parishioners. Certainly the period saw clergy in many areas engaged in tithe disputes, but this should not necessarily be seen as evidence of a breakdown in the relations between the clergy and their flock.

In France in particular something of a crisis developed in disputes between the lower members of the profession and the senior dignitaries, in the movement known as RICHERISM, which developed from the work of E. Richer (1559–1631). Its adherents argued that the parish priests' right to administer the sacrament did not depend on episcopal authority, and that they ought to have an economic status commensurate with their spiritual dignity. Indeed the poverty of the rural clergy throughout Europe illustrated the most serious weakness of the churches in this period. In some countries the clerical profession seems to have also suffered from the development of new and rival professional opportunities.

P. T. Hoffman, *Church and Community in the Diocese of Lyon, 1500–1789* (New Haven, Conn.: Yale University Press, 1984).
B. Plongeron, *La Vie Quotidienne du Clergé Francais au XVIIIè* (Paris, 1974).
T. Tackett, *Priest and Parish in Eighteenth-Century France* (Princeton, NJ: Princeton University Press, 1977).

JEREMY GREGORY

Clive of Plassey, Robert, baron (1725–1774)   English colonial administrator, popularly regarded as one of the founding fathers of British India. After arriving at Madras in 1744, he served for several years as an East India Company writer before being thrown into the thick of the action during the Anglo-French conflict. He made a name for himself as a military hero, most notably at the siege of Arcot in 1751. He later helped to mastermind the Bengal revolution after the BATTLE OF PLASSEY, although his acceptance of 'presents' worth £234,000 from native ministers later caused him difficulties when his actions were subjected to parliamentary scrutiny in 1773. In 1765 he consolidated the British position by signing the Treaty of Allahabad with the Mughal emperor, and his administrative arrangements as governor of Bengal established the East India Company as the main political and economic agent in the region. Clive returned to Britain for the third and final time in 1767, and devoted the remainder of his life to political activity at Westminster and India House. His death in 1774 may well have been as a result of suicide.

P. Spear, *Master of Bengal: Clive and his India* (London: Thames & Hudson, 1975).

HUW BOWEN

clocks The mechanical innovations in horology in the second half of the seventeenth century meant that clocks became relatively common domestic items in the eighteenth century, and encouraged the growth of the clock-making trade. The most common clocks of the period were spring-driven mantel clocks, spring- or weight-driven wall clocks and tall weight-driven clocks with full second pendulums (pedestal clocks in France, long-case clocks in England). Timekeeping was regulated by a balance wheel or a pendulum, and the common escapements were the verge and the anchor. The latter is indicated by the characteristic 'recoil' observed in the beat of the second hand of a pendulum clock. There were wide national variations in design and decoration, the more utilitarian English clocks, for example, contrasting with the often elaborate French ornaments which are clocks almost incidentally. The technical improvements in the century were inspired by astronomy and navigation. George Graham ($c.1674–1751$) introduced two features that turned a long-case clock into an astronomical measuring-instrument: the dead-beat escapement, which eliminated recoil, and the mercury pendulum, whose centre of gravity was unmoved by changes in temperature. The quest for a viable marine chronometer, to solve the long-standing problem of determining longitude, also contributed to a general improvement in accuracy and reliability in timekeeping. The prize offered by the British government for a solution to the longitude problem was won by John Harrison (1693–1776) whose marine chronometer proved exceptionally accurate (*see* MEASUREMENT OF LONGITUDE).

D. S. Landes, *Revolution in Time* (Cambridge, Mass.: Harvard University Press, 1983).

J. A. BENNETT

Clootz, Anacharsis [Jean Baptiste du Val de Grâce, baron] (1755–1794) One of the most enthusiastic cosmopolitan supporters of the French Revolution. A wayward itinerant German nobleman with an interest in literature, he settled in France in 1789. In radical journalism and speeches in the Paris Jacobin Club (*see* JACOBINS) he emphasized the Revolution's cosmopolitan potential, preaching a war of liberation in *ancien régime* Europe. On 26 August 1792 the Legislative Assembly awarded this self-styled 'orator of mankind' honorary French citizenship, alongside other 'foreign philosophers and writers who courageously maintained the cause of freedom', including Washington, Priestley, William Wilberforce, Bentham, Paine and Schiller. He was elected to the Convention, but Robespierre came to mistrust his foreign connections, his association with Hébert and other Parisian radicals, and his militant atheism (he played a leading role in the DECHRISTIANIZATION campaign in Paris). In December 1793 he was expelled from the Paris Jacobins, then excluded from the Convention. In March 1794 he was sent before the Revolutionary Tribunal as an Hébertist, and was executed with them.

A. Clootz, *Oeuvres*, 3 vols (Munich: Kraus, 1980).

COLIN JONES

clubs The word 'clubbable' was coined by Johnson whose *Dictionary* defined a club as 'an assembly of good fellows meeting under certain conditions'. The Georgian clubs of London ranged from the Sublime Society of Beefsteaks, which nourished the image of a meat-eating British bulldog, to the rakish Mohawks and the libertine Society for the Propagation of Sicilian Amorology. Clubs for men of letters flourished, including the coterie of Scriblerians founded by Swift, and the Kit-Cat Club, the creation of Christopher Cat, a cook who excelled in pork pies and was more renowned for his culinary skills than for his literary talents. The Liberty or Rumpsteak Club founded by Horace Walpole's enemies satisfied both the stomach and the higher faculties.

Political clubs were popular. These included the Calves' Head, whose annual banquet was dedicated to the rather unappetizing memory of the beheading of King Charles I. The Hanover and the Green Ribbon'd Caball were also clubs of a political shade, while there was no mistaking the hue of the 150 Staunch Tories Club. Another club with political leanings was the Wet Paper Brigade, whose members read the newspapers not hot off the press but damp from the printers before the ink had been given time to dry out. The Lying Club, for which tergiversation was essential for admission, was open to those of any political persuasion provided they were proficient in the arts of mendacity. Many clubs were short-lived, and in order to combat this, the Everlasting Club was set up expressly to last for ever; since this was its only appeal it soon closed down. Clubs that did thrive included the Ugly Club, which had no shortage of recruits. The more exotic Mollies Club catered for male enthusiasts of cross-dressing, while in contrast the Roaring Boys cultivated an image of exaggerated masculinity. Debauchees could join the Hell-Fire Club or the Dilettanti Society, whose entrance requirement was to have visited Italy, but, according to Walpole, the real qualification was to get drunk. The clubs and COFFEE-HOUSES frequented by wits and rakes were almost exclusively male preserves.

The legacy of this gregarious and fraternal spirit of eighteenth-century England has persisted, prompting the brothers Goncourt to observe that if two Englishmen were to be cast ashore on an uninhabited island, their first consideration would be to form a club. In contrast most of the clubs that developed on the Continent, particularly those which flourished during the period of the French Revolution, were devoted to political rather than social purposes.

See also SECRET SOCIETIES.

Robert J. Allen, *The Clubs of Augustan London* (Cambridge, Mass.: Harvard University Press, 1933).

MARIE MULVEY ROBERTS

coal   The fuel of the future was coal. It made possible the characteristic technologies of nineteenth-century industrialization: the stationary steam engine and railway locomotive, mass production of iron, gas lighting and, finally, organic chemistry (synthetic dyes and other coaltar products). All this rested on several centuries' development of coal-mining and coal-using techniques but in the eighteenth century coal was still in its infancy: only in Britain was it mined and burned on any scale. Elsewhere demand was small, mines tended to be shallow or driven horizontally into the hillside (as in China), and consequently posed fewer technological challenges.

It remains controversial whether Britain's shift towards mineral fuel was a response to a timber famine caused by population pressure and the rising demand for wood for both fuel and structural purposes (particularly shipbuilding), or merely the outcome of possessing huge, accessible reserves from which landowners could profit. By 1700 the annual output of British mines had risen to 3 million tons and the problems of substituting coal for wood in all but one fuel-burning industry had been solved. Yet the biggest user remained the urban domestic hearth: a fleet of Tyneside colliers kept London's fires burning, and they in turn created the air pollution that already caused concern.

Further expansion depended on the solution of problems encountered as mines were driven deeper, principally drainage and ventilation, but also on improved transportation for this heavy, bulky material. Newcomen's (1663–1729) invention of the STEAM ENGINE provided both a means of effective drainage and an important source of demand. Ventilation was improved through the development of existing methods of 'coursing the air' but the dangers of 'firedamp' and 'chokedamp' remained. Horse haulage along wooden rails above and below ground, winding by horse-gins and, later in the century, by steam reduced the cost of short-distance transportation. Water provided the only economical means of long-distance carriage, and it was coal that chiefly prompted the construction of the canal network after 1760 (*see* CANALS).

Coal output grew to over 15 million tons by 1800, at constant or slightly falling prices thanks to such productivity increases. It represented over 9 per cent of the value of total industrial output. The upsurge in demand came principally from the IRON industry, where the solution to the one outstanding technical problem of coal usage permitted massive expansion in the face of rising charcoal prices from mid-century.

Coal-viewers, the technical managers of the larger collieries, provided the expertise, and coalowners (mostly large landowners but also iron companies), the capital; much of it was drawn from agricultural rents and some borrowed on mortgage. Mounting capital requirements squeezed out the small partnerships of working miners. The coal was won by male faceworkers hewing with picks and hauled and carried hundreds of feet to the surface in many pits by women and children. Mining communities were largely closed and self-sustaining: miners were born to the job and inducted early. In Scotland until 1799 whole families were bound for life to coalowners. Miners' relatively high wages and short hours reflected their arduous, unhealthy and dangerous conditions.

See also MINING.

Michael W. Flinn, *The History of the British Coal Industry*, vol. 2 (Oxford: Clarendon, 1984).

                                                    CHRISTINE MACLEOD

Code Napoléon The French civil code, which was promulgated in 1804 and from 1807 referred to as the Code Napoléon, or Napoleonic Code, has proved a document of world-historical importance. It was implemented in all the parts of Europe under direct French domination down to 1815; certain areas, notably Belgium and the Netherlands, retained it thereafter; and it became the basis for many national civil codes throughout and outside Europe later in the nineteenth century. The establishment of a uniform civil code had been a constant ambition of the revolutionary assemblies since 1789, and much credit for its achievement is due to NAPOLEON BONAPARTE. While it retained the liberal gains of 1789 (individual freedom, civic equality, religious toleration and so on), the code also reflected the conservative and bourgeois values of post-revolutionary France: its concern for property was focused on land; it provided for partible inheritance of property (rather than primogeniture); and it gave the head of the family extensive powers over family members, thereby ensuring inferior status for women. The code was, finally, part of a whole programme of legal uniformization: a Code of Civil Procedure was inaugurated in 1806, a Commercial Code in 1807, a Criminal Code in 1808 and so on.

COLIN JONES

coffee-houses After their first appearance in Venice and Constantinople, coffee-houses opened throughout Europe in the seventeenth century. They were to play an important part in European social and political life from then on and were for the eighteenth-century Scottish and English intelligentsia, in particular, what the *salons* were for the *philosophes*. The *Encyclopédie* entry on coffee provides a summary of the arguments for and against the drink and concludes with a sentence defining coffee-houses as 'the places whose establishment gave rise to the use of coffee and where all manners of strong liquors are consumed. They are also manufactures of ideas, good as well as bad.' Most famous in Paris were the Café Procope (which Diderot frequented), the Café Gradot, the Café Laurent, the Café de la Régence (where chess and draughts were played) and the Café Buci, where the *Gazette* and the *Mercure de France* could be read and tobacco came free with the coffee. In Italy the most influential journal of the period was *Il Caffè*.

Nicholas Phillipson, 'The Scottish Enlightenment', in Roy Porter and Mikuláš Teich (eds), *The Enlightenment in National Context* (Cambridge: Cambridge University Press, 1981) pp. 19–40.

SYLVANA TOMASELLI

Coleridge, Samuel Taylor (1772–1834) English poet and philosopher. Coleridge occupies an unusual position in nineteenth-century British culture, in that he single-handedly tried to put together a system of philosophical idealism based on German writings with a description of a new kind of academic class – the intelligentsia or clerisy – who should propagandize for it. He was also a poet and in his early life initiated in collaboration with William WORDSWORTH a revolution in the forms and subject-matter of English verse. Part of the novelty of this achievement lay in both men endorsing democratic beliefs that they later abandoned.

The bane of Coleridge's life was that he damaged his own vision by a lifelong addiction to opium and that he spoke of his plans rather than completing them in his writings. His influence was as much by his personal reputation, his table talk and his correspondence as through works such as *Biographia Literaria* (1817) which came to be seen as deliberately obscure. For many of his admirers, Coleridge had prophesied the nature of this confusion and isolation in his *Rime of the Ancient Mariner* (1798), one of the great poems of the ROMANTICISM that Coleridge was a part of in England.

S. T. Coleridge, *Collected Letters*, 6 vols, ed. E. L. Griggs (Oxford: Clarendon, 1956–71).

MICHAEL NEVE

Collins, Anthony (1676–1729)   English theologian. Born in Heston in Middlesex and educated at Eton and King's College, Cambridge, he was a leading deist thinker. He was much influenced by John Locke. In his *Essay concerning the Use of Reason* (1707) he denied the usual distinction between things that are above and those that are against reason to assert the use of reason in all areas. His *Discourse of Freethinking* (1713) was his most controversial work. In it he condemned clergy of all denominations, believing that clerical traditions and dogmas misled the intellect and that truth could be found only through totally free enquiry, which he found support for in Scripture. His *Inquiry concerning Human Liberty* (1715) argued in support of determinism and his *Discourse of the Grounds and Reasons of the Christian Religion* (1724) argued against the idea that the Old Testament contained prophecies of the New, denied that the New Testament was canonical and rejected the immateriality and immortality of the soul. In this work, in particular, he found himself in dispute with another freethinker, William Whiston (1667–1752). Whereas Whiston had argued that the Scriptures ought to be understood literally, Collins favoured an allegorical approach.

See DEISM, FREETHINKING.

John Redwood, *Reason, Ridicule and Religion: The Enlightenment in England, 1660–1750* (Cambridge, Mass.: Harvard University Press, 1976).

JEREMY GREGORY

Colombia   Spanish-controlled Colombia was repeatedly reorganized in the eighteenth century, definitively as the viceroyalty of the new kingdom of Granada (Nueva Granada, 1739) consisting at its most extensive of present-day Colombia, Panama, Venezuela and Ecuador. It was an economically diverse, largely self-sufficient colony. Its viceroys, who were mainly energetic, capable reformers, faced problems of coastal defence against the British, widespread smuggling, administrative corruption and the challenge of economic modernization. Their attempts at reform were often opposed by rich creoles – bureaucrats, professional men, merchants, miners and landowners – who felt that their wealth and political influence were under threat, while the masses of Indians, poor whites, mestizos, and blacks and mulattos (free and slave) hated the increasingly authoritarian, centralized government, with its taxes and oppressive monopolies. A series of risings culminated in the Comunero revolt (1781), one of the most widely supported in Spanish colonial history. The Comunero army of nearly 20,000, led by well-off creoles and uniting virtually all groups, threatened to capture the capital, Santa Fe de Bogotá. Following defeat by the diplomacy and arms of the authorities, both masses and elite remained quiescent until the definitive break from Spain in 1810.

See also SPANISH AMERICA.

J. L. Phelan, *The People and the King: The Comunero Revolution in Colombia, 1781* (Madison, Wisc.: University of Wisconsin Press, 1978).

CHARLES C. NOEL

colonization The eighteenth century saw great movements of people and the interaction of cultures and religions in all quarters of the globe, as trade and discovery pushed back the frontiers of the known world. Added to the long-standing ebb and flow of Islamic imperial fortunes in the Near East, Asia and north Africa was the establishment of European hegemony in many new areas. European colonization of the Americas had been taking place steadily for many years, and the Spanish and Portuguese had established huge territorial empires in South America. On a more limited scale, settler colonies had been established by Britain, France, Holland and Spain in North America and the Caribbean.

Superior military technology and organization now gave the Europeans a decisive edge in conflicts with Asian powers, and the EAST INDIA COMPANIES began to establish and expand territorial holdings on the Indian subcontinent. The European presence in Asia after 1750 was increasingly characterized by dominion rather than by simple trading activity, and control was established, especially by the British, over indigenous states and rulers. In this process Europeans were undoubtedly assisted by internal weaknesses within the region's geopolitical systems, and in the long term the Marathas, Mughals and Ottomans proved to be incapable of withstanding the development of a new imperial world order.

The European presence in AFRICA remained a limited one, and was restricted to the coast, where slaving stations and strategic naval bases had long been established, particularly by the Portuguese. The interior, which was known to be unsuitable for settlement, remained largely unexplored. Similarly, central Asia remained beyond the scope of the European powers, although further to the east in the Pacific and South China Sea the Dutch, Portuguese and British had established a network of 'factories' and trading stations which stretched from Japan south to Indonesia (*see* EAST INDIES).

By 1800 the long-standing Dutch, French and Portuguese empires were, for a variety of complex reasons, in decline, and this process accelerated during the Napoleonic wars. Outwardly at least, the Spanish empire remained the largest and most impressive, yet by 1830 the breakdown of the Spanish–American imperial connection caused by warfare in Europe, and the subsequent development of South American independence movements, meant that Spain's days as a major imperial power were over (*see* SPANISH AMERICA).

In spite of the loss of its thirteen American colonies in 1782 (*see* NEW ENGLAND COLONIES), Britain was in a position by 1815 to embark on a century of imperial ascendancy. The main focus of British attention was now directed towards Asia, for while the rump of the old North Atlantic empire based on settlement and emigration in CANADA, Newfoundland and the West Indies (*see* CARIBBEAN) was still of supreme importance, great territorial advances were being made as a new empire developed in the East. The dynamics of this process are difficult to determine and they have engaged the attention of historians over many years, but it is clear that impulses, economic or otherwise, emanating from Britain itself were weak. It is not possible to discern the consistent application of any coherent imperial policy from London. In the main, strategic considerations, the development of trade and involvement in regional politics drew Britain further and further into the expansionist process (*see* CHARTERED TRADING COMPANIES). Specific examples of this were to be found in the seizure of the islands of CEYLON (1796–1818) and MAURITIUS (1810), and in the steady extension of control in India, Burma, Java and the Cape. At the same time, important exceptions to this rule, such as the establishment of Sierra Leone in 1787 as a refuge for freed slaves and the development of New South Wales as a penal colony in 1788, pointed the way forward to important new areas of imperial activity for Britain in the nineteenth century.

See also IMPERIALISM.

C. A. Bayly, *Imperial Meridian: The British Empire and the World, 1780–1830* (London: Longman, 1989).

H. Bull and A. Watson (eds), *The Expansion of International Society* (Oxford: Oxford University Press, 1984).

D. K. Fieldhouse, *The Colonial Empires: A Comparative Study from the Eighteenth Century* (London, 1966).

HUW BOWEN

commercial society   Leading social analysts of the Enlightenment often deemed their age that of commercial society, perhaps viewed, in a 'conjectural history' of the progress of civilization, as the successor to an original state of nature, to pastoral society, and to a feudal, agrarian order. But a society dominated by commercial values seemed to pose severe threats, according to powerful strands of moral and political thinking deriving from antiquity and associated with the civic humanism of the Renaissance. Taken in conjunction with its natural partner, LUXURY, commercial WEALTH was often diagnosed as the mortal enemy of virtue in both its classical republican and transcendental senses. Commercial society, it was feared, would promote personal vanity and private vices associated with corruption, fraud, deceit and inequality; it was thus thought to be inimical to public spirit and the long-term well-being and security of the body politic.

Counter-claims were developed, however, arguing for the socio-moral benefits of commercial society. Most provocatively, Bernard Mandeville in his *Fable of the Bees* (1714) defended luxury, arguing that private vices like acquisitiveness and covetousness were in truth public benefits, because they were the only means to ensure employment, industry and prosperity. Mandeville argued that classical virtue was a sure recipe for poverty, and implied that those who defended it were hypocrites. The moral?

> Then leave complaints; Fools only strive
> To make a great an honest hive ...
> Fraud, luxury and pride must live
> While we the benefits receive.

Others, including David Hume in his *History of England* (1762), argued more temperately that commercial society brought with it the great advantages of personal liberty and safety of property under the disinterested rule of law. A trading kingdom was thus a bulwark against despotism and arbitrary rule. An extension of this reasoning, put forward, among others, by Joseph Addison and Adam Smith, argued that a commercial society increased the sociability and humanity of subjects, demanded polished manners and civil calm, and thus promoted the progress of true CIVILIZATION and the refinement of the arts and sciences. In France Montesquieu, in *L'Esprit des lois* (1744), argued that commerce encouraged frugality and labour, order and rule. Internationally too it encouraged peace and accord. Arguments of this kind became standard to the 'sociology' developed by the leaders of the Scottish Enlightenment, Adam Ferguson and John Millar (1735–1801) – though Ferguson was also troubled by the corresponding decline of the martial spirit.

A further key vindication of commercial society was offered by

Smith's *Inquiry into the Nature and Causes of the Wealth of Nations* (1776). Smith underscored the valuable growth of interdependency created by the division of labour. By capitalizing on social emulation and the pursuit of vanity and refinement, commercial societies could direct the human yearning for self-betterment to collective advantage. In Smith and his fellows, the new discourse of political economy offered a vindication of commercial society, thereby cleverly meshing a discourse of wealth with theories of liberty, political moderation, the relations of individual to the whole, and historical progress.

Istvan Hont and Michael Ignatieff (eds), *Wealth and Virtue: The Shaping of Political Economy in the Scottish Enlightenment* (Cambridge: Cambridge University Press, 1983).

J. G. A. Pocock, *Virtue, Commerce and History: Essays on Political Thought and History* (Cambridge: Cambridge University Press, 1985).

ROY PORTER

Committee of General Security Together with the COMMITTEE OF PUBLIC SAFETY, this was one of the great executive committees of government that directed the TERROR from the summer of 1793 down to the overthrow of Robespierre on 9 Thermidor (27 July 1794). While the Committee of Public Safety concentrated on the war effort and general policy, the Committee of General Security, which was formed in October 1792, constituted a virtual police ministry with sweeping powers in regard to security and law and order. Its effectiveness was initially limited by political squabbles over its size and composition. On 14 September 1793 the Committee of Public Safety appointed twelve fellow *conventionnels* who constituted the 'Great Committee of General Security' of Year II (1793–4). Maintaining close correspondence with departmental and district authorities, municipalities and revolutionary committees, it was responsible for tens of thousands of imprisonments and numerous trials before revolutionary tribunals. By the spring of 1794, however, disharmony had emerged within the Committee and in its relations with the Committee of Public Safety. Robespierrists such as Lebas (1765–94) and the painter David clashed with anti-Robespierrists such as Amar (1755–1816) and Vadier (1736–1828), who conspired in Robespierre's overthrow. The Committee's powers were signally reduced after Thermidor.

COLIN JONES

Committee of Public Safety The basis of government from 6 April 1793 until the end of the NATIONAL CONVENTION, the Committee of Public Safety was instituted to ensure the execution of the war effort through policies of TERROR. It achieved its notorious form only in July 1793, when ROBESPIERRE was elected to it. The twelve members of the

Convention who composed the 'Great Committee' formed a war cabinet with semi-dictatorial powers (for example authority over ministers, generals and constituted authorities; right to dismiss state officials at will; conduct of foreign policy). Robespierre was its most visible member within the Convention, in which he expounded the Committee's strategy. 'Ideological' members of the Committee (Saint-Just (1767–94), Billaud-Varenne (1756–1819) and Collot-d'Herbois (1750–96)) were outnumbered by 'technicians' of the war effort such as Carnot and Jean Bon Saint-André (1749–1813), effective army and navy ministers and Robert Lindet (1743–1825), who operated the Maximum (the terroristic policies of managing the economy). Once the Committee had repelled foreign armies, its terroristic and *dirigiste* policies seemed less necessary. This was the context for the THERMIDOR *coup* (27 July 1794), which overthrew Robespierre and his followers and reduced the powers and importance of the Committee.

Robert R. Palmer, *Twelve who Ruled* (Princeton, NJ: Princeton University Press, 1941).

COLIN JONES

concerts, public   Although concerts for the aristocracy were sometimes open to the common people, public concerts were, in general, part of the rise of middle-class culture in the eighteenth century. Performances for a limited, non-paying audience were held in Hamburg as early as 1660. Concerts open to a paying audience seem to have been first held in England, where they were organized by the violinist John Banister (1630–79) in the 1670s. The first concert hall was built in London in 1678. After 1775 the Hanover Square Rooms were used. There were various subscription concerts in eighteenth-century London, notably those organized by JOHANN CHRISTIAN BACH and Karl Friedrich Abel. In Leipzig the Great Concerts were started in 1743, becoming the Gewandhaus Concerts 1781. In France the Concerts des Amateurs were introduced in 1769, and renamed Concerts de la Loge Olympique in 1780. In Vienna MOZART organized subscription concerts of his own music from 1782.

Many of the early concert series were organized by amateur groups, such as the Academy of Ancient Music in England (1710) and the Concerts Italiens in Paris (1713). In Germany such groups were called 'collegia musica'. Music societies were first established in central Europe: Musikübende Gesellschaft in Berlin, in 1749; Tonkünstlersozietät and Gesellschaft der Musikfreunde in Vienna, in 1771 and 1812 respectively. A particular bourgeois development occurred in revolutionary France after 1789, when concerts were held in the open air as part of organized entertainment for the masses.

G. Abraham (ed), *Concert Music (1630–1750)* (Oxford: Oxford University Press, 1986) [New Oxford History of Music, vol. 6].

M. S. Morrow, *Concert Life in Haydn's Vienna: Aspects of a Developing and Social Institution* (Stuyvesant, NY: Pendragon Press, 1989).

W. Weber, *The Rise of Musical Classics in Eighteenth-Century England: A Study in Canon, Ritual and Ideology* (Oxford: Clarendon, 1992).

FRITZ WEBER

Concordat of 1802 The agreement between the first consul Napoleon Bonaparte and Pope Pius VII which ended the breach between the revolutionary state and the Catholic Church that had originated in the CIVIL CONSTITUTION OF THE CLERGY was known as the Concordat. Papal hostility, foreign war, the emigration of much of the *ancien régime* higher clergy, and 'church and king' peasant insurrection in western France had all envenomed relations between church and state. The Concordat now recognized Catholicism as the religion of the great majority of Frenchmen (though not as official state religion: religious toleration was assured); committed the state to pay ecclesiastical salaries; regulated appointments within the church (the first consul nominated bishops, the pope consecrated them); permitted the establishment of seminaries; and confirmed the sale of church lands since 1790. Negotiated and signed in secrecy in 1801, the document was officially promulgated only on Easter Day 1802 with 'Organic Articles' which buttressed Napoleon's position. It restored a measure of religious harmony, reunited the clergy, took the wind out of the sails of religiously inspired counter-revolution, won massive support from peasant and bourgeois purchasers of church lands and remained the basis of church–state relations throughout the nineteenth century.

COLIN JONES

Condillac, Étienne Bonnot de (1715–1780) French philosopher and psychologist. He believed that the rigour and certainty of mathematics could be extended to the human sciences. A great admirer of Locke, he traced the development of the mind in the *Essai sur l'origine des connaissances humaines* (Essay on the Origin of Human Knowledge, 1746) and went further than Locke in arguing that not only ideas, but the mind's very faculties originated in sensation (*see* SENSATIONALISM). These views were expanded in *Traité des sensations* (Treatise on Sensations, 1754). In *Traité des systèmes* (Treatise on Systems, 1749) he criticized abstract and speculative systems like that of Descartes (1596–1650). *Traité des Animaux* (Treatise on Animals, 1755) attacked Buffon and Descartes for their account of animals as mere automatons, devoid of cognitive powers. The *Logique* (1780) considered the origins of ideas again and the means to facilitate the acquisition of knowledge. He was elected to the Académie Française in 1768.

The many references to his works in the *Encyclopèdie* attest to the esteem in which he was held, but his religious orthodoxy and staunch rejection of materialism placed him outside the *philosophes'* circle, and he became increasingly estranged from those who, like Diderot, had once been his friends. In the late eighteenth century the *Idéologues* were to look to him for inspiration.

John W. Yolton, *Locke and French Materialism* (Oxford: Clarendon, 1991).

SYLVANA TOMASELLI

Condorcet, Marie-Jean-Antoine-Nicolas de Caritat, marquis de (1743–1794) French mathematician, historian of science, political theorist and feminist. He was born in Ribemont in Picardie and educated at the Jesuit College of Navarre. Admitted to the Académie des Sciences in 1769 for his mathematical work, he was elected its perpetual secretary in 1776 and became a member of the Académie Française in 1782. A friend of Voltaire, D'Alembert (1717–83) and Turgot, he married Sophie de Grouchy (1764–1822) in 1786 whose *salon* was among the most brilliant of the period.

In 1785 he published *Essai sur l'application de l'analyse à la probabilité des décisions rendues à la pluralité des voix*, which investigated through the calculus of probability the conditions under which majority decisions proved correct. It was part of his more general argument for the validity of a mathematical approach to ethics and politics. Elected to the Legislative Assembly in 1791, he devoted much effort to planning a system of public education. He addressed the issue of the rights of women in *Essai sur l'admission des femmes au droit de cité* (On the Admission of Women to the Rights of Citizenship, 1790). His defence of his liberal constitution for the new republic against that drawn by the Jacobins forced him to take flight in July 1793. While in hiding, he worked on his famous *Esquisse d'un tableau historique des progrès de l'esprit humain* (Sketch for a Historical Account of the Progress of the Human Mind), published posthumously in 1795. Captured in 1794, he died during his first night in prison.

Keith Michael Baker, *Condorcet: From Natural Philosophy to Social Mathematics* (Chicago: University of Chicago Press, 1975).

SYLVANA TOMASELLI

Constantinople *see* ISTANBUL.

Constituent Assembly The Third Estate of the Estates General proclaimed itself the NATIONAL ASSEMBLY on 17 June 1789, inviting the representatives of the other two orders to merge with them. Following the TENNIS COURT OATH of 20 June, the king agreed to the merger of the three estates as (from 9 July) the National Constituent Assembly, whose task was to draw up a new constitution for France. It passed the DECLARATION OF THE RIGHTS OF MAN AND THE CITIZEN on 26 August 1789, which provided the foundations on which the constitution (agreed in September 1791) was to be built. The Constituent Assembly ceded to the new LEGISLATIVE ASSEMBLY on 1 October 1791, after achieving perhaps the most remarkable legislative programme in French history: besides founding the constitutional monarchy, it established the liberal freedoms (of press, speech, religious opinion, equality before the law and so on); totally reorganized the church (through the CIVIL CONSTITUTION OF THE CLERGY of July 1790); laid the basis for economic freedom; and introduced structural administrative changes, including the creation of the departments and major financial and judicial reforms. These reforms reflected the social composition of the assembly, over two-thirds of whom were from the liberal professions (especially the law).

COLIN JONES

Constitution of 1791 France's first written constitution, and one of the first in world history, the 1791 Constitution was the achievement of the CONSTITUENT ASSEMBLY. It was ratified by Louis XVI on 13 September 1791 but many of its proposals had been voted in progressively since mid-1789. France became a constitutional monarchy which enshrined indirect, representative democracy: the electoral process was multitiered and a property franchise distinguished between less well-off 'passive citizens' who enjoyed civil but not political rights and 'active citizens' who enjoyed both. The new system operated within the framework of the DECLARATION OF THE RIGHTS OF MAN AND THE CITIZEN, which served as preamble to the constitutional document, and was characterized by a thoroughgoing separation of powers (judiciary, legislature, executive). The monarch, now only 'king of the French', appointed ministers and headed the armed forces, but had no powers to pass decrees and only a suspensive veto on legislation passed by the unicameral legislature, the LEGISLATIVE ASSEMBLY, which first sat on 1 October 1791. The signal reduction in the monarch's powers caused much dissension down to the overthrow of Louis XVI in 1792, when the dispositions of the 1791 Constitution were ended.

COLIN JONES

Constitution of 1793 The democratic constitution voted by the Convention in June 1793, which received popular assent by referendum that summer, was, however, never implemented. The emergency regime of 'revolutionary government' necessitated by foreign and civil war in 1793–4, then the decision to create a less democratic, more classically liberal constitution (the Constitution of 1795) prevented this. Formulated following the expulsion of Girondin deputies (*see* GIRONDINS) from the Convention (31 May–2 June 1793) by the more radical MONTAGNARDS, and viewed partly as a means of rallying popular support behind the war effort, the constitution embodied far more radical dispositions than any former political system. Universal manhood suffrage was envisaged; the right to work was recognized, as were rights to education and to public assistance; sovereignty was lodged in the people rather than the nation; and forms of referendum were instituted to allow something like direct democracy. The implementation of this constitution was demanded by radicals following the fall of Robespierre, and though the Constitution of 1795 ended its applicability, it served as a blueprint and guide for many social revolutionaries in nineteenth-century western Europe.

COLIN JONES

Constitution, United States The written constitution by which the UNITED STATES OF AMERICA is governed today arose from the peculiar circumstances of the country following the War of Independence. Influential men believed that America's financial, economic and diplomatic problems could be tackled only by national policies which could not be enacted under the existing Articles of Confederation. Accordingly, congress called a convention of state delegates to meet in Philadelphia in May 1787 to revise the articles, and by September the delegates had agreed on an entirely new document, drafted largely by James MADISON. Within a year, the constitution had been ratified by eleven state conventions, and it came into operation in 1789.

The constitution gave the federal government the power to execute its wishes directly within the states, but only in defined areas of common concern, while the states retained extensive powers over their internal affairs. To prevent the federal government from becoming tyrannical, its various functions were separated and different methods of election ascribed for each branch. A complex amending process allowed changes to this fundamental law, and by 1791 a Bill of Rights had been added establishing principles of individual liberty beyond the reach of statute law.

R. B. Morris, *The Forging of the Union, 1781–1789* (New York: Harper & Row, 1987).

DONALD J. RATCLIFFE

consumerism In recent years, historians analysing the dramatic economic upswing noticeable especially in north-western parts of Europe from the second third of the eighteenth century have paid increasing attention to consumption (traditionally neglected in favour of production). It was a surge in home demand, many now believe, that played a (possibly *the*) crucial role in economic revitalization, particularly in encouraging brisker sales of standardized personal and domestic items manufactured in large quantities: textiles, furniture, tools, watches, mirrors, crockery, tableware, simple domestic appliances, books and prints, trinkets and ornaments. This activation, common to north-west Europe, occurred because the middle classes, broadly defined, were growing in numbers and prosperity, and so were able to afford not just necessities but 'decencies' and 'luxuries' too. It was also facilitated by more efficient economic infrastructures: better roads, canals and haulage services; a growing number of retail outlets, especially customer-conscious shops, newly light and airy with an eye to display; and improved advertising and publicity. Not least, taste and fashion played a major role. In a society increasingly concerned with appearances and possibly more socially mobile, emulation attained heightened importance, and successful social climbing depended on the acquisition of the right novelties and possessions. Manufacturers certainly grew adroit at cashing in on emulation and at angling for wider markets. The metal-master Matthew Boulton believed it critical to win the aristocratic market first, because 'the lower ranks will imitate them as soon as they have discovered the innovation'.

See also COMMERCIAL SOCIETY.

Neil McKendrick, John Brewer and J. H. Plumb, *The Birth of a Consumer Society: The Commercialization of Eighteenth-Century England* (London: Europa, 1982).

Carole Shammas, *The Pre-industrial Consumer in England and America* (Oxford: Clarendon, 1990).

ROY PORTER

contraception   According to demographic data, contraception, or the employment of natural or artificial means to prevent conception, began to be practised on an unprecedented scale in the eighteenth century, by the notables of France and to a lesser extent elsewhere in western Europe. Late marriage, periodic continence and the spacing of births by extended nursing had, of course, always been available as tactics to which Europeans could turn to avoid over-large families. Recourse to herbal potions, which from ancient times had been consumed with the intention of repressing lust, preventing conception and inducing miscarriage, had declined by the beginning of the century. Coitus interruptus was increasingly practised, if the rising chorus of disapproval expressed by such writers as S. A. A. D. Tissot (1728–97) and the author of *Onania* (1723) is anything to go by. Withdrawal would remain the most important method of fertility control up to the twentieth century. The sponge, mentioned by Bentham, does not appear to have been widely employed, while the expense and unreliability of the condom restricted its use to the patrons of prostitutes like Boswell and Casanova.

Angus McLaren, *Reproductive Rituals: The Perception of Fertility in England from the Sixteenth Century to the Nineteenth Century* (London: Methuen, 1984).

ANGUS MCLAREN

Cook, James (1728–1779)   English explorer. He volunteered into the navy as an able seaman in 1746 after a period in the North Sea coal trade. He served in America during the Seven Years War and in 1763 was appointed surveyor of Newfoundland. His success on this service led to his promotion to first lieutenant and in August 1768 he left Plymouth in command of the *Endeavour* for an expedition to the Pacific. This was to be the first of three voyages which became epics of European exploration. On the first Cook observed the transit of Venus at Tahiti and then circumnavigated and charted New Zealand before discovering the eastern coast of Australia. The second voyage, from 1772 to 1775, finally laid to rest the myth of the SOUTHERN CONTINENT and opened up vast areas of the PACIFIC. The final voyage, from 1776 to 1780, in search of a NORTH-WEST PASSAGE to the Pacific, charted the Canadian Pacific coast and discovered the Hawaiian Islands. There, in one of the great moments of European tragedy, Cook met his death at the hands of the islanders.

J. C. Beaglehole (ed.), *The Life of Captain James Cook* (London: Hakluyt Society, 1974).

DAVID MACKAY

Corelli, Arcangelo (1653–1713)   Italian composer, violinist and conductor. Little is known about his early years. In 1670 he became a member of the Accademia Filarmonica in Bologna, and in 1675 he appeared in Rome, at the start of a brilliant career. He became director of music to Cardinal Benedetto Pamphili and in 1690 also to Cardinal Pietro Ottoboni. In 1706 he was admitted to the Accademia Arcadi, an exclusive circle of scientists, philosophers and artists still in existence today.

Corelli's musical *œuvre* comprises chamber and church sonatas and twelve *concerti grossi* (op. 6), one of which, the famous 'Christmas' Concerto, remains popular even today. More than a hundred pieces have been ascribed to him, but their origins are uncertain. His well-balanced, symmetrical works show an extreme economy of means, and represent the opposite of baroque opulence. Some scholars see him as the inventor of the *concerto grosso* form. His style influenced composers like Telemann, Handel and Johann Sebastian Bach.

M. Pincherle, *Corelli et son temps* (Paris, 1954); trans. as *Corelli: his life, his work* (New York: Da Capo, 1979).

FRITZ WEBER

Corsica An outpost of the Genoan Republic from the fourteenth century, Corsica fought against Genoan hegemony in the so-called 'Forty Years War' (1729–69). Under Pasquale de Paoli (1725–1807) autonomy was virtually achieved. However, in 1768 Genoa made the island over to France in return for an annual subsidy of 200,000 livres over ten years. Louis XV decreed the union of the island with France, and French troops occupied it, defeating Corsican resistance at Pontecorvo and forcing Paoli to flee. The French effected a typical Bourbon compromise between centralization (introduction of an intendant, a military governor, royal presidial courts and so on) and maintenance of local liberties in justice and finance. The Corsican nobility received recognition: the lawyer Carlo Buonaparte (1746–85) was thus able to send his son Napoleon BONAPARTE to the military college at Brienne in 1779 which catered for the French nobility. In 1789 the Constituent Assembly invited Paoli to return to Corsica, but in 1793 he declared the island's independence, securing British protection, and in 1795 he turned it over to a British viceroy. The British evacuated the island in 1796, and under the Directory and Consulate the island was brought back under French control.

COLIN JONES

corvée The *corvée* was a form of forced labour service. Seigneurial forms of it – rarely amounting to more than four days' unpaid labour or cartage per year – were most widespread in France prior to 1789 in areas like Franche-Comté where feudal servitude still existed, and these were destroyed through the abolition of feudalism in August 1789. A royal *corvée* was established progressively throughout France from about 1730. It normally took the form of work to build or maintain roads. Nobles, clerics and other privileged groups were exempt from it. Although there was a royal regulation on the matter in 1737, there was no uniformity in its application. In many areas, especially from the 1760s, royal intendants progressively commuted it into cash payment to the royal treasury, and its commutation on a national scale was envisaged in 1787. Although even in the nineteenth century, apologists for a system of *corvées* maintained that the service provided the only means of maintaining local roads, in fact France's best roads

– as in Languedoc – were often built and maintained without recourse to this system.

See also SEIGNEURIALISM.

COLIN JONES

Cosimo III *see* MEDICI, COSIMO III.

cosmetics Mammals groom continuously, but human groups also decorate the body through artifice. The ancient urban civilizations of Asia, Africa, the Middle East and southern Europe employed sophisticated cosmetic arts for the purposes of beautifying and preserving the body, and enhancing the elaborate ritual surrounding all ceremonial occasions. Many of these archaic techniques and natural products have remained unchanged world-wide and were merely modified in Europe. The traditional medieval cosmetic art scoured and anointed the externals – 'dry-cleaning' the extremities (teeth, hair, face, hands and feet) using the ancient pharmacopoeia of humoral medicine purveyed by barber-surgeons, of paints, powders, pomades, perfumes and vegetable and mineral pastes. Hot-tubs or 'stews' in Europe were more for pleasure than cleanliness, but not so the increasing use of linen underwear to dry and dispose of the body's unclean humours, or perspiration. But by the eighteenth century older practices were slowly being overlaid by the 'hygienic' methods of the self-styled moderns. In post-revolutionary Europe the *ancien régime* of 'high' cosmetic care so beloved of the nobility had become outmoded. Health-conscious bourgeois elites at the end of the century (both men and women) shed their powders and corsets, wore lighter clothes and perfumes, used their new bathrooms frequently, ate less and exercised more and (in Britain especially) were probably devotees of the cold-spa craze.

Georges Vigarello, *Concepts of Cleanliness: Changing Attitudes in France since the Middle Ages*, trans. Jean Birrell, *Le propre et le sale* (Paris: Maison des Sciences de l'Homme; Cambridge: Cambridge University Press, 1988).

VIRGINIA SMITH

cosmology Cosmological speculation in the eighteenth century revolved around a few perennial questions, such as the nature of the Milky Way, the universality of gravitation (particularly in relation to the fixed stars), the evolution of the solar system, and the nature of the milky patches in the sky known as nebulae and their relation to systems – solar or interstellar – closer to earth. There was little evidence to constrain this speculation: contemporary astronomy was not designed to provide data of particular relevance to cosmology, and theoreticians were by no means confined to the ranks of astronomers.

Some who have attracted historical interest are relatively obscure, such as Johann Heinrich Lambert (1728–77) from Alsace and the Englishman Thomas Wright (1711–86); best known is Immanuel Kant, who proposed an account of the formation of the solar, and similar, systems, through an evolutionary process involving both attractive gravitational and repulsive forces.

One astronomer who did venture into the field was Pierre Simon de LAPLACE, who towards the end of the century envisaged the solar system condensing from a rotating, incandescent nebula, which as it cooled and contracted threw off rings of matter, which in turn condensed into planets, themselves leaving rings to form satellites or to remain as rings around Saturn. Also late in the century more directed empirical input came from William HERSCHEL, who pursued an extensive observational programme aimed specifically at such cosmological subjects as the distribution of stars in space and the nature of nebulae. Even though his theoretical accounts were shaped by the observations he made with his extraordinary telescopes, his writings retained a good measure of the creative speculation that had characterized cosmology and distinguished it from ASTRONOMY.

M. A. Hoskin, *Stellar Astronomy: Historical Studies* (Chalfont St Giles: Science History Publications, 1982).

J. A. BENNETT

cosmopolitanism 'It is the duty', wrote Edward Gibbon of the individual in *The Decline and Fall of the Roman Empire*, 'to prefer and promote the exclusive interest and glory of his native country: but a philosopher may be permitted to enlarge his views, and to consider Europe as one great republic, whose various inhabitants have attained almost the same level of politeness and cultivation.' Such sentiments were typical of the *philosophes*. Eighteenth-century intellectuals saw themselves as members of a republic of letters, a perception that was reinforced by their Grand Tours of Europe and their meeting of kindred spirits in every country.

Cosmopolitanism thus went hand in hand with enlightenment. The rule of reason admitted neither parochialism nor particularism of any kind, and the *philosophes* wrote as if the whole of mankind were their concern. 'Only the true cosmopolitan can be a good citizen', argued Christoph Wieland, for only he 'could do the great work to which we have been called: to cultivate, enlighten and ennoble the human race'. For Kant the cosmopolitan ideal was part of a sustained vision of the history of mankind; indeed, it was its culmination, and though it was still far off, he thought that 'it nonetheless seems as if a feeling is beginning to stir in all its members, each of which has an interest in maintaining the whole. And this encourages the hope that, after many revolutions, with all their transforming effects, the highest human purpose of nature, a universal *cosmopolitan existence*, will at last be realised as the matrix within which all the original capacities of the human race may develop.'

See also CIVIL SOCIETY, POLITENESS.

Immanuel Kant, 'Idea for a Universal History with a Cosmopolitan Purpose', in *Kant's Political Writings*, ed. H. Reiss (Cambridge: Cambridge University Press, 1971).
Thomas Schlereth, *The Cosmopolitan Ideal in Enlightenment Thought* (Notre Dame, Ind.: University of Notre Dame Press, 1977).

SYLVANA TOMASELLI

Coulomb, Charles Augustin de (1736–1806) French engineer. He influenced the move towards combining mathematical and experimental techniques as the new scientific discipline of physics emerged, and is famous today for his work in electricity, magnetism and applied mechanics, particularly friction and torsion. Until 1781 Coulomb served as a trained military engineer, supervising various construction projects in France and in Martinique, where he spent eight years. But after winning a prize competition for measuring magnetism, he moved to Paris, where he concentrated on a scientific career at the Académie des Sciences and the post-revolutionary French Institute, of which he became president. He still acted as a consultant engineer and contributed to hundreds of committee reports on a variety of topics including machines, instruments, canal improvements and educational reform. A skilled and precise experimenter who established the value of a mathematical approach to quantitative empirical research, he developed delicate instruments, most importantly those utilizing the torsion of a twisted thread, to demonstrate that the Newtonian gravitational inverse-square law could be extended into electricity and magnetism.

Charles Gillmor, *Coulomb and the Evolution of Physics and Engineering in Eighteenth-Century France* (Princeton, NJ: Princeton University Press, 1971).

PATRICIA FARA

Couperin, François (1668–1733) French composer. Known as 'Couperin le grand', he was a member of a family of musicians. His uncle Louis Couperin (1626–61) was a composer, violinist and keyboard player who wrote seventy pieces for organ and 130 for harpsichord. From him Francois's father, Charles Couperin (1638–79), inherited the post of organist at the Church of St Gervais in Paris. François entered the same position in 1685 and was appointed court organist in 1693. Ennobled in 1696, he was appointed Chevalier de l'Ordre de Latran in 1702. In his later years he suffered from illness and retired from musical life. One of his daughters, Marguerite-Antoinette (1705–c.78) became the first female *ordinaire de la chambre pour le clavecin*, a post she inherited from her father.

Couperin, who also composed church music of an intimate character, is most famous for his harpsichord suites. He wrote 240 pieces, collected in four books (*Pieces de clavecin*), and a manual, *L'Art de toucher le clavecin*. The pieces are of very lively character, with marked rhythms borrowed from dance music, but show surprising harmonic changes, complex accompaniment and rich ornamentation. They usually bear programmatic or picturesque titles.

W. Mellers, *François Couperin and the French Classical Tradition* (2nd ed.) (London: Faber, 1987).
D. Tunley, *Couperin* (London: BBC, 1982).

FRITZ WEBER

crime   With the expansion of CAPITALISM in Europe, crime in the modern Western sense of the term became an increasingly familiar (and increasingly debated) social problem. Over much of the world, however, both definitions of crime and methods of dealing with it were very different from those obtaining in the more economically advanced parts of Europe. Even there, law codes demonstrated a much less clear-cut distinction between criminal and civil law than that obtaining in modern legal theory. Moreover, the Christian culture of Europe made distinction between sin and crime difficult. This distinction was even more difficult to sustain in some other areas (notably the Islamic world), while everywhere, then as now, 'crime' was an umbrella term, covering acts as disparate as murder and cheating in the local market.

Many areas suffered from that characteristic form of pre-industrial criminality, banditry (or its maritime equivalent, piracy). Extensive territories experienced endemic banditry: the imperial Chinese law, for example, recognized 'brigand areas' such as the provinces of Szechwan, Honan, Anhwei, Hupeh, Shansi and parts of Kiangsu and Shantung, while in Europe bandits flourished in a number of rural areas, notably Calabria, Apulia, Sicily and Jülich. Frontier zones, such as the area where the borders of the Dutch Republic, the Austrian Netherlands and the adjacent German states met, or the Christian–Ottoman borderlands in south-eastern Europe, were especially prone to banditry, and the related problem of smuggling.

Although banditry was to remain endemic in the Middle East and Asia well into the next century, in Europe the gradual firming-up of state systems made it less of a problem as the eighteenth century progressed. Conversely, Europe moved towards a more 'modernized' form of criminality, arguably paralleling the shift towards a more capitalist and more class-based society. This development should not be over-simplified: few historians would now accept the model which portrays a simple transition in Europe from a 'feudal' criminality based on violence to a 'capitalist' one based on crimes against property. Even so, two broad developments can be traced. The first was the general identification of criminality with the poor (*see* POVERTY AND POOR RELIEF). The second was the development of organized crime: it is no accident that Europe's first criminal entrepreneur, Jonathan Wild (1683–1725), should flourish in its largest city, London. A further development which demonstrated how crime was being redefined to keep step with commercial advance was the emergence of concepts equivalent to what the twentieth century would describe as 'white collar' crimes, notably fraud.

The existence of 'modern' forms of criminality in some parts of Europe by 1800 should not obscure the point that, taken on a world basis, crime was a very complex phenomenon which presents the historian with considerable problems of definition and interpretation.

See also ADMINISTRATION OF JUSTICE, PUNISHMENT.

Eric Hobsbawm, *Bandits* (London: Allen Lane, 1972).
Olwen Hufton, 'Crime in Pre-industrial Europe', *International Association for the History of Crime and Criminal Justice Newsletter*, 4 (July 1981), 8–35.

J. A. SHARPE

Crompton, Samuel (1753–1827)   English inventor of the 'mule', the spinning-machine favoured by the British cotton industry for two centuries. Born near Bolton (Lancashire) to a farming family, he attended a local school, excelled in mathematics and was an accomplished violinist; in adolescence he became a handloom weaver and jenny spinner. His invention, completed in 1779, was designed both to speed up yarn production and to improve its quality. The mule combined the roller-drawing principle of ARKWRIGHT'S water frame with the twisting and winding-on motions of Hargreaves's spinning-jenny; it proved to be versatile and invaluable for fine spinning.

Crompton's inventiveness was not matched by business acumen. Handicapped by shyness and naivety, he obtained no patent, exhibited the mule to leading manufacturers for a derisory sum, and rejected Sir Robert Peel's (1750–1830) offer of a partnership in favour of his own cottage-based business. A relatively small parliamentary grant of £5,000 in 1812 was invested in an unsuccessful bleaching concern; a second appeal to parliament in 1826 failed. Crompton joined the Swedenborgian Church in the 1790s, and acted as organist and choirmaster in Bolton.

Gilbert J. French, *Life and Times of Samuel Crompton*, ed. S. D. Chapman (Bath: Adams & Dart, 1970).

CHRISTINE MACLEOD

Cuba   A Spanish colony since 1511, Cuba became Spain's strategic shipping centre in the CARIBBEAN. At first a relatively poor land of small-scale livestock and tobacco farmers, the Cuban economy and society were transformed from the mid eighteenth century by its sugar revolution. Encouraged by reformed Spanish trading regulations, the collapse of sugar production in French Saint Domingue after 1791 and the greater availability of slaves, planters and merchants built an innovative, highly capitalized agro-industry, enriching themselves and Cuba. The capital, Havana, (population 96,000 by 1810) flourished, particularly following capture and occupation by British troops and merchants during the Seven Years War. The latter event encouraged Madrid to impose military, administrative and fiscal reforms, some of which became models for other Spanish colonies. The planter-merchant elite led by intellectuals and economic reformers established new or revitalized old institutions including the famous Economic Society (1792), encouraging a lively culture and promoting the slave-owners' economic and political interests. Continuing prosperity and fear of revolt by their brutally treated slaves helped keep the Cuban elite loyal to Madrid when other Spanish colonies seized their independence (1810–26).

See also SPANISH AMERICA.

J. Suchlicki, *Cuba: From Columbus to Castro* (Washington, DC: Pergamon, 1986).

CHARLES C. NOEL

Culloden, Battle of (16 April 1746)   Fought on Drummossie Moor, south of Culloden House, the Battle of Culloden marked the decisive defeat of Prince Charles Edward STUART, with 5,000 men, by the duke of Cumberland (1721–65), with 9,000. The unsuitable site was chosen by Charles Edward: flat and partly waterlogged, the terrain gave no help to the fearsome 'Highland charge'. The Jacobite right wing was partly obstructed by park walls, and the rebel line was angled, the left having furthest to advance through withering fire. The battle began with a short cannonade, in which Cumberland's artillery were much more effective. Within minutes the rebel forces charged, to escape the grape-shot, and faced a hail of disciplined musket fire. The Jacobite right wing engaged the Hanoverian left, but was repulsed with bayonets, and cut off in retreat by mounted dragoons. Its centre and left failed even to break the firing rhythm of the massed infantry, and retreated with heavy losses, not having come closer than a hundred yards. In little more than thirty minutes the JACOBITES lost some 1,500–2,000 dead, against around 300 for Cumberland. No Highland army took the field again, and for the next three months Cumberland destroyed and terrorized the region.

J. M. Black, *Culloden and the '45* (Gloucester: Alan Sutton, 1990).

PHILIP WOODFINE

customs and tariffs Taxes levied on trade – on goods imported and, less often, exported across international or internal borders – are known as tariffs. The relative ease of collection made them an important source of 'customary' government revenue from the earliest times. In the eighteenth century costly wars and the expansion of international trade provided both the need and the opportunity to increase European tariff revenues. In Britain annual tax revenue increased almost eightfold and about a quarter was provided by customs. However, increased import substitution and smuggling meant revenue rose less fast than tariff levels and provoked some of the earliest explicit discussion of the effects of elasticity of demand. Moreover, lobbying for special treatment resulted in numerous modifications and increasing complexity. Restraints on the free flow of trade stimulated the rise of the doctrine of LAISSEZ-FAIRE and FREE TRADE, although the fiscal needs of government delayed reform until the nineteenth century.

In Europe economic liberalism found expression in a drive to eliminate internal tariff barriers, but although tariffs were primarily fiscal in intent they did have a second role of providing protection, notably for infant industries. This ensured their retention and found systematic expression in Napoleon's Continental system and in Alexander Hamilton's celebrated 'Report on Manufacturers' for the US Congress in 1791.

See also TAXATION.

NUALA ZAHEDIEH

D

d'Alembert, Jean Le Rond *see* ALEMBERT, JEAN LE ROND D'.

Danton, Georges Jacques (1759–1794)   One of the most rumbustious radical politicians of the French Revolution. A lawyer before 1789, he achieved notoriety in the radical Cordeliers Club, then the Paris Commune. Appointed justice minister in the provisional executive council set up on the overthrow of Louis XVI in August 1792, he famously rallied the capital for the war effort, but was also implicated in instigating the SEPTEMBER MASSACRES aimed at clerical and aristocratic prisoners. He was elected to the Convention, but his violent background and his known penchant for venality and the good life made him the target for right-wing attacks. He was instrumental in establishing the framework of the TERROR (including the Revolutionary Tribunal and the peoples' armies), and he served on the Committee of Public Safety from April to July 1793. After a spell of ill health in autumn 1793, he became increasingly disenchanted with the Terror which he had helped to establish and became associated with proposals to move from terror to clemency. This won him the enmity of Robespierre and left-wing radicals, and he was arrested and executed for excessive moderation.

Norman Hampson, *Danton* (London: Duckworth, 1978).

COLIN JONES

Danzig [Gdańsk]   The principal port of the Polish-Lithuanian Commonwealth, Danzig commanded access to the Baltic from the Vistula. The great bulk of the state's exports (mainly primary commodities, particularly grain and timber) and imports (finished, luxury and colonial goods) passed through it. Although by the eighteenth century it had (along with the volume of Polish trade) declined from the peak of its early-seventeenth-century prosperity, it remained the most populous city (c.46,000 inhabitants in 1750) in the Commonwealth until the expansion of Warsaw after 1760. About half of the population and the ruling classes were Lutheran and German-speaking. Danzig's determination to preserve its old staple privileges made it particularly closely involved in Polish politics. The best-defended city in Poland, it held out against a Russian siege for four months in 1734 in support of Stanislas LESZCZYŃSKI's claim to the Polish throne. Its acquisition was a long-standing objective of the kings of Prussia. The first partition cut it off territorially from Poland and its trade suffered badly as a result of Prussian tariff policies. Prussia finally annexed the city in 1793.

See also POLAND.

J. T. Lukowski, *Liberty's Folly: The Polish-Lithuanian Commonwealth in the Eighteenth Century* (London: Routledge, 1991).

J. T. LUKOWSKI

Darwin, Erasmus (1731–1802)   English physician, scientist and poet. Educated at Cambridge and Edinburgh, Darwin practised all his life as a physician in the West Midlands. A conviction that disease could be classified in terms of its precipitating physiological function (sensation, volition and so forth) informed his major medical work, the *Zoonomia* (1794–6). A lively polymath, Darwin became a scientist of some eminence (Fellow of the Royal Society 1761) and was celebrated as an ardent inventor of ingenious machines, including a mechanical voicebox. He popularized the Linnaean System in botany, and set forth in verse in his *Temple of Nature* (1803) an early theory of organic evolution (embracing the evolution of man and society), which depended on the hypothesis of the inheritance of acquired characteristics later rejected by his grandson Charles Darwin (1809–82) (*see* EVOLUTIONISM). A close friend of Matthew Boulton, Josiah Wedgwood, James Watt and Joseph Priestley, he was one of the founders of the Lunar Society in Birmingham and later of the Derby Philosophical Society (1783). A deist in religion and a liberal in politics, he delighted in the outbreak of the French Revolution; Darwin's reputation plummeted in the reactionary atmosphere after his death.

M. McNeil, *Under the Banner of Science: Erasmus Darwin and his Age* (Manchester: Manchester University Press, 1987).

ROY PORTER

David, Jacques Louis (1748–1825)   French painter. He achieved an illustrious reputation with his *Oath of the Horatii* (1785), which contributed to the triumph of NEOCLASSICISM over rococo styles. In 1789 he threw himself into the Revolution with gusto, joining the Paris Jacobin Club, painting the Tennis Court Oath and, from 1791, acting as director and pageant-master for the great revolutionary festivals held in Paris. Elected to the Convention by Paris, he sat as one of the Montagnards, with whom he voted for the king's death; played an important part in the liquidation of the artistic and academic establishment of the *ancien régime* (universities, colleges, academies and so on); and was a keen artistic propagandist for the patriotic cause. From September 1793 he served on the Committee of General Security and, a Robespierrist, narrowly escaped death at Thermidor (though he endured spells of imprisonment). From 1797 he became increasingly linked with Bonaparte, for whom he painted some of his finest works (such as *Napoleon's Coronation*). He tried to rally to the Bourbons in 1815, but was exiled as a regicide and died in Brussels.

See also HISTORY PAINTING.

Anita Brookner, *Jacques-Louis David* (London: Chatto & Windus, 1980).

COLIN JONES

death   At the opening of the eighteenth century, European urban burial grounds were over-full. Imagery on street literature, funerary ephemera and tombs harked back to the *memento mori* tradition of skulls, crossbones and grisly depictions of the figure of Death with arrow raised. Traditional cultures of death are very resilient and slow to change. In many places people followed what had been considered decent by their forebears. In Roman Catholic areas purgatory continued to exercise its comforting but costly sway over the afterlife, while in the more austere religious atmosphere of parts of northern Europe, great stress was placed on the good death, hell-fire and personal redemption during life. Among the intelligentsia, however, a growing rationalism and interest in the customs of other nations and times led to a recognition that obsequies are culturally variable, and hence, capable of change.

The heraldic funeral collapsed under commercial pressure from the developing profession of undertaking, and superstitions concerning the inviolability of the grave and of the body were challenged by anatomists, who explored the bodies of the unearthed dead with increasing zeal, and established commercial schools and great anatomical collections during this period (*see* ANATOMY). But although rationalism banished mental images of death and physical decay, from the 1760s these found a new lease of life in the GOTHIC NOVEL. Then, as now, nostalgia and humour played important roles in questioning human vanity and rendering bearable the contemplation of mortality.

In France the closure of old graveyards led to a process of clearance, starting with the burial ground of Les Innocents in central Paris. Old quarry workings which honeycomb the stone strata on which Paris was built were put to use, and thus an Enlightenment version of the medieval ossuary was created under Paris (from 1785). These catacombs rapidly became a tourist attraction. They did not, however, set a trend as did the new cemetery of Pere-La-Chaise (planned 1790s, opened 1804), heavily influenced by the early-eighteenth-century *jardin anglais*, whose romantic landscapes and irregular plantings were punctuated with monuments to the dead.

By 1800 the skeletal figure of Death had become attenuated into the benign figure of Old Father Time, while charnel-house imagery had been largely displaced by flowers, cherubs, willows and draped urns. Most European and many colonial cities had established suburban cemeteries. Designed for the financially fortunate, they offered fashionable and hygienic repose, with the clean lines of architectural styles revived from the past.

In Britain changes in death imagery followed a similar pattern, but partly due to reaction to the French Revolution, and then to isolation during the Napoleonic wars, the British were slow to adopt burial reform. The idea of the suburban cemetery modelled on Pere-La-Chaise did not really take off there until the third decade of the nineteenth century.

Richard Etlin, *The Architecture of Death* (Cambridge, Mass.: MIT, 1984).
Ruth Richardson, *Death, Dissection and the Destitute* (London: Penguin, 1989).

RUTH RICHARDSON

dechristianization   Both a contentious term for the alleged decline of religious belief and practice during the eighteenth century and a more particular name given to the vigorous attempt to replace Roman Catholicism with new forms of civic religion during the most radical phase of the French Revolution, dechristianization was promoted by representatives of the Committee of Public Safety on mission duty, beginning in the Nièvre in September 1793. It was then imported into Paris and given a degree of legitimacy by the Convention. Its roots lay in the difficulties experienced by the French Catholic Church before 1789 which were then exacerbated by tensions between church and state in the first year of the Revolution.

Among the most noteworthy features of dechristianization was the implementation of a new republican calendar with twelve thirty-day months and three ten-day weeks (*décades*) ending with a rest day (*décadi*). Supporters of the process of dechristianization included the genuinely idealistic and the religiously disaffected out to settle old scores against the Catholic clergy and their churches. It is generally agreed that the whole process was more successful in damaging the old religion than in establishing the new cults (*see*, for example, CULT OF THE SUPREME BEING). Despite the theatrical choreography surrounding the new ceremonies and liturgies, they failed to have the emotional resonance required for mass appeal. Although forced dechristianization failed to achieve its objectives, it bequeathed a powerful legacy in the shape of unremitting conflict between CATHOLICISM and ANTICLERICALISM in nineteenth-century France.

J. McManners, *The French Revolution and the Church* (London: SPCK, 1969).

DAVID HEMPTON

Declaration of the Rights of Man and the Citizen (1789)   Passed by the CONSTITUENT ASSEMBLY on 26 August 1789, the declaration set the blueprint for constitutional debate in the French Revolution. A composite document which reflected the varying influences of the American revolutionaries, the *philosophes*, natural law theory and even *ancien régime* constitutionalism, the declaration has had a powerful impact on world history, strongly influencing the United Nations' Universal Declaration of Human Rights (1948). A liberal, if hardly democratic document, it itemized as man's natural and imprescriptible rights liberty, property, security and freedom from oppression – not equality, though it was stated that 'men are born free and remain free and equal in rights'. Rights of the individual included equality before the law, religious toleration, freedom of expression and of the press, freedom from arbitrary arrest, equal opportunity and fiscal equality. Sovereignty was said to reside in the nation, which expressed its wishes through elected assemblies, and had power to tax. The monarch was to be subordinate to the law and to observe a strict separation of the judicial, executive and legislative powers. The declaration was placed as a preamble to the CONSTITUTION OF 1791 and, appropriately modified, added to other constitutions of the revolutionary era.

COLIN JONES

Defoe, Daniel (1661–1731)   English writer. He is now best known as a novelist, the author of *Robinson Crusoe* (1719, with sequels in 1720 and 1721), *A Journal of the Plague Year* (1721), *Moll Flanders* (1722) and several other fictional autobiographies. Usually these are the penitent memoirs of sinners or miscreants. Defoe's contemporaries, however, did not know him as a novelist. (Indeed, all these texts were anonymous, and most were not attributed to him until several decades after his death.) His career is notable for the sheer variety of genres in which he worked: political polemic, travel, satirical poetry, journalism and religious instruction being the most prominent. Like his parents, he was a Protestant Dissenter, and he first became widely known as a writer for his *Shortest Way with Dissenters* (1703), a satirical defence of his co-religionists. Before this publication, he had failed in a variety of business ventures; after it, he became a full-time writer, in the pay of succeeding ministries. Only late in his career did he turn to 'novels'. Once treated as primitive by literary historians, these texts have recently enjoyed a greatly enhanced reputation.

Laura Ann Curtis, *The Versatile Defoe* (London: George Prior, 1979).

JOHN MULLAN

deism A notoriously eclectic term, 'deism' generally embraces belief in one supreme being, a reliance on reason and NATURAL RELIGION, a distrust of revelation, a commitment to moral virtue and a repudiation of religious intolerance, dogma and superstition. Although it was never a coherent intellectual movement, it reached the peak of its influence in late-seventeenth- and early-eighteenth-century England in the writings of John Toland and Matthew Tindall (1655–1733) and in eighteenth-century France in the writings of Rousseau and Voltaire. French deists (or theists as Voltaire insisted on calling himself) were particularly severe on the corruptions of the church and the evils of priestcraft. Deism also attracted vibrant intellectual minorities in Germany and the American colonies. For men like Benjamin Franklin and Thomas Jefferson, religion was essentially a utilitarian moral code with the supernatural and coercive elements left out.

Deism was one of the most powerful intellectual solvents of the eighteenth century, for it undermined both clerical authority and the state's right to prescribe and enforce religious orthodoxy. Tom Paine's *Rights of Man* and *Age of Reason* were appropriate *fin de siècle* demolitions of the old order. Although deism as a distinctive intellectual creed is largely confined to the eighteenth century, its legacy, especially in the growth of a spirit of TOLERATION, has been much more extensive.

J. C. D. Clark, *English Society 1688–1832* (Cambridge: Cambridge University Press, 1985).

DAVID HEMPTON

democracy In Enlightenment political thought, democracy was considered one of the two forms which republican government could assume, the other being aristocracy. In a democracy, Montesquieu explained, sovereignty was vested in the whole of the people; under an aristocratic regime, it was vested in only a part of the people. His *L'Esprit des lois* showed how VIRTUE is the spirit peculiar to democracies and how important true equality and education were to them; for democracies required of their citizens a continual preference for the common interest. Frugality and strict laws governing mores were also vital. Democracy was not, therefore, a form of government suitable to large modern states characterized by a system of luxury, and in which individuals were ruled by their self-interest or sense of honour.

This opinion was shared by David Hume. Far from idealizing ancient democracies, however, Hume wrote in 'Of Some Remarkable Customs' (1754): 'The Athenian Democracy was such a tumultuous government as we can scarcely form a notion of in the present age of the world. The whole collective body of the people voted every law, without any limitation of property, without any distinction of rank, without controul from any magistracy or senate; and consequently without regard to order, justice, or prudence.'

For all that was said about their impracticability in the modern world, the democracies of the ancient world were to prove inspirational during the French Revolution. So, too, were the ideals embodied in the American Revolution. The proclamation of the principle of popular sovereignty in 1789 was the first step towards a reconsideration of the question of political representation. Given the demographic and economic reality of France, direct or participatory democracy was ruled out, leaving a system of elected representation as the only viable alternative. In the absence of a clear division of power and of a tradition of popular election, the implementation of the democratic ideals of the Revolution was at best chaotic and was to culminate in the Terror.

Biancamaria Fontana, 'Democracy and the French Revolution', *Democracy after 2500 years* (Oxford: Oxford University Press, 1992).

Robert R. Palmer, *The Age of Democratic Revolution: A Political History of Europe and America, 1760–1800*, 2 vols (Princeton, NJ: Princeton University Press, 1959–64).

SYLVANA TOMASELLI

demography   There were few subjects in the seventeenth and eighteenth centuries on which there was so high a degree of agreement as the topic of population. The cameralists, the mercantilists, the physiocrats and the political economists were all agreed that the size of a nation's population was a clear index of its well-being. Whether from considerations of the defence of their countries, out of fear of shortages of manpower or simply because it was deemed the tell-tale sign of domestic felicity, eighteenth-century political theorists, rulers and civil servants alike thought that increasing the size of a nation's population ought to be a prime consideration of governments. Even Jean-Jacques Rousseau, who had no wish to see economic expansion and for whom the military preoccupations of large European states were of no concern, was of the opinion that population increase was the most certain yardstick of the happiness of a people.

Such views help account for the very great interest in the eighteenth century in the question of whether the ancient world was more populated than that of the moderns. Thus Montesquieu had one of the characters of his *Lettres persanes* claim that the present population of the earth was one-tenth what it had been in ancient times, and that given the present rate of decline the globe would be entirely deserted within the next thousand years. However, in his famous essay 'Of the Populousness of Ancient Nations' (1754) Hume argued that 'it seems impossible to assign any just reason, why the world should have been more populous in ancient than in modern times'. In fact, on the basis of calculations he made from the figures given by various ancient authors, Hume thought the opposite more likely to be true.

However good they deemed population increase to be in and of itself, a number of thinkers, most notably Malthus, did argue that there were limits to population growth. Greatly influencing Malthus, Robert Wallace's (1697–1771) *Various Prospects of Mankind, Nature and Providence* (1761) contended that a utopian state would destroy itself, since under an ideal system of government there would be no check to population, and this could only lead to a population explosion. To this William Godwin ultimately answered that the nightmare which was being conjured by Wallace was too distant to be frightening. Condorcet, for his part, placed his trust in the practice of birth control to resolve the problem. From Malthus's point of view, the population problem was imminent and insurmountable.

See also POPULATION GROWTH.

Joseph J. Spengler, *French Predecessors of Malthus: A Study in Eighteenth-Century Wage and Population Theory* (Durham, NC: Duke University Press, 1942).
Sylvana Tomaselli, 'Moral Philosophy and Population Questions in Eighteenth-Century Europe', in Michael S. Teitelbaum and Jay M. Winter (eds), *Population and Resources in Western Intellectual Traditions* (Cambridge: Cambridge University Press, 1989), pp. 7–29.
E. A. Wrigley, 'The Limits to Growth: Malthus and the Classical Economist', ibid., pp. 30–48.

SYLVANA TOMASELLI

demonology With the general decline in WITCH-HUNTING, it was inevitable that the academic study of witchcraft and demonism would gradually lose its appeal. Demonology had also been sustained by patterns of thought that were now in retreat – a natural philosophy that allowed demons to interfere in the natural world, theocratic notions of political and social order, expectations of the end of the world and, above all, a theology based on providential intervention in human affairs and a literal interpretation of the Bible. What had previously been attributed to devils and witches was now explained in terms of medical and psychological pathology, legal injustices and 'SUPERSTITION'.

The two authors who did most to challenge traditional beliefs in witchcraft were the Dutch pastor Balthasar Bekker (1634–98) and the German academic Christian Thomasius (1655–1728). Bekker's *De Betoverde Weereld* (The Enchanted World, 1691–3) was not original in its arguments but it effectively questioned the corporality of devils. In 1712 Thomasius wrote powerfully against inquisitorial methods, especially the use of torture, in witchcraft trials. Both authors provoked long and bitter controversies and Bekker was removed from office by the Dutch Reformed Church.

See also EVIL/THEODICY.

William Monter, *Ritual, Myth and Magic in Early Modern Europe* (Brighton: Harvester, 1983), ch. 7.

STUART CLARK

Denmark   In the eighteenth century Denmark was an important second-rank state which included Norway (until 1814), Ireland, Greenland, the Faeroe Islands and colonies in the West Indies and on the west African coast. Overshadowed by Sweden, which successfully invaded in 1700, it relied for its security for most of the eighteenth century on a Russian alliance and followed a policy of profitable neutrality in many of the conflicts, such as the Seven Years War. Danish attempts to restore the Union of Kalmar and have a Danish heir elected king of Sweden failed in 1743, and attempts to maintain a neutralist line during the Napoleonic period led to attacks on the Danish fleet by the British in 1801 and 1807. In the eighteenth century the country was ruled by Christian V (1670–99), Frederik IV (1699–1730), Christian VI (1730–46), Frederik V (1746–66) and Christian VII (1766–1808). Its population rose from 798,000 in 1769 to 929,000 in 1801.

The second half of the century saw reforms in a number of spheres. There was a move towards large-scale farming, while enclosure and agrarian reform brought about a general rise in the standard of living, including new and better housing. Serfdom for most Danish peasants was abolished in 1788. The first of the two major periods of reform, in 1770–2, was associated with STRUENSEE, which provoked a backlash. The other occurred after 1784 when Crown Prince Frederik (later Frederik VI) became regent for his schizophrenic father. Censorship was abolished in 1771. Protestant North German culture was very influential in the golden age of Danish painting (1770–1850), which saw the work of Nicola Abildgaard (1743–1809), Bertel Thorwaldsen

(1768–1844), Carl Gustaf Pilo (1711–93) and Jacob Carstens (1754–98). The rebuilding of Copenhagen after the English bombardment in 1807 provided opportunities for neoclassical architects.
See BALTIC.

J. Baack, *Agrarian Reform in Eighteenth-Century Denmark* (Lincoln, Nebr.: 1977).
T. Munck, 'The Danish Reformers', in H. M. Scott (ed.), *Enlightened Absolutism* (London: Macmillan Educational, 1990).
S. P. Oakley, *The Story of Denmark* (London: 1972).

JEREMY BLACK

Descartes, René (1596–1650)   French philosopher and man of science. Born at La Haye, Descartes went to school at the Jesuit college of La Flèche, showing great promise in mathematics, and quickly winning the friendship of the natural philosopher Marin Mersenne (1588–1648). After seeing military service and leading a wandering life in his twenties, he lived for a time in Paris but settled in the Netherlands in 1629, where he was befriended by Isaac Beeckman (1588–1637). Descartes made just three brief visits back to France thereafter. In 1649 he went to the court of Queen Christina in Stockholm, where he died the following year.

It was in his *Discours de la méthode* (Discourse on Method, 1637) that he announced his revolution in thinking, notably a commitment to clear and distinct reasoning derived from first principles: 'I think, therefore I am.' He contended that, though the senses were deceptive, logical and consistent ratiocination was able to generate basic truths about the physical world. Interested in medicine, Descartes was an early convert to the ideas of William Harvey (1578–1657). His *La Géometrie* (Geometry, 1637) made distinguished advances in coordinate geometry and algebra. In the 1630s Descartes increasingly dedicated himself to the study of physics and mathematics, producing *La Dioptrique* (Dioptrics, 1637), *Les Météores* (Meteors, 1637), *Les Principes de la philosophie* (Principles of Philosophy, 1644) and other writings in which he promoted a MECHANICAL PHILOSOPHY based on rigid mind–body dualism and on the notion of universal natural law with God as first cause. His mechanical thinking emphasized cause-and-effect contact action, and offered a vision of the solar system kept in motion through a swirl of vortices (*tourbillons*).

Descartes's rational philosophy (CARTESIANISM) achieved enormous popularity in late-seventeenth- and early-eighteenth-century France, partly because it could be squared with orthodox Christianity, before being swept away by Newtonianism.

J. Cottingham, *Descartes* (Oxford: Blackwell, 1986).

ROY PORTER

Desmoulins, Camille (1760–1794) Revolutionary journalist and agitator. He was a scholarship boy at the College Louis-le-Grand, where Robespierre became his friend. His pronounced stutter ruined his career prospects as a barrister, but the 1789 crisis allowed him to spring to notoriety as a radical street-figure: he harangued the crowd from the Palais Royal on 12 July, urging them to take up arms and storm the BASTILLE. His newspaper, *Les Révolutions de France et de Brabant* (The Revolutions of France and Brabant), also won him notoriety. He served as secretary to Danton, a fellow-member of the Cordelier Club and in the ministry of justice after the overthrow of Louis XVI, and was elected by Paris to the Convention. A Montagnard, he violently attacked the more moderate Girondin faction and voted for Louis XVI's death. By December 1793, however, he was having second thoughts about the Terror. In his new newspaper, *Le Vieux Cordelier* (The Old Cordelier), he moved from unstinting support of Terror to demands for its relaxation. Taxed with 'indulgence' along with DANTON, he was tried by the Revolutionary Tribunal and executed as a Dantonist.

Jean-Paul Bertaud, *Camille et Lucile Desmoulins* (Paris: Renaissance, 1986).

COLIN JONES

despotism *see* ABSOLUTISM.

determinism The view that every event is determined or necessitated by a prior cause, and that by another, has come to be known as determinism, or necessitarianism. Enlightenment philosophers were generally agreed that all physical events were necessitated by prior causes, but they were divided on the question as to whether human actions were so determined. Samuel Clarke (1675–1729) and other Newtonians held that human and divine actions were free, but they were opposed by thinkers such as Antony Collins and David Hume who argued that there was as much reason to attribute necessity to human actions as to physical events. According to Hume, our only evidence for ascribing necessity in either case was that the effect regularly followed the cause in time. He argued that there was indeed such a regularity to be found between human character and motives on the one hand and human behaviour on the other, and that if it were not possible to find such a basis for necessity in human behaviour there would be no reason to hold people responsible for their actions.

David Hume, *A Treatise of Human Nature*, ed. L. Selby-Bigge, rev. P. Nidditch (Oxford: Clarendon, 1978), pp. 399–412.

JOHN P. WRIGHT

dictionaries and encyclopaedias   Dictionaries, which were already very popular in the seventeenth century, were to continue to be considered as the most useful of books in the eighteenth century. The alphabetical arrangement of knowledge became ever more attractive, and dictionaries developed from simple compilations of words to encyclopaedias, which either were on specific subjects, such as Pierre Bulliard's *Dictionnaire élémentaire de botanique* (Elementary Dictionary of Botany, 1783), or, like the *Encyclopédie*, sought to encompass no less than the totality of human knowledge.

Among the important seventeenth-century examples of the genre were Louis Moreri's *Le Grand Dictionnaire historique* (The Great Historical Dictionary, 1674), which was greatly expanded over the years and reached its twentieth edition in 1759; *Dictionnaire de l'Académie française* (Dictionary of the French Academy, 1694), which saw four editions during the eighteenth century; and Pierre Bayle's *Dictionnaire historique et critique* (1697), which the *Encyclopédie* entry on Bayle described as the ancestor of Diderot's great monument to the Enlightenment.

The many significant dictionaries that were first published in the eighteenth century included the *Dictionnaire universel françois et latin* (French and Latin Universal Dictionary, 1704), also known as the *Dictionnaire de Trévoux*, and compiled by the Jesuits, who accused the *encyclopédistes* of plagiarism; Rousseau's *Dictionnaire de musique* (Dictionary of Music, 1768), containing his *Encyclopédie* articles on music and based on Sébastien de Brossard's *Dictionnaire* on the same subject, translated into English in 1740; Voltaire's *Dictionnaire philosophique portatif* (Portable Philosophical Dictionary, 1764), a collection of short articles on, for example, 'Amitié' (Friendship), 'Batême' (Baptism), 'Tout est bien' (All is well) , 'Job', 'Joseph', 'Vertue' (Virtue), which waged war against the church and dogmatism, was condemned to be burnt in Geneva, The Hague and Paris, and was proscribed by the Holy Office at Rome; and Panckoucke's *Encyclopédie méthodique* (Methodical Encyclopaedia, 1781–1832).

Of the influential English-language dictionaries and encyclopaedias, John Harris's *Lexicon Technicum, or An Universal English Dictionary of Arts and Sciences* (1704), Ephraim Chambers' *Cyclopedia, or An Universal Dictionary of Arts and Sciences* (1728) and William Smellie's *Encyclopaedia Britannica, or Dictionary of Arts and Sciences* (1768–71) were the greatest. It was the publication of Chambers' *Cyclopedia* that provided the impetus for the publication of a French equivalent, which became the ENCYCLOPÉDIE. In 1747 JOHNSON published the *Prospectus* for what remains one of the most liked works of the period, his *Dictionary of the English Language* (1755). Asked how he could hope to produce a dictionary in three years single-handedly when it had taken the forty members of the Académie Française forty years to produce theirs, he replied: 'Let me see; forty times forty is sixteen hundred. As three to sixteen hundred, so is the proportion of an Englishman to a Frenchman.' It was to prove a labour of eight years.

Leibniz drafted the outlines of both a dictionary of philosophy and a general encyclopaedia. His disciple Johann Georg Walch's *Philosophisches Lexikon* (Philosophical Lexicon, 1726) is considered to be the first dictionary of philosophy, properly speaking, in a modern language. The great Kantian critic Solomon Maimon was the author of another, *Philosophisches Wörterbuch* (Philosophical Dictionary, 1791). Many of the period's works included the word 'dictionary' or 'encyclopaedia' in their titles even when they were nothing of the kind, as their authors, for example Kant and Hegel, were in fact discussing philosophy or history as encyclopaedic disciplines.

William Gerber, 'Philosophical Dictionaries and Encyclopedias', in Paul Edwards (ed.), *The Encyclopedia of Philosophy*, 8 vols (London: Macmillan; New York: Free Press, 1967), vol. 6, pp. 170–99.

SYLVANA TOMASELLI

Diderot, Denis (1713–1784)   French man of letters. The son of a successful cutler of Langres, he was educated by the Jesuits and expected to enter the church, but after obtaining a Master of Arts from the University of Paris in 1732 he abandoned the idea of joining any of the established professions. Cut off by his family and having to live on his wits, he taught, translated and went on to edit, with Jean le Rond d'Alembert, the work he is best known for, the *Encyclopédie*. Besides numerous entries for the latter, he wrote extensively on a wide variety of subjects. Several months of imprisonment in Vincennes after his *Lettre sur les aveugles* (An Essay on Blindness, 1749), in which he questioned the argument from design, together with the difficulties the *Encyclopédie* encountered with censorship, taught him prudence; he withheld from publication his increasingly bolder philosophical speculations.

His literary works include *Les Bijoux indiscrets* (1748), a highly successful licentious tale; a number of plays exploring ethical issues within the context of bourgeois life, such as *Le Fils naturel* (1757); his masterpiece, *Le Neveu de Rameau* (The Nephew of Rameau, 1891), a disturbing dialogue whose translation into German (1823) by Goethe attracted the attention of Hegel and which, along with *La Religieuse* (The Nun, 1796) and *Jacques le Fataliste* (1796), was published posthumously; and many shorter stories and critical essays. His *Salons* (1759–81) established art criticism as a literary genre, while his letters to Sophie Volland (1716–84) make for one of the most interesting correspondences of the period.

After the *Pensées philosophiques* (1746) he gradually moved from deism to atheism, espoused determinism and developed a sophisticated theory of materialism, which revolved around the notions that motion is inherent to matter, that sensitivity is a property latent in all matter and that the difference between inorganic and organic matter was simply one of organization (quantitative changes in the one making for the qualitative transformation into the other). *De l'Interprétation de la nature* (1753), concerned primarily with the experimental method and guide-lines to scientific research, also considered the question of the evolution of species. Influenced by Maupertuis, Buffon and Louis-Jean-Marie Daubenton (1716–99), Diderot conceived of a process of natural selection and transformation. His originality is most evident in *Le Rêve de d'Alembert* (D'Alembert's Dream). Written in 1769, it sets forth an account of heredity, of the unit of the self, of memory and of the mechanism of the association of ideas. His determinism and materialism notwithstanding, Diderot had little patience with simplistic psychological theories, as is made clear by his *Réfutation de 'L'Homme' d'Helvétius* (begun in 1773).

A member of the Academy of Berlin since 1751, he was elected to the Academy of Arts in St Petersburg in 1767. In 1773 he travelled to Russia to thank Catherine II for her patronage. His political views ranged from reformism to radicalism, depending on the context in which they were voiced.

Élisabeth de Fontenay, *Diderot, Reason and Resonance*, trans. Jeffrey Mehlman (New York: G. Braziller, 1982).
Arthur M. Wilson, *Diderot* (New York: Oxford University Press, 1972).

SYLVANA TOMASELLI

Diplomatic Revolution (1756)   The Diplomatic Revolution referred to two treaties in the first half of 1756, that between Britain and Prussia of 27 January (Convention of Westminster) and that between France and Austria of 1 May. The first, not an alliance but a non-aggression pact, was the product of Frederick II's fear that British subsidies to Russia and Sweden would enable them to attack in east Prussia, while his defensive treaty with France might provoke a British attack from Hanover to the west. Yet the expiration of this treaty in 1757 was a foregone conclusion because of Louis XV's dislike of Frederick, and Louis's and Madame de Pompadour's growing respect for Maria Theresa. At the same time, Britain attempted to assure the empress that Prussia's professed desire to see Germany neutral in a future war must afford it security to the north.

The Franco-Austrian treaty, strongly desired by Louis XV, meant that France need not fear invasion from south Germany, that Bourbon Spain and Italy would be strengthened and that an Austrian neutrality in the Anglo-French colonial struggle would not provoke Britain into invading the Austrian Netherlands. But France would not countenance a dismemberment of Prussia as planned by Kaunitz, only the recovery of Silesia. Though it started the Seven Years War, Frederick's overrunning of France's ally Saxony in August–October 1756 seemed to him a prerequisite for Prussia's defence.

R. Waddington, *Louis XV et le renversement des alliances* (Paris: Firmin-Didot, 1896).

D. D. ALDRIDGE

Directory   The Directorial regime introduced by the French revolutionary Constitution of 1795 lasted until the establishment of the Consulate in 1799. Reacting against the radical authoritarianism of the Terror, the Directory revived the liberal spirit of the CONSTITUTION OF 1791. A property franchise was preferred to manhood suffrage, the separation to the concentration of powers. The legislature was bicameral – the Council of Five Hundred initiated laws, the Council of Ancients ratified them – and the executive was entrusted to five directors, elected by the councils and one of whom was to be replaced annually. This system of checks and balances aimed at avoiding democratic or royalist extremes proved unable to cope with the political turbulence, economic disarray, religious dissension and military demands of the late 1790s. The course of its history was a reckless series of zigzags to left and right, punctuated by coups and counter-coups. Significantly, the regime's most successful politician, Barras (1755–1829), was renowned for his political slipperiness and venality. The Directory also witnessed the growth of the power of the army as an independent political force, a development enshrined in Napoleon BONAPARTE's final *coup d'état* of November 1799.

Martyn Lyons, *France under the Directory* (Cambridge: Cambridge University Press, 1975).

COLIN JONES

discovery *see* EXPLORATION.

disease   For much of the eighteenth century disease continued to be understood in a Galenic framework, that is as caused by an imbalance in the body's humours, the four fluid components (black and yellow biles, blood and phlegm) which formed the basis of medical thought since classical antiquity. This imbalance was shaped by an individual's constitution and circumstances; disease was not a specific unchanging entity. People regulated what they ate and drank, what they evacuated, sweated and vomited, to restore and maintain a bodily balance of intake and outgo. Closely tied to humoral theory was the interpretation of disease in environmental terms – seeing air, water and other factors as promoting or protecting against disease.

While a humoral view remained dominant, three additional perspectives complemented and extended ideas about disease. The first was that of natural history. Followers of Thomas Sydenham (1624–89) sought to organize diseases as if they were botanical specimens, claiming that diseases had specific and distinct identities. Others sought to discover unifying themes in disease causation; William Cullen (1712–90) organized disease processes around concepts of nervous force. These elaborate nosologies, or classifications of illness, have sometimes led historians to dismiss eighteenth-century medicine as the product of relentless systematizers.

A second approach was to see disease in physical terms. Such 'iatromechanism' reflected doctors' attempts to develop a Newtonian mathematical medicine. Albrecht Haller grounded his influential understanding of the body on the physical properties of irritation and SENSIBILITY.

Thirdly, and most consequentially, medicine began to interpret disease in solidistic and localistic terms, as the product of malfunctions in specific body parts. Such a perspective derived in part from surgery, which emphasized specific organs rather than the overall fluid balance of the body. Giovanni Morgagni's (1682–1771) monumental work of pathological anatomy, De sedibus et causis morborum (On the Seats and Causes of Disease, 1761), analysed the relationship between disease processes and anatomical change. By the end of the century, developments usually associated with Parisian clinical medicine were beginning to institutionalize such views of disease in the hospital. Clinicians in the large teaching HOSPITALS of Paris, London, Vienna, Edinburgh, Berlin and elsewhere sought to classify diseases by correlating symptoms with pathological changes discovered in post-mortem dissection (see ANATOMY). Despite such innovation, humoral theories of disease continued to be the basis of much therapeutics.

Patterns of disease in the eighteenth century were structured by increased long-distance travel which meant greater potential transmission of disease. For the original inhabitants of the New World such exchange was deadly; even at the beginning of the century, the native population of North America was a tiny fraction of what it had been pre-contact. The costs of imperialism were borne to a lesser degree by armies and settlers who encountered new diseases in the unfamiliar climates of India, South and North America, the Caribbean and Africa.

See also MEDICINE.

W. F. Bynum, 'Health, Disease, and Medical Care', in G. S. Rousseau and Roy
Porter (eds), *The Ferment of Knowledge: Studies in the Historiography of
Eighteenth-Century Science* (Cambridge: Cambridge University Press, 1980),
pp. 211–53.

R. Shryock, *The Development of Modern Medicine* (Madison, Wisc.: University of Wisconsin Press, 1979).

MARY E. FISSELL

Dissenters   The Dissenters were Protestants who worshipped outside
the communion of the established churches in Britain and who were
therefore both beneficiaries and victims of the so-called Toleration Act
of 1689 (*see* TOLERATION). This Act exempted trinitarian Protestants
from the penalties of certain laws, but also excluded them from holding office and required them to pay tithes and other parochial duties.
In the early eighteenth century religious dissent comprised Presbyterians, Independents, General and Particular Baptists, and Quakers, and
accounted for less than 10 per cent of the population of England and
Wales. The Presbyterian Church in Ireland, which was heavily concentrated in the ancient province of Ulster, was also a dissenting church
subject to legal disabilities including the sacramental test clause of
1704 (*see* TEST ACTS). Uniquely among dissenting churches in the British
Isles, the Presbyterian Church in Ireland received, through the *regium
donum*, a state contribution to the cost of its ministry. This attempt
to secure loyalty and to bolster the Protestant ascendancy in Ireland
was not entirely successful. An influential minority of Irish Presbyterians was implicated in the rebellion of the UNITED IRISHMEN in 1798.

A higher proportion of Dissenters than of the population at large
were urban dwellers engaged in manufacturing, commerce and skilled
trades. But the alleged causal relationship between Protestant dissent
and capitalism probably has less to do with the notorious work ethic
than with the social, political and educational parameters within which
Dissenters were required to live.

From a religious perspective, the two most significant changes within
the dissenting community were the growth of antitrinitarian opinions,
especially within Presbyterianism (*see* UNITARIANISM), and the spread of
evangelical religion (*see* EVANGELICALISM). The former made sections of
Old Dissent more rationalistic and ultimately more radical, while the
latter revived an older evangelistic tradition which increased numbers
and made Nonconformity a major force in nineteenth-century society
throughout the British Isles. The Methodists who inspired this revival did
not regard themselves as Dissenters in the eighteenth century. It was
not until the period 1795–1820 that Methodists throughout the British
Isles took formal steps to separate themselves from the ecclesiastical and
sacramental disciplines of the established church (*see* METHODISM).

P. Brooke, *Ulster Presbyterianism: The Historical Perspective 1610–1970* (Dublin: Gill & Macmillan, 1987).

M. R. Watts, *The Dissenters: From the Reformation to the French Revolution* (Oxford: Clarendon, 1978).

DAVID HEMPTON

dixième [tithe]   This tax was first imposed in France in 1710 during the War of the Spanish Succession, when the country was suffering a severe financial crisis. The great military engineer Marshal VAUBAN had earlier expounded the virtues of such a *Dixme royale*. In theory at least, the tax of one-tenth on revenues was to be levied on all Louis XIV's subjects, and it therefore represented a radical departure from the accepted principle that members of the First and Second Estates, as well as other privileged groups, should be exempt from direct taxation. For that reason it was introduced as a temporary wartime measure. Nevertheless, large sections of the community succeeded in evading payment. The tax was reintroduced in 1733 for three years, during the War of the Polish Succession; and in 1741 during the War of the Austrian Succession. It was abolished in 1749 but the principle was later reintroduced in the form of a twentieth (*vingtième*) tax.

See TAXATION.

Marcel Marion, *Dictionnaire des institutions de la France aux XVIIe et XVIIIe siècles* (Paris: Auguste Picard, 1923).

J. H. SHENNAN

Dobrovsky, Joseph (1753–1829)   Czech scholar. From a Germanized Czech family, he was responsible for pioneering work in Slavonic philology, and played a major role in the rediscovery of literary Czech. Born and educated in Bohemia, he became a Jesuit and, after the dissolution of the order in 1773, an educationist and lecturer in theology. He enjoyed the patronage of the noble Nostitz family. In 1792 he was commissioned by the Bohemian Academy of Sciences to travel in Russia and Scandinavia to trace lost Slavonic manuscripts. He played a major role in the restoration of the Czech language, which had declined since the Thirty Years War. He also undertook important research into the history of Bohemia. His main works include *History of the Bohemian Language and Older Literature* (1792) and *Glagolitica* (1807), a reconstruction of the old Church Slavonic liturgy.

F. Palacky, *J. Dobrowskys Leben und gelehrtes Wirken* (Prague: 1833)

MICHAEL HUGHES

domestic industry   Defined as industrial work carried on in the household, domestic industry is usually associated with dispersed production processes in rural areas before the rise of the factory system, but in fact it continued to be the predominant form of industrial organization until the latter half of the nineteenth century in Britain and into the twentieth century in Europe. The workforce was the family labouring at home. Each household purchased its raw materials or secured small quantitites of materials on credit, worked these up and sold them. Artisan producers had independent access to markets; those working under the putting-out system were dependent for materials and markets on merchants. Debt rather than wage labour defined the social relations of this industrial organization.

Domestic industry spread rapidly in the later sixteenth and seventeenth centuries in the woollen spinning, stocking-knitting, button-making, pin- and nail-making, ribbon- and lace-making, and linen-weaving trades. At this time it was frequently, but not always, associated with areas of pastoral farming, partible inheritance and common rights, but later expanded to many areas. Domestic industry's main disadvantage was the merchants' lack of control over the production process, hence the constant complaints of bad spinning, dirty yarn and embezzlement of raw materials. But it had even greater advantages including its flexibility in the face of economic fluctuations, development of specialized division of labour and creative skills, and capacity to provide product choices for localized tastes.

See also ARTISANS, HOUSEHOLD STRUCTURE.

M. Berg, *The Age of Manufactures*, second edn (London: Routledge, 1994).

MAXINE BERG

drama World drama existed in the eighteenth century, in the sense that plays were being performed in all corners of the earth, as they had been for many centuries. But world history did not impact directly on much of this; and inevitably it was European drama which reached the consciousness of the world-shapers and the participants in major historical events. Much of the Orient was still cut off from the West, and news from remoter places (let alone untopical information such as the dramatic repertoire) took months to reach Europe. At the time of the Seven Years War, or the Napoleonic wars, there were still relatively few major centres of intense dramatic activity, even though a growing number of cities in Europe, and eventually North America, supported professional companies. The most prominent of such centres were at first London, Paris, Venice and, increasingly, Vienna. The decline in economic and political power of Spain was matched by a relative lull in drama after the triumphs of the golden century; Russia with its cultural expansion under Catherine II took time to achieve international attention for its theatre, and French influences remained strong in St Petersburg. The foundation of the National Theatre, now the

Pushkin Theatre, in 1756 marked an incipient nationalist movement, with the versatile writer Aleksandr Petrovich Sumarokov (1717–77) appointed as the first director. A more lasting contribution was made by Fedor Grigorievich Volkov, who wrote plays and operas and ran an innovative company of players. Most of the minority languages produced respectable neoclassical dramatists, deft in observing the unities and in turning out well-constructed verse tragedies. Perhaps the only figure from this background to leap the language barrier was a citizen of the Dano-Norwegian monarchy, Ludvig HOLBERG, a widely travelled and academically distinguished man of letters. Born in Bergen in 1684, Holberg spent most of his career in Copenhagen (where he died in 1754), and wrote distinguished works in Danish covering most of the literary genres. He did more than anyone else to create an authentic Danish theatre with his intensely realistic comedies, such as *The Political Tinker* (1723). Many of his plays owe a debt to Molière, but they also contain a vein of fantasy and wild invention which gives them an almost surreal quality.

Inevitably it was drama in English, French, Italian or German which most easily crossed national barriers. The main evolution here was the increasing prominence of German theatre as the century progressed. Gotthold LESSING was one of the first authors to help effect this shift, with tragedies such as *Emilia Galotti* (1772), comedies such as *Minna von Barnhem* (1767) and the widely admired 'dramatic poem' *Nathan der Weise* (1779), which was translated into English by the author of *Baron Munchausen*, R. E. Raspe (1737–94). Lessing struggled to make a living in Berlin and Leipzig, but within a generation the revival in German literature was in full flower: its dramatic expression ranged from the major historical and mythological tragedies of GOETHE and SCHILLER to the popular stage-pieces of August Kotzebue (1761–1819) and, just into the new century, the strange poetic creations of Heinrich KLEIST.

A high proportion of the most prolific men and women of letters attempted drama, and some (including Voltaire, Fielding and even Diderot with his *Le Fils naturel* (1757), one of the new domestic dramas) were better known in that capacity during their lifetime than they have been since. This is often not because these authors wrote good stage plays, though they occasionally did; more usually, it is because they were able to take their polemical skills on to the stage and use the theatre as a medium to discuss ideas abroad in society. Sometimes their plays were the springboard for pamphleteering and journalistic exploitation of issues which had been brought to the attention of the public in the playhouse. The vogue for 'domestic' or sentimental drama tended to renounce the grandiose subjects of traditional tragedy in favour of topical, familiar and accessible material. This is not altogether true of the most famous early work of bourgeois tragedy, George Lillo's *The London Merchant* (1731), with its quasi-Elizabethan setting, melodramatic events and high-flown language; but it was increasingly true of sentimental comedies featuring the distresses of humdrum citizens battling with social conventions in a recognizably modern world of money and marriage laws.

The comedy of manners, working through wit and satire, produced more vigorous critiques of the prevailing order. There may have been no Molière in France, and after the energy of Restoration comedy drained away in England no real successor to Congreve (1670–1729), but Venice saw the sharp and scathing plays of Goldoni (1707–93), London the articulate exchanges of GOLDSMITH and SHERIDAN, and Paris the works of the quintessential eighteenth-century playwright, BEAUMARCHAIS. That his *Le Mariage de Figaro* has not been totally overshadowed by the operatic masterpiece to which it gave birth six years later is testimony to its abiding qualities. Lively, irreverent and eminently actable, it gives us an intrigue of ideas and a serious farce of emotions. Not surprisingly, Beaumarchais was arrested for his pains in exposing the *ancien régime* to exquisite ridicule. Indeed, the themes of *Figaro* were among the ideas that contributed eventually to the Revolution.

Living drama is always in touch with history, and if the eighteenth century produced few unchallenged masterpieces in drama its theatre consistently felt the impress of an age of convulsive change. Closet drama, opera seria and mythological rodomontade continued to be staged, but they were gradually crowded out by more open treatment of the urgent social and political agenda of the day. In the early part of the century, it had been normal to attack corrupt ministers obliquely, through parallel stories drawn from classical legends, or through other kinds of displacement (as when the opposition to Walpole sponsored plays ostensibly based on King Alfred or Edward III). By the time of the French Revolution a new dramaturgy had arrived, which could present the contemporary Jacques on stage, as good as his master.

See also THEATRE.

PAT ROGERS

Dresden   The capital of the electorate of SAXONY, Dresden contains major art collections and a number of splendid buildings, which make it a jewel of baroque and classical architecture and have earned it the name of 'Florence on the Elbe'. It owed its beauty mainly to the electors Frederick Augustus I (1670–1733), known as 'the Strong', and Frederick Augustus II (1696–1763), who rebuilt large parts of the city destroyed by fire in 1695 and created a brilliant court there. It was their ambition to make the city the artistic capital of Germany and they attracted renowned artists and architects. Perhaps the finest buildings are the Zwinger palace, built by Pöppelmann and decorated with paintings by Permoser (1651–1732), the Catholic court chapel and the Church of Our Lady. In the years between the Great Northern War and the Seven Years War it blossomed and its population grew rapidly to reach some 63,000. Dresden declined after 1763 when the Saxon government, concentrating on rebuilding the country, sharply cut expenditure on artistic and architectural projects. The city was devastated in allied air-raids in 1945, but has been rebuilt.

E. Hempel, *Baroque Art and Architecture in Central Europe* (Harmondsworth: Penguin, 1965).

MICHAEL HUGHES

dualism In the eighteenth century the term 'dualism' was used to designate the cosmological theory that the universe consists in two independent and original principles – one of which is evil and the other of which is good. This view, which was treated sympathetically by Pierre Bayle and David Hume, was opposed to orthodox Christianity.

The word has since come to be used for a theory of human nature which was also much disputed in the eighteenth century – that human beings consist of two substances, an immaterial soul and a material body. Following Descartes, many eighteenth-century thinkers considered the essential property of the soul to be thought or perception, and that of the body to be extension or divisibility into parts. (*See* RELATIONSHIP BETWEEN MIND AND BODY.)

Cartesian dualists were opposed by materialists who argued that thought or perception could be a property of matter structured in a certain way, that is, as it is in a human brain. John Locke, who clearly laid out the rival theories, argued that both views were possible and that we have no certain way of deciding between them.

J. Yolton, *Thinking Matter: Materialism in Eighteenth-Century Britain* (Minneapolis: University of Minnesota Press, 1983).

JOHN P. WRIGHT

Dumouriez, Charles François du Périer (1739–1823) French Revolutionary general. An adventurous career soldier and diplomat prior to 1789, he developed a local power-base in Cherbourg before moving to Paris, where he established links with Mirabeau and Lafayette and joined the Jacobin Club. In March 1792 he was appointed foreign minister, but when he was dismissed in June 1792 resumed his military career. Commander of French troops in the momentous victories at Valmy (September 1792) and Jemappes (November 1792), he led the French invasion and occupation of Belgium. He had maintained political links with the GIRONDINS in Paris, and when military reverses, including the defeat at Neerwinden in March 1793, led to the evacuation of the Low Countries, he secretly negotiated with the commanders of the allied forces, then tried to lead his army on Paris to crush the anti-Girondin Jacobins. The coup flopped, and he deserted his post, crossing behind enemy lines. Rejected when he offered his services to the *émigrés*, he travelled widely before ending up in England.

COLIN JONES

Dupleix, Joseph François (1697–1764)   French colonial administrator. He arrived in India in 1720 to take up a post at PONDICHERRY. He later moved to Bengal, before returning to Pondicherry as governor in 1742. A shrewd strategist, Dupleix sought to reinforce the French position in southern India at the expense of the British. Taking advantage of Anglo-French hostilities in Europe, and of a series of disputed local successions, he was initially successful and Madras was captured in 1746. However, British supremacy at sea allowed them to besiege Pondicherry, and at the Treaty of Aix-la-Chapelle Madras was returned to its former owners. Involvement in local politics saw Dupleix extend French influence in the Deccan and Carnatic, but a new pattern of alliances saw the British enter the fray in decisive fashion in support of rival powers. As a result, significant defeats were inflicted on Chanda Sahib and his French allies. Beset with difficulties, Dupleix continued the struggle in the face of mounting opposition from home, and in due course he was removed from his post and accused of financial mismanagement. He spent the rest of his days fighting to clear his name in France, and died in poverty.

H. Dodwell, *Dupleix and Clive: The Beginning of Empire* (London: Frank Cass, 1967).

HUW BOWEN

Dutch Republic *see* UNITED PROVINCES.

E

East Friesland   A geographically remote principality of about 100,000 people in the north-western corner of Germany, East Friesland was culturally, politically and socially different from most of its neighbours. It celebrated a tradition of Frisian liberty and was characterized by an absence of serfdom, a weak nobility and powerful parliamentary estates. It was dominated by the city of Emden. In the 1720s an attempt was made by the prince to undermine the estates' power and install an absolutist system of government. This precipitated a serious constitutional crisis which culminated in civil war. The case came before the Imperial Aulic Council (*Reichshofrat*), one of the two high courts of the Holy Roman Empire, and external powers, including Prussia, Hanover, Münster, Denmark and the Dutch, also became involved. No settlement was reached. In 1744 the native ruling house, the Cirksena, died out and the territory was inherited by PRUSSIA. Hanoverian and Dutch claims to the territory were abandoned. After 1744 Prussian rule became popular. The administration was reformed to remove corruption and it was spared forced recruiting. It retained its separate identity and enjoyed a long period of tranquillity.

M. Hughes, *Law and Politics in Eighteenth-Century Germany* (Woodbridge: 1988).

MICHAEL HUGHES

East India Company, Dutch   In 1602 a large number of trading companies merged to form the Dutch East India Company, the Vereenigde Oostendische Compagnie. By 1700 the Company dominated the Indonesian archipelago; trading stations were founded in Indo-China, the Malacca peninsula, Japan, Ceylon, India and the Persian

Gulf; and strategic bases were established at the Cape of Good Hope and Mauritius. This far-flung commercial network produced pepper, cinnamon, tea, coffee and textiles for the Amsterdam market, and Dutch investors in the Company were rewarded with a return of not less than 12.5 per cent until 1781. However, the Company over-stretched its capital resources, and expansion had to be funded by enormous loans. These difficulties, which were serious by the 1760s, were compounded by Anglo-Dutch warfare in which the Company suffered a number of set-backs in the 1780s. The important settlement of Negapatam in southern India was lost, and this enabled the British to mount a successful attack on Ceylon. In the 1790s the Company's position deteriorated further, and, after being taken over by the BATAVIAN REPUBLIC in 1795, the organization was wound up in 1798.

See also CHARTERED TRADING COMPANIES.

C. R. Boxer, *The Dutch Seaborne Empire 1600–1800* (London: Hutchinson, 1965).

HUW BOWEN

East India Company, English   The United Company of Merchants trading to the East Indies came into being in 1709 following the merger of the 'old' East India Company (founded in 1600) with the 'new' Company (formed in 1698). In return for payments to the crown, this joint-stock company secured chartered monopoly trading rights east of the Cape of Good Hope. Most of its efforts were devoted to commercial activity in India, although important trading posts were also established on the island of Sumatra and at Canton on the Chinese coast.

The Company developed a large army to counter the threat posed by European rivals, but increasingly this force was used in support of favoured Indian powers against their enemies. By the 1760s the Company had extended its role to include widespread political and administrative activity as well as revenue collection. These developments caused concern at Westminster, which led to greater government supervision of British Indian affairs. The process began with Lord North's Regulating Act of 1773, continued with Pitt's India Act of 1784 and culminated with the Charter Act of 1813. The last measure ended the trading monopoly, and thus precipitated the long-term decline of the Company.

See CHARTERED TRADING COMPANIES.

J. Keay, *The Honourable Company: A History of the English East India Company* (London: Harper Collins, 1991).

HUW BOWEN

East India Company, French   The French East India Company had a chequered history. Several companies had failed in the seventeenth century, but this did not deter those who in 1719 promoted the Edit of Reunion which merged the Compagnie des Indes Orientales (founded in 1664 by Colbert) with John LAW's Compagnie des Indes, the aim being to direct all of France's overseas commerce in the national interest. In India the Company centred its activities on the Coromandel coast, although an important foothold was maintained in Bengal at Chandernagore. Trade development was steady if unspectacular, and much energy was devoted to diplomatic and military activity which resulted in economic difficulties becoming acute by the 1750s. This weakness, together with poor leadership, was underlined in 1760 when twenty years of hostilities were brought to an end by the British defeat of the French at the Battle of Wandiwash. Although a recovery was attempted in the 1760s, the Company was wound up in 1769 and French trade with India was thrown open. A short-lived Company was founded by Calonne in 1785, but this did not survive the Revolution, and in 1790 French trade with India was opened once more.

See CHARTERED TRADING COMPANIES.

H. Furber, *Rival Empires of Trade in the Orient, 1620–1750* (Minneapolis: 1976).

HUW BOWEN

East Indies   Although employed loosely by eighteenth-century writers to refer to India and South-east Asia as a whole (for example in Raynal's *Histoire des deux indes*), the term 'East Indies' is now normally restricted to Indonesia, the group of more than 2,000 islands between the Malay peninsula and northern Australia. In the seventeenth century the DUTCH EAST INDIA COMPANY had established itself as the dominant power in the archipelago, with a virtual monopoly (unbroken till 1784) of the trade in pepper, spices, coffee and sugar – commodities which it shipped home for profitable sale in Europe. Control was exercised through a handful of trading bases (including Batavia, the Company's headquarters in Java) and by treaties imposed on the indigenous rulers, whose warriors the Company employed but whose authority it generally left intact. In Amboyna and the Banda Islands, however, Dutch rule was direct; and it was here and in nearby Ceram that the worst brutalities occurred, with slave-labour plantations and annual armed expeditions to destroy unlicensed spice orchards.

Until the nineteenth century, Dutch interest in the East Indies remained almost exclusively commercial. Missionary activity and colonization were minimal. Intermarriage tended to be with women of

Indo-Portuguese descent, though the Buginese of Celebes (reputedly 'much handsomer than any other Indian nation') were preferred as concubines. Only with the foundation of the Batavian Society of Sciences (1778) did the wider culture and history of the Indonesian peoples begin to be studied.

See also DUTCH IN JAVA.

C. R. Boxer, *The Dutch Seaborne Empire 1600–1800* (London: Hutchinson, 1965).

HUGH DUNTHORNE

economics   The discipline of 'political economy', or economics, was a product of the emergent capitalist economy of western Europe (*see* CAPITALISM) and embodied its ideology; it also bore the liberal stamp of the Enlightenment. Much writing on economic issues was partisan, the lobbying of mercantile and agrarian interests for tariffs, import and export bans, or bounties on particular items of trade, justified by appeal to national interests – an approach dignified by Adam Smith's hostile coinage of the term 'MERCANTILISM'. Governments responded only where such policies coalesced with wider aims of raising revenue or maintaining social peace. In Continental Europe, however, enlightened despots embraced the programme of agricultural improvement and legislative reform advanced by the French PHYSIOCRATS, led by François Quesnay.

Although mercantilist authors sometimes offered novel insights, the discovery of generalizable laws of economic behaviour was not their goal. It did begin, however, to exercise political philosophers, whose primary concern was the role of the state and concomitant issues of morality and justice. The impact of the late-seventeenth-century financial revolution in Britain – banking, stockjobbing and the national debt – promoted reflection on the fundamentally different and superior social relations of commercial over landed society, a 'stages of growth' theory which Marx would develop. The natural laws of Newtonian physics offered a paradigm of order and explicability to which the social sciences aspired. Economists' methodology, however, was inductive and historical, with virtually no quantitative analysis.

As the conviction that economic systems were naturally self-regulatory grew among theorists, so did condemnation of particularist intervention by the state. The most complete and influential expression of this doctrine of LAISSEZ-FAIRE was Adam Smith's *Inquiry into the Nature and Causes of the Wealth of Nations* (1776): individual pursuit of self-interest would produce the optimal outcome for society, creating wealth through the 'invisible hand' of market mechanisms. This would allow the actual price of a commodity to approach its 'natural' price (or value) determined by long-term competitive forces. This doctrine bolstered those who dismissed paternalism as harmful: a prime example was the mounting reluctance to regulate grain markets through price-setting, public granaries and prosecution of speculators, despite popular pressure to continue. Smith, however, remained conscious of the need for the legislator to repair the moral damage and injustices of COMMERCIAL SOCIETY.

How far Smith was aware of the INDUSTRIAL REVOLUTION remains a matter of controversy. The classical economists generally placed little faith in technology's capacity to extend the margins of production and expected growth ultimately to be halted by exhaustion of resources. Most pessimistic and influential was Thomas Malthus's *Essay on the Principles of Population* (1798) with its overprecise formula: 'population when unchecked increases in a geometrical ratio. Subsistence increases only in an arithmetical ratio.' Poor relief by nullifying the natural checks on overpopulation would hasten the day of reckoning. Such minimalist prescriptions of the state's role were most in tune with British and American political ideology.

Phyllis Deane, *The State and the Economic System: An Introduction to the History of Political Economy* (Oxford: Oxford University Press, 1989).

CHRISTINE MACLEOD

Edinburgh   A Celtic fortress originally, Edinburgh had become the effective capital of Scotland by 1403. During the Reformation it became the source of a radical Presbyterian culture. The Union of the Crowns (1603) turned it into a provincial capital with an uneasy relationship with the court in London. In 1638 it became a centre of resistance to the government of Charles I. A century later it had become one of the most fertile sources of Enlightenment in the Western world with a university that became one of the most important influences on Western higher education in the later eighteenth and early nineteenth centuries.

Its subsequent history has been one of *embourgeoisement* set against the background of declining political and social status. Its has remained a centre of government, professional and financial life, and culture. It remains one of the oldest and best-established ports of call for European and American tourists, the catalyst for a mythology of Scotland as a land of technology, Enlightenment and romance that remains as durable as it was when it was first created, in the Edinburgh of Sir Walter Scott (1771–1832).

See also SCOTLAND.

A. J. Youngson, *The Making of Classical Edinburgh* (Edinburgh: Edinburgh University Press, 1966).

NICHOLAS PHILLIPSON

education In the eighteenth century western Europe, aided by its science, technology and systems of formal education, had begun to dominate the entire globe. Despite doctrinal differences between the Catholic south of Europe and the Protestant north, Western education was basically a continuation of classical culture. In the fourth century BC the Greeks had developed a programme for privileged males which sought to cultivate the supposed innate knowledge of the mind. Beginning with the elementary school which taught religion, reading and writing, progression was made to a secondary school of literature – known as 'grammar' – and mathematics. For a further tiny privileged minority a third level of rhetoric, history and philosophy (including mathematics) was provided in academies. (*See* ELITE CULTURE.) This pattern, reconstructed with a Christian emphasis on 'divine illumination' as the source of knowledge, continued virtually unchanged into the eighteenth century, both in Protestant regions where elementary and grammar schools were supported by religious foundations, town councils and philanthropic groups, and in the Catholic south where schools were conducted by dioceses under direction of their bishops, or, in more limited cases, by religious orders and monasteries.

By the eighteenth century increasing numbers of religious societies had been founded, specifically as teaching congregations, often for the poor, both boys and girls. Even so, illiteracy was still the general rule, covering at least 70 per cent of the population, and even more in Iberia, Italy and eastern Europe. For the world in general, LITERACY was probably less than 1 per cent overall. Teaching was invariably in LATIN, based on the memorization of grammars or 'accidences', followed by the close study of classical and religious authors.

Western thought, especially in northern Europe, was dynamic, and led to the Enlightenment, which asserted the priority of the human mind and experience in opposition to the doctrine of 'divine illumination' of the medieval religious tradition, and was to affect education radically in the major centres of France, Switzerland, Germany and, to an extent, England. Dominating educational and political thought were John Locke in England and Jean Jacques Rousseau in Geneva. Locke's 1690 *Essay concerning Human Understanding* profoundly influenced the eighteenth century with its attack on both the traditional doctrine of innate ideas which were held to be implanted by God, and the belief that the function of education is to bring these ideas to consciousness. Locke argued that all perception is the result of the direct operation of external phenomena, or 'reality', on the senses and knowledge comes from the power of the mind to organize such sensory impressions into coherent, operative concepts. (*See* EMPIRICISM.)

Following this approach, Rousseau wrote the most influential works on education and society since Plato's *Republic* of the fourth century

BC. These were *Émile* of 1762, and its sequel, *Du contrat social*. Not only, he asserted, is our mind, and hence our knowledge of the phenomenal world, built empirically, but society itself is a cultural construction – a 'contract' – and not a divinely designed organic whole in which all persons have a providential and therefore unchangeable role. Rousseau argued that for the individual and for society, education must therefore be the paramount activity. Rousseau stimulated progressive educators to implement the ideas of *Émile* which, for the time, were both revolutionary and threatening. He asserted the priority of nature, the inherent goodness of the child, the unfolding in natural sequence of the conceptual powers of the mind and the fact that all education should be based on direct experience and activity learning, and conducted in the vernacular. His major disciples, Johann Heinrich Pestalozzi (1746–1827) in Switzerland, Johann Bernard Basedow (1724–90) in Dessau and Philipp von Fellenberg (1777–1844) at Hofwyl all conducted progressive schools which attracted many visitors and helped to propagate Rousseau's ideas. In Catholic countries *Émile* was banned, although attempts were made to produce similar progressive methods while retaining the essential doctrine of original sin and the magisterial authority of the church.

As the eighteenth century progressed formal schooling became increasingly extended as more bodies made voluntary provision, chiefly for boys and to some extent for girls. In addition, there was a significant increase in private-venture schools which taught such practical skills as navigation, bookkeeping, writing and various technical crafts. As well, private 'academies' began to offer cultural pursuits such as dancing, singing, musical-instrument playing and languages.

Compulsory education, and systematic state funding and regulation, however, were yet to come in the nineteenth century, although a beginning was made in the USA where Pennsylvania in 1776 and Delaware in 1792 enacted two of the world's first compulsory attendance ordinances. Revolutionary France followed with the Loi Danou of 1795. Similarly, the wider extension of education, especially to girls, blacks, minority races and the poor, as well as a pedagogy based on Rousseau's principles of progressive, activity-based learning, and taught in the vernacular were developments still a century ahead.

See also CHILDREN, SUNDAY SCHOOLS.

JAMES BOWEN

Egypt The OTTOMAN EMPIRE began to decline from the end of the sixteenth century. The history of Egypt from that period onwards mirrored that decline. At the beginning of the eighteenth century Egypt, under the rule of the Ottomans, was torn by warring overlords (called beys) and military factions: the JANISSARIES stationed in Cairo were a potent source of trouble. During the eighteenth century the viceroys appointed by the Ottomans lost considerable power while the beys became stronger. In particular, the Qasimi beys established themselves as leaders for a time but were later overthrown. The most notable of all the beys to achieve real power in the second half of the eighteenth century was 'Ali Bey al-Kabir (d 1773). He became almost like a king in Egypt, virtually denying the authority of the Ottoman sultan there. However, eventually even 'Ali's power crumbled and he died a week after being wounded and captured in battle in May 1773. Perhaps the most significant event of late-eighteenth-century Egyptian, and, indeed Middle Eastern, history was the invasion of Napoleon Bonaparte in 1798.

P. M. Holt, *Egypt and the Fertile Crescent 1516–1922: A Political History* (London: Longman, 1966).

IAN NETTON

electricity   Exploring static electricity was a new and popular practice in the eighteenth century. Demonstrating their control over the active powers of nature, natural philosophers entertained polite audiences with spectacular electrical displays, performed electric medical therapy and safeguarded buildings from lightning storms. Static electricity was commonly generated by machines first developed at London's Royal Society by exerting friction on a rotating evacuated glass globe, and from the middle of the century large charges could be produced – sometimes lethally – by the newly invented Leyden jar from Holland. Early studies at London on conduction, followed by more systematic examination in Paris of the electrical properties of different substances, suggested the existence of either one or two electric fluids, but none of the competing theories satisfactorily explained all the effects being obtained during an intensive programme of internationally conducted research. In the last third of the century Continental investigators – particularly in Paris – adopted far more quantitative theoretical and experimental approaches. After the Italian introduction of batteries to produce electric currents (*see* VOLTA), in the early nineteenth century electricity was linked first with HEAT and CHEMISTRY, and then with magnetism.

J. Heilbron, *Electricity in the Seventeenth and Eighteenth Centuries* (Berkeley, Calif.: University of California Press, 1979).

PATRICIA FARA

elite culture   It may be more accurate to speak of elite cultures than of an elite culture. It is true that the sons of the upper classes all over Europe (from Dublin to Warsaw, if not St Petersburg) had a more or less uniform education in the classics at grammar school, continued for some in the arts course at university. The classical tradition gave them a common frame of reference, while the continuing use of LATIN facilitated learned communication across linguistic frontiers. (*See* EDUCATION.) Scholars in this period continued to follow new developments in the sciences ('natural philosophy') as well as in the humanities. The *philosophes* were not alone in this respect. However, upper-class women were still virtually excluded from the world of the universities and expected to read little more than works of piety, novels or, at most, popularizations of science like the dialogues by Francesco Algarotti expounding 'Newtonianism for ladies' (1734). The three major professions – the church, the law and medicine – may be regarded as subcultures, intellectual worlds difficult of access by outsiders. As a consequence of the division of Europe into Catholic, Lutheran, Calvinistic and Orthodox, elite culture was fissured, if not fragmented.

PETER BURKE

Elizabeth (1709–1761)   Empress of Russia (1741–61). The fifth child of PETER I and CATHERINE (I), she was repeatedly bypassed for the throne, but in December 1741 she overthrew the infant Ivan VI and his German retinue with the support of Guards regiments. Pious and pleasure-loving, Elizabeth ruled through favourites, including the Shuvalovs and the Vorontsovs. Count A. Bestuzhev-Riumin maintained Russia's prominence in Europe. Territory was gained from Sweden (1743), and in 1756 Russia joined Austria and France against FREDERICK II of Prussia. The Seven Years War saw Russian victories, but gains were repudiated by PETER III. Elizabeth was no intellectual, but she sponsored education and the arts. In 1755 Moscow University, Russia's first, was founded, followed by the Academy of Arts in 1757. Her court was famed for its lavish entertainments, with French influence predominant. Bartolomeo Rastrelli (1700–71), building in the 'Elizabethan baroque' style, was her chief architect. Early marriage plans (into the houses of France and Holstein) foundered, but Elizabeth may later have morganatically married the Cossack Aleksei Razumovskii. She died childless on 25 December 1761, having nominated her nephew Peter (III) as her successor.

James Brennan, *Enlightened Absolutism in Russia: The Reign of Elisabeth (1741–62)* (New York: Lang, 1987).

LINDSEY HUGHES

embryology   Eighteenth-century natural philosophers inherited lingering problems about reproductive generation and regeneration in animals from their intellectual forebears. There remained questions such as distinguishing between inert and animate matter, the point when the soul becomes integrated into the body, the possibility of spontaneous generation and explanations for both foetal development and monstrous births. The predominant theory of generation in the early eighteenth century was preformation. This theory proposed that the embryo existed in a fully preformed, yet miniature state prior to conception. Embryonic development occurred by an increase in size of the pre-existent embryo. Arguments arose between preformationists who believed that the preformed entity existed in the ovum (ovists included Spallanzani, Haller and Bonnet) or in the sperm (animalculists included van Leeuwenhoek, Buffon, J. F. Blumenbach (1752–1840), C. L. F. Andry (1741–1829), Boerhaave, J. Lieutaud (1703–80), Leibnitz, M. F. Ledermueller (1719–69) and J. Astruc (1684–1766)).

In mid-century C. F. Wolff (1734–94) introduced experimental findings that chick embryos arose, after fertilization, from a homogenous living matter which gradually unfolded in a regularly observed order and combined to form the full foetus (that is epigenesis). Many materialists opposed the epigenesis account of embryonic creation which implied that an essential or vital force was inherent in living matter (*see* VITALISM). By the close of the century, however, epigenesis had gained support in many midwifery writings as well as from natural philosophers, including Kant.

E. B. Gasking, *Investigations into Generation, 1651–1828* (London: Hutchinson, 1967).

PHILIP K. WILSON

émigrés A salient feature of the French Revolution was the way in which each new regime produced a new crop of enemies. One consequence of this was emigration by those who lost in the successive power struggles. In the years 1792 to 1800 150,000 to 160,000 people fled France, of whom only 42 per cent were noble. *Émigrés* were as heterogeneous politically as they were socially. The first, most famous, *émigrés* were Louis XVI's brothers, the comtes de Provence and d'Artois, together with several great court families. They were soon followed by the *monarchiens* Mounier (1758–1806) and Malouet (1740–1814). Lesser nobles, clerics and army officers soon followed in the period 1789–92. Royalist *émigrés* clustered around the courts in exile, first in Turin and Coblenz, then in London, and there were small *émigré* communities scattered all over Europe and America. Some took part in counter-revolutionary actions, as at Quiberon Bay.

After them came Girondin survivors (*see* GIRONDINS) of the Terror like Madame de Stael and the Federalists of Toulon. Indeed, the trend seems to have intensified after 1792, in parallel to the harsh series of anti-*émigré* laws following the outbreak of the war. The properties of *émigrés* were confiscated in April 1792 and first put up for sale in August; on 25 October they were banished in perpetuity; and finally, in April 1793, a decree imposed the death penalty for any *émigré* found in France. These laws were temporized under the Directory, but remained in force until the general amnesty granted by Napoleon in 1802, when a gradual return began, although sold *émigré* property was not returned.

M. Boffa, 'Émigrés', in F. Furet and M. Ozouf (eds), *A Critical Dictionary of the French Revolution* (Cambridge, Mass.: Harvard University Press, 1989), pp. 324–36.
J. Godechot, *The Counter-Revolution: Doctrine and Action, 1789–1804* (London: Routledge & Kegan Paul, 1972).
D. Greer, *The Incidence of Emigration during the French Revolution* (Cambridge: Cambridge University Press, 1951).

MICHAEL BROERS

empiricism   John Locke published his *Essay concerning Human Understanding*, the classic Enlightenment statement of empiricism, in 1690. He intended to end intellectual controversy, particularly marked in mid-seventeenth-century England, by delimiting a domain of reliable ideas, namely those founded in sense experience, and rejecting Cartesian and other rationalists' claims to innate or intuitive ideas about the principles of creation. Locke's programme was continued by other 'British empiricists', with David Hume famously arguing that even ideas of causality were unwarranted constructions imposed on repeatedly conjoined sense experiences. Empiricism also underwrote the eighteenth-century growth of experimental sciences (*see* EXPERIMENTAL METHOD).

Some intellectuals associated Britain's progressive and tolerant society with its empiricist temper. To them, empiricism had negative and positive appeals. Negatively, it was used to undermine traditional systematic philosophy (pejoratively called 'metaphysics'), and the dogmatics of revealed theology. Positively, it encouraged applied science, and the social attitudes of bourgeois INDIVIDUALISM, for example the value of education. From Locke to the French revolutionary ideologues, pedagogical programmes of rich, ordered and useful experiences were produced and consumed in the pursuit of rational self-improvement.

John Yolton, *John Locke and the Way of Ideas* (New York: Oxford University Press, 1956).

STEPHEN PUMFREY

enclosures   Areas of land separated by permanent boundaries, and individually owned and occupied were known as enclosures. Unlike the open fields, only the occupier had rights of use. Their main advantage was the freedom given the occupier to cultivate the land as he wished, an important advantage as agriculture became more specialized, with a greater variety of crops being grown, and valuable livestock reared. Enclosures existed from early times, and gradually replaced open fields and those commons and wastes worth cultivating (*see* OPEN-FIELD SYSTEM). Enclosures were carried out by the owners, sometimes privately by mutual agreement, and often on a small scale, and later more generally with the sanction of government. In England the major part of the farmland had already been enclosed by the middle of the eighteenth century, and subsequently over 7 million acres, nearly a quarter of the whole, were enclosed by private Acts of Parliament. This resulted in a major addition to the cultivated acreage, but had effects on very small farmers and cottagers which are disputed, but may have been harmful in some circumstances.

See also EUROPEAN AGRICULTURE.

Michael Turner, *English Parliamentary Enclosure* (Folkestone: Dawson, 1980).

G. E. MINGAY

encyclopaedias   *see* DICTIONARIES AND ENCYCLOPAEDIAS.

Encyclopédie   The Enlightenment work *par excellence*, the *Encyclopédie, ou Dictionnaire raisonné des sciences, des arts, et des métiers par une société de gens de lettres* remains a fascinating book, if only because it was never a mere compendium of knowledge. It was first conceived as a rather modest project, namely as the French translation of Ephraim Chambers' *Cyclopaedia* of 1728. To be sure, such a translation was to have been a revised and extended version of the original English text, but the publisher, André-François Le Breton (1708–79), and his associates never envisaged the kind of monument to the Enlightenment that DIDEROT was to produce. Although he was assisted in this enterprise by D'ALEMBERT until 1758, and received the help of friends such as d'Holbach and of indefatigable contributors such as the chevalier de Jaucourt (1704–79), the *Encyclopédie* was in some senses a single-handed achievement. Seeing the work through to its completion was itself a major feat, but Diderot also wrote very many of its controversial and lengthy articles, including most of the ones on the history of philosophy, and he often made substantial additions to the entries of other writers.

A privilege for its publication was obtained in 1748. The *Prospectus* appeared in 1750, while seventeen volumes of text along with eleven volumes of plates were published between 1751 and 1772. Seven further volumes appeared between 1776 and 1780, but not under Diderot's editorship. The aims of the work were delineated in d'Alembert's

Discours préliminaire (1751). The intention was not only to assemble all available knowledge, but to do so in such a way as to show the connection between different areas of knowledge and to expose the foundation of each of these as well as their substantive content. Besides exhibiting the influence of Francis Bacon (1561–1626), the *Encyclopédie* was indebted to the empiricism of Locke, parts of whose writings can be found scattered verbatim throughout the text.

There were numerous difficulties in the course of its production. Apart from the conflicts between Le Breton and Diderot, it was prohibited twice, once in 1752, when the Jesuits allied themselves with members of the court and succeeded in having an *Arrêt du Conseil du Roy* issued; and more seriously in 1759, when the *Encyclopédie*'s privilege was revoked due to the pressure exerted by the *parlement*. The work was also placed on the INDEX in the same year. That publication was resumed was due in part to the benign censorship of Malesherbes. It was to be a great commercial success for its publishers, their profits being something of the order of 2,400,000 livres.

The *Encyclopédie* has been seen to be the embodiment of the aspirations and views of the rising *bourgeoisie*. Many of its articles were written anonymously, though the names of 142 contributors are given in the text. Those who are known to have written for it include Montesquieu, Voltaire, Turgot, Quesnay, Raynal, Condillac and Rousseau.

See also DICTIONARIES AND ENCYCLOPAEDIAS.

Jacques Proust, *Diderot et l'Encyclopédie* (Paris: Slatkine, 1982).

SYLVANA TOMASELLI

England Eighteenth-century England was a much-applauded nation, yet highly puzzling too. It formed a polity and society that were, in most respects, the envy and example of the Continent. Religious toleration and freedom of speech had largely, though not completely, been secured, thanks to the constitutional settlement following the Revolution of 1688 (*see* GLORIOUS REVOLUTION), which had expelled the would-be absolutist and Roman Catholic James II (1633–1701) for a more constitutional monarch, William III. Britain's mixed constitution, in which the powers of the monarch were legally balanced against the people represented in parliament, avoided the extremes both of despotism and of democracy, and secured crucial freedoms of the person and property. England boasted a fluid, dynamic social system, which was admired by those who condemned the ossified strata of nobles and clergy typical, for instance, of Spain or Poland. England was highly inventive in science and was developing a national literary tradition, while economic freedom and a thriving bourgeoisie spelled

the conditions for successful commercial development and industrialization. Many of the features of progress celebrated by the *philosophes*
found their embodiment in England.

Yet commentators, at home and abroad, also found much to de-
plore in England. Its parliamentary politics appeared quarrelsome and
corrupt; *virtù*, or public spirit, was markedly deficient. Neither monarchy nor parliament was prepared to fund those grand programmes
of building and schemes of artistic and scientific patronage that were
the glories of Bourbon Versailles or even of Habsburg Vienna. In
various fields of culture England lagged: its chief composers, like
HANDEL, were imported from abroad, as were most artists before
Hogarth. England had few profound thinkers to match, say, Kant
abroad or even Scotsmen like David Hume and Adam Smith. Hence
England wore a somewhat enigmatic air, and the English were a
puzzle: wealthier and enjoying greater liberty than their Continental
fellows, yet (it was said) notoriously melancholy (it was known as the
'English malady') and given to suicide.

The explanation for this riddle is that England under the Hanoverians
(from 1714) was, by European standards, a genuinely new type of
nation. It had established that mixed constitutional government, with
a division of powers between monarchy, House of Lords (aristocracy)
and House of Commons, which was the envy of commentators such
as Montesquieu. Sir Robert WALPOLE, the Whig prime minister for
practially the whole of the 1720s and 1730s, succeeded in imposing
political stability by party management in parliament and shameless
corruption in the constituencies. Thereafter, with the exception of the
temporarily troublesome but in the long run futile second Jacobite
invasion of 1745, no serious dynastic or political crisis threatened to
shake the political foundations. Unlike many European nations, England discovered techniques of financial management, through the Bank
of England, a national debt and deficit finance, and largely indirect
taxation. Public confidence in the state's financial viability increased.
Not least, England was blessed by success in all major wars during the
century, except the revolt of the American colonies (*see* AMERICAN WAR
OF INDEPENDENCE). The result was a huge boost of national pride and
a telling increase of naval power and imperial possessions (India,
Canada, additional Caribbean islands) which in turn promoted trade.
In short, success bred success, and by the standards of almost every
other European nation, a sizeable proportion of English people grew
genuinely more prosperous, more self-possessed and more patriotic.
By luck and judgement, England, unlike France, found ways of successively generating wealth while carrying through essential reforms.

Georgian England produced an ideology and a culture to match its
distinctive institutional disposition and its needs. John LOCKE set out

the principles of political liberalism, philosophical empiricism, practical education and religious toleration. Daniel DEFOE and Bernard MANDEVILLE spelled out the basis of modern economic liberalism on which others later elaborated. The third earl of SHAFTESBURY developed psychological aesthetics, and thus launched the cult of feeling that became so powerful after 1750; a handful of deists, such as Anthony COLLINS, established the principles of rational religion. Many of these ideas and outlooks, moreover, were popularized by ADDISON and STEELE in *The Spectator*, perhaps the world's first large-circulation high-quality magazine, whose function was to serve up a palatable and polite version of the Enlightenment to the educated public.

England's chief contribution to Enlightenment culture lay in translating ideals into action. It was the key concern of English thinkers to find practical and applied ways of ensuring the successful working of a polite civilized society dedicated to the pursuit of private interest and happiness within the framework of economic prosperity and under the rule of law. For example, Jeremy BENTHAM applied the basic philosophy of utilitarianism (the greatest happiness of the greatest number viewed as the yardstick of good) to the realistic reform of the legal system, and to the administration of schools, workhouses, prisons and the like. Pioneer industrialists such as Josiah WEDGWOOD, brimful of the liberal confidence of the Enlightenment, used scientific groups such as the Lunar Society of Birmingham as forums for developing the institutions and attitudes appropriate to an industrial society. Edward GIBBON adopted a secular, naturalistic outlook on history, utilizing it for interpreting the collapse of the world's greatest empire. Through *belles lettres* and letters English novelists and essayists attempted to formulate new codes of interpersonal behaviour requisite in a civil society marked by stability and politeness. Not least, the emergence of classical political economy, absorbing the original population theories of MALTHUS, sought to explain the market mechanisms of a capitalist economy in which individual profit-seeking contributes to the good of the whole, but also evaluated the social costs brought by *laissez-faire*. Not least, England, especially LONDON, provided a matrix for a new consumer culture, grounded on a world of fine objects at prices that made them available to the many not just the few, and featuring the rise of the NOVEL to a high art form, through Richardson, Smollett, Sterne, Fanny Burney and Jane Austen (1775–1817), the emergence of first-rate artists, such as Reynolds and Gainsborough, a popular THEATRE and the development of a high level of literacy.

This emergent consumer culture helps explain the final paradox of England. At a time, in the 1790s, when revolution was alight over most of Europe, England played a counter-revolutionary role, combating first the Jacobins and then Napoleon. Why? Because England had long ago achieved most of the gains and goals for which the French were striving, and which French success would have imperilled.

Roy Porter, 'The Enlightenment in England', in R. Porter and M. Teich (eds), *The Enlightenment in National Context* (Cambridge: Cambridge University Press, 1981), pp. 1–18.

R. Porter, *English Society in the Eighteenth Century* (London: Allen Lane, 1982).

J. Redwood, *Reason, Ridicule and Religion* (London: Thames & Hudson, 1976).

ROY PORTER

enlightened absolutism   The term 'enlightened absolutism' was applied retrospectively to the theory and practice of rulership adopted by a number of European monarchs and statesmen in the later eighteenth century. (The term 'enlightened despotism' is also current, but has been less favoured in recent scholarship.) It was coined by the German scholar Wilhelm Roscher in 1847 in reference to FREDERICK II of Prussia (1740–86) and JOSEPH II of Austria (1780–90), and was later extended to CATHERINE II of Russia (1762–96), Duke LEOPOLD of Tuscany (1765–90), GUSTAV III of Sweden (1771–92), CHARLES III of Spain (1759–88), to rulers of some of the minor German states and to certain ministers, for example marquês de POMBAL in Portugal (1750–77), J. F. STRUENSEE (1770–2) and A. P. Bernstorff (from 1784) in Denmark and B. TANUCCI in Sicily (1734–76). (Rulers such as PETER I of Russia (1682–1725) fit many of the categories but fall outside the chronological limits.)

Enlightened absolutism was influenced both by ideas and the practical realities of international politics and local conditions, the Seven Years War (1756–63), in particular, underlining the need for fiscal and administrative reform. The Enlightenment provided an ideological framework, especially in the emphasis on the replacement of custom, tradition and God's will by reason and natural law, but there was no blueprint, nor were all thinkers equally influential. German ideas were as important as those of the French *philosophes* (Voltaire, Montesquieu, Diderot et al.), for example CAMERALISM with its emphasis on the welfare of the population achieved through a well-regulated state, and theories of secular NATURAL LAW based on a social contract whereby citizens proffered loyalty in return for the ruler's protection and efforts on their behalf (Frederick II: 'The king is the first servant of his people').

Individual works had a disproportionate influence, for example Cesare Beccaria's *Dei delitti e delle pene* (1764) on Frederick II, Catherine II, Gustav III and Duke Leopold. Common elements in the programmes of 'enlightened' rulers included religious toleration and rejection of 'fanaticism'; subordination of established churches (for example Joseph II's curbing of the Catholic Church, Catherine II's secularization of ecclesiastical estates); milder penal policies (especially abolition of torture and minimal use of the death penalty); patronage of arts, science and education (school reforms of Joseph II and Catherine II, university reform in Spain); sponsoring of industry, trade and agriculture; concern for law and order (reformed codes in Prussia and Austria) and public welfare; limitations on censorship. Overall, these rulers shared a belief in progress through human agency and a preference for integrated plans over *ad hoc* measures, implemented by a well-oiled state apparatus manned by trained bureaucrats. (*See* ADMINISTRATION.) HUMANITARIANISM and enlightened paternalism were the watchwords: government for the people but not by the people. Elements of consultation were admissible (for example Catherine II's LEGISLATIVE COMMISSION; Leopold's constitutional project (1782); Joseph II's tours of the Empire), but implementation was in the hands of an educated elite inspired by the monarch. The latter, as legislator, needed the fullest powers in order to do good. State power had to be maximized, not lessened, in order to give scope for improving welfare. Most of the enlightened absolutists were dedicated and energetic individuals, often penning their own legislation and consciously avoiding uncultured 'despotic' behaviour, even though most were concerned with their own image.

In the 1960s and 1970s enlightened absolutism was out of favour with historians, who stressed the 'hypocrisy' and cynicism of rulers whose priority was maintaining their own power and that of the 'ruling class'. 'Enlightenment' was dismissed as mere window-dressing. Failures such as those of Catherine II or Frederick II to abolish serfdom or of Catherine to invite serfs to attend her Legislative Commission were underlined, as was the discrepancy between civilized behaviour at home and aggression abroad, the Partitions of Poland being a particularly blatant example. More recently scholars have reconsidered what rulers did rather than what they did not do, making a conscious effort to avoid modern concepts of 'liberalism' and 'democracy'. Mobilization of state resources in order to maintain national status and, ultimately, their own thrones may have been a prime motivator, but much of lasting value was achieved by advocates of enlightened absolutism.

T. C. W. Blanning, *Joseph II and Enlightened Absolutism* (London: Longman, 1970).
H. M. Scott, 'Whatever Happened to Enlightened Despotism?', *History* (June 1983), 244–57.
H. M. Scott (ed.), *Enlightened Absolutism: Reform and Reformers in Later Eighteenth-Century Europe* (London: Macmillan, 1990).

LINDSEY HUGHES

Enlightenment　Eighteenth-century critics and thinkers liked to think of themselves as bringing light to a world long shrouded in gloom by the forces of ignorance, superstition, political and ecclesiastical despotism and censorship, and so the term 'the Enlightenment' is highly appropriate to describe such currents of thought, although it had little currency in the English language till the twentieth century. The older phrase 'the age of reason' is now rightly discarded, since many of the *philosophes* or *Aufklärer* were themselves fierce critics of the kind of 'rationalism' earlier advanced by Descartes, with his belief that man was endowed with 'innate ideas', or by Leibniz, which, in their view, merely replaced the dogmatism of the church with the dogmatism of *a priori* philosophy.

'Was ist Aufklärung?' (What is Enlightenment?) asked the German intellectual Immanuel Kant in the title of a booklet published in 1784; and historians ever since have echoed him, trying to divine the essence of the movement. In truth, however, it was extremely wide-ranging and diverse. It spanned a full century or more, from its early heroes like Locke, Bayle and Newton, through to such thinkers as Condorcet, Erasmus Darwin, Herder, Tom Paine and Thomas Jefferson, who lived to see the FRENCH REVOLUTION which (all agreed, friend and foe alike) was one of the fruits, possibly bitter, of the Enlightenment's politico-ecclesiastical criticism. During the course of the century the movement changed, arguably became more radical, culminating in the democratic political programme of Paine's *Rights of Man*.

Moreover, the Enlightenment was also geographically diverse. Despite a popular stereotype which sees it primarily as a French movement, focusing on Montesquieu, Voltaire, Diderot, d'Alembert, Helvétius, Condillac, the Genevan but French-speaking Rousseau and others, it should be emphasized that practically all other regions of Europe enjoyed a ferment of ideas and policies of their own, but often very distinctive in nature. The French Enlightenment was preoccupied with the critique of despotism, aristocratic feudalism and the evils of the Roman Catholic Church (*écrasez l'infame* became Voltaire's watchword). The Enlightenment in England and Scotland set greater store by tracking the conditions under which a liberal, free, constitutionally governed capitalist society could successfully operate. In most German states and in Spain, Portugal and Scandinavia champions of Enlightenment were chiefly concerned to educate existing and generally absolutist rulers, with a view to improving the efficiency of ADMINISTRATION, modernizing old-fashioned economies and fostering a governing class of experts. There was, in any case, no homogeneity within Enlightenment circles. If the PHILOSOPHES were a family, they had family rows. Disagreements were occasionally violent; Rousseau managed to alienate most of his erstwhile friends among the *philosophes*. And others – rebels like the materialist La Mettrie and the sexual nihilist Sade – defy easy categorization. The Enlightenment should be seen less as a rigid party-political programme than as a mood, a climate of criticism, a new conception of the relations of consciousness and society.

Nevertheless, certain elements were widely held in common. All men of the Enlightenment (and it should be noted in passing that women played second fiddle) believed in a fundamental duty of intellectual and personal autonomy. Every person had to take responsibility for his own destiny, for his own thinking. (*See* INDIVIDUALISM.) Truth could not be taken on authority. The acquisition of fresh knowledge was the key to truth and progress, for, following the maxim of Francis Bacon (1561–1626), 'knowledge was power'; and experience was the key to valid *a posteriori* knowledge. Hence, truth could not be accepted *ex cathedra* from the church, the Bible or any other so-called definitive book, and CENSORSHIP was unacceptable. Intellectual freedom and enquiring minds were essential. That is why almost all *philosophes* applauded the scientific revolution of the seventeenth century as the greatest act of intellectual emancipation in the history of mankind. The science of Bacon, Galileo (1564–1642), Boyle (1627–91), Newton and others, with its accent on observation and experiment, had provided a model for intellectual enquiry of all kinds and provided a blueprint for progress unlimited.

Science had showed the grandeur and uniformity of nature, governed by the natural laws of physics, astronomy and chemistry. Men of the Enlightenment gloried in this vision of nature as harmonious, orderly, intelligible. It challenged Christian pessimism about original sin and the decay of nature. This is not to imply that all or even most *philosophes* were atheists. Only a very few deserve that name, notably the baron d'Holbach and perhaps Diderot and Voltaire (in his later years). Many wanted a more rational form of faith, with the miracles and absurdities stripped away, as for instance Locke in his *Reasonableness of Christianity* (1695). Others rejected the Christian God, but – like Erasmus Darwin – warmly insisted on the reality of some benign creator, a divine mechanic, who would underwrite the order and justice of the universe. All *philosophes* applauded religious tolerance and execrated bigotry and the spirit of religious persecution. (*See* NATURAL RELIGION.)

The glories of the SCIENTIFIC REVOLUTION suggested that man could improve himself by improving nature. Hence science offered a programme of progress through enquiry, labour, industry and technology, the transformation of nature for the benefit of mankind. Applied knowledge – in the form of economics, technology, public administration – thereby became crucial to Enlightenment strategies. For the *philosophes* wished to create new social sciences on the basis of established natural sciences. To be the 'Newton of the moral sciences' was the great aim of David Hume. This encapsulated the hope of establishing the human sciences on a sure, scientific epistemological foundation: man would be viewed as a product of his environment, of social conditioning, of a mechanical psychology in which all knowledge, opinions and affect arose through the senses by empirical experience. If man were thus machine-like, amenable to cause–effect analysis, he could be reprogrammed or re-educated to behave in more socially responsible and advantageous ways, pursuing peace, social harmony, economic productivity, and achieving individual happiness. EDUCATION was a common plank in the platform of *philosophes* like Locke, Condillac and Helvétius. Rousseau in particular insisted on learning by doing, as the antidote to all authoritarianism. Jeremy Bentham, with his utilitarian philosophy (embracing the greatest HAPPINESS of the greatest number) believed populations could be conditioned by government, via the law, to maximize private and public enjoyment.

Morally and socially, the Enlightenment looked back to Graeco-Roman antiquity for its models of dignified conduct and responsible CITIZENSHIP: Socrates, Cicero and the Stoics were especially admired, and to a lesser degree Plato. Politically, the *philosophes* were more divided. Some, like Rousseau, admired small city-states like Geneva, where all could participate and enjoy active freedom as citizens. Pragmatists like Voltaire assumed the future lay with enlightened absolutist rulers, the only sure bulwark against the pope and a reactionary aristocracy (*see* ENLIGHTENED ABSOLUTISM). American activists like Benjamin Franklin and Jefferson were fortunate enough to have a whole new world in which to construct a new political order, based on the inviolability of life and property and the pursuit of happiness. The attempt to translate Enlightenment principles into reality through the 'liberty, equality and fraternity' of the French Revolution was, alas, to prove more equivocal. Nevertheless, the Enlightenment had the most profound long-term consequences for the development of the Western polities. The rise of the modern secular intelligentsia, belief in basic liberal and personal freedoms, the role of the press and the media, and the fundamental conviction that man must forge his own destiny through industry and intellect – all these are the legacies of the Enlightenment.

Ernst Cassirer, *The Philosophy of the Enlightenment* (Princeton, NJ: Princeton University Press, 1951).

L. G. Crocker, *An Age of Crisis: Man and World in Eighteenth-Century French Thought* (Baltimore, Md.: Johns Hopkins University Press, 1959).

William Doyle, *Origins of the French Revolution* (Oxford: Oxford University Press, 1980).

Peter Gay, *The Enlightenment: An Interpretation*, 2 vols (New York: Knopf, 1966–9).

Norman Hampson, *The Enlightenment* (London: Penguin, 1968).

R. Porter and M. Teich (eds), *The Enlightenment in National Context* (Cambridge: Cambridge University Press, 1981).

ROY PORTER

enthusiasm Samuel Johnson memorably defined 'enthusiasm' as 'a vain belief of private revelation; a warm confidence of divine favour or communication'. Both contemporaries and subsequent commentators have employed an eclectic definition of the word to include characteristics such as claims of special spiritual insight, personal assurance of salvation, a return to the primitive simplicity of the early church, ecstatic experiences, a belief in special providences and miracles and an undue emphasis on the religion of the heart not the head. In his classic treatment of the subject, R. A. Knox describes it as a tendency towards 'ultrasupernaturalism' and includes within his definition studies of Quakerism, Jansenism, the Camisards, the Moravians and Methodism.

In its eighteenth-century context the word also carried with it associations of social and ecclesiastical subversion, and was thought to be antithetical to Christian ethics and moral duty. Not surprisingly, women and children were regarded as particularly susceptible to enthusiastic forms of religion. With characteristic ingenuity John Wesley turned the conventional usage of the word on its head by stating that all those who falsely imagined themselves to be Christians without any observable evidence to support it were in fact the real enthusiasts.

See also EVANGELICALISM, METHODISM, PIETISM.

R. A. Knox, *Enthusiasm: A Chapter in the History of Religion* (Oxford: Clarendon, 1950).

DAVID HEMPTON

environment Today the word 'environment' evokes notions of damage and abuse of NATURE by mankind, and when we speak of nature as other than despoiled, we think of it as being preserved and protected from the consequences of the activities of various human agencies. Apart from the few remaining areas that have as yet not been touched, the natural environment is increasingly perceived as the product of some human artifice or other. Although their perception of nature was different from ours, and the term 'environment' was not then used in the sense it is now, Enlightenment men and women were no stranger to the idea that mankind was usurping its place within the natural order. The Enlightenment was, on the whole, far from complacent about its views of nature and of the species' relationship to it. The period produced a wide range of insightful reflections on the concept of nature and the natural. Even the view that nature is good, or at least benign, which is often seen as a quintessential Enlightenment position, was questioned. Long before the LISBON EARTHQUAKE shook the confidence of men like Voltaire in the operation of nature, others, such as Diderot, spoke of nature as a mother who could be heartless and cruel, and of the relation between man and his environment as one of relentless struggle. Every day in the life of the species was a victory scored against nature. Indeed, as Diderot saw it, society owed its origins to this perpetual antagonism, for men had to unite to fight against their common enemy. But if he was far from sentimental about nature, he did not by any means conceive of this combat as one without rules or limitations: man was not at liberty to act in any way he pleased. Diderot was highly critical of what he considered to be man's going beyond the quest for survival: in *Réfutation d'Helvétius* he wrote, 'he was not content with defeating it, but has wanted to triumph over it'.

The theme of man's exploitation of nature was taken up by a number of writers, most notably ROUSSEAU, whose predominant concern was what it did to man in immediate terms, for example under the conditions in which some men laboured in mines, and how this attitude to nature was part and parcel of a social organization that alienated man from his own self and from other men. Thus his concern was not for what the destruction of his habitat would mean for man, let alone for the environment in itself. In this respect, Rousseau's views reflected those of his age.

Alfred W. Crosby, *Ecological Imperialism: The Biological Expansion of Europe 900–1900* (Cambridge: Cambridge University Press, 1989).
John Passmore, *Man's Responsibility for Nature: Ecological Problems and Western Traditions* (London: Duckworth, 1980).

SYLVANA TOMASELLI

equality   That inequality was not the concern of only the more radical political theorists of the period may be seen in the fact that the most famous work on the subject was an entry in an essay competition set by the Académie of Dijon. Rousseau's second *Discours* answered a set question: What is the origin of inequality among men and is it authorized by natural law? His claim in that work and in *Du contrat social* that men were born equal was a commonplace. What caused considerable disagreement was whether men and WOMEN were equal, and whether the growing social inequality between the rich and the poor, which was thought to be characteristic of modern commercial society according to conceptions such as that of Adam Smith, could be justified by appealing to liberty and freedom and/or to the improved standard of living that the poor were said to be enjoying in absolute terms under a system of inequality. To Mary Wollstonecraft, the two issues were related. To those who criticized women for failing in their duties as mothers, she wrote: 'we shall not see women affectionate till more equality be established in society, till ranks are confounded and women freed.' Such statements should, nevertheless, not obscure the fact that the issue of equality, political or material, was not the predominant subject of Enlightenment political theory. This is true even of Rousseau, who was far more preoccupied with analysing the effects of the civilizing process on mankind than on eradicating social inequalities.

See also FEMINISM, RIGHTS.

Janet Todd and Marilyn Butler (eds), *The Works of Mary Wollstonecraft*, vol. 5: *A Vindication of the Rights of Men; A Vindication of the Rights of Woman* (London: William Pickering, 1989).

SYLVANA TOMASELLI

Estates General   France's national representative body under the *ancien régime*, the Estates General comprised delegates of the three estates (or orders) of the realm: the First Estate (clergy), the Second Estate (the nobility) and the THIRD ESTATE (the remainder of society). Its origins lay in the fourteenth century, though before the financial crisis in 1788–9 it had remained unconvened since 1614. There was uncertainty even in government about the procedures the assembly should adopt in 1789. In December 1788 it was agreed that the Third Estate should have numerical parity with the other two orders combined, but the question of voting procedures was unresolved. The decision to opt for voting by order when the estates met sparked opposition in the Third Estate which risked being outvoted by the two 'privileged orders'. Louis XVI's attempts to shake free from the resultant political deadlock triggered the Third Estate into declaring itself on 17 June the NATIONAL ASSEMBLY. The crisis was resolved after the storming of the Bastille on 14 July, when Louis XVI finally agreed to the remodelled Estates General functioning as the CONSTITUENT ASSEMBLY.

William Doyle, *Origins of the French Revolution* (Oxford: Oxford University Press, 1980).

COLIN JONES

Eugene of Savoy [François Eugène de Savoie Carignan] (1663–1736)   Austrian general. Austria owed its great territorial gains in the early eighteenth century, in large part, to his skill. The youngest son of a member of the royal house of Savoy, he was born and brought up in France but his attempts to enter French military service were rejected and he was advised to become a priest. Encouraged by his anti-French mother, he followed his brother into Austrian military service. A brilliant and inventive commander, he rose rapidly during the Turkish and French wars of the 1680s and 1690s, becoming a field marshal at the age of 32. In 1703 he was appointed head of the Aulic War Council, which administered Austria's forces, and carried through major reforms. He was an important member of the reforming 'Young Party' around Leopold I's son Joseph during the emperor's last years. He was also an able diplomat and a leading member of the Austrian government. At the faction-ridden court of Charles VI he faced jealousy and plots to discredit him but he survived them. He was remembered in popular memory as 'the noble knight'.

D. McKay, *Prince Eugene of Savoy* (London: 1977).

MICHAEL HUGHES

Euler, Leonhard (1707–1783)   Swiss mathematician. A prolific writer and energetic administrator who applied his skills in many fields, he was obviously gifted from childhood. In 1727 he was recruited by the newly organized Academy of Sciences at St Petersburg, where he published extensively about his discoveries in mathematical analysis, the theory of numbers and mechanics. He also served on committees investigating geographical, navigational and technological topics. Already internationally famous, in 1741 he went to Berlin, where, while simultaneously maintaining many Russian commitments, he expanded the Academy into a prestigious organization. Continuing his research into various problems of mathematical physics, including planetary motion, hydrodynamics, optics, electricity and magnetism, he also gave advice on the state lotteries, insurance and demographics, and ballistics. He was publicly involved in controversial philosophical and scientific debates, and his extremely popular introductory text on natural philosophy, written in the form of letters, was translated into many languages. In 1766 increasing friction with the king caused him to return to St Petersburg, where he continued to work intensively even after becoming blind.

Jeremy Gray, 'Leonhard Euler 1707–1783', *Janus*, 72 (1985), 171–92.

PATRICIA FARA

Evangelical Awakening   *see* GREAT AWAKENING.

Evangelicalism   There was a revival movement within late-eighteenth-century ANGLICANISM, in reaction against prevailing rational Latitudinarianism. Many forces were at work in eighteenth-century England for religious renewal including, of course, METHODISM, which began within the Church of England before being driven out. The spiritual awakening most permanently associated with Anglicanism is called the Evangelical movement. Drawing obliquely on John Wesley and his brother Charles, and on the lives and writings of earlier advocates of spiritual regeneration, notably William Law (1686–1761), the Evangelicals embraced an Arminian theology that set special store by personal faith and conversion experience. They developed modes of faith characterized by impassioned (but highly controlled) inner emotional intensity rather than by an intricate theology. The Evangelical revival involved eminent churchmen, conspicuously Thomas Clarkson (1760–1846), but many of its leading lights were laymen: William WILBERFORCE; Henry Thornton (1760–1815); Zachary Macaulay (1768–1838), father of the Victorian historian; and T. B. Macaulay (1800–59). These latter formed a circle of wealthy professional Anglicans (several were bankers) known, from their domicile, as the 'Clapham Sect'. Such activists aimed to translate spiritual Christianity into pious and practical ways of life. They declared war on aristocratic and plebeian vice alike, condemning drunkenness, sexual promiscuity and cruel sports, and advocating the life of sober, do-gooding rectitude nowadays popularly associated with middle-class Victorian respectability. Clarkson and Wilberforce, particularly, put their Evangelical convictions to the service of the movement to end the slave trade and to emancipate slaves.

F. K. Brown, *Fathers of the Victorians: The Age of Wilberforce* (Cambridge: Cambridge University Press, 1961).

Boyd Hilton, *The Age of Atonement: The Influence of Evangelicalism on Social and Economic Thought, 1750–1865* (Oxford: Clarendon, 1988).

ROY PORTER

evil/theodicy Ancient problems of trying to defend the goodness and omnipotence of God against objections arising from the existence of moral evil and human pain were given a new impetus in the philosophy of the Enlightenment. The word 'theodicy' (literally the justification of God) was first used by G. W. Leibniz in the title of a book published in 1710. In general terms, the Augustinian explanation of evil in the dogma of original sin was antithetical to Enlightenment humanism and scepticism.

Answers to this old dilemma varied from the OPTIMISM of Leibniz, Shaftesbury and Pope to the complex realism of Voltaire who accepted both the reality of evil and its apparently indissoluble relationship with more agreeable human aspirations and attributes (*see* PESSIMISM). In the writings of Rousseau the problem of evil became less a metaphysical puzzle and more a human problem rooted in political and social ethics, and therefore more amenable to human solution. Such intellectual developments need to be held in tension with a resurgent populist belief in original sin and divine grace in the GREAT AWAKENING and with the complex handling of evil in the popular beliefs and practices of the uneducated (*see* DEMONOLOGY).

E. Cassirer, *The Philosophy of the Enlightenment* (Princeton, NJ: University Press, 1951).

DAVID HEMPTON

evolutionism   Before nineteenth-century Darwinism, many theories had been proposed which implied that living beings had, historically and hereditarily, developed according to a natural, progressive process that may be called evolutionism. Buffon, for example, disregarded fixed artificial classification schemes of the natural world like that of Linnaeus which were founded on minute differences between species. Instead, he claimed the likenesses between all living beings provided a natural order from which interrelationships within the natural world may be ascertained. Erasmus DARWIN, the intellectual and hereditary forebear of Charles Darwin (1809–82), claimed that the appearance of species, as a result of their adjustment to external environmental influences, had changed over time. Others claimed that external influences produced adaptive, progressive affects on the mind (Locke), embryology (Maupertuis) and human anatomy (Blumenbach). Theories of directional, adaptive change were also espoused by progressive-minded French Enlightenment thinkers including Condorcet, who held to an uninterrupted history of progressive humanity, and Diderot, who believed that nature was constantly undergoing universal change. Response to environmental change was also central to Lamarck's pre-Darwinian explanation of the mutability and 'degradations' seen in a variety of living, organic beings.

P. J. Bowler, *Evolution: The History of an Idea* (Berkeley, Calif.: University of California Press, 1984).

B. Glass (ed.), *Forerunners of Darwin, 1745–1859* (Baltimore, Md.: Johns Hopkins University Press, 1968).

PHILIP K. WILSON

experimental method   Some of the most influential models for how SCIENCE should be conducted, bequeathed by the seventeenth century, were based on experimentation. Even if this claim had at times been more rhetorical than real, the notion was influential in an age that sought to eschew the constraints of traditional authority; experiment was potentially available to all, and could be seen as the unbiased arbiter in sterile disputes or the safeguard against dogmatic systems. As Newtonian came to replace Aristotelian and Cartesian views, Newtonian experimental practice and rhetoric established a widespread methodological consensus. The consensus even permeated society more generally, for lectures based on experimental demonstration became fashionable, and popular books of Newtonian natural philosophy were published with great success in England, France and the Netherlands. This fashionable activity was scarcely an instance of experimental method, for the well-rehearsed demonstrations formed an established repertoire of scientific theatre – no item of natural philosophical theory was at stake in these performances. However they do indicate a widespread assent to the notion of the experimental foundation of natural knowledge. It is ironic that the most impressive achievements of the Newtonian programme in the eighteenth century – for example in planetary theory – were mathematical rather than experimental, and that in chemistry, for example, the most influential developments involved importing quantification into a practice that had been experimentally based for centuries.

T. L. Hankins, *Science and the Enlightenment* (Cambridge: Cambridge University Press, 1985).

J. A. BENNETT

exploration   Eighteenth-century exploration was distinguished by five main features: it was inspired by renewed public interest in new lands, which was reflected in the popularity of books on travel and discovery; it manifested a link between science and navigation which made seaborne discovery more technical and safe; it saw Britain take the lead in maritime discovery; it saw the destruction of some of the most persistent geographical myths of the *ancien régime*; and its emphasis on the Pacific projected that ocean and its inhabitants on to the European imagination.

The publication of Dampier's (1652–1715) *New Voyage round the World* (1697) and *A Voyage to New Holland* (1703–9) inaugurated a new era of both official and public interest in discovery. Fictional accounts such as Swift's *Gulliver's Travels* and Defoe's *Robinson Crusoe* enlivened the imagination of the reading public, creating a receptive environment for the geographical theorists with proposals for voyages of discovery. Political economist and historian John Campbell (1708–75) argued in 1744–8 for government-sponsored expeditions to search out both the NORTH-WEST PASSAGE and the SOUTHERN CONTINENT, since the discovery of these would stimulate British commerce. The Frenchman Charles de Brosses (1709–77) was one of the most articulate advocates for the search for the southern continent, arguing in *Histoire des navigations aux terres australes* (1756) that such an endeavour would be more profitable to France than costly European wars. Later, antiquary John Callander (*d* 1789) and hydrographer Alexander Dalrymple (1737–1808) sought to stimulate British government interest in such a quest.

In the course of the eighteenth century there were steady if undramatic changes in the practices of seafaring and navigation which aided the process of exploration. For the most part these changes derived from a more scientific approach to seamanship, aided by the development of more accurate navigational instruments. Foremost among these was the solution to the problem of determining longitude at sea, which was accomplished with the development of accurate and reliable chronometers (*see* MEASUREMENT OF LONGITUDE), and Maskelyne's (1732–1811) perfection of accurate astronomical tables. There were no fundamental innovations in hull design or rigging, but the use of copper sheathing for ships extended their capacity to operate between refits and provided greater speed. Towards the end of the century the devastating consequences of scurvy on long voyages were brought under control through better shipboard management and the use of fresh fruits and vegetables. In a more general sense, the example of Captain Cook served as a model for the way in which maritime exploration should be conducted.

Although French trappers and *coureurs des bois* (forest traders) contributed most to the land-based exploration of North America in the first half of the eighteenth century and Russian explorers in the same period opened up eastern Siberia, it was British travellers who contributed most to eighteenth-century exploration. While European exploration of AFRICA was in abeyance for most of the century, between 1769 and 1773 the travels of James Bruce (1730–94) in Ethiopia and Egypt re-enlivened interest. The African Association coordinated the British effort after 1788 and was concentrated on the north and west with the expeditions of Lucas (*fl* 1789), Hornemann (1772–1801) and PARK. In central and southern Africa the most remarkable expedition was that of the little-known Portuguese doctor Francisco José de Lacerda (1753–98), who travelled up the Zambesi River in 1798 from Mozambique to Lake Mweru on the present border between Tanzania and Zaïre.

The main focus of eighteenth-century exploration was on the Pacific, and, to a lesser extent, the Arctic. To some degree the PACIFIC represented the last great unknown – a vast expanse only tentatively penetrated by the European world before 1700. It also contained the possibility of holding the last great unclaimed land mass – the elusive southern continent – and the possibility of an open sea route through to China. These two great objects, along with commercial and strategic motives, were behind the majority of eighteenth-century voyages in the Pacific from Roggeveen (1659–1729) to VANCOUVER. Although interest in Pacific exploration was strong from the beginning of the eighteenth century, it was from the end of the Seven Years War in 1763 that momentum picked up. In a forty-year period French, Spanish and, above all, British explorers stripped away its remaining mysteries and mapped its furthest recesses. In the voyages of CARTERET, LA PEROUSE, Malaspina (1754–1809), Vancouver and above all James Cook the eighteenth century witnessed triumphs of exploration unequalled even by the Tudor navigators.

J. C. Beaglehole, *The Exploration of the Pacific* (London: A. & C. Black, 1966).
J. H. Parry, *Trade and Dominion* (London: Weidenfeld & Nicolson, 1971).

DAVID MACKAY

F

factories There is no agreed definition for 'factories'; they were seen in the eighteenth century as textile mills which centralized previously dispersed production processes (*see* DOMESTIC INDUSTRY). These mills could include a power source connected to machinery, but not necessarily. The size and organization of factories varied enormously from sheds bringing together several handloom weavers in the woollen industry, and the cotton factory of Cheadle Hulme in 1777 which contained two carding-engines and six jennies, to the New Lanark spinning-mill which employed 1,600 to 1,700 in 1816. The Derby silk mill in 1719 contained machinery driven by a complex maze of gearings fed by one large water-wheel. It employed 200 hands, mostly children. The mills to accommodate Arkwright's water frame from 1769 were built to contain 1,000 spindle frames, and were the first great cotton factories. If technology was not the deciding feature, then centralized and hierarchical management, division of labour and labour discipline were. The factory brought together capitalist ownership with direct managerial control of the production process.

Contemporaries in the eighteenth and early nineteenth centuries perceived the factory system in terms of power, machinery and large-scale production with an unskilled labour force. They debated over its social effects, and tried to curb the exploitation of factory labour in a series of Factory Acts.

See also MACHINES, TEXTILES.

M. Berg, *The Age of Manufactures*, second edn (London: Routledge, 1994).

MAXINE BERG

Fahrenheit, Gabriel Daniel (1686–1736) German physicist. Born in Danzig, he became a scientific-instrument maker in Amsterdam. Although his significant designs included a hypsometer and a hydrometer, he is best remembered for his most important work – a standard thermometric scale. There was a recognized need for such a scale, for without it readings taken from the arbitrary divisions of one thermometer could not be compared with measurements with any other. Fahrenheit took his lower fixed point, which he called 32 degrees, as the temperature of a mixture of ice and water, and the upper (96 degrees) as the temperature of the normal human body. The resulting interval of 64 degrees could be divided into single degrees by repeated bisection. He published a value of 212 degrees as the boiling point of water on his scale, and when this figure, which is a little too high, was subsequently used as the upper fixed point, normal body temperature became 98.6 degrees.

W. E. Knowles Middleton, *A History of the Thermometer and its Use in Meteorology* (Baltimore, Md.: Johns Hopkins University Press, 1966).

J. A. BENNETT

Falkland Islands The explorer John Strong gave the South Atlantic islands their English name in 1689, while the French claimed discovery by ships from St Malo, hence their name 'Iles Malouines', in Spanish the Islas Malvinas. Spain claimed exclusive rights over the whole hemisphere, and though in 1764 a French settlement was established on East Falkland, it was yielded to the Spanish in 1767. In 1765 a British naval base, Port Egmont, was set up on West Falkland, garrisoned in 1766. On 10 June 1770 a Spanish naval force compelled this garrison to quit the island. For a while, as Samuel Johnson commented, European peace was in danger 'for a few spots of earth, which, in the deserts of the ocean, had almost escaped human notice' (*Thoughts on the Late Transactions respecting Falkland's Islands*, 1771). The British ministry threatened war and began raising a fleet. Spain failed to get naval help from France, and on 22 January 1771 Spain and Britain concluded an agreement. Spanish sovereignty was restated, but the British garrison was restored, subject to a verbal agreement that it would later be abandoned, which, ostensibly on grounds of cost, it was in 1775.

N. Tracy, 'The Falklands Islands Crisis of 1770: Use of Naval Force', *English Historical Review*, 90 (1975), 40–75.

PHILIP WOODFINE

families The eighteenth century is held by some historians to have witnessed significant changes in family life. These changes, however, are largely attitudinal and concern the emotional bonds within families rather than more tangible questions of structure and internal composition. Debate on the European family centres less on questions of family or household structure (which altered little in this period), or on composition and size (which changed only slowly), and more on the nature of marital relations, on attitudes to children, on the relative importance attached to the conjugal family and on the sexual division of labour.

Particularly influential has been the work of historians who see the family becoming a more private and domestic institution, with relationships between its members being more 'affective' and less calculating or mercenary. Lawrence Stone has argued that the eighteenth century witnessed, among the social elite of eighteenth-century England, the arrival of the 'closed domesticated nuclear family', in which the patriarchal power of the husband was tempered by close and companionate relations with the wife, and greater emphasis was placed than before on individual personal aspirations. Families became more self-contained and less influenced by neighbours and relatives. This new family type was marked out by mate selection 'determined more by free choice than by parental decision', on grounds of love and affection rather than financial considerations. Child-rearing became more permissive and considerate rather than a brutal suppression of what was considered to be the child's innate sinfulness. Accompanying this change in family sentiment was a new emphasis on sexual fulfilment, within and outside marriage. Stone conceded that changes in familial behaviour occurred only very slowly among particular social groups.

Stone's thesis has been criticized widely. Some argue that evidence for affectionate and romantic relationships from earlier periods had been ignored, that literary evidence deployed was misleading and that demographic statistics were misinterpreted. Especially unconvincing was Stone's notion that 'the omnipresence of death coloured affective relations at all levels of society, by reducing the amount of emotional capital available for prudent investment in any single individual'. After all, it was claimed that attitudinal changes had taken place when there had not been any significant improvement in mortality rates in eighteenth-century Britain. Moreover, the new family type was supposed to have developed first among wealthy city merchants and tradesmen in the late seventeenth century, yet recent work has highlighted the very high mortality rates of urban centres in this period, as well as identifying unusually materialistic marriage markets, where courtship was dominated by financial rather than emotional concerns.

Other historians have similarly seen changes in the eighteenth-century family. Edward Shorter has argued for a shift in the eighteenth century from a basically calculative and emotionally attenuated peasant family life to one in which individual emotional ties and bonds became more important. For Shorter, as for Stone, the family was seen as becoming a more discrete and private entity, with growing interest and concern for child care and development and new freedom of individual expression in emotional and sexual relationships. As with Stone's view of family life, however, much of this work has been criticized on the grounds of misuse of literary evidence and unwarranted inferences from demographic statistics. Recent work on parent–child relations has stressed the continuity in attitudes to children and has tended to play down the incidence of corporal punishment in the early modern home. There is considerable evidence, too, that many of the European peasantry retained a calculative attitude to courtship well into the nineteenth century.

The determinants of family behaviour are also unclear. Some have argued that the eighteenth century saw industrial and economic changes that altered the family economy, thus affecting the relationships and behaviour of its members. Industrialization and urbanization is sometimes believed to have broken down the family's role as a productive unit and increased opportunities for working outside the home. The growth of capitalist relations eroded communal restraints on sexual behaviour and inspired a desire, according to Shorter, for freer sexual expression. The growth of wage labour is said to have freed the young from the parental control over their choice of partners exercised by virtue of their control over the family property. Others have identified the declining influence of the church over aspects of family life as conducive to significant behavioural change. Recent work, however, has questioned many of these causative factors. Working outside the home was experienced by many family members well before industrialization. In early-eighteenth-century London only about 10 per cent of working wives complemented the trade of their husbands, questioning the notion that the urban family was ever a self-contained productive unit. (*See* DOMESTIC INDUSTRY.)

There is some evidence of change in family life in the eighteenth century. It may well be, for example, that the English social elite experienced more companionate and friendly relations between the sexes than their social counterparts in eighteenth-century Europe. One contemporary observer reported that three-quarters of middle- and upper-class marriages were based on companionship and friendship in England but this formed a minority in France. Moreover, recent work has identified a decline in the incidence of remarriage in parts of Germany, attributable to changes in attitudes rather than to alterations in survival chances. Similarly, divorce petitions heard in American courts began stressing the emotional content of relationships in the late eighteenth century, another sign that some genuine changes in the accepted ideal of family relations may have been occurring. The dictionary definitions of the very word 'family' in the later eighteenth century increasingly emphasized the conjugal couple and their children rather than an institution consisting of servants or a wider kinship group. Despite such evidence, however, many historians believe that there has been little fundamental change in family relationships and attitudes since well before the eighteenth century.

See also CHILDREN, HOUSEHOLD STRUCTURE, MARRIAGE.

M. Anderson, *Approaches to the History of the Western Family* (London: Macmillan, 1980).

R. Houlbrooke, *The English Family 1450–1700* (London: Longman, 1984).

M. Mitterauer and R. Sieder, *The European Family* (Chicago: University of Chicago Press, 1982).

L. Stone, *The Family, Sex and Marriage in England, 1500–1800* (London: Weidenfeld & Nicolson, 1977).

JEREMY BOULTON

Family Compact (1733, 1743, 1761)   Three secret engagements between the Bourbon dynasties of France and Spain were called Family Compacts. The first was really an expression of common aims, signed early in the WAR OF THE POLISH SUCCESSION, on 7 November 1733. Louis XV and Philip V promised eternal friendship and mutual aid in their future schemes: Spain would help France against Britain, and France would help Spain to regain territories in Italy. The second compact was aimed against England, and signed during the WAR OF THE AUSTRIAN SUCCESSION, on 25 October 1743. It included a secret agreement to mount an invasion to restore the Pretender. The third Family Compact, signed on 15 August 1761 between Louis XV and Charles III, was drawn up at the nadir of French fortunes in the SEVEN YEARS WAR. In an accompanying secret agreement, Spain agreed to enter the war by 1 May 1762, and both the powers' grievances and claims were merged. Militarily the compact was a failure, but closer national cooperation did result, though Spain wanted colonial defence against Britain, while France wanted a more aggressive alliance. Until 1790, in the aftermath of the French Revolution, the two powers had few subjects of dispute, and presented a united front to European diplomats.

J. Lynch, *Bourbon Spain* (Oxford: Blackwell, 1989).

PHILIP WOODFINE

famine   Death from starvation became increasingly rare in eighteenth-century Europe. Serious famines occurred in many countries in 1693–4, 1709–10 and 1740–1 but thereafter famines were experienced only at a local level. Sweden suffered exceptional loss of life as late as 1772, parts of Spain in 1809, Switzerland and southern Germany in 1816 and Ireland as late as the 1840s. By contrast, the last significant famine in England occurred in 1622–3. Explaining the escape from famine has not proved straightforward. The English experience suggests that improving agricultural productivity, more integrated and efficient marketing and transport systems, rising real income and more effective welfare policies played a large part. In the European context less destructive warfare and the introduction of the POTATO were also important.

Most deaths in famine years were caused by diseases such as dysentery rather than by hunger, and those most at risk were those who lacked purchasing power to buy food. Recent work has underlined the fact that flight from famine areas provoked increases in death rates, as rural refugees were exposed to urban diseases to which they lacked immunity.

J. Walter and R. Schofield (eds), *Famine, Disease and the Social Order in Early Modern Society* (Cambridge: Cambridge University Press, 1989).

JEREMY BOULTON

Farmers General   The Farmers General was a syndicate of forty financiers who leased the right to collect indirect taxes from the French crown on a six-year basis. They were the most powerful members of a larger network of tax farmers who collected government revenue at all levels, drawing a profit from the sums collected (*see* TAX FARMING). This practice grew up in the course of the eighteenth century, but intensified rapidly. The opposite of this system was the *régie*, when taxes were collected by royal officials who did not draw a profit, which was what most ministers preferred, but the farmers proved too powerful to oust, as one controller, d'Ormesson (1751–1808), found in 1783 when he tried to convert the *Ferme* into a *régie* and soon lost office. In 1785 they reached the height of their power when they built a ten-foot-high wall around Paris to prevent evasion of their tolls. The farmers were efficient in raising taxes, but they charged the government a high commission for their work. The general hatred they inspired throughout French society is well attested to, but this did not prevent many of them acquiring noble status or marrying into the aristocracy. Their ruthlessness produced widespread smuggling to avoid their duties on commodities.

Many of their most hated duties, such as those on wine, salt and tobacco, were abolished early in the Revolution and the Farmers General was abolished in March 1791, its functions reverting to the civil service.

J. F. Bosher, *French Finances, 1770–1795* (London: Cambridge University Press, 1970).

MICHAEL BROERS

farming *see* AGRICULTURE, EUROPEAN.

feeling *see* SENTIMENT.

Feijoo, Benito Jerónimo (1676–1764)   Spanish Benedictine monk and scholar, commonly regarded as the father of the Spanish Enlightenment. His career as professor of theology at the University of Oviedo (Asturias) spanned four reigns. An avid reader of foreign books (mainly in their French versions), he began at the age of 50 to produce his seminal writings. Through the nine volumes of his *Teatro crítico* (1726–39) and the five of his *Cartas eruditas* (1742–60), he reached a Spanish public in the early eighteenth century to whom he introduced Newtonian science and a spirit of criticism of superstition. His work provoked considerable attacks and controversy, but in 1750 Ferdinand VI prohibited any further attacks on his works, which were declared to enjoy royal favour. He continued writing till 1759 and died five years later, aged 88. His work as an early diffuser of the Enlightenment was complemented by other writers in the mid-century, notably Mayans y Siscar, but he enjoyed unrivalled popularity among the elite, and numerous editions of his works were issued in the generation after his death.

Richard Herr, *The Eighteenth-Century Revolution in Spain* (Princeton, NJ: Princeton University Press, 1958).

HENRY KAMEN

feminism   Though 'feminism' is a rather recent term, the movement it refers to was well under way by the eighteenth century. There was in that century no single unified answer to the question of WOMEN; no more so than there is a single twentieth-century feminist critique of society and its treatment of women. The condition of women was a subject that many eighteenth-century women and men addressed in earnest. Many works pleaded their case for greater independence and for better education; some writers, especially those, like Olympe de Gouge (1755–93), Théroigne de Méricourt (1762–1817), Condorcet and Mary Wollstonecraft, who were writing in the context of the French Revolution, argued for the necessity of granting them full citizenship. If by feminism one means a discourse which tackles the issues of EQUALITY and difference in the relations between the sexes, then such a discourse was one of the important strands of the Enlightenment.

What must be remembered when approaching the subject, is that the idea of eighteenth-century women is as meaningless as that of twentieth-century women. The condition of women varied to an enormous extent depending on their rank, wealth and nationality. Generally speaking, women outside Europe were deemed to live under far more oppressive conditions than European women. Among the so-called 'savages', the lives of women were thought to be almost, if not altogether, intolerable and the reports of travellers to South America describing how mothers killed their daughters at birth to spare them from the tyranny of men exerted an important influence on the European perception of the history of women. Similarly, the condition of women in the Middle and Far East tended to be conceived as one of unmitigated slavery. However, some writers were far more discerning in their judgements. When Lady Mary Wortley Montagu travelled through Europe and in the Middle East, she was struck by the differences which prevailed even within the very small elite of Austrian, German, French and English aristocratic women, and was able to appreciate the unexpected freedom which the veil afforded Eastern women, having herself adorned one. She noted with amazement the power which Viennese noblewomen held, thanks to their financial independence from their husbands. As for French aristocratic women, everyone was agreed that they enjoyed a degree of liberty known only to men elsewhere in the world.

The alleged licentiousness, idleness and futile accomplishments of aristocratic women came under fire in the writings of Mary Wollstonecraft and Elizabeth Hamilton (1758–1816). Far from seeing the sexual freedom which some women had as a step towards emancipation, Wollstonecraft and like-minded theorists joined the ranks of Rousseau and his followers in their attacks on the wantonness of the sex. Under Rousseau's influence, they saw the power which *salon* women exercised in a negative light (*see* SALONS), and chose instead to defend the sex against his accusations by claiming that only *some* women were, as he contended, failing in their duties as mothers, and by arguing that if women were adequately educated (and not just left to read novels, which Wollstonecraft thought, generally speaking, to be detrimental to a moral upbringing) as well as given the same RIGHTS as men, they would no more deviate from the path of civic virtue than men.

To understand why the debate about women assumed the form it did in the eighteenth century, it is important not to lose sight of the fact that women (and men who elected to side with them) were by and large on the defensive when they wrote about themselves. In other words, they did not so much rail against the tyranny of men and the inequities of their situation as seek to prove, in response to the charges brought against the sex, that they were the equal of men in intelligence, virtue, courage and moderation. Thus, following on from the battles of the previous two or three centuries about women, a good part of Enlightenment feminism centred around minimizing the difference between women and men, and, on that basis, the demand for more or less extensive rights to EDUCATION, property, CITIZENSHIP and so on. Those who sought to come to terms with the question of the difference between the sexes tended to do so by trying to understand the origins of this difference in historical terms, and endeavoured to produce a history of woman to match the history of man which was so crucial to the period's political philosophy. Such histories described how the condition of women improved with the end of the state of nature and the growth of civilization.

Ruth Perry, *The Celebrated Mary Astell: An Early English Feminist* (Chicago: University of Chicago Press, 1986).
François Poulain de la Barre, *The Equality of the Sexes*, trans. and ed. Desmond M. Clarke (Manchester: Manchester University Press, 1990).
Elisabeth Roudinesco, *Théroigne de Méricourt: A Melancholic Woman during the French Revolution*, trans. Martin Thom (London: Verso, 1991).
Mary Lyndon Shanley and Carole Pateman (eds), *Feminist Interpretations and Political Theory* (Cambridge: Polity, 1991).
Sylvana Tomaselli, 'Reflections on the History of the Science of Woman', *History of Science*, 29 (June 1991), 185–205.

SYLVANA TOMASELLI

Fénelon, François de Salignac de la Mothe (1651–1715) French clergyman and writer who made a significant contribution to the political and pedagogical thinking of his day. In 1689 he was appointed tutor to Louis XIV's eldest grandson, the duke of Burgundy, and continued to exercise a great influence over the prince until the latter's premature death in 1712. However, he lost the king's favour in 1695 so that his appointment to the archiepiscopal see of Cambrai marked less a preferment than the beginning of an exile. Later he suffered a further disgrace as a result of his connection with the Quietist movement, and he never regained his earlier public reputation.

His writings include a treatise on the education of girls, and a number of other works which, directly or indirectly, reveal his political beliefs, the best-known among them being *Les aventures de Télémaque* (The Adventures of Télémaque, 1690). Fénelon opposed despotic government as the negation of the rule of law, and on foreign-policy matters in particular his criticisms were clearly directed against Louis XIV. He was a moderate rather than a radical reformer who strongly supported the nobility's role as a defence against royal arbitrariness.

Nannerl O. Keohane, *Philosophy and the State in France* (Princeton, NJ: Princeton University Press, 1980).

J. H. SHENNAN

Ferdinand IV (1751–1825) King of Naples (1759–99, 1799–1806, 1815–16); king of Sicily (1759–1816), as Ferdinand III; King of the Two Sicilies (1816–25), as Ferdinand I. He assumed power in 1767 and until 1776 his government was dominated by TANUCCI. This period was marked by largely unsuccessful attempts through legal reforms to curb the power of the feudal baronage and of the church. Tanucci was followed in power by John Acton (1736–1811), a man of Franco-Irish origin who was appointed on the advice of the queen, Maria Caroline (1752–1814). The 1780s were an active if ill co-ordinated period of reform both on the mainland, where it was led by FILANGIERI, Grimbaldi and other pupils of GENOVESI, and in Sicily where it centred on Caracciolo (1752–99), the governor-general. The French invasion of Italy in 1794 saw Ferdinand reverse all these policies, depose most of the reformers and sanction a reactionary policy throughout the 1790s. Briefly driven into exile in Sicily by the French and their Jacobin supporters in 1799, Ferdinand supported a ruthless reconquest of the mainland directed by the queen and Cardinal Ruffo (1744–1827). Until he was again deposed by the French in 1806, he pursued a vindictive, reactionary course. The period 1806–15 was spent in Sicily where his traditional, centralizing policies brought the court into conflict with the Sicilian baronage and the British. Restored only in 1815, after Murat's support for Napoleon in the Hundred Days, he now showed great restraint, retaining many of the men and measures of the period of French rule. His chief minister, Dei Medici, balanced this with a continued belief in centralized absolutism and a refusal to grant a constitution, which led to a revolution by liberal army officers in 1820–1. Restored to power by Austrian arms, Ferdinand ruled until his death in 1825.

S. J. Woolf, *A History of Italy, 1700–1860* (London: Methuen, 1979).

MICHAEL BROERS

Ferdinand VI (1713–1759) king of Spain (1746–59). He played no active role in the government of his country, which was occupied throughout his reign in resisting English aggression in both Europe and the colonies. He had the good fortune to be served by able ministers, notably Zenón de Somodevilla, marqués de Ensenada (1702–81), who from service in the military administration rose to become chief secretary of state (1743–54). His term in office was, however, balanced by the appointment in 1746 as secretary of state of José de Carvajal, scion of old nobility and supported by noble interests. Carvajal believed in a rapprochement with England, which he carried through in 1750; after his death in 1754 his policies were continued by the Irishman Ricardo Wall. Ensenada, whose lasting historical monument is the great survey (*catastro*) of Castile carried out in 1749, was removed from power in 1754, shortly after Carvajal's death, as a result of English intrigues. In 1758 Ferdinand's wife, Bárbara of Braganza died; the king was deeply affected, and died mad the next year.

John Lynch, *Bourbon Spain 1700–1808* (Oxford: Blackwell, 1989).

HENRY KAMEN

Ferdinand VII (1784–1833)   king of Spain (1808, 1814–33). He played a crucial part in the downfall of the old regime in his country, at the time balanced between the pretensions of England and of revolutionary France. Heir to his reigning father, Charles IV (1784–1819), the prince was bitterly opposed to the chief minister Godoy (1767–1851) and led numerous plots against the throne (1807). English success over the Franco-Spanish navy at Trafalgar (1805) induced both Godoy and Ferdinand to place their hopes in Napoleon. In March 1808 a palace revolution ('the riot of Aranjuez') obliged Charles IV to sack Godoy and abdicate in favour of his son; but the change was short-lived and in May Ferdinand was obliged to hand back the crown, which his father then ceded to Napoleon. During the subsequent period of uprisings against the French, Ferdinand remained as a national symbol, the 'desired one' (el Deseado). He returned as king in 1814, after the Napoleonic period, and restored an absolutist regime which changed its character from year to year and most decisively after the liberal revolution of 1820, which was followed by the emergence of the influential conservative Carlist movement.

Raymond Carr, *Spain 1808–1939* (Oxford: Oxford University Press, 1966). John Lynch, *Bourbon Spain 1700–1808* (Oxford: Blackwell, 1989).

HENRY KAMEN

Ferguson, Adam (1723–1816)   Leading social philosopher of the Scottish Enlightenment. He enjoyed a long life and a varied career. Born at Logierait in Perthshire, he was educated at the University of St Andrews and became deputy chaplain of the Black Watch regiment, fighting at the Battle of Fontenoy in 1745. In 1754 he abandoned the church for the world of letters, succeeding David Hume as librarian to the Edinburgh faculty of advocates. In 1759 he was appointed professor of natural philosophy at Edinburgh University, five years later transferring to the moral philosophy chair. His chief work was the *Essay on the History of Civil Society* (1767), though his *History of the Progress and Termination of the Roman Republic* (1783) and his *Principles of Moral and Political Science* (1792) – both developing themes first stated in the *Essay* – also proved highly popular. Ferguson was an analyst of social evolution, tracing the various stages of civil development from savagery to commercial society. Repudiating the notion of a fixed human nature, he traced the interlinkage of economic, social, political and psycho-cultural development. Emotionally attached to the Highlands, Ferguson believed that 'progress' entailed loss as well as gain: traditional society had possessed valuable community ties that the rise of capitalism dissolved. Ferguson is also remembered for championing the method known as 'conjectural history', the rational reconstruction of what must logically have happened in the past in the absence of empirical data. Many have thus seen him as the father of sociology.

W. C. Lehmann, *Adam Ferguson and the Beginning of Modern Sociology* (New York: Columbia University Press, 1930).

ROY PORTER

feudalism The system of government that prevailed in Europe during the Middle Ages, and which was based on the relation of lord and vassal arising out of holding land in feud was described at some length by Adam Smith in his university lectures and used as a contrast to modern commercial societies in the *Wealth of Nations*. In his lectures on jurisprudence, for instance, he examined the feudal system of inheritance and traced the origins of primogeniture; he noted how feudal customs had been significant in shaping contemporary libel law. More generally, he showed how the allodial form of government, the first form of government in western Europe following the fall of the Roman Empire, was replaced by the feudal one, and how the latter in turn came to an end.

Among the most salient differences between feudal and opulent European nations was the extent to which modern agriculture required capital investment. In contrast, Smith argued, 'during the prevalency of the feudal government, a very small portion of the produce was sufficient to replace the capital employed in cultivation. It consisted commonly in a few wretched cattle, maintained altogether by the spontaneous produce of uncultivated land, and which might, therefore, be considered as part of that spontaneous product.' The same applied in manufactures, which required very little capital in feudal times. Along with other Enlightenment writers, Smith thought of the feudal age as a period of great internal strife and maintained that even after the introduction of feudal subordination, the king was incapable of restraining the violence of feudal lords, and described the 'open country' as 'a scene of violence, rapine, and disorder' which only 'the silent and insensible operation of foreign commerce and manufactures' could and did bring to an end.

Whether feudalism was peculiar to European history has been the subject of debate since the eighteenth century. Montesquieu thought so, whereas Voltaire thought it was the prevalent form of government throughout the world. Though the term 'feudalism' is often used by Europeans to describe political relations outside Europe, it often requires so many qualifications as to be useless in most contexts. Thus, whatever the seeming similarities between decentralized governmental power in Europe and that in the Middle East, the status of vassal in Europe, for instance, had no true equivalent in the latter. Though it was possible, as Ira M. Lapidus has remarked, for a governor to be a personal dependent of the sultan, 'The vassal was a free man who contracted his dependency, while dependents in the Muslim world were slaves or freedmen.' Nor was an iqta' identical to a fief. The former did not, for example, confer legal rights and privileges, and the status of its holder was not related to LANDOWNERSHIP. While the term 'feudal' has been used somewhat pejoratively in some writings about Japan where it is employed in contrast to 'modern' or 'democratic', the comparison between the Japanese and the European manorial system is not entirely unfruitful, even if it is not uncontroversial. In Perry Anderson's view, 'The Japanese feudalism which emerged as a developed mode of production from the 14th–15th centuries onwards, after a long period of prior incubation, was characterized by essentially the same essential nexus as European feudalism: the fusion of vassalage, benefice and immunity into a fief system which constituted the basic politico-legal framework in which surplus labour was extracted from the direct producer.'

See also SEIGNEURIALISM.

Perry Anderson, *Lineages of the Absolutist State* (London: Verso, 1984).

Ira M. Lapidus, *A History of Islamic Societies* (Cambridge: Cambridge University Press, 1988).

Adam Smith, *Lectures on Jurisprudence*, ed. R. L. Meek, D. D. Raphael and P. G. Stein (Oxford: Clarendon, 1978).

SYLVANA TOMASELLI

Fichte, Johann Gottlieb (1762–1814)   German philosopher. He aimed to complete Kant's work, and in effect established a theory of ROMANTICISM. As professor of philosophy at Jena from 1794, he exerted a compelling influence on the younger generation, notably on NOVALIS and HÖLDERLIN, but was driven out in 1799 because of his alleged atheism.

His philosophy, or *Wissenschaftslehre* (Science of Knowledge), written in 1794 and often expanded, was a system of 'subjective idealism' on which he grounded his understanding of nature, society, ethics and religion. According freedom to the subject, his first principle was a primary act (*Thathandlung*) by which 'the Ego originally posits its own self'; conversely, a 'Non-Ego opposes the Ego'. These oppositions unite in a dialectic synthesis, whereby the absolute Ego maintains priority, as a creative being, bringing forth the world in the imagination.

Fichte's social philosophy centred on 'duty'. In politics he was a republican, and supported the French Revolution. Opposed to Napoleon, after the humiliation of Prussia he became active politically, notably with his highly nationalistic *Reden an die Deutsche Nation*

(Addresses to the German Nation, 1808). He was closely involved in university reform and became rector of the new University of Berlin in 1810.

JEREMY ADLER

Fielding, Henry (1707–1754)   English man of letters and novelist. Born into a West Country gentry family, he was educated at Eton before studying law at Leiden. He quickly set up as a London man about town, and from 1728 made a name for himself as the author of lively comic works for the theatre, including *Tom Thumb* (1730) and *Pasquin* (1735). His satires against Walpole provoked the passing of the Licensing Act (1737), which introduced censorship of stage plays by the lord chamberlain. Abandoning the theatre, Fielding returned to the law, being called to the Bar in 1740.

Three pursuits dominated the later stages of a brief career increasingly blighted by drink and illness. He turned to political journalism, embracing a populist, anti-government Toryism in *The Champion* (1739–41), *The True Patriot* (1745–6), the *Jacobite's Journal* (1747–8), and *The Covent Garden Journal* (1752). He became interested in legal issues, serving as a justice and writing on the causes of the mid-century crime wave and the reform of the criminal law, notably in his *Enquiry into Causes of the Late Increase of Robbers* (1751). Above all, he won fame in developing the new genre of the novel. *Tom Jones* (1743) was the age's great epic novel; *Shamela* (1741) and *Joseph Andrews* (1742) mocked the works of Samuel Richardson, *Jonathan Wild* (1743) was a criminal biography, while *Amelia* (1751) was his venture into a more sentimental mode. In painting the comedy of manners with a broad brush Fielding has found few peers.

Pat Rogers, *Henry Fielding: A Biography* (London: Elek, 1979).

ROY PORTER

Filangieri, Gaetano (1752–1788)   Neapolitan writer. Born into an illustrious family, he entered the law in 1774 and was a leading figure of what Franco Venturi has called the 'high summer of the Neapolitan Enlightenment'. In *Political Reflections* (1774) he defended a much opposed royal ordinance whose aim it was to reform legal practice. The first two volumes of his highly acclaimed, as well as virulently attacked, *La scienza della legislazione* (Science of Legislation) appeared in 1780. Writing within the natural law tradition, Filangieri thought himself the first to reduce legislation to 'a certain and regular science', though he professed his admiration for Montesquieu. He argued that 'preservation and tranquillity' were the sole and universal objects of legislation and that laws must not only be just in themselves, but appropriate to the circumstances of each nation, for example its climate and the fertility of its soil. He thought that governments ought not only to remove obstacles to commerce, but to encourage national industries, and see not only to increasing riches, but also to their equitable distribution throughout society; he defended luxury as a means to achieve this. Although true to his faith and emphatic about the role of Christianity in inculcating public and private virtue, he thought the church in no less need of reform than any other institution.

Franco Venturi, *Italy and the Enlightenment: Studies in a Cosmopolitan Century*, ed. Stuart Woolf, trans. Susan Corsi (London: Longman, 1972).

SYLVANA TOMASELLI

finance Britain and France had incurred huge national debts by the beginning of the eighteenth century, caused by the long series of wars between them. From 1715 they initiated similar financial reforms, based on speculation in colonial trade, France through the Louisiana Company and Banque Royale of John LAW, and Britain through the SOUTH SEA COMPANY, supported by Stanhope's (1675–1721) ministry. In both cases it was hoped that the release of credit and an increase in the currency supply would stimulate the economy and reduce the debt. Over-speculation and lack of regulation destroyed both schemes within months; Law's Royal Bank and its paper currency were defunct by 1720, as was the South Sea Company (*see* SOUTH SEA BUBBLE). The responses of the two governments were very different. In Britain Walpole used the crisis to re-establish the Bank of England's control over the debt. Throughout the eighteenth century the Bank of England underpinned the sprawling, chaotic banking system as a lender of last resort; by 1797 it was allowed to abandon cash payments in gold, making its notes *de facto* legal tender. As prosperity grew, by the 1730s the national debt was regarded as a source of investment, not a burden and Walpole's 'Sinking Fund', which had been established to reduce it, was increasingly diverted to other uses. In France 1720 saw a wholesale return to the previous system of tax farming by the FARMERS GENERAL, the complete discrediting of paper currency and a permanent reluctance to create a national bank. Government finance remained in the hands of the Farmers General until the Revolution.

See also BANKS AND BANKING.

J. F. Bosher, *French Finances, 1770–1795* (London: Cambridge University Press, 1970).

A. Cobban, *A History of Modern France*, vol. 1: *1715–1799* (Harmondsworth: Penguin, 1963).

P. G. M. Dickson, *The Financial Revolution in England, 1688–1756* (London: Macmillan, 1967).

MICHAEL BROERS

Finland A thinly populated part of the Swedish state. Finland was exposed to military pressure from the increasingly powerful Russia. Conquered in 1713–14 during the Great Northern War, it was restored to SWEDEN at the Treaty of Nystad, though Russia retained the strategic regions of Kexholm and part of Karelia. The Swedes were again unsuccessful during war with Russia in 1741–3. In 1742 the Russians urged the Finns to establish an independent state to serve as a buffer between Russia and Sweden, invaded Finland and routed the Swedes. By the Treaty of Åbo of 1743 Finland was returned to Sweden with the exception of Karelia. Under the Tilsit division of spheres of influence between Napoleon and Russia, Russia drove the Swedes from Finland in 1808. Its annexation was recognized in the Treaty of Hamina of 1809. Finland became a grand duchy and the capital was moved from Turku to Helsinki. Most of the population was involved in farming, fur-trapping or fishery. The Lapps in the north were still nomadic. Henrik Porthan (1739–1804), founder of modern studies in Finnish history and folklore, studied Finnish traditional literature and language. The population rose from 300,000 (1700) to 705,623 (1790).

JEREMY BLACK

Fleury, André Hercule de (1653–1743) French prelate, chief minister to Louis XV. He became bishop of Fréjus in 1698, the first step in a remarkable public career which reached its apogee only after his seventieth birthday. He was named in Louis XIV's will as tutor to the new king, and the regent, Orléans, respected that choice. In 1726 he was made a cardinal and became Louis XV's chief minister. Following the dramatic collapse of John Law's fiscal experiments during the regency, Fleury concentrated on restoring economic stability. That policy required a circumspect approach to foreign affairs since war would quickly unbalance the budget. His subtle diplomacy enabled him to maintain British neutrality (in the spirit of the Triple Alliance) even when France was drawn into the War of the Polish Succession. After a minimum show of force he negotiated a most advantageous peace (Vienna, 1738). In return for French recognition, at last, of the Emperor's Pragmatic Sanction, Lorraine was handed over to Louis XV's father-in-law, Stanislas Leszczyński, as a sop for his loss of the Polish throne, to be absorbed finally into France upon Leszczyński's death in 1766. Fleury thus succeeded, where Louis XIV had failed, in securing that vulnerable eastern entrance to the kingdom.

A. M. Wilson, *French Foreign Policy during the Administration of Cardinal Fleury, 1726–43* (Cambridge, Mass.: Harvard University Press, 1936).

J. H. SHENNAN

flight *see* AVIATION.

Florence One of the oldest cities in Italy, Florence was the capital of
TUSCANY. Despite its old and proud history, Florence was most characterized by stagnation in this period; its population of 71,000 in
1701 had hardly changed by the 1740s and had risen to only 81,000
by 1795. Although still an important local centre of several industries,
such as textiles, it had lost its international standing in commerce and
banking. By the mid eighteenth century, the church had become the
most prominent factor in Florentine life, most evident in the fact that
it undertook the only significant public building in this period. Until
the reign of Peter Leopold II (1765–90) the city retained most of its
privileges such as the *Annona*, which ensured the town its cheap grain
supplies, and its powerful guilds, the corporations. Peter Leopold dismantled both of these in the course of his rule, as well as carrying out
an inquiry into the titles of the Florentine nobility, which resulted in
its official restriction to 238 families, a great reduction. In general, his
rule saw the city brought under a more centralized government at
every level; it also saw a marked revival of intellectual life centred on
the enlightened, reforming court of the grand duke. Most of these
reforms were deeply resented; the abolition of the *Annona* – coupled
with a poor harvest – led to violent riots in 1790 and the withdrawal
of most of the reforms by Ferdinand III (1769–1824), Peter Leopold's
successor. Even during his reactionary rule in the 1790s, the political
autonomy enjoyed by Florence prior to 1765 was never fully restored.

E. Cochrane, *Florence in the Forgotten Centuries, 1527–1800* (Chicago:
University of Chicago Press, 1973).

MICHAEL BROERS

Florida The explorer Juan Ponce de León (1460–1521) discovered and
claimed Florida for Spain in 1512. In the absence of any easily found
gold, Spain ignored Florida until the French built a small post there.
Reasserting their claims, the Spanish constructed a strong fort at St
Augustine (from 1565 the oldest permanent European settlement in
North America). As with their other New World possessions, after
brutalizing and enslaving many native Indians the Spanish established
a series of missions to convert the survivors to Christianity.

In 1763, as a result of the Treaty of Paris, East Florida (the peninsula) and West Florida (the panhandle, including modern Mobile,
Alabama) were ceded to England. The Floridas became a safe haven
for loyal American guerrillas during the War for Independence. An
American effort to wipe out St Augustine failed and, partially in retribution, the British launched an invasion of Georgia. It succeeded,
and Florida played an important role in the British attempt to reconquer
and pacify the south. In West Florida, however, America's Spanish
allies sailing out of NEW ORLEANS captured British forts at Mobile and

Pensacola. Following the war, the Floridas reverted to Spain under whose control they remained until becoming American territory in 1819.

Charlton W. Tebeau, *A History of Florida* (Coral Gables, Fla.: University of Miami Press, 1971).

JOHN MORGAN DEDERER

folklore The word 'folklore', like its equivalents in other languages, is a nineteenth-century term, but the interest taken by European elites in what they called the culture of 'the people' was increasingly visible in the second half of the eighteenth century, to some extent as a reaction against classicism and the Enlightenment. Intellectuals such as the German clergyman Johann Gottfried Herder collected what they called 'folk-songs' or observed and noted down the beliefs, the customs and the costumes of the local peasants, whom they saw (often inaccurately) as the custodians of ancient traditions, as well as models of virtuous behaviour free from the corruption of the cities.
See also MYTH.

P. Burke, *Popular Culture in Early Modern Europe* (London: Temple Smith, 1978), ch. 1.

PETER BURKE

Fontenelle, Bernard le Bovier de (1657–1757) French writer. Born in Rouen and educated by the Jesuits, he wrote a number of unsuccessful poems, librettos and comedies before discovering his real talent, for popularizing science. His first contribution to the genre was a comedy, *La Comète* (The Comet, 1681) in which he ridiculed the notions the ancients entertained about comets. The theme of ancients versus moderns dominated his writings, including his best-selling and widely translated *Entretiens sur la pluralité des mondes* (A Plurality of Worlds, 1686) – dialogues on astronomy between a man of science and an intelligent but uneducated marquise which reveal his Cartesian tendencies.

Fontenelle settled in Paris around 1687 and for the next ten years wrote mostly plays and literary criticism, but from 1699 – when he became permanent secretary of the Académie des Sciences – to 1740 he devoted himself to writing the memoirs of Académie members past and present. Sixty-nine of these *eloges* were published in forty-two volumes of the *Histoire de l'Académie*. Despite his long-term exposure to and sympathy with the ideas of Newton, Fontenelle's preference for mechanical over 'occult' explanations anchored him to Cartesian thought. Though his views were well known, the appearance of his last major work, *Théorie des tourbillons cartesiens* (1752) caused astonishment.

Alain Niderst, *Fontenelle* (Paris: Plon, 1991).

M. L. BENJAMIN

Fontenoy, Battle of (11 May 1745)   The Battle of Fontenoy was fought between the allied army of the PRAGMATIC SANCTION, composed of British, Hanoverian, Austrian and Dutch troops led by the duke of Cumberland (1721–65), and a French army under Marshal SAXE. Cumberland's intention was to force the French away from Tournai and raise the siege. Saxe was able to prepare a strong defensive wedge-shaped position with its apex resting on the village of Fontenoy. Cumberland, only 24 years old, with about 47,000 men, faced one of the most resourceful and experienced commanders of the age, with a more advantageously placed and larger force, probably totalling 60,000 men. Cumberland disdained to manœuvre and launched two frontal assaults against the French, on the centre with Dutch and Austrians, and on a section between Fontenoy and a wooded area with British and Hanoverians. The main British column advanced into Saxe's prepared killing-ground and drove deeply into the position, from which they were at length forced back by a series of counter-attacks. They then retreated slowly back for a considerable distance without losing their formation, having suffered perhaps 20,000 casualties. Saxe, whose casualties totalled 7,000, then captured Tournai and a large area of Flanders.

Charles Grant, *The Battle of Fontenoy* (London: Luscombe, 1975).

TONY HAYTER

food riots   Food riots took place in years of bad harvests. They were attempts to defend local food supplies, either by preventing the movement of grain out of a community (the *entrave* in France) or by forcibly selling corn at what were conceived to be fair or just prices (*taxation populaire*). A particular target of rioters were middlemen in the GRAIN TRADE. Riots were often orderly, disciplined and frequently involved women. They tended to take place either in areas of grain production, such as Flanders, which supplied major cities or in areas of rural industry. In England most protesters were industrial workers but in France independent peasants played a major role.

Rioters were defending the 'moral economy' according to which the capitalist profit motive was to be subordinated to the communal good, and local markets supplied at reasonable prices. Governments were expected to regulate the grain trade along similar lines but, increasingly, paternalistic intervention gave way to active encouragement of free grain markets. Food riots were gradually replaced by new forms of industrial and political protest in the later eighteenth and early nineteenth centuries.

See also GRAIN RIOTS.

R. B. Outhwaite, *Dearth, Public Policy and Social Disturbance in England, 1550–1800* (Basingstoke: Macmillan, 1991).

JEREMY BOULTON

Fox, Charles James (1749–1806)   English statesman. A brilliant orator and a man of magnetic personal charm, Fox was dogged in his career by frustration. For only three brief periods, in 1782, 1783 and 1806, did he hold office as foreign secretary, the post to which he was best suited. During the American War of Independence he favoured granting independence to the Americans and attacked the influence of the crown as the source of political corruption. After 1783 he was in opposition until the last few months of his life. He supported economic and parliamentary reform, defended civil and religious liberties, advocated Catholic emancipation, and throughout the French wars called for a negotiated peace. Sympathetic to the ideals of 1789, he was appalled by the reign of Terror. On becoming foreign secretary in 1806, he found it impossible to negotiate a satisfactory peace. His last months were consoled by the knowledge that the Commons had passed resolutions condemning the slave trade. Fox was an inspiration to his followers, but his political judgement was erratic and his career was blighted by a tendency to take gambles which ended disastrously.

J. W. Derry, *Charles James Fox* (London: Batsford, 1972).

JOHN W. DERRY

Fragonard, Jean Honoré (1732–1806)   French painter of genre and portraits. He was born in Grasse, and a taste for Mediterranean colouring was a consistent feature of his work. He went to Paris at the age of 16 and, after a brief period with Chardin (1699–1779), became a pupil of Boucher. In 1756 he went to Rome, funded by the prestigious Prix de Rome, and travelled around Italy. He returned there in the 1770s, and throughout his career the influence of Tiepolo was very marked. In 1765 he presented a history painting, *Coresus Sacrificing Himself*, to the annual *salon*. It established his career, but was not a style which he continued to use: thereafter he concentrated mainly on the erotic scenes of love and seduction that were so much in vogue. However, he was much more than a painter of pretty nudes; he also produced a series of *portraits de fantasie*, which reveal an almost romantic approach to both technique and characterization. The grand moralities that the Revolution encouraged were completely outside his range. His career collapsed after 1789 and he spent the rest of his life working for the Louvre.

Pierre Rosenberg, *Fragonard* (New York: Metropolitan Museum of Art, 1988).

IAIN PEARS

France At the beginning of the eighteenth century the French population numbered some 20 million, the highest in Europe. They lived in a fertile land of great diversity and economic potential but within a social and political system which prevented the majority of people from profiting from it, for the tax structure continued to favour the privileged estates of the clergy and nobility and to bear down heavily on the members of the Third Estate. In the rural areas few peasants could afford to invest in land improvement, so most remained vulnerable from year to year to the vagaries of the weather. The eighteenth century also witnessed a significant rise in population, to about 26 million by 1800, and in prices, two factors which further exacerbated the problems of the poor.

Nevertheless, France remained the most powerful state in Europe during the first half of the century despite the scaling down of Louis XIV's ambitions at the TREATY OF UTRECHT. With handsight, however, it is possible to view that settlement as the harbinger of a shift in the balance of power with France's loss of Nova Scotia and Newfoundland to Great Britain. The SEVEN YEARS WAR, in which France was forced to fight on two fronts, in Europe against Prussia and overseas against Britain, confirmed the change. The need to defend its vulnerable land frontiers had always led France to channel the wealth of its human and natural resources into the army; and its political culture, based on the alliance of crown and Second Estate, gave priority and honour to the military nobility. Consequently, France held its own in Europe. However, its overseas territories were vulnerable precisely because its domestic security, unlike Britain's, did not depend upon its being a strong maritime power. The superior British navy was able to prevent the French colonies from being adequately supplied. The result was the humiliating TREATY OF PARIS, by which France ceded to Britain Canada, the West Indian islands of Tobago, Grenada, St Vincent and Dominica, most of its trading stations in India and a number in west Africa. Subsequently, the French navy was strengthened and national honour restored when France played a major role in bringing about the loss of Britain's American colonies. However, the cost of financing that war was one of the factors leading to the fatal political crisis of the 1780s.

Throughout the eighteenth century France remained the cultural leader of Europe. French was the language of diplomacy and of educated society. VERSAILLES became the model for the palaces of aspiring kings and princes; the original, under the cultivated if extravagant tutelage of Madame de Pompadour, continued to set standards of fashion and taste. More significant still was the influence of the French Enlightenment on European ideas. Philosophers and propagandists like Voltaire, Diderot and Rousseau crusaded in favour of improving the quality of life by the application of laws based on human reason rather than on state-supported Christian revelation.

In the final decades of the century such ideas were helping to undermine the established secular order in France, challenging the king's authority as God's lieutenant. However, the old order was already vulnerable. To add to the financial bankruptcy which followed the War of American Independence and the longer-lasting inflationary and demographic pressures, came years of bad harvests in the 1770s and 1780s with accompanying social distress and disorder. It was becoming increasingly clear that without fundamental reform to the country's social and economic structure the crown was in danger of losing control of the situation. Yet its authority was based on its role as guarantor of the legal order, and that included the long-held privileges of the first two estates. If the government sought to modify those rights the crown would face the accusation of despotism and the forfeiture of its authority. Out of this impasse came the decision to summon the ESTATES GENERAL in May 1789. The political crisis represented by that convocation, combined with the widespread disorders caused by famine, triggered the FRENCH REVOLUTION. The lessons and inspiration that have since been drawn from that social and political upheaval constitute eighteenth-century France's chief legacy to the modern world.

The future patterns of European political organization could all be discerned in the tumultuous decade of the 1790s. The constitutional revolution of 1789–92 offered a model for property-owning middle-class democracy. In 1793 representatives of the SANS-CULOTTES demanded a greater share in political and economic decision-making in the name of popular sovereignty. That movement was followed during the period of the DIRECTORY (1795–9) by a communist utopian conspiracy devised by François Babeuf. The FRENCH REVOLUTION also provided a new political vocabulary, that of Left and Right, representing a spectrum of opinion from radical to reactionary, which was to become universal. Most significantly, during the TERROR (1793–4) the principle was established that in times of crisis civic virtue would consist of unquestioning loyalty to the state under siege. That idea provided the impetus which allowed the young French republic to survive. Counterrevolutionary risings, like that in the VENDÉE, were defeated, and by the middle of 1794 the revolutionary armies were on the offensive. In 1796 NAPOLEON BONAPARTE was appointed to command the French army of Italy.

Subsequently Napoleon became First Consul and ultimately, in 1804, emperor of the French. As military dictator he embarked upon the conquest of Europe, exporting aspects of the French Revolution to those areas under his direct, or his family's, control. In particular the new civil code, the CODE NAPOLÉON, enshrined the principles of equality before the law, freedom of conscience and individual liberty. However, the domination of French arms prompted the growth of anti-French national sentiment in Germany and Italy. After Napoleon's defeat in 1814–15 the Bourbon dynasty was restored in the person of LOUIS XVIII. But the old order of which the royal house had once formed an integral part had been destroyed; and the restoration was therefore an artificial and doomed device.

C. B. A. Behrens, *The Ancien Régime* (London: Thames & Hudson, 1967).
F. Braudel and E. Labrousse (eds), *Histoire économique et sociale de la France, 1660–1789* (Paris: Presses Universitaires de France, 1970).
Alfred Cobban, *A History of Modern France,* vol. 1: *1715–1799* (Harmondsworth: Penguin, 1963).
William Doyle, *Origins of the French Revolution* (Oxford: Oxford University Press, 1980).
D. M. G. Sutherland, *France, 1789–1815: Revolution and Counterrevolution* (London: Fontana, 1985).

J. H. SHENNAN

Francis I (1708–1765) Holy Roman Emperor (1745–65). Francis Stephen, duke of Lorraine, married Archduchess MARIA THERESA, heiress of Emperor Charles V, in 1736, creating the house of Habsburg-Lorraine. He held a large number of military and civil titles and offices, culminating in his election as Holy Roman Emperor in 1745 but his actual involvement in command and government was always limited and he was happy to leave decision-making to his wife. He was not one of the eighteenth century's great achievers but he had a talent for economic management and accumulated a large personal fortune. In 1763 he took charge of Austria's financial management and achieved considerable improvements. He was responsible for the abandonment by the Vienna court of the Spanish ceremonial and the adoption of the more informal French system. His formidable procreative vigour was his greatest asset: he gave the Habsburg house, of which two male lines had died out, an amplitude of new blood: he and Maria Theresa had sixteen children, of whom ten survived. During his later years he suffered from bouts of depression. He died suddenly in August 1765.

P. G. M. Dickson, *Finance and Government under Maria Theresa 1740–80* (Oxford: Oxford University Press, 1987).

MICHAEL HUGHES

Francis II (1768–1835)   Holy Roman Emperor (1792–1806), emperor of Austria (1804–35). The eldest son of Emperor LEOPOLD II, he succeeded to the Habsburg lands on his father's premature death. In his ideas he was sharply different from Leopold, who was one of the greatest enlightened rulers in Europe. Although he had been well educated for his role, he was dull, stubborn, narrow-minded and suspicious of those with greater intelligence than his. His natural conservatism and fear of change were increased by the French Revolution. He believed firmly in the virtues of monarchical absolutism and religious orthodoxy and his reign was the most repressive period in Austria's modern history. He relied heavily on the advice of the reactionary Prince METTERNICH. In 1804 Francis assumed the title of emperor of Austria, a sign of Austria's increasing detachment from Germany. On 6 August 1806 he ended the existence of the HOLY ROMAN EMPIRE by abdicating from the throne. In spite of his repressive policies, he became very popular with his subjects, who called him 'Francis the Good'.

W. C. Langsam, *Francis the Good: The Education of an Emperor* (New York: 1949).

MICHAEL HUGHES

Franklin, Benjamin (1706–1790)   American businessman, politician and natural philosopher. He was idolized in contemporary France as the personification of Enlightenment ideals and is still upheld in America as exemplifying the rewards of industry and sober moderation. With little schooling, he devoted the first part of his life to developing a flourishing printing company in Philadelphia, simultaneously pursuing an intensive programme of educational and moral self-improvement. Already occupied with local politics, civic amenities and scientific experiments, he terminated his active business participation in 1748, and became deeply engaged in natural philosophy, particularly in experimental and theoretical work on electricity and lightning. From 1754 he played an increasingly important role in diplomatic affairs and, after gaining an international reputation for his handling of the repeal of the Stamp Act in 1766, frequently represented the American colonies in negotiations with Britain and France, contributing to the drawing up of the Declaration of Independence. He spent many years in London and Paris, where he was admired for his political, commercial and scientific expertise as well as his numerous philanthropic activities and humanitarian outlook.

Esmond Wright, *Franklin of Philadelphia* (Cambridge, Mass.: Belknap, 1986).

PATRICIA FARA

Frederick I (1657–1713)   Elector of Brandenburg (1688–1713), as Frederick III; king of Prussia (1701–13). His father's will divided the Prussian lands between him and his half-brothers, but he bought them out, preserving the unity of his territories. Their indivisibility was made permanent when he declared himself the first king of PRUSSIA on 18 January 1701. His reign is traditionally regarded as a dull interval between the more significant and creative reigns of his father, the Great Elector (1620–88), and his son, Frederick-William I. A more balanced view of his reign now prevails, but he was certainly no innovator and relied heavily on his able first minister, Eberhard Christoph Danckelmann (1643–1722). He is best remembered for his lavish court. His foreign policy was strongly influenced by his desire to obtain the Emperor's consent to his royal title and he provided substantial forces for the imperial armies. In 1703 he established a high court of appeal in Berlin for all his territories, an important step in their consolidation as a single state. He also founded the University of Halle, the Berlin Academy of Arts and the Academy of Sciences.

H. W. Koch, *A History of Prussia* (London: Longman, 1978).

MICHAEL HUGHES

Frederick II [Frederick the Great] (1712–1786)   King of Prussia (1740–86). He was the most successful Prussian ruler in the eighteenth century and the dominating German figure of the age. Nationalist myth exaggerated but did not invent his genuine achievements. He united a multitude of talents in his person: he was an audacious military commander, a prolific author and correspondent and an innovative modernizer strongly influenced by enlightened ideas. He had great strength of character, which enabled him to overcome disasters. At the same time he had very contemptuous view of his fellow-men and conservative social ideas. Frederick's achievement was considerable but ambivalent in its effects. He considerably enlarged his kingdom and modernized its government but also retarded its political and social development.

Many of Frederick's attitudes were formed during his early years, marked by growing friction with his authoritarian father, FREDERICK-WILLIAM I, who had no time for Frederick's artistic and literary interests. Their bad relations culminated in the prince's attempted flight in July 1730, after which he was court-martialled for desertion. His punishment, an enforced stay in the garrison at Küstrin, gave him a beneficial period of separation from his father. This produced an improvement in relations and Frederick devoted himself to military matters. On his marriage in 1733 he was allowed to maintain his own court at Rheinsberg, where he could indulge his interests. He absorbed the basic ideas of the Enlightenment by reading and in conversations with a circle of friends. He supported toleration, rationalism and the notion of the ruler as first servant of the state. His intellectual interests remained strong throughout his life. His faith in Enlightenment waned only in his last years when he became increasingly misanthropic as his friends died or left.

He had great personal ambition and a desire to make a name for himself. He was convinced that his father had created but not used the instruments by means of which PRUSSIA could become a great power, field a strong army and maintain a full treasury. In 1740 he decided to change this and to end what he described as the 'hermaphrodite' nature of Prussia, too big for a mere electorate but too small to be a great power. He revived shadowy Prussian claims to the rich Austrian province of SILESIA and, when the new ruler of Austria, Maria Theresa, refused to cede it, he invaded and annexed it. Military victories and his clever manipulation of diplomacy allowed him to retain Silesia, which revolutionized the international situation. The acquisition of the province made Prussia a great power of European significance. Frederick enlarged his state further by his gains from the first partition of Poland in 1772, which took place largely at his initiative.

By 1756 Prussia's international position had deteriorated sharply, and it faced a powerful coalition of France, Austria, Sweden and Russia determined to destroy her, with only Britain and a few smaller German states as allies. Frederick seized the initiative and launched a pre-emptive strike in August before his enemies were ready, beginning the SEVEN YEARS WAR. He was very fortunate: Prussia won great victories but on several occasions during the war came close to total defeat. Frederick also made brilliant use of propaganda, which contributed to his growing reputation as a German hero, even though most of the German states were allied to Austria against him.

Frederick's reconstruction of his country after the devastation of the war was very successful. Economic growth was encouraged and Prussia developed the most successful economy in Germany. In spite of major judicial and educational reforms, Frederick maintained the privileged position of the nobility and the institution of serfdom, though measures to protect the peasantry from abuse by their lords were enforced. As he stated in his *Political Testament* of 1752, he believed it was essential for the survival of the Prussian state to maintain the structure of society as it was.

During Frederick's reign Prussia emerged as Austria's equal in German politics but he had no ambitions to adopt a leadership role in

Germany, as later nationalist myth claimed. His policy was to preserve the Holy Roman Empire and to prevent any substantial change in the distribution of power within it. In 1785 he took over headship of the League of Princes, an alliance of German rulers devoted to the preservation of the *status quo* in Germany.

C. Duffy, *Frederick the Great: A Military Life* (London: Routledge, 1988).
G. Ritter, *Frederick the Great: A Historical Profile* (Berkeley, Calif.: University of California Press, 1968).

MICHAEL HUGHES

Frederick II (1720–1785)   Landgrave of Hesse-Kassel (1760–85). He was the most successful eighteenth-century ruler of HESSE-KASSEL. In 1749, after increasing disillusionment with Calvinism, he became a secret convert to Roman Catholicism. This was portrayed by Frederick the Great in his propaganda as the first step in an Austrian campaign to recatholicize Germany. In fact his conversion was purely personal and Hesse remained a leading Calvinistic state. In 1756 he entered Prussian military service, rising after considerable experience to the rank of field marshal. His reputation was traditionally bad, especially in German nationalist historiography, because he hired out mercenary troops, most notoriously to Britain for use in the American War of Independence. He is now viewed more favourably. A tolerant and humane ruler, he was strongly influenced by enlightened ideas and carried through important measures of modernization, especially in education and welfare. He was responsible for the reconstruction of his state after it suffered serious devastation in the Seven Years War. He also contributed to the beautification of his capital, Kassel, commissioning major new buildings. He was unusual in that he co-operated throughout with representatives of his subjects in the parliamentary estates.

C. W. Ingrao, *The Hessian Mercenary State* (Cambridge: Cambridge University Press, 1987).

MICHAEL HUGHES

Frederick Charles Joseph, baron von Erthal (1719–1802)   Elector and archbishop of Mainz. Born into a family of Mainz imperial knights, he embarked on a career in ecclesiastical administration immediately after concluding his university studies. Prebendaryships in Mainz, Bamberg and Würzburg led to the rectorship of Mainz University (1764) and an ambassadorship to the imperial court (1769). On the death of the enlightened reformer Elector Emmerich Joseph in 1774, he was elected by a chapter hoping for a reaction. After two years, however, he embarked on an ambitious programme of reform more wide-ranging even than that of his predecessor.

In imperial politics he sought to enhance the status and independence of the electorate. He supported efforts to reform the Reich and after 1785 participated in the Prussian-led League of German Princes. He also clashed with the papacy over his desire to curtail the influence of Rome. Ultimately, however, his ambitions were undermined by reality. In 1792 he was driven out of Mainz by the French. Although he later returned, the city never again became a secure base. The Treaty of Lunéville (1801) finally destroyed all his plans.

T. C. W. Blanning, *Reform and Revolution in Mainz 1743–1803* (Cambridge: Cambridge University Press, 1974).

JOACHIM WHALEY

Frederick-William I (1688–1740)   King of Prussia (1713–40). Traditionally known as 'the Soldier King' or 'the Sergeant-Major King', he played a major part in building the military and financial foundations of Prussia's eighteenth-century power. He also did much to create the characteristics traditionally associated with the word 'Prussian' – authoritarianism, militarism and frugality. He had a great fondness for the military life and a deep Calvinistic religious faith, which gave him a love of order, discipline and economy. He was tyrannical and violent but also a hard-working ruler. He personally supervised government, especially in financial and military matters. During his reign the size of the Prussian army doubled to some 83,000. He carried through important administrative reforms designed to increase the yield of taxation, especially the creation of the General Directory in 1723. As a result of his frugal spending, he left a substantial reserve to his son (Frederick the Great). He continued his predecessors' policies of religious toleration to encourage people to settle in Prussia, and of weakening the parliamentary estates in order to strengthen monarchical power. His foreign policy was very cautious and he had no spectacular successes.

R. A. Dorwart, *The Administrative Reforms of Frederick William I of Prussia* (Cambridge, Mass.: Harvard University Press, 1953).

MICHAEL HUGHES

Frederick-William II (1744–1797)   King of Prussia (1786–97). He was the nephew and successor of FREDERICK II, who disliked him and took little interest in his education. A dull and lazy man, ill prepared for his role, he has traditionally suffered from unfavourable comparisons with his illustrious predecessor. Although he continued some of Frederick's work, for example in educational reform and the publication of a law code in 1794, his reign was marked by reaction, caused by growing fear of the French Revolution and the influence of the Rosicrucian movement represented by his reactionary ministers Wöllner and Bischoffswerder. In order to prevent the spread of new ideas, he strengthened censorship and increased the powers of the church. In foreign policy he exploited Prussia's status as a great power, for example by his military intervention in the Netherlands and in the second and third partitions of Poland. After 1792 he co-operated with Austria in war against revolutionary France, but this alliance was never congenial and in 1795 Prussia withdrew into neutrality under the Treaty of Basle in order to concentrate on extending its power in Germany and Poland.

H. Brunschwig, *Enlightenment and Romanticism in Eighteenth-Century Prussia* (Chicago: University of Chicago Press, 1974).

MICHAEL HUGHES

Frederik V (1723–1766) King of Denmark (1746–66). The son of King Christian VI (1699–1746) and Sophie-Magdalene of Brandenburg-Cülmbach (1700–70), he married first Louise, daughter of George II, king of England, and then Juliana Maria of Brunswick-Wolfenbüttel. In marked contrast to his father, he was indolent and pleasure-seeking. Rejecting the puritanism of the previous reign, he presided over the establishment of a new public theatre (1747) and founded the Royal Academy of Art (1754). He was a keen patron of the arts, although an ambitious project to construct an elegant new suburb for Copenhagen ultimately came to nothing. Although he approvingly quoted Frederick the Great's dictum that the monarch was the first servant of the state, he left government largely in the hands of his able ministers, especially Adam Moltke and Johan Bernstorff. Trade flourished and Denmark continued its policy of friendship with France and Russia. Relations with Adolf Fredrik of Sweden were regularized in 1750 and Denmark stayed neutral in the Seven Years War, until the accession of Peter III, from the rival family of Holstein-Gottorp, as tsar of Russia. The danger of a Russian invasion was ended by Peter's overthrow in July 1762.

S. Oakley, *The Story of Denmark* (London, 1982).

ROBERT I. FROST

Fredrik I (1676–1751) King of Sweden (1720–51) Born as hereditary prince of Hesse-Kassel, he succeeded as landgrave in 1730. He married a Brandenburg princess in 1700 who died in 1708. Fredrik proved a gifted soldier in the War of the Spanish Succession, and had an outgoing manner which won him many friends. In 1715, with CHARLES XII's approbation, he married the latter's only surviving sister, Ulrika Eleonora (1688–1741), but the marriage was childless. He remained scrupulously loyal to Charles, although he never troubled to learn Swedish. In 1718 he ensured his wife's election to the crown, overriding the stronger claim of her 18-year-old nephew, Charles Fredrik of Holstein-Gottorp (1700–39). Following her abdication in his favour in 1720, he succeeded to a throne to which he had no hereditary right and which, in any case, had been constitutionally deprived of power by Sweden's new political leaders. The reign saw Fredrik increasingly lose interest in government, devoting his time to hunting and to his mistresses, especially Hedvig Taube. He ensured that she and their four children were imperially ennobled as 'Hessenstein'. After the war with Russia (1741–3) Sweden was compelled to accept ADOLF FREDRIK as Fredrik's heir, and for a time (1746–47) this made Fredrik's position rather precarious.

W. Holst, *Fredrik I* (Stockholm: Wahlström & Widstrand, 1953).

D. D. ALDRIDGE

freedom In *An Essay on Human Understanding* John Locke explained that only an agent could be said to be free; to call any mental power or faculty free was misleading, 'For *Powers* are Relations, not Agents: And *that which has power, or not the power to operate, is that alone, which, is or is not free*, and not the Power it self: For Freedom, or not Freedom, can belong to nothing, but what has, or has not a power to act.' '*Freedom*', he went on to explain, 'consists in the dependence of the Existence, or not Existence of any Action, upon our Volition of it, and not in the dependence of any Action, or its contrary, on our preference.' It was Locke's belief that the confusion surrounding the philosophical issue of man's freedom would be dispelled if the word were used to refer to nothing other than 'our being able to act, or not to act, according as we shall chuse, or *will*'. Despite Locke's clarification and the enormous influence which the *Essay* exercised over eighteenth-century philosophy, the age-old debate about free will was by no means resolved.

The philosophers and theologians of the day contributed to it, and the theme made its way from universities and studies to coffee-houses and dinner-tables. Thus it was a topic that recurred in the conversations of Boswell and Johnson, although they were very much agreed on the freedom of what, regardless of Locke, they continued to call the human will. In the article 'De la liberté' in his *Dictionnaire philosophique* (1764), Voltaire has one interlocutor tell another the Lockean position: 'Your will is not free, but your actions are. You are free to act when you have the power to act.' Because of the centrality of the question of the freedom of volition to theology, the issue assumed, in an age of militant anticlericalism an importance it might not otherwise have had outside of the philosopher's study. Outstanding among the century's many works on the subject are Hume's *Treatise of Human Nature* and Kant's response to it in *Kritik der reinen Vernunft* (1781) and *Grundlegung zur Metaphysik der Sitten* (1785). Both philosophers also made distinguished contributions to the political discussion of the question of freedom or LIBERTY, the two terms being used interchangeably in this period. Freedom, moreover, was a notion that was increasingly extended from single to composite agents in this period. Events such as the American Revolution, as well as the struggle led by men like Toussaint L'Ouverture in Haiti, and developments like FEMINISM not only took the debate about freedom beyond the European context, but made nations, races and the female sex as a whole the subjects of this debate. The question was thus no longer only what it meant for an individual agent to be free, but what was necessary for various bodies of people to be so.

David Hume, *A Treatise Of Human Nature*, ed. L. A. Selby-Bigge, rev. P. H. Nidditch, second edn (Oxford: Clarendon, 1978).

Immanuel Kant, *Foundations of the Metaphysics of Morals*, trans. Lewis White Beck, with critical essays ed. Robert Paul Wolff (Indianapolis: Bobbs-Merrill, 1969).

Raymond Polin, 'John Locke's Conception of Freedom', in John W. Yolton (ed.), *John Locke: Problems and Perspectives* (Cambridge: Cambridge University Press, 1969), pp. 1–18.

SYLVANA TOMASELLI

Freemasonry Bound together by rites of initiation, the secretive fraternity of Freemasons evolved a system of allegory and symbolism based on the building of King Solomon's Temple and medieval stone-masonry. Its origins have remained obscure but the likelihood is that the lodge system was started by operative craftsmen in Scotland around 1600 and then imported into England where non-operatives, like Elias Ashmole, were initiated from 1646 onwards. In 1717 the first grand lodge of England was formed out of four London lodges. By 1743 Masonic conviviality had become so notorious that Horace Walpole remarked that nothing but a persecution could bring Freemasonry into vogue again. Blending the teachings of the Renaissance Neoplatonists with the ideals of the Enlightenment, the Freemasons formed 'one close system of benevolence', attracting freethinkers, deists and radicals such as Voltaire and Paine. The lodges in France and America during the revolutionary period inculcated the principles of liberty, equality and fraternity. Notwithstanding its egalitarian aims, this universal brotherhood of man excluded women. Subject to suppression by governments and condemned by religious bodies, the resilience and protean character of Freemasonry have ensured its continued survival.

See also SECRET SOCIETIES.

Margaret Jacob, *The Radical Enlightenment: Pantheists, Freemasons and Republicans* (London: Allen & Unwin, 1981).

MARIE MULVEY ROBERTS

freethinkers   The English word 'Freethinkers' is first recorded in the 1690s. Freethinkers were widely separated individuals and groups whose opinions formed a diffuse way of thought rather than an organized party, although their intellectual resources and political connections gave them an influence far beyond their numbers. Drawing on classical and Renaissance interpretations of religion, they rejected the authority of revealed Christianity as bolstered only by dubious biblical texts and foisted on an ignorant populace by self-interested priests. Freethought was regularly denounced as ATHEISM, but many freethinkers believed that a benevolent creator existed, had revealed himself in the scientific harmonies of the natural world and had endowed men with rational powers to comprehend this revelation. VOLTAIRE was characteristic of freethinkers both in his adoption of biblical criticism and in the accusations of DEISM levelled against him. Freethinking flourished in some intellectual circles in early eighteenth-century England, strongly influenced by the writings of John TOLAND, and in mid-century Prussia. It was an important element of the French Enlightenment and a form of deism re-emerged in the work of Thomas PAINE.

J. S. Spink, *French Free-Thought from Gassendi to Voltaire* (London, 1960).

G. M. DITCHFIELD

free trade   Commerce, wrote Montesquieu in *L'Esprit des lois,* 'cures destructible prejudices and it is almost a general rule that wherever there are gentle mores, there is commerce; and that wherever there is commerce, the mores are gentle'. That theirs was a commercial age was a fact that no one in the eighteenth century would have disputed (*see* COMMERCIAL SOCIETY). What it entailed became a topic of debate, which revolved around the questions, What is the impact of commerce on a nation? Is commerce compatible with virtue, with any or only a specific form of government, with the martial spirit of a people, with equality? What were its relations to luxury, to wealth, to population, to war and peace?

  Montesquieu's writings afforded one of the earliest and most systematic analyses of the pros and cons of commerce in ancient and modern times. Though he thought commerce nefarious where mores had to remain pure (*see* DEMOCRACY), he considered it to have a benign effect on barbarism. He argued that commerce made for peace between nations by encouraging interdependence, but also noted that it had the opposite effect on individuals in civil society. In those countries such as Holland where, in his view, only the spirit of commerce prevailed, everything acquired a price, including what would normally be regarded as humanitarian services. Commerce thus heightened and hardened perceptions of self-interest and a sense of exact or perfect justice. As a result, hospitality was a rare feature of commercial society, according to the baron, yet it was characteristic of brigands. He also argued that commerce was closely linked to LUXURY, wherever government was in the hands of one who was opposed to a part or the whole of the people. In the latter case, commerce tended to provide for the real need of the population rather than for the superfluities of the court. In general, Montesquieu thought that the security of property typical of republican states was more favourable to commerce than regimes in which such confidence was always somewhat qualified. He therefore saw the rule of law as an index of commercial prosperity, and England as the ideal modern commercial nation, praising it for the manner in which it dealt with the three interconnected issues of religion, commerce and liberty.

These themes were taken up by subsequent generations of Enlightenment writers throughout Europe. Discussions emphasizing the close connection between the spirit of toleration and that of commerce flourished more particularly in France, where the Revocation of the Edict of Nantes and the persecution of the Jews were nearly always counted as decisive factors in the country's commercial backwardness, especially in contrast to Holland and England. Another issue, which taxed the Scots and the English perhaps more than other economists, was whether the commercial superiority of a nation could be maintained indefinitely or whether it was part of a cyclical phenomenon. Whether trade should be allowed to be entirely or only partially free within a given country as well as between nations was a matter of dispute between mercantilists, physiocrats and other advocates of the philosophy of LAISSEZ-FAIRE.

TRADE was obviously not only a theoretical matter. The eighteenth century witnessed a notable commercial expansion. Commercial rivalries that had in previous centuries existed mostly between towns were by the eighteenth century major national concerns. Naval power, and the colonial trade which ensued from it, played a crucial part in this, to the detriment of some of the German states, for instance. Competition did, however, also lead to special relationships. Political or dynastic ties could be crucial to trade relations, as was the case between Hanover and England since the early part of the century or between France and Poland.

In England, which supplanted Holland as the foremost commercial European nation, exports rose from £6.4 million in 1711, to £7.5 million in 1721, £8.4 million in 1731 and £9.1 million in 1741, due principally to an increase in manufacturing output. Exports of iron and steel rose from 16,770 tons in 1765–74 to 30,7171 in 1795–1804. With the Act of Union of 1707, free trade was established with Scotland, which, like the colonies, became a market for English manufactured goods. Colonial trade was a significant factor in English trade. Though the overall value of English and, say, French trade was more or less comparable, more than half of English trade was colonial and this world trade provided the basis of English exports to Europe. French commerce, on the other hand, was predominantly European. Moreover, taking the size of their respective populations into consideration, English foreign trade was four times that of France.

The East India companies of the seventeenth century maintained their importance in the eighteenth century. European trade extended beyond India to China and Japan and return trips via Africa and America often partook in the slave trade. Between 1660 and 1800 an estimated 4,000 English, 3,750 Dutch, 1,200 Portugese and 650 French trips took place. It was therefore with good reason that, as Hume explained, one of the most striking features of modern political theory was the prominence it gave to commerce. What this entailed in terms of commercial policy was, however, to remain a topic of great controversy.

While mercantilists urged rulers to protect their economy by restricting foreign imports (see MERCANTILISM), the PHYSIOCRATS and Scottish political economists clamoured for a policy of *laissez-faire*. Adam Smith's *Wealth of Nations*, much of which was devoted to this subject, argued that the greatest encouragement a sovereign could give to domestic production was 'to grant the most perfect freedom of trade to the artificers, manufacturers and merchants of all other nations'. As Smith was well aware and as the attempt of Sir Robert Walpole to implement a new excise scheme in relation to wine and tobacco made clear, such changes were by no means easy to bring about. Burke was also to make himself very unpopular with his constituents in Bristol for the support he gave to the abolition of restrictions on Irish trade. Then, as always, the interest of a country's consumers and that of its inhabitants involved in various aspects of production led to radically opposed responses to the establishment of free trade.

W. H. Bruford, *Germany in the Eighteenth Century: The Social Background of the Literary Revival* (Cambridge: Cambridge University Press, 1965).

Istvan Hont, 'The "Rich Country–Poor Country" Debate in Scottish Classical Political Economy', in Istvan Hont and Michael Ignatieff (eds), *Wealth and Virtue: The Shaping of Political Economy in the Scottish Enlightenment* (Cambridge: Cambridge University Press, 1983), pp. 271–315.

R. Picard, J.-P. Kerneis and Y. Bruneau, *Les Compagnies des Indes* (Paris: 1966).

Elizabeth Body Schumpeter, *English Overseas Trade Statistics 1697–1808* (Oxford: Clarendon, 1960).

SYLVANA TOMASELLI

French Revolution The French Revolution of 1789 was a world-historical event which has had a massive influence on subsequent European history. It represented (until the Russian Revolution of 1917) the paradigm of a REVOLUTION which through radical means could achieve wide-ranging social and political transformation. Much of the vocabulary of liberal Western politics (including the very word 'revolution') derives from the French experience between 1789 and 1799.

Although the storming of the BASTILLE on 14 July 1789 is usually accounted the beginning of the Revolution, historians normally start their narratives with the 'pre-Revolution', the state bankruptcy and 'noble revolt' against the monarchy in 1787–8 which led to the convocation of the ESTATES GENERAL in 1789. Similarly, although the Revolution is usually conceptualized as a unitary and unifying act, there is a sense of the diversity and complexity of the 1789 events: following Georges Lefebvre, perhaps the most influential historian of the Revolution in the twentieth century, historians distinguish the political revolution centred on the NATIONAL ASSEMBLY from the popular revolution in Paris, the 'municipal revolution' taking place in the townships of provincial France and the peasant revolution sweeping the countryside, each of which had a degree of autonomy.

Three main stages in the Revolution from 1789 are usually delineated. First, there was the period of constitutional monarchy from 1789 to 1792, when the DECLARATION OF THE RIGHTS OF MAN AND THE CITIZEN and the CONSTITUTION OF 1791 established the liberal freedoms and when the CONSTITUENT ASSEMBLY (1789–91) in particular introduced major legislative reforms (administrative reorganization, church reform, abolition of feudalism, economic freedom and so on). The overthrow of King Louis XVI on 10 August 1792 inaugurated a second, more radical phase, marked in particular by the application of Jacobin methods of centralized authoritarian government. This was embodied in the rule of the COMMITTEE OF PUBLIC SAFETY, characterized by the implementation of policies of TERROR, which were arguably justified by the critical state of the war with European powers and by the civil war which was raging in western and southern France. The overthrow of the Robespierre faction within the Committee of Public Safety in the THERMIDOR coup of 27 July 1794 inaugurated the third phase of the revolutionary decade. The Thermidorian Convention and then, from October 1795, the regime of the DIRECTORY attempted to revivify the liberal, constitutional values of 1789–92, albeit within a republican framework. The rule of law proved too difficult to maintain in such a politically turbulent period, however, and the regime fell to a military *coup d'état* in November 1799 engineered by Napoleon BONAPARTE.

The advent of Napoleon in 1799 is usually viewed as marking the 'end' of the Revolution. Napoleon's contribution to stabilizing (though also deforming) the revolutionary achievement is, however, acknowledged. The importance of both the political achievements of the revolutionary decade (the liberal freedoms, constitutionalism and so on) and its socio-economic impact (destruction of the influence of the aristocracy, abolition of feudalism, property transfers and so on) has long been acknowledged. The concept of the Revolution as a 'bourgeois revolution', borrowed from Marx, with 1789 allegedly marking a key date in the transition from feudalism to capitalism in France, was adapted and elaborated in the twentieth century by a line of socialist historians including Jean Jaurès, Albert Mathiez, Georges Lefebvre and Albert Soboul, and by the 1950s it constituted the paradigm through which professional historians viewed the Revolution. From 1955, however, the so-called 'Marxist interpretation' was roundly attacked on largely empirical grounds by the British historian Alfred Cobban, and from the 1960s the influential work of François Furet questioned many of the presuppositions on which it was based. A 'revisionist' approach to the Revolution developed which by the time of the bicentenary of the Revolution in 1989 dominated historiographical debate: the socio–economic significance of the Revolution was widely contested; the bourgeois–aristocratic struggle was no longer viewed as a helpful perspective on political change; the revolutionary credentials of the bourgeoisie were doubted; and 1789 was viewed, notably in Furet's work, as marking less a social 'advent' of the bourgeoisie than a political 'event' in its own right with its own generative logic and dynamism.

François Furet and Mona Ozouf, *A Critical Dictionary of the French Revolution* (Cambridge, Mass.: Harvard University Press, 1989).
Alice Gérard, *La Révolution française: mythes et interprétations, 1789–1970* (Paris: Flammarion, 1970).
Georges Lefebvre, *The French Revolution*, 2 vols (New York: Columbia University Press, 1962; London: Routledge, 1964).

COLIN JONES

Fuseli, Henry [Füssli, Johann Heinrich] (1741–1825)   Swiss painter. He became one of the most influential of the romantic school in England. His painter father intended him for the church, but this proposed career collapsed after he joined Johann Kaspar Lavater (1741–1801) in attacking a local magistrate and was forced to leave the country. He went to London in 1764, where he translated Winckelmann into English and helped develop interest in the German STURM UND DRANG movement. He trained as a painter in Italy for nine years from 1770. Back in London he collaborated on the Shakespeare Gallery, aimed at developing history painting in England, and followed with illustrations for Milton's *Paradise Lost*, *Siegfried* and English fairy-tales. As professor of painting at the Royal Academy after 1800, he greatly influenced the next generation of English painters.

Although he was devoted to HISTORY PAINTING, Fuseli had more in common with Blake and Goya than with the neoclassical school. His work is characterized by an almost impressionistic approach centred on the human figure. He frequently depicted the irrational – spirits and goblins – and his work is above all characterized by a distaste for women.

Henry Fuseli (London: Tate Gallery, 1975).

IAIN PEARS

G

⎯⎯⎯⎯⎯⎯◆⎯⎯⎯⎯⎯⎯

gabelle   The *gabelle* was the much hated salt tax levied in *ancien régime* France. Collected by the private syndicate of FARMERS GENERAL responsible for most indirect taxes, the *gabelle* represented the highest source of state tax revenue after the TAILLE. The use of salt for food preservation made it a commodity of prime necessity, but hostility to its taxation also focused on the arbitrariness of its imposition and the bureaucratic efficiency of its collection. Although it was in theory an indirect tax, the fact that individuals were taxed at a certain amount per head made it seem closer to a direct tax. From 1680 the kingdom was divided into six areas, in each of which salt was taxed at a different level: the tax was a half-sou in so-called *pays exempt* like Brittany, 13 sous in some *pays de grande gabelle* like the Paris region. These disparities encouraged widespread smuggling as well as fraud, and to keep both in check the excise officials of the Farmers General were allowed wide-ranging powers of search, while punishments against smuggling were ferocious. The tax was denounced in the CAHIERS OF 1789, widely evaded from the summer of that year and abolished in 1790.

See also TAXATION.

COLIN JONES

Gainsborough, Thomas (1727–1788)   English painter. With Joshua REYNOLDS he dominated the English art world for much of the mid eighteenth century. Although he regarded himself mainly as a landscape painter – being influenced particularly by seventeenth-century Dutch and Flemish painters – like most of his contemporaries he had to earn a living as a portraitist. Unlike them, however, he established a successful career outside London, in his native Suffolk and then in Bath, before moving to London in 1774. Early in his career he produced innovative works such as *Mr and Mrs Andrews* (1749), in which a landscape of the sitters' estate received as much prominence as the sitters. His Bath period (1759–74) was influenced by paintings of Van Dyck (1599–1641) and produced works such as the *Blue Boy*. Although neither as productive as Reynolds – he employed no assistants to help him in his work – nor as successful socially, he was greatly admired for his intelligence, and was enormously popular with the public both for his carefully observed portraits and his meticulously composed landscapes. Technically he was also more accomplished – his paintings have survived in much better condition than those of most of his contemporaries.

John Hayes, *Thomas Gainsborough* (London: Tate Gallery, 1981).

IAIN PEARS

Galiani, Ferdinando (1728–1787)   Neapolitan economist. He was secretary at the embassy in Paris from 1759. He entrusted the publication of his *Dialogues sur le commerce des blés* (Dialogues on the Grain Trade, 1770) to Denis Diderot and Madame D'Épinay (1726–83) when recalled, at France's request, in May 1769. An early work on money (1749) shows him to have been originally close to the physiocrats, but he grew to be fearful of the consequences of the implementation of the decree of 19 July 1764, permitting the free export of grain from France.

The *Dialogues*, which even Turgot acknowledged to be full of wit, caused a great stir. In them Galiani used historical evidence to criticize government policy as well as to argue that in affairs of state everything was interconnected. The abbé Morellet and Le Mercier de la Rivière were among those who took up the pen to refute Galiani. Diderot, whose defence of Galiani was not published in his lifetime, Friedrich Melchior von Grimm and others among the *philosophes* were to become more cautious in their support of free trade partly as a result of reading the *Dialogues*. Rather than being against the free export of grain *per se*, Galiani contended that France's priority should be the removal of its internal tariff barriers and that the decree of 1764 did not achieve its intended effect.

See also GRAIN TRADE.

Steven L. Kaplan, *Bread, Politics and Political Economy in the Reign of Louis XV*, 2 vols (The Hague: Nijhoff, 1976).

SYLVANA TOMASELLI

Gallicanism   The nineteenth-century label 'Gallicanism' was applied to a set of French doctrines and attitudes originating in King Philip the Fair's (1285–1314) conflicts with the papacy and the Conciliar movement in the late Middle Ages. Its most striking definition is found in the Declaration of Four Articles, framed in 1682 by Bishop BOSSUET for Louis XIV, which asserted the independence of the monarch in temporal matters; the superiority of an ecumenical council over the pope's pronouncements; and the unity of the French church and king in the protection of customary rights (for example the king's right to nominate bishops, as asserted in the Concordat of Bologna, 1516), thus limiting the authority of the papacy to spiritual matters. The articles were specifically revoked in 1693 but the spirit they represented lived on in the eighteenth century and was embodied in royal pronouncements and also in the claim of the *parlements* to deal with church affairs affecting the fundamental laws of the kingdom. Gallicanism's most famous success was the expulsion of the JESUITS from France in 1764. The CIVIL CONSTITUTION OF THE CLERGY was strongly influenced by it, as was the CONCORDAT OF 1802.

COLIN JONES

Galvani, Luigi (1737–1798) Italian physiologist and physician. He invented 'animal ELECTRICITY', or galvanism, when he found that muscular contractions elicited by application of static electricity in frog preparations, could be induced even when the frog was distanced and insulated from the electrical machine. In *De viribus electricitatis* (1791) he detailed further experiments where he obtained contractions simply by placing brass hooks against frog preparations on an iron plate. He concluded that a subtle and vital electrical fluid existed within animal nerves and muscles which, in generating currents, was responsible for animal motion. He compared muscle to the Leiden jar.

By 1793, Alessandro VOLTA, who had initially been sympathetic to galvanism, had become Galvani's chief rival. He developed a theory of 'contact' by which certain metals excited electrical fluid on contact with each other. Galvani and his nephew Giovanni Aldini mounted a counter-campaign in defence of animal electricity, the success of which was still in the balance when Galvani died. Popular belief in galvanism, however, outlived its inventor, and influenced F. H. A. Humboldt, Lorenz Oken, Charles Henry Wilkinson and Percy B. Shelley.

John F. Fulton and Harvey Cushing, 'A Bibliographic Study of the Galvani and Aldini writings on Animal Electricity', *Annals of Science*, 1 (1936), 239–68.

M. L. BENJAMIN

gardens By the eighteenth century the original concept of the garden, as a 'guarded' space enclosed by a fence, hedge or wall, had changed to include the landscape beyond. Horace Walpole in *The History of* *the Modern Taste of Gardening* (1771–80) wrote of William KENT that he first 'leaped the fence, and saw all nature was a garden'.

While formal garden design continued well into the 1750s, the influence of seventeenth-century Italian, French and Dutch landscape painters had inspired landowners and designers to recreate natural and pastoral landscapes. Alexander Pope observed that 'all gardening is landscape painting'. Man's relationship with nature was no longer one of imposition, but of emulation. William Hogarth's dictum of the serpentine 'line of beauty and grace' was reflected in the creation of parkland landscapes with flowing, informal lines applied to lakes, tree planting, earth modelling and drives. This manner of garden-making achieved world renown, and was referred to as 'le jardin Anglais' or 'der Englische Garten'. In England few estates escaped some degree of 'landscaping'. European gardens included Stowe, Stourhead (English) Ermenonville, Desert de Retz (French), Wörlitz and Schwetzingen (German).

See also 'CAPABILITY' BROWN.

John Dixon Hunt and Peter Willis, *The Genius of the Place: The English Landscape Gardens 1620–1820* (London: Paul Elek, 1975).

MARYLLA HUNT

Garrick, David (1717–1779) English actor. He was the most famous actor of the eighteenth century, and also a successful playwright and theatre manager. He wrote almost forty dramatic pieces, which included adaptations of Shakespeare, and many romantic and social comedies. In his own lifetime he became a cultural icon – both of the powers of dramatic expression, and of the desirability of literary fame. He was painted perhaps more often than any other personality of the century (by Hogarth, Reynolds and Gainsborough among others) and earned respectful mention from many famous writers (he makes appearances in *Tristram Shandy* and *Tom Jones*). His role as an emblem of naturalistic powers of expression is preserved in a number of theatrical conversation pieces: paintings of him in his most renowned roles. His first appearance on the London stage was as Richard III in 1741, and his success was almost immediate. He became co-manager of the Theatre Royal, Drury Lane in 1747, and both he and the theatre enjoyed considerable prosperity until his retirement in 1776.

Alan Kendall, *David Garrick* (London: Harrap, 1985).

JOHN MULLAN

Gay, John (1685–1732) English poet and playwright is now best known for *The Beggar's Opera*, a musical drama blending political satire and popular songs. It was first performed in 1728, and was hugely successful. Earlier in his career, he wrote mostly poetry, including *The Shepherd's Week* (1714), *Trivia* (1716) and *Fables* (1727). The best of this work is parodic, like that of his friends and associates, Pope and Swift. These three, together with John Arbuthnot (1667–1735), were the leading members of the Scriblerus Club, dedicated to works of mock-learning. Gay is likely to have contributed to several 'Scriblerian' texts whose authorship remains uncertain. Despite some important friends (including Mrs Howard, George II's mistress) and successful books, he sought patronage to little avail, and was frequently short of money (he lost a large sum in the South Sea Bubble). Committed to advancement within the court, he obtained nothing better than the minor post of commissioner of the English state lottery. Gay enjoyed literary fame for only the last four years of his life; he died shortly after completing the libretto of Handel's *Acis and Galatea*.

Peter Lewis and Nigel Wood (eds), *John Gay and the Scriblerians* (London: Vision, 1988).

JOHN MULLAN

general will The term 'general will' was common in political discourse long before the Enlightenment, especially in the plural form *volontés générales*. It was employed in several senses by various authors in the eighteenth century, including Montesquieu, Diderot and Kant. However, it is now most readily associated with Jean-Jacques Rousseau, who used the term in his *Encyclopédie* article on 'Économie' (1755) to mean the totality of all particular wills, and then, in *Du contrat social* (1762) in a radically different sense, to answer the question of how men can be free in a society where their FREEDOM is of necessity constrained by laws. He argued that men could be morally free only in a society whose laws were the expression of the general will, that is the will of the people taken as a whole and constituting an artificial being, one which they had brought into existence through surrendering their natural RIGHTS, thereby transforming themselves into citizens (*see* CITIZENSHIP). In obeying such laws men would be obeying laws of their own making.

Robert Wokler, 'The Influence of Diderot on the Political Theory of Rousseau: Two Aspects of a Relationship', *Studies on Voltaire and the Eighteenth Century*, 132 (1975), 55–111.

SYLVANA TOMASELLI

Geneva Until Napoleonic annexation (1798), Geneva was an independent city-state allied to SWITZERLAND, ruled by a Francophile patriciate which attracted successive protest revolts (notably 1707, 1734–8, 1766–8 and 1782) aimed at correcting oligarchy and restoring an 'ancient constitution'. Its economic strengths rested on the luxury trades and banking; later came tourism. Culturally it was an important international centre for the Calvinistic church, education and publishing, mediating between trends in English, Dutch, German, Italian and French thought. The Academy's modernized curriculum was strong in science and law: luminaries included Cramer (1704–52), Calandrini (1703–58), Bonnet, H. B. de Saussure (1740–99) and Burlamaqui. The entire population was highly literate. Geneva's rational Christianity was notoriously misconstrued as Socinian in d'Alembert's *Encyclopédie* article. Voltaire in nearby Ferney was both a magnet and a gadfly; the Genevan context is crucial for understanding Rousseau. His *Émile* popularized the Lake Léman countryside, while Albertine Necker de Saussure's (1766–1841) views on female education rebuked Rousseau's misogyny from the perspective of Geneva's relative egalitarianism towards its citizenesses.

Maurice Cranston, *Jean-Jacques: The Early Life and Work of Jean-Jacques Rousseau, 1712–1754* (London: Allen Lane, 1983).

CLARISSA CAMPBELL ORR

genius Who was and who was not a genius was as much a subject of conversation in the eighteenth century as it is today. Moreover, the concept was used in two rather contradictory ways. On the one hand, it was used to denote talent which, though seemingly exceptional, would be found in vast numbers of people given the right environment; on the other, it was ascribed to individuals who were thought to be unique. This double usage is well reflected in the writings of Mary Wollstonecraft. In a review of the book *Hints on Producing Genius* (1790) she wrote: 'The word *genius*, which has commonly been used to describe a peculiar disposition of nature, expresses, we think, in a rather vague manner, this writer's meaning . . . we agree with him, that much *understanding* might be . . . propagated . . . if the body were strengthened by exercise, chastity, and temperance, and the mind by learning to think, were allowed to attain the perfection that they seem capable of reaching, when not weakened by vice. The sins of the fathers would not then be visited upon the children, and the race, improved gradually, during many successive generations, might all be men of genius, compared with the present dwarfish, half-formed beings, who crawl discontented between earth and heaven.' In the *Vindication of the Rights of Woman* she argued that 'a person of genius is the most improper person to be employed in education', because 'Minds of this rare species see things too much in masses, and seldom, if ever, have a good temper.'

When reflecting on this subject, she thought of Shakespeare and

Milton. So did the author (who may be Diderot) of the *Encyclopédie* article 'Génie', who ranked them with Horace, Homer and other ancient authors. Surprisingly, it also compared John Locke and the earl of Shaftesbury, deeming the latter a genius and describing the former as simply possessed of a vast, penetrating and just mind.

In an altogether different genre, Diderot's *Le Neveu de Rameau* contains one of the most arresting discussions of the nature of genius. Most interesting of all was his description of a failed genius, the second-rate musician, Rameau's nephew. Although he was far from excelling at anything, he was supposedly capable of some striking insights. Diderot demonstrated the importance of coming to terms with one's own mediocrity. Indeed, he intimated that such a process could in itself be a form of art, in which some might reveal something akin to genius. However, this might be at the cost of one's virtue.

Herbert Dieckmann, 'Diderot's Conception of Genius', *Journal of the History of Ideas*, 2 (Apr. 1941), 151–82.

SYLVANA TOMASELLI

Genoa The republic of Genoa was one of the oldest states in Italy, comprising the port itself, a narrow strip of coastline and a poor mountainous hinterland. The rebellious island possession of CORSICA was sold to France in 1768. By the 1740s the city's population was 75,000, its highest level since the plague of 1656. The republic continued to be dominated by its narrow elite of old noble families, led by the Dorias, Grimbaldis and Brignoles, who controlled the Casa di San Giorgio, the great banking-house which effectively financed the state. A large, active middle class emerged in the course of the century to challenge the patricians, but their hold remained unbroken until the French Revolution, thanks to their paternalistic policies such as the *Annona* which ensured cheap food for the urban poor, and numerous charitable foundations. Popular support for the republic was clear in 1746, when the urban poor and the peasantry rose in a furious revolt against an attempt to impose Austrian rule; there was a similar revolt against the French in 1798.

Genoa faced economic difficulties early in the eighteenth century, suffering a loss in trade to Marseilles and the new Tuscan port of Livorno, which even its conversion into a free port did not reverse. By mid-century its maritime activity had increased again, mainly in trade with the Levant, Spain and Naples. The financial activities of the patricians also expanded after the War of the Austrian Succession and between 1771 and 1792, especially, large sums were advanced to creditors abroad. It was an artificial wealth, based on past investments, for while the city's commercial activities grew, they did not keep pace with other ports and industry remained artisanal and insignificant.

D. Carpanetto and G. Ricuperati, *Italy in the Age of Reason, 1685–1789* (London: Longman, 1987).

MICHAEL BROERS

Genovesi, Antonio (1713–1769)   Italian philosopher and political economist. Ordained in 1737, he turned to the study of political economy when his hopes for a chair in theology were thwarted by the authorities. In 1754, he was appointed to the newly created chair of political economy at the University of Naples. His *Discourse on the True End of the Art and Sciences* (1753), which has been called 'the manifesto of the Neapolitan Enlightenment', emphasized the importance of education and the need for reform. Genovesi juxtaposed the philosophical and theological ideas of his native culture with those coming from Britain and France for heuristic as well as critical purposes.

Like Ferdinando Galiani, he was deeply shocked by the terrible famine of 1764 and what it highlighted, the enormity of the gap between the impoverished and illiterate peasantry and the privileged classes in Naples itself. He argued for the removal of the principal barriers to economic development and saw English commercial society as a model for Neapolitan society. The first volume of *Lezioni di commercio o sia di economia civile* (Lessons on Commerce) appeared in 1765, followed by another in 1767. His many disciples made up the second wave of Enlightenment figures in southern Italy in the latter part of the century.

Richard Bellamy, '"Da metafisico a mercatante" – Antonio Genovesi and the Development of a New Language of Commerce in Eighteenth-Century Naples', in Anthony Pagden (ed.), *The Languages of Political Theory in Early-Modern Europe* (Cambridge: Cambridge University Press, 1987), pp. 277–99.

SYLVANA TOMASELLI

gentry   The term 'gentry' refers to the middle group of English land-owners, those standing between the great owners and the minor country gentlemen (*see* LANDOWNERSHIP). In the eighteenth century the gentry may have numbered some 3,000 families, enjoying annual incomes rising from a few hundred pounds to several thousands, though with considerable regional variations. A proportion of them held titles as knights or baronets, while higher titles were largely confined to the great landowners. Gentry estates probably occupied over a third of the area of England and Wales, with a concentration in the Home Counties, the south-west and southern England, and in Wales. Locally the gentry were influential as magistrates, exercising numerous judicial and administrative functions, especially in relation to petty crime, roads, the Poor Law and alehouses. Some important families long controlled county seats and in parliament formed a group of 'country members', jealous of their independence of crown and government. They were closely associated with support for the Church of England, and were especially concerned with agriculture and other county interests; early in the century numbers espoused the Jacobite cause.

G. E. Mingay, *The Gentry* (London: Longman, 1976).

G. E. MINGAY

George I (1660–1727)   King of Great Britain and Ireland (1714–27). Born at Osnabrück, the son of Ernest Augustus, elector of Hanover (1629–98), he inherited the throne under the 1701 Act of Settlement, through his mother Sophia, granddaughter of James I of England (1566–1625), when Queen Anne, the last Stuart ruler, died on 1 August 1714. George brought with him a skilled team of Hanoverian advisers and a decided Hanoverian bias, yet made only five return visits to his electorate, and was an active and important British ruler. A soldier himself, he promoted army reform and reorganization. He was also a rationalist and progressive, in sympathy with early Enlightenment thought, who endowed the regius professorships at Oxford and Cambridge to promote knowledge of modern history, diplomacy and languages. He supported inoculation against smallpox, encouraged religious toleration, patronized music and architecture, and permitted open political and social criticism. He appeared publicly with little formality in London's streets, churches, theatres and meeting-places. In diplomacy he did much to rebuild Britain's standing in Europe after the collapse of the Grand Alliance in 1713. In domestic politics he promoted political stability and did much to secure his novel and foreign dynasty.

R. Hatton, *George I: Elector and King* (Cambridge, Mass.: Harvard University Press, 1978).

PHILIP WOODFINE

George II (1683–1760)   Elector of Hanover, king of Great Britain and Ireland (1727–60). The son of George I, he was born at Herrenhausen, and in 1705 married the intelligent and influential CAROLINE OF ANSPACH, who promoted the policies of Walpole. An active diplomat and biased towards Hanover, he did distort foreign policy, most obviously in July 1741, when he broke with his alliances and made Hanover neutral without consulting the British ministry. He supported the army and had himself led an army into battle, successfully, at Dettingen on 27 June 1743. He actively favoured promotion through seniority and merit, not purchase or influence. Courtiers and politicians had an informal club of those who had been 'rumped' (George publicly turning his back on them). He resented the limits of power in Britain compared with Hanover, yet the royal closet was the focus of ministerial politics, and his influence and patronage were significant. In domestic affairs he favoured compromise and stability, consistently supporting the 'Old Corps' of Whigs, WALPOLE and then Pelham (c.1695–1754) and Newcastle. Underrated because he left few papers and worked through the spoken word and terse written comment, he was shrewd and successful.

J. Brooke (ed.), *Horace Walpole: Memoirs of King George II,* 3 vols (Harvard: Yale University Press, 1985).

PHILIP WOODFINE

George III (1738–1820) King of Great Britain and Ireland (1760–1820), and of Hanover (1815–20). As a young man he was immature and politically naive, but from the mid-1760s he was a consummate politician. A sincere Anglican, and devoted to the constitution, he believed that the Revolution Settlement left him with two inalienable prerogatives: the right to choose ministers and to veto legislation. During the American dispute he upheld the sovereignty of the British parliament. Detesting Fox, he exploited the India Bill crisis in 1783 to install the younger PITT as first minister. The first British-born Hanoverian, George became a popular monarch. His prejudices were shared by many of his subjects, and his patriotism and sense of public duty were impressive. He opposed Catholic emancipation, believing it to be a violation of his coronation oath, and loathed the French Revolution. From 1788 he suffered recurring attacks of porphyria, becoming permanently incapacitated in 1810 and spending his remaining years in retirement. During the French wars he became the focus for loyalist sentiment. His integrity in public and private life helped to popularize the monarchy as a national institution.

J. Brooke, *King George III* (London: Constable, 1972).

JOHN W. DERRY

George IV (1762–1830) Prince regent of Great Britain and Ireland (1811–20), king (1820–30). The eldest son of George III was a man of intelligence, aesthetic discernment and wit; he was also irresponsible, devious and selfish. Once he came of age he associated with the Foxite opposition, much to his father's disgust. His life-style and debts were controversial, while his secret marriage to Maria Fitzherbert, a Catholic widow, laid him open to the charge of violating the Act of Settlement and the Royal Marriages Act. His official marriage to Caroline of Brunswick was disastrous. Attempts to convict her of adultery and to exclude her from the privileges of queen-consort embarrassed several ministries. As he aged, George became estranged from the Foxite party, supporting the war against Napoleon and resisting Catholic emancipation. He was unpopular with the London mob, but he revived the coronation as a public spectacle and his visits to Scotland and Ireland were successful exercises in public relations.

C. Hibbert, *George IV: Regent and King* (London: Allen Lane, 1973).

JOHN W. DERRY

Germany   In the eighteenth century Germany existed within the HOLY ROMAN EMPIRE as a state of sorts, and as a cultural nation which had no political expression. The Empire after 1648 has suffered from an almost universally bad press, especially in Germany. Nationalist propaganda in the nineteenth century consistently portrayed it as a barrier to the rise of Prussia, with its supposed mission to unite and lead Germany. There has also been a tendency to emphasize the fragmentation of Germany and to write off the imperial constitution as no more than the codification of weakness. Although there were great debates on it in the eighteenth century, many contemporaries believed that the Empire could still behave like a proper state, to preserve internal peace and external defence, and that the imperial constitution was perfect for Germany, as it combined the diversity that allowed each state to develop in its own way and at same time gave a measure of unity to the German nation. A balance had been found which it would be dangerous to disturb, expressing as it did the true nature of the Germany that had evolved over the centuries. The Empire was also seen as a European necessity, a vital component in the European BALANCE OF POWER, the disappearance of which would lead to an orgy of wars, partitions and conquest.

The balance in the imperial constitution between imperial and princely power was still fluid, although clearly the princes possessed virtual sovereignty. The early eighteenth century saw the imperial reaction, an attempt by the emperors Joseph I and Charles VI to recover something of their authority in Germany using the few powers they still possessed. Joseph took advantage of a wave of German national solidarity arising from hatred of the French to persuade the imperial diet to ratify a decree of outlawry against the electors of Bavaria and Cologne. This provoked fear that the emperor was becoming too powerful among the German princes. The deep religious divisions that had afflicted Germany since the Reformation also continued to cause division and suspicion.

The German political scene changed briefly when the elector of Bavaria became Emperor CHARLES VII in 1742, the only non-Habsburg elected to the title between 1438 and 1806. This raised hopes among the smaller states of a reform and revival of the Empire free from Austria's dynastic control. Prussia floated the idea of enlarging Bavaria to give the WITTELSBACHS a more substantial basis for a long occupation of the imperial throne. All these hopes and plans came to nothing with the premature death of Charles in 1745, when the title reverted to the Habsburgs in the person of Francis I, husband of Maria Theresa. She and Joseph II saw the imperial title as little more than an adjunct of Habsburg dynastic power, but still a significant one, as Joseph showed by his attempts to increase Austrian influence in the Empire using what was left of the Emperor's powers.

German political life until the Empire ended in 1806 was dominated by the rise of dualism – the emergence by the mid eighteenth century of two German states powerful enough to dominate the whole country, Austria and Prussia – and by foreign influence. In 1740 PRUSSIA became the second German great power when FREDERICK II seized Silesia from Austria. Thereafter each saw the other as the main enemy; German issues became central to German politics. Both had major non-German interests and both increasingly behaved like foreign powers, seeking to build up clientage blocs among the smaller German rulers as France had in the past. Each tried to stop any increase of power in Germany by the other. Foreign influence, political and cultural, remained very important in the eighteenth century. Only in the last decades of the century was there a marked reaction against the cultural dominance of France. At the same time many states sought an extension of their power outside Germany, the Habsurgs in Hungary and the Balkans, SAXONY in Poland, and HANOVER in Britain. BAVARIA dreamed of re-creating the Burgundian state by exchanging German territory for the Netherlands. Only Prussia among the larger states saw serious opportunities for expansion in Germany, but in the eighteenth century Prussia also looked to Poland for territorial expansion.

The SEVEN YEARS WAR accelerated many processes at work within the German political structure. Dualism hardened. This was seen clearly in the WAR OF THE BAVARIAN SUCCESSION and the establishment of the League of Princes (*Fürstenbund*) in 1785, by which Prussia blocked Austrian attempts to expand into southern Germany and preserved the *status quo*. After 1763 the fragmentation of the country into a collection of virtually sovereign states continued and the Empire seemed to be losing what little unifying power it had possessed. This led to the emergence of movements among the smaller states for the reform and strengthening of the Empire to prevent its destruction or exploitation for the narrow interests of Austria and Prussia. Another manifestation of this imperial patriotism was Febronianism, a movement which began in the Catholic Church in 1786 to eliminate papal control and establish a German national church (*Reichskirche*). This had the support of Joseph II and was, inevitably, opposed by Prussia and Bavaria, which suspected, rightly, that it was a device to increase Austrian power in Germany. This was another example of how dualism preserved the Holy Roman Empire by freezing it and preventing any change in it.

A decisive turning-point came in 1792, with the outbreak of the French Revolutionary wars. After that, as a result of her victories, France decided the future shape of Germany. The French supervised a series of major territorial reorganizations which swept away the small and ecclesiastical states and in 1806 compelled Francis II to abandon the imperial crown. Germany ceased to exist, except as a geographical and cultural expression.

J. Gagliardo, *Reich and Nation: The Holy Roman Empire as Idea and Reality 1763–1806* (Bloomington, Ind.: Indiana University Press, 1980).
M. Hughes, *Law and Politics in Eighteenth-Century Germany* (Woodbridge: Boydell, 1988).
J. J. Sheehan, *German History 1770–1866* (Oxford: Clarendon, 1989).

MICHAEL HUGHES

Giannone, Pietro (1676–1748) Italian historian. He studied law in Naples and devoted twenty years to his great work *Storia civile del Regno di Napoli* (1723), a critical philosophical history of civil society, much admired by Gibbon. Giannone's systematic treatment of the relationship between state and church, in the course of which he not only sided strongly with the civil authorities but was overtly critical of Rome, led to his persecution and imprisonment; the book was soon placed on the INDEX. Excommunicated, he was forced to leave Naples for Vienna. There he began another antipapal work, *Il Triregno, ossia del regno del cielo, della terra, e del papa*, which he never completed. He left Vienna for Venice, which he was later also compelled to quit. Tricked into celebrating the Easter service in a village under the jurisdiction of the king of Sardinia in 1736, he was apprehended and spent the last twelve years of his life in a Turin prison.

Giuseppe Ricuperati, *L'Esperienza Civile e Religiosa di Pietro Giannone* (Milan: Riccardo Ricciardi, 1970).

SYLVANA TOMASELLI

Gibbon, Edward (1737–1794) The most reflective English historian of the Enlightenment. The son of a country gentleman and a lifelong bachelor, he was sufficiently affluent to indulge his tastes as a gentleman scholar. A sickly and lonely child, he became bookish, and after a disastrous spell at Oxford University, where he briefly converted to Roman Catholicism, travelled widely on the Continent before setting himself up in London, where for some years he was a member of parliament and a pensionary of Lord NORTH, although he never spoke in the Chamber. Increasingly antagonistic to Christianity, Gibbon viewed history in a secular, philosophical manner. His barbed attempt to offer a naturalistic (rather than providential) account of the rise of the church within the Roman Empire, and his belief that the Christian faith had sapped the Roman will to rule and thus contributed to the decline of the empire, angered many churchmen. Although religiously radical and friendly with many *philosophes*, he grew increasingly politically conservative, and deplored the French Revolution, as tending to democracy or despotism. He is the author of the most famous history book in the English language, *The History of the Decline and Fall of the Roman Empire*, which began to appear in 1776 and was completed in 1787.

R. Porter, *Edward Gibbon: Making History* (London: Weidenfeld & Nicolson, 1988).

ROY PORTER

Gibraltar   At the foot of the Spanish peninsula and in a commanding position at the entrance to the Mediterranean, the Rock rises to 1,330 feet at its highest. It is sheer to the east but less so to the west, where its dockyard lies fronting the Bay of Algeciras. It is hardly a sheltered anchorage, and its springs for watering a fleet were Gibraltar's one natural resource. Taken by Britain from Spain in 1704, it was ceded to Britain by Spain at the TREATY OF UTRECHT only on the insistence of Louis XIV, and on condition that contraband was barred, corsairs denied a haven and the Roman Catholic religion tolerated. Although at times the British government, out of concern for Anglo-Spanish relations, would have been ready to respond favourably to pleas from Madrid for its return, parliament remained steadily opposed. The Rock was held in time of war with Spain, pre-eminently during its long siege (1779–83) during the American War of Independence, under the governorship of George Augustus Eliott, Lord Heathfield (1717–90), but also throughout the Napoleonic wars. It required continual supply and replenishment of dockyard stores from home; much naval opinion preferred Minorca as a base and anchorage.

G. Hills, *Rock of Contention* (London: Hale, 1974).

D. D. ALDRIDGE

Gillray, James (1756–1815)   Chief founder of the English school of political caricature. The idea of attaching caricature to politics was initiated by George Townshend (1724–1807) in the 1750s, but Gillray combined this strategy with symbolic interiors of the sort HOGARTH employed in his 'modern moral subjects', mock-baroque compositions, and the free style of ROWLANDSON's early etchings. His mature caricatures began to appear in the 1780s, and most memorably comment on the French Revolution, the Napoleonic period, and the struggles of William Pitt the younger and Charles James Fox inside England (with a gaudy cast of characters including Richard Brinsley Sheridan). His career came to an end in 1810 when he lapsed into a state of insanity. The progeny of Gillray include the main line of British caricaturists from George Cruikshank in the nineteenth century to Vicky, Gerald Scarfe and Ralph Steadman in the twentieth century.

Draper Hill, *Mr Gillray the Caricaturist* (London: Phaidon, 1965).

RONALD PAULSON

Girondins   The Girondins comprised the loose grouping (rather than party) which in the Legislative Assembly (1791–2) supported a vigorous war policy. A good number were elected by the Gironde department (including Vergniaud (1753–1793), Guadet (1758–94), Gensonné (1758–93)), though the grouping included deputies from other localities, individuals associated with the *salon* run by the celebrated bluestocking Madame Roland (1754–93) and others linked to Brissot's emancipationist Amis des Noirs (Friends of the Blacks). Their war policy gave them political ascendancy and from March to June 1792 they composed the so-called 'patriot ministry'. Outraged by the September Massacres of 1792, however, which they blamed on their more radical Montagnard fellow deputies like Danton, Robespierre and Marat, they became more moderate in the NATIONAL CONVENTION. Their attacks on the MONTAGNARDS became increasingly shrill in the context of the military crisis of early 1793. On 31 May and 2 June 1793, popular demonstrations led to twenty-two Girondin deputies being purged from the Convention. Some tried to raise revolt in the provinces but the so-called 'Federalist Revolt' fizzled out and the Girondins who had not managed to escape Paris were guillotined in late 1793.

Michael J. Sydenham, *The Girondins* (London: Athlone, 1960).

COLIN JONES

Glasgow   The city of Glasgow found its identity in 1707 when the Act of Union gave its merchants access to British colonies. They quickly gained a monopoly on the Virginia tobacco trade and, at home, began rebuilding Glasgow to classical proportions. By 1783 they had founded Britain's first chamber of commerce. Through the stimulus of the philosopher Francis HUTCHESON, Glasgow University underwent a similar infusion of energy, hosting figures as diverse as Adam Smith, James

Reid (1798–1851), Joseph Black, James Watt and William Cullen (1710–90).

While SMITH produced *The Wealth of Nations* and *The Theory of Sentiments* his contemporaries Joseph BLACK and William Cullen helped to found the faculties of medicine and chemistry respectively. Black later discovered the theory of latent heat which James WATT used to develop the separate condenser and perfect the steam engine. Another university professor, John Anderson (1726–96), left a will providing for the creation of the Andersonian Institute for the training of 'mechanics', and established the concept of technical colleges. The arts flourished under the Foulis brothers, who were printers of European standing and the founders of an original but ill-fated academy of arts. London still remained the centre of power, however, and continued to lure such figures as Tobias Smollett (1721–71) and William (1718–83) and John Hunter from the city.

David Daiches, *Glasgow* (London: André Deutsch, 1977).

FRANCIS MCKEE

Glorious Revolution (1688) James II (1633–1701) was replaced as ruler of Britain by his son-in-law and nephew William of Orange (*see* WILLIAM III), in 1688. James's Catholicizing, autocratic and apparently pro-French policies aroused opposition and on 5 November 1688 William landed at Torbay, Devon with an invasion force. A failure of nerve on James's part led him to abandon his attempt to resist William's approach on London, and he fled to France. The Bill of Rights (1689) declared that James had abandoned the throne and offered it to William and his wife, Mary. The Revolution led to civil war in both Scotland and Ireland, but after the Treaty of Limerick (1691), William was in secure control. The Revolution Settlement, the name given to the constitutional changes of 1688–1701, established parliamentary monarchy. Under the Triennial Act (1694), it was necessary to have elections at least every three years. Catholics were debarred from the throne. The Protestant future of Britain was secured. William III's enemy, Louis XIV recognized James II as king, and the revolution was followed by war between Britain and France (1689–97, 1702–13).

J. I. Israel (ed.), *The Anglo-Dutch Movement: Essays on the Glorious Revolution and its World Impact* (Cambridge: Cambridge University Press, 1991).

JEREMY BLACK

Gluck, Christoph Willibald (1714–1787) German-Bohemian composer. Born at Erasbach, Bavaria, he developed his musical talents while earning a living as church organist and music teacher in Prague. After working with Černohorský (?1684–?1742), he proceeded to study in Vienna, before going to work in Italy alongside G. B. Sammartini (*c.*1700–75). There Gluck picked up the modern Italian style that is the hallmark of his early compositions. Success in Milan, Venice and Turin led to a London debut in 1745. Gluck was there introduced to Arne and Handel, who was not, however, very impressed. In 1750 Gluck returned to settle in Vienna as court musician to Maria Theresa, winning applause for his popular light operas. A switch from Italian to French style is evident in his first major work, *Orpheo ed Euridice* (1762), notable for the abandonment of threadbare conventions and Italianate vocal fireworks. *Iphigénie en Aulide*, which followed soon, was also in a more simple French manner, and Gluck went on to produce a French version of his earlier success, *Orphée et Eurydice*. There ensued *Alceste* (1776), *Armide* (1777), *Iphigénie en Taudide* and *Echo et Narcisse* (both 1779). Gluck's promotion of the 'reformed' French OPERA – demoting the ballet, accentuating the overture, and eliminating facile vocal brilliance – provoked the hostility of partisans of the Italian opera but gained him lasting renown.

P. Howard, *Gluck and the Birth of Modern Opera* (London: Barrie & Rockliff, 1963).
[herausgegeben von] Klaus Hortschansky, *Christoph Willibald Gluck und die Opernreform* (Darmstadt: Wissenschaftliche Buchgesellschaft, 1989).
Bruce Alan Brown, *Gluck and the French theatre in Vienna* (Oxford: Clarendon, 1991).

ROY PORTER

Godwin, William (1756–1836)   English political writer and novelist. Educated at Hoxton Academy, he eventually abandoned his early career as a dissenting minister for atheism and the ministry of the rational Enlightenment. His reputation as a philosopher of anarchical views was ensured by the publication of the *Enquiry concerning Political Justice* in 1793, in which he espoused the supremacy of truth and the perfectibility of mankind. His philosophical principles and protests against injustice are dramatized in the psychological novel *Things as They Are, or The Adventures of Caleb Williams* which appeared in 1794. During the same year he defended members of the radical London Corresponding Society from charges of high treason in the pamphlet *Cursory Strictures*. He married Mary WOLLSTONECRAFT in 1797, and following her death from puerperal fever after the birth of their daughter, Mary (who was to marry Shelley), wrote his *Memoirs of the Author of a Vindication of the Rights of Woman* (1798). Wollstonecraft was idealized in his Rosicrucian novel *St Leon* (1799), which was parodied by 'Count Reginald de St Leon' in *St Godwin* (1800). Other novels include *Fleetwood* (1805), *Mandeville* (1817), *Cloudesley* (1830) and *Deloraine* (1833). In 1801 he married Mrs Clairmont whose daughter Claire (1798–1879) bore a daughter, Allegra, to Byron in 1817 when she returned from her travels on the Continent with Mary (1797–1851) and Percy Shelley (1792–1822).

William St Clair, *The Godwins and the Shelleys: The Biography of a Family* (London: Faber, 1989).

MARIE MULVEY ROBERTS

Goethe, Johann Wolfgang von (1749–1832)   Goethe was the undisputed genius of German letters. Ever striving for human 'wholeness', his diverse *œuvre* encompasses practically every theme and form of literary expression, including poems, letters, essays, aphorisms, plays, fairy-tales, *Novellen*, novels, travel writing, translations, autobiographical works and scientific treatises. In his multifarious activities as pedagogue, administrator, inspector of mines, painter, theatre director and natural philosopher, he embodies the ideal of Renaissance man. By his learning, he imbued himself with contemporary thought and recast it in a personal synthesis which stretched back to Baconian empiricism, Neoplatonism, and pre-Socratic philosophy. Throughout, truth to 'life', to nature and growth, lay at the heart of his developing wisdom. Born into a solidly middle-class family in Frankfurt am Main, he was introduced to the main currents of Enlightenment thought in his student days at Leipzig from 1765. These were cut short by illness in 1768, and it was during his convalescence that he was profoundly affected by mysticism and the occult sciences. He resumed his studies in Strasbourg in 1770. His love for Friedericke Brion (1752–1813) and the decisive influence of HERDER inaugurated his first major phase of STURM UND DRANG writings. Early love poems like 'Wilkommen und Abschied' (Welcome and Farewell, 1771) brought a new freshness to German literature; for the first time, in this *Erlebnislyrik*, subjective authenticity became the undisputed hallmark of poetry. The great free-verse hymns like 'Prometheus' and 'Ganymede' (1774) transformed this restless subjectivity into philosophical images; and his first major drama, *Götz von Berlichingen* (1771, revised 1773), imitates Shakespeare: the German past offers the matter for a tragic paean to freedom. In *Die Leiden des jungen Werthers* (The Sufferings of Young Werther, 1774) he took subjectivity to its limit, exploring the contradictions which thrust his hero from pantheistic nature-worship and overwhelming love into the abyss of existential despair and suicide. The novel brought him instant fame and a European reputation.

In 1775 he moved to Weimar, where he spent the rest of his life. From 1776 he was a member of the cabinet of the young duke of Saxe-Weimar. Court life and the influence of his beloved Charlotte von Stein (1742–1827) mellowed his personality, but although he wrote some perfect lyrics, notably 'Wandrers Nachtlied' (Wanderer's Night-Song, 1780), he completed no major projects, and in 1786 he decamped to Italy until 1788. Described in *Italienische Reise* (Italian Journey, 1816–17), the trip meant a reversal in orientation as he now discovered the classical ideal; it bore fruit in the two neoclassical dramas, *Iphigenie auf Tauris* (Iphigenia in Tauris, 1787) and *Torquato Tasso* (1790).

Meanwhile, guided by his belief in the unity of nature, he had already started work on natural philosophy, beginning with geology and comparative anatomy; in 1784 he discovered the intermaxillary bone in man, which he interpreted as a sign of nature's continuity; and he complemented this view in *Metamorphose der Pflanzen* (The Metamorphosis of Plants, 1790), which defines an 'archetypal plant' (*Urpflanze*) of which all existing plants are modifications. These studies founded the science of morphology. His greatest energies were expended on his *Zur Farbenlehre* (Colour Theory, 1810), which attempts to demolish Newton's *Opticks*: colour arises from the interaction of light and dark by means of 'polarity and intensification', 'the two great driving forces of all nature'. No less important were his reflections on experiment and method; his 'gentle empiricism' entails constant methodological self-awareness to steer between competing hypotheses in order to discover a symbolical *Urphänomen*.

A new sense of harmony was epitomized by his setting up house with Christiane Vulpius (1765–1816) on returning from Italy, a love celebrated in the frank *Römische Elegien* (Roman Elegies); and by friendship with SCHILLER, from 1794; this brought a new philosophical self-awareness, some immensely productive criticism and the promulgation of a shared classical ideal.

His second novel, *Wilhelm Meisters Lehrjahre* (Wilhelm Meister's Apprenticeship, 1795–6), brought the full scope of his science and experience to fruition in an ironic *Bildungsroman* that suffuses realism with poetic symbolism to chart the organic growth or *Bildung* of an individual. *Die Wahlverwandtschaften* (The Elective Affinities, 1809) expands the focus to a group of four characters, trapped by the tragically conflicting demands of love and duty; while *Wilhelm Meisters Wanderjahre* (Wilhelm Meister's Travels, 1821–9) widens out yet further to encompass society as a whole; locating the modern dilemmas of a technological society, the book opens the boundaries of the novel form and, by concluding with maxims, involves the reader directly in making meaning and discovering wisdom.

The inexhaustible profusion of his poetry was crowned by two cycles, *Westöstlicher Divan* (West-Eastern Divan, 1819), a joyously ironic imitation of the fourteenth-century Persian poet Hafiz which records

Goethe's love for the young Marianne von Willemer in sensuously transparent verse, and the *Chinesisch-deutsche Jahres- und Tageszeiten* (Chinese-German Book of Hours and Seasons, 1830). Such books embody his concept of a single *Weltliteratur*.

One project spans and epitomizes the whole of his creative life, from the *Urfaust* of his *Sturm und Drang* days via the *Fragment* of 1790 to *Faust I* (1808) and *Faust II*, concluded shortly before his death. This Protean play, which defies categorization by combining all poetic categories, pursues the ceaseless strivings of its divided hero towards a positive conclusion, and thereby rehearses and symbolically resolves the paradoxes of modern Western man.

N. Boyle, *Goethe: The Poet and the Age*, 2 vols (Oxford: Oxford University Press, 1991–).

T. J. Reed, *Goethe* (Oxford: Oxford University Press, 1984).

E. M. Wilkinson and L. A. Willoughby, *Goethe: Poet and Thinker* (London: Arnold, 1962).

JEREMY ADLER

Goldsmith, Oliver (1730–1774)   Irish playwright, novelist and poet. He became a writer after starting a career as a physician. Born in Ireland, the son of a clergyman, he studied medicine at Edinburgh and Leiden, and, after supporting himself in London as a physician, he turned to hack-work. Initially he worked for Ralph Griffiths' (1720–1803) *Monthly Review*, and then for *The Critical Review* and other journals. In 1759 he produced his own periodical, *The Bee*, and in 1760 his *Chinese Letters* began appearing in *The Public Ledger*. He befriended JOHNSON in 1761, and became a founder member of his club. (Boswell's *Life of Johnson* includes a vivid characterization of Goldsmith.) As an impecunious writer for a shifting market who did not enjoy lasting success, Goldsmith attempted various genres: poetry (the major poems are *The Traveller* of 1764, and the anti-commercial and nostalgic *The Deserted Village* of 1770), history (he published histories of Rome in 1769, England in 1771 and Greece in 1774), drama (his most successful play was *She Stoops to Conquer*, first performed in 1773) and fiction (*The Vicar of Wakefield*, published in 1766, was the most frequently republished novel of the century).

R. M. Wardle, *Oliver Goldsmith* (Lawrence, Kan.: University of Kansas Press, 1957).

JOHN MULLAN

Gordon Riots (1780)   For a week in June 1780 London was terrorized by the mob. The Protestant Association, led by the fanatical and eccentric Lord George Gordon (1751–93), presented petitions to parliament protesting against the Catholic Relief Act of 1778, which had made limited civil rights concessions to Catholics. But enthusiastic popular support became violent. Catholic chapels were attacked and soon private houses were being ransacked. The Bank of England was besieged, prisoners released from gaols, distilleries and breweries looted and at least 450 lives were lost. George III took the initiative in restoring order by calling in the army. Several hundred rioters were arrested, twenty-one of whom were executed. The riots left an indelible impression on the propertied classes, and memories of the Gordon Riots heightened British fears of violence during the French Revolution. It is significant that the worst outbreak of public disorder in the eighteenth century was inspired by the traditional slogan 'No popery', and the riots demonstrated the prevalence of anti-Catholic prejudice among the populace and the virtual absence of adequate means for the maintenance of public order.

C. Hibbert, *King Mob* (London: Longman, 1958).

JOHN W. DERRY

Gordon, Thomas (*d* 1750)   Whig journalist. He began his polemical career in the 1710s with tracts against high churchmen in the Bangorian Controversy. He collaborated with the veteran parliamentarian John Trenchard (1662–1723) to produce *The Independent Whig* (1720–1) and *Cato's Letters* (1720–3). There were eight collected editions of the former in Gordon's lifetime; it was translated into French by d'Holbach and widely read by the American revolutionaries. Gordon voiced country Whig refrains against ministerial corruption, stockjobbing, standing armies and placemen. Latterly, however, he became Walpole's press adviser and was appointed commissioner of wine licences.

He regularly assaulted Toryism, Jacobitism, religious credulity and 'pulpit incendiaries'. In *The True Picture of a Modern Tory* (1722) he wrote, 'A Tory is a monster . . . a tool of Rome, an emissary of the Pretender's, a friend of priestcraft.' He echoed Locke on natural rights and consent, but recent scholarship emphasizes his 'neo-Harringtonian' preoccupation with money and credit, and debates the extent of his hostility to commerce. This 'English Cato' is a pre-eminent example of the classicizing tendency of Augustan political thought; his edition of Tacitus (1728) remained a standard.

Marie P. McMahon, *The Radical Whigs, John Trenchard and Thomas Gordon* (Lanham, Md.: University Press of America, 1990).

MARK GOLDIE

Gothic novel   The Goths were the post-Roman German tribes whose name had become synonymous with philistine barbarism. During the eighteenth century, which saw a revival of Gothic architecture (*see*

GOTHIC REVIVAL), the term 'Gothic' had become associated somewhat derisively with medievalism. Its most notable exponent was Horace WALPOLE who produced *Castle of Otranto* (1764), a landmark in Gothic fiction, which was followed by William Beckford's (1760–1844) Oriental tale *Vathek* (1786). The emergence of classic Gothic was polarized by Ann Radcliffe (1764–1823), whose sentimental approach included a rationalization of the supernatural, and Matthew Lewis (1775–1818) who exploited the more lurid aspects of Gothicism in his best-selling novel *The Monk* (1796). While Lewis generated horror in order to achieve his effects, Radcliffe drew on terror as a source for the SUBLIME, particularly in her descriptions of landscape in *Mysteries of Udolpho* (1794). In addition to being a tribute to Radcliffe, Jane Austen's (1775–1817) *Northanger Abbey* (1818), like Thomas Love Peacock's (1785–1866) *Nightmare Abbey* (1818), parodies the Gothic novel. In the same year Mary Shelley's *Frankenstein* (1818) appeared as a modern 'scientific' variation on the Faustian pact. A later and more traditional version was Charles Maturin's *Melmoth the Wanderer* (1820) which is perceived as marking the end of the period of the Gothic novel.

MARIE MULVEY ROBERTS

Gothic Revival The various medieval styles subsumed under the term 'Gothic' were still around in the eighteenth century. A modern Gothic was used for the repair or expansion of buildings for which a *retardataire* air was thought appropriate. WREN designed a Gothic doorway (1669) for the Oxford Divinity School and Louis XIV required it for the new west front of Ste Croix, Orléans (1704). VANBRUGH could build in a castle style; in this tradition Robert ADAM designed country houses whose forbidding battlements suggested that the elegance of their neoclassical interiors had been hard won. William KENT used a pointed-arch 'Gothick' without fussing over exactitude; it was Horace WALPOLE's work at his villa Strawberry Hill, at Twickenham, London (begun 1748), that initiated the Gothic Revival's distinctive alliance of archaeology, historical sentiment and the PICTURESQUE. The French were taking a serious interest in medieval structure by mid-century – J. G. Soufflot's (1713–80) Ste Geneviève, Paris (the Panthéon), begun in 1759, was constructed around thrusts and counter-thrusts, some miscalculated, in classical dress. It was this 'rational' (or even neoclassical) Gothic that would shape later architecture's preoccupations with logical construction and truth to materials.

Howard Colvin, 'Gothic Survival and Gothick Revival', *Architectural Review*, 103 (Mar. 1948), 91–8.

CHRISTINE STEVENSON

Göttingen, University of Next to the UNIVERSITY OF HALLE, Göttingen was the focal point of new teaching in the German Protestant lands. Indeed, it was expressly modelled after Halle, exceeding that university only in its decisive emphasis on the natural sciences. These areas were shared between the philosophy faculty and medicine. Göttingen was also influential in law and in its innovative support for new subjects: it combined the study of Oriental languages (Arabic, Hebrew, Greek) with philological interests (Homer) to create archaeology and to shape German classicism (Goethe, Winckelmann). The university library was exemplary in its holdings and classification system, containing 60,000 books by 1761. HALLER, professor of medicine from 1736 to 1753, established a European reputation and also founded two important academic institutions connected with the university, the learned journal *Göttinger Journal* of 1747, which from 1753 became the *Göttinger Gelehrten Anzeigen*, and the Sozietät der Wissenschaften (1751), the first learned society attached to a university.

Teaching at Göttingen commenced in 1734, with the inauguration of the university held in 1737. It was named the Georga Augusta after George II of Great Britain and Ireland, who was also responsible for the territory of Brunswick-Lüneburg. The king provided the finances while Baron Gerlach Adolph von Münchhausen's (1688–1770) administrative genius structured the university.

G. Meinhardt, *Die Universität Göttingen: Ihre Entwicklung und Geschichte von 1734–1974* (Frankfurt: Musterschmidt Göttingen, 1977).

JOHANNA GEYER-KORDESCH

Gottsched, Johann Christoph (1700–1766) German man of letters. He was an advocate of WOLFF's rationalism. Having been professor of poetry at Leipzig since 1730, he was elevated to the chair of logic and metaphysics there in 1734. As publicist and scholar, he propounded rational 'principles'. He edited two moral weeklies in the style of Addison and Steele, translated Bayle's *Dictionary*, and published books on metaphysics, language and rhetoric. His *Poetics* (1729, fourth edition 1751) advocated the neoclassical 'rules' that he also observed in plays like *Sterbender Cato* (The Death of Cato, 1732). He demanded of literature 'plausibility' and 'a useful moral truth', while 'imagination' was essentially 'reason': this led to conflict with BODMER and Breitinger (1701–76) in the 1740s. His importance was already declining when LESSING effectively terminated his influence by savaging him in his celebrated *17 Literaturbriefs* (17th Literary Letter, 1759).

G. L. Jones, 'Johann Christian Gottsched', in A. Natan and B. Keith-Smith (eds), *German Men of Letters*, vol. 6 (London: Wolff, 1972), pp. 45–69.

JEREMY ADLER

government *see* ADMINISTRATION.

Goya y Lucientes, Francisco José de (1746–1828)   Spanish artist. Born at Fuendetodos (Aragon), he showed early signs of artistic gifts. He went to Madrid to study under the painter Francisco Bayeu (1734–95), marrying his sister in 1773. Establishing himself in Saragossa, he produced frescos in the cathedral, before being called to Madrid to work on designs for the royal tapestry works. A serious illness in 1792 left him deaf, and the after-effects of this in turn accentuated idiosyncratic character traits, including a tendency to coarseness and a rather gross sexuality. Charles IV (1748–1819) appointed him court painter in 1799, a post that he retained under Ferdinand VII (1788–1838) and Joseph Bonaparte, though from 1824 he chose to live as an exile in France, dying at Bordeaux.

Toweringly imaginative as an artist, Goya was profoundly creative and almost unrivalled for the expressive power of his vision. Influenced in his youth by Tiepolo, he exhibited in his early paintings a delicate, charming, colourful rococo style. But his work grew increasingly weighty, personal and psychologically charged. The mature Goya frankly expressed his disgust at human brutality, stupidity and vanity. His savagely nightmarish sequence of etchings *Los Caprichos* satirized moralistic and religious pieties. The harrowing *Disasters of War* (1810–14) was inspired by the atrocities engendered by the Napoleonic occupation of Spain. Recurrent images of sorcery and demons and bloody bullfighting scenes betray his obsession with the dark, unconscious and horrifying sides of human existence. Goya was also a supreme portraitist. The bold brushwork he cultivated in his later years, in some respects prefiguring Impressionism, won admiration from nineteenth-century French painters.

F. Klingender, *Goya in the Democratic Tradition* (London: Sidgwick & Jackson, 1948).

ROY PORTER

grain riots   Early modern governments throughout Europe typically regulated the GRAIN TRADE. The motives were mixed. Political expediency dictated that grain staples should be stable in price and affordable. And there was some paternalistic desire to protect the peasantry and urban poor from middlemen, millers and merchants, who were proverbially rapacious. National and local ordinances specified the conditions under which grain should be brought to market and publicly sold at fixed prices, under the direction of magistrates. What E. P. Thompson has called a 'moral economy' reinforced the notions of fair prices and just trading. When, for whatever reasons, normal market regulation broke down – perhaps because of scarcity or profiteering – price riots commonly followed; in England these occurred especially in the 1760s. Grain or bread protests could be radical – often blood was shed – but they were conservative in orientation, being designed to restore *old* prices. For this reason they sometimes commanded the support of conservative forces with a stake in continuity. The gradual desuetude of grain regulation in Georgian England as part of free trade and the 'political economy' advocated by Adam Smith's *Inquiry into the Nature and Causes of the Wealth of Nations* did not, in reality, lead to massive disturbance, partly because absolute grain shortages were rare. The deregulation of the grain trade in France, in accordance with the policies of the physiocrats, proved, however, far more unsettling, and contributed to the erosion of confidence between town and country that formed part of the background to the French Revolution.

See also FOOD RIOTS.

Ian Gilmour, *Riot, Risings and Revolution* (London: Hutchinson, 1992).
Steven L. Kaplan, *Provisioning Paris: Merchants and Millers in the Grain and Flour Trade during the Eighteenth Century* (Ithaca, NY: Cornell University Press, 1984).
W. J. Shelton, *English Hunger and Industrial Disorder: A Study of Social Conflict during the First Decade of George III's Reign* (London: Macmillan, 1973).
E. P. Thompson, *Customs in Common* (London: Merlin, 1991).

ROY PORTER

grain trade   With agricultural techniques changing little in most areas and with a growing population, Europe as a whole rarely had an overabundance of grain. Although rye, maize and a few other grains were consumed, wheat was the primary grain. The major part of each harvest was consumed on the estates where it was grown or in nearby towns. By the eighteenth century regular land and water transportation networks had been developed for conveying grain to the major urban areas in each region. In addition, there was also a fast-growing international grain trade. The chief exporting areas were Hungary, Russia and territories around the Baltic. In years of poor harvests, governments and speculators in the rest of Europe competed to import grain from those areas, but by the second half of the century the United Provinces, England and France had become dependent on imports even in average years. Government reformers and economic writers such as the physiocrats in France succeeded in relaxing controls on domestic trade in several countries, but the international grain trade remained heavily regulated in most areas.

See also FREE TRADE, GRAIN RIOTS.

Steven L. Kaplan, *Provisioning Paris: Merchants and Millers in the Grain and Flour Trade during the Eighteenth Century* (Ithaca, NY: Cornell University Press, 1984).

THOMAS J. SCHAEPER

Grande Peur *see* GREAT FEAR.

Grand Tour   A lessening of religious tension played a major part in the expansion of travelling for pleasure in the eighteenth century. The expansion of foreign tourism was also part of not only a general growth in travel and tourism, but a more widespread consumerism throughout both the social elite and the middling orders. The Grand Tour involved essentially a trip to Paris and a tour of the principal Italian cities, namely Rome, Venice, Florence and Naples, although a variety of possible itineraries could be devised. Although classically associated with the British elite, whose wealth and security encouraged tourism as never before, an increase in tourism was general across much of Europe.

French, Germans, Poles, Russians and Scandinavians also travelled to Paris and Italy. A large number of tourists met and conversed with foreigners as social equals and attended ceremonies or visited institutions which it was more difficult to encounter at home, for example Italian opera. Predisposed by an education in the classics to take an interest in the past achievements of Italian society, the elite, through tourism, became aware of the current achievements of Continental society and culture. Social emulation and a belief in foreign travel as a means of education and, particularly, of social finishing, were crucial. This conflation of social and educational aspects was central to the development of the concept of the Grand Tour in its classical mould – education for aristocratic youth – but during the course of the eighteenth century the stress on educational aspects declined. Finishing remained important, but leisure became more of an accepted aspect of foreign travel. Foreign tourism was curtailed by the Revolutionary and Napoleonic wars and travellers after 1815 were conscious that they were visiting a different world from that toured by their pre-Revolutionary predecessors.

See also COSMOPOLITANISM.

J. M. Black, *The British Abroad: The Grand Tour in the Eighteenth Century* (London: Alan Sutton, 1992).

W. Griep and H. Jager (eds), *Reise und Soziale Realität am Ende des 18. Jahrhunderts* (Heidelberg, 1983).

T. Grosser, *Reiseziel Frankreich: Deutsche Reiseliteratur vom Barock bis zur Französischen Revolution* (Opladen, 1989).

L. Schudt, *Italienreisen im 17. und 18. Jahrhundert* (Vienna, 1959).

JEREMY BLACK

graveyards *see* DEATH.

Gray, Thomas (1716–1771)   English poet. He was a fellow of Peterhouse and then of Pembroke College, Cambridge. He was renowned in his own day, as now, for *his Elegy Written in a Country Church-Yard*, published in 1751, and perhaps the most popular poem of the eighteenth century. His other substantial poems (the 'Odes' published from 1747–8, and *The Progress of Poesy* and *The Bard*, published by Horace Walpole in 1757) are somewhat sterile experiments in form and subject-matter.

JOHN MULLAN

Great Awakening   A powerful religious revival swept the New England colonies in the 1740s. A broad Evangelical movement was begun in the British colonies of North America in the 1730s by the preaching of George Whitefield (1714–70) in the south, especially in the newly founded Georgia, and by Jonathan Edwards (1703–58) in Massachusetts. Their work was taken up in the early 1740s by clergy and laymen alike, preaching in a dramatic style and rousing their hearers to a pitch of emotional frenzy that often included convulsions, writhing, shrieking and hysteria. Some made much of the contrast between the regenerate reborn and the 'dead men', that is incumbent parsons. Fearful of revivalist religious anarchy, the general court of Massachusetts in 1742 forbade itinerant preaching and in the next year issued a condemnation of errors targeted at lay preachers. Touring America in 1744–5, Whitefield found that the Universities of Harvard and Yale had testified against him and he was denied access to many pulpits.

One consequence of the Great Awakening was the foundation of various separatist churches, some of which later joined the Baptists. *See also* EVANGELICALISM.

S. R. L. Clark, *God's World and the Great Awakening* (Oxford: Clarendon, 1991).

ROY PORTER

Great Fear (July–August 1789)   The Great Fear, or *Grande Peur*, of July–August 1789 was a panic reaction which seized rural France and mobilized the peasantry for revolution. The period prior to the harvest, when stocks from the previous year were low, was particularly tense because of high bread prices caused by bad harvests in 1787 and 1788. The peasantry was, moreover, exceptionally politicized thanks to the drawing up of CAHIERS for the ESTATES GENERAL. Six panics swept through most of France from 20 July 1789: a belief that noble seigneurs were hiring 'brigands' to attack the harvest following the Paris rebellion in an 'aristocratic plot' combined with fear that seigneurs were hoarding grain to profit from the ensuing high prices. Peasants formed armed militias to defend themselves against brigands. When these failed to materialize, they attacked chateaux, often burning feudal charters and documents referring to seigneurial and feudal rights whose abolition they had demanded in their *cahiers*. Peasant action destroyed the legal basis of the seigneurial regime in many regions; on 4 August the new Constituent Assembly ratified their action and formally abolished feudalism.

See also JACQUERIES.

G. Lefebvre, *The Great Fear of 1789: Rural Panic in Revolutionary France* (London: New Left Books, 1973).

COLIN JONES

Great Northern War (1700–1721) The war was begun by an anti-Swedish coalition of Denmark, Russia and AUGUSTUS II of Saxony-Poland, which saw the accession of CHARLES XII of Sweden as an opportunity to destroy Swedish power. Initially, however, it was Charles who triumphed. With Anglo-Dutch help, Denmark was invaded and put out of the war at the Treaty of Travendal (1700). Charles destroyed a Russian army at Narva (November 1700) and then invaded Poland. By 1706 Augustus II had been defeated and removed from the Polish throne, to be replaced by the Swedish client Stanislas LESZCZYŃSKI.

Swedish success was short-lived. Defeat at POLTAVA swung the balance to Sweden's enemies. Augustus II was restored in Poland (1709), Russia overran Finland and Sweden's Baltic provinces, while Denmark re-entered the war (1710). Despite renewed military successes after Charles XII's return from his Turkish exile (1714), Sweden was unable to recover. Although Finland was restored in the Treaty of Nystad (1721), Russia kept the rest of Sweden's eastern Baltic empire. The war was a triumph for Russia, not least because of the establishment of Russian dominance over Polish politics after 1710.

R. M. Hatton, *Charles XII of Sweden* (London: Weidenfeld & Nicolson, 1968).

ROBERT I. FROST

Greece From the conquest of Constantinople in 1453 up to the Greek struggle for independence in the early nineteenth century, the area that we know today as Greece was administered in greater or lesser part by the OTTOMAN EMPIRE. By the beginning of the eighteenth century the empire was well in decline, and the Greeks, like other Ottoman territories, shared in the vicissitudes of Ottoman political life. Russia, which as an Orthodox Christian country felt special links with the Greeks, took advantage of this and tried to undermine the Ottomans in various ways. For example, Catherine the Great sent a fleet to foster an uprising in the Peloponnese in 1770. But the desultory Greek rebellion was still-born; an Albanian army sent by the Turkish governor defeated the small joint Greek and Russian army and the Albanians were permitted to terrorize the Peloponnese for the next ten years. In 1783 Catherine won for the Greeks the right to trade under the Russian flag, and Greek merchant activity expanded.

C. M. Woodhouse, *Modern Greece: A Short History*, fifth rev. edn (London: Faber, 1991).

IAN NETTON

Greek Revival Attempts to recreate Greek taste appeared intermittently in European art in the early eighteenth century, but the Greek Revival is properly associated with the more systematic appreciation that began in the 1750s with the opening of Greece to Western travellers. Aesthetically, it was an aspect of the neoclassical movement, stimulated in particular by the theories and writings of WINCKELMANN and others who wished to turn art away from the frivolity of the rococo back to what was considered a nobler, purer, more moral style. One of the most influential works was a French account of Greek architecture by J. D. LeRoy (1758) followed by the English James Stuart (1713–88) and Nicholas Revett's (1720–1804) *Antiquities of Athens* (1762), which influenced the architecture of Nash (1752–1835) and Soane (1753–1837) in England. But in architecture, a full-blown Greek Revival did not appear until the nineteenth century, with Smirke (1781–1867) in England, Schinkel (1781–1841) in Germany and Strickland (1787–1854) in the United States. In other arts the vogue for Greek subject-matter was less exact. While Canova (1757–1822), Schiller and David were all influenced by the fashion, they were never dominated by it.

See also CULT OF ANTIQUITY, NEOCLASSICISM.

J. Mordaunt Crook, *The Greek Revival* (London: John Murray, 1977).

IAIN PEARS

Greuze, Jean Baptiste (1725–1805) French portrait and genre painter. His immense popularity and success lasted from the mid-1750s, when he began exhibiting in Paris, to the 1780s, when changing tastes and the rise of neoclassicism demanded a stern seriousness that his studies of family groups and individual emotion could not satisfy. Although he attempted different forms of painting, he was most successful as a genre painter, in which he was influenced by seventeenth-century Dutch domestic painting, and most gifted as a draughtsman and portraitist. Engravings after his works enjoyed enormous success in the 1770s. His attempts at the more reputable HISTORY PAINTING led to a ferocious dispute with the Académie Royale, and he never exhibited in the annual *salons* after 1769.

Despite welcoming the French Revolution and attempting to change his style to fit public demand from the 1780s onwards, Greuze spent the last decade of his life virtually forgotten. His attempts at history pieces were little more than genre pictures in antique clothes, depicting family relations with psychological acuity.

Anita Brookner, *Greuze: Rise and Fall of an Eighteenth-Century Phenomenon* (London: Paul Elek, 1972).

IAIN PEARS

Gribeauval, Jean Baptiste Vaquette, comte de (1715–1789) Reformer and theorist of ARTILLERY in late *ancien régime* France, whose ideas were enormously influential on the conduct of war in the revolutionary and Napoleonic periods. A valiant soldier whose services were put at the disposal of France's Austrian ally during the Seven Years War, his career was initially blighted by Choiseul's disfavour, but in 1776 he was appointed inspector-general of artillery. He completely overhauled the service, standardizing gun calibres, weight and length, introducing a greater interchangeability of parts, increasing the size of the horse teams pulling the guns, fixing the ratio of artillery to the other arms and reforming artillery training. The result was that the artillery (in which Bonaparte trained) had the highest morale of any of the arms in 1789, and the reputation as the best artillery service in Europe. A light, tactically mobile and efficient artillery was then in place which would have a devastating impact on the battlefields of revolutionary and Napoleonic Europe.

COLIN JONES

Grimm, Friedrich Melchior von (1723–1807) German diplomat, writer and critic. The son of a Lutheran clergyman, he represented Russia, Austria and other German states at Paris and elsewhere. He was at first influenced by the leader of the German literary and theatrical revival movement, GOTTSCHED, and wrote poetry in German. In 1745 he went to Paris to become a secretary of the duke of Orléans. There he became a friend of Rousseau and was accepted into enlightened literary circles. He contributed to the *Encyclopédie*. He wrote in French on a variety of topics, although it was in the field of literary criticism that he made his reputation. Together with Diderot, he corresponded on a massive scale with a number of German and other rulers, including Frederick II and Catherine II, on intellectual and cultural developments in France. His *Correspondance littéraire, philosophique et critique*

(Literary, Philosophical and Critical Correspondence, 1753–92) with the duke of Saxe-Gotha is a particularly valuable source. As a result of his work, many French literary productions became known in Germany. He was ennobled by the emperor in 1777.

E. Lizé, 'Voltaire, Grimm et la Correspondance littéraire', *Studies on Voltaire and the Eighteenth Century*, 180 (1979).

MICHAEL HUGHES

Grimm, Jacob Ludwig Carl (1785–1863) and **Wilhelm Carl** (1786–1859)   German brothers who pioneered FOLKLORE research, best known as collectors and publishers of German folk stories. Jacob, an academic philologist, became a university librarian and academic. William was of a more artistic or poetic nature. Their best-known work was the three volumes of children's stories published between 1812 and 1822, which was only a small part of their large output of scholarly works on the history of language, literature, mythology and folklore. They recovered and published a substantial number of ancient German texts. The Grimms were ardent German nationalists. Their etymological studies contributed substantially to the rise of the German romantic movement (*see* ROMANTICISM). They believed that it would be possible, through the study of authentic folk literature in all its forms, to reach an uncorrupted natural German world free of artificial sophistication and foreign influences. There is some suspicion that where the authentic texts were incomplete they may have used their imagination to supply the gaps.

J. M. Ellis, *One Fairy Story Too Many: The Brothers Grimm and their Tales* (Chicago: University of Chicago Press, 1983).

MICHAEL HUGHES

Grub Street   In eighteenth-century London, Grub Street was both an actual place and a metaphor. Situated in the part of the city now covered by the Barbican development, it was a street that acquired a reputation as the haunt of those who hired themselves as writers, or 'hacks' in contemporary parlance. It thus became a metaphor for a new commerce of writing: rapid, transient and mercenary. Grub Street was a world of authors who owed nothing to patrons or posterity and everything to the market-place. Its productions were most famously satirized in Pope's *Dunciad* and Swift's *Tale of a Tub*. These writers used Grub Street to lament the decay of a culture fallen upon commercial times, but – abiding though their visions have been – it should not be presumed that their views were representative. Less patrician accounts were offered by authors like Defoe, Goldsmith and Johnson, each of whom pursued part of his career in Grub Street. As a metaphor, Grub

Street stands both for the real changes taking place in PUBLISHING in the eighteenth century, and for the anxieties of writers about those changes.

Pat Rogers, *Hacks and Dunces* (London: Methuen, 1980).

JOHN MULLAN

Guadeloupe The French CARIBBEAN colony of Guadeloupe was founded in 1635, and for a long time it was the poorer relation of its near-neighbour Martinique. However, its fortunes picked up with an influx of slaves following its capture by Britain in 1758 so that, although the anticipated permanent British occupation never materialized (Guadeloupe was returned to France after a vigorous debate with those who urged the retention of Canada instead), the boost kept its population higher than that of Martinique up to the French Revolution, at which point it totalled 16,760 whites and free coloureds and 89,823 slaves. Captured again by the British in 1794, it was speedily retaken by the energetic commissioner of the French republic, Victor Hugues (*d* 1826), who turned Guadeloupe into the Caribbean head-quarters of the French Revolution, including the full panoply of the TERROR. Hugues emancipated the slaves but then conscripted them to carry the revolution into the other islands. Eventually thwarted by massive British reinforcements, Hugues turned his efforts instead to the far more profitable field of privateering until he was recalled to France in 1798. In the meantime, however, the prosperous plantation economy of Guadeloupe had been devastated and Napoleon's bloody restoration of slavery in 1802 did little to help its recovery.

MICHAEL DUFFY

Guiana, Dutch Extending along the 'Wild Coast' of South America between the Orinoco and the Amazon, Dutch Guiana consisted of four agricultural colonies producing sugar, coffee and cotton. Essequibo and Demerara were under direct control of the Dutch West India Company, while Berbice and Surinam were run by private societies. In contrast to the usual monopolistic restrictions, Surinam was open to all Dutch citizens, and contained a prosperous community of Sephardic Jews. Furthermore, in the course of the eighteenth century all four territories developed representative institutions which gave the white settlers real influence in their administration – and which were retained when Essequibo, Demerara and Berbice were transferred to Britain in 1814.

In other respects, however, Guiana's record in this period was deplorable. Production depended heavily on SLAVERY – over 30,000 slaves laboured on Surinam's 400 plantations in 1750 – and, despite the humanitarian efforts of Moravian missionaries, the Dutch planters cruelly mistreated their work-force. Rebellions were endemic, and slaves regularly fled to the jungles of the interior, setting up egalitarian communities which the colonists' punitive expeditions tried unsuccessfully to destroy.

C. Ch. Goslinga, *The Dutch in the Caribbean and the Guianas 1680–1791* (Assen: Van Gorcum, 1985).

HUGH DUNTHORNE

Guibert, Jacques Antoine Hippolyte de (1743–1790) Military theorist in late *ancien régime* France. A distinguished soldier, he became obsessed with the success of the Prussian army, against whom he fought in the Seven Years War, and from the 1760s undertook theoretical studies which bore fruit in his *Essai général de tactique* (General Essay on Tactics, 1772). A massive literary success, the work was translated into all the major languages (including even Persian), and he was received by both Frederick II of Prussia and Joseph II of Austria. Contradictory in several ways, Guibert emphasized quality over quantity in military power, but his view that massed columns could break through the linear formations adopted by the Prussians and others, and his emphasis on tactical mobility and mass mobilization, foreshadowed the conduct of war by the revolutionary armies and by Napoleon, who was one of his most avid readers. In 1787–8 he served on the military council which made sweeping Prussian-style reforms in the French army, albeit at the cost of alienating much of the officer corps.

Matti Lauerma, *J. A. H. de Guibert* (Helsinki: Suomalainen Tiedeakatemia, 1989).

COLIN JONES

Gustav III (1746–1792) King of Sweden (1771–92). Born into the house of Holstein-Gottorp, he became king on 12 February 1771 on the death of his father, ADOLF FREDRIK. On 19 August 1772 he staged a bloodless military *coup* to reverse the constitutional provisions of the 'age of liberty'. The powers of the crown were restored, the senate arrested and the Riksdag reconvened. A new constitution, with greater powers for the crown, was approved on 21 August 1772, by which the king regained the power to summon and dismiss the Riksdag, to appoint ministers and to propose legislation. An enlightened despot, he introduced reforms including reform of the currency (1776–7), reduction in the number of capital offences and limited religious toleration. His difficult, restless temperament made Gustav prefer to work with favourites rather than through his council. In later years he became increasingly interested in a bolder foreign policy. Prevented from invading Norway in 1784 by Russian pressure, he attacked Russia in 1788, but the war, which ended in 1790, did not live up to his expectations, and precipitated domestic tension in Sweden, especially among the Finns. To break his opponents, he staged a new constitutional *coup* in 1789, pushing through an Act of Union and Security under which the estates lost all their legislative initiative and the crown's power to introduce laws was considerably extended. Most public offices were opened to commoners, and peasants' rights to purchase land were extended. Gustav was greatly affected by French Revolution and made plans to act against France. An aristocratic conspiracy led to the mortal wounding of Gustav at a masked ball by Johan Jakob Anchorstrom on 16 March 1792. He died on 29 March. He was one of the more talented of the enlightened despots, but, like Joseph II, he paid insufficient attention to the need to win elite support.

H. A. Barton, *Scandinavia in the Revolutionary Era, 1760–1815* (Minneapolis: University of Minnesota Press, 1986).
C. Nordmann, *Gustave III* (Lille: Presses Universitaires de Lille, 1986).

JEREMY BLACK

H

Habsburg Empire   The Habsburgs were an old and distinguished German dynasty, which had ruled Austria from the thirteenth century. On the abdication of Charles V (1519–66), their empire was partitioned into two, ruled by the senior Spanish and the junior Austrian branches. At the beginning of the eighteenth century the Spanish line died out. Thereafter the Habsburg or Austrian empire was, in reality, not a state but a collection of kingdoms and provinces accumulated over the centuries through conquest and inheritance by the Austrian branch of the family. Lacking a collective name, it was often referred to in the eighteenth century as Casa d'Austria (House of Austria), which emphasized its dynastic nature. It had no common language, laws or constitution. It included the Austrian hereditary lands, the kingdoms of Hungary and Bohemia and their dependencies, the Austrian Netherlands (Belgium) and territories in Germany and Italy. Its development as a state was retarded by the survival of powerful local loyalties and institutions and by the Habsburgs' constant involvement in external affairs. They also suffered from a confusion of roles between the universalist pretensions arising from the imperial title and the narrower demands of the Austrian state. Between 1438 and 1806, with one brief interval, they occupied the throne of the HOLY ROMAN EMPIRE, which brought them great prestige but little else. Only in the later seventeenth century did a distinct Austrian consciousness begin to emerge among the upper classes, associated with the dynasty and the Catholic faith. There was always a powerful confessional basis to the Habsburg state, deliberately cultivated in the form of *Pietas Austriaca* (Austrian Piety), representations, in the form of baroque art and public rituals and displays, of the alliance between the house and the church. As a result, Italy also exercised a fascination on them and they were eager to extend their influence there.

The foundations of the institutional basis of a state were created in the sixteenth century. Ferdinand II's defeat of rebellion and elimination of religious diversity in his lands in the Thirty Years War made possible further building in the seventeenth century, but the work remained incomplete. LEOPOLD I's reign saw long and bitter wars against France and the Turks which denied Austria the creative pause in which to undertake internal state-building and modernization. Large territorial gains were made in these wars, which turned Austria into a great power, but it also took on great commitments in many parts of Europe, to which its resources were not equal. Even at the apparent pinnacle of its power, the insecure foundations of the Austrian state were clear. Wars against France and the Turks in the 1730s showed up the flaws in the structure of the state. JOSEPH I and CHARLES VI, under the influence of Prince EUGENE and other members of the 'Young Party', initiated moves towards further centralization but little progress was achieved. The situation was made worse by Charles VI's failure to produce a male heir and growing obsession with the PRAGMATIC SANCTION, which made Austria's international position very vulnerable in the fluid diplomatic circumstances of the 1720s. The sanction was significant in that it proclaimed, for the first time, the indivisibility of all Charles's possessions even if, as seemed likely, the male Habsburg line died out.

The basic weakness of the empire was starkly revealed in the WAR OF THE AUSTRIAN SUCCESSION, when it came close to dismemberment at the hands of its enemies, led by France. In 1741 Elector Charles Albert of Bavaria occupied large parts of Austria and Bohemia and in December was crowned king of Bohemia. In 1742 he was elected Holy Roman Emperor. In 1740 Frederick II of Prussia seized Silesia and later Austrian efforts to reverse this grievous loss in the SEVEN YEARS WAR were unsuccessful. Apart from Silesia and Parma in Italy, the empire survived intact. Further territorial growth took place later in the century with the acquisition of Galicia in the first partition of Poland in 1772 and Bukovina from the Turks in 1775, both backward areas.

Thereafter under MARIA THERESA a programme of long-overdue major reforms, proposed by HAUGWITZ, was carried out in the Austrian-Bohemian core of the 'empire', against the opposition of powerful vested interests. This included the establishment of central institutions of government and a large standing army. Although Austria was not as militaristic as Prussia, the needs of the army were paramount, especially under JOSEPH II. The powers of the provincial estates in taxation and recruiting were sharply reduced and a new local government system installed. Measures were also taken to modernize the economy and to place the church under tighter state control. The improvement was remarkable, though it fell short of Haugwitz's intentions. When his mother's restraining hand was removed, Joseph tried to accelerate the reforms to achieve more centralization and standardization. The improvements he achieved in his subjects' welfare were considerable but he also trampled on their susceptibilities, especially in religious matters. This was an unwise move for a dynasty whose authority had traditionally rested on its alliance with the church. He also disregarded the privileges of the Hungarians, which his mother had been careful to respect. As a result, he brought many of his lands to actual or near-revolt and shortly before his death he began to dismantle many of his own policies. His brother LEOPOLD II continued to scrap his more extreme policies but retained the solid core of beneficial changes. These reforms enabled the state to survive as a European great power, though it had to accept the rise of Prussia in Germany and of Russia, replacing Turkey, in eastern Europe.

The premature death of Leopold II in 1792 was a disaster for Austria. At a time when the country was entering a very difficult period because of the French Revolution, the throne was occupied by the narrow-minded and reactionary FRANCIS II. Austria entered a period of stagnation and obscurantism which was to last until 1848.

R. A. Kann, *A History of the Habsburg Empire 1526–1918* (Berkeley, Calif.: University of California Press, 1974).

E. Wangermann, *The Austrian Achievement 1700–1800* (London: Thames & Hudson, 1973).

MICHAEL HUGHES

Hales, Stephen (1677–1761) English clergyman and plant physiologist. He published his first scientific work at the age of 50 and went on to become a leading champion of Newtonianism. He left Cambridge in 1709 to become minister of Teddington, a post that he held for the rest of his life. Teddington also served as the base where he performed the experiments that were to become the backbone of his *Vegetable Staticks* (1727), in which he denied the long-held notion that sap circulated like blood; he measured transpiration, sap pressure and root pressure, and concluded that the sap's motion was due to the attracting power of the fine capillary vessels. His comparative studies of sap and blood led to *Haemastaticks*, published in his *Statical Essays* (1731).

His contributions to PNEUMATICS were both theoretical and practical. His pneumatic trough for collecting air allowed him to measure the amount of air 'fixed' in various substances, and his ventilators were designed to improve the air by removing noxious fumes. For Hales, air was a homogeneous substance comprised of possibly elastic particles.

D. E. G. Allen and R. E. Schofield, *Stephen Hales: Scientist and Philanthropist* (London: Scolar, 1980).

M. L. BENJAMIN

Halle, University of With the inaugural ceremony of 11 July 1694, the University of Halle was established as a powerhouse of early Enlightenment thinking and teaching. It became as influential as the University of Leiden (founded 1575) had been in the seventeenth century, by attracting faculty and students of international calibre. As a bastion of progressive and contentious ideas, it later influenced the founding of GöTTINGEN (1734–7), the other important university of the German Enlightenment. The hallmark of all these universities was their abandonment of scholastic traditions. At the beginning of the eighteenth century interest in Halle focused on the meaning of mechanical philosophy (whether immediate physical causes rather than invisible, spiritual forces governed nature), the introduction of natural law theory (whether common sense and community instead of canonical law and Bible-based morality should govern society) and the contentious issue of theological orthodoxy versus Pietistic activism.

If Leiden had in the seventeenth century introduced the *philosophia nova* of Descartes, Halle came to intellectual blows on the subject. The professor of medicine, Friedrich Hoffmann (1660–1742), advocated the mechanical philosophy. He was supported by Christian WOLFF, who taught mathematics and natural philosophy in Halle from 1706. Wolff was one of the best-known Enlightenment philosophers of pro-Cartesian leanings, but he was expelled from the university in 1723 by an anti-Cartesian coalition, only to be reinstated in 1740.

Opponents of dualism and the mechanical philosophy were strongest in the theological faculty, but also, surprisingly, in medicine, with the professor of medicine, STAHL, in his *Theoria medica vera* systematizing a unique Enlightenment theory on the union of the body and soul. This anti-Cartesian approach in the natural sciences and the formation of the Stahlian school in medicine influenced the eighteenth-century definitions of the sentiments, pathology, psychology and practical therapeutics. Stahl's search for new principles governing observed nature also determined his views on chemistry, his phlogiston theory being adopted throughout Europe until disproved by Lavoisier. Hoffmann and Stahl were the moving forces behind practical chemical advance in Europe, laying the groundwork for the analysis of mineral waters, chemically based remedies, research on drug use in case histories and industrial chemistry (textile dyes and porcelain).

High attendance rates, and consequentially the large number of professionals who advocated ideas taught in Halle, characterized not only the medical, but also the law and the theological faculties. In the eighteenth century Halle was by no means a provincial university with local clientele. It drew Protestant students from Hungary, Poland, Protestant southern Germany, the Scandinavian countries, the Baltic and Russia. It was the first university to admit an African, Anton

Wilhelm Amo, who taught as a lecturer. It also admitted the first Jewish medical students in large numbers.

In law the attraction centred on THOMASIUS, who successfully divided canonical law from secularized natural law, and fought a campaign against witchcraft trials and the use of torture which culminated in the criminal law reform of Frederick the Great (1740). Thomasius became the figurehead for early Enlightenment causes such as the assertion of professional competence in competition with aristocratic rights to civic office. His was also indisputably the sharpest pen in the new periodical literature on moral and polite reform. His law faculty colleagues Samuel Stryck, Johann Peter von Ludewig (1668–1743) and N. H. Gundling (1671–1729) advanced change through their expertise on Roman law, constitutional law and common law. Within the Prussian context (and beyond, since the law reforms of Prussia affected Bavaria and Austria towards the end of the century), the impetus of law opinion created a firmer civil basis for law enactment and enforcement, disestablishing it from religious constraints.

Curiously, Enlightenment liberalism, although at loggerheads with the more pious demands of 'active Christianity' (*Thätiges Christentum*) combined well with early Pietism. This branch of Lutheranism began by opposing the clericism of the Orthodox Church by supporting lay interpretation of the Bible. To promote these aims (of Christian social justice and charity), the indefatigable Pietist August Hermann Francke (1663–1727) established the pedagogical institutions of the *Waisenhaus* (orphanage) which fed into the university. These comprised schools not only for the poor, but also for noblemen's sons and the first effort at a girls' school. Tutors for these schools were often impoverished university students and thereby the Waisenhaus provided support in training future clergy and civil servants. Pedagogy was not then a concern of universities; Halle, however, set the pace for the educational aims of the period. (The first chair of pedagogy was created in 1779.) The liberalism of Halle also led to the first doctoral degree granted to a woman, Dorothea Christiane Erxleben-Leporin (1715–62), in medicine, in 1754. In the latter half of the century, until it was closed by Napoleon in 1806 (it was reinstated in 1813), the university excelled in the practical initiatives of the Enlightenment: rational theology (Johann Salomon Semler (1725–91)), secular philosophy and aesthetics (Alexander Baumgarten), philanthropy (J. B. Basedow (1723–90)), philology, in particular of the classical and Oriental languages (Friedrich August Wolf (1759–1824)) and the sciences. Thus, in the best sense, Halle stood for the education and controversies of the Enlightenment.

C. E. McClelland, *State, Society and University in Germany 1700–1914* (Cambridge: Cambridge University Press, 1980).

JOHANNA GEYER-KORDESCH

Haller, Albrecht von (1708–1777) Swiss polymath, poet and scientist. Born in Berne, he studied in Tübingen and with Boerhaave in Leiden. In 1736 he became professor of anatomy, surgery and botany at Göttingen, where he remained until 1753, when he returned to Berne in the hope of a political career. He was the leading poet of his generation. His *Versuch Schweizerische Gedichten* (Essay in Swiss Poetry, 1732, eleventh edition 1777) contains philosophical verse, satires and his great nature poem *The Alps*. The volume brought a new seriousness to German verse and was defended by Bodmer against Gottsched. Haller made numerous contributions to physiology and anatomy, such as his distinction between muscle and nerve and his description of the mechanical automatism of the heart, and he established the highly influential doctrine of 'irritability'. His *Elementa physiologiae* (8 vols, 1757–66) provided the basis for modern physiology. His method was empirical and systematic: incorporating exhaustive bibliographical research, he based his results on observation, dissection (preferably vivisection), experiment and quantitative analysis. In botany, he gave a seminal account of Swiss plants (1742, second edition 1768) characterized by the search for a natural system and a reliance on plant geography.

D. R. Wiswall, *A Comparison of Selected Poetic and Scientific Works of Albrecht von Haller* (Berne: Peter Lang, 1981).

JEREMY ADLER

Hamann, Johann Georg (1730–1788) German philosopher and theologian, known as the 'magus of the north'. He abandoned his studies in Königsberg for a dissolute life, and on a visit to London in 1757–8 had a religious revelation. After this 'descent into the hell of self-knowledge', he launched his attack on reason in a series of highly charged and obscure writings on aesthetics, literature, language, religion and philosophy. In his *Sokratische Denkwürdigkeiten* (Socratic Memorabilia, 1759) Socrates points the way to a truth 'hidden in the darkness' and accessible only through faith and sensibility. Sexuality, too, cannot be divorced from heart and brain, as the *Aesthetica in Nuce* (Aesthetics in a Nutshell, 1762) affirms. Hamann similarly privileged language, and treated poetry as 'the mother-tongue of the human race'. In opposition to his friend and mentor KANT, he launched his own *Metakritik* (Metacriticism, 1784), according to which knowledge always existed in language, since cognition depended on words. Goethe famously celebrated Hamann as the thinker of 'the whole man'; his influence extended from HERDER and the *Sturm und Drang* movement down to the existential philosophy of Kierkegaard (1813–55).

J. C. O'Flaherty, *Johann Georg Hamann* (Boston: Twayne, 1979).

JEREMY ADLER

Hamburg The Lutheran imperial city of Hamburg, whose population rose from 75,000 in 1715 to 100,000 in 1790, was one of Germany's most dynamic and prosperous commercial centres in the eighteenth century. In 1712 a new constitution ended a long period of internal unrest and became the foundation for political stability and economic growth. Even before 1700 Hamburg had been a significant cultural centre. After 1720 the city became a breeding-ground for progressive, enlightened ideas. The first Patriotic Society (founded in 1724) stood at the centre of the early literary Enlightenment in Germany, inspired by Locke, Thomasius and Christian Wolff. The second Patriotic Society (founded in 1765) was a model of a society devoted to practical enlightened reform. Both societies were influential, since their members were recruited from the urban elite. This often led to friction with the orthodox Lutheran clergy, particularly over religious toleration, which was introduced for non-Lutheran Christians only in 1785. During the 1790s Hamburg steered a neutral course. Between 1806 and 1814 the city was occupied by the French and from 1810 governed by a French *mairie* (town council). After the liberation of the city, the 1712 constitution was restored.

Joachim Whaley, *Religious Toleration and Social Change in Hamburg, 1529– 1819* (Cambridge: Cambridge University Press, 1985).

JOACHIM WHALEY

Handel, George Frideric [Händel, Georg Friedrich] (1685–1759) Naturalized British composer of German origin. After the death of Henry Purcell (1659–95) English music suffered from a lack of fresh talents. The gap was to be filled by a composer born Georg Friedrich Händel in Halle, but who took the name George Frideric Handel when he became a naturalized British citizen in 1727.

He started his career in Hamburg in 1703 as a violinist at the famous Theater am Gänsemarkt. He became friendly with the singer and composer Johann Mattheson (1681–1764), and wrote his first opera, *Almira*, in 1705. He moved to Italy in 1706, where he met composers such as Arcangelo Corelli and Alessandro and Domenico Scarlatti, and composed a number of successful works: the psalm-setting *Dixit Dominus* (1707); oratorios, including *La ressurezione* (1708); and operas, including *Agrippina* (1709).

In 1710 he was appointed kapellmeister to the elector of Hanover (who later became George I), but soon left for London. There he wrote the opera *Rinaldo* (1711). After having composed the *Te Deum* and the *Jubilate* to celebrate the Treaty of Utrecht, he was granted a pension of £200 by Queen Anne, which was increased by her successor, George I. For him Handel composed the *Water Music* (1717). On the occasion of the coronation of George II he presented *Four Anthems*, including *Zadok the Priest*, which has been performed at every British coronation since. He was appointed music director of the Royal Academy of Music, a commercial opera venture of aristocratic entrepreneurs, for which he composed fourteen operas, including *Radamisto* (1720), *Giulio Cesare* (1724) and *Rodelinda* (1725).

The success of John Gay's *Beggar's Opera* in 1728 foreshadowed the end of the opera boom. The Academy closed down, but Handel set up a venture of his own, and wrote several new operas, among them *Orlando* (1733), *Alcina* (1735) and *Giustino* (1737), and started composing oratorios (*Deborah, Athaliah*, both in 1733).

He suffered a stroke in 1737, and following his recovery he concentrated on composing oratorios, producing *Saul* in 1738, *Israel in Egypt* in 1739, *Messiah* in 1741 (which had been commissioned by the Charitable Musical Society in Dublin), *Samson* in 1743 and *Judas Maccabaeus* in 1746. His physical condition detoriated rapidly after 1745, but he still wrote the *Music for the Royal Fireworks* (1749) and the oratorios *Theodora* (1750) and *Jephtha* (1751). He had to give up composing when he became virtually blind in 1752. In April 1759 he had a fainting fit during a performance of the *Messiah* and died soon after.

Handel left behind him about forty operas and thirty-two oratorios, the Concerti Grossi Op. 3 and 6, organ concertos and chamber music. His oratorios inspired Haydn's *Creation*; Mozart, too, appreciated Handel's oratorios and reorchestrated some of them.

W. Dean, *The New Grove Handel* (London: Macmillan, 1982).
J. Keates, *Handel: The Man and his Music* (London: Gollancz, 1985).
R. Strohm, *Essays on Handel and Italian opera* (Cambridge: Cambridge University Press, 1985).

FRITZ WEBER

Hanover The Protestant state of Hanover, or Brunswick-Lüneburg, was an important medium-sized one in North Germany. In 1750 its population was about 700,000. Its power was established by the able Duke Ernest Augustus (1680–98), who built it up by collecting territories as other branches of the Welf house became extinct. In 1692 he was elevated to an electorate by Emperor Leopold I in return for support in German and European affairs, and Hanover became an indivisible primogeniture. In 1714 Elector George Louis succeeded to the British throne as GEORGE I, establishing a personal union that was to last up to 1837. This distracted the electors from involvement in German politics. Hanover's potentially prominent role in German affairs was not exploited but, as a result of the 'Hanoverian factor' in British foreign policy, it remained important in European diplomacy. It had an able prime minister in Gerlach Adolph von Münchhausen (1688–1770). After 1714 it was well governed but stagnant and conservative. Its economy was undeveloped because of poor communications and the decline of the Harz metal and the Lüneburg salt industries. The university founded by Münchhausen at GÖTTINGEN in 1734 quickly established a reputation as the best in Germany.

U. Dann, *Hanover and Great Britain* (Leicester: Leicester University Press, 1991).

MICHAEL HUGHES

happiness   When Madame du Châtelet wrote her *Discourse sur le bonheur* (1746–8, published 1779), she was one of many eighteenth-century *philosophes* to address the subject. Happiness, she contended, required VIRTUE, health and the capacity for pleasure and passion. It also necessitated the difficult task of ridding oneself of prejudices and yet remaining open to illusion. She recommended study as a source of happiness, particularly for women. So did Mary Wollstonecraft, though in her *Vindication of the Rights of Man* (1790) she thought 'that true happiness arose from the friendship and intimacy which can only be enjoyed by equals' and asserted that 'the business of the life of a good man should be, to separate light from darkness; to diffuse happiness, whilst he submits to unavoidable misery'. Speaking of the relationship between the happiness of an individual and that of society as a whole, she claimed: 'The happiness of the whole must arise from the happiness of the constituent parts, or the essence of justice is sacrificed to a supposed grand arrangement.' 'To endeavour to make unhappy men resigned to their fate', she argued further, 'is the tender endeavour of short-sighted benevolence, of transient yearnings of humanity; but to labour to increase human happiness by extirpating error, is a masculine godlike affection.'

Eighteenth-century thinkers were not the first to think of themselves as contributing to the happiness of mankind through their enlightenment. Nor were they particularly original in their various recipes for individual felicity; it was, after all, a subject as old as philosophy. What remains identified with the Enlightenment, however, is the utilitarian attempt to quantify happiness. Though it was to come under vigorous attack, most notably by Immanuel Kant, the view that the aim of political activity should be conceived in terms of the promotion of the happiness of the population became a commonplace of the period's political theory. Thus, what might be deemed a quintessentially private pursuit was increasingly seen as a public matter. As the language of happiness invaded political discourse and policies, and laws were judged in relation to their tendency to increase or diminish a people's happiness, the need to quantify it increased. To measure happiness so as to be able to ascertain the merit or demerit of any action was one of the first objects of BENTHAM's writings. His '*greatest happiness* or *greatest felicity* principle', as stated in *his Introduction to the Principles of Morals and Legislation*, is that 'the greatest happiness of all those whose interest is in question, as being the right and proper, and only right and proper, and universally desirable, end of human action; of human action in every situation, and in particular in that of a functionary or set of functionaries exercising the powers of Government'. The happiness of individuals consisted, according to Bentham, in their pleasures and their security. 'Pleasures then,' he wrote, 'and the avoidance of pains, are the *ends* which the legislator has in view: it behoves him therefore to understand their *value*.' To aid legislators, Bentham produced a pleasure–pain calculus analysing, comparing and measuring the various pleasures and pains. Thus Bentham's own contribution to the happiness of the species resided in reducing it in this way to a simple and universally applicable yardstick.

Robert Mauzi, *L'Idée du bonheur dans la littérature et la pensée française au XVIIIième siècle* (Paris: Armand Colin, 1960).

SYLVANA TOMASELLI

Hastings, Warren (1732–1818) English administrator who was a key figure in the development of British India. He arrived in India in 1750, and gradually worked his way up the East India Company's administrative hierarchy until he became governor of Bengal in 1772. The following year Lord North's Regulating Act named Hastings as the first governor-general of the presidency, partly in recognition of his recent reform of revenue and judicial practices. Thereafter, he ran into political difficulties as charges of mismanagement and malpractice were levelled against him, and his position was further weakened by sustained attacks mounted on him by colleagues such as Philip Francis (1740–1818). Although he orchestrated several successful military campaigns in the late 1770s and early 1780s, his unscrupulous tactics were called into question, and he had to defend his actions at length when he returned to Britain in 1785. Burke took the leading part in pressing for an inquiry into Hastings' conduct, and the subsequent impeachment proceedings lasted nine years until 1795 when Hastings was acquitted of all charges of misrule. He was an effective administrator whose methods were not always sound, but he was also a man of wide-ranging scholarly interests, particularly in the field of Orientalism.

K. G. Feiling, *Warren Hastings* (London: Macmillan, 1954).

HUW BOWEN

Haugwitz, Wilhelm count von (1700–1765)   Austrian administrative reformer. The son of a Saxon general, he entered Austrian service in 1725. From 1736 he held a high position in the administration of Silesia. In 1742 he was appointed to head the government of the small part of the province retained by Austria, and carried through a major remodelling of its government. He quickly won the confidence of MARIA THERESA, who commissioned him to make recommendations for reforms that would enable Austria to maintain an army of 108,000 men. He proposed the creation of new organs of centralized government, the abolition of tax exemptions and a decisive weakening of the parliamentary estates. The empress accepted his plan in 1748 and it was pushed through against the opposition of the majority of his fellow ministers and the noble-dominated estates of Bohemia and Austria. He then carried out a thorough and long-overdue reorganization of the Austrian administrative system. It was largely due to his efforts that the Habsburg Empire survived the serious crisis at the accession of Maria Theresa and retained its position as a European great power.

P. G. M. Dickson, *Finance and Government under Maria Theresa 1740–1780* (Oxford: Clarendon, 1987).

MICHAEL HUGHES

Hawksbee [Hauksbee], **Francis** (*c.*1666–1713)   English instrument-maker. Particularly renowned for his surgical cupping-glasses, air pumps and barometers, in 1704 he inaugurated the financially rewarding practice of giving public lectures in London on experimental natural philosophy. Appointed by Newton to the demanding post of curator of experiments at the Royal Society, he prepared spectacular weekly demonstrations, often based on original work. Research topics included capillary action, magnetism and light, but his most successful and influential experiments were in ELECTRICITY. Following the popularity with his audience of luminescent displays of phosphorus, he proceeded to investigate the flashes of light seen in a barometer over mercury, and discovered that rubbing a spinning evacuated glass globe caused it to glow brightly as well as produce electricity. Under Newton's guidance, he carried out an important series of experiments exploring the nature of electrical attraction and repulsion and its relation to gravity. His machines made from spinning globes or plates turned by a large wheel were the standard electrostatic generators throughout the century.

J. Heilbron, *Physics at the Royal Society during Newton's Presidency* (Los Angeles: University of California Press, 1983).

PATRICIA FARA

Haydn, (Franz) Joseph (1732–1809) Austrian composer who, together with Mozart and Beethoven, represented the so-called first or classical Viennese school of music. He was born in a village on the Austro-Hungarian border. His father, a craftsman, sent him to a church school, where his musical talent was discovered. In 1740 he joined the boys' choir at St Stephen's Cathedral in Vienna, where he received his basic musical education. After leaving the choir in 1749, he lived in poverty in Vienna. However, his life changed in the mid-1750s when he met the famous Italian librettist METASTASIO and the singer and composer Niccola Porpora (1686–1768). Up to then Haydn had been self-taught, but Porpora gave him a grounding in the fundamentals of composition.

In 1759 he was appointed musical director to the Bohemian count Morzin. Previously, he had composed only small pieces and a (lost) opera, but during this period he wrote his First Symphony. He was then engaged by Prince Paul Anton Esterházy (*d* 1762) as assistant to his kapellmeister, Gregorius Joseph Werner (1693–1766). He succeeded Werner in 1766 and remained formally in the service of the Esterházy family for the rest of his life.

Haydn reached the height of his career after the death of Prince Paul Anton. The art-loving Prince Nikolaus Esterházy, a skilled baryton player, considerably expanded the orchestra at his castle in Eisenstadt and in many respects stimulated the composer's talents. Haydn's fame soon extended beyond Austria: his symphonies were known all over Europe, and in 1785 he was commissioned to write six symphonies (nos. 82 to 87) for the Parisian society Concert de la Loge Olympique.

Prince Nikolaus died in 1790. His successor, who was not interested in music, dismissed the musicians and considerably reduced Haydn's obligations to a mere formality. The composer moved to Vienna, and during the next years visited London twice (1791–2, 1794–5) on the invitation of the German impresario, violinist and composer Johann Salomon (1745–1815). For these occasions he composed the 'London Symphonies' (nos. 93 to 104) and the opera *L'anima del filosofo*.

During the Viennese interlude (1792–4) Haydn taught Beethoven among other students. From 1795 he settled in Austria for good, and wrote six great masses (among them the *Missa in tempore belli* and the *Nelson Mass*) for the new Prince Nikolaus Esterházy. Influenced by the works of Handel, which he had encountered in England, he composed the oratorios *Die Schöpfung* (The Creation, 1798) and *Die Jahreszeiten* (The Seasons, 1801). The String Quartets Op. 76 and 77 also belong to this period. In 1803 he committed to paper his last (unfinished) work, the String Quartet Op. 103. He died in 1809, during the Napoleonic occupation of Vienna.

Haydn as a composer has been underestimated. His name has been synonymous with charming, colourful but unexciting music (the 'Papa Haydn' image). He stood in the tradition of Philipp Emanuel and Johann Christian Bach. In the late 1760s (his *Sturm and Drang* period), however, he developed a style of his own. His *Sonnenquartette* (Sun Quartets) Op. 20 (1772) and the *Russischen Quartette* (Russian Quartets) Op. 33 (1781), which he described as 'written in a new and special manner', show him at the height of his talent as a composer. In the field of the string quartet his merits have never been challenged. They were an influence on Mozart, who dedicated his quartets published in 1785 to him. Haydn also contributed to the development of the symphony. His later symphonies show a mastery of the formal approach. The 'London Symphonies' rank with the symphonies of Mozart or Beethoven. Haydn left behind him a great variety of musical compositions: twenty-four operas, 106 symphonies, fifty-nine divertimenti, 126 baryton trios, fifty-two piano sonatas, fourteen masses and 445 arrangements of Scottish, Irish and Welsh folk-songs (1791–1805).

R. Hughes, *Haydn* (London: Dent, 1989).
H. C. Robbins Landon and D. Wyn Jones, *Haydn: His Life and Music* (London: Thames and Hudson, 1988).

FRITZ WEBER

health *see* DISEASE; HOSPITALS; MEDICINE; PUBLIC HEALTH.

heat Many eighteenth-century scientists regarded heat, like electricity and other phenomena, as a subtle fluid. Chemical in origin, like phlogiston, the theory succeeded the mechanical notion of heat as rapid atomic motion. Much work concerned how the fluid combined with gross matter and how it could be measured. Joseph BLACK distinguished between temperature and heat, arguing that thermometers recorded the density of (and capacity for) heat in a body, not the quantity. He also showed that, when melting or boiling a substance, the added heat produced no temperature rise. Similar physico-chemical changes were taken as evidence for hidden or latent heat.

Two problems persisted. First, could the fluid be independently detected, for example did hot bodies weigh more? Doubts were allayed by the sophisticated French theory of caloric, a fluid allegedly measurable by the calorimeter. Secondly, limitless heat could apparently be generated by friction. But the useful concepts of heat flow and heat conservation developed by fluid theorists sustained the programme into the nineteenth century. There were also powerful practical developments, notably of the steam engine by Black's associate James WATT.

R. Fox, *The Caloric Theory of Gases from Lavoisier to Regnault* (Oxford: Oxford University Press, 1971).

STEPHEN PUMFREY

Hébert, Jacques René (1757–1794)   French revolutionary. An obscure literary hack prior to 1789, he found his niche after 1789 when he began publishing the famous radical journal *Le Père Duchesne* (1790–4), which became his mouthpiece. It offered a scatological commentary on politics in a style that claimed to be authentic street argot, but was in fact closer to music-hall patter. A member of the Cordelier Club and, after the overthrow of Louis XVI, a key figure in the Paris Commune, he maintained a democratic, extraparliamentary critique of the National Convention. He was instrumental in the purge of the Girondins from the Convention on 31 May–2 June 1793, and helped to co-ordinate the demonstrations of 4–5 September 1793 which obliged the Convention to make Terror the order of the day. In the autumn of 1793 he and his allies led the DECHRISTIANIZATION movement in Paris, which aroused the hostility of Robespierre, who felt that militant atheism served the cause of counter-revolution. In March 1794 the committees of government had the Hébertists arrested, tried by the Revolutionary Tribunal on trumped-up charges and executed.

Louis Jacob, *Hébert, le Père Duchesne, chef des sans-culottes* (Paris: Hachette, 1960).

COLIN JONES

Hegel, Georg Wilhelm Friedrich (1770–1831)   German philosopher. He was born at Stuttgart and entered the theological seminary at the University of Tübingen in 1788. In 1818 he was appointed professor at the University of Berlin where he became extremely influential. A philosophical idealist, he sought to understand the nature of human subjectivity and the relationship between thought and the real world. As its most profound critic, he was the true heir to the Enlightenment. His greatest works were *Phänomenologie des Geistes* (Phenomenology of the Mind, 1807), *Wissenschaft der Logik* (Science of Logic, 1812–16), *Encyclopädie der philosophischen Wissenschaften* (Encyclopedia of the Philosophical Sciences, 1817), *Naturrecht und Staatswissenschaft im Grundrisse* (Philosophy of Right, 1821) and *Die Philosophie der Geschichte* (The Philosophy of History, 1833–6). He died during a cholera epidemic.

Within the eighteenth century, his greatest debt was to KANT, whose conceptions of rationality, will and freedom he went on to develop. Like Kant, Hegel thought that reason required men to be treated as rational subjects, as ends and not as means. Similarly, the political implications of his philosophy were that the state had to respect the rights of autonomous individuals, including the right to property and freedom of conscience. Well known for his account of 'dialectic' or pattern that thought followed, Hegel argued that thought proceeded through processes of thesis, antithesis and synthesis or *Aufhebung* of the thesis and its contradiction, preserving what is rational in both.

Charles Taylor, *Hegel* (Cambridge: Cambridge University Press, 1978).

SYLVANA TOMASELLI

Helvétius, Claude-Adrien (1715–1771) French philosopher of Swiss origin He was also a literary patron and tax farmer for a period, thanks to the patronage of Queen Marie Leszczyńska (1703–68), to whom his father had been first physician. In 1758 he published *De l'esprit*. The privilege first granted to it was soon revoked and the book burnt by order of the *parlement* on 10 August 1759. It argued that sensation was the ultimate source of all mental activity, that the human mind did not essentially differ from that of animals, that 'normally constituted' individuals had equal mental abilities and that differences between them were due only to environmental factors. These views were expounded in *De l'homme, de ses facultés intellectuelles et de son éducation* (1772). Diderot's *Réfutation*, written in the mid-1770s, ridiculed all aspects of Helvétius's thought, from the epistemology and analysis of the nature of the mind to the boundless confidence in the powers of education and account of man as entirely subservient to the pleasure–pain principle. Helvétius influenced the ideologues and Bentham.

Irving Louis Horowitz, *Claude Helvétius: Philosopher of Democracy and Enlightenment* (New York: Panie-Whitman, 1954).

SYLVANA TOMASELLI

Herculaneum The ancient city of Herculaneum at the foot of Mount Vesuvius was buried under lava after the eruption of the volcano in AD 79. Its rediscovery in 1713 was of immense consequence not only for the science of archaeology (for which it has been said to have acted like a cradle), but also for history, literature, painting and architecture (*see* CULT OF ANTIQUITY). Some of the earliest reflections on the rediscovery of the city are to be found in Charles de Brosses's (1709–77) *Lettres familières écrites d'Italie en 1739 et 1740*.

Appalled by the manner in which the excavations were being conducted by the local authorities, J. J. WINCKELMANN wrote *Sendschreiben von den Herculanischen Entdeckungen* (Open Letter on the Discoveries made at Herculaneum, 1762) and *Nachrichten von den neuesten Herculanischen Entdeckungen* (Report on the Most Recent

Excavations at Herculaneum, 1764). These sentiments were shared by Goethe who thought it 'a thousand pities that the site was not excavated methodically by German miners, instead of being casually ransacked as if by brigands' (*Halienische Reise*). Horace Walpole and Thomas Gray were among Herculaneum's numerous eighteenth-century visitors.

In 1756 the Academy of Herculaneum was founded, and one of its members, the abbé Galiani, contributed to its first volume of plates, *Le Pitture ed i bronzi d'Ercolano* (The Antiquities of Herculaneum; 8 vols., 1757–92). See also, Ch. N. Cochin and Bellicard's *Observations sur les antiquités et la ville d'Herculanum* (1754).

SYLVANA TOMASELLI

Herder, Johann Gottfried (1744–1803)   German critic and philosopher. He studied in Königsberg in 1762–4, where he was befriended by Kant and HAMANN; the latter especially shaped his views. His own inspirational philosophy was expressed in the *Journal meiner Reise im Jahre 1769* (Journal of my Journey in the Year 1769), an outburst against rationalism and abstraction which invoked his central categories of nature, immediacy, feeling, organic development and education. The *Fragmente über die neuere deutsche Literatur* (Fragments On Recent German Literature, 1766–7) had already aimed to outdo LESSING, pointing the way to a new native German literature based not on imitation of the French or the Greeks but on Germany's own circumstances, and these thoughts took definitive and practical form in *Über Ossian und die Lieder alter Völker* (Ossian and the Songs of Ancient Peoples) and *Shakespeare* which, included in *Von deutscher Art und kunst* (Of German Art, 1773), proved seminal for the young and the whole STURM UND DRANG movement. Shakespeare and folk-song were the natural forms of, and appropriate to, northern feeling; and feeling, as *Plastik* (Sculpture, 1770) explains, is the prime faculty through which we become in touch with the world.

Pluralism is central to Herder's frequently expounded philosophy of history: each nation follows nature according to its own geographical, cultural and temporal circumstances; indeed, as *Auch eine Philosophie der Geschichte zur Bildung der Menschheit* (Another Philosophy of History for the Education of Humanity, 1774) and *Ideen zur Philosophie der Geschichte der Menschheit* (Ideas for the Philosophy of the History of Mankind, 1784–91) explain, history itself pursues a teleological path of organic growth, like a natural body.

Locating mankind as an ethical being in the cosmos, Herder's philosophy culminates in the *Briefe zur Beförderung der Humanität* (Letters for the Advancement of Humanity, 1793–7). In later life Herder was isolated, and distanced from Goethe's classicism. His ideas on literature were overtaken by those of the romantics, for whom he had helped prepare the way; and his views on nationhood contributed to a rise in NATIONALISM, far removed from his own ideals.

Wulf Koepke, *Johann Gottfried Herder* (Boston: Twayne, 1987).

JEREMY ADLER

heresy   The word 'heresy' is of Greek derivation and originally denoted choice; it acquired its derogatory connotation with the rise of the Christian church and its literature. Over time it came to mean the formal denial, doubt or profanation of the Catholic faith. As the records of the Italian and Spanish Inquisitions show, this could mean a wide variety of offences, including the doctrinal 'errors' of Protestantism, Judaism, magic, witchcraft and blasphemy. In the period 1700–20 'illicit magic' was the most common offence punishable by the Italian Inquisition, whereas in the Iberian peninsula New Christian Judaizers bore the brunt of religious persecution. The Italian Inquisition slackened off considerably during the course of the eighteenth century, but the Spanish and Portuguese Inquisitions retained some of their vigour first against New Christians and then against crimes such as blasphemy and bigamy. (*See* INQUISITION.) In more general terms, Freemasons were also regarded as heretics in many Catholic countries.

While physical persecution for religious deviance began to decline in the eighteenth century, some of the advocates of enlightened opinions found themselves accused of heresy and some reformed churches implemented their own heresy trials against the heterodox. Accusations of religious heresy thus survived the Enlightenment, but the coercive powers of churches and states steadily declined.

See also TOLERATION.

G. Henningsen et al., *The Inquisition in Early Modern Europe* (De Kalb, Ill.: Northern Illinois University Press, 1986).

DAVID HEMPTON

Herschel, Sir **William** (1738–1822)   Naturalized British musician and astronomer of German birth. He moved to Bath in 1766 to become organist of the Octagon Chapel. Gradually, his interest in harmonics was supplanted by optics, so that by the time his sister Caroline (1750–1848) joined him in 1772 he was making telescopes. The astronomer royal, Neville Maskelyne (1732–1811), was later to concede their superiority to those at the Royal Observatory. Herschel's crowning achievement came at the beginning of his career when on 13 March 1781 he discovered Uranus; within a year he was elected a fellow of the Royal Society and awarded an annual stipend of £200 by George III. In 1787 a further £50 a year was granted to Caroline who had discovered a comet in 1786. In 1783 he completed what was to become his favourite telescope, a 20 foot reflector, and when he moved to Slough in 1785 the king financed a 40 foot design to eclipse its predecessor. Herschel published several catalogues of double stars and nebulae as well as papers on the construction of the heavens.

In 1788 he married the widow Mary Pitt; their only son, John (1792–1871), was to follow in his father's footsteps.

Constance Lubbock, *The Herschel Chronicle* (Cambridge: Cambridge University Press, 1933).

M. L. BENJAMIN

Hesse-Kassel   A landgraviate in western central Germany, Hesse-Kassel was an important middle-ranking state and, after 1604, a major centre of Calvinism. It overshadowed the smaller and less assertive Hesse-Darmstadt, with which it shared control of the Calvinist university at Marburg. In the seventeenth century it entered into a close connection with Sweden – and indeed in 1720 the landgrave became King Frederick I of Sweden – but this did not bring the hoped-for increase in power in Germany, as Sweden was in decline. In the eighteenth century Hesse-Kassel moved into the Prussian orbit. As Prussia's ally in the Seven Years War, it suffered French occupation and serious damage but was successfully rebuilt by the landgrave FREDERICK II. Its rulers gained a reputation for strong government and maintained substantial armed forces, which they hired out as mercenary troops. They were not unique among German rulers in this, but their habit of it became notorious. None the less, they were very popular with their subjects. Landgrave Charles (1670–1730) began the ornate rebuilding of his capital, Kassel, and the promotion of the arts and sciences, policies that were continued by his successors, William VIII (1751–60) and Frederick II.

C. W. Ingrao, *The Hessian Mercenary State* (Cambridge: Cambridge University Press, 1987).

MICHAEL HUGHES

history   On hearing a remark as to the usefulness of reading history, Johnson remarked: 'We must consider how very little history there is; I mean real authentick history. That certain Kings reigned, and certain battles were fought, we can depend upon as true; but all the colouring, all the philosophy of history is conjecture.' This was said in the presence of GIBBON, of all people, whose *Decline and Fall of the Roman Empire* is the most celebrated history written in English. Other notable histories of the eighteenth century were David Hume's *History of England*, William Robertson's *History of Scotland 1542–1603* (1759) and *History of Charles V* (1769) and Catherine Macaulay's *The History of England from the Accession of James I to that of the Brunswick Line* (1763–83). As Boswell remarked, on Johnson's view of things, one 'would reduce all history to no better than an almanack, a mere chronological series of remarkable events'.

The disagreements between Boswell and Johnson, who himself wrote histories, as to what kind of history ought to be written and how it should be narrated were symptoms of the importance of history in the eighteenth century. Hundreds of histories were published, many of which were works of great scholarship. The kind of healthy scepticism Johnson loved to exhibit enhanced the self-consciousness of historians about the nature of their source material, which led Boswell to note, for instance, how William Gutherie (1708–70) was 'the first English historian who had recourse to that authentick source of information, the Parliamentary Journals'. What counted as evidence was a topic that exercised many a mind, especially in debates concerning religious history and reports of miracles and exceptional deeds. Doubt was also cast on how much insight could ever be had into the real intentions of historical agents. As Johnson remarked: 'We may know historical facts to be true, as we may know facts in common life to be true. Motives are generally unknown. We cannot trust to the characters we find in history, unless when they are drawn by those who knew the persons; as those, for instance, by Sallust and by Lord Clarendon.'

Such incredulity did not dampen eighteenth-century enthusiasm for history, however. Not only were a great number of histories written in the period, but a great variety of subjects received historical treatment, for example music, language and women. Nor was the interest confined to Europe. In China a very important publishing project, the *Official History of the Ming Dynasty*, was begun in 1679 and completed in 1735. In the Ottoman Empire, the establishment of the position of an official court chronicler in the seventeenth century was to strengthen historiography. Mustafa Naima Efendi (1665–1716) was to be the first of many great historians who not only wrote about the court and its history but reflected on the art of history writing and the task of the historian, as did Ahmet Ásim Efendi (1755–1819), the first Ottoman historian to use some of the methods of Western historians.

Much in demand in Europe was the history of mores, what Voltaire called 'l'histoire des moeurs'. Even Johnson clamoured for it: 'I wish much to have one branch well done, and that is the history of manners, of common life.' The century also witnessed a profusion of philosophical histories, such as those of Vico, Giannone, Rousseau, Condorcet, Adam Ferguson (1723–1816) and John Millar (1735–1801). Enlightenment history, however rich in conjecture, was by no means poor in 'fact'. If it was the age of embroiderers like the comte de

Volney (1757–1820), it was also that of MURATORI, the great Italian historian of the Middle Ages, often hailed as the founder of modern scientific history.

John Kenyon, *The History Men* (London: Weidenfeld & Nicolson, 1983).
Nicholas Phillipson, *Hume* (London: Weidenfeld & Nicolson, 1989).
Roy Porter, *Edward Gibbon: Making History* (London: Weidenfeld & Nicolson, 1988).

SYLVANA TOMASELLI

history painting According to Renaissance theorists, history painting was the highest form of painting. The depiction of historical subjects was considered to be the best visual method of expressing ideas to an audience. The genre was at the beginning of the century in great vogue, following the success of Poussin (1594–1665) and Le Brun (1619–90), and by the end of the century the neoclassical revival begun by Mengs and Winckelmann had found full expression in the work of DAVID. In between, its popularity declined due to an increased emphasis on the individual as a fitting object for study and the development of private, as opposed to institutional, patronage. In England, where commissions by state and church were of small significance, history painting never gained much of an audience, and even in France individual buyers were increasingly drawn to landscape and genre pieces such as those produced by Boucher and Greuze. Throughout the century there was a dispute as to how broad a range of subjects history painting could embrace. On the one hand, painters like Benjamin West (1738–1820) portrayed modern-day heroes like General Wolfe, while the more doctrinaire privileged the deeds of classical heroes and biblical subjects.

M. Levey, *Rococo to Revolution: Major Trends in Eighteenth-Century Painting* (London: Thames & Hudson, 1966).

IAIN PEARS

Hogarth, William (1697–1764) English painter and engraver. The most prominent English painter between Lely (1618–80) and Reynolds, he founded the 'English School' and created a genre that combined paintings with engravings, which he called 'modern moral subjects', and which Fielding dubbed 'comic history-paintings'. Examples of this genre are *A Harlot's Progress* (6 pictures, 1732), *A Rake's Progress* (8 pictures, 1735) and *Marriage à la Mode* (6 pictures, 1745.) It revised the tradition of HISTORY PAINTING, adapting it to contemporary English events and assumptions. In the late 1740s Hogarth reached out to a wider audience with *Industry and Idleness* (1747), and *Beer Street*, *Gin Lane* and *The Four Stages of Cruelty* (1751). In the 1750s he formulated his aesthetic theory in *The Analysis of Beauty* (1753). He also pursued portraiture, first in conversation pictures (1728–40) and, from the late 1730s, in single portraits, most notably the monumental *Captain Thomas Coram* (1740). He was active in advancing the prestige and profits of English artists, taking a prominent role in the passing of the Copyright Act of 1735, founding the St Martin's Lane Academy, both in 1735, and developing new exhibition spaces for paintings.

Ronald Paulson, *Hogarth*, 3 vols (New Brunswick: Rutgers University Press, 1991–3).

RONALD PAULSON

Holbach, Paul Heinrich Dietrich, baron d' (1723–1789) French philosopher of German birth. Born at Hildesheim in Baden, he lived most of his life in France and became a French subject in 1749. He studied at the University of Leiden, where he met John Wilkes. One of the *philosophes* and an intimate friend of Diderot, d'Holbach was a major contributor to the ENCYCLOPÉDIE and his help was especially acknowledged in its second volume. Described by Marmontel as having 'read everything and never forgotten anything of interest', he was said to have contributed 1,100 articles to the last ten volumes, mostly anonymously and in a wide variety of fields, including chemistry, technology, geology, mineralogy and metallurgy (for which his mastery of German was particularly useful), politics and religion.

D'Holbach's name was associated with MATERIALISM, ATHEISM and DETERMINISM. His most widely read work, *Le Système de la nature, ou des lois du monde physique et du monde moral* (1770) denied the existence of the soul and advanced a materialist conception of man. Matter and motion constituted the world, which in his system was self-created and eternal. Motivated by self-love, which he equated with gravitation, 'the gravitation of the individual upon himself', man was necessarily drawn towards the pursuit of happiness, which, on his view, was comparable to health. *Le Bon Sens, ou Idées naturelles opposées aux idées surnaturelles* (1772) is a shortened version of the *Système*.

Few among his contemporaries were as dogmatic and constant in their materialism and atheism, or in their condemnation of religion and the church. He considered ignorance of natural causes to be the source of belief in the supernatural, and true virtue to be incompatible with religion. Politically, he advocated the abolition of privileges and was essentially a utilitarian. His other works include *Le Chritianisme dévoilé* (1761–6), *Politique naturelle* (1733), *Le Système social ou Principes naturels de la morale et de la politique, avec un examen de l'influence du gouvernement sur les moeurs* (1773) and *Morale Universelle, ou Les Devoirs de l'homme fondés sur la nature* (1776).

D'Holbach was a generous and hospitable man. He and his wife held dinners every Sunday and Thursday for up to twenty men of letters and foreign visitors, including Horace Walpole who was taken there by David Hume in 1765. Grandval, where the d'Holbachs had their country estate, was also a famous meeting-place for the *philosophes*. In their efforts to show that morality did not depend on religious conviction, the *philosophes* made much of d'Holbach's exemplary moral life. He is thought to have served as the model for the altruistic unbeliever M. de Wolmar in Rousseau's *La Nouvelle Héloïse* (1761).

A. C. Kors, *D'Holbach's Circle: An Enlightenment in Paris* (Princeton, NJ: Princeton University Press, 1977).

Virgil Topazio, *D'Holbach's Moral Philosophy: Its Background and Development* (Geneva: Institut et Musée Voltaire, 1956).

SYLVANA TOMASELLI

Holberg, Ludvig, baron (1684–1754) Norwegian man of letters. The bachelor professor in Copenhagen enjoyed a European reputation for a large body of legal, philosophical, historical and satirical writing. The most widely translated was *Nicolai Klimii Iter subterraneum* (Niels Klim's Underground Journey, 1741), whose hero falls on to Nazar, a planet occupied by ambulatory trees. Niels's antecedents are obvious, but Nazar has nice idiosyncrasies, including a country whose inhabitants, incapable of sleep, irritably write huge books instead. Holberg's work was underpinned by erudition, wide travel on a shoestring (he had walked 2,000 kilometres in France and Italy by 1716) and the conviction that God in His mercy equips us to distinguish good from evil. The means by which ignorance, passion and custom could dim this light gave rise to great comedies of character. His plays are still popular in Scandinavia and Germany, for example *Jeppe paa Bierget* (Jeppe of the Hill, 1722) and *Erasmus Montanus* (1731). He looked increasingly further back for inspiration – the last plays, he claimed, revived ancient Greek drama. Molière (1622–73) is the obvious comparison, but Holberg's earnest and spectacularly deluded heroes reach lunatic fringes not reached by Molière and his school. He was proud of the money he earned from his pen, which allowed him, like Voltaire, to end his days as an estate-owner. His last publication was a sharp correction of Montesquieu on absolute monarchy; among the last was an essay on cattle plague.

F. Billeskov Jansen, *Ludwig Holberg* (New York: Twayne, 1974).

CHRISTINE STEVENSON

Hölderlin, Johann Christian Friedrich (1770–1843)   German poet. He occupied a unique position between the classicism of Goethe and Schiller and romanticism. He studied theology at Tübingen from 1788 to 1793, where he made friends with Schelling and Hegel. In 1796–7 the three collaborated on a document, now hailed as 'the oldest system-programme of German idealism'. Hölderlin soon saw his destiny as following 'Pindar's flight' and 'Klopstock's greatness' (1787), but came under Schiller's influence, writing idealistic rhymed poems like the 'Hymne an die Schönheit' (Hymn to Beauty, 1791), before he developed his true voice. He found the Greek ideal embodied in his employer's wife, Susette Gontard, whom he called 'Diotima' and celebrated in poems in classical metres and in the lyrical novel *Hyperion* (1797–9). His unfinished tragedy *Empedocles* (1797) and his translations of Sophocles' *Oedipus Rex* and *Antigone* (1804) similarly testified to his attempt to re-create a sacred, classical, republican world. As the elegy 'Brot und Wein' (Bread and Wine, 1800) revealed, this involved a synthesis of Greek and Christian religion.

He enriched his poetry by applying to it the principles of his philosophical poetics, and subsequently strengthened it by the lessons learned from his translations of Pindar. The poetry of his final phase returned to unrhymed free rhythms with poems that combined great beauty with sustained intellectual intensity, such as 'Der Rhein' (The Rhine, 1801) and 'Patmos' (1802–3). After 1804 he increasingly fell prey to madness, and from 1807 spent his years in care at Tübingen.

D. Constantine, *Hölderlin* (Oxford: Oxford University Press, 1988).

JEREMY ADLER

Holy Alliance (26 September 1815)   The Holy Alliance was the treaty signed by the rulers of Russia, Prussia and Austria, to which the other crowned heads of Europe were invited to accede. It resulted from the long-held idealistic aspirations of Tsar ALEXANDER I for a European brotherhood, now reinforced by Christian sentiments and stimulated by the influence of Baroness Krüdener (1764–1824). The signatories solemnly declared their fixed resolution, in both internal administration and external relations with other governments, to be guided solely by the precepts of holy religion, 'namely, the precepts of Justice, Christian Charity and Peace'. Compared to the precise treaty obligations of the QUADRUPLE ALLIANCE, it amounted more to a general declaration of intent. Metternich called it 'sonore et vide' and Castlereagh thought it 'sublime mysticism and nonsense'. Only Britain, the pope and the heathen sultan of Turkey failed to sign it. When Alexander suggested assembling the signatories at the Congress of Aix-la-Chapelle in 1818, Metternich and Castlereagh managed instead to confine discussions to the great powers, but when the latter intervened against the liberal revolts of the early 1820s despite British wishes, it was convenient to call this an action by the Holy Alliance, which Britain had never joined.

MICHAEL DUFFY

Holy Roman Empire With the papacy, the Holy Roman Empire was the most important constitutional survival from the Middle Ages. The area of, roughly, modern Germany, Austria and Bohemia comprised the empire, under an elected emperor and with a number of common institutions, such as a diet (assembly) at Ratisbon (Regensburg) and an imperial court at Wetzlar. From 1438 to 1740 and 1745 to 1806 the emperors were always members of the Habsburg family, the rulers of Austria, Bohemia and Christian Hungary (*see* HABSBURG EMPIRE). In 1742, in the absence of a male Habsburg, Charles Albert of Bavaria was crowned as Charles VII. In 1806 the Holy Roman Empire was dissolved. The last emperor, Francis II, became emperor of Austria; while much of Germany was joined in the Confederation of the Rhine, a body that excluded Austrian influence. These changes were made in response to Napoleon's wishes. Prior to this collapse, the power and authority of successive emperors had been limited, especially in northern Germany and particularly after the Thirty Years War (1618–48), by the strength of the major principalities, such as Prussia, Hanover, Saxony and Bavaria. A measure of unity could be obtained in the face of common adversaries – the Turks in 1683–99, Louis XIV in 1702–14 – and in the late 1710s and early 1720s Charles VI had some success in reviving imperial authority, but thereafter it declined. Austro-Prussian animosity from 1740 weakened Maria Theresa, and Joseph II's policies and intentions were widely feared. German unity required a new forum if it was to have much of a future.

M. Hughes, *Early Modern Germany, 1477–1806* (London, Macmillan, 1992).

JEREMY BLACK

homosexuality In the first generation of the eighteenth century (1690–1730) homosexual relations between men in western Europe underwent a profound transformation which produced the modern pattern of homosexuality that has lasted until today. By the end of the eighteenth century a similar change had begun to occur (but less markedly) in homosexual relations between women. Before 1700 Europeans had presumed that all men desired both men and women but that sexual behaviour would occur within the prescribed limits of Christian doctrine and patriarchal power. Only in marriage was sex regarded as not sinful, but for men it could honourably be enjoyed in two other circumstances:

with female prostitutes and with adolescent men. This is best documented in the cities of Renaissance Italy, where in Florence, for instance, prostitution was legal (if sinful) and one man in four was arrested for sodomy at least once between the ages of 15 and 30. Male homosexual behaviour must therefore have been widespread. It was, however, structured according to age. Men in their twenties took the active or penetrator's role in intercourse with adolescents. These young men also went to female prostitutes and in their early thirties married and raised families. Their sexual relations with adolescents did not mark them as effeminate, but were, rather, a sign of manly self-assertion.

A similar pattern of homosexual behaviour was found in seventeenth-century Spain and Portugal, where adolescent men often dressed as women and were joined by a much smaller number of passive adult transvestite men. Something like these two southern European patterns also prevailed in northern Europe before 1700 but is harder to document since there were fewer trials than in the south. European homosexuality before 1700 therefore conformed to one of the two patterns prevalent in the rest of the world, in which men had relations both with women and with either a majority of adolescent males or with a minority of passive transvestite adult men.

While this pattern continued to prevail in southern and central Europe, after 1700, in France, the Netherlands and England a new pattern appeared. In these three modernizing societies waves of arrests revealed the existence of a new subculture of passive effeminate men who desired only men, whether adult or adolescent. They were classified as a third, deviant, gender, which combined aspects of male and female behaviour. They moved and spoke like women, took women's names and were in varying degrees transvestite. It was now presumed that the majority of men desired only women and never other men, and that legitimate masculine status was founded on this exclusive desire. The modern distinction between homosexuality and heterosexuality had come into existence.

Dennis Altman et al., *Which Homosexuality?* (London: GMP, 1989).

Kent Gerard and Gert Hekma (eds), *The Pursuit of Sodomy: Male Homosexuality in Renaissance and Enlightenment Europe* (New York: Haworth, 1988).

R. P. Maccubbin (ed.), *'Tis Nature's Fault: Unauthorized Sexuality during the Enlightenment* (New York: Cambridge University Press, 1987).

RANDOLPH TRUMBACH

honour   In his essay 'Of the Independency of Parliament' (1741) Hume wrote, 'Honour is a great check upon mankind: But where a considerable body of men act together, this check is, in a great measure, removed; since a man is sure to be approved of by his own party, for what promotes the common interest; and he soon learns to despise the clamours of adversaries.' 'Serious attention to the sciences and liberal arts', he claimed in 'The Sceptic' (1742), 'softens and humanizes the temper, and cherishes those fine emotions, in which true virtue and honour consists.' In an *Encyclopédie* article on the subject (1765) the chevalier de Jaucourt (1704–79) described honour as self-esteem and the legitimate feeling that one was entitled to be esteemed by others because one led a life of virtue. He went on to criticize the arbitrariness and inequity with which distinctions and honours were conferred by society, and made what might be deemed a self-contradictory plea for a system of honours linked to the performance of duty for its own sake. Three rules governed honour, in Montesquieu's analysis: first, one should value one's fortune but never one's life; secondly, having acquired a certain status, one should never give the least indication that one held oneself unequal to it; and finally, the dictates of honour were all the more binding in the absence of laws to enforce them.

Charles de Secondat, baron de Montesquieu, *The Spirit of the Laws*, ed. Anne Cohler, Basia Carolyn Miller and Harold Samuel Stone (Cambridge: Cambridge University Press, 1989).

SYLVANA TOMASELLI

Horne-Tooke, John *see* TOOKE, JOHN HORNE.

hospitals In the later eighteenth century hospitals became increasingly important to MEDICINE. In England a wave of hospital foundation started in the 1730s, and the American colonies followed with their first hospital in 1751. In Continental Europe a variety of old institutions – orphanages, asylums, prisons and poorhouses – often contained medical components, which evolved into hospitals. Medical science, emphasizing the classification of DISEASE, began to separate the institutionalized poor from the sick, and medical education came to include a period of 'walking the wards', observing illness and treatment. The French Revolution led to the restructuring of medicine, and French doctors began to study large numbers of hospital patients, routinely dissecting the bodies of those who died in hospital, seeking to correlate changes before and after death.

Contrary to popular myth, such places were not death traps. Although only the poor entered hospitals (most people were treated at home even for severe illnesses), they were seen by leading medical men and received nursing care. Hospital stays were lengthy by our standards, but the vast majority of patients recovered and many were cured.

C. Jones, *The Charitable Imperative* (London: Routledge, 1989).
G. B. Risse, *Hospital Life in Enlightenment Scotland* (Cambridge: Cambridge University Press, 1986).

MARY E. FISSELL

Houdon, Jean-Antoine (1741–1828)   French sculptor. He trained in Paris with Jean-Baptiste Lemoyne (1704–78) and Jean-Baptiste Pigalle (1714–85). He won the Prix de Rome in 1761 and spent the years 1764–8 in Rome. There he created well-known figures of *St Bruno* and of a *Flayed Man*; the latter is widely used in art schools. In 1777 he became a member of the Académie Royale de Peinture et de Sculpture on presentation of a statue of *Morpheus*. Although he created a number of successful funerary monuments in a neoclassical style, such as that for the *Heart of the Comte d'Ennery*, as well as some fine statues on classical themes, among them *Diana the Huntress*, he was best known as a portrait sculptor.

The superb series of busts of his contemporaries that made him the pre-eminent portrait sculptor of the eighteenth century, with a reputation that extended to Russia and the United States, began with *Denis Diderot*, exhibited at the 1771 Paris *salon*. The writer was shown in the antique manner, with his own hair and his shoulders naked. His pose, with head turned slightly to one side and lips parted as if listening, was typical of Houdon's lively and naturalistic approach to characterization. Among his busts of *ancien régime* figures were those of the economist *Turgot*, the composer *Gluck* and a brilliant portrait of Louis XV's aunt *Mme Victoire*. The latter was a virtuoso demonstration of his abilities as a marble carver. Other works of the period included busts of *Rousseau*, *D'Alembert*, *Franklin*, *Washington* and *Voltaire*. These existed in a number of different types and versions, Houdon being among the first artists to exploit fully the market for portraits of famous men.

Although he portrayed many of the prominent figures of the French Revolution, he gradually fell out of favour in the 1790s. His herm bust of *Napoleon I* marked a revival in his fortunes. His most successful statues were those of *Voltaire Seated* and *George Washington*. In both of these antique costume was rejected. Voltaire appeared in a dateless loose dressing-gown and Washington in contemporary dress, the only classical reference being a ploughshare in allusion to Cincinnatus.

H. H. Arnason, *The Sculptures of Houdon* (London: Phaidon, 1975).

MARC JORDAN

household structure   Since the 1960s historians of the family have discovered a great deal about the household structure of pre-industrial Europe. Using the limited number of surviving listings of the population, they discovered, contrary to expectations, that mean household size in much of western Europe was relatively small. Mean household size in England from 1650 to 1749 was 4.2, rising to 4.6 in the period 1750–1821. Moreover, the predominant structure was simple: three-quarters of English households consisted solely of the nuclear family (defined as a husband and wife, with or without children) and only about 15 per cent contained resident relatives. It appeared, too, that historically there had been distinct regional patterns in European household structure. Whereas nuclear families predominated in north-west Europe, complex multiple households predominated in eastern and southern Europe.

The north-western nuclear family system was associated with the presence of large numbers of unmarried life-cycle servants, with a relatively late age at first marriage for women and large numbers of people never marrying at all. Couples expected to form their own independent households at marriage. In Denmark, Norway, Flanders and England, where nuclear families predominated, at least a third of men and women aged 15–24 were in service.

Until recently, it was believed that eastern or southern European complex household structures were associated with early and near-universal marriage and few life-cycle servants. Where complex households predominated, young married couples lived and worked within the household of one of the groom's parents. Research on southern Europe, however, has recently questioned the validity of such associations.

Early criticism of this approach to the study of the household focused on the classification system developed by Laslett, which analysed households by internal kin relationships: a nuclear family consisted of a husband and wife with or without children; extended households were those containing in addition any relatives who were neither married nor members of a parent-child group; and multiple households were those containing two or more related married couples or parent-child groups. It was pointed out that high death rates placed an artificial constraint on the possibility of forming multiple households and that household structures vary naturally over the life course. Thus a multiple family consisting of a married couple and one married son (one definition of a 'stem family') is only one stage in a cycle which begins with a nuclear family and children, becomes a stem family when a son marries and stays at home, is extended when a parent dies, and becomes nuclear again when the second parent dies. It was also felt that analysis exclusively in terms of kin relationships gave undue prominence to relationships that may not have been important as structural features, such as the presence of servants.

Recent analyses of household structure have adopted new classification systems. One is the calculation of headship rates. These bring out the very different familial experiences represented by different household structures. Thus in one nineteenth-century Russian community only 10 per cent of men in their thirties headed their own households compared to as many as 80 per cent in early modern England.

Much effort has also been expended recently in analysing the determinants of household structure. In eighteenth-century England both servant-keeping and the degree of household complexity varied according to the occupation of the household head. In eastern Europe landlord control over serf populations and limited geographical mobility underpinned multigenerational peasant households. In general, limited resources and a large pool of wage labour were associated with nuclear structures while family farms or businesses often encouraged the formation of multiple households. Consequently, rapid economic change in Europe has been associated with changes in household structure. Industrialization in southern France in the early nineteenth century is thought to have been mainly responsible for the demise of the stem family in that region. In other parts of Europe inheritance practices have been associated with particular family forms. It should be said, however, that enduring and little-understood cultural norms, seemingly unaffected by social and economic change, sometimes underpin household structure.

The eighteenth century saw some alteration in the composition of households. In England the late eighteenth and early nineteenth centuries saw a fall in resident servants and a rise in the number of offspring, due, respectively, to a decline in the use of live-in agricultural servants and a rise in fertility.

See also FAMILIES.

P. Laslett and R. Wall (eds), *Household and Family in Past Time* (Cambridge: Cambridge University Press, 1972).

R. Wall, J. Robin and P. Laslett (eds), *Family Forms in Historic Europe* (Cambridge: Cambridge University Press, 1983).

JEREMY BOULTON

Hudson's Bay Company The Hudson's Bay Company was chartered by King Charles II on 1 May 1670 to trade and settle in a vast wilderness known as Rupert's Land, on the North American continent around Hudson Bay. From the outset, the organization was run by a tightly knit board of Scottish adventurers who relied heavily on labour from the Orkneys to man the ships and posts of the company, which dealt in furs with the Indian nations. The problems of the company between 1688 and 1820 were threefold: attacks on its monopoly, an inability to expand and competition from a rival organization based in Montreal called the North-West Company. The Hudson's Bay Company dealt with the first problem successfully in a protracted press and parliamentary campaign between 1688 and 1756. The problem of expansion proved more intractable not only because of French hostility to the company's interests before 1760 but also because the severity of the climate mitigated against settlement on a large scale. Such dilemmas made the company vulnerable to competition from the North-West Company, and the two waged a highly competitive and, for a time, profitable trade war in furs over the whole continent until they merged in 1821.

Peter C. Newman, *Company of Adventures*, vol. I: *The Story of the Hudson's Bay Company* (Harmondsworth: Viking, 1985).

PHILIP LAWSON

Huguenots The Calvinist French Protestants who were involved in the French wars of religion in the sixteenth century were popularly known as 'Huguenots'. Their limited and erratic TOLERATION was effectively ended by the REVOCATION OF THE EDICT OF NANTES in 1685. Although there was considerable Huguenot emigration before 1685, Louis XIV's brutality against them led to the largest forced migration in early modern Europe. Some 300,000 made their way to Holland, Switzerland, Prussia, the British Isles and North America. Their speed of assimilation into host cultures varied from place to place, but it seems to have proceeded most slowly in parts of Germany and most swiftly in the more fluid ethnic and social structure of colonial America.

Although the prime motivation for the Huguenot diaspora was religious freedom, Huguenots made a considerable economic contribution to their adopted countries in banking, trade and textile production. Huguenot industriousness was generally welcomed by host countries, but their increased economic competitiveness was sometimes resented by indigenous populations. Ironically, these sturdy religious exiles did not always gravitate to specifically Calvinist churches and there is now growing evidence of their distinctive contribution to the new religious movements generated by the international evangelical revival.

R. D. Gwynne, *Huguenot Heritage* (London: Routledge & Kegan Paul, 1985). A. D. Lavender, *French Huguenots* (New York: Peter Lang, 1990).

DAVID HEMPTON

humanitarianism A multifarious movement in late-eighteenth- and early-nineteenth-century western Europe, humanitarianism drew on a number of different and sometimes divergent sources which condemned cruelty and intolerance and urged more humane social practices. Whereas in eastern and southern Europe it was often coextensive with ENLIGHTENED ABSOLUTISM, in the socially more advanced north-western states it was championed by groups within the social elite: in England, for example, devotional religious groups such as the Methodists and the Evangelicals were important (see EVANGELICALISM; METHODISM); in France the key role was played by the *philosophes*. The range of objectives of the humanitarian movement included religious toleration;

less discriminatory policies towards Jews; the abolition of the slave trade, then of slavery; the removal of harsh, humiliating and disabling punishments within the criminal code; better provision for the sick and needy in the form of hospitals and lunatic asylums; better facilities for needy children, including orphanages and foundlings' homes; charity schools for the children of the poor; public health measures; and better prison conditions.

See also CHARITY, PHILANTHROPY.

Shelby T. McCloy, *The Humanitarian Movement in Eighteenth-Century France* (Lexington, Ky.: University of Kentucky Press, 1957).

COLIN JONES

Hume, David (1711–1776)   Scottish philosopher, historian and writer of popular essays. He also played a central role in the upsurge of scientific and cultural activity in mid-eighteenth-century Edinburgh. He held various government offices but his central activities were always literary and philosophical. He grew up in a Scotland that had recently lost its independence due to the 1707 Act of Union. In 1723 he entered the University of Edinburgh where he was destined for the study of law, but before leaving university he had already projected his major philosophical work, *A Treatise of Human Nature*. He wrote much of the book during a sojourn in France from 1734 to 1737. It was published in 1739–40 when he was only 28 years old. However, it 'fell dead-born from the press' and he rewrote and republished each of its three parts over the following two decades. In it he aimed to show how all human belief and action was rooted in certain principles of human psychology (for example the association of ideas and feelings) and that reason played only a secondary role. Hume developed significant theories concerning the origin of our idea of causality, of the nature of human will (*see* DETERMINISM), of the basis of our moral judgements (a 'moral sense') and of the origin of justice.

His first literary success was his *Essays* of 1741 where he set out to be an ambassador from the world of learning to that of polite society. These essays, which he supplemented considerably in 1742 and 1752, were popular not only in Britain, but especially in France. They covered topics in politics, economics, aesthetics as well as morals. He attempted twice (1745, 1751) to obtain a teaching position in a Scottish university, but without success: a major obstacle was his reputation for scepticism and ATHEISM. In the *Enquiry concerning Human Understanding* (1748), originally entitled *Philosophical Essays*, he argued systematically that reason could undermine both natural and revealed religion. This criticism of religion continued in his writings and publications of the 1750s. In the *Enquiry concerning the Principles of Morals* (1751) he sought to show that morality could be established on a purely secular basis. In the six volumes of his *History of England* (1754–62) he argued that the social and political effects of religion were usually bad, and that the worst crimes of humanity were committed in the name of religion. In *The Natural History of Religion* (1758) he argued that religion had its origins in the natural human tendency to anthropomorphize the harmful unknown causes in nature. His posthumously published *Dialogues concerning Natural Religion* (1778) attacked the design argument for the existence of God.

D. Hume, *Enquiries concerning Human Understanding and concerning the Principles of Morals*, ed. L. Selby-Bigge, rev. P. H. Nidditch (Oxford: Clarendon, 1978).

D. Hume, *The History of England from the Invasion of Julius Caesar to the Revolution of 1688*, 6 vols (London: A. Millar, 1762).

D. Hume, *A Treatise of Human Nature*, ed. L. A. Selby-Bigge, rev. P. H. Nidditch, second edn (Oxford: Clarendon, 1978).

JOHN P. WRIGHT

Hungary The kingdom of Hungary was the largest and most unruly of the territories of the Habsburg, or Austrian, monarchy (*see* HABSBURG EMPIRE). Fierce fighting raged there in the decades around 1700, as a successful crusade to liberate large parts of the country from Turkish control turned into a war between the forces of the Austrian government in Vienna and Hungarian insurgents under Prince Francis [Ferenc] Rákóczi (1676–1735). This rebellion in defence of the traditional liberties of the kingdom was settled by a compromise peace at Szatmár in 1711: the Hungarian nobility, the dominant political force within the country, obtained guarantees that the historic constitution, based on a regularly convoked diet, a distinct and native administrative structure, and a separate legal system, would be observed. In return, they recognized the hereditary rights of the Habsburg dynasty and the indissolubility of the link between Hungary and the rest of the monarchy.

On this basis, eighteenth-century Hungary made an impressive recovery, both material and cultural, from the sorry state to which it had earlier been reduced. The population more than doubled, to reach 8 or 9 million by 1800. The overwhelmingly agrarian economy expanded vigorously, helped by a major recolonization of the great Danube plain. It remained centred on the cattle and wine trades, but grain and tobacco production also increased. Though urban development was slow, many artisans prospered, and the rich copper, silver and iron mines continued to be among the most important in Europe. The Catholic Church exploited its privileged position to engage in a lavish but determined mission of spiritual renewal, directed not least against the large Protestant and Orthodox minorities. Educational reform became more marked towards the end of the century, and a larger reading public began to support new literary and journalistic endeavours in the spirit of the Enlightenment.

The process of rapid change placed new strains upon the political fabric of the country, especially when Habsburg rulers came to encourage it as part of a general absolutist reform programme for the monarchy as a whole. Although the Hungarian nobility rallied to the military defence of MARIA THERESA during the 1740s and 1750s, her government resented their refusal to pay taxes and their oppression of the peasantry. It sought to outflank them carefully by ruling through decrees, notable among them a major revision of feudal dues (the *Urbarium* of 1767). In the 1780s Maria Theresa's son JOSEPH II threw caution to the winds: refusing even to be crowned, this 'hatted king' abolished the constitution and introduced radical changes throughout public life. Embittered Hungarian resistance was a chief factor in the overall failure of his policies. Yet enough common ground survived for a further compromise to be reached in the 1790s, which was reminiscent of that of 1711. Hungary's leaders and the Habsburgs came together once more through a common fear of popular revolution, though the seeds of new social and national tensions were to bear fruit in the nineteenth century.

Domokos Kosáry, *Culture and Society in Eighteenth-Century Hungary* (Budapest: Corvina, 1987).

Henrik Marczali, *Hungary in the Eighteenth Century* (Cambridge: Cambridge University Press, 1910).

R. J. W. EVANS

Hunter, John (1728–1793) Eminent Scottish surgeon, naturalist and anatomist. Born in Lanarkshire, Scotland, he went to London in 1748 as an assistant to his brother William Hunter (1718–83). William taught anatomy, and John spent eleven years making preparations and performing dissections while learning and practising surgery at St George's Hospital. After a spell as an army surgeon, he returned to build a successful London practice. He pursued research and teaching in various aspects of medical science, assembling a huge collection of 13,682 pathological and physiological specimens before his death in 1793.

This collection has been called Hunter's 'great unwritten book' because its organization embodied significant aspects of his contribution to medical science. Hunter stressed the function as well as structure of anatomical parts. He moved away from classifying animals on a single chain of complexity, focusing instead on the ways different organs and organ systems varied between and among groups of animals. His book on inflammation and gunshot wounds exemplifies his experimental and scientific approach to surgery for which subsequent generations have revered him.

S. J. Cross, 'John Hunter, the Animal Oeconomy, and Late Eighteenth-Century Physiological Discourse', *Studies in History of Biology*, 5 (1981), 1–110.

MARY E. FISSELL

Hutcheson, Francis (1694–1746) British philosopher. Born into a Scottish Presbyterian family in Northern Ireland, he attended the University of Glasgow from 1711 to 1717. After becoming a Presbyterian minister, he ran a private academy in Dublin from 1721 to 1730. During this time he published his *Inquiry into the Original of our Ideas of Beauty and Virtue* (1725) in which he defended the moral theory of Shaftesbury against the egoistic morality of Mandeville. He also published his *Essay on the Nature and Conduct of the Passions and Affections* (1728). He was appointed professor of moral philosophy at Glasgow in 1729. Through his lectures and writings he came to have enormous influence on Scottish philosophy in the eighteenth century.

He thought that reason could never be a stimulus to action and that all action must arise from feeling. He argued that all moral judgement must be based on a 'moral sense': this makes us feel approval of persons to the extent that they are benevolent. From this point of view he derived one of the first formulations of the principle of utilitarianism, that 'that action is best, which procures the greatest happiness for the greatest numbers'.

W. Scott, *Francis Hutcheson* (Cambridge: Cambridge University Press, 1900).

JOHN P. WRIGHT

I

Iceland Since 1380, Iceland had been a dependency of the crown of Denmark-Norway. The country imported essentials such as timber, iron and cereals, and exported its rich resources of fish, hides and fur. However, its trade was conducted through Danish monopolists who operated under the favour of a monarchy with almost unlimited power after 1660. The population, of 47,000 in 1800 was lower than it had been a century earlier; it was prone to epidemics and natural disasters such as the eruption of Skaptarjökull in 1783. In 1807–8 Iceland was cut off from Denmark, which had joined Napoleon's Continental System, by British sea power. For a time after 1810 free trade between Britain and Iceland worked to the benefit of the latter. Sweden annexed Norway in 1814 by the Treaty of Kiel, but the cession of Iceland and Greenland appears not to have been required or even considered. Iceland re-entered Danish tutelage, and in 1816–18 saw something of a cultural renaissance with the founding of the Icelandic Literary Society and a national library.

K. Gjerset, *History of Iceland* (London: Allen & Unwin, 1923), pp. 314–47.

D. D. ALDRIDGE

ideologues The word *idéologie*, or 'ideology', was coined by Antoine-Louis-Claude Destutt de Tracy (1754–1836) in a paper delivered to the Deuxième Classe (the future Académie des Sciences Morales et Politiques) of the Institut National, to designate the science whose object it was to study the origin and nature of ideas (in the sense of conscious phenomena) and of their relations to one another and to language. Reports of Destutt de Tracy's paper and of his new term for the philosophy of mind in *The Monthly Review* (1796) and *The Monthly Magazine* (1797) soon spread the use of the word outside France.

The ideologues included CONDORCET; Constantin, comte de Volney (1757–1820), the author of *Voyage en Syrie et en Égypte* (1787) and *Les Ruines, ou Méditations sur les révolutions des empires* (1791); and Georges Cabanis (1757–1808), a physician and philosopher whose materialism was first expounded in *Traité du physique et du moral de l'homme* (1798–9). They were disciples of CONDILLAC and were indebted to his study of the origins of human knowledge and his sensationalist interpretation of John Locke's epistemology. The tenets of the group's philosophy were put forward in Destutt de Tracy's *Éléments d'Idéologie* (1801–5).

S. Moravia, *Il Pensiero degli idéologues: scienza e filosofia in francia, 1780–1815* (Florence: La Nuova Italia, 1974).

F. Rastier, *Idéologie et théorie des signes: analyse structurale des Élément d'Idéologie d'Antoine-Louis-Claude Destutt de Tracy* (Paris: Mouton, 1972).

SYLVANA TOMASELLI

illegitimacy The eighteenth century saw a marked increase in the proportion of illegitimate births. In England the percentage of illegitimate births rose from about 2 per cent of all births in the late seventeenth century to 3.4 per cent by 1750, over 5 per cent by 1800 and 6.5 per cent by 1850. In France illegitimacy rose from around 2.9 per cent before 1750 to 4.1 per cent in 1740–90 and 4.7 per cent in 1780–1820. In Germany it rose from 2.5 per cent before 1750 to 3.9 per cent in 1740–90 and as high as 11.9 per cent in 1780–1820. Such figures are subject to regional variation, with the figure being much higher in some cities.

It is not clear why illegitimacy increased. Peter Laslett has argued that the cause was an increase in the number of children born to members of the 'bastardy-prone sub-society', but there is little convincing evidence for his theory. Bastard-bearers were women whose MARRIAGE plans were unexpectedly frustrated following conception during courtship, so that the true explanation for the increase is that, for some reason, the level of sexual activity during courtship increased and that factors such as urbanization made the dislocation of marriage plans more likely.

P. Laslett, K. Oosterveen and R. M. Smith (eds), *Bastardy and its Comparative History* (London: Edward Arnold, 1980).

JEREMY BOULTON

illuminati The term 'illuminati' refers to the members of diverse, often secret, societies and sects – considered as a single phenomenon or movement – who claim to be specially enlightened. Although the designation is not specific to any eighteenth-century group – it has been used of various Enlightenment enthusiasts, including the French and Russian Martinists and followers of SWEDENBORG – it is most commonly used to refer to the German *Illuminaten,* a secret society founded in Bavaria in 1776 by Adam Weishaupt (1748–1830). A professor of canon law in Ingolstadt, Bavaria and an ex-Jesuit, Weishaupt called his followers Perfectibilists, promulgated deism as well as republican principles, and believed that political freedom was best served by the moral education of the people. He was confident that rulers could be enlightened, as long as they could be shown that the pursuit of virtue and justice was in their interest. Goethe and Herder were members of the illuminati, as were a number of noblemen and officials, including prominent figures such as the Bavarian reformer Count Maximilian Montgelas (1759–1838), and the archbishop-elector of Mainz, Karl von Dalberg (1744–1817). The order had links with FREEMASONRY and was alleged to have ties with the JACOBINS. Its illustrious membership did not prevent it from being persecuted in Bavaria in the 1780s.

Richard von Dülman, *Der Geheimbund der Illuminaten* (Stuttgart: Frommann Holzboog, 1975).

SYLVANA TOMASELLI

imagination   The imagination has at times appeared to be the special province of Romantic authors, like Blake and Coleridge, who celebrated and analysed it for the first time. It is a word on whose redefinition much of what we call ROMANTICISM turns, but the imagination was already an important concept in eighteenth-century discussions of aesthetics and of literature.

Throughout the eighteenth century, discussions of the imagination owed much to Hobbes's (1588–1679) empiricist notion of the faculty: 'Imagination . . . is nothing but decaying sense' (*Leviathan*). Locke, Hume and Hartley (1705–57) discussed it in terms of a power of retention and recombination. Hume in his *Treatise of Human Nature* saw it as the power 'to transpose and change . . . ideas', where 'ideas' are all themselves copies of 'sensations and emotions'. For the empiricist, all ideas derived from sensory experience; the imagination separated and recombined these ideas in ways that could flout the rules of experience.

The concept of the imagination was important in critical and aesthetic texts of the early part of the century, because it seemed to bridge the gap between the new mechanical EMPIRICISM (the major text being Locke's *Essay concerning Human Understanding*) and the polite discourse of TASTE. The text that most effectively bridged it was a series of essays by Addison in the *Spectator*, later much reprinted as 'The Pleasures of Imagination'. Silently supported by Locke, Addison described how, tutored in the correct associations, a gentleman could view 'Scenes and Landskips' with tasteful delight. (For him, as for others, 'landscape' usefully conflated 'nature' and 'painting'.) The description was the basis of Mark Akenside's (1721–70) rhapsodic poem 'The Pleasures of Imagination' (1744).

Addison and Akenside attempted to rescue imagination from the pejorative connotations that the word often had in empiricist philosophy. Locke and Hume saw it as the triumph of fantasy over reason and experience. This sense lived on through the century, notably and surprisingly in novels. Works as diverse as Johnson's *Rasselas* and the fiction of Ann Radcliffe (1764–1823) depicted the imagination as a disabling appetite requiring cure rather than release, even as literary critics seized on the word as a reaction against neoclassicism. 'It is a creative and glowing imagination, and that alone that makes the poet', wrote Joseph Warton (1722–1800) in his revisionist *Essay on Pope* of 1756. From the imagination came what was 'original' (a vogue word after Edward Young's *Conjectures on Original Composition* of 1759). Such writers attempted to change its denotation from reproduction to creation – Addison called reproduction the skill of 'the man of polite imagination'. However, it was not until the beginning of the nineteenth century that empiricist models of perception were challenged and organic metaphors found for the activity of imagination.

M. H. Abrams, *The Mirror and the Lamp* (Oxford: Oxford University Press, 1953).

James Engell, *The Creative Imagination* (Cambridge, Mass.: Harvard University Press, 1981).

W. K. Wimsatt and C. Brooks, *Neo Classical Criticism* (London: Routledge & Kegan Paul, 1970).

JOHN MULLAN

imperialism   The terms 'imperialism' and 'empire' were not widely used during the eighteenth century; indeed, the former was not coined until the second half of the nineteenth century. The word 'empire' had a wide and flexible range of meanings, which did not embrace the modern concept of economic and political control over subordinate peoples and societies. In Britain the term was usually applied to the idea of a unified commercial and maritime system, and only slowly did the notion of domination over weaker societies emerge. Even today it is impossible to invest the words with universal meanings, but despite the problems of definition, it is broadly acceptable to equate imperialism with the coercion of weaker societies by stronger geopolitical systems. In this sense, the eighteenth century may be said to have witnessed a number of different forms of imperialism or imperial activity.

In general terms, the established world imperial order was thrown into disarray during the course of the eighteenth century: long-established systems were superseded by new and different empires. The great Muslim empires of the Mughals, Ottomans, Safavids and Uzbeks all disintegrated to varying degrees, while the European overseas empires of Britain, France, Portugal, Spain, and the United Provinces experienced fluctuating fortunes. (*See* MUGHAL EMPIRE, OTTOMAN EMPIRE.) Only the British maintained any sort of steady territorial growth, and that came only in Asia during the last years of the century, following the calamitous loss of the American colonies in 1782.

The reasons for this transformation are complex, yet at the heart of the issue lies the very nature of the interaction between Europe and the wider world. For while the Muslim empires suffered from crucial internal political and administrative weaknesses, their capacity to resist European advances was undermined by three important external factors. First, a constant flow of precious metals from South America to Asia and the East occurred through the medium of the European trading companies, and this helped to fuel the inflationary process, which in turn placed great strain on a number of regional economies. Secondly, the European search for commercial profit at both a corporate and an individual level was often aggressive and accompanied by the deployment of military and naval strength. Finally, Europeans had gained an important technological lead over the rest of the world, and when this was allied with the use of well-disciplined troops it proved to be a decisive advantage in the military sphere.

Beyond these factors, it is difficult to identify general European imperialist impulses, and it is often a fruitless task to try to ascertain the extent to which domestic influences manifested themselves in the acquisition of overseas territory. While historians have attempted to impose broad frameworks of interpretation on the expansionist process, these efforts have been largely unsuccessful, and it is only through a close examination of specific examples that the dynamics of imperialism can be discerned and analysed. Such an examination reveals a wide range of motivating factors, most of which do not fit into any neat historical pattern. Local political factors, strategic considerations and the unregulated initiatives of merchants, military commanders and private individuals all played their part in creating an environment in which expansion could occur.

Equally, it is clear that the European presence overseas embraced many different forms of imperial relationship. In only a few cases did European governments accept direct responsibility for the administration of overseas territory in the way that the Spanish did throughout much of South America (*see* SPANISH AMERICA). In an important number of instances large tracts of territory were left in the hands of organizations such as the East India Companies, which governed them in a semi-official representative capacity on behalf of their home government (*see* CHARTERED TRADING COMPANIES). The weaknesses of such imperial relationships became all too clear as the century progressed, and increasingly close central supervision was exercised over companies such as the English East India Company. Even then, it is not possible to argue that metropolitan governments developed coherent imperial policies which were consistently and effectively applied to subordinate societies in the wider world. In this sense, European imperialism was only partly developed, and it was not yet recognizable in its later, twentieth-century form.

See also COLONIZATION.

C. A. Bayly, *Imperial Meridian: The British Empire and the World, 1780–1830* (London: Longman, 1989).
D. K. Fieldhouse, *The Colonial Empires: A Comparative Study from the Eighteenth Century* (London: Weidenfeld & Nicolson, 1966).
R. Koebner, *Empire* (Cambridge: Cambridge University Press, 1961).

HUW BOWEN

Index The Index Librorium Prohibitorum (List of Prohibited Books) was the official list of books that members of the Roman Catholic Church were forbidden to read. It was issued in 1557 by the INQUISITION, in an attempt to preserve the faith from writings considered to be heretical or in some way dangerous to orthodoxy, and was put on a firm footing in 1571. During the seventeenth century works such as Galileo's *Dialogues concerning the Two Principal Systems of the World* (1632) were put on the Index, where it remained until the mid nineteenth century. During the eighteeth century many of the works of leading Enlightenment thinkers were likewise prohibited, although Benedict XIV took the works of Copernicus off the list in 1758. Clement XIII put the *Encyclopédie* and Helvétius's *De l'esprit* on the list in 1759, and Rousseau's *Émile* in 1763. Nevertheless, as the power of the papacy declined during this period, the Index was often flouted by the spreading publishing networks, and its authority was challenged by more secular forms of CENSORSHIP.

JEREMY GREGORY

India *see* BENGAL; CALCUTTA; MADRAS; MUGHAL EMPIRE; PONDICHERRY.

Indian Ocean By the eighteenth century Asian civilizations were well developed in cultural, economic and social terms, and K. N. Chaudhuri has made a compelling case for them to be regarded as the 'first world' of human societies. While these civilizations remained diverse in many different ways, they were given a coherence and unity by their relationship with, and dependence on, the Indian Ocean. The ocean, which incorporated the present-day Persian Gulf, Bay of Bengal and South China Sea regions, carried a large volume of seaborne trade which served to sharpen a common sense of identity between the Arabic, Chinese, Indian and Indonesian civilizations. Bullion and material goods, as well as ideas, information and experience, moved between peoples of different origins and religious backgrounds, and regional economies were integrated into a complex pattern of trade and commerce. This maritime commercial process complemented the long-established inland caravan-based movement of goods across Persia and central Asia, and dependence on long-distance trade became a fact of everyday life.

Important centres of trade had been developed around the Indian Ocean, and these port-towns provided meeting- and market-places for financiers, seamen, merchants and traders. However, a number of larger trading emporia gave shape and structure to the pattern of inter-Asian commercial exchange. Trade operated in a series of natural zones, and at the junction of these zones the emporia provided facilities and safe havens for merchants and seamen. In the west, Basra, Gombroon, Jedda, Mocha and Surat fulfilled this function, while in the east, Bantam, Canton, Hugli, Malacca and Masulipatam performed similar roles. The development of these emporia was in part determined by a climate in which wind systems dictated journey times and destinations, but local political conditions, the availability of competitively priced goods and access to caravan routes also helped to establish and sustain them.

The introduction of western European influence into the region in the fifteenth century had served to redefine long-standing commercial patterns, and new centres of trade such as Goa gained in wealth and prestige as the Portuguese made full use of excellent commercial and strategic facilities. While the Portuguese had to a large extent integrated themselves into the existing regional economic framework, the later arrivals – the DUTCH, ENGLISH AND FRENCH EAST INDIA COMPANIES – were more seriously disrupting inter-Asian trade patterns by the eighteenth century. Their efforts to supply northern European markets with products such as silk, spices, tea, coffee and piece-goods brought them into conflict with traditional Asian commercial practices as well as with each other. The trade link with Europe was diverted from Persia and the Red Sea to the sea route around the Cape of Good Hope, and this undermined the status of several important ports in the west of the region. European companies established new trading settlements of their own, and from towns such as Calcutta and Negapatam goods were shipped direct to London and Amsterdam. As the network of European trading contacts spread, so too did the involvement of the East India Companies in the inter-Asian carrying trade, and of particular importance by the second half of the eighteenth century was the English East India Company's large-scale transfer of bullion and goods from Bengal to Canton to fund the fast-growing trade in tea. In the final analysis, the European companies regarded their trade as an armed trade, and they were not reluctant to use force against either indigenous traders or one another. Commercial privileges could be secured by the tactical deployment of troops or ships, and wars in Europe increasingly took on an Asian dimension. The result of this was that the Indian Ocean became an arena for military conflict in which the European presence gradually became the dominant one. Few Asian powers could offer a serious naval challenge to the British, Dutch or French. By the end of the century the net result of this European activity was that the Indian Ocean no longer existed in isolation as a self-contained economic and commercial unit. It had become woven into an elaborate system of intercontinental economic relations which embraced Asia, Europe and the Americas.

See also CHARTERED TRADING COMPANIES, COLONIZATION, IMPERIALISM.

K. N. Chaudhuri, *Trade and Civilization in the Indian Ocean. An Economic History from the Rise of Islam to 1750* (Cambridge: Cambridge University Press, 1985).

D. Kumar (ed.), *The Cambridge Economic History of India*, vol. 2: *c.1757–c.1970* (Cambridge: Cambridge University Press, 1983).

T. Raychaudhuri and I. Habib (eds), *The Cambridge Economic History of India*, vol. 1: *c.1200–c.1750* (Cambridge: Cambridge University Press, 1982).

HUW BOWEN

Indians, North American   Indians, or Native Americans or American Indians as they are known today, were the aboriginal inhabitants of North America. Thousands of tribes, groups and subgroups existed across present-day Canada and the United States of America. They were culturally, ethnically and socially diverse from one another: members of the Iroquois confederacy of New York and south-east Canada lived in stone and wooden homes according to a warrior's code; Indians of the Great Plains, such as the Blackfoot and Cheyenne, were nomadic hunters of buffalo who set up tepees; and in the North American south-west, natives grew grain and constructed their dwellings of adobe clay. Generally, Indians lived in accord with nature, which led Rousseau to dub them 'noble savages' (*see* CULT OF THE NOBLE SAVAGE).

Relations between European settlers and the Indians were equally diverse. French fur-hunters in Canada lived among the Indians, the Spaniards converted and enslaved them, while Englishmen variously fought against and in alliance with them. Along the ever-changing frontier, contact between the two cultures was regular and often violent. The Indians held land that the white settlers coveted, and treaties were often abrogated.

James Axtell, *The European and the Indian* (New York: Oxford University Press, 1981).

JOHN MORGAN DEDERER

Indians, South and Central American   According to the imperial census of 1792, Indians comprised 60 per cent of the population of Mexico and Peru; but the figure gives no indication of their distribution. There was a heavy preponderance of Indian peasants in the Andean highlands and Mesoamerica, while in the cities, the tropical coastlands and zones of frontier settlement Spaniards, mestizos, mulattos and African slaves formed the majority of the population. Although most Indian villagers remained in possession of their communal lands, the growing population placed increasing pressure on resources, since all vacant land of worth had been appropriated by the Spanish. In Peru Indians were still subjected to a labour levy for the mines, paid heavy tribute to the crown and were obliged to pay for merchandise, especially mules and woollen cloth distributed by district magistrates. In Mexico forced labour had ended, but the Indians continued to be exploited through tributes and the enforced distribution of goods and cash. In the Andean highlands and Mesoamerica the Indian nobility retained its influence and often its wealth. Peru was disturbed by a series of Indian revolts which culminated in the Tupac Amaru rebellion of 1780–1, but Mexico enjoyed relative peace until the advent of independence in the next century gave rise to bitter social conflict.

Charles Gibson, 'Indians Societies under Spanish Rule', *The Cambridge History of Latin America*, ed. Leslie Bethell, vol. 2 (Cambridge University Press, 1984), pp. 381–419.

D. A. BRADING

individualism   If individualism refers to the doctrine that privileges the individual, his RIGHTS and needs, over and above all social institutions, and maintains that the individual can be meaningfully considered independently of his or her community or social framework, the term must be used with circumspection in the context of Enlightenment political thought. Philosophers of the social sciences and historians of the romantic movement have tended to present Enlightenment theorists as considering social institutions to be aggregates of individuals and individuals not to be constituted by the social institutions and groupings of which they are members. But for every Helvétius expounding a rather crass version of hedonism and a mechanistic view of the formation of personality, there was a Diderot refuting him by stressing the complexity of personhood, or an Adam Smith with a profound analysis of the nature of sympathy. The concept of individualism plays a crucial role in descriptions of the Enlightenment which

present it as having created a wedge between reason and feeling, understanding and the imagination, and as having subordinated a culturally
acceptable notion of the self to purely utilitarian considerations proper
to its macro-economics and political reformism. Such an interpretation
does not even rank as a one-sided view of the movement.

S. Lukes, *Individualism* (Oxford: Blackwell, 1973).
Alistar MacIntyre: *After Virtue: A Study in Moral Theory* (London: Duckworth,
   1985).

SYLVANA TOMASELLI

Indonesia *see* EAST INDIES.

industrial revolution   The industrial revolution is generally perceived
as a major discontinuity in history, the period of transition from a
rural, agrarian past to an urban, industrial present. However, its precise definition excites much controversy, and some historians would
prefer to consign the term to oblivion. The industrial revolution usually refers to the process and period of industrialization in Britain,
where it first occurred, but is sometimes used more widely to encompass any case of industrialization. It was coined by early-nineteenth-
century French commentators who drew a parallel between economic
changes in Britain and their contemporary political revolution. British
observers of immense new blast furnaces, factories, locomotives and
townscapes restricted their description to an 'age of machinery' but
spoke in awestruck terms using supernatural metaphors – 'Prometheus
unbound', 'Pandemonium' or 'the huge demon of Mechanization
... changing his shape like a very Proteus' (Thomas Carlyle).
   It was not until the 1880s that British historians began to concep-
tualize the half-century after 1780 as the 'industrial revolution': their
dramatic and generally pejorative imagery coloured popular conceptions and set the agenda for a century's academic debate. To Arnold
Toynbee, suffused with middle-class guilt and disillusionment at continuing mass poverty, the industrial revolution was 'a period as disastrous and as terrible as any through which a nation ever passed;
... production on a vast scale, the result of free competition, led to
a rapid alienation of classes and to the degradation of a large body of
producers' (*Lectures on the Industrial Revolution in England*, 1884).
Interwar historians, notably Sir John Clapham, began to redress the
balance, treating British industrialization more sympathetically and as
a gradual, long-term process. As Western economies boomed in the
post-war period, this gave way to a new, optimistic interpretation and
missionary zeal to discover and distribute world-wide the secrets of
sustained economic growth. The concept of a short, swift transition

again held sway; W. W. Rostow narrowed the period of British 'take-off' (a suitably technocratic metaphor) to 1783–1802, though few others went so far. He saw it as driven by the 'leading sector' of cotton (allied to steam, iron and engineering), financed by unprecedented levels of capital formation and facilitated by contemporary revolutions in agriculture and transport. It was primarily a technological revolution, inspired by the advances of post-Newtonian science.

Since the 1970s the historical tide has turned again, in the light of new research and against a background of economic downturn and the catastrophic failure of most high-technology, capital-intensive development programmes. British industrialization is now widely perceived as gradual and evolutionary, beginning much earlier than 1780 and hardly under way by 1830. This paradoxical view is based both on recalculations of national income data and on a more sophisticated understanding of technological change which recognizes the frequently long intervals between an invention and its widespread diffusion.

Crucially, the latest figures of gross domestic product, calculated by N. F. R. Crafts, reveal only a gentle acceleration of economic growth and a rate of 2 per cent per annum reached only after 1830. Yet there is evidence to suggest that already by 1700 as much as 30 per cent of the labour force was employed at least part-time in industry, implying considerable restructuring away from agriculture. Evidence for major improvements in agricultural techniques in the seventeenth century or earlier undermine the claims for a late-eighteenth-century 'agricultural revolution', while a new regard for turnpike roads and river improvements has reduced the emphasis on canals.

In the other direction, the slow substitution of the STEAM ENGINE for water, wind and muscle power (see WATER POWER) and the virtual confinement of mechanized factory production to textile-spinning indicate that industrialization was far from having reached its peak in 1830. Moreover, the cotton industry's spectacular growth and eye-catching technology may be considered as exceptional and regional; its impact was confined to Lancashire and Lanarkshire and its contribution barely shifted the national output figures. (See TEXTILES.)

Increasingly, British industrialization is perceived as a gradual advance across a broad front, with modernized textile and metallurgical industries counterbalanced by a weight of traditional ones whose technology was neither stagnant nor changing rapidly; a large supply of labour (forced off the land by highly productive commercial agriculture) inhibited the need for labour-saving innovations.

Alternatively, and unsurprisingly in our energy-conscious age, the COAL industry has been accorded a new importance. It fulfilled the criterion of gradual growth and development since before 1700, yet without it the massive expansion of the iron industry, the railways and steam power in the nineteenth century are unthinkable. E. A Wrigley's recent interpretation of the industrial revolution as two overlapping phenomena categorizes the period to 1830 as one of traditional growth on the seventeenth-century Dutch model of commercial agriculture, trade and textiles; it was saved from stagnation and resource exhaustion only by the fortuitous possession of enormous coal reserves and a coal-based technology developed during the preceding three centuries.

The problems of definition pale beside those of explanation. Only a positive role for the state can be excluded, since all these developments were spontaneous and privately financed. Yet for some historians the very absence of state intervention is the key to Britain's early start; others look to the spin-offs from legislation that granted religious toleration or excluded Dissenters from public life or to other aspects of the social structure favourable to enterprise. Such explanations are plausible but generally lacking in proof. Those who single out the stimulus of population growth or technological ingenuity have still to provide convincing explanations for these; neither was unique to Britain. No single cause has been satisfactorily isolated. Multicausal explanations are more realistic but quickly shade into description.

A more fruitful line of explanation may lie in considering European industrialization as a whole, recognizing interdependences, an essentially common cultural background, including overseas expansion and trade, and the retardative or forwarding role of political factors. In this context and over the long term, Britain's short lead begins to look less momentous.

See also FACTORIES, INDUSTRY, MACHINES, TECHNOLOGY.

David Cannadine, 'The Present and the Past in the English Industrial Revolution, 1880–1980', *Past and Present*, 103 (1984), 131–72.

N. F. R. Crafts, *British Economic Growth during the Industrial Revolution* (Oxford: Clarendon, 1985).

Peter Mathias, *The First Industrial Nation: An Economic History of Britain, 1700–1914*, second edn (London: Methuen, 1983).

W. W. Rostow, *The Stages of Economic Growth* (Cambridge: Cambridge University Press, 1960).

E. A. Wrigley, *Continuity, Chance, and Change: The Character of the Industrial Revolution in England* (Cambridge: Cambridge University Press, 1988).

CHRISTINE MACLEOD

industry In the eighteenth century 'industry' meant the virtue of hard work. The word has since become synonymous with the manufacturing sector of the economy, and it is discussed in that sense here. Perhaps as much as three-quarters of the world's industrial output was produced in Asia, principally China and the Indian subcontinent, but this proportion slowly fell as both manufacturing output and population grew in Europe. Europeans were learning to copy the high-quality TEXTILES and PORCELAIN imported from Asia and would soon undermine their dominance through mechanization and factory production.

Many forms of industrial organization coexisted. There was still much subsistence production for home consumption, particularly in rural areas where peasants made their own clothes, shoes, household items and tools, except for metalwares. In towns it had long been usual to buy such goods from specialist producers. Paid industrial employment was the occupation of a minority, although a substantial one in England and the Netherlands.

The larger the town and therefore the market, the greater the range of craftsmen it boasted: London contained nearly 500 different trades in 1792, each narrowly specialized but varying widely in the degree of skill and capital investment required. Some, such as watchmaking and coach-building, had pushed the division of labour to extremes, the master craftsman doing little more than assemble the parts made by semi-skilled specialists. Urban artisans were organized in guilds that regulated entry to the trade through apprenticeship, aimed to maintain quality of production and provided insurance for their members in times of hardship. They guarded their privileges fiercely but many guilds were reverting to purely ceremonial functions as they were challenged by new enterprises established outside their control, in the countryside or in new, unincorporated towns. Except where a high level of skill was necessary, merchant-entrepreneurs were able to by-pass artisan producers and attune production to market conditions. (*See* ARTISANS.)

Large-scale enterprises were rare and mostly urban. Breweries served a concentrated market, sugar and tobacco were processed at the port of entry, complex finishing processes in the textile industry brought together teams of dyers and printers, and a few pioneer potteries and metalware manufactories, such as Wedgwood's and Boulton's, centralized production. The largest collieries began to count their workforce in hundreds, as did some building sites. Otherwise, large enterprises were almost all controlled and funded by the state: naval dockyards, arsenals and the royal manufactures of luxury goods established by European monarchs (foreshadowed by the royal and noble karkhanas of Mogul India.)

Power-intensive industries were generally restricted to rural sites by their requirement of fast-falling water until the rotative STEAM ENGINE became available. The charcoal IRON industry was further constrained by its fuel supply, which was both friable and heavy, making transportation beyond a few miles untenable.

Industrial employment was overwhelmingly rural, small-scale and part-time. The fastest growing type of industry was that organized on the domestic, proto-industrial or putting-out system, characterized by the employment of workers in their own cottages. It was labour-intensive, requiring quickly learned skills and little fixed capital: wool-, linen-, and cotton-spinning and weaving, hosiery, lacemaking and simple metalware production (such as nail-making) were most suitable. Urban merchants supplied the raw materials and collected the finished goods to sell them in national and international markets. By-employment in agriculture effectively subsidized labour costs; putting-out was established in the most marginal farming regions. A less common variant occurred typically where cottage-producers had greater resources of land, which gave them more independence: they dealt on the open market themselves. The whole family was often thus employed, though in areas of arable agriculture it was the wives and children of farm labourers who supplemented the family income in this way. In India, European merchants, pursuing tighter control over production, began to substitute the putting-out system, with its advance of materials, for the customary advance to artisans of capital.

That some of these proto-industrial regions proceeded to factory production has led some historians to offer an explanation of industrialization based on their accumulation of factors of production, their experience in international marketing and the stimulus to population growth of earlier marriage among wage-earners. However, the model's explanatory power is weakened by the subsequent deindustrialization of many such regions and by its neglect of the heavy industries, which played a significant role but were never thus organized.

Water-powered silk mills had spread from Italy during the sixteenth to eighteenth centuries. Of the domestic industries, however, only cotton-spinning and its preparatory processes had been reorganized into factories by 1800, and even that to no great extent outside Britain. Factory production required unprecedented levels of fixed capital investment in buildings and machinery: the domestic system gave manufacturers the flexibility to divert liquid capital into other, more profitable channels. The rapid expansion of demand for cotton cloth, both domestic and export (particularly in North America) lay behind this shouldering of new risks: it stimulated the search for mechanization and gave manufacturers the incentive to discipline their part-time workforce and reduce the transaction costs of their widening putting-out circuits. It was principally the massive increase in productivity offered by powered machinery that made the factory attractive. Labour was hard to recruit, since WATER POWER sites were usually remote and factory conditions unappealing to independent, self-timetabling domestic workers. Some factory owners hired batches of pauper children from city workhouses. The steam engine brought relief by permitting access to urban labour. Capital was raised from family and friends, and profits ploughed back into growth. It was possible to start modestly, with rented 'room and power', by equipping the mill over several years, or with second-hand machinery.

Mechanization brought redundancy to thousands of rural spinsters and was forcibly resisted in many places. However, the enormous expansion in yarn output created a huge, if temporary, new demand for domestic handloom weavers, and women invaded this traditionally male preserve.

See also DOMESTIC INDUSTRY, FACTORIES, INDUSTRIAL REVOLUTION, MACHINES, TECHNOLOGY.

K. N. Chaudhuri, The Trading World of Asia and the English East India Company, 1660–1760 (Cambridge: Cambridge University Press, 1978).
Jordan Goodman and Katrina Honeyman, Gainful Pursuits: The Making of Industrial Europe, 1600–1914 (London: Edward Arnold, 1988).

CHRISTINE MACLEOD

inheritance   Eighteenth-century Europe had an enormously wide range of inheritance patterns, grounded in varying local legal arrangements. PRIMOGENITURE, which favoured the eldest son at the expense of siblings, and equal inheritance among children were the two extremes of a very broad spectrum. Western European landed aristocracies tended to maintain a system of primogeniture, which made the preservation of a landed domain across several generations more manageable. Links are sometimes suggested between inheritance patterns and household size and complexity, but broad generalization in this area is dangerous, since social practice and legal norms were often widely divergent. The Enlightenment attack on primogeniture as contrary to the natural RIGHTS of siblings, led to legislation in the revolutionary assemblies to generalize partible inheritance. In the egalitarian phase of the Revolution under the Terror, illegitimate sons even had equal rights recognized, although these were withdrawn shortly afterwards. The Code Napoléon's endorsement of partible inheritance is sometimes linked to the spread in the nineteenth century of coitus interruptus among French peasants anxious to restrict their family size so as to prevent the fragmentation of holdings.

COLIN JONES

inoculation   Intentional infection with smallpox in order to confer immunity, or inoculation, was a folk practice in many parts of the world before it was introduced to European medicine in the eighteenth century. Lady Mary Wortley MONTAGU, wife of the British ambassador to Turkey, brought the practice to the West from Constantinople and had her daughter inoculated in London in 1721. The interest of Hans Sloane (1660–1753), president of the Royal Society, and other leading medical men led to a trial being carried out on prisoners: six felons in Newgate were inoculated and all recovered to receive royal pardons.

Inoculation was not, however, universally or speedily adopted. Religious anxieties shaped some opposition; Boston Puritans argued about interference with divine providence and with God's covenant, as well as the possibility that inoculation could spread smallpox. In France inoculation overcame medical indifference and opposition only in the mid-1750s. In the 1760s the Englishman Robert Sutton (1707–88) perfected a new method and began a career as a mass inoculator with his six sons, eventually claiming 40,000 inoculations with only five deaths. Inoculation was largely abandoned with the advent of VAC-CINATION.

G. Miller, *The Adoption of Inoculation for Smallpox in England and France* (Philadelphia: University of Pennsylvania Press, 1957).

MARY E. FISSELL

Inquisition The so-called Spanish Inquisition, for which there are a number of medieval precedents, was set up with papal approval in 1479 and became the most notorious means by which the Catholic Church attempted to persecute those it considered to be heretics (*see* HERESY). It was first used against the Moriscos, Jews who had converted to Christianity, and many of these New Converts/Christians were treated with suspicion. With the decline of the papacy in the eighteenth century the power of the Inquisition was limited and frequently ignored. It was not only frowned upon by secular powers, but also treated with suspicion in reformist clerical circles, and in 1768 the distinction between Old and New Christians was abolished. The Inquisition was also used against Protestants and atheists. It was abolished by Joseph Bonaparte in 1808 and, after a brief resurrection in 1814 as part of the counter-revolution, was finally dissolved in 1820.

JEREMY GREGORY

insanity At the beginning of the eighteenth century insanity was regarded essentially as a disorder of man's higher faculties (those of judgement and REASON in particular). It was thought to be associated with the passions but located primarily in physiological imbalances, and was characteristically defined as a vitiation of that which distinguished man from beast. Animality as the fundamental corollary of insanity informed a therapeutics and provision of resources orientated emphatically towards the control, repression and custodial care of the insane. Coexisting with such notions, however, were alternative attitudes to insanity: as a psychological affliction and a pitiable calamity; as delusion or misassociation of ideas, capable of comfort and remedy by moral or psychological therapy. Through the influence of natural philosophy, a broadening Enlightenment culture and a growing appreciation of the sensibility of the insane, these attitudes gained ground as the period progressed. The insane had been exhibited as freaks of nature before the public from Bethlem to Charenton, but the spectacle came under increasing attack and by the end of the century had been radically curtailed.

It was the laity rather than medical men who identified and managed the insane. Not until the latter third of the century was the diagnosis and treatment of insanity recognized by law as a medical matter. The 'medicalization' of insanity was itself mitigated, however, by the lay orientations of moral management. Only gradually was insanity defined as a distinct type of deviance, and the insane distinguished as a separate category of the disabled and disorderly poor and furnished with specialized accommodation. In France, Germany and elsewhere, state-sponsored public provision saw the large-scale sequestration of insanity. In Britain and America institutional solutions were initiated primarily through private enterprise and voluntary subscription, while the vast majority of the insane remained at large, boarded out or locally provided for.

Roy Porter, *Mind-Forg'd Manacles: A History of Madness in England from the Restoration to the Regency* (London: Athlone, 1987).

JONATHAN ANDREWS

intendants By the eighteenth century, intendants, who had charge of the thirty-six *généralitiés* (the main administrative units of France), had become established as key internal administrators. The office, which had a long history under the French monarchy, was a direct royal appointment, accountable only to the king and the controller-general. By the the reigns of Louis XV and Louis XVI intendants were all nobles, if often of recent origin, usually drawn from the *maîtres des requêtes*. Many, like Turgot and Calonne, went on to occupy high ministerial office.

The intendants had very wide powers and during the eighteenth century many tried to introduce physiocratic (*see* PHYSIOCRATS) reforms into local agriculture and industry, as TURGOT did while he was intendant of Limoges. Assisted by their *sous-délégués*, they intervened in most aspects of local life, often coming into conflict with the *parlements* and provincial estates. However, they also co-operated with these bodies on day-to-day affairs. They enjoyed good personal relations with the *parlementaires* with whom they shared equal social status and similar cultural tastes. They were, in short, the backbone of local government under the old regime. Their extensive powers were effectively limited by the only armed force directly under their control being the undermanned *maréchaussée*. The office of intendant was abolished, along with the *généralitiés*, in 1789, but the new office of Napoleonic prefect was similar in many ways. An almost identical office existed in Piedmont-Sardinia in the same period.

G. Chuassiand-Nogaret, *The French Nobility in the Eighteenth Century* (Cambridge: Cambridge University Press, 1984).
D. Dakin, *Turgot and the Ancien Regime in France* (New York: Octagon, 1965).
W. Doyle, *The Oxford History of the French Revolution* (Oxford: Oxford University Press, 1989).

MICHAEL BROERS

Ireland John Bull's other island had suffered waves of often brutal colonization from the Tudor period, through the Cromwellian era, up to William III's hounding of the Catholic supporters of the deposed James II (1633–1701) which culminated in the Battle of the Boyne (1690). Ireland was inhabited predominantly by a Catholic peasantry, who were governed and exploited by a frequently absentee Protestant landlord class. Landlords' incomes trebled during the century, largely at the expense of their small tenantry, and by 1750 three-quarters of a million pounds in rent was leaving Ireland annually. Ireland was always a potential trouble spot for Westminster, and a large proportion of the British army was stationed there in peacetime. There was full-scale insurrection in the 1790s, fomented by the Society of UNITED IRISHMEN under Wolfe Tone (1763–98), which was sympathetic to the ideals of the French Revolution and looked to French support; this was energetically crushed. Catholics, although a large majority, suffered legal disabilities, including being disfranchised from the Irish parliament which had met briefly in Dublin from 1782 up to the inclusion of Ireland in the Union in 1801. Irish commerce and industry was sacrificed to English manufacturers, the export of Irish wool and cloth, except to England, being banned. By mid-century, Ulster was already establishing its industrial edge over the pastoral south, which was suffering worsening subsistence crises. Famine struck, particularly in 1726–9 and 1739–41, the latter killing 400,000. Even so, aided by the POTATO and the parcelling of holdings, the population continued to grow, outpacing the English. In 1800 there were over two Irish mouths to feed for every one in 1700, and the great famines of the 1840s were looming on the horizon.

E. M. Johnston, *Ireland in the Eighteenth Century* (Dublin: Gill & Macmillan, 1974).
T. W. Moody and W. E. Vaughan (eds), *A New History of Ireland*, vol. 4: *Eighteenth-Century Ireland 1691–1800* (Oxford: Clarendon, 1984).

ROY PORTER

iron The importance of iron as a structural material grew, especially in those parts of Europe where timber supplies were under pressure. Employed at the beginning of the century for tools, cooking-pots, nails, cannon and shot, by 1800 its uses had extended to bridges, buildings, rails, machinery parts, water pipes and boats. The major producers were Sweden and Russia, where iron ore, wood for fuel (charcoal) and water power were all plentiful, and labour relatively cheap. Britain, substituting mineral fuel for charcoal and steam power for water, challenged this dominance and by 1800 was approaching self-sufficiency. British ironworks produced approximately 220,000 tons per annum (ten times more than a century before), and production shifted from forests to coalfields.

In 1709 Abraham Darby (1677–1717) smelted iron ore with coke (desulphurized coal) in a blast furnace, and the process was generally adopted in Britain after 1750 as charcoal prices rose. Refining this pig-iron to produce the more malleable wrought iron required repeated heating and hammering. The puddling and rolling process, patented by Henry Cort (1740–1800) in 1783–4, allowed large-scale coal-fired refining and greatly reduced production costs. Antecedents of these (and other) techniques have been identified in medieval Asia, particularly China, but there is no evidence of their transmission. Europe was replacing Asia as the centre of iron production, while the American Revolution hastened the (charcoal) iron industry's development in the eastern United States.

See also COAL.

C. K. Hyde, *Technological Change and the British Iron Industry, 1700–1870* (Princeton, NJ: Princeton University Press, 1977).

CHRISTINE MACLEOD

Islam For a long time scholarly opinion has maintained that, after the Mongol conquests in the Middle East in the thirteenth century, and the rise to prominence and power of the OTTOMAN EMPIRE in the fifteenth and sixteenth centuries, a period of stagnation set in which affected all areas of life, including the religious. According to this view, Islamic law became stultified and precedent replaced independent judgement. But it may be questioned how deep and real this alleged stagnation was. Whatever the truth of the matter, however, it is clear that the roots of the nineteenth-century revival in all walks of Islamic life are readily perceptible in the eighteenth century. In Arabia, for example, Muhammad ibn 'Abd al-Wahhab (1703–92), a puritanical adherent of the strictest school of Islamic law, the Hanbali, enlisted the political support of a local chieftain named Muhammad b. Su'ud, and the Wahhabi movement, thus born, marched forth in Arabia.

Wahhabism preached a strict Islamic fundamentalism, forbidding, *inter alia*, the intercession of the saints, the visiting of their tombs and the use of tobacco.

In West Africa the militant reformer 'Uthman dan Fodio (1754–1817) embarked on a holy war and spread a reformed, if somewhat legalistic, Islam throughout the region. In India the decline of the Mughal Empire at the beginning of the eighteenth century was paralleled by the career of such figures as the theologian Shah Wali Allah (1703–62) who founded a powerful fundamentalist school of religious thought which stressed the study of Islamic tradition and exegesis of the Koran, and had an extraordinary impact on succeeding generations of scholars up to the twentieth century.

P. M. Holt, *Egypt and the Fertile Crescent 1516–1922: A Political History* (London: Longman, 1966).

IAN NETTON

Istanbul After its capture in 1453 by the Ottoman Turks, the city of Constantinople was renamed Istanbul by its conquerors who made it the centre and capital of their great empire. In the eighteenth century, while it was sometimes the focus for rebellions by such groups as the JANISSARIES, it was also the centre of a cultural renaissance. Following the building of a new pleasure palace for his sultan in Istanbul by one grand vizier, numerous imitations sprang up, and a new age of building in Istanbul was inaugurated. Cultural and artistic links with the West were strengthened and Western furniture began to be used. A Turkish-language printing-press was set up in Istanbul with the freedom to print books on all subjects except the Islamic religious sciences. This age of renaissance became known as the 'Tulip Period' because of the widespread cultivation of the bulb. In 1720 a Frenchman established a fire brigade in Istanbul. The city was also the diplomatic centre of the empire where foreign ambassadors lived. Despite their presence, the Christians of Istanbul remained by and large unaffected by the ideas of the French Revolution.

See OTTOMAN EMPIRE.

Stanford J. Shaw, *History of the Ottoman Empire and Modern Turkey*, vol. 1: *Empire of the Gazis: The Rise and Decline of the Ottoman Empire, 1280–1808* (Cambridge: Cambridge University Press, 1976).

IAN NETTON

Italy During the eighteenth century the Italian peninsula was divided into several states, most of which survived the wars and diplomacy of the first decades of the century with their traditional territories more or less intact. The southern half of the peninsula comprised the kingdom of NAPLES; to its north, the Papal States stretched across central

Italy; north-central Italy was divided between several small states, the largest among them being PARMA, Modena, Lucca and TUSCANY. In the north were the two maritime republics of GENOA and VENICE, the territories of the Savoyard monarch and the duchy of Milan, which passed from Spanish to Austrian rule in 1713. The duchy of Milan was the only part of Italy under direct foreign rule for most of the century; Parma was the only state among them to lose its independence, between 1738 and 1748, in the course of the century. Following the French conquest of 1796–1814, Napoleon greatly reshaped the map of Italy, but all the states, with the important exception of Venice and Genoa, were restored largely unchanged in 1814.

The territorial integrity of the Italian states is central to the history of the peninsula in this period, but it stands in contrast to their dynastic histories. The wars of the Spanish, Polish and Austrian Successions led to important changes in who ruled these states; the division became one between the states on which France or the Habsburgs imposed dynasties, and those that remained untouched by the changes. The Papal States, the Savoyard domains and the two maritime republics fell into the second category, the kingdom of Naples and the central duchies into the first. In Naples a branch of the Bourbons replaced Austrian rule although the state was now technically – and increasingly *de facto* – independent of control from Madrid; elsewhere, the pattern was one of Spanish satellite states giving way to Austrian ones, as the house of Lorraine replaced the Medicis in Tuscany; only Parma joined Naples in the Bourbon orbit. All three major islands changed hands in the course of the century: SICILY passed from Spanish to Savoyard (1713–20), and then to Austrian rule (1720–35), until it came definitively under Neapolitan rule in 1735; Sardinia passed from Spain to the house of Savoy in 1720; CORSICA was sold by Genoa to the French in 1768. All these shifts and changes took place before 1748; the first half of the century had seen the course of military and diplomatic events follow patterns established in the seventeenth century, that of Italy as a major battlefield and source of territorial compensation, for the great powers; after the end of the War of the Austrian Succession, however, the peninsula entered a period of peace and political stability which was broken only by the Revolutionary wars of the 1790s.

This political and dynastic stability was not matched by social and economic developments, which were characterized by a series of structural crises that were to continue into the next century and beyond. The total population of the peninsula numbered approximately 13 million in 1700; by the 1790s it had grown to about 17 million, an increase of just over 34 per cent, compared to the European average of 62 per cent for the period. This growth represents Italy's recovery from the wars, plagues and famines of the previous century – for although famines and plagues still occurred, they were much more localized than before; for the first time the cycle of demographic expansion continued unbroken. However, two important aspects of this growth made it a source of tension. First, it was most dynamic in the countryside rather than in urban centres (which was very different from the rest of western Europe), and in those parts of the countryside least able to absorb it. In general, this meant upland areas, and in regional terms it was the kingdom of Naples that saw the greatest expansion. It was in the early eighteenth century that the demographic preponderance of the south over the north first established itself. Secondly, this growth was not accompanied by an expansion of agricultural resources or production, except in the lowlands of the Po valley in LOMBARDY and eastern Piedmont, where the only area of truly commercial agriculture emerged. Throughout most of rural Italy competition for land within the peasantry increased, strengthening the grip of landlords and their agents at the expense of tenants. The eighteenth century became the golden age of the rack-renter, and generally the condition of the peasant subsistence farmer worsened as the century progressed. Absenteeism by large landowners – still mainly nobles and the church – led to the emergence of a numerous, increasingly powerful rural middle class engaged in letting and subletting to the peasantry, rather than engaging in commercial activities, either agricultural or industrial. The Po lowlands were the only major exception to this pattern, where an entrepreneurial rural bourgeoisie emerged as the driving force behind the development of commercial agriculture. Elsewhere, social tensions worsened at every level of society.

The governments of the Italian states were, for the most part, deeply aware of these problems, and throughout the century, especially between 1760 and 1790, they embarked on ambitious attempts at administrative, financial, economic and social reform. The problems they faced were not only social or economic; the great landlords had been able to consolidate their political and economic power at a local level during the unsettled early years of the century and they usually proved impossible for reforming rulers to dislodge. This did not deter contemporary rulers from undertaking reforms. The most determined and sustained among them were the two Habsburg rulers of Lombardy, MARIA THERESA and her son JOSEPH II. Their rule saw public administration and finance greatly improved in the Habsburg lands, but this success was bought at the price of alienating the local elites. In Tuscany, Peter Leopold's ecclesiastical reforms infuriated the Church, producing conflict with the Vatican and much of the local hierarchy. The pattern was repeated when similar reforms were attempted in Parma and the kingdom of Naples. Peter Leopold tackled the economic crises at their roots in his attempts to reform land tenure in favour of the peasantry, but although these projects were admired by contemporary rulers, they were also his most unsuccessful. By the 1780s the impetus for reform had exhausted itself, the major social and economic problems of the period remaining unresolved. The French invasion of the 1790s saw them almost wholly rejected in the face of the challenge of the French Revolution.

Throughout the period of reform the Italian rulers were progressively replaced by native ministers, products of the Italian Enlightenment who directed their rulers' projects while developing their own. The list of such men is impressive, and testifies to the role of Enlightenment thought in eighteenth-century Italy and the re-entry of the peninsula into the mainstream of European intellectual life. Chief among them were TANUCCI, a Pisan legist and chief minister at Naples between 1730 and 1771; GENOVESI, an economist at the University of Naples whose pupils, in turn, provided the core of the economic reformers who succeeded Tanucci; Pompeo Nerri (1706–76) who served the Habsburgs in Lombardy and Tuscany; and Gianni (1728–1801), chief minister to Peter-Leopold II. Equally influential was the Milanese jurist BECCARIA, whose book Dei delitti e delle pene was among the most widely read of the century. None the less, for all its intellectual brilliance, the work of the Italian Enlightenment, like the regimes it served remained ineffective and marginalized.

In contrast to these trends, the two maritime republics, the Papal States and the lands of the house of Savoy, remained politically and culturally conservative throughout the century. The Savoyard state experienced a fundamental process of reform early in the century under VICTOR AMADEUS II, which was modelled on seventeenth-century Bourbon absolutism; it was a system that his successors refined rather than altered. Genoa and Venice remained under their traditional oligarchies of old noble families, and their states, like those of the papacy, took little part in the mainstream of Italian intellectual life. None the less, they were the best established of the Italian states and, particularly Piedmont and Genoa, continued to command the loyalty of the popular classes to an extent that more reforming regimes no longer did by the end of the century.

The consequences of the French Revolutionary and Napoleonic wars for the Italian states were enormous. In the course of the period 1796–9, the French army of Italy, under Napoleon BONAPARTE, overran the peninsula, although the islands of Sardinia and Sicily remained under their respective rulers, the house of Savoy and the Neapolitan Bourbons. On the mainland the French overthrew most of the established rulers and created a series of new states, modelled on revolutionary France, and the mainland territories of the house of Savoy were placed under a pro-French provisional government; those of the Neapolitan Bourbons became the Parthenopean Republic, and the Papal States the Roman Republic. The most significant changes were the creation of a wholly new territorial entity, the Cisalpine republic, based broadly on Lombardy and Emilia-Romagna, and the definitive disappearance of the Venetian republic, in 1797, when it was awarded to the Habsburgs in compensation for the loss of Lombardy.

Following a brief reconquest by the Austro-Russian armies of the Second Coalition in 1799–1800, Napoleon, now first consul, re-established French hegemony over the Italian peninsula. In the period 1800–14 he reorganized Italy until, by the end of his rule, every indigenous ruler had been expelled, and three large blocks of territory existed. The first consisted of the parts of Italy directly annexed to France, comprising the former territories of Piedmont, the republic of Genoa, the duchies of Parma and Piacenca, Tuscany and, by 1810, the Papal States. Secondly, the Italian republic, which became the kingdom of Italy in 1805, an expanded reincarnation of the Cisalpine republic, with Napoleon's stepson, Eugene de Beauharnais, as its viceroy and Napoleon himself as king. The kingdom of Naples, comprising the mainland territories of the Neapolitan Bourbons, who were deposed by Napoleon, in 1805, was ruled first by Napoleon's elder brother Joseph (1805–8), and then by his brother-in-law Marshal Murat (1808–15).

These territorial changes brought a greater degree of unity to Italy, but it was achieved by force of French arms, and the peninsula remained firmly under Napoleonic domination until 1814. Important legal and administrative reforms were carried out by the French, but few survived the fall of Napoleon in 1814, when, once again, the state order in Italy was reorganized, this time by the Congress of Vienna.

S. J. Woolf, *A History of Italy, 1700–1869* (London: Methuen, 1979).
D. Carpanetto and G. Ricuperati, *Italy in the Age of Reason, 1685–1789* (London: Longman, 1987).

MICHAEL BROERS

J

Jacobins The Jacobin Club of Paris originated in meetings of deputies of the THIRD ESTATE during the crisis of the summer of 1789. It became institutionalized in 1790 when liberal deputies and wealthy non-parliamentarians started to hold their meetings in the former monastery of the Jacobin monks in Paris. The club acted as a parliamentary pressure group, deciding a political line before a matter was discussed in the National Assembly. The club's complexion was transformed from mid-1791 as more democratic elements came to the fore, and from late 1792 ROBESPIERRE's influence increasingly predominated. It was also an instrument of revolutionary consciousness-raising in France as a whole: at the height of Jacobin influence under the Terror there were about 2,000 clubs affiliated to the Paris club, with a total of 100,000 members. The term 'Jacobin', which became synonymous with 'radical activist', was a term of abuse used by counter-revolutionaries and conservatives well into the nineteenth century. The Jacobin network declined after Thermidor: the Paris Club was closed in November 1794, and provincial branches in August 1795.

Michael L. Kennedy, *The Jacobin Clubs in the French Revolution: The First Years* (Princeton, NJ: Princeton University Press, 1982).
Michael L. Kennedy, *The Jacobin Clubs in the French Revolution: The Middle Years* (Princeton, NJ: Princeton University Press, 1988).

COLIN JONES

Jacobites The Jacobites were the adherents of the Catholic Stuart king James II (1633–1701) who was deposed in 1688, and of his heirs (see James Francis Edward and Charles Edward STUART). Since parliament had determined that the monarch must be a Protestant, Britain was ruled from 1714 by a Hanoverian prince, George I, while the

Stuarts remained in exile. The Whig party dominated politics, determined to uphold the Hanoverian succession and the established church of England. Jacobites were therefore always TORIES, although by no means all Tories were Jacobites, and not all Jacobites were Catholics. The most open Jacobite resistance came in the rebellions of 1715 and 1745 (see BATTLE OF CULLODEN), but there were a number of other planned invasions or risings, in 1708, 1714, 1722, 1744, 1752 and 1759. For twenty years Walpole spent much on the surveillance of Jacobites in Europe and Britain, fearing that they might overthrow the Hanoverians. Less violent support for the Stuarts ran through British political life, and Jacobite writings constantly stressed law, constitution, heredity and right. Protesting mobs made use of Stuart emblems and imagery, and Jacobite songs, slogans and writings also underpinned radical challenges to the dominant order. But by the 1780s Jacobitism had become insignificant in political life and belief.

P. K. Monod, *Jacobitism and the English People 1688–1788* (Cambridge: Cambridge University Press, 1989).

PHILIP WOODFINE

jacqueries No peasant revolt in France approached the savagery of the original *jacquerie* in northern France in 1358 when discontented peasants slaughtered their seigneurs. In the West peasant discontent tended to be contained within forms of violence that were individualistic (rick-burning, banditry, poaching), relatively docile and legitimized by custom (grain and bread riots), or were channelled through the courts in antiseigneurial litigiousness. The great exception to this was the peasant revolution of 1789 in France, which was characterized by attacks on property rather than persons (*see* GREAT FEAR). In the East more atavistic outbreaks of collective peasant violence did occur, notably the Rákóczi revolt in Hungary (1705–11); disturbances in the west Ukraine in 1734–7, 1750 and especially 1768; and revolts in Bohemia in 1775 and in Transylvania in 1784. Antiseigneurial feeling was often overlaid with ethnic and xenophobic grievances, as when southern Russia was racked by the Bulavin revolt of 1707, and then by the PUGACHEV revolt of 1773–5, which seemed at one stage likely to topple Catherine II.

See also REBELLIONS, SEIGNEURIALISM.

Y. M. Bercé, *Revolt and Revolution in Early Modern Europe* (Manchester: Manchester University Press, 1987).

COLIN JONES

Jamaica The jewel of Britain's eighteenth-century empire, Jamaica saw its population rise from 7,768 whites and 9,504 slaves in 1673 to 25,000 whites and 210,894 slaves in 1787, by which time its trade was greater than that of all the other British West Indian islands put together and that of any one of the former American mainland colonies. Great Jamaican planters such as the Beckfords were major political and social figures in Britain too: William Beckford (1709–70) was lord mayor of London (1762, 1769), MP (1754–70) and the builder of Fonthill Giffard, while his son William (1759–1844), MP, was the author of *Vathek* and creator of Fonthill Abbey. Although it was overtaken by French Saint-Domingue in the 1720s as the richest CARIBBEAN colony, it regained that position by nearly doubling production (and slave imports) in the 1790s when Saint-Domingue was torn apart by slave revolt, only to lose its lead to Cuba in the 1830s. Its own history was turbulent, with nine slave uprisings and two wars with the Maroon population of nativized runaway slaves between 1673 and 1798. The Jamaican assembly was no less jealous in defence of its rights than those of the North American colonies, but Jamaica was more dependent on British sea power for its protection, and it lacked the internal divisions of the larger white populations further north which led many there to see independence from Britain as the best way to triumph over local rivals. Consequently, it refused to join the rebels in 1776.

MICHAEL DUFFY

janissaries The word 'janissary', in Turkish *Yeniçeri*, derives from two Turkish words, *yeni* and *çeri*, which mean 'new troops' or 'new force'. The janissaries had their origins in the forcible conscription of Christian boys from areas under the control of the OTTOMAN EMPIRE, for example the BALKANS. The youths were trained in Ottoman culture, including the Turkish language and ISLAM, and provided with a military education. The janissary corps became the elite backbone of the Ottoman army, but were also prone to revolt. For example, in 1703 there was a janissary rebellion over the issue of back pay: Istanbul fell into rebel janissary hands and the ruling sultan was deposed. Again, in 1730, an Albanian janissary instigated a revolt which led to the sultan's abdication. Attempts to reform the janissaries were often resisted. However, towards the end of the century a lieutenant of the grand vizier instituted a number of military reforms in an attempt to modernize the Ottoman army. Large numbers of janissaries were dismissed, while the remainder had their salaries raised. The Bektashi order of dervishes became associated with the janissaries and acquired considerable political importance.

Stanford J. Shaw, *History of the Ottoman Empire and Modern Turkey*, vol. 1: *Empire of the Gazis: The Rise and Decline of the Ottoman Empire, 1280–1808* (Cambridge: Cambridge University Press, 1976).

IAN NETTON

Jansenism A radical movement within the Catholic Church in the seventeenth and eighteenth centuries, Jansenism derived its basic propositions from the *Augustinus* (1640) of Cornelius Otto Jansen (1585–1638), bishop of Ypres. It parted company with the doctrinal formulations of the Council of Trent by asserting the individual's absolute reliance upon divine grace for the Christian life. The allegedly heretical implications of the five propositions of Jansenism were condemned by Pope Innocent X in 1653. The Jansenists became involved in bitter controversy with the JESUITS at the heart of which was a conflict between other-worldly asceticism and lax casuistry. Their position was made yet more vulnerable in the early eighteenth century as a result of the destruction of the abbey at Port-Royal in 1709 and the issue of the strongly condemnatory papal bull UNIGENITUS DEI FILIUS in 1713.

By the middle of the eighteenth century the term 'Jansenism' was used to embrace both the religiously devout and those who, in association with the *parlement* of Paris, carried out a campaign against Jesuitry and ultramontanism which resulted in the effective dissolution of the Jesuit order in France in 1762. Thus from its origin as a movement of theological dissent, Jansenism became a term that was used to describe moral asceticism and rigorism, popular religious enthusiasm, and antipapal and anti-Jesuit sentiment. Such features became more pronounced when Jansenism spread to other parts of Europe.

D. Van Kley, *The Jansenists and the Expulsion of the Jesuits from France 1757–1765* (New Haven, Conn.: Yale University Press, 1975).

DAVID HEMPTON

Japan In the eighteenth century Japan was effectively closed to the outside world except for Dutch traders. This peaceful and prosperous period was presided over by the Tokugawa dynasty as heads of state through administrative reform, limits on the power and property of individual feudatories, the establishment of Edo (Tōkyō) as capital and class stratification. There was also a gradual rise in the standard of living, in the size of the population and in national wealth. A newly powerful merchant class oversaw the growth of industry and commerce as well as the transition from a rice economy to a money economy. Nevertheless, there were also times of considerable hardship throughout the century.

Xenophobia and conservatism made the period seem outwardly stagnant but, domestically, it was a time of intellectual stimulation and cultural development. Buddhism was in decline and Christianity had been effectively eradicated. Feudal morality was codified as Bushidō under the revival of secular learning. Confucianism was still a powerful force, while Shintō, partly as a result of antiquarian interest, developed as a nationalistic philosophy and popular religion, especially after 1728 and a plea for 'nutritional learning' by Kada Azumamoto (1669–1736).

Through the interest and influence of the merchant class, literature and the arts flourished. These achievements reached their peak in the so-called Genroku period (1688–1704), which marked the apogee of the ebullient self-expression patronized by the merchants. Among the great names of the vigorous culture at the beginning of the century were Chikamatsu Monzaemon (1653–1725), probably Japan's greatest playwright, and Hishikawa Moronobu (1638–1714), a master of ukiyo-e painting. In time, however, the artistic spirit was attenuated through the gradual amalgamation of the merchant and warrior classes.

With the reign of the Ienobu shōgun (1709–12) a series of much needed financial reforms was inaugurated with the aid of the enlightened Confucian scholar Arai Hakuseki (1657–1725). Other necessary reforms were envisaged but were not carried out because of the shōgun's death and the succession of the infant Ietsugu, whose reign (1713–16) was no more than an interlude. In 1715 the number of Dutch vessels trading at Nagasaki was reduced to two a year.

The next shōgun, Yoshimune (1716–45, d 1751), was perhaps, after the founder of the dynasty, the greatest of the Tokugawa line. He attempted economic reforms, but these tended to restore the class distinctions of previous periods. His encouragement of Confucian scholarship confirmed his conservatism. From the intelligentsia came the able adviser Muro Kyūsō (1658–1734). Nevertheless, the seed of future disasters was sown, as economic and social ills gradually became more acute: the farm population was declining because of infanticide and mass migration to the towns; to save the warrior class from ruin as a result of their enormous indebtedness to the merchants, a series of laws favouring debtors was instituted, which undermined the social stratification begun under the first shōguns. These problems were complicated in 1732–3 by a great famine which, fortunately, met with positive action from Edo. The main political achievement of the reign was the codification of criminal law in 1742, initially for the benefit of judges and administrators. The reform became the basis for the legal system throughout the rest of the Tokugawa period.

Culturally, while Yoshimune maintained a xenophobic stance, he did remove the ban on the importation of foreign books, except for theological treatises. This small gesture opened up Dutch culture to the Japanese, especially medical knowledge. A Dutch–Japanese dictionary was published in 1745, and a text on anatomy translated into Japanese in 1774. This modest beginning in Western scientific method ultimately produced works of cartography and military science that were of great value after 1868.

The rule of the incompetent Ieshigi shōgun (1745–60) saw a rapid decline in administration and further weakening of the economy, complicated by the revolt of Takenouchi Shikibu (1714–68), who attempted an imperial restoration at Kyōto but was arrested and punished, along with his followers. Asada Gōryū (1734–99), the century's foremost astronomer and mathematician, flourished, however.

The Ieharu shōgun (1760–86), though able, was dominated by the tyrannical Tanuma Okitsugu (called Mototsugu) (1719–88), and Tokugawa rule continued its downward course, with natural disasters, like the eruption of Mount Asama and great famine in the north, contributing to serious riots in Edo in 1787.

The reign of the child shōgun Ienari (1786–1837), under the government of Matsudaira Sadanobu (1759–1829), saw the promulgation of some necessary reforms, but with publication of the Kansei Edict (1790) opposition to the regime continued to grow until Ienari's majority in 1793. Awareness of a possible Western threat intensified with the arrival of Russian (1793), British (1795) and American (1798) vessels, which did not, however, succeed in opening up Japan.

Although the personal rule of the shōgun after 1793 was characterized by extravagance and inefficiency in the administration, accompanied by the breakdown of isolationism and military rule, the reign was nevertheless notable for the publication of novels by Ueda Akinari (1734–1809) and Kyokutei (Takizawa) Bakin (1767–1848) and for the world-famous woodblock prints of Katsushika Hokusai (1760–1849) and Andō (Utagawa) Hiroshige (1797–1858). In 1798, after thirty-five years labour, the *Kojikiden* (a commentary on the *Kojiki*, *c.*712) by Motoori Norinaga (1730–1801), the greatest of the Shinto scholars, was published. This work, which continues that of Kamo Mabuchi (1697–1769) and anticipates Hirata Atsutane (1775–1843), is important for the revival of Shintō and the imperial cause in the nineteenth century.

Gerstle, C. Andrew (ed.), *Eighteenth Century Japan: Culture and Society*, (Sydney: Allen & Unwin, 1989).

BASIL GUY

Java, Dutch in The mountainous and densely populated island of Java (3.5 million inhabitants in 1780) was the hub of Dutch trading activity in south-east Asia. The governor-general of the DUTCH EAST INDIA COMPANY and his staff resided in splendour at the western port of Batavia (present-day Jakarta), which was the commercial entrepôt for the region. There were sugar plantations nearby, worked by Chinese immigrants, while rice, coffee and indigo were cultivated in central and eastern Java.

In 1677 Governor Maetsuyker (1606–78) had intervened reluctantly in a succession dispute in the Muslim empire of Mataram, the loose union of sultanates that ruled most of Java at the time. This increased the regime's dependence on the company, and over the next century a series of similar, though unplanned, interventions gradually extended Dutch hegemony over the whole island. By the 1770s the sultanates were vassal states of the company, and most of the Javanese, somewhat unwillingly, were subject directly to Batavia.

See EAST INDIES.

B. H. M. Vlekke, *Nusantara: A History of the East Indian Archipelago* (Cambridge, Mass.: Harvard University Press, 1945).

HUGH DUNTHORNE

Jefferson, Thomas (1743–1826) Architect, diplomat, author, philosopher and third president of the United States (1801–9). A wealthy Virginia planter, he had received a classical education at the College of William and Mary. His clear, forceful writing style impressed fellow congressmen and in 1776 it was he who drafted the Declaration of Independence. After serving as Virginia's wartime governor and ambassador to France (1784–9), he became Washington's first secretary of state. He advocated individual liberty, separation of church and state (he wrote the Virginia statute for religious freedom) and preferred agriculture to manufacture, which set him at odds with the leader of the Federal Party Alexander Hamilton (1757–1804); Jefferson's and MADISON's faction evolved into the Republican Party (present-day Democrats). Elected president in 1801, he purchased LOUISIANA from France in 1803, dispatched Lewis and Clark on their famous expedition and successfully avoided embroiling America in the Napoleonic wars.

In 1809 he returned to his beloved Monticello where he wrote and experimented with agriculture and architecture. He had a lifelong interest in the arts and sciences, and helped to found the University of Virginia. His *Notes on Virginia* was published in 1782. He died on the date he had helped to immortalize, 4 July.

Dumas Malone, *Jefferson and his Time*, 6 vols (Boston: Little, Brown, 1948–81).

JOHN MORGAN DEDERER

Jena, Battle of (14 October 1806) The Battle of Jena was a decisive opportunist victory by Napoleon BONAPARTE over the Prussian army, after which the famed Prussian military machine was routed, its fortresses yielded and most of PRUSSIA occupied within a month. Expecting an imminent declaration of war, Napoleon entered Saxony in early October 1806 with an army of 180,000, and sought out the main

Prussian forces, let by Frederick-William III (1770–1840). He made contact with them at Jena, on the river Saale, east of Erfurt, and at 10 a.m. on 14 October attacked with over 50,000 men, and 70,000 more expected in support, against 53,000 Prussians. Both sides had around 120 guns, and bombardment caused many of the Prussian casualties, which numbered 25,000 against the French total of 5,000. On 13 October Napoleon had ordered Marshal Davout (1770–1823), with 27,000 men and 40 guns, to outflank the enemy to the north and cut off their retreat. He himself did not, however, engage the main army, which had retired north with 63,500 men and 230 guns and met Davout at Auerstädt. Desperate French attacking was rewarded by a Prussian collapse. Frederick-William, believing Napoleon to be his opponent, ordered a retreat which became a rout, and in effect gave France the whole of Prussia west of the Elbe.

O. Connelly, *Blundering to Glory: Napoleon's Military Campaigns* (Wilmington, Del.: Scholarly Resources, 1987).

PHILIP WOODFINE

Jerusalem The ancient city of Jerusalem is known as al-Quds in Arabic. The Ottomans took Jerusalem in 1516–17, when its population was around 4,000, but it was to grow considerably. Throughout much of the period of Ottoman rule, including the eighteenth century, Jerusalem suffered from problems of security, as visitors to the city found to their cost. For example, both Christian and Muslim pilgrims were often obliged by the bedouin to pay a tribute or tax. Formally, Jerusalem was ruled from ISTANBUL through a series of resident military governors of greater or lesser strength, but the governor of Damascus often had more actual control. A judge of the Hanafi school of Islamic law was also imported from Istanbul. The rise to power of certain families in Jerusalem had parallels to some extent with the rise of the powerful beys in EGYPT during this period. In 1808, after the destruction by fire of part of the Holy Sepulchre, a revolt followed attempts by the JANISSARIES in the city to inhibit the necessary repairs. The rebellion was quelled by the governor of Damascus.

K. J. Asali (ed.), *Jerusalem in History* (Buckhurst Hill: Scorpion, 1989).

IAN NETTON

Jesuits The Society of Jesus was founded by Ignatius Loyola (?1491–1556) in 1534 and approved by Paul III in his 'Regimini militantis ecclesiae' (1540), with the aim of reforming the church, undertaking missionary work and leading the offensive against the Protestants. Over the centuries it acquired a reputation for education, training and missionary work. Apart from the three usual religious vows, Jesuits pledged to go wherever the pope sent them and were regarded as principal papal agents. They were largely responsible for the spread of Catholicism to the New World, especially South America, China, India and Persia. The order's 600 colleges, which provided education to the elites of various states, and the often high social status of its members meant that it was one of the most powerful sections of the church.

From the late seventeenth century the Jesuits met with serious opposition within the Catholic Church, most notably from the Jansenists (*see* JANSENISM) who disputed with them on the question of free will and grace, and from the Franciscans and Dominicans who debated the propriety of the Jesuits permitting pagan rites in China in spreading the Christian message. The Jesuits, who had won the confidence of Chinese rulers and educated classes by their knowledge of science, believed that if Christianity were to be accepted in China there had to be some accommodation of Chinese customs such as ancestor-worship. They argued that these social customs were not incompatible with Christianity, but their accommodation was condemned by a number of papal pronouncements, including those of 1704 and 1715 by Clement XI. Anti-Jesuit propaganda received more secular support from the mid-century, largely because of fears of the undue political influence of royal confessors. In 1759, under the influence of the marquês de POMBAL, who claimed that they were responsible for an attempt on the life of King José I, the order was banished from Portugal. In 1764 it was expelled from France, in 1767 from Spain and the Holy Roman Empire, and its lands and endowments were taken over by governments, often for religious purposes. France, Spain and Naples then demanded that Clement XIII suppress the order, but he died before he could do so. In 1773 the order was officially dissolved by Clement XIV, although it continued to operate in Prussia, Russia and parts of Germany and Austria. The Society founded a school at Stonyhurst in England, in 1794, and the Society was officially restored in 1814.

W. V. Bangert, *A History of the Society of Jesus* (St Louis: Institute of Jesuit Sources, 1972).
D. Mitchell, *The Jesuits* (London: Macdonald, 1980).

JEREMY GREGORY

Jews There were about 2 million Jews in Europe in the eighteenth century; over half of them lived in Poland, and there was a growing community in North America. There had been some large-scale defections from the traditions of Jewry after the collapse of the Shabbatean movement in 1666, leading to significant demographic decline in Italy and Germany. The two major groups were the Sephardic Jews (originally from Spain or Portugual) and the Askenazi (from Germany or

Poland). The Sephardics were on the whole the more cultured and sophisticated and were treated with respect in the major ports, like London, Amsterdam and Hamburg, where they played a crucial economic role.

During the eighteenth century in Germany, Holland, Britain and France they received increasing, if at times grudging, legal and civil toleration. Joseph II attempted to integrate Jews into Austrian life, abolishing sumptuary legislation in 1782, and they received civil freedom in France from 1791. TOLERATION was largely reserved for the groups that respected European traditions; the price was the gradual whittling away of traditional Jewish identity, through the abandonment of the synagogue and the abolition of fast customs. Nevertheless, they continued to bear the stigma of popular anti-Semitism and bursts of mass outrage, for example the national outcry caused by the British government's unsuccessful attempt in 1753 to pass a Jewish naturalization bill, and the 1768 peasant massacre of Jews in the Ukraine. Attacks on Jews came not only from orthodox Christian quarters, like the abbé Grégoire (1750–1831), who advocated the need to convert them to Christianity in 1783, but, perhaps more surprisingly, from the supposed leaders of toleration, the English deists and the French philosophes. Writers like William Whiston (1667–1752) and Matthew Tindal (1657–1733) who were proponents of natural religion, saw Judaism as a perversion of the truth, and in the longest entry in his Dictionnaire philosophique (Philosophical Dictionary, 1764) Voltaire denounced the Jews of his day.

Some of the most influential Jewish figures were incorporated into the mainstream of political and intellectual life. These included the diplomatic and political activities of Menasseh ben Israel (1604–57) in the mid seventeenth century and the influence of the so-called 'court Jews' in the late seventeenth century, as well as to the philosophical writings of the Jewish heretic Spinoza, and Isaac de Pinto (1717–87) who replied to Voltaire's criticisms. Also important was the intellectual and cultural influence of Moses MENDELSSOHN. Mendelssohn can be seen as a forerunner of the early-nineteenth-century Jewish Enlightenment, with his attempt to combine Jewish learning with the newer intellectual developments of the period. He encouraged Christian Wilhelm Dohm to write Über die bürgerliche Verbesserung der Juden (On the Civil Betterment of the Jews, 1781). Mendelssohn was also a friend of the dramatist LESSING whose sympathetic portrayal of a Jew in Nathan der Weise was commonly taken to be based on Mendelssohn. The history of the Jews in this period has often been understood as their gradual acceptance into Western culture. More probably, it represented the gradual erosion of Jewish ideology and identity by a Western political and cultural hegemony.

Jonathan I. Israel, *European Jewry in the Age of Mercantalism, 1550–1750* (Oxford: Clarendon, 1985).

Leon Poliakov, *The History of Anti-Semitism*, vol. 3: *From Voltaire to Wagner*, trans. M. Kochan (London: Routledge & Kegan Paul, 1972); orginally published as *Histoire de l'Antisemitisme* (1968).

JEREMY GREGORY

John V (1689–1750)   King of Portugal (1706–50). PORTUGAL under John V (João V) was the eighteenth-century rationalist's stereotypical example of lack of rationalism. John spent vast sums of Brazilian gold to persuade Rome to create a patriarchate in Lisbon (1716), to build his great palace-monastery at Mafra, and to acquire the title 'most faithful' from the Pope in 1748. Ironically, his reign also saw an intense debate on fundamental questions of philosophy, education and political economy.

The most important writers during this period included Martinho de Mendonça de Pina e Proença, who attempted to introduce Locke to Portugal; Jacob de Castro Sarmento, who introduced Newtonian ideas to Portugal; and António Nunes Ribeiro Sanches, a collaborator with the French encyclopaedists, who wrote on medicine, pedagogy and economics. Most influential was the orator Luís António Verney (1713–92), whose *O Verdadeiro Método de Estudar* (The True Method of Studying) was published in 1746.

In addition to the philosophical debate, there was discussion on governance, economy and diplomacy among a small but influential group of John's overseas representatives and government ministers. They were sometimes called *estrangeirados* (foreigners) because of their supposed infatuation with foreign models, but their preoccupations were a product of a Portuguese milieu. D. Luís da Cunha, the most formidable of these thinkers, wrote a comprehensive analysis of Portugal's weaknesses and the means to remedy them.

C. R. Boxer. *The Portuguese Seaborne Empire 1415–1825* (London: Hutchinson, 1969).

Jay A. Levinson (ed.), *The Age of the Baroque in Portugal* (New Haven, Conn.: Yale University Press, 1993).

KENNETH MAXWELL

Johnson, Samuel (1709–1784)   English writer, critic, lexicographer and poet. His reputation has been shaped by BOSWELL's *Life of Johnson*, which depicts him – blunt, contrary and aphoristic – after he had become a famous man of literature (he was in his mid-fifties when Boswell first met him). This status came, however, quite late in a life of writing. Johnson had arrived in London in 1737, after failing to establish a school in his native Lichfield. For two decades he worked mostly as a high-class hack: composing parliamentary debates for Edward Cave's *Gentleman's Magazine*, entries for a medical dictionary, and prefaces for any text proposed by a publisher. In this period he produced the poems *London* (1738) and *The Vanity of Human Wishes* (1749), and the sententious, melancholy essays of *The Rambler* (1750–2). His fame began with his *Dictionary*, published in 1755 after eight years of labour, and probably his most influential work. There followed *Rasselas*, an Eastern tale, in 1759, his edition of Shakespeare's *Works* in 1765 and *The Lives of the English Poets* in 1779. He was the first important English writer to work primarily as a critic and editor.

W. J. Bate, *Samuel Johnson* (London: Chatto & Windus, 1978).

JOHN MULLAN

joint-stock companies A joint-stock company is a business enterprise whose capital is divided into transferable shares subscribed by a number of investors many of whom are uninvolved in either promotion or management. Most early modern business activity was small-scale and conducted by sole proprietorships or partnerships, but the joint-stock company had advantages in areas with substantial capital requirements or risks. Division into shares enabled companies to draw on large pools of capital and spread risks. Transferability of shares ensured the company an existence independent of a particular partnership, which provided flexibility. Many companies obtained a charter which regulated activity and often provided a monopoly, which was an incentive to venture capital but also attracted heavy criticism, for example from Adam Smith.

The first English joint-stock company, the Russia Company, emerged in 1553, and in 1688 there were fifteen companies involved in trade, COLONIZATION, utilities and new industries. In the early 1690s promoters found that they could float companies without a formal grant, and the number of companies rose dramatically, embracing a wide range of projects – many of them ephemeral. A speculative frenzy culminated in the South Sea crisis in 1720, which was blamed on stockjobbing and there were efforts to suppress it (*see* SOUTH SEA BUBBLE). The Bubble Act required companies to obtain a charter or Act of parliament, which was expensive and restricted joint-stock flotation in industry and commerce until it was reformed a century later. However, as most businesses had small capital requirements, this does not seem to have retarded economic development. Meanwhile, the great trading companies and a few new joint-stock companies for risky or expensive ventures like insurance and canals served as a reminder of the earlier creative speculation.

William Robert Scott, *The Constitution and Finance of English, Scottish and Irish Joint-Stock Companies to 1720* (Cambridge: Cambridge University Press, 1910–12).

NUALA ZAHEDIEH

José I (1714–1777) King of Portugal (1750–77). His reign was dominated by his prime minister, the marquês de POMBAL. Pombal's decisiveness during the traumatic days of the LISBON EARTHQUAKE in 1755 vastly increased his authority within the Portuguese state and made his influence over the monarch and the nation almost absolute. It is estimated that the earthquake destroyed about one-third of the city and killed at least 15,000 people out of a population of almost 250,000. Under Pombal's direction, a group of engineers and surveyors developed the economical 'Pombaline' architecture, the grid-iron pattern of streets and the great waterfront square that make Lisbon to this day a classic example of eighteenth-century town planning.

Pombal was a nationalist. He attributed his country's problems in large part to the state of semi-colonial dependency on Great Britain. He devised an approach which, while seeking to diminish British influence, avoided open confrontation over the terms of the treaties between the two countries. In essence, he employed a variety of administrative and legislative means, including tariffs, to shift capital formation away from foreigners to national merchant groups in Portugal and the colonies.

Kenneth Maxwell, *Pombal: An Enlightenment Paradox* (Cambridge: Cambridge University Press, 1994).

KENNETH MAXWELL

Joseph I (1678–1711) Holy Roman Emperor (1705–11). Having been elected king of the Romans in 1690, he succeeded to the throne automatically on the death of his father, Leopold I. During the last years of his father's long reign, in preparation for his assumption of power, he began to build his own party of younger men, which included Prince EUGENE of Savoy who favoured a more assertive policy. This 'Young Party' was installed in government when Joseph came to the throne. A vigorous ruler, he was determined to reassert imperial rights in Germany and Italy, which his father had neglected. This involved the imposition of the ban of the empire against the electors of Bavaria and Cologne, who had allied with France in the War of the Spanish Succession. This and other examples of his energetic imperial policy aroused growing suspicion among the German rulers. He also reasserted his rights over the German Catholic Church and this, together with his territorial ambitions in Italy, brought him into conflict with the papacy.

A lively and talented man with a love of ceremonial and an elevated concept of his office, he died suddenly from smallpox in 1711. He was known as the Austrian Sun-King.

C. W. Ingrao, *In Quest and Crisis: Joseph I and the Habsburg Monarchy* (West Lafayette, Ind.: Purdue University Press, 1979).

MICHAEL HUGHES

Joseph II (1741–1790)   Holy Roman Emperor (1765–90). He became Holy Roman Emperor and joint ruler of the Austrian lands with his mother, MARIA THERESA, in 1765, on the death of his father, Francis I. From his youth he had been stubborn, opinionated, violent, impatient, cold and intolerant, and his relationship with his mother had always been troubled; he was keen to carry through radical changes which she was reluctant to accept. In 1763 he produced a memorandum, his *Rêveries*, in which he set out his political views: given total power for ten years, he was confident that he could reform the administration root and branch, restore Austria's finances and build a powerful army. He was an ardent admirer of his greatest rival, Frederick II of Prussia, whom he met twice. His main objective was to build a formidable military power to defeat Prussia and win back Silesia. He was greedy for land and in the interests of Austria, exploited imperial rights in Germany, stirring up considerable opposition among the German rulers.

He also faced mounting opposition from his own subjects. While he was strongly influenced by enlightened ideas, he also believed in absolute monarchical power (*see* ENLIGHTENED ABSOLUTISM). After his mother's death he rushed through a series of major reforms in government, which he considered were essential for Austria to survive as a great power. He disregarded the views of those who disagreed with him, and created a secret police to deal with opponents of his policies. Although he had the welfare and happiness of his subjects at heart, he could also trample on their susceptibilities and infringe well-established rights. For example, he ignored Hungarian privileges, centralized power in Vienna and interfered with the church. On his death many parts of his empire were in or close to open revolt. He left a permanent legacy in the centralizing Josephine party in the Austrian bureaucracy in the nineteenth century.

D. Beales, *Joseph II*, vol. 1: *In the Shadow of Maria Theresa* (Cambridge: Cambridge University Press, 1987).

T. C. W. Blanning, *Joseph II and Enlightened Despotism* (London: Longman, 1970).

MICHAEL HUGHES

Josephine de Beauharnais *see* BONAPARTE, JOSEPHINE.

Justi, Johann H. G. von (1720–1771) a German exponent of CAMERALISM and theorist of enlightened government. In 1751, after a mixed career in various German states, which established his reputation, he accepted the chair of cameralism in Vienna. He was also a practical administrator, running mines and the silk industry in Austria until his fall from favour in 1754. Thereafter he served in Hanover and Denmark and in 1766 he obtained a long-promised post in Prussia as supervisor of mines and steelworks. By then he was already going blind. Following the discovery of irregularities in his accounts, he was thrown into prison in Prussia, where he died. Always a restless spirit, he travelled widely and published on a broad range of subjects. He was an early advocate of economic individualism, freeing the economy from restrictions, and is credited with the first systematic exposition of cameralism, the science of administration and state management of the economy, in his *Grundfeste zu der Macht und Glückseligkeit der Staaten* (The Foundations of the Power and Happiness of States, 1760–1). He believed that the main objective of government should be the welfare of the people.

K. Tribe, 'Cameralism and the Science of Government', *Journal of Modern History*, 56 (1984), 263–84.

MICHAEL HUGHES

justice, administration of Most eighteenth-century regimes paid lip-service to the ideal of justice. In practice, however, standards of the administration of justice, especially on a local level, varied enormously. The most centralized system of justice in a major state was that of the Chinese, where the administration of justice depended heavily on the local magistrate. Chinese magistrates (apart from a few petty officials promoted for exceptional service) were commoners who had bought titles or men who had passed a civil service examination. They had powers to try civil and minor criminal cases, more serious cases being reported to superior officials. Cases involving the death penalty had to be retried before the provincial governor-general and governor, while regular reports of punishments inflicted had to be returned to the board of punishments in Peking. In theory, Chinese magistrates were subject to strict supervision, and could suffer severe penalties (even demotion) if they failed to capture murderers and robbers within a given period; penalties for a wrong legal decision by a magistrate or his clerk were also severe.

English practice demonstrated how a relatively decentralized system of administering justice could work, at least with criminal and administrative justice. It relied heavily on the justice of the peace, who was usually (especially in rural areas) a gentleman of some standing for whom holding office was a mark of prestige. Justices might attend quarter sessions, the body that governed their county, but much of their work took place locally, at petty sessions or even, given the dependence on summary jurisdiction, in a justice's parlour. As in China, however, trial of serious offenders was reserved for centrally appointed officials, the assize judges. These were sent out in pairs from Westminster twice a year, each riding a circuit or group of counties, to try prisoners and determine civil suits in the localities. The eighteenth-century English criminal trial was essentially a short and ramshackle affair, but it is noteworthy that the most consistent feature of the assize judges' activities was the amelioration of a harsh penal code in favour of offenders. Mercy was regarded as being as useful a way of maintaining the law as terror, while the ability to obtain pardons for offenders extended a gentleman's patronage.

A number of complications hindered the administration of justice. The first (perhaps most prevalent in Europe) was a multiplicity of courts, for example the French town of Angers, with about 34,000 inhabitants late in the century, had fifty-three law courts. The existence of such a hierarchy of tribunals both impeded speedy justice and encouraged litigation. Secondly, notions of equality before the law were limited. Over much of Europe, noblemen had privileges before the law (indeed, in rural Poland they administered it locally), in addition to the *de facto* advantages of wealth. Other legal systems were explicitly attached to inequality. In Japan civil and criminal legislation mirrored the inequalities of the social system: different marriage and inheritance laws obtained for commoners and samurai, and it was accepted that criminal offences were punished according to social status. This led to samurai being lightly punished for offences for which commoners suffered severe penalties, and, conversely, to samurai being sentenced to banishment or suicide for dishonourable acts that were regarded as petty among commoners. The Chinese penal system exhibited a similar regard for social hierarchy. A third difficulty was ensuring that officials were efficient and not corrupt. It is impossible to discover if one culture's system of judicial administration was more successful than another's in this respect. There were at one time or another rulers in Japan, China and many European states who attempted to purge the judicial system of corruption and to appoint able officials. Modern ideals of public service were, however, absent, and even relatively professionalized systems, like that of the Chinese, suffered continual problems.

Systems of administering justice, dependent as they often were on amateur officials, underpaid petty agents and public goodwill, were ramshackle by modern standards. The social inequalities that were built into these systems seem alien to modern eyes, while the delays and inefficiencies of legal process in the period were a constant source of contemporary complaint. Yet many of these systems worked well, not least because diligent officials from Szechwan to Yorkshire laboured to ensure that they did.

See also CRIME, PUNISHMENT, TORTURE.

Tung Tsu Ch'u, *Local Government in China under the Ch'ing* (Stanford, Calif.: Stanford University Press, 1969).
Douglas Hay, 'Property, Authority and the Criminal Law', in Douglas Hay et al. (eds), *Albion's Fatal Tree* (London: Allen Lane, 1975), pp. 17–63.

J. A. SHARPE

K

Kant, Immanuel (1724–1804)   Pre-eminent German philosopher of the later eighteenth century. He was professor of logic and metaphysics at the university in Königsberg, where he lived all his life. His best early work was in natural philosophy, the *Allgemeine Naturgeschichte und Theorie des Himmels* (General Natural History and Theory of the Heavens, 1755), which added to Newtonianism a theory of the origins of the stars. His major ('critical') phase began only in 1769, when the reading of Hume awoke him from 'dogmatic slumber', and he prepared his *magna opera*, the *Kritik der reinen Vernunft* (Critique of Pure Reason, 1781), the *Kritik der praktischen Vernunft* (Critique of Practical Reason, 1788), the *Kritik der Urteilskraft* (Critique of Judgement, 1790) and other major texts. To clarify the first *Critique*, he wrote the brilliantly lucid *Prolegomena zu einer jeden Künftigen Metaphysik* (Prolegomena to Any Future Metaphysics, 1783), and this ensured his success.

In these works Kant went beyond the philosophies of Leibniz and Newton; in an attempt to find a ground for knowledge, his 'transcendental idealism' established a grand synthesis of EMPIRICISM and RATIONALISM. The first *Critique* summarized his questions thus: 'What can I know?' 'What should I do?' 'What can I hope?' The answers were less simple.

He reformulated the first question technically: 'How are synthetic judgements *a priori* possible?' These judgements, which were 'synthetic' because the subject did not contain the predicate and '*a priori*' because they preceded experience, were exemplified in mathematics. The 'Copernican revolution' of Kant's answer lay in reversing the accepted relation between thought and its objects: the objects of the senses did not determine perception (*Anschauung*), but perception determined the objects. Kant examined the meaning of this reversal by analyses that defined the sphere and limits of reason. Knowledge was produced by the understanding from both perception and thought; space and time were forms of human consciousness, essential to our sensory perception; while the understanding employed 'categories' (such as quantity, quality, causation) to make sense of the world. Thus we know appearances ('phenomena'), but cannot penetrate 'things in themselves' ('noumena'). If empiricism hereby reached a boundary, so did reason, which, trapped by 'antinomies', could not decide the major issues of freedom, immortality, God and cosmology. However, if an absolute could not be known, it could be thought, and as such functioned as a 'regulative idea'.

In the *Grundlegung zur Metaphysik der Sitten* (Fundamental Principles of the Metaphysic of Ethics, 1783) and the second *Critique* Kant turned to his next question, which he also approached through the subject. Action and morality should be dictated not by happiness, but by the 'moral law' of the 'categorical imperative': 'Act as if you wished the maxim by which you act to become a universal law.'

Kant's third question related to a philosophy of religion. Moral action led 'necessarily to religion', to the ideas of immortality and God. These were insights and postulates, not imperatives and truths, but reason necessarily posited them as practical guides to the highest good.

The trajectory of Kant's philosophy extended from aesthetics in the third *Critique* to politics, encompassing such practical utopian treatises as his republican *Zum Ewigen Frieden* (On Perpetual Peace, 1795). His thought effectively crowned the philosophy of the Enlightenment in Germany; it influenced contemporaries like Goethe and Schiller and unwittingly paved the way for the idealism of Fichte, Schelling and Hegel.

E. Cassirer, *Kant's Life and Thought* (New Haven, Conn.: Yale University Press, 1981).
R. Scruton: *Kant* (Oxford: Oxford University Press, 1982).

JEREMY ADLER

Karlowitz, Treaty of *see* CARLOWITZ, TREATY OF.

Kaunitz-Rietberg, Wenzel Anton, prince von (1711–1794) Austrian statesman. A member of a Moravian noble family, he was the dominant figure in the diplomacy of Austria in the second half of the eighteenth century. He rose quickly in the Austrian state service through a series of diplomatic and administrative posts. He played a major role in bringing about the so-called DIPLOMATIC REVOLUTION, by which the age-old enemies France and Austria became allies. This alliance remained the basis of Austrian foreign policy until the French Revolution. He was convinced that Austria did not benefit from its traditional alliance with the Dutch and Britain, as its main enemy was no longer France but Prussia. As ambassador in Paris from 1750 and chancellor in charge of foreign policy from 1753, he worked to achieve the French alliance but was successful only after Frederick II had precipitated the Seven Years War. Strongly influenced by enlightened ideas, he had an important position in domestic as well as foreign policy under Maria Theresa. Under Joseph II his influence declined. An able but eccentric man, he owed his power to the consistency of his ideas, which were original.

K. A. Roider Jr, *Austria's Eastern Question 1700–1790* (Princeton, NJ: Princeton University Press, 1982).

MICHAEL HUGHES

Kay, John (1704–1779) English inventor of the flying shuttle. Born into a yeoman family near Bury, Lancashire and apprenticed to a reed-maker (maker of weavers' tools), he patented the flying shuttle in 1733. It was intended to reduce the labour of broad-loom weaving from two men to one, by enabling the weaver to flick the shuttle across the loom on rollers. It proved best suited, however, to the narrow looms and stronger yarns of the Lancashire cotton industry, where it spread quickly in the 1750s and raised productivity, probably by 50 per cent. Kay found partners in the Essex woollen industry, but the patent was widely evaded and he was ruined by the cost of un-resolved litigation. Following an unsuccessful appeal to parliament for support, he went to France in 1747 and negotiated a government pension to instruct French weavers in the shuttle's use. He was similarly rewarded for card-making machinery invented in 1754 to improve the carding of woollen yarn. Other textile inventions followed but, lacking any talent for business, he remained poor and financially dependent on the French government. (*See* TEXTILES.)

A. P. Wadsworth and Julia de Lacy Mann, *The Cotton Trade and Industrial Lancashire, 1600–1780* (Manchester: Manchester University Press, 1931).

CHRISTINE MACLEOD

Kent, William (1685–1748) English architect, designer and decora-tor. The patronage of fellow Yorkshiremen enabled Kent, who was of modest origins, to spend nine or ten years studying painting in Rome. There he met Richard Boyle, third earl of Burlington (1694–1753), who brought him back to England in 1719 to complete the painted decorations of Burlington House in London, which had recently been remodelled according to the tenets of PALLADIANISM. Thus began a happy association of thirty years, which had enormous significance for English – and Western – architecture, landscape gardening and interior design. Holkham Hall, Norfolk (begun 1734) is an early, and great, Palladian country house; its broad masses are recapitulated in London's Horse Guards, which were begun to Kent's designs c.1751. His gardens at Stowe, Buckinghamshire (1736) and Rousham, Oxfordshire (1738–41) articulated a new, picturesque and sentimental relationship between architecture and landscape. It was Kent who abstracted the GOTHIC REVIVAL from its idiosyncratic outcrops in the work of Vanbrugh and others into a pretty vocabulary – mostly used in a classical syntax – which was current in Britain for over a century. Barely literate, he was a superb designer whose intellectual range remains uncharted.

Michael I. Wilson, *William Kent: Architect, Designer, Painter, Gardener, 1685–1748* (London: Routledge & Kegan Paul, 1984).

CHRISTINE STEVENSON

Kleist, Heinrich von (1777–1811) German writer of the second romantic generation. He abandoned military service for his studies in 1799, and in March 1801 his so-called 'Kant crisis' shattered his world-view: 'We can never be certain that what we call truth is truly true, or whether it only appears to be.' Doubt drove him to devote himself to literature. His eight plays and as many *Novellen* explore 'the enigma of the heart' and 'the fragile constitution of the world'. In them reality proves violent, gruesome and perverse, the human senses too weak to apprehend it, language too ambiguous to convey it and God too fickle to uphold it. His classically constructed tragedies burst with violent energy: in *Amphityron* (1807) Jupiter deceives Alkmene's 'innermost feelings', the guarantor of identity; in *Penthesilea* (1807) the eponymous heroine devours her lover. The *Novellen* are similarly dramatic, notably *Das Erdbeben in Chili* (The Earthquake in Chili (1807). However, some characters win through, as do the MARQUISE *von O . . .* (1808) and his last dramatic hero, *Prinz Friedrich von Homburg* (1810), who accomplishes 'the journey round the world'. Rejected by Goethe, whom he revered, and broken by social, political and financial failure, Kleist committed suicide. It was not until the twentieth century that his achievement was universally recognized.

Ilse Graham, *Heinrich von Kleist* (Berlin: De Gruyter, 1977).

JEREMY ADLER

Klopstock, Friedrich Gottlieb (1724–1803) German poet. He introduced the fashion for subjectivity into eighteenth-century German poetry. Born in Quedlinburg, Saxony, he received a Pietist education at Schulpforta, where he was inspired to begin a religious epic to rival Milton's *Paradise Lost*; when the first cantos of his epic *Messias* (Messiah) appeared in 1748, his powerful German hexameters, sublime style and evocative imagery caused a sensation; however, his vision lacked concreteness and the epic, which was concluded in 1773, did not live up to its promise. In his *Oden* (Odes), begun in 1747 and first collected in 1771, he pioneered the use of free verse. In one of his most influential poems, 'Die Frühlingsfeier' (The Spring Celebration, 1759), he energetically affirms the presence of God in nature. Elsewhere, he meditates sentimentally on death, as in 'Die frühen Gräber' (The Early Graves, 1764). Love, history and politics are also important themes in his work. Altogether, Klopstock gave new dignity to the vocation of poetry, and exerted an important influence on the *Sturm und Drang*, on the young Goethe and on Hölderlin.

K. M. Kohl, *Rhetoric, the Bible, and the Origins of Free Verse* (Berlin: De Gruyter, 1990).

JEREMY ADLER

Kościuszko, Tadeusz (1746–1817) Polish soldier and patriot. Of middling Polish noble stock, he was one of the first beneficiaries of King Stanislaw Augustus Poniatowski's military academy, which opened in 1765. After study in France, he went to America in 1776 to fight for the cause of independence. His military engineering skills earned him the rank of brigadier-general before his return to Poland in 1784. He distinguished himself in the Russo-Polish war of May–July 1792. After the second partition of Poland, he was made commander-in-chief of the insurrection which broke out in March 1794. His defeat of a Russian force at Raclawice (near Krakow) on 4 April allowed the rising to survive. Kosciuszko was caught between the desirability of emancipating the largely enserfed peasantry and the need to placate the conservative Polish nobility. Between 6 July and 6 September he repulsed the Prussian siege of Warsaw, only to be captured at the Battle of Maciejowice (10 October) by the Russians. He was released by Tsar Paul I in November 1796, to spend much of the remainder of his life in America, France and Switzerland (where he died). He rejected all offers of service under Napoleon and Tsar Alexander I.

J. T. Lukowski, *Liberty's Folly: The Polish-Lithuanian Commonwealth in the Eighteenth Century* (London: Routledge, 1991).

J. T. LUKOWSKI

Kristian V *see* CHRISTIAN V.

Kristian VII *see* CHRISTIAN VII.

L

Lacondamine, Charles Marie de (1701–1774) French mathematician and scientist. Born in Paris, he served in the cavalry before entering the Académie des Sciences. After a general scientific training he embarked on a naval squadron for the Levant in 1731, gathering information on meterology, natural history and antiquities. In 1735 he set out with a party of scientists for equatorial Peru on a geodesic mission to measure the arc of 1 degree from the meridian. In spite of disputes between him and the mathematician Bouguer (1698–1758) about their respective contributions, the achievements of the expedition were considerable, particularly in investigation of the earth's magnetic field. Lacondamine returned to France in 1743 to general acclaim.

He later travelled to Italy and England, following interests as diverse as the measurement of the Roman foot to smallpox inoculation. His irrepressible enthusiasm for experiment was not matched by solid achievements, however, and his chief contribution was as a publicist for science and the Enlightenment. His fascination for new knowledge precipitated his own death when he encouraged a young surgeon to experiment on him for the removal of a hernia. The operation killed him.

I. Todhunter, *The Figure of the Earth* (New York: Dover, 1962).

DAVID MACKAY

Lafayette, Marie Joseph Paul Yves Roch Gilberr Motier, marquis de (1757–1834) French reformer. He was born into a wealthy old noble family. In 1774 he entered a dragoon regiment and was a courtier at Versailles. In 1777 he went to America, where he served under Washington in the War of Independence, returning to lobby for the American cause at Versailles in 1780. He commanded the French forces at YORKTOWN in 1781. Between 1782 and 1787 he campaigned for many liberal causes, chiefly Protestant emancipation and the abolition of slavery. He was a member of the Assembly of Notables in 1787 and was elected to the Estates General, for the Second Estate, in 1789. He was among the liberal nobles who joined the new Constituent Assembly and was elected its vice-president and commander of the Paris NATIONAL GUARD in July 1789. It was in the latter capacity that he was unable to prevent the March of the Women which brought the king to Paris by force, in October. In 1789–91 he was a leader of the moderate Feuillants, a club of deputies who were committed to retaining both the monarch and the narrow electoral franchise of the CONSTITUTION OF 1791. But his reputation suffered in this period, first by his suppression of the mutiny at Nancy in August 1790, then by the king's attempted flight in June 1791 and, finally, when he ordered the Massacre of the Champs de Mars on 17 July 1791. After resigning from the National Guard, he was defeated in the Paris municipal elections. He was given a command when war broke out in March 1792 but played no part in the Napoleonic regime. He was a leading liberal during the restoration. In the revolution of 1830 he again commanded the Paris National Guard and helped secure Louis Philippe (1773–1850) in power.

L. R. Gottschalk, *Lafayette*, 5 vols (Chicago: University of Chicago Press, 1937–73).

P. Gueffiney, 'Lafayette', in F. Furet and M. Ozouf (eds), *A Critical Dictionary of the French Revolution* (Cambridge, Mass.: Harvard University Press, 1989), pp. 224–33.

MICHAEL BROERS

Lagrange, Joseph Louis (1736–1813)   French mathematician. Born in Turin of a French family, he early proved himself an exceptional mathematician, submitting work that won the approval of Leonard EULER. Before his twentieth birthday he was appointed professor of mathematics at the Artillery School in Turin, and in 1759 he was elected a foreign member of the Berlin Academy. The progress of his career was soon interrupted, however, by severe breakdowns in his health. On the initiative of Euler, he was invited to Berlin in 1766 by Frederick the Great. On the king's death, he removed to Paris in 1787. In 1795 he was made a member of the Académie des Sciences, and two years later elevated to a chair at the new École Normale.

After Euler, the leading practitioner of mechanical mathematics of his century, Lagrange's masterpiece was the *Mécanique analytique* (1788). In the first part of that work statical questions were addressed, discussion of virtual velocities being followed by dazzling applications to rigid and fluid mechanics. The second part was devoted to dynamics. Lagrange gloried in the fact that his tome was entirely algebraic, containing no diagrams and no geometrical and mechanical reasoning. Lagrange also made substantial contributions to physical astronomy, and worked on the theory of equations, though his attempts to establish the calculus without using infinitesimals or Newton's limits proved a failure. Partly in reaction, late in life he moved away from mathematics and developed an interest in metaphysics, chemistry, botany and the history of language.

ROY PORTER

laissez-faire, philosophy of   The philosophy of laissez-faire, which was shared by the physiocrats, all the advocates of economic liberalism and the Scottish political economists, embraces all the critics of mercantilism and of the interventionist policies associated with the ministry of Jean-Baptiste Colbert (1619–83). The formula *laissez faire, laissez passer* was coined by Jean-Claude Vincent de Gournay (1712–59). His opposition to the intervention of the state in the economy (typical of the financial policies of absolutist monarchies in seventeenth- and eighteenth-century Europe) is not, however, to be confused with that of the physiocrats, for whom *laissez-faire* was only one element of a much larger and complex political and economic doctrine.

Gournay became *intendant de commerce* in 1747 and began his campaign for FREE TRADE and perfect competition. In 1755 he attacked the support that the French government granted to the Compagnie des Indes, arguing that France's trade with the East would flourish if trading monopolies were suppressed and all state subventions withheld. His disciples included Turgot and the abbé de Morellet, whose *Mémoire sur la situation actuelle de la Compagnie des Indes* argued that the company's difficulties were inherent rather than temporary; both men were also sympathetic to physiocracy. Gournay's views became especially influential during the 1760s, not least because one of his followers, Manyon d'Invau became controller-general in September 1768.

The most eminent and clear-minded eighteenth-century advocate of the benefits of free trade, and hence of economic *laissez-faire*, was Adam SMITH, but his political philosophy was not simply that of *laissez-faire*. Perfect freedom of trade and the removal of duties on imported commodities, he argued in *The Wealth of Nations*, was the means for predominantly agricultural nations to raise the value of their 'surplus produce, for encouraging its increase, and consequently the improvement and cultivation of their own land', and 'the most advantageous method in which a landed nation can raise up artificers, manufacturers and merchants of its own, is to grant the most perfect freedom of trade to the artificers, manufacturers and merchants of all other nations'. He also considered monopolies to be the enemies to good management: they distorted the natural distribution of the stock of society and were supported by unjust and cruel laws. But Smith believed that the legislator had a duty to attend to any unjust outcome of market distribution, to remedy the consequences of the intensification of the division of labour, not least by making provisions for education, and to adapt to changing circumstances.

Donald Winch, 'Adam Smith's "Enduring Particular Result": A Political and Cosmopolitan Perspective', in Istvan Hont and Michael Ignatieff (eds), *Wealth and Virtue: The Shaping of Political Economy in the Scottish Enlightenment* (Cambridge: Cambridge University Press, 1983), pp. 253–69.

SYLVANA TOMASELLI

Lamarck, Jean-Baptiste Pierre Antoine de Monet, chevalier de (1744– 1829) French botanist and zoologist. In *Flore française* (1778) he challenged the notion of a single CHAIN OF BEING, and posited two separate series for plants and animals, organizing plants in accordance with their reproductive systems. Supported by the comte de Buffon, he became a member of the Académie Française in 1779 and keeper of the Jardins du Roi. On the foundation of the Museum d'Histoire Naturelle in 1793, he was appointed to the chair of zoology. In *Philosophie zoologique* (1809) he outlined his theory of transformation, that life had developed from simpler to more complex forms and that new species evolved because of the need to adapt to new environmental conditions, for these encouraged new habits that gave rise to structural changes, which were passed on to their offspring (the theory of the inheritance of acquired characters). Lamarck's other works included *Histoire naturelle des animaux sans vertèbres* (1815– 22), *Système analytique des connaissances positives de l'homme* (1820) and *Hydrogéologie* (1802), which defined biology as the study of life and hence as concerned with more than CLASSIFICATION. He was also interested in meteorology.

Ludmilla Jordanova, *Lamarck* (Oxford: Oxford University Press, 1984).

SYLVANA TOMASELLI

La Mettrie, Julien Offray de (1709–1751) French physician and philosopher, best known for his conception of man as a machine. He studied medicine in Paris, but in 1733 moved to Leiden where he completed his training under BOERHAAVE. The latter's iatromechanism, a mechanical model of life, had a profound influence on him. In 1742 he became surgeon to the Guardes Françaises, whom he followed into battle. He wrote several medical treatises, including *Observations de* *médecine pratique* (1743). He favoured strong remedies and copious bleeding. His *Histoire naturelle de l'âme* (1745), later renamed *Traité de l'âme*, argued that the brain was the seat of mental activity. This work, together with his satire against doctors, turned the medical profession as well as the religious authorities against him. He took refuge in Leiden, but the scandal caused by *L'Homme machine* (1746) made it impossible for him to remain there, and he fled to the court of Frederick the Great. The book developed the thesis that matter thinks, but moved from a purely mechanistic to a more organic conception of man. *L'Homme plante* (1749) pursued a similar argument and emphasized the uniformity of nature. He died of an overdose of pheasant pâté, which was interpreted by his enemies as a just desert for his life of hedonism.

John W. Yolton, *Locke and French Materialism* (Oxford: Clarendon, 1991).

SYLVANA TOMASELLI

landownership Land was the most important source of wealth in the eighteenth century, giving its owners a significant role in politics, government and society. The incomes of the largest landowners were rivalled only by those of a small number of leading merchants and contractors, while below the ranks of the great landowners stood the numerous lesser owners, down to the modest country gentleman and the landowning peasantry. There was much regional diversity: larger owners tending to have their estates in more remote districts or areas of poorer soil, while lesser owners were concentrated on better land which could yield a sufficient income from a relatively small area. In many regions large estates were owned by the crown, the church, colleges and other bodies.

Land yielded an income for its owners which was derived primarily from farm rents or the profits of farming, but large revenues were sometimes also obtained from timber and minerals, and from feudal survivals such as tenants' customary payments and rights over mills and wine presses. In western Europe the majority of larger owners had given up direct farming of their lands in favour of a parcelling out in farms held by tenants, occupiers who paid a rent and provided all or part of the working capital themselves. In central and eastern Europe, by contrast, large areas were dominated by estates worked by serfs, and here the owners were directly involved in agricultural production and sales of surpluses to near and distant markets.

Land conferred social status, and generally the larger his estate the greater the landlord's title and influence. In most European countries land supported a numerous ARISTOCRACY whose political power rivalled or exceeded that of the monarch. Many functions of central and local government were carried out by landowners, whose services were rewarded by control of patronage and an extended influence over the population at large.

Such was the economic, social and political power of land that owners of all kinds sought to extend their property, even when the return in money terms did not justify the cost of purchase. Precautions were taken to ensure that land remained in the family, and carefully arranged marriages between landed families became a means of adding to a family's wealth and of cementing political alliances. The larger estates sustained mansions which were frequently newly built, rebuilt or added to in the course of the century, while landscaped parks and gardens enhanced their grandeur, and woodlands provided amenities for hunting and shooting. Even the small but locally important squires achieved a degree of exclusiveness by building houses surrounded by walled grounds which shut out the neighbouring community.

The value of landed estates, which represented the largest accumulations of capital of the time, necessitated careful management to maintain and improve their resources and the income derived from them. Estate management developed as a new profession as the larger properties were seen to merit full-time specialist attention. Particular care was given to the safeguarding of soil fertility and the value of woodlands, the increased exploitation of minerals and the development of transport facilities for the marketing of agricultural and other produce. In Britain a logical extension of this was a growth of landowners' interest in agricultural improvement and transport developments. While many owners were too heavily involved in government, politics or sport to concern themselves with the minutiae of agriculture, there were some who became leading figures in experimental farming. The fifth duke of Bedford and Thomas Coke of Holkham (1752–1842) are well-known examples, while the duke of Bridgwater (1736–1803) built his famous canal to market the coal of his estate. Although the Continental aristocracy showed less interest in these matters, some of them were sufficiently enthusiastic to visit the great English pioneers and to correspond with leading figures such as Arthur YOUNG. In general, however, landed estates were seen only as a means of supporting an elevated life-style and of sustaining their owners' position in society.

In the Americas, Africa and parts of Asia land was allocated to families by the tribe, although in some cases the nomadic character of their life and the migration of tribes over long distances worked against close attachment to particular areas of land. Attempts by Europeans in North America to introduce the institution of the large estate broke down in favour of family farming and small owner-occupiers, while in Central and South America very large areas were appropriated as private estates by owners of European origin.

See also SEIGNEURIALISM.

J. V. Beckett, *The Aristocracy in England 1660–1914* (Oxford: Blackwell, 1986).

A. Goodwin (ed.), *European Nobility in the Eighteenth Century* (London: A. & C. Black, 1953).

Sir John Habakkuk, 'The Rise and Fall of English Landed Families, 1600–1800', *Transactions of the Royal Historical Society*, fifth series, 29 (1979), 187–207; 30 (1980), 199–221; 31 (1981), 195–217.

G. E. MINGAY

landscape The word 'landscape' refers to both an actual view of natural scenery and to an artistic representation of a view. Landscape emerged as an important subject for art in the seventeenth century with the 'poetry of place' of Ben Jonson (1572–1637) and Andrew Marvell (1621–78), the paintings of Claude Lorraine (1600–82), Nicolas Poussin (1594–1665), Salvator Rosa (1615–73) and Jacob van Ruïsdael (*c.*1628–82), and the gardens of LE NÔTRE. However, it was not until the eighteenth century that landscape poetry, painting and gardening developed, particularly in England, into major modes of artistic, political and cultural expression. Early in the century the celebration of rural life by the classical Latin authors Virgil and Horace appealed to the influential circle attached to Richard Boyle, third earl of Burlington (1695–1753) which included the poets Alexander Pope and James Thomson (1700–48) and the artists and garden designers Charles Bridgeman (*d* 1738) and William KENT. To their eyes nature and landscape represented a 'natural', contemplative life of virtuous simplicity. At the same time as nature was being discovered by poets, painters and garden designers, the natural landscape was undergoing an economic transformation. The process of enclosing commons, open fields and wastes and improving them through hedging and draining accelerated in the second half of the century, raising the price of land by increasing its agricultural yield. As a result of this, land acquired new social and political value. In France, in the middle of the century, many of the moral themes of Augustanism and the arguments for land improvement came together in the writings of the PHYSIOCRATS, whose founder, Quesnay, claimed that land was the source of all wealth and value. Quesnay's ideas influenced Adam Smith's economic ideas and Thomas Jefferson's agrarian republicanism.

The eighteenth-century discovery of landscape was echoed in the many artistic works of the period. James Thomson's *The Seasons* (1730) evoked a variety of natural scenes by drawing on images of landscape found in seventeenth-century Italianate landscape paintings as well as on contemporary landscape gardens such as Stowe. His exploration of the connections between NATURE and human IMAGINATION was a major preoccupation of other eighteenth-century writers, for example Addison, Burke, Rousseau and the young Wordsworth.

While landscape painting had long been held to be an inferior branch of art, eighteenth-century artists like Richard Wilson (1714–82), Gainsborough and Pierre Henri de Valenciennes (1750–1819) devoted themselves to it, producing landscapes remarkable for their naturalism. Their work anticipated the romantic landscape paintings of J. M. W. Turner (1775–1851), John Constable (1776–1837) and Caspar David Friedrich (1774–1840). Finally, important aesthetic theories arose in the second half of the century which had significant bearing on the practice of landscape painting and gardening and on landscape touring. Burke's *A Philosophical Enquiry into the Origin of our Ideas of the Sublime and the Beautiful*, the many tour books of William Gilpin (1700–1802) and Uvedale Price's (1747–1829) *Essay on the Picturesque* (1794) categorized both artistic and natural landscape as either beautiful, SUBLIME or PICTURESQUE. These terms were used in turn by artists and critics to describe various landscape styles and by tourists exploring natural scenery such as that of the Lake District, the Alps and the Italian Campagna.

John Barrell, *The Dark Side of the Landscape: The Rural Poor in English Painting* (Cambridge: Cambridge University Press, 1980).

Ann Bermingham, *Landscape and Ideology: The English Rustic Tradition 1740–1860* (London: Thames & Hudson, 1987).

Kenneth Clark, *Landscape into Art* (London: John Murray, 1949).

John Dixon Hunt, *The Figure in the Landscape: Poetry, Painting, and Gardening during the Eighteenth Century* (Baltimore: Johns Hopkins University Press, 1976).

Raymond Williams, *The Country and the City* (London: Chatto & Windus, 1973).

ANN BERMINGHAM

language Eighteenth-century attitudes to language are best seen as a series of shifting perspectives that began in the mid seventeenth century. The focus moved from the seventeenth-century concern with individual words, through revivals in the study of syntax and grammar, to an interest in language as a 'natural' consequence of the human drive towards sociability. This shift was due to the succession of intellectual fashions, from rational and materialist philosophy, through the impact of the Lockean philosophy of mind, to the later-eighteenth-century concern with human communication, sensibility and sentimentality. Strains of earlier interests continued to be registered in later writings on language, but in general emphasis on the word was replaced by emphasis on the sentence, and then by the relationship between human sentiments or passions and the different language forms that articulated them in the various languages and cultures.

Mid-seventeenth-century writers on language were concerned to find the language of universal communication, which was identified with the language that humankind was assumed to have spoken first in paradise (the original language) or with the true interrelationship of things in the physical universe (the natural language). It was thought that knowledge of these languages would bring men closer to the ultimate truth and perfection of God's language. In his *Essay towards a Real Character and a Philosophical Language* (1668) John Wilkins (1614–72) created a system of universal notation, with the intention of establishing a conventional language that was commensurate with the true nature of objects in the natural world. Wilkins and other language innovators were particularly interested in pictorial language forms like ideographs and hieroglyphs. For them grammar was necessary, but the controlling principle was the meaningfulness of basic language units.

The interest in cognition was common to thinkers like Hobbes, the Port-Royal group, and LOCKE produced an account of language as an extension of mental activity. The structure of language, and in particular its syntactic features, was seen as an embodiment of human reason and judgement. Writing became as important as speech, and correct spelling – as a way of determining the syntactic function of a word – was a significant concern.

The third movement, which can be traced back to the early eighteenth century, stressed the social function of language. Reading and writing were separable from ratiocination, and were more properly rooted in functions connected with social status and communication. According to the theoretical writings of James Harris (1709–80), the elements of different languages conformed to the general laws of nature, enabling the human soul to be viewed 'in the light of a Crucible, where Truths are produced by a kind of logical Chemistry'. The Italian thinker VICO saw ideas and language developing at an equal pace in any one society. Robert Lowth (1710–87) pursued more practical aims, seeking to establish a grammar that would match the stylistic refinement he saw in contemporary English. Language being seen as an instrument of social cohesion, its powers could be prescriptively refined by a proper investigation of language usage. The history of languages was no longer governed by a consideration of their origins but by the need to produce an account of language change through time. In this connection, later-eighteenth-century writers of language, like PRIESTLEY, regarded attempts to enforce language change as inappropriate: time would permit the best forms and usages to emerge from the morass of differing customs.

Hans Aarsleff, *From Locke to Saussure* (London: Athlone, 1982).
Murray Cohen, *Sensible Words: Linguistic Practice in England 1640–1785* (Baltimore: Johns Hopkins University Press, 1977).

J. Knowlson, *Universal Language Schemes in England and France 1600–1800* (Toronto: University of Toronto Press, 1975).
S. K. Land, *From Signs to Propositions: The Concept of Form in Eighteenth-Century Semantic Theory* (London: Longman, 1974).

N. SMITH

La Pérouse, Jean François de Galaup, comte de (1741–1788)   French navigator. Born in Guo, near Albi in southern France, he entered the navy at the age of 15 and served with distinction in both the Seven Years War and the American War of Independence. Because of his interest in navigation and oceanography, he was given command of a French scientific expedition to the Pacific to emulate the achievements of COOK. Sailing from Brest in August 1785, the *Boussole* and *Astrolabe* made the American coast in southern Alaska. After coasting south as far as Monterey, the expedition crossed the Pacific to Macao, discovering in transit Necker Island in the Hawaiian group. During the summer of 1787 he explored the Korean coast, Sakhalin and Hokkaido before refreshing at Kamchatka. The final stage of the voyage took him south to Samoa and Tonga, and then to Botany Bay, where he arrived six days after Governor Phillip's (1738–1814) convict fleet. Departing New South Wales in March 1788, the ships then disappeared. Two vessels under Bruny d'Entrecasteaux (1737–1793) were sent in search of the expedition but it was not until 1828 that Dumont d'Urville (1790–1842) established that La Pérouse had perished on the island of Vanikoro.

Catherine Gaziello, *L'Expédition de Lapérouse 1785–1788* (Paris: Comité des Travaux Historiques et Scientifiques, 1984).

DAVID MACKAY

Laplace, Pierre Simon, marquis de (1749–1827)   French mathematician and astronomer. His aim was to unify celestial and terrestrial physics within a determinist and mechanical cosmology. He established his scientific pedigree in papers published between 1785 and 1788 in which he proved the stability of the solar system by demonstrating that 'secular variations' in planetary motion were long-term periodic inequalities that could be accounted for by gravitation. His secular theory of the origins of the universe was christened the 'nebular hypothesis'. His comprehensive mechanical system of the world, the *Traité de méchanique céleste* (5 vols, 1799–1825) contained the fruits of his research into molecular mechanics. By 1796 Laplace was already convinced that optical refraction, capillary action, the cohesion of solids and chemical reactions were the result of attractive forces between particles of matter. His concept of molecular forces, like Newton's before him, relied on chemistry, in his case Berthollet's (1748–1822) conception of chemical affinity. Although Laplace's treatment of molecular phenomena was mathematical, he never found a law relating molecular force to distance as Newton had for gravity. Despite support from eminent graduates of the École Polytechnique, the Laplacian programme was superseded by newer physical approaches after 1810.

R. Fox, 'The Rise and Fall of Laplacian Physics', *Historical Studies in the Physical Sciences*, 4 (1974), 89–136.

M. L. BENJAMIN

La Rochefoucauld-Liancourt, François Alexandre, duc de (1747–1827)   French courtier. On 12 July 1789 he entered the chamber of Louis XVI to report on events in Paris. 'It's a revolt, then?' the king said. 'No, Sire, it is a revolution.' The duke was worth more than the anecdote, however. A liberal aristocrat, Anglophilic and patriotic in his outlook, he was appointed chair of the Constituent Assembly's committee of mendicity which, in a series of reports in 1790–1, elaborated a remarkable scheme of public assistance tantamount to a kind of 'welfare state', in which a variety of government pensions funded out of state taxation aimed to relieve a wide variety of categories of the needy. His plan was taken further by the Convention in 1793–4, but by then he was in exile, following an attempt to aid the escape of Louis XVI in 1792. He returned to France from England in 1799 and for the rest of his life was associated with a wide list of 'improving' and liberal causes (including vaccination, dispensaries, friendly societies, prison reform, slave emancipation, technical education and soup kitchens).

J. D. de la Rochefoucauld, C. Wolikow and G. Ikni, *Le duc de la Rochefoucauld-Liancourt, 1747–1827* (Paris: Perrin, 1980).

COLIN JONES

Latin   The lament of the Italian philosopher-historian Vico over the fall in the demand for Latin books in Naples is well known. A decline in the importance of Latin as a learned language was evident in the eighteenth century, but reports of its death were somewhat exaggerated. It survived as the liturgical and administrative language of the Catholic Church, as the medium of instruction in universities and grammar schools and as a lingua franca (Dr Johnson was not the only Englishman to speak Latin in France). Learned journals such as the *Acta eruditorum* of Leipzig continued to use Latin for articles and book reviews. No fewer than nine Latin poems on Newton's system of the universe were published in the course of the century. Even translations from the vernacular into Latin continued to be made, ranging from Addison's description of his travels in Italy to Gray's *Elegy* and Freind's history of medicine.

P. Burke, 'Heu Domine, adsunt Turcae: A Sketch for a History of Post-Medieval Latin', in P. Burke and R. Porter (eds), *Language, Self and Society* (Cambridge: Polity, 1991), pp. 23–50.

PETER BURKE

latitudinarianism   The term 'latitudinarianism' was from the 1660s applied to a tendency within Anglicanism towards theological liberalism, especially the downgrading of arcane doctrine, of liturgical formality and of ecclesiastical hierarchy. Latitudinarians emphasized 'holy living' and reconciliation with the Puritans. The term was initially used with opprobrium to denote religious turncoats, particularly the Cambridge Platonists, who accepted both Cromwell and the restored monarchy. In the 1680s the term was applied to those, like John Tillotson (1630–94), who worked with Presbyterians for comprehension (that is, inclusion in the Anglican Church). High churchmen condemned them as 'trimmers', and were horrified when they became bishops after the 1688 Revolution.

Comprehension implied rejection of divine-right episcopacy, and the word 'latitudinarian' soon became equated with 'low church', which took the view that particulars of church government were indifferent to God and subject to the civil power. To high churchmen this was an Erastian slavery of religion to the state. In theology, Restoration latitudinarians upheld Christian mysteries and were 'rationalist' only in their reaction against fanatical ENTHUSIASM. But from the 1690s 'latitudinarian' became associated with heresies that denied the Trinity and regarded Jesus Christ more as an ethical model than as a miracle-worker or as the Son of God who atoned for sin. There was no distinct latitudinarian movement, as they were distinguished more by what they opposed than by particular tenets of belief, and the term became progressively vague.

John Gascoigne, *Cambridge in the Age of Enlightenment* (Cambridge: Cambridge University Press, 1989).

Richard Kroll, Richard Ashcraft and Perez Zagorin (eds), *Philosophy, Science, and Religion in England 1640–1700* (Cambridge: Cambridge University Press, 1992).

MARK GOLDIE

Lavoisier, Antoine Laurent (1743–1794)   French chemist, prime architect of the 'chemical revolution'. His *Traité elémentaire de chimie* (Elements of Chemistry), in which he announced that the gaseous state was the third state of matter, was, aptly, published in 1789. Many found the 'new chemistry', like its political counterpart, difficult to accept; even Priestley defended phlogiston to the end. Ironically, it was Priestley's isolation of 'dephlogisticated air' in 1775 that inspired

Lavoisier's experiments. He found that animals living in this pure air produced 'fixed air', thus vitiating it, and since all acids contain it he called it the 'oxygen principle'. By June 1783, aided by LAPLACE, he burned this air with 'inflammable air' (hydrogen) and synthesized water. A more sophisticated version of decomposing and resynthesizing water was performed in 1785 before witnesses at the Paris arsenal. A year later Lavoisier attacked the phlogiston theory. He now began to win eminent supporters; his defenders Berthollet (1748–1822), Fourcroy (1755–1809) and Guyton de Morveau (1736–1816) collaborated with him on the *Méthode de nomenclature chimique* (1787), the forerunner of his *Traité*. (*See* CHEMISTRY.)

Lavoisier supported the French Revolution but was arrested during the Terror when the National Assembly abolished the Farmers General, for whom he had worked since 1768. He was guillotined in 1794.

Frederick L. Holmes, *Lavoisier and the Chemistry of Life* (Madison, Wisc.: University of Wisconsin Press, 1985).

                                                            M. L. BENJAMIN

law No human society has regarded chaos as a desirable end and, sociologically speaking, it is the existence of rules that makes human society possible. In any reasonably developed society (or, perhaps more accurately, any society with a developed state structure) the law is one of the sets of rules by which that society is governed. Differentiating law from other types of rule (notably, in the eighteenth century, custom) can be difficult. Broadly, however, law involves a notion of power: the law is enforced, normally by the state or by state-appointed agents in a way in which, for example, rules of etiquette are not. But law is not simply imposed: it is something that people develop a need for and make use of. Thus, in addition to criminal law, there existed what modern terminology describes as civil law, which is most often concerned with economic affairs and rights of property, although this distinction was not as clear in the eighteenth century as it now is.

Western and central Europe possessed complex legal structures and a developed legal ideology. Royal or state justice was normally based on Roman law, but in many places this coexisted with other types of law, which was in some places vestigial and in others quite strong. Customary law codes, sometimes enshrined as noble, civic or even peasant privileges, were widespread. Ecclesiastical courts continued to supervise marital, religious, moral and testamentary affairs. In some areas seigneurial jurisdictions were still important, although by the eighteenth century they rarely tried matters of life and death. England provided an interesting variation on the western European theme, for its unique common law tradition was regarded as a central element in the constitution after the Glorious Revolution (1688–9). Over much of Europe the law developed in line with social and economic change, and was regarded as something that defined personal and property RIGHTS.

Other civilizations manifested rather different concepts of law. In China ethics rather than laws were regarded as the main arbiters of human conduct. The law-making power theoretically rested in the emperor alone, although in practice laws were frequently proposed by ministers and approved by the emperor. Despite the presence of numerous, and often elaborate, law codes, much of the type of social regulation which would depend on the law in Europe was carried out by other types of rules: those emerging from patriarchal social institutions, for example, or paternal political ones, or non-legal means of dispute settlement. Even so, each province in China had a hierarchy of four grades of courts, overseen by the 'three supreme tribunals' in Peking. Such concepts as equality before the law or due legal process, which were establishing themselves precariously in Europe, were absent from Chinese legal thinking.

Another legal system that was grounded in ethics was the Islamic system, where the fundamental moral basis of the law was the teaching of the Koran, which contains most of the ethical notions on which a civilized society could be based. This remained at the centre of Islamic legal thinking, and judges (*qadis*) interpreted and administered the qur'anic law throughout the eighteenth century. From an early date, however, the development of a number of schools of Islamic law pointed to its complexity, while the need to govern widespread territories meant that in the Ottoman Empire serious offences were increasingly dealt with by provincial governors or their officials. The expansion of Islam also meant that qur'anic or Ottoman state law had to coexist with local customary law codes.

Outside of the major civilizations, the variety of legal arrangements was wide. Africa, outside of the Islamic sphere of influence, probably depended for its law on tribal law codes similar to those described by twentieth-century anthropologists. Some of the larger African states, however, developed sophisticated legal systems to complement their complex administrative structures: indeed, the Ashanti became so attached to their law that an attempt to subvert it in favour of Islamic law by King Osei Kwame was partly responsible for his deposition at the end of the century. In eastern Europe, law codes might echo earlier legal systems that had been superseded in the West. Thus the code of King Wakhtang VI of Georgia (1711–24) included trial by single combat, a system of wergild or blood money, and the ordeals of boiling water and red-hot iron. Western Europe's colonies used the laws of the colonial power, sometimes with adaptations: the 'Laws of the Indies' in Spanish and Central America were based on Spanish models, while New England colonists were happy to transpose English common law precepts to the New World.

One concomitant of the existence of the law is the existence of a legal profession. Cross-cultural comparisons are difficult here, but although skilled and specialized legal practitioners existed in China and the Islamic world, the professional lawyer was essentially a product of Europe. (*See* LAWYERS.)

Another European development was the emergence of legal reform at the end of the eighteenth century, which reflected possibly deeper differences between Europe and the other great civilizations. Perhaps partly in response to the writings of such commentators as the Tuscan jurist BECCARIA, a number of rulers promulgated reformed law codes, including Catherine the Great of Russia (1767), Grand Duke Leopold of Tuscany (1786) and Joseph II of Austria (1787). Other important codes were introduced in Sweden (1779), France (1791) and Prussia (1794). What difference such codes made to the everyday ADMINISTRATION OF JUSTICE remains unclear.

William J. Bouwsma, 'Lawyers and Early Modern Culture', *American Historical Review*, 78 (1973), 303–27.

N. J. Coulson, *A History of Islamic Law* (Edinburgh: Edinburgh University Press, 1964).

Bruce Lenman and Geoffrey Parker, 'The State, the Community and the Criminal Law in Early Modern Europe', in V. A. C. Gatrell, Bruce Lenman and Geoffrey Parker, *Crime and the Law: The Social History of Crime in Western Europe since 1500* (London: Europa, 1980), pp. 11–48.

J. A. SHARPE

Law, John (1671–1729)   Scottish financier. He was the most influential economic adviser in France during the regency of Philippe duc d'Orléans. Born in Edinburgh, he had a chequered career, which included a spell in a London prison for killing a duelling opponent, before he settled in France in 1714. He was a strong advocate of the use of paper money as a stimulus to trade and industry, and the regent, faced with a severe economic recession, was captivated by the boldness of his ideas. In 1716 Law established a private bank in Paris which in 1718 became the Banque Royale, and the trading company the Compagnie des Indes (1719). This company was the successor to the Compagnie de l'Occident, or Mississippi Company, established in 1717 to develop the French colony of Louisiana in part through the founding of New Orleans. In January 1720 Law became controller-general of finance, and in the following month the bank and the Compagnie des Indes were united, thereby forming a monopolistic commercial enterprise and a bank empowered to raise taxes and print money. But in May 1720 his so-called 'system' collapsed and in the following December he was forced to flee the country. Law failed to control the inflationary spiral caused by the availability of large amounts of paper money for the purchase of a steadily increasing number of company shares. The result was a crisis of confidence. However, he was no mere adventurer but an innovative economic thinker whose failure was due in part to the precociousness of his ideas.

Edgar Faure, *La banqueroute de Law* (Paris: Gallimard, 1977).

J. H. SHENNAN

lawyers Private legal practice was effectively forbidden in imperial China, while the metropolitan authorities made less successful efforts to exclude the disruptive presence of lawyers from French and Spanish colonies in the New World. But large numbers of secular specialist legal advisers could be found throughout eighteenth-century western Europe and other parts of the world where the institution of private property was well developed, and a knowable body of rules, administered by more or less autonomous tribunals, constrained the actions of government.

Law was the second oldest learned profession, but most practitioners acquired their knowledge of legal doctrine and forms by example and experience rather than by academic study. The more numerous and lower-ranking attorneys, solicitors, proctors, notaries and clerks, who rarely appeared in court, were the first point of contact for clients, providing advice, drafting contracts, wills and other legal instruments, and preparing cases for trial. Only the professional and social elite, who argued cases before the judges as advocates in civil (or Roman) law jurisdictions, and as barristers in the English common law courts, required a university law degree or a call to the bar of an inn of court.

These qualifications were in any case primarily tests of socio-economic status rather than of legal learning. In a slightly broader context, although a few individual jurists and some corporate bodies of lawyers, such as the Scottish Faculty of Advocates, continued to play a significant role in the arts, literature and scholarship, the legal profession was generally less central to the cultural and intellectual preoccupations of the Enlightenment than to those of the Renaissance and Reformation. Men of the law remained prominent in the political sphere, however; one estimate suggests that over two-thirds of the delegates to the French Constituent Assembly in 1789 were lawyers or legally trained officers.

See also LAW.

WILFRID PREST

Leeuwenhoek, Anton van (1632–1723)   Dutch scientist. Throughout his long life the merchant and amateur scientist of Delft undertook investigations into a large number of natural historical subjects, and experimented with many instruments, but it was his microscopical investigations that brought him fame. Shortly before 1673, Leeuwenhoek began to construct his own single-lens microscopes with a stronger magnification than had previously been available: one extant instrument has a magnification of up to 266 times. With such lenses he began an extensive examination of micro-organisms, using ingenious techniques and exciting his learned colleagues in Delft. The Delft physician Reinier de Graaf (1641–73) included some of Leeuwenhoek's observations in a letter of 28 April 1673 to Henry Oldenburg (1615–77) of the Royal Society. From then until his death, 116 of Leeuwenhoek's letters were published in the *Philosophical Transactions*. He professed a clear and strong allegiance to empirical observation, and placed little trust in academic learning, but he also held strong religious convictions and adopted a number of simple mechanistic principles. His most famous observations, recorded in a letter of November 1677, were on human sperm. In 1680 he was elected fellow of the Royal Society.

Clifford Dobell, *Antony van Leeuwenhoek and his 'Little Animals'* (New York: Russell, 1958).

HAROLD J. COOK

Legislative Assembly   The successor to the Constituent Assembly met first on 1 October 1791. Most of the deputies were men of property or lawyers. The Assembly declared war against Austria, but was bitterly divided, and enjoyed the support of neither Louix XVI nor the Paris radicals. The storming of the Tuileries and overthrow of the monarchy by the radicals on 10 August 1792 was followed by constitutional change. The Legislative Assembly had to invite the people to form a convention elected by manhood suffrage.

C. J. Mitchell, *The French Legislative Assembly of 1791* (Leiden: 1988).

JEREMY BLACK

Legislative Commission (Russian) (1767–1768)   In a manifesto of 14 December 1766 CATHERINE II invited the free estates of her empire to send representatives to a commission for the composition of a plan for recodifying the laws, a task last undertaken in 1649. The commission was convened in Moscow on 30 July 1767, when Catherine's *Great Instruction* was read out, and met 204 times, moving to St Petersburg in February 1768. The last session took place in December 1768, after which many deputies left to serve in the Turkish war. A rough breakdown according to social composition – numbers fluctuated between 518 and 580 – reveals 205 nobles, 167 merchants, 42 homesteaders, 29 free peasants, 44 Cossacks, 7 industrialists, 54 non-Russian tribesmen and miscellaneous categories. The serfs and clergy were not represented. Sometimes dismissed as an exercise in publicity and power-building (at the third session Catherine was offered the titles 'Great' and 'All-wise Mother of the Fatherland'), the commission is best seen as an attempt at national dialogue which was hampered by conflicts of interest. It failed to recodify the laws, but it spawned committees that incorporated the information gleaned into later reforms.

K. Morrison, 'Catherine II's Legislative Commission: An Administrative Inter-pretation', *Canadian Slavonic Studies*, 4 (1970), 464–84.

LINDSEY HUGHES

Leibniz, Gottfried Wilhelm (1646–1716) German philosopher and mathematician. He was born in Leipzig in the second last year of the Thirty Years War, which left Germany highly fragmented, and educated at the Universities of Leipzig, Jena and Altdorf, where he obtained the degree of doctor of law in 1666. In the same year he entered the service of the elector of Mainz who initially sought his aid in reforming the law code. In the early 1670s he went on an extended diplomatic mission to Paris and London where he met and began corresponding with some of the leading scientists and philosophers of his day. During this period he did much work on mathematics and physics and was elected a member of the Royal Society in 1673.

In 1676 he entered the service of the elector of Hanover as librarian and eventually became court historian. Thus began the most productive period of his life. Some of his papers appeared in the journals of the day, though many of his ideas were simply conveyed through his extensive correspondence. In 1684 he founded a scientific journal called *Acta eruditorum*, in which he first published his independent discovery of the infinitesimal calculus, which had been discovered by Newton earlier.

In 1686 he wrote *Discours de métaphysique*, in which he sought to provide the philosophical basis for his plan to reunite Christendom. The central principle of his metaphysics was the principle of sufficient reason: 'Nothing happens without a reason why it should be so, rather than otherwise.' From this he derived the idea that the universe consisted of 'monads', or supersensible substances, each of which reflected the universe from its own point of view. Each unique substance had its own principle from which its whole historical development was derived. The total set of monads was the best of all possible sets because it was chosen by a perfect Deity. In developing his metaphysics, Leibniz sought to reconcile the scholastic philosophy of substantial forms with the modern philosophy which sought to reduce everything to mechanical terms. While he held that all phenomena needed to be explained mechanically, he saw his metaphysics as showing the supersensible reality that underlay such phenomena.

He wrote on a wide range of subjects, including jurisprudence, history, physics, mathematics, theology, linguistics and metaphysics. In much of his work his aim was to provide a universal view that would unite disparate factions. His *Essais de théodicée* (Essays on Theodicy, 1710) was the only book he wrote that was published during his lifetime, and it became the source of the popular conception of his philosophy. In it he espoused the view, which was later attacked by Enlightenment thinkers, that this was the best of all possible worlds.

Leibniz laid the foundations for scientific academies in Vienna and St Petersburg. In 1700 he founded the Prussian Academy of Sciences in Berlin and became its first president.

S. Brown, *Leibniz* (Minneapolis: University of Minnesota Press, 1984).

G. Leibniz, *Philosophical Papers: A Selection*, ed. G. Parkinson (Oxford: Clarendon, 1969).

C. Wilson, *Leibniz's Metaphysics* (Manchester: Manchester University Press, 1989).

JOHN P. WRIGHT

Le Mercier de la Rivière, Pierre Paul François Joachim Henri (1719–1801) French physiocrat and writer. He became counsellor to the *parlement* of Paris in 1747 and was intendant of Martinique from 1759 to 1764. He was the author of *L'Ordre naturel et essentiel des sociétés politiques* (1767) which clarified QUESNAY's views, attracted international interest and brought him to the attention of Catherine the Great. His trip to visit the empress was, however, a failure. He attacked the abbé Galiani in *L'Intérêt général de l'état* (1770), which Galiani, in turn, parodied. Le Mercier's other works include *De l'instruction publique* (1775) and *Essai sur les maximes et les lois fondamentales de la monarchie française* (1789).

Steven L. Kaplan (ed.), *La Bagarre: Galiani's Lost Parody* (The Hague: Martinus Nijhoff, 1979).

SYLVANA TOMASELLI

Le Nôtre, André (1613–1700) One of the most influential French garden designers. His name became synonymous with the symmetrical, formal garden. An early work, Vaux-le-Vicomte, led to his appointment with Louis XIV from 1657 and assured him of work at royal properties such as Versailles, the Tuileries and Fontainebleau. His only work in England was plans for Greenwich Park, which were partly executed.

His style of design continued to influence garden-making throughout the eighteenth century. Typically, a central vista or axis extended
from the centre of the house to the horizon, with a grand canal set at
right angles to it. Level terraces around the house, ornamented with
parterres, were bounded by *bosquets* (wildernesses).

Le Nôtre's theory and practice were codified by Dezaillier D'Argen-
ville (1680–1765) in his *La Théorie et la pratique du jardinage* (The
Theory and Practice of Gardening, 1709) which went into several
editions. The English editions of 1712 and 1728 were translated by
John James. Le Nôtre's influence extended through the work of pupils
and designers in France and abroad, including his nephew Claude
Desgots and the Huguenot Daniel Marot.

Kenneth Woodbridge, *Princely Garden* (London: Thames & Hudson, 1986).

MARYLLA HUNT

Leopold I (1640–1705) Holy Roman Emperor (1658–1705). The
second son of Emperor Ferdinand III (1608–57), he was intended for
the church until the death of his elder brother. In 1665 the Tyrolean
Habsburg line died out and all the Austrian lands came into his hands.
He had a colourless personality and is little known in history but his
long reign was significant for the rise of Austria. It was dominated by
wars against Sweden, France and the Turks, in which Austria gained
substantial territories. A major turning-point came in 1683 when a
Turkish army besieging Vienna was defeated, after which Leopold's
armies swept into Hungary and the Balkans, winning victory after
victory. His foreign policy was increasingly dominated by the question
of the Spanish succession. In 1702 he entered the WAR OF THE SPANISH
SUCCESSION against France, hoping to acquire part of the Spanish empire
after the Spanish Habsburg line died out. Although the wars made
Austria a great power, they also made it difficult to carry through the
fundamental internal reorganization that would have consolidated its
status. Nevertheless, the emergence of a distinct Austrian state, separate from the Holy Roman Empire, continued under Leopold.

J. P. Spielman, *Leopold I of Austria* (London: Thames & Hudson, 1977).

MICHAEL HUGHES

Leopold II (1747–1792) Grand duke of Tuscany, as Peter Leopold
(1765–90); Holy Roman Emperor (1790–2). On the death of his
father, Francis I, he took over the Habsburg territory of Tuscany. The
country was very run-down and he carried through a programme of
major reforms which earned him a reputation as one of the greatest
of the enlightened absolutists (*see* ENLIGHTENED ABSOLUTISM). He restored economic prosperity, cleaned up the administration of justice,

replaced the armed forces with a citizens' militia and introduced local self-government. His attempts to reform the church were less popular with the conservative Tuscans. To crown his work he planned to give Tuscany a written constitution, which would have placed major restrictions on the ruler's power. This was vetoed by his brother, JOSEPH II. In 1790 he inherited Austria after it had been reduced to near-chaos by Joseph's rule. It took months to restore order. He reversed many of Joseph's more extreme policies but retained the valuable administrative and financial reforms introduced by him and Maria Theresa. Leopold's premature death in March 1792 robbed Austria of a moderate, intelligent and experienced ruler just as it was entering a very difficult period.

A. Wandruszka, *Leopold II*, 2 vols (Vienna: Herold, 1965).

MICHAEL HUGHES

Lessing, Gotthold Ephraim (1729–1781) German writer, the supreme exponent of the German Enlightenment. The work of this poet, dramatist, critic, antiquarian and theologian was underpinned by his 'quest for truth'; he turned literature into debate of the highest order. In *Laokoon* (1766) he attacked Winckelmann's aesthetics and, overturning the Horatian doctrine *ut pictura poesis*, clarified the distinction between poetry and painting. His drama criticism, for example the *Hamburgische Dramaturgie* (Hamburg Dramaturgy, 1767–8), reorientated the theatre away from Gottsched and towards English drama. His plays founded modern German drama: the sentimental comedy *Minna von Barnhelm* (1767) was Germany's first political play; *Emilia Galotti* (1772) its first major bourgeois tragedy; and *Nathan der Weise* (1779), a bold defence of Judaism and tolerance built around an affectionate portrait of Moses Mendelssohn, its first great drama of ideas. With dialectic wit and verve, Lessing asked 'how rational is . . . reason?', demolished prejudice and spread his ideals: rationality tempered by feeling, right action and brotherhood – in short *Humanität*. His publication of fragments by the freethinker H. S. Reimarus (1694–1768) provoked a bitter polemic with the orthodox and dogmatic pastor J. M. Goeze (1717–86). Side-stepping censorship, Lessing finally settled the feud in *Nathan* and *Die Erziehung des Menschengeschlechts* (The Education of the Human Race, 1780), which sought to reconcile revelation and reason by an optimistic philosophy of history, anticipating a time when people 'will do good, because it is good'.

F. J. Lamport, *Lessing and the Drama* (Oxford: Oxford University Press, 1989).

JEREMY ADLER

Leszczyński, Stanislas (1677–1766)   King of Poland (1704–10, 1733–6), duke of Lorraine (1736–66). Scion of a Polish magnate family, he was set up by Charles XII of Sweden as an anti-king to AUGUSTUS II in 1704, during the GREAT NORTHERN WAR. He had to flee Poland in the aftermath of Charles's defeat at Poltava in 1709. From 1719 he resided in France, where infighting at Versailles led to the unexpected marriage of his daughter Maria (1703–68) to Louis XV in 1725. The death of Augustus II allowed Leszczyński, bolstered by the myth of an exiled patriot-king, to be re-elected to the Polish throne on 12 September 1733. He was almost immediately forced to flee Warsaw by the approach of Russian forces in support of his rival, Augustus III. The War of the Polish Succession between France and Augustus's other sponsor, Austria, was ended by the peace Preliminaries of Vienna of 3 October 1735. Leszczyński abdicated (but was allowed to keep his royal title) and was compensated with the duchy of Lorraine which on his death was to pass to France.

J. T. Lukowski, *Liberty's Folly: The Polish-Lithuanian Commonwealth in the Eighteenth Century* (London: Routledge, 1991).

J. T. LUKOWSKI

letters, profession of   Writers became a more coherent group in eighteenth-century Europe, and the existence of such a group is often held to be crucial for the spread of Enlightenment ideas. However, the trade had not become concerted enough to form its own union, and so there are no hard figures on the size and composition of the literary profession. Perhaps the fullest guide to the structure of authorship is to be found in the lists of authors drawn up by an official inspector of the book trade, Joseph d'Hémery, in the period 1748–53. Robert Darnton has used this material to compile an 'anatomy of the republic of letters', as viewed from the policing end. The reports of d'Hémery are useful in several ways: they concern France, the cradle of the Enlightenment and – along with Britain – the country in which the profession was developing most rapidly; and they centre on the years when some of the key books of the century were making their appearance (volumes by Montesquieu, Buffon, Rousseau and Diderot figure in the reports, along with the great *Encyclopédie*). Moreover, d'Hémery reported on precisely 501 individuals, a nicely round figure for broad statistical purposes. It should be added that the people under scrutiny mostly worked in Paris, although their birthplaces were scattered around the whole of France; but in this respect the survey simply reflects the intellectual predominance of the capital.

The authors covered had a median age of 38, the biggest single cohort being those in their thirties. Lawyers, private teachers and lesser officials comprise the largest occupational groupings: there are only nine identified as journalists. According to Darnton, 'The aristocratic writers generally appear in the reports as power brokers, channelling patronage toward more lowly *littérateurs*.' There were also a few artisans and shopkeepers, actors, one musician (presumably not Rousseau) and one servant, but the biggest single group is that of the lower clergy, a figure that may have been boosted in France by the debates over clericalism which surfaced less often in Protestant countries. Only sixteen women are identified.

While this is little more than a snapshot of what was observable to the authorities in a single city at a single juncture, it is broadly representative of what we know elsewhere. In France and England especially, the eighteenth century saw a steady expansion in the outlets for writing of all kinds, whether salacious popular fiction or solemn tomes of antiquarian lumber. The ancillary trades of book production and distribution grew in measurable ways, as gauged by such things as the annual output of titles. It is harder to document the increase in the number of authors, since they operated in a more dispersed manner and did not take out indentures. It is abundantly clear that this was none the less an 'age of authors', as JOHNSON termed it, and that a newly self-conscious category of 'author by trade or profession' was in the making. Johnson was one of those who needed the proceeds of his pen to live (his royal pension was a kind of official honour, bestowed in 1762 when the greater part of his major work was already published). It would be rash to claim that the pen was mightier than the sword when wars continued to settle the destinies of nations, but eighteenth-century history came more and more to include wars of ideas, where paid authors were the foot-soldiers and sometimes the generals.

See also PUBLISHING.

R. Darnton, 'A Police Inspector Sorts his Files', in *The Great Cat Massacre* (London: Allen Lane, 1984), pp. 145–89.

R. Saisselin, *The Literary Enterprise in Eighteenth-Century France* (Detroit: Wayne State University Press, 1979).

PAT ROGERS

lettres de cachet   *Lettres de cachet* in *ancien régime* France were closed letters signed by the king, countersigned by a secretary of state and authenticated by the king's personal seal. The procedure governing their issue was thorough and well defined. They contained orders that allowed for imprisonment without trial and without term. There were two sorts of *lettres de cachet*: those dealing with political matters, which were served, for example, against suspected salt or tobacco smugglers, or to imprison outspoken dissidents like Voltaire and Diderot; and those dealing with family disputes. The latter, *lettres de petit cachet*, were the more common. The use of *lettres de cachet* was diminishing in the latter part of the eighteenth century. Nevertheless, their secretive and arbitrary nature, which posed a threat to individual liberty, provoked increasing hostility which culminated in the strong criticism contained in the list of grievances presented to the Estates General in 1789 (*see* CAHIERS). The employment of *lettres de cachet* was abolished in 1790 by the Constituent Assembly.

Roland E. Mousnier, *The Institutions of France under the Absolute Monarchy, 1598–1789*, vol. 2, trans. A. Goldhammer (Chicago: University of Chicago Press, 1984).

J. H. SHENNAN

Levant   The Levant comprised what are now Lebanon, Syria, Jordan and Israel. After the conquest by the OTTOMAN EMPIRE of the Mamluks in 1516, the Levant came under Ottoman rule. By the beginning of the eighteenth century the empire was in decline and its weakness was frequently mirrored in the lack of control exercised by its governors in the various provinces. As in EGYPT, a number of local families came to power. In Damascus the al-'Azm family were prominent for a while, one of them becoming governor of Damascus in 1725. The Sunni Muslim family of the Shihabs held sway in the Lebanon. The Ottoman decline had its impact on trade; for example the English Levant Company, which had a factory in Aleppo that traded in raw Persian silk, faded in the eighteenth century. Following his invasion of Egypt in 1798, Napoleon undertook a Levantine campaign, capturing Jaffa, but was ultimately forced to retreat from Acre back to Egypt. This brief incursion into the Levant in 1799 did not have the impact on the later politics of the region as did the invasion of Egypt. The general history of the Levant in the eighteenth century is one of instability and change which was due to the growing power vacuum at the heart of the Ottoman Empire.

P. M. Holt, *Egypt and the Fertile Crescent 1516–1922: A Political History* (London: Longman, 1966).

IAN NETTON

Lewis and Clark expedition (1804–1806)   The expedition commanded by Army Captain Meriwether Lewis (1774–1809) and Lieutenant William Clark (1770–1838) was the first American overland expedition to the Pacific coast. It was planned and expertly organized by President JEFFERSON. The forty-man party included men trained in botany, meteorology, zoology, celestial navigation and with practical skills such as boat-handling. Leaving St Louis in three boats, in 1804, the expedition progressed up the Missouri to what was to become North Dakota. Wintering with the Mandan Indians, they hired

Toussaint Charbonneau and his wife, Sacajawea, as guides and interpreters. Poling upriver into Montana, they switched to horses to cross
the 'Shining Mountains' (the Rockies), and then paddled down the
Snake to the Columbia River in canoes they had built themselves,
reaching its mouth in November 1805. They returned by the Yellow-
stone River, arriving in St Louis in September 1806.

The exploration and mapping of the LOUISIANA Purchase did much
to advance knowledge of what had been a largely unknown territory,
dispelling many myths, including that of an easy crossing of the
continent by water (the fabled NORTH-WEST PASSAGE). Lewis and Clark's
Journal is a fascinating narrative, including accounts of many stirring
adventures. Remarkably, despite hostile Indians, grizzly bears, and
accidents, only one man died *en route*.

The Journals of Lewis and Clark, ed. Frank Bergon (Harmondsworth: Penguin,
    1989).

                                                    JOHN MORGAN DEDERER

liberalism   In the eighteenth century the term 'liberalism' may be used
to refer to the body of political theories whose object it was to curtail
governmental powers and protect the rights and liberties of individuals
considered independently or as members of the various ranks and
classes of society. Following Locke and his *Two Treatises of Government* (1690), the principal expositors of aspects of liberalism in the
eighteenth century were the baron de Montesquieu, whose influential
Esprit des loix discussed the nature of moderate government and the
English constitution, and argued that political liberty was anchored in
the division of powers; Kant, who took up the latter theme in his
account of the republican constitution and whose writings provided
the most appealing philosophical foundation of liberalism; Bentham,
whose utilitarianism constituted the other important philosophical
strand within liberal political thought; Jefferson, who advocated bicameral government, a bill of rights and various checks on power;
James Madison who, like Jefferson, saw the necessity of a division of
power and the merits of federalism; and Benjamin Constant (1767–
1830), who provided one of the major reassessments of the nature of
political principles in the aftermath of the French Revolution.

Biancamaria Fontana, *Benjamin Constant and the Post-Revolutionary Mind*
    (New Haven, Conn.: Yale University Press, 1991).

                                                    SYLVANA TOMASELLI

liberty   Much was written in the eighteenth century about what
was conducive or detrimental to liberty, and as with many other
subjects, the debate acquired a historical dimension and the issue became

in part whether liberty was growing with the progress of civil society. Some of the best insights were from those who were more readily associated with conservative political thought. Thus, Hume, who in spite of his own political inclinations exerted a major influence on LIBERALISM, argued in 'Of Refinement in the Arts' (1754) that 'a progress in the arts is rather favourable to liberty, and has a natural tendency to preserve, if not to produce a free government'. Under feudalism, or what Hume termed 'rude and unpolished nations', lords raised themselves up as petty tyrants forcing their vassals or tenants to live in complete subjection. 'But where luxury nourishes commerce and industry the peasants, by a proper cultivation of the land, become rich and independent; while the tradesmen and merchants acquire a share of the property, and draw authority and consideration to that middling rank of men, who are the best and firmest basis of public liberty. These submit not to slavery, like the peasants, from poverty and meanness of spirit; and having no hopes of tyrannizing others, like the barons, they are not tempted, for the sake of that gratification, to submit to the tyranny of their sovereign. They covet equal laws, which may secure their property, and preserve them from monarchical, as well as aristocratical tyranny.' Hume contended against those who thought modern commercial society inimical to liberty, and claimed that 'liberty is the perfection of civil society', but he was insistent that in the inevitable conflict between authority and liberty, the former should prevail, for the threat to security and the rule of law, on which liberty itself depended, was the greater evil.

Not so for Adam Ferguson, who argued that liberty required far more than the government of laws and believed that the fear of political turmoil was the greatest threat to liberty: 'Liberty is a right which every individual must be ready to vindicate for himself, and which he who pretends to bestow as a favour, has by that very act in reality denied.' Like other Enlightenment thinkers, not least Montesquieu, Ferguson was sceptical of the idea of freeing a servile people but, unlike a growing number of his contemporaries, he believed the willingness to bear arms to be crucial to liberty. Far from it being irrelevant to modern society, Ferguson reiterated the humanist conception of virtue and agitated for a militia. In his view, tranquillity was not the true friend of liberty. 'The sovereign', he wrote, 'may protect his subjects in the enjoyment of every animal advantage or pleasure; but the benefits arising from liberty are of a different sort; they are . . . the communication of virtue itself to man; and such a distribution of functions in civil society, as gives to numbers the exercises and occupations which pertain to their nature.'

See also FREEDOM.

Duncan Forbes, *Hume's Philosophical Politics* (Cambridge: Cambridge University Press, 1985).

Gary Wills, *Inventing America: Jefferson's Declaration of Independence* (Garden City, NY: Doubleday, 1978).

SYLVANA TOMASELLI

Lichtenberg, Georg Christoph (1742–1799)   German physicist and satirical writer. He would have savoured the irony that whereas his contemporaries knew him as Germany's first professor of experimental physics at Göttingen, he is today better remembered for the penetrating aphorisms posthumously published in his *Scrapbooks*. He contributed to geodesy, vulcanology and astronomy, and in his electrical experiments hit on the principle of xerography, discovering the so-called 'Lichtenberg figures'. His canny scepticism was demonstrated in his questioning of Euclidean geometry, as in his maxim that one should 'doubt everything at least once'. He published successful satires on the physiognomy of Johann Caspar Lavater (1741–1801) and, as Germany's most astute observer of the English social scene, wrote five instalments of the *Ausführliche Erklärung der Hogarthischen Kupferstiche* (Complete Explanation of Hogarth's Etchings, 1794–9). As a private aphorist, he experimented with ideas, casting a caustic eye at the world. Neither Goethe nor Kant escaped. Nor do we: 'A book is a mirror: if an ass peers in, you can't expect an apostle to look out.' Lichtenberg's admirers ranged from his pupil Alexander von Humboldt (1769–1859) to Musil (1880–1942) and Wittgenstein (1889–1951).

Nicholas Boyle, 'Georg Christoph Lichtenberg', in A. Natan and B. Keith-Smith (eds), *German Men of Letters*, vol. 6 (London: Wolff, 1972), pp. 171–206.

JEREMY ADLER

linguistics   The nature and origins of LANGUAGE as well as the relationship of languages to one another were important concerns of the Enlightenment. Following on from the work of seventeenth-century linguists and grammarians such as Father Mersenne (1588–1648) and the Port-Royal scholars Antoine Arnauld (1612–94) and Pierre Nicole (1625–95), who wrote *Grammaire générale* (1660), and those associated with the Royal Society, such as John Wilkins (1614–72), author of the *Essay towards a Real Character and a Philosophical Language* (1668), and William Holder (1616–98) author of *Elements of Speech* (1699), the study of language continued to blossom in the eighteenth century.

Among many similar works, mention must be made of Condillac's *Essai sur l'origine des connaissances humaines* (1746) whose influential discussion of language inspired the IDÉOLOGUES in particular. In the

German-speaking world *Abhandlung über den Ursprung der Sprache* (Treatise on the Origin of Language, 1772) argued for the total interdependency of language and thought. Noteworthy among British studies were James Harris's (1709–80) *Hermes, or A Philosophical Enquiry concerning Language and Universal Grammar* (1751), Lord Monboddo's (1714–99) *Of the Origin and Progress of Language* (1773–92) and Lindley Murray's (1745–1826) *English Grammar* (1795). In 1786 the Orientalist Sir William Jones (1746–94) discovered the kinship between Sanskrit and Latin, Greek and the Germanic languages.

Stephen K. Land, *From Signs to Propositions: The Concept of Form in Eighteenth-Century Semantic Theory* (London: Longman, 1974).

SYLVANA TOMASELLI

Linnaeus, Carolus [Linné, Carl von] (1707–1778)   Swedish botanist. The son of a parish pastor, he studied medicine briefly at Lund and then at Uppsala, where he started to lecture. In the summer of 1732 he went on a trip to Lapland to collect plants and make observations; his diary of this trip was later published as *Iter lapponicum* (1889).

To finish his medical studies he went abroad in 1735. He took his doctor's degree in the Netherlands with a dissertation on the ague. His *Systema naturae*, which contained a new CLASSIFICATION system based on the sexuality of plants, was published in 1735. It became a classic for botanists, and he met Boerhaave and other leading botanists. He was appointed director of George Clifford's garden at Hartecamp near Haarlem, where he stayed for two years and published a number of books. After visits to England and Paris, he returned to Sweden, where he worked as a doctor and gave public lectures on botany and mineralogy. Together with five colleagues, he founded the Royal Swedish Academy of Sciences in 1739 and became its first president. He married in the same year, and in 1741 was appointed professor of medicine at Uppsala University. He settled in Uppsala for the rest of his life.

Linnaeus was a prolific author and a popular lecturer. The foundation of all his work was his classification system, which he developed and applied to a variety of floras. His systems for zoology and mineralogy, which were included in *Systema naturae*, were less successful, but he was the first to call man *Homo sapiens* and to include him in a zoological system. He provided a firm foundation for Swedish natural history with *Flora svecica* (Swedish Flora, 1745) and *Fauna svecica* (Swedish Fauna, 1746). In *Philosophia botanica* (1751) ha developed his ideas about theory and terminology, and his binomial nomenclature was brought to perfection in *Species plantarum* (1753), where he described 8,000 species, using only two names to classify plants.

Linnaeus was a leading figure in his time. He was sent out by the parliament to different parts of Sweden to make an inventory of the natural resources, and he himself dispatched assistants to different parts of the world to study and bring back exotic plants. In his scientific work he used a rationalist method, based on empirical observation and strict classification. He has even been described as a late scholastic in his systematic thinking. He subscribed to ideas of economic utility that were popular in Sweden. At the same time he expressed a deep religious feeling for nature, but he was not religiously dogmatic and he had his clashes with the theologians. After his death his collections and archives were sold to England, where they formed the basis of the Linnean Society in London, founded in 1788.

W. Blunt, *The Complete Naturalist: A Life of Linnaeus* (London: Collins, 1971). T. Frängsmyr (ed.), *Linnaeus, the Man and his Work* (Berkeley, Calif.: University of California Press, 1983).

TORE FRÄNGSMYR

Lisbon earthquake (1 November 1755)   The city of Lisbon was virtually destroyed by fire following the earthquake in November 1755. At least 30,000 people were thought to have lost their lives. The city was reconstructed under the supervision of the marquês de POMBAL, and became, like St Petersburg, one of the most architecturally distinguished cities of the century. The disaster led some of the *philosophes* to question the notion of Providence and their own spirit of optimism (*see* PESSIMISM). In May 1756 Voltaire composed *Poèmes sur le désastre de Lisbonne et sur la loi naturelle*, which greatly disturbed Rousseau and prompted him to reply with *Lettre sur la Providence* (1756), which argued that it was not Providence that had designed an ill-built and overcrowded city.

Thomas Downing Kendrick, *The Lisbon Earthquake* (London: Methuen, 1956).

SYLVANA TOMASELLI

literacy   In the eighteenth century literacy was the privilege of a minority. In Africa the minority was very small and was concentrated in Muslim areas. In the Middle East the spread of literacy was hindered by the absence of a printing press in the Islamic world. In the Far East the minority of the literate was larger. It has recently been argued that, despite the difficulty of learning ideograms, some artisans and shopkeepers in Chinese cities could read simple messages at least. In Japan, where syllabic systems coexisted with Chinese ideograms, some women and some farmers as well as a substantial part of the urban population could read and write.

In Europe in 1800, however, it is unlikely that more than a minority of the population were able to read and write. European literacy varied widely according to region, religion, gender and what was beginning to be called 'class'. Townspeople were more likely to be literate than peasants because schools were more accessible and because the ability to read and write was more useful in the town than it was in the countryside. In central London in the 1750s, for example, 92 per cent of grooms and 74 per cent of brides signed their names in the marriage register (despite controversy, the ability to sign is generally considered to be a reliable indicator of the ability to read and write). Literacy was relatively high in Protestant regions, notably Scandinavia, Switzerland, the Netherlands, Scotland and Prussia. In Sweden over 90 per cent of adults of both sexes were at least able to read. On the other hand, literacy was very low in Orthodox Russia and the Balkans. Catholic Europe came in between, with the French more literate than the Italians and the Italians more literate than the Spaniards.

Most WOMEN were unable to write. Whether they were equally unable to read is much less certain, since reading was often taught separately from writing. Reading was encouraged by Protestant churches to enable individuals to study the BIBLE for themselves, and by some of the Catholic clergy in order to communicate the rudiments of doctrine to the faithful. Once learned, reading skills could of course be put to other uses, and in the eighteenth century they certainly were, as the expanding output of chap-books, pamphlets and newspapers (in northwestern Europe, for example) shows clearly enough. Indeed, some officials saw the spread of literacy as a threat, on the grounds that reading newspapers encouraged ordinary people to criticize the regime. It was also feared that the ability to read would make ordinary people dissatisfied with their lot. However, other officials saw literacy as the key to economic and military efficiency. Hence elementary EDUCATION was made compulsory in Prussia in 1717.

R. A. Houston, *Literacy in Early Modern Europe: Culture and Education 1500–1800* (London: Longman, 1988).

PETER BURKE

Lithuania *see* POLAND.

Liverpool In 1700, with a population of about 5,000, Liverpool just made it into the list of the thirty largest towns in England and Wales. By 1800, with 90,000 inhabitants, it was second only to London in the urban hierarchy. It had changed from a retail centre of little more than regional importance into one of the world's great ports. In the last third of the century improvements in road and water transport allowed Liverpool to serve as the place from which the manufactured goods of Lancashire and the west Midlands were exported and through which raw cotton entered the country.

The first dock was opened in 1715 but as the triangular trade between Africa, America and Britain in slaves, sugar, cotton and manufactures brought more ships to the port, the system was extended with the Coburg (1753), Kings (1781) and Queens (1796) docks. The docks were in the official charge of the corporation, which handled the interests of the free burgesses of the borough, although it was actually run by a self-nominated clique in common council. It vigorously defended the propriety of the slave trade, making a grant of £100 to the Reverend Raymond Harris for his attack on the abolitionist William Roscoe (1753–1831).

Towards the end of the century large chunks of the corporation estate were sold off and, in contrast to what was happening in contemporary Edinburgh, virtually no control was exercised over the way this land was developed. It fell to the less wealthy parish authorities to deal with the poor. As many as one in eight of the population of the city lived in filthy and damp cellars at the close of the century. While the Liverpool merchant class was beginning, with such institutions as the Liverpool Athenaeum (1799), to acquire some of the trappings of polite culture, it had done little to address the social and environmental problems created by its dash for growth.

GERRY KEARNS

Livonia   From 1721 Livonia (Livland in German, or Inflanty in Polish) was a province of the Russian empire. Comprising the area of modern Latvia north of the Daugava River, it had been created in 1561 following the secularization of the crusading Order of the Knights of the Sword. It was originally part of Poland-Lithuania before its conquest by Sweden in the 1620s. Overrun by Russia in 1710, it was ceded to Peter I at the Treaty of Nystad (1721). In contrast to his treatment of the Ukraine, Peter on the whole respected the traditional rights and privileges of the Livonian elite, largely German, who represented a useful channel for Western influences owing to its close links with Germany and Scandinavia. Many Livonians and Estonians served the tsars as bureaucrats and army officers throughout the eighteenth century. Livonian trade was, however, threatened by the rise of St Petersburg; as Russia expanded and became more Westernized, the special status of Livonia was undermined. Its autonomy was ended by Catherine II; although Paul I and Alexander I restored the rights and privileges of the Livonian elites, the province continued to be ruled from St Petersburg.

See also BALTIC.

E. C. Thaden, *Russia's Western Borderlands, 1710–1870* (Princeton, NJ: Princeton University Press, 1984).

ROBERT I. FROST

Locke, John (1632–1704)   English philosopher. He was a formative influence on British empiricism and on theories of liberal democracy. He was born into a Somerset Puritan family and was attending Westminster School at the time of Charles I's death in 1649. He became a scholar at Christ Church, Oxford in 1652, and stayed on to take up various teaching positions. From the early 1660s he became involved in the new experimental science, especially through his friend Robert Boyle (1627–91), and also pursued the study of medicine. His political writings from this time give no hint of the radical positions on toleration and authority that he was to adopt in his later writings.

It was during his association with Anthony Ashley Cooper, later first earl of Shaftesbury, that Locke's radical liberal views began to take shape. He moved to London in 1667 and became physician and personal secretary to Shaftesbury, then chancellor of the exchequer and later lord chancellor. He wrote notes concerning his support for religious TOLERATION and his belief that political authority was founded on popular consent. He was elected fellow of the Royal Society in 1668 and began writing on the theory of knowledge in the early 1670s.

Locke continued his close association with Shaftesbury after the latter fell from power in 1673 and mounted an opposition to the Catholic succession of Charles II's brother James (1633–1701). His political activities led to extended sojourns abroad, in France (1675–9) and, after the Rye House Plot, in Holland (1683–9). His *Two Treatises of Government*, which was not published until after the Glorious Revolution, was written in the early 1680s when Shaftesbury was plotting with other radical Whigs to overthrow the monarchy of Charles II (1630–85). Seen in context, Locke's book not only put forward a labour theory of property and a theory of popular sovereignty, but also encouraged REVOLUTION.

In 1689, the year of his return to England in the entourage of William and Mary, he published not only the *Two Treatises*, but also the first *Letter concerning Toleration*, and *An Essay concerning Human Understanding*. In the latter, which is now a philosophical classic, he set out to show what we can be certain about and how we should regulate our agreement in the matters which are merely probable. The book also contains important discussions on the experiential origin of ideas, the sources of irrational belief, the distinction between faith and reason, the relation between words and reality. (*See* EMPIRICISM.)

The remainder of Locke's life was spent as a close adviser to the

Whig government and in publishing and revising his writings. New works included *Some Thoughts concerning Education* (1693), the works on Money (1692, 1695, 1696) and *The Reasonableness of Christianity* (1695). He was a commisioner on the board of trade from 1696 to 1700.

R. Ashcraft, *Locke's Two Treatises of Government* (London: Unwin Hyman, 1987).

J. Locke, *Two Treatises of Government*, ed. P. Laslett (Cambridge: Cambridge University Press, 1963).

J. Locke, *An Essay concerning Human Understanding*, ed. P. Nidditch (Oxford: Clarendon, 1975).

J. Yolton, *Locke: An Introduction* (Oxford: Blackwell, 1985).

JOHN P. WRIGHT

logic The analysis of the human mind to discover the correct operation of its native powers – reason, memory, imagination and sense – in acquiring knowledge was known as logic. The new philosophers René Descartes (1596–1650) in *Regulae ad directionem ingenii* (Rules for the Direction of the Mind, 1684), Antoine Arnauld (1612–94) and Pierre Nicole (1625–95) in *La Logique, ou l'art de penser* (Logic, or The Art of Thinking, 1662) and Locke in *An Essay concerning Human Understanding* had refocused thinking about inference and the acquisition of knowledge.

Although students of formal logic, like Christian Wolff, continued to work in the eighteenth century, the interest of modern European philosophers generally shifted from an Aristotelian- and Stoic-inspired study of the validity of inference forms to the normative study of cognition and experience of drawing inferences. No longer was the main role of logic taken to be providing the means of justifying knowledge claims; it was to explain how the mind should be used to acquire knowledge. This was typically effected in analyses of the origin of ideas, the nature of judgement, reason, and demonstration and method.

See also REASON.

James G. Buickerood, 'The Natural History of the Understanding: Locke and the Rise of Facultative Logic in the Eighteenth Century', *History and Philosophy of Logic*, 6 (1985), 157–90.

JAMES G. BUICKEROOD

Lombardy The province of Lombardy was centred on the duchy of Milan, which the Austrian Habsburgs acquired from Spain in 1713, to which Mantua was added and various western parts subtracted, giving the new Austrian province its territorial shape until 1796, when Napoleon made it the centre of the new Cisalpine republic. No other part of Italy underwent as much dynamic political and economic change in the eighteenth century, which left Lombardy with a society and economy that were, in many ways, very different from the rest of Italy. Under Maria Theresa and Joseph II, extensive administrative reforms were carried out, particularly in the field of taxation, which began with the completion of a comprehensive land register, the *catasto*, by Nerri in the 1750s. All the work was done with close co-operation between the government and the Milanese intelligensia, a thriving group which by the 1760s centred on the Milanese journal, *Il Caffè* and its leading lights, Pietro and Alessandro VERRI. The crowning intellectual achievement of the Milanese Enlightenment was BECCARIA's *Dei delitti e delle pene*, the most influential book produced by the Italian Enlightenment. Maria Theresa's reforms had been pragmatic and piecemeal, but those of Joseph II were more sweeping; his administrative changes included the abolition of the senate of Milan and the wholesale destruction of the old provincial and municipal structures for which he substituted eight uniform provinces under one administrative structure. The reforms, although efficient, caused a great deal of ill feeling, even within enlightened circles. Economically, Lombardy produced the only true captialist agriculture in Italy, centred on the Po valley and fuelled by investment from a growing urban bourgeoisie, which created a vibrant unique economic structure.

M. S. Anderson, 'The Italian Reformers', in H. M. Scott (ed.), *Enlightened Absolutism* (London: Macmillan, 1990), pp. 55–74.

S. J. Woolf, *A History of Italy, 1700–1860* (London: Methuen, 1979).

MICHAEL BROERS

Lomonosov, Mikhail Vasilievich (1711–1765) Russian scientist and writer. When he joined the St Petersburg Academy of Sciences in 1742, he was already an accomplished linguist, poet and philosopher, as well as an embryonic chemist. Critical interest in him focuses on his concept of 'physical monads' expounded in his 'On the Weight of Bodies' (1748) as a corporeal equivalent to LEIBNIZ's spiritualist ontology. In 1745 he became professor of chemistry and oversaw the construction of Russia's first chemical research laboratory, which opened in 1748, and which housed his early experiments on saltpetre and solvents. In 1756 he repeated Boyle's (1627–91) experiments on heating metals in sealed containers and found that, in the absence of air, weight was constant, thus proving the law of conservation of matter.

Lomonosov combined theory with practice, his interest in mining, glass- and mosaic-making not only inspired his poetry but led him to open a mosaic factory in 1758 with adjacent optical and chemical laboratories. His encyclopaedic writings – including works on Russian history, language and literature – led Pushkin (1799–1837) to call him Russia's first university.

Ilya Z. Serman, *Mikhail Lomonosov: Life and Poetry* trans. Stephany Hoffman (Jerusalem: Centre of Slavic and Russian Studies, Hebrew University of Jerusalem, 1988).

M. L. BENJAMIN

London   In the eighteenth century London was the largest city in Europe. With about three-quarters of a million inhabitants in 1700, and around 900,000 by 1800, it easily outstripped Naples and Paris. The century also saw it grow in wealth and prestige as a result of a concatenation of favourable circumstances. It was the centre of the court, of parliament, of the law courts, and was the premier port in the nation. Its financial institutions grew rapidly, especially after the foundation of the Bank of England in 1694 and the expansion of the business of the stock exchange around the same time. It remained a key centre of manufacturing and marketing, although modern heavy industry was to develop in the Midlands and the north, where coal and iron resources were available. Not least, Georgian London consolidated its position as the focus of fashion, display, shopping, consumption and culture, theatres and galleries. The city also housed the ROYAL SOCIETY and the ROYAL ACADEMY – although most literary and artistic activity was organized on a market basis rather than through royal or aristocratic patronage. London's GRUB STREET became a metaphor for hack journalism. The ever-busy city acted as a honeypot. Johnson, a Midlander who had come to the metropolis to make his fortune, famously quipped, 'When a man is tired of London, he is tired of life; for there is in London all that life can afford.'

Its most spectacular growth was in the West End (St James's, Piccadilly, Mayfair, Bloomsbury, Marylebone), where aristocratic landowners laid out their estates in the form of high-grade town housing, in a style that gave the area an air of classical regularity unlike any other district. This movement culminated in the development by the prince regent and his architect, John Nash (1752–1835), of the ribbon of major thoroughfares (notably, Regent Street.) leading from Pall Mall to the newly-laid-out Regent's Park. Increasingly, the West–East division differentiated the world of fashion from the world of commerce, the latter being concentrated primarily within the ancient bounds of the City of London. To the east of the City, London's first artificial docks began to be constructed around 1800, leading to the rapid growth of the East End as a working-class waterfront area.

London was considered remarkable by foreigners not merely for its size and wealth, but for its social integration, and for pioneering aspects of modernity: street-lighting by gas was introduced just after 1800. Yet in important ways the town remained highly traditional. The corporation of the City of London remained hidebound; the districts developing beyond the City typically had no effective government at all, apart from the purely parochial. The policing of the great city remained piecemeal and archaic, and London was notorious, in reality and in the popular imagination, as the headquarters of CRIME and vice. One consequence was that the city remained politically volatile, with a tradition of artisan and apprentice demonstrations, culminating in the GORDON RIOTS of 1780 – nominally an expression of Protestant solidarity – which lasted nearly a week and cost some 500 lives. In the 1790s London became the centre of the 'rights of man' radicalism sparked by the French Revolution, though fears of bloody revolution in the metropolis were never realized.

M. D. George, *London Life in the Eighteenth Century* (Harmondsworth: Penguin, 1966).
E. A. Wrigley, 'A Simple Model of London's Importance in Changing English Society and Economy, 1650–1750', *Past and Present*, 37 (1967), 44–70.

ROY PORTER

London Corresponding Society Founded in 1792, the London Corresponding Society was the most significant of the radical associations inspired by the example of the French Revolution. It was a democratic society, organized by artisans for artisans, with the radical shoemaker Thomas Hardy (1752–1832) as its secretary. It advocated universal male suffrage, annual parliaments and a programme of public economy. The society sought to sustain the reform movement throughout the country, called for a British reform convention and affirmed its sympathy with the French republic. All this was seen as sinister by the government. At its peak, membership was probably around 5,000. Most of the society's supporters were men of persuasion not violence, although a small minority contemplated the use of force. After the outbreak of war in 1793 the society suffered from the escalation of loyalist opinion as well as legal action by the authorities. By the time the Anti-Combination Act was passed in 1799 it was in decline. It marked the emergence of popular RADICALISM as a permanent element in politics, as well as typifying a shift in thinking to an ideology of natural RIGHTS.

A. Goodwin, *The Friends of Liberty* (London: Hutchinson, 1979).

JOHN W. DERRY

longitude, measurement of Differences in longitude between locations are measured by differences in local time, the almost uniform rotation of the earth ensuring that places 15 degrees apart in longitude will differ in time by one hour. By choosing one location as conventionally 0 degrees, measuring longitude reduces to finding standard time (local time at 0 degrees) and comparing that with local time. Astronomers on land could manage this, but it was a different matter to make an urgent and accurate measurement on a ship at sea. Finding a longitude method was the most pressing navigational problem of the eighteenth century, and its economic and political importance was demonstrated by the offer in 1714 of a huge reward (£20,000) by the British government for a practical solution. The prize stimulated much of the effort to solve the problem in the eighteenth century.

Eventually two methods were prosecuted. The position of the moon against the fixed stars could provide the basis of a celestial clock, given adequate lunar theory and stellar positions, a portable instrument of sufficient accuracy (the sextant) and tables calculated in advance giving times at the standard meridian. The observation was delicate and the calculation complex, but thanks largely to the efforts of Nevil Maskelyne (1732–1811) at Greenwich, the 'lunar distance method' was viable by the end of the century. The alternative was simpler – to carry a watch reading standard time – but the mechanical challenge was immense. Important advances were made in France by Pierre Le Roy (1717–85) and Ferdinand Berthoud (1729–1807), but the longitude prize was eventually awarded for a watch by the English horologist John Harrison (1693–1776).

D. Howse, *Greenwich Time and the Discovery of Longitude* (Oxford: Oxford University Press, 1980).

J. A. BENNETT

Lorraine   The duchy of Lorraine, traditionally part of the Holy Roman Empire, became a pivot of Louis XIV's policy of eastward expansion from 1661 onwards. Duke Charles IV was driven into exile in 1670. The native dynasty returned after the Treaty of Ryswick in 1697, under Charles V, although France retained effective military control of the duchy. In 1729 Francis Stephen became duke, and his planned marriage to Maria Theresa, heir to the Habsburg Empire, which eventually took place in 1736, put Lorraine at the centre of European diplomacy. It was clear to many that he would be pressed to renounce the duchy on his marriage, for the French minister Fleury wanted Lorraine for France. This was France's main goal in the WAR OF THE POLISH SUCCESSION, and its troops occupied Lorraine in 1733. At the Third Treaty of Vienna (1738) Lorraine was given to Stanislas LESZCZYŃSKI as compensation for the loss of the Polish throne; the new duke was the father of the French queen, and the duchy passed to her heirs – the French Bourbons – on his death in 1766. Francis Stephen was compensated with the archduchy of Tuscany, but the loss of Lorraine made him permanently hostile to France. His reluctant willingness to relinquish Lorraine had the important consequence of French recognition of the PRAGMATIC SANCTION, which allowed his wife to succeed to the Habsburg patrimony. Under Leszczyński, between 1736 and 1766, Nancy, the capital of the duchy, became the centre of a culturally and artistically enlightened court, although Lorraine was administered by French officials. By the time of its final integration into France in 1766, the duchy was already *de facto* a French administrative unit.

M. S. Anderson, *Europe in the Eighteenth Century*, second edn (London: Longman, 1976).

D. McKay and H. M. Scott, *The Rise of the European Powers, 1679–1793* (London: Arnold, 1990).

MICHAEL BROERS

Louis XIV (1638–1715) King of France (1643–1715). His seventy-two-year reign was the longest in modern European history. He remains a controversial figure, since his great European reputation, based on the triumph of French arms and culture, was achieved at the expense of his neighbours and at considerable cost to his own subjects.

As head of the Bourbon dynasty Louis believed that his authority was God-given and also soundly based in French law. That personal authority remained at the heart of government throughout his reign, though greater efficiency in the organization of central and local government through the use of professional administrators tended gradually to reduce the king's involvement in day-to-day affairs. Nevertheless, Louis remained directly responsible for the fundamental policies of the reign: the efforts to limit religious dissent, to elevate the prestige of the ruling house and to secure France's frontiers. The French Protestants, or HUGUENOTS, were seen to represent a challenge to his authority and an affront to his self-esteem, for it was still generally accepted that in the interest of security subjects should share their ruler's religious beliefs. In 1685 he expelled the Huguenots from France and proscribed their religion. One of the effects of this decision, which was brutally implemented by the minister Louvois (1639–91), was to convince other European states that Louis's ambitions were boundless and would have to be resisted. Even the fellow French Catholics, the Jansenists, were persecuted (*see* JANSENISM). Though their theological beliefs scarcely placed them outside the Catholic Church, like the Huguenots they could be identified as a politically distinct group. In 1711 their headquarters, the convent of Port-Royal, was razed to the ground.

A short distance from Port-Royal stood Louis's great palace of VERSAILLES, the symbol and focus of French and Bourbon power, which acted as a magnet for the social and political establishment. There the king assembled an impressive group of writers, musicians, sculptors and painters, including Racine (1639–99), Lully (1639–87), Coysevox (1640–1720) and Le Brun (1619–90), who lent an aura of grandeur and high culture to his court that was designed to impress both visiting diplomats and his own subjects.

Louis's foreign policy was marred by excess, for example in his treatment of the Dutch (1672–9), the bombardment of Genoa (1684) and the devastation of the Palatinate (1688). He also vacillated between support for traditional doctrines of dynastic inheritance and emerging considerations of *realpolitik*, both elements being present, for example, in the War of Devolution (1667–8). Towards the end of his life Louis made serious miscalculations as a formidable European coalition was mounted against him. He was fortunate that the War of the Spanish Succession did not leave his country gravely weakened. At the TREATY OF UTRECHT his once vulnerable frontiers on the east and northeast were made more secure and the shape of modern France virtually settled.

J. F. Bluche, *Louis XIV*, trans. Mark Greengrass (Oxford: Blackwell, 1990).
R. M. Hatton (ed.), *Louis XIV and Europe* (London: Macmillan, 1976).
Roger Mettam, *Power and Faction in Louis XIV's France* (Oxford: Blackwell, 1988).

                                                        J. H. SHENNAN

Louis XV (1710–1774)   King of France (1715–74). He succeeded his great-grandfather Louis XIV and reigned for fifty-nine years. He differed considerably in character and temperament from his predecessor, being withdrawn and irresolute. He ruled at a time when the belief in the divine right of kingship was coming under attack and the increasing complexity of government made the exercise of personal authority more difficult.

He served his apprenticeship under a regent, Philippe, duc d'ORLÉANS, who died shortly after Louis reached his majority in 1723. Subsequently, his former tutor, Cardinal FLEURY, became chief minister and effectively controlled affairs of state until his death in 1743, although Louis continued to perform his public duties conscientiously. Louis then came under the influence of Madame de POMPADOUR, the most important of his numerous mistresses, who dominated his court between 1745 and her death in 1764. Through her patronage and taste Pompadour contributed more than anyone else to the effulgence of the Louis XV style, which was the most impressive and enduring memorial to the reign. After Fleury's departure Louis had determined to pursue his own foreign policy, the so-called *secret du roi*, independently of his government's official diplomacy, and Pompadour played a key role in the appointment and dismissal of ministers and in the formulation of foreign policy, culminating in the DIPLOMATIC REVOLUTION which united the rival houses of Habsburg and Bourbon against Britain and Prussia.

The most successful foreign policy initiative of the reign was Fleury's achievement in securing the reversion to France of the strategically important province of Lorraine which took place in 1766. Neither the War of the Austrian Succession nor the Seven Years War, which followed the Diplomatic Revolution, added to France's reputation. Indeed the TREATY OF PARIS signalled the humiliating collapse of the French empire overseas with the loss to Britain of most of France's colonies in Canada, India and the West Indies.

In domestic affairs Louis became embroiled intermittently with his chief law court, the *parlement* of Paris, ostensibly over issues of finance and religion but more fundamentally over constitutional matters. The magistrates' political conservatism made them oppose any change that cut across established rights and privileges, for example in the tax system. In pursuing such initiatives, the crown could be accused of acting despotically even though the need for reform was becoming ever more apparent. Louis disbanded the *parlement* in 1771 but it was restored immediately after his death in 1774.

Louis XV, 'the well-beloved', was popular with his subjects during the first half of his reign, but in his later years the extravagance of his mistresses and his own self-indulgence contributed to the legacy of anger and bitterness that he bequeathed to his successor.

M. Antoine, *Le conseil du roi sous le règne de Louis XV* (Geneva: Droz, 1970).
J. Egret, *Louis XV et l'opposition parlementaire, 1715–1774* (Paris: Armand Colin, 1970).
J. H. Shennan, 'Louis XV: Public and Private Worlds', in A. G. Dickens (ed.), *The Courts of Europe* (London: Thames & Hudson, 1977), pp. 305–24.

J. H. SHENNAN

Louis XVI (1754–1793) King of France (1774–93). He acceded to the throne on the death of his grandfather Louis XV, amid enthusiasm in a spirit of national renewal, and enjoyed considerable dynastic success through France's involvement in the American War of Independence. However, he never mastered court faction or the state's financial problems. Consummately well intentioned but fickle and badly advised, he vacillated throughout the pre-revolution of 1787–8 and, crucially, in 1789. After popular demonstrations ended his residence in Versailles in October 1789 he was effectively a prisoner in Paris. He paid only lip-service to constitutional monarchy, and seems to have developed a serious depressive illness. His attempt to flee from Paris to Varennes in June 1791 ended in ignominious failure, but he held on to his throne by speedily agreeing to the 1791 constitution. His attitude provoked growing hostility, especially once France was at war with

Austria from April 1792, and he was finally overthrown on 10 August. He defended himself with dignity in his trial before the Convention, but his execution was by then inevitable. It took place on 21 January 1793.

John Hardman, *Louis XVI* (New Haven, Conn.: Yale University Press, 1993). Evelyne Lever, *Louis XVI* (Paris: Fayard, 1979).

COLIN JONES

Louis XVIII (1755–1824)   King of France (1795–1824). The younger brother of Louis XVI, he was the comte de Provence until the death of his nephew Louis XVII (1785–95), who never reigned. In the years immediately preceding the French Revolution, his relations with Louis XVI and their younger brother the comte d'Artois (1757–1836) (the future Charles X) were marked by distrust, stemming mainly from his dislike of the queen, Marie Antoinette. He fled to Brussels in 1791, being one of the first leading aristocrats to do so. Louis XVI continued to distrust him, and his escape plans, which were foiled at Varennes in 1791, were aimed to avoid dependence on him. He was the nominal head of the *émigré* resistance; his court moved first to Brunswick and then to England in 1807. (*See* ÉMIGRÉS.) King in exile after 1795, he promised to undo the work of the revolution, to restore all church and noble properties to their original owners and to execute the regicides. He retracted all this in 1814, when he accepted both a constitution, the Charter, and the major reforms of the revolutionary period. From 1814 to 1824 Louis XVIII ruled as a constitutional monarch, showing great skill at operating within a parliamentary system. He was not a disinterested figurehead but never exceeded the limitations placed upon him. Politically, he was opposed to the Ultra-Royalists, led by d'Artois, and ruled through two moderate ministers, first the duc de Richelieu (1766–1822) and then the duc Decazes (1780–1860). Following the murder of the duc de Berry in 1820, the government moved to the right, but remained within the framework of the Charter. Louis XVIII's reign was crucial in establishing a stable parliamentary system in France and in healing the wounds of the revolution.

G. Bertier de Sauvigny, *The Bourbon Restoration* (Philadelphia: University of Pennsylvania Press, 1966).
A. Jardin and A.-J. Tudesq, *Restoration and Reaction, 1815–1848*, trans. E. Forster (Cambridge: Cambridge University Press, 1983).
P. Mansel, *Louis XVIII* (London: Blond & Briggs, 1981).

MICHAEL BROERS

Louisiana   The eighteenth state to enter the union, in 1812, the Louisiana Territory stretched from the Gulf of Mexico to the Canadian border. Discovered and claimed for France by La Salle (1643–87) in

1682, Louisiana became a crown colony in 1731. Its population was a mixture of French, French Canadian (Acadian), African and, when it was ceded to Spain in 1763, Spanish. It reverted to France in 1800.

Control of Louisiana meant control of the mouth of the Mississippi. As Americans advanced over the Appalachian mountains, they needed an outlet for their grain and produce and free passage along the Mississippi River. From 1800 Louisiana was under the rule of Napoleon, a fearful prospect for American expansion. He sent an army to put down a Haitian slave rebellion, then occupy Louisiana. However, yellow fever wiped out the army, and facing financial problems in Europe, Napoleon sold Louisiana to the United States for $3 million. Jefferson then dispatched an expedition under Lewis and Clark to explore and map this new addition that would constitute one-third of the land area of the United States (see LEWIS AND CLARK EXPEDITION). Through the Louisiana Purchase the United States gained the states of Louisiana, Arkansas, Missouri, Nebraska, North and South Dakota, Montana and parts of several other states.

See also NEW ORLEANS.

Alexander De Conde, *This Affair of Louisiana* (New York: Charles Scribner's Sons, 1976).

JOHN MORGAN DEDERER

Lunar Society The Lunar Society of Birmingham was an informal group of fourteen friends in the English Midlands with a wide range of shared interests, particularly the practical application of science to industry. In the last quarter of the eighteenth century they started to meet regularly on the Monday nearest the full moon – hence their name – to discuss recent scientific research and to conduct experiments. The group included prominent industrialists like the engineer Matthew Boulton and the pottery manufacturer Josiah Wedgwood, as well as men more noted for their scientific and medical interests, such as Joseph Priestley and Erasmus Darwin. Like many of their contemporaries in other provincial societies, they tended towards religious dissent and political radicalism. Most of them belonged to the Royal Society and participated in an international network of scientific communication. Overriding individual research projects were their collective investigations of a wide range of topics, including ballooning, standardizing weights and measures, heat, colours and chemical changes. Their close co-operation illustrates the intimate and complex interdependent relationships between science, industry and commerce during the early industrial revolution. The society gradually waned and was effectively dead by 1790.

See also SCIENTIFIC SOCIETIES.

R. Schofield, *The Lunar Society of Birmingham* (Oxford: Clarendon, 1963).

PATRICIA FARA

Lutheranism A religious tradition based on the teachings of Martin Luther, particularly the centrality of grace, justification by faith alone and the authority of the Scriptures in all matters of faith and conduct, Lutheranism made its most substantial gains in northern Germany, Scandinavia and among some ethnic minorities in central Europe during the Protestant Reformation of the sixteenth century. These remained centres of Lutheran strength in the succeeding two centuries, but a combination of the Thirty Years War and an arcane scholasticism, centred on the University of Wittenberg, undermined its strength and progress.

The two most important developments in the eighteenth century were the rise of PIETISM in some of the old heartlands of German Lutheranism and the creation of a transplanted Lutheran tradition among German, Swedish and Dutch immigrants in the American colonies. That Lutheranism could survive both as a state-endorsed establishment in Scandinavia, replete with episcopal government, legal privileges and financial exactions, and as an independent self-regulating religious community in the American colonies demonstrates its ecclesiological flexibility.

C. Bergendoff, *The Church of the Lutheran Reformation: A Historical Survey of Lutheranism* (St Louis: Concordia, 1967).

DAVID HEMPTON

luxury Whether luxury corrupted a nation and destroyed the spirit of LIBERTY was a frequent subject of conversation in the eighteenth century. When Goldsmith suggested that it was responsible for degeneracy, Johnson replied 'Sir, . . . I believe there are as many tall men in England now, as there ever were. But . . . supposing the stature of our people to be diminished, that is not owing to luxury; for, Sir, consider to how very small a proportion of our people luxury can reach.' His defence went further: 'You cannot spend money in luxury without doing good to the poor. Nay, you do more good to them by spending it in luxury, than by giving it: for by spending it in luxury, you make them exert industry, whereas by giving it, you keep them idle.'

While Rousseau and Godwin were only two of many writers who continued the age-old war against luxury, other influential thinkers, such as Adam Smith and Malthus, joined Johnson in defending the economic system that produced 'superfluities'. It was a complex debate, however, which can be fully understood only by reference to the wider framework in which it took place, the assessment of the merit of the progress of CIVILIZATION and its cost in terms of the increasing inequality it fostered. Godwin, for one, was not against luxury *per se*. He did not object to the enjoyment of goods other than bare necessities. Indeed, he did not think that a state of equality necessarily entailed one of 'Stoical simplicity'. Luxury was a vice only when it was the privilege of some 'at the expense of undue privations, and a partial burthen upon others'.

The relative nature of the notion of luxury led Smith to define basic necessities as 'not only those things which nature, but those things which the established rules of decency have rendered necessary to the lowest rank of people'. It was his purpose to show in *The Wealth of Nations* that even the meanest labourer in a civilized and thriving country benefited from the intense division of labour that characterized modern commercial nations, and that while the gap between rich and poor was ever widening, in absolute terms the living standards of the poor were much improved: 'Compared, indeed, with the more extravagant luxury of the great, his accommodation must no doubt appear extremely simple and easy; and yet it may be true, perhaps, that the accommodation of an European prince does not always so much exceed that of an industrious and frugal peasant, as the accommodation of the latter exceeds that of many an African king, the absolute master of the lives and liberties of ten thousand naked savages.'

See also WEALTH.

John Sekora, *Luxury: The Concept in Western Thought, Eden to Smollett* (Baltimore: Johns Hopkins University Press, 1977).

SYLVANA TOMASELLI

M

Mably, Gabriel Bonnot de (1709–1785) French historian and moralist. The elder brother of Condillac, he became secretary to the minister Cardinal Pierre de Tencin (1679–1758), whom he accompanied on his travels from 1741 to 1746. In the late 1750s he wrote *Des Droits et des devoirs du citoyen* (1789), in which he discussed the nature and cause of the political condition in France and entered into the well-established historical polemic about the alleged constitutional relationship between the *parlements* and the crown. His *Observations sur l'histoire de France* (1765–88) revised his views on the subject, tracing the rise of despotic power in French history and challenging the *parlements'* self-description as the champions of liberty. He was an advocate of the necessity of an understanding of ancient history to the comprehension of the modern political predicament. His other works include *Parallèle des Romains et des Français par rapport au gouvernment* (1740), *Observations sur les Grecs* (1749), *Observations sur les Romains* (1751), *Entretiens de Phocion sur le rapport de la morale avec la politique* (1763) and *De la législation ou Principes des lois* (1776). He was a staunch critic of luxury and of physiocracy, for example in *Doutes proposés aux philosophes économistes sur l'ordre naturel et essentiel des sociétés politiques* (1768). He has been dismissed as a retrograde utopian on more than one occasion.

Keith Michael Baker, *Inventing the French Revolution: Essays on French Political Culture in the Eighteenth Century* (Cambridge: Cambridge University Press, 1990).

SYLVANA TOMASELLI

Macartney, George, first earl (1737–1806) Irish diplomat. The son of an Antrim landowner, he gained social advancement through diplomatic service. In 1764 he was sent as envoy to Russia for three years, and on his return entered parliament. He was governor of Grenada from 1775 to 1779, after which he was governor of Madras (1781–5). In July 1792 he was charged with his most celebrated mission, the embassy to the emperor of China, to negotiate for freer trade with China, breaking the monopoly of Canton and the restrictions on foreign travel and residence. Nothing came of it; despite his depiction of England as a tolerant, progressive country, the imperial court appears to have regarded the mission as a tribute from a distant barbarian culture. Macartney considered Chinese society and politics to be degenerate and endangered. He was a humane, intelligent observer, widely read and broad-minded. His entourage published valuable new accounts of CHINA, which were free of the anti-Buddhist bias of standard Jesuit writings.

E. H. Pritchard, *The Crucial Years of Early Anglo-Chinese Relations 1750–1800* (Pullman, Wash.: Research Studies, State College of Washington, 1936; repr. New York: Octagon, 1970).

PHILIP WOODFINE

machines In the eighteenth century the word 'machine' was used interchangeably with 'engine' to refer to the different complex combinations of the mechanical powers and sometimes extended to simple hand tools. The most intricate mechanical device known was the clock, brought to a new degree of accuracy in the chronometer, invented by John Harrison (1693–1776) to measure longitude at sea (*see* MEASUREMENT OF LONGITUDE). CLOCKS provided a model of perfect workmanship, and were used as a metaphor for divine creation, while understanding of the human body and of society was also coloured by mechanical analogies.

Machines were welcomed where they eased the burden of labour or released men and women from degrading or dangerous work, such as manual mines-drainage. More controversial but increasingly common were machines that displaced workers and diluted skills. Machine-breaking became a well-established tactic of workers threatened by unemployment due to mechanization, for example sawmills.

Demand for machinery was sufficient to give rise to specialist makers and the invention of machine tools to cut and plane metal parts. However, the majority of people encountered machines no grander than a plough or a spinning-wheel, and even in Britain human muscle provided the energy for most occupations well into the nineteenth century.

Christine MacLeod, *Inventing the Industrial Revolution: The English Patent System, 1660–1800* (Cambridge: Cambridge University Press, 1988).

CHRISTINE MACLEOD

Mackenzie, Henry (1745–1831)   Scottish writer, known as 'the Man of Feeling'. He enjoyed a successful career as an Edinburgh lawyer before producing, in the 1770s, a series of sentimental novels, the first and most successful being *The Man of Feeling* (1771). He also contributed extensively to the periodicals *The Mirror* (1779–80) and *The Lounger* (1785–7), and prepared a report on the authenticity of Macpherson's 'OSSIAN'.

JOHN MULLAN

Macpherson, James *see* OSSIAN.

Madison, James (1751–1836)   Fourth president of the United States (1809–17), best remembered as 'the father of the Constitution'. He was born in Virginia and classically educated at the College of New Jersey (later Princeton University), where he was introduced to Enlightenment ideas and eighteenth-century republicanism, becoming a lifelong champion of personal freedom and the separation of church and state. Illness precluded him from military service, but he quickly became a leader of the Continental Congress.

He supported centralized federal government that respected individual rights. He was diminutive and weak in voice, but through his writings, his knowledge of ancient and modern law and his strength of character he played a pivotal role in the Constitutional Convention of 1787. His Virginia Plan furnished the basic framework and principles for the Constitution (*see* UNITED STATES CONSTITUTION). To ensure ratification, he, Alexander Hamilton (1757–1804) and John Jay (1745–1829) co-authored *The Federalist Papers* (1787–8) which explained and defined the benefits of constitutional government. Under his sponsorship, the first ten Constitutional Amendments (Bill of Rights) were passed which delineated individual freedoms. In the 1790s he and JEFFERSON split with Hamilton over ideological differences. He later served as Jefferson's secretary of state (1801–9), and was president during the War of 1812.

Jack N. Rakove, *James Madison and the Creation of the American Republic* (Glenview, Ill.: Scott, Foresman, 1990).

JOHN MORGAN DEDERER

madness *see* INSANITY.

Madras   Following a grant from a local ruler to Francis Day, the ENGLISH EAST INDIA COMPANY founded Madras in 1639, and Fort St George was built. In 1652 Madras superseded Masulipatnam as the Company's headquarters on the Coromandel coast, and the town became the centre of British operations in south India. It also developed into an important market for the textile trade. By 1711 the 'white' town inside the fort housed 250 Europeans, while the 'black' town outside the walls provided a home of sorts for a native population of about 40,000.

Throughout the century Madras found itself in the military front line. The French captured the city in 1746, only to exchange it for Louisbourg (Canada) at the TREATY OF AIX-LA-CHAPELLE, while in 1758 another lengthy but ultimately unsuccessful siege took place. Between 1769 and 1782 Madras was repeatedly threatened by the incursions into the Carnatic of Haidar Ali of Mysore. After 1773 it was forced to play a secondary role to CALCUTTA in the Company's administrative framework of operations, although this was not always accepted by those who still regarded the city as the Company's premier Indian settlement.

H. D. Love, *Vestiges of Old Madras, 1640–1800*, 4 vols (London: John Murray, 1913).

HUW BOWEN

magazines The appeal of the printed word in the eighteenth century was reflected in the popularity of periodical publications, containing articles, essays and reviews by various hands and intended for a general readership, especially in Britain, where there were relatively few restrictions on the press compared to the rest of Europe. These publications, which were usually monthly, sold at around 6*d*, and were important in shaping tastes and public opinion.

Thus ADDISON and STEELE, who effectively defined the genre of the periodical essay, sought to bring learning out of the closets and universities into the COFFEE-HOUSES, CLUBS and drawing-rooms by promoting literature and philosophy through the pages of *The Spectator*. It had a circulation of around 3,000. *The Gentleman's Magazine*, which was founded in 1731 by Edward Cave (1691–1754), and was the first to have the word 'magazine' in its title, described itself as 'a monthly collection, to treasure up as in a magazine'. It reported on crimes, riots and the like, commented on English usage (for example, it listed ninety-nine ways of describing drunkenness) and pioneered parliamentary reporting (JOHNSON became its parliamentary reporter in 1740). In the 1730s its circulation was 10,000. Johnson published his own periodical, *The Rambler*, from 1750, which was modelled on *The Tatler*, *The Spectator* and *The Guardian*.

The essence of a magazine, remarked Goldsmith, was 'never to be long dull upon one subject'. Magazines in the eighteenth century had to be well written and entertaining. Their aim was not simply to diffuse knowledge, but to do so in a diverting manner. Some of them became specialized. There were magazines devoted to reviews, for example *The Analytical Review* (1788–99), which attempted to comment fully on every book published. Mary Wollstonecraft contributed to it and served for a time as editorial assistant. There were many magazines aimed at women, for example the *Ladies' Diary* (1704–1840), which contained mathematical problems and articles on history and geography. Others were of a religious nature. By 1800, 250 periodicals had been published in England, including the *Matrimonial Magazine*, the *Macaroni*, the *Sentimental Magazine*, the *Westminster*, *The Evangelical Magazine*, the Wilkite *Middlesex Journal*, the *Monthly Review* and the *Critical Review*.

In 1776 the word 'magazine' returned to the French language in its new meaning, though it did not appear on any well-known title-page. *Le Pour et Contre*, a literary magazine started by the abbé Prévost in 1733 which resembled the periodicals of Addison, Steele and Johnson, kept its readers abreast of developments in English literature. The more famous *L'Année littéraire* was created in 1754 by Élie Fréron (1718–76), who had already founded one periodical, *Lettres sur quelques écrits de ce temps*, in 1749. Like the monthly *Journal de Trévoux* which was begun in 1701 by the Jesuits, it ran attacks on the *philosophes*. Among the semi-official periodicals was *Le Mercure galant*, whose editor was appointed by the government; founded in 1672, it was renamed *Le Mercure de France* in 1724. In 1702 the state bought the oldest French literary and scientific periodical, *Le Journal des savants*, which had been established in January 1665 just before the Royal Society launched its *Philosophical Transactions*.

Patricia Phillips, *The Scientific Lady: A Social History of Woman's Scientific Interests 1520–1918* (London: Weidenfeld & Nicolson, 1990).

SYLVANA TOMASELLI

magic In the eighteenth century, as now, the word 'magic' was applied to an enormous range of phenomena. Even its simplest definition – 'effects which are marvellous to those who do not understand their causes' (*OED*) – begs questions such as whether the causes are natural or supernatural, material or spiritual. It is tempting to take Enlightenment assertions about vanquishing magic – stigmatized as 'superstition' – at their face value. That would be wrong. First, far from being disinterested descriptions, they were polemical assertions. Secondly, magic was in fact constantly used by philosophical and scientific interests (as it had long been by religion) to define themselves against; indeed, it is not too much to say that if magic had not existed, it would have had to have been invented. Thirdly, in that process, magic became to a significant extent the self-conscious creation of the very forces that opposed it.

That is particularly true of the change in meaning of the word 'occult' from merely 'hidden' to becoming virtually synonymous with 'magic'. At a popular level, the meaning of 'magic' continued a degradation begun in the sixteenth century, when religious persecution loosened its hermetic and Neoplatonic associations and identified it rather with necromancy and diabolism, that is, 'conjuring'. In the eighteenth century, however, 'conjuring' came increasingly to mean merely technical feats that produced marvellous effects by concealed material and natural (rather than supernatural) means. This development was uneven and coexisted with older traditions of popular magic, for example fortune-telling, table-turning and quack medicine (*see* QUACKERY).

Equally ancient traditions of high or metaphysical magic – Neoplatonic correspondences of sympathy and antipathy, the cabbala, cosmological astrology, philosophical alchemy and the like – found new expression too, principally in the work of SWEDENBORG and in FREEMASONRY. The former made some headway in Scandinavia and in England, where a Theosophical Society was formed in 1783, which exercised considerable influence on William Blake.

Freemasons, who were also active in England, emphasized deism and political radicalism, but there was also a principally magico-occult strand, which was represented by Manoah Sibly (1757–1840) and his brother Ebenezer (1751–99) (*see* ASTROLOGY). On the Continent radical and occult Freemasonry (and parallel groups) flourished after the mid eighteenth century. The latter included the secretive *Illumines* in France, who, with their metaphysical and quasi-religious revolutionary ideology, became closely involved with the revolution. They did not survive much beyond the late 1790s. In German-speaking countries Freemasonry identified itself closely with ROSICRUCIANISM, and had an influence on Goethe and Mozart. There too it largely went underground at the end of the century. Both countries were to see a major revival of Freemasonry in the early nineteenth century.

Along with Swedenborgianism, Freemasonry influenced MESMERISM. Freemasonry also figured strongly in the career of perhaps the most representative magician of the age, the mysterious Count Alessandro di CAGLIOSTRO whose notorious occultism, reputedly supernatural abilities and involvement in contemporary social and political intrigues, led to his ending his days languishing in a papal prison – a fate reminiscent of another magus possessed of similar ideas two centuries earlier, Giordano Bruno (*c*.1548–1600).

See also SECRET SOCIETIES.

Richard Cavendish, *Encyclopedia of the Unexplained* (London: Routledge & Kegan Paul, 1974).

Robert Darnton, *Mesmerism and the End of the Enlightenment in France* (Cambridge, Mass.: Harvard University Press, 1968).

M. K. M. Schuchard, 'Freemasonry, Secret Societies, and the Continuity of the Occult Traditions in English Literature' (Ph.D. dissertation, University of Texas, 1975).
W. R. H. Trowbridge, *Cagliostro* (London: Chapman & Hall, 1910).

PATRICK CURRY

Maistre, Joseph Marie comte de (1753–1821)   French ultramontane political philosopher. Born at Chambéry, the ancient capital of Savoy, he was the elder brother of the novelist Xavier de Maistre (1763–1852). He pursued legal studies at the University of Turin, obtaining a doctorate in 1771. From 1772 to 1792 he practised law and was involved in Masonic activities, but led an otherwise uneventful existence until he fled Chambéry as the French army was approaching. He became one of the great counter-revolutionary writers and has been called the French Edmund Burke. His first pamphlet, *Adresse de quelques parents des militaires savoisiens à la Convention Nationale des Français* (1793) was a vindication of the Sardinian monarchy. It was followed by *Lettres d'un royaliste savoisien* (1793), which also expounded the benefits of monarchical rule over the disorder brought by the revolutionary army. *Considérations sur la France* (1796) presented his metaphysical interpretation of the French Revolution, which he considered to be a divine punishment as well as a purification. *Du pape* (1819) and his masterpiece *Les Soirées de Saint-Pétersbourg* (1821) were written during his fourteen-year stay as Sardinian envoy in St Petersburg. The latter consists of eleven brilliant dialogues on the subjects of evil, Providence and the efficacy of prayer. He was a great critic of the idea of progress and human perfectibility.

Richard A. Lebrun, *Joseph de Maistre: An Intellectual Militant* (Kingston: McGill-Queen's University Press, 1988).

SYLVANA TOMASELLI

malaria   A parasitic disease transmitted by anopheles mosquitoes, malaria has been a major global health problem since ancient times. In the eighteenth century the Fens and marshes of England were notorious for the 'agues' and 'intermittent fevers' that they gave rise to, as were the Dutch polders and other low-lying regions of northern Europe. A severe form of malaria was endemic around the Mediterranean, the southern colonies of North America and tropical Africa, Asia and South America. The connection between malaria and mosquitoes was not to be established until the late nineteenth century. In the eighteenth century many believed that the foul vapours, or miasmata, emanating from the marshes were the cause of the disease – hence the Italian name, *mal'aria*, meaning literally 'bad air'. Different forms (for example quartan, tertian) were identified according to the periodicity of the fever crises. Cinchona bark, the source of quinine, was imported to Europe in the seventeenth century from Peru by the Spanish as a remedy. Charms, magic, opium and alcohol were also used to combat the debilitating shakes and shivers of malarial fevers, but the disease remained firmly entrenched in many low-lying regions, with profound consequences for their demographic character in the eighteenth century.

L. J. Bruce-Chwatt, 'History of Malaria from Prehistory to Eradication', in W. H. Wernsdorfer and Sir I. McGregor (eds), *Malaria: Principles and Practice of Malariology* (Edinburgh: Churchill Livingstone, 1988), pp. 1–59.
M. J. Dobson, 'History of Malaria in England', *Journal of the Royal Society of Medicine*, supplement no. 17, 82 (1989), 3–7.

MARY J. DOBSON

Malebranche, Nicolas (1638–1715)   French philosopher and theologian. He studied first at the Sorbonne and then at the Oratory, where he became a priest in 1664. He was strongly influenced by the thought of St Augustine, but found his philosophical vocation only in 1664 when he read Descartes's (1596–1650) posthumous work *L'Homme*, which proposed mechanical hypotheses to explain human behaviour. Malebranche developed these hypotheses in his *De la recherche de la vérité* (Search after Truth, 1673–8), and also presented his theory of occasional causes – God was the only real cause in the universe and all finite causes were merely regular conjunctions of events. While his philosophy was initially inspired by Descartes, he came to differ from the latter on central points, especially his theory that we see all things in God.

Malebranche made important contributions to the sciences of optics and mechanics. He became a member of the Académie des Sciences in 1699. His significant influence in the eighteenth century has only recently been acknowledged by historians of ideas in the English-speaking world.

See also MATERIALISM, RELATIONSHIP BETWEEN MIND AND BODY.

C. McCracken, *Malebranche and British Philosophy* (Oxford: Clarendon, 1983).

JOHN P. WRIGHT

Malesherbes, Chrétien Guillaume de Lamoignon de (1721–1794) French statesman. One of the most enlightened magistrates of the *ancien régime*, he was *premier président* of the Paris Cour des Aides and minister of the Maison du Roi as well as director of the library from 1750 to 1763. He protected the *philosophes* and was a staunch believer in the freedom of the press. He outlined administrative abuses for the magistrates of the Cour des Aides in *Très humbles et très* *respectueuses remontrances que présentent au roi notre très honoré et souverain seigneur les gens tenants sa Cour des Aides* (1775), which criticized the system of taxation and warned that the monarchy was turning into despotism. Louis XVI had these confiscated and prevented their publication until 1778. Malesherbes argued for the restoration of the traditional right of representation at all levels and for a resumption of public debate. He thought the press had a crucial role to play in the administration of justice and wrote a *Mémoire sur la liberté de la presse* (1790). He defended the king before the Convention in 1793 and died on the scaffold.

Keith Michael Baker, *Inventing the French Revolution: Essays on French Political Culture in the Eighteenth Century* (Cambridge: Cambridge University Press, 1990).

SYLVANA TOMASELLI

Malthus, Thomas Robert (1766–1834)   English political economist. He is best known for his denial that a large and growing population necessarily indicated the prosperity of a nation and for the doubt he cast on the notion of the inevitability of improvement. He was educated at Cambridge, where he studied mathematics, before becoming an Anglican clergyman. His first publication, *An Essay on the Principle of Population as It Affects the Future Improvement of Society, with Remarks on the Speculations of Mr. Godwin, M. Condorcet, and Other Writers* (1798), was followed by a much enlarged edition of the same work, the product of more extensive research and bearing another subtitle, *A View of its Past and Present Effects on Human Happiness, with an Inquiry into our Prospects respecting the Future Removal of the Evils which It Occasions* (1803). Though his writings often appear to mark a radical break with Enlightenment thought on the subject, they in fact developed the ideas on population that had been put forward by David Hume, Adam Smith, Robert Wallace (1697–1771) and others. He argued that since demographic increase was exponential (it could double every twenty-five years) while food production could only ever be increased by a constant factor, no system of distributive justice could defy the constraints that nature placed on human felicity. Critical of theorists such as the marquis de Condorcet and William Godwin, Malthus was also far less optimistic than Smith and other political economists he admired, who believed that modern commercial society, whatever its drawbacks, could ensure an improvement in the condition of even the poorest of labourers. However, he believed that if population growth were kept in line with food production a nation with a properly managed economy could sustain a much larger population as well as enjoy a higher standard of living in the long term.

In the second version of the *Essay* he advocated moral restraint, that is, sexual restraint, as the necessary and only morally acceptable response to demographic pressure and the misery and vice it entailed. MARRIAGE ought to be delayed until it became clear that children born within it could be provided for by their parents. He also maintained that the Poor Laws should be abolished, for they added to the problem that they were designed to alleviate; such permanent (as opposed to provisional) schemes kept prices high and encouraged the population to increase.

Besides seeing his *Essay* through six editions, he wrote on the Corn Laws, rent and various other topical issues. His *Principles of Political Economy considered with a View to their Practical Application* (1820), *Measure of Value* (1823) and *Definitions in Political Economy* (1827) challenged the views of his friend David Ricardo (1772–1823), whom he had greatly influenced. He also had a notable impact on James Mill (1773–1836), John Stuart Mill (1806–73) and Charles Darwin (1809–82).

See also DEMOGRAPHY.

Patricia James, *Population Malthus: His Life and Times* (London: Routledge & Kegan Paul, 1979).
J. R. Poynter, *Society and Pauperism: English Ideas on Poor Relief, 1795–1834* (London: Routledge & Kegan Paul, 1969).
Donald Winch, *Malthus* (Oxford: Oxford University Press, 1987).

SYLVANA TOMASELLI

Mandeville, Bernard (1670–1733)   British satirist of Dutch origin. A physician, he moved to London in the 1690s and established a medical practice in which he treated patients suffering from hypochondria, hysteria and other nervous disorders. He pursued a parallel career as a writer and first gained attention in 1706 with a poem called 'The Grumbling Hive', a satire on the corruption of early-eighteenth-century England. Its success was quickly followed by a trilogy of prose works – *The Virgin Unmask'd* (1709), A *Treatise of the Hypochondriack and Hysterick Passions* (1711) and *The Fable of the Bees* (1714), in which he combined medical theories of digestion with the literary tradition of imitation as he explored the fluid concepts of personal identity evolving in England's new consumer society.

In 1723 he achieved notoriety when an expanded edition of *The Fable of the Bees* was published during a public controversy over the value of charity. *The Fable*'s subtitle, *Private Vices, Public Benefits*, exemplified the book's mocking argument that a nation could be poor and virtuous or prosperous and corrupt. This dark celebration of early capitalism inflamed the imagination of a public already shaken by the SOUTH SEA BUBBLE scandal. Throughout the eighteenth century

Mandeville's anatomy of SELF-INTEREST remained an important alternative to the idea that humans were bonded in society by an innate sense of benevolence.

Richard I. Cook, *Bernard Mandeville* (New York: Twayne, 1974).
Malcolm Jack, *The Social and Political Thought of Bernard Mandeville* (New York: Garland, 1987).

FRANCIS MCKEE

Mansfield, William Murray, first earl (1705–1793) English judge. Hailed as the father of commercial law, he became solicitor-general in 1742, attorney-general in 1754 and was chief justice of the King's Bench from 1756 to 1788. His opinions made him very unpopular, and his house was burned during the GORDON RIOTS in 1780.

Along with fellow reforming judges like Lord Kames (1696–1782), he insisted on the superiority of courts over parliaments as instruments for developing legal rules. His court appealed to NATURAL LAW, which he regarded as the foundation of common law. A critic of mercantilist policies who was well acquainted with the merchant community, he made a significant contribution to the development of commercial law, which he treated under its own system, known as 'law-merchant', separate from common law. The 'complete code of jurisprudence' which he brought about in this area did not involve legislation, but proceeded gradually through judicial means alone. He endorsed the cause of religious toleration by arguing that Nonconformity was not a crime against common law, which he defined as being 'only common reason or usage', and which was superior to statutes.

David Lieberman, *The Province of Legislation Determined: Legal Theory in Eighteenth-Century Britain* (Cambridge: Cambridge University Press, 1989).

SYLVANA TOMASELLI

Marat, Jean Paul (1743–1793) French revolutionary, physician and journalist of Swiss birth. He was born in Neuchâtel, of obscure parentage. His pre-revolutionary career began with medical studies, which took him on lengthy visits to Holland and England; his writings on medical problems and optics had a mixed reception from the intellectual establishment. From 1777 to 1783 he was physician to the guards of the comte d'Artois. He then turned to journalism which led him into the world of the hacks of the late *ancien régime*. At the outbreak of the French Revolution he founded his paper *L'ami du peuple*, which was subsequently renamed *Journal de la Révolution française* (1792) and then *Publiciste de la Révolution française* (1793). He quickly gained a reputation as a radical who was outspoken in his opposition to the CONSTITUTION OF 1791 and in his belief in a widespread reactionary plot against the Revolution. His paper was closed after the Massacre of the Champs de Mars and he was temporarily driven into hiding, during which time he may have contracted a skin disease. He is regarded as the driving influence behind the prison massacres of September 1792, for which he alone among the leading revolutionaries showed no remorse. Elected to the Convention in 1792, he was brought to trial by Girondin deputies for a violent circular directed against them but was acquitted by the Revolutionary Tribunal. Later he was prominent in their overthrow in May–June 1793. He was murdered by Charlotte Corday (1768–93), a Girondin sympathizer, in July 1793. After his death he was celebrated as a popular martyr and became the focus of a republican cult, immortalized by David's painting *The Death of Marat*.

R. Darnton, *The Literary Underground of the Old Regime* (Cambridge, Mass.: Harvard University Press, 1982).
M. Ozouf, 'Marat', in F. Furet and M. Ozouf (eds), *A Critical Dictionary of the French Revolution* (Cambridge, Mass.: Harvard University Press, 1989), pp. 244–51.
J. M. Thompson, 'Marat', in *Leaders of the French Revolution*, (Oxford: Blackwell, repr. 1932), pp. 163–85.

MICHAEL BROERS

Marathas The Marathas were an aggressive and warrior-like Hindu people whose homeland was on the west coast of India. They sought to extend their control into the Deccan and northern India, which brought them into conflict with the Mughals, Afghans and eventually the British. They enjoyed a period of considerable success after 1730: the Mughal capital, Delhi, was attacked in 1738; part of Orissa was occupied; and several devastating raids were launched into Bengal. Much feared, the Marathas survived by collecting chauth, a forced tribute, from the areas they dominated. But as their influence spread so central control weakened, and five quasi-independent army commands emerged. Infighting and leadership contests did not help the Maratha cause, and a catastrophic defeat was suffered at the hands of the Afghans at the Battle of Panipat in 1761. This led to a decade of relative inactivity, but the Marathas were still able to offer serious challenges to the British in wars in 1775–82, 1803–5 and 1817–18. Even so, defeat in the third Anglo-Maratha war marked the final reduction of Maratha influence and the extension of British control over much of India's western seaboard.

S. Gordon, *The Marathas, 1600–1818* (Cambridge: Cambridge University Press, 1993).

HUW BOWEN

Maria Theresa (1717–1780)　Archduchess of Austria, queen of Hungary and Bohemia (1740–80); Holy Roman Empress (1745–65). She succeeded her father, Charles VI, as an inexperienced young woman faced with a coalition of enemies determined to partition her lands in spite of his efforts to preserve their unity by the Pragmatic Sanction. In 1740 her state, which was still little more than a collection of provinces with different laws and constitutions and whose weaknesses were made worse by financial mismanagement, came close to dismemberment. Inspiring great devotion and helped by able advisers like HAUGWITZ, she undertook long-overdue substantial reform of the administrative, financial, legal and military organization of the realm, rejecting advice to give away part of her possessions to her enemies to buy them off. Government income was increased by improved administration and the abolition of tax exemptions. Power was concentrated in five new central departments under the supervision of a council of state, local government was subjected to greater central control, and the functions of the parliamentary estates were reduced. After the Seven Years War a second wave of reform brought about improvements in education and welfare. Serfdom was abolished on state lands. A standing army of 200,000 was created. As a result, Austria's status as a great power was restored. After the death in 1765 of her husband, FRANCIS I, she faced constant friction with her son JOSEPH II, with whom she shared power and who wished to embark on more radical reforms. She was not motivated by theories but by pragmatism, common sense and a deep religious conviction that it was her God-given duty to act as a mother to her people. By far the most able of the modern Habsburg rulers of Austria, she was a realistic and moderate reforming conservative.

P. G. M. Dickson, *Finance and Government under Maria Theresa 1740–1780* (Oxford: Clarendon, 1987).

C. A. Macartney, *Maria Theresa and the House of Austria* (London: English Universities Press, 1969).

MICHAEL HUGHES

Marie Antoinette (1755–1793)　Queen of France (1774–92). She was the youngest daughter of Maria Theresa and Francis I, and the sister of the Habsburg emperors Joseph II and Leopold II. In 1770 she married the French dauphin and future LOUIS XVI, after several years of difficult negotiations; it was the pinnacle of the new Bourbon–Habsburg alliance, born after the War of the Austrian Succession. Louis XV saw the marriage as a means of controlling the Habsburgs, while Maria Theresa saw it as part of a wider strategy of alliance; the dauphin's parents belonged to the anti-Austrian court faction and did all they could to prevent it. Marie Antoinette had almost no formal education and found life at Versailles difficult. The marriage was not consummated until 1777, which sparked ceaseless rumours about the couple's personal life. It was not until 1781 that a son was born (the dauphin, 1781–9), followed by the future Louis XVII (1785–95) and the future Duchess d'Angouleme (1786–7).

She became queen in 1774, on the accession of Louis XVI. Her reputation was worsened by the Diamond Necklace Affair of 1785–6; public opinion refused to accept her innocence. She played a key role in the final ministerial crisis of the *ancien régime*, first in the replacement of CALONNE by BRIENNE in 1787–8, and then in the recall of NECKER. She always advocated the use of force against the Third Estate and was a figure of hatred from 1789 onwards; the march of the women on Versailles in October 1789 was largely directed against her. Throughout 1789–91 she pleaded for foreign intervention to halt the Revolution and urged the king to flee, well before he attempted to do so in June 1791. Imprisoned with her husband after the fall of the monarchy on 10 August 1792, she was tried and executed in October 1793.

R. Browne, 'The Diamond Necklace Affair Revisited', *Renaissance and Modern Studies*, 33 (1989), 21–39.

A. Cobban, *Aspects of the French Revolution* (London: Jonathan Cape, 1968), ch. 4.

J. Revel, 'Marie Antoinette', in F. Furet and M. Ozouf (eds), *A Critical Dictionary of the French Revolution* (Cambridge, Mass.: Harvard University Press, 1989), pp. 252–63.

MICHAEL BROERS

Marivaux, Pierre Carlet de Chamblain de (1688–1763) French novelist and dramatist. An admirer of La Motte (1672–1731) and Fontenelle, he was immersed in the battle between the ANCIENTS AND MODERNS, making his mark with a number of polemics against the ancients, principally Homer. His early theatrical works were tragedies, but he soon renounced the genre for comedy and produced many plays for the Comédie-Française which starred the celebrated Madame Balletti.

He claimed that his drama was natural rather than mannered, reflecting the real life intrigues of love. Frustrated love was a recurring theme, in particular the obstacles and torments that self-esteem put in the way of love – concealment, uncertainty, timidity, deference to honour and convention. Chief among his works were *La Surprise de l'amour* (1722) and *Le Jeu de l'amour et du hasard* (1730), as well as the novels *La Vie de Marianne* (1731–6) and *Le Paysan parvenu* (1735). Despite his popularity, fortune eluded him; he lost much of his inheritance through bad speculation but was saved from ruin by obtaining pensions from Helvétius and Madame de Pompadour. He was harshly treated by the generation of writers who succeeded him; they employed the term 'Marivaudage' to describe a rather affected, precious style of writing.

MARINA BENJAMIN

Marlborough, John Churchill, first duke of (1650–1722) English soldier. Created duke of Marlborough in 1702, he was the most able European soldier during the WAR OF THE SPANISH SUCCESSION. Appointed captain-general of the British army and master-general of the Ordnance on the accession of Queen Anne, he also became commander of the Anglo-Dutch forces in the Low Countries, in which role he served as the diplomatic and military linchpin of the Grand Alliance against France. He was dismissed from his commands in December 1711, although these were restored by George I in 1714.

His military success was based on a well-developed intelligence service, attention to organization and supply, and acceptance of the compromises demanded by coalition warfare. He frequently sought battle, in which he employed flexible tactical formations. He was an exponent of strategic and tactical surprise, as demonstrated by his march into Bavaria in 1704 and by his forcing the French lines in 1705 and 1711. The victory at Blenheim (1704) prevented a Franco-Bavarian raid into Austria, while the Battle of Ramillies (1706) led to the recapture of most of the Spanish Netherlands. Later successes at Oudenarde (1708) and Malplaquet (1709) were less significant, as the allied army became enmeshed amid the fortresses guarding the French frontier.

D. G. Chandler, *Marlborough as Military Commander* (London: Batsford, 1973).

JOHN CHILDS

Marmontel, Jean François (1723–1799) French writer. A Jesuit education gave the humbly born Marmontel the opportunity to follow his literary vocation. At the age of 23 he settled in Paris and with Bauvin established the journal *L'Observateur littéraire*. Voltaire encouraged him to write for the stage, and he duly produced *Denys le Tyran* (1748), *Aristomène* (1749) and *Cléopaire* (1750), three tragedies that brought him recognition. His principal output in the 1750s and 1760s were operas, though his series of 'Contes moraux' (1756) in the official journal *Le Mercure* was extremely successful. However, his radicalism invited controversy and made him an easy target for the duc D'Aumont who named him as the author of the scandalous *Cinna*, which led to his serving time in the Bastille. His political novel *Bélisaire* (1767), in which he defended individual liberty, was the cause of a pamphlet war between the religious establishment who condemned its impiety and *philosophes* like Voltaire who jumped to its defence. He emerged triumphantly from the quarrel to be named royal historiographer of France, a title that he justified in 1775 with his *Lettre sur le sacre de Louis XVI*. In 1783 he became permanent secretary of the Académie Française. He also wrote articles on poetry and literature for the *Encyclopédie* and the six-volume *Éléments de littérature* (1787). He held a number of offices in revolutionary France before he died of apoplexy.

M. L. BENJAMIN

marriage Historical demographers now accept that in many European countries the timing and incidence of marriage determined the level of fertility and hence the rate of population growth. In addition to interest in the demography of marriage, attention has also recently been directed towards the social and economic context of eighteenth-century marriages, in an attempt to achieve a fuller understanding of the determinants of marital behaviour.

In north-west Europe the expectation was that couples formed independent households on marriage. This usually involved a long period of service in other households and extensive, although predominantly local, mobility. Marriage was therefore delayed until well after puberty by the need to acquire sufficient resources, and a significant number of individuals were never able to marry at all. Fertility levels were therefore restricted to well below their biological maximum.

Work based on parish registers has been crucial to a new understanding of marriage. One of the techniques employed, aggregative analysis, is used to generate annual counts of births, marriages and deaths. A procedure developed for England, known as generalized inverse projection, or back projection, has been used to convert the results of aggregative analysis into national birth, death and marriage rates. Another technique, family reconstitution, involves the reconstruction of family genealogies from parish register entries, and supplies important demographic measures of age at first marriage, marital fertility, and infant and child mortality.

Age at first marriage for both men and women was late in north and west Europe. In England the mean age at first marriage for men stood at 28.1 in the later seventeenth century, at 27.2 in the early eighteenth century and fell to 25.7 in 1750–99. For women the mean marriage age was 26.2 in 1650–99, 25.4 in 1700–49 and 24.0 in the period 1750–99. In other European countries, however, the mean age at marriage appears to have risen in the eighteenth century. In France the female marriage age rose from 24.6 before 1750 to 26.0 in the period 1740–90 and 26.7 between 1780 and 1820. In Germany it rose from

26.4 before 1750 to 27.5 in the later eighteenth century, and in parts of Scandinavia, from 25.5 in 1740–90 to as high as 29.8 between 1780 and 1820. It should be noted that such figures are provisional, given the small number and possibly unrepresentative nature of available reconstituted parishes, and that there are significant regional variations.

Calculating the proportion of the population who ever married is difficult, but recent estimates for England suggest that throughout the eighteenth century 10 per cent of individuals never married. In France the proportion of women who had not married by the age of 50 may have risen from 8 per cent for those born in the early eighteenth century to as high as 13 per cent one hundred years later. In Sweden and Norway, too, celibacy rates rose over the eighteenth and early nineteenth centuries.

Such demographic changes were often crucial in determining rates of population growth. It has been argued that the fall in marriage age in late-seventeenth- and eighteenth-century England was chiefly responsible for rapid population growth in the eighteenth century. Conversely, later and less frequent marriages help to explain the slowing down of population growth rates in eighteenth-century France.

However, it is difficult to explain why changes in the timing and incidence of marriage occurred. Most theories link available resources to the rate of marriage formation and to that extent they owe a considerable debt to the writings of MALTHUS, who proposed that prudential restraint on marriage would operate to restrict population growth to the resources available. In France the rising marriage age has been linked to increasing land shortages and subdivision of peasant holdings. In England, Wrigley and Schofield have argued, it was the movement of real wages, with a time-lag of some thirty years, that determined the rate of entry into marriage and hence the fertility of the population.

Other research has focused on the timing and incidence of marriage among particular social groups. Especially influential has been the belief that wage-earners married earlier and with greater frequency than those in more traditional agrarian and craft sectors where marriage formation continued to be delayed by apprenticeship and service, and by communal controls and customs. As employment opportunities for such workers expanded in the later eighteenth century the marriage age fell. Those involved in proto-industry, rural workers involved in industrial production for distant markets, such as the framework knitters of Shepshed, England, experienced a marked fall in marriage age as rural industrialization proceeded in their village. Such explanations, however, fail to show why the marriage age rose in industrializing countries such as England in the early

nineteenth century and in periods known for the spread of rural industry such as the late seventeenth and early eighteenth centuries.
Recent evidence from Germany and Scandinavia also casts doubt on
the notion that wage-earners married significantly earlier than other
social groups.

Other recent theories point to the possible effects of a decline in
farm service in the later eighteenth century as a cause of earlier entry
into marriage. Female employment patterns may also explain changes
in the marriage age. It has been argued that declining opportunities for
agricultural work in parts of late-eighteenth-century England propelled
women into earlier marriages when all other economic opportunities
were absent. Where female employment opportunities expanded, however, marriages were delayed. This was especially so where unequal
employment opportunities skewed the sex ratio of those in the marrying age groups and distorted local marriage markets. It has also been
suggested that in England the increasingly generous Poor Law in the
later eighteenth century encouraged early and imprudent marriages, as
Malthus had feared.

See also DEMOGRAPHY, FAMILIES, HOUSEHOLD STRUCTURE.

M. W. Flinn, *The European Demographic System 1500–1820* (Brighton:
    Harvester, 1981).
J. Knodel, *Demographic Behaviour in the Past* (Cambridge: Cambridge Uni-
    versity Press, 1988).
D. Levine, *Family Formation in an Age of Nascent Capitalism* (London:
    Academic Press, 1977).
E. A. Wrigley and R. S. Schofield, *The Population History of England* (London:
    Edward Arnold, 1981; repr Cambridge: Cambridge University Press, 1989).

                                                    JEREMY BOULTON

Marseilles [Marseille]   One of France's oldest cities, situated at the
mouth of the river Rhône on the Provençal coast, Marseilles enjoyed
increasing prosperity during the last century of the *ancien régime*. It
was granted the status of a free port by Colbert in 1669, and its rise
was only briefly checked by an outbreak of plague in 1720. This was
the last such visitation to affect France and it reduced the city's population by some 50 per cent. By the end of the century the population
had risen again, from under 50,000 to nearly 100,000. The basis of
the port's prosperity was the Levant trade. Good-quality cloth from
Languedoc was the staple export, matched from the mid eighteenth
century by grain imports from the eastern Mediterranean. Marseilles
also looked westwards towards the Atlantic, developing an import and
re-export trade in sugar and coffee. Towards the end of the century
the Levant trade began to falter but the city remained famous for a

different reason. In 1792 Rouget de Lisle's (1760–1836) 'War Song for the Rhine Army' was taken up by the revolutionary troops marching from Provence to Paris, and became 'La Marseillaise'.

G. Duby (ed.), *Histoire de la France urbaine*, vol. 3 (Paris: Seuil, 1981).

J. H. SHENNAN

materialism   The most important Enlightenment debate concerned the nature of the relationship between mind and body. The issue, which was as old as philosophy itself, ceased to be addressed by only theologians and philosophers and became a subject of public debate between the *philosophes* and the clergy. The question of whether man was composed of a single substance, namely matter, and whether matter could be said to be endowed with mental properties, was a crucial intellectual concern. It was analysed under various headings in the *Encyclopédie*, discussed by Voltaire, Diderot, the abbé de Condillac and the baron d'Holbach, and taken up by their reviewers in publications like the Jesuits' *Journal de Trévoux*, and by physicians and physiologists.

In his 'Lettre sur Locke', the thirteenth of the *Lettres philosophiques*, Voltaire briefly sketched the philosophical history of the idea of the soul. Dismissing Descartes's rationalism and dualism (the view that man is composed of two substances, mind and matter) and Malebranche's particular version of mind–body relations, which claimed that God intervened to cause all physical events in the world, he saw the answer in Locke, who showed that the proposition that matter can think was not logically incoherent. Locke's approach to epistemology confounded innate theories of knowledge by showing how ultimately all ideas derive from sensory perception. Following his suggestion that there was no reason to assume that God might not have endowed matter with thought, Voltaire went on to parody Descartes's famous dictum, 'I think therefore I am' by stating: 'I am body and I think: that is all I know'. Why, he asked, attribute to an unknown cause what could easily be explained by knowable ones?

Although materialism was almost automatically linked to ATHEISM by its opponents, the one did not necessarily entail the other. The difficulty for materialists arose in the context of meditations on the nature of the self. Diderot was happy to argue that man was no more than matter organized in a certain manner, but was troubled by his inability to produce a satisfactory account of personhood. As he owned in the *Rêve de D'Alembert*, speaking of the unity of the self: 'Obviously, the fact of the matter is clear, but the reason for the fact isn't in any way, especially for those who hold the hypothesis that there is only one substance.'

See also ATOMIC THEORY, RELATIONSHIP BETWEEN MIND AND BODY.

Sylvana Tomaselli, 'The First Person: Descartes, Locke and Mind–Body Dualism', *History of Science*, 22 (1984), 185–205.

John W. Yolton, *Thinking Matter: Materialism in Eighteenth-Century Britain* (Oxford: Blackwell, 1984).

John W. Yolton, *Locke and French Materialism* (Oxford: Clarendon, 1991).

SYLVANA TOMASELLI

mathematics The eighteenth century has been described as Newtonian in its development of the physical sciences; it could well be called Leibnizian in terms of its mathematics. Among the most industrious mathematicians who developed the infinitesimal calculus (which was discovered independently by NEWTON and LEIBNIZ), were the Bernoullis. Jakob BERNOULLI pioneered the use of polar co-ordinates, and produced basic studies of curves like the catenary, lemniscate and logarithmic spiral. He was interested in isoperimetric problems, discovered the isochrone and studied the theory of probability. In his *Ars conjectandi* 'Bernoulli numbers' made their appearance for the first time. His brother Johann (1667–1748) contributed to the understanding of the brachystochrone and tautochrone, which led him to the cycloid. Johann's sons Nicolaus (1695–1726) and Daniel were also gifted mathematicians. The former studied probability theory, the latter mathematical physics. In addition to hydrodynamics, Daniel BERNOULLI studied the kinetic theory of gases and, most importantly for the history of mathematics, ordinary and partial differential equations, including the properties of vibrating strings.

The calculus was also greatly advanced by the writings of EULER. In his *Introductio in analysin infinitorum* (1748) infinite series, trigonometric functions and the well-known identity $e^{ix} = \cos x + i \sin x$ all are treated in detail. The book contains analysis of prime numbers and introduces the zeta function. The *Introductio* was followed by a volume on the differential calculus (1755), including a theory of differential equations. Euler is similarly well known for his many contributions to number theory in general, in particular for the law of reciprocity for quadratic residues. In addition to fundamental work in rational mechanics, astronomy and optics, he is also remembered for the formula relating the number of vertices V, edges E, and faces F of closed polyhedra: $V + F - E = 2$.

It has often been said that Euler was frequently careless or failed to exercise enough rigour in his mathematics, particularly in infinite series. While Euler lacked many of the criteria to test convergence or divergence of series, for the most part, he dealt with series that were convergent, which saved him from many errors that he might otherwise have made. Even so, as counter-examples to many of his theorems became known, and as difficulties with his use of infinitesimals and infinite series became increasingly apparent, new approaches were studied and a new age of rigour was brought to mathematics (largely in the nineteenth century). Much of the most important work was done by mathematicians in France.

Early in the eighteenth century the French mathematician CLAIRAUT published a treatise on the analytical and differential geometry of space. He also made important contributions to the study of line integrals and differential equations. By mid-century the great comprehensive work of the French Enlightenment – the *Encyclopédie* – had begun to appear, and editors Diderot and D'Alembert saw to it that entries on mathematics were included.

Among the most influential of the French mathematicians was Joseph Louis Lagrange (1736–1813), who was concerned with developing the calculus on rigorous foundations, and was particularly suspicious of relying on any geometric 'intuition' of space and continuity. Scrupulously avoiding such assumptions, he once boasted that his *Mécanique analytique* (1788) contained not a single diagram. His widely read textbooks, especially the *Théorie des fonctions analytiques* (1797) and the *Leçons sur le calcul des fonctions* (1801), similarly rejected geometric intuition and sought to develop the calculus in wholly algebraic terms, using infinite series.

The English mathematician Brook Taylor (1685–1731) had also introduced such series in his *Methodus incrementorum* of 1715. Taylor's work was subsequently taken up by Colin Maclaurin (1698–1746), but it was again Euler who recognized the value of Taylor's series for advancing the calculus. Unfortunately, Lagrange paid insufficient attention to the problem of the convergence of Taylor series, and eventually this led to other difficulties. Discovery that some functions did not have a Taylor series expansion raised serious questions about the general applicability of Lagrange's work. Nevertheless, his approach underscored the value of doing mathematics without recourse to geometric or physical intuitions, which all too often proved misleading. Mathematicians in the nineteenth century were to pursue this attitude of Lagrange's to its logical conclusions.

The last of the great mathematicians of the eighteenth century was LAPLACE. Best known for his *Mécanique céleste* (1799–1825), he provided a comprehensive presentation of Newtonian celestial mechanics using the mathematical advances made in the eighteenth century. He applied the impressive results of another of his important works, *Théorie analytique des probabilités*, with great ingenuity to establish the physical stability of the solar system.

In the aftermath of the French Revolution the École Polytechnique was founded to provide the best possible scientific education. It directly supported the best of the nation's mathematicians, who were employed to teach students recruited from all over France. It encouraged both theoretical research and practical application. The model provided by the École Polytechnique for scientific education, especially the central role of mathematics in scientific instruction, was influential the world over. Public education became more egalitarian, and new textbooks accompanied the professionalization of mathematics. Many of the great works of the nineteenth century were written as instructional manuals.

JOSEPH W. DAUBEN

matter theory *see* ATOMIC THEORY.

Maupeou, René Nicolas Charles Augustin de (1714–1792)   French politician. Born into a distinguished noble family, he was successively councillor, president *à mortier* and first president in the PARLEMENT OF PARIS. In 1768 be became chancellor of France and in that capacity took drastic action against his former court and colleagues. His relations with the *parlement* had deteriorated as a result of manœuvrings aimed at removing the dominant figure of the duc de CHOISEUL from the government. In 1771 he took the extreme measure of dissolving both the *parlement* of Paris and the provincial *parlements*, and replacing them with courts staffed by magistrates who were no longer the owners of their office but salaried officials.

His actions provided the crown with the opportunity for root-and-branch reform, for these sovereign courts, the *parlements*, were by their nature committed to the legal status quo, and their opposition to fundamental changes in the law was buttressed by their members' independence as venal office-holders. However, Maupeou did not introduce further radical reforms, and when Louis XVI succeeded his grandfather in 1774 the chancellor was dismissed and the old judicial order promptly restored. Maupeou played no further part in public affairs.

William Doyle, 'The Parlements of France and the Breakdown of the Old Regime, 1771–1788', *French Historical Studies*, 6 (1970), 415–58.

J. H. SHENNAN

Maupertuis, Pierre Louis Moreau de (1698–1759)   French scientist and mathematician. A precocious talent for mathematics saw him elected to the Académie des Sciences at the age of 25. In London in 1728 he discarded Cartesian for Newtonian doctrines which he returned to France to champion. *Discours sur les différentes figures des astres* (1732) was the first of several defences of Newton. In 1736 he led an expedition to Lapland to measure the length of a degree along the meridian, while LACONDAMINE did the same in Peru. Comparison of their findings proved that the earth was oblate, as Newton had predicted. Frederick the Great offered Maupertuis the presidency of the Academy of Science in Berlin which he took up in 1746 after marrying. In 1745 he published his *Venus physique* (1745) where he applied his mechanistic ideas to counter pre-formation theory, and in 1749 his *Essai de philosophie morale*. After publishing *Essai de cosmologie* (1750) he became embroiled in intellectual quarrels with Samuel König (1712–57) and Haller, and with Voltaire who satirized him in his *Micromégas* (1752). Crushed by Voltaire's invectives, he left Berlin in 1756 but died in 1759 before reaching France.

J. H. S. Fourmey, *Éloge de M. de Maupertuis* (Berlin, 1760).

M. L. BENJAMIN

Maurepas, Jean Frédéric Phélippeaux, comte de (1701–1781)   One of Louis XV's most influential administrators and ministers. From a family distinguished for state service (his father was Pontchartrain, minister to Louis XIV), he became minister for the royal household in 1718, and in 1723 moved on to the navy ministry, where he introduced major reforms, upgrading port facilities, embarking on naval construction, suppressing the outmoded galleys (1748) and favouring scientific expeditions. Disgraced in 1749 as a result of court intrigues involving Madame de Pompadour, he returned to power only in 1774 when the new monarch, Louis XVI, called on him to transform the corrupt and unpopular ethos of the last years of Louis XV. A steadying if unimaginative aide for an inexperienced monarch, he promoted able and technocratic administrators such as Turgot, Vergennes (1719–87), Malesherbes, Saint-Germain and Sartine (1729–1801), but remained a background figure who intrigued for the dismissal as well as the appointment of the principal ministers Turgot and Necker and others. Moreover, his re-establishment of the PARLEMENTS, which had been suppressed by Terray and Maupeou, has been accounted a fateful step on the road to revolution.

COLIN JONES

Mauritius   Also known as Île de France, Mauritius was of great strategic importance in the eighteenth century. Its location 500 miles east of Madagascar offered an ideal naval base for those seeking to control the main sea route to India and the Spice Islands; and it also offered a safe haven for shipping in times of conflict in the INDIAN OCEAN. The island, initially occupied by the Dutch, was settled by the French in 1712, and it played a key part in the long-running Anglo-French contest for supremacy in the East. It was almost impregnable, but was dependent on supplies from the Cape of Good Hope and Madagascar, which proved to be a great weakness during times of conflict. The island was eventually taken by the British in 1810 and retained by them, with possession being confirmed by the Vienna peace settlement of 1814–15.

F. Madden with D. Fieldhouse (eds), *Imperial Reconstruction, 1763–1840: The Evolution of Alternative Systems of Colonial Government* (New York: Greenwood, 1987).

HUW BOWEN

Maximilian II [Maximilian Emanuel] (1662–1726)   Elector of BAVARIA (1680–1726). An ambitious ruler who dreamed of becoming Holy Roman Emperor and king of a revived independent Burgundy, he maintained a lavish court which absorbed most of the state's income. He sought to gain advantage and to enhance the status of Bavaria by shifting between an Austrian and a French alliance. In the early part of his reign he adhered to the Habsburg camp and commanded imperial forces on the Rhine in the war of the League of Augsburg. He was the king of Spain's governor of the Netherlands. In the War of the Spanish Succession he and his brother, the archbishop-elector of Cologne, entered an alliance with France. This was a disastrous mistake and led in August 1704 to a crushing defeat by British and Austrian forces at Blenheim (Höchstädt). Bavaria was occupied by Austrian troops and the two electors stripped of their lands and titles. Maximilian and a small Bavarian force fought on with the French army in the Netherlands. French support ensured that his possessions were restored to him in 1714 and his experiences did not lessen the attractiveness of the French connection, from which he continued, in vain, to expect great things.

M. Spindler (ed.), *Handbuch der bayerischen Geschichte*, second edn, 4 vols (Munich: Beck, 1967–75).

MICHAEL HUGHES

Maximilian III [Maximilian Joseph] (1727–1777)   Elector of BAVARIA (1745–77). He succeeded to a country devastated by the War of the Austrian Succession and heavily in debt. One of his first acts was to make peace with Austria and formally to abandon claims to the Austrian lands. He shelved the long-standing great-power ambitions of his house and devoted himself to improving the economy and administration of his state. He was the first ruler of Bavaria to be strongly influenced by enlightened ideas but his reform efforts came up against the opposition of powerful vested interests. State-sponsored improvements in agriculture were more successful and his subjects did not suffer as much as those in some neighbouring states in a severe famine in 1770. While he appreciated the political value of religious uniformity, he opposed the excessive power of the clergy. In 1771 he introduced compulsory education and removed schools from clerical control. In later years he returned to more traditional attitudes on religion. A sign that he did not make great changes was that he remained popular with the Bavarians, the majority of whom were very conservative.

M. Spindler (ed.), *Handbuch der bayerischen Geschichte*, second edn, 4 vols (Munich: Beck, 1967–75).

MICHAEL HUGHES

mechanical philosophy   The mechanical philosophy, which was developed in the seventeenth-century, challenged established Aristotelian teachings. By rejecting teleological explanation in favour of mathematical explanation and by interpreting natural phenomena solely in terms of matter and motion, it ushered in the SCIENTIFIC REVOLUTION.

The dominant world view of the early mechanists was Cartesian. In his *Principia Philosophiae* (1644) Descartes denied the existence of a void and thus rejected the corpuscularian theories of Galileo (1564–1642) and Pierre Gassendi (1592–1655) in favour of a plenum universe. In order to preserve an account of contact action whereby impact was the transmitter of motion, he posited a subtle matter, or ether. Vibrating ether accounted mechanically for celestial motion, gravity, electricity, heat, light and much more.

Mechanical philosophers, except for Thomas Hobbes (1588–1679) and Spinoza, agreed on the explanation of physical but not mental phenomena in mechanical terms, in accordance with the mind–body dualism of Descartes (1596–1650), but the precise definition as to what matter consisted of and how it was set and kept in motion were issues of contention. For Descartes matter was defined by extension alone, while for Robert Boyle (1627–91) – to whom we owe the term 'mechanical philosophy' – the primary qualities of matter included size, shape and number. Such divergence in opinion is only to be expected within a philosophy premised on the idea that the reality of nature is not identical to the appearances that sense experience affords.

NEWTON rejected Descartes's invocation of a watchmaker God who, having set the universe in motion, left it to its own devices. Newtonian mechanics, by contrast, was underpinned by a commitment to God's intervention in sustaining the status quo. Thus Newton embarked on a quest to understand the problem of the 'ghost in the machine'. (The pineal gland had been the sum of Descartes's solution to this problem of his own devising!) Newton's theological commitments led to his intimating that divinely empowered active principles caused forces like gravity and interparticulate attractions – a far cry from Descartes's spiritless world-machine. It was perhaps in response to LEIBNIZ's charge of occultism that Newton in his *Opticks* attributed to a subtle quasi-material ether all the phenomena that he had earlier attributed to active principles. In this way, and despite his own insistence on the inert nature of matter, Newton furnished his followers with a metaphysical basis for an immanentist philosophy.

In Newton's wake, mechanistic philosophies were most rigorously developed by French *philosophes*, like Diderot and Voltaire, La Mettrie and the baron d'Holbach, whose *Système de la nature* (1770) was dubbed 'the atheist's Bible'. In Britain immanentism dominated matter theory, though the mechanical philosophy survived in the physiology of physicians belonging to the Pitcairne-Gregory circle who explained bodily operations in terms of the actions of short-range forces analogous to gravity. A mechanically orientated physiology of mind was revived by David Hartley (1705–57) in his influential *Observations on Man* (1746), later publicized by Joseph Priestley.

See also MATERIALISM, RELATIONSHIP BETWEEN MIND AND BODY.

Robert E. Schofield, *Mechanism and Materialism: British Natural Philosophy in an Age of Reason* (Princeton, NJ: Princeton University Press, 1970).
Simon Schaffer and Steven Shapin, *Leviathan and the Air-Pump: Hobbes, Boyle and the Experimental Life* (Princeton, NJ: Princeton University Press, 1985).

M. L. BENJAMIN

mechanics The mathematical science of motion, or mechanics, lay at the heart of the European Enlightenment, both as a pure science and as a metaphor. NEWTON's *Principia* had provided the laws for a cosmic machine whose parts were moved by attractions and repulsions. By 1750 his followers had marginalized the fluid mechanics tradition inspired by Descartes's (1596–1650) whirlpool model of the cosmos. Working on theoretical problems such as the proper measure of force, exponents of MATHEMATICAL ANALYSIS effectively systematized and extended Newtonian mechanics using the techniques of LEIBNIZ. They were, with a few exceptions like the remarkable Émilie du Châtelet-Lomont, professional academic men supported by royal patronage.

Their successes were given wider significance when deployed by Enlightenment *philosophes* like Voltaire to promote an image of all nature as a machine, obeying a law-like harmony comprehensible by human reason. *Philosophes* argued that mechanics exploded the supernatural interventions or caprices of traditional religious beliefs although, a few atheists apart, they grounded cosmic laws in a Christian or deistic God. They were encouraged to search for similar principles of motion for human agents and political societies.

Thomas L. Hankins, *Science and the Enlightenment* (Cambridge: Cambridge University Press, 1985).

STEPHEN PUMFREY

Medici, Cosimo III (1642–1723) Grand duke of Tuscany. The son of Ferdinando II and Vittoria della Rovere (daughter of the duke of Urbino), and father of Gian Gastone, the last of the Medicis. In his youth he travelled around Europe studying different forms of government and political systems. In 1661 he married Marguerite Louise d'Orléans, niece of Louis XIII. Their relationship proved to be extremely troubled and ended with Marguerite's return to France. Cosimo's accession (1670) was followed briefly by a period of personal rule, but he soon switched to a traditional management which left the state in the hands of a patrician oligarchy. Attempts at reforming the administration of justice and the fiscal system met with resistance and had minimal lasting effects. He stuck to a protective mercantilist policy, favouring urban economy and in particular the interests of Florence. More daring was his policy towards the city of Livorno, which was made a free port. In the countryside he continued the efforts of his predecessors to promote the drainage of the marshes and the construction of irrigation channels. Deeply religious, he gave indiscriminate support to the church and its policy towards culture and science. He promoted the reorganization of Tuscan artistic and cultural heritage and brought to completion the Medicean galleries.

SANDRA CAVALLO

medicine Eighteenth-century medicine is often portrayed by historians of ideas as stagnant or lacking a central developmental focus. However, in the past fifteen years social historians have revitalized the study of the eighteenth century, medicine included. Dramatic changes, such as the development of Inoculation and the rise of the man-midwife, can now be interpreted in the context of gradual shifts in professional structure, medical institutions and Enlightenment optimism about the potential for improving health.

Central to eighteenth-century medical life was the primacy of the patient. Most health care took place in the home under the direction of the patient and his or her family, and frequently did not involve professional practitioners. This structure reflected the relatively weak organization of the profession, which was divided into physicians, surgeons, midwives, apothecaries and a host of others, including quacks (*see* QUACKERY). Over the course of the century the status of surgeons gradually improved as they aped the gentlemanly behaviour of university-trained physicians; they became involved with charitable institutions and trained in Hospitals as well as through apprenticeship. The increased utilization of men as midwives, which was related to the willingness and ability of surgeons to use forceps, can be seen as part of this process.

During the eighteenth century medical men increasingly found themselves practising in institutions. Many a young practitioner got his start in the military; others trained in hospitals or dispensaries. Numbers of charitable medical institutions grew, creating a new bureaucratic hospital medicine. So too, the development of clinical medicine, involving education at the hospital bedside, began to forge a professional identity and to exclude female healers.

In as much as the Enlightenment reshaped medicine, its impact lay as much in prevention as in cure. New public health measures sought to improve conditions in prisons and the military. Johann Peter Frank (1745–1821) created a system of 'medical police', or medical planning, which involved state administration and regulation of numerous factors to promote health. This public aspect of Enlightenment medicine was balanced by an emphasis on individual responsibility for health. Doctors like Simon-André Tissot (1728–97) and William Buchan (1729–1805) wrote unprecedented numbers of popular health books, attempting to convince their better-off patients to adopt healthier lifestyles, and to promote new methods of child-rearing. Edward Jenner's (1749–1823) discovery of VACCINATION and William Withering's (1741–99) discovery of digitalis were both based on folk wisdom. Such empiricism characterized an Enlightenment response to the endless theoretical wrangling of learned physicians, but also served to demarcate folk knowledge from scientific medicine. In sum, Enlightenment medicine was characterized by what one historian has called 'the recovery of nerve', an optimism that medicine could and would improve life chances.

See also DISEASE, OBSTETRICS, PUBLIC HEALTH.

W. F. Bynum, 'Health, Disease, and Medical Care', in G. S. Rousseau and Roy Porter (eds), *The Ferment of Knowledge: Studies in the Historiography of Eighteenth-Century Science* (Cambridge: Cambridge University Press, 1980), pp. 211–53.

Peter Gay, *The Enlightenment: An Interpretation*, vol. 2 (New York: Knopf, 1966–9), pp. 12–23.

Roy and Dorothy Porter, *In Sickness and in Health: The British Experience 1650–1850* (London: Fourth Estate, 1988).

MARY E. FISSELL

Mediterranean In the eighteenth century, after two millennia of Mediterranean dominance, Europe's economic centre of gravity shifted to the Atlantic seaboard. The Italian cities, which had been powerhouses of the world economy in the sixteenth century, were in poor shape by 1700, while Spain was also in relative decline. The dynamic cities of Europe (for example London, Amsterdam, Paris, Nantes and Bordeaux) were located in the north-west. Seville and VENICE stagnated; Italian and Spanish elites preferred to invest in land rather than in trade or industry.

The torpor of the Mediterranean may, however, have been exaggerated. In global terms, NAPLES, Cairo and Constantinople (*see* ISTANBUL) were massive cities. Trade within the Mediterranean was considerable: the amount of internal grain movement (notably out of Sicily) was enormous; and exports of salt, alum, wines and olive oil remained high. European relations with the Islamic states on the southern and eastern shores of the Mediterranean were not insignificant (*see* BARBARY STATES). The Austrian Habsburgs made important inroads into the Ottoman Empire over the century, while in 1798–9 Napoleon's Egyptian expedition marked a new beginning in colonial penetration. Trade with the LEVANT was critical for French and English textile industries, and Oriental fashions were much in vogue.

COLIN JONES

Mendelssohn, Moses (1729–1786)   Key Jewish thinker of the German Enlightenment. Rabbinically trained at Dessau, he moved to Berlin where, overcoming indigence, he taught himself German, studied Shaftesbury, Locke and Wolff, made friends with Lessing and soon gained acceptance as a philosopher.

Developing BAUMGARTEN's aesthetics, he argued for a distinction between beauty and metaphysical perfection; aesthetic feelings differed from intellect and desire, belonging to a third mental faculty of 'approval' (*Billigungsvermögen*), a doctrine which Kant accepted in his third *Critique*. His many publications included a translation of Rousseau's second *Discours* (1764) and the highly popular *Phädon* (1767), where he updated Plato's treatment of immortality. His *Jerusalem* (1783), which elaborated the limits of the state and the necessity for tolerance, promulgated the highly influential view of Judaism as a rational religion and the non-mystical religion of law. His translation of the *Pentateuch* (1780–3) into German and proposals for Jewish educational reform contributed to the emergence of Reform-Judaism, and, together with his exemplary career and character, facilitated the emancipation of the Jews in Germany and throughout Europe.

A. Altmann, *Moses Mendelssohn: A Biographical Study* (London: Routledge & Kegan Paul, 1973).

JEREMY ADLER

Mengs, Anton Raphael (1728–1779)   German painter. The German pioneer of neoclassicism in painting, he had a successful career, mainly in Italy and Spain. Greatly influenced by WINCKELMANN, he was a teacher of considerable influence. Although his decorative works experiment with new styles, his many pastel portraits were largely conventional.

IAIN PEARS

mercantilism According to Adam SMITH, one of the principal effects of the discoveries of America and of a passage to the East Indies by the Cape of Good Hope was to have raised 'the mercantile system to a degree of splendor and glory which it could never otherwise have attained to'. The commercial, or mercantile, system of political economy was the school of thought which Smith was predominantly concerned to undermine in *The Wealth of Nations*, since physiocracy had, in his view, comparatively little practical influence.

Prevalent from the mid-sixteenth century onwards, mercantilism was favourable to the intervention of government in regulating the economy. Some of its leading exponents had been Sir Thomas Mun (1571–1641), a director of the East India Company who wrote *England's Treasure by Forraign Trade* (1664); Gerald Malynes (1586–1641), an English merchant, government official and author of *The Maintenance of Free Trade* (1622); and Edward Misselden (1608–54) who wrote *The Circle of Commerce* (1623) and argued that the flow of international trade determined the movement of specie and the exchange rate. Though their claims admitted of qualifications, and men like Mun argued against the prohibition of the export of bullion because of the backlash such restrictions engendered, mercantilists generally conceived the wealth of a nation principally in terms of the generation of a surplus of exports in the balance of trade, and argued for the maintenance of high levels of bullion, thereby equating WEALTH and money.

According to political economists like Hume and Smith, the view that wealth consists in money, and hence that all that was conducive to its accumulation through a favourable balance of trade was the proper object of government policy (for example encouraging exports, especially of manufactured goods, discouraging imports and granting monopolies), was a great fallacy which they sought to expose partly by explaining its origins. Smith thus explained that the aforementioned territorial discoveries had transformed the commercial towns of Europe from being the provider of a rather limited market to becoming 'the manufacturers for the numerous and thriving cultivators of America, and the carriers, and in some respects the manufacturers too, for almost all the different nations of Asia, Africa, and America'. Such developments had contributed to obscure the true nature of wealth, a truth unattainable, according to Smith, by any system which eclipsed agriculture and failed to recognize the benefits of FREE TRADE. 'It cannot be very difficult', he remarked, 'to determine which have been the contrivers of this whole mercantile system; not the consumers, we may believe, whose interest has been entirely neglected.'

Adam Smith, *An Inquiry into the Nature and Causes of the Wealth of Nations*, ed. R. H. Campbell, A. S. Skinner and W. B. Todd, 2 vols (Oxford: Clarendon, 1976).

SYLVANA TOMASELLI

Mercier, Louis-Sébastien (1740–1814)   French dramatist, novelist, historian and critic. Associated with the Girondins, he was deputy for Seine-et-Oise at the Convention, where he voted against the death penalty for Louis XVI. He was arrested in 1793 but escaped the guillotine, and went on to become a member of the Institut.

He was a prolific writer and his works included *Songes et visions philosophiques* (1768), *L'An 2440* (1770), *Nouvel essai sur l'art dramatique* (1773), *De la littérature et des littérateurs* (1778) and *Néologie* (1801). His most interesting and best-known work is the twelve-volume *Tableau de Paris* (1782–8), which is a collection of short philosophical reflections, satirical comments on the mores of the day, journalistic pieces and gossip. For example, volume 5 opens with a depiction of the arrival in Paris of someone from the provinces, and describes the shops and their contents, discusses midwifery, considers some religious and economic matters and ends with a sketch on bailiffs. He founded and edited *Les Annales patriotiques et littéraires* (1789–97).

Fawzi Boubia, *Theater der Politik, Politik des Theaters: Louis-Sébastien Mercier und die Dramaturgie des Sturm und Drang* (Frankfurt am Main: Peter Lang, 1978).

SYLVANA TOMASELLI

mesmerism   One of the new healing sciences of the Enlightenment, mesmerism, or hypnotism as it is usually known today, was derived from the work of the Swabian-born, Vienna-trained physician Franz Anton Mesmer (1734–1815). He discovered in the early 1770s that he could cure hysterical patients by passing magnets over their bodies. He soon found that stroking with a finger imparted the same therapeutic benefits. These he explained in terms of his ability to channel a cosmic, ethereal force, which he called 'animal magnetism'. In time he perfected his technique using tubs (*baquets*), in which animal magnetic forces could be stored and concentrated. After being driven out of Vienna as a quack in 1778, he settled in Paris, where he built up a fashionable clientele before a commission of inquiry scientifically discredited the philosophy of animal magnetism, and forced him once more on his travels. He spent his last years quietly by Lake Constance.

Although he regarded animal magnetism as a Newtonian physical force, his followers developed mesmerism as a psychological technique for psychosomatic disorders.

R. Darnton, *Mesmerism and the End of the Enlightenment in France* (Cambridge, Mass.: Harvard University Press, 1968).

ROY PORTER

Metastasio, Pietro [Trapassi, Antonio] (1698–1782) Italian poet and librettist. A grocer's son, Metastasio worked his way up to become court poet of the Habsburgs, and he was the most significant librettist of the eighteenth century. He wrote his first drama for the opera in 1724, inspired by the singer La Romanina (Marianna Benti-Bulgarelli): *Didone abbandonata* was set to music by Domenico Sarri (1679–1744). From 1730 he lived in Vienna. His elegant and charming verses found favour among his contemporaries, and his librettos were used by virtually all the major composers of the time, including Handel, Haydn, Gluck and Mozart. The German composer Johann Adolf Hasse (1699–1783) set almost all his twenty-seven librettos. Some of his texts were set as many as sixty or seventy times.

His aim was to purify and to heighten the drama by omitting elements of seventeenth-century opera, like the excessive use of stage machinery and the interpolation of comic elements into tragedies. Nevertheless, his characters remained artificial and the dramatic process was repeatedly interrupted by virtuoso arias. It was against this kind of opera that the GLUCK reform reacted.

E. S. Di Felice, *Metastasio: ideologia, drammaturgia, spettacolo* (Milano: F. Angeli, 1983).
M. T. Muraro, *Metastasio e il mondo musicale* (Firenze: Olschki, 1986).
D. Neville, 'Metastasio, Pietro' in S. Sadie (ed.), *The New Grove Dictionary of Opera* (London: Macmillan, 1992).

FRITZ WEBER

Methodism Originally a term of abuse applied to the so-called 'Holy Club' in Oxford, 'Methodism' came to be used as a generic term for the system of religious faith and practice promoted by the Wesleys and later that of George Whitefield (1714–70) and other evangelical leaders in the British Isles and North America. It began as a religious movement within the established church and was usually characterized by evangelical Arminian theology (although Calvinistic Methodism, as preached by Whitefield, was strong in Wales), itinerant preaching, a cell structure, and a disciplined commitment to holy living and social duty. Its distinctive beliefs and practices inevitably led to tensions within the Church of England and to a *de facto* separation in 1795.

In the 1780s Wesley had already taken steps to secure the future of American and Scottish Methodism and seems to have envisaged an itinerant episcopal oversight for Methodists in the English-speaking world. By the end of the century the world-wide membership of Methodist societies approached a quarter of a million, and many more came within the sphere of Methodist influence. Much of the historical debate surrounding Methodism has focused on the complex task of explaining the origins of the evangelical revival and on relating Methodist growth to contemporaneous changes in the economic and social structure.

R. Davies and G. Rupp (eds), *A History of the Methodist Church in Great Britain*, vol. 1 (London: Epworth, 1965).

DAVID HEMPTON

Methuen Treaty (27 December 1703) The Methuen Treaty was a three-clause commercial treaty named after its two negotiators, John Methuen (1650–1706), ambassador extraordinary to Portugal, and his son Paul Methuen (1672–1757), who had been envoy to Portugal since 1697. It is to be distinguished from two political treaties with Portugal that preceded it in May, which deprived France of its Portuguese ally in the War of the Spanish Succession. When it had been set up in September 1701, the Grand Alliance against France had not been committed to unseating the French-born Philip V from the Spanish throne. Now, at Portugal's insistence, the Grand Alliance's objectives were widened to include the deposition of Philip V in favour of the archduke Charles of Austria, titular Charles III of Spain and, after 1710, the emperor Charles VI. The British had considerable property in Portugal, but the opening of Portuguese ports to Britain would now facilitate British operations in the Mediterranean against France. Portugal's own concern for relations with Britain, and Portuguese military needs, explain its agreement to import British textiles exclusively, to the detriment of its own textile industry. But, since Portugal was fully aware of British hopes of future commercial gains from Spain, the Portuguese government reciprocally prescribed that its wine exports to Britain pay a third less duty than French wines imported by Britain.

A. D. Francis, *The Methuens and Portugal* (Cambridge: Cambridge University Press, 1966).

D. D. ALDRIDGE

Metternich, Prince **Clemens Lothar Wenzel** (1773–1859) Austrian statesman. Born into a family of imperial counts which had long provided servants for the Habsburgs and other German dynasties, he rose quickly in the Austrian diplomatic service, becoming foreign minister in 1809. He strongly influenced the young emperor FRANCIS II. In his early years he followed enlightened ideas but his experience of the effects of the French Revolution, while studying at Strasburg and Mainz, coloured his views for the rest of his life. His methods and concepts were rooted in the eighteenth century and he was unable to progress intellectually beyond ENLIGHTENED ABSOLUTISM. He had a mechanistic view of international relations and saw himself as the great physician whose ministrations were vital to the health of the Austrian state and of Europe as a whole. He believed that a powerful Austria was essential for the stability of the continent. He was the dominant European statesman of the early nineteenth century and his name became a byword for rigid conservatism. In recent years this traditional negative image has been revised and some historians now see him as a pioneer of European integration.

A. Palmer, *Metternich* (London: Weidenfeld & Nicolson, 1972).

MICHAEL HUGHES

Mexico   Alexander von Humboldt (1769–1859), who visited Mexico in 1803, described a great empire stretching northwards from Guatemala to Texas and California which supported a rapidly growing population of over 5 million. Mexico City, with a population of 130,000, was the greatest city in the Americas, distinguished by a majestic cathedral, many baroque churches and convents, and palaces of the nobility. The new Academy of San Carlos promoted the neoclassical style in art and architecture, and the Mining College educated future managers in metallurgy and mineralogy. The colony's prosperity derived from the SILVER boom: production rose from 5 million pesos in 1700 to 22 million pesos by the 1790s. Humboldt visited the Valenciana mine at Guanajuato, which employed over 3,000 workers and had invested 2 million pesos in shafts 600 yards deep. The boom, which created a new class of millionaires, allowed the Spanish crown to remit revenue to the Caribbean and to fund the maintenance of a regular army of 10,000 men in Mexico, and gave rise to a dramatic increase in transatlantic trade.

However, the export boom did not alleviate the gross inequality of income and status among the population. The rural masses lived close to the margins of subsistence, and during the eighteenth century thousands died from the periodic onslaughts of epidemic disease (plague and smallpox) and famine caused by harvest failure. The population was sharply divided into ethnic castes, each distinguished by differing fiscal obligations and legal rights. Although most Indian villages preserved communal lands, population increase exerted pressure on

resources. In central and northern Mexico the countryside was dominated by haciendas, great estates which at times controlled entire districts. The latifundia housed resident peons, impoverished tenants and
squatters, and often recruited seasonal labour from an assortment of
mestizos, mulattos, poor Spaniards and acculturated Indians.

When Charles III expelled the Jesuits in 1767, over 500 Mexican
priests were exiled to Italy. The popular riots that this measure provoked were repressed with great harshness. The Spanish crown exacted
a heavy fiscal tribute from Mexico, through the new tobacco monopoly and increased excise duties, and the greater yield from taxes on
silver production and overseas trade. By the 1790s remittances
amounted to over 10 million pesos a year. The creole elite, Spaniards
born in Mexico, bitterly resented these measures, especially when the
Bourbon revolution in government was enforced by officials and soldiers
drafted in from Spain. The clergy were alienated by the amortization
of church property and landowners by annuities charged on haciendas. This resentment, coupled with news of the American and French
Revolutions, impelled the creoles to seize the opportunity presented by
the French invasion of Spain in 1808 to launch an insurrection against
colonial rule.

See also SPANISH AMERICA.

D. A. Brading, *Miners and Merchants in Bourbon Mexico 1763–1810*
   (Cambridge: Cambridge University Press, 1971).
Alexander von Humboldt, *Political Essay on the Kingdom of New Spain*, trans.
   J. Black, 4 vols (London: Longman, Hurst, Rees, Orme & Brown, 1811).

                                                           D. A. BRADING

Middle Ages   The Enlightenment tended to think of history as divided between the ancients and the moderns while, at best, neglecting
the period in between. More often than not the Middle Ages were
described in the most contemptible of terms. Condorcet spoke of it as
a 'disastrous era', and the author of 'Histoire' in the *Encyclopédie*
asserted that after the fall of the Roman Empire 'a new order of things
began, and that is what is called the history of the Middle Ages; a
barbaric history of barbaric people, made none the better for becoming Christians'. Vico considered the words 'vassal' and 'fief' to be
barbarous, and repeatedly praised learned feudalists for replacing them
'with Latin elegance and propriety' by substituting 'clientes' and
'clientelae'.

The eighteenth century also witnessed some very important scholarship on, and reassessment of, the Middle Ages. The author of
Antiquitates italiae medii aevi (1732–42), Ludovico Muratori, for one,
proved an 'incomparable guide' through the Dark Ages for Edward

Gibbon. Scottish historians and political theorists, including William Robertson and Adam Smith, took a great interest in the origins of feudal law and government. In France the battle between the advocates of the *thèse nobiliaire*, who argued for a restoration of aristocratic power and mixed government, and the defenders of the *thèse royale*, who upheld absolutism, kindled scholarly debate about the precise nature of the relationship between the first French kings and the nobility as well as the character of the transition between Roman and feudal forms of rule.

J. Q. C. Mackrell, *The Attack upon 'Feudalism' in Eighteenth-Century France* (London: 1973).
Arnaldo Momigliano, 'Gibbon from an Italian Point of View', in G. W. Bowersock, John Clive and Stephen R. Graubard (eds), *Edward Gibbon and the Decline and Fall of the Roman Empire* (Cambridge, Mass.: Harvard University Press, 1977).

SYLVANA TOMASELLI

millenarianism The expectation of a second coming of Christ and his reign on earth for a thousand years, or millenarianism, was inspired mainly though not exclusively by the book of Revelation. Millennialists usually belonged to one of two broad categories: premillennialists, who believed that the millennium would follow the second coming; and postmillennialists, who, more optimistically, predicted that it would predate the second coming and were convinced that human affairs were already moving in that direction. The millenarian dimension to Newtonian thought has been recognized by recent scholarship. In the eighteenth century, social and political upheavals, with their apparent confirmation of prophetic writings, were a powerful stimulus to apocalyptic ideas. A millenarian element existed among some German Pietists and groups of exiled Huguenot communities (*see* HUGUENOTS, PIETISM), while the War of American Independence and, more emphatically, the French Revolution and the temporary overthrow of the papacy seemed in some quarters to herald the fall of antichrist. In Britain millenarian ideas stimulated such popular cults as the Irvingites and the followers of the self-styled prophet Joanna Southcott (1750–1814).

Clarke Garrett, *Respectable Folly: Millenarians and the French Revolution in France and England* (Baltimore: Johns Hopkins University Press, 1975).

G. M. DITCHFIELD

mind and body, relationship between Following René Descartes (1596–1650), many eighteenth-century thinkers believed that man consisted of two distinct substances: an immaterial mind or thinking substance, and a material extended body. Descartes himself held that these two substances were combined in a 'substantial union' which was evident through our sense experiences or our passions, but he did not explain the precise nature of this union.

Three metaphysical theories regarding the relationship between mind and body were commonly cited in the eighteenth century: the 'occasionalist' theory of Cartesians like MALEBRANCHE; the 'pre-established harmony' theory of LEIBNIZ; and the theory of physical influence, commonly ascribed to LOCKE. According to the occasionalists, there could be no causal relationship between two distinct finite substances; rather God, the only genuine power in the universe, would cause a change in ideas when there was a physical change in the relevant part of the brain. Similarly, when a certain action was willed, God would bring about appropriate changes in the body. Leibniz, who also held that there could be no real interaction between independent substances, maintained that the soul was created to represent the changes that occurred in the material body. The sequence of perceptions and desires that occurred in the soul followed each other according to an order that had been established by God when it was created. Thus, there was a pre-established harmony between events in the soul and the body. Finally, the theory of physical influence maintained that there was a causal influence of the body on the mind. This theory was commonly thought to reduce to materialism.

Eighteenth-century physicians were concerned with a more practical problem, namely the influence of the mind on the life processes of the body. BOERHAAVE defined the mind as a thinking conscious substance and denied that it had any influence on life processes such as digestion and the beating of the heart. These occurred completely automatically, through mechanical causes. But other influential thinkers like STAHL argued that the rational mind constantly acted unconsciously in the body, fighting off disease and maintaining a healthy state. The dispute between the Stahlians and those who believed that the body was a self-maintaining physical automaton raged throughout the eighteenth century. The Scottish physiologist Robert Whytt (1714–66) sought a compromise between these views: while he agreed, with Stahl that the mind was involved in the vital motions of the body, he denied that its actions were voluntary; and he argued against Boerhaave that these motions arose from the sensibility of the vital parts rather than from their mechanisms.

Physicians generally agreed that the passions and imagination could cause bodily illness, and many disputed the Cartesian view that these faculties could operate purely mechanically. Passions like grief were thought to cause serious bodily illness.

See also MATERIALISM.

J. Wright, 'Metaphysics and Physiology', in M. Stewart (ed.), *Studies in the Philosophy of the Scottish Enlightenment* (Oxford: Clarendon, 1990), pp. 251–301.

J. Yolton, *Locke and French Materialism* (Oxford: Clarendon, 1991).

JOHN P. WRIGHT

mining The extraction of minerals from the ground was pursued almost world-wide. It furnished everything from the medium of international exchange (gold and silver) to the materials for tools, machines and warfare (primarily iron). Mineral deposits were generally found through chance, where a vein outcropped on the surface, and faith in folklore 'symptoms' persisted. Geological science in the eighteenth century was too rudimentary to help, but test-boring increasingly assisted prospectors. Consequently, profitability was hard to predict; there were spectacular successes but also frequent disappointments. Most mines were open-cast or driven horizontally into the hillside: few were very deep, although this was changing.

Different techniques were used to mine metallic ores and COAL. The technology for the former was most advanced in central Europe, where gunpowder for boring shafts, fire-setting to break hard rock and numerous drainage devices were pioneered. Transferred to America, underground blasting and powerful whims for drainage and ore-raising facilitated Mexico's emergence as the world's chief producer of SILVER, and gave rise to a century-long (and final) boom at the heart of Spain's imperial revival in North America and the Caribbean.

Coal seams ran horizontally, requiring underground haulage. There was also the danger of poisonous and explosive gases in coal-mining, which necessitated a more cautious technique. This was developed principally in Britain. Several European governments opened mining schools to train their engineers and publish instructional literature but in Britain, as in America, technologists continued to acquire their expertise down the mine.

Charles Singer et al. (eds), *A History of Technology*, vol. 4 (Oxford: Clarendon, 1958).

CHRISTINE MACLEOD

Mirabeau, Honoré Gabriel Riqueti, comte de (1749–1791) French revolutionary politician and orator. The son of a prominent Provençal noble and physiocrat, Victor Riqueti Mirabeau, he spent the first forty years of his life producing unremarkable writing on a wide range of subjects, and in loose living which twice earned him imprisonment under LETTRES DE CACHET.

Although he was a noble, he was elected to the Third Estate for Aix in 1789. During the sessions of the Estates General he emerged as a leading spokesman for the rights of the new National Assembly against royal opposition. His ambition unsettled many deputies and it was partly due to this that the decree of 9 November 1789, which forbade deputies to be ministers, was passed so easily. During the debates on the new constitution he supported a strong executive, the crown, and influenced the vote in favour of the king's suspensive veto. In May 1790 he became a secret adviser to the court on political matters in return for the payment of his extensive debts and a monthly stipend. The result was a series of fifty 'Notes' to the king, in which he tried, initially, to persuade the latter to work with the constitution, believing that its reforms would strengthen rather than weaken the power of the monarchy. The later notes were more pessimistic, however, advising the king to undermine the assembly and quit Paris for a provincial centre. These facts did not emerge until 1792, and outwardly Mirabeau continued to seek the support of Lafayette and other liberal nobles, but to no avail. He died on 2 April 1792, still a popular hero, and was the first person to be buried in the Panthéon.

F. Furet, 'Mirabeau', in F. Furet and M. Ozouf (eds), *A Critical Dictionary of the French Revolution* (Cambridge, Mass.: Harvard University Press, 1989), pp. 265–72.

J. M. Thompson, 'Mirabeau', in *Leaders of the French Revolution* (Oxford: Blackwell, 1929), pp. 17–40.

MICHAEL BROERS

Mirabeau, Victor Riqueti, marquis de (1715–1789) French economist. Born to a newly ennobled Provençal family, he was the father of the revolutionary politician Honoré Mirabeau. After a youth spent in the army, he became a prolific if unoriginal writer on political economy. He emerged as one of the most devoted followers of QUESNAY, the leading figure among the physiocrats, with whom he collaborated on the influential essay *La Philosophie rurale* (Rural Philosophy). In common with other physiocrats like Turgot and Gournay (1712–59), he saw agriculture as the only true source of economic wealth. His dogmatic attachment to this idea reached its height in his *Théorie de l'impôt*, where he argued that the non-agricultural sectors of the economy were almost outside the political nation. He was a poor stylist, despite the clarity of his views, and his contemporary reputation as the friend of the people rested on his belief in the primacy of public opinion in political life – 'la regina del mundo' as he called it – and of property over privilege in public life, as expressed in his *L'Ami des hommes*. These views earned him rustication to remote Provençal villages and it was during one such spell that his son was born. His last years are best remembered for his quarrels with his son, and his use of LETTRES DE CACHET against him, but his contemporary reputation was a favourable one among enlightened opinion in Provence as the elections to the Estates General approached. He died in 1789, at the dawn of his son's rise to prominence.

K. M. Baker, 'Representation', in *The French Revolution and the Creation of Modern Political Culture*, vol. 1: *The Political Culture of the Old Regime*, ed. K. M. Baker (Oxford: Pergamon, 1987).

E. Fox-Genovese, *The Origins of Physiocracy: Economic Revolution and Social Order in Eighteenth Century France* (Ithaca, NY: Cornell University Press, 1976).

P. Gay, *The Enlightenment: An Interpretation*, vol. 2: *The Science of Freedom* (London: Weidenfeld & Nicolson, 1979).

MICHAEL BROERS

missionaries   The eighteenth century saw the decay of Roman Catholic missions and the beginning of Protestant ones. Catholic activity was complicated by the papal division of the Catholic world mission between Spain and Portugal, by the Portuguese *padroado* (royal patronage) over the church in much of Africa and Asia and by the Jesuit strategy of accommodation to native cultures, originally endorsed by Rome. Catholic missions in India, begun in the seventeenth-century, were sustained by the Venetian Costanzo Giuseppe Beschi (1680–1747), who wrote a celebrated Tamil epic in honour of St Joseph and created the study of Tamil grammar. The Vietnamese mission set up by Alexander de Rhodes (1591–1660) through lay catechists was maintained by the French Society of Foreign Missions. In China, despite anti-Christian imperial edicts, the Jesuit presence survived the society's dissolution. The Catholic mission in Ceylon, suppressed by the Dutch, was revived, despite persecution, by the 'apostle of Ceylon', the Venerable Joseph Vaz (1651–1711). The evangelization of the Philippines and of South and Central America continued, and the eighteenth century was also the principal era of the missions to the Indians of California. But nothing permanent was achieved by the Portuguese Capuchin and Jesuit missions in Angola and Mozambique, and cultural accommodation was rejected by Cardinal Charles-Thomas Maillard de Tournon (1668–1710), papal legate *a latere* to India and China, and by Benedict XIV's bulls of 1742 ('Ex quo singulari') and of 1744 ('Omnium sollicitudinum'), confirming Tournon's measures against conformity with ancestor-veneration in China and Brahminism in India. A bishop and priests in China were martyred after 1747 and some died in prison after arrest in 1784.

The crisis of the Catholic missions, however, came with the dissolution of the Society of Jesus (*see* JESUITS) between 1759 and 1773, resulting in the severe depletion of the Indian clergy, and in 1767 in the destruction of the Indian Reductions in Paraguay. The military assistance secured by Pierre-Joseph Pigneaux, vicar apostolic in Cochin China to the emperor pretender Nguyen-an, confirmed the prosperity of the Vietnamese Catholic Church, but the French Revolution completed the eclipse of the Catholic mission, with the near-destruction of the great French missionary orders St Vincent de Paul's Lazarists, the Society of Foreign Missions and the Fathers of the Holy Ghost. (*See also* CATHOLICISM.)

The Protestant missions were late starters to the Catholic ones. The chief Anglican missionary agency, the Society for the Propagation of the Gospel in Foreign Parts (1701), was largely confined to ministering to the needs of English colonists in North America and the Caribbean, while the English East India Company employed chaplains but frowned on missionary activity. When Frederick IV (1671–1730) of Denmark sought missionaries for his Indian possession of Tranquebar he turned to the German Lutheran Pietists of Halle, whose missioner Bartholomäus Ziegenbalg (1683–1719) translated the New Testament into Tamil in 1714. Following Ziegenbalg, Protestant missionaries stressed the need for vernacular Scriptures and an educational system to enable converts to read them. The mission's work was taken over by the Anglican Society for Promoting Christian Knowledge, still using German missionaries. Larger-scale Protestant enterprise began with the organization, in 1722, of Moravian refugees at Herrnhut in Saxony by the Pietist ZINZENDORF who perpetuated the mission of the Danish Hans Egede (1686–1758) to the Greenlanders, begun in 1722, and established missions in the West Indies, Dutch Guiana and the American colonies. (*See* MORAVIANS.) The flowering of Protestant missionary activity, however, came out of the evangelical revival only at the end of the century, with the establishment in 1792 of the Baptist Missionary Society by the Northamptonshire cobbler William Carey (1761–1834), followed in 1795 by the non-denominational London Missionary Society, which later became Congregationalist, and in 1799 by the Anglican Evangelical Church Missionary Society. The glory of these societies was to come during the era of European expansion in the nineteenth century.

Some missions, like the Norwegian and the Scots, evangelized pagans or semi-Christians on the periphery of Europe. From 1702 Filofey Leschinski, Orthodox bishop of Tobolsk, laboured to convert the Ostiaks, Voguls and Yakuts of western Siberia, assisted by Peter the Great's exemption of converts from taxation. Other eighteenth-century Russian missions evangelized the Kalmucks of the steppes, the Chuvashes, Tchermisses and Ostiaks of the Middle Volga, the Tungus people of Dauria in eastern Siberia, and the natives of the Kamchatka peninsula and the Aleutian Islands. They also confirmed Russian influence over an ever-growing proportion of the earth.

S. Delacroix (ed.), *Histoire universelle des missions Catholiques* (Paris: Grund, 1956).

K. S. Latourette, *A History of the Expansion of Christianity* (London: Harper, 1937–45).

Stephen Neill, *A History of Christian Missions* (Harmondsworth: Penguin, 1974).

SHERIDAN GILLEY

Moderns *see* ANCIENTS AND MODERNS.

Mollwitz, Battle of (10 April 1741)   The Battle of Mollwitz was the baptism of fire of the young Prussian king FREDERICK II, who on 16 December 1740 had invaded the rich Austrian province of SILESIA. Early in April 1741 an Austrian army of 19,000 advanced on the Prussian army of around 22,000, still in its winter quarters. Frederick met the enemy outside Mollwitz (Matujowice), south-east of Breslau (Wroctaw). He marched his army in line of battle from noon, and finally engaged the enemy, head-on, at 1.30 p.m.: directly contrary to his usual idea of an oblique approach in columns. In the confused order of battle, the Prussian cavalry staggered at first under the weight of the experienced Austrian horse – around 8,000 to Prussia's 4,500 – and morale collapsed. At 4 p.m. Field Marshal von Schwerin (1684–1757) urged Frederick to leave the field, on his fast horse, the 'Mollwitz Grey', which was promptly given privileged retirement. The fortunes of battle turned, however. Schwerin brought order into the cavalry, pushed forward with the infantry and drove the Austrians back from Mollwitz. Prussian casualties were around 4,800 to Austria's 4,500, but the day was won.

C. Duffy, *Frederick the Great: A Military Life* (London: Routledge, 1985).

PHILIP WOODFINE

monarchy   One of three main forms of rule in the eighteenth century, monarchy was arguably the most dynamic. Even the arch-critic Rousseau conceded that 'no kind of constitution can be imagined in which a less amount of effort produces a more considerable amount of action' (*Du contrat social*, 1762). Large areas of the world were governed by a central dynasty exacting obedience or co-operation from regional lords. Notable examples were Manchu China, Tokugawa Japan, the Ottoman Empire, Mughal India, the Habsburg Empire and Russia. Empires found it difficult to introduce rapid change, and dangerous to do so. Their strength lay in the appeal to tradition and continuity. Republics, which were advocated by Rousseau, were mostly small and oligarchical. The United Provinces, still wealthy but torn by rivalries, was a second-class power. The once-great naval power, the republic of Venice, where Rousseau first conceived his writing on politics, was a symbol of decay. Geneva, like Venice ruled by a handful of wealthy families, was riven by constitutional disturbances. The only successful large republic was the United States of America after 1776, with stable but conservative and decentralized rule by the propertied. The French republic set up after 1789 disintegrated into terror and absolutism. (*See* REPUBLICANISM.)

Monarchy was the norm for middle-sized states, and for most small ones as well. The authority of European monarchs, greatly increased by their overseas possessions, was often used to inititate reform and change. In Spain, although reforms in the administration, tax and agricultural systems had been proposed since 1646, it was only with the accession of Charles III that a distinct trend of reform began. In Germany, cameralist reforming thought was promoted in the universities and courts, but ideas alone were not enough. The character of the numerous princely rulers made a crucial difference to how quickly and completely reforms penetrated the ranks of bureaucrats and nobles. Where a monarch was influenced by enlightened thought, policies could change in ways uncalled for, perhaps not understood by, the mass of the population (*see* ENLIGHTENED ABSOLUTISM). For this reason, *philosophes* tended to overlook the shortcomings of monarchs like Frederick II and to praise their aspirations. Even a regent such as Crown Prince Frederik, after 1784 the effective ruler of Denmark, could initiate wide-ranging change.

In all societies, monarchy could be constrained by elite factions. British and Swedish monarchs were constitutionally limited by a powerful noble class, while in eastern Europe nobles frustrated serfdom reforms. In West Africa kingship in Oyo and Benin was significantly limited by the claims of descent groups. Dahomey, by contrast, was a kingdom set up by conquest, in which rights and obligations came from the king rather than from birth and family relationships. In Europe Prussia came closest to this pattern, and was also the most complete example of a state transformed by the dynamic agency of monarchy. (*See* ARISTOCRACY.)

See also ABSOLUTISM.

J. M. Black, *Eighteenth Century Europe 1700–1789* (London: Macmillan, 1990).

H. M. Scott (ed.), *Enlightened Absolutism: Reforms and Reformers in Late Eighteenth-Century Europe* (London: Macmillan, 1990).

PHILIP WOODFINE

monasteries Monastic life disappeared during the sixteenth century in Reformed churches, but remained a fundamental and flourishing part of Orthodox and Catholic life and practice. During the eighteenth

century many monasteries continued to attract large numbers of adherents and several were lavishly rebuilt according to the baroque and roccoco tastes of the age. Some of the older orders were refounded and new orders were established. In 1731 Alphonso Liguori (1696–1787) set up a new congregation of nuns, and the Passionists, founded by St Paul of the Cross (1694–1775), received canonical approval. The religious orders, which were responsible for much of the pastoral and social work of the church, engaged in education and poor relief. But monasticism received increasing criticism not only from anticlerical thinkers (*see* ANTICLERICALISM) and those concerned to limit the power of the papacy, but also from within the church, for being centres of perverse practices and a drain on the economy of the church. The great wealth of many monasteries, which were often leading landowners, attracted the attention of hard-pressed rulers and many were suppressed to provide funds for state programmes and educational development. Joseph II suppressed 738 monasteries in the Austrian Netherlands in the 1780s, to fund other areas of church life. This seemed to constitute such an attack on the church that Pope Pius VI went to Vienna in the hope of restraining the emperor, but to no avail. Monasteries were suppressed in Russia after the general secularization of 1764, and in France the contemplative orders were abolished in 1789, resulting in the closure of 400 monasteries and the disappearance of orders such as the Servites and the Brigittines from France.
See also CATHOLICISM.

J. Derek Holmes and Bernard W. Bickers, *A Short History of the Catholic Church* (Tunbridge Wells: Burns & Oates, 1983).

JEREMY GREGORY

Monge, Gaspard (1746–1818) French mathematician, chemist, metallurgist and republican senator. He began his teaching career in 1765 at the Royal Corps of Engineers, succeeding Nollet (1700–70) as instructor of experimental physics in 1770. His major contribution to mathematics lay in the fields of descriptive and infinitesimal geometry, and of partial differential equations. He helped to found the École Polytechnique in 1794. In chemistry his greatest achievement was the synthesis of water, independently of LAVOISIER, in 1783, and in 1784 he achieved, with Clouet (1751–1801), the first liquefaction of a gas.

He played a considerable political role in the aftermath of the revolution. From being minister of the navy he proceeded to work for the committee on arms, and the commissions on weights and measures and on the arts. In 1796 he was one of six men commissioned to select the war trophies that France would claim from Italy. There followed three years of such work for Napoleon, to whom he was a loyal friend, for which he was rewarded by being made a life senator. As other honours and duties came his way his scientific output diminished. Soon after Napoleon abdicated, he fled France. When he returned in 1816 he was expelled from the Institut de France.

Paul V. Aubry, *Monge, Le Savant Ami de Napoléon Bonaparte 1746–1818* (Paris: Gauthier-Villars, 1954).

M. L. BENJAMIN

Montagnards   The volatile nature of French revolutionary politics was such that terminology varied and political groupings were not rigid. It is therefore appropriate that the Montagnards derived their name from where they sat, first in the Legislative Assembly and later in the Convention. These left-wing deputies sat on benches that were high up on the left side of the hall. They were united by their opposition to the Girondins in the Convention and by their use of the Paris Jacobin Club as a centre for organization. The radical policies of the Montagnards were very influential from late 1792 and dominated the period from the purge of the Girondins on 2 June 1793 to the fall of Robespierre on 27–28 July 1794. Proclaiming the rule of the people, they had little time for their views. The Montagnards (or Mountain) dominated the COMMITTEE OF GENERAL SECURITY, a revolutionary agency for surveillance established on 2 October 1792, and were responsible for the creation of the Revolutionary Tribunal in Paris on 10 March 1793.

JEREMY BLACK

Montagu [née Pierrepont], Lady **Mary Wortley** (1689–1762)   English essayist, poet and letter writer. She was equally at home among the aristocracy and the literati, in England and abroad. In 1712 she secretly married Edward Wortley (*d* 1761), a Whig member of parliament and courtier, and accompanied him when he went to Constantinople as ambassador in 1716. There she wrote her *Embassy Letters* (1763). She returned to London in 1718 after bearing her second child whom she bravely and famously submitted to the new smallpox inoculation.

Self-taught in Latin, she moved easily among the London wits Addison, Arbuthnot (1667–1735), Pope and Gay, who were more enamoured of her than she of them. POPE's infatuation with her seems to have soured with rejection, however, and he published a number of spiteful attacks on her. Though some of her poems were pirated, she preferred to publish anonymously, including a nine-issue periodical *The Nonsense of Common-Sense* in 1737–8. A passion for the Italian dandy Francesco ALGAROTTI inspired her move to the Continent in 1739 where she remained for over twenty years, estranged from her husband even after her ardour had cooled. She is renowned for her letters home to her daughter, Lady Bute (1718–94).

The Complete Letters of Lady Mary Wortley Montagu, ed. Robert Halsband, 3 vols (Oxford: Clarendon, 1965).

M. L. BENJAMIN

Montesquieu, Charles de Secondat, baron de la Brède et de (1689–1755) French philosopher and jurist. President of the *parlement* of Bordeaux from 1727, a member of the Academy of Bordeaux from 1716 and of the Académie Française from 1728, he was to exercise a great influence on the Enlightenment.

In his *Lettres persanes* (1721), which made him famous overnight, he commented on political events, social, economic and religious issues, and the mores of his age from the perspective of imaginary visiting Persians. *L'Esprit des lois* (1748), which David Hume described as 'the best system of political knowledge that, perhaps, has ever yet been communicated to the world', endorsed the notion of NATURAL LAW and sought to show the causal relations between the spirit of a people, its culture, mores, economy, geographical location, religion and its form of government and laws. It also presented an account of French history which demonstrated that a moderate monarchy, in which the nobility balanced the power of the crown and that of the people, was best suited to the French nation. A great admirer of what he took to be the English constitution, he was an eloquent advocate of the separation of powers, religious toleration and liberty.

His work was acclaimed throughout Europe and was praised even in official circles, but it incurred the hostility of ecclesiastical authorities. Montesquieu responded to the mutually contradictory claims that he was a Spinozian and a deist in a skilful and elegant *Défense de l'Esprit des lois*. The work was placed on the Index in 1751.

Robert Shackleton, *Montesquieu: A Critical Biography* (Oxford: Oxford University Press, 1961).

SYLVANA TOMASELLI

Montreal The city of Montreal took its name from a mountain on the Isle of Montreal which forms the heart of the city today. This island is the largest and most important of the Hochelaga archipelago, which lies at the confluence of the Ottawa and St Lawrence rivers. First settlement took place in 1542, but development of the site proved slow and haphazard at first owing to native hostility and indifference on the part of the French government. After the signing of the 1701 treaty with the Iroquois, however, the situation improved considerably. The fur trade to Europe sparked development of the city's natural advantages of good harbours and access to the interior. Montreal merchants came to control a vast interior network, stretching from the

Gulf of Mexico to the Great Lakes. This pattern of economic growth had enlarged the population to 5,000 by the time of British conquest in 1760. Under the new regime the traditional trade in furs continued, enhanced by the growth of Montreal as the port of entry for new immigrants, and by the development of farming. By 1820 Montreal's population of mixed French and British descent had reached 20,000, within which certain Scottish families formed the city's mercantile elite.

See also CANADA.

PHILIP LAWSON

Moravians   The Moravian Brethren, or *Unitas Fratrum*, were a pre-Reformation religious community that had been rooted out of its old heartlands in Bohemia and Moravia by the Thirty Years War and by the repressive measures of the Counter-Reformation. The revived movement took shape among religious refugees on the Berthelsdorf estate of ZINZENDORF in lower Saxony. The resultant village settlement at Herrnhut became a focal point of religious disputes between Lutherans and separatists, a centre of popular revivalism and ultimately a model community which was reproduced in settlements from the Wetterau to the American colonies.

The eighteenth-century Moravian diaspora is one of the most complex and intriguing stories in the history of popular Protestantism. By the end of the 1730s there were Moravian missions in the West Indies, Greenland, North and South America and South Africa. Part ancient church, part revivalistic sect and part interconfessional movement, Moravianism played a pivotal role in the Great Awakening of the eighteenth century, in spite of its small numbers.

W. R. Ward, 'The Renewed Unity of the Brethren: Ancient Church, New Sect or Interconfessional Movement', *Bulletin of the John Rylands University Library of Manchester*, 70/3 (1988), 77–92.

DAVID HEMPTON

Morellet, André (1727–1819)   French man of letters. He contributed to the *Encyclopédie*, mostly on theological subjects, and translated Beccaria's *Dei delitti e delle pene* into French. A member of the Académie Française, he collaborated on its *Dictionnaire* and was to save the work from destruction during the revolution. The sharpness of his tongue led Voltaire to call him 'mords-les' (bite them). He was well acquainted with the leading *philosophes*, and was as ready to attack as to defend his friends in print. He retaliated against Charles Palissot's (1730–1814) satire on the *philosophes* with an anonymous pamphlet, *Le Vision de Charles Palissot*, written in mock-scriptural style, which led to his imprisonment in the Bastille for eight weeks in

1760. He also undertook a refutation of the abbé Galiani's *Dialogues* at the request of Trudaine de Montigny (1703–69), head of commerce, for whom he had composed a critical *Mémoire sur la situation actuelle de la Compagnie des Indes* (1769), of which Jacques Necker was a syndic. The *Réfutation*, which was not allowed to be published until 1774 although it was widely circulated before then, highlighted the differences among the *philosophes* on economic matters.

Steven L. Kaplan, *Bread, Politics and Political Economy in the Reign of Louis XV* (The Hague: Martinus Nijhoff, 1976).

SYLVANA TOMASELLI

Morelly, abbé (?1715–1778)   French theoretician and novelist. Little is known about the life of the author of what Franco Venturi called 'the most important communist book of the eighteenth century', *Le Code de la nature, ou Le Véritable Esprit de ses lois* (1755). Claiming that societies throughout the world were prey to only one vice, avarice, it argued that the abolition of property, not its redistribution, would put an end to all social ills. Published anonymously, the work was persistently attributed to Diderot despite the latter's disclaimers. It was by no means unique in its radicalism or its utopian ideas, but its availability in print and its attribution to Diderot help to explain why Morelly proved more influential than other utopians of the period. *Le Code* inspired men such as Babeuf and Pierre-Joseph Proudhon (1809–65). In addition, Morelly wrote two works on education, *Essai sur l'esprit humain* (1743), *Essai sur le coeur humain* (1745); a dialogue concerning aesthetics, *Physique de la beauté* (1748); a critique of Montesquieu, *Le Prince* (1751); a critique of civilization in the form of an epic poem, *Naufrage des isles flottantes, ou La Basiliade* (1753) and a mythological poem, *L'Hymen vengé* (1778). He also edited *Lettres de Louis XIV* (1755).

Richard N. Coe, *Morelly: Ein Rationalist auf dem Wege zum Sozialismus* (Berlin: Rütten & Loening, 1961).

SYLVANA TOMASELLI

Morocco *see* BARBARY STATES.

mortality crises   Historical demographers define mortality crises as periods in which the death rate is suddenly and markedly higher than the norm, although they do not agree on the magnitude at which it constitutes a crisis. Formerly, FAMINE was identified as the key to crisis, while recent scholars have focused on waves of epidemic disease.

Eighteenth-century Europe saw the end of a demographic regime in which mortality crises were common, although there was unusually high mortality in the late 1720s, early and late 1740s and early 1770s. Crises caused by military action ceased with the seventeenth century. Subsistence crises – those in which deaths were caused by absolute want of food – became less common after the 1690s, due to improved transport and trade, welfare systems and better crop mixes. PLAGUE became less of a threat after 1720. SMALLPOX and other epidemic killers, with the exception of TYPHUS, tended to become endemic, reducing their potential for crisis. Although population growth rates changed little before 1780, patterns of mortality had shifted towards endemic disease and old age.

M. W. Flinn, *The European Demographic System 1500–1800* (Brighton: Harvester, 1981).

MARY E. FISSELL

Moscow   The capital of RUSSIA until 1712 and again from 1918, Moscow became the second city with the rise of ST PETERSBURG. Although the court again resided there in 1728–32 and the Kremlin Cathedral of the Dormition continued to be used for coronations, it fell into decline until PETER III's 1762 manifesto freed the nobles from obligatory state service, encouraging many to return. It remained a major centre of commerce, industry (textiles), education (Moscow University, founded in 1755) and intellectual life. City plans drawn up in 1739 and 1755 led to some rationalization, and there was major rebuilding after the great fire of 1812. A number of leading architects devoted their careers to Moscow, notably Matvei Kazakov (1738–1812), who inaugurated a golden age of classical architecture which lasted up to the mid nineteenth century. Moscow remained Russia's biggest city for much of the century, despite the plague of 1771, which killed over one-third of the population of city and province. It numbered about 200,000 in 1785, and perhaps 300,000 by 1800, although there were seasonal variations. Moscow was regarded as more Russian, less Westernized, than St Petersburg, with more merchants and OLD BELIEVERS and fewer foreign residents.

Kathleen Berton, *Moscow: An Architectural History*, second edn (London: Studio Vista, 1990).

LINDSEY HUGHES

Möser, Justus (1720–1794)   German legal and historical writer. A high-ranking lawyer, he was the senior administrator in Osnabrück. He edited *A Moral Weekly* from 1746 and contributed to *The German Spectator* (1748). The preface to his *Osnabrückische Geschichte* (History of Osnabrück, 1768) was included by Herder in his manifesto of the STURM UND DRANG, *Von deutscher Art und Kunst* (Of German

Character and Art). Exploring Tacitus's image of the Germans, he utilized his knowledge of the past to apprehend and improve modern culture and customs. His major work, *Patriotischen Phantasien* (Patriotic Phantasies, 4 vols, 1774–86), is a collection of almost 300 essays on virtually every aspect of society – social, economic and historical. He wisely and humorously affirmed the unique historical particularity of social circumstances and the validity of every social class, aiming to achieve change through overall political consensus.

W. F. Sheldon, *The Intellectual Development of Justus Möser* (Osnabrück: Wenner, 1970).

JEREMY ADLER

Mozart, Wolfgang Amadeus (1756–1791) Austrian composer. The son of Leopold Mozart (1719–89), kapellmeister to the archbishop of Salzburg, he started composing at the age of 5, wrote his first operas as a teenager and toured Europe as a wunderkind. His second trip led him through Germany to Paris and London, where he met JOHANN CHRISTIAN BACH and, under his influence, wrote his first symphonies. Three journeys to Italy followed (1769–72), during which he met composers like Giovanni Battista Martini (1706–84) and Niccolò Jommelli (1714–1744), famous for Neapolitan opera, and composed three operas. In one of these, *Lucio Silla* (1772), his distinctive style is already discernible. Another tour through Germany and France (1777–9) included visits to Mannheim, with its famous orchestra, and Paris, where he encountered the music of GLUCK, whose influence can be seen in *Idomeneo* (1780).

His travels and contact with other European musicians gave rise to an impatience with the narrow provincialism of Salzburg, and in 1781 he broke with the archbishop. He settled in Vienna, where he married Constanze Weber, and made friends with HAYDN, to whom he dedicated the six String Quartets published in 1785. After the *Singspiel Die Entführung aus dem Serail* (The Escape from the Seraglio, 1782) he made his living by giving piano lessons and by performing and composing. His next commission, in 1786, initiated a working relationship with the Venetian librettist Lorenzo da Ponte. *Le Nozze di Figaro* (The Marriage of Figaro), based on Beaumarchais's play, was coolly received in Vienna but enthusiastically acclaimed in Prague where it was produced the following year.

The success led to the commission of a new opera, *Don Giovanni* (1787), which again was well received in Prague, but not in Vienna, despite the insertion of some raucous scenes in an attempt to appeal to Viennese taste. His last three symphonies were composed in 1788 and the opera *Cosi fan tutte* in 1789, which was commissioned by

Emperor Joseph II. When the emperor died in 1790, Mozart lost an important potential patron. With growing financial difficulties, he accepted the offer of the actor, librettist and theatre manager Emanuel Schikaneder (1751–1812) to compose *Die Zauberflöte* (The Magic Flute, 1791). Mozart's last opera was an opera seria after Metastasio, *La Clemenza di Tito* (The Clemency of Titus, 1791), written for the coronation of Emperor Leopold II as king of Bohemia. His last works were the Clarinet Concerto and the unfinished Requiem. He died of typhus on 5 December 1791 and was buried in a pauper's grave. The Requiem was finished by his pupil Franz Xaver Süssmayr (1766–1803).

Mozart left behind him forty-one symphonies, twenty-seven piano concertos and several concertos for other instruments, twenty-three string quartets and six quintets, thirty-five piano sonatas, and a series of masses, concert arias and songs. His operatic works range from opera seria to Singspiel and the opera semibuffa, which he developed in collaboration with da Ponte. Mozart's works have been put in order by the Austrian musicologist Ludwig Ritter von Köchel (1800–1877), and are therefore indicated with the Köchel-Verzeichnis (KV).

Mozart's attempt to live as a freelance composer in socially backward Vienna was doomed to failure, although his financial difficulties were probably due at least partly to mismanagement. He was a 'free' composer also in the sense that he liberated musical language from traditional formulas and continued the process of radical individualization that CARL PHILIPP EMANUEL BACH had initiated with his piano fantasies. Mozart was a dramatic as well as melodious talent. In his music everything seems to be directed to singing and to stream along in a natural flow.

M. Levey, *The Life and Death of Mozart*, rev. ed. (London: Cardinal, 1988).
H. C. Robbins Landon, *Mozart: The Golden Years, 1781–1791* (London: Thames and Hudson, 1989).
H. C. Robbins Landon, *The Mozart Compendium: A Guide to Mozart's Life and Music* (London: Thames and Hudson, 1990).
S. Sadie, *The New Grove Mozart* (London: Macmillan, 1982).

FRITZ WEBER

Mughal Empire At the height of its influence the Muslim Mughal Empire embraced most of the Indian subcontinent, having penetrated south and east from its heartland in Kabul and Kashmir. By the middle of the eighteenth century, although the Mughal imperial order in India remained outwardly intact, with provincial governors still dependent on the favour of the emperor, the empire was already losing much of its coherence. The Afghans and MARATHAS posed a constant military threat; important provinces such as Awadh, BENGAL and Hyderabad were becoming autonomous; and warfare from 1740 onwards disrupted the all-important flow of tribute to the imperial capital at Delhi. Yet few were prepared to deny the theoretical authority of the Emperor, and even the British went to elaborate lengths to acknowledge the sovereignty of the Mughals. Indeed, by the Treaty of Allahabad (1765) the East India Company formally integrated itself into the Mughal system when it accepted the office of diwan of Bengal from the emperor Shah Alam II. But despite continued outward displays of pomp and splendour, the empire had become little more than a fiction by the end of the century. Real power in India now lay with the successor states and the British.

J. F. Richards, *The Mughal Empire* (Cambridge: Cambridge University Press, 1993).

HUW BOWEN

Murat, Joachim (1767–1815) Napoleon BONAPARTE's best-known cavalry leader, king of Naples (1808–14). Born the son of an innkeeper, he joined a light cavalry regiment before the revolution. In October 1795 he organized the dispatch of cannon from the Sablons artillery park for Napoleon's counterstroke against a Parisian rising, became aide-de-camp to the rising general and confirmed his position in the Italian campaign (1796–7). He distinguished himself further in the Egyptian expedition (1798–9), and returned to France with Napoleon to assist in the *coup d'état* of 18 Brumaire (1799). His link with the new leading family of France was then strengthened by his marriage to Napoleon's sister Caroline (1782–1839). From then on he commanded the cavalry at most of the great Napoleonic battles in Europe. His political ambitions grew from 1808, and after the dashing of his hopes for the Spanish throne, Napoleon made him king of NAPLES, where he instituted a programme of useful reforms in a previously backward country. His star waned with that of the emperor, and following a desperate attempt to invade and recover his former kingdom of Naples he was shot in October 1815.

D. Chandler, *Napoleon's Marshals* (London: Weidenfeld & Nicolson, 1987).

TONY HAYTER

Muratori, Lodovico Antonio (1672–1750) Italian historian and theological scholar. The father of Italian history, sometimes also described as the founder of modern scientific history, he was an important figure of the Catholic Enlightenment, being an advocate of religious and legal reforms. Ordained in 1695, he was appointed to the Ambrosian library at Milan. In 1740 he discovered the 'Muratorian Canon', a list of New Testament writings. He was a prolific writer, and his publications included *Rerum italicarum scriptores* (28 vols, 1723–51), *Annali d'Italia* (12 vols, 1744–9), *Antiquitates italicae medii aevi* (1738–43) and *Novus thesaurus inscriptionum* (1739–43). He commented on the shortcomings of the legal system in an essay entitled *De' difetto della giurisprudenza* (1742) while his *Della Regolata Divozione dei Cristiani* (1747) became an inspiration for leading Italian and Austrian religious reformers.

Aldo Andreoli, *Nel mondo di Lodovico Antonio Muratori* (Bologna: Il Mulino, 1972).

SYLVANA TOMASELLI

museums Eighteenth-century museums were basically of two types, with distinctive, if overlapping, roots. One followed the tradition of private collections of works of art which dated back to the princely patrons of Renaissance Italy, and was emulated throughout Europe. The other derived from the 'cabinet of curiosities', collections of a variety of natural and artificial phenomena, often inspired by the growing interest in the natural world that was associated with the scientific revolution. The earliest public museum, the Ashmolean Museum at Oxford (1683), was of the latter type, and was based on the collections of the Tradescant family as extended by Elias Ashmole (1617–92). The British Museum, created by Act of Parliament in 1753 and opened in 1759, also derived from a private collection, that of Sir Hans Sloane (1660–1753). The other route to public museums was through the opening up and subsequent nationalization of formerly private art collections of princes and monarchs. This occurred in various European countries in the eighteenth century, the classic example being the Louvre in Paris, which was nationalized in the French Revolution. This, the first great public art gallery, pioneered the arrangement of works of art by schools and their exposition to a non-learned public.

F. H. Taylor, *The Taste of Angels* (London: Hamish Hamilton, 1948).

MICHAEL HUNTER

music Where the seventeenth century might be described as the age of opera, the eighteenth century witnessed the rise of the symphony. The transition from baroque to classical styles saw the emergence of what is commonly called tonality, that is an exactly defined relationship between chords as well as keys. At the same time traditional forms like the concerto grosso, suite and trio sonata gave way to new genres like the sonata, string quartet and symphony. The centre of European musical activity shifted from Italy, France (although both countries remaining important for opera) and England to central Europe, in particular Vienna. In areas where music had formerly been dominated by the court and aristocracy a musical life grew up among the middle classes.

Early-eighteenth-century opera reflected the world of courts and kings, and, apart from commercial productions in Italy and England, provided entertainment for a small aristocratic elite, which also dominated taste by paying and employing the composers. New, popular elements sprang up in Italy and England during the first half of the century. Handel's success was overshadowed by *The Beggar's Opera,* and opera buffa began its triumphant march as intermezzo to the Neapolitan opera seria. The salient feature, however, was the emancipation of orchestral music from opera and court life. PUBLIC CONCERTS and *collegia musica* grew in popularity from the late seventeenth century, stimulated by the Protestant idea of musical self-government and by commercial interest.

During the eighteenth century an international music market emerged. Printed scores were circulated, spreading the names of Vivaldi and Haydn throughout Europe. In England JOHANN CHRISTIAN BACH promoted public concerts; Johann Peter Salomon organized Haydn's London concerts in the 1790s; and a Parisian music society had commissioned Haydn symphonies even earlier. The existence of an international market helped to free musicians from aristocratic patronage, even in economically backward areas. This development can be seen in the careers of Haydn, Mozart and Beethoven, who was the first composer not to be exclusively employed by a patron.

The century also saw technical and formal innovations that contributed to musical developments: Carl Philipp Emanuel Bach and other composers explored the possibilities of the PIANOFORTE as a means of expressing inner feelings. A similar spirit can be felt in Mozart's da Ponte operas, where the orchestra is already able to 'comment' on the play on stage, a step forward hard to imagine without the progress of the Mannheim School. The prescription of an exactly defined orchestral apparatus by Johann Stamitz and his pupils was equivalent in importance to the new instruments of the eighteenth century, as was the string quartet, which was developed as a field of symphonic experimentation by Haydn.

The symphony, with its origins in the operatic overture, began to assert its independence in the middle of the eighteenth century. Here *Empfindsamkeit* (sentimentality) was amalgamated with intellectual strain to create the highest structural density possible within a new formal framework. Sonata form, which was the heart of the symphony, required a specific technique of developing musical material. Similar to the philosophy of Hegel, musical ideas were explicated in a quasi-antagonistic process. By the end of the period, these symphonic achievements were transplanted back to opera by Cherubini (1760–1842) and Beethoven.

Increased expressivity demanded rising technical standards in performance and therefore involved the separation of amateur bands from professional orchestras. In a similar way audiences were split into two factions, in effect the fans of light and of serious music. At the same time as composers tended to increase their demands on the listener, the middle classes were asking for musical performances as social events. At the end of the eighteenth century – at least in central Europe – concert attendances declined, while there was a great demand for the popular loud Singspiels. The process of leading audiences to accept higher artistic standards of music – though set about in the eighteenth century – remained a task for the future.

A. Carse, *Eighteenth Century Symphonists: A Short Story* (London: Augener, 1951).

Peter Schleuning, *Das 18. Jahrhundert: Der Bürger erhebt sich* (Reinbek: Rowohlt, 1984).

W. Weber, *The Rise of Musical Classics in Eighteenth-Century England: A Study in Canon, Ritual and Ideology* (Oxford: Clarendon, 1992).

E. Wellesz and F. Sternfeld (eds), *The Age of Enlightenment, 1745–1790* (London: Oxford University Press, 1973) [New Oxford History of Music, vol. 7].

FRITZ WEBER

mysticism　The tradition of mysticism, in which the believer apprehends God through personal religious experience, had a number of notable followers in the eighteenth century. Madame Guyon (1648–1717), the French quietist author, lived a life of mysticism which was applauded by Madame de Maintenon (1635–1719), the mistress of Louis XIV, but was suspected of heresy by Bishop Bossuet and defended by Bishop Fenélon, who placed himself under her spiritual direction. William Law (1686–1761), a Nonjuror, wrote one of the devotional classics of the age, *A Serious Call to a Devout and Holy Life* (1729), which was influenced by the teachings of J. Tauler (c.1300–61) and Thomas à Kempis (1380–1471). His later writings, especially *The Spirit of Prayer* (1749–50) and *The Spirit of Love* (1752–4), were influenced by the German mystic J. Boehme (1575–1624), in their emphasis on the indwelling of Christ in the soul. John Byrom (1692–1761) was a spiritual poet who attempted to express in verse the mysticism of Law and Boehme. SWEDENBORG was noted for his *Worship and the Love of God* (1745), and for his visions of heaven and hell, which were influential particularly in the mystical writings and poetry of BLAKE.

Michael Cox, *Mysticism* (Wellingborough: Aquarian, 1983).
R. A. Knox, *Enthusiasm: A Chapter in the History of Religion, with Special Reference to the Seventeenth and Eighteenth Centuries* (Oxford: Clarendon, 1950).

JEREMY GREGORY

myth 'It is absurd', wrote Adam Ferguson in *An Essay on the History of Civil Society* (1767), 'to quote the fable of the Illiad or the Odyssey, the legends of Hercules, Theseus, or Oedipus, as authorities in matter of fact relating to the history of mankind; but they may, with great justice, be cited to ascertain what were the conceptions and sentiments of the age in which they were composed, or to characterise the genius of that people, with whose imaginations they were blended, and by whom they were fondly rehearsed and admired.' Ferguson's belief that where historical records were wanting myths were a valuable source of information about antiquity reflected a widely shared opinion in the eighteenth century. The study of mythology was part of a great interest in the origins of religious beliefs, which was pursued by many Enlightenment figures, including Charles de Brosses (1709–77), Hume, Diderot and Gibbon, often though by no means always for the purpose of undermining Christianity or monotheism.

Ferguson's remarks are the more arresting in view of his appreciation of the Greek 'talent for fable'. He distinguished between nations that had their own myths and those that had borrowed theirs: in the first 'The passions of the poet pervaded the minds of the people, and the conceptions of men of genius being communicated to the vulgar, became the incentives of a national spirit'; by contrast, 'A mythology borrowed from abroad, a literature founded on references to a strange country, and fraught with foreign allusions, are much more confined in their use: they speak to the learned alone; and though intended to inform the understanding, and mend the heart, may, by being confined to a few, have an opposite effect: they may foster conceit on the ruins of common sense, and render what was, at least innocently, sung by the Athenian mariner at his oar, or rehearsed by the shepherd in attending his flock, an occasion of vice, and the foundation of pedantry and scholastic pride.'

Building on the results of a well-established study of myths and especially on the comparative approach that evolved in the seventeenth century, Vico, Gianvicenzo Gravina (1664–1718), Jean-François Lafitau (1681–1746), Bernard de Fontenelle (1657–1757) and others stressed the similarities between various mythologies and explained myths in anthropomorphic terms. For them, as for Ferguson, the study of myths afforded the possibility of understanding the mentality of various cultures.

According to Johnson, modern sensibilities were utterly unresponsive to mythology: 'The machinery of the Pagans is uninteresting to us: when a Goddess appears in Homer or Virgil, we grow weary', he claimed, adding what Richard Wagner (1813–83), for one, was to disprove: 'It is evident enough that no one who writes now can use the Pagan deities and mythology.'

See also ANTHROPOLOGY.

Frank Manuel, *The Eighteenth Century Confronts the Gods* (Cambridge, Mass.: Harvard University Press, 1959).

The New Science of Giambattista Vico, trans. from third edn (1744) by T. Goddard Bergin and Max H. Fish (Ithaca, NY: Cornell University Press, 1948).

SYLVANA TOMASELLI

N

Nantes, revocation of the Edict of (1685)   The Edict of Nantes (1598) had recognized the right of French Protestants (HUGUENOTS) to practise their faith without persecution. However, the dictates of security and the consciousness of the affront to his dignity as the 'most Christian king' persuaded Louis XIV that all his subjects should share his Catholicism. Events conspired to sharpen this perception around the end of the 1670s. He came under the influence of his second wife-to-be, the devout Madame de Maintenon, and of the minister of war, Louvois (1639–91), who favoured a policy of conversion by force. Louis signed the Edict of Fontainebleau in October 1685. It proscribed the practice of Protestantism, introducing the death penalty for those who acted in defiance of the new law. Some 200,000 people, 10 per cent of the Huguenot population, fled the country. The adverse effects on French trade and industry of this defection have been exaggerated, but they were not insignificant. Neither was the impact of Louis's intolerant act on his European neighbours who were persuaded to seek security in an anti-French coalition.

Seventeen years after the revocation a Protestant revolt broke out in the Cévennes mountains in south-eastern France (*see* CAMISARDS). Paradoxically, its failure reinvigorated Huguenotism, although the movement remained officially banned in France until 1787.

W. C. Scoville, *The Persecution of the Huguenots and French Economic Development, 1680–1720* (Berkeley, Calif.: University of California Press, 1960).

J. H. SHENNAN

Naples, city of   The city of Naples, the capital of the KINGDOM OF NAPLES, was the largest city in Italy in the eighteenth century and one of the largest in Europe. Its population numbered 220,000 in 1707, had risen to 315,000 by 1742 and to well over 400,000 by 1791. The phenomenal rate of expansion made it a densely populated, poverty-ridden city, with an essentially parasitic economy. Among the lower classes, popularly known as the *lazzaroni*, this manifested itself in begging and heavy reliance on public charity, while among the educated it has been estimated that almost 26,000 men formed 'the legal class', who were almost a group apart. The nobility, too, had either become wholly dependent on state employment or lived a parasitic existence, funded by their rural estates. The main industry was textiles but commerce and industry remained very limited in scope, partly due to Charles III's failure to gain local acceptance for the admission of foreign merchants to the port. Naples enjoyed many privileges, with its powerful *Annona*, the civic body that ensured cheap grain supplies for the city, and its council, the *Sedili,* composed of 130 families, a virtual nobility within the nobility. These prerogatives were always jealously protected against the central government, resulting in the paralysis of municipal government. The plague of 1764 ravaged Naples, killing around 20,000 and exposing the weakness of the administration. Paradoxically, Naples, with an important university and an intelligentsia deeply involved in politics, literature and the arts, was a centre of the Italian Enlightenment.

D. Carpanetto and G. Ricuperati, *Italy in the Age of Reason, 1685–1789* (London: Longman, 1987).

S. J. Woolf, *A History of Italy, 1700–1860* (London: Methuen, 1979).

MICHAEL BROERS

Naples, kingdom of   The kingdom of Naples had been under Spanish rule until the Treaty of Utrecht placed it under the Austrian Habsburgs. In 1734 it was returned to the Spanish Habsburgs (who were now nominally no longer tied to Spain) under Charles III (from 1734 to 1759) and then, when he became king of Spain, his son Ferdinand IV (from 1759 to 1825). The kingdom comprised the southern half of the Italian peninsula and had a population of around 4,925,000 by 1791, with its capital at the CITY OF NAPLES. Recent dynastic changes notwithstanding, it was one of the oldest territorial states in Europe.

Its economy was very backward and its economic and social structures underwent a prolonged crisis which intensified in the last years of the century. There were very few proper roads, little industry and a backward agricultural sector hampered by rapacious landlords (ecclesiastical, noble and bourgeois), and even relatively successful sectors of the economy, such as the Calabrian silk trade, were stagnant rather than expansionist. The Calabrian earthquake of 1783 further disrupted the region. Social relations in the countryside were marked by banditry, frequent litigation and general lawlessness throughout the period. A series of reforming ministers confronted these problems: TANUCCI until 1771 and then FILANGIERI, Pagano (1748–99) and other pupils of the economist Genovesi into the 1790s. Indeed, the century produced a highly cultivated, enlightened intelligentsia working closely if incoherently with the government, but the resistance of the church and the feudal baronage prove too strong.

D. Carpanetto and G. Ricuperati, *Italy in the Age of Reason, 1685–1789* (London: Longman, 1987).

S. J. Woolf, *A History of Italy, 1700–1860* (London: Methuen, 1979).

MICHAEL BROERS

Napoleon I *see* BONAPARTE, NAPOLEON.

National Assembly (French) The French National Assembly emerged directly from the ranks of the deputies already elected to the Estates General sitting at Versailles in the spring of 1789. Following a long series of disputes over the voting procedure to be adopted by the Estates General, the 641 deputies of the THIRD ESTATE, that is, those of non-clerical and non-noble status, seceded from the Estates General, declaring themselves to be the National Assembly on 17 June 1789, explicitly claiming the right to represent the whole of the French people as its only elected representatives. This stand was reaffirmed at the famous TENNIS COURT OATH of 20 June, when the deputies swore to remain united until they had devised a new constitution for France, but Louis XVI did not give the other two estates formal orders to unite with them until 27 June 1789. This act represented the king's legal, though reluctant, acceptance of the *fait accompli* of 17 June. Henceforth, the National Assembly was the effective national government of France until it dissolved itself on 30 September 1791. Among its deputies were to be found almost all the major political figures who were to dominate the next ten years of revolutionary government in France, including Mirabeau, Robespierre, Barnave and Lafayette.

The National Assembly named itself the CONSTITUENT ASSEMBLY, in its capacity as a constitution-making body. It was the most powerful and influential institution of government at national level. Faced with serious rural disturbances throughout these months, on 4 August the Assembly abolished all feudal rights and dues, at least in principle. Although the sweeping, radical nature of the original declaration was diluted when its detailed terms were dealt with after the crisis had passed, the 'Night of the Fourth of August' represented the first in a series of seminal acts by the Assembly that reached far beyond the narrow work of framing a constitution. The first was the voting of the DECLARATION OF THE RIGHTS OF MAN AND THE CITIZEN on 26 August, which laid down the general principles on which the new constitution would rest. Its two central themes were the clear guarantee of personal liberties and the enunciation of the principle that the national government was the exclusive source of legitimate authority. These two concepts would become central to the political system that emerged in the course of the Revolution. Building swiftly on these principles, the Assembly next nationalized all church property, thereby removing the church's quasi-autonomous place in French political life, a step that led to the voting of the Civil Constitution of the Clergy on 12 July 1790 which made the church virtually a branch of the civil service and provoked deep resentment at many levels of society, from Louis XVI down. On 16 August 1790 the semi-independent law courts, the *parlements*, were abolished and replaced by a national system of courts with elected judges. The single most durable achievement of the Assembly was the creation of eighty-three new administrative units, the departments, in place of the old provinces, a system that is still in use today.

The constitution that came into effect on 1 October 1791 was based on an electorate of propertied citizens, the 'active citizens', who chose a single chamber of deputies, drawn from still wealthier citizens. This new LEGISLATIVE ASSEMBLY shared power with the king, who had been granted a suspensive veto over legislation (*see* CONSTITUTION OF 1791). On 6 November 1789 the deputies of the National Assembly voted to refrain from entering the new legislature for three years. None of their work had been achieved without rancour, and deep divisions had been sown in the course of its debates, particularly over the restricted franchise and the religious reforms, which enraged radicals and reactionaries, respectively.

W. Doyle, *The Oxford History of the French Revolution* (Oxford: Oxford University Press, 1989).

D. Richet, 'Revolutionary Assemblies,' in F. Furet and M. Ozouf (eds), *A Critical Dictionary of the French Revolution* (Cambridge, Mass.: Harvard University Press, 1989), pp. 529–37.

MICHAEL BROERS

National Convention (French) The National Convention was the longest lived of the representative bodies produced by the French Revolution. It came into being on 21 September 1792, following the overthrow of the monarchy and the Constitution of 1791, and dissolved itself on 2 November 1795, to make way for the Directory. It was elected on the basis of universal suffrage, but in practice participation in the elections differed little from those for its predecessor, the Legislative Assembly, being confined to the propertied classes. Most of its 749 deputies had served in previous assemblies and included some of the most famous figures of the Revolution – Robespierre, Brissot, Marat and Danton.

The Convention had two main tasks, to govern France during the crisis created by the war and counter-revolution, and to frame a new constitution for the country. It produced the radical Constitution of Year II (*see* CONSTITUTION OF 1793), which was never enacted and then the conservative Constitution of Year III, which replaced its rule. The period of the Convention witnessed the creation and dismantling of the two great COMMITTEES OF PUBLIC SAFETY AND GENERAL SECURITY, the Revolutionary Tribunal and the whole structure of the TERROR, encapsulating the most radical, violent period of the Revolution. It was purged of its last radical members after the *coup* of Thermidor in 1794, but the Law of Two-Thirds perpetuated its survivors' rule into the Directory.

W. Doyle, *The Oxford History of the French Revolution* (Oxford: Oxford University Press, 1989).

R. R. Palmer, *The Twelve who Ruled* (Princeton, NJ: Princeton University Press, 1941).

D. Richet, 'Revolutionary Assemblies', in F. Furet and M. Ozouf (eds), *A Critical Dictionary of the French Revolution* (Cambridge, Mass.: Harvard University Press, 1989), pp. 529–37.

MICHAEL BROERS

national guard The term 'national guard' was first used by the citizens' militia of Paris when it made itself a permanent body during the crisis of July 1789. The new National Assembly gave it formal recognition soon afterwards and then ordered the creation of a national guard for every commune. In practice, this simply legalized the municipal militias that had sprung up in many provincial towns during the summer of 1789, in response to widespread rural disorder.

The terms of membership in the national guard, and therefore its social and political composition, corresponded to the pattern of revolutionary politics. At its inception, the guard was restricted to the propertied classes, as guardsmen had to buy their own weapons and uniforms. The Paris Guard, commanded by LAFAYETTE in the period 1789–92, was used against the republican radicals at the Massacre of the Champs de Mars. During the war emergency of the summer of 1792, however, membership was opened to all citizens and arms were distributed; its character changed and the guard became the arm of radicals in the Commune and the Convention. It was dominated by the SANS-CULOTTE, many of whom served in the *armées revolutionaires* against the Federalists in 1793–4 and in the Vendée as well as in the *grandes journées*. After Thermidor the guard reverted to a propertied membership and helped to suppress popular risings in 1795. In the countryside it was largely urban in composition, active against peasant revolts and in the enforcement of conscription.

R. C. Cobb, *The Peoples' Armies* (New Haven, Conn.: Yale University Press, 1984).

G. Rudé, *The Crowd in the French Revolution* (Oxford: Oxford University Press, 1959).

S. Scott, 'Problems of Law and Order during 1790, the 'Peaceful' Year of the French Revolution', *American Historical Review*, 80 (1975), 859–88.

D. M. G. Sutherland, *France, 1789–1815: Revolution and Counter-revolution* (London: Collins, 1985).

MICHAEL BROERS

nationalism   Before the French Revolution there was very little in Europe that could be called nationalism as it is understood today. There was certainly a passive awareness of national distinctiveness – people knew they were French not German, for example – but other criteria of self-definition (class, region, religion and occupation) remained far more important. Concepts like national freedom and unity, which were to become so important in the nineteenth century, were of little significance.

It is equally hard to find nationalism outside Europe. In the Ottoman Empire the existence of separate 'nations' (*millet*) was legally recognized but these were based on religious rather than ethnic divisions. In the Far East the Chinese, the Japanese and the Koreans believed that they had reached a pinnacle of civilization beyond which it was impossible to progress and tried to close themselves off from all external influences. Perhaps the rebellion of the American colonists against British rule could be seen as a nationalist rising. They claimed to be acting to recover their national rights as Englishmen, which had been stolen from them by the crown, and at the same time to be founding a new nation based on the advanced principles embodied in the Declaration of Independence (*see* AMERICAN WAR OF INDEPENDENCE).

The American example also accelerated developments in Europe that were later to contribute to the growth of modern nationalism. The centralizing and standardizing policies of absolute monarchs had begun to break down traditional regional and local loyalties, though it would be dangerous to exaggerate the effects of this: before the advent of mass communications, an essential tool of modern nationalism, the horizons of most Europeans remained very limited and they identified with localities rather than nations. Only a minority of Frenchmen spoke French and in Germany the state was much more immediate to the lives of ordinary people than the nation. Among the educated middle classes new ideas and movements were growing up in the later eighteenth century that contributed to the development of the concept of the nation but only rarely did this become the political movement that nationalism essentially is. Enlightened ideas gave rise to rational criticism of religious and class distinctions that artificially divided society. The Patriot movements, which grew up in many countries, helped to break down old class barriers and to spread the belief that all men have a duty to serve their nations but they were minority movements and essentially cosmopolitan in nature. Rising middle-class consciousness, based on a rejection of noble models of behaviour, often fuelled antiforeign national cultural revivals. The German Society in Leipzig in the early eighteenth century promoted the use of German rather than French as a literary language. HERDER defined the nation as a living linguistic and cultural community; but his contribution to nationalism has been exaggerated as he remained thoroughly cosmopolitan in his attitudes.

Nationalism in the modern sense, that is a political movement employing national symbols and aspirations to mobilize mass support, developed after 1789, first in France and later elsewhere, as the effects of the gigantic release of national energy in the French Revolution made themselves felt on the battlefields of Europe. A desire to obtain the benefits of the Revolution or, more usually, to defeat the French and throw off their control, led other governments to adopt similar policies to involve the people.

See also PATRIOTISM.

P. Alter, *Nationalism*, trans. Stewart McKinnon-Evans (London: Edward Arnold, 1989).

O. Dann and J. Dinwiddy (eds), *Nationalism in the Age of the French Revolution* (London: Hambledon, 1989).

MICHAEL HUGHES

natural history   The eighteenth century was an age of natural history as much as an age of Newtonianism. It laid the foundations for a science concerned with CLASSIFICATION, description and anatomical analysis of living forms, and developed the institutional structures for its disciplinary development. It saw the publication of the foundational works of systematic classification in zoology and botany, especially the writings of LINNAEUS: *Systema naturae* (13 edns, 1735–88), *Genera plantarum* (1737), *Classes plantarum* (1738), *Philosophia botanica* (1751) and *Praelectiones in ordines naturales plantarum* (1792). Linnaeus also expounded more speculative views on physical anthropology, the 'economy of nature' and on the descent of forms from primordial species, through dissertations written by his students under his supervision at the University of Uppsala *(Amoenitates Academicae, 7 vols, 1749–69)*. His assistants conducted extensive expeditions to

remote parts of the world to collect botanical and zoological specimens for him. British Linnaeanism was developed particularly through
the efforts of James E. Smith (1759–1828), a founder of the Linnean
Society of London.

Linnaean science carried on the tradition of *historia naturalis* as a
description and classification of natural objects, after the writings of
Francis Bacon (1561–1626) and the Renaissance encyclopaedists. In
the eighteenth century there developed another meaning of the term,
which came to designate 'a history of nature', that is the understanding of organisms within the context of the historical development of
the earth and cosmos operating by the action of natural forces over
time. Exponents of this approach included Benoît de Maillet (1656–
1738; *Telliamed*, 1748), Kant *Allgemeine Naturgeschichte und Theorie
des Himmels*, 1755) and, posthumously, Leibniz (*Protogaea*, 1749).
Fundamental to the theoretical development of this tradition were the
writings of BUFFON (*Histoire naturelle, générale et particulière*, 1749–
88), who proposed novel theories regarding the former connection
of continents, and the migration and degeneration of forms, from
primordial sources. He integrated the history of the earth and the
history of life in an ambitious work, *Les Époques de la nature* (1778).
Aspects of this integrated historical and biogeographical approach
to natural history were explored in France through the writings of
Buffon's associates at the Jardin du Roi, Bernard de Lacépède (1756–
1825) and Jean Baptiste Lamarck, and in Germany through the writings of the Göttingen professor Johann Blumenbach (1752–1840) and
the geographer E. A. W. Zimmerman (1743–1815). The creative
tensions between descriptive and historical approaches to natural history
were important for the development of nineteenth-century natural
history.

S. Atran, *Cognitive Foundations of Natural History* (Cambridge: Cambridge
University Press, 1990).
J. Larson, 'Not without a Plan: Geography and Natural History in the Late
Eighteenth Century', *Journal of the History of Biology*, 19 (1986), 447–88.
P. Sloan, 'Natural History', in R. C. Olby et al. (eds), *Companion to the History
of Modern Science* (London: Routledge, 1990), pp. 295–313.
F. Stafleu, *Linnaeus and the Linnaeans* (Utrecht: A. Oosthoek, 1971).

PHILLIP R. SLOAN

natural law In his *Encyclopédie* entry on the subject Diderot remarked that 'natural law' was so familiar a term that everyone would
imagine that they knew its meaning, but even philosophers were hard
put to define it. The difficulty resided, in his view, in the notion of
natural law itself. Natural law theories sought to find a moral basis for

justice, and were so many attempts to produce a universal criterion by which various laws and institutions could be assessed, but, Diderot argued, such efforts were vain if determinism were true and men were not possessed of a free will. Appeals to natural law would only ever convince those who wished to be fully human and who recognized that their humanity consisted in the exercise of reason. Granted this, the content of natural law could be discovered by consulting the general will of the human species as a whole. Its terms ought to govern the relations between individuals as well as between nations. It was knowable to man as it was 'a pure act of the understanding reasoning in the silence of the passion about what man can exact of his fellow being, and what his fellow being has a right to exact from him'.

Although the Enlightenment is generally identified with utilitarianism, the importance of the natural law school should not be underestimated. While it had no advocates of the stature of Hugo Grotius (1583–1645) or Samuel Puffendorf (1632–94), it none the less provided the framework within which much of the period's political and economic writings was conceived, for example Rousseau's critique of civilization and *Du contrat social,* Adam Smith's political economy, Kant's political reflections and more mainstream natural law theories such as Lord Kames's (1696–1782) *Essays on the Principles of Morality and Natural Religion* (1751). The tradition was also kept alive by Montesquieu, not only in his *De l'esprit des lois,* but in the communications he made to the Académie de Bordeaux and in his *Essai touchant les lois naturelles et la distinction du juste et de l'injuste* (1725), *Analyse du traité des devoirs* (1725) and *Discours sur l'equité qui doit régler les jugements et l'éxécution des lois* (1725), which was published for the first time in 1771 and subsequently sold at the doors of the Palais on the opening day of sessions. Likewise, one of his greatest admirers, the chevalier de Jaucourt (1704–79), displayed his conversance with the natural law school in numerous articles for the *Encyclopédie,* which did much to acquaint readers with the works of Grotius, Puffendorf, Thomasius, Guillaume Budé (1467–1540), John Selden (1584–1654), Richard Cumberland (1631–1718), William Wollaston (1659–1724) and Locke.

Diderot's early and somewhat sceptical discussion of 'Droit naturel' found a counterpart in Jaucourt's 'Naturelle, loi (Droit naturel)'. In contrast to Diderot's secular account, Jaucourt's view of natural law was anchored in a theocentric perspective: 'One defines *natural law* as a law which God imposes on all men, and which they can discover through the power of reason, by carefully considering their nature and their condition. *Natural* law is the system of the said laws and *natural* jurisprudence is the art of elaborating these laws of nature and of applying them to human actions.' Following Montesquieu almost to the word, Jaucourt claimed obedience to God to be the most important, though not the first, law of nature to reveal itself to man. In the state of nature, peace was the first natural law man acceded to, self-preservation the second, sexual attraction the third and the desire to live in society the fourth. Hobbes's view of the original condition of humanity as a state of war of all against all was thus firmly rejected. Montesquieu's view was that the idea of dominion and subjugation was too complex to occur to humankind in its early years. Only with the beginnings of society did men lose their sense of weakness and, with natural equality ceasing to prevail amongst them, the state of war began.

Duncan Forbes, 'Natural Law and the Scottish Enlightenment', in R. H. Campbell and A. S. Skinner (eds), *The Origins and Nature of the Scottish Enlightenment* (Edinburgh: Edinburgh University Press, 1982), pp. 186–204.
James Moore and M. Silverthorne, 'Gershom Carmichael and the Natural Jurisprudence Tradition in Eighteenth-Century Scotland', in I. Hont and M. Ignatieff (eds), *Wealth and Virtue: The Shaping of Political Economy in the Scottish Enlightenment* (Cambridge: Cambridge University Press, 1983), pp. 73–87.
Mark H. Waddicor, *Montesquieu and the Philosophy of Natural Law* (The Hague: Martinus Nijhoff, 1970).

SYLVANA TOMASELLI

natural religion   The concept of natural religion was essentially of a primary, universal religion that bound humanity in a common moral law. Revelation was not necessarily redundant but it had to be harmonized with REASON to ensure that it did not result in selective dogma and superstition, which was thought to be the cause of religious wars, persecutions, intolerance and viciousness. Such views both depended on and created a more anthropocentric view of religion in which social utility and moral virtue took precedence over revelation and dogma. The concept of natural religion also embraced the related notions of a more beneficent deity, a harmonious natural order and the welfare of man in society.

Ultimately, natural religion rested on the presupposition that there was such a thing as a universal human nature, endowed with reason, conscience and knowledge. Such a hypothesis, if not a dogma in its own right, was relentlessly attacked by HUME who regarded human nature as a chaotic mixture of instincts, appetites and passions. In this way, Enlightenment scepticism eroded natural religion as the latter had itself eroded revealed religion (*see* CHRISTIANITY).

N. Hampson, *The Enlightenment* (Harmondsworth: Penguin, 1968).

DAVID HEMPTON

nature The later eighteenth century saw earlier mechanistic notions of nature replaced by a more substantive, active idea of nature. Prior to the mechanistic philosophies of the seventeenth century, nature (*phusis, natura*) was usually understood either in the Aristotelian sense of an internal principle of growth and purposiveness, which acted as an internal formal and final cause, or in the Platonic-Stoic sense of a superintending world-soul. The latter was common in the classical and Renaissance medical tradition, especially in the writings of Galen.

With the advent of the MECHANICAL PHILOSOPHY in the seventeenth century, particularly as inspired by Descartes, the traditional conceptions of nature were rejected. Nature was now seen as a system of bodies created by God and operating by contact action. Similar views were espoused by other leading theorists of the mechanical philosophy, for example Robert Boyle (1627–91; *A Free Inquiry into the Vulgarly Received Notion of Nature*, 1696).

These assumptions were challenged by several eighteenth-century philosophers. The English natural philosopher NEWTON, particularly in the second edition of his *Principia* (1713), identified the reality of absolute space and time with God's extension and duration and made universal gravitation a manifestation of a substantive divine presence. The writings of the earlier Cambridge Platonists, especially Henry More (1614–87) and Ralph Cudworth (1627–88), had defended the Platonic-Stoic notion of nature as an intermediary world-soul between God and matter against Cartesian notions. Their views were resurrected, in 1703, through a series of discussions by Jean LeClerc (1657–1736), editor of the influential *Bibliothèque choisie*. The German philosopher LEIBNIZ had revived the Aristotelian-scholastic conception of nature as an inherent teleological principle and these views were further developed by his disciple Christian WOLFF. In his *Ethica* the Dutch philosopher Spinoza identified God with nature in a system of rational pantheism.

Thus eighteenth-century philosophers and naturalists were confronted with several alternatives to mechanical nominalistic views of nature. Greek and Platonic-Stoic notions of an intermediate animating and curative nature were made part of the mainstream of mid-century medical theory through the writings of the animist school, which were centred on the University of Halle, under the influence of STAHL. Stahlian medical theory was introduced in the the medical school of the University of Montpellier in France, and disseminated by the writings of Théophile de Bordeu and François Boissier de Sauvages (1706–67). The notions of the Montpellier medical school theorists were particularly important for the philosophical development of the concept of nature by the French encyclopaedists, especially DIDEROT, who applied them to issues of ethics and used them to constitute an atheistic natural philosophy in *Rêve d'Alembert*. The assumption of an active, vitalizing and constructive nature, drawn from the French medical tradition, was important for further developments in natural philosophy, particularly in the early transformist views of the French naturalist LAMARCK.

Newtonian-Leibnizian interpretations of nature influenced significant developments in natural philosophy in the writings of BUFFON. In two important essays, *De la nature: premier vue* (1765) and *De la nature: seconde vue* (1766), he expounded upon the concept of nature as an 'immense living power which animates the universe', serving as the foundation for an autonomous, self-activating nature in which the life and death of species and the naturalistic formation of the world takes place under the action of Newtonian forces.

The revival and reformulation of substantive conceptions of nature, with the addition of an inherent teleological purposiveness, provided fertile soil for the German *Naturphilosophen*, led particularly by Friedrich Schelling inspired by Leibniz and Immanuel Kant, to develop a speculative philosophy of nature at the end of the century.

J. Ehrard, *L'Idée de nature en France dans la première moitie du 18ᵉ siècle* (Paris: SEVPEN, 1963).

J. E. McGuire, 'Boyle's Conception of Nature', *Journal of the History of Ideas*, 33 (1972), 523–42.

B. Willey, *The Eighteenth-Century Background: Studies in the Idea of Nature in the Thought of the Period* (New York: Columbia University Press, 1941).

PHILLIP R. SLOAN

navies The possession of a fleet of warships, which had long been the mark of serious military power in the Mediterranean, had spread in the sixteenth and seventeenth centuries to the rising powers of northern Europe, and during the eighteenth century it became the key to participation in the world beyond Europe. Success in creating a navy, however, was costly and elusive, presenting financial, technical and managerial challenges which strained the resources of the eighteenth-century state to the limit. To sustain an effective fleet required heavy investment in dockyards, stores and industrial plant over many years; it called for a ceaseless effort of shipbuilding to match the continual decay of wooden ships, and for a large seafaring population to provide skilled crews for the ships.

In the naval arms race of the late eighteenth century Britain – with the largest merchant navy, the most resilient system of public credit in Europe and, above all, the political will consistently to support the only effective defence of a fragile regime with an inadequate army – was able to win a decisive victory. Having beaten off a dangerous challenge from the united fleets of France and Spain during the American War of Independence, the Royal Navy enabled Britain during the

Revolutionary and Napoleonic wars not merely to survive but to prosper while every other European state was more or less devastated.

The other major navies of the eighteenth century suffered from a lack of one or more of the basic components of sea power. The Dutch fleet, still in the first rank in 1688, declined rapidly after 1715 for want of adequate funds. The French navy grew rapidly to a peak in the 1690s, then suffered much neglect, was painfully rebuilt in the 1770s and 1780s, only to suffer a disastrous collapse of morale and efficiency during the Revolution. At its best it was always beset by industrial and financial weaknesses, inconsistent state policy and inadequate skilled manpower. The Spanish fleet grew in size and capability between the 1740s and 1780s and became a formidable force in many respects, but it was always crippled by a shortage of seamen. Other navies, notably those of Russia, Sweden, Denmark, Turkey, Algiers and the Two Sicilies, belonged to the second rank, exercising an important influence on events only in particular areas and periods.

The basic unit of sea power was the ship of the line or battleship, mounting a minimum of 40 or 50 guns (in 1688), and 64 or 70 guns (by 1815), and capable of lying in the line of battle in action. Because warships mounted almost all their guns on the broadside, and were vulnerable to fire from ahead or astern, actions were usually fought in line ahead. This was a formidable defensive formation, and the meeting of two competent fleets in roughly equal numbers almost always resulted in an inconclusive action. Victory tended to go to the power that could mobilize and deploy overwhelming numbers fastest, which placed a premium not only on numbers of ships, but on logistical and technical resources, reserves of manpower and the means to draw on them, and the political will to begin the very lengthy mobilization process in good time. Only in the Revolutionary and Napoleonic wars did the development of new tactical methods (notably by NELSON), coupled with the sharp decline in the professional qualities of the French and Spanish fleets, allow equal or even inferior fleets to win overwhelming victories.

Fleets and squadrons were employed to escort convoys of merchant ships, to cover raiding, expeditionary and invasion forces and, in the case of Britain in particular, to defend the country against threats of invasion. Lesser squadrons and individual ships fulfilled some of the same functions, besides cruising for the defence and harrying of trade, attacking or co-operating with armies on the coast and assuring supplies to any place accessible by sea. Smaller warships such as frigates and sloops were employed as cruisers, escorts and scouts for the battle squadrons; bomb vessels deployed heavy mortars for shore bombardment; schooners and cutters maintained communications; while gunboats of various types operated inshore and a huge fleet of store-ships, transports, hospital ships and other auxiliaries supplied and sustained the seagoing fleets.

Naval warfare was above all the warfare of technology and capital. The costs of maintaining even a small fleet greatly exceeded those of a large army ashore, and they had to be borne over a much longer period to achieve useful results – which called for the resources of an advanced economy. The number of men in a fleet, although not negligible (a fleet of thirty sail in the 1780s called for about 25,000) was small by comparison with that of an army, but the men were highly skilled and hard to replace. The fire-power of even a single battleship exceeded that of all the artillery of a large army, and on the occasions when naval gunfire could be laid down in direct support of military operations ashore the results were usually decisive. The flexibility and power of navies, which were capable of being deployed at high speeds and over huge distances, presented problems of strategy, command and communications many of which were never satisfactorily solved in the eighteenth century.

For states with the capacity to develop effective naval power, it offered opportunities as a diplomatic instrument in peacetime, as well as a means of waging war, which even the largest army could not equal. While they were limited or altogether useless against landlocked powers, navies could be used effectively, often decisively, against any state with a sea coast, and especially one that depended to any extent on foreign trade or colonies. As the world economy grew more inter-dependent and sophisticated during the century it relied increasingly on seaborne trade as an engine of prosperity in general, and a generator of liquid investment capital in particular. Naval power provided states with access to this means of economic growth, and eventually enabled Britain to dominate the world economy in the nineteenth century.

J. Black and P. Woodfine (eds), *The British Navy and the Use of Naval Power in the Eighteenth Century* (Leicester: Leicester University Press, 1988).
G. J. Marcus, *Heart of Oak: A Survey: of British sea Power in the Georgian Era* (London: Oxford University Press, 1975).
N. A. M. Rodger, *The Wooden World: An Anatomy of the Georgian Navy* (London: Collins, 1986).

N. A. M. RODGER

Navigation Acts   Passed between 1651 and 1733, the Navigation Acts provided that certain goods from Europe must be imported in ships belonging to England or the country of origin. All colonial trade was reserved to English or colonial ships and 'enumerated' colonial products must be exported to England or an English colony. European goods could be sent to the colonies only via England (Scotland was incorporated with England after 1707). The legislation aimed to strike a blow at Dutch commercial supremacy by promoting England's carrying and entrepôt trade. It also aimed to reserve the benefits of colonization for the mother country, which had provided the people and capital for settlement of the colonies, and the defence forces to maintain the Empire. After initial difficulties, enforcement procedures improved and by 1713 colonial trade seems to have conformed broadly to the Navigation system. A blatant exception was smuggling to North America from the non-English Caribbean, where returns outweighed risks.

Although any burdens that the Acts imposed on the colonies were probably offset by the benefits of membership of the British Empire, they were increasingly seen as a means of enforcing subservience, which fuelled the independence movement. Meanwhile, with the rise of FREE TRADE ideology, they were increasingly criticized at home. Yet the aim of their engineers had not been to increase world trade but to increase England's share of it and consequently her wealth, strength and security, and in this they seem to have succeeded.

See also TRADE.

L. A. Harper, *The English Navigation Laws: A Seventeenth Century Experiment in Social Engineering* (New York: Columbia University Press, 1939).

NUALA ZAHEDIEH

Necker, Jacques (1732–1804) French statesman and banker. Born in Geneva, he settled in Paris when he was 18, and established the bank of Thellusson and Necker in 1756. He was involved in the Compagnie des Indes between 1763 and 1773; appointed one of its syndics from 1765 to 1767, he wrote *Réponse au mémoire de M. l'abbé Morellet sur la Compagnie des Indes* (1769) in its defence. In 1773 he published *Éloge de Colbert*. Falsely accused of mercantilism by the physiocrats, he was, however, an advocate of state intervention and rejected the view that property rights were anchored in natural law. He published *Sur la législation et le commerce des grains* in 1775. He was appointed director of the royal treasury in 1776 and director-general of finance in 1777. His famous *Compte rendu* (1781) exposed the government's finances to public scrutiny and led to his resignation. He wrote a defence of his conduct while in office, *De l'administration des finances de la France* (1784). Vilified by his enemies, he nevertheless succeeded in swaying public opinion in his favour and was recalled in 1788. His dismissal in July 1789 was very unpopular and he was recalled soon after. Finally resigning in 1790, he retired to Geneva. His wife, Suzanne (1737–94), née Curchod, hosted an important *salon*. Their daughter was Madame de Staël.

Robert D. Harris, *Necker, Reform Minister of the Ancien Régime* (Berkeley, Calif.: University of California Press, 1979).

SYLVANA TOMASELLI

Nelson, Horatio, viscount (1758–1805) English naval commander. As a commodore at the Battle of St Vincent (1797) he turned out of line on his own initiative, without orders, personally boarding two large Spanish ships, and gained a victory. In 1798 he commanded the British squadron that pursued Napoleon's expedition to Egypt, and in a night battle took or destroyed eleven of the thirteen battleships of the French fleet (*see* BATTLE OF ABOUKIR BAY). At Copenhagen in 1801 he achieved an equally crushing victory over an anchored Danish fleet, and at TRAFALGAR in 1805 he died in the hour of a complete victory over the Franco-Spanish combined fleet.

To an age accustomed to indecisive naval battles, or at best modest successes, he brought annihilating victories. His tactical methods were eclectic, but he always took his captains completely into his confidence and encouraged them to use their initiative to carry out his intentions. Officers and men followed him with devotion, and few contemporaries were untouched by his charm, while his complex character and notorious liaison with Lady Hamilton (*c.*1765–1815) have made him a celebrated historical figure for both his public and private lives.

Carola Oman, *Nelson* (London: Hodder & Stoughton, 1947).

N. A. M. RODGER

neoclassicism In the eighteenth century neoclassicism as a literary mode, that is, the imitation of classical poets and dramatists and subscription to their ideals, began to lose its vitality. The old idea that truth to nature involved truth to authority had become questionable: the boundaries of what were considered 'natural' emotions, for example, were expanding very fast. The same changes of emphasis were eventually to undermine neoclassicism in the visual arts.

Neoclassicism is often used to define the visual arts of the second half of the century, but that is misleading inasmuch as at the heart of the latter was the realization – fuelled by historical, archaeological and geographical enquiry – that the quest for the entirely rational, the 'natural', could not end in human history: there had never been a golden age. The idea of a return to constituent origins remained a powerful one, and priggishness about archaeological exactitude is increasingly detectable in the arts towards the end of the century. However, no one advocated simple-minded copying of antique art: origins were to be sought in the realm of universal and eternal human needs, not history. This philosophy admitted both a variety of authorities – the GOTHIC, for example, in building construction – and the abstract reductionism of the architect Friedrich Gilly (1772–1800) and the sculptor John Flaxman (1755–1826).

The most flexible readings of classical architecture could not offer prototypes for the new buildings that were in demand after mid-century.

As the most utilitarian of the high arts, the one most obviously tied to need, ARCHITECTURE attracted the earliest, the most extreme and the most influential theoreticians of neoclassicism. J. L. de Cordemoy's *Nouveau traité de toute l'architecture* (A New and Comprehensive Treatise on Architecture, 1706) called for the abandonment of façades that merely imitated architecture, in a return to the first principles of column-and-lintel. He was followed in mid-century by the demands of Marc Antoine Laugier (1713–69) and the Venetian priest Carlo Lodoli (1690–1761) for an architecture entirely based on *besoin*, man's need for shelter. After 1750 the systematic archaeological investigation and recording of sites as diverse as POMPEII, Paestum and Palmyra revealed the primitiveness of some classical civilizations: indeed, the Greeks were barbarians once. It was also thought that clues to the wellsprings of architecture might be found in that of present-day 'barbarians' in central Asia and the New World, and the PICTURESQUE vernaculars of Europe.

Although the century saw the first surveys of many monumental remains in Attica, Asia Minor and southern Italy, contemporary architectural neoclassicism had relatively little to do with Greece, except insofar as some conceptualized Greece as the ultimate source of the art. The more accessible Italian remains were continuing sources of inspiration: PIRANESI evoked Etruria and Egypt (neoclassicism was also preclassicism, seeking origins earlier than classical antiquity) in his defence of Italian primacy. Other countries defined their positions with reference to the Roman Empire. For example, the sometime architect Thomas JEFFERSON, inspired by French friends, concluded that antique construction had reached rational perfection not on Greek or Italian soil, but at the Maison Carrée, Nîmes; his contemporary the Danish painter Nicolai Abildgaard (1743–1809), on the other hand, explored Nordic myths, for Scandinavia had never seen the Roman legions. Neoclassicism was the first international art movement, not least because its principles were easily communicated verbally, but it was not homogeneous.

Like architecture, PAINTING could look to only a limited number of antique formal models. Greek vase painting, rather than Roman murals, offered visual conventions that seemed elegant and challengingly restrictive. Painting, the most narrative of the visual arts, chose subjects from classical antiquity, for example Mengs's *Parnassus* (1760–1) and David's *Oath of the Horatii* (1784–5), which are exemplary for their serious exhortative themes, and for their linearity and lucidity of composition, in contrast to the complexity and the illusionistic devices and colouristic bravura of BAROQUE painting. Neoclassical paintings were often statements about the evils of tyranny and luxury, notions that were scarcely contentious even under the *anciens régimes* for which most of the works were produced.

Mengs's mural *Parnassus* was painted for the villa in Rome that housed Cardinal Alessandro Albani's (1692–1779) collection of antique sculpture, which after 1758 came under the curatorship of WINCKELMANN. There Winckelmann, who had already written *Gedanken über die Nachahmung der griechischen Werke in der Malerei und Bildhauerkunst* (Reflections on the Imitation of Greek Art in Painting and Sculpture, 1755), wrote *Geschichte der Kunst des Altertums* (History of Ancient Art, 1764). His precepts are easily reconcilable with the work of the best contemporary sculptors, Antonio Canova (1757–1822) for example. Winckelmann's evolutionary model for the progress of antique sculpture towards the perfection of a Lysippus or a Praxiteles was conventional, but his relative lack of interest in the relationship between nature and the ideal was not. His concern was with the viewer's reaction to the best Greek sculpture, its 'noble simplicity and calm grandeur' and the contact it provided with the 'great and grave soul' of the Greeks. Reading Winckelmann, Goethe wrote, 'one does not learn anything but one becomes somebody'; the same could be said of the best neoclassical art.

See also CULT OF ANTIQUITY, GREEK REVIVAL.

The Age of Neo-classicism, Catalogue of the Fourteenth Exhibition of the Council of Europe (London: Arts Council of Great Britain, 1972).
Hugh Honour, *Neo-classicism* (Harmondsworth: Penguin, 1968).
Anthony Vidler, *The Writing of the Walls: Architectural Theory in the Late Enlightenment* (New York: Princeton Architectural Press, 1987).

CHRISTINE STEVENSON

nervous system   Following Descartes's view that the nerves were the medium by which sensation and motion were transmitted, and John Locke's account of the mind as the product of sensation, Enlightenment thinkers believed that the nervous system played a mediating role between man and the environment. In the first half of the century physicians like George Cheyne (1671–1743) made nervous disorders fashionable. Agitation or lowness of spirits were described as a nervous disease, 'the English malady', and were regarded as the price of advanced civilization. Mid-century medical authors such as Albrecht von Haller and William Cullen (1710–90) claimed that a precondition of sensation was a nervous property, SENSIBILITY. The concept of sensibility was used to explain how mental abilities were determined by such physical factors as heredity, constitution and mode of life. 'Refined', 'delicate' and 'sensible' were terms applied to both nerves and mind. This model was employed by Scottish social theorists like David Hume and Adam Smith in their accounts of the origins and development of society. It was implicit in the writings of the sentimental novelists (*see* SENTIMENT). In 1776 Cullen coined the term 'neuroses' to refer to all non-febrile disorders of the nervous system. At the end of the century, partly under the influence of ROMANTICISM, the nervous system began to be remodelled in hierarchical terms. It remained, however, the fundamental structure in which differences between social classes, men and women, and man and the animal world were naturalized.

J. D. Spillane, *The Doctrine of the Nerves: Chapters in the History of Neurology* (Oxford: Oxford University Press, 1981).

CHRISTOPHER LAWRENCE

Netherlands, Austrian The circumstances surrounding the transfer of the Netherlands from Spanish to Austrian rule at the Treaty of Utrecht (*see* SPANISH NETHERLANDS) determined much of its history up to the DIPLOMATIC REVOLUTION of 1756. The Dutch always regarded the region as a rampart for their republic's defence against France, and jealously retained their rights to garrison its leading fortresses, which composed the notorious 'Barrier'. However, despite designated annual subsidies from Vienna, which did not cease until 1756, the Dutch failed to maintain the fortresses, which fell to French assaults in 1745–7. To compound the problem, they obdurately held to the continued closure of the Scheldt, which cut off almost all supplies to and from the port of Antwerp; this stranglehold was only partially eased by improved canal communications with Ostend. Charles VI bitterly resented the suspension and abolition of his Ostend Company (1727–31) which only confirmed for Vienna how intolerable were the provisions of Utrecht. Austria's strident maintenance of Catholicism and papal authority in the Netherlands may have made the Dutch even more insistent on Protestant minority rights and their garrisons' freedom of worship.

The provincial structure of the Netherlands was complex, dating back to before the sixteenth century, but only Brabant had a written constitution. Yet Netherlandish economic strength rendered this region the Habsburgs' best financial asset, and Charles VI and his daughter Maria Theresa were wary of tampering with jealously guarded rights, however unaccountable and self-confessedly anachronistic they might be. During the eighteenth century the Netherlands population grew, and agricultural production became more efficient. Liège, an independent principality on the eastern periphery of the country, developed a reputation for coal-smelted iron and weapon production, as did its dependency Verviers as a textile centre.

This period of comparative tranquillity ended in November 1780, with the death of Maria Theresa, when Joseph II became the sole ruler of the Habsburg Empire. His reforms cut across the grain of Netherlandish institutions, and incited a national revolt unprecedented since the era of Philip II (1527–98). The next emperor, Leopold II, endeavoured to return the Netherlands to the *status quo ante*, which he largely achieved by the time of his unexpected death in March 1792. But within three years the Netherlands and the Dutch provinces had been overrun by revolutionary France which, in 1795, incorporated both as the BATAVIAN REPUBLIC. In 1806 Napoleon converted this into a kingdom under the rule of his youngest brother, Louis Bonaparte, but in 1815 the rulership was conveyed to the Dutch prince of Orange. In 1830 this quarter-century of union between the Dutch and the one-time Austrian Netherlands was violently terminated, with the latter becoming the modern kingdom of Belgium.

See also UNITED PROVINCES.

H. Pirenne, *Histoire de Belgique*, vol. 5 (Brussels: M. Lamertine, 1926).
E. Kossmann, *The Low Countries 1780–1940* (Oxford: Clarendon, 1978).

D. D. ALDRIDGE

Netherlands, Spanish Historically, the Spanish Netherlands formed the north-western part of the fifteenth-century duchy of Burgundy. The Hispano-Dutch peace settlement of 1648 (Westphalia) established the northern Netherlands as the independent Dutch Republic (*see* UNITED PROVINCES). The southern Netherlands remained under Spanish sovereignty, their northern bounds marching with north Brabant. The Hispano-French peace settlement of 1659 defined the southern bounds of the Spanish Netherlands in relation to French territory, so that the Netherlandish provinces of Flanders, Hainaut, Namur and Luxemburg constituted Spanish territory marching with French. For the remainder of the seventeenth century the southern boundaries of the Spanish Netherlands were infringed by Louis XIV through war or dynastic pretext; but by 1697 both Louis XIV and William III, in their search for a solution to the Spanish succession question, accepted the elector of Bavaria's governorship of the Spanish Netherlands as an appropriate prelude to offering the Netherlands to the elector in exchange for Bavaria, which would become Austrian-Habsburg. However, the War of the Spanish Succession intervened; and by 1712 French weakness, combined with Austrian-Habsburg determination to obtain the Spanish Netherlands as some compensation for not acquiring Spain's transoceanic possessions, assured the transfer of Netherlands sovereignty from Bourbon Spain to Habsburg Austria under the terms the Treaty of Utrecht. The continued *de jure* closure of the Scheldt to the advantage of Dutch commerce, extensive Dutch garrisoning rights and Dutch championship of Austria's newly acquired Protestant subjects all ensured the long continuance of Austro-Dutch tensions.

F. van Kalken, *La fin du régime espagnol aux Pays-Bas* (Brussels: Lebègue, 1907).

D. D. ALDRIDGE

Neumann, (Johann) Balthasar (1687–1753) German architect and teacher of architecture. He designed the palace of the bishop of Würzburg, the Residenz, which is regarded by some as the finest example of eighteenth-century secular architecture in Europe. Largely self-taught – he trained as a bell and canon founder – he was a man of phenomenal energy and productivity. He owed his fame to the patronage of the Schönborns, a family of imperial counts who, through their service and loyalty to the Habsburgs, rose high in the German Catholic Church and wished to leave permanent memorials, in the form of spectacular buildings, of their reigns as bishops and archbishops. In 1719 the bishop of Würzburg, Johann Philip Franz von Schönborn, gave him a free hand to transform the city. Other Schönborns were so impressed by Neumann's work that they commissioned him to design palaces, churches and fortifications in Bamberg, Speyer and Trier. He was later put in charge of all building work and urban planning in Würzburg and Bamberg, and in 1731 he became professor of civil and military architecture at Würzburg.

E. Hempel, *Baroque Art and Architecture in Central Europe* (Harmondsworth: Penguin, 1965).

MICHAEL HUGHES

New England colonies The origins and development of the New England colonies – Connecticut, Massachusetts, New Hampshire and Rhode Island – were rather different from those of the other North American settlements. Unlike VIRGINIA, which was started as an exploratory commercial venture in 1607, the New England colonies were created as communities by men and women who braved the Atlantic seas in search of an ideal. By the eighteenth century commerce and trade would be their life-blood, but it had been the quest for religious freedom that had driven them to the New World.

English settlement of North America had a late start. In the 1580s a small colony founded at Roanoke Island off North Carolina failed and the colonists disappeared. After the founding of Jamestown, colonizing efforts slowed down until 1620 when English religious Dissenters, called Separatists, sailed aboard the *Mayflower*. Landing south of Cape Cod, the pilgrims established Plymouth Colony according to their Calvinistic religious ideas. In 1630 a larger and better-organized contingent of Dissenters (Puritans) landed near modern-day Boston, and formed the Massachusetts Bay Colony.

Unlike the adventurers and gold-seekers of Jamestown, the Puritans were hard-working people with clearly defined ideas about religion, education, work and defence, a philosophy well suited to carving out new communities from the wilderness. Fiscally and philosophically opposed to regular troops, the Puritan fathers made every male citizen from 16 to 60 a part-time soldier, with compulsory attendance at military drills and musters. They founded Harvard College in 1636, in order to train ministers, modelling it on Cambridge; in New Haven Yale College was founded in 1701. Full participation in community life, religious and political, required a literate populace, so all their children were taught to read and write. A historian later noted that in a community so well supplied with ministers, schoolmasters and birch trees their education was assured.

These practical settlers also had a paradoxical nature which they harmonized within themselves. Intelligent and well educated, they also feared forest spirits and executed fellow colonists for witchcraft. Avowedly Christian, their God was the fierce warrior chieftain of the Old Testament; thus, while they arrived seeking peace, at war they fought unrestrained by any law save His. In England, until the advent of Cromwell (1599–1658), the Puritans, as dissenters from the Church of England, had been poorly treated. They emigrated for religious freedom, but proved intolerant of deviation from the orthodoxy of their creeds and structured, well-ordered life. Idlers, malcontents, the frivolous and, of course, religious dissenters were punished and then banished from the colony. Among those who questioned the leadership were the eventual founders of Rhode Island, New Hampshire and Connecticut.

Life was hard for the new Englanders in the seventeenth century. The summer heat brought repeated outbreaks of deadly malaria, dysentery and typhoid fever. Winters were particularly fierce, and summer crop failure meant starvation in the winter. Only the colonists' shared sense of community, substantial immigration from Europe and a high birth rate ensured population growth.

Another problem was that of relations between the white settlers and the Indians. The Puritans had arrived with an olive branch in one hand and a sword in the other. They desired to live at peace with the Indians, but their growing hunger for land and the significant cultural differences between them made conflict inevitable. The Indians, tough warriors skilled in woodcraft, routinely ambushed and slaughtered colonial militiamen. To counter this, the colonists adopted tactics that had been learned in Ireland, attacking Indian villages, burning crops and killing indiscriminately. In the eighteenth century the situation was reversed: urged on by their French allies, the terror wrought by Indian raids from northern New York and Canada made colonial frontier life one of constant low-intensity conflict. (*See* NORTH AMERICAN INDIANS.)

Eighteenth-century New England remained closely tied to its Puritan roots, but change was evident. The ships that carried people and cargo from Europe to Boston also carried Enlightenment ideas. Increased trade between West Indian sugar plantations, West Africa and New England added to the wealth of the region as a whole. As England took a larger role in the governance of its colonies, New Englanders began serving alongside British regulars on military expeditions against French Canada and the French and Spanish Caribbean. The religious fervour of the Great Awakening, which began in 1735, opened up schisms among the orthodox. The physical size of New England remained unchanged, although Massachusetts claimed Maine, and New Hampshire battled New York over claims to the Hampshire Grants (modern Vermont). The fresh, invigorating ideas of the Enlightenment and the stimulus of the Great Awakening broadened colonial minds. The end of French rule in North America opened up the west, and New Englanders had the time to consider their relationship with England.

New England, and particularly Massachusetts, became the hotbed of sedition and revolutionary foment in the 1760s and 1770s. After the Revolutionary War (see AMERICAN WAR OF INDEPENDENCE) and gradual flowering of manufacture, discord between commercial and increasingly industrial New England and the agricultural south became noticeable. The great-grandsons of the Puritans were to outlaw slavery and to begin to criticize the 'peculiar institution' of the south while they paid their own factory workers a pittance.

Daniel J. Boorstin, *The Americans: The Colonial Experience* (New York: Random House, 1958).

John Morgan Dederer, *War in America to 1775* (New York: New York University Press, 1990).

Michael Kammen, *People of Paradox* (New York: Knopf, 1972).

Perry Miller, *The New England Mind*, new edn (Boston: Beacon, 1961).

Samuel Eliot Morison, *Intellectual Life of Colonial New England* (Ithaca: Cornell University Press, 1936; New York: New York University Press, 1956).

JOHN MORGAN DEDERER

Newgate London's main criminal gaol, Newgate came to symbolize all that was wrong with eighteenth-century English prisons. Located near the Old Bailey, it was a five-storey structure measuring 85 feet by 50 feet. The original fifteenth-century building was damaged in the Great Fire of London (1666), and the subsequent refurbishments cost the City of London £10,000. The resultant elegant exterior contrasted with its interior, which was a warren of gloomy rooms (or wards) divided between the Common Side and the Master Side. Poor prisoners inhabited the Common Side, often experiencing severe overcrowding and squalor: Newgate could accommodate 150 prisoners in comfort, but normally held at least 250. Richer prisoners lived in relative comfort on the Master Side. Officialdom's control within the prison was minimal, most internal affairs being run by the prisoners, whose families, friends and other associates had ready access to them. The demolition of Newgate and subsequent building of a new prison began in 1767, although the burning of the new gaol by the Gordon rioters (*see* GORDON RIOTS) in 1780 delayed its completion until 1785.

See PUNISHMENT.

W. J. Sheenan, 'Finding Solace in Eighteenth-Century Newgate', in J. S. Cockburn (ed.), *Crime in England 1550–1800* (London: Methuen, 1977), pp. 229–45.

J. A. SHARPE

New Orleans   Established in 1718 as Nouvelle-Orléans by John LAW's Company of the West, the Paris-based proprietors of LOUISIANA, New Orleans was situated in a strategic position near the mouth of the Mississippi, which made it pivotal in the struggle for North American dominance. Whoever controlled New Orleans dominated the rich trade of the vast Mississippi-Missouri river system. In 1731 New Orleans and Louisiana returned to French rule, and in 1762 it was ceded to Spain (finalized in the 1763 Treaty of Paris).

American frontiersmen sailing cargoes down the Mississippi often clashed with Spanish officials, and bitter discord over treaties on free passage on the Mississippi through New Orleans further divided the American congress. In 1800 Spain returned Louisiana to Napoleonic France. French control of the Mississippi forced President Jefferson to consider a British alliance. Napoleon dispatched 40,000 troops under General LeClerc (1772–1802) to quell a slave revolt on French Haiti, and then proceed to New Orleans. Yellow fever decimated the force, and Napoleon sold the city and the Louisiana Territory to the United States in 1803. Out of the city's polyglot population of Africans, Americans, Canadians, French, Indians and Spanish evolved a unique culture.

JOHN MORGAN DEDERER

Newton, Sir Isaac (1642–1727)   English scientist and mathematician. While based at Cambridge he was a fellow of Trinity College. He became a fellow of the Royal Society in 1675 and president in 1703. In 1796 he moved to London to become warden of the Royal Mint and in 1700 he became keeper. He was knighted in 1705.

Whether Newton is regarded as the father of modern science or as the last of the alchemists, it is clear that he stood at the most significant crossroads in scientific history, the parting of the ways between the ancients and moderns. His achievement was monumental: in his rigorously mathematized mechanical system of the world he succeeded in uniting the mathematico-deductive tradition of Galileo (1564–1642) with the mechanical philosophy of Descartes.

The key to his cosmology lay in his introduction of a third variable, force, to the science of matter and motion. He transformed force from being merely a property of moving bodies into an abstract entity with ontological reality. Nevertheless, how he spoke about force depended on whether he was attempting to describe its effects, when mathematics sufficed, or its workings, when he invoked an ether.

These differing discourses on force are indicative of the problems he encountered in trying to reconcile the mechanist's concept of inert matter with the alchemical concept of active principles. Isaac Barrow (1630–77), the teacher whom he succeeded as Lucasian professor of mathematics in 1669, and the Cambridge Platonist Henry More (1614–87), were both committed to the view that a subtle spirit pervaded and enlivened matter. Newton also conducted his own alchemical experiments and made detailed notes on Ralph Cudworth's (1617–88) *True Intellectual System of the Universe* (1678).

It was in his optical experiments and his speculations on the nature of light that his mechanical thinking was most conspicuously tinged with alchemy. In 'An Hypothesis Explaining the Properties of Light' of 1675 (which includes a description of the periodic phenomenon of 'Newton's rings') he introduced an aether and distinguished light from air and aether by defining it as 'something or other capable of exciting vibrations in the aether'. At this stage he did not claim universality for this ether since it would have contradicted his definition of matter. By the time he wrote the *Philosophiae naturalis principia mathematica* (The Mathematical Principles of Natural Philosophy, 1687), inter-particulate forces had replaced the aether. In the General Scholium of 1713 and in the *Opticks* (1717) he resolved the ontological problem of his aether by claiming that short-range forces acted between its constituent non-inertial particles. In the *Principia* he had no need of an aether, for what he was offering was mathematical proof of a universal force, namely gravity.

In book 1 of the *Principia* he stated his laws of motion, the principle of inertia (a change in motion is proportional to the force impressed) and the principle of action and reaction. Replacing Huygens's (1629–95) centrifugal force with his centripetal force, he applied these laws to bodies orbiting attracting centres, and proved that if the central force varied in proportion to the inverse of the square of the distance of the body then the orbit would be an ellipse. He thus proved that Kepler's (1571–1630) laws of planetary motion could be derived from dynamics. In book 2 he demolished Cartesian cosmology by showing that a vortex could not be a self-sustaining system (see CARTESIANISM). And in book 3 he universalized the law of gravitation by correlating the centripetal acceleration of the moon with the acceleration of gravity on the earth's surface. (He had approximated this last calculation in 1666 shortly after graduating from Trinity College.)

His career was not free from dispute. When the *Principia* was in progress, Hooke (1635–1702) claimed that Newton had plagiarized him. A longer-lived dispute concerned whether he or LEIBNIZ was the inventor of calculus. This dispute began in the 1690s and outlived Leibniz, who began a second dispute which was to colour matter theory for decades; he claimed that gravity was occult. It may have been partly in response to him that Newton revived his aether hypothesis in 1717.

The aether revival allowed Newton's materialist followers to equate the ether with active principles and thereby attribute activity to matter, a position Newton did his utmost to disprove for theological reasons: if matter were active then there would be no room for God in nature. As president of the Royal Society, Newton, along with Hauksbee and Desaguliers (1683–1744), sought to demonstrate through electrical and pneumatic experiments the existence of a repulsive virtue, and proselytizing itinerant lecturers brought home the theological and moral lessons to be drawn from Newtonian science. During the eighteenth century Newtonian science became increasingly heterogeneous as Enlightenment philosophers cited Newton's authority as a synonym for truth. His reputation grew considerably after his death.

See also ATOMIC THEORY.

Betty Jo Teeter Dobbs, *The Foundations of Newton's Alchemy, or the Hunting of the Greene Lyon* (Cambridge: Cambridge University Press, 1975).

Henry Guerlac, *Newton on the Continent* (Ithaca, NY: Cornell University Press, 1981).

Margaret Jacob, *The Newtonians and the English Revolution 1689–1720* (Hassocks: Harvester, 1976).

Richard Westfall, *Never at Rest: A Biography of Isaac Newton* (Cambridge: Cambridge University Press, 1980).

M. L. BENJAMIN

New York In 1626 the Dutch founded the colony of New Netherland on the North (now Hudson) River, placing their capital, New Amsterdam, on the tip of Manhattan Island. They had purchased it for $24 worth of trinkets from Indians who did not even live there. Captured in 1664 by the English who renamed the colony and the city New York, the city soon became a leading colonial port. Upstate farmers sold their grain alongside pirates such as Captain Kidd (c.1645–1701) who were bartering pilfered goods.

Strategically located on the North River, New York City had a superb deep-water port, easy access up the North River–Lake Champlain corridor and control of Long Island and the surrounding waters. During the War of Independence Washington tried to defend the city and failed. The British quickly turned New York into their principal North American base, remaining there until late in 1783. Many important battles were fought in New York state, including the pivotal rebel victory at Saratoga. After the war New York was chosen as the first temporary capital under the new constitution. This helped to attract many of the new banking ventures. By 1810 it was the most populous state as well as the manufacturing, trade and transportation centre of the new nation.

JOHN MORGAN DEDERER

New Zealand   European visitors to New Zealand in the eighteenth century encountered a culture that had developed in isolation over the previous millenium, whose origins were in eastern Polynesia. Although the Maori displayed regional diversity, particularly in dialect and means of subsistence, theirs was basically a homogeneous culture separated into tribal groups. When Cook made contact with them on the east coast of the North Island in 1769, he found a people unaffected by European contact and with no memory of the fleeting but disastrous visit of Abel Tasman (c.1603–59) in 1642.

Although European contact increased steadily after 1769, New Zealand remained essentially a Maori society for the remainder of the eighteenth century. Cook refitted his ships there on each of his three voyages and the islands were visited by French, Spanish and other British explorers. In the 1790s Europeans began to exploit some of its basic resources, particularly seals, whales, timber and flax. These economic forays did not lead to permanent settlements, although temporary bases were established for a few months in the two main islands and the Maori eagerness to trade became apparent.

W. H. Oliver (ed.), *The Oxford History of New Zealand* (Wellington: Oxford University Press, 1981).

DAVID MACKAY

Nile, Battle of the *see* ABOUKIR BAY, BATTLE OF.

nobility   The concept of nobility was based on the idea of living nobly, in turn derived from the stoical code of the patrician elite of classical Rome, and meant being lofty in spirit and ambitious, and giving leadership. This civic humanism, revitalized in the Renaissance, was still a potent ideal for the classically educated ruling elite, most of whom assumed that the lower orders could not develop such qualities. As a rank, nobility was, like servitude, largely a hereditary status, but one that was defined differently in almost every country. In Britain title and land passed generally only to the eldest son, whereas the numerous Polish nobility were largely illiterate and poor. Many French *hoberaux* and Spanish *hidalgos*, though nobles, had no more land than small peasant farmers; and in Prussia many unemployed nobles lived on the hospitality of their wealthier fellows. The distinguishing mark of nobility was abstention from work, and a noble who engaged in trade or industry could lose his rank by law. Military and government employment, on the other hand, preserved or even imparted rank. This was sometimes embodied in an official Table of Ranks, as in Russia, which was designed to link nobility to service to the state.

See also ARISTOCRACY, LANDOWNERSHIP.

J. M. Black, *Eighteenth Century Europe 1700–1789* (London: Macmillan, 1990).

PHILIP WOODFINE

noble savage, cult of the   The concept of the noble savage, which arose from the encounter between American Indians and Europeans and the growth of ANTHROPOLOGY, played an important part in eighteenth-century discussions of the history and merit of CIVILIZATION. It was by no means a novel subject, for the idea of the savage can be traced back to the ancients.

Its idealization is most readily associated with the writings of ROUSSEAU, whose *Discours sur l'origine et les fondements de l'inégalité parmi les hommes* was an extreme instance of the glorification of natural or savage man and the denigration of its antithesis, civilized man. Natural man as depicted by Rousseau was a healthy, robust, unreflective and fearless creature; he was indolent and had no cause to be otherwise, since nature was bountiful and man's needs few. Above all, he was happy, not least because of a striking feature of Rousseau's vision of the infancy of mankind: its solitariness. Natural man, in the conception of this troubled *philosophe* whose own relationships with his fellow beings were difficult at the best of times, lived alone and met others rarely. The chance encounters between men and women were short; women raised children on their own and parted with them as soon as the latter could survive independently.

Among those who had no time for the cult of the noble savage was Samuel Johnson. Boswell reported that when he argued for the superior happiness of the savage life, Johnson sought to delude him: 'The savages have no bodily advantages beyond those of civilized men. They have no better health; and as to care or mental uneasiness, they are not above it, but below it, like bears.'

Although women were often portrayed as having played a crucial part in bringing the state of nature to an end, and as the principal beneficiaries of this change, the image of the savage was also deployed by some eighteenth-century writers to depict the deplorable conditions under which women lived in modern society. Here the notion of the savage was far removed from ideas of natural dignity and nobility. Thus in her *Vindication of the Rights of Woman* Mary Wollstonecraft claimed that 'An immoderate fondness for dress, for pleasure, and for sway, are the passions of savages; the passions that occupy those uncivilized beings who have not yet extended the dominion of the mind, or even learned to think with the energy necessary to concatenate that abstract train of thought which produces principles. And that women from their education and the present state of civilized life, are in the same condition, cannot, I think, be controverted.'

See also PRIMITIVISM, SAVAGERY, WILD MEN.

V. G. Kiernan, 'Noble and Ignoble Savages', in G. S. Rousseau and Roy Porter (eds), *Exoticism in the Enlightenment* (Manchester: Manchester University Press, 1990), pp. 86–116.

Anthony Pagden, *The Fall of Natural Man: The American Indian and the Origins of Comparative Ethnology* (Cambridge: Cambridge University Press, 1988).

SYLVANA TOMASELLI

noblesse d'épée A section of the Second Estate in *ancien régime* France, the *noblesse d'épée* saw themselves as providing the natural leadership of the French NOBILITY. The claim was based on the assertion that true nobility depended on an original act of military valour rather than on the possession of high office. Hence their emphasis was on the sword rather than the professional gown, or *robe*. Indeed, unlike the NOBLESSE DE ROBE, the *noblesse d'épée* always insisted that their members passed the crucial test of heredity. However, the theoretical distinctiveness of the *noblesse d'épée* did not always match the reality, for *robe* and sword both claimed the privileges of noble status, and that preeminent fact was more significant than the different traditions on which their nobility was based. Besides, the attraction of intermarriage between the scions of ancient but impoverished noble houses and the daughters of affluent *robe* noblemen proved on occasion to be irresistible. However, Louis XIV succeeded in strictly limiting the number of these liaisons, unlike his successor, Louis XV.

Roger Mettam, *Power and Faction in Louis XIV's France* (Oxford: Blackwell, 1988).

J. H. SHENNAN

noblesse de robe The possession of French NOBILITY under the *ancien régime* was either hereditary or personal. It generally took three generations of personal nobility to acquire a hereditary title, and one of the chief routes to hereditary noble status, achieved either immediately or in the third generation, was through the acquisition of high office in the law or administration. Successful families thereby became members of the *noblesse de robe*. However, the phrase is imprecise, for the possession of nobility was more important than its origins. Some members of the *noblesse de robe* came from families that had already gained noble status in some other fashion, while intermarriage continued to blur the distinctiveness of noble origins.

F. L. Ford, *Robe and Sword: The Regrouping of the French Aristocracy after Louis XIV* (Cambridge, Mass.: Harvard University Press, 1953).

J. H. SHENNAN

Nonconformity *see* DISSENTERS.

Nonjurors The term 'Nonjurors' refers to the members of the Church of England who, after the Glorious Revolution (1688), were ejected from office for refusing to take the oaths of allegiance and supremacy to William and Mary, because it would mean breaking their previous oaths to James II (1633–1701) and his successors. They included Archbishop William Sancroft (1616–93) and eight bishops, some 400 clergy and a few laymen, in England; nearly all the Episcopalian clergy in Scotland; and one bishop in Ireland. They had little personal devotion to James: five of the bishops were among the seven bishops tried for seditious libel in 1688. Their Anglican principles were balanced uneasily against the divine right of kings.

As well as their 'state point' they also had a 'church point': they repudiated the parliamentary sacking of bishops for a political crime. After the crown filled the vacant bishoprics in 1691 a Nonjuror sect was perpetuated; new bishops were secretly consecrated, the last of whom died in 1805. During Queen Anne's reign there were fifty Nonjuror chapels in London. The abjuration oath (1701) and accession of George I replenished their ranks but, with the death of the last ejected bishop in 1711, some returned to the established church. Among influential Nonjurors were the journalist Charles Leslie (1650–1722), the mystic William Law (1686–1761), the hymnologist Robert Nelson (1665–1715) and the historians Thomas Carte (1686–1754), Jeremy Collier (1650–1726) and Thomas Hearne (1678–1735).

J. H. Overton, *The Nonjurors* (London: Smith, Elder & Co., 1902).

MARK GOLDIE

Nootka Sound incident Nootka Sound is an inlet on the Pacific coast of Vancouver Island, at which a British trading entrepôt, with markets across the Pacific, had been established in the mid-1780s. From 1789 to 1794 it was the focus of an Anglo-Spanish dispute, which led to fleet mobilizations in 1790. Spanish warships from Mexico seized British vessels at Nootka in 1788 on the grounds that, through its presence there, Britain was challenging Spain's historic sovereignty in the Pacific. The Dutch, who were Britain's ally, and the French, owing to the Family Compact with Spain, were also drawn into the fray. The British cabinet were as bellicose as the Spanish *junta*; but the moderation of Pitt and Floridablanca (1728–1808), who was realistic about the weakness of his ally France (Nootka occasioned a debate in the National Assembly concerning future powers to make peace or war, crown or nation), defused the tension. Freedom of whale-fishing throughout the Pacific was accepted, as well as mutual abstention from territorial claims in northern California and Alaska. It may have been Pitt's greatest diplomatic success in peacetime, and it paved the way for the establishment of British Columbia.

C. de Parrel, 'Pitt et l'Espagne', *Revue d'histoire diplomatique*, 64 (1950), 58–98.

D. D. ALDRIDGE

North, Frederick, eighth Lord North and second earl of Guilford (1732–1792) English statesman. His reputation has been tarnished by the loss of the American colonies, but he was a politician of considerable skill and a prime minister of some talent. His greatest gifts lay in public finance, where he proved his worth as chancellor of the exchequer, and in parliamentary debate, where he was a formidable performer. Like most British politicians, he upheld the sovereignty of the British parliament in North America. His instincts were conciliatory, and in the early 1770s his efforts met with some success, but a crisis in the finances of the East India Company reopened the American dispute. Once the BOSTON TEA PARTY had taken place, he felt compelled to pass the Coercive Acts and the situation deteriorated thereafter. He was aware that he was temperamentally unsuited to the conduct of a major war. Military defeat eventually led to the country gentlemen withdrawing their support, and he resigned in March 1782. The disastrous coalition with FOX antagonized the king and a substantial body of opinion. After the dismissal of the coalition his health declined. By 1788 he had virtually retired from politics.

P. D. G. Thomas, *Lord North* (London: Allen Lane, 1976).

JOHN W. DERRY

north-west passage The search for a passage to Cathay through an ice-free Arctic Sea across the top of Canada began with Cabot in the fifteenth century but was resumed more systematically in the eighteenth century. Early attempts, such as the fatal Knight expedition of 1719, focused on a route through Hudson Bay joining up with the mythical Strait of Anian. In the 1740s the search was resumed as a result of the enthusiasm of a publicist, Arthur Dobbs (1689–1765), who master-minded the voyages of Christopher Middleton (*d* 1770), William Moor and Francis Smith. These attempts were defeated by ice and contrary flood tides. Overland routes were pursued by Samuel Hearne (1745–1792) between 1769 and 1771 and by Alexander McKenzie (?1755–1820) in 1789, who reached the Arctic Ocean via the Coppermine and McKenzie Rivers respectively.

The search from the Pacific coast was one of John Byron's (1723–86) objects in 1764 but it was not until Cook's third voyage that it was seriously pursued. His discoveries on his voyage to the north-west coast of America seriously reduced the possibility of a navigable passage, and the subsequent survey by Vancouver finally destroyed the credibility of the mythical straits.

G. Williams, *The British Search for the Northwest Passage in the Eighteenth Century* (London: Longman, 1962).

DAVID MACKAY

Norway In 1397 the Union of Kalmar had formally joined Norway with Denmark and Sweden, and the union with Denmark persisted until 1814. Norway was, however, very much a junior partner: in demographic, economic and political terms. Its population rose from 550,000 in 1770 to 843,000 in 1795, and about 10 per cent of the population was urban in 1801. The Norwegian economy was based on fishing, forestry, mining and farming; timber, fish and metals were exported. The peasantry were directly or indirectly involved in pro-duction for export, which formed about 30 per cent of the country's aggregate production around 1801.

Swedish pressure was an important feature of Norway's international position. Charles XII was killed besieging a Norwegian fortress in 1718. Gustav III sought to gain Norway, which was protected by the Danish-Russian alliance, especially in 1784 when Catherine II made it clear that she would oppose such a policy with force. Norway and Denmark were increasingly divided by their respective economic links: Norway traded with Britain, while Denmark traded principally with Germany, France and North America. This tension increased when Denmark allied with Napoleon. Swedish support against Napoleon led to international acceptance of its acquisition of Norway, which was ceded by Denmark under the Treaty of Kiel of 1814. The Norwegians were persuaded to accept union with Sweden under the Swedish crown. *See also* BALTIC.

JEREMY BLACK

Novalis [Hardenberg, Friedrich von] (1772–1801) German romantic poet and novelist. Novalis, which means 'pioneer', 'newsbringer', was the pen-name of Friedrich von Hardenberg, a poet and inspector of the government salt-works at Weissenfels, Saxony. With the brothers Friedrich (1772–1829) and August Wilhelm Schlegel (1767–1845) and Ludwig Tieck (1773–1853), he formed the first Jena Romantic school. Inspired by Schiller and Goethe, Fichte and Werner (1768–1823), he regarded himself as a prophet: 'The world must be romanticized. Then we will discover its original meaning.' The death of his young fiancée, Sophie, in 1797, led to a spiritual crisis, which was resolved in a mystical experience he subsequently poeticized in *Hymnen an die Nicht* (Hymns to the Night, 1800). This strengthened the religious, inward tendency of his work. His fragments, collected in *Pollen* (1798) and the *Das allgemeine Brouillon* (The General Brouillon, 1798), as well as other works, also project an encylopaedic vision of 'magic idealism' in which poetry and science should unite. Sympathy as love provided the basis for knowledge, as the fragmentary novel of science *Die Lehrlingeszu Sais* (The Novices of Saïs, 1798) confirmed; so, too, did the unfinished novel *Heinrich von Ofterdingen* (1800), which vied with Goethe's *Wilhelm Meister* to describe the development of a poet. For Novalis, language and nature provided the poet and scientist with a system of signs and hieroglyphs to be penetrated and interpreted; and their common goal was to realize the Golden Age as a political reality.

J. Neubauer, *Novalis* (Boston: Twayne, 1980).

JEREMY ADLER

novel The novel as a recognizable modern form came into being in the eighteenth century. There was naturally a long prehistory, with prose fiction surfacing in ancient Greece and Rome as well as medieval Japan. The confluent energies that ran into the mainstream of the form included epic poetry, romance, the Italian *novella*, the moral essay (such as those in *The Spectator*) and certain elements of stage drama. Prose satires by writers such as Erasmus (?1466–1536), Thomas More (1478–1535) and Robert Burton (1577–1640) were another source of influence, while Puritan autobiographies and the lives of criminals, rogues and pirates (both forms flourishing in the second half of the seventeenth century) offered yet another narrative model. In spite of all this, comparatively little had emerged that we should readily call a novel. Cervantes' (1547–1616) comic masterpiece *Don Quixote* (1605–15), and the classic psychological study by the comtesse de La Fayette (*c.* 1634–1693) *La Princesse de Clèves* (1678), properly qualify for this description, and at a lower level of attainment this might be said of the early picaresque novel in Spain, notably *Lazarillo de Tormes* (1553) and Mateo Alemán's (1547–c.1610) *Guzmán de Alfarache* (1599–1602). In England the most impressive achievement in fiction had been Aphra Behn's (1640–89) *Oroonoko* (1688); but even this moving and morally searching narrative of a slave rebellion looked back rather than forwards in its technique. Behn had died before many of the elements that contributed to the development of the novel had fallen into place.

A long-lasting debate on the rise of the novel has not produced any widespread agreement on exactly how, let alone why, the novel proper finally emerged at the start of the eighteenth century. Some propitious circumstances have been isolated, including the growth of urban living, the possibility of greater privacy afforded by new architectural styles, alleged signs of greater sexual equality and of a new degree of privacy in everyday life, and even what had been seen as an access of individualism at the political and economic level. These make limp explanatory factors, although they may supply an informative context.

The older manuals were inclined to fall back on the simple proposition, *enfin Defoe vint*, and there is much to be said for this way of looking at matters. DEFOE was himself a repository of almost all the tendencies that brought the novel into being. A Dissenter from London merchant stock, he had been intended for the ministry and was deeply versed in the theological forms of the late seventeenth century. He had been a businessman and was to be the author of the archetypal guide to becoming 'the complete English tradesman' (his own bankruptcies notwithstanding). In addition, he had fought at Sedgmoor, served as a political spy and written a regular newspaper of comment and polemic. Above all, he had practised in poetry, satire, biography, domestic conduct manuals, history, topography and economics. This background as a writer was crucial for the figure who was to pioneer the most eclectic and all-consuming form of literature. The first part of *Robinson Crusoe* (1719) is the most representative work of early fiction, as well as one of the greatest. It was the first and almost the only book Rousseau would allow Émile to get his hands on, and it was explored by Marx as a test case of political economy. In the Victorian era it became an epic of colonial expansion, and in recent times it has been read as an allegory of the capitalist ethic. Similarly, *Moll Flanders* (1722) has been interpreted as a study of the female urban proletariat (although Moll's love-life is even more untypical than her criminal career), and *Roxana* (1724) found to illustrate the economic base of sexual politics in early Hanoverian England. Such readings are seldom fully convincing, but they point to a historical resonance in Defoe's texts that is absent from those of his contemporaries.

In England the most interesting figure in the formative period is perhaps Eliza Haywood (c.1693–1756), one of a number of able women

novelists who extended the scandalous memoir into a potentially serious art form. In France, the only other country where the novel
developed with comparable energy, a different accommodation was
made by writers like the abbé PRÉVOST, creator of Manon Lescaut;
Crébillon *fils* (1707–77), with his licentious but polished tales of high
life; and MARIVAUX, with lighter, more delicate and recognizably French
stories of sentimental courtship. There are a few echoes of Marivaux
in Richardson, Fielding and Sterne, but he is closer in spirit to the
major French novelists later in the century: the subject-matter and
epistolary form of ROUSSEAU's *La Nouvelle Héloïse* (1761) and Pierre
Choderlos de Laclos's (1741–1803) *Les Liaisons dangereuses* (1782)
may derive from Richardson, but the combination of emotional intensity with a kind of ruthless philosophical probity looks forward rather
to the marquis de Sade, especially to *Justine* (1791).

It was RICHARDSON who gave the novel a distinct expressive voice
and a special realm of intimacy, not so much in his earlier best-seller
Pamela (1740–1) as in its much greater successor, *Clarissa* (1747–8),
the deepest portrayal of sex, love and death that prose had yet produced. FIELDING began by parodying Richardson, and his best work
retained a strong element of Scriblerian satire and learned wit. But
Joseph Andrews (1742) went beyond its model into a vivid form of
social caricature and a breezy portrait of England at the end of the
Walpole era. His masterpiece *Tom Jones* (1749) helped to codify the
art of fiction, both by its brilliant interpolated critical essays and its
superbly managed plotting, which turned narratology into a rhetorical
demonstration of the providential order governing human life. Fielding's influence can be seen most directly in the work of Tobias SMOLLETT,
with an equally broad social canvas and a coarsened brushstroke. A
more original and ultimately more seminal contribution to the novel
was that of STERNE, whose idiosyncratic and self-conscious style in
Tristram Shandy (1759–67) subverted many of the conventions that
had helped to establish polite fiction in the preceding two or three
generations. His other major work, *A Sentimental Journey* (1768),
satirized and at the same time indulged the fashionable fad for sensibility, a pan-European cult of feeling which is thought by some to
have heralded romanticism and by others to have indicated by its
decadence the need for a new movement of creativity and energy.

By this time the leading writers were drawn into the new medium,
although VOLTAIRE and JOHNSON confined themselves to the *conte* or
short philosophic tale. DIDEROT composed one brilliantly witty novel in
dialogue form, *Le Neveu de Rameau* (written *c.*1770, published 1823),
which was translated by Goethe. And the fact is significant, for GOETHE
was the only writer outside England and France to produce an internationally influential work of fiction in the whole century. This was

Die Leiden des jungens Werthers (1774), a novel in the form of letters describing the tragic career of a sensitive young aesthete; it is one of those books that define an age not because they portray what was already happening but because they caused similar things to happen by way of imitation and response.

Well before the century, the cross-currents that helped to make for both social revolution and literary revival were in full flow. Spain had produced its first considerable novelist since Cervantes in the Jesuit padre José Francisco de Isla (1703–81), with his satirical *Historia del famoso predicador Fray Gerundio de Campazas* (1757–68). The Gothic had raised its sensationalist head with horror stories such as Anne Radcliffe's (1764–1823) *Mysteries of Udolpho* (1794). England had its first great woman novelist in Fanny BURNEY, who produced incisive studies of contemporary urban life, for example *Cecilia* (1782). The novel form had approached the preromantic poem in the idyllic fantasy of *Paul et Virginie* (1787) by Bernardin de Saint-Pierre (1737–1814). By the time the revolutionary barricades were erected, the novel had helped to transform consciousness by the range and depth of its penetration into the fabric of life under the old regime.

See also GOTHIC NOVEL.

J. P. Hunter, *Before Novels* (New York: Norton, 1991).
V. Mylne, *The Eighteenth-Century French Novel: Techniques of Illusion* (Manchester: Manchester University Press, 1965).
J. Spencer, *The Rise of the Woman Novelist* (Oxford: Blackwell, 1986).
I. Watt, *The Rise of the Novel* (London: Chatto & Windus, 1957).

PAT ROGERS

nutrition Historians generally agree that the basic cereal diet of eighteenth-century Europe was nutritionally poor, even if it sometimes provided adequate calories (2,700 calories are required by an adult male, with more needed for hard physical labour). A diet composed largely of bread and peas in Caen in 1725 supplied some 3,000 calories per day but lacked vitamins C and D. Another study of the southern Netherlands suggests that the diet of the poor lacked adequate supplies of animal proteins, fats and vitamin A. The English poor in 1795 also experienced a calorific intake hovering around the bare minimum and an inadequate supply of meat or dairy produce. English data also illustrate the huge regional variations in diet: those living in high wage areas of northern England ate more and better food than those in the low-waged south.

The eighteenth century saw significant changes in both the type and quantity of food eaten in Europe and America. Potatoes began to form an increasingly large part of the diets of the poor after 1750 (*see* POTATO). RICE and maize were introduced in parts of Europe in the same period. Most notably, the century saw the beginnings of the mass consumption of TOBACCO and groceries like SUGAR, TEA and coffee. Per capita consumption of sugar in England grew to some 24 lb. per year by 1775 and tea was already central to the diet of the adult population of the English-speaking world by the middle of the century.

Estimates suggest that families spent more than half their total income on food, with the poorest social groups spending up to three-quarters. Therefore nutritional intake was determined as much by purchasing power as it was by location and climate. There is some evidence of a deterioration in the diet of particular social groups when living standards declined in parts of Europe after the mid eighteenth century. Such experiences may have been particularly severe in cities. Antwerp's poor suffered a 44 per cent loss of calories between 1780 and 1850, with falling consumption of grain, meat, fish and beer. Elsewhere in both rural and urban Europe the poor probably ate less meat and dairy produce after the middle of the century.

Since the 1980s historians have begun to use age and height data to shed light on levels of nutrition. Such data indicate that, as expected, modern stature had not yet been achieved by Europeans in the eighteenth century. Moreover, evidence from London suggests that falling living standards, as expected, coincided with a fall in the heights of adolescent children. By contrast, American soldiers had achieved modern final heights by the later eighteenth century (they were as much as 4 inches taller, on average, than European troops) confirming the higher nutritional status of colonial Americans.

R. I. Rotberg and T. K. Rabb (eds), *Hunger and History: The Impact of Changing Food Production and Consumption Patterns on Society* (Cambridge: Cambridge University Press, 1985).
R. Floud, K. Wachter and Annabel Gregory, *Height, Health and History: Nutritional Status in the United Kingdom, 1750–1980* (Cambridge: Cambridge University Press, 1990).

JEREMY BOULTON

O

obstetrics The practice of obstetrics underwent great change during the eighteenth century as, from around 1720, doctors began to attend more deliveries. This triggered off competition and often acrimonious debate between the midwife, the traditional birth attendant, and her new rival, the obstetrician or 'man-midwife', who was schooled in the latest techniques and the use of instruments. In 1733 the design of the obstetric forceps, which had been kept secret for over a hundred years by the influential surgical family the Chamberlens, was made public, and forceps came into more frequent use. A great many obstetric text-books appeared during the century, especially in Britain, France and Holland, outlining obstetric theory and techniques of delivery. A number of European states had training schemes for midwives, organized on a local basis; elsewhere they were licensed by the church and taught by apprenticeship. Standards of training and practice, and professional status varied greatly among both midwives and men-midwives. Infant and maternal deaths remained high, however, particularly in the lying-in hospitals set up across Europe in a surge of philanthropic effort in the late eighteenth century, when childbed fever was rife.

See also MEDICINE.

J. Towler and J. Bramall, *Midwives in History and Society* (London: Croom Helm, 1986).

HILARY MARLAND

Old Believers The members of the Russian ORTHODOX CHURCH who refused to accept the patriarch Nikon's (1605–81) liturgical reforms were known as Old Believers, schismatics (*raskol' niki*), dissidents or Old Ritualists. The schism originated in the 1650s with Nikon's reform of corrupt texts and rituals. Opponents to the reform were anathematized by the church council of 1666–7, dissent against the church being equated with rebellion against the state. The 1680s saw cruel persecutions of the dissenters; whole communities responded with flight and self-immolation. Peter I adopted different methods of bringing them into line. An Act of February 1716 imposed registration and double taxes on 'non-confessors', and Old Believers were banned from state service and from giving evidence in court. Strictures were accompanied by attempts at moral persuasion of those who erred out of 'blindness and ignorance'. But their numbers grew so that they constituted up to 20 per cent of the population. Peter III made some concessions to them, but greater toleration was initiated by Catherine II: old rituals were permitted if the church was acknowledged, the designation 'schismatic' was withdrawn and rights to enter state service and to give evidence were restored. Many Old Believers returned to Moscow, where with their close-knit communities and puritanical lifestyle they were influential in trade and commerce.

Robert Crummey, *The Old Believers and the World of Antichrist: The Vyg Community and the Russian State, 1694–1855* (Madison, Wisc.: University of Wisconsin Press, 1970).

LINDSEY HUGHES

open-field system   The open-field system, also known as the common-field system, was in its various forms a major feature of EUROPEAN AGRICULTURE from before the Middle Ages, surviving in some countries down to the twentieth century. Characteristically, the arable land of a community was laid out in a number of large fields, which were subdivided into strips. The fields, or furlongs within the fields, formed the basis of the crop rotation, and generally the strips occupied by an individual farmer were widely scattered across each field, for reasons which remain highly speculative. Each farmer had rights to graze livestock in the fields after harvest, and to graze the meadows, common and waste land while the crops were growing. The limitations of the system, involving some restrictions on the crops that could be grown, a possible inadequacy of grazing land, the rapid spread of animal disease and long-term decline in the fertility of the arable, were factors in its gradual replacement by ENCLOSURES.

Alan R. H. Baker and Robin A. Butlin (eds), *Studies of Field Systems in the British Isles* (Cambridge: Cambridge University Press, 1973).

G. E. MINGAY

opera   The dramaturgical turning-point of eighteenth-century opera in the 1760s was marked by the death of Jean Philippe RAMEAU in 1764, the reform work of Christoph Willibald GLUCK (*Orfeo ed Euridice* and

Alceste) and the growing success of the opera buffa as a form in its own right (for example Niccolò Piccinni's (1728–1800) *La buona Figliuola*, 1761). Therewith the age of the castrato, to whom the opera seria was dedicated and to whom Handel paid reverence, came to an end.

Gluck's reform programme initiated a return to the very beginnings of opera at a higher level: opera seria had given the singer pre-eminence over the music. Gluck subordinated the singer to the dramaturgical concept, in order to bring true feelings on to the stage, as he stated in his famous preface to the printed score of *Alceste* (1770).

During the eighteenth century opera had established itself as the most important musical genre. The decades between 1680 and 1750 saw the triumph of Alessandro Scarlatti in Naples, of Handel in London and of Rameau in France. Above all, this was the golden age of the opera seria, or the Neapolitan School, which depended on the librettos of Apostolo Zeno (1668–1750) and Pietro METASTASIO. Opera seria was a formalized drama consisting of dramatic recitatives and virtuoso arias expressive of emotions. There were hardly any ensemble scenes and no chorus. In France, where ballet, the chorus, spectacle and scenery had been paramount since Lully (1632–87), the *Tragédie lyrique* reached its height with the work of Rameau.

The opera seria had eventually to give way to new developments. The popular opera buffa in Italy (PERGOLESI), the French *opéra comique* and the German *Singspiel* (of which the first example was Johann Adam Hiller's (1728–1804) *Der Teufel ist los* (1766)) undermined its position probably to a greater extent than Gluck's reform project. They brought to the stage fleshed-out characters, and thus prepared the way for the opera semiseria, and in particular MOZART's da Ponte operas, with their delicate balance between comic and tragic elements (*Don Giovanni* is called a dramma giocoso – comic drama), and their greater depth of characterization.

The French Revolution gave rise to a new type of opera, the rescue opera. The first example of this genre was *Le Rigeurs du cloître* (1790), set to music by Henri-Montan Berton (1767–1844). Cherubini's (1760–1842) *Lodoiska* (1791) and *Les Deux Journées* (1800) anticipated BEETHOVEN's *Fidelio* (1805–14), which was based on a libretto by the revolutionary public prosecutor Jean Nicolas Bouilly (1763–1842). It was first set to music by the French composer Pierre Gaveaux (1761–1825) in 1798.

A. Lewis and N. Fortune (eds), *Opera and Church Music, 1630–1750* (London: Oxford University Press, 1975).

S. Sadie (ed.), *History of Opera* (London: Macmillan, 1989).

E. Weimer, *Opera Seria and the Evolution of Classical Style, 1755–1772* (Ann Arbor, Mich.: UMI Research Press, 1984).

FRITZ WEBER

optics The study of light and vision, optics, was redirected in the eighteenth century by Newton's *Opticks* (first edition 1704). His experiments on coloured rays and his theories of force and matter suggested a projectile theory of light: luminous sources emitted microscopic cannon-balls, which could be variously refracted and reflected by short-range attractive and repulsive forces. His writings, especially on the forces, allowed various interpretations, leaving eighteenth-century opticians the far from sterile task of experimental and theoretical development, which was most successfully carried out by the French school of Laplace. Projectile theorists succeeded those who, emphasizing the analogy with sound, saw light as a pressure or vibration transmitted through an ether. Franklin and, more rigorously, Euler were exceptions: their interventions highlighted problems with the projectile model (for example, why did stars not lose weight? why was the momentum of light undetectable?). By 1830 classical wave theory had replaced it.

During the century scientists ceased to privilege the theological view of light as a divine agent, although it remained a feature of early Newtonianism and inspired several unorthodox works of 'sacred physics'. Instead, the Enlightenment extracted from optics emblems of the spread of rational illumination.

G. Cantor, *Optics after Newton* (Manchester: Manchester University Press, 1983).

STEPHEN PUMFREY

optimism A spirit of optimism and an uncritical belief in the progress of society have frequently been ascribed to the eighteenth century. The picture that is now emerging shows the period to be no cruder than any other and, if anything, more acutely aware of the pros and cons of civilization and of the complexity of social phenomena. Two of the best-known positive pronouncements about the state of the world, by Leibniz (that this was the best of all worlds), and by Pope ('whatever is, is right'), were challenged by many Enlightenment writers, often at the cost of gross over-simplification of the two authors' positions. Most notorious among them was Voltaire who attacked supporters of the view that 'Tout est bien' (All is well) in a article of that title, claiming that they represented God as a malicious king who cared not what means He used to achieve His end.

See also Lisbon earthquake, Pessimism.

Charles Henry Vereker, *Eighteenth-Century Optimism: A Study of the Interrelations of Moral and Social Theory in English and French Thought between 1689 and 1789* (Liverpool: Liverpool University Press, 1967).
Voltaire, *Philosophical Dictionary*, trans. and ed. Peter Gay (New York: Harcourt, Brace & World, 1962).

SYLVANA TOMASELLI

Orangeism In the United Provinces of the Netherlands the main provincial office was that of stadtholder (literally lieutenant). Monopolized by the house of Orange-Nassau, the country's leading noble family, the office acquired national importance because the princes of Orange generally held it in several provinces simultaneously: WILLIAM III in five, WILLIAM IV and WILLIAM V in all seven. (There were also two periods of republican reaction against Orange, 1650–72 and 1702–47, when the stadtholder's office was left unfilled.) Orangeism, therefore, was the creed of those who supported the prince/stadtholder of the day, seeing him as a necessary focus of unity in the otherwise fragmented Dutch state and as the protector of the citizens against the local oligarchs. There was never a proper party organization, Orangeist support coming from a miscellaneous assortment of social groups: officers of the Dutch army, and civilian officials in Utrecht, Gelderland, Overijssel, Zeeland and rural Groningen, many of whom depended on the prince's patronage for their livelihood; ministers of the Calvinistic church; the Amsterdam Jews; and the lower-middle and working classes generally (or at least the Protestant majority within those classes). The ablest publicist for Orangeism was Elie Luzac (1721–96), whose *Hollands Rijkdom* (1780–3) praised the Dutch state and the stadtholder's role in it as embodiments of Montesquieu's constitutional principles.

Further light is shed on Orangeism by considering the two political movements opposed to it. The older and more traditional of these was the republican States party, so called because of its insistence (following the writings of Johan and Pieter de la Court in the 1660s) on the absolute sovereignty of the provincial states. Its adherents were mainly urban oligarchs of the province of Holland, who tended to mistrust the princes of Orange as would-be monarchs bent on fighting dynastic wars which would harm the republic's trade.

The Patriot movement, on the other hand, which challenged Orangeism in the 1780s, originated outside Holland and drew on support from the broader social spectrum of the middle and lower classes, whose former Orangeist sympathies had declined as the stadtholder's growing power of patronage bound the Orange dynasty more closely to the ruling elite and less to the Dutch nation as a whole. The Patriots held three national conventions at Utrecht (1784–5) and in a torrent of print pressed for the democratization of urban government within the existing federal structure of the republic. Their founding father was the Overijssel nobleman, J. D. van der Capellen (1741–84), whose *Aan het Volk van Nederland* (*To the People of the Netherlands*, 1781) was the most influential Dutch pamphlet of its time.

E. H. Kossmann, 'Enlightened Conservatism: The Case of Elie Luzac', *Acta Historiae Neerlandicae*, 6 (1973), 67–82.

I. L. Leeb, *The Ideological Origins of the Batavian Revolution* (The Hague: Nijhoff, 1973).

HUGH DUNTHORNE

Orientalism   The rise of Orientalism in the eighteenth century was largely the outgrowth of previous developments, particularly in relations with China, Japan and India.

CHINA was the best known of the exemplars. Partly because of earlier travel literature, and misguided efforts to convert the largest, most flourishing and most populous empire in the world to Christianity, Europe's knowledge of the Middle Kingdom was reasonably full and accurate, but Western concerns – some egregious, some subtle – retarded evaluation of that knowledge. The wonder of the first Europeans who visited China generally continued to inspire successive generations. The MISSIONARIES were different, however, for their work among the people brought to light more reliable information about the language, the customs and the people. Missionary zeal, as well as jealousy between the different orders, prevented them and their European audience from realizing how important were their observations.

There was some progress in cultural exchange as linguists, scientists and other intellectuals, especially among the JESUITS, communicated their experiences to their counterparts in the West. The correspondence between Fr Bouvet (*d* 1732) and Leibniz, Fr Prémare (*d c.*1734–5) and Fréret (1688–1749) and Fourmont (1683–1745), Fr Parrenin (1665–1741) and Mairan (1678–1771), and Fr Gaubil (1689–1759) and the cartographer de l'Isle (1675–1726) and Fréret are significant in this respect. So, too, are the three great publications of the Jesuits, *Lettres édifiantes* (1702–73), Du Halde's *Description* (1735) and the *Mémoires concernant . . . les Chinois* (1776–1814). From these high-minded undertakings, the knowledge of the vast empire filtered down, via the physiocrats, to the point as which it was absorbed and misrepresented in the art of *chinoiserie*, probably the one lasting contribution of sinology to the Enlightenment. With the end of the century, previous misconceptions were corrected by overland travellers from Germany and Russia, but their contributions were too late to be effective.

The case of JAPAN was different. After its first contacts with the Portuguese and the expulsion of Christian missionaries, trade was confined to the Dutch, at Nagasaki and with only two ships a year. Limited linguistic and cultural cross-fertilization whetted the curiosity of savants in Holland and literati in Japan, but by the end of the eighteenth century there was still nothing to compare with the fruits of Jesuit labours in China, and the culture remained almost as closed as before.

Interest in Indian language, customs and culture did not lag far behind the first commercial contacts. But in the eighteenth century due appreciation was thwarted while the native political system was destabilized by Anglo-French rivalries. Only in the 1770s did Anqueteil-Duperron's (1731–1805) interest in the Vedas inspire curiosity in Europe, reinforced by the British conquest and the genial spirit of Sir William Jones (1746–94), who helped to found the Asiatic Society of Bengal (1784) and oversaw translations from the Sanskrit that were of signal importance to philology, history and literature.

The artistic heritage of Japan and India, unlike that of China, had to wait until the late nineteenth century to be generally appreciated.

B. Guy, *The French Image of China before and after Voltaire* (Geneva: Institut et Musée Voltaire, 1963).

Edward W. Said, *Orientalism* (New York: Pantheon, 1978).

BASIL GUY

Orissa *see* BENGAL.

Orléans, Philippe, duc d' (1674–1723)   Regent of France during Louis XV's minority (1715–23). His deserved reputation as a roué should not obscure his political talents which enabled him to protect the authority of his young charge, LOUIS XV, and to pursue innovative foreign and financial policies. His regency, unlike most preceding ones, passed off in relative tranquillity despite his inheritance of a country debilitated by war and threatened with a disputed succession. His foreign policy involved the creation of a series of security alliances of mutual guarantee both with France's former enemies, the Holy Roman Emperor, Britain and the Dutch republic, and with Bourbon Spain. In economic affairs his policy was to support the ideas of the Scottish financier John LAW. Law's belief in the value of paper money as a means to prosperity through rapid circulation eventually foundered on the rock of inflation, although not before France had shown real signs of economic recovery.

Orléans, though a flawed personality, was an intelligent man and an important patron of the arts. In the last months of the regency, as boredom and excess took their toll, he allowed his first minister, Dubois (1656–1723), to conduct the day-to-day running of government, but he was careful not to relinquish the authority as regent that he had always exercised on the king's behalf.

J. H. Shennan, *Philippe, Duke of Orléans, Regent of France, 1715–23* (London: Thames & Hudson, 1979).

J. H. SHENNAN

Orthodox Church   Throughout the eighteenth century most of the Orthodox world was under the rule of the OTTOMAN EMPIRE. The head of the *Rum Millet* (the Roman nation, that is Orthodox Christians) was the Ecumenical Patriarch of Constantinople. In the eighteenth century he came increasingly under the influence of the wealthy (and ancient) families of the Greek quarter of Istanbul, the Phanariots, and his concerns became more narrowly Greek. As a consequence, the churches of Serbia and Bulgaria lost their autocephalous status and were governed by exarchs appointed by the patriarch (in 1766 and 1767, respectively).

Russia was beyond the sway of the Ottomans, but there the church was subject to the reforms of the emperor Peter the Great (see PETER I). These wide-ranging reforms were intended to make Russia part of the modern Western world. For the church they meant that it lost its spiritual independence and became part of the state bureaucracy. By the *Spiritual Regulation* (1721), the patriarchate of Moscow and all Russia was abolished and the church governed by an ecclesiastical college, which managed, however, to acquire the more ecclesiastical title of the Most Holy All-Ruling Synod. Seminaries were set up and an attempt made to produce a learned clergy. Although the *Regulation* was Protestant in inspiration, the seminaries were run on Catholic lines, with Latin as the language of instruction, largely because much of the staff was drawn from the Ukraine, which had long been subject to Catholic influence. Monasticism was subject to many restrictions: in the course of the century most monastic estates were confiscated and many monasteries closed down. One result of the Petrine reforms was to make the clergy even more of a priestly caste, cut off from both peasants and gentry.

Towards the end of the century, there was an extraordinary spiritual revival in Orthodoxy, stemming from the monastic settlement on the Holy Mountain of Athos. The most important figure was St Nikodimos of the Holy Mountain (1749–1809) who published a great deal of patristic literature and, together with St Makarios of Corinth (1751–1805), an influential collection of texts, mainly concerned with the Jesus Prayer, called the *Philokalia* (published in Venice in 1782; English translation 1979 ff.). At around the same time the Ukrainian St Paissy Velichkovsky (1722–94), after a period on Mount Athos, established monasteries in Moldavia and reintroduced much of the spirit and practice of traditional monasticism, as well as translating much monastic literature into Slavonic, especially the *Philokalia* (the *Dobrotolubiya*, 1793). Paissy's influence was widespread in the Slav countries and was the inspiration for much of Russia's religious and cultural revival in the nineteenth century.

J. Cracraft, *The Church Reform of Peter the Great* (London: Macmillan, 1971).
G. L. Freeze, *The Russian Levites: Parish Clergy in the Eighteenth Century* (Cambridge, Mass.: Harvard University Press, 1977).
S. Runciman, *The Great Church in Captivity* (Cambridge: Cambridge University Press, 1968).

ANDREW LOUTH

Ossian [Oisín Mac Fhinn Mhic Cumhail Mhic Tréanmóir Uí Baoisne] Ossian was a fabled Gaelic bard, son of Fingal, a Highland chieftain whose deeds he was reputed to have recorded. He was given as the author of *Fingal: An Ancient Epic Poem, in Six Books*, supposedly discovered by James Macpherson (1736–96) in journeys to remote parts of Scotland, and then translated and published by him (1762). His travels and his publications were undertaken with the encouragement of Hugh Blair (1718–1800), professor of rhetoric at Edinburgh University. A second Ossianic epic, *Temora*, followed in 1763, and a collected edition of Ossian's works was published in 1765. *Fingal* at least made some use of ballads that Macpherson had transcribed; *Temora* appears to have come entirely from his imagination. Argument about the texts' provenance continued through the last decades of the eighteenth century: Blair believed Ossian to be a latter-day Homer; Johnson, in his *Journey to the Western Islands* (1775), declared him a trickster's invention. The Highland Society of Scotland established a committee to decide on the authenticity of Ossian's poetry; its report was published in 1805. Although Johnson's judgement now seems correct, 'Ossian' was not merely a fraud. Macpherson's compositions and their widespread acceptance bespeak a fashion for PRIMITIVISM that was highly influential in the late eighteenth century.

Fiona Stafford, *The Sublime Savage: A Study of James Macpherson and the Poems of Ossian* (Edinburgh: Edinburgh University Press, 1988).

JOHN MULLAN

Otaheite *see* TAHITI.

Ottoman Empire By the beginning of the eighteenth century, the long decline of the Ottoman Empire was well under way. Six Sultans held power during this century – Ahmed III (1703–30), Mahmud I (1730–54), Osman III (1754–7), Mustafa III (1757–74), Abdülhamid I (1774–89) and the reformist Selim III (1789–1807) – of whom only the last can lay any real claim to greatness. From a cultural, horticultural, architectural and intellectual point of view, the early decades of the century witnessed a renaissance, particularly in ISTANBUL; this became known as the 'Tulip Period'. Politically, however, the Ottomans did rather less well and the period from the end of the seventeenth century and through the eighteenth century saw a steady decline in real power and loss of territory; for example, by the TREATY OF CARLOWITZ, the Ottomans finally lost Hungary and Transylvania to the Austrians, and by the Treaty of Kuchuk-Kainardji (1774), they lost their suzerainty in the Crimea (*see* BALKANS).

Stanford J. Shaw, *History of the Ottoman Empire and Modern Turkey*, vol. 1: *Empire of the Gazis: The Rise and Decline of the Ottoman Empire, 1280–1808* (Cambridge: Cambridge University Press, 1976).

IAN NETTON

P

Pacific In the late seventeenth century the Pacific existed largely as an empty expanse in the minds of European geographers. Little of its detail, geographic or ethnographic, had been filled in, even though it had been traversed by explorers from Magellan (1480–1521) to Tasman (1603–59). Navigators had traced fragile lines across its immensity and Spanish galleons had plied it in narrow and blinkered bands. Its peoples were scarcely known to Europeans and its economic potential remained confined in the realms of fantasy.

By 1800 the principal islands of the Pacific and its main ethnic groups were known and its commercial exploitation was under way. The ocean and its inhabitants, from being objects of mystery and fascination, became subjects of romantic speculation and then a field for missionary endeavour. Where the Spanish and Dutch had dominated sixteenth- and seventeenth-century exploration of the Pacific, eighteenth-century exploration was dominated by the British. The motivation behind the Georgian voyages of exploration was a mixture of strategic concerns, commercial enterprise and scientific curiosity. Underlying it was the continuing fascination in the possibility of a SOUTHERN CONTINENT, which might produce enormous benefits for its discoverer. The virtues of this continent were proclaimed by numerous voyagers and armchair geographers whose works found an expanding market among a European public avid for travel literature both descriptive and fantastical.

William Dampier's (1652–1715) *New Voyage round the World* of 1697 was the first such work to stir the eighteenth-century imagination, and was the stimulus for his second voyage to western Australia and New Guinea which left England in 1699. Although this achieved little, it kept the Pacific in the minds of the reading and investing public. The floating of the SOUTH SEA COMPANY in 1711 owed much to this impulse, although it never actually exploited the resources of the ocean.

The first eighteenth-century voyage that contributed to knowledge of the Pacific was a last fling by the Dutch. Sailing from the Texel in August 1721, Jacob Roggeveen (1659–1729) discovered Easter Island and touched at parts of the Tuamotus and Samoan group on his passage to Batavia. Commodore ANSON crossed the Pacific as part of a military expedition against Spain in 1741–4, but this voyage, with its catastrophic loss of human life, added nothing to European knowledge of the ocean. When Commodore John Byron (1723–86) sailed for the Pacific on 21 June 1764 he initiated the most sustained and intensive period of exploration in the history of maritime discovery. The subsequent voyages of CARTERET and Wallis (1728–95), BOUGAINVILLE, COOK, LA PÉROUSE, d'Entrecasteaux (1737–93), Malaspina (1754–1809) and VANCOUVER dispelled the remaining myths of the southern continent and the NORTH-WEST PASSAGE and revealed the Pacific fully to the eighteenth-century public. Before this era of exploration was completed, sealers, whalers, fur-traders and other merchants had begun the process of economic transformation that was to be a feature of the nineteenth-century history of the ocean.

O. H. K. Spate, *Paradise Lost and Found* (Minneapolis: University of Minnesota Press, 1988).

DAVID MACKAY

paganism The eighteenth-century church had to deal with two sorts of what could loosely be called 'paganism'. The post-Tridentine Catholic and the Protestant churches maintained their attack on various forms of religious ignorance, notably among the rural masses (the Latin word for 'pagan', *pagus*, also signified 'peasant'). Educational and missionary orders were ever active, while JANSENISM gave a fresh boost to the drive to purge Catholicism of pre– or non-Christian excrescences. Overseas, too, missionary endeavour continued unabated wherever European flags were planted (*see* MISSIONARIES).

The Christian churches also had to cope with a new form of paganism from the social elite. The anticlerical writings of the *philosophes* in France are the best-known example of forms of religious indifference making inroads, especially among men, town-dwellers, and middling and bourgeois milieux in western Europe. The French Revolution, notably in its militantly atheistical phase of 1793–4, took this process of DECHRISTIANIZATION even further. By 1800 European beliefs were in general far more secular and pluralistic than they had been in 1700.

Jean Delumeau, *Catholicism from Luther to Voltaire* (London: Burns & Oates, 1977).

COLIN JONES

Paine, Thomas (1737–1809)   English-born American revolutionary philosopher and writer. He came to prominence as a publicist during the American crisis. In 1776 his *Common Sense* urged the colonists to separate themselves from Britain and many of them were persuaded of the benefits of independence. When the French Revolution broke out he welcomed it as an extension to Europe of the ideas of the English and American Revolutions. In 1791 and 1792 he published the two parts of *Rights of Man*, in reply to BURKE, as a justification of the French Revolution and an exposure of the hypocrisy of British public life, but his proposals for social welfare were widely regarded as an attack on property. Elected to the French Convention in 1792, he opposed the execution of Louis XVI and was imprisoned during the Reign of Terror. His *Age of Reason* (1794–6) purported to defend deism against atheism, but the extremism of his assault on orthodox Christianity shocked many who had previously sympathized with him. On his return to America he was ostracized as an atheist and his final years were unhappy. No one did more to popularize radical ideas and an optimistic belief in progress in the eighteenth century.

A. O. Aldridge, *Man of Reason* (London: Cresset, 1960).

JOHN W. DERRY

painting   The development of painting in the eighteenth century was characterized above all by the emergence of a mass market. Where the art market had previously been dominated in much of Europe by commissions from the church and a circle around the courts in various countries, it now expanded to include a much wider range of society. The auction took hold in much of northern Europe and this, combined with the emergence of art dealers, enabled paintings to be distributed to buyers throughout the continent. Public exhibitions, which began on a regular basis in France in the 1740s and in England in the 1760s, also played a part in stimulating public interest. Finally, technological developments allowed the mass production of prints and therefore gave artists access to a much larger clientele.

The expansion of the market largely dissolved the tight control previously exercised over artistic production and encouraged stylistic developments. In particular, commissions for large-scale decorative frescos diminished, although TIEPOLO continued to paint such expensive works until the 1760s. In France the death of Louis XIV in 1715 led to the decline of the official style associated with painters like Lebrun (1619–90), while the larger number of private buyers sought the more intimate and emotional work of painters like WATTEAU. In eighteenth-century England court and church exercised almost no influence, with painters like HOGARTH developing a style aimed at a wide market. In Italy economic decline meant that many of the best artists were forced to work abroad or to sell to foreigners, and only in Spain and some parts of Germany did court patronage continue to dominate artistic production.

The relative importance of different genres of painting remained wedded to the hierarchy established during the Renaissance, that is with history painting at the top, descending by degrees through landscape and portraiture down to the lowest forms of domestic scene. This structure prevailed despite the enormous popularity of seventeenth-century Dutch art in the period, the emergence of genre painters like Chardin (1699–1779) in France, the dominance of portraitists in England and the triumph of the essentially French ROCOCO style in the first half of the century.

The belief that painting had a moral and didactic role to play resurfaced with the neoclassical movement in the latter part of the century, in a reaction against what was seen as the triviality and decorative emptiness of rococo. Aided by the theories of WINCKELMANN and the teaching of MENGS, NEOCLASSICISM spread from Rome to become the dominant style from the 1770s onwards.

In general, however, whatever the style of the moment, eighteenth-century painting increasingly sought to cast off artificiality in favour of a type of naturalism. This can be noted in the increased vogue for landscape, beginning with Claude Lorraine (1600–82) through to Constable (1776–1837) and Caspar David Friedrich (1774–1840). There was also a growing interest in the individual as an object of study in itself, not merely as a cipher representing an abstract principle. Portrait painters began to explore the psychology of their sitters, notably in the English school exemplified by REYNOLDS, and also among the most vehement of neoclassicists like David.

Not all eighteenth-century painters can be easily categorized by movement and style. Indeed, most of the paintings produced during this period were at best workmanlike, and bore little relation to theory. A large proportion were portraits or mundane hunting and domestic scenes designed for a large clientele of modest means. In any case, the categories have been created by later generations of art historians.

There was also a growing tension in the notion of the role of the artist. He was widely regarded as a teacher, with duties and obligations to see and present moral truths to the audience. This perception was accentuated through state supported institutions like the academies in France and England (*see* ACADEMIES OF ART), and culminated in the relation between DAVID's neoclassical paintings and the French Revolution. There was an equally strong perception of the artist as the continuer of a tradition that stretched back through the Renaissance to the ancient world. Opposing these conceptions was the more introspective notion, later to be characterized as romantic, that the duty of artists was to present their inner vision, and to discover for themselves the best means of achieving this.

See also HISTORY PAINTING, LANDSCAPE PAINTING, PORTRAIT PAINTING.

M. Levey, *Rococo to Revolution: Major Trends in Eighteenth-Century Painting* (London: Thames & Hudson, 1966).

IAIN PEARS

Palatinate   Known in German as 'Pfalz', the Palatinate consisted of various territories belonging to the many branches of the Palatinate WITTELSBACHS, the most significant of which were those of the elector palatine. After defeats in the Thirty Years War, the Palatinate did not play as prominent a role as before in German and European politics. The territories, scattered on both banks of the upper Rhine, were vulnerable and lacked geographical cohesion. They were severely ravaged by the French in the wars of the 1670s and 1690s. In 1685 the territory was inherited by a Catholic branch of the house, which began to promote Catholicism and to persecute the Calvinists. This contributed to a major religious crisis in Germany in the 1720s, which came close to war. In 1710 venality of offices on the French model was introduced, which led to a sharp decline in the standard of administration. In 1720 the capital was moved from Heidelberg to Mannheim. After a period of stagnation, the territory began to revive under the reforming elector CHARLES THEODORE but in 1777 he inherited Bavaria and moved his residence to Munich, after which the Palatinate again fell into neglect.

H. Grundmann (ed.), *Gebhardt Handbuch der deutschen Geschichte*, vol. 2, ninth edn (Stuttgart: Union, 1970).

MICHAEL HUGHES

Palladianism   The influence of Andrea Palladio (1518–80) is detectable in earlier architecture, but Palladianism as a style began in 1715, with the first volume of Colen Campbell's (*c*.1676–1729) *Vitruvius Britannicus*, which contained engravings of British classical architecture and Nicholas Dubois's (*c*.1665–1735) translation of Palladio's *I quattro libri dell' architettura* (Four Books of Architecture), with plates redrawn by Giacomo Leoni (*c*.1686–1746). Campbell and Leoni were avowedly dedicated to the absolute authority that Palladio had attributed to the buildings of Roman antiquity, and Inigo Jones (1573–1652) had attributed to those of Palladio. Jones, the first British architect to understand Italian Renaissance architecture, was Palladianism's real inspiration.

The style became associated with a generation of Whig gentry who objected, politically as well as aesthetically, to the English court architecture of the previous half-century (as exemplified by WREN) and its

Continental flavour, and who had the resources to build the porticoed country houses that are Palladianism's most typical manifestation. Richard Boyle, third earl of Burlington (1694–1753) was the most influential exponent of Palladianism, which is epitomized by his Chiswick House (begun 1725), for which William KENT designed the interiors. In its public function and antique inspiration (mediated by the sixteenth century), Burlington's York Assembly Rooms (begun 1730), a realization of a design which Palladio had extrapolated from a Vitruvian description, pointed the way to architectural NEOCLASSICISM. Over the century Palladianism was to spread as far afield as America and Russia.

R. Wittkower, *Palladio and English Palladianism* (London: Thames & Hudson, 1974).

CHRISTINE STEVENSON

Panckoucke, André-Joseph (1700–1753) French publisher. Born at Lille, he wrote burlesque poems and compiled various dictionaries including one of proverbs, *Dictionnaire des proverbes et des façons de parler comiques, burlesques et familières* (1748). His son Charles-Joseph (1736–98) moved to Paris in 1760 and acquired the *Mercure* and the *Journal des savants* as well as other periodicals. He published the *Supplément* to the ENCYCLOPÉDIE from 1776, founded the *Moniteur universel* in 1789 and was also famous for his *Encyclopédie méthodique, ou Par ordre de matières, par une société de gens de lettres, de savans et artistes* (1781–1832), which reorganized the contents of the *Encyclopédie* by subject-matter. Louis-Sébastien Mercier made much of the fact that Panckoucke described himself as the 'entrepreneur de l'encyclopédie méthodique', and deplored the emergence of a world in which such men were to writers what entrepreneurs of building works were to bricklayers and labourers; he owned the usefulness of the work, however, and consoled himself with the thought 'Let Panckoucke make his money as *Entrepreneur* of this massive Encyclopedia, which he won't read.' Panckoucke was also loathed by Diderot, who thought him 'swollen with the arrogance of a newly successful upstart'.

Robert Darnton, *The Business of Enlightenment: A Publishing History of the 'Encyclopédie', 1775–1800* (Cambridge, Mass.: Harvard University Press, 1979).

SYLVANA TOMASELLI

papacy The papacy was in many ways the most tangible aspect of the international organization of the Catholic Church and, claiming to be the centre of Christian unity, was responsible for the maintenance of orthodoxy. The popes of the eighteenth century were usually appointed

in old age, and were sometimes infirm and therefore open to manipulation, for example Benedict XIII (1649–1730) who was advised
by an unscrupulous circle dominated by Niccolo Coscia. Most popes
were appointed for political reasons, for example the French ambassador in Rome was largely responsible for the elections of CLEMENT
XIV and PIUS VI. As well as being the spiritual leaders of the Catholic
Church, popes were also temporal rulers of the Papal States. These
were generally badly administered, largely because for most of the
seventeenth and eighteenth centuries the papacy suffered from immense
financial problems, and although several popes attempted economic
reforms they did not pursue their policies with enough rigour. Nevertheless, there was reforming activity that demonstrated that the
papacy was not the moribund and corrupt institution of Enlightenment satire. In 1692 Innocent XII (1615–1700) made the revolutionary move of striking at the roots of nepotism which had been a feature
of the Renaissance and Tridentine papacy, by decreeing that the pope
should never grant estates, offices or revenues to relatives. The
eighteenth-century popes followed his example, although at the end
of the century Pius VI revived nepotism, assigning substantial allow-
ances to his relatives and building the Palazzo Braschi for his nephew
Luigi.

The period after the mid seventeenth century also saw a significant
decline in the ability of the papacy to play a part on the stage of
international diplomacy. Papal representatives were excluded from the
negotiations leading to the Treaty of Westphalia in 1648, and again
from the 1697 Treaty of Ryswick and the 1713 Treaty of Utrecht. At
the start of the eighteenth century CLEMENT XI was unable to stop VICTOR
AMADEUS II from disputing papal jurisdiction in his lands. The dispute
was not settled until 1742 when the papacy yielded to most of his
claims. The Treaty of Vienna in 1735 completely ignored the feudal
rights of the pope and gave Naples and Sicily to Spain. Papal feudal
rights were ignored again in 1748 at the Treaty of Aachen. JOHN V of
Portugal broke with the papacy over his demand for a patriarchate in
Lisbon, diplomatic relations being severed in 1728–32, and again in
1760–9 when Pombal was angered by CLEMENT XIII's continued support of the Jesuits. Clement XI, who clashed with all the Catholic
powers, pursued, somewhat unsuccessfully, papal claims to supremacy
in Italy. All this demonstrated that although popes claimed to be the
arbiters of Europe, in reality, without military backing, the papacy
was very weak.

The power of the papacy was also threatened by trends towards nationalism and political absolutism within Catholic countries
(see ULTRAMONTANISM). The powers of the papacy were limited in
the Gallican Church in France, where the French crown had long

controlled ecclesiastical appointments (*see* GALLICANISM). From the 1760s the antipapal offensive gained ground with the development of Febronianism, which was based on *De statu ecclesiae et legitima potestate Romani pontificis* (Present State of the Church and the Legitimate Power of the Roman Pontiff, 1763) by Bishop J. N. von Hontheim (1701–90), who published it under the pseudonym 'Justinus Febronius'. He attacked papal power, and asserted the claims of a church council against papal primacy, defending the rights of bishops and secular rulers. In 1769 at Koblenz and at the 1786 Punctation of Ems the German archbishop elect declared that only a general council of the church could wield supreme power, and denounced unjustifiable extensions of papal activity. The most telling illustration of the weakness of the papacy in this period was the suppression of the JESUITS in 1773, a society established to support the papacy, as a direct result of the pressure of secular governments.

The end of the century saw the nadir of the papacy when Napoleon invaded the Papal States in 1796 and forced Pius VI to surrender Ferrara and Bologna as well as valuable manuscripts, at the Treaty of Tolentino. In 1798 General Louis Berthier (1753–1815) entered Rome, proclaimed the Papal States a republic and deposed Pius, who died a prisoner in Valence in 1799. He had, however, left instructions that in an emergency the senior cardinal should convene a conclave to elect his successor. In 1800 Pius VII (1742–1823) was elected, who did much to revitalize the papacy during the first two decades of the nineteenth century.

See also CATHOLICISM.

F. Heyer, *The Catholic Church from 1648 to 1870* (London: A. & C. Black, 1969).

J. Derek Holmes and Bernard W. Bickers, *A Short History of the Catholic Church* (Tunbridge Wells: Burns & Oates, 1983).

JEREMY GREGORY

Paraguay A thriving region of farms surrounding Asunción where the governor resided, Paraguay was famous above all for its Jesuit missions (*see* JESUITS). These missions, which were founded in the early seventeenth century, differed from both Jesuit and Franciscan missions elsewhere in Spanish America, in that no Spaniards, other than Jesuits, were allowed to enter the mission zone and the missions maintained their own armed militia. Governors and bishops could visit but not interfere in the missions. The ministers of Charles III found this increasingly intolerable, especially since a joint expedition of Spanish and Portuguese troops had been required to enforce a transfer of mission territory to Brazil in 1754. In 1767 the Jesuits were expelled, leaving around 100,000 Guarani Indians to the mercy of Asunción and its elite. By then the Jesuits owned 850,000 cattle and 240,000 sheep and were competing with local farmers in the export of hides and the production of yerba maté; and the Jesuit state was being compared to Plato's Republic and the Inca empire. It was the combination of their wealth and virtual independence that brought about their downfall, for neither the Spanish crown nor Paraguayan landowners could tolerate the challenge to their pre-eminence.

See also SPANISH AMERICA.

Philip Caraman, *The Lost Paradise: An account of the Jesuits in Paraguay 1607–1768* (London: Sidgwick & Jackson, 1975).

D. A. BRADING

Paris By 1789 the city of Paris had a population of over half a million people. Between the mid seventeenth and late eighteenth centuries its area had expanded threefold. By any criterion it was one of Europe's major cities. It remained the religious and administrative centre of the kingdom. In the heart of the capital, on the Île de la Cité the Palais de Justice challenged the Cathedral of Notre Dame for pre-eminence, and opposite, on the left bank of the Seine, the Latin Quarter testified to its status as the world's largest university city.

But the university had lost much of its reputation and the city some of its dynamism. The proximity of Versailles, the centre of the French political world, with its royal court, diminished its standing, as did the rise of LONDON, a thriving port and market with a comparable population and a wider commercial and manufacturing base. Paris was owned largely by the nobility, and their elegant town houses reflected traditional landed values. Commercial and fiscal regulations hampered the development of trade, but Colbert (1619–83) allowed the controls to be lifted in one area, the *faubourg* St Antoine, which consequently expanded rapidly as a commercial centre. Industrialization in Paris began around 1760 and was concentrated on the production of luxury goods, glassware, porcelain and wallpaper. Such products were beyond the purses of the poor, who lived permanently in fear of famine like that visited on the city in the terrible year of 1709. The lieutenant-general of police and the intendant of Paris were responsible for countering the consequent threat of public disorder.

The establishment of the office of lieutenant-general in 1667 marked the beginning of an improvement in the environment of the capital, and the introduction of street lighting made it a safer place after dark. In the 1670s Louis XIV decided to convert Paris into an open city by replacing the old defensive ramparts stretching from the *porte* St Honoré to the Bastille with tree-lined walks: the origin of the *grands boulevards* of the nineteenth century. During the eighteenth century efforts were made to give Paris an air of public grandeur worthy of a capital city. The king's principal architect, Ange-Jacques Gabriel (1698–1782), planned the Ecole Militaire and the Place Louis XV, now the Place de la Concorde. Soufflot (1713–1780), the protégé of the king's superintendent of buildings, Marigny (1727–81), built the church of Ste Geneviève, renamed the Panthéon after the Revolution, on the highest point of the Left Bank. Marigny's sister, Madame de Pompadour, lived for a number of years in the most celebrated of Parisian town houses, the Hôtel d'Evreux, later to become the Elysée Palace.

On the eastern edge of the city the *faubourg* St Antoine contained by 1789 some 40,000 people. The decision taken by some of them to attack the most prominent local landmark, the BASTILLE, precipitated the Revolution. At that moment Paris regained its dynamic leading role in France and Europe.

P. Gaxotte, *Paris au XVIIIᵉ siècle* (Paris: Arthaud, 1968).
Orest Ranum, *Paris in the Age of Absolutism* (New York: John Wiley, 1968).
Paris de la préhistoire à nos jours (St-Jean-d'Angély: Bordessoules, 1985).

J. H. SHENNAN

Paris, *parlement* of The *parlement* of Paris was the chief law court in eighteenth-century France, with jurisdiction over about one-third of the kingdom. It was essentially a court of appeal but its political significance had increased as a result of its practice of registering royal enactments and pointing out objections to proposed legislation before registration. This so-called right of remonstrance provided the judges with an opportunity to influence policy and to aspire to a constitutional role. Although the crown always rejected such claims, a symbiotic relationship did develop which, except in moments of crisis, enhanced the authority of both king and *parlement*. However, the judges were not elected to office; indeed, with the growth of venality membership of the *parlement* became a quasi-hereditary right, conferring nobility on a wealthy oligarchy.

The court's opposition to the royal government became more persistent and challenging during the eighteenth century. It was ostensibly concerned with issues of religion and finance, but its supporters interpreted its stance as the defence of law against tyranny. Later it was viewed as a reactionary body that sought to prevent necessary reform. Louis XV abolished the *parlement* in 1771. It was restored by his successor three years later and finally abolished in 1790.

See also PARLEMENTS.

J. H. Shennan, *The Parlement of Paris* (London: Eyre & Spottiswoode; Ithaca, NY: Cornell University Press, 1968).

J. H. SHENNAN

Paris, Treaty of (10 February 1763)   Anglo-French talks towards the end of the costly global SEVEN YEARS WAR led to preliminaries of peace being signed at Fontainebleau on 3 November 1762, and the Treaty of Paris on 10 February 1763. For France, financially exhausted and militarily drained, the terms were moderate, including the regaining of such valuable Caribbean islands as Guadeloupe, Martinique and St Lucia, as well as lost Indian territory. Britain's allies, Hanover, Brunswick and Hesse-Kassel, regained territories invaded by France; and France's ally, Spain, regained Havana and Manila. British gains were substantial. With the cession of Canada by France, the North American colonies were no longer in danger of encirclement, France retaining only a foothold in the Newfoundland fisheries. In addition, Britain took back Minorca, and gained Grenada, Dominica, St Vincent, Tobago and Senegal. The peace did not restore trading relations between Britain and Spain, and was denounced by Britain's late ally Frederick II of Prussia, but was generally seen as a British success. It was violently criticized only by the elder Pitt, the architect of victory now out of office, and by John Wilkes, for whom it was 'like the peace of God, which passeth all understanding'.

Z. E. Rashed, *The Peace of Paris 1763* (Liverpool: Liverpool University Press, 1951).

PHILIP WOODFINE

Park, Mungo (1771–1806)   Scottish explorer. Born in Selkirk, he trained as a surgeon before seeking employment in London in 1791. There he was introduced to Sir Joseph BANKS who secured him a position as a surgeon on an East Indiaman bound for Sumatra. Returning to England in 1793, he was commissioned by Banks to explore the Gambia and the region east towards Timbuktu under the auspices of the African Association. He set out for the interior in December 1795 with six African assistants. They were continually diverted and pillaged by Moors, and his life was frequently under threat as he headed northeast towards the town of Jarra. Turning south he joined the Niger at Segu, there deciding to abandon the search for Timbuktu. He returned to the Gambia in June 1797. An account of the expedition was published in 1799.

He then practised medicine in Scotland for a few years but remained restless. Turning down an opportunity to explore Australia, in 1805 he set out on another expedition for the elusive city of Timbuktu, with the additional object of finding the mouth of the Niger. The expedition ended with his death in mysterious circumstances early in 1806.

Robin Hallett, *The Penetration of Africa to 1815* (London: Routledge & Kegan Paul, 1965).

DAVID MACKAY

parlements The *parlements* of France were the chief courts of appeal under the *ancien régime*. The senior *parlement*, the PARLEMENT OF PARIS, originally claimed judisdiction over the whole kingdom. However, as the extent of the kingdom grew a number of provincial courts were set up with sovereign powers over their own areas of judisdiction. *Parlements* were established in Toulouse (1443), Grenoble (1453), Bordeaux (1462), Dijon (1476), Rouen (1499), Aix-en-Provence (1501), Rennes (1554), Pau (1620), Metz (1633), Besançon (1676), Douai (1686) and Nancy (1775), while five supreme councils, which were *parlements* in all but name, were set up in Dombes (1523), Arras (1530), Colmar (1657), Perpignan (1660) and Bastia in Corsica (1768).

In the eighteenth century the *parlements* attempted to develop a degree of constitutional solidarity among themselves by invoking the argument that each of them formed a constituent part of a single national body. Louis XV's ministers rejected this view of a union of *parlements* in the 1750s and 1760s but the theme was restated in 1787–8. In between, in 1771, the courts had been abolished by Chancellor MAUPEOU, only to be restored in 1774. None of the *parlements* survived the storm of the French Revolution.

Bailey Stone, *The French Parlements and the Crisis of the Old Regime* (Chapel Hill, NC: University of North Carolina Press, 1986).

J. H. SHENNAN

Parma The duchy of Parma, Piacenza and Guastalla was the epitome of a weak *ancien régime* petty state, which owed its existence to the dynastic ambitions of the Habsburgs and the French and Spanish Bourbons. At the start of the century Parma was ruled by the near-extinct Farnese dynasty and it was preserved by the diplomatic skill and dynastic ambitions of Elizabeth Farnese (1692–1766), wife of Philip V of Spain, and her minister, Cardinal Alberoni (1664–1752), who linked the duchy through marriage to the Bourbons. Although it emerged enlarged from the Treaty of Utrecht (1713), its fundamental precariouness was shown in 1735, at the end of the WAR OF THE POLISH SUCCESSION when Parma was absorbed by the Habsburgs, disappearing altogether as an independent state until it was restored to Don Philip (1720–65), Elizabeth Farnese's second son, in 1748, at the end of the War of the Austrian Succession. Henceforth, there was no doubt of the duchy's status as a Franco-Spanish satellite. It remained under this cadet branch of the Bourbons until Napoleon annexed it directly to France in 1805; in 1814 it was given to Marie Louise (1791–1847), the Habsburg princess who had been Napoleon's second wife.

The only period of reform in the eighteenth century came under DU TILLOT, a minister 'imported' from France, who created a glittering if artificial court until his overthrow in 1771. Even during this period, the reforms were limited to ecclesiastical matters – producing the expulsion of the Jesuits in 1768 and a bitter dispute with the papacy – and education, which particularly enhanced the university. Real power within the duchy lay with the nobles and the church, however; Parma reverted to parochial reaction after du Tillot's fall.

S. J. Woolf, *A History of Italy, 1700–1860* (London: Methuen, 1979).
D. Carpanetto and G. Ricuperati, *Italy in the Age of Reason, 1685–1789* (London: Longman, 1987).

MICHAEL BROERS

Partitions of Poland (1772, 1793, 1795)   Political and military weaknesses rendered the Polish state incapable of defending itself against its neighbours. Prussia had the longest-standing designs on Polish territory, reaching back to at least the mid seventeenth century, but its ambitions were held in check primarily by Russia, which, from the reign of Peter the Great, preferred to exercise a self-interested *de facto* protectorate over the Polish state in its entirety. The possibility of Russian expansionism into the Balkans during the Russo-Turkish war of 1768–74 aroused the anxiety of Austria and Prussia, generating tensions between the three powers that were peaceably resolved, at Poland's expense, only in the first partition (Conventions of St Petersburg, 5 August 1772). Political reforms in Poland after 1788 provoked Russia and Prussia into imposing a second partition (Treaty of St Petersburg, 23 January 1793) in which Austria, deluded by the prospect of substantial territorial gains from revolutionary France, did not participate. The third partition, a direct response to the KOŚCIUSZKO insurrection, was finalized in St Petersburg on 24 October 1795; it gave Russia, Prussia and Austria shares in what remained of the Polish state.

See also POLAND.

J. T. Lukowski, *Liberty's Folly: The Polish-Lithuanian Commonwealth in the Eighteenth Century* (London: Routledge, 1991).

J. T. LUKOWSKI

Passarowitz, Treaty of (21 July 1718)   This treaty was signed under Anglo-Dutch mediation at Passarowitz, 30 miles south-east of Belgrade, and it concluded some three years of war between the Austrian Habsburgs and the Turks (*see* AUSTRO-TURKISH WARS). The signatories included representatives of the Venetian republic, which had lost the Morea to the Turks in 1715. The gains made by Austria were substantial: southern Hungary was recovered, and the Banat of Temesvar, as well as considerable areas of Serbia (including Belgrade) and Wallachia, annexed. The anxiety of George I, in his electoral capacity, to place the emperor Charles VI in his debt stood revealed in the treaty's consequences. Above all, Austrian troops were released from the Danubian territories to counter the designs of Philip V of Spain in Italy, off the coasts of which the emperor could expect British naval support. Of no less consequence for Hanover, Austrian reinforcements could now be posted northwards to back up the 'Imperial Execution' against Mecklenburg, a task given Hanover by Charles VI so that a possible return of Russian troops to that duchy could be prevented.

O. Redlich, *Das Werden einer Grossmacht: Österreich von 1700 bis 1740* (Vienna: Rudolf M. Rohrer, 1962).

D. D. ALDRIDGE

Patiño, José (1667–1736) Chief minister of Spain (1726–36). He rose to prominence during the War of the Spanish Succession, and in 1726 was entrusted with the ministries of the navy and finance; he subsequently also assumed those of war (1730) and foreign affairs (1733), areas that he had in practice controlled for some time. The first notable minister of the Bourbon monarchy in Spain, he centred his efforts on the armed forces, the economy and foreign policy. His lasting achievement was the creation of the Spanish navy, which was used to counter the unfavourable international position forced on Spain by the TREATY OF UTRECHT. Steps were taken to assure the interests of the royal family in Italy, particularly the rights of Don Carlos (later Charles III) to the duchy of Parma (1731). During the War of the Polish Succession, and taking advantage of the first FAMILY COMPACT which ensured agreement between the Bourbon states of France and Spain against Austria, Spanish forces successfully ensured the succession (1734) of Carlos to the kingdom of Naples. Spain was obliged, however, to cede Parma to Austria, a failure that was severely criticized in Madrid, where a pamphlet war was unleashed against the minister and embittered his last years.

John Lynch, *Bourbon Spain 1700–1808* (Oxford: Blackwell, 1989).

HENRY KAMEN

patrician families, urban The nature of the urban patriciate varied according to urban typology. In capital cities, which usually accommodated the royal court and multifarious organs of central administration, the principal families would be drawn from a pool of powerful nobles, courtiers, bureaucrats, and spiritual, judicial and military leaders. Such families would assert their status by the sophisticated social and cultural life they engaged in, and by the grand dwellings they occupied; the princes and great amirs of Shahjahanabad built magnificent mansions, which were the central institutions of the city, and the French nobility resided in splendid *hôtels* in quarters like the *faubourg*

St Germain and *faubourg* St Honoré in Paris. If a capital was also a major commercial centre, then there might be several elites, as in the case of London, with the courtly families (whose presence was generally seasonal) of the burgeoning squares and streets to the west, and the business plutocrats of the City to the east. Outside the capital the nature of the urban patriciate depended on a town's mixture of economic, social and administrative functions, but here there was far greater scope for middling families to play a leading role.

See also ARISTOCRACY, NOBILITY.

PETER BORSAY

patriotism COSMOPOLITANISM was a tenet widely espoused within the thought of the Enlightenment republic of letters; but many *philosophes* also believed that love of one's country was a virtue, inimical to factionalism and corruption, conducive to internal civil cohesion and breeding an admirable spirit of liberty. Early in his career Gibbon attempted to write a history of the Swiss republic, to exemplify the essential connections between civic freedom and patriotism: Geneva was widely admired for its patriotism, as were the North American patriots who rebelled against George III. Later in the century HERDER and others sought to root patriotic feelings in shared history, the soil, language and myth.

Although, after the mid nineteenth century, patriotism became associated with a mindless, flag-waving jingoism, in the eighteenth century patriotic sentiments were often radical, serving as veiled critiques of corruption at court and as expressions of community feeling against despotism and dynasticism. In English political thinking the term 'patriot', however, also took on a different connotation. Following the publication of Lord Bolingbroke's *The Idea of a Patriot King*, 'patriotism' could also mean the repudiation of party and faction in the name of monarchical loyalism. The widespread distrust of Bolingbroke's opportunism explains Johnson's remark that patriotism was the last refuge of a scoundrel.

See also NATIONALISM.

L. Colley, 'Radical Patriotism in Eighteenth-Century England', in R. Samuel (ed.), *The Making and Unmaking of British National Identity*, vol. 1 (London: Routledge, 1989), pp. 169–87.

J. G. A. Pocock, *The Machiavellian Moment* (Princeton, NJ: Princeton University Press, 1975).

ROY PORTER

patronage The relationship between patron and client was a recurrent theme in Western society during the eighteenth century. The dependence of one group on the other was not just a matter of an abstract caste system: it supplied the mechanism for getting deals done, bargains struck, commissions executed, appointments made, wars funded, warehouses stocked and parliaments elected. The arts were not at all special in being subject to a complex ramification of favours, bribes and more or less subtle pressures, by which artists could make a living and the wealthy could claim possession of a beautiful object or else the vicarious 'ownership' of a work dedicated to them. Most patrons were men, even though it might have been a woman in the family who had a greater interest in and knowledge of art and who sought out promising executants to fulfil a commission with credit.

The old system of patronage was starting to break down as the century progressed, but it never totally lost its hold on the sponsorship of art. In architecture and landscape gardening the private patron retained almost all his historic influence. There were still few public commissions, apart from churches and occasional municipal buildings such as playhouses and assembly rooms. Government building was normally centrally controlled: thus in England the board of works had its own in-house architect (at one time, Sir William Chambers (1726–96), creator of Somerset House) to superintend official building. Such commissions were dwarfed by the number of private commissions for architects, emanating either from royalty (as when Fischer von Erlach (1656–1723) worked for Joseph I of Austria), or from rich grandees (as when Robert Adam worked for the earl of Mansfield). Capability Brown was once consulted by members of Cambridge University with a view to improving the Backs by means of diverting the River Cam from Newnham to Magdalene College, but this came to nothing. As it was, his work was all carried out on behalf of rich individuals. An army of craftsmen, artisans and providers were needed for each large-scale building work, but there was generally only the one paymaster.

Music and THEATRE saw a small shift towards public patronage, in the growth of regular PUBLIC CONCERTS and the establishment of permanent playhouses outside the metropolitan centres. But composers were still mostly employed either by churches or by aristocratic households. Perhaps the most independent of the major composers in the period was Handel, who spent years presenting to the public, first, opera (often at a loss) and then, more successfully, oratorio. But he too had enjoyed the subsidies of great private supporters of the arts, notably Cardinal Pietro Ottoboni in Rome and then the duke of Chandos and the earl of Burlington in England. By contrast, J. S. Bach and Haydn spent most of their careers in the service of more or less appreciative masters.

It was in literature that the first stirrings of revolt were seen. Both Alexander Pope, by the shrewd manipulation of his published output, and Voltaire, by his cunning exploitation of business opportunities, made themselves independent of ordinary patronage. Both had made capital from the briefly dominant subscription mode of publication. More slowly and fitfully, some visual artists took advantage of the market for popular engravings to evade some of the restrictions of the system, though even Hogarth found that paintings could not be disseminated in large numbers like books. It is often said that the booksellers were the new patrons of the eighteenth century, and it is certainly true that the development of a relatively small trade into a large industry with a huge turnover each year did mean that authors could look to sources outside the traditionally wealthy classes (*see* PUBLISHING). It is to the trade that we owe the inception of the *Encyclopédie* and of Johnson's *Dictionary*, for instance.

This did not mean that men like Ottoboni, Chandos or Burlington disappeared overnight. Burlington (1695–1753), the great 'Apollo of the Arts', was a practising architect as well as a supporter of the Palladian movement, a director of the opera company and a friend of leading literary men like Pope and John Gay. His monument is not just the house and garden he created at Chiswick, but also the eloquent praise of Pope in an *Epistle* addressed to him by the poet, which celebrated his munificent contribution to the artistic life of the nation. In an attenuated form, Burlington's role was replicated late in the century by Sir George Beaumont (1753–1827). Similar stories can be told in other countries. Only a very determined ideologue of the modern would want to dispense with this level of enlightened patronage and indeed, for as long as it was economically viable, the private patron lived on, until altruism and vanity alike proved no match for taxes and the monolithic state.

M. Foss, *The Age of Patronage* (Ithaca, NY: Cornell University Press, 1972).
F. Haskell, *Patrons and Painters: A Study in the Relations between Italian Art and Society in the Age of the Baroque* (London: Chatto & Windus, 1963).
J. Lees-Milne, *Earls of Creation: Five Great Patrons of Eighteenth-Century Art* (London: Hamish Hamilton, 1962).
F. Owen and D. B. Brown, *Collector of Genius: A Life of Sir George Beaumont* (New Haven, Conn.: Yale University Press, 1988).

PAT ROGERS

Peninsular War (1808–1814)   In 1808 Napoleon BONAPARTE invaded Spain and Portugal and deposed the Spanish Bourbons in order to deny the ports of Spain and Portugal to British commerce. His intervention provoked massive popular resistance in both countries. The British government responded to requests for help by the dispatch of an expeditionary force to Portugal, but hopes for speedy success were disappointed. The war was prolonged and bitter. From 1809 onwards the Anglo-Portuguese forces used Portugal as a base from which they challenged the French. In Spain guerilla warfare wore down French strength. The Lines of Torres Vedras compelled the withdrawal of the French army from Portugal in 1811. In 1813 the allies took the initiative and the Vittoria campaign expelled the French from Spain. In 1814 France was invaded. The Peninsular War saw the first truly national resistance to Napoleonic France. The drain on French resources decisively contributed to the final defeat of Napoleon, while Spanish defiance and Anglo-Portuguese co-operation showed that despite difficulties coalition forces could be sustained in opposition to the might of imperial France.

D. Gates, *The Spanish Ulcer* (London: George Allen & Unwin, 1986).

JOHN W. DERRY

Pennsylvania   When Charles II of England awarded a proprietary charter to William Penn (1644–1718) in 1681, Pennsylvania became a colony. Penn was a member of the Society of Friends, or Quakers, founded by George Fox (1624–91). Like the New England Puritans, he had a utopian vision of transforming his colony by 'holy experiment'. He offered peace, religious pluralism and prosperity to the many members of small religious sects who braved the Atlantic crossing. Immigrants came from Ireland (including many Scots Irish), Scotland and the German principalities. The Germans established rich farms and became known as the Pennsylvania Dutch. Unlike many colonists who, in spite of good intentions, regularly cheated Indians of their land, Penn was honest and sought cordial relations. It was thus ironic that much of the French and Indian War (1754–63; in Europe the Seven Years War, 1756–1763) was fought along the Pennsylvanian frontier. The capital, PHILADELPHIA, with its port, libraries and philosophical society, became the most important colonial city.

During the Revolution the colony was a principal source of men and matériel for the Americans and the site of several important battles. Afterwards Philadelphia served as the nation's first capital. Anger over federal government tax policy led to the short-lived Whiskey Rebellion in 1794.

Hildegard Dolson, *William Penn, Quaker Hero* (New York: Random House, 1961).

JOHN MORGAN DEDERER

perfectibility   That man was perfectible was central to the social and political theories of many eighteenth-century thinkers. 'By perfectible', Godwin stressed in *An Enquiry concerning Political Justice*, 'it is not meant that he is capable of being brought to perfection. But the word seems sufficiently adapted to express the faculty of being continually made better and receiving perpetual improvement.' Earlier in the century Rousseau, who is thought to have coined the word *perfectibilité* in his *Discours sur l'inégalité*, had made perfectibility the distinguishing characteristic of mankind. Far from seeing man's capacity to perfect himself in a positive light, however, he used it to explain why and how the species had been slowly dragged out of its original and happy condition and made to endure the physical and moral misery that the advent of society and the gradual progress of civilization necessarily inflicted on men and women. Considering history from an entirely different perspective, Kant argued that 'the proposition that the human race has always been progressively improving and will continue to develop in the same way . . . is tenable within the most strictly theoretical context'.

R. V. Sampson, *Progress in the Age of Reason* (London: Heinemann, 1956).

SYLVANA TOMASELLI

Pergolesi, Giovanni Battista (1710–1736) Italian composer. He was frail as a child, and died of consumption at the age of 26. Educated at the Conservatorio dei Poveri di Gesu Christo in Naples, he was appointed maestro di capella to the Neapolitan prince Stigliano in 1732. He composed fifteen operas, including the comic *Lo fratre' nnamorato* (1732), based on a libretto in Neapolitan dialect, the opera seria *Salustia* (1731), *Il prigoniero superbo* (1733), *Adriano in Siria* (1734), *L'Olimpiade* (1735) and the opera buffa *Flaminio* (1735). His most successful work was the buffonesque intermezzo *La serva padrona* (to Il prigioniero superbo), which became the model for the French *opéra comique*. A Paris performance in 1752 provoked the so-called Querrelle des bouffons between the defenders of the French opera tradition and the supporters of the 'natural' and more popular Italian opera. He also wrote church music. His *Stabat mater* (1729) established the ideal of frugal, moving sacred music. A good deal of music has been erroneously attributed to Pergolesi, including most of the pieces Igor Stravinsky recomposed for his ballet *Pulcinella*.

H. Hucke, 'Pergolesi' in S. Sadie (ed.), *The New Grove Dictionary of Music and Musicians* (London: Macmillan, 1981)

FRITZ WEBER

periodicals *see* MAGAZINES.

persecution, religious The REVOCATION OF THE EDICT OF NANTES in France in 1685, which outlawed Protestantism on French soil and led to the emigration of nearly a quarter of a million Huguenots, was to prove a watershed in the history of religious persecution in Europe. Although similar moves were later made on a smaller scale – the prince-bishop of Salzburg expelled 17,000 Protestants in 1732, for example – there was a clear decline in religious intolerance throughout the eighteenth century. Sometimes (as in Poland) this was testimony to government weakness, sometimes it showed government pragmatism – many rulers counted the economic cost of emigration of valuable manpower. Frederick II of Prussia followed dynastic tradition in endorsing toleration, and many minor German states followed suit. Joseph II introduced toleration even for Jews in the 1780s, and Catherine II allowed a measure of toleration to Muslim communities. In France fierce battles over *causes célèbres* such as the CALAS case (1761–5), led to *de facto* tolerance, a partial toleration edict in 1787 and the introduction of full toleration after 1789, while in England statutes against Dissenters were waived. In the United States the 1787 Constitution envisaged toleration, in contrast to the strongly denominational fervour of individual states. Many regions, however, notably Spain and Italy, remained relatively untouched by the spirit of religious *détente*.

See also TOLERATION.

COLIN JONES

Persia The beginning of the eighteenth century in Persia saw the effective end of rule by the great Safavid dynasty, in 1722. Three dynasties followed, exercising power to a greater or lesser degree in all, or parts of, Persia: the Afsharids, the Zands and the Qajars. Nadir, a Turkoman chieftain of the Afshar tribe, removed the Ottomans from Azerbaijan in 1730 and had himself proclaimed Nadir Shah in 1736. He tried unsuccessfully to force the abandonment of the Twelver Shi'ism branch of ISLAM practised in Persia, allegedly to try to effect a *rapprochement* with the OTTOMAN EMPIRE, but this has been disputed by scholars and other reasons are given. After Nadir's murder in 1747, Persia degenerated into chaos. The Zands briefly gained power and were in turn overthrown by the Turkoman Qajars who assumed control of all of Persia towards the end of the eighteenth century. This century was thus an age of considerable instability and breakdown in Persia on the political front. On the religious front, the eighteenth century witnessed the return of a number of Sufi groups from India to Persia, and this, not surprisingly, created friction between the existing religious establishment and the Sufis. Many of the former also fled to Iraq to escape the religious tyranny of Nadir Shah.

P. M. Holt, A. K. S. Lambton and B. Lewis (eds), *The Cambridge History of Islam*, vol. 1: *The Central Islamic Lands* (Cambridge: Cambridge University Press, 1970).

IAN NETTON

Peru   Once Spain's richest colony in America, Peru eventually experienced economic stagnation and political crisis. Population decline reached its nadir in the plague of 1719 and silver production during the 1730s, but subsequent recovery was modest and slow. The system of *repartimientos de comercio*, whereby district magistrates, who were invariably recruited from Spain, sold mules from the Argentine pampas, locally produced woollens and European merchandise to the Indian inhabitants of the highland zone at inflated prices, caused great hardship among the Indians and led to several revolts. When tributes and excise duties were more rigorously collected, an Indian lord, Tupac Amaru, headed a general insurrection in 1780–1 which stretched from Potosí to Cuzco. The crisis was accentuated by the creation of the viceroyalty of Río de la Plata in 1776, which meant that upper Peru (modern Bolivia) was governed from Buenos Aires. This contributed to the stagnation of Lima, a capital shorn of its empire and housing a population of only 52,000. In the 1790s the creole elite of Lima published *Mercurio Peruano*, a journal of Enlightenment ideas, but, fearful of Indian rebellion, they failed to respond to the revolutionary fever of these years and remained loyal to the Spanish crown.

See SPANISH AMERICA.

J. R. Fisher, *Government and Society in Colonial Peru: The Intendant System 1784–1814* (London: Athlone, 1970).

D. A. BRADING

pessimism   In the eighteenth century the word 'optimism' had a wider currency than 'pessimism'. The latter entered the French vocabulary in 1759, and the English (through Coleridge) only in 1794. However, this is by no means indicative of the spirit of the times, since for every Condorcet or William Godwin who, towards the end of the century, expressed confidence in the ability of men and women to shape a happy future, there was a Malthus insisting on the natural constraints within which humanity had to learn to exist. Earlier in the period Rousseau responded to the supporters of modernity by stressing the human cost of the progress of civilization and the system of luxury it brought in its wake. In an altogether different vein, Voltaire's *Candide, ou L'Optimisme* was written to ridicule Leibniz's theory that ours is the best possible world or, in Boswell's phrase, 'the system of Optimism', which Johnson also attacked in *Rasselas*. Boswell noted that 'Notwithstanding my high admiration of *Rasselas*, I will not maintain that the "morbid melancholy" in Johnson's constitution may not, perhaps, have made life appear to him more insipid and unhappy than it generally is; for I am sure that he had less enjoyment from it than I have.'

See also LISBON EARTHQUAKE, OPTIMISM.

SYLVANA TOMASELLI

Peter I [Peter the Great] (1672–1725)   Tsar and first emperor of Russia (1682–1725). The son of Tsar Alexis (1629–76) and his second wife, Natalia Naryshkina (1651–94), he became tsar in April 1682, and reigned jointly with his handicapped elder half-brother Ivan (1666–96) until 1696 and under the regency of his half-sister Sophia (1657–1704) until 1689. The adolescent Peter enjoyed sailing and drilling his 'play' regiments of boy troops who formed the basis of the elite Preobrazhensky and Semenovsky guards. His first success came in 1696 with the capture of the Turkish fortress of Azov. In 1697–8 his grand embassy visited the West, publicizing the anti-Turkish league while he broadened his education. On his return, he commanded the boyars to shave their beards and don Western dress, as a symbolic prelude to measures aimed at strengthening Russia's military status in Europe. This was achieved during the Great Northern War against Sweden, especially after Poltava (1709). In 1703 he founded St Petersburg, Russia's Baltic 'window on the West' and its capital from 1712. In 1721 the Treaty of Nystadt ratified Russia's possession of Livonia, Estonia and Ingria, and Peter became emperor. The war against Persia (1722–3) gained him a Caspian shore-line. However, Turkey regained Azov after the Battle of Pruth (1711).

Military considerations determined most of Peter's reforms. He created a huge standing army (210,000 regular troops by 1725) and a navy, which were based on conscription and modern equipment and training, as set out in the Military Statue of 1716. The Senate was created in 1711, supervised by the procurator-general from 1722, and administrative colleges were set up in 1718. The country was divided into fifty provinces. Even the Orthodox Church was rationalized, the patriarchate being replaced by the Holy Synod in 1721. Fund-raising for the war effort culminated in 1722–4 with the introduction of the annually levied poll tax. State-sponsored mining and industry were developed to supply the armed forces. Foreign specialists, especially mercenaries, were hired, and Russians sent abroad to study. Education was compulsory for the nobility, who served for life. In 1722 promotion in military and civil service based on merit was enshrined in the Table of ranks. Peter, who regarded himself as 'the first servant of the state', worked his way up through the military and naval ranks, but his power remained absolute. His influence was wide-ranging: he reformed the calendar and simplified the Russian alphabet, encouraged publishing, improved the status of women, commissioned Western-style painting and architecture.

In 1689 Peter married Evdokia Lopukhina (1669–1731), but later banished her to a nunnery. In 1718 he disinherited Evdokia's son Alexis, and in 1722 issued a succession law by which the monarch designated his successor. However, he died on 28 January, 1725, without having nominated an heir. His second wife, Catherine I, succeeded him. Peter was not a revolutionary – he built on foundations laid by his seventeenth-century predecessors – but he has long been regarded as such. Larger than life, energetic and cruel, he aroused both adulation and fierce opposition during his lifetime. The controversy continues, especially over the relative costs and gains of the Petrine 'system' and the rift it created between the elite and the peasant masses.

M. S. Anderson, *Peter the Great* (London: Thames & Hudson, 1978).
James Cracraft (ed.), *Peter the Great Transforms Russia*, third edn (Lexington, Mass.: D. C. Heath, 1990).

LINDSEY HUGHES

Peter II (1715–1730)   Emperor of Russia (1727–30). He was the son of Tsarevich Alexis and Princess Charlotte of Blankenburg-Wolfenbüttel. On the death of his grandfather Peter I, in 1725, he was the only male heir, but the 1722 law of succession allowed him to be passed over in favour of Peter's wife, Catherine I. Subsequently, influenced by Peter I's favourite, Alexander Menshikov (1673–1729), she nominated Peter as her heir. He succeeded on 6 May 1727, with Menshikov acting as regent in all but name, but in September 1727 the latter was banished by rival factions of the old nobility, headed by the Dolgorukii clan. In November 1729 Peter was betrothed to Catherine, the daughter of Prince Aleksei Dolgorukii, but he died of smallpox on 18 January 1730, shortly before his wedding. The Dolgorukii clan was itself ousted as the new empress, ANNA, promoted her own favourites. Peter II's reign has sometimes been associated with a reversal of Peter I's reforms, as symbolized by the temporary abandonment of the new capital, St Petersburg, but in fact Peter I's new institutions survived intact and relations were maintained with European powers.

A. Yanov, 'The Drama of the Time of Troubles', *Canadian-American Slavic Studies*, 12 (1978), 1–59.

LINDSEY HUGHES

Peter III (1728–1762)   Emperor of Russia (1761–2). The only son of Peter I's daughter Anna and Duke Charles Frederick of Holstein-Gottorp, Karl Peter was brought to Russia as heir apparent in 1742 by his childless aunt, empress Elizabeth. In 1745 he married the future CATHERINE II, and succeeded Elizabeth on 25 December 1761. Peter was well educated. His short reign saw the Manifesto of Freedom to the Nobility (abolishing compulsory state service), the secularization of church estates and decrees on religious toleration. However, his Prussophile views, neglect of Orthodoxy, demotion of the senate and immature, impulsive personality alienated the Russian elite, who were horrified by the restoration to Prussia of Russia's territorial gains from the Seven Years War and the preparations for war against Denmark. On 28 June his wife Catherine staged a *coup* with the aid of the Guards. Peter died on 6 July, dispatched by colic, according to the official version, but probably by Catherine's supporters. The mysterious circumstances of his death and unfulfilled promise of his reign encouraged the emergence of many false Peter IIIs, notably PUGACHEV.

L. Hughes, 'Peter III', in *Modern Encyclopedia of Russian and Soviet History*, vol. 27 (Gulf Breeze, Fla.: Academic International Press, 1982), pp. 238–44.

LINDSEY HUGHES

Philadelphia Called the 'City of Brotherly Love' by its founder and architect, William Penn (1644–1718), Philadelphia was the principal British North American port until the late eighteenth century. Situated on the banks of the deep-water Delaware River, it was laid out by Penn in 1682. Ships from Europe carrying manufactured goods and immigrants enriched its merchants and peopled PENNSYLVANIA's rich farmlands. Drawn by its wealth, religious freedom and intellectual open-mindness were colonial luminaries such as Benjamin FRANKLIN.

In the 1770s Philadelphia became the meeting-place for colonial representatives (the Continental Congresses) grappling with worsening relations with England. In Philadelphia the young Thomas JEFFERSON wrote the American Declaration of Independence, which was proclaimed on 4 July 1776, and which made the city America's first capital. Occupied briefly by the British during the War of Independence, Philadelphia was the site of the constitutional convention of 1787. Meeting throughout that summer, delegates from the thirteen states hammered out the fundamental laws of the nation and the make-up of its new centralized government. After the war merchants from Philadelphia initiated trade with Asia. The city served as the nation's capital until the move to the newly built city of Washington in the District of Columbia.

JOHN MORGAN DEDERER

philanthropy An offshoot of the HUMANITARIANISM that characterized late-eighteenth-century Europe, philanthropy varied in its forms and inspirations. In France the Enlightenment critique of traditional Catholic CHARITY produced a call for a more secular type of assistance – *bienfaisance* – which was rationally calculated to cater to proven need. In southern and eastern Europe, dominated by enlightened absolutists, philanthropic endeavours were usually linked to the state and were pragmatic in their objectives. In England in particular, but also elsewhere in western Europe, the revival of devotional forms of piety produced humanitarian efforts to improve the lot of the poorer classes, albeit in ways that conformed to a bourgeois value system and promoted public welfare. English societies for the reformation of manners and charity schools originated in the 1690s and provided the model of voluntary organization that was taken up by numerous similar and related ventures (for example HOSPITALS, foundling homes) from the 1740s onwards. In France the Revolution provided the government with the opportunity to effect a kind of philanthropic welfare state grounded in the values of Enlightenment *bienfaisance*, although financial pressures and political turbulence led to its failure.

See *also* POVERTY AND POOR RELIEF.

COLIN JONES

Philip V (1683–1746)   Duke of Anjou and first Bourbon king of Spain (1700–46). He occupied the throne twice, abdicating briefly in 1724 in favour of his son, Louis I (1707–24), who died within a few months. He became king at the age of 17 and was never given the opportunity to assert himself as a ruler. At the beginning of his reign, which was dominated by the WAR OF THE SPANISH SUCCESSION, policy was determined by his grandfather, Louis XIV of France. He was devoted to his first wife, Marie Louise (1688–1714) of Savoy. When she died in 1714 he married Elizabeth Farnese (1692–1766) of Parma, an imperious woman who completely changed the political complexion of the court, placing in charge of affairs her confidant, the priest Giulio Alberoni (1664–1752). For the rest of the reign she effectively imposed on ministers her obsession with securing the dynastic interests of her family in her native Italy, and specifically in PARMA. Philip remained a background figure, whose psychological problems came to the fore during the period of his abdication. His reign marked an important phase of readjustment to Spain's new role in Europe, and the importation of foreign tastes showed itself in the construction of new royal palaces in Madrid and Aranjuez.

John Lynch, *Bourbon Spain 1700–1808* (Oxford: Blackwell, 1989).

HENRY KAMEN

philosophes   A term best used very loosely as an alternative to 'thinkers', 'writers', 'figures' of the eighteenth century, '*philosophes*' is more often than not made to designate those whose ideas constituted the Enlightenment, a movement of ideas which in its turn is defined by establishing the common ground amongst those intellectuals who could not possibly be excluded from it, that is, Montesquieu, Diderot, Voltaire, d'Holbach, Helvétius, A. R. J. Turgot, François Quesnay, Condorcet, Condillac and Rousseau.

Were one to think of the *philosophes* as the company of men of letters who, along with Diderot, were engaged in the publication of the *encyclopédie*, one would need to consider whether those who, like d'Alembert, deserted the enterprise, should be considered true *philosophes* or simply as fellow travellers. Moreover, many of the *Encyclopédie*'s most illustrious contributors wrote but one or two entries each, and a great many articles were such as to commit their authors to very little in terms of reform or a philosophical outlook for which the *Encyclopédie* as whole might be deemed to have been the vehicle.

The desire to diffuse knowledge, or to encourage a critical spirit, both of which were aims of the *Encyclopédie*, was not exclusive to the eighteenth century, nor to the French *encyclopédistes*. And in view of the cosmopolitan spirit of the age and the extent to which ideas crossed linguistic and geographical frontiers, any definition that necessarily excludes Scottish or Italian intellectuals, or indeed thinkers outside France, is less than satisfactory. Diderot had more in common with, say, David Hume than with most of the contributors to his great work. Similarly, Cesare Beccaria was intellectually closer to men like Sir William Blackstone and Jeremy Bentham than to most of his learned countrymen.

An international perspective precludes any description of the *philosophes* that would tie them to clearly parochial concerns, and makes one wary of identifying them with what may appear to be more wide-ranging compaigns such as that of *écraser l'infâme*. A crusade of this nature was almost non-existent in England, yet would one necessarily wish to exclude the likes of Bentham or Mary Wollstonecraft from the Enlightenment project? Within the Neapolitan context, some, Pietro Giannone for instance, did combat the church, and the papacy in particular. But throughout Italy and elsewhere, there were many Catholics who, like Lodovico Muratori, sought to reform the church from within rather than attack it from without. Indeed, the notion of the Catholic Enlightenment is gaining greater currency, and its study is at last receiving the attention it merits.

If neither nationality nor religious conviction barred one from joining the ranks of the *philosophes*, gender proved even less of a handicap. For while women were excluded from institutions such as the Académie Française, some, like Madame de Lambert (1647–1733), were extremely influential in determining who was admitted to its membership. Moreover, most of the activity of the Enlightenment took place in the *salons*, which were held by women, and was disseminated through books, many of which were written by women. Madame du Châtelet cannot but be regarded as a *philosophe*. She wrote on scientific subjects and on happiness, produced a critical commentary on the Bible and disseminated knowledge, not least through her translation of and commentary on Newton's *Principia*, which was published in 1759.

Tempting thought it might be, making Madame du Châtelet the measure of all *philosophes* might lead one to give too much emphasis to what might be assumed to be the *philosophes'* obvious common denominator, namely, espousal of all things English. For if their various ideas about methodological and social and political reforms differed radically, the *philosophes* seem to have been agreed in their endorsement of the Baconian approach to learning, Lockean epistemology and Newtonian physics. To define them along these lines, however, would require some considerable qualifications, if only so as to accommodate the rationalism of the German Enlightenment and the author of *Was ist Aufklärung?*, Immanuel Kant, in particular, not to mention the likes of Rousseau who had few illusions about the English political system. Thus it would seem, that, used in a narrow sense, *philosophes* could be made to mean something, but to little purpose, while in a wider sense, it might be of greater use, but would then embrace almost every eighteenth-century thinker, with the exception perhaps of the Jesuits and Charles Palissot de Montenoy (1730–1814) whose comedy *Les Philosophes* (1760) much angered the *Encyclopédistes*. But even he was to be reconciled with the philosophical party.

Ernst Cassirer, *The Philosophy of the Enlightenment*, trans. F. C. A. Koellen and J. P. Pettegrove (Princeton, NJ: Princeton University Press, 1979).

A. C. Kors and Paul J. Korshin (eds), *Anticipations of the Enlightenment in England, France and Germany* (Philadelphia: University of Pennsylvania Press, 1987).

Roy Porter and Mikuláš Teich (eds), *The Enlightenment in National Context* (Cambridge: Cambridge University Press, 1981).

SYLVANA TOMASELLI

phlogiston   Where today's chemist sees oxygen absorbed in combustion or respiration, eighteenth-century phlogiston theorists saw the liberation of this 'fire-substance'. They held that substances like coal or metals burned because they contained phlogiston, that flames or heat accompanied its release – leaving an ashy residue – and that combustion ceased when the surrounding air became fully saturated, or 'phlogisticated'.

The concept was developed by STAHL in Germany, where chemists studied the techniques of metal extraction. Although never universally or uniformly held, phlogiston theory had gained currency by mid-century as natural philosophers concerned themselves with industrial processes and accepted the existence of similar subtle fluids.

Concerted opposition to the theory grew in Paris's Académie des Sciences, led by LAVOISIER. His analytical methods and his physicist's concern with weight conservation were offended by phlogiston's elusive and protean nature. Focusing on the anomalous weight gain of combusted metals, French chemists developed oxygen theory. There persisted a 'sect of phlogistonists', led by PRIESTLEY, who elaborated sophisticated defences. They feared that French domination of chemistry, particularly of its language, would foreclose that debate. They were to be proved right.

J. B. Conant, *Harvard Case Histories in Experimental Science*, vol. 1 (Cambridge, Mass.: Harvard University Press, 1964).

STEPHEN PUMFREY

physiocrats Also known as the *économistes* or economists, the physiocrats were advocates of what Adam SMITH called 'the agriculture system of political economy' in *The Wealth of Nations*: 'That system which represents the produce of land as the sole source of the revenue and wealth of every country, has, so far as I know, never been adopted by any nation, and it at present exists only in the speculations of a few men of great learning and ingenuity in France.' He explained how physiocracy, with its emphasis on the country, had evolved in response to MERCANTILISM, with its emphasis on the industry of the towns. Physiocrats saw each society as consisting of three orders: those who owned the land, those who cultivated it and the artisans, manufacturers and merchants. They regarded the cultivators of the land as the productive class and the last group as the unproductive one. 'The capital error of this system', Smith could see, lay in the physiocrats' blindness to the usefulness of the third class to the other two, especially under the conditions of free trade. But despite 'all its imperfections', he considered physiocracy to be 'the nearest approximation to the truth that has yet been published upon the subject of political economy'.

According to physiocracy, the wealth of agricultural nations, like England and France, could be increased only by increasing agricultural production, while the wealth of predominantly trading nations, like Holland, could be enlarged only through restraints on consumption and parsimony. It thus followed from their notion of agriculture as the only source of wealth that in agricultural countries there should be a single tax levied on the land.

Alongside their critique of mercantilism and everything that favoured the production of luxury goods, physiocrats were passionate about the need to remove all restrictions on the GRAIN TRADE. In their view, the government's regulation of grain prices contributed to, rather than alleviated, shortages: only the removal of controls on the price of grain and a policy of *laissez-faire* would provide the incentives necessary to the expansion of agriculture, and only the freedom to export would ensure that the poor could purchase bread and that farmers would increase production.

The founder of physiocracy was QUESNAY. His *Tableau économique* sought to demonstrate how the annual produce of the land was distributed among the three classes and how the unproductive class did no more than replace the value of its consumption. Le Mercier de la Rivère's *L'Ordre naturel et essentiel des sociétés politiques* clarified Quesnay's views and drew international attention to the tenets of physiocracy. Pierre Samuel Dupont de Nemours (1739–1817) also popularized its doctrines in *Origines et progrès d'une science nouvelle* (1768).

The physiocrats were by no means modest about their 'discovery'. In *La Philosophie rurale* the marquis de MIRABEAU named the three great inventions that had lent stability to political societies as 'writing, money and the *Tableau économique*'. Some of the tenets of physiocracy were, *pace* Smith, put into practice, first in the 1760s, and again under the ministry of TURGOT, whose experiments in the free trade of grain were ill-fated; the restrictions, which had been lifted on these occasions, were reinstated. The *Ephémérides du citoyen, ou Chronique de l'esprit national*, founded in 1765, by the abbé Nicolas Baudeau (1730–92) and edited by him, first with Mirabeau, then with Dupont de Nemours, was the organ of the physiocrats.

Among physiocracy's numerous critics were Necker and Mably. The latter's *Doutes proposés aux philosophes économistes sur l'ordre naturel et essentiel des sociétés politiques* attacked Le Mercier de la Rivière's political thought and in particular his trust in the unbridled operation of enlightened self-interest. Another important critic, the abbé Galiani, who had witnessed the Neapolitan famine of 1764, argued that no one with a sense of responsibility could argue for anything but the most cautious approach to the lifting of controls on grain prices. He and Le Mercier de la Rivière entered into a much publicized dispute, known as 'la bagarre'.

Keith M. Baker, 'State, Society, and Subsistence in Eighteenth-Century France', *Journal of Modern History*, 50 (1978), 701–11.

Elizabeth Fox-Genovese, *The Origins of Physiocracy* (Ithaca, NY: Cornell University Press, 1976).

Ronald Meek (ed.), *The Economics of Physiocracy* (Cambridge, Mass.: Harvard University Press, 1962).

SYLVANA TOMASELLI

pianoforte   Although the pianoforte first appeared in Florence around 1709, it did not become a serious rival of the traditional keyboard instruments, the harpsichord and clavichord, until the last decades of the century. The invention of Bartolomeo Cristofori (1665–1731), it was copied by the German organ-builder Gottfried Silbermann (1683–1753), one of whose apprentices, Zumpe, changed its shape when he invented the square pianoforte in England. The compass of the instrument was gradually extended from four and a half (Cristofori) to six octaves by the 1790s. The upright pianoforte was introduced simultaneously in Austria and in America around 1800.

The earliest known piece written specifically for the pianoforte dates back to 1732. C. P. E. BACH was the first to recognize fully the revolutionary potential of the piano, for example, different techniques of touching the keys, and its ability to produce long-lasting tones and to 'sing' melodies; in short, it offered greater opportunity for expressiveness. The pre-eminence of the melody and the growing preference for the piano went hand in hand: Muzio Clementi (1752–1832) was the first composer for the pianoforte, and his piano sonatas were admired by Beethoven. Mozart's late and Beethoven's early sonatas marked the transition in keyboard composition from the harpsichord and clavichord to the new pianoforte.

C. F. Colt, *The Early Piano* (London: Stainer and Bell, 1981)
K. Wolff, *Masters of the Keyboard: Individual Style Elements in the Piano Music of Bach, Haydn, Mozart, Beethoven and Schubert* (Bloomington: Indiana University Press, 1983)

FRITZ WEBER

picturesque Until the aesthetic was codified in the 1790s the picturesque was generally understood to refer to landscapes and buildings that were reminiscent of those depicted by painters like Claude Lorraine (1600–82) and Gaspar Dughet (1615–75). Richard Payne Knight's (1750–1824) *Landscape: A Didactic Poem* and Uvedale Price's (1747–1829) *Essay on the Picturesque*, which, amplifying Knight, defined it as a category distinct from Burke's Sublime and Beautiful, were both published in 1794. In 1795 appeared Humphry Repton's (1752–1818) influential *Sketches and Hints on Landscape Gardening*. The picturesque *jardin anglais*, which had been initiated by an Augustan literary revolt against the formal garden, had already swept Europe: Pope had advised that one 'Consult the Genius of the place', and 'strike from chance'. As an aesthetic based on boundlessness, informality and locality, the picturesque was seemingly antithetical to classicism's self-containment, symmetry and universality; but Pope saw his own contribution as a return to the authentic simplicity of the classical garden, and the aesthetic's accommodation with architecture, by Payne Knight above all, made it clear that the picturesque building manifested an important species of NEOCLASSICISM. Irregular it may have been, and eclectic in materials and style, but its 'accidental' accretions over time were based entirely on rational need, and the result was no less natural than the surrounding LANDSCAPE.

David Watkin, *The English Vision: The Picturesque in Architecture, Landscape, and Garden Design* (London: John Murray, 1982).

CHRISTINE STEVENSON

Pietism From the late seventeenth century, through the eighteenth and into the nineteenth centuries, Pietism was a pervasive force not only in Holland (where it began in the Dutch Reformed Church) and the German sovereign territories, but also in Scandinavia, Switzerland and the United States. (Catholicism had its own pietistic movements, in, for example, JANSENISM.) It was characterized not so much by the formation of churches – although Quakers, Presbyterians and other Dissenters forged their own communities in Great Britain following the 1689 and 1712 (Scotland) Acts of Toleration – as by an inward spirituality, which was practised within established churches or (as with the radical Pietists) a visible personal piety that was also critical of the established churches, which they saw as lifeless and corrupt. As a movement, Pietism began when like-minded men and women, who were highly educated and often had private means at their disposal, implemented ideas of personal piety contained in the great classics of devotional and mystical literature, among them Johann Arndt's *Wahres Christentum*, Johannes Tauler's *Theologia Deutsch* and Thomas à Kempis's (1380–1471) *Imitatio Christi*.

German Lutheran Pietism originated in Frankfurt where SPENER was minister from 1666 to 1686. Together with Johann Jakob Schütz (?1640–90), a lawyer who had strong connections with Calvinistic Holland (and in particular with Jean de Labadie, 1610–71), he instituted regular private discussions on biblical and devotional texts. This did not find favour with the orthodox clergy, who saw it as an affront to church discipline and authority. Private active spirituality was given a wider currency through Spener's *Pia Desideria* (1675), in which he outlined the aims of church reform: the teaching of the church was correct, but the lives Christians led were corrupted through drink, litigation, striving for capital gain and disregard for the plight of the poor. (Radicals, on the other hand, pointed to corruption in the teaching of the church leading to corrupt lives.) To counter the evident decline of piety in the church, Spener proposed more thorough instruction in Christian principles (he held that church attendance on Sundays and the hearing of the sermon was insufficient), and promoted catechismal teaching for children and private religious discussion for lay people. In these *collegia pietatis* they could voice their doubts and questions. Spener was also an advocate of the priesthood of all believers and strongly upheld the idea that Christians were characterized not by their learning but by their actions. Practical Christianity should replace dogmatic dispute and a style of preaching versed in baroque refinement. Plain-speaking and a strong belief in the 'simplicity' of truth were to become a badge of Pietism.

Spener's advocacy of active Christian renewal was taken up by August Hermann Francke (1663–1727), a skilled Hebraic scholar, who had translated the Old Testament six times during his studies. Francke experienced a crisis of faith in 1687 when he realized that his formidable knowledge in theology had robbed him of belief. The crisis was resolved through an emotional reassurance he received, while praying, of God's living presence. This *Bekehrungserlebnis* (conversion experience) became a prototype of Pietistic conversion (*Wiedergeburt*): many Pietists recorded the hour and day of their spiritual rebirth. This preoccupation with the life of the soul was to influence autobiographical literature in Germany, especially the *Bildungsroman*.

Pietism as practised by Francke and his friends was also eminently active. After eviction from the Universities of Erfurt and Leipzig due to Orthodox opposition, Francke became minister (appointed by the crown) in Glaucha (near Halle) and professor of Oriental languages at the nascent University of Halle (he became professor of theology shortly thereafter). With Pietist colleagues, he began the most visible work of Pietism, the building of the *Waisenhaus* (orphanage) in 1689, a long row of houses which included a library, a natural history cabinet, living quarters for scholars and pupils, a hall, kitchens and an infirmary. The emphasis of the *Waisenhaus* was on education, and it contained three schools, one for children of craftsmen and farmers (*Deutsche Schule*), one for pupils entering university (Latin School) and a *paedagogium regium* for those pursuing a career in the civil service or officer corps. The *Waisenhaus* also accommodated a publishing house and bookselling agency (run by Heinrich Julius Elers, 1667–1728), which printed many of the university's books. Its other major enterprises included an inexpensive edition of the Bible (*Cannsteinbibel*) and a mail-order dissemination of the panacea *essentia dulcis*, which was innovative in that it turned drug-selling into a capitalist enterprise.

Besides Halle, the movement was affiliated with major communities in which persecuted separatists found tolerance. Prominent among these was Herrnhut, which was protected by ZINZENDORF, whose members became the Moravian Church (*see* MORAVIANS), some of whom went on to found Bethlehem, Pennsylvania. Radical Pietists often came under the wing of the 'Pietist counts', whose small sovereign territories, for example Sayn-Wittgenstein (Berleburg and Laasphe) and Ysenburg-Büdingen, were significant centres of radical ideas and publications.

J. Wallman, *Der Pietismus* (Göttingen: Vandenhoeck & Ruprecht, 1990).

JOHANNA GEYER-KORDESCH

Piranesi, Giovanni Battista (1720–1778)   Italian etcher, archaeologist and architect. He studied stage design, together with architecture, and his fantastic *Carceri d'invenzione* (Imaginary Prisons) etchings, begun c.1745, have transcended art-historical classification as a species of stage design to become the eighteenth century's most famous representations. A respected antiquarian, he defended Etruscan priority and Roman excellence against new voices then arguing that the Greeks had taken classical art to perfection, in *Della magnificenza ed architettura de' Romani* (Roman Magnificence and Architecture, 1761). His *Antichità romane* (Roman Antiquities, 1756) consists of 135 etchings in which the Roman views, through careful selection of viewpoint, elision of detail and exaggeration of shade and stereometry, played their part in his larger historical project. His only executed building was the reconstructed Church of Sta Maria del Priorato in Rome (1764–5). As a pamphleteer, a printmaker (with over 1,000 prints to his name) and an adviser to some of the hundreds of foreign artists who began coming to Rome in the 1740s (among them Robert Adam), he was one of the most important figures in eighteenth-century architecture.

John Wilton-Ely, *The Mind and Art of Giovanni Battista Piranesi* (London: Thames & Hudson, 1978).

CHRISTINE STEVENSON

Pitt, William, the elder, first earl of Chatham (1708–1778)   English statesman and orator. Following a controversial earlier career, his reputation as a great war leader was established during the Seven Years War. He successfully pursued a policy of attacking French colonies and commerce while collaborating with Prussia. His brilliant oratory dominated the Commons, and he had links with commercial and financial interests in the City of London, but he was an outsider in British politics. A patriot with a respect for the crown, he was arrogant and uncooperative in dealing with other politicians. Resigning in 1761 when the cabinet refused to endorse his pleas for a preemptive attack on Spain, he became more wayward and unpredictable. As a prime minister (1766–8) he was a failure. He lost popularity by going to the House of Lords, as earl of Chatham, and illness prevented him from controlling his ministerial colleagues. He was willing to accept limitations on the sovereignty of the British parliament in North America, and opposed the Declaratory Act and policies of coercion, pleading for conciliation with the colonists, but he never accepted

American independence and died urging reconciliation with the Americans to enable Britain to fight its Continental enemies more effectively.

J. Black, *Pitt the Elder* (Cambridge: Cambridge University Press, 1992).

JOHN W. DERRY

Pitt, William, the younger (1759–1806)   English statesman. The second son of PITT the elder, he was an outstanding finance minister and brilliant orator. Combining a regard for the prerogatives of the crown with a dislike of party, he believed economical reform to be necessary to improve public administration, but while favouring parliamentary reform he did not take a doctrinaire stance on the issue. When he became premier in 1783 he restored the national finances, initiated commercial and fiscal reforms and ended Britain's diplomatic isolation. He negotiated a commercial treaty with France, but was defeated on parliamentary reform and Irish free trade. During the French Revolution his main desire was for peace, but after the outbreak of war in 1793 he sought to build up coalitions against France. After carrying the Irish union, he resigned in 1801 when George III thwarted his bill for Catholic emancipation. Recalled as first minister in 1804, he created the third coalition against France, but his health was in decline and he died in 1806. He became the symbol of national defiance, his blend of conservatism and reformism influencing the development of British politics long after his death.

J. Ehrman, *The Younger Pitt*, 2 vols (London: Constable, 1969–83).

JOHN W. DERRY

Pius VI [Giovanni Angelo Braschi] (1717–1799)   Pope (1775–99). Born into an aristocratic family, he was treasurer of the Roman chamber in 1766, cardinal in 1773 and pope from 1775. He was notorious for his nepotistic activities (he built the Palazzo Braschi for his nephew) and became a significant patron of the arts. His reign saw the power and prestige of the papacy effectively challenged by developments in France and the empire. He was unable to prevent the emperor Joseph II from favouring Febronianism, which advocated toleration and the subjection of church to state (*see* PAPACY), despite previous papal attacks. Nor was he able to stop the Jesuits from continuing in Russia and Prussia despite the abolition of the order. He was likewise ineffective against the French Revolution, although he condemned the Civil Constitution of the Clergy of 1791, which subjected French clergy to civil authorities. He supported the first coalition against France, but when Napoleon invaded the Papal States in 1796 he was forced to surrender Ferrara and Bologna together with valuable manuscripts, at the Treaty of

Tolentino. In 1798 General Louis Berthier (1753–1818) entered Rome and proclaimed the Papal States a republic. Pius was deposed and died a prisoner in Valence.

JEREMY GREGORY

plague   The plague ceased to be a significant threat to western Europe in the eighteenth century; the last great plague occurred in Marseilles in 1720. Epidemics of bubonic plague, which was caused by a virus transmitted by rat fleas, continued in eastern Europe until the mid nineteenth century and later elsewhere. Historians have advanced a variety of arguments to explain the disappearance of the plague from Europe. Some focus on changes in the vector of transmission, claiming that the black rat, which lived closely with humans, was ousted by the brown rat, which kept its distance. Others look to improved immunity in humans or in rats, possibly as a consequence of better nutrition or improved habits of cleanliness. Finally, it has also been proposed that quarantine measures, which were taken by Mediterranean ports from the mid seventeenth century, may have been effective. After the 1719 peace treaty between the Ottoman and Habsburg Empires, a huge *cordon sanitaire* was erected by the latter: 4,000 men controlled the 1,200 mile frontier, supported by several thousand more when the intelligence service noted plague in the east. Travellers, their animals and goods were then quarantined and disinfected.

In the Islamic world plague was viewed as a natural catastrophe, like war, flood or famine. As in Europe, it was often seen as God-given, but not necessarily as a sign of God's displeasure; its meaning was unknowable. Hence, the keynote of responses to epidemics was resignation rather than prevention. In contrast to the European example of the 1770–2 Moscow plague, where rioting broke out and an archbishop lost his life, people were forbidden to flee cities, and civil disorder rarely ensued.

A. Appleby, 'The Disappearance of the Plague', *Economic History Review*, 33 (1980), 161–73.
M. W. Flinn, *The European Demographic System 1500–1820* (Brighton: Harvester, 1981).

MARY E. FISSELL

Plains of Abraham, Battle of (13 September 1759)   The Plains of Abraham, just outside the gates of Quebec, was the site of a battle fought between the attacking British and defending French, in 1759. In this round (in America, the French and Indian War, 1754–63; in Europe, the Seven Years War) of the second Hundred Years War (1689–1815), Britain had suffered a series of early defeats, including the rout of Braddock (1695–1755) in 1755 and Abercromby's (1740–1827) assault on Fort Carillon (Ticonderoga) in 1757. By 1759 the tide was turning, but Quebec, the centre of the French North American empire, which was commanded by the marquis de Montcalm and de Vaudreuil, was proving a tough nut to crack. British General James Wolfe's army and fleet lay at anchor for months, unable to breach the city's walls. Finally he rowed his men past Quebec's guns, sent them scrambling up a supposedly unscalable cliff and, on the morning of 13 September, stood awaiting the surprised French on the Plains of Abraham. In a fierce battle both Montcalm and Wolfe were mortally wounded, but not before the latter had learned of his splendid victory. History has shown, however, that the battle had less of a dramatic impact on subsequent events than earlier historians had believed.

Christopher Hibbert, *Wolfe at Quebec* (Cleveland, Oh.: World Publishing, 1959).

JOHN MORGAN DEDERER

plantations An agricultural system stretching from Brazil to Maryland, plantations produced SUGAR, TOBACCO, coffee and cotton (in that order of importance) for export to Europe. The cultivation of these crops was labour-intensive and, as their scale of production rapidly expanded beyond the ability of local native labour or imported white indentured servants to sustain, the system became totally dependent on slave labour imported from Africa. In consequence, an estimated 10 million slaves were imported into the Americas throughout the period of the SLAVE TRADE. The largest profits were to be had from sugar, which made men like Richard and William Beckford fabulously wealthy, but sugar also required the largest investment both in slaves and in industrial plant by way of crushing-mills and boiler-houses. The Jamaican planter Bryan Edwards (1743–1800) estimated the value of a medium-sized sugar plantation of 650 acres and 250 slaves at nearly £30,000, an average coffee walk of 300 acres and 100 slaves at nearly £11,000 and a 50-acre cotton plantation with 12 slaves at just over £1,000 (a water-powered cotton mill in England could cost £3,000 to £5,000 in the 1780s).

M. Craton and J. Walvin, *A Jamaican Plantation* (London: W. H. Allen, 1970).

MICHAEL DUFFY

Plassey, Battle of (24 June 1757) The Battle of Plassey had a profound long-term effect on the British position in India. The nawab of BENGAL, Siraj-ud-daula (c.1729–57), had seized Calcutta in June 1756, but the city was retaken by East India Company forces eight months later. The British were then drawn into a complex power struggle between the nawab and a group of disaffected ministers who offered enormous financial rewards in return for deployment of Company troops in support of a *coup*. A deal was struck, and on 24 June 1757 Company forces commanded by CLIVE engaged the nawab's army at Plassey. The battle consisted of no more than a few artillery exchanges and the British won a comfortable victory. Siraj-ud-daula, who was murdered during his flight from the battlefield, was replaced by Mir Jafar as nawab. British involvement in what became known as the Bengal 'revolution' demonstrated that they could no longer stand aloof from local politics. At the time, the ends were held to justify the means, but later the methods of Clive and his colleagues were called into question by those in Britain who regarded Plassey as a disreputable and sordid affair.

M. Edwardes, *The Battle of Plassey and the Conquest of Bengal* (London: Batsford, 1963).

HUW BOWEN

Platonic dialogue   Just as ancient literary genres like the tragedy and the epic were modified in the eighteenth century to suit neoclassical tastes, the hybrid genre of Platonic dialogue, which combined literary, semi-dramatic style and philosophical content, was also adapted to contemporary needs. Dialogue writers in the eighteenth century, while seeking to emulate Plato, nevertheless rejected what was considered to be Socratic hair-splitting and over-intrusive dialectic, in favour of reproducing the flow of cultivated and broad-minded conversation. Neoclassical taste required that logical reasoning be subordinated to urbane conversation, while retaining its philosophic rigour.

The Moralists (1709) by the third earl of SHAFTESBURY, closely followed such a prescription, but his Platonic dialogue paradoxically advocated contemplation of 'Nature' in order to arrive at 'inward colloquy', or the communing of the soul with itself. Much closer to Plato's Socratic model in its dazzling dialectic was *Three Dialogues between Hylas and Philonous* (1713) by BERKELEY, which argued, through civilized conversation between two friends, 'that there is no such thing as what philosophers call *material substance*'. Berkeley's aim was to gain a wider audience for the controversial views first adumbrated in his more formally philosophical work, *A Treatise concerning the Principles of Human Knowledge*. His elegant dialogue, as befitted the future bishop of Cloyne, was directed 'in opposition to sceptics and atheists'.

The greatest masterpieces of the genre in the Enlightenment, Hume's *Dialogues concerning Natural Religion* and Diderot's *Le Neveu de Rameau*, however, were so subversive that they both appeared only posthumously. The former cast doubt on the existence of God, and the latter questioned traditional Christian morality. HUME's dialogue brilliantly reproduced the twists and turns of lively conversation at its most dynamic, the protagonists being Philo, a 'careless sceptic', Demea, rigidly orthodox in his views, and Cleanthes, a 'moderate Christian'. All the arguments were carefully balanced, and the mastery of dialectic is at least equal to Plato's. DIDEROT stretched Platonic dialogue even further. The dialogue is between Diderot himself ('Mr Philosopher') and an eccentric. Set in a Paris café, their conversation resembles Diderot's opening description of his own thought processes: 'I hold discussions with myself on politics, love, taste or philosophy, and let my thoughts wander in complete abandon, leaving them free to follow the first wise or foolish idea that comes along, like those young rakes we see in the Allé de Foy who run after a giddy-looking little piece with a laughing face, sparkling eye and tip-tilted nose, only to leave her for another, accosting them all, but sticking to none. In my case my thoughts are my wenches.' Another dialogue of Diderot's, *Le Rêve d'Alembert*, was similarly inventive.

Denis Diderot, *Rameau's Nephew; D'Alembert's Dream*, trans. L. W. Tancock (Harmondsworth: Penguin, 1966).

David Hume, *Dialogues concerning Natural Religion*, ed. Norman Kemp Smith, second edn (London: Thomas Nelson & Son, 1947).

MARIO RELICH

playing-cards, political and geographical Political playing-cards most probably first appeared in Britain during the 1680s. Restoration packs, such as *The Horrid Popish Plot 1678* and *Reign of James II 1685–1688*, the former designed by Francis Barlow (1626–1704), who was probably also responsible for the latter, were at the service of Whig politics. Barlow's engravings, which were reminiscent of political cartoons, satirized both Puritans and Roman Catholics. The political effectiveness of a later pack, *Marlborough's Victories 1702–1707*, which glorified the great duke, may be gauged by the fact that no pack is known to have been sold after his fall in 1711. *All the Bubbles 1720* and *The South Sea Bubble 1720* provided wry comment on the great financial scandal.

Geographical playing-cards reflected a spirit of enquiry rather than partisanship. In the pack known as the *Winstanley Geographical Cards* (*c.*1675) the suits represent different continents, and each card is graced by a copper-engraved scene and geographical information. Never imitated, they were designed, engraved and published by Henry Winstanley from his home in Littlebury, Essex. Other packs from the Restoration contain miniature maps on each card. This latter design was widely imitated in various geographical packs throughout the eighteenth century, both in Britain and in France.

Virginia Wayland, *The Winstanley Geographical Cards* (Pasadena, Calif.: Virginia and Harold Wayland, 1967).
J. R. S. Whiting, *A Handful of History* (Dursley: Alan Sutton, 1978).

MARIO RELICH

Pluche, Noël-Antoine (1688–1761) French writer. A professor of rhetoric in his native city of Reims, he became director of the College of Laon. He refused to sign the papal bull UNIGENITUS DEI FILIUS, and became a private tutor on relinquishing his post. He moved to Paris where he taught geometry and history. Often regarded as the best-known representative of the teleological school in natural history, he was the author of the very widely read *Spectacle de la nature* (1732–50). This eight-volume work presented new ideas in science and history within a Christian framework and rendered them accessible to a wide readership. He also wrote *La Mécanique des langues* (1751) and *Concorde de la géographie des différents âges* (1765). He left a number of manuscripts including two treatises on prophesies and one on the human heart.

Jean Ehrard, *L'Idée de nature en France dans la première moitié du dixhuitième siècle* (Paris: SEVPEN, 1963).

SYLVANA TOMASELLI

pneumatics The study of pneumatics, or the science of the mechanical properties of air and other gases, built on the work of Torricelli (1608–47), Pascal (1623–62), Boyle (1627–91) and Hooke (1635–1703) – most notably the experiments *in vacuo* using air pumps and the notion of air as an elastic fluid – and attracted Newtonians in search of a 'repulsive virtue'. HALES and BLACK heralded a realization of the chemical nature of air. Hales showed that air was 'vitiated' when rebreathed and that gaseous exchange in plants which 'fixed' air reinvigorated vitiated air. Black, beginning with the principle of conservation of matter, isolated 'fixed air' (carbon dioxide). However, air was still considered to be an element. It was LAVOISIER who embarked on resolving air into its component parts, having been inspired by PRIESTLEY's isolation of the 'dephlogisticated air' (oxygen) which was responsible for combustion and respiration (*see* PHLOGISTON).

Determining the respirability of different kinds of air became something of a vogue in the second half of the century; philosophers used eudiometers to gauge the 'goodness' of air until Humboldt (1769–1859) and Gay-Lussac (1778–1850) showed that the percentage of oxygen in unvitiated air was independent of its source.

Simon Schaffer, 'Measuring Virtue: Eudiometry, Enlightenment and Pneumatic Medicine', in Andrew Cunningham and Roger French (eds), *The Medical Enlightenment of the Eighteenth Century* (Cambridge: Cambridge University Press, 1990), pp. 281–318.

M. L. BENJAMIN

poetry In poetry the eighteenth century marked a seismic shift in taste and sensibility from a dominant neoclassicism, with its emphasis on order, decorum and the rules, to ROMANTICISM, with its belief in individual expression, sublimity and the visionary powers of the IM-AGINATION. Throughout the century the poets and critics most eloquent in their defence of the classical rules of composition (derived from Aristotle's *Poetics* and given fuller formulation in Horace's *Ars poetica*) were in no doubt that a remedial process of literary refinement was necessary to discipline the immature and 'Gothic' irregularities of earlier verse. In his *Preface to Shakespeare* (1765) Samuel Johnson asserted that 'nations, like individuals have their infancy . . . the English nation, in the time of Shakespeare, was yet struggling to emerge from barbarity'. By thus extenuating Shakespeare's 'faults' (the 'lowness' and extravagance of his diction and the waywardness of his plots), Johnson gave expression to the same cultural imperatives which motivated countless poets and dramatists, from John Dryden (1631–1700) to Colley Cibber (1671–1757), who sought to 'improve' Shakespeare's plays, refining their dialogue and regularizing their plots in accordance with the classical unities of action, time and place.

At the beginning of the century the ageing BOILEAU in France and the young POPE in England were the chief poetic advocates and representatives of this rage for literary refinement and order. Known as the *legislateur du Parnasse* on the strength of his *Art poétique* (1674), Boileau not only prescribed rules for other poets to follow, but also provided a model, in his satiric poem *Le Lutrin* (The Lectern), of the delicately formal social comedy in which the age excelled. The symmetrical patterns of Pope's heroic couplets, driven by a dynamo of ironic antitheses and built on a framework of classical motifs, are perhaps the perfect expression of neoclassicism in verse. There is scarcely a line of Pope which does not contain some classical echo or allusion, giving his satiric vision of his society the imaginative backdrop of a mythopoeic evocation of the idealized values of Greece and Rome, as represented by Homer, Virgil and Horace. Satire, particularly mock-heroic satire, became the dominant poetic genre in the early eighteenth century, as a fondness for classical motifs found an uneasy accommodation with the values and institutions of an increasingly mercantile culture. Pope's *Rape of the Lock* and *The Dunciad*, Boileau's *Le Lutrin* and Gay's *Trivia* provided the models for a host of later imitations, and established the characteristically ambivalent tone towards the grandiose pretensions of a self-styled 'Augustan' age.

In his *Essay on Criticism* Pope asserted a cardinal principle: 'First follow Nature, and your judgment frame / By her just standard, which is still the same.' But this is not nature as the sublime elemental force of Wordsworth, but nature as a divine plan, a grand providential mechanism whose balanced laws and reciprocating forces were explained by

Newton. Hence there was no conflict between following nature and following Aristotle's rules: 'Those Rules of old, discover'd, not devis'd, / Are Nature still, but Nature methodiz'd' – 'Nature methodized' is the hallmark of neoclassical art. In JOHNSON's *Rasselas* the teacher Imlac asserts that 'The business of the poet is to examine not the individual, but the species; to remark general properties and large appearances: he does not number the streaks of the tulip, or describe the different shades in the verdure of the forest.' The reduction of both poetry and nature to a series of generalized categories was emphatically rejected by BLAKE, the most individualistic of the romantic poets. 'To generalize is to be an idiot', he asserted. The poet who could see 'a World in a Grain of Sand' and who wrote in 'Auguries of Innocence', 'Each outcry of the hunted Hare / A fibre from the Brain does tear', was not a man content to dwell in generalities.

The first cracks in the neoclassical façade appeared early in the century. In *The Spectator* (1711) ADDISON praised the old border ballads 'Chevy Chase' and 'The Two Children in the Wood', although he still found a 'despicable simplicity' in their verse. The publication of Bishop Thomas Percy's (1729–1811) *Reliques of Ancient English Poetry* in 1765, gave a new respectability to the taste for these early ballads, providing a literary pedigree for an emerging sensibility which preferred such 'Gothic' simplicity to the polished, formal idioms of classical verse. In poems like 'The Bard' (1757), 'The Fatal Sisters' and 'The Descent of Odin' (1761) GRAY affected to imitate the prophetic voice of a northern bard, while William Collins (1721–59) in his odes 'To Simplicity' and 'To Fear' (1747) cultivated a poetic style of reflective simplicity. Many of these early evocations of a Gothic or romantic style were undertaken in a spirit of historical make-believe or pastiche. Thomas Chatterton's (1752–70) 'Rowley' poems (1778), though containing sparks of original genius, were fraudulently presented as authentic medieval works, while James Macpherson (1736–96) fabricated two epic poems, *Fingal* and *Temora* (1763), both much admired by Goethe, claiming them to be translations of ancient Gaelic works (*see* OSSIAN). In Germany WIELAND wrote a number of verse-tales drawn from medieval and Oriental sources. Another inspirational source for the new poetic mood was religion. Christopher Smart's (1722–71) *Song to David* (1763) is imbued with a spirit of mystical celebration, while in Germany KLOPSTOCK's *Messias*, inspired by Milton's *Paradise Lost*, was characterized by a pietistic delight in religious sentiment.

Gradually, a new critical vocabulary developed which, rejecting the formal categories of French neoclassicism, placed a new emphasis on the sensations of sympathy and awe generated by works of art. BURKE's *Philosophical Enquiry into . . . the Sublime and Beautiful* examined the sublime qualities of such unpleasurable sensations as pain and fear;

LESSING's essays, including the *Laokoon*, challenged the old Horatian certainties concerning poetry's status as a mimetic art; and ROUSSEAU, throughout his writings, celebrated the poet as a prelapsarian *naïf*, the voice of a primitive spirit of freedom, rejecting all formal constraints. However, it was not until the last decade of the century that the poetry which we now call Romantic came into its own. In Germany the collaboration of GOETHE and SCHILLER, who came together in 1794, led to such lyrical poems as 'Das Ideal und das Leben', 'Der Taucher' and 'Die Glocke', while in England that of WORDSWORTH and COLERIDGE resulted in the publication of the *Lyrical Ballads* in 1798. In the Preface to this celebrated work, which included 'The Ancient Mariner' and 'Tintern Abbey', Wordsworth set out a poetic manifesto, rejecting the 'poetic diction' of the Augustans in favour of a poetry that was 'the spontaneous overflow of powerful feelings' expressed 'in the real language of men'.

Walter Jackson Bate, *From Classic to Romantic* (Cambridge, Mass.: Harvard University Press, 1946).
Margaret Anne Doody, *The Daring Muse: Augustan Poetry Reconsidered* (Cambridge: Cambridge University Press, 1985).
Roger Lonsdale (ed.), *The New Oxford Book of Eighteenth-Century Verse* (Oxford: Oxford University Press, 1985).
James Sutherland, *A Preface to Eighteenth-Century Poetry* (Oxford: Oxford University Press, 1948).

DAVID NOKES

Poland Officially styled 'the Commonwealth of the two nations, the Polish and the Lithuanian' to reflect the political union between the Polish kingdom proper and the grand duchy of Lithuania, the state of Poland-Lithuania covered some 733,500 square miles, with a population of around 12 million in 1700, and 14 million by 1772. It was dominated by a Polish and polonized nobility, the *szlachta*, which made up 6 to 7 per cent of the total population.

The peasant majority of Poles, Lithuanians, Ukrainians and Belorussians were enserfed, with little or no right of appeal from seigneurial jurisdiction. Urban commercial prosperity was massively impaired by noble economic privilege and by the *szlachta*'s self-interested exploitation of Poland's Jews (some 7 per cent of the population).

A number of great magnate families dominated the political scene, manipulating their clienteles and a shared republican ideology in the guise of protecting their 'liberty', which was generally conceived of in terms of concrete privileges exclusive to the *szlachta*, including the right to elect their own monarch and to participate in all legislation, immunity from arrest without trial and freedom of speech. These privileges were taken to such extremes that by the later seventeenth century every envoy sent to the Polish parliament, the *Sejm*, had the right to annul its proceedings through his individual protest – the so-called *liberum veto*. The same right applied at the local assemblies that elected representatives to the *Sejm*. The result was legislative impotence and constitutional chaos. Neighbouring powers regularly intervened in Polish domestic affairs, which became an extension of their foreign policies. Polish impotence was compounded by the restriction on the size of the army in 1717 to 24,000 pay units, which in practice meant around 12,000 men. A significant expansion of the army took place only after 1788, but even then it never exceeded 52,000.

Attempts at reform only inspired fears of royal absolutist designs. King Stanislaw Augustus PONIATOWSKI's efforts at reform helped provoke virtual civil war between 1768 and 1772, which culminated in the first partition by Russia, Prussia and Austria; this cost Poland a third of its population and territory. Between 1775 and 1788 a degree of enforced stability followed under a *de facto* Russian protectorate, which tolerated only marginal reform. Major change, however, did come between 1788 and 1792 when Russia was sufficiently distracted by conflicts with Turkey and Sweden to allow the so-called 'Four Years *Sejm*' to engineer a radical constitutional overhaul. Such a show of independence finally provoked Russian armed intervention, and the partition of 1793. The defeat of the KOŚCIUSZKO insurrection of 1794 brought about the political extinction of the commonwealth in 1795.

See also PARTITIONS OF POLAND.

J. T. Lukowski, *Liberty's Folly: The Polish-Lithuanian Commonwealth in the Eighteenth Century* (London: Routledge, 1991).

J. T. LUKOWSKI

police   The history of the police in the eighteenth century is complicated by terminology. For most Europeans 'police' meant something like 'public administration' rather than the modern concept of a force for crime control. Indeed, the most admired police force of the century, that of Paris (essentially set up in 1667), was involved in supervising markets and ensuring that the streets were clear of rubbish, as well as in repressing crime, prostitution and vagrancy. By 1789, however, the guard, a paramilitary crime-prevention element, numbered 1,200. The Parisian model was widely admired (notably by Frederick the Great of Prussia), although its paramilitary overtones, together with the supposed French dependence on undercover agents and informers, rendered it unacceptable to English observers. In England, despite the piecemeal emergence of paid police officials in London, policing by amateur parish constables continued.

The most developed police force outside Europe was perhaps that of China, where police officials were a category of government runner. As in Europe, 'policing' in China was part of a wider administrative project, and recruiting and retaining reliable and uncorrupt officers was a constant problem.

Clive Emsley, *Policing and its Context 1750–1870* (London: Macmillan, 1983).

J. A. SHARPE

Polish Succession, War of the (1733–1735) In its Polish aspect this struggle involved a successful effort by Russia and the Habsburg Empire to establish AUGUSTUS II, elector of Saxony, as ruler of Poland, and to defeat the rival French-backed candidate, Stanislas LESZCZYŃSKI, the father-in-law of Louis XV. France sought compensation from the Habsburgs for its Polish failure in the Rhineland and also in Italy, where it had the support of Spain and where the most serious fighting of the war took place. When peace was made in October 1735 (the definitive treaty was signed in Vienna only in November 1738) Naples and Sicily were surrendered by the Habsburgs to Don Carlos (later Charles III), the son of Philip V of Spain, and they received in exchange the smaller Italian territories of Parma and Piacenza. The grand duchy of Tuscany was given to Francis, duke of Lorraine, the husband-to-be of the Habsburg archduchess Maria Theresa, while Lorraine itself was handed over to Stanislas Leszczyński and became French territory on his death in 1766. During the war a Russian army penetrated for the first time into western Europe and reached the River Neckar in west Germany.

J. O. Lindsay (ed.), *The New Cambridge Modern History*, vol. 7 (Cambridge: Cambridge University Press, 1957), chs 9, 16.

M. S. ANDERSON

politeness In *Clarissa*, a novel much concerned with the difficulties of judging character on the basis of outward appearances, Richardson was at pains to distinguish between politeness and flattery as well as other forms of insincerity. In keeping with contemporary usage, he tried to employ the notion to denote a quality which went beyond good manners and respect for decorum. Peculiar to modern men and women, politeness was a consequence of the civilizing process on the human psyche. While civility was part of its external manifestation, 'true politeness' was a character trait which disposed one to treat other human beings with humanity and consideration. Such ideas were dismissed out of hand by those who, like Rousseau, thought civilization brought nothing but the alienation of man from his real self and only engendered a dichotomy between being and appearance.

Although much was said and written about the true nature of politeness, its relation to civility, propriety, virtue, honour and hypocrisy, it would be foolish to imply that the term was used with much consistency even by one Enlightenment author, let alone all of them. Reproaching Edmund Burke for his treatment of Dr Price (1723–91), Mary Wollstonecraft reminded him in her *Vindication of the Rights of Man* (1790) that 'Even in France, Sir, before the revolution, literary celebrity procured a man the treatment of a gentleman; but you are going back for your credentials of politeness to more distant times. – Gothic affability is the mode you think proper to adopt, the condescension of a Baron, not the civility of a liberal man. Politeness is, indeed, the only substitute for humanity; or what distinguishes the civilised man from the unlettered savage?'. However in the *Vindication of the Rights of Woman* (1792) Wollstonecraft spoke of the 'slippery graces of politeness' as well as 'the courtly robe of politeness', and argued: 'Were boys and girls permitted to pursue the same studies together, those graceful decencies might early be inculcated which produce modesty without sexual distinctions that taint the mind. Lessons of politeness, and that formulary of decorum, which treads on the heels of falsehood, would be rendered useless by habitual propriety of behaviour.'

Nicholas Philipson, 'Politics and Politeness in Early Eighteenth Century Britain', in John Pocock (ed.), *Varieties of Political Discourses in Early Modern Britain* (Cambridge: Cambridge University Press, 1994).

SYLVANA TOMASELLI

political economy   *see* ECONOMICS.

political thought   Enlightenment political theorists worked very much within the framework set by their seventeenth-century predecessors, especially, though not exclusively, by those within the NATURAL LAW tradition. Thus eighteenth-century political philosophers, from the baron de Montesquieu to the founding fathers of the American Revolution, often referred to the writings of Hugo Grotius (1583–1645), Thomas Hobbes (1588–1679), John Locke and Samuel Pufendorf (1632–94); and Rousseau, Beccaria and Kant employed the theoretical apparatus of a state of nature and a social contract, while Hume and Bentham made their critique of these notions central to their own conceptions. While Burlamaqui and Blackstone, for instance, contributed in more straightforward ways to jurisprudential thought, other theorists, like Wollstonecraft and Olympe de Gouges (1755–93), took the concepts of natural rights and liberty into new discourses. That all human beings, regardless of status, wealth, religion, sex or race, were the bearers of natural and inviolable RIGHTS was a view which gained increasing acceptance as the century wore on.

Next in importance was the influence exercised by the political writings of MONTESQUIEU. His *Considérations sur les causes de la grandeur des Romains et de leur décadence* (1734) and *L'Esprit des lois* (1748) contrasted the political life of the ancients with that of the moderns. The latter work, in particular, showed that, however attractive ancient politics might be, the principle on which ancient republics rested, namely virtue, was no longer prevalent in the large commercial nations of eighteenth-century Europe, whose monarchies were characterized instead by considerations of honour and conspicuous consumption. His analysis of law in *L'Esprit des lois* sought to demonstrate not only the manner in which laws were the product of certain historical and political constraints, but also the extent to which they could be modified in order to deal best with the three great and interrelated subjects of legislation: religion, commerce and liberty. For a country to flourish economically and the happiness of its people to prevail, it had to secure LIBERTY from the encroachments of despotism, which was latent in all monarchies, and to guarantee religious toleration. In contrast to those who, like many of the liberal reformers of his age, advocated piecemeal policies, such as that of *laissez-faire*, Montesquieu stressed that the legislator had to consider society as a whole and that securing one end, say the defence of the land, required the orchestration of all the necessary and causally related legislative means, from religious toleration (so as to prevent the emigration of skilled workers, for instance) to the maintenance of the division of power essential to the preservation of liberty, which was vital to commerce and prosperity. The physiocrats and the Scottish political economists, especially Adam SMITH, similarly conceived of their economic theories within overarching social and political philosophies.

Unlike them, ROUSSEAU had relatively little to say about the issues of scarcity and the nature of the wealth of modern trading nations, although he contributed the *Encyclopédie* entry on political economy. What interested him was the conditions under which membership in a political society would not only not subjugate man, but enable him to attain a form of freedom, unknown to him in nature, namely moral freedom. Man, he argued in *Du contract social* (1762), would be morally free under the laws of his polity if these laws were the expression of the GENERAL WILL; for he would then be obeying laws of his own making and to these self-imposed laws he would, as a citizen, owe liberty and justice. Such laws would not only require political equality, but would also favour economic equality. Indeed, the ideal polis he had in mind was a small, independent, economically self-subsistent and predominantly agrarian community, whose members could enjoy face-to-face relations and whose culture was homogeneous, in other words the antithesis of the countries that were the subject of Montesquieu's and Smith's great works.

Although the political ideas of Rousseau remain of interest to twentieth-century political philosophers and are, for instance, at the heart of Robert Wolff's discussion of democracy and autonomy, the Enlightenment political thinker whose philosophy is the object of the greatest consideration today is KANT. He is noteworthy not only because of the importance his views assumed within Hegelian political theory, but because his philosophy constituted the soundest foundation for LIBERALISM. Like Rousseau, Kant thought moral freedom necessarily tied to the rule of law. Unlike Rousseau, however, he conceived of the state of nature in Hobbesian terms, that is, as a state of war. Civil society was the context within which man could become fully human and be treated as an end rather than as a means. It was the domain in which he could transcend his appetites and inclinations to obey the dictates of his own reason, commanding him to act in accordance with maxims that could be universalized. The more enlightened a society the freer a man could be in it, for such a society, Kant explained in *Was ist Aufklärung* (An Answer to the Question: 'What is Enlightenment?', 1784), being governed by rational laws, would be the guarantor of the 'freedom to make *public use* of one's reason in all matters'. Thus while he firmly denied the right of resistance, he staunchly defended freedom of expression. In opposition to the utilitarians, he did not consider HAPPINESS to be the proper end of politics. 'Men have different views', he argued in *Theorie und Praxis* (Theory and Practice, 1793), 'on the empirical end of happiness and what it consists of, so that as far as happiness is concerned, their will cannot be brought under any common principle nor thus under any external law harmonising with the freedom of everyone.' Whether at the national or international level, the aim of politics was rational legislation to ensure freedom and afford the possibility of leading a moral life.

From the point of view of European political theorists, the rest of the world was essentially divided between the natural societies of savages and the despotic regimes of the East. Despite the efforts of travellers like Lady Mary Wortley MONTAGU who sought in her *Turkish Letters* to convey a more balanced view of life in the Ottoman Empire, the latter tended to be considered as a land of unmitigated tyranny. China, on the other hand, was the object of some admiration despite the absolute power of its emperors. Diderot, however, had little patience with favourable descriptions of Chinese rule, for example Quesnay's in *Le Despotisme de la Chine* (1767), and virulently attacked its arguments in a chapter of the abbé Raynal's *Histoire philosophique et politique des deux Indes*, a work which inspired the Haitian revolutionary Toussaint L'Ouverture in his fight against slavery and colonianism.

Thomas A. Horne, *Property Rights and Poverty: Political Argument in Britain, 1605–1834* (Chapel Hill, NC: University of North Carolina Press, 1990).

Nannerl O. Keohane, *Philosophy and the State in France: The Renaissance to the Enlightenment* (Princeton, NJ: Princeton University Press, 1980).

Mary Lyndon Shanley and Carole Pateman (eds), *Feminist Interpretations and Political Theory* (Cambridge: Polity, 1991).

Charles Taylor, 'Kant's Theory of Freedom', in *Philosophy and the Human Sciences*, vol. 2 (Cambridge: Cambridge University Press, 1985), pp. 318–37.

Robert Paul Wolff, *In Defense of Anarchism* (New York: Harper Torchbooks, 1976).

SYLVANA TOMASELLI

Poltava, Battle of (8 July 1709)   The Battle of Poltava was the decisive battle of the GREAT NORTHERN WAR, in which 40,000 Russians under Peter I defeated 22,000 Swedes under CHARLES XII. Charles had invaded Russia in 1708, turning south-east in 1709 into territory unaffected by the Russian scorched-earth policy to join up with rebel Cossack forces under Mazeppa (*c.*1644–1709) in the Ukraine. In June the Swedes besieged Poltava, the key to the southern route to Moscow. Mazeppa failed to provide large-scale support and, with the position of the Swedish party in Poland under threat, Charles needed a decisive victory. Wounded just before the battle, he was unable to take full charge. The Swedish frontal assault on the prepared Russian positions was repulsed with heavy losses: 10,000 men, including 6,901 dead, compared with 1,345 dead and 3,290 wounded for the Russians. The surrender of 15,000 Swedes at Perevolochna on 11 July sealed the Russian victory, as Charles fled into a five-year exile in Turkey. Poltava ended Swedish ascendency in north-eastern Europe and marked the establishment of Russia as a major military power.

R. Hatton, *Charles XII of Sweden* (London: Weidenfeld & Nicolson, 1968), ch. 5.

P. Englund, *The Battle of Poltava: The Birth of the Russian Empire* (London: Victor Gollancz, 1992).

ROBERT I. FROST

Pombal, Sebastião José de Carvalho e Mello, marquês de (1699–1782)   Despotic Portuguese statesman who ruled Portugal for three decades. He came from rural gentry and studied law at the stagnant

University of Coimbra. He was then appointed to diplomatic posts in London and Vienna, which experience convinced him that Portugal was suffering from an undeveloped economy, out-of-date education and racial prejudice. His opportunity to change all this came in 1750 when he became the favourite and chief minister of King José I. After the LISBON EARTHQUAKE in 1755 he masterminded the rebuilding of the ruined capital. In 1759 he expelled the JESUITS, whom he saw as the main obstacle to educational reform; Jesuit manuals were prohibited in schools and the Jesuit University of Evora abolished. At Coimbra he replaced Aristotelianism with Newtonian physics. He encouraged trade by founding companies and schools of commerce, abolished statutes that discriminated against those of Jewish origin and legislated against racial prejudice in Goa. He was ennobled by the king in 1770. By the time he fell from power when his royal protector died, he had effectively transformed the face of the kingdom through sweeping social and institutional reforms.

C. R. Boxer, *The Portuguese Seaborne Empire 1415–1825* (London: Hutchinson, 1969).

DAVID GOODMAN

Pompadour, Jeanne Antoinette Poisson, marquise de (1721–1764) Mistress of LOUIS XV. The daughter of the steward to the wealthy, powerful banking family the Paris, who dominated government finances after the demise of John Law, she entered Parisian society through her marriage to the nephew of an influential farmer-general, who was her mother's lover. In the early 1740s she was the hostess of an important literary *salon* which was frequented by Voltaire and Montesquieu. She formed a liaison with Louis XV (of which the details are unknown) following the death of the marquise de Nesle, the king's recognized mistress, in 1744. By 1745 she was installed at Versailles, and given a country seat and the title of marquise. Together with her brother Marigny (1727–81), who became *intendant des batiments*, she was a major influence on the development of the artistic and cultural *style Louis XV*. In 1752 she and Louis ended their sexual relationship, but she remained at court as his confidant and friend; no one replaced her as his recognized mistress in her lifetime.

She had little influence on politics, but in 1749–51 the mutual antipathy between herself and the clergy led her to back Machault's (1701–94) unsuccessful attempt to tax the church. On a personal level, she acted as a counterweight to the king's pious, pro-Jesuit daughters. Although she was seldom a direct protagonist in court politics, her presence initially helped the Paris brothers to oust their rival, Orry, by 1745. By contrast, CHOISEUL – a personal favourite – survived in power long after her death in 1764. Her political role was negligible compared to that of the king's last mistress, Madame du Barry (*c*.1743–93), from 1771.

A. Cobban, *A History of Modern France*, vol. 1: *1715–1799* (Harmondsworth: Penguin, 1957).
N. Mitford, *Madame de Pompadour* (London: Hamish Hamilton, 1954).

MICHAEL BROERS

Pompeii An ancient town of Campania, Pompeii came under the influence of the Greek colonies from the eighth century BC and was destroyed through the eruption of Mount Vesuvius in AD 79, an event described by Pliny the Younger in his *Letters* (100–9). Its discovery in 1748 added to the impetus that the discovery of HERCULANEUM in 1713 had given to ARCHAEOLOGY. The gradual recovery of these towns was to transform perceptions of the ancient world, especially with regards to its domestic life, and to be a great source of inspiration to artists, architects and writers.

Many Enlightenment figures were to travel to Italy, visiting these and other ancient sites and monuments; they paved the way for neoclassicism. Among those who gave an account of their impressions on seeing Pompeii's ruins was Goethe, who had 'seldom seen anything so interesting'.

See also CULT OF ANTIQUITY.

Wolfgang Leppmann, *Pompeii in Fact and Fiction* (London: Elek, 1968).

SYLVANA TOMASELLI

Pondicherry Situated 85 miles south of Madras on the Coromandel coast, Pondicherry was the principal French settlement in India. A factory or trading station was first established there in 1674 by François Martin (*c*.1640–1706), and the village was purchased in 1683. The settlement was virtually refounded by Martin in 1703 when the original site was fortified and 500 looms were installed for the manufacture of piece goods. Steady growth and development occurred in the subsequent half-century. However, with the advent of the Anglo-French wars in the 1740s, Pondicherry found itself playing an increasingly important strategic role as DUPLEIX's headquarters. The settlement was besieged several times by the British, most notably in 1760–1 following the Battle of Wandiwash when the garrison, under the command of comte de Lally (1702–66), resisted attacks for eight months. After Lally's capitulation in January 1761, it was decided that the French presence in the Carnatic should be eradicated once and for all, and Pondicherry was systematically dismantled. The TREATY OF PARIS restored Pondicherry to the French and the settlement was rebuilt, although it again fell prey to military action in 1778 when it was taken by the British once more following French intervention in the American War of Independence.

H. Furber, *Rival Empires of Trade in the Orient, 1620–1750* (Minneapolis: University of Minnesota Press, 1976).

HUW BOWEN

Poniatowski, Stanislaw (1732–1798)   King of Poland (1764–1795). Though of comparatively modest gentry background, the Poniatowskis were closely related to the Czartoryski family, one of the most powerful political groupings in POLAND and closely committed to a programme of national reform. With Russian military support, Stanislaw August (his assumed regnal name) was elected king on 6 September 1764. His determination to effect a thoroughgoing reform of the Polish state brought him into conflict with Catherine II, who had cast him in the role of a passive instrument of Russian policy. In 1767–8, Catherine engineered a rebellion of malcontent nobility to block substantive reform, only to create a situation of near civil war which culminated in the first partition of 1772. Until 1788, Stanislaw August was obliged to restrict himself mainly to cultural patronage and educational reform and it is in these fields that his greatest achievements lie. Fresh Russian intervention crushed the constitutional reforms of 1788–92, and brought on the second and third partitions. The king was forced to abdicate in 1795. He died in enforced exile in St Petersburg.

A. Zamoyski, *The Last King of Poland* (London: Cape, 1992).

J. T. LUKOWSKI

Pope, Alexander (1688–1744)   English poet. He was the dominant literary figure in England in the first half of the eighteenth century. His person and his poetry were celebrated and reviled in equal measure, but few writers – and no poets – of the period could escape his influence. Yet his fame was paradoxical, for he was in many ways an outsider from his culture. He was a Roman Catholic, a Tory in a time of Whig ascendancy, and physically stunted due to a childhood illness (a fact that few of his attackers failed to use). Barred by his religion from the universities, he was largely self-educated. After a childhood in London, he lived at Binfield, near Windsor, and spent most of his adult life at Twickenham, where he designed his own Palladian villa. He cultivated a select circle of literary and political friends, including Swift, Arbuthnot and Lord Bolingbroke. These and other friends, and many enemies, populate his poems.

Pope was a rare example of a poet who made large sums of money from writing poetry: his translation of Homer's *Iliad* (1715–20) gave him material security as well as literary status. Before this he had produced pastoral poetry, the agile *Essay on Criticism* (1711) and the sparkling, mock-heroic *Rape of the Lock* (1712–14). In 1725 he published an edition of Shakespeare's *Works*, whose most severe critic, Lewis Theobald (1688–1744), was made the antihero of his mock epic *The Dunciad* (1728). This, his most extraordinary work, was rewritten radically, and reappeared in 1743. In the 1730s he wrote a variety of satires, including *Imitations of Horace*, and a lengthy philosophical poem, *An Essay on Man* (1733–4). His major poems were all in the form of heroic couplets, which he brought to a new and witty perfection.

Maynard Mack, *Alexander Pope: A Life* (New Haven, Conn.: Yale University Press, 1985).

JOHN MULLAN

population growth In the eighteenth century most countries experienced population growth. Europe had 83.9 million inhabitants in 1700, 98.4 million in 1750 and 124.8 million by 1800. The North American colonies had a population of 360,000 in 1713, 1.6 million in 1760, 3.9 million in 1790 and 5.3 million by 1800. In England population increase was caused by a rise in the birth rate but in other countries, such as Sweden, falling death rates played a larger role. North American growth was fuelled partly by natural increase but principally by immigration.
See also DEMOGRAPHY.

M. Anderson, *Population Change in North-Western Europe, 1750–1850* (London: Macmillan, 1988).

JEREMY BOULTON

porcelain A chic and expensive type of pottery, porcelain graced the tables of the rich and was valued for its delicacy of form and elegance of design. It was invented in China during the T'ang dynasty (618–908), and its manufacture was concentrated around Jingdezhen, near Nanking. A large export trade developed: cargoes to Europe consisted principally of dinner services and sets for drinking tea, coffee and chocolate. Shapes and designs were adapted to European tastes and habits: blue-and-white, polychrome, and plain white were the most popular; 'armorial' porcelain was commissioned to include coats of arms.

The first attempts to imitate 'China' ware resulted in the fragile soft-paste porcelain, made of white clay and ground glass at many European factories until *c.*1800. Hard-paste or true porcelain awaited the discovery in Europe of kaolin (china clay) deposits. Meissen, in Saxony, began production in 1710 and set technical and artistic standards for half a century: rococo tablewares delicately painted with Chinese landscapes and naturalistic statuettes of people, birds and animals were its hallmark. Leadership passed in the 1760s to Sèvres, the French national factory, which excelled in rich colours and elaborate gilding in the newly fashionable neoclassical style.

Robert J. Charleston (ed.), *World Ceramics* (London: Hamlyn, 1968).

CHRISTINE MACLEOD

portrait painting   Throughout most of the eighteenth century portrait painting was considered as less respectable than HISTORY PAINTING or even LANDSCAPE PAINTING; it involved simply representation in contrast to the communication of great moral ideas in other types of painting. In spite of this, portraiture reached its peak in the century, with the English school in particular raising the form to such a level of achievement that the old hierarchy began to crumble.

In seventeenth-century portraits, for example those by Lebrun (1619–90), facial and bodily expressions had been used to convey ideas – heroism, nobility – rather than to say anything about the person represented. Eighteenth-century artists like Reynolds, Gainsborough, David and Goya imbued their portraits with a self-conscious psychological insight which marked a complete departure from the formal representations of most of their predecessors. In essence, this deliberate attempt to portray character derived from the Enlightenment interest in the individual, as seen in the work of philosophers like Locke. The new social informality also allowed the painter a much wider range of settings, costumes and attitudes in which to explore his subject. There were also parallels with the growing interest in the study of physiognomy.

M. Levey, *Rococo to Revolution: Major Trends in Eighteenth-Century Painting* (London: Thames & Hudson, 1966).

IAIN PEARS

Portugal   The first economic characteristic of eighteenth-century Portugal was the importance of colonial (mainly Brazilian) staples (sugar, tobacco, cacao, hides, cotton) and specie (Brazilian gold and silver obtained by contraband trade with Spanish South America) in underwriting Portuguese prosperity. Secondly, the period was marked, domestically, by the rise of viticulture, especially port wine, and by the capture of the British wine market. British merchants in Oporto had initiated the port-wine trade in 1678 as a substitute for the re-export trade in Brazilian sugar and tobacco, which they had lost to British West Indian competition. Parliament gave them a beneficial tariff in 1697, and under the terms of the METHUEN TREATY of 1703, Portuguese wines paid a rate one-third below those of French wines. By the end of the century, nine-tenths of all port wine exported went to England, where Portuguese wine had cornered 70 to 75 per cent of the market. Thirdly, Portugal remained a chronic grain importer, from northern Europe at the beginning of the century and from North America (especially Virginia and the Carolinas) towards the end – which also helped North Americans to develop a taste for Portuguese wines.

Social, institutional, and geostrategical questions were influenced by the importance of Portugal's empire in South America. Gold from Brazil, for example, allowed the Portuguese monarchs the luxury of avoiding recourse to the nation's ancient representative (and tax-granting) institution, the *Cortes*, which did not meet between 1698 and 1820. The century, therefore, saw the apogee of the absolutist state in Portugal.

The period from the late 1660s through to 1807 also saw the presence of influential foreign merchant communities in Lisbon and Oporto, protected by treaties and enjoying religious toleration. Through their entrepreneurial skills and access to capital, foreign merchants penetrated the whole fabric of the metropolitan and colonial economy directly (for example, port-wine merchants) or indirectly (for example merchants interested in commerce with Brazil). The British merchants in Lisbon and Oporto were organized within so-called 'factories', which were in effect legally recognized commercial corporations. With their privileges guaranteed by the Cromwellian treaty of 1657 and reinforced by the Methuen Treaty of 1703, the British were the most prominent foreign merchants in Portugal.

The century was also characterized by the continuing struggle between France and England. Lisbon tried to accommodate both but, because of its dependence on maritime lines of communication, was tied inextricably to Britain, the dominant naval power of the epoch. It was rarely able to maintain neutrality for long, during either the Seven Years War or the Napoleonic wars. The need for external political and military support was at the core of the commercial concessions Portugal had made in the seventeenth century and it continued throughout the eighteenth century to set the parameters within which Portuguese policy had to be conducted.

See also BRAZIL.

C. R. Boxer, *The Portuguese Seaborne Empire 1415–1825* (London: Hutchinson, 1969).

H. E. S. Fisher, *The Portugal Trade: A Study of Anglo-Portuguese Commerce 1700–1770* (London: Methuen, 1971).

Kenneth R. Maxwell, *Conflicts and Conspiracies: Brazil and Portugal 1750–1808* (Cambridge: Cambridge University Press, 1973).

Kenneth R. Maxwell, *Pombal: An Enlightenment Paradox* (Cambridge: Cambridge University Press, 1994).

KENNETH MAXWELL

potato   The potato is known to have been cultivated in South America some two thousand years before the Spanish Conquest. It was exported to Spain from Peru, probably around 1570. Its introduction to England (*c.*1590) was not connected with Drake (*c.*1540–96) or Ralegh (1552–1618), but with John Gerard (1545–1612), an amateur botanist and gardener. The spread of the potato as a field crop was very slow, partly because of its novelty, but mainly because of the long process of adaptation to a temperate climate; originally the crop did not mature in northern Europe until the late autumn. It became widely grown and eaten only from about the middle of the eighteenth century, and it subsequently became a staple element of diet of industrial workers in Europe, providing a nutritious alternative to bread, of particular value when bread grains were dear following a bad harvest. Its role in the rapid growth of the Irish population, and the subsequent famine and mass emigration from that country, is celebrated and controversial (*see* IRELAND).

R. N. Salaman, *The History and Social Influence of the Potato* (Cambridge: Cambridge University Press, 1949).

G. E. MINGAY

Potemkin, Grigorii Aleksandrovich (1739–1791)   Russian statesman and favourite of CATHERINE II. In 1762, as an officer in the horse guards, he participated in the *coup* that brought Catherine to power, later, in the 1760s serving as assistant procurator of the Holy Synod and on the LEGISLATIVE COMMISSION. He won fame as a cavalry commander in the first Turkish War (1768–74) and in March 1774 was installed as official favourite with the title of adjutant-general. His passionate affair with Catherine lasted only until 1776, but he remained her trusted friend and adviser for which he was rewarded with honours. He may even have married her, although this did not preclude her from having other lovers. From 1776 he supervised Russia's new territories in the south, building towns and fortresses and encouraging settlers. In 1781 he and Catherine devised the abortive 'Greek project'. In 1783 he secured the annexation of the Crimea to Russia, and in 1787 he arranged Catherine's southern tour, the lavish theatricality of which gave rise to the myth of 'Potemkin villages'. From 1784 he headed the war department, initiating reforms of army and fleet. He died in the south on 5 October 1791.

George Soloveytchik, *Potemkin: Soldier, Statesman, Lover and Consort of Catherine of Russia* (New York: Butterworth, 1947).

LINDSEY HUGHES

poverty and poor relief   Poverty was a problem of growing concern for states in the eighteenth century. Population growth outstripped economic development in many regions, and even where the 'Malthusian trap' was less in evidence the benefits of growth were not equally shared among all members of society, with the poorest groups doing worst. The capitalistic forms of economic development also contributed to growing concern by throwing up new forms of poverty – more and more, a worker's position in the labour market determined his or her state of wealth or poverty. The cyclical character of capitalist development produced parallel waves of poverty. There was much evidence that the decline of voluntary charity in Catholic countries, possibly in connection with the secularization of attitudes, was reducing the capacity of this traditional standby in times of crisis to cope adequately. Finally, governments were increasingly sensitive to mercantilistic arguments that the poor represented an untapped source of productive wealth and, later, to physiocratic notions of the prosperity of a society being founded on the well-being of its peasantry.

Contrary to a widely held view, economic growth did not bring better NUTRITION for most people; indeed, evidence from average heights even suggests some decline in nutritional levels. The poor suffered from dietary deficiencies which may have led to a greater proneness to epidemic disease. Plague had disappeared from most places in western Europe by the 1670s, and from most of eastern Europe and Russia by the early decades of the eighteenth century, although there were some later freak outbreaks – at Marseilles in 1720, Messina in 1743 and Moscow in 1771. However, other diseases – for example SMALLPOX, TYPHUS, dysentery – took over its role as the scourge of poverty. Although the eighteenth century witnessed the decline of the great MORTALITY CRISES associated with epidemic disease, there was a continuing – possibly worsening – picture of mass morbidity.

Fear of FAMINE – the other great demographic scourge of pre-industrial societies – was also largely exorcised. Britain had known its last famines in the late sixteenth century, and in France and elsewhere in the West the pan-European famines of 1692–7 and 1709–10 brought the series to a close. When famine threatened again in 1739–42 following a string of bad harvests, a diverse set of government welfare policies – public granaries, the buying in of grain, bread doles, assistance to hospitals and welfare agencies and the like – prevented famine conditions emerging; only in Ireland and Scandinavia were governments unable to keep the problem in check.

State intervention was an established part of poor-relief provision throughout Europe by the mid eighteenth century. Its origins lay in major reforms undertaken in the last third of the previous century. In England the parish poor-relief system was institutionalized and made more effective after the 1660s. In France, as well as in many areas of Italy, west Germany, the Low Countries and Spain, policy took the form of confinement of the needy and dangerous poor in so-called 'general hospitals' (*hôpitaux généraux*). A network of over a hundred of these institutions was established in France from the 1660s and 1670s, and by the eighteenth century they housed over 100,000 paupers. This policy of confinement was usually accompanied by a range of other government initiatives, including a commitment to the containment of epidemic disease and the regulation of the GRAIN TRADE in times of crisis.

State intervention thus became an important and tried component of welfare organization. As the century wore on, however, governments tried to lighten their grip. A critique of institutionalization of the poor discredited the notion of 'general hospitals', and forms of relief that kept the worker in the labour market, notably through the provision of work schemes and home-based relief, found favour. Greater liberalization of the grain trade was part of the same package of measures. The apparently more humane aspect of relief policies (which were not, however, without negative repercussions, as popular disturbances caused by free trade in grain bore witness) was propagated by many of the enlightened absolutists and reached its apogee in the attempts of the revolutionary assemblies in France in the 1790s to create a kind of welfare state.

At the household level, Olwen Hufton has emphasized the growing importance in the eighteenth century of family structures in the incidence of poverty. An 'economy of makeshifts' determined whether a family stayed above the breadline: given that population pressure and agrarian capitalism were reducing peasant holdings below the level of family viability, supplementary sources of income were required (such as work in cottage industry or for wealthier landowners, petty theft, crime, begging) or else some members of the family had to absent themselves, by temporary or seasonal migration, in order to relieve pressure on resources. A similar pattern prevailed among the urban labouring classes too. The pattern of poverty tended therefore to be dictated by this family strategy. The largest numbers of the poor were single mothers (married and unmarried), abandoned children and aged widows – precisely those who had fallen out of the family economy. Migration too swelled the numbers of wandering paupers and vagrants who often ended up in hostile and overcrowded towns outside the protective network of family and kin. Growing state concern with vagrancy and delinquence thus led to the tempering of the humanitarian streak in welfare provision with more Draconian attempts to repress the crimes and rootlessness of the poor. In France, for example, *dépôts de mendicité* established in 1767 led to the forcible incarceration of beggars, vagrants and other deviant groups.

See also BEGGARS, CHARITY, WORKHOUSE.

O. Hufton, 'The Rise of the People: Life and Death among the Very Poor', in A. Cobban (ed.), *The Eighteenth Century: Europe in the Age of Enlightenment* (London: Thames & Hudson, 1969), pp. 279–310.
O. Hufton, *The Poor in Eighteenth-Century France, 1750–1789* (Oxford: Oxford University Press, 1974).
J. D. Post, *Food Shortage, Climatic Variability and Epidemic Disease in Preindustrial Europe: The Mortality Peak in the Early 1740s* (Ithaca, NY: Cornell University Press, 1985).

COLIN JONES

power The leading countries of eighteenth-century Europe were often called 'powers' and the concept of power is indispensable to understanding their nature. At least two strands can be detected in state power: military might, and political and social control. The power of states was closely linked to the success with which governments raised large forces, or the money to hire them, but the use of this force carried political risks. The financial collapse and military decline of France after the American War of Independence was one example of the dangers of military deployment and an over-ambitious foreign policy. States varied in their capacity to support armed power by effective ADMINISTRATION and fiscal measures. The decentralized anarchy of Poland, hamstrung by its numerous nobility and in clientage to Russia, left it open to partition and extinction between 1772 and 1795. The attempted centralization of Austria-Hungary and Russia, and the still more successful control exerted in Prussia, provided those states with money for the weaponry of war and also with systems of recruitment and manpower deployment. Each raised an army at levels set by the example and ambitions of France, the model of governmental absolutism. Britain's power rested on the ability to finance war disproportionately to the size of the country, permitting large naval spending, the hiring of mercenaries and the subsidizing of allies to fight on the Continent. In explaining power rivalries and politics, the role of financial management and of administration is important. So, too, is the role of sea power in a century in which increasingly overseas possessions became the focus of interpower rivalries. The French navy, like that of Spain after the 1720s, was no negligible force, but the dominance of the British fleet, certainly after the mid-century, was a fact of great power relationships even if it could not prevent one of the greatest reverses of the era, the independence of the American colonies. (*See* ARMIES, NAVIES.)

Both naval and military power, however, were vulnerable to simple constraints that were outside the control of the eighteenth-century state. Contrary winds could prevent fleets sailing, and the largest ships of the line were laid up during the winter, while the shortage of forage and problems of weather meant that the army campaigning season lasted usually only from April to October. These constraints were part of a limiting reliance on wind and water power and human and animal muscle. COAL offered liberation from costly organic energy, but was exploitable only in certain areas of Europe such as the Sambre-Meuse region, the Scheldt valley of Belgium and the flourishing coal-mining area around Valenciennes. The greatest concentration of such coalfields, linked to specialized manufacturing traditions, and with good transport, was found in Britain, where the landowning classes were eager to exploit mineral resources. There, fuel power and political and economic power met to create a dominant state.

See also BALANCE OF POWER.

J. Brewer, *The Sinews of Power: War, Money and the English State 1688–1783* (London: Unwin Hyman, 1989).
J. M. Black, *The Rise of the European Powers 1679–1793* (London: Edward Arnold, 1990).

PHILIP WOODFINE

Pragmatic Sanction   The Pragmatic Sanction was devised in 1713 by the emperor CHARLES VI to secure the prior succession to the Austrian Habsburg dominions in his future children, male or female, rather than in the two surviving children of his brother Joseph I. Joseph's children, both daughters, were hence required to renounce their rights when they married into Bavaria (1719) and Saxony-Poland (1724) respectively. Charles's employment of the traditional Habsburg device of renunciation here proved particularly contentious, since both nieces produced sons whereas his only son died in infancy. In 1723 he formally settled the Habsburg patrimonial lands on the 6-year-old Maria Theresa, between 1720 and 1725 obtaining the consent of the representative assemblies of all these lands to the changed order of succession. It was not until 1732, when the Pragmatic Sanction received a *Reichsgarantie*, that the international tensions it was generating became clear: significantly, neither Bavaria (and its Palatinate dependency), nor Saxony, associated themselves with the *Reichsgarantie*. In 1714 France had secretly undertaken to support a Bavarian candidature to the emperorship, and after 1726 was even ready to support Bavaria's claim to so integral a Habsburg patrimony as Bohemia. Hence when, in 1737, France, having obtained Lorraine at the end of the War of

Polish Succession, gave her guarantee to the sanction it was stated to be without prejudice to third parties. Although Saxony did acknowledge Maria Theresa on her father's death in October 1740, that electorate had refrained from participation in the *Reichsgarantie* in the hope of receiving Silesia as an inducement, and the knowledge that Saxony would have Charles's support against France in the imminent competition over the Polish succession.

While Bavarian and Saxon refusals to guarantee may have been predictable, other guarantees were also conditional. Philip V of Spain guaranteed in 1725 but, as heir to the Spanish Habsburgs, he later claimed succession to the Austrian branch should Charles VI remain without sons. It may have been mere pique at the rebuffs his marriage proposals had sustained at Vienna, but Protestant guarantors did not hesitate to exact their prices, using Catholic repression of Protestant minorities within the empire as a general pretext. British and Dutch commercial considerations required Charles to terminate his profitable Ostend Company (1727–31) (*see* AUSTRIAN NETHERLANDS), and he had also to agree to Spanish garrisons in Parma and Tuscany (as part of the 1728 Anglo-Spanish peace). Hanover finally obtained the investiture of Bremen and Verden, but also realized an old ambition, imperial permission to keep the peace in neighbouring Mecklenburg (*see* TREATY OF PASSAROWITZ). Brandenburg-Prussia, in turn, obtained the investiture of Stettin and recognition of its sovereignty in Jülich and Berg, but refused to assist in the defence of Habsburg territories beyond the Alps, confining military undertakings under its guarantee to Silesia and Bohemia. If Frederick II's invasion of Silesia in December 1740 has usually been seen as the *coup de grâce* to Charles's sanction policies, the innate credulity of the policies and the spirit of cynicism in which they were concurred with across Europe require no less emphasis.

O. Redlich, *Das Werden einer Grossmacht: Österreich 1700–1740*, ch. 8. (Vienna: Rudolf M. Rohrer, 1962).

D. D. ALDRIDGE

Pretender, Old *see* STUART, JAMES.

Pretender, Young *see* STUART, CHARLES EDWARD.

Prévost, abbé (Antoine François) (1697–1763) French novelist and cleric. He spent his life vacillating between monasticism and the *beau monde*. At 16 he left his order of Saint Ignace and joined the army. Following an unhappy love affair, he entered a Benedictine monastery in 1720, and took his vows the following year. He began composing his largely autobiographical *Mémoires d'un homme de qualité* (1728–32). After seven years with the order he requested a transfer to Cluny, where the rules were gentler, but while Rome agreed his superiors refused to allow it. He fled in 1727, first to London and then to Holland where he finished the memoirs.

He returned to England following another amorous liaison and wrote the novels *Cleveland* (1732–9) and *L'Histoire de Manon Lescaut* (1733), and started a new kind of periodical, *Le Pour et contre* (The Pros and Cons, 1733–40), based on *The Spectator*. On returning to France, he rejoined the Benedictine order. He continued to produce novels prolifically, as well as undertaking a translation of the works of Hume and Richardson. In old age he became a passionate defender of religious truth and regretted his earlier forays into society. In 1763 he suffered an attack of apoplexy in the the forest of Chantilly. His body was discovered and taken to the nearest village where a surgeon began a post-mortem; Prévost awoke with a cry, but it was too late to save his life.

M. L. BENJAMIN

Price, Richard (1723–1791)   Welsh dissenting minister, moralist and political pamphleteer. He was educated at Moorfields Academy. Most of his adult life was spent as minister to various congregations in London, where he also taught at the short-lived Hackney College. His professional approach to the economics of public finance, exemplified in his work on reversionary payments, led to his being consulted by leading politicians, and being drawn into the circle of Lord Shelburne. His most celebrated publications were his *Observations on the Nature of Civil Liberty* (1776), which, drawing on natural rights theory, took the colonial side in the American War of Independence, and his *Discourse on the Love of our Country* (1789), a sermon, subsequently published, which sympathized with the early stages of the French Revolution and drew a counterblast from Burke. Although in the year of his death he joined the Unitarian Society, he retained his belief in the pre-existence of Christ and, preserving his Arian theology, shared neither the Socinianism nor the materialistic determinism of Joseph Priestley.

D. O. Thomas, *The Honest Mind: The Thought and Work of Richard Price* (Oxford: Clarendon, 1977).

G. M. DITCHFIELD

Priestley, Joseph (1733–1804)   English scientist, historian and Unitarian theologian, polymath and polemicist. Born in Yorkshire and trained for the dissenting ministry, he repudiated the Calvinism of his youth and adopted a fundamentally antitrinitarian position. Serving successively as minister at Leeds, librarian to Lord Shelburne and minister to New Meeting congregation, Birmingham, he published important research into the nature of electricity and contributed to the discovery of oxygen. His *History of the Corruptions of Christianity* (1782) led him into controversy with Samuel Horsley and made him the best-known Dissenter of his day. However, his theology, which challenged Christian orthodoxy, his materialistic 'doctrine of necessity' which seemed to deny the freedom of the will, and his political radicalism incurred the hostility of the religious and political establishment and of Church and King mobs. The destruction of his property in the Birmingham riots of July 1791 obliged him to emigrate to Pennsylvania, where he spent the last decade of his life. Although his theological legacy was abandoned by nineteenth-century Unitarians, he remains an outstanding figure in their history (*see* UNITARIANISM).

R. G. W. Anderson and Christopher Lawrence, *Science, Medicine and Dissent: Joseph Priestley (1733–1804)* (London: Wellcome Trust/Science Museum, 1987).

G. M. DITCHFIELD

primitivism 'The savage nations of the globe are the common enemies of civilised society; and we may enquire with anxious curiosity, whether Europe is still threatened with a repetition of those calamities, which formerly oppressed the arms, and institutions of Rome', declared Gibbon at the end of the third volume of *The Decline and Fall of the Roman Empire*. He was not a follower of the CULT OF THE NOBLE SAVAGE, and reassured his readers that they would not return to the state of 'the *human savage*, naked both in mind and body, and destitute of laws, of arts, of ideas, and almost of language. From this abject condition, perhaps the primitive and universal state of man, he has gradually arisen to command animals, to fertilise the earth, to traverse the ocean, and to measure the heavens. His progress in the improvement and exercise of his mental and corporeal faculties has been irregular and various . . . Yet the experience of four thousand years should enlarge our hopes, and diminish our apprehensions: we cannot determine to what height the human species may aspire in their advances towards perfection; but it may safely be presumed, that no people, unless the face of nature is changed, will relapse into their original barbarism.'

In contrast, other Enlightenment thinkers, most notably Rousseau, believed in the superiority of primitive man. Though primitivism rarely went as far as he did in his unqualified praise for the life of original man, several writers presented the early condition of mankind as an enviable one. Diderot's *Supplément au voyage de Bougainville* (1796), for instance, belonged to the tradition that, from Michel Eyquem de Montaigne (1533–92) onwards, represented primitive man as naturally good and corrupted by civilization. The Tahitians, according to Diderot's argument, were free of the taboos that plagued civilized man's sexuality and happier than their European visitors (*see* TAHITI). The abbé Raynal's *Histoire des deux Indes*, to which Diderot contributed, also compared natural and modern man, and concluded that the former suffered only from natural pains.

Robert Wokler, 'Perfectible Apes in Decadent Cultures: Rousseau's Anthropology Revisited', in 'Rousseau for our Time', *Daedalus*, 107 (3) (summer 1978), 107–34.

SYLVANA TOMASELLI

primogeniture   Of the wide range of conventions governing INHERITANCE in eighteenth-century Europe, primogeniture – whereby the bulk of an individual's immovable property passed to his eldest son – was at the furthest extreme from equal partible inheritance among heirs. It was practised at all levels of society in certain regions, but was particularly widespread among Europe's landed aristocracies: primogeniture, together with the rules of 'strict settlement' introduced after 1650 which restricted an heir's power to dispose of his inheritance, were usually accounted of critical importance in maintaining the integrity of the large estates of the English aristocracy. There was, however, a strong current of legal and ideological thinking critical of primogeniture in the eighteenth century, on the grounds that it was inimical to the natural RIGHTS of siblings and subverted family affection. This thinking received most effective implementation in the French revolutionary assemblies which in 1790 abolished the *droit d'aînesse* (the right of nobles to confer their manor plus between half and four-fifths of their property on their eldest son) and proceeded to extend partible inheritance to commoners. The Code Napoléon of 1804 confirmed the abolition of primogeniture.

COLIN JONES

printing   The only mass medium of the eighteenth century was printing. In 1700 it was largely though not entirely confined to Europe, but by 1800 it was to be found throughout the parts of the world where European influence was becoming paramount. There had been printers on the American continent since around 1540, when a press was established by the Spanish colonial rulers of Mexico. Stephen Daye (?1610–68) had begun to print in Cambridge, Massachusetts in 1638, and the art gradually spread throughout the parts of the North American continent where Europeans established permanent settlements. In Asia, too, printing largely followed European colonial influence, in the Dutch East Indies (*c.*1668), and among the Portuguese (1556), Danish (1712) and British (1778) settlements in India and elsewhere. In the

Islamic world there were doctrinal and political objections to the mass reproduction of texts by mechanical means, and almost all printing in the Arabic alphabet actually took place in Europe for the benefit of Western scholars.

During the eighteenth century, in western Europe at least, printed matter became an increasingly familiar part of life. Newspapers, which had originated in Germany in the late sixteenth century, proliferated; together with magazines and periodicals, they were important sources of economic as well as political information. Printing was also used to produce the administrative documents needed by increasingly complex societies. Such ephemeral material, as it is termed by some historians and librarians, was critical to the financial success of the printing trade, as well as being an important engine of economic, social, cultural and political development and change.

Despite the importance of the art, however, there were comparatively few technical developments: for printing from type – the normal process – the wooden hand-press in use throughout the century was fundamentally unchanged from that invented in the mid fifteenth century. Operated by two skilled men – one handling the ink and the other the paper – it could produce some 250 printed sheets per hour. The size of the sheet was necessarily limited by the size of the press itself. This was, in turn, determined by the fact that the platen, the wooden block that was lowered on to the paper to impress it on to the inked type, had to be planed to a perfectly flat surface. Even if this could be achieved, there was a constant danger of warping, since the paper was damped before printing to allow it to absorb the ink more effectively. Consequently, sheets were small by later standards, further inhibiting the speed of book production.

The few technical developments that did take place were largely concerned with illustration processes. Although the basic techniques of hand-printed illustration – woodcut and engraving – had been in use since the fifteenth and sixteenth centuries respectively, both were somewhat refined. The adoption of processes such as mezzotint and various other sophisticated versions of conventional engraving improved both the quality and subtlety of reproduction. Illustrated books became somewhat more common, although technical problems still restricted the number. Engraved prints, on the other hand, were widespread, and were of considerable importance in Britain, France and Britain's North American colonies as a mechanism for the expression of political dissent. In typographic printing there were few developments. Stereotyping – the production of a page of type as a single plate rather than as individual pieces of type – was invented by William Ged (1690–1749) in 1740, but although it was used a little, mainly in the Low Countries, it was of no commercial significance, and had effectively to be reinvented in the first decade of the nineteenth century.

The suppliers of the printing trade benefited from its continued growth. The two principal groups were typefounders and papermakers. The great Dutch typefounding house of Enchede flourished throughout the century, while in England a long-established tradition of typefounding, largely in a single family, was augmented by the notable addition of the talent and skill of William Caslon the elder (1692–1766) and his descendants. There were few technical innovations, but a number of crucial developments in type design. In particular, the English type designers Willian Caslon the younger (1720–78) and John Baskerville (1706–75) introduced new standards into a country where printing had never aspired to great heights of aesthetic achievement. Even the Dutch and the French, the leading European printers, were impressed by the work of these two Englishmen.

In papermaking there were some changes towards the end of the century, leading to the introduction of higher quality, but very expensive, wove papers to supplement the traditional laid paper. The real problem, however, was that growing demand for paper for printing (and other purposes) was forcing papermakers to be less selective in choosing materials for making the pulp from which paper was manufactured, and at the same time allowed them to increase their prices. By the late 1780s there was a serious crisis, and attempts were being made to design and build a papermaking machine and to seek new materials suitable for papermaking. Neither was achieved before 1800, but the first machine was to be built in the first decade of the nineteenth century.

Despite its conservatism in technical matters, the printing trade underwent considerable economic change during the century. In particular, the typical printing-house was larger in 1800 than it had been in 1700, although there had been substantial houses since the sixteenth century, especially in the Low Countries, France, Italy and Germany. Some of the major European printing-houses already had a long history by 1700, and survived for long thereafter; these included the Elzevir and Plantin firms in the Low Countries, and the Imprimerie Royale in France. In England, too, there were a few firms that had several decades of history behind them by the middle of the century. Large printing-houses employing many workmen provided a very different environment from the small family businesses out of which most of them had developed. The relationship between masters and men was increasingly to typify the industrial economies of the nineteenth century. The men were, by definition, literate and more than capable of organizing themselves. Traditional craft-guild practices evolved into something akin to trade unions in the London printing trade before the end of the eighteenth century, and despite repressive legislation there was collective bargaining between employers and employees. By 1800 a 300-year-old craft was in the process of transformation into a modern industry.

Giles Barber and Bernhard Fabian, *Buch und Buchhandel in Europa im achtzehten Jahrhundert* (Wiesbaden: Ernst Hauswedell, 1981).
Colin Clair, *A History of Printing in Britain* (London: Cassell, 1965).
Colin Clair, *A History of European Printing* (London: Academic Press, 1972).

JOHN FEATHER

prisons *see* NEWGATE; PUNISHMENT.

privilege   A pervasive feature of eighteenth-century life, privilege was by no means restricted to the elite, and sometimes the only claim on property that the poor possessed. In Prussia, under Frederick the Great, army veterans, especially the disabled, had a special claim to low-grade civil service jobs as postmasters and teachers. The privilege of the vote, or a share in local administration or politics, often went with membership of some urban elite, as craftsman or merchant. In several countries those who could read and write enjoyed immunity from the death sentence for a first offence, the so-called 'privilege of clergy' which was a hangover from the medieval period when literacy was a rarer attainment. Whole categories of the population in Russia serving in the college of war, the navy or various civil colleges enjoyed special jurisdictional treatment. In Prussia apprentices to a wide range of trades were exempt from military service. For the peasant mass of Europe's population there scarcely existed advantages specific to their class, apart from the pauper's dubious privilege of not having to contribute to poor relief. Yet even for the poor some special right, advantage or immunity was a common way of differentiating one group from another. Even the privileges of upper servants, such as receiving used candles or clothes, could be status-markers, giving the poor an interest in preserving hierarchy and distinctions. At the local level these distinctions were typically more complex and fluid than at the national.

In Ch'ing dynasty China provincial hierarchies were open to those with wealth and talent. At regional and national levels administrative posts and rewards went to holders of higher degrees, the official imperial passport to privilege. In Germany the growing insistence on education and training for administrators effectively made bureaucratic careers a special preserve of the elites who already enjoyed good educational facilities. (*See* ADMINISTRATION.) More noticeable across Europe were the rights granted to the landed ARISTOCRACY and the CLERGY, the privileged castes or 'estates' of the age (*see also* LANDOWNING,

NOBILITY). Nobles enjoyed accelerated promotion in, and privileged entry to, careers in administration and the army. Both nobles and clergy enjoyed access to their own courts, or direct access to royal courts, although rank mattered here too. In Russia the lower clergy could find themselves arrested at will, whereas members of the hierarchy enjoyed immunity.

In Austria-Hungary the church, the major landowner, was for most of the century exempt from taxes on land, even though these were a vital source of revenue for the state. In Britain the land tax was artificially low, and assessment criteria outdated, so that even major landowners sometimes paid no more than 3 per cent of their income in TAXATION. French aristocrats were exempt from the *taille*, the kingdom's basic direct tax, up to at least the first four *charrues* of their land: often the only difference between the impoverished but tax-free *hoberaux* and their less privileged neighbours.

G. Chaussinand-Nogaret, *The French Nobility in the Eighteenth Century* (Cambridge: Cambridge University Press, 1985).

PHILIP WOODFINE

probability Previously thought of as 'well-founded opinion', probability as calculation emerged around 1650 from questions of equity: when was a game of chance, an annuity or a commercial risk fair? when was legal testimony credible? The essence of rational decision-making for many *philosophes*, it was extended to assess belief in scientific theories and even in God.

Jakob BERNOULLI analysed the now archetypal problem: given an urn containing known numbers of differently coloured balls, how to calculate the probability of drawing a particular colour. Later workers addressed the more useful and complex reverse calculation – how probable is an explanatory hypothesis, given known facts (balls drawn, laboratory results and so on)?

This so-called 'classical probability' was not fully modern. It focused not on objective probabilities of events, but on subjective mental expectations of them, which contemporary associationist psychology held to be equivalent. Furthermore, as its typical questions reveal, it assumed that the mental processes of elite men were universalizable. Finally, doctrinaire 'social mathematicians' used it to reduce human behaviour to quantitative laws. All these positions were to be rejected in the nineteenth century.

See also STATISTICS.

Lorraine Daston, *Classical Probability in the Enlightenment* (Princeton, NJ: Princeton University Press, 1988).

STEPHEN PUMFREY

professions Most communities accord some measure of respect and material reward to those undertaking socially useful tasks that require mastery of a body of esoteric knowledge. CLERGY, LAWYERS and physicians have occupied a distinctive niche in European societies and their colonial offshoots since medieval times. While similar functional equivalents may be identified in many non-Western societies, the European learned professions appear unique in the relatively high status and autonomy of their membership and the role played by the academy in their training and certification.

The term 'profession' comes from the Latin *profiteri*, 'to avow, or profess' – whether religious belief or secular vocation. Its usage has always been ambiguous, no less in the eighteenth century than today. Broadly construed, 'profession' simply meant job or occupation, as it still often does. But the noun had also acquired a more specific connotation in relation to callings claiming higher status than mere 'mechanical' or 'servile' trades, mainly because their practice involved the exercise of mental rather than manual skills.

Sociologists, and some historians, once depicted the pre-industrial professions as essentially subordinate and relatively insignificant components of societies dominated by aristocratic landowning elites. Recent research has cast doubt on this view. Industrialization seems not to have made very much difference to the proportion of the population following professional careers, their well-developed sense of vocational identity or the existence of a mass market for professional services. The eighteenth-century professions were, on the whole, less highly organized and institutionally regulated than their modern successors but, to quote E. W. Hughes, a pioneering student of the eighteenth-century English professions, 'Most . . . had a long history before ever they were organised in professional associations.'

In much of Continental Europe the state apparatus was often the major direct employer of professional expertise (almost exclusively male, until very recent times), including not only public administrators and officers of the armed forces, but also clergy, university professors and school teachers, as well as lawyers and physicians. In the British Isles the role of government was more circumscribed. But besides tacitly upholding particular monopolies of practice in the hands of a core of institutionally affiliated practitioners (such as barristers of the Inns of Court and fellows of the Royal College of Physicians), the state also sought to control the training and recruitment of attorneys and solicitors, while Britain's burgeoning military and naval commitments created corresponding opportunities for followers of the profession of arms.

The church (and chapel), the law and medicine all required a minimum of educational attainment, if not necessarily an academic qualification. But most professional training was acquired on the job, via some kind of apprenticeship. This ranged from the relatively short-term and informal, such as would-be barristers served in a special pleader's office, to the extended relationship established by articles of indenture and sealed with a substantial premium, which was customarily imposed on young men seeking to become apothecaries or attorneys. The newer professions, including those of actuary, architect, banker, engineer, estate steward, landscape gardener, man of science, musician and surveyor, were particularly reliant on practical, hands-on education. Theoretical or bookish learning was not altogether neglected but tended to be supplied by private study, or in institutions other than the ancient universities, such as dissenting academies and training colleges run by the armed services.

While professional men stood apart from and above the labouring classes and aspired to the status, if not always the life-style, of the landed elite, their social origins, vocational prestige and opportunities for economic advancement varied enormously. One of the most important functions of the professions was to provide a meritocratic channel of upward mobility for the poor but talented 'lad of parts', as well as a respectable living for younger sons from more elevated family backgrounds. Capital and connections were both desirable, albeit not essential ingredients of professional success; but the lower slopes and fringes of the professions were far more thickly populated than their commanding and lucrative heights. Contemporaries were well aware of this and frequently if ineffectually deplored the proliferation of genteel parasites, who appeared to produce nothing substantial and lived by baffling hapless clients with obfuscatory jargon.

See also PROFESSION OF LETTERS.

E. Hughes, 'Professions in the Eighteenth Century', *Durham University Journal*, 13(1) (1951), 46–55.
W. Prest (ed.), *The Professions in Early Modern England* (London: Croom Helm, 1987).

WILFRID PREST

progress, Enlightenment doctrine of While there was no single Enlightenment doctrine of progress, the question of whether mankind was progressing and what progress consisted in was one of the great issues of the time. 'I am always angry', Johnson is reported to have said, 'when I hear ancient times praised at the expense of modern times. There is now a great deal more learning in the world than there was formerly; for it is universally diffused.' Nor was Johnson more tolerant of the idea of the superiority of savages: as he told Boswell, 'there can be nothing more false. The savages have no bodily advantages beyond those of civilised men. They have no better health; and as to care or mental uneasiness, they are not above it, but below it, like bears. No, Sir; you are not to talk such paradox... It cannot entertain, far less can it instruct.'

Instruction was, however, what writers like Rousseau thought could be gained by the suggestion that the seeming advancement of society was only a façade hiding the gradual depravation of humanity. Though he did not instigate such debates, Rousseau certainly fuelled them on both sides of the Channel. Among those who responded to his argument, Adam Ferguson was one of the most interesting. He saw it as a distinguishing characteristic of the species that it 'has a progress as well as the individual; they build in every subsequent age on foundations formerly laid; and, in a succession of years, tend to a perfection in the application of their faculties, to which the aid of long experience is required, and to which many generations must have combined their endeavours'.

Yet it would be highly misleading to imply that the eighteenth-century intellectual scene divided neatly between the party of modernity and their opponents. There were few among the former who did not stress that the advancement of CIVILIZATION engendered very real social and psychological problems unknown in preceding ages. The impact of luxury and of the intensification of the division of labour were only two of the topics that exercised thinkers. Some, like Diderot, argued for or against the notion of progress depending on the context in which they were writing. When thinking about this subject from woman's point of view, however, Diderot, like many other eighteenth-century men and women, argued that her present condition, whatever its shortcomings, showed a very marked improvement on that of her ur-mother. Women, according to this view, were both the instigators and the beneficiaries of the progress of society.

Adam Ferguson, *An Essay on the History of Civil Society 1767*, ed. Duncan Forbes (Edinburgh: Edinburgh University Press, 1966).
David Spadafora, *The Idea of Progress in Eighteenth-Century Britain* (New Haven, Conn.: Yale University Press, 1990).
Sylvana Tomaselli, 'The Enlightenment Debate on Women', *History Workshop*, 20 (1985), 101–24.

SYLVANA TOMASELLI

property Whether the right to private property was a legitimate one had long been central to natural jurisprudence, when the events of the French Revolution seemed to give the issue an unprecedented importance and Burke rose to remonstrate against the violation of private property in his *Reflections on the Revolution in France*. Most influential was Locke's account of the rise of private property and the conditions of its legitimacy, despite the fact that God had initially given the earth to mankind in common. He argued that it was a positive duty of mankind, by virtue of being God's creatures, to preserve itself; this made labour an obligation, and the acquisition of things necessary to self-preservation by mixing one's labour with them a natural right grounded in natural law. He also considered INHERITANCE to be a right of children and charity a right of the needy (providing they were not so as a result of idleness) and a duty of the rich (see PHILANTHROPY). Prior to the invention of money, men could barter their surpluses but never accumulate food in such a way as to allow it to spoil. With the introduction of money, the spoiling of God's gifts ceased to be a limitation to accumulation and greed, and the state of nature came to an end as political society was needed to settle the disputes which inevitably arise out of covetousness.

Locke's account provided the framework for most subsequent discussions of the rise of private property, but it did not go unchallenged. In *A Treatise of Human Nature* HUME attacked the notion that property could exist outside civil society and the institution of justice: 'A man's property is some object related to him: This relation is not natural, but moral, and founded on justice. 'Tis very preposterous, therefore, to imagine, that we can have any idea of property, without fully comprehending the nature of justice, and shewing its origin in the artifice and contrivance of men.'

The debate about property was not confined to the subject of its creation. Writing in mid-century, the abbé Morelly contended that, for all the arguments of political theorists, nothing could be achieved if property was not uprooted; he thought it a demonstrable truth that 'any distribution, equal or unequal' of property was the cause of all social evils. He was not alone in this belief, but a more common view, held by Rousseau for example, was that the unequal distribution of property, rather than property in itself, was the true cause of man's unhappiness, especially as the history of the divide between rich and poor was linked to the rise of LUXURY. In a similar vein, Godwin argued that: 'Property is sacred: there is but one way in which duty requires the possessor to dispose of it, but I may not forcibly interfere, and dispose of it in the best way in his stead ... The principle that attributes to every man the disposal of his property, as well as that distributes to every man his sphere of discretion, derives its force in both instances from the consideration that a greater sum of happiness will result from its observance than its infringement.' That not only property but also its unequal distribution and luxury were part and parcel of a system in which the poorest members of society were better off than they would otherwise be was the case that political economists sought to make.

William Godwin, *Enquiry concerning Political Justice*, ed. Isaac Kramnick (Harmondsworth: Penguin, 1976).

James Tully, *A Discourse on Property: John Locke and his Adversaries* (Cambridge: Cambridge University Press, 1980).

SYLVANA TOMASELLI

prostitution   In eighteenth-century England prostitution was regarded as an inevitable response to certain social conditions rather than as a moral pollutant or symptom of woman's deviant sexuality. It was rife in London, where Saunders Welch estimated that in mid-century there were 3,000 active prostitutes in a city whose population was between 500,000 and 900,000. Knowledge of prostitution tends to be limited to legal records, libertine literature and the proposals made by reformers. In his *Dictionary* Johnson defined a 'whore' variously as 'a woman who converses unlawfully with men; a fornicator, an adultress; a strumpet' and as 'a prostitute, a woman who receives money from men'.

Together with London's sodomites, who targeted male homosexuals, female prostitutes plied their trade at public places where crowds gathered, such as fairs, theatres, parks and even churches. Erotic catalogues, like *A List of Sporting Ladies* (1717) which made ribald comparisons between whores and horses, served as consumer guides in which prostitutes were stratified according to social status and priced accordingly. A shilling was the standard payment for the Boswellian white-thread-stockinged 'nymph' who tramped along the Strand, while higher class madams were able to demand 50 guineas a night. BOSWELL once boasted of purchasing the delights of an actress called Louisa at the knock-down price of 18 shillings, but he did not get away so lightly since she left him with the 'scourge of Cupid' – an infection on his member. As an early advocate of 'safe sex', he used condoms not to prevent unwanted pregnancy but as a protection against venereal disease.

Prostitutes risked the ravages of disease and drink as depicted by HOGARTH in his moral cycle *The Harlot's Progress* (1732). More fortunate were those who were able to retire into marriage like John Cleland's (1709–89) Fanny Hill, the heroine of his *Memoirs of a Woman of Pleasure* (1748–9). Within popular fiction, the economic necessity for prostitution solicited sympathetic treatment as in DEFOE's *Moll Flanders* who, according to the title-page, was 'Twelve years a Whore', and *Roxana, or The Fortunate Mistress* who could be classified as a courtesan. In contrast, Defoe's non-fictional *Some Considerations upon Street-Walkers* (1726) recommended harsh punishments for 'strumpets', such as the workhouse, whipping-post, transportation to the colonies and matrimony.

The Society for the Suppression of Vice, along with campaigners like Hannah More (1745–1833), welcomed the publication of black-lists of convicted prostitutes and brothel-owners who were prosecuted under the Disorderly Houses Act of 1751.

Some reformers envisaged magdalen houses as havens of rehabilitation for renegade prostitutes. Reformist tracts that provided popular reading included Mandeville's proposal in *A Modest Defence of Publick Stews, or An Essay upon Whoring* (1724) that public brothels be established in order to regulate the trade so as to enable men to 'exercise their lewdness in a proper place'.

Because prostitution was not perceived as a social evil, the prostitute was not pitied as a fallen woman but seen instead as a victim of economic deprivation. The Enlightenment view of the oldest of professions continued to sanction the hiring of women's bodies by men, while embracing the changing social construction of gender which rested on the more recent assumption that not all women were whores, just a select few.

G. S. Rousseau and Roy Porter (eds), *Sexual Underworlds of the Enlightenment* (Manchester: Manchester University Press, 1987).
Peter Wagner, *Eros Revived: Erotica of the Enlightenment in England and America* (London: Paladin, 1990).

MARIE MULVEY ROBERTS

Protestantism   The term 'Protestant' comes from the 'Protestatio' of the reforming members of the Diet of Speyer in 1529 and has come to be used as a generic term covering all the churches that have separated from the Roman Catholic Church since the Reformation. It thus embraces the major traditions – Reformed, Lutheran, Anglican, Methodist and Baptist – and scores of many smaller religious groups. Protestantism is nothing if not fissiparous. Theological coherence is not to be expected in such diversity, but Protestantism's inner core has traditionally been an emphasis on the authority of Scripture, justification by faith and the priesthood of all believers.

In the eighteenth century the main developments within Protestantism were the rise of antitrinitarian and rationalist religion, the great international religious revival from the Urals in the East to the Appalachians in the West, the growth of Protestant missions and the development of 'the most Protestant of Protestant cultures' in the American colonies.

Protestant orthodoxy probably suffered more than Catholic orthodoxy from the intellectual challenges of the Enlightenment. In the British Isles DEISM, ARIANISM and Socinianism all made headway among Presbyterians and Independents, and battles between defenders of old confessions and advocates of independent judgement were fought out among Protestants throughout the English-speaking world. In England so-called rational DISSENTERS were at the forefront of criticisms of the English state and its established church and can thus lay claim to be at the heart and centre of early political radicalism.

A still more influential movement within eighteenth-century Protestantism was the growth of PIETISM and revivalism. From its roots in the displaced and persecuted minorities of Habsburg-dominated central Europe, this revival was partly a reaction against the confessional absolutism of much of early-eighteenth-century Europe and was also an attempt to express religious enthusiasm outside the stranglehold of politically manipulated established churches. From such roots sprang METHODISM in England and Wales and the Great Awakening in the American colonies. Thus if the eighteenth century was an age of reason it was also, in a more profound sense, an age of ENTHUSIASM. It was also an age that brought hymn-singing into the centre of the Protestant tradition and further confirmed its commitment to literacy and education. Above all, it stimulated a remarkable surge of Protestant missionary enthusiasm and brought forth the ubiquitous voluntary societies to reclaim the lost and reform the wicked.

Many of these trends not only affected Protestantism in the American colonies, but also helped create one of the most powerful cultural traditions in the modern world. Through its colonial origins, great awakenings and revolutionary struggles, American Protestantism, by its immense diversity, helped forge a voluntaristic, pluralistic and libertarian religious culture. It was in the United States, therefore, that Protestantism first put an end to religious establishments and enshrined religious freedom as a constitutional right.

R. T. Handy, *A History of the Churches in the United States and Canada* (Oxford: Clarendon, 1976).

E. G. Rupp, *Religion in England 1688–1791* (Oxford: Clarendon, 1986).

DAVID HEMPTON

proto-industrialization   The term 'proto-industrialization' has been much used in recent years by historians attempting to define the stage of economic growth preceding the phase of heavy industrialization associated with the classic INDUSTRIAL REVOLUTION. It has been argued that, especially from around 1600 to 1750 (and later still in certain Continental regions), manufacture migrated away from the traditional great cities into the countryside. Capitalists wished to avoid the high-wage, high-control economies of the guild-dominated towns; production costs were lower outside city walls; and the rural setting was often convenient for raw materials and by-employments. The value of the concept of proto-industrialization lies in its breaking down of the sharp agricultural/industrial dichotomies; its weakness lies in apparently suggesting a town/countryside divide. Critics maintain that it is better to emphasize the economic symbiosis of town and country; they would also stress the continued flowering of manufactures in the majority of towns. Along these lines, recent historians of the industrialization process in Britain (for instance, E. A. Wrigley) have drawn attention to the significance for the modernizing process of the growing proportion of the workforce employed within manufacturing towns and the urban sector in general. Whether 'proto-industrialization' will enter the historical vocabulary remains unclear.

L. A. Clarkson, *Proto-industrialisation: The First Phase of Industrialisation?* (Basingstoke: Macmillan, 1985).
E. A. Wrigley, *The Character of the Industrial Revolution in England* (Cambridge: Cambridge University Press, 1988).

ROY PORTER

Prussia The collective name 'Prussia' was increasingly used in the eighteenth century for the various possessions of the Hohenzollerns. The rise of Brandenburg-Prussia from a weak and unimportant German electorate of some 900,000 people to a great European power with a population of 6 million at the end of the eighteenth century was, even allowing for the distortions of later nationalist historiography, a major development in German and European history.

The main ingredient in Prussia's success was a series of able and energetic rulers, who pursued consistent state-building policies, the creation of a powerful army, the elimination of intermediate power-sharing bodies and the centralization of power in Berlin. The foundations of this were laid by Frederick William, the Great Elector (1620–88), but the major credit belongs to two eighteenth-century rulers, FREDERICK-WILLIAM I and FREDERICK II. They concentrated their efforts on the creation of a powerful army, which grew from some 38,000 in 1713 to 200,000 in the 1760s, and a centralized state apparatus to finance and maintain it. They also worked to build up the economic potential of their territories, attracting new settlers, clearing and draining land (Prussia was fortunate to have ample sparsely populated land available for development), building canals and establishing manufactures. Particularly successful examples of state-directed economic improvement were Frederick William I's resettlement (*Rétablissement*) of east Prussia in the 1720s, after it was ravaged by plague, and Frederick II's development of new land acquired in the first partition of Poland in 1772. The decline or distraction by non German ambitions of potential rivals like Sweden, Saxony and Hanover was also important, as were religious factors. The rulers pursued a policy of toleration in order to attract new subjects, such as the Huguenots, and this also extended, with restrictions, to Jews and Catholics. The Calvinist and Pietist movements within German Protestantism, which emphasized the value of hard work and personal commitment, played a role in the emergence of a distinct Prussian consciousness.

Geography was important in the growth of Prussia. The scattered nature of their possessions, which consisted of a series of blocks of territory from Cleves-Mark on the Rhine to East Prussia, an enclave inside Poland, led its rulers logically to a policy of acquiring more land to round off what they had. The period after 1648 saw a steady increase in the size of the state as new territories were added by conquest or inheritance. As the Great Elector made clear in his *Politische Testament* (Political Testament) for his son, it was only by acquiring more land and population that a state could become 'considerable'. In 1740 Frederick II, in a bold stroke, decided to use the army and funds that his more cautious father had accumulated to make the most important such gain, the rich and populous province of Silesia, conquered from Austria. This gave Prussia 1.5 million additional subjects and the resources to become a substantial European power strong enough to challenge and defeat other major powers.

For all its success, the creation of a powerful Prussia was an ambivalent achievement. On the one hand, it was one of the most modern states in eighteenth-century Germany, served by a professional bureaucracy, influenced by enlightened ideas and increasingly seeing itself as a distinct order in society whose function it was to promote the common welfare. Universal primary education was introduced in 1763. The code of civil law, the *Allgemeine Landrecht*, begun under Frederick II and introduced in 1794 as the culmination of a programme of judicial reform, was seen as a model in Germany. Economically and intellectually, Prussia was a leader among German states. It was also a noted centre of enlightened thought. In the early eighteenth century the University of Halle was the most respected in Germany and the home of leading intellectuals like Christian Thomasius and Christian Wolff. BERLIN was a beacon for enlightened intellectuals throughout Germany.

On the other hand, however, Prussia's behaviour towards its weaker neighbours was predatory: it ignored borders, kidnapped men for enforced military service and plundered fields. Although Frederick II abolished judicial torture, he retained savage punishments in the army. Prussia was authoritarian and militaristic. Its disproportionately large army was the *raison d'être* of the state and everything was subordinated to its needs. It was characterized by an all-powerful nobility, weak towns and a largely unfree peasantry, who bore the main burdens of taxation and conscription. The parliamentary estates remained in existence but had no powers. Urban self-government was nonexistent. In order to buy off the political opposition of the noble *Junkers*, the rulers confirmed and strengthened their social and economic predominance. By the reign of Frederick II their resistance had waned and they saw service to the state as a badge of their noble status. Frederick reversed his father's policy of employing non-nobles in high positions and reserved high rank for nobles, whose privileges he further extended. Absolute monarchy at the top was sustained by total noble control at the lower levels of Prussian society.

Another ambivalence lay at the heart of Prussia's great-power status. It was based on barely adequate financial and military resources and by the end of the eighteenth century the strains of maintaining it were beginning to show. Participation in the War of the First Coalition against revolutionary France exhausted Prussian finances. The centre of interest had also shifted decisively to Poland as a result of the three partitions. As a result, in 1795 Prussia by the Treaty of Basle came to separate terms with France. It withdrew into neutrality, ten years of cultural and economic flowering and further territorial growth which concealed the basic stagnation of the state in the reign of Frederick William II. This was, however, revealed clearly in 1806 when Prussia was decisively defeated at Jena by Napoleonic France. It marked a new beginning but the authoritarian, militaristic legacy of Prussia was to prove remarkably resilient.

C. B. A. Behrens, *Society, Government and the Enlightenment: The Experiences of Eighteenth-Century France and Prussia* (London: Thames & Hudson, 1985).
L. Feuchtwanger, *Prussia: Myth and Reality* (London: Wolff, 1970).

MICHAEL HUGHES

psychology   While there was no discipline corresponding to modern psychology in the eighteenth century, parallel lines of enquiry can be traced. The epistemological preoccupations of philosophy led to a variety of accounts of the human mind, including associationist SEN-SATIONALISM (Berkeley, Hume, Hartley (1705–57), Condillac, La Mettrie), faculty models (Wolff, Baumgarten, Tetens (1736–1807), Kant) and antireductionist EMPIRICISM (notably Reid (1710–96), Stewart (1753–1828) and other Scottish Enlightenment thinkers). In physiology, neurological pioneers (notably Haller, Unzer, Prochaska and Whytt (1714–66)) laid the foundations for physiological psychology, while Gall's (1758–1828) 'craniology' (later called 'phrenology'), which appeared in the 1790s, espoused an extreme version of the localization of functioning in the brain. From the mid-century there was increasing interest in education, stimulated by Rousseau's *Émile* (1762), although social developments were in any case inevitably prioritizing the issue. This provided a basis for later European developmental psychology. Anticipations of social psychology may be discovered in many texts, from Mandeville's *Fable of the Bees* (1711) to Scottish social philosophical works (for example Smith's *Theory of Moral Sentiments*, 1759). Medical concern with INSANITY generated various nosologies of mental illness, but for the most part drew its theoretical frameworks from philosophy or neurology. Lavater's best-selling physiognomical essays (1775–87) and the 'animal magnetism' craze initiated by Mesmer also deserve a mention. The emergence of ANTHROPOLOGY in Germany and France may be additionally noted as frequently touching on social psychological matters. Finally, the linguistic thought of writers such as Condillac, Herder, Harris (1709–80), Monboddo (1714–99) and Horne Tooke adumbrated modern concerns with the relationship between language and thought.

The relationship between Enlightenment psychological thought and the modern discipline of psychology is currently undergoing a major reappraisal. Orthodox general histories of psychology have, until recently, provided schematic accounts centred primarily on British associationism and German 'rationalism' (now widely felt to be a misnomer) at the expense of Scottish Enlightenment writers and subjects such as education, physiology, physiognomy and linguistics. In the context of these, the roots of modern psychology appear to be far more diverse, while the central role often accorded to British associationism seems somewhat exaggerated. (More recent historians have tended to trace the origins of psychology to mounting social management pressures in the latter decades of the nineteenth century, creating a demand for psychological expertise in such realms as education, insanity and crime.) The effective absence of experimental psychology in the modern sense has nevertheless not been fully explained, given the ubiquitous rhetoric calling for a 'science of the mind' or a 'science of man'. The term 'psychology' was most widely used by German philosophers, following Wolff, but their interests remained primarily metaphysical. Its (rare) use in English during this period has been reviewed by Christopher Fox. In the event, the discipline was not to materialize until the late 1850s, or, arguably, the 1890s even, and its diverse lines of descent from eighteenth-century 'psychological' thought remain to be unravelled.

Christopher Fox, 'Defining Eighteenth Century Psychology: Some Problems and Perspectives', in Christopher Fox (ed.), *Psychology and Literature in the Eighteenth Century* (New York: AMS, 1987), pp. 1–22.
Graham Richards, *Mental Machinery: The Origins and Consequences of Psychological Ideas, Part I 1600–1850* (London, Athlone Press, 1992).

GRAHAM RICHARDS

public health With the retreat of plague from western Europe from the early 1700s, the eighteenth century witnessed rising levels of endemic sicknesses which occasionally became epidemic, such as malaria, smallpox and gastro-enteric diseases. The age of Enlightenment was a period of reflection upon the health of populations, and socio-scientific analyses of DISEASE; it witnessed significant innovations in sanitary prevention and immunization (*see* INOCULATION, VACCINATION).

Through popular advice-books, Enlightenment doctors promoted the Hippocratic philosophy of prolonging life and preserving individual health through a regimen of diet and exercise. Equally, concern with environmental-health regulation led health reformers, such as the English Quaker cloth-merchant John Bellers (1654–1725), to identify a link between dirt and disease and to propose the hygienic improvement of towns. In *laissez-faire* England the campaign to avoid disease became a voluntary and commercial enterprise through the creation of improvement commissions in towns and the rise of various trades such as scavenging, night-soil collection and the design of 'airy' dwellings.

On the Continent, by contrast, the people's health was identified as the responsibility of Enlightened absolute monarchy. Johann Peter Frank (1745–1821), physician of the late-eighteenth-century Habsburg court and director of the general hospital in Vienna, designed a comprehensive system of medical police for regulating public hygiene and managing individual behaviour that might spread or engender disease. Frank's system was a product of the political philosophy of CAMERALISM. Comprehensive health reform in eighteenth-century Sweden was made possible through the creation of the first national census in 1749.

The Victorian age of public-health revolutions in Europe owed much to Enlightenment theories of social improvement through the promotion of the health of populations which flowered in the sanitary ideas of the later period.

See also MEDICINE.

James C. Riley, *The Eighteenth Century Campaign to Avoid Disease* (Basingstoke: Macmillan, 1987).

DOROTHY PORTER

public opinion   Whether governments in modern societies were more sensitive to public ópinion than those of previous ages, and whether or not that was a good thing, were frequently debated questions in the eighteenth century. Statesmen and political commentators alike enquired into the nature of public opinion, the extent of its influence and how to bridle it. Could it be trusted as the voice of the true interest of the nation, it was wondered, or was it no more than the clamour of SELF-INTEREST and factious dissent? Such concerns were not new, and educated men and women were well versed in classical articulations of the issue. The growing awareness of the real and latent power of the printed word, and the spread of literacy, however, pushed the ancient topic ever closer to the top of the political agenda.

'Nothing appears more surprizing to those, who consider human affairs with a philosophical eye, than the easiness with which the many are governed by the few', noted Hume in an essay entitled 'Of the First Principles of Government' (1741), adding, 'When we enquire by what means this wonder is effected, we shall find, that, as *force* is always on the side of the governed, the governors have nothing to support them but opinion'; this and only this was the foundation of all governments, be they despotic or free. In another essay discussing 'Whether the British Government Inclines More to Absolute Monarchy, or to a Republic' (1741) he remarked: 'though men be much governed by interest; yet even interest itself, and all human affairs, are entirely governed by *opinion*. Now, there has been a sudden and sensible change in the opinions of men within these last fifty years, by the progress of learning and of liberty.' As a result, he found, people were less submissive to authority of any kind, and he claimed that had such a spirit prevailed in the seventeenth century monarchical rule would have come to an end.

Necker's considerations on the subject are of particular interest, for he had been in turn the plaything of public opinion and its manipulator. In the words of Wollstonecraft's translation of his *De l'importance des opinions religieuses* (1788), 'the opinion of the public is an approbation or censure, exercised in the name of the general interest; thus it ought only to be applied to actions and to words, which either directly or indirectly affect this interest'. Necker went on to comment that 'The world is often mistaken in its judgment' and there are moments when it 'loses its force, and becomes enervated or governed by a servile spirit, it searches to find faults in the oppressed, and attributes grand intentions to powerful men, that it may, without shame, abandon one, and celebrate the other'. It followed that 'the opinion of the world, whose influence I have seen increase, which unites so many motives to excite men to distinguished actions, and to exalt them even to the great virtues, still ought never to be compared with the universal, invariable influence of religion, and with those sentiments which its precepts inspire men of all ages, of all condition, and every degree of understanding'. There was cause to be apprehensive about the growth of the power of public opinion, according to Necker. He insisted that it could never replace religion as a check on princes and their ministers and was only too conscious that while the just complaints of the people often never reached those in authority, corporations and institutions could harness public opinion and impede the rule of enlightened government. Such had been his experience while in office in the face of the recalcitrance of the *parlements*.

Among those who expressed faith in the benign influence of public opinion was Mercier. Puzzling over the many aspects of this intangible entity in the *Tableau de Paris*, he wrote of 'Monsieur le Public' and asked whether *he* existed: lacking a focal point and a single unified voice, this 'indefinable composite' nevertheless spoke the truth, which inexplicably emanated from the clash of all opinions.

There is no doubt about the power that public opinion exerted in the eighteenth century. The *Encyclopédie*, for example, noted more than once that it could never have been completed without the support of public opinion. Certainly, Diderot and his friends used every means to sway it in their favour.

Keith Michael Baker, 'Public Opinion as Political Invention', in K. M. Baker (ed.), *Inventing the French Revolution: Essays on French Political Culture in the Eighteenth Century* (Cambridge: Cambridge University Press, 1990), pp. 167–99.

The Works of Mary Wollstonecraft, ed. Janet Todd and Marilyn Butler, vol. 3: *Of the Importance of Religious Opinions, translated from the French of Mr. Necker* (London: William Pickering, 1989).

SYLVANA TOMASELLI

publishing   In the eighteenth century publishing was widely practised within the book trade, although it was only at the very end of the century that the English term took on its modern meaning. As a concept, however, it was well known, and could be found wherever a commercial trade in books had developed. The publisher is essentially the co-ordinator of the processes of book production: he or she commissions or accepts the book, arranges for it to be illustrated or otherwise augmented, causes it to be printed and bound, promotes its sale and organizes its distribution.

At the beginning of the eighteenth century these processes were often undertaken by the same trader, or within the same business. There was, however, a growing tendency towards a separation of the various functions within the book trade. In particular, because printers had specialized skills, needed both equipment and the capital to acquire it and were employers of skilled and semi-skilled labour, theirs became a distinctive branch of the trade. In the more highly developed book trades of north-western Europe printers had lost the primacy in the trade that their skills and facilities had commanded since the fifteenth century. This process began early in Britain, where it was well advanced before the end of the sixteenth century, but somewhat later elsewhere. Printers became the paid agents of publishers, but operated independently of them, a position that they have substantially retained ever since. In England, by the beginning of the eighteenth century a few printers still had retail shops, or were still involved in the publishing of books, and some were wholesalers or distributors, but most worked on commission for booksellers and publishers. The leadership role in the trade that had been theirs in the sixteenth and early seventeenth centuries had passed to others.

The members of the trade who were not printers thus became principally involved in the organization and co-ordination of book production, but they were booksellers and distributors, rather than producers. Some terminological explanation is needed here. At the beginning of the eighteenth century the word 'publisher' was used in English only to describe the distributors of (often illicit) pamphlets. The members of the book trade who performed the publishing function called themselves 'booksellers', but men such as Jacob Tonson the younger (1682–1735) and Robert Dodsley (1703–64) were publishers in the modern sense in all but name. They commissioned books from authors, accepted or rejected manuscripts submitted without commission, paid authors for their copyrights, arranged and paid for printing and organized the advertising, sale and distribution of books. They differed from modern publishers only in also having retail bookshops through which they sold their products directly to the public, although they also sold at trade prices to other retailers in London, as well as to booksellers in the provinces, in Scotland, Ireland and overseas. Perhaps ten large firms and twenty smaller ones existed in mid-eighteenth-century London, where publishing was a significant activity.

The separation of printing and publishing was not as marked elsewhere as it was in England. In most other European countries and in north America printers continued to dominate the trade, although in the more advanced book trades of France, the Low Countries and Switzerland the pattern was not unlike that which developed in England. Similar changes can be observed in the United States before the end of the century.

The development of the concept of copyright was critical to the emergence of the publisher as the key figure in the English book trade. Copyright was legally recognized in a number of European states in the eighteenth century, although not always under that name, but it was in Great Britain that the law of copyright was most highly developed. In 1710 the British parliament confirmed the existing practices of the London book trade, and provided the first comprehensive legal guarantees of copyright protection. Although the law was obscure in some particulars, the 1710 Copyright Act was an important stage in the development of publishing as a distinctive branch of the book trade, for it protected the investment of the publishers in books that they 'owned' and produced. After many courtroom battles, it was established in 1774 that after the expiry of the protected period (at that time a maximum of twenty-eight years), a text passed into 'public domain' and could be reprinted without formality by anyone. This forced members of the book trade to look for new titles which they could 'own' for twenty-eight years in order to maximize profits and minimize competition. In turn this forced them to adopt a more entrepreneurial attitude towards the conduct of business and, perhaps, a more adventurous attitude towards the selection and commissioning of material for publication. At the same time, it meant that publishers needed to invest more time and money in new titles, and thus reinforced the other factors that were pushing the trade towards a transformation into a capital-intensive publishing industry.

After 1774 the booksellers could no longer rely on endless reprints of popular favourites that they 'owned'. The need to find new books to publish and to recruit authors to write them forced them to take a different attitude to their work. Some firms virtually abandoned their retail bookselling, and concentrated entirely on publishing, as happened to the long-established Longman firm in the 1780s and 1790s. The first Thomas Longman (1699–1755) had indeed published books, but he and his immediate successors were also retail booksellers. Thomas Longman the younger (1730–97) and his son Thomas Norton Longman (1771–1842) turned the successful family business into an equally successful publishing-house, and even brought in partners from outside the family to supply the capital that was necessary for entrepreneurial publishing. Others confined themselves to retailing, or became wholesale booksellers; this happened to the Rivingtons at the same time as the Longmans were becoming publishers. New entrants to the trade began to set themselves up as publishers, and never had signficant retail businesses at all; John Murray (1778–1843) was perhaps the first significant example. Thus by the end of the century the familiar tripartite division between publisher, printer and bookseller was well established as the pattern for the future.

See also PRINTING.

Giles Barber and Bernhard Fabian (eds), *Buch und Buchhandel in Europa im achtzehten Jahrhundert* (Wiesbaden: Ernst Hauswedell, 1981).
John Feather, *A History of British Publishing* (London: Croom Helm, 1988).
David Foxon, *Pope and the Early Eighteenth-Century Book Trade* (Cambridge: Cambridge University Press, 1991).
Kathleen M. Lynch, *Jacob Tonson, Kit-Kat Publisher* (Knoxville, Tenn.: University of Tennessee Press, 1971).
James E. Tierney (ed.), *The Correspondence of Robert Dodsley 1733–1764* (Cambridge: Cambridge University Press, 1988).

JOHN FEATHER

Pugachev, Emel'ian Ivanovich (?1742–1775) Russian Cossack rebel, the most famous of several pretenders claiming to be PETER III. An illiterate veteran of the Seven Years and Turkish Wars, he deserted in 1771, appearing on the Iaik River in 1773 to fan local Cossack discontent and exploit grievances over increased taxation and recruitment burdens. His first manifesto (September 1773) was issued in the name of Peter III, the true tsar reclaiming his throne and bringing justice to the downtrodden. Later manifestos exhorted peasants to massacre landowners. Traditionally defined as a 'peasant war' (*see* JACQUERIES) by Soviet historians, the Pugachev rebellion, or *Pugachevshchina*, attracted diverse supporters – Ural factory serfs, Cossacks, non-Russian tribes-people, OLD BELIEVERS, as well as serfs and assorted fugitives – and encompassed a vast territory from the Volga (Kazan was stormed in July 1774) to the Urals, with many local leaders. The end of the Turkish war allowed a concerted onslaught on the poorly co-ordinated rebels. Pugachev was betrayed and executed in Moscow on 10 January 1775, dismemberment being preceded by beheading on the secret orders of Catherine II.

John T. Alexander, *Emperor of the Cossacks: Pugachev and the Frontier Jacquerie of 1773–1775* (Lawrence, Kan.: Coronado, 1973).

LINDSEY HUGHES

punishment   The punishment of criminals was everywhere regarded as one of the responsibilities of rulers; and as states and empires developed, punishment at the hands of officials came gradually to replace earlier systems based on compensation or the conventions of the feud. This process was far from universally complete by the early nineteenth century.

In most systems, insofar as we can reconstruct the rationale behind them, the main objectives of punishment were retribution and deterrence. The sovereign power (or the society that it claimed to represent) needed to be avenged on those who infringed the criminal code. Moreover, it was felt that the punishment of criminals should be used as a means of deterring other potential wrongdoers: this objective was assisted by the nearly universal practice of punishing wrongdoers in public.

The eighteenth century had at its disposal a repertoire of punishments which, in their emphasis on corporal or capital penalties, initially seem barbarous to the modern observer. Certainly, such punishments as that inflicted on Damiens (1715–57), who was mutilated and then torn apart by horses for the attempted regicide of Louis XV, the Chinese practice of slicing criminals in pieces, and the Georgian custom of cutting off the feet of thieves for a third offence seem very alien. In practice, however, they made sense to their societies, which believed strongly in retribution against criminals, and which, lacking the means to catch all offenders, needed to make examples of such as were apprehended.

Despite the harshness of many penal codes, most systems assumed a flexible use of punishments. This reflected the truism that petty crime was statistically more prevalent than serious crime, and that punishment should be fitted to the nature of the offence and of the offender. Thus Lord MACARTNEY, British ambassador to China in the 1790s, noted six forms of capital punishment there, including being burned to death with green faggots and being cut into ten thousand pieces, but he also observed that the punishments of fining, imprisonment, flagellation and exile were far more common. In Europe, too, despite the impact that the spectacle of public execution had on contemporary observers and later historians, punishments like fines, whippings and short terms of imprisonment inflicted on petty criminals by magistrates, town authorities and seigneurs were much more common.

Despite the virtues of some extra-European penal systems (for example, Macartney noted that Chinese gaols were well administered, and approved of the practice of holding debtors and felons in separate places), it was Europe that experienced large-scale innovations in penal techniques. In the long term these had their origins in the desire to find effective alternatives to CAPITAL PUNISHMENT for serious offenders. The very desire could be regarded as reflecting an important shift in the attitudes of the elite. Arguably, in the later seventeenth century judges and jurists felt less inclined to execute large numbers of offenders, and sought other means of punishing them. In France, for example, increasingly systematic use had been made of sentencing convicted criminals to serve as rowers in the royal galleys. As the use of galley fleets declined over the eighteenth century the galleys essentially became prison hulks, the prisoners sleeping on them and working on shore during the day. Other forms of state service were also used as punishment: thus in the Habsburg Empire, when the number of condemned criminals exceeded the needs of the galley fleet at Naples in 1728, the emperor sent them to work in the mines of Hungary.

In England from 1718, in response to a crime wave which followed the War of the Spanish Succession, convicted criminals were regularly sent as indentured servants to the American colonies: by 1776 some 30,000 had gone from England, 13,000 from Ireland and 700 from Scotland. After the loss of the American colonies, an alternative destination had to be found, and in January 1788 the first convict fleet arrived in Australia. Transportation there ended in 1868, by which time 160,000 convicts had been sent from Britain and Ireland.

The last years of the eighteenth century witnessed the emergence of an important innovation in penal policy, the penitentiary prison. Hitherto, prisons had been used occasionally to hold important political prisoners apart, but mainly to hold suspects before trial. Now reform of the criminal was seen as feasible and desirable, and the use of prisons also meant that punishment was removed from the public to a private sphere. It has been argued that this shift was connected with the rise of industrial capitalism and the need of the emergent industrial bourgeoisie to find new means of disciplining the proletariat. While the broader socio-economic context should not be ignored, Evangelical and Nonconformist Christianity probably provided a more important impetus for change than economic developments: this certainly appears to have been the case in Britain and the United States.

It should be stressed that in most penal systems penal codes provided a framework within which judicial discretion could be applied to the punishment of offenders. Often, judges decided to apply a lesser or greater punishment according to the age, sex, past record or reputation of the offender, or according to how far they felt the circumstances of the times or the offence dictated the need to make an example of him or her. This flexibility operated surprisingly often to the advantage of the offender, and helped give a distinctive rationale to eighteenth-century penal systems.

See also CRIME, ADMINISTRATION OF JUSTICE.

Michel Foucault, *Discipline and Punish: The Birth of the Prison*, trans. A. Sheridan (London: Allen Lane, 1977).

Dario Melossi and Massimo Pavarini, *The Prison and the Factory: Origins of the Penitentiary System* (London: Macmillan, 1977).

J. A. Sharpe, *Judicial Punishment in England* (London: Faber, 1990).

Pieter Spierenburg, *The Spectacle of Suffering: Executions and the Evolution of Repression: From a Preindustrial Metropolis to the European Experience* (Cambridge: Cambridge University Press, 1984).

J. A. SHARPE

Q

quackery The term 'quackery' is often used to refer to the variety and profusion of medical practitioners in the eighteenth century, but its boundaries are vague. Virtually any practitioner may have been a quack in someone else's eyes. Quackish characteristics of medical practice that disgusted later practitioners, such as travelling from town to town, advertising, selling drugs dramatically or prescribing by mail, were not closely linked with levels of education, income, social standing or medical reputation. Thus John 'Chevalier' Taylor (1703–72), an oculist whose itinerant practice was seen as quackery by subsequent generations, trained as an orthodox surgeon and received medical degrees from the Universities of Basle, Liège and Cologne.

Some of the styles of practice labelled 'quackery' reflect the process of commercialization that dominated eighteenth-century medical practice. MEDICINE was a consumer good, and practitioners' lack of professional authority forced them to advertise their wares like other tradesmen. Patients were eager to purchase; by our standards, people in the eighteenth century consumed large quantities of medicines. Some doctors revelled in the potential for publicity and advertisement. For example, James Graham (1745–94) invented and marketed a 'celestial' bed which provided its occupants with spectacular sex or offspring as required. Through the century, a range of patent medicines were developed which became standard remedies.

This commercialization depended on the power of patients to govern their own health care. Historians and sociologists argue that eighteenth-century practitioners were far less powerful than twentieth-century counterparts; patients treated themselves and called in different medical practitioners according to what they perceived to be their particular needs. Hence all practitioners had to market and promote themselves, whether quacks or not.

So-called quackery also reflected a different structure in the medical profession from what we have today. One of the practitioners most often called a quack was the specialist, who was often an itinerant. These men and women specialized in treating a specific disease, such as cancer or venereal disease, or specific parts of the body, such as eyes, ears or teeth. Others specialized in a therapeutic modality, such as electrical healing or MESMERISM.

Governments regulated medicine to different extents, with corresponding variations in quackery from country to country. Great Britain represented the pinnacle of a free-market economy in which all manner of practitioners flourished. The same was true for its American colonies. The French controlled medicine more tightly; travelling practitioners and secret remedies were supposed to be licensed by the government.

Quackery was thus a product of the structures of medical practice; a mirror-image twin often barely distinguishable from its orthodox sibling. While the roots of some forms of nineteenth-century 'alternative' medicine lie in eighteenth-century quackery, the political meanings of the two are diametrically opposed. Quackery was an integral part of the market-place of medicine; alternative medicine was created in opposition to an increasingly powerful profession.

W. F. Bynum and R. Porter (eds), *Medical Fringe and Medical Orthodoxy 1750–1850* (London: Croom Helm, 1987).

R. Porter, *Health for Sale: Quackery in England 1660–1850* (Manchester: Manchester University Press, 1989).

M. Ramsey, *Professional and Popular Medicine in France, 1770–1830* (Cambridge: Cambridge University Press, 1988).

MARY E. FISSELL

Quadruple Alliance (2 August 1718) The Quadruple Alliance was signed by Britain, France and the emperor CHARLES VI. It was the climax of Stanhope's (1675–1721) 'peace plan for the south', foreshadowed in the TRIPLE ALLIANCE, and was based on an Anglo-French partnership compelling PHILIP V of Spain to relinquish his Bourbon ambitions in Italy – as distinct from those of his second wife, Elizabeth Farnese (1692–1766) – and to cajole Charles into surrendering his Habsburg claims to Spain. Through the alliance the emperor could expect British naval assistance to enable him to wrest Sicily back from Philip, while he gave up Sardinia to Savoy. He accepted the latter's claims to Spain in the event of Philip's line dying out, and undertook to end his support for the Jacobite claim to the British crown. Austrian Habsburg suzerainty over Parma, Piacenza and Tuscany was established, on the understanding that the successions in these duchies lay with the Farnese house. Although he was distrustful of Anglo-French motivation,

Charles had to settle for the advantages he was gaining from their brokerage. The alliance was misnamed at its inception, for the Dutch, who were determined to avoid war with Spain, were never admitted. Savoy acceded as a fourth party in October 1718 and Spain itself after a year of war, in January 1720.

O. Weber, *Die Quadrupel-Allianz vom Jahre 1718* (Vienna: F. Tempsky, 1887).

D. D. ALDRIDGE

Quebec The province of Quebec underwent several transformations in the period 1688 to 1820. Under the French regime, Quebec became the capital of the colony of New France. After the British conquest in 1760, the whole colony became known as the province of Quebec. When the Constitution Act of 1791 became law, however, the province became known as Lower Canada until 1867. The principal economic activity of the area was agricultural, supplemented with some timber and iron production, and the peltry trade with Europe. The population of Quebec expanded steadily from the original 100 settlers in 1627 to some 180,000 or so by 1820.

What makes the history of the province since the seventeenth century unique is its staunch adherence to the French-language legal system, and its deep-rooted Catholicism. Up to the conquest of 1760 these factors had kept the colony from withering away in the face of neglect by France. After the conquest, Quebec was unique in the British Empire by virtue of its statutory protection as a French-speaking, Catholic society, with its own civil courts based on French law – amid Anglo-centric Canadian settlement elsewhere, and with the English-speaking American republic to the south.

See CANADA.

PHILIP LAWSON

Quesnay, François (1694–1774) French surgeon, later physician, and founder of the physiocratic school of economic theory. Despite his humble origins, he rose to become the secretary of the newly created Academy of Surgery (1740–8) and a member of the Académie des Sciences in 1751. He was Madame de Pompadour's physician, as well as first physician to Louis XV. In 1752 he was ennobled in recognition of his services during the illness of the crown prince. Well respected as a practitioner, he wrote in defence of surgeons in their battle against physicians, and helped to improve the standing of scientific medicine.

He contributed the articles 'Évidence', 'Fermiers' and 'Grain' to the *Encyclopédie*. The first dealt with the relationship between mind and body and the problem of freedom and determinism, while the other two, both lengthy and influential, provide a sketch of his economic position, with their critique of luxury, their argument in favour of liberty of the grain trade and their emphasis on land and agriculture as the true source of a nation's wealth. From 1766 onwards, he was to consider these to be the only rightful basis for taxation. (*See* PHYSIOCRATS.) His writings include *Tableaux économiques* (1758) and *Le Droit naturel* (1765).

Gianni Vaggi, *The Economics of François Quesnay* (Basingstoke: Macmillan, 1987).

SYLVANA TOMASELLI

R

race According to both Scripture and science in the eighteenth century, mankind had arisen monogenetically from a common source, a pair of ancestors of the whole human race. Most anthropological thinkers deemed that the prototype of our species must have been white, and that the complexion, facial features and diverse physical characteristics of other races were due to the dispersion of peoples in different climates and conditions. Although that doctrine could and would eventually be pursued to racist conclusions which justified the world supremacy of nations closest to God or Eden, its subscribers in the Enlightenment generally deplored SLAVERY, not least because the successful interbreeding of races was thought to prove that all the varieties of mankind formed a single species. But numerous problems with this interpretation of race were also pursued in the eighteenth century. Kames (1696–1782), who thought that the relative lightness of equatorial Amerindians and other evidence established that climate did not determine skin pigment, subscribed to a polygenist belief in the separate creation of races. Jefferson, for all his opposition to slavery, could not bear to regard Negroes as truly human, and the first republic of the New World, unlike that of France which it inspired, found itself unable at birth to extend all the rights of man to blacks.

See also BLACKS.

W. Jordan, *White over Black: American Attitudes toward the Negro 1550–1812* (Chapel Hill, NC: University of North Carolina Press, for Institute of Early American History and Culture, 1968).

ROBERT WOKLER

radicalism   The late eighteenth century saw radicalism establish itself as a permanent feature of British politics. WILKES provoked a popular movement which went beyond his original objectives, and the American crisis raised questions about the nature and purpose of representation on both sides of the Atlantic, while stimulating demands for public economy and parliamentary reform. Civil and religious liberties, the freedom of the press and anxiety about the powers of the executive dominated radical thinking. The French Revolution reinvigorated a movement that was becalmed in the late 1780s, while PAINE disseminated an ideology which stressed natural rights, civil and religious liberties, and parliamentary reform. The loyalist reaction blighted the radical movement in the 1790s, but radicalism remained a feature of public controversy. BENTHAM formulated a radical, utilitarian ideology which was free from associations with Jacobinism (see JACOBINS). The radical creed was often summed up as 'peace, retrenchment and reform', but the range of beliefs among radicals was remarkably wide. The movement was evidence of a growth in political awareness among tradesmen, shopkeepers, artisans and craftsmen, and was often identified with religious dissent, especially in its Unitarian form (see DISSENTERS, UNITARIANISM).

A. Goodwin, *The Friends of Liberty* (London: Hutchinson, 1979).

JOHN W. DERRY

Radicati di Passerano, Alberto (1698–1737)   Italian writer and thinker. Born into the Piedmontese aristocracy, he developed into an original if eccentric thinker. During early visits to France and England he was greatly influenced by deism, Calvinism and secular thinkers such as Bayle. He came briefly to prominence during VICTOR AMADEUS II's conflict with the papacy, when his view of papal authority as illegitimate momentarily found favour with the king (1725–6). By 1727, however, Victor Amadeus and the papacy had resolved their quarrel and Radicati, whose unease at the attitude of the Inquisition had already made him flee to England, found himself in permanent exile after a brief return to Turin when the new king, Charles Emanuel III, rebuffed him. In 1736 he was forced to flee England too. He died in poverty in Amsterdam, having returned to Calvinism.

Radicati's thought was rooted in a radical, evangelistic theology which rejected the temporal wealth of the church; by the 1730s he had become a freethinker. His religious ideas led him to very specific support for egalitarian forms of government – in a legal dispute between his family and their peasant tenants he sided with the latter – which led him to an outright condemnation of monarchy as a system of government. His major work, *Douze discours moraux, historiques et politiques* (The Discourses), probably written in the mid-1720s for Victor Amadeus II, grew until its final publication in 1736; it set out a programme, both religious and political, for a prince. Radicati stands with Alfieri (1749–1803), the Vasco brothers and Vico, all radical thinkers driven into exile by the conservative Savoyard state in the eighteenth century.

D. Carpanetto and G. Ricuperati, *Italy in the Age of Reason, 1685–1789* (London: Longman, 1987).
G. Symcox, *Victor Amadeus II* (London: Thames & Hudson, 1983).

MICHAEL BROERS

Ramazzini, Bernardini (1633–1714)   Italian physician who wrote the first book on occupational health. Born in Carpi, he studied medicine at the University of Parma. After practising in Carpi and nearby Modena, he was appointed professor of the theory of medicine at the newly founded University of Modena in 1682 under the patronage of the Este family. In the 1690s he investigated the health of workers. Allegedly, his interest was sparked off by a conversation with a cesspit cleaner who had trouble with his eyes. His *De morbis artificum* (Diseases of Workers) was published in 1700, when he moved to a professorship at Padua. He lectured until his death in 1714, and also wrote on epidemics of rinderpest in cattle and of malaria.

His work on occupational health is extensive; he examined the health of male and female workers in forty-two occupations, including nuns. He interviewed workers, examined their homes and did autopsies, analysing both the materials used in work and the distortions of the body occasioned by work. Sadly, there is little modern historical work of quality on Ramazzini.

B. Ramazzini, *Diseases of Workers*, trans. W. C. Wright (New York: Hafner, 1969).

MARY E. FISSELL

Rameau, Jean Philippe (1683–1764)   French composer, organist and music theorist. After studying in Italy he worked as an organist in various French cities, and from 1722 lived in Paris, where he opened a private school for the teaching of composition (1737), was granted a royal pension and appointed chamber music composer to Louis XV (1745).

He left a large number of harpsichord pieces, but is today best remembered as an opera composer. He started writing stage works of a different kind when he was 50, the most famous being *Les Indes galantes* (1735), *Castor et Pollux* (1737), *Dardanus* (1739) and *Platée* (1745). Some of his operas anticipate those of Gluck.

In his *Traité de l'harmonie reduite à ses principes naturels* (1722) and *Nouveau système de musique théorique* (1726) he presented findings which were far ahead of his time and point forward to classical tonality, such as the inversions of chords and the principles of chord progression.

Rameau's standing among his contemporaries was not undisputed. He was attacked by the conservative defenders of Jean-Baptiste Lully (1632–87) as well as by the *encyclopédistes*, who were in favour of 'progressive' Italian opera.

D. Paquette, *Jean-Philippe Rameau, musicien bourguignon* (Saint-Seine-l'Abbaye: Eds. de Saint-Seine-l'Abbaye, 1984).

FRITZ WEBER

rationalism   The term 'rationalism' has come to be applied to certain philosophies which sought to deduce a set of philosophical and scientific truths from a few basic principles which were self-evident. The rationalist philosophers held that they could determine the nature of objective reality by appeal to principles that were established independently of sense experience.

According to Descartes, the first truth that one discovers is that one exists as a thinking being. In his *Meditationes de prima Philosophia* (Meditations on First Philosophy, 1641) he proceeded from this truth to establish the existence of God, the distinction of the mind of human beings from their bodies (*see* RELATIONSHIP BETWEEN MIND AND BODY) and the existence of a material world. In his *Principia Philosophiae* (Principles of Philosophy, 1644) he claimed to derive the laws of motion from the attributes of the Deity.

In his *Ethics* (1677) Baruch Spinoza went even further than Descartes in presenting his philosophy as an organized set of deductions from axioms and definitions. But it was the rationalist system of LEIBNIZ as organized by WOLFF that had the most widespread influence in the eighteenth century, especially in Germany.

Generally speaking, later philosophers of the Enlightenment were critical of rationalism.

See also REASON.

J. Cottingham, *The Rationalists* (Oxford: Oxford University Press, 1988).

JOHN P. WRIGHT

Raynal, Guillaume Thomas François (1713–1796)   French writer. He frequented the *salons* of d'Holbach and Necker, and was paid by the Ministry of Foreign Affairs to write a number of works. It may be at Choiseul's instigation that he turned to the subject of colonialism and wrote the very successful *Histoire philosophique et politique des établissements et du commerce des Européens dans les deux Indes*

(1770), usually referred to as *Histoire des deux Indes*. Between 1772 and 1780 it went through seventeen editions, and something like 25,000 copies. Though Diderot may have had a hand in the first edition, it is the third edition (1780) that bears his stamp. The work was condemned in 1781, the year of the third edition's diffusion. The book contains an account of the mores of peoples like the Chinese and the Peruvians, discussing and challenging comparisons between 'civilized' and 'savage' men; a critique of slavery and colonialism; and after 1780 an attack on many French institutions and policies, including fiscal ones – but Raynal's declared interest was in the history and nature of commerce, and its impact on various European as well as non-European nations. Thus the wealth of information was provided partly with a view to facilitate and encourage French commercial relations overseas. Engagingly written for the most part, the *Histoire* is one of the period's most important texts. Raynal is also remembered for starting, in 1747, the *Correspondance littéraire* which Friedrich Melchior Grimm took over in 1753.

Yves Benot, *Diderot, de l'athéisme à l'anticolonialisme* (Paris: François Maspero, 1981).

SYLVANA TOMASELLI

reason In the eighteenth century the word 'reason' was commonly used to designate the natural faculty or power of the mind that discovered what was true, or at least what was probable. This faculty was considered to be the source of science and philosophy, and as such was often distinguished from memory and imagination, which were thought to give rise to history and poetry respectively.

Following Descartes, eighteenth-century philosophers advocated a natural kind of LOGIC which dispensed with the artificial rules of scholastic reasoning – those related to the use of the syllogism. For the Cartesians, the basis for all reasoning was an act of comparison by which the relation of one idea to another was perceived. In his *Essay concerning Human Understanding* LOCKE described reasoning as a process whereby the intermediate ideas between two extremes were discovered and ordered: these ideas were conceived as links in a chain of reasoning. Modern philosophers sought to formulate a logic that would help to discover new truths rather than reorder old ones.

For Descartes the model of all reasoning had been the absolutely necessary connections dealt with in mathematics. Locke and earlier English writers differed from him in as much as they stressed the importance of probable reasoning. The use of testimony in law and history provided them with a model for such reasoning: even if the necessary connection of ideas could not be directly perceived, the testimony of others could be reasoned from, for example by taking into account expertise and intentions. According to Locke, even reasoning about particular matters of fact in science was based on probable reasoning, albeit of the most certain kind: in order to establish a matter of fact for which there was no direct perception, one had to reason from the uniform experience of oneself and others.

A central aim of HUME's philosophy was to show the limits of human reason and the need for natural principles, which were derived from the senses and imagination. In his *Treatise of Human Nature* he maintained that reason could have no direct influence on action and could only discover the means to satisfy feelings that arose from human nature. Following Hutcheson and Shaftesbury, he argued that judgements of morality had to be based on a moral sense, and not on reason. In the part of the *Treatise* concerning human understanding he argued that even the metaphysical principle that underlay the use of reason in experimental science – the principle that every event had a cause – was ultimately rooted in imagination, and not in any rational insight into nature.

KANT thought that Hume's arguments showed that previous philosophers had misconstrued the role of reason in metaphysics. He himself argued that reason provided structuring principles – like that of causality – which allowed one to conceive of an objective world of experience apart from the senses. He also held that reason operated independently of the data of the senses (for example, in moral argument) in order to produce principles that were unconditioned. But he denied that knowledge of this unconditioned realm – the purely intelligible realm of freedom, God and immortality – was possible: any attempt to establish these principles on the basis of reason would lead to contradictions. He saw himself as denying the possibility of knowledge of these principles in order to make way for faith.

Eighteenth-century philosophers differed in their views on the respective domains of reason and faith. Sceptics like Bayle sought to show the contradictions of reason, even in scientific matters, and thus to undermine the critical function of reason in matters of religion (*see* SCEPTICISM). Locke, on the other hand, argued that faith could never contradict the truths that were established by reason, and that reason could be used to establish the veracity of revelation and the signification of the words of witnesses. In this way he sought to establish a reasonable form of Christianity which required only a few simple beliefs. Hume, on the other hand, argued systematically that reason was opposed to both natural and revealed religion. (*See* CHRISTIANITY, NATURAL RELIGION.)

Pierre Bayle, 'Pyrrho', in R. Popkin (trans. and ed.), *Historical and Critical Dictionary: Selections* (Indianapolis: Bobbs-Merrill, 1965).

David Hume, *A Treatise of Human Nature*, ed. L. Selby-Bigge, rev. P. H. Nidditch (Oxford: Clarendon, 1978), pp. 76–82, 413–18, 455–76.

Immanuel Kant, *Critique of Pure Reason*, trans. N. K. Smith (London: Macmillan, 1933), pp. 17–29.

John Locke, *An Essay concerning Human Understanding*, ed. P. H. Nidditch (Oxford: Clarendon, 1975), pp. 654–696.

JOHN P. WRIGHT

Réaumur, René Antoine Ferchault de (1683–1757)   French experimenter and natural philosopher. He gained international renown as he rose to eminence at the Académie des Sciences. He was from a bourgeois background, and initially studied mathematics, but after 1709 pursued diverse interests in natural philosophy and its utilitarian applications. Participating in an international correspondence network, he transmitted foreign discoveries, such as the electrical Leyden jar and physiological characteristics of polyps, and also devised a much copied new thermometer scale using spirit instead of mercury. In his role as supervisor of the bureaucratically inspired project of an industrial encyclopaedia to be published by the Académie, he examined several technological processes, including ceramics and tin-refining, but his most influential investigations were into the properties and manufacture of iron and steel. He maintained his early fascination with molluscs and published six volumes on invertebrates, classifying them by their occupations; the work also included his substantial research into bees and applied topics like pest control and the production of silk and wax. He conducted experiments on the digestive systems of birds, but, influenced by contemporary preformationist ideas, his biological studies focused on the problem of generation.

William Smeaton, 'Réaumur: Natural Historian and Pioneer of Applied Science', *Endeavour*, 7 (1983), 38–40.

PATRICIA FARA

rebellions   The term 'rebellion' is here taken to mean a localized revolt against an established order. While reference is made to the commonly called 'Jacobite Rebellion', there is none to rebellions within an American revolutionary, French revolutionary or Napoleonic context, or to *coups d'état*, riots or mutinies. Jacobite attempts to unseat the British monarchy as it had been established in 1689 occurred in 1689, 1696, 1708, 1715, 1719, 1722, 1745–6 and 1759. There were substantial differences between these, but French commitment to the cause remained constant. Defeat was due, variously, to the elements (1744–5, 1719), government vigilance (1696, 1722), lack-lustre leadership (1715) and British military/naval superiority (1689, 1708, 1719, 1759). The combination of the latter, French hesitation and public indifference in England condemned the most serious attempt in 1745–6 to failure. (*See* JACOBITES.)

In 1698 Tsar Peter I repressed a discontented elite civic guard (*Streltsi*); and in 1707–8 faced a Don Cossack rebellion. Catherine II faced the most far-reaching of Russia's eighteenth-century internal rebellions under PUGACHEV (1773–4). Peasant unrest in Bohemia and Transylvania between 1760 and 1785 affected Habsburg reforms, though the weakness of the Polish government made such unrest in the commonwealth insoluble. Rebellions in Corsica (1734–68) and Switzerland (1720–80) were against Genoese rule and patrician rule, respectively (in the case of Geneva in 1738, it was against more democratic rule). The Swedish crown put down a peasant rebellion in Dalecarlia against conscription and overseas service, in 1743, and from 1772 to 1778 there was unrest in south Sweden and Finland over labour services. In 1788 the League of Anjala sought to force Finland's secession from Sweden but failed to enlist the support of Catherine II. In southern Norway in 1765 there was a rebellion over the poll tax levied by central government in Copenhagen, and 1787–8 saw a rising in the same region under C. J. Lofthuus (1750–97), which was directed against bureaucratic abuses and commercial privilege. The preservation of abuse and privilege, threatened by the authority of Governor William Bligh (1754–1817), gave rise to the 'Rum Rebellion' in New South Wales (1808–10).

In North America there was resistance, in Massachusetts, New York and Maryland, to the 'Glorious Revolution'. In 1763–4 the Indian chief Pontiac (*c.*1720–69) led a rebellion against encroachment on Indian lands from the east. In Virginia, South Carolina and Georgia there were periodic slave rebellions between 1713 and 1775. Portuguese South America saw several Jesuit-inspired rebellions during the ministry of POMBAL, while the Spanish lost their South American colonies to the independence movement led by Simon BOLÍVAR between 1813 and 1820.

See also JACQUERIES.

H. Aptheker, *American Negro Slave Revolts* (New York: Columbia University Press, 1943).

H. A. Barton, *Scandinavia in the Revolutionary Era 1760–1815* (Minneapolis: University of Minnesota Press, 1986).

E. Bonjour, H. S. Offler and G. R. Potter, *A Short History of Switzerland* (Oxford: Clarendon, 1955).

H. V. Evatt, *Rum Rebellion* (Sydney: Angus & Robertson, 1938).

F. McLynn, *The Jacobites* (London: Routledge & Kegan Paul, 1985).

I. de Madariaga, *Russia in the Age of Catherine the Great* (London Weidenfeld & Nicolson, 1981).

G. Sherwell, *Simon Bolivar* (Washington, DC: B. S. Adams, 1921).

D. D. ALDRIDGE

refugees   In the early eighteenth century, as in the previous 200 years, most refugees were victims of RELIGIOUS PERSECUTION. The last Sephardic JEWS driven from Spain and Portugal by the Inquisition embarked for the north in the 1720s, although anti-Semitic campaigns (and consequent migrations) continued in eastern Europe. Among Protestant refugees, the best known were the 200,000 to 250,000 HUGUENOTS who left France at the Revocation of the Edict of Nantes, enriching northwestern Europe with their technical and professional skills and furthering the spread of capitalism. Another of their destinations was North America, to which many German Protestants also fled. Meanwhile, some 40,000 to 50,000 British and Irish JACOBITES, who were loyal to the Catholic James II (1633–1701), followed him into Continental exile in the half-century after 1689, many to settle as soldiers or entrepreneurs. They were in part political refugees, a type that became increasingly common as the century continued. Defeat in the American War of Independence caused 100,000 colonial loyalists to leave for Canada, the West Indies and Britain. In the Old World the convulsions of 1789–1815 created still more exiles – from assorted radicals seeking asylum and hope in revolutionary France to royalist ÉMIGRÉS living on foreign charity.

J. -A. Lesouard and M. Hutt, 'Refugees, Exiles, Émigrés', in D. Johnson et al. (eds), *Britain and France* (Folkestone: Dawson, 1980), pp. 115–36, 372–3.

HUGH DUNTHORNE

Reid, Thomas (1710–1796)   Scottish philosopher. He was the leading exponent of the philosophy of 'common sense' (later known as the 'Scottish School'), which directly confronted Hume's scepticism. In his principal work, *An Inquiry into the Human Mind on the Principles of Common Sense* (1764), he questioned the notion that reality consisted simply of 'ideas', arguing that belief in an external reality is intuitive, and not mediated by sensory perceptions. The impact of this work was immediate, leading within the year to his appointment to succeed Adam Smith as professor of moral philosophy at Glasgow. When Reid retired, he published his lectures on the intellectual (1785) and the active powers (1788) of man.

He kept abreast of developments in chemistry and the Newtonian physical sciences: he took an interest in his colleague Black's concept of latent heat, and in Watt's steam engine, for he believed that scientific methods should be brought to philosophy. His successor, Dugald Stewart (1753–1828), accepted much of his philosophy, as did French spiritualist philosophers such as Victor Cousin (1792–1867) and Jouffroy (1796–1842).

Keith Lehrer, *Thomas Reid* (London: Routledge, 1989).

M. L. BENJAMIN

religion　The place of religion in eighteenth-century society has received fresh consideration in recent years. Traditionally, the century has been conceived of as an age of increasing secularization or – as French scholars in particular have stressed – a period of dechristianization and desacralization, where the role of religion in politics, in the world of ideas and in society more generally was increasingly marginalized, overtaken by secular and more modern assumptions, attitudes and practices that were galvanized by the anti-clerical Enlightenment. Such a process could be seen in both Protestant and Catholic countries where the power of the churches to govern the lives of the people became increasingly ineffective.

Recent research, however, has suggested that the confident assertions of the older histories are questionable, that concentration on the writings and beliefs of a handful of French *philosophes* has exaggerated the extent to which religious modes of thought and habits of mind were superseded by enlightened ideas. Above all, the recognition of tremendous regional differences, not only between countries but also within countries like France, has tempered too easy generalizations. For example, one can readily find groups of people who held millennial beliefs which ran counter to the Enlightenment stress on reason, such as the Camisards who came to England in 1709, the German Pietists, the Moravians, the Freemasons, the Methodists and Evangelicals in England, the participants in the Great Awakening in America and the Swedenborgians. As long ago as 1932 Carl Becker argued in his still-underestimated *Heavenly City of the Eighteenth Century Philosophers* that even the *philosophes* inherited patterns of thought that were more Christian than pagan or secular. Faith in nature, for example, replaced the authority of Christ and the Bible, and a belief in the redeeming power of grace was replaced by one in the inspiration to be drawn from virtue.

It would be wrong to polarize the forces of religion and those of the Enlightenment. Historians who have interpreted the relationship between religion and the Enlightenment as one of inevitable conflict have missed the many areas of overlap. For a start, *philosophes* had no coherent position on religion. While the more radical, such as d'Holbach, espoused materialist views that effectively denied the supernatural, much of the most vehement satire of *philosophes* like Voltaire was aimed not at religion or Christianity, but at the church, and in particular what was perceived to be the corrupt nature of the Catholic Church.

In many ways – for example the spread of learning and literacy and the emphasis on reason – Enlightenment ideals found a home not only in Protestant churches in England, Scotland, Germany, Holland and North America but also through the movement known as the CATHOLIC

ENLIGHTENMENT, especially in Italy and Spain. The Catholic Enlightenment was an attempt to reform the church and to improve its pastoral work. It shared the contempt of the *philosophes* for superstition and their hostility towards monasteries, which were regarded as useless. Joseph II of Austria suppressed monasteries to finance new bishoprics, seminaries and parishes, while in Portugal the Marquês de Pombal sponsored a series of reforms within the church.

The churches adopted various strategies to increase their influence, such as pastoral work and religious education. A major preoccupation of movements such as the Catholic Enlightenment was to purify what historians have labelled 'popular religion', the religion of the masses, which consisted of beliefs and assumptions that dated back to the Middle Ages. Scholarly opinion is as yet divided over whether popular religion represented a cultural system quite separate from the religion of the clergy or the latter were able to operate in tandem with it. Certainly, in this period the behaviour of the populace, the growth of urban centres and the spread of alehouses called for renewed clerical efforts to reform the aspects of popular culture that appeared to impede the spread of more godly living.

Both within and outside Europe this was the great period of Christian missions (*see* MISSIONARIES), which served to spread Christianity, and in addition became one of the principal forces, under Evangelical influence, for the abolition of the slave trade at the end of the eighteenth century. These missionary efforts also gave Christians a greater awareness of other religions and other types of clergy. Depending on the stance of the writer, it could be used to bolster the position of Christianity as the only true faith, or to attack it. Enlightenment critics were particularly interested in ISLAM which they considered to be a superior religion, and in Confucianism, because it did not not require a clergy.

The emphasis on the process of secularization in the eighteenth century is a product of liberal Anglo-American thinking which has interpreted the period largely through Western eyes. In other parts of the world no such process has been discerned and other faiths continued to hold sway over people's lives. The period was in many ways one of the most glorious in the history of Chinese civilization, in which there was widespread observance of the Confucian tradition. In Japan, under the Tokugawa system, religious militancy led to the persecution of Christians, and renewed vigour in both Buddhism and Shintoism. The period also saw attempts to reconstruct the Islamic faith, which were in part sparked off by the recognition of the weakening of the Islamic world in the face of European expansion. The Wahhabi movement, led by 'Abd al-Wahhab (1703–92), was a call for a return to the original basis of Islam. In India the period saw the further development of Sikhism from a syncretic and peaceful way of combining the Hindu and Muslim faiths into a militant organization, under the leadership of Gobind Singh (1666–1708). In eastern Europe the Jewish religion experienced the great awakening known as Hasidism, which brought the Jewish cabbala to a popular audience. Viewed from such perspectives, what used to be seen as an age of reason, may very well have been an age of renewed faith.

See also CHRISTIANITY, NATURAL RELIGION.

Sheridan Gilley, 'Christianity and Enlightenment: An Historical Survey', History of European Ideas, 1 (1981), 103–21.
Kaspar von Greyerz (ed.), Religion and Society in Early Modern Europe, 1500–1800 (London: German Historical Institute, 1984).
Stephen Neill, A History of Christian Missions (Harmondsworth: Penguin, 1974).
Ninian Smart, The World's Religions (Cambridge: Cambridge University Press, 1989).

JEREMY GREGORY

religious persecution see PERSECUTION, RELIGIOUS.

religious toleration   The theoretical underpinning of religious toleration was set out in Locke's *Letters concerning Toleration* (1689–92) and Voltaire's *Treatise on Toleration* (1764). Under the Toleration Act of 1689, the worship of Trinitarian Protestant DISSENTERS was, subject to the fulfilment of certain conditions, tolerated in England, but dissenting preachers and teachers were still obliged to subscribe to all but three of the Thirty-nine Articles. This obligation was removed in 1779 and replaced by an oath of fidelity to the Scriptures. The Tudor and Stuart laws against Catholicism remained on the statute-book, but were not rigorously enforced even in Ireland where the perceived threat was more urgent. Acts of Parliament in 1778, 1791 and 1793 removed some of the disabilities placed on Catholics, but full equality of civil status for adherents of all faiths was not realized in the eighteenth century. The established church retained its political, social and legal privileges and served as a theological and organizational pillar of the state. (See CATHOLIC EMANCIPATION, TEST ACTS.)

Nine of the thirteen American colonies also had established churches, but by 1700 *de facto* religious toleration had become the norm in Connecticut and Massachusetts, and spread from there. In the Habsburg lands Joseph II granted toleration to Lutherans, Calvinists and Greek Orthodox believers in 1781 and a measure of civil relief to JEWS in 1782. Catherine II of Russia began the process of granting toleration to Muslims in 1764. In 1785 she opened public office to OLD BELIEVERS and in 1786 granted civil equality to the Jews. Similarly, Frederick the

Great made Prussia one of the most tolerant states in eighteenth-century Europe.

The motivation for such acts varied from ruler to ruler and from place to place, but foremost among them were economic self-interest, political expediency, principled humanitarianism and a growing awareness that state security did not necessarily depend on religious uniformity. Toleration was, nevertheless, far from a universal tendency in eighteenth-century Europe. It made little headway in either the Iberian peninsula or the Italian states (*see* INQUISITION). Toleration was also highly selective and hedged with restrictions. Joseph II, while tolerating various expressions of Christianity, felt it to be his duty to persecute atheists and deists. (*See* ATHEISM, DEISM, FREETHINKERS.) Similarly, a royal edict in 1786 forbade Prussian Protestant clergy from straying from strictly orthodox beliefs in their sermons. Nor was religious toleration necessarily a popular policy. Mob action against religious minorities was a recurring feature of eighteenth-century life.

The DECLARATION OF THE RIGHTS OF MAN AND THE CITIZEN promulgated by the French National Assembly in August 1789 proclaimed freedom of expression, including that of religious belief. However, what effectively amounted to persecution of Catholics was later undertaken by the revolutionary government. In North America Jefferson's famous Virginia Bill for Establishing Religious Freedom (1786) was a classic statement of freedom of religion and civil equality, which was reiterated in article 1 of the Amendments to the Constitution forbidding congress from making any law 'respecting an establishment of religion, or prohibiting the free exercise thereof'. Thus in parts of the world influenced by theories of natural RIGHTS, religious toleration was beginning to be replaced by more progressive notions of religious equality.

H. M. Scott (ed.), *Enlightened Absolutism* (London: Macmillan, 1990).
J. M. Black, *Eighteenth Century Europe 1700–1789* (London: Macmillan, 1990).

DAVID HEMPTON

republicanism   The terms 'republic' and 'republican' were freely used in the eighteenth century to describe not only kingless states (the republics of Venice, Genoa and Lucca, the Swiss cantons, the Dutch United Provinces) but also certain monarchies whose parliamentary constitutions appeared to make government the common business (*res publica*) of all patriotic citizens (Britain, Sweden, Poland). In practice, republican rule was often oligarchical, faction-ridden and corrupt, and several of the states subject to it were in obvious decline. Yet its very survival as a working system – combined with its classical and Renaissance pedigree – gave it continuing vitality as a theme in Western thought. In portraying Britain's independent landed gentry as upholders of republican virtue against the moneyed interest of the court, 'country party' publicists drew on Machiavelli's (1469–1527) republicanism as well as that of seventeenth-century writers like Harrington (1611–77). The same tradition, enriched by MONTESQUIEU's critique of the Graeco-Roman republics and praise of modern Britain, also influenced the federalist founders of the United States. It was North America's successful 'experiment of an extended republic', more than the patriotic egalitarianism of Rousseau and the French Revolution, that gave republicanism a new lease of life and helped to spread the tradition to Latin America.

J. G. A. Pocock, *The Machiavellian Moment: Florentine Political Thought and the Atlantic Republican Tradition* (Princeton, NJ: Princeton University Press, 1975).
J. N. Shklar, 'Montesquieu and the New Republicanism', in G. Bock et al. (eds), *Machiavelli and Republicanism* (Cambridge: Cambridge University Press, 1990), pp. 265–79.

HUGH DUNTHORNE

Restif [Rétif] de la Bretonne, Nicolas Edme (1734–1806) French writer. His precocity first manifested itself when, as a printer's apprentice, he seduced his boss's wife. In 1755 he moved from his native Sacy to Paris where he joined the royal printers, and began the life of libertinism that was later to make him notorious. At 23 he published his first novel and the ease with which it had been written made him decide on writing as his *métier*. He made his name with *Le Pied de Fanchette* (1769), and capitalizing on it he published his views on prostitution, the law, government, theatre and language. The success that *Le Paysan perverti* (1775) met with made him a celebrity, swelled his vanity as well as his pocket and earned him the name 'Rousseau des halles'. *Les Contemporaines* (1780–5), which aroused controversy with its indecent passages, presented a vivid picture of a society in decay. For a time he was the darling of the *salon* world, but the Revolution plunged him into obscurity and poverty. Even the publication of his memoirs in 1794 failed to rescue him. Eventually, and ironically, he was offered work at the ministry of police. Ill-health soon forced his retirement but he lived to see his massive corpus ridiculed and brushed aside.

M. L. BENJAMIN

revolution The FRENCH REVOLUTION has had an enormous impact on subsequent ideas about revolution, and is often credited with inventing the term, particularly as denoting a radical break with the past accompanied by a thoroughgoing social transformation.

The term 'revolution' was in use before 1789. Its primary sense was the broadly astronomical one of a cyclical return to a former state or point of departure. Dictionaries also reported usage of the term as denoting abrupt changes in human affairs, startling, unpredictable and often regrettable vicissitudes of fortune. From here it developed a political dimension, in the sense of striking changes in the political order of a state. As such the plural form was usually used: Joseph d'Orléans's *Histoire des révolutions d'Angleterre depuis le commencement de la monarchie jusqu'à présent* (History of the Revolutions of England from the Beginnings of the Monarchy to the Present Day, 1693) is an early example. From mid-century the word came to be used in the singular, with a strong cultural or socio-cultural flavour: Voltaire contrasted the pettiness of political revolutions with the revolution in the human mind, the cultural transformation springing out of the profound change in civil society through which his contemporaries were living. Symptomatically, Mercier saw the emergence of public opinion as a political force as constituting 'a great and important revolution in our ideas'. The English 'Glorious Revolution' and the American Revolution broadened the context in which the term was used; but, although 1688 was seen as a revolution in the singular, it was conceptualized in terms of a constitutional restoration to a *status quo ante* rather than as a breakthrough to a new constitutional state, while the American Revolution, although it was welcomed as a harbinger of a happy change in human affairs, was viewed as essentially foreign to the European experience (*see* AMERICAN WAR OF INDEPENDENCE).

What was added to the term from 1789 was, first, a sense of the specificity and grandeur of the French experience: 'revolutions' became '*the* Revolution', whose importance for the whole of humanity was soon taken for granted. Secondly, there was a greater sense of human agency: revolution was no longer passive and restitutive ('revolutions' in the broadly astronomical sense) or invisible (in the cultural transformation sense), but was rather the result of the intentional acts of groups of men. Thirdly, revolution opened up a sphere of social and political transformation which aimed totally to recast society and polity and mark a complete break with what had gone before: thus the term *ancien régime* was created at the same time as 'revolution' was invested with its new meaning. Finally, as Keith Baker has pointed out, once the meaning of 'revolution' had become stabilized in this way, a domain of transformative activity was opened up, a kind of historic present of lived experience with its own dynamic and chronology. So, too, the revolutionaries came up against the more difficult question of how a revolution could be ended.

See also INDUSTRIAL REVOLUTION, SCIENTIFIC REVOLUTION.

Keith M. Baker, *Inventing the French Revolution: Essays on French Political Culture in the Eighteenth Century* (Cambridge: Cambridge University Press, 1990).

Mona Ozouf, 'Revolution', in F. Furet and M. Ozouf (eds), *A Critical Dictionary of the French Revolution* (Cambridge, Mass.: Harvard University Press, 1989), pp. 806–17.

COLIN JONES

Reynolds, Sir Joshua (1723–1792) English painter. The foremost portraitist of his day, he dominated the visual arts in England for almost forty years. He studied in Italy and France and rapidly established his pre-eminence in London after his return in 1753. He did more than anyone to raise the status of the artist to a new level of respectability in England. He was instrumental in the founding of the ROYAL ACADEMY, of which he was the first president, and was knighted in 1769. He also gained a reputation as a man of letters and, unlike Hogarth, moved easily in the circles of the rich and powerful.

Professionally, he faced the dilemma that history painting was considered the most intellectually exacting, and respectable, form of painting at a time when no one in England wanted to buy it. Despite his artistic integrity and his admiration for Michelangelo, he had to make a living primarily as a portraitist (*see* PORTRAIT PAINTING). Many of his works, however, were workshop pieces, produced largely by assistants. The best of his portraits – his self-portraits and that of Giuseppe Baretti – contain a psychological insight into the sitter previously unknown in English art. His *Discourses*, which were delivered to the Royal Academy, became one of the prime textbooks of English aesthetic theory for nearly a century.

Nicholas Penny (ed.), *Reynolds* (London: Tate Gallery, 1986).

IAIN PEARS

rice Originally from the borders of India, Burma and China, rice was probably first domesticated in south-east Asia. Adaptation to semi-aquatic cultivation increased yields and it became the staple food of southern east Asia, spreading to Europe, Africa and the Americas.

China developed high-yielding strains, including a variety maturing in forty days cultivated in Hunan province in the eighteenth century which contributed to a substantial increase in the population in that period. In rice-growing areas like the economically dominant Yangtze delta, large landholdings were rare and smallholder or tenant cultivation was the norm. The economy of imperial China depended heavily on the transport of rice to the north via the Grand Canal. Bureaucratic inefficiency and corruption led to silting, and in 1826 there was an attempt to bypass this by using coastal junks.

In Japan the rural poor ate mixed grains, and a diet of rice alone was restricted to the ruling samurai. Rice served as a form of currency and by the eighteenth century markets in Osaka and Edo were dealing in rice futures.

Joseph Needham, *Science and Civilisation in China*, vol. 6, pt 2: *Agriculture*, by Francesca Bray (Cambridge: Cambridge University Press, 1984).

MICHAEL DILLON

Richardson, Samuel (1689–1761) English printer, man of letters and novelist. Derbyshire-born and intended for the church, Richardson instead rose to prominence as a London printer, bringing out the *Journals* of the House of Commons. Always a pious and moralizing man, his early writings were works of self-improvement directed to the young. He won lasting fame for three novels, *Pamela* (1740), *Clarissa* (1747–8) and *Sir Charles Grandison* (1753–4), all epistolary in form. The tale of a servant girl who won her master's hand by preserving her virtue, *Pamela* was widely mocked, notably in Fielding's *Shamela* (1741), but it proved influential in creating the genre of the domestic problem novel. In dramatizing the conflicts of female sexuality and sensibility in a world of domineering families and predatory males, *Clarissa* created a remarkable tragic heroine. Overall Richardson is noteworthy for his precocious recognition of the appropriateness of the novel form for portraying inner female conflicts.

E. Bergen Brophy, *Samuel Richardson* (Boston, Mass.: Twayne, 1987).

ROY PORTER

Richerism The set of beliefs propounded by Edmond Richer (1559–1631), syndic of the faculty of theology in the University of Paris, was known as Richerism. His ideas were contained in two books, *De Ecclesiasticae et politica potestate libellus* (1611) and *Demonstratio libelli de ecclesiastica et politica potestate* (1622). He gave special emphasis in his writings to the role of the lower CLERGY, particularly the *curés*, in the government of the church. During the eighteenth century this democratic tone attracted a number of *curés* who were embroiled in the Jansenist controversy, and stiffened their opposition to their episcopal superiors (*see* JANSENISM). Richerism also contributed to informing the attitude of the lower clergy in the early days of the French Revolution.

Pierre Goubert, *Louis XIV and Twenty Million Frenchmen*, trans. Anne Carter (Harmondsworth: Penguin, 1970).

J. H. SHENNAN

rights The eighteenth century closed with a proliferation of assertions of the rights of men and women, not only in France, where in
1789 the DECLARATION OF THE RIGHTS OF MAN AND THE CITIZEN had been
published, but also throughout Europe and its colonies. The Declaration
attributed all social ills and political corruption to the neglect or violation of the natural rights of man, and maintained that such inalienable and sacred rights should be solemnly proclaimed. They included
the rights to liberty, property, security, resistance to oppression and
freedom of expression.

The language of rights, which was based on the natural rights theories of the seventeenth century, gradually became one of the most
commonly used of political languages. It was the language of the
replies to Burke's *Reflections on the Revolution in France*, for example
Paine's *The Rights of Man* and Wollstonecraft's *Vindication of the
Rights of Man*. It was also the language which feminists of the period
seemed to draw on, for example Olympe de Gouges in *Les Droits de
la femme et de la citoyenne* (1791) and Wollstonecraft in *A Vindication
of the Rights of Woman* (1792). More often than not, however, the
language of rights was mixed, in those debates, with that of public
utility. The theory of rights found radically different advocates in the
persons of Kant and Hegel.

Immanuel Kant, *Political Writings,* ed. Hans Reiss (Cambridge: Cambridge
University Press, 1990).

SYLVANA TOMASELLI

roads The eighteenth century witnessed the first road-building programmes since the Roman period, but the vast majority of roads remained mule trails or vacant ribbons of land between fields. Road
transport was preferred to water for short or urgent journeys and
where a high value-to-volume ratio could sustain the greater cost.

In 1716 the French government established the Corps des Ponts et
Chaussées. Its engineers rebuilt over 12,000 miles of highway, achieving a firm surface through good drainage and graded-stone construction. With routes determined more by political and military than
commercial goals, it is hardly surprising that many remained empty –
a fate shared by General Wade's (1673–1748) military roads in
Scotland and other state-funded projects.

In England the mounting pressure of traffic on major routes prompted
private turnpike trusts to assume the parishes' responsibility for road
maintenance, levying a toll on users. By 1770 15,000 miles had been
turnpiked: most were kept in good repair. Journey times shrank, stage-
coaches ran throughout the year and the legal maximum tonnage of
freight doubled (assisted by improved vehicle design, stronger horses
and better organization).

Charles Singer et al. (eds), *A History of Technology*, vol. 4 (Oxford: Clarendon, 1958).

CHRISTINE MACLEOD

Robertson, William (1721–1793)   Scottish historian. One of the most admired historians of the Scottish Enlightenment, he was often cited by Gibbon as an example of a philosophical historian who was not a religious sceptic. He was a minister of the Church of Scotland, a noted ecclesiastical politician and principal of Edinburgh University (1762–93). His *History of Scotland* (1759) was read as a polite cleric's reply to Hume's sceptical account of the Reformation. His *History of the Reign of Charles V* (1764) provided an account of the origins of the modern state system and established him as a philosophical historian of the first rank. His *History of America* (1776) provided a classic account of a pagan, savage society on the eve of colonization. His *Historical Disquisition concerning . . . India* (1791) demonstrated his lifelong interest in the natural history of religion.

He was admired by contemporaries for his mastery of narrative, for his Plutarchian eye for characterization and for using the history of civilization to illuminate the truths of natural theology. More recently, he has been seen as an intelligent if scarcely original exponent of the 'conjectural history' of the Scottish Enlightenment, but a modern re-appraisal is needed.

R. Sher, *Church and University in the Scottish Enlightenment* (Edinburgh: Edinburgh University Press, 1985).

NICHOLAS PHILLIPSON

Robespierre, Maximilien Marie Isidore de (1758–1794)   French revolutionary. The most vilified of the leading politicians of the revolutionary era, he was, prior to 1789, a small-time lawyer from Arras, which he represented in the Estates General. In the Constituent Assembly his unswervingly democratic, Jacobin views gained him the title 'the Incorruptible'. He was a key member of the Commune at the time of Louis XVI's overthrow, and was elected to the Convention by Paris. He fell out with the Girondins over the political role of Parisian SANS-CULOTTES, the king's trial and the establishment of the institutions of the Terror, and supported the Girondins' expulsion in May–June 1793. Elected to the COMMITTEE OF PUBLIC SAFETY in July 1793, he played a general role in determining and presenting policy, and was particularly associated with religious policies. His fear that the Revolution was being subverted by a 'foreign plot' led him to support purges of Dantonist and Hébertist factions and the acceleration of the TERROR. His apparent wish for further purges brought his enemies together in the successful THERMIDOR *coup* which led to his execution.

N. Hampson, *The Life and Opinions of Maximilien Robespierre* (London: Duckworth, 1974).

COLIN JONES

robot The term *robot*, derived from the Czech *robota* ('work'), was used throughout the Austrian Habsburg lands from at least the 1550s to denote peasant labour services. Their extent varied enormously, from a few days per year to several days per week, especially in Bohemia, Moravia and Hungary. *Robot* provided a means of working the extensive seigneurial demesnes so that the chief costs were borne by the peasant rather than by the landlord. The larger the peasant holding the greater were the services usually demanded, so that very large holdings may have had to keep (or employ) more than one plough team to discharge their obligations, whereas smallholders may have been asked to work just half a day a week. Demands tended to be higher in the spring and summer than in the autumn. *Robot* could be commuted for cash but, in general, was regarded as indispensable to the economic survival of the landowning classes. Joseph II's attempts at limited abolition of *robot* in 1789 provoked uproar among the nobility, threatening the Habsburg monarchy with widespread revolt and even political disintegration. Similar labour services under different names were the rule wherever SERFDOM prevailed.

See also CORVÉE, SEIGNEURIALISM.

J. Blum, *The End of the Old Order in Rural Europe* (Princeton, NJ: Princeton University Press, 1978).

J. T. LUKOWSKI

rococo A style of French origin that held sway for much of the first half of the eighteenth century, rococo derived its name from a pejorative term coined long after the style had gone out of favour, *rocaille*, or rock-work, stressing the use of elaborate, often asymmetrical, curves in much of the interior decoration of the period. In all the arts the rococo style was a reaction against the formal classicism that held sway under Louis XIV. The style was developing early in the century, and one of the earliest full examples was the interior of the Chapel of Versailles by Pierre Le Pautre (*c.*1648–1716), finished in 1716, a year after Louis's death. The declining importance of Versailles under the Regency and the consequent refurbishment of Paris town houses, gave rise to a burst of interior design along more intimate and domestic lines, for example by Germain Boffrand (1667–1754) at the Hôtel Soubise, Paris (1738). From there the style spread to porcelain, silver and furniture in the sinuous forms known as the Louis XV style. In architecture the rococo found its most complete expression in light and fanciful works such as Héré's (1705–63) Place de la Carrière in Nancy (1753).

For all its convenience, however, the term is apt to be misused. Rococo was far from being a universal phenomenon and its application as a general term for art produced in the first half of the eighteenth century – in music, for example – can be more confusing than enlightening. While painters like WATTEAU and BOUCHER can be called rococo artists, others, like Tiepolo and Hogarth, produced works in which rococo themes were only one of many elements. Rococo made little direct impact in England and was only partly adopted in Italy. Outside France it had its greatest influence in Germany, where architects like Zimmermann (1685–1766) and Neumann (1687–1753), and porcelain manufacturers like Meissen, evolved a distinctly regional and elaborate version of the style.

It is also possible to overstress the distinction between rococo and later artistic styles. Rococo came increasingly under attack after the 1740s by theorists like Diderot and Winckelmann. Its emphasis on the elaborate and the attractive for its own sake incurred the disapproval of the developing school of neoclassical theorists who advocated a return to a purified form of the grand style of Louis XIV. Both styles were wedded to a form of naturalism, even though they differed over what this should be. Some parts of Europe – Spain, Portugal and Venice ware the main examples – were immune to the strictures of neoclassicism and produced works in the rococo style up to almost the end of the century.

Germain Bazin, *Baroque and Rococo* (London: Thames & Hudson, 1964).
A. Blunt (ed.), *Baroque and Rococo* (London: Granada, 1978).

                                                                    IAIN PEARS

romanticism   Mercier's comment in his *Neology or Vocabulary of New Words* (1801) about the term 'romantic' – 'you can feel it but you cannot define it' – aptly conveys the caution with which historians currently approach the term 'romanticism'. If there is a consensus as to what romanticism signifies it is that it cannot be defined as a unified, pan-European movement bound by time and space. But there are central themes associated with romanticism that can be discerned by considering the profound shifts in literary sensibility, scientific epistemology, political ideology and aesthetic value that began in specific countries towards the end of the eighteenth century. These include an extreme assertion of the self and of the authenticity of individual experience, a preoccupation with the creative imagination and a search for harmony between man and nature.

The emergence of romanticism from the demise of the old order was violently symbolized by the revolutions in America and France, and by the wars of independence in Spain, Greece and Poland, which represented the triumph of liberty over arbitrary power (*see* REVOLUTION). Conservative romantics shared with their radical peers a disillusionment with the established social order as epitomized by the academies which they identified with convention and decay. Both rebelled against the tyranny of reason and classicism, seeing Western Enlightenment traditions as narrow and limited. Although few romantics directly championed the causes of oppressed peoples everywhere as Shelley (1792–1822) did, many advocated a multiculturalism which recognized the shortcomings of colonialism.

The desire to embrace diversity and challenge existing authority found expression in a fascination with the past. The impetus to mine the past for its ancient wisdom and mythologies came from various quarters: the Gothic traditions popularized by Horace Walpole, 'Monk' Lewis (1775–1818) and Ann Radcliffe (1764–1823); the primitivism of Rousseau which found a literary incarnation in the poetry of Macpherson, Chatterton and Gray; the renewed interest in folklore that made a classic of Thomas Percy's (1729–1811) *Reliques of Ancient English Poetry* (1765) and became a lifelong enterprise for the brothers Grimm. The drive towards greater self-understanding inspired new genres in history – institutional history, local history and the history of language – which in turn fed an interest in origins which found its most passionate expression in the myths of creation and re-creation that became central to romanticism – Faust, Prometheus and Frankenstein. The nostalgic harking back to former ages of glory was dignified by its appeal to the sublime and ennobled by the heroism popularized in the epics of Sir Walter Scott (1771–1832).

In their disillusionment with a corrupt modern society that had debased humanity with its materialist values and severed mankind's link with nature, romantic thinkers self-consciously positioned themselves as outcasts, wanderers and exiles. Rousseau's belief in man's quest for virtue through communion with NATURE was echoed in the nature poetry of William Cowper (1731–1800) and Wordsworth, and in the *Naturphilosophie* of Schelling (1775–1854) and Hegel. The wild, the natural and the organic took on spiritual significance, while the SUBLIME, the infinite and the transcendental took on moral significance. A more despairing outsider perspective was developed in STURM UND DRANG literature. In Goethe's *Leiden des jungen Werthers* the hero's feelings of alienation led to his tragic suicide. While Chatterton and Kleist sought escape from the world through suicide, others nurtured their feelings of solitariness and alienation: Wordsworth 'wandered lonely as a cloud', Byron lived in self-imposed exile, Coleridge and De Quincey (1785–1859) lost themselves in a haze of opium. In a more optimistic vein travel writings proliferated as romantics looked abroad for inspiration. The foreign, and particularly the Orient, was regarded as exotic, and where travel was impossible, fantasy substituted; every good romantic journeyed to Samarra and Xanadu.

Romanticism rebelled against the neoclassical values of the Enlightenment, challenging the supremacy of reason as the foundation of knowledge and the authority of society over that of the individual. Science, the handmaid of reason, came in for particular criticism: Keats (1795–1821) complained that reductive Newtonian science demystified the rainbow, while Blake's 'dark, Satanic mills' were an apocalyptic vision of the industrial revolution. At the same time, the irrational attained prominence on the cultural agenda as witnessed by the reification of terror, mystery and the sublime in Gothic literature, ghost stories and tales of the living dead. There was a burgeoning of mystical cults such as Swedenborgianism, Rosicrucianism and Freemasonry, as well as subjective sciences such as mesmerism, electrotherapy and physiognomy, and an insistence on the unfathomable nature of human genius. Romanticism generated a cultural climate in which feelings, dreams and imagination had authority and validity. It sanctioned the pursuit of INDIVIDUALISM by promoting the view that an understanding of the world began with self-understanding, and it valued insight over external observation. The introspective and egotistical poetry of Wordsworth, culminating in *The Prelude*, as well as the autobiographical and confessional prose of De Quincey, Hazlitt (1778–1830) and Lamb (1775–1834) captured the mood of self-reflection. The creative IMAGINATION had never stood in such high regard. Shelley's view, in his *Defence of Poetry* (1840), that the exercise of the imagination qualified poets to be the 'unacknowledged legislators of the world', was shared by Coleridge whose 'clerisy' consisted of poets, writers and critics.

M. H. Abrams, *The Mirror and the Lamp: Romantic Theory and the Critical Tradition* (Oxford: Oxford University Press, 1953).
J. J. McGann, *The Romantic Ideology: A Critical Investigation* (Chicago: University of Chicago Press, 1983).
Roy Porter and Mikuláš Teich (eds), *Romanticism in National Context* (Cambridge: Cambridge University Press, 1988).
Andrew Cunningham and Nicholas Jardine (eds), *Romanticism and the Sciences* (Cambridge: Cambridge University Press, 1990).

M. L. BENJAMIN

Rosicrucianism   The term 'Rosicrucianism', which is derived from the Latin *rosa* (rose) and *crux* (cross), refers to an enigmatic brotherhood supposed to have been founded by a certain Christian Rosenkreutz, and based on the veneration of the rose and the cross as symbols of Christ's resurrection and redemption. The real founder is believed to have been Johann Valentin Andreae (1586–1654), a Lutheran theologian who produced the spoof manifestos *Fama Fraternitatis* (Rumour of the Fraternity, 1614) and *Confessio Fraternitatis* (Confession of the Fraternity, 1615), which heralded the appearance of the Brotherhood of the Rosy Cross. Ensuing searches for the Rosicrucians turned out to be a false trail, their existence a hoax and their name a metonymy for enthusiasm. More tangible was their literary influence, for example in abbé de Montfaucon de Villars's (1635–73) *Le Comte de Gabalis* (1680) and the Rosicrucian machinery of Pope's *The Rape of the Lock* (1714). As an identifiable way of thinking, Rosicrucianism is related to hermetic traditions, and eventually gave rise to a number of alchemical and Masonic societies. The original Rosicrucians, who were reputed to possess the philosopher's stone, were also known as the 'Immortals' and the 'Invisibles'. Their alleged invisibility tended to be confirmed by the fact that no one had ever caught sight of a member of this elusive brotherhood.

See SECRET SOCIETIES.

Frances Yates, *The Rosicrucian Enlightenment* (London: Routledge & Kegan Paul, 1972).

MARIE MULVEY ROBERTS

Rossbach, Battle of (5 November 1757) The Battle of Rossbach, fought near Merseburg in Saxony, was one of the most complete of the victories of FREDERICK II. In it a Prussian army of 22,000 completely defeated 36,000 French soldiers commanded by the prince de Soubise (1715–87) and a badly trained and poorly disciplined composite force of 12,000 raised by the small states of south-west Germany to support the empress Maria Theresa against Frederick. The battle was decided by a Prussian surprise attack while the allies were on the march in an attempt to turn Frederick's flank and cut his communications. In the short and one-sided struggle (it lasted less than two hours and the allies lost in all about 8,000 men against only about 550 on the Prussian side) the Prussian cavalry under General von Seydlitz (1721–73) particularly distinguished itself. The humiliating defeat helped to produce in France feeling in favour of drastic military reform, which bore considerable fruit in the decades before the Revolution.

R. Waddington, *La Guerre de Sept Ans*, vol. 1 (Paris: Firmin-Didot, 1899), ch. 11.

M. S. ANDERSON

Roubiliac [Roubillac], Louis François (*c*.1702–1762) English sculptor of French birth. He is said to have been apprenticed to Balthazar Permoser (1651–1732) in Dresden and to have worked in the Paris studio of Nicolas Coustou (1652–1733). By 1730 he was in London where his remarkably lively and informal marble statue of *Handel* (Victoria and Albert Museum, London) attracted considerable attention when it was erected in Vauxhall Gardens in 1738. He rapidly established himself as the most accomplished sculptor working in England in the mid eighteenth century. His dramatic funerary monuments, characterful portrait busts and his brilliant handling of terracotta and marble were an important contribution to the development of the English ROCOCO style. His early busts include portraits of many of the literary and artistic figures who frequented Slaughter's coffee-house. Among them are *Pope* (City Art Gallery, Leeds) and *Hogarth* (National Portrait Gallery, London). His first major funerary monument was that to *John Campbell, second Duke of Argyll* (1745–9) in Westminster Abbey, which introduced to England many of the formal and dramatic ideas current in European tomb sculpture. His most admired monument is that to *Joseph and Lady Elizabeth Nightingale* (1758–61), also in Westminster Abbey. In this he adopted a number of devices he had seen in the work of Gianlorenzo Bernini (1598–1680) during a trip to Rome in 1752. They are, however, transformed by a pathos that is his own: Lady Elizabeth's husband tries vainly to protect her from the spear of the skeletal figure of Death which emerges from a vault within the tomb. Among his later portraits are a classicizing bust of *Lord Chesterfield* (1755; National Portrait Gallery, London) and posthumous marble statues of *Newton* (1754–5; Trinity College, Cambridge) and *Shakespeare* (1757–8; British Museum, London).

K. A. Esdaile, *L. F. Roubiliac* (Oxford: Oxford University Press, 1928).
M. Whinney, *Sculpture in Britain, 1530–1830*, rev. edn (Harmondsworth: Penguin, 1988), pp. 198–226.

MARC JORDAN

Rousseau, Jean-Jacques (1712–1778)   Genevan political thinker and man of letters. His writings constitute one of the powerful critiques of CIVILIZATION. Following the death of his mother at his birth, he was brought up by various relations, and later apprenticed to an engraver from whom he ran away in 1728. He converted to Catholicism and became the lover and *protégé* of Madame de Warrens, who encouraged him to study. Although Rousseau took pride in presenting himself as an independent man, this was the first of a series of client–patron relations most of which ended acrimoniously.

At the age of 30 he set off for Paris in quest of fortune and fame. Welcomed in various *salons*, he soon became acquainted with most of the *philosophes*, including Diderot, to whom he was to be especially close for some years. Rousseau tried to earn a living giving music lessons and wrote a *Dissertation sur la musique moderne*. After a spell in Venice where he was attached to the French Embassy, he returned to Paris. While he seemed never to have been entirely satisfied with his opera *Les Muses galantes*, his next major musical endeavour, *Le Devin du village*, was very well received when it was performed before the king and his court in 1752. With his *Lettre sur la musique française*, Rousseau partook in the *querelle des bouffons*, siding with those who argued that Italian opera was naturally superior to French opera, as Italian was a melodious language whereas French was a harsh and nasal tongue. He also contributed a number of articles on musical subjects to the *Encyclopédie*.

But Rousseau had already secured his fame outside the world of composition and musical theory, by winning the Academy of Dijon essay competition with his *Discours sur les sciences et les arts* (1750). His attack on civilization had begun. NATURE was the measure of all things for Rousseau. Central to his thought, therefore, were such dichotomies as between nature and society, the natural and the artificial, and being and appearing. These concepts acquire their meaning in his writings through a history of society, tracing the latter's development from the state of nature to modernity. Such a history reveals the ever-increasing number of man's material and affective needs. In trying to secure these, men alienate themselves from nature, their true selves and each other. Perfectibility, which is a potential in natural man, prompted the advent of the arts and sciences, of society and its attendant, inequality. Thus the *Discours sur l'origine de l'inégalité* (1755) reads not so much as an account of human potentiality as a history of human corruption and fall.

Du contrat social (1762), Rousseau's treatise on liberty, developed the notion of the general will and afforded a model for the theoretical prevention, rather than the cure, of existing social ills. At the level of the individual, it is to *Émile, ou, De l'éducation* (1762) that we must turn for Rousseau's proposed remedy for mankind's psychological troubles. Here again, the 'natural' holds the key to human felicity. Hence, swaddling was condemned and mothers were admonished for sending their children to wet-nurses. The body of the work outlined a 'natural' education for Émile while his future wife, Sophie, was to be subjected to what amounted to an impoverished version of conventional female upbringing. Further insight into his views about marriage and love can be gained from his novel *La Nouvelle Héloïse* (1761), which was partly based on his platonic love for a married woman, Madame d'Houdetot.

As a result of his lifelong quest for his true self, Rousseau wrote a number of biographical texts, including *Confessions, Rousseau juge de*

Jean-Jacques and *Rêveries*. He sought to distance himself from the *philosophes* and to vindicate some of his morally most offensive actions, such as orphaning his children.

Maurice Cranston, *Jean-Jacques: The Early Life and Work of Jean-Jacques Rousseau 1712–1754* (London: Allen Lane, 1983).
Maurice Cranston, *The Noble Savage: Jean-Jacques Rousseau (1754–1762)* (London: Allen Lane, 1991).

SYLVANA TOMASELLI

Rowlandson, Thomas (1756–1827)   English caricaturist. After training as an artist in London and Paris he sought to establish himself as a portrait painter, but financial embarrassments caused by gambling induced him to turn to the illustration of books and the production of satirical prints and watercolours. His fluent and vigorous style, bawdy humour and keen eye for the follies of humanity fitted him for the craft of the caricaturist. He exposed conventional hypocrisy, political ineptitude and the absurdities of contemporary society with a sure command of his idiom. Often modelling his work on the example of other artists, he depicted the turmoil and tumult of seaports, race meetings, cock-fights, the gaming-table, the pleasure gardens and even the university, with vitality and honesty. The dissipations of youth and the foibles of age inspired his brush and pen. While his work has done much to enhance understanding of the social life of his time, he was, as an artist, as much concerned with the production of accomplished pieces of art as with scathing and amusing satire.

R. Paulson, *Rowlandson: A New Interpretation* (London: Studio Vista, 1972).

JOHN W. DERRY

Royal Academy of Arts   On 10 December 1768 George III agreed to give royal patronage to the first regular school of art in England. The Royal Academy of Arts expected from the outset that the teachers were to advise and instruct, while also cultivating taste. The first meeting of the general assembly of the originally nominated academicians was held on 14 December 1768, when officers, council and visitors (teachers) were elected. Three days later, appointments were made: Edward Penny (1714–91) became painting professor (1768–82), Samuel Wale (*d* 1786) professor of perspective (1768–86) and Dr William Hunter (1718–83) professor of anatomy (1768–83). The first president of the academy, REYNOLDS, heralded the dawn of the Royal Academy with his opening address on 2 January 1769, to visitors, students and the dilettante. Although there appears to have been no set period of studentship, it was usual for students to attend the academy for between six and seven years. Female artists such as foundation member Angelica Kauffmann (1741–1807) and Mary Moser (d 1819) were the exceptions rather than the rule at the academy.

S. Hutchison, *The History of the Royal Academy, 1768–1986* (London: Robert Royce, 1980).

ANNE DARLINGTON

Royal Society The Royal Society of London for the Promotion of Natural Knowledge was founded in 1660, and dedicated to BACONIANISM. It never consistently achieved its modern quality and leadership in science. Royal in name only, it lacked the funds and professionalism of the Parisian Académie des Sciences. It relied on voluntary contributions, both scientific and financial, from its amateur fellows, many of whom belonged for reasons of sociability and status.

NEWTON reversed an early decline, using his presidency to enforce competent, continuous and, of course, Newtonian scientific activities, such as the electrical researches of his paid assistant, Jean Desaguliers (1683–1744). Its reputation in this period, together with Newton's own, and that of its journal, *Philosophical Transactions*, secured it the admiration of and collaboration from foreign SCIENTIFIC SOCIETIES that it did not have at home. In the 1740s it declined into a gentleman's club, but it was revived in the 1780s under the naturalist Joseph Banks.

Peripherally involved in state concerns, such as research into the measurement of longitude, its real power lay in the control of British science. It excluded radicals and tradesmen, and resisted the foundation of new societies.

Sir Henry Lyons, *The Royal Society, 1660–1940* (Cambridge: Cambridge University Press, 1944).

STEPHEN PUMFREY

ruins In the context of the PICTURESQUE garden, the classical or GOTHIC REVIVAL artificial ruin, like the hermitage or the grotto, was halfway between architecture and landscape, and allowed the viewer to shift between appreciation for the artifice and wilful suspension of historical common sense. The ambiguities ran deeper. 'Ruins' could be equated with 'antiquities' – witness the title of such key documents of neoclassicism as Robert Adam's *Ruins of the Palace of . . . Diocletian* (1764) – and antiquarianism, not antiquity, could determine the form of such magnificent fakes as the 'Roman Ruin' (1778) at Vienna's Schönbrunn Palace, which imitated not so much the originals as Piranesi's representations of them. Moreover, a structure ruined after completion was, arguably, indistinguishable from one that was never finished: the Temple to Modern Philosophy at Ermenonville, north of Paris (1770s) was not 'ruined' but 'incomplete'. The unfinished antique column in Athens drawn by James 'Athenian' Stuart (1713–88) inspired those on the primitivist Shepherd's Monument at Shugborough, Staffordshire (c.1758), which aroused delicately fearful speculation about the interruption of the ancient mason's work.

See also CULT OF ANTIQUITY.

Diana Balmori, 'Architecture, Landscape and the Intermediate Structure: Eighteenth-Century Experiments in Mediation', *Journal of the Society of Architectural Historians*, 50 (1991), 38–56.

CHRISTINE STEVENSON

Rumford, Thompson, Benjamin, Count (1753–1814) Anglo-American officer, gentleman and dilettante scientist. He divided his time between America, England and Bavaria. His zeal for municipal reform was matched only by his fondness for explosives. In 1799 he founded the Royal Institution in Albemarle Street.

W. J. Sparrow, *Knight of the White Eagel: A Biography of Sir Benjamin Thompson, Count Rumford* (London: Hutchinson, 1964).

M. L. BENJAMIN

Russia In the eighteenth century Russia became a European power. There were European dimensions to Russia's seventeenth-century diplomacy, but victory over Sweden at Poltava (1709) in the Great Northern War marked Russian ascendancy. In 1721 PETER I became emperor. Previously virtually landlocked, Russia gained territory on the Baltic by the Treaties of Nystadt (1721) and Åbo (1743), and on the Black Sea by the Treaties of Kuchuk-Kainardji (1774) and Jassy (1791), and incorporated much of Poland-Lithuania by the Partitions of 1772, 1793 and 1795. The exploitation of the population and natural resources for military ends largely determined government activity throughout the century.

The Russian monarchy was unlimited by representative institutions, although sovereigns such as Catherine II ruled in the spirit of ENLIGHTENED ABSOLUTISM. Court politics were coloured by Peter I's Law of Succession (1722) which required the reigning monarch to designate a successor. This gave scope for the promotion of factional interests and prompted numerous 'constitutional' crises: the death of Peter I and the accession of his wife CATHERINE I; the death of PETER II and the invitation to ANNA; the overthrow of Ivan VI (reigned 1740–1) by ELIZABETH and of PETER III by his wife CATHERINE II. Paul I (1754–1801; reigned 1796–1801) restored male primogeniture in 1797, but was himself assassinated. The sovereigns ruled as much through persons as through institutions, of which the senate (founded 1711) was the most resilient. The government 'colleges' ran the bureaucracy. Outside the capital, authority was thinly spread. The 1775 Provincial Statute rationalized local government, encouraging the nobles to participate more actively.

Eighteenth-century Russia was a service state, in which subjects belonged to hereditary 'estates' with associated obligations and, occasionally, privileges. Under Peter I, the nobility (*dvorianstvo*) served for life. Promotion was regularized by the TABLE OF RANKS, which also provided for ennoblement of talented commoners. After Peter's death the nobles won concessions, for example in 1736 service was reduced to twenty-five years. The 1762 Manifesto of Freedom removed the service requirement altogether, but many nobles continued to serve for salary and honours. The Charter to the Nobility (1785) ratified freedom from service, corporal punishment, dishonour and taxation, and gave guarantees on ownership and exploitation of property. But the persecution of the nobility by Paul showed that even the elite were subject to the sovereign's arbitrary power. Assassination rather than the law remained their last resort.

The nobles' crucial privilege was the ownership of peasants, although only 16 per cent of them owned more than 100 serfs. Landlords wielded almost unlimited power over their serfs. There were restrictions on open sale and purchase for factories and reiteration of the Sunday rest rule (1797), but central authority preferred not to intervene. Serfs in fertile 'black-soil' regions mainly performed labour service (*barshchina*), on poorer soils they paid quit-rent (*obrok*). State peasants, comprising about 50 per cent of the peasant population, were better off, but could be conscripted on to state projects and, like serfs, into the army. All peasants paid the poll tax (1724). But there were huge local variations in living standards and it would be wrong to think that Russian peasants were uniformly worse off than their European counterparts. Revolt – from local riots to massive outbreaks like the PUGACHEV rebellion – provided a safety valve.

Russia's economy and culture were overwhelmingly rural, with subsistence agriculture predominating. Peasants constituted about 90 per cent of the total population, which rose from about 15 million in 1725 to more than 37 million (including about 7 million on new territories) by the end of the century. About 3 per cent lived in towns at the beginning of the century, and little more than 4 per cent by the end. The urban middle class was tiny, although there were substantial merchant communities, and even dynasties, such as the Demidovs and Stroganovs. The Charter to the Towns (1785) sought to promote urban institutions and enterprise. Manufacturing and mining increased greatly in Peter I's reign, notably in the Urals, making Russia the world's leading iron producer by mid-century, but most enterprises were state-run, based on the bound labour of 'possessional' serfs. Flax and hemp were exported and, increasingly by the end of the century, grain.

The Orthodox clergy, both married parish priests and monks, formed a sizeable category. The church, although weakened by the Old Believer schism (*see* OLD BELIEVERS), had dominated culture and morals, but under Peter I its status changed dramatically. When the patriarch died in 1700 he was not replaced, and in 1721 the office was abolished and administration passed to the Holy Synod. In 1762–4 about 2 million serfs on church and monastery lands were secularized. The clergy became state employees who served like everyone else.

For the arts this was an age of apprenticeship and Westernization, led from the new capital, ST PETERSBURG. Before Peter I culture was overwhelmingly religious; thereafter Russia produced its own variants of the styles of the age – Petrine and Elizabethan baroque, and classicism under Catherine II. Russian architects and painters worked alongside foreigners – Kazakov (1738–1812), Bazhenov (1738–99), Starov (1743–1808), Rokotov (1730–1810), Levitskii (1735–1822), Borovikovskii (1757–1825), Trezzini (1670–1734), Rastrelli (1700–71), Quarenghi (1744–1817), Cameron (*c.*1740–1812). National literature developed, along with a literary language, only in the second half of the century, under the influence of poet and scientist Mikhail Lomonosov (1711–66). The poetry of Derzhavin (1743–1816), prose of Karamzin (1765–1826), journalism of Novikov (1744–1816) and Chulkov (1743–92), plays of Fonvizin (1745–92) and Sumarokov (1717–77) were popular with contemporaries, but their work is virtually unknown outside Russia. The Moscow Academy (founded 1687) was seventeenth-century Russia's only school. Peter forced education on his nobles, but attempts to establish a national network (the 'cipher' schools of 1714) soon collapsed. The Academy of Sciences, whose first professors were all Germans, was founded in 1724, Moscow University in 1755, the Academy of Arts in 1757, but Catherine's 1786 National Schools Statute was the first systematic attempt to extend secondary education to the provinces. Despite these shortcomings, the eighteenth century saw the birth of the Russian intelligentsia, nurtured on the ideas of the Enlightenment and a race apart from the mass of the population.

Paul Dukes, *The Making of Russian Absolutism 1613–1801*, second edn (London: Longman, 1990).

M. Raeff, 'Imperial Russia', in R. Auty and D. Obolensky (eds), *An Introduction to Russian History* (Cambridge: Cambridge University Press, 1976), pp. 121–95.

LINDSEY HUGHES

Ryswick, Treaty of (20 September 1697) Mediated by Sweden under an innovatory protocol, the Treaty of Ryswick was signed at Ryswick in south Zeeland by France, the Dutch, Britain and Spain. While it brought the Nine Years War, or the War of the League of Augsburg, to an end, it was only reluctantly endorsed by Austria on 30 October because the emperor Leopold I did not want to see Austria's allies disarm with the Spanish succession issue still outstanding. Among its more important terms was French recognition of Britain's Protestant succession, restoration to Spain by France of Luxemburg, Charleroi, Mons, Courtrai and Barcelona, French retention of Strasbourg and lower Alsace, and joint Dutch-Bavarian garrisoning of some Spanish Netherlands frontier towns. Especially fraught for the future was the article 4 stipulating that the Catholic religion was to be left undisturbed in all territories outside Alsace gained by France through its acquisitions policy, which it was now returning.

A. Legrelle, *Notes et documents sur la paix de Ryswick* (Lille: Desclée de Brouwer et Cie, 1894).

D. D. ALDRIDGE

S

Sade, Donatien Alphonse François, comte de [marquis de] (1740–1814)   French novelist and pornographer. Like Mesmer (1734–1815), he was a figure on the edge of the Enlightenment who gave his name to a philosophy, sadism. He had an unhappy education and a mixed career as a cavalry officer in the Seven Years War. His diplomat father insisted on an arranged marriage to which he was strongly opposed: the experience contributed to his aristocratic disdain for the mores of the pre-revolutionary French bourgeoisie. He deliberately spurned his wife's family to spend time with prostitutes and servant girls.

He spent long periods in prison between 1778 and 1790, and was again imprisoned during the French Revolution before being committed to a mental asylum. During these years he wrote his pornographic novels, notably, in 1791, *Justine*. In these he distilled a mechanical philosophy of a standard eighteenth-century kind but transferred it to the world of the orgy, group flagellation and collective sodomy. His philosophical point was that cruelty was the fundamental human activity, and was best observed in sexual conduct. Sade believed that the sciences of perversion and the worlds where they were acted out were the logical outcome of Enlightenment philosophy in its previous respectable forms.

Œuvre Complète de Marquis de Sade, ed. Annie Le Brun and Jean-Jacques Pauvert (Paris: Pauvert, 1986–7).

MICHAEL NEVE

St Petersburg   The capital of Russia from 1712 to 1728 and from 1732 to 1918, St Petersburg was renamed Petrograd in 1914 and Leningrad in 1924, only to return to its original name in 1991. PETER I founded the city on an island on the Neva delta in the Gulf of Finland, which had been captured from the Swedes, on 16 May 1703. The first buildings (Peter-Paul Fortress) were defensive, but after the victory at Poltava in 1709 Peter envisaged St Petersburg as his administrative capital, as it was more European in location and style than Moscow. The Cathedral of SS Peter and Paul housed the imperial mausoleum. Officials and foreign trade were relocated by imperial decree and masonry construction banned throughout Russia. Planning – the straight lines of Nevskii Prospekt and the grid plan of Vasil'evskii Island – reflected Peter's passion for regularity. The chief architect was the Swiss Italian Domenico Trezzini (1670–1734). By 1725 the population was around 40,000, growing to 180,000 by the 1760s. Tsarina Elizabeth added many baroque buildings, including Rastrelli's (1675–1744) Smol'nii Convent and Winter Palace, but the city's second architect was Catherine II, who commissioned the granite embankments and numerous public buildings in the classical style.

James Cracraft, *The Petrine Revolution in Russian Architecture* (Chicago: University of Chicago Press, 1988).

LINDSEY HUGHES

Saint-Simon, Louis de Rouvroy, duc de (1675–1755) French writer and courtier. He spent a significant part of his life at the court of Versailles where he was inordinately proud of his membership of the French peerage whose interests he fiercely defended. He also held public office as an undistinguished member of the regency council (1715–23). The impression left by his long life would have been negligible but for his having been a writer of genius.

He bequeathed an unpublished collection of memoirs, the definitive edition of which (by A.de Boislisle, 1879–1928) runs to forty-one volumes. The memoirs provide a colourful and revealing picture of high life and politics in the closing years of Louis XIV's reign and during his successor's regency. It is not a dispassionate, measured account, for Saint-Simon preferred to explore the eccentricities of his dramatis personae, the excesses of their behaviour and the absurdities governing the human condition. He was himself an extraordinary personality, a highly moral man, narrowly preoccupied with his social status yet capable of maintaining a close friendship with the unconventional regent the duc d'Orléans, a notorious roué. His witty, compelling prose is one of the most enduring legacies of that febrile, cultivated age.

Historical Memoirs of the Duc de Saint-Simon, 3 vols, ed. and trans. Lucy Norton (London: Hamish Hamilton, 1967–8).

J. H. SHENNAN

salons In her *Histoire des Salons de Paris* (1836–8) Laure Permon, duchesse d'Abrantès (1735–1838) explained that the rise of the *salons* was the unintended consequence of Cardinal Richelieu's (1585–1642) policy of drawing the French nobility away from their provincial seats to surround the king at court. WOMEN, she explained, were quick to exploit the potentials that residing in the capital afforded them. Like the clubs of the French Revolution, the *salons* became places of political intrigue, where women wielded more power than they had ever known. After the Fronde, cabals gave way to literary coteries, and in time *salons* opened their doors to men of letters and artists, who found themselves received by, or mingling with, members of the aristocracy or of the *haute bourgeoisie*.

Famous eighteenth-century *salons* included those of Madame du Deffand (1697–1780) which Montesquieu attended; Mademoiselle de Lespinasse (1732–76) which D'Alembert, Turgot and Condorcet frequented after their hostess's break with Madame du Deffand; as well as Madame Necker's (1737–94) Friday dinners to which Diderot, Buffon and the abbé Raynal were invited.

Roger Picard, *Les Salons littéraires et la société française (1610–1789)* (New York: Brentano, 1943).

SYLVANA TOMASELLI

sans-culottes The epithet *sans-culotte* – literally, 'without knee-breeches', that is, an individual who wore straight workman's trousers rather than more genteel breeches – was at first used pejoratively by the Right in the French Revolution to describe popular radicals in Paris. The term became a badge of pride worn by individuals drawn from the *petite bourgeoisie* and labouring classes (petty clerks, shopkeepers, master artisans, journeymen and so on), who attended club meetings, engaged in sectional political activity (for example membership of revolutionary committees, hoarding committees), read radical newspapers and demonstrated in *journées* when necessary. A type of dress characterized the group: besides the trousers, a red bonnet (or Phrygian cap) was always *de rigueur*. They were at their most powerful in 1793–4, when they pushed the Convention to accept political, economic and religious TERROR as the prime instrument of revolutionary government. Their influence declined even before the Thermidor *coup* of 27 July 1794, which had the effect of further reducing their effectiveness and making them targets for vigilante action by the Right.

A. Soboul, *Les Sans-culottes parisiens en l'an II: Mouvement populaire et gouvernement révolutionnaire, 2 juin 1793–9 thermidor an II* (La Roche-sur-Yon: Henri Potier, 1958).

COLIN JONES

savagery In a cosmopolitan age of culture, savagery was deemed by missionaries and explorers to be unchristian, and by philosophers to be uncivilized; in either case heathen Amerindians, Hottentots, pygmies and other wild men were judged fit for conversion or improvement by Europeans who were well disposed towards them, and for repression by those who were not. Their mental inferiority seemed to be confirmed by their barbarism, their pagan rituals and their polygamy; and while many enlightened thinkers followed Montesquieu and Voltaire in condemning the institution of slavery in both the Old World and the New, progressive thinkers were largely persuaded that the moral development of savages would follow the transformation of their backward hunting and nomadic modes of life into pastoral, agrarian and eventually commercial societies. However, especially in the late eighteenth century, anticolonial and romantic commentators came to find the state of savagery superior to CIVILIZATION. Rousseau and his disciples argued that primitive men were more robust than effete citizens, because they were closer to nature, and Diderot, Raynal and other exponents of the idea of a state of noble savagery praised the gentle delights of a world in which free love and simplicity reigned, in contrast with the bigotry and hypocrisy of truly savage Christendom.

See also CULT OF THE NOBLE SAVAGE, PRIMITIVISM.

R. Meek, *Social Science and the Ignoble Savage* (Cambridge: Cambridge University Press, 1976).

F. Tinland, *L'Homme sauvage* (Paris: Payot, 1968).

ROBERT WOKLER

Savoy-Piedmont The house of Savoy ruled over a composite state centred on north-western Italy, comprising the duchy of Savoy, the county of Nice and the principality of Piedmont; in 1713 it gained territories in Lombardy and the island of Sicily, which was exchanged for Sardinia in 1720 and from which its rulers took the title 'king'. The succession passed from father to son through VICTOR AMADEUS II, CHARLES EMANUEL III, VICTOR AMADEUS III and Victor Emanuel I (1759–1824). Victor Amadeus II created an efficient, centralized absolutism modelled on France which his successors retained and strengthened. The king ruled through provincial intendants and magistrates (*prefetti*) appointed by himself; he also controlled the senates of Nice, Chambery and Turin, the high courts. The army and the diplomatic corps were regarded as among the best in Europe. Internally, the monarchy reduced the aristocracy to a service nobility, which process was completed with a series of ruthless enquiries into titles, taxation and land tenure (the *Perequazione*), coupled to a comprehensive land survey (the *catasto*), which was periodically updated. All these steps were well in advance of other Italian states, but the monarchy did not enter into the general trends of enlightened reform later in the century, remaining conservative and Catholic in its ideology. Many leading intellectuals, from Radicati in the 1720s to Denina (1731–1813) and Alfieri (1749–1803) in the 1790s, fled abroad. The monarchy maintained a rigidly mercantilist economic policy; by the 1770s an agricultural revolution had swept the countryside, destabilizing the peasantry, and the regime's social base was eroded by the 1790s.

M. G. Broers, 'Revolution as Vendetta, Patriotism in Piedmont, 1794–1821: Part I', *Historical Journal*, 33 (1990), 573–97.
G. Symcox, *Victor Amadeus II* (London: Thames & Hudson, 1983).
S. J. Woolf, *A History of Italy, 1700–1860* (London: Methuen, 1979).

MICHAEL BROERS

Saxe, Maurice, comte de (1696–1750)   French military commander and military theorist. The illegitimate son of Frederick Augustus I of Saxony (who became Augustus II of Poland), he served in the armies of Saxony and Savoy, after which his father purchased for him a German regiment in the French army in 1719. He distinguished himself in the War of the Polish Succession, and in the War of the Austrian Succession rose to the highest rank, being made marshal in 1744. After capturing Prague in 1741, he was put in charge of the abortive expeditionary force to invade England in conjunction with the Young Pretender, then became effective commander-in-chief of French forces. Victor at Fontenay (1745), perhaps the last great French victory before the French Revolutionary wars, he conquered the Austrian Netherlands before the end of the war. His influential reflections on the science of war, *Mes rêveries*, which he had written in 1732, were published posthumously in 1756–7.

COLIN JONES

Saxony   A region of northern central Germany ruled by branches of the Wettin family, Saxony consisted of two parts: the tiny fragmented Saxon duchies in Thuringia and the compact electorate of Saxony, an important medium-size state. In 1697 the elector Frederick Augustus I, known as 'the Strong', was elected king of Poland (as AUGUSTUS II) after becoming a convert to Catholicism. Thereafter, the ambition of the Saxon rulers to become hereditary kings of Poland diverted their attention from German affairs. The personal union between Saxony and Poland lasted until 1763. Saxony was a major manufacturing centre and the union brought increased trade opportunities but, on balance, it represented a drain on Saxon resources. Augustus also tried to impose absolutism but he was unable to eliminate the Saxon parliamentary estates. Invaded and occupied by Prussia at the outset of the Seven Years War, the country was, by its end, in ruins. After 1763, under the influence of enlightened ideas, the regent-electress Maria Antonia and elector Frederick Augustus III (1768–1827) carried out a substantial internal reconstruction. Prosperity was restored but Saxony played no further significant role in German or European politics.

H. Grundmann (ed.), *Gebhardt Handbuch der deutschen Geschichte*, vol. 2, ninth edn (Stuttgart: Union, 1970).

MICHAEL HUGHES

Scarlatti, Alessandro (1660–1725) Italian composer. His first known opera, *Gli equivoci nel sembiante* was performed in Rome in 1679. In the same year he was appointed maestro di cappella to Queen Christina of Sweden (1626–89), and in 1706 he became a member of the Accademia degli Arcadi, as did Corelli, with whom he shared the patrons Cardinals Pietro Ottoboni and Benedetto Pamphili. He moved to Naples in 1684, where he became maestro di cappella to the viceroy, and stayed there for the next eighteen years. In 1702 he left Naples for Florence and Rome, returning in 1708; after another absence (1717–23) he remained in Naples for the rest of his life.

He wrote 114 operas, of which seventy have survived. His masterwork is considered to be *Il Mitridate Eupatore* (1707). He also composed more than twenty oratorios and about 800 chamber cantatas. His work was dismissed as old-fashioned soon after his death. Not until the twentieth century was he acknowledged to be one of the most important baroque composers. His innovations were the three-movement sinfonia form of the overture and the da capo aria.

His son Domenico Scarlatti (1685–1757) was famous for his harpsichord music, which he developed in Spain in the 1730s.

R. Pagano, *Scarlatti: Alessandro e Domenico: due vita in una* (Milano: Mondadori, 1985)

FRITZ WEBER

scepticism The philosophical sceptic seeks to induce a state of doubt, or scepticism, by showing the uncertainty or incomprehensibility of claims to knowledge or opinion. This ancient philosophical sect underwent a revival in the seventeenth and eighteenth centuries. Sceptics like BAYLE and HUME sought to show the paradoxes involved in scientific ideas – such as matter, space and causality – as well as religious beliefs, for example in the Trinity, the Incarnation and a benevolent all-powerful creator of an evil world.

It is difficult to determine the ultimate aims of the sceptical philosopher. While Bayle had an immense influence on later Enlightenment thinkers who were opposed to all religions, it is generally agreed that he sought to reveal the paradoxes of reason in order to support faith.

Hume adopted a form of academic or 'mitigated' scepticism which sought to show the dependence of fundamental scientific notions on 'natural instinct', and so to restrict enquiries to those grounded in everyday reasoning. Yet, paradoxically, he produced devastating rational critiques of both revealed and natural religion.

R. Popkin, *The History of Scepticism from Erasmus to Spinoza* (Berkeley, Calif.: University of California Press, 1979).

JOHN P. WRIGHT

Schelling, Friedrich Wilhelm (1775–1854)   German romantic thinker. Born in Leonberg, Württemberg, he studied at the University of Tübingen, alongside Hölderlin and Hegel. From 1798 he gave lectures alongside Fichte at the University of Jena, and later rose to become professor at Würzburg, Munich and Berlin. He won a reputation as a leading spokesman of the romantic movement (*see* ROMANTICISM), elevating art to the status of a religion, and seeing it as the true union of nature and spirit. No mean poet, Schelling regarded his poetic instincts as finding their true fulfilment in philosophy. In his *System des transcendentalen Idealismus* (System of Transcendental Idealism, 1800) and *Zur Geschichte der neueren Philosophie* (Towards a History of Modern Philosophy, 1826) he represented true philosophy as the blending of inner intuitive drives with the progressive thought-tendencies of the universe, and projected the human mind reaching a harmony with the divine. True freedom, he argued, lay in the objective rapport between mind and nature. Schelling whole-heartedly championed the superiority of the mental and spiritual over the merely material, pioneered investigations into unconscious forms of thought and regarded his philosophy as the true union of Idealism and Realism.

E. D. Hirsch, *Wordsworth and Schelling: A Typological Study of Romanticism* (New Haven, Conn.: Yale University Press, 1960).

ROY PORTER

Schiller, Johann Christoph Friedrich von (1759–1805)   German poet, dramatist, historian and philosopher. As a youth he experienced at first hand the autocratic rule of a petty tyrant, Duke Charles Augustus of Württemberg, which furnished him with his dominant theme: the quest for freedom. His early plays were in the rebellious mode of the STURM UND DRANG: *Die Räuber* (The Robbers, 1781) was a stirring if puzzling protest, while *Fiesko* (1782) and *Kabale und Liebe* (Intrigue and Love, 1784) were similarly iconoclastic. From the start he raised philosophical questions regarding revolt, which he saw as ambivalent. These concerns were to come increasingly to the fore, as in the more subtle verse play *Don Carlos* (1787).

After publishing his *Geschichte des Abfalls der vereinigten Niederlande* (History of the Revolt of the Netherlands, 1788), he was appointed to the chair of history at Jena. His friendship with GOETHE began in 1794 and they launched their project of Weimar Classicism. His study of KANT from 1791 onwards bore fruit in several major essays: *Über Anmut und würde* (On Grace and Dignity, 1794) modified Kant's moral rigour; *Über naïve und sentimentalische Dichtung* (On Naive and Reflective Poetry, 1795–6) objectified his relation to Goethe; and *Über die ästhetische Eltiehung des Menschen in einer Reihe von Briefen* (Letters on the Aesthetic Education of Man, 1795), reacting to the Terror, sought to reinstate human 'wholeness' by locating the role of beauty and the aesthetic sense in political life.

Enriched by philosophy and disillusioned by politics, he returned to drama with the tragic *Wallenstein* (1796–8), *Maria Stuart* (1800) and *Die Jungfrau von Orleans* (The Maid of Orleans, 1801). Now, however, as Goethe observed, it was not physical but spiritual freedom that counted. None the less, in *Wilhelm Tell* (1804) Schiller found for once a revolt that produced an idyll.

T. J. Reed, *Schiller* (Oxford: Oxford University Press, 1991).

JEREMY ADLER

schools *see* EDUCATION; SUNDAY SCHOOLS.

science   The modern use of the term 'science' dates from the early nineteenth century, the term 'scientist' as a description of a cultivator of natural knowledge being coined by William Whewell in 1840. Raymond Williams has argued that until the seventeenth century the term 'science' remained largely faithful to its Latin connotation of knowledge in general. Important refinements of its meaning took place in the seventeenth century when a separation between science and art, which expressed the distinction between theoretical and practical skills, lent it greater specificity. In the eighteenth century an overriding distinction between experiment as theoretical knowledge and experience as practical knowledge further reinforced the polarization of science and art, which began to be institutionalized over the course of the century. The new emphasis on experimental and empirical knowledge of reality also distinguished science from the older studies of metaphysics and logic.

The EXPERIMENTAL METHOD, which became central to the meaning of science and symbolic of the height of rational achievement, developed hand in hand with natural philosophy. NEWTON's philosophy, in particular, was seen as the pinnacle of an experimental tradition associated with Bacon (1561–1626), Galileo (1564–1692) and Boyle

(1627–91), in which natural laws were rationally deduced from phenomena and were mathematically demonstrated. There was no room for speculation, or, as Newton most famously put it in 1713: 'I feign no hypotheses.' Natural philosophers discriminated against mere belief as they increasingly defined their own work as the pursuit of truth.

The palpable explanatory successes of experimental scientific investigation turned science into a principal resource for sceptics intent on employing reason to challenge the authority of faith. The rise of NATURAL RELIGION during the Enlightenment spawned a variety of creeds each positioning God in a different relationship to nature. The deist philosopher John Toland coined the term 'pantheism' to describe a cosmology that placed God and nature on an equal footing, while for atheists like Diderot NATURAL LAW represented the ultimate authority. Even the argument from design – the proof of God's existence from a scientific appreciation of nature's intricacies – could be pressed into the service of scepticism if articulated within the MECHANICAL PHILOSOPHY, which implied that God's activity was constrained by the natural order.

Faith in the ability of science to uncover truth inspired attempts to fashion a science of man using methods analogous to those developed within natural philosophy. Locke's *Essay concerning Human Understanding* (1690), self-consciously founded on Newtonian principles, paved the way for scientific studies of human nature like Hume's *Treatise on Human Nature* (1739) and Montesquieu's *Esprit des lois* (1748). The study of man could also be moulded in accordance with the precepts and methods of NATURAL HISTORY, as Buffon demonstrated in his *Histoire naturelle*. While science overtly provided models for moral philosophy, it covertly embodied moral lessons of its own. Newtonian philosophy, for example, was used to recommend a specific system of moral and political authority by Boyle lecturers, coffeehouse lecturers who deployed nature as theatre and most conspicuously in texts like Desaguliers's *The Newtonian System of the World: The Best Model of Government* (1728). At the opposite end of the spectrum, Rousseau blamed the sciences for the corruption that plagued modern society and held man's natural virtue in chains.

The pursuit of science remained for the best part of the Enlightenment a non-professional affair; with the exception of medical science, the sciences were not accommodated in university curricula. However, it was organized at an institutional level with academies like the Royal Society (1660), the Académie des Sciences (1666) and those established along the same lines in Berlin (1700), St Petersburg (1724), Edinburgh (1783) and elsewhere. Although French academicians were salaried, full-time scientific careers remained largely the privilege of men of substance or beneficiaries of progressive patrons like Frederick the Great. Outside the societies, the study of science was cultivated in *salons* and in provincial groups like the LUNAR SOCIETY of Birmingham or the literary and philosophical societies which were formed in the latter part of the century. At a popular level, it captured the imagination through public lectures and popular texts; microscopy and botany aroused especially widespread interest. With the founding of the Royal Institution in 1799, a new kind of scientific society was brought into being, which provided salaried posts for natural philosophers to carry out experimental research as well as to present public lectures. (*See* SCIENTIFIC SOCIETIES.)

The Enlightenment also witnessed an increasing specialization of science into different disciplines, although the hardening of disciplinary categories through institutionalization and professionalization was not to take place until the nineteenth century. In addition to natural philosophy, natural history, MATHEMATICS and ASTRONOMY, new disciplines such as botany, geology and CHEMISTRY emerged as fields of enquiry in their own right. Trying to negotiate the scientific topography of the Enlightenment entails recognizing that even within a particular disciplinary field there was not one science but a plurality of competing sciences; vitalist, materialist and mechanical versions of matter theory, for example, were incommensurable, and in botany advocates of sexual classification waged an intellectual battle with advocates of natural classification.

Enlightenment science in all its diverse and non-linear forms – including MESMERISM, galvanism (*see* GALVANI) and physiognomy, which have traditionally been defined as pseudo-sciences – nourished attempts to realize the perfectibility of mankind through the use of reason.

See also SCIENTIFIC REVOLUTION.

Thomas L. Hankins, *Science and the Enlightenment* (Cambridge: Cambridge University Press, 1985).
G. S. Rousseau and Roy Porter (eds), *The Ferment of Knowledge: Studies in the Historiography of Eighteenth-Century Science* (Cambridge: Cambridge University Press, 1980).
S. J. Schaffer, 'Natural Philosophy and Public Spectacle', *History of Science*, 21 (1983), 1–43.
Raymond Williams, *Keywords* (London: Croom Helm, 1976).

MARINA BENJAMIN

Sciences, Académie des *see* ACADÉMIE DES SCIENCES.

scientific revolution The seventeenth-century transformation in European thought about NATURE, which overthrew scholasticism and replaced it with the 'new philosophy', is generally known as the scientific revolution (after Fontenelle and D'Alembert (1717–83)). The face of nature was changed principally by developments in astronomy and the physical sciences. On a macrocosmic level, the sun-centred cosmology of Copernicus (1473–1543) marked the end of the anthropocentric view of the natural world characteristic of Greek thought. The new ASTRONOMY was championed by Galileo (1564–1642), who went on trial for anticlericalism, and mathematically vindicated by Kepler (1571–1630) and Newton. On a microcosmic level, the mind –body dualism of Descartes (1596–1650) stripped nature of the vitality and divinity that Renaissance thinkers had accorded it – a process that Carolyn Merchant has called the 'death of nature' – and severed the links between man and nature (though not between woman and nature). Nature, objectified and inert, was subjected to the scrutiny of MATHEMATICS and to the EXPERIMENTAL METHOD recommended by Francis Bacon (1561–1626), and institutionalized by the Royal Society.

The scientific method of mathematically deducing laws of nature from the evidence of experimental observation generated a faith in the power of REASON that crescendoed during the Enlightenment. Reason replaced theological doctrine as the key to understanding nature; and, by extension, understanding nature was seen to be tantamount to understanding God. John Ray (1627–1705) clearly articulated the argument from design in his *Wisdom of God in Creation* (1691).

The scientific revolution is generally represented as a frenzied growth of natural knowledge sandwiched between the work of Copernicus and that of Newton. Yet Enlightenment thinkers felt that they were taking part in the revolution: the mathematical astronomy that peaked with the work of Lagrange (1736–1813) and Laplace was of a piece with the Copernican revolution; and with respect to matter theory Newton's philosophy represented more of a beginning than an end – his success in putting God back into nature without conceding any activity to matter provided Enlightenment philosophers with an entirely new agenda which centred on the concept of force. The scientific revolution has tended to be understood with exclusive reference to astronomy and the physical sciences, but it also involved developments in other disciplines: the medical achievements of William Harvey (1578–1657) and Malpighi (1628–94), the microscope-inspired work of Robert Hooke (1635–1702), the precision instruments made by Christian Huygens (1629–95), the chemistry of Robert Boyle (1627–91) and the calculus of Leibniz.

See also SCIENCE.

Herbert Butterfield, *The Origins of Modern Science, 1300–1800*, second edn (London: Bell & Hyman, 1957).
Arthur Koestler, *The Sleepwalkers: A History of Man's Changing Vision of the Universe* (London: Hutchinson, 1959).

Carolyn Merchant, *The Death of Nature: Women, Ecology and the Scientific Revolution* (New York: Harper & Row, 1980).
Simon Schaffer and Steven Shapin, *Leviathan and the Air-Pump: Hobbes, Boyle and the Experimental Life* (Princeton, NJ: Princeton University Press, 1985).

M. L. BENJAMIN

scientific societies   As science became a fashionable component of polite urban culture, scientific societies proliferated, from a handful in 1700 to some seventy official and even more private ones in the 1780s. Every progressive ruler or city wanted one, and scientists found them more rewarding than universities. They spread like the Enlightenment in general: quickly in France, then to northern Europe, later America and last and least in Iberia; they declined in the post-French Revolutionary turmoil.

The Parisian ACADÉMIE DES SCIENCES and the ROYAL SOCIETY in London provided the two institutional models for the few government-funded, professional academies and the poorer amateur societies respectively. They began by promoting science in the battle against 'ignorance', but by mid-century they were confidently celebrating and applying it, although rarely with economic success. Active members presented papers or experiments for discussion, read other societies' journals in a library, corresponded and vied for prizes (some for the few salaried posts). The emergence of features of nineteenth-century professional scientific practice should not be exaggerated. Instances of successful major projects, mainly in mathematical sciences (such as the Parisian expeditions to measure the shape of the earth in 1735), were outweighed by those of upwardly mobile windbaggery.

James E. McLellan III, *Science Reorganized* (New York: Columbia University Press, 1985).

STEPHEN PUMFREY

Scotland   In 1700 Scotland was an independent kingdom connected to the linked thrones of England and Ireland by a personal union in the shape of a joint monarch. Its political class had even contrived after 1688 to assert a substantial degree of independence of action for the previously tame Scots legislature, the estates (a unicameral body in which nobles, barons or lairds, and burgesses sat together). William III resented this development, hoped to reverse it by the effect of an incorporating union with England and died in 1702 still urging such a union. In the early years of Queen Anne's reign pressure for union from Westminster abated. Scotland was illegally taken into the War of the Spanish Succession by executive action, and Westminster policy was to secure Scottish acceptance of the English Act of Succession and of the Hanoverian dynasty. Most Scots hoped to use the succession issue to force a drastic renegotiation of the terms of association with England. Overplaying their hand after 1704, and undercut by English bribery of the nominal 'country' leader, the duke of Hamilton (1658–1712), they found themselves by 1707 in an unpopular incorporating union.

An abortive Franco-Jacobite invasion in 1708, designed to exploit the unpopularity of the Treaty of Union of 1707, would have been dangerous if it had been executed. There was a hard core of Jacobite Episcopalian aristocratic opposition to the 1707 union, and the 1690 Presbyterian settlement in the Kirk by Law Established with which it was identified. A rising in 1715 led, or misled, by the earl of Mar (1675–1732) and coinciding with unrest in the north of England should have succeeded, but it failed. A small-scale joint invasion of the northern Highlands by a Spanish and Jacobite force in 1719 was a fiasco. General Wade embarked on a programme of fort- and road-building in the Gaelic-speaking Highlands. With Jacobites excluded from public politics, the field was dominated by Hanoverian factions, of which by far the most potent was the Argathelian Party, or followers of the duke of Argyll, chief of clan Campbell. Under the wily Archibald Campbell, first earl of Islay, later third duke of Argyll (1682–1761), the Argathelian ascendancy at the local level in Scotland could be so absolute as to drive opponents into support for the 1745 Jacobite rising. Despite its army having reached Derby, the rising was always more of a *coup* by a militant minority than a national rising like the one in 1715. It was helped by widespread apathy towards the Westminster regime; its failure doomed the clan system. (*See* JACOBITES.)

Scotland became a quiescent province in an Atlantic-wide Hanoverian monarchy. Three developments dominated its history. One was the integration of its elites, including ex-Jacobites, into a new British ruling class. By 1762 the prime minister of Great Britain, to the fury of many of the English, was a Scot, the earl of BUTE. The second phenomenon of note was the international recognition of the flowering of a Scottish Enlightenment whose roots lay deep in Restoration Scotland. The most-cited figures in the high Enlightenment of the third quarter of the century – the philosopher HUME and the political economist Adam SMITH – were in fact thoroughly atypical of an Enlightenment that was always conservative and dominated at its apogee by Church of Scotland divines like William ROBERTSON, historian of Scotland and America, and principal of Edinburgh University.

The third development was the basic shift in productive techniques which produced, although not widely before the 1780s, an agricultural revolution, and an earlier industrial revolution based on textiles. Urbanization, the emergence of a much larger and richer middle class disproportionately addicted to secessionist bodies that had left the

Kirk by Law Established, and a current of radical ideas threatened the conservative, landed political establishment run by Henry Dundas (1742–1811), first Viscount Melville, the younger Pitt's crony and in his own way the patriotic 'satrap of Scotland'. Skilful exploitation of the backlash from the French Revolution carried it past 1800 intact.

H. Hamilton, *An Economic History of Scotland in the Eighteenth Century* (Oxford: Clarendon, 1963).
Bruce Lenman, *Integration, Enlightenment and Industrialization: Scotland 1746–1832* (London: Edward Arnold, 1981).
Thomas Christopher Smout, *A History of the Scotlish People, 1560–1830* (London: Collins, 1969).

BRUCE P. LENMAN

sculpture Throughout the eighteenth century the tomb and the equestrian statue were the most important public manifestations of the sculptor's art, and the most challenging. The portrait bust, the staple of many artists' activities, assumed an increasing importance in secular and domestic settings around the mid-century. With the renewal of interest in the psychology of the individual, the bust in the work of ROUBILIAC in England and HOUDON in France reached a high point in its history for the capture of personality and expression. Decorative carving of all kinds and stucco-work were in great demand, particularly in France and central Europe, much of it executed, or at least designed, by sculptors rather than craftsmen. Garden sculpture, too, inspired by the example of the park at the palace of Versailles, was much in vogue. It assumed various guises to suit the tastes and aspirations if its patrons: mythological, as at La Granja de San Ildefonso in Spain; political, as at Stowe House in England; or moral, as at Kuks in Bohemia.

The dominant stylistic trend in large-scale public sculpture in the first half of the century was the BAROQUE. While in Italy and central Europe the influence of Bernini and his followers remained paramount in the work of such sculptors as the Italian Camillo Rusconi (1658–1728) or the Bohemian Matthias Braun (1684–1738), in the Netherlands figure sculpture was still conditioned by the painted types of Rubens (1577–1640). In France, by the 1730s, there was a move away from the exaggerated plasticity, rhetorical gestures and theatrical *mise-en-scène* of baroque sculpture towards the more graceful forms, delicately modelled surfaces and more tender emotions of the ROCOCO. Such sculptures as Etienne-Maurice Falconet's (1716–91) marble statuettes of nude female bathers were the perfect complement to the curvilinear decoration of carved wooden panelling and modelled stucco ceilings typical of French interiors of the Louis XV period. With the growth of French cultural hegemony, this style spread to most parts of Europe, including Germany, Russia and Scandinavia. Only Italy remained largely exempt from rococo influence, while in England it was modified by nationalist distrust of French style and a preference for a dignified naturalism inspired by ancient Roman sculpture.

From around 1770 the reverence for antiquity, which had been given an additional impetus by a more systematic study of Greek and Roman remains and by a more serious moral and intellectual climate, found sculptural expression in the neoclassical style. In the neoclassicist John Flaxman (1755–1826) England produced its only internationally famous sculptor of the eighteenth century. Although the circumstances of patronage in England meant that much of his work consisted of relatively small church monuments, he produced some striking pieces of free-standing marble sculpture on both mythological and religious themes, the most important subject-matter in the academic hierarchy. Far more fortunate in this respect were the two other great sculptors of the international movement, the Italian Antonio Canova (1757–1822) and the Dane Bertel Thorwaldsen (1768–1844), both of whom spent their working lives in Rome, the traditional centre of the art world. NEOCLASSICISM continued to be the dominant sculptural style until the mid nineteenth century, and it was the idiom of the first important native-born American sculptors, Horatio Greenough (1805–52) and Hiram Powers (1805–73).

Eberhard Hempel, *Baroque Art and Architecture in Central Europe* (Harmondsworth: Penguin, 1965).

Wend Graf Kalnein and Michael Levey, *Art and Architecture of the Eighteenth Century in France* (Harmondsworth: Penguin, 1972).

Fritz Novotny, *Painting and Sculpture in Europe 1780–1880,* rev. edn (Harmondsworth: Penguin, 1970).

Margaret Whinney, *Sculpture in Britain, 1530–1830*, rev. edn (Harmondsworth: Penguin, 1988).

John Wilmerding, *American Art* (Harmondsworth: Penguin, 1976).

Rudolf Wittkower, *Art and Architecture in Italy 1600–1750* (Harmondsworth: Penguin, 1958).

MARC JORDAN

scurvy A deficiency disease resulting from too little vitamin C, scurvy was in the early eighteenth century regarded as an abnormal acidity or alkalinity of the blood. Various remedies were recommended, including fresh vegetables, and an elixir based on sulphuric acid. Scurvy caused more loss of life to the eighteenth-century British navy than did enemy action, and it was in the navy that cures were pioneered.

The naval surgeon James Lind (1716–94) established the curative value of citrus fruit. He conducted one of the first clinical trials on voyages in 1747, testing six remedies on twelve sailors with scurvy.

Those who received two oranges and a lemon a day recovered fastest. However, Lind's published findings (1753) had little immediate impact on medicine or naval administration. Debate continued on the causes of the disease and preventive measures. Captain Cook's exploration of the Pacific (1768–71) showed that long voyages could be free from scurvy deaths but did not establish the efficacy of one preventive over another. Only with Gilbert Blane's (1749–1834) advocacy of citrus juices did they become routine in the Royal Navy from 1796, dramatically reducing the incidence of scurvy.

K. J. Carpenter, *The History of Scurvy and Vitamin C* (Cambridge: Cambridge University Press, 1986).

MARY E. FISSELL

secret societies Among the plethora of eighteenth-century clubs there were clandestine organizations like the Freemasons and Rosicrucians (*see* FREEMASONRY, ROSICRUCIANISM). Many of these were kept secret for reasons of political expediency, for example the Italian Carbonari who were fighting for national independence. In the wake of the French Revolution clubs enlisting radicals and social reformers, such as the LONDON CORRESPONDING SOCIETY, were persecuted as seditious by the authorities and forced to go underground. The conspiratorial Bavarian ILLUMINATI were condemned in 1785 as politically subversive by the Bavarian elector. Founded in 1776 at the University of Ingoldstadt by Adam Weishaupt (1748–1830), the Illuminati were dedicated to egalitarianism and the moral regeneration of the world. In contrast, the degenerate Hell-Fire Club (founded in 1720) had a reputation for diabolic carousing and Bacchanalian abandonment which led to a royal proclamation in 1721 banning 'blasphemous clubs in London'. Twenty years later Francis Dashwood (1708–1781) founded a Rabelaisian brotherhood at Medmenham Abbey which inspired John Hall-Stevenson's (1718–85) Demoniacs. The obscurantism of secret societies, which supplied Gothic novelists with a popular motif, was anathema to the spirit of the Enlightenment.

J. M. Roberts, *The Mythology of the Secret Societies* (London: Secker & Warburg, 1972).

MARIE MULVEY ROBERTS

seigneurialism The term 'seigneurialism' referred to the complex of jurisdictional and other rights that landowners, mainly in Continental Europe (although vestiges remained in the British Isles), exercised over their landed properties. Comprising their judicial competence (which, in Poland or Naples, could extend, at least in theory, to capital crimes), the levying of various dues in cash and/or kind (*see* SHARECROPPING,

TAXATION), the command of labour services (*see* CORVÉE, ROBOT) – in frequently bewildering permutations – seigneurialism derived from medieval FEUDALISM, when such dues had represented a rational way of organizing a simpler and comparatively non-monetized economy.

It was indeed *le régime féodal* that the National Assembly formally suppressed in France on 4 August 1789. By the late eighteenth century, these rights represented a major economic burden even on the non-enserfed peasantry of western Europe and a serious constraint on the expansion of the economy as a whole, although they preserved many individual landlords from economic ruin. Landlords remained attached to them as much for that reason as for the sense of ruling over 'subjects' which seigneurialism conferred.

See also SERFDOM.

J. Blum, *The End of the Old Order in Rural Europe* (Princeton, NJ: Princeton University Press, 1978).

J. T. LUKOWSKI

self-interest   Godwin's view on the question of whether or not self-interest was the true motivation behind all our actions was that the French tended to argue that it was, while the British believed that some actions were 'disinterested'. He thought the French position crude and considered its crassest exponent to be La Rochefoucauld, believing that only those who failed to reflect on the complexity of human agency could hold such a hypothesis. In his view, if self-love were the sole principle of action, there would no such thing as virtue; but the virtuous did exist. They were those who, by dint of habit and education, possessed such characters as to wish to perform benevolent acts for their own sake.

Although Godwin's point about French ethical theorists was not entirely devoid of merit, Diderot, for one, was a strong critic of those who, like Helvétius, reduced every human activity to the pursuit of self-interest. Truth and beauty, he argued, were sought by many as ends in themselves and it was ludicrous to think of Leibniz, for instance, as motivated only by the prospect of riches or fame.

In Scotland the pupils of Hutcheson attempted to reconcile self-interest and benevolence in various ways. Recalling Hume's famous comment that ' 'Tis not contrary to reason to prefer the destruction of the whole world to the scratching of my finger', Smith asked: 'When we are always so much more deeply affected by whatever concerns ourselves, than by whatever concerns other men; what is it which prompts the generous, upon all occasions, and the mean upon many, to sacrifice their own interests to the greater interest of others?' Describing the impartial spectator in each of us, Smith argued that it was not the love of mankind, but rather 'a stronger love, a more powerful affection, which generally takes place upon such occasions; the love of what is honourable and noble, of the grandeur, and dignity, and superiority of our own characters'. Self-love, in other words, was the means to VIRTUE.

While the question of the exact nature of the relation between self-interest and benevolence was central to eighteenth-century ethical theories, it was relegated to the periphery of political thought by utilitarians such as Bentham: societies could only benefit from being ruled by lawgivers who did not probe into the complexity of human motivation and took it for granted that individuals sought pleasure and avoided pain. At the level of the market, Smith's *Inquiry into the Nature and Causes of the Wealth of Nations* endures as a powerful analysis of the system of unintended consequences of the pursuit of self-interest and the prosperity which, he claimed, resulted from it.

A. O. Hirschman, *The Passions and the Interests* (Princeton, NJ: Princeton University Press, 1977).

SYLVANA TOMASELLI

sensationalism   That knowledge is acquired entirely through sense perception and that every idea has its origin in sense data is a view which many philosophers in the eighteenth century studied at great length and some whole-heartedly espoused. Inspired by Locke's *Essay concerning Human Understanding*, writers like Helvétius and the abbé de Condillac renewed the attacks of seventeenth-century philosophers on those who held that some ideas were innate. Thus in his *Essai sur l'origine des connaissances humaines* Condillac criticized the followers of Descartes, Malebranche and Leibniz for the scepticism with which they considered knowledge derived from the senses. Not only could the senses be trusted, according to Condillac, but the mind's faculties were themselves nothing over and above acts of perception.

Hume, who also sought the origin of ideas, came to realize the limits of EMPIRICISM. In A *Treatise of Human Nature*, which greatly influenced Kant, he showed that some of the most important concepts could not be explained by simple appeal to sense perception.

John W. Yolton, *Perceptual Acquaintance from Descartes to Reid* (Oxford: Blackwell, 1984).

SYLVANA TOMASELLI

sensibility   Early in the eighteenth century the word 'sensibility' denoted specifically physical sensitivities, but by the mid eighteenth century it was being used to denote an emotional, even moral, faculty: it now meant a special, and admirable, susceptibility to feelings that were not physical. What was important, and surprising, was the ease of transition from a connotation of emotional sensitivity (introduced in the early eighteenth century) to one of laudable delicacy; by this transition, a capacity for feeling became a capacity for fellow feeling. This capacity was most powerfully displayed by characters in novels of the period, especially those of Samuel Richardson, and later Rousseau and Goethe. It was frequently represented as a peculiarly feminine quality: sensibility and virtue were often conjoined in depicting a suffering heroine. (Sensibility frequently seemed to disable, as well as to dignify, its possessors.) The stereotype found a new lease of life in Gothic fiction, particularly in the novels of Anne Radcliffe (1764–1823). Towards the end of the century the idea of sensibility as a virtue began to be attacked. Some, like Wollstonecraft, saw it as an enervating female stereotype; others, like Jane Austen (1775–1817), considered it as indulgent individualism. The importance of the concept can be gauged by the pressing need of writers to debunk it.

See also SENTIMENT, SYMPATHY.

Janet Todd, *Sensibility: An Introduction* (London: Methuen, 1986).

JOHN MULLAN

sentiment The eighteenth-century fashion for 'sentiment' – a word closely allied with 'SENSIBILITY' – is usefully understood with respect to the fortunes of the adjective 'sentimental'. While its pejorative implications are uppermost today, for most of the latter half of the eighteenth century it was used in approbation or celebration. The shift in meaning can be felt in the uncertain resonances of the title to Sterne's novel of 1768, *A Sentimental Journey*. Quite rapidly, however, the word moved from designating a special refinement of emotion to its still-current sense of mawkishness or self-indulgence. By the early nineteenth century the latter sense was dominant.

In the mid eighteenth century the word seems to have been been employed for its useful ambivalence. On the one hand, it referred to visceral emotion, as displayed in novels like Mackenzie's *Man of Feeling* and Henry Brooke's (1703–83) *Fool of Quality*, and, on the other hand, it meant an (often ethical) opinion or judgement, for instance in the titles of Adam Smith's *Theory of Moral Sentiments* and Samuel Richardson's (1689–1761) *Collection of Moral and Instructive Sentiments*. 'Sentiment' denoted both feeling and morality and 'sentimental' displays were thus considered as evidence of unusual private virtue: to be 'sentimental' was to have acquired an access to the feelings that made morality natural.

John Mullan, *Sentiment and Sociability* (Oxford: Clarendon, 1988).

JOHN MULLAN

September Massacres The September Massacres were a panic reaction to a sense of treason at home and the enemy at the gate. On 2 September 1792 news reached Paris that the Austro-Prussian forces advancing on the city had passed Verdun. That afternoon a convoy of prisoners was attacked by SANS-CULOTTES and seventeen were butchered. The prisons were full of those arrested on suspicion of treasonable activities and on the 2nd and 3rd all but two of Paris's prisons were broken into, makeshift tribunals erected and 'people's justice' dispensed. There were acquittals but on 2–7 September 1,100 to 1,400 people were killed. Most were politically innocuous, many common criminals. Over 200 priests were killed. The massacres helped to unite much European opinion against the Revolution. Searching the classical world for comparisons, the earl of Dalkeith thought they outstripped 'the massacres of Rome in its most abandoned style' and revealed an 'innate love of blood'. He wrote of 'the hell devils already celebrating their orgies at that great cauldron of the world'.

JEREMY BLACK

serfdom A general term describing various degrees of peasant dependency on landed seigneurs, serfdom was, above all, associated with legally sanctioned attachment to the soil, combined with the performance of obligatory labour dues on the demesne (home farm) of the seigneur (*see* CORVÉE, ROBOT). The precise conditions of serfdom varied enormously from country to country and from one property to another: indeed, at the margins, it is very difficult to distinguish 'serfs' from so-called 'free' peasants. In general, the further east in Europe, the more onerous were the conditions, for the much lower degree of urbanization and much less sophisticated patterns of economic activity made tying peasants to the land much more practicable and necessary than in western Europe.

In parts of western Germany serfs may have performed only a few days' compulsory labour for their seigneurs each year and been entitled to a high degree of security of tenure, with rights of redress in state courts. East of the River Elbe they were far more likely to owe several days' service per week (the amount was usually related to the size of the peasants' own landholdings), and in Poland or Russia serfs had for the most part no access to state courts against seigneurial decisions. At the extreme, seigneurs could sell their serfs as chattels, independently of the land (as in Poland and Russia), although in Prussia and the Habsburg lands the government increasingly tried to prevent this. The Austrian Habsburgs in particular were anxious to regulate seigneurial authority over the serfs, largely through placing limits on the amount of labour service that the seigneur could extract (usually a maximum of three days per week) and facilitating appeals from serfs to state courts, but such reforms really began to be effective only from the 1770s and 1780s.

Economically, serfdom was grossly inefficient: so much of their labour was creamed off that serfs had little incentive to work productively and no interest in agricultural improvement; at the same time, seigneurs could exercise control only through often elaborate and inflexible management structures, which offered opportunities for abuse by demesne officialdom. Alternatively, landlords leased their estates to tenants whose main aim was to squeeze as much as they could out of them, regardless of the consequences. Numerous calculations to demonstrate the inefficiency of the system made little impression on landowners who appreciated that many of them would be driven to bankruptcy by the operation of a free agricultural labour market – which accounts for the immense resistance to Joseph II's experiments in the abolition of labour services in 1789. For all the enlightened propaganda in favour of serf emancipation, there was no certainty that, in pre-industrialized societies, life would be any better for the peasants. In reality, eastern European peasants were not necessarily worse off than many of their western counterparts.

See also FEUDALISM, SEIGNEURIALISM.

J. Blum, *The End of the Old Order in Rural Europe* (Princeton, NJ: Princeton University Press, 1978).

J. T. LUKOWSKI

Seven Years War (1756 –1763)   This complex struggle fell into two distinct parts. On the one hand, the Habsburg Empire, helped by France, Russia and Sweden, confronted Prussia under Frederick II. On the other, France, supported from January 1762 by Spain, struggled with Britain for colonial empire. The war in Germany began when Frederick, alarmed by the prospect of imminent attack by powerful enemies, attempted in August 1756 to strike at the Habsburg dominions through Saxony. This soon involved Prussia in a struggle for survival against an apparently overwhelming hostile coalition. Although he won some great victories, Frederick also suffered great defeats, and his territories were severely strained by the demands of the war. Nevertheless, when it was ended by the Treaty of Hubertusburg (February 1763) he retained Silesia, the recovery of which had been the essential Habsburg war aim. The Anglo-French struggle saw Britain win decisive successes in Canada (the capture of Quebec in 1759), in India (Battle of PLASSEY), and at sea. The TREATY OF PARIS of February 1763 destroyed the French position in North America and established Britain clearly as the leading European imperial power.

J. O. Lindsay (ed.), *The New Cambridge Modern History*, vol. 7 (Cambridge: Cambridge University Press, 1957), chs 20, 22, 23.

M. S. ANDERSON

Shaftesbury, Anthony Ashley Cooper, third earl of (1671–1713) English moral and aesthetic philosopher, politician and writer. His education was supervised by Locke, who was secretary to his grandfather, the first earl (1621–83), a leading Whig. He broke with Locke in his *Inquiry concerning Virtue* (1699), in which he defended a theism based on the conviction that everything that existed was for the best and nothing was owing to chance – a natural religion in which VIRTUE (concern with the good of the whole), which was grounded in feeling, was as basic to human nature as self-interest: one was morally good only when the good of the whole was 'the immediate object of some passion or affection moving him', without any thought to reward or punishment. This germ of 'moral sense' ethics, complemented by optimistic intuition of 'the whole', was linked to the emergent discipline of aesthetics.

The affinity blossomed in his *Letter concerning Enthusiasm* (1708) and *The Moralists* (1709; early version 1703–4, *The Sociable Enthusiast*). For him ENTHUSIASM was participation in what was greater than the self; it was to be countered only with raillery and good humour, which separated true enthusiasm from false. This theory of social discourse was elaborated in *Sensus Communis: An Essay on the Freedom of Wit and Humour* (1709) and applied to the self in *Soliloquy* (1710). All these works were collected in *Characteristics* (1711).

R. Voitle, *The Third Earl of Shaftesbury, 1671–1713* (Baton Rouge, La.: Louisiana State University Press, 1984).

JEFFREY BARNOUW

sharecropping A form of agricultural tenure, sharecropping was much resorted to by the poorer peasantry of southern France (*métayage*), northern and central Italy (*mezzadria*) and parts of the Rhineland. The landlord provided a landholding, a house and around half of the working capital and, in return, the sharecropper delivered a substantial portion (usually around half) of his crop (often the gross rather than the net) and of any other returns to the landlord. The agreement may have covered arrangements for the payment of TAXES and the provision of additional agricultural services (*see* CORVÉE, ROBOT), increasingly to the detriment of the tenant. Contracts could be written or verbal: around Toulouse, in France, a term of six to nine years was usual.

While such arrangements provided a basic security of tenure, sharecroppers who failed to discharge their obligations – which was very likely after a poor harvest – found themselves increasingly indebted to the seigneur, and were then forced to renew their leases under ever more disadvantageous conditions in order to discharge their debts. Sharecropping readily degenerated into the 'free' agricultural labour market's equivalent of SERFDOM.

R. Forster, *The Nobility of Toulouse in the Eighteenth Century* (Baltimore: Johns Hopkins University Press, 1960).

J. T. LUKOWSKI

Shcherbatov, Prince **Mikhail Mikhailovich** (1735–1790)   Russian historian, writer and critic of Catherine II. Of ancient noble descent, he was privately educated and commissioned in 1756 in the Semenovskii Guards, resigning with the rank of captain in 1762. He was one of the most vocal delegates at the 1767–8 LEGISLATIVE COMMISSION, speaking as deputy for the nobility of Yaroslavl' in support of the rights of the hereditary ruling class. Thereafter he held minor posts such as heraldmaster and chamberlain, but never received a major office of state. His appointment in 1768 as official historiographer led to the publication of seven volumes of his *History of Russia* (1770–90). Works unpublished in his lifetime include his essay *On the Corruption of Morals in Russia* (1787; first published 1858), which attributed the decay in moral standards to the poor example offered by the extravagant, favourite-ridden court, and his utopian novel *Journey to the Land of Ophir* (1783–4). Earlier historians dismissed him as a reactionary, but his reputation has since been rehabilitated. Admirers point to his well-informed views on science, education and foreign policy, and to his library of 15,000 volumes.

M. M. Shcherbatov, *On the Corruption of Morals in Russia*, ed. A. Lentin (Cambridge: Cambridge University Press, 1969).

LINDSEY HUGHES

Shelburne, William Petty, second earl of (1737–1805)   English statesman. He was one of the most original thinkers among eighteenth-century British politicians, but was widely distrusted for being difficult to deal with. A disciple of Chatham (*see* PITT the elder) he was influenced by the French physiocrats and patronized radicals such as Price and Bentham. In 1782 he favoured a generous peace with the Americans, hoping that this might preserve a common foreign policy and commercial links. When Rockingham (1730–82) died George III appointed Shelburne as premier. He defended the king's right to choose ministers and this, together with disagreements over the peace negotiations, led to conflict with FOX. Fox and North threw out the draft peace treaty, enforcing his resignation. He never held office again. An advocate of economic and parliamentary reform and of religious and civil liberties, he sympathized with the ideals of 1789 and opposed the war with France. A fascinating mixture of conservatism and radicalism, he did not fit any conventional category. His career demonstrated that intellect and insight could not ensure political success without good judgement and the ability to win the confidence of others.

J. Norris, *Shelburne and Reform* (London: Macmillan, 1963).

JOHN W. DERRY

Sheridan, Richard Brinsley (1751–1816)   Irish playwright and politician. He wished to be esteemed as a political orator, and was active as a playwright only briefly. Posthumously, however, he became the most highly regarded of eighteenth-century dramatists. He was born in Ireland, the son of Thomas Sheridan (1719–88), actor and teacher of elocution, and Frances Sheridan, novelist and dramatist. In his mid-twenties he produced his major works, *The Rivals* (1775), *The School for Scandal* (1777) and *The Critic* (1779). This period also saw *St Patrick's Day*, *The Duenna* (both 1775) and *A Trip to Scarborough* (1777). From 1776 he was principal manager and part owner of the Theatre Royal, Drury Lane (which was destroyed by fire in 1809). Apart from *Pizarro*, an adaptation of a play by Kotzebue (1761–1819), in 1799, he stopped writing plays before he was 30. Thereafter, he pursued a career in politics, becoming renowned as a parliamentary orator. He became member of parliament for Stafford in 1780, as a supporter of Fox (whom he succeeded as member for Westminster in 1806), and held various posts in liberal ministries during the 1780s, and again after 1806. He lost his seat in parliament in 1812, and was arrested for debt a year later. He died in 1816.

J. Loftis, *Sheridan and the Drama of Georgian England* (Cambridge, Mass.: Harvard University Press, 1977).

JOHN MULLAN

Sicily   The island of Sicily changed hands several times following the TREATY OF UTRECHT (1713) which ended Spanish rule there. It went first to the house of Savoy until 1718, when the Spanish retook the island easily and turned it over to the Austrian Habsburgs who ruled until 1735, when Sicily came definitively under the Neapolitan Bourbons. Each of the rulers initiated ambitious reform programmes – the Savoyards in 1713, the Austrians in the 1720s and Charles III in the 1740s – which aimed to break the power of the feudal nobility, to reform taxation and to improve the economy in general and the lot of the peasantry in particular. They all failed, in the face of intransigent, effective resistance by the baronage, whose domination of the island's parliament was never broken. Reform was attempted for the last time under Caracciolo (1715–89) and Caramanico (1738–95), the royal viceroys of the period 1782–9, whose work met with some success but was halted by the French Revolution.

The population of Sicily was approximately 4.5 million by the late 1780s, a huge increase concentrated in the poorer rural areas. Some of the rural population growth was absorbed by Palermo, whose 200,000 inhabitants made it second in size only to Naples. Over 3 million Sicilians lived in communities controlled directly by the barons, whose power strangled the economy, preventing the building of any real roads outside Palermo, Their absenteeism allowed the rise of ruthless middlemen who in turn worsened the lot of the peasantry and fostered the conditions for banditry and other forms of disorder which plagued Sicily throughout this period.

M. I. Finley, D. Mack Smith and C. Duggan, *A History of Sicily* (London: Chatto & Windus, 1986).

S. J. Woolf, *A History of Italy, 1700–1860* (London: Methuen, 1979).

MICHAEL BROERS

Sieyès, Emmanuel Joseph, abbé (1748–1836)   French revolutionary statesman and constitutional theorist. He made his name with the pamphlet *Qu'est-ce que le Tiers État?* (What is the Third Estate?), which made a great impact in the run-up to the Estates General in 1789. Sacrificing a vocation as an ecclesiastical bureaucrat, he became a back-room plotter and constitutional expert. This 'monk of Revolution', as Robespierre called him, helped to draft the Constitutions of 1791, 1795 and 1799. Elected to the Estates General in 1789, he urged the decision to adopt the title 'National Assembly', composed the TENNIS COURT OATH, contributed to the drafting of the DECLARATION OF THE RIGHTS OF MAN AND THE CITIZEN and made major contributions to administrative changes in the Constituent Assembly. Elected to the Convention, he lay low during the Terror, served on the post-Thermidorian Committee of Public Safety, and after a spell in the Council of Five Hundred, was chosen as ambassador to Berlin in 1798, and then elected director in 1799. He plotted the Brumaire *coup* with Napoleon, who chose him as a member of the provisional consulate. He then saw his influence reduced by Napoleon, who did, however, make him president of the senate.

COLIN JONES

Silesia   A large and wealthy province on Germany's north-eastern border, Silesia was consolidated in the later Middle Ages from a collection of small principalities and duchies. Although part of the Bohemian lands, its population was totally German when the Habsburgs inherited it in 1526. Only part of it was ruled directly by the crown, the rest being autonomous, and the Habsburgs were unable to prevent the consolidation of Protestantism there. Protestant rights were guaranteed in the Treaties of Westphalia and in 1707 Charles XII of Sweden forced the emperor to accept the Altranstadt Convention reaffirming them. Silesia was very important to Austria's power in Germany and eastern Europe, for it was strategically located and had a thriving economy. It was therefore a severe blow when in 1740 Frederick II of Prussia invaded the province and successfully defended it against Austrian attempts to recover all but a small part of it (*see* SEVEN YEARS WAR). Its acquisition made Prussia a great power of European stature. The inhabitants were initially anti-Prussian, especially after Frederick II abolished the parliamentary estates and introduced Prussian administrative methods, but after 1763 it experienced substantial economic growth and the population became reconciled to Prussian rule.

H. Bartsch, *Geschichte Schlesiens* (Würzburg: Weidlich, 1985).

MICHAEL HUGHES

silver   Given the still relatively limited use of paper money, silver retained the importance it had had since the Middle Ages as the basic currency of exchange, along with copper, in most of Europe (gold was rarely used for mundane purposes). There was some silver-mining within Europe – notably in the Harz mountains, Saxony, Bohemia, the Tyrol, Slovakia and Bosnia. This was swamped in significance, however, by silver production in the New World, notably in the eighteenth century in MEXICO. Mexican supplies, together with increased gold production from Brazil and Colombia, had taken up the slack when Japan's prohibition of silver exports at the end of the seventeenth century threatened Europe with a bullion deficiency, and permitted a relative stabilization of currency in most states. The production and exchange of silver was a notable component in the increasingly integrated pattern of world trade. Europe needed silver in huge amounts to meet the demands for payment in coin for Asian luxury goods which European consumers required in ever-increasing quantities through the eighteenth century. Silver thus formed a critical link in a chain of interdependence, joining together Europe, the New World and the Far East.

COLIN JONES

sisters of charity   Religious communities of active life, engaging in education and poor relief, had developed throughout Catholic Europe in the wake of the Council of Trent. The organizational archetypes were, for education, the Ursulines founded in Brescia in 1516 by Saint

Angela Merici (1474–1540), and, for poor relief, the Daughters of Charity founded by Saints Vincent de Paul (1581–1660) and Louise de Marillac (1591–1660) in Paris in 1633. Numerous communities of sisters of charity on the latter model developed in the late seventeenth and eighteenth centuries, and played a major part in educational and poor-relief provision, particularly in France. They provided scope for a career and social esteem through work afforded few other women in the eighteenth century. By 1789 the Daughters of Charity numbered over 4,000 and ran 175 hospitals and several hundred home-relief institutions. Their administrative and medical expertise was considerable: when most communities were dissolved during the French Revolution, their absence contributed to a massive managerial crisis in poor relief and hospital institutions, and Napoleon allowed them to regroup even before the Concordat of 1802.

See also CHARITY, POVERTY AND POOR RELIEF.

Colin Jones, *The Charitable Imperative: Hospitals and Nursing in Ancien Régime and Revolutionary France* (London: Routledge, 1989).

COLIN JONES

slavery Pioneering settlements in the Americas initially used free, indentured or Indian labour. That changed with the creation of the labour-intensive sugar PLANTATIONS in Brazil. From Brazil (which absorbed more Africans than any other New World region), the use of black slaves spread northwards in the seventeenth century, into the CARIBBEAN and North America. Plentiful land, European capital and enslaved Africans, plus the burgeoning European demand for tropical staples, made possible the rise of black slavery in the Americas.

The eighteenth century was the apogee of black colonial slavery. Between 1700 and 1800 some 5.5 million Africans were shipped across the Atlantic and deposited primarily in the Caribbean islands where they worked on sugar plantations in field gangs and in the sugar factories. Slaves were not imported into North America in significant numbers until after 1730. By the time of abolition in 1807, the North American share of the total importation was 6 per cent (over half a million), compared to 20 per cent in the West Indies. American slaves grew tobacco, rice, indigo and cotton in the region between Savannah and Virginia. Most were owned and worked in small groups, whereas West Indian sugar slaves worked in gangs of upwards of 300.

Unlike their American counterparts, West Indian slaves did not reproduce easily, as a result of unequal sex ratios, intensive gang labour and the disease-ridden environments in which they had to live; only in Barbados did the population reproduce itself. The Caribbean, unlike North America, thus continued to depend on the Atlantic SLAVE TRADE for its labour force, and Africans hence continued to play a more formative role in the shaping of Caribbean society than in North America, where locally born slaves were more quickly acculturated to white society. This may also explain the greater frequency and violence of Caribbean slave rebellions.

Slaves were valued initially for their strength in the fields (although most Africans were severely debilitated by the Atlantic crossing). The maturing economies demanded more than brute strength, and a hierarchy of slave skills developed in the fields, factories, workshops and planters' homes. Slavery spread from the plantations to the towns and ports. Social control and the law were ill at ease with urban slavery, which allowed slaves levels of freedom uncommon in the country. In both town and country slaves began to develop economic independence, trading their crops, goods and skills on the open market. Some even travelled great distances, notably as enslaved sailors. By the late eighteenth century there was a community of slaves and free blacks in London. Slavery thus reached into the metropolitan heartlands of eighteenth-century Europe.

Planters initially demanded strong young men but in time they employed the sexes equally in the fields. It was within the slave community that slave women made their mark: as creators and defenders of the slave family and as interpreters of slave culture (much of it African) to the young. By the late eighteenth century black slavery began to collide with a new European sensibility. Ultimately, the European attachment to slavery was undermined by the ideals of the age of revolution. Ironically, slavery was to be revived, in the United States and Brazil, in the nineteenth century, at a time when the Europeans had abolished it.

R. W. Fogel, *Without Consent or Contract: The Rise and Fall of American Slavery* (New York: Norton, 1989).

JAMES WALVIN

slave trade   In the eighteenth century 5.5 million Africans crossed the Atlantic as slaves. The Dutch, the French and the Americans were important slave-traders, but it was the British who dominated the century's trade. The Caribbean absorbed 40 per cent of all imports to work the lucrative sugar plantations.

Africans were exported as slaves from the coast between Senegambia and Angola, but most of them came from the Guinea coast. Many were drawn from the African interior, along complex trading systems which took European (and Asian) goods into Africa in exchange for slaves. Recruited through local warfare and sometimes through indigenous slavery, slaves formed the most significant African export in the eighteenth century. (*See* AFRICA.) Initially, Africans had been relatively cheap and planters preferred to import rather than to breed slaves, but rising prices in the course of the century persuaded them to pay greater attention to slave-breeding.

The monopoly of slave-trading companies was replaced in the early eighteenth century by a more open trade. Thereafter, the slave trade boomed. The major British trading ports were London, Bristol and Liverpool, but many smaller ports also dispatched slave ships. Profits from the voyages were rarely higher than for other speculative maritime ventures, but the slave trade gave a major economic fillip to the slave ports' hinterland. Textiles and metalware, foodstuffs and re-exported goods were fed into the slave ships for trade and barter in Africa. It was rarely a triangular trade. While the slave ships traded goods for slaves, shipping them to the Americas and returning with tropical staples, the slave colonies thrived on a much more complex trading nexus: between colonies, and to and from Europe.

Slavers, often financed by a collection of local business interests, normally had to wait on the African coast before accumulating a sufficient cargo, but the longer they waited on the coast the greater the risk to the slaves and sailors from disease. The level of slave mortality and illness was determined by the time spent waiting on the coast and at sea. Neither could be accurately predicted. The crossing, of two months or more, could be made much worse by storms. Mortality levels were sometimes very high, the average being 12 per cent. Survivors were often enfeebled and sick and generally required a 'seasoning' period to convalesce on arrival. Many died within the early years of arrival, victims of their enslavement as much as of conditions in the Americas.

The British refined the eighteenth-century slave trade: their ships were custom-built, voyages became quicker and more efficient, and shipboard routines (of exercise and feeding) were designed to minimize losses. However, the sailors had to remain alert to the dangers of slave revolt, violence and suicide. Landfall involved cleaning and preparing the slaves for sale, making them appear healthier and fitter. The enfeebled and sick were described as 'refuse' slaves. Sale on arrival took a variety of forms. Some slaves were assigned to particular owners, while others were sold at public auctions or at terrifying 'scrambles', one ordeal thus replacing another.

See also SLAVERY.

Philip D. Curtin, *The Rise and Fall of the Plantation Complex* (Cambridge: Cambridge University Press, 1990).

JAMES WALVIN

smallpox   In the eighteenth century smallpox remained endemic and epidemic: as a German proverb had it, 'From love and smallpox but few remain free.' In the early eighteenth century, 10 to 15 per cent of all deaths in many countries were supposedly due to the disease. Most of those who died were children; adults would have already been exposed to the disease and have succumbed or become immune. In areas such as the New World, populations that had never before encountered the disease suffered terrible mortality.

Among the most significant effects of INOCULATION was a shift in ideas about the cause of the disease. The origins of smallpox no longer lay in an individual's constitution, or in poisonous seeds within the body, but in contagion, the spread of disease by a specific material cause. However, it was only with VACCINATION that the three-century-old European wave of smallpox deaths began to come to an end.

G. Miller, *The Adoption of Inoculation for Smallpox in England and France* (Philadelphia: University of Pennsylvania Press, 1957).

MARY E. FISSELL

Smith, Adam (1723–1790)   Scottish economist and philosopher. A pupil of Francis Hutcheson at Glasgow University from 1737, he went to Balliol College, Oxford in 1740 as a Snell exhibitioner. In 1751 he was appointed to the chair of logic at Glasgow and in the following year to that of moral philosophy. He resigned his chair on becoming tutor to the young duke of Buccleuch (1746–1812) whom he accompanied on a Grand Tour (1764–6), during which he met Quesnay, Turgot, and other physiocrats and *philosophes*.

His first book, *The Theory of Moral Sentiments*, was published in 1759; he was to continue revising it, the sixth edition appearing shortly before his death. Combining Stoic and Christian outlooks, the book afforded a sophisticated account of the nature of SYMPATHY and the formation of selves in modern society. *An Inquiry into the Nature and Causes of the Wealth of Nations* (1776) was, in Dugald Stewart's (1753–1828) opinion, 'the most comprehensive and perfect work that has yet appeared, on the general principles of any branch of legislation'. It endorsed FREE TRADE, demonstrating the benefits of the division of labour and the interdependency between manufacture and agriculture, and argued that the function of government was to protect the perfect right to property, rather than to police the provision of subsistence goods, and that, for all its inequality, modern market society would, in the long term, best meet the basic needs of the labouring poor.

Istvan Hont and Michael Ignatieff (eds), *Wealth and Virtue: The Shaping of Political Economy in the Scottish Enlightenment* (Cambridge: Cambridge University Press, 1983).

SYLVANA TOMASELLI

Smollett, Tobias (1721–1771) Scottish surgeon, novelist and man of letters. Born of a long-established Dumbartonshire family, Smollett studied at Glasgow University and practised as a ship's surgeon, in the merchant marine and in the royal navy. In 1744 he set up as a London surgeon, but soon primarily settled on a literary career, becoming one of the most prolific all-round writers of the age, turning his hand to satire, history, essays and journalism. He wrote a *History of England* (1758), and a major travelogue, *Travels through France and Italy* (1766). He edited the *Critical Review or Annals of Literature* (1755–63) and in 1762 began a political weekly, *The Briton*, to defend George III and his Scottish first minister, Lord Bute – John Wilkes's notorious *North Briton* was the response. But he is best remembered today for his novels, including the largely autobiographical *Roderick Random* (1748), *Peregrine Pickle* (1751) and *The Expedition of Humphry Clinker* (1771). Blessed with a cruel streak, Smollett excelled in hard, masculine, satirical humour and knockabout farcical scenes.

L. M. Knapp, *Tobias Smollett: Doctor of Men and Manners* (Princeton, NJ: Princeton University Press, 1949).

ROY PORTER

socialism It is not clear who first used the terms 'socialism' and 'socialist'. Early usages of these terms did not bear a straightforward relation to their subsequent meanings. One of Beccaria's most violent critics, Father Ferdinando Facchinei (*c*.1725–1812), of the order of Vallambrosa, coined the word 'socialist' in his *Notes and Observations on the Book entitled Of Crimes and Punishment* (1765) to describe those who considered the origins of society to reside in a voluntary contract between free and equal men; by 'socialist' he meant a disciple of Rousseau, such as Beccaria. During the eighteenth century the term 'socialist' was also employed in Italy and France to refer to the followers of Hugo Grotius (1583–1645) and Samuel Pufendorf (1632–94), and to members of the school of NATURAL LAW who made the idea of sociability the cornerstone of their political theory. Whether the abbé Morelly, the abbé Mably, the Jacobins, Babeuf and others were socialists or communists has been a subject of lively debate.

Franco Venturi, *Italy and the Enlightenment: Studies in a Cosmopolitan Century* (London: Longman, 1972).
Ference Fehér, *The Frozen Revolution: An Essay on Jacobinism* (Cambridge: Cambridge University Press, 1987).

SYLVANA TOMASELLI

society The advantages and disadvantages of society, its history and the conditions necessary to its maintenance were of great concern to eighteenth-century philosophers. Then as now, the term 'society' was used in a number of related senses. It was often employed in opposition to the notion of the individual. Thus, Johnson and Boswell agreed that daughters should not, whatever their feelings, follow their inclinations and allow themselves to marry men beneath them: 'I think it of the utmost consequence to the happiness of society, to which subordination is absolutely necessary', Boswell remarked. 'Society' was also used to denote the collective body of the people in contrast to government, its instrument; as for example in Johnson's explanation of toleration: 'Every society has a right to preserve publick peace and order, and therefore has a good right to prohibit the propagation of opinions which have a dangerous tendency. To say the *magistrate* has this right, is using an inadequate word: it is the *society* for which the magistrate is agent.' Such views on the liberty of expression did not prevent him from thinking that 'Without truth there must be a dissolution of society. As it is, there is so little truth, that we are almost afraid to trust our ears; but how should we be, if falsehood were multiplied ten times? Society is held together by communication and information; and I remember this remark of Sir Thomas Browne's "Do the devils lie? No; for then Hell could not subsist." ' In this view society was the network of relations between individuals from which everyone benefited, and which had to be based on trust; a society of liars would be unsustainable. Being trustworthy, keeping one's word and hence being in a position to enter into contracts with other individuals, as well as being capable of self-denial for the happiness of the whole, were thus vital to society. 'All societies, great and small', Johnson dictated to Boswell, 'subsist upon this condition; that as the individuals derive advantages from union, they may likewise suffer inconveniences.'

That mankind had never known life outside society was the general view, for not even the natural law philosophers conceived of the state of nature as a solitary one. It was not, however, taken for granted that man was by nature a social creature. Lengthy arguments were presented in defence of society, mostly in reaction against ROUSSEAU's notorious depiction *Discours sur l'origine de l'inégalité parmi les hommes* of natural man and woman, living solitary existences. Clans, tribes and groupings were unknown in the state of nature as he conceived of it. Not even families existed; men and women met only through chance encounters, after which they parted company, and mothers remained with their offspring only until they could be independent. Rousseau regarded society as being artificial: in his view, it was only owing to great natural calamities and the scarcity which followed them that men and women were brought together into society.

Many writers refuted Rousseau's account of the infancy of the species, arguing that even in the state of nature men, however aggressive and competitive, lived in groups, as did lions and wolves. But a good number of them continued the tradition, of tracing the progress of society and civilization from its earliest stages to modernity. Among them some, like Rousseau himself, thought it helpful to conceive of society, as opposed to the earlier hordes or clans, as the product of a social contract, giving rise to government through the surrender by every individual of some, or all, of his natural RIGHTS.

Here a distinction can be drawn between the notion of society, generally speaking, and that of CIVIL SOCIETY. Used with increasing frequency in the eighteenth century, the term 'civil society' could refer to societies that knew a notable degree of civilization and refinement in contrast to primitive or savage societies (see SAVAGERY); it could also be used more narrowly to denote only the societies of nations governed by laws and not by the despotic wills of their rulers. Thus, one could speak of various Oriental societies of the eighteenth century and of the sophistications of their art or culture, but not deem them part of the history of civil societies. The concept of 'civil society', therefore, had a political facet or implication which 'society' did not.

Among those who did not consider the idea of a social contract to be beneficial to political thought was HUME. He was also one of the many Enlightenment philosophers who believed the family to be the most natural society of mankind. Thus, in *A Treatise of Human Nature* he argued: 'in order to form society, 'tis requisite not only that it be advantageous, but also that men be sensible of its advantages; and 'tis impossible, in their wild uncultivated state, that by study and reflexion alone, they should ever be able to attain this knowledge. Most fortunately, therefore, there is conjoin'd to those necessities, whose remedies are remote and obscure, another necessity, which having a present and more obvious remedy, may justly be regarded as the first and original principle of human society. This necessity is no other than that natural appetite betwixt the sexes, which unites them together, and preserves their union, till a new tye takes place in their concern for their common offspring ... In a little time, custom and habit operating on the tender minds of the children, makes them sensible of the advantages, which they may reap from society, as well as fashions them by degrees for it, by rubbing off those rough corners and untoward affections, which prevent their coalition.'

Outside Europe, the reflections of Japanese thinkers of the Tokugawa era (1600–1868) on the nature of society are of interest. For Ogyū Sorai (1666–1728) – who was to be compared to Bentham by Nakae Chōmin (1847–1901) because social utility constituted the underlying principle of his thought – it was society and its history, rather than nature, that held the key to social and political ideals. It has also been argued that this led him to seek in historical studies the support he wanted for the view that government should be in the hands of the gifted few ruling in the interest of society as a whole.

Maurice Cranston, *The Noble Savage: Jean-Jacques Rousseau 1754–1762* (Harmondsworth: Penguin, 1991).

John Dunn, 'From Applied Theology to Social Analysis', in Istvan Hont and Michael Ignatieff (eds), *Wealth and Virtue: The Shaping of Political Economy in the Scottish Enlightenment* (Cambridge: Cambridge University Press, 1983), pp. 119–35.

Tetsuo Najita, *Visions of Virtue in Tokugawa Japan: The Kaitakudo Merchant Academy of Osaka* (Chicago: University of Chicago Press, 1987).

SYLVANA TOMASELLI

Sonnenfels, Joseph baron **von** (1733–1817) Leading figure of the Austrian Enlightenment. The greatest authority in the field of administrative science, he combined an administrative career with vigorous academic, literary and journalistic activities, like many prominent contemporaries. He was the son of a professor at the University of Vienna, a Jewish convert to Catholicism who was ennobled by Maria Theresa. In 1762 he became professor of administrative science (*Cameralwissenschaft*) at Vienna. He enjoyed considerable influence over Emperor Joseph II and was a leading member of a number of legislative commissions which carried through reforms of education and the criminal law, including the abolition of torture in 1776. He also chaired the book and theatre censorship commissions and was secretary of the Viennese Academy of Arts. He published a large number of works on political, financial and administrative matters, building on the work of JUSTI. His most important work was the three-volume *Grundsätze der Polizei- Handlungs- und Finanzwissenschaft* (Basic Principles of the Science of Administration, Business and Finance, 1765–76). He also launched a number of periodicals, including a women's journal.

See also CAMERALISM.

K. Tribe, 'Cameralism and the Science of Government', *Journal of Modern History*, 56 (1984), 263–84.

MICHAEL HUGHES

Sorbonne One of the most celebrated of the colleges attached to the University of Paris, the Sorbonne, whose name was synonymous with the faculty of theology, was the traditional guardian of Catholic orthodoxy. In the first part of the eighteenth century the Paris faculty was deeply divided over the bull UNIGENITUS DEI FILIUS. The bull, issued by the pope in 1713, condemned as heretical 101 propositions in the *Réflexions morales* of the Jansenist Pasquier Quesnel (1634–1719). The bull met with widespread opposition from the Augustinian and

Gallican wing of the French Church because it seemed to discourage an austere morality and implied that the pope had power over temporal rulers.

As the resultant controversy monopolized the minds of Paris theologians for the next half-century, the faculty initially ignored the new threat to Christianity from the *philosophes*. It was not until 1751, when a dissertation sustained by the abbé de Prades (1720–82) suggested that the *philosophes*' critique of the Bible had infected the ranks of the faculty, that eighteenth-century materialism and deism became a central concern. Among the works subsequently censured were Pope's *Essay on Man*, Helvétius's *De l'esprit*, Rousseau's *Émile* and Marmontel's *Belisaire*.

In 1793 the revolutionaries permanently closed the Paris faculty and the colleges of the University of Paris became state property, but it was not the end of the Sorbonne as a centre of learning. In the early nineteenth century it became the home of the Paris faculty of letters and henceforth its name became synonymous with philosophical, literary and historical studies.

L. W. B. Brockliss, *French Higher Education in the Seventeenth and Eighteenth Centuries: A Cultural History* (Oxford: Clarendon, 1987).

LAURENCE BROCKLISS

South America   *see* AMERICA, SPANISH.

southern continent   Much of eighteenth-century oceanic exploration was devoted to the search for the southern continent, *Terra Australis Incognita*. The notion of a land mass counterbalancing those of the northern hemisphere originated with the Greeks but was later supported by geographers such as Mercator (1512–94) and Ortelius (1527–98). In the eighteenth century its chief promoters were John Campbell, Alexander Dalrymple (1737–1808) and Charles de Brosses (1709–1777). The most likely locations were seen as the Pacific, somewhere between New Zealand and South America, and the south Atlantic. To geographers like Dalrymple, the southern continent would balance the northern hemisphere in peoples and materials, as well as in mass, and was therefore a worthwhile imperial object.

The first eighteenth-century voyage in pursuit of the continent was by the Dutchman Jacob Roggeveen (1659–1729) in 1721–2. A succession of British and French expeditions subsequently chipped back the perimeters of any likely land mass. Byron (1723–86) in 1764–5, Wallis (1728–95) and CARTERET in 1767 and BOUGAINVILLE in 1768 all had the discovery of the continent as their principal objectives. With COOK's magnificent second voyage, the myth of a habitable Terra Australis was systematically destroyed.

J. C. Beaglehole, *The Exploration of the Pacific* (London: A. & C. Black, 1966).

DAVID MACKAY

South Sea Bubble (1720)   Corrupt mismanagement of the SOUTH SEA COMPANY gave rise to the South Sea Bubble, a financial crisis which hit Britain in the summer of 1720. As it operated under an international treaty (the Treaty of Utrecht), the company appeared to be an organ of state; in fact, it was overcapitalized and critically underemployed due to the deterioration in Anglo-Spanish relations between 1716 and 1719. Through the chancellor of the exchequer, John Aislabie (1670–1742) it won parliamentary support for taking over £30 million of unsecured debt. George I, who had been appointed governor of the company in 1718, gave the royal assent to the conversion on 7 April 1720. The company's stock value was falsely quoted when it accepted government obligations in lieu, and so the stock rose dramatically. Influx of foreign (especially Dutch) money made it rise from 360 on 18 May to 870 on 2 June. A week later the king assented to the Bubble Act, a criminal statute to suppress mushroom companies taking their cue from the South Sea Company. The stock peaked on 24 June at 1,050 but, with foreign withdrawals, was slipping inexorably by August. In September assets were written down by 50 per cent, and on 5 October the government intervened with fresh supplies of coinage. The government was only temporarily shaken by the crash, but until the 1760s JOINT-STOCK COMPANIES were discredited in Britain.

J. Carswell, *The South Sea Bubble* (London: Cresset, 1961).

D. D. ALDRIDGE

South Sea Company   Notorious through the SOUTH SEA BUBBLE of 1720, the South Sea Company was founded by the Tory leader Robert Harley (1661–1724) in 1711 to compete with the Whig-dominated Bank of England and East India Company. Like them it was a chartered company, operating with royal and parliamentary approval (*see* CHARTERED TRADING COMPANIES), but, unlike them, its total capital consisted of funded government obligations, and a working capital had essentially to be raised through trading privileges within the Spanish empire. These were critically limited by Spain at Utrecht, within the terms of the forty-year ASIENTO. Harley acted with culpable misjudgement and party bias in employing a directorate without any knowledge of trade, half of whom were bent on revenge against the Bank of England for past slights. By the end of 1719, a year of war between Britain and Spain, the company had had to turn to stockjobbing. With parliamentary and court support, it outbid the Bank of England in an offer to convert £30 million of unsecured national debt, and through false quotations of stock value the company made substantial initial profits from exchanging stock for government obligations. The speculation it invited led to its crash. It held the Asiento until 1749. In 1854 the company was wound up with a capital of £10 million.

J. G. Sperling, *The South Sea Company* (Boston: Kress, 1962).

D. D. ALDRIDGE

Spain Eighteenth-century Spain made few efforts to break with its past, and change was less significant than historians once believed. Political changes came early, as a result of the WAR OF THE SPANISH SUCCESSION, which marked the disappearance of its European empire (*see* TREATY OF UTRECHT) and the political unification of the peninsula (abolition of the autonomy of Aragon and Valencia in 1707, of Catalonia in 1714). These developments brought with them substantial administrative and political innovation, including a restructuring of the tax system, the army and the navy, and the introduction of intendants. But there was little movement away from the past in society or economy, and the grave subsistence and fiscal crises of the 1790s were clear testimony to the absence of effective reform.

Historians used to cite a sharp increase of population in the second half of the century as a fundamental stimulant to progress, but recent research has emphasized that the population – already rising early in the century – in fact grew slowly and faced major reverses in the last decade of the century, so that the 'vital revolution' experienced in northern Europe did not occur here. The persistence of traditional structures, not only demographic but also social and economic, was a basic fact which dampened the endeavours of reformist intellectuals like CAMPOMANES and Jovellanos (1744–1811). In the early part of the century the state encouraged industrial projects, mainly textiles, because they helped to raise taxes, but by the 1760s the evident problems of the rural economy and the plight of commerce forced a search for more long-term solutions. Numerous projects were drawn up for an 'agrarian law' which would bring more land into productive use: by Olavide (1725–1803), Campomanes and Jovellanos (the celebrated *Informe* of 1794). Legislation for economic reform was continually proposed but never brought effectively into play.

The political union of Spain after 1714 facilitated the slow evolution of a bureaucracy, created in part through the military administration and in part through the judicial system. Reforms in the army were completed by ordinances of 1768. Civil administration was developed through the recruitment of officials chosen from the university-trained elite. The state assumed greater initiatives in the 1780s with a number of acts of legislation, which also took in a programme for the American colonies. Central control throughout the century was, however, always marginal, since the local oligarchies of nobles and landlords remained firmly in command of provincial administration. Until the 1800s Spain retained its traditional structures unchanged both in the economy and in politics.

Enlightened absolutism was at best a concept rather than a reality. The most positive aspect of the Enlightenment was the intellectual achievement of the elite minority, which drew heavily on the thought of England, France and Italy. Figures such as Feijoo in the early part of the century and Mayans y Siscar (1699–1781) in mid-century paved the way for an appreciation of the liberal elements in European thought. Later thinkers always expressed their ideas in concrete schemes for reform, as in the published *Discourses* of Campomanes, the rise of the economic societies and the attempt by Olavide to colonize the Sierra Morena. Parallel to a growth in press activity, there was a significant rise in learned publications (notably on the natural sciences) and in medical studies. An important development was growing criticism of the political and economic role of the church: the former took shape in the expulsion of the Jesuits in 1767, the latter could be seen in the programmes proposed by ministers like Campomanes which were not put into effect until the following century.

The French Revolution provoked a conservative reaction in upper circles and exposed the traditional character of Spanish society. War abroad and popular agitation within, culminating in the events of 1808, led to the fall of the monarchy, the dissolution of the social order and the independence of the American colonies (*see* SPANISH AMERICA). Only with the programme of the Cortes of Cadiz (1810–13) did Spaniards seize the opportunity to break with their country's past.

Richard Herr, *The Eighteenth-Century Revolution in Spain* (Princeton, NJ: Princeton University Press, 1958).
John Lynch, *Bourbon Spain 1700–1808* (Oxford: Blackwell, 1989).

HENRY KAMEN

Spallanzani, Lazaro (1729–1799)   Italian natural philosopher. He was renowned for his wide-ranging contributions to natural history, geology, zoology, chemistry, meteorology, vulcanology and reproductive generation. Abandoning jurisprudence studies in Bologna, he obtained a doctorate in philosophy and became an ordained priest. He followed an academic career which led to professorships at Modena and Pavia, while priesthood provided him with a professional and moral base from which he could more freely investigate aspects of God's natural world.

During his investigations of nature he verified the origin of mountain springs, determined the composition of volcanic lava and pursued such diverse studies as sensation in bats, the solvent properties of gastric juices and deep-sea marine phosphorescence. He constructed geological and marine specimen exhibits in many Italian museums from his own collections and established a laboratory of marine zoology at Portovenere. His greatest fame rests on his experiments in the reproductive generation of both animals and plants. He disproved van Leeuwenhoek's and J. T. Needham's (1713–81) claims of spontaneous generation, demonstrated that particular organisms could survive without air and identified partial regeneration capacities in many lower animal species. As a preformationist, he was convinced of ovism (*see* EMBRYOLOGY), which stance gave rise to vehement disputes with contemporary epigeneticists, Needham and Buffon.

C. E. Dolman, 'Spallanzani', in C. C. Gillispie (ed.), *Dictionary of Scientific Biography*, vol. 12 (New York: Charles Scribner's Sons, 1975), vol. 12, pp. 553–67.

PHILIP K. WILSON

Spanish Succession, War of the (1701–1714) The War of the Spanish Succession, which was fought nominally over the throne of Spain, involved world-wide interests in trade and the colonies. The succession, which had been in dispute for a generation due to the lack of an heir to CHARLES II, the last Habsburg ruler of Spain, had initially been resolved by partition treaties between the major European powers. The will of Charles II aimed to avoid any carve-up of the monarchy by settling the throne on Louis XIV's grandson, Philip duke of Anjou, who in 1700 became King PHILIP V of Spain, thereby provoking a declaration of war by the other disappointed powers. The Grand Alliance of The Hague (1701) united England, the Holy Roman Empire and the United Provinces against France and Spain. The main centre of land operations was in the Netherlands, where the duke of Marlborough inflicted major defeats on the French at BLENHEIM (1704) and Ramillies (1706), but there were also crucial spheres of conflict in Italy and the Iberian peninsula. In Italy the successful imperial forces, commanded by Eugene of Savoy, defeated the French at Turin (1706) and subsequently drove the Spanish out of the greater part of Italy, forcing the papacy, which had tried to be neutral, to recognize as king of Spain the allied pretender, the archduke Charles of Habsburg (1685–1740).

In the Iberian peninsula Portugal joined the allies (METHUEN TREATY) and facilitated a base for operations. Imperial and English troops made landings on the Mediterranean coast and secured Barcelona. In 1710 the gains of the antiwar Tories in the English elections, and the failure of the archduke to consolidate his position in the peninsula, together with his succession to the imperial crown, made peace inevitable.

Negotiations were opened and agreement eventually reached through the TREATY OF UTRECHT and the subsequent Treaty of Rastadt (1714), in which the Spanish Netherlands and the Italian possessions of Spain passed to the Empire, England occupied Gibraltar and Minorca, and Spain with its American colonies was guaranteed to Philip V.

Louis XIV, who confided that the war was really about control of trade to the New World, was the ruler who gained least, although the accession of a branch of his family to the throne of Spain was very prestigious. By its successful deployment of naval power in the Mediterranean, England emerged as the commercial victor, and also gained a foothold in America through securing the slave-trade ASIENTO, and permission to send an annual ship for trade. The Empire, to counterbalance its retreat from the traditional German lands, dominated northern Italy for the next century. Spain lost all its European empire but was now able to dedicate itself to internal renewal.

Henry Kamen, *The War of Succession in Spain 1700–1715* (London: Weidenfeld & Nicolson, 1969).

HENRY KAMEN

Spener, Philipp Jakob (1635–1705)   Lutheran clergyman. He was one of the most quiet but effective influences on PIETISM as it emerged *c*.1675 in Protestant northern Europe. When he died he had written more than 200 books and innumerable letters of expert spiritual and moral advice, which were published as *Theologische Bedencken* (1700–2) and *Letzte theologische Bedencken* (1711). His publications were able defences of Pietism and guides to a Christian life showing his deep concern with reforming the Lutheran Church. He saw this in a different light from his orthodox opposition, who insisted on church discipline, via secular and clerical authority from above.

Spener's purpose, clearly outlined in his seminal *Pia Desideria* (1675), was to renew an inner commitment to religion ('thaetiges Christenthum'). The means to this end were the *collegia pietatis*, founded during his time in Frankfurt (from 1666). The *collegia* were discussion circles based on readings from the Bible and devotional literature and open to lay men and women. They included aristocrats, members of the urban elite and skilled craftsmen. Through his encouragement and his wide circle of friends, these conventicles implemented Lutheran Pietist ideas and improvements (better education, charitable institutions, spiritual renewal through personal piety). Spener never left the church as did a number of his separatist friends; he supported fellow Pietists through his excellent connections with the court when he became rector of the Nikolaikirche in Berlin (1691). His very significant influence on Pietism was channelled through personal advice, letters, a discriminating and thorough training in theology reflected in his writings, and the wide used of these writings by those who valued a spiritual rather than a nominal Christianity.

J. Wallman, *Der Pietismus* (Göttingen: Vandenhoeck & Ruprecht, 1990).

JOHANNA GEYER-KORDESCH

spice trade   The trade in costly Asian spices greatly expanded with the European discovery of the Cape route to India at the turn of the sixteenth century. Although they failed to dislodge the existing Levant trade, the Portuguese did establish dominance in the new seaborne trade until they lost ground to the English and the Dutch in the seventeenth century. Driving their competitors out of the Indonesian archipelago and Ceylon, the DUTCH EAST INDIA COMPANY managed to monopolize the lucrative trade in the 'famous four' – cloves, mace, cinnamon and nutmeg – but continued to share pepper, which originated in a wider area, with European and Asian merchants. Throughout the seventeenth and eighteenth centuries enormous quantities of spices were thus purchased for bullion and cloth and shipped to Europe as well as to China and Persia.

After a peak in the late seventeenth century, the share of spices in the activity of the maritime companies gradually diminished. The Dutch lost their monopoly and ceded pre-eminence to the ENGLISH EAST INDIA COMPANY and private traders. With the decline of the Companies in the late eighteenth century, new participants, especially the United States, entered the spice market.

Holden Furber, *Rival Empires of Trade in the Orient, 1600–1800* (Minneapolis: University of Minnesota Press, 1976).

RUDI MATTHEE

Spinoza, Baruch [Benedictus de] (1632–1677)   Dutch philosopher. Born into the Amsterdam community of Sephardic Jews, refugees from Spanish-Portuguese persecution, he worked as a grinder of optical lenses while pursuing his philosophical studies. Excommunicated for heterodoxy by the synagogue in 1656, he was welcomed by the Collegiants, an ecumenical Protestant group, and developed contacts among the theorists of the States party (*see* ORANGEISM). Laying the foundations of enlightened biblical criticism (with roots in Sephardic scholarship), his *Tractatus Theologico-politicus* (Theological and Political Treatise, 1670; French translation 1678) treated the Old Testament as fallible history, dismissed its miracles as superstition and argued that the purpose of theology was to instil obedience rather than to discover truth. Not surprisingly, it got a hostile reception, and his other works were published only after his death. His unfinished

Tractatus Politicus (Political Treatise, 1677) used Italian as well as Dutch thought and practice to analyse the best forms of monarchy, aristocracy and democracy – the last being his preference, although he excluded servants and women from citizenship. His *Ethica* (1677) developed a pantheistic view of nature as a single entity, identifiable with God. Though at first generally condemned, Spinoza's work appealed to later philosophers such as Herder and Hegel – and, in our own time, to the inimitable Jeeves.

E. O. G. Haitsma Mulier, *The Myth of Venice and Dutch Republican Thought in the Seventeenth Century* (Assen: Van Gorcum, 1980).
R. Scruton, *Spinoza* (Oxford: Oxford University Press, 1986).

HUGH DUNTHORNE

Staël, Anne Louise Germaine Necker, Madame de [baroness of Staël-Holstein] (1766–1817) French writer. The only child of Jacques Necker, she made a precocious entrée to Parisian intellectual life in the *salon* of her mother Suzanne, née Churchod (1739–94). Marriage to Eric Magnus de Staël (1749–1802), Sweden's French ambassador, led to her own *salon*. She later used her diplomatic immunity courageously to help friends escape from France. Her circle at Necker's Vaudois chateau, Coppet, was the focus of liberal constitutionalist opposition to the Jacobins and Napoleon, who exiled her, as well as of cultural and political significance. The circle included her lover and intellectual intimate, Benjamin Constant (1767–1830), and A. W. Schlegel (1767–1845). Her writings on culture and society followed in the tradition of Montesquieu and the Scottish Enlightenment. Her famous exploration of German culture, *De l'Allemagne* (On Germany, 1813), was banned in France by Napoleon; *Considérations sur la Révolution française* (Considerations on the French Revolution, 1818), an early attempt to understand it, was a tribute to her beloved father. In her own life and through her fictional persona *Corinne* (1807) she was a significant model to women in the nineteenth century.

Madelyn Gutwirth, *Madame de Staël, Novelist* (Urbana, Ill. University of Illinois Press, 1978).

CLARISSA CAMPBELL ORR

Stahl, Georg Ernst (1660–1734) German physician. He was born in Anspach, Franconia, an enclave of Lutheranism in Catholic southern Germany, the son of an official of the church, and was thus sent to the Protestant University of Jena. His family was not rich and he was an example of the professional meritocracy at work in eighteenth-century Prussia. At his death in 1734 he had reached the highest medical office as first physician to Frederick-William I, and was president of the

Collegium Medicum-Chirurgicum, the body regulating medical affairs in Brandenburg-Prussia. In 1725 he had, together with Johann Theodor Eller (1689–1760), written the first effectively binding rules for the education, practice, reimbursement and conduct of medical practitioners in the monarchy.

He was a man of originality and principle. When he graduated from Jena in 1684 his interest was already clear: as a pupil of Georg Wedel (1645–1721) and together with his fellow student and later colleague in Halle, Friedrich Hoffmann (1660–1742), he became adept at the new science of medical chemistry. His training made him well aware of the inadequacy of classics-based medical teaching. In answer to the new circulation theory and the mechanical philosophy, he sought an entirely new systematization of physiology and pathology. These ideas were worked out fully in his *Theoria medica vera* (1708) and encompassed a practical medical reform based on dynamic processes (circulation of the fluids, activity of the fibres and organs) regulated by intelligence. This intelligence or soul activated the body in health and disrupted the psyche and body in disease. Therapeutics, whether drug-based or diatetic, were to be minimal and applied through expertise gained in case observations. His influence as professor of medicine at the University of Halle (1694–1715) was marked; many of his students published on the Stahlian method, which became a recognized school and the only antithesis to the Boerhaavian idea of somatic mechanism (the animal economy) in medicine. His emphasis on the crucial significance of soul and emotion was bitterly opposed, but resurfaced in psychiatry, ROMANTICISM and VITALISM.

JOHANNA GEYER-KORDESCH

Stamitz, Carl Philipp (1745–1801) German violinist and composer. He was the brother of the composer Anton Stamitz (1750–96) and the son of the Bohemian musician Johann Wenzel Anton Stamitz (1717–57), who founded the Mannheim School, which played an essential role in developing the early stages of the symphony. With the Mannheim School, the symphony orchestra replaced the random *ad hoc* ensemble of the aristocratic court, and the minuet was introduced as the third movement of the now four-movement symphony. The melody became dominant *vis-à-vis* the general bass, and determined the harmonies and structure of the music. New means of contrast were introduced (Mannheim crescendo), and the wind section was given a new importance and independence within the orchestra.

Carl Stamitz was a pupil of his father and of Christian Cannabich (1731–98). A member of the Mannheim court orchestra from 1731 to 1798, he then moved to Strasburg and Paris. From 1778 to 1793 he engaged in extensive concert tours through Europe, and in 1794 he settled in Jena as director of the academic concerts. His significance lay in his development of the sinfonia concertante form. He composed around fifty symphonies, fifty solo concertos and chamber music.

FRITZ WEBER

Stanislas Leszczyński *see* LESZCZYŃSKI, STANISLAS.

states general From 1579 the states general had constituted the UNITED PROVINCES' central representative assembly. Sovereignty within the Dutch state lay, however, with the seven units which comprised it, each of which had its own estates and administrative machinery, plus a hereditary head of the executive (stadtholder). This was a system that guaranteed inertia except in times of national emergency, or when the house of Orange, which provided the stadtholder in five of the provinces, was in the ascendant. William III of Orange (William III of England) was an effective monarch from 1672 until 1702, but there followed four decades in which republican oligarchies from the provinces based in the states general dominated. William IV provided a brief Orangeist episode between 1747 and 1751 but his death left the post in the hands of the 3-year-old William V. The states general held the upper hand up to 1787, when a political crisis led Prussia to intervene militarily on William V's behalf. The Netherlands were prey to French Revolutionary armies from 1792, and in 1795 the states general were abolished in the new BATAVIAN REPUBLIC, although the title was reinstated for the parliament of the kingdom of the Netherlands in 1814.

COLIN JONES

statistics The term 'statistics', derived from the Latin *status*, originally meant enquiries into the condition of a state. The seventeenth century saw the lively pioneering pursuit of 'political arithmetic' in the work of John Graunt (1620–74) of London, notably his *Natural and Political Annotations Made upon the Bills of Mortality* (1666), which was the first serious attempt to tabulate the changing mortality of the metropolis. His work was continued by Sir William Petty (1623–87), who published *Five Essays in Political Arithmetick* (1683), and by the astronomer and polymath Edmond Halley (1656–1742). But statistics in something like the modern sense of the word originated with J. P. Süssmilch's (1707–67) *Die göttliche Ordnung in den Veränderungen des menschlichen Geschlects aus der Geburt, dem Tode, und der Fortpflanzung desselben erwiesen* (1741). A Prussian pastor, Süssmilch expanded the earlier tradition of political arithmetic and attempted to apply what was later to be called the 'law of large numbers' to broad questions of national vital statistics: birth, death and marriage rates, taxation returns, military recruitment and so forth. (*See* DEMOGRAPHY, POPULATION GROWTH.)

In the second half of the eighteenth century especially, the arithmetical manipulation of data was developed by medical men attempting to correlate epidemic mortality with climate, population and other variables. It was also attractive to political economists like Mirabeau and Arthur Young, because numerical expressions suggested that economic forces were not subject to personal whim but obeyed scientifically discernible and universal natural laws. Enlightenment philosophers, like Hume, who denied the possibility of epistemological certainty were, on the whole, well disposed to the probabilistic mode of thinking entailed by the way of statistics (*see* PROBABILITY).

Gerd Gigerenzer et al., *The Empire of Chance* (Cambridge: Cambridge University Press, 1989).

Ian Hacking, *The Taming of Chance* (Cambridge: Cambridge University Press, 1990).

ROY PORTER

steam engine   In the eighteenth century steam engines provided a new source of energy, particularly in Britain where COAL was plentiful and cheap. They offered flexibility of location and year-round operation, but lower maximum power and poorer reliability than contemporary water-wheels. By 1800 one-fifth of Britain's mechanical energy was steam-generated: approximately 1,500 engines produced an average 23 horsepower, principally in mines, ironworks, flour and textile mills, breweries, waterworks and canals.

While the scientific properties of steam had been investigated by the Greeks, they were first intensively explored in the seventeenth century. The need of English mining industries for drainage at unprecedented depths stimulated Thomas Savery (*c*.1650–1715) and Thomas Newcomen (1663–1729) to invention. Newcomen's invention prevailed: in his 'atmospheric engine', first erected in Staffordshire in 1712, atmospheric pressure depressed a piston into a cylinder evacuated by the condensation of steam. Its fuel efficiency was trebled by WATT's invention of the separate condenser (patented 1769). His rotative engine promoted wider use in industry after 1782. High-pressure engines were under experimentation in Britain and the United States: greater power from smaller engines and less fuel made the locomotive and the steam boat feasible.

Richard L. Hills, *Power from Steam: A History of the Stationary Steam Engine* (Cambridge: Cambridge University Press, 1989).

CHRISTINE MACLEOD

Steele, Sir Richard (1672–1729) Irish man of letters and Whig propagandist. He was born in Dublin, educated at Oxford and joined the Life Guards in 1692. He wrote 'The Procession' (1695) on the death of Queen Mary (1662–94) and published *The Christian Hero: An Argument proving that no Principles but those of Religion are Sufficient to make a great Man* in 1701. His comedies, *The Funeral, or Grief à la Mode* (1701), *The Lying Lover* (1703) and *The Tender Husband* (1705), were not very successful. In 1706 he became gentleman waiter to Prince George of Denmark and in the following year was appointed editor to the *London Gazette*. He started *The Tatler* (1709–11), *The Spectator* (1711–12) with ADDISON, *The Guardian* (1713) and *The Englishman* (1713–14, 1715). He became a member of parliament in 1713, but was expelled the following year as a result of his pamphlet defending the Hanoverians, *The Crisis*. A member again in 1715, when he was knighted, he was appointed governor of the Theatre Royal, Drury Lane. His last play, *The Conscious Lovers* (1722), was highly successful. He sought to demonstrate how to lead a life of virtue within modern society, and presented domestic life as the source of true felicity.

Richard H. Dammers, *Richard Steele* (Boston: Twayne, 1982).

SYLVANA TOMASELLI

Sterne, Laurence (1713–1768) English novelist. Like other English pioneers of the novel, he came late to the writing of fiction. He was in his mid-forties when he began composing *The Life and Opinions of Tristram Shandy, Gentleman*, arguably the most inventive, and unarguably the most idiosyncratic, novel of the century. He was already committed to an (occasionally troubled) career in the church, and when the first two volumes of *Tristram Shandy* were published in 1759 he was a Yorkshire vicar. In 1760 he was licensed to the living of Coxwold, near York. *Tristram Shandy* was a huge and immediate success; it also scandalized critics and moralists, more because of its frequent sexual innuendo than its experiments with chronology and pictorial device. Sterne wrote further volumes of the book, published in four more stages up to 1767. It continued to enjoy notoriety – it was frequently parodied or imitated – and its author became a celebrity. Trading on his fame, Sterne published his *Sermons of Mr Yorick* in 1760 and 1766. 'Yorick', his transparent pseudonym, was the name of a character in *Tristram Shandy*, and of the narrator of his final work, *A Sentimental Journey* (1768). This novel too was ripe for continuation, but Sterne died only days after its publication.

Arthur Cash, *Laurence Sterne: The Later Years* (London: Methuen, 1980).

JOHN MULLAN

Struensee, Johann Friedrich, count (1737–1772)   German-born Danish doctor and statesman. Born in Halle to a pious but not illiberal family, he pursued medical studies, followed by medical journalism. He acquired influential Danish friends and in 1768 was installed as personal physician to CHRISTIAN VII, to whose extravagant and, later, insane fantasies Struensee seems, unusually, to have listened attentively. Back in Copenhagen after the king's European tour (1768–9), he quickly gained an authority possible only in Europe's most absolute monarchy. Cabinet orders from the autumn of 1770 record a series of reforms, beginning with freedom of the press and embracing Struensee's special interest, public health, among many other changes. Still surprising today for their range and the speed with which they were promulgated, these resolutions infuriated vested interests and, more seriously, various court factions. The latter may also have realized that Struensee's liaison with Queen Caroline Mathilde (1751–75) was, if anything, a stabilizing factor for Christian. A *coup* brought about his downfall in January 1772, and three months later his execution as a traitor (by hanging, followed by quartering and the wheel) became the subject of a hundred prurient penny prints.

Stefan Winkle, *Johann Friedrich Struensee: Ärzt, Aufklärer, Staatsmann: Beitrag zur Kultur-, Medizin-, und Seuchengsgeschichte der Aufklärungzeit* (Stuttgart: Gustav Fischer, 1983).

CHRISTINE STEVENSON

Stuart, Charles Edward Louis Philip Casimir (1720–1788)   Son of James Francis Edward STUART, claimant to the British throne. Known variously as the 'Young Pretender' and 'Bonnie Prince Charlie', he was born on 31 December 1720 at Rome. He led the attempts to invade Britain and restore the Stuart dynasty, beginning with the abortive French naval invasion planned in the spring of 1744. In July 1745 Charles sailed from France to land in Scotland, raising the Stuart standard on 19 August at Glenfinnan. By 21 September his Highland army had occupied Edinburgh and beaten the superior force of Sir John Cope (*d.* 1760) at Prestonpans. The handsome and victorious prince enjoyed adulation in Scotland, but the invasion of England begun on 8 November 1745 brought disaster. His army reached as far as Derby, spreading panic through England, but retreated northward in early December. On 16 April 1746 he was decisively defeated at CULLODEN and was a fugitive until his escape to France on 20 September. The last practicable Jacobite invasion plan was the short-lived French scheme of 1759. When 'James III' died on 1 January 1766, even the pope did not recognize Charles Edward as 'Charles III'. His physical and mental health deteriorated quickly: asthmatic, dropsical and a chronic alcoholic, he died in Rome on 30 January 1788.

See also JACOBITES.

F. McLynn, *Charles Edward Stuart: A Tragedy in Many Acts* (London: Routledge, 1988).

PHILIP WOODFINE

Stuart, James Francis Edward (1688–1746) Claimant to the British throne. The son of James II (not the warming-pan baby of legend), he succeeded his father as Stuart claimant in 1701, being proclaimed James III of England and James VIII of Scotland. He sailed to the Firth of Forth in the 1708 invasion attempt, and again landed in Scotland in December 1715. Establishing his court at Scone Palace in January 1716, he made preparations for a coronation, but had to flee in the face of the advancing troops of George I's general, the duke of Argyll. He never again visited Britain. He married Maria Clementina Sobieski in 1719 and was the father of Charles Edward STUART (Bonnie Prince Charlie) and Cardinal Henry. Politically inept and lacking in charisma, he nevertheless showed bravery at the Battle of Malplaquet (1709). While Louis XIV was at war with Queen Anne, he lived at St Germain-en-Laye, near Paris, but thereafter at Bar-le-Duc in Lorraine, Avignon and, thanks to British diplomatic pressure, from 1728 continually in Italy, first at Bologna and then at the Palazzo Muti in Rome. He had a papal pension from 1727, and remained a firm Catholic, refusing to consider conversion to Protestantism in order to gain Britain.

JEREMY BLACK

Sturm und Drang [Storm and Stress] The mainly literary revolutionary movement that began in Germany in the 1770s with an explosion of subjective energy which swept aside the restraints of the rational Enlightenment now takes its name *Sturm und Drang* from the title of a play by F. M. Klinger (1752–1831). The young generation, inspired by figures like Hamann and Klopstock at home, by Rousseau and by English writers like Young, Macpherson and, above all, Shakespeare, cast aside accepted social and literary norms and put their faith in NATURE. HERDER was the movement's theoretician, and the volume of essays he edited entitled *Von deutscher Art und Kunst* served as its manifesto. 'Nature' was the watchword: for the individual it meant reliance on feeling and 'genius'; and for society it meant liberty and social justice. The plays of J. M. R. Lenz (1751–92), H. L. Wagner (1747–79), F. M. Klinger (1752–1831) and the young GOETHE and SCHILLER characteristically dispensed with the unities, giving a sense of 'life'. In poetry the new emphasis on subjectivity inspired Goethe's early lyrics; other achievements ranged from the songs of Mathias Claudius (1740–1814) to G. A. Bürger's (1747–94) ballads. The meteoric movement burned itself out in a decade, having dramatically changed the face of German literature and set the scene for European ROMANTICISM.

Roy Pascal, *The German Sturm und Drang* (Manchester: Manchester University Press, 1953).

JEREMY ADLER

sublime While the adjective 'sublime' was used from the sixteenth century to describe grand or elevated writing, it was only in the early eighteenth century that 'the sublime', as a substantive, became a common topic of critical discussion. In his highly influential *Philosophical Enquiry into the Origin of our Ideas of the Sublime and the Beautiful* BURKE wrote: 'whatever is in any sort terrible . . . is a source of the *sublime*; that is, it is productive of the strongest emotion which the mind is capable of feeling.' The sublime in nature or literature (the word connected appreciation of the two) was that which was pleasurably awesome, frightening or overwhelming. Most frequently, the sublime was an effect of visual perception. In descriptive texts, in paintings or in nature itself, it was produced by all that surpassed human scale and comprehension.

Burke brought to his analysis of the sublime a Lockean rigour. The idea was derived from Longinus's treatise *On the Sublime*, first made widely available in Boileau's French translation of 1674, and then in Welsted's (1688–1747) English version of 1712, followed by William Smith's (1711–87) translation and commentary of 1739. The latter drew samples from the Bible, Shakespeare (1564–1616) and Milton (1608–74), texts which, by transcending elegance, continued as exemplars of the sublime. Theories of the sublime were the first systematic attempts to transform AESTHETICS into what we would call psychology.

S. H. Monk, *The Sublime* (New York: MLA, 1935).

JOHN MULLAN

sugar In the 2,500-year history of the sugar industry the eighteenth century stands out as the period during which the island colonies of the CARIBBEAN played the pivotal role in a tricontinental trading system, based on an exchange of sugar, molasses and rum for African slaves, European manufactured goods and North American foodstuffs and timber. In the late 1700s Caribbean sugar exports in the order of 200,000 tonnes accounted for about three-quarters of recorded world trade, most of the rest coming from South America. Annual per capita consumption in Britain rose from 4 pounds (1.8 kilograms) in 1700–9 to 18 pounds (8.2 kilograms) a hundred years later, turning sugar from a luxury into a household staple. Satisfaction of the growing demand for sugar in Europe and North America entailed the transportation to the western hemisphere of millions of Africans who put their distinctive mark on the societies of tropical America (*see* SLAVE TRADE).

At the close of the century the Haitian Revolution, the advent of the steam engine and successful experiments with beetroot as a source of sugar in temperate regions foreshadowed a new era.

J. H. Galloway, *The Sugar Cane Industry* (Cambridge: Cambridge University Press, 1989).
S. W. Mintz, *Sweetness and Power* (New York: Viking Penguin, 1985).

G. B. HAGELBERG

suicide In both Catholic and Protestant nations suicide, or 'self-murder', was traditionally designated as a crime and a heinous sin, incited by the Devil. Suicides were buried in unconsecrated ground and their belongings forfeit. From the late seventeenth century the secularizing currents of the Enlightenment began to soften attitudes towards the nefarious deed. In practice, those who killed themselves were increasingly judged to have been disordered in mind. When suicide was seen not as a deliberate violation of the commandment against murder, but as the impulse of an unbalanced mind, it could be largely exonerated.

The moral philosophizings of the Enlightenment, notably Montesquieu's *Lettres persanes*, went further to offer defences of the right to suicide. The *Encylopédie*'s article on the subject dutifully summarized the Christian arguments, but closed with a vindication of the right to take one's own life. Increasingly, the great suicides of antiquity, notably Seneca, were admired as examples of the triumph of nobility of mind, and, especially after 1750, with the arrival of the age of SENSIBILITY, the man or woman who committed suicide out of love, melancholy or despair became the new hero or heroine of popular novels, particularly following the scandalous success of *Werther* by Goethe.

M. MacDonald and T. Murphy, *Sleepless Souls: Suicide in Early Modern England* (Oxford: Clarendon, 1990).

ROY PORTER

Sunday schools The first Sunday school was said to have been founded by an evangelical Gloucester printer named Robert Raikes (1735–1811) in 1781. It was part of a widespread, interdenominational, lay-controlled burgeoning of philanthropic institutions of the late eighteenth century, and more specifically of a new concern for CHILDREN motivated by a combination of the desire to remove them from the corrupting influence of their parents, to teach them to read the Gospels and simply to better their lives.

The largest and most famous of the early schools, in Manchester, Stockport and Leek for example, were not attached to any church or chapel, but by 1800 few such institutions had survived the suspicion of dissent bred by the French Revolution. In 1801 over 1,200 schools were under the direction of the Church of England, and over 1,000 more were loosely connected with chapels, while only a handful of very large schools, some with over 1,000 students, remained independent. Some 200,000 children were attending these schools.

Although Sunday schools were to some extent an effort by the 'middling sorts' to mould the characters of the poor, teachers at the schools came largely from the same social strata as the children being taught. Instruction in reading, largely from a wide range of biblical texts with an overt social message, was the core of the curriculum; some schools also taught writing to older children and a few offered evening classes in other subjects. By 1831 over a million students, more than half of them at schools associated with dissent, were enrolled in an institution that was central to the making of English working-class 'respectability'.

THOMAS W. LAQUEUR

superstition 'That the corruption of the best things produces the worst', HUME remarked in his essay 'Of Superstition and Enthusiasm' (1741), 'is grown into a maxim, and is commonly proved, among other instances, by the pernicious effects of *superstition* and *enthusiasm*, the corruptions of true religion.' Although the distinction between superstition or fanaticism and true religion was by no means a novel one, it was one of the favourite sports of the *philosophes* to investigate, or pretend to investigate, the psychological origins of superstition. This often led to their casting ridicule on the central tenets of Judaism and Christianity in more or less explicit terms.

For Hume, 'Weakness, fear, melancholy, together with ignorance' were the true sources of superstition, while 'Hope, pride, presumption, a warm imagination, together with ignorance' were the true sources of ENTHUSIASM. Although he regarded both as pernicious, he argued that the effects of each 'species of false religion' were not only different, but contrary, and offered three reflections on the subject: firstly, 'That superstition is favourable to priestly power, and enthusiasm not less or rather more contrary to it, than sound reason and philosophy'; secondly, 'that religions, which partake of enthusiasm are, on their first rise, more furious and violent than those which partake of superstition; but in a little time become more gentle and moderate'; and finally, 'that superstition is an enemy to civil liberty, and enthusiasm a friend to it'.

The *Encyclopédie* defined superstition as 'any religious excess'. Its author, the chevalier de Jaucourt (1704–79), like Hume, considered it to be the product of fear. For him, as for Enlightenment thinkers in general, superstition was the antithesis of reason and hence of everything that they stood for; indeed, he wrote of it as a kind of mental derangement: those who were ill or unhappy were particularly prone to superstition. But even those who were sound of mind and body soon ceased to be able to resist it once they were touched by it: it was 'mankind's most terrible scourge', worse than atheism, since atheism did not obscure an individual's perception of his own self-interest and hence did not constitute a threat to public order. Superstition, on the other hand, could, and indeed had, undermined empires. This was a point or 'paradox' which BAYLE had made famous and which many Enlightenment writers subsequently took up. For instance, it was one of the themes in Gibbon's *Decline and Fall of the Roman Empire*, although he was careful to distinguish between superstitious cults, like those of the Romans, that had bolstered civil society, and those within monotheistic religions that, in view of monotheism's tendency towards intolerance and fanatism, undermined good government. In their writings on the psychological origins and the impact of religion on the human mind and society, eighteenth-century authors like Gibbon and Jaucourt drew inspiration from Titus Lucretius Carus's poem *De rerum natura* and identified with the 'mighty one of Greece', Epicurus, Lucretius' hero:

> ... Long time Men lay opprest with slavish Fear,
> Religion's Tyranny did domineer,
> Which being plac'd in Heaven look'd *proudly* down,
> And frighted abject Spirits with her Frown.
> At length a mighty one of *Greece* began
> T'assert the natural Liberty of Man,
> By senseless Terrors and vain Fancies led
> To slavery; streight the conquer'd Fantoms fled, ...

Drawing on Hume's distinction between superstition and enthusiasm, we can say that the Enlightenment's victory over the former only enhanced the latter's powers as the century came to its terrible end. Enthusiasm, *pace* Hume, proved no better friend to liberty than any other species of irrationality.

Lucretius, His Six Books of Epicurean Philosophy, trans. Thomas Creech (1700), in Peter Gay (ed.), *The Enlightenment: A Comprehensive Anthology* (New York: Simon & Schuster, 1973).

David Hume, *Essays: Moral, Political and Literary*, ed. Eugene F. Miller (Indianapolis: Liberty, 1985).

Roy Porter, *Gibbon* (London: Weidenfeld & Nicolson, 1988).

SYLVANA TOMASELLI

Supreme Being, Cult of the   The Cult of the Supreme Being, which was associated with ROBESPIERRE, represented an attempt to institute a secular, deistic religion grounded in support for the values of the

French Revolution. Although the Revolution had been initially favourable to the Catholic Church, the schism caused by the Civil Constitution of the Clergy and the suspicion that attached to refractory
clergy once war had broken out made patriotism and Catholicism
increasingly incompatible. Anticlericalism became widespread, and
in autumn 1793 Hébertist radicals in Paris, assisted by like-minded
représentants en mission in the departments, began militantly atheistic
'DECHRISTIANIZATION' campaigns. Robespierre mistrusted the revolutionary fidelity of the Hébertists, and to counter their appeal devised
a Rousseauist state cult which was founded on belief in a Supreme
Being and immortality of the soul. Once the Hébertists had been purged
(March 1794), Robespierre persuaded the Convention to accept the
cult as the state religion (7 May 1794), and went on to celebrate the
Festival of the Supreme Being. The slightly ridiculous cult was attacked by both Catholics and non-believers. It was too closely associated with Robespierre to survive his fall. However, attempts to
formulate a cult of patriotism continued under the Directory.

                                                        COLIN JONES

Sweden In the eighteenth century, with the rise of Russia, Sweden
lost most of its empire: as a result of the GREAT NORTHERN WAR, it lost
Kexholm, Ingria, Estonia and Latvia to Russia, Bremen and Verden to
Hanover, and part of Pomerania to Prussia; after a war in 1741–3 it
lost Karelia to Russia; and in the Napoleonic conflicts it lost Finland
(1809) and the rest of Pomerania (1815), although Norway was gained
(1814). The conflicts placed major demographic and economic burdens on the country, and war and foreign policy disputes were a
central theme in Swedish political disputes, being exacerbated by external intervention. The failures of the Great Northern War and the
disputed succession after the death of CHARLES XII led to a new political
order, the 'age of liberty' (1719–72), which was a period of limited
constitutional monarchy under Ulrika Eleonora (1718–20); FREDRIK I
and ADOLF FREDRIK, with the powerful estates dominated by the rivalry
of the two major political groupings, the Hats and the Caps. GUSTAV
III restored a stronger monarchy in 1772, introduced reforms, alienated
the nobility and pursued a daring foreign policy. The Napoleonic
period was a confused one, with the end of the royal dynasty and the
loss of Finland. In 1810 the French marshal Jean Baptiste Bernadotte
(1763–1844) was elected heir to the throne and became Protestant. He
turned against Napoleon and in 1813 campaigned against him. Sweden was rewarded with Norway and Bernadotte ruled as Charles XIV
from 1818 to 1844.

The population of Sweden numbered 1,500,000 in 1700, and rose
to 2,281,137 by 1790. Its economy was dominated by farming, forestry

and mining. There was a growing national cultural consciousness, and the Swedish Academy was founded in 1786. Olof von Dalin (1708–63) wrote a scholarly HISTORY OF SWEDEN, refuting Gothicist myths of Sweden's early history. LINNAEUS and SWEDENBORG acquired international scientific reputations. In the late seventeenth century Sweden had been a major European power; by 1830 it was an inconsequential player in the international field, but it was far more vigorous economically and culturally.

See also BALTIC.

H. A. Barton. *Scandinavia in the Revolutionary Era, 1760–1815* (Minneapolis: University of Minnesota Press, 1986).

R. M. Hatton, *Charles XII of Sweden* (London: Weidenfeld & Nicolson, 1968).

M. Roberts, *The Age of Liberty: Sweden 1719–1772* (Cambridge: Cambridge University Press, 1986).

JEREMY BLACK

Swedenborg, Emanuel (1688–1772)   Swedish philosopher, scientist and mystic. He worked as an engineer and scientist on the Swedish board of mines from 1716. He became increasingly concerned to demonstrate, by scientific methods, that the universe had an essentially spiritual structure. Following a personal religious crisis in 1743–4, he resigned his post in 1747 and devoted himself to disseminating his doctrines. He claimed to have conversed with angels and to have experienced waking visions, regarding himself as the prophet of a theosophic system, in which God was Divine Man, from whom the two worlds of nature and spirit emanated. A prolific scientific and theological writer, he devoted himself, from 1745, to biblical exegesis.

His philosophy had a profound influence on BLAKE, which is evident in the latter's *Marriage of Heaven and Hell* (*c.*1790–3). Swedenborg's Dantesque spiritual odyssey, *Wisdom of Angels concerning Divine Love and Divine Wisdom* (*c.*1789), charted the geography of paradise and contained a vision of hell which prompted Strindberg to comment, 'Except Rabelais and Dean Swift, nobody had ever [such] science of filth and corruption'. His admirers ranged from the French Symbolists and followers of Jung to members of the Swedenborgian New Church.

Kathleen Raine, *Blake and Tradition* (Princeton, NJ: Princeton University Press, 1968).

MARIE MULVEY ROBERTS

Swieten, Gerhard van (1700–1772)   Dutch physician A student of BOERHAAVE, he graduated from Leiden in 1725. As a Dutch Catholic, he had no future in a Protestant country; in 1734 he was stopped from teaching on cases in a *privatissimum* (private lecture) in Leiden. In

1745 the empress Maria Theresa invited him to become the first physician at court, with responsibility for medical matters in the Habsburg lands. Thus began his sweeping medical and cultural reforms in the wake of Maria Theresa's own reorganization of Austrian bureaucracy in 1749. In that year he became head of the medical faculty of the University of Vienna and usurped the faculty's right to appoint professors. He initiated hospital clinical teaching in Austria, by appointing Anton de Haen (1704–76) from Leiden to the city hospital and other teaching clinicians in Pavia, Prag and Pest. He helped to extend the botanical gardens and recruited Nikolaus Jacquin (1727–1817) to look after the natural history collections that had been gathered from the West Indies between 1755 and 1759. He was responsible for the Hofbibliothek, later the Austrian National Library. He helped to curb the PLAGUE in 1765 and 1770 and took drastic public health measures against venereal disease.

His studies and exchanges with Boerhaave gave rise to one of the basic medical texts of eighteenth-century Europe, his *Commentaria*, translated into English as *Commentaries upon the Aphorisms of Dr Hermann Boerhaave concerning the Knowledge and Cure of Several Diseases Incident to Human Bodies* (18 vols; London, 1744–72, Edinburgh, 1776). The work comprised notes on Boerhaave's lectures with Van Swieten's own observations.

E. Lesky and A. Wandruszka, *Gerhard van Swieten und seine Zeit* (Vienna: Böhlau in Komm, 1973).

JOHANNA GEYER-KORDESCH

Swift, Jonathan (1667–1745)   Anglo-Irish poet and satirist. Born and educated in Dublin, he always insisted on his Englishness, and his career was marked by a restless oscillation between the assumption of English and Irish identities. He took holy orders in 1694 but was always more attracted by a literary than a clerical career, beginning as secretary to the former diplomat and self-styled philosopher Sir William Temple (1628–99). During Queen Anne's reign he was a leading figure in literary London, contributing to *The Tatler* and *Spectator* and forming the satiric fraternity the Scriblerus Club with his like-minded friends POPE, John Arbuthnot (1667–1735) and John GAY. His career as a political journalist began in 1710 when the new Tory leader, Robert Harley (1661–1724), recruited him, a former Whig, to mastermind a propaganda campaign promoting government policies. His series of *Examiner* essays (1710) and his magisterial pamphlet *The Conduct of the Allies* (1711), raised the art of political journalism to new heights of polemical brilliance. In his private *Journal to Stella*, an intimate daily record of these years sent to his young protégée and

friend in Dublin, he presented himself as a man at the centre of political events, maintaining the equilibrium of the Tory ministry by
mediating between its two rival leaders, Harley and St John (1678–
1751). But his reward for all this loyal service was a severe disappointment, and he regarded his appointment in 1713 as dean of St Patrick's
in Dublin as a virtual exile to that 'isle of slaves'.

With the accession of George I the following year, he sank into a
prolonged silence, oppressed by political surveillance and complications
in his private life. In the 1720s he embarked on a new career as a
'Hibernian patriot' championing the cause of Irish liberty, and denouncing exploitation by absentee English landlords and English
government placemen. His series of *Drapier's Letters* successfully defeated a scheme to impose a devalued currency in Ireland, and his
Modest Proposal (1729), with its ironic recommendation of cannibal-
ism as the only solution to Ireland's economic ills, was a masterpiece
of political indictment.

As a satirist, he offered no easy solutions, and the ironic masks he
habitually assumed deliberately provoked misreadings of his tone.
Thackeray (1811–63) denounced his most celebrated work, *Gulliver's
Travels* (1726), as 'filthy in word, filthy in thought, furious, raging,
obscene', finding in its violent and disturbing imagery an obsessive
fascination with human physicality. All of Swift's major satires, *A Tale
of a Tub* (1704), *Gulliver's Travels* (1726) and his ironic poem *Verses
on the Death of Dr Swift* (1731) are deeply paradoxical works, de-
ceiving us with false premises and teasing us with the prospect of
illusory utopias. He remains one of the greatest satirists in English
because his writings offer a continual challenge to the reasoning process
itself, and to our notions of identity.

D. Nokes, *Jonathan Swift, a Hypocrite Reversed: A Critical Biography* (Oxford:
Oxford University Press, 1985).

DAVID NOKES

Switzerland The Swiss Confederation, like the Holy Roman Empire,
which recognized its independence in 1648, was a complex political
entity. Most Swiss were German-speaking, with a multitude of dialects;
German was the official language. The Suisse Romande mostly had
dependent status: Jura was a fief of Basle; Berne ruled the Pays de
Vaud; Neuchâtel was a Prussian principality; but Geneva was an independent, allied city-state. The confederation comprised thirteen
cantons: the original 'forest' cantons, Uri, Schwyz and Unterwalden;
Zurich, Berne and Basle (the three most important by the eighteenth
century); Lucerne, Fribourg, Schaffhausen, Zug, Glarus, Solothurn and
Appenzell. Permanent allies included the rich abbey of St Gallen with

its rural hinterland; the city-state of St Gallen, a flourishing textile centre; and the Graubünden (Grisons), a microcosm of Switzerland, being a trilingual federation of three leagues, ruling the Valtellina. Some cantons possessed fiefs outside Switzerland. Federal institutions were weak.

Politically, the reputation of Swiss liberty stood high, but it really meant freedom from external control. Oligarchic rule was pervasive, through rural landowners in the forest cantons, or city patriciates, such as elective aristocracies (Berne) or guilds (Zurich). Each unit from canton to village had its own constitutional forms sanctioned by custom and tradition; the Valais and the Graubünden enjoyed unique forms of patriarchal direct democracy.

The social structure everywhere embodied the privileges of the *ancien régime*, consolidated after the failed peasant revolt of 1653. The Helvetic Society, founded in 1762, discussed enlightened reform but action was usually hindered by the ruling oligarchies, who while capable of ruthless suppression of dissent, as in Berne (1749), were able, economical and incorruptible in their fashion. Switzerland had no secular princes imposing enlightened reform, and thus lacked courtly patronage for opera, ballet and architecture, but wealthy patricians adapted the baroque and rococo for their discreetly opulent residences, and the prince-abbot of St Gallen embellished his principality spectacularly.

Religious conflict was settled in the Treaty of Aarau (1712), which recognized confessional coexistence. Geneva and Lausanne remained international centres of Calvinism. The balance of power favoured Protestant Zurich and Berne, which with the university city of Basle were the most dynamic cantons. Generally, religious dogmatism relaxed its grip. Catholic prince-prelates resembled their urbane south German counterparts, while in cantons like Fribourg, formerly centres for the Counter-Reformation, pious tradition vied with stagnation.

The 1798 Napoleonic invasion forced reconstruction to a confederation with a stronger federal constitution, and the privileges and religious discriminations of the *ancien régime* began to disappear, often under the aegis of newly empowered 'patriots' from the Helvetic Society.

The confederation and its allies played a formative role in the creation, modification and transmission of the Enlightenment. Swiss publishing facilities were invaluable for original publication, translation and popularization – sometimes clandestinely. Crousaz (1663–1750) mediated Leibnizian optimism to Francophone Europe; the elder Lesage (1676–1759) introduced Newtonianism. HALLER, BONNET and Trembley (1710–84) made advances in biology; S. A. Tissot (1728–97) and Théodore Tronchin (1709–81) in medicine, the BERNOULLI and EULER dynasties in mathematics; and H. B. de Saussure (1740–99) and J. A. Deluc (1727–1817) in geology. BURLAMAQUI, Barbeyrac (1674–1729) and Vattel (1714–67) developed the natural law tradition. Pestalozzi (1745–1827) was an influential educational innovator while Albertine Necker de Saussure (1766–1841) advocated a rational, scientific upbringing for women. BODMER's circle in Zurich fostered pre-romantic aesthetics while Muller's (1752–1809) historiography blended piety and classical republicanism. Many Swiss staffed new German academies, typifying the Swiss export of talent at all social levels, including mercenary service and regular or seasonal migration of artisans and labourers. The Swiss excelled in the luxury trades, mainly textiles and watchmaking, often undertaken as secondary occupations in winter, while merchant capitalists and bankers were operating on a Continental scale. As a taste for wild mountain scenery developed, the Grand Tour often included the Grindelwald glaciers and other scenic spots.

Christopher Hughes, *Switzerland* (London: Ernest Benn, 1975).
Clarissa Campbell Orr, 'The Romantic Movement in Switzerland', in R. Porter and M. Teich (eds), *Romanticism in National Context* (Cambridge: Cambridge University Press, 1988), pp. 134–71.
Jonathan Steinberg, *Why Switzerland* (Cambridge: Cambridge University Press, 1976).
Samuel S. B. Taylor, 'The Enlightenment in Switzerland', in R. Porter and M. Teich (eds), *The Enlightenment in National Context* (Cambridge: Cambridge University Press, 1981), pp. 72–89.

CLARISSA CAMPBELL ORR

sympathy One of the oldest concepts of Western medicine, sympathy was primarily a physiological notion in the eighteenth century. It referred to the natural harmony prevailing between the different parts of the body as a result of the nervous system. Jacobus Benignus Winslow, Robert Whytt, Xavier Bichat and Johann Christian were among those who attempted to explain the nature of the relation between the sympathetic and central nervous systems.

In the course of the eighteenth century the notion of sympathy came to play a key role in moral and aesthetic theories. It was closely linked to the notions of fellow-feeling, compassion and pity prominent in seventeenth-century political texts as well as in the writings of men like Rousseau. Most social theorists, with the notable exception of Godwin, claimed that pity, or some feeling or instinct akin to it, was innate in man.

The most influential and insightful examination of the mechanism of sympathy, however, is to be found in Adam Smith's *Theory of Moral Sentiments* which opens as follows: 'How selfish soever man may be supposed, there are evidently some principles in his nature, which interest him in the fortune of others, and render their happiness necessary to him, though he derives nothing from it except the pleasure of seeing it.' While pity and compassion were occasioned by seeing the sorrow of others, 'sympathy', he noted, could be used to 'denote our fellow-feeling with any passion whatever'. He argued that we derived pleasure on becoming aware that others sympathized with us and showed how crucial the notion was to our sense of propriety, in which cases it could be expected (for example grief and injury) and which not ('a certain reserve is necessary when we talk of our own friends, our own studies, our own professions'). Sympathy also played a key role in explaining 'all the toil and bustle of this world' as well as the consideration shown to the rich and powerful: 'A stranger to human nature, who saw the indifference of men about the misery of their inferiors, and the regret and indignation which they feel for the misfortunes and sufferings of those above them, would be apt to imagine, that pain must be more agonizing, and the convulsions of death more terrible to persons of higher rank, than to those of meaner stations.'

In *A Philosophical Enquiry into the Origin of our Ideas of the Sublime and the Beautiful* Burke argued that sympathy, imitation and ambition were the three main links of society. It was owing to the working of sympathy that others could perceive the intentions and feelings of artists as expressed through their works. So important was the notion of sympathy to the social and political imagination of the day that even Godwin claimed that human beings are placed in a system of things whose parts were tightly connected together and exhibited 'a sympathy and unison, by means of which the whole is rendered familiar, and, as it were, innate to the mind'.

See also SENSIBILITY, SENTIMENT.

Adam Smith, *The Theory of Moral Sentiments*, ed. D. D. Raphael and A. L. Macfie (Oxford: Clarendon, 1976).

SYLVANA TOMASELLI

T

Table of Ranks [*Tabel' o rangakh*]   The Table of Ranks was a system of promotion based partly on Prussian, Danish and Swedish models, introduced in Russia on 14 February 1722 by PETER I. The main branches of service – army, guards, navy, bureaucracy and court – were divided into fourteen classes, the fourteenth corresponding to the lowest commissioned rank in the army (ensign). Entering the table conferred noble status on non-aristocratic servitors and their families, which was hereditary for all military ranks and from rank 8 in the civil service, and personal for civilian ranks 9–14. Military ranks enjoyed precedence over civilian ranks. The table reflected Peter's principle of a career open to talent. On the other hand, 'old' nobles who failed to gain commissioned rank were not deprived of their status and the royal family enjoyed precedence over all others, even though Peter himself insisted on starting from the bottom. The table established equivalent ranks across the branches of service, facilitating transfers and clarifying precedence at functions. It was to change over the centuries – for example, access for commoners was restricted, and several ranks disappeared – but it remained the basis of promotion until the Bolsheviks abolished it in 1917.

B. Meehan-Waters, 'The Russian Aristocracy and the Reforms of Peter the Great', *Canadian-American Slavic Studies*, 7 (1974), 288–302.

LINDSEY HUGHES

Tahiti [Otaheite]   The island of Tahiti, which was known as Otaheite in the eighteenth century, had a profound effect on the European imagination. Its lush beauty, the simplicity of Polynesian life and its apparent sexual freedom were suggestive of an Arcadian past which was useful as an image for Enlightenment philosophers.

Wallis (1728–95) first sighted Tahiti in 1767 and on his recommendation it was chosen as a site for the observation of the transit of Venus. This was accomplished during Cook's first voyage. Between these visits Tahiti was explored by Bougainville, whose paradisal account of 'Nouvelle Cythère', as he styled it, found its way into Diderot's *Supplément au voyage de Bougainville* of 1772. The island was portrayed as having a 'natural' society driven by instinct rather than by reason or convention – the home of the true noble savage (*see* CULT OF THE NOBLE SAVAGE).

Subsequently, Tahiti became a base for the discovery and commercial exploitation of the PACIFIC. Cook touched there on all three voyages, as did VANCOUVER. Spain attempted to establish a mission in 1774, as did England in 1797, with scarcely more success. The lure of Tahiti was the precipitating cause of the mutiny of the *Bounty* in 1789.

O. H. K. Spate, *Paradise Lost and Found* (Minneapolis: University of Minnesota Press, 1988).

DAVID MACKAY

taille   Created in 1439, the *taille* was the main royal direct tax of the *ancien régime* French monarchy. The burden of the tax fell on the peasantry, since nobles were held to pay their taxes in blood on the field of battle, while the clergy and a great many urban groups enjoyed tax exemptions and privileges. The administrative district known as the *généralité* provided the framework for its assessment and distribution. Collectors were at the level of fiscal districts known as *élections*, although in the *pays d'état* local elective assemblies imposed it. Most northern areas were areas of *taille personnelle*, that is, assessment was according to the collector's opinion of the taxpayer's wealth. Southern areas were, in contrast, *pays de taille réelle*, where the tax was payable on the basis of whether a person's landed property was designated noble or non-noble in (usually antiquated and out-of-date) cadastral surveys. Attempts to reform the glaring inadequacies of this tax barely scratched the surface, and the serious efforts of Calonne (1787) and Brienne (1788) to change the basis of direct taxation to a universal and unitary land tax sparked noble revolt. It was left to the Constituent Assembly to abolish the *taille* outright.

See TAXATION.

COLIN JONES

Talleyrand-Périgord, Charles Maurice de (1754–1838)   French statesman. Born into a noble family, he entered the church only because a childhood accident had made him unfit for the army; he became an abbot before being ordained a priest and was made bishop of Autun in 1788. He seldom visited his diocese but became an active liberal deputy in the First Estate and then in the National Assembly. His intervention was influential in passing the decree nationalizing all church properties during the debates on the CIVIL CONSTITUTION OF THE CLERGY. One of only two bishops to take the oath to the constitution, he said mass at the famous Fête de la Fédération in July 1790.

In 1792 he was entrusted with a futile diplomatic mission to London, in an attempt to prevent war; he spent most of the period of the Terror in exile in England and America. Re-entering political life under the Directory, he became foreign minister in 1797, a post he retained under Napoleon until 1807. These ten years probably saw him at the apex of his influence in affairs of state, but even after his dismissal Napoleon continued to rely heavily on his advice, as in 1807–8 when he directed the Congress of Erfurt between Napoleon and Tsar Alexander I to settle German affairs.

In 1814, together with Fouché (1759–1820), he played a crucial part in organizing the deposition of Napoleon by the imperial senate, and resumed as foreign minister under Louis XVIII. His work at the Congress of Vienna was crucial in restoring France's place in Europe, and he continued to serve both the Bourbons and the July Monarchy until his death in 1838.

J. Orieux, *Talleyrand ou le Sphinx incompris* (Paris: Plon, 1970).

MICHAEL BROERS

Tanucci, Bernardo di (1698–1783) Neapolitan reformer. He dominated the government of the KINGDOM OF NAPLES between 1734 and his fall from office in 1776. Born in Tuscany, he was a prominent jurist at the University of Pisa. Taking service under the new Bourbon dynasty in Naples, he pursued a series of reforming policies throughout his long tenure of office but few of them achieved much success, baronial and clerical opposition proving far too strong for him to overcome, even with the consistent support of the crown. His reforms, mainly legal rather than economic, were criticized by contemporaries such as Genovesi and Joseph II as being too narrow in scope to meet the problems facing Naples.

Although the great famine of 1764 led him into a brief period of attempted reforms influenced by physiocratic ideas, he was openly sceptical of French-influenced theorizing, preferring a more pragmatic approach to reform. His two chief interests were legal and clerical reform. In the first sphere, in 1759 and again in 1773, he tried to limit the autonomy of baronial jurisdictions, but with no success; his attempts to root out corruption within the royal magistrature in the 1730s also failed. His last years in office, from 1768, were marked by anticlerical legislation which led him into direct conflict with the papacy by 1776. In these years he expelled the Jesuits from the kingdom, gave support to their Jansenist opponents and attempted to secularize many areas of public education, particularly the University of Naples.

D. Carpanetto and G. Ricuperati, *Italy in the Age of Reason, 1685–1789* (London: Longman, 1987).

S. J. Woolf, *A History of Italy, 1700–1860* (London: Methuen, 1979).

MICHAEL BROERS

taste The nature of taste, and the means to its acquisition, were among the main topics of literary criticism and aesthetic theory in the eighteenth century. This now much diminished word once bore the burden not only of aesthetic judgement, but also of moral discrimination. (Eighteenth-century discussions of taste often conflated aesthetic and moral sensitivities.) Taste was the ambition of the gentleman, and the special object of enquiry of the philosopher. Not only did it mark the refinement of the polite classes, but it was also the subject of several theoretical texts.

The Oxford English Dictionary cites Milton's *Paradise Regained* of 1671 for the first use of 'taste' to mean 'The sense of what is appropriate, harmonious, or beautiful', and in particular 'the faculty of perceiving and enjoying what is excellent in art, literature, and the like'. The definition repeats the paradox implicit in the word's metaphorical root: on the one hand, it is a responsiveness to the products of culture and, on the other, it is a natural 'faculty'. The discussions of taste as a general quality from the early eighteenth century onwards found the force of the concept in just this paradox. It was apparent in an early and influential discussion in *The Spectator* of 1712, where Addison described how, while taste 'must in some measure be born with us, there are several Methods for Cultivating and Improving it, and without which it will be very uncertain, and of little use to the Person that possesses it'. It is telling that this periodical, dedicated to fashioning polite sociability, should feature taste, for taste was becoming a new kind of social bond among gentlemen. In the absence of shared political and religious values, taste was becoming the common ideal of the propertied classes.

Such idealization was deflated in the satire of the period. Pope's *Epistle to Burlington* (1731) mocked the vulgar displays of supposed taste of the wealthy, but itself subscribed to the importance of taste, suggesting what Shaftesbury, in his *Characteristick*s, had also implied: that good men will have good taste. Shaftesbury made moral judgement itself an exercise of taste. His arguments were supported and developed by the Scottish philosopher Hutcheson in his *Inquiry concerning Beauty, Order, Harmony, Design* (1725). He continued to use aesthetic judgement as a model for moral judgement: 'The Author of

Nature has . . . made virtue a lovely form, that we might easily distinguish it from its contrary.'

The theme was influentially sustained in Alexander Gerard's (1728–95) *Essay on Taste* (1759) which, together with Hume's *Of the Standard of Taste* (1757), Burke's *On Taste* (1759) and Lord Kames's (1696–1782) *Elements of Criticism* (1762), made AESTHETICS into the analysis of 'those simple powers of human nature, which are its principles'. Writers on taste were anatomists of what Kames called the 'wonderful uniformity' of human 'feelings'; yet they could not forget that, while its principles may have been 'natural', the development of taste was a sign of CIVILIZATION. It is this notion of 'a *taste* for poetry' as a badge of refinement that Wordsworth attacked in his Preface to the *Lyrical Ballads* of 1798. Scepticism about codes of taste distinguished the early phase of Romanticism.

See also SENSIBILITY, SENTIMENT.

B. Sprague Allen, *Tides in English Taste* (New York: Pageant, 1937).
H. A. Needham, *Taste and Criticism in the Eighteenth Century* (London: Harrap, 1952).
Joan Pittock, *The Ascendancy of Taste* (London: Routledge & Kegan Paul, 1973).
René Welleck, *A History of Modern Criticism 1750–1950* (London: Jonathan Cape, 1955).

JOHN MULLAN

taxation   The principal taxes in the eighteenth century were land taxes, poll taxes, excise taxes and customs duties (*see* CUSTOMS AND TARIFFS). The heaviest burden fell on peasants and ordinary townspeople. In most areas of Europe nobles and state churches had, as part of their privileges, exemptions from certain taxes, but nowhere were the nobility and clergy exempt from all taxes (*see* PRIVILEGE). British peers, for example, paid the land tax. In most provinces of France nobles were exempted from the heaviest direct tax, the *TAILLE*, but in general they were subject to other impositions. Throughout the century the governments of Austria, Prussia, Russia, France and other countries challenged some of the remaining noble exemptions. In addition to paying taxes to the state, peasants in most of Europe paid seigneurial dues to their landlords (*see* SEIGNEURIALISM) and, in Catholic countries, tithes to the church. Although they were less numerous than in previous centuries, tax revolts by all levels of society continued to erupt sporadically throughout Europe.

See also AIDES, DIXIÈME.

J. F. Bosher, *French Finances, 1770–1795: From Business to Bureaucracy* (Cambridge: Cambridge University Press, 1970).

P. G. M. Dickson, *The Financial Revolution in England: A Study of the Development of Public Credit, 1688–1756* (London: Macmillan, 1967).

THOMAS J. SCHAEPER

tax farming Every government in early modern Europe practised tax farming at one time or another. This was a system whereby a state leased the collection of sales taxes, customs dues or other indirect impositions to private individuals. Each year the tax farmers paid the government an agreed rental fee. The tax farmers then collected the taxes, keeping for themselves any revenues above the amount owed to the government. The advantage to the state lay in it receiving a stable amount of money each year. The disadvantage (to the taxpayer) was that tax farmers could sometimes be ruthless, for it was in their interest to collect as much as possible above the lease charge. The most famous example of tax farming was France's company of FARMERS GENERAL.

As governments became stronger, they were able to replace tax farmers with state employees. England abolished tax farms in the late seventeenth century. With the exception of France, other countries in Europe witnessed significant curtailment of tax farming by the latter half of the eighteenth century.

George T. Matthews, *The Royal General Farms in Eighteenth-Century France* (New York: Columbia University Press, 1958).

THOMAS J. SCHAEPER

tea Long consumed and cultivated in the Far East, tea was introduced into seventeenth-century Europe and North America as an exotic health drink; it soon became China's staple export to the West. Peasant proprietors cultivated the bushes, roasted the leaves to produce either black or green varieties and sold them to merchants who dealt in Canton with European trading companies. Tea remained fashionable, but falling prices throughout the eighteenth century hastened its descent of the social scale – to become a 'necessity' in the British working-class diet, eked out by repeated brewings and well sugared. By 1800 British annual consumption of 'legal' tea averaged 2 pounds per head; large-scale smuggling had been dealt a death-blow by Pitt's Commutation Act of 1784, which drastically reduced excise duty.

Tea was also a catalyst of revolution. Already infuriated by the British parliament's imposition of duty on various goods without their consent, American colonists responded to the 1773 Tea Act with pledges not to drink tea, and mass meetings that culminated in the BOSTON TEA PARTY, when 342 full tea chests were thrown into Boston harbour. Relations deteriorated into war in 1776, and Americans deserted *en masse* to coffee.

William H. Ukers, *All about Tea* (New York: Tea and Coffee Trade Journal Company, 1935).

CHRISTINE MACLEOD

technology   A new consciousness of the 'mechanical arts' had arisen among European scholars since the Renaissance. Descriptions of crafts, their tools and skills appeared in print, culminating in Diderot's ENCYCLOPÉDIE, with its illustrations of contemporary best practice. Tourists gazed in awe at STEAM ENGINES and at textile FACTORIES, while artists and poets found in them examples of the sublime. In North America much technological interest was stimulated by the goal of import substitution, particularly independence from British manufactures. Private societies aimed to promote invention and its diffusion through the offer of prizes, and most states in Europe and North America rewarded inventors with patents of monopoly or financial privileges. Oriental techniques of cloth manufacture and printing (*see* TEXTILES), CERAMICS and steel-making were keenly investigated and imitated. The West was beginning to contest Asia's dominance of manufacturing, and through mechanization would soon overturn it. (Asia's already advanced technology did not share the new dynamism emerging in the West.)

Inventions were made in the workplace by men seeking to lighten their workload or to increase their profits (*see* MACHINES). Only in chemistry did scientists begin to make a direct contribution. Yet scientists and 'practical men' exchanged ideas, and inventions conceived by the latter challenged the former to provide explanations. Technology was transferred most effectively by personal demonstration. Recognizing this, states tried to prevent the emigration of skilled craftsmen and the export of machinery, but generally in vain: mobility among craftsmen was extensive, industrial espionage rife and patent protection weak. Consequently, production techniques differed little across Europe and North America.

See also INDUSTRIAL REVOLUTION.

Ian Inkster, *Science and Technology in History; An Approach to Industrial Development* (Basingstoke: Macmillan, 1991).

CHRISTINE MACLEOD

Telemann, Georg Philipp (1681–1767)   German organist and composer. He studied law at Leipzig, but soon changed to a musical career as an organist. He became kapellmeister at the court of Sorau (Zary, Poland) in 1704, and at Eisenach in 1709, where he made friends with Johann Sebastian Bach. In 1712 he was appointed kapellmeister at the Barfüsser- und Katharinenkirche in Frankfurt am Main, and from 1721 he was musical director and cantor in Hamburg.

He was a very active promoter of music. In 1728 he founded the first German musical journal, *Der getreue Musicmeister*. He was director of the Hamburg opera, and arranged amateur concerts in several cities. Part of his music was written for the new musical culture of the middle classes.

A prolific composer, he was one of the most successful musicians of the eighteenth century, but his reputation has since declined. He composed more works than Handel and JOHANN SEBASTIAN BACH together. His orchestral works have been estimated at around 1,000 suites and 120 concertos; he also wrote forty operas, thirty-five oratorios, forty Käpitansmusiken and a great deal of church and chamber music.

K. Grebe, *Georg Philipp Telemann* (Reinbek: Rowohlt, 1970).
W. Menke, *George Philip Telemann: Leben, Werke und Umwelt in Bilddokumenten* (Wilhelmshaven: Noetzel, 1987).
Petzoldt, Richard, *Georg Philipp Telemann*, trans. Horace Fitzpatrick (London: Benn 1974).

FRITZ WEBER

Tennis Court Oath (20 June 1789)   The famous French revolutionary oath of 20 June 1789, by which the THIRD ESTATE vowed to remain in session until the drafting of a new constitution for France, was made in an empty tennis court because the assembly's normal meeting-place had inadvertently been locked.

COLIN JONES

Terray, Joseph-Marié (1715–1778)   French minister during the last years of the reign of Louis XV. An ecclesiastical administrator and lawyer attached to the Paris *parlement*, he was brought into government as controller-general by Chancellor MAUPEOU in 1769. He intrigued with his patron to oust CHOISEUL from government, which they achieved in 1770. With Maupeou and the minister for foreign affairs, d'Aiguillon (1720–88), he now formed the much lambasted 'Triumvirate' which undertook important reforms aimed at restoring the financial health of the state. When the *parlements* objected, he effected a virtual *coup d'état*, introducing sweeping judicial and administrative reforms which nullified the political influence of the PARLEMENTS. This and his financial reforms alienated much of the social and judicial elite; he was also the target for attacks over his policy of grain-price regulation, from which he was accused of making huge profits through the so-called 'famine plot' (*pacte de famine*). The death of Louis XV adventitiously removed the Triumvirate's essential support, and when the young Louis XVI called on Maurepas to oversee his government, Terray's dismissal was assured.

COLIN JONES

Terror The repressive and intimidatory measures aimed at commanding obedience in the course of the French Revolution, which were known as the Terror, formed an essential part of the strategy of 'revolutionary government' in operation between the overthrow of Louis XVI on 10 August 1792 and the establishment of the Directory on 26 October 1795. Four stages of the Terror may be discerned. The first, down to the meeting of the Convention on 21 September 1792, was marked by the September Massacres. In the second period, down to June 1793, the major instruments of Terror were established: *représentants en mission* on 9 March, the Revolutionary Tribunal on 10 March and the COMMITTEE OF PUBLIC SAFETY on 6 April. The 'Great Terror' lasted from the summer of 1793 down to the THERMIDOR *coup* of 27 July 1794. The height of the Terror saw the *levée en masse* (23 August), the Law of Suspects (17 September), the General Maximum (29 September), the Law of 22 Prairial (10 June 1794), the proscription of Girondin, Hébertist and Dantonist deputies, and the repression of the VENDÉE rising. Finally, the Thermidorian reaction, down to the autumn of 1795, saw the dismantling of the institutions of Terror and the authorities conniving with royalist vigilantes against former terrorists in the so-called 'White Terror'.

COLIN JONES

Test Acts By imposing the oaths of allegiance and supremacy, the sacramental test and the declaration against transubstantiation on all office-holders (1673) and on members of both houses of parliament (1678), the Test Acts sought to safeguard the Anglican regime against feared Catholic infiltration. The Acts were repealed in 1828–9.

See also CATHOLIC EMANCIPATION.

J. P. Kenyon, *The Stuart Constitution* (Cambridge: Cambridge University Press, 1966), ch. 13.

JOHN W. DERRY

textiles The making of cloth from animal and vegetable fibres, primarily for clothing, constitutes a basic feature of every economy apart from the most primitive. In China, India, the Levant and Europe the textile industry became early on a major source of employment, for it was highly labour-intensive. Medieval and Renaissance Europe had been dominated by woollen textiles. Silks and other costlier fabrics, chiefly imported from Asia, were reserved, sometimes by sumptuary laws, for the genteel. The textile industries of eighteenth-century Europe underwent change in two fundamental ways.

First, there were notable additions to the favoured fabrics: cottons joined woollens as a widely available cloth. Growing trade links facilitated the importation of raw cotton, first from Egypt, the Levant and

India, and then increasingly from plantations in the New World. In Britain a series of statutes at the close of the seventeenth century prohibited the importation of Indian calicoes and other cotton cloths, thereby giving domestic manufacturers a monopoly of the market in made-up cottons. Technical innovation followed. Calico-printing was pioneered in late-seventeenth-century France and Germany; it took a generation more to establish itself in Britain. Readily available and hence cheaper cottons had distinct advantages when used for garments worn next to the skin and for bedlinen, being less susceptible to vermin than woollens and easier to wash. Thus the spread of cottons boosted the eighteenth-century drive towards personal hygiene and greater personal refinement (when Johnson professed himself no great lover of clean linen, he was on the defensive). The exportation of cotton goods to Europe and to America was to give a singular boost to the British INDUSTRIAL REVOLUTION. In the thirty years after 1765, exports of cottons went up from £236,000 to £5,371,000, while exports of woollens went up from £4,356,000 to £6,323,000. Some two-thirds of the output of the fast-growing cotton industry was shipped abroad.

Secondly, the dramatic expansion in textile manufacture, especially cottons, was made possible largely by technological innovations. Mechanical yarn spinning was developed by Lewis Paul (d 1759) who obtained a patent in 1738. In 1769 Richard ARKWRIGHT obtained a patent for his water frame, which derived its inspiration from Paul's drawing-rollers. Around the same time, James Hargreaves (c.1720–78) invented the spinning-jenny, by which sixteen or more threads could be spun simultaneously by the same person. Hargreaves' device was unsuitable for fine spinning; a solution came with the mule developed by Samuel CROMPTON in the years after 1774, combining the rollers of Paul with the stretching technique pioneered by Hargreaves. Despite the invention of the flying shuttle, spinning technology outstripped advances in weaving technology, providing employment for vast numbers of handloom weavers into the 1820s and 1830s. The invention of the Jacquard loom around the beginning of the nineteenth century enabled complicated patterns to be woven from patterns by relatively low-skilled workers. Factory-sited power looms were essentially a development of the nineteenth century.

Productivity improved immensely and unit costs dropped. Thanks to Arkwright's water frame and Crompton's mule, between the 1770s and 1810 the cost of spinning cotton yarn was reduced to around one-sixth of its former price. In sheer output, Europe led the rest of the world. To process 100 pounds of cotton took an Indian hand-spinner 50,000 operative man-hours, a Crompton mule (1780) 2,000, a 100-spindle mule (1790) 1,000, a power-assisted mule (1795) 300, and by 1825 Richard Roberts's (1789–1864) automatic mule took just 135 man-hours.

The cotton industry gave industrialization a great boost, although talk of its being a 'leading sector' is probably exaggerated. Not until 1785 was steam harnessed to a cotton mill, at Papplewick in Nottinghamshire. In 1800 the cotton industry was still largely using wooden machinery and WATER POWER. It was only later that steam-powered machinery became widely used. (*See* MACHINES, TECHNOLOGY.)

S. D. Chapman and S. Chassagne, *European Textile Printers in the Eighteenth Century* (London: Heinemann, 1981).

N. B. Harte and K. G. Ponting (eds), *Textile History and Economic History: Essays in Honour of Miss Julia de Lacy Mann* (Manchester: Manchester University Press, 1973).

ROY PORTER

theatre DRAMA is as ancient as civilization, and plays continued to be performed throughout the world in the eighteenth century as they had always been. In Japan, for example, the well-established Noh play continued to flourish, while some of the classics of the newer, less sombre and more spectacular kabuki theatre were also performed. In all countries folk drama survived, along with court theatre in the more cosmopolitan centres. But it was in the West that drama was most closely related to urgent topical issues, and both affected and was affected by the course of history. European norms filtered out to a wider world, and the first American professional companies came into being in the second half of the century, with a repertoire that was at first imported (the first all-American comedy, by Royall Taylor (1757–1826), dates from the mid-1780s).

Like everything else, the theatre was felt to be in need of improvement. A major movement of moral 'reformation' took place in England in the 1690s, and the theatrical profession began to acquire a respectable face. Voltaire noted acerbically in his *Lettres philosophiques* that the great French tragic actress Adrienne Lecouvreur (1692–1730) was refused a proper burial while her English contemporary Anne Oldfield (1683–1730) was given a pompous funeral at Westminster Abbey in the same year (1730). The actor David Garrick (1717–79) and the actress Sarah Siddons (1755–1831) did most to legitimize what had previously been a calling for vagrants and outcasts, by the sobriety of their private life, as well as the dignity of their stage presence. From then on, life on the stage was considered to be less wicked, although eyebrows were still raised when popular comic actresses married into the aristocracy and when 'serious' writers made a career of writing for the theatre.

The eighteenth-century theatre was a lively, varied and busy place. With Italian opera came mass adulation of highly paid stars, the castrato serving as a *monstre sacré* to be both admired and scorned. There were ramshackle touring troupes, puppet companies, every variety of coarse acting and hammy production in contrast to the ponderous neoclassical austerities of closet tragedy, which spread from France to Scandinavia, Russia and further afield. Venice saw the surreal fantasies of Gozzi (1720–1806) and the realistic urban comedy of Goldoni (1707–93), while France and England, in the van of cultural progress and degradation, witnessed a vigorous alternative theatre in fairgrounds and show-booths. This street theatre presented a range of entertainments which may have included conjurors, harlequins, menageries and freak-shows; and also fostered spectacular stage-effects which filtered back into mainstream theatre. Out of this mix of the legitimate and illegitimate there evolved freer ways of staging traditional drama. Contemporary moralists deplored the activities of these vulgar institutions, the *théâtre de la foire* and the Smithfield drolls, not least on account of their presumed infection by the rabble of criminals and drop-outs who were seen as their natural audience. But it was in such 'low' surroundings that some characteristic modes of modern dramaturgy first came into being; for example it was in a suburban vaudeville theatre in Vienna that *The Magic Flute* was first staged.

In Europe the legitimate theatre tended to move out of the protection of royal support and aristocratic sponsorship. As with so many eighteenth-century institutions, drama shifted from the court to the market-place, relying on either public subscription or box-office takings. A new playhouse became a source of municipal pride, if not of profit, and theatres sprang up around the provincial centres of northern Europe. The behaviour of audiences became more decorous than it had been in earlier centuries. From 1759 spectators were no longer allowed to sit on the edge of the stage at the Comédie Française (a position they had long been free to enjoy despite Voltaire's complaints). The stage became a more respectable place, and in the process also more prim and conventional. But alongside mainstream theatre there were always the far from respectable fringe theatres which were able to evade licensing laws, censors and moral policemen; and there were always those who were prepared to challenge the established order, as Beaumarchais did in a private performance under the patronage of the comte d'Artois (1757–1836) at Versailles. The *ancien régime* was not immune to the barbs of dissident drama.

L. Hughes, *The Drama's Patrons: A Study of the Eighteenth-Century London Audience* (Austin, Tex.: University of Texas Press, 1971).

R. M. Isherwood, *Farce and Fantasy: Popular Entertainment in Eighteenth-Century Paris* (New York: Oxford University Press, 1986).

C. Price, *Theatre in the Age of Garrick* (Oxford: Blackwell, 1973).

D. Thomas (ed.), *Restoration and Georgian England 1660–1788* (Cambridge: Cambridge University Press, 1989).

PAT ROGERS

theodicy *see* EVIL/THEODICY.

Thermidor The *coup d'état* of 27 July 1794, or 9 Thermidor Year II in the revolutionary calendar, by which ROBESPIERRE and his supporters were ousted from government, was a major victory for the NATIONAL CONVENTION. The latter had established the COMMITTEE OF PUBLIC SAFETY in April 1793 to revive the war effort. In theory, the Convention renewed appointments to the committee on a monthly basis, but in practice there was no change in the 'Great Committee' from September 1793 onwards, so that from being the instrument of the Convention, the committee appeared to have become its dictator. By the spring of 1794, the war was going well, but the machinery of TERROR was becoming ever more repressive. Deputies endured the purge of Girondins (2 June 1793) and Hébertists and Dantonists (March–April 1794), but when Robespierre in early Thermidor threatened a further purge, those in the Convention on left and right who felt under threat conspired to overthrow him. In the long term, Thermidor marked a lurch to the right, as many of the radical welfare policies associated with the Terror were consequently dismantled.

M. Lyons, 'The 9 Thermidor: Motives and Effects', *European Studies Review*, 5 (1975), 123–46.

COLIN JONES

Third Estate In France the term 'Third Estate' denoted all commoners. In practice and especially in the events leading up to the French Revolution, the Third Estate was dominated by lawyers, bankers and professional men, rather than by peasants and workers. Enlightenment thought and economic expansion gave the Third Estate's elites a new sense of worth. The refusal of the nobility and clergy at the ESTATES GENERAL in May 1789 to treat them as equals, symbolized by the decision to vote 'by order' rather than 'by head', which allowed the two privileged orders to outvote the Third Estate, led it to secede and to set itself up as the NATIONAL ASSEMBLY on 17 June 1789. This was dramatic vindication of the claim made earlier in abbé Sieyès's *Qu'est-ce que le Tiers Etat?* that only the Third Estate truly made up the French nation.

Outside France, 'Third Estate' essentially denoted the urban and commercial classes, and this was what reformers in Russia, Germany and Poland meant by the term. It was more usual to refer to the 'estates' in a narrower sense, for example *Bürgerstand*, *Bauernstand* (estates of townsmen and peasants respectively).

J. M. Black, *Eighteenth Century Europe 1700–1789* (London: Macmillan, 1990).

J. T. LUKOWSKI

Thomasius, Christian (1655–1728) German jurist and philosopher, leader of the early Enlightenment in Germany. His work on natural law theory contributed to the development of enlightened absolutism. An enemy of superstition and unreason, he was an early advocate of religious toleration.

P. H. Reill, *The German Enlightenment and the Rise of Historicism* (Berkeley, Calif.: University of California Press, 1975).

MICHAEL HUGHES

Tiepolo, Giovanni Battista [Giambattista] (1696–1770) Italian decorative painter in the rococo style. He worked in northern Italy and as a court painter in Würzburg and Spain. The last exemplar of the Venetian school of painting, he was unable to work much in his native city due to its economic decline. All the key elements of his style – strong lines, high colour, inventive planning and the ability to control large areas – can be seen in his frescos for the Palazzo Labia, painted in Venice in the 1740s. He is known largely for his decorative works, including works in Milan, the Residenz in Würzburg and projects for the royal palace in Madrid from 1762 onwards. He also painted a large number of easel pieces, and left behind numerous drawings and etchings. In his youth he was a rebel against the formality of baroque classicism, and in old age he came under assault from advocates of neoclassicism, especially Mengs, who challenged his position in Madrid.

Michael Levey, *Giambattista Tiepolo: His Life and Art* (New Haven, Conn.: Yale University Press, 1986).

IAIN PEARS

Tillot, Guillaume du (1711–1774) Italian statesman of French origin. The son of one of Louis XIV's officials, he was chief minister of Bourbon-ruled PARMA in the late 1750s and 1760s, where he created an enlightened court centred on CONDILLAC, tutor to the young duke, and introduced a series of administrative reforms which were largely abandoned due to noble and clerical resistance. His ecclesiastical reforms brought him into conflict with the papacy when he abolished mortmain in 1764, an act which led him to go beyond traditional assertions of state authority in church matters and to enact a series of anticlerical laws in 1765–8. His fall from power in 1771 was due partly to growing opposition to his reforms, and partly to his patron, Choiseul, having lost power in France in 1770. As a foreigner, he had always been resented in Parma.

D. Carpanetto and G. Ricuperati, *Italy in the Age of Reason, 1685–1789* (London: Longman, 1987).
S. J. Woolf, *A History of Italy, 1700–1860* (London: Methuen, 1979).

MICHAEL BROERS

timekeeping *see* CALENDARS; CLOCKS.

tobacco The use of tobacco, chewed or smoked, has long been recorded in various cultures. Tobacco-smoking was common among the Turks in the early modern era. Travellers to America found it consumed by native Indians, and from the early seventeenth century the leaf was being imported into Europe from several parts of the New World, especially Virginia; by the eighteenth century it had become the mainstay of Virginia's economy. Tobacco cultivation was initiated in west and south Africa by the Portuguese.

The tobacco habit became especially popular in the Low Countries and England, among both men and women. In the poorer classes tobacco was mainly chewed or taken in clay pipes. During the eighteenth century more elegant pipes came into use, which used meerschaum, a hydrous silicate of magnesia found in central Europe. In high society tobacco was ground into the powdered form known as snuff, and inhaled. Elaborate rituals made elegance in handling the snuff-box a requisite for the well-bred man. Cigarettes and cigars were later developments.

Tobacco still had its medical advocates, as it was believed to clear the head and to correct digestion. It was also widely taken in enema form as a laxative. By the close of the century, however, some doctors, such as Thomas Trotter (1760–1832), were suggesting that it could be addictive, and the English man of letters Sir John Hill (1716–75) noticed a connection between heavy snuff-taking and nose cancer.

Carole Shammas, *The Pre-Industrial Consumer in England and America* (Oxford: Clarendon, 1990).
V. Kiernan, *Tobacco: A History* (London: Hutchinson, 1991).

ROY PORTER

Toland, John (1670–1722) Irish deist and controversialist. Brought up a Catholic in Ireland, he converted to Protestantism, and studied in Glasgow, Edinburgh, Leiden and Oxford. Notoriety came with *Christianity not Mysterious* (1696), which initiated the deist controversy (*see* DEISM), and was burned by the Middlesex justices. Locke was embarrassed by its affinity with his *Reasonableness of Christianity*. Toland next established a quasi-republican 'commonwealth' Whiggery, serving the 'country' opposition against the Junto government and recalling Whigs to their erstwhile radicalism. He reprinted James Harrington's (1611–77) *Oceana* (1700); Edmund Ludlow's (1617–92) *Memoirs* (1698), excising its biblical Puritanism; a *Life of Milton* (1698); and tracts on standing armies and mercenary parliaments.

In *Amyntor* (1699) he questioned the exclusive authority of the Bible by showing that there were many rival apocryphal gospels. He defended the Protestant succession in *Anglia Libera* (1701) and, on several Continental visits, added the Hanoverian court to his patrons, who included the earl of Shaftesbury and Robert Harley (1661–1724). *Letters to Serena* (1704) and *Nazarenus* (1718) continued his investigation of priestcraft and superstition, and in 1705 he coined the word 'pantheism'. His materialism drew on Bruno (*c*.1548–1600) and Spinoza, his critique of miracles foreshadowed Hume and his scriptural hermeneutics anticipated modern German scholarship. Ruined by the South Sea Bubble, he died in poverty.

See also FREETHINKERS.

Robert Sullivan, *John Toland and the Deist Controversy* (Cambridge, Mass.: Harvard University Press, 1982).

MARK GOLDIE

toleration Religious toleration is usually understood as the concession by governments of some measure of freedom of worship and other civil benefits to religious groups excluded from political power. The term also describes more local and informal relations between different religious movements or sects. In neither sense should its extent or progress in the eighteenth century be exaggerated. In practice, toleration was applied in negative terms of absence of restriction and as a privilege to be conferred or withheld, rather than as a right. Excessive influence should not be ascribed to the theories of Locke, whose *Letters concerning Toleration* were published in 1689–92, or Leibniz. As they wrote, there was a vast Huguenot diaspora (*see* HUGUENOTS); OLD BELIEVERS in Russia were severely persecuted; Protestants were under threat in the Habsburg lands; and toleration had little impact in Spain (*see* INQUISITION), Portugal and Italy. Even the celebrated English Toleration Act of 1689 was a very limited measure, excluding Catholics, Unitarians (*see* UNITARIANISM) and JEWS, and originally designed for only a few recalcitrant DISSENTERS who would not join an (abortive) scheme for comprehension within the Anglican Church. (*See* CATHOLIC EMANCIPATION, TEST ACTS.) Other Protestant states (Brandenburg-Prussia, the United Provinces, Sweden) usually tolerated their Protestant nonconforming subjects but were more restrictive towards Catholics.

Politics remained a branch of theology, and relations between states and their religious nonconformists hinged on the implications of the religious beliefs of the latter for the security of the former. During the century Protestants in Catholic states became less associated with rebellion; Catholics in Protestant states became less associated with the international claims of the papacy. In addition, following the Huguenot experience, religious minorities came to be seen as potential economic assets, to be encouraged (or even integrated) rather than persecuted. Hence the emperor Joseph II extended toleration to Jews and Protestant minorities including (unusually) Unitarians (although not deists), the Prussian monarchy tolerated its Catholic subjects in Silesia, and Britain passed a significant measure of toleration for its new French Catholic subjects in Canada with the Quebec Act of 1774. From around 1770, toleration certainly seemed to be advancing. Old Believers in Russia were relieved from many burdens; the civil status of French Protestants was improved; the short-lived Polish constitution of 1791 proclaimed religious liberty; there were relief Acts for English, Scottish and Irish Catholics and for Scottish Episcopalians; while several of the independent North American states, notably Virginia, with its Statute of 1786, adopted libertarian principles. The work of such exceptional individuals as Sir William Jones (1746–94) even suggested the beginnings of a more sympathetic European perception of the religions of India. These developments did not necessarily result from or produce religious indifference. The beneficiaries of toleration tended to demand full civil equality; previously dominant religious groups often reacted defensively, detecting threats to their own positions. The governmental enactment of toleration frequently exacerbated, rather than eased, relations between religious sects at a popular level, and the missionary impulse at the end of the century often indicated a sense of superiority over, rather than a greater understanding of, non-Christian religions.

See also ATHEISM, DEISM, FREETHINKERS.

Johannes van den Berg, *The Idea of Tolerance and the Act of Toleration* (London: Friends of Dr Williams's Library Annual Lecture, 1989).
Peter Gay, *The Enlightenment: An Interpretation*, vol. 2: *The Science of Freedom* (London: Weidenfeld & Nicolson, 1970).

G. M. DITCHFIELD

Tooke, John Horne [Horne, John] (1736–1812) English radical politician and etymologist. He thrived on controversy and, although his opponents kept him out of elective office, they could not keep him out of the public eye. A supporter of John WILKES and an inflammatory pamphleteer, in 1777 he was convicted of seditious libel for an advertisement in support of American colonists killed at Lexington. In a much publicized trial in 1794, he was acquitted of charges of treason for his organizing role in a network of democratic societies suspected of agitating for a revolution in England.

As an etymologist, he was no less polemical. His first language study argued that he would have been acquitted of sedition charges had the court understood the proper use of conjunctions. In his great etymological study *The Diversions of Purley* (1786–1805) he attacked the ontological status of political and metaphysical abstractions. Arguing that Locke's philosophy of knowledge was better understood as a philosophy of language and that the clarity that Locke sought in simple ideas could be attained by an analysis of word roots, Horne Tooke demystified terms such as 'spirit' and 'rights' which he showed to be derived from the concrete (and compromising) terms 'breath' and 'commands'. His influence can be seen in fields as diverse as philosophy (James Mill (1773–1836)), literature (Coleridge) and natural science (Erasmus Darwin).

D. Rosenberg, '"A New Sort of Logick and Critick": Etymological Interpretation in Horne Tooke's *The Diversions of Purley*', in Peter Burke and Roy Porter (eds), *Language, Self and Society* (Cambridge: Polity Press, 1991), pp. 300–29.

DANIEL ROSENBERG

Tories Deriving from the name of Irish Catholic bandits, 'Tory' was originally used in the late 1670s as a term of abuse, being employed by the WHIGS to suggest that their opponents, who supported Charles II, were un-English and crypto-Catholic. The linchpin of Tory policy was in fact support for the Church of England. In the Exclusion Crisis (1679–81) the Tories supported Charles against what they saw as the factiousness of the Whigs, and in the 'Tory Reaction' of 1681–5 their influence rose. The Catholicizing policies of Charles's successor, James II (1685–8), however, lost him Tory support. The Tories were divided by the Glorious Revolution, some thereafter becoming JACOBITES. After the ministry of 1710–14 the Tories never controlled the government. George I and George II preferred to rely on the Whigs. The Tories remained as a coherent political group but atomized from 1746, and, increasingly, after the accession of George III (1760), as the Whig–Tory divide broke down. George III, who did not see himself as a monarch of party, was willing to employ Tories. As a result, the term came to be applied both to his North American supporters and to the ministry of William Pitt the younger (1783–1801, 1804–6). His conservative legacy was maintained by subsequent Tory prime ministers, Perceval, Liverpool, Canning, Wellington and Peel.

J. M. Black, *Robert Walpole and the Nature of Politics in Early Eighteenth-Century Britain* (London: Macmillan, 1990).
Frank O'Gorman, *The Emergence of the British Two-Party System 1760–1832* (London, 1982).

JEREMY BLACK

torture, abolition of By the beginning of the eighteenth century most European legal systems (with the notable exception of England) had incorporated torture into their legal process. Its function was to help establish proof in criminal investigations by obtaining confessions from suspects, and also to encourage suspects to incriminate accomplices. Standard forms of torture included the rack, strappado, thumbscrew and legscrew. Its application as part of legal process was, in theory at least, governed by strict rules aimed at enhancing the quality of the confession.

During the second half of the eighteenth century judicial torture was abolished over much of Europe. In 1740 Frederick the Great of Prussia abolished torture except in cases of treason and mass murder, full abolition following in 1754. Similar measures followed in Saxony (1770), Austria (1776), France (1780) and Tuscany (1786). This process is traditionally portrayed as one of the major triumphs of Enlightenment thinking. Conversely, it has been argued that the development of secondary punishments allowed judges to deal with uncertain cases (that is, those in which torture may have been appropriate) without recourse to torture, thus rendering it largely redundant in practical terms long before formal abolition.

See also ADMINISTRATION OF JUSTICE, PUNISHMENT.

John H. Langbein, *Torture and the Law of Proof* (Chicago: University of Chicago Press, 1977).

J. A. SHARPE

Toussaint L'Ouverture, Pierre Dominique (1746–1803) Haitian leader of the only successful slave revolt in history. A slave descended from an African chieftain, he was educated in San Domingo by his godfather, Pierre Baptiste, who was literate. Originally surnamed Bréda, he reputedly acquired his *nom de guerre* from French generals astounded by his military genius. San Domingo at the time was France's richest colony. When the black slaves, stimulated by the French Revolution, revolted in 1791, he became their leader. Inspired by a prophecy from the abbé Raynal, historian and *philosophe*, he saw himself as the 'courageous chief' destined to free the African slaves in the West Indies. Years of intermittent warfare against the French followed, varied by conflicts with the British and Spanish. Despite vicissitudes, he became the *de facto* ruler of San Domingo, and continually endeavoured to conciliate the French and the free mulattos.

In 1802, lulled by apparent goodwill from the French, he was arrested on Napoleon's secret orders and sent to France, where he died of systematic ill-treatment as a prisoner in solitary confinement. His tragic fate was commemorated in a sonnet by Wordsworth. His lieutenants, Jean Jacques Dessalines (*c*.1748–1806) and Henry Christophe (1767–1820), however, finally drove out the French in 1804, and founded the independent state of Haiti.

C. L. R. James, *The Black Jacobins: Toussaint L'Ouverture and the San Domingo Revolution* (London: Allison & Busby, 1980).

MARIO RELICH

town planning Eighteenth-century views on the importance of Ar-
CHITECTURE to physical and spiritual health specified the building types
necessary to enlightened urban culture, but had less to say about their
integration into existing urban fabrics, and about planning problems.
However, Vitruvius's injunctions on clean water and healthy air still
made sense, and not much theory was required when it came to the
'improvement' of cities, the extension of tidiness, which is what most
planning was concerned with.

Annapolis, Maryland (*c.*1700), Karlsruhe, Germany (1715), Hamina,
Finland (1721) and Chaux, France (1775) were laid out on the centralized polygonal plans of Vitruvius and Renaissance fortifications.
Most plans for new towns or quarters were grids punctuated by
monumental buildings and open spaces in a variety of shapes: poly-
gons, squares, crescents and circuses. The extension of 'civilization'
presupposed that of its town-planning norms: Philadelphia, Pennsylvania (1681–3) was laid out on a huge grid, 1 mile by 2; Catherine II's
commission approved 416 plans for foundations and rebuildings in
her own empire (1763–96). The edges of the Western world offer the
best examples of large-scale planning, in the new capitals of St
Petersburg (1704), Washington (1789) and Helsinki (1812).

Urban life was understood to offer particular delights, not just practical advantages: new building types like assembly rooms, theatres and
race-track stands catered for the town-dweller's leisure hours, and
fortification lines and palla-a-maglio alleys were converted to urban
walks. Quays and open-sided esplanades fronting rivers and harbours
provided not only healthy walks, but the pleasing spectacle of commerce, whose improvement was another great desideratum. 'New towns'
like Copenhagen's Frederiksstad (begun 1749), which abuts the harbour, and those in Edinburgh (1767) manifest the efforts of royal and
civic authorities to stimulate wealth, in part by attracting the productive middle classes to prestigious quarters. Similarly, the St Petersburg
Bourse (completed 1816) was placed on a prominent site at the tip of
an island on the Neva. The monument was redefined: no longer merely
a commemoration, it was now an outstanding building whose relative
position signalled the importance of its function. The control of civil
disorder was another factor in planning: converging on the river bank
opposite the Bourse were the three great prospects, of which two ran
straight into barracks.

Measures to improve public health centred on the dissolution of
knots of congestion, the improvement of 'circulation' – an old trope
which had considerable life in it yet – as well as the removal of such
noxious activities as tanning and fishmongering from the town centres.
A new, more sophisticated, regard for the city's problems and prospects was reflected in a growing appreciation for its older fabric. The

Bavarian and Danish architects preparing the village of Athens as a new capital in the 1830s first surveyed and designated for preservation its antique, Byzantine and Ottoman buildings.

See also TOWNS AND CITIES.

Alistair Rowan, 'Neo-classical Town Planning', in *The Age of Neo-classicism* (London: Arts Council), pp. 656–60.

CHRISTINE STEVENSON

towns and cities In pre-modern times only a minority of people lived in towns. It has been estimated by de Vries that at the end of the eighteenth century 5 per cent (45 million) of the world's population (900 million) lived in 1,200 cities of 10,000 or more inhabitants. How far this represents the true size of the urban population depends on the reliability of the statistics used and the definition of a town employed. Settlements of under even 1,000 people could exercise urban functions, and it was the smaller and medium-sized communities (of under 10,000) that made up the majority of the world's towns.

Urban civilization was not spread evenly across the globe. China and Japan were imperial states in which towns had historically played a major role. In 1800 China contained twenty-four of the seventy great cities of the world with populations of over 100,000, and Japan five. But whereas during the long eighteenth century the proportion of the population living in Chinese towns remained relatively static, Japan underwent rapid urban growth so that by the mid-nineteenth century it was over twice as urbanized as its neighbour.

Europe was another region in which towns had long enjoyed a position of pivotal importance. By 1800 one in ten of its inhabitants lived in cities of over 10,000, although this masks much lower levels of city-living in the Scandinavian and eastern fringes. During the early modern period Europe had witnessed substantial, but not steady or uniform, demographic urbanization. The principal beneficiaries were the larger centres, particularly port cities and capitals, although recent evidence from England and Spain points to the vitality of many smaller towns in the seventeenth and eighteenth centuries. These centuries also saw a decisive change in the profile of urban Europe, with the focus of growth shifting from the Mediterranean to the north and west.

By the eighteenth century the most dynamic area of urbanization in Europe – and probably in the world – was the United Kingdom: in 1800 one in five of the inhabitants of England, Wales and Scotland lived in cities of over 10,000, and during the century the proportion of the English and Welsh population in towns of over 2,500 increased from 19 to 30 per cent. Significantly, this growth was achieved not just through the continued expansion of LONDON, but also by the dramatic rise of a number of originally small ports and 'industrial' towns, such as LIVERPOOL, Birmingham and Manchester. This foreshadowed a major shift in the pattern of European urbanization, which was to become more evident in the following century, away from a phase of consolidation to one of creation.

To the east of Europe stretched the sparsely urbanized Russian empire: in 1800 only 3 per cent of its peoples lived in settlements of over 10,000, although it is suggested that in 1780 about 8 per cent occupied cities in general. To the west of Europe, and a key geographical factor behind the urban expansion of the continent's western periphery, lay the Atlantic and America. Eighteenth-century North America was a predominantly rural society. At the end of the revolutionary era around 5 per cent of its population dwelt in twenty-four towns of 2,500 people or more. Most of these people were located in the north, for urban development in the south had been retarded by the prominence of the tobacco trade (with its limited call on urban services), a weak middle class and a work-force containing a high proportion of agricultural slave labour with restricted consumer power. However, despite its apparent rurality, North America was an area of huge urban potential; and this was already evident in the eighteenth century, with the rise of Atlantic ports like Boston, PHILADELPHIA and NEW YORK (the last had 21,000 inhabitants in 1771, 33,000 in 1790 and over 800,000 by 1860), and the emergence of patterns of social and political life that prefigured those of the modern city.

See also CAPITAL CITIES, URBAN PATRICIAN FAMILIES.

P. Corfield, *The Impact of English Towns 1700–1800* (Oxford: Oxford University Press, 1982).
R. A. Mohl (ed.), *The Making of Urban America* (Wilmington, Del.: Scholarly Resources, 1988).
G. Rozman, *Urban Networks in Ch'ing China and Tokugawa Japan* (Princeton, NJ: Princeton University Press, 1973).
J. de Vries, *European Urbanization, 1500–1800* (London: Methuen, 1984).

PETER BORSAY

trade Assessed in terms of gross national products, domestic trade was traditionally far larger in scale and more significant for most national economies than the export trade. The bulk of commercial activity always occurred within the circuits of the home market. It is believed, for instance, that in the first three-quarters of the eighteenth century over 90 per cent of British output was absorbed domestically. Particularly with the acceleration of urbanization after mid-century (in the half-century after 1750, some 200 additional cities achieved a population of between 5,000 and 10,000 in Europe alone), there is abundant evidence of buoyant home markets in most regions of Europe, associated with the growth of CONSUMERISM.

In the sixteenth and seventeenth centuries exports from the European economies had typically been directed to other European markets. Mediterranean outlets, for instance, were still extremely important for England in the post-1660 commercial boom: cloth was sent to the Levant, and raw silk, spices and luxuries imported from Turkey (the silk was worked up by Huguenot refugee silk-weavers in Spitalfields). Trade patterns began to change, however, with the growing importance of transoceanic markets. With the rise of empire, the proportion of English exports shipped to Europe halved between 1700 and 1770, while in the same period the share going to America rose from 10 per cent to over 30 per cent. Overall, with the growth of the Atlantic economies, the Mediterranean gradually declined, ceasing to operate as the nucleus of European trade as it had done since Roman times. As transatlantic trade grew, there was also a decline in the importance of east central Europe in the international trading system.

In the eighteenth century international commerce rapidly expanded in scale and achieved an astonishing complexity. Many historians have argued that a commercial 'world system' became fully operational, thanks, not least, to the expansion of COLONIZATION, with its plantation monocultures, utterly dependent on the SLAVE TRADE, and with attendant leaps forward in mercantile organization (for example the rise of insurance and similar businesses). European trade with America, Asia and Africa had been growing rapidly from around 1600, thanks largely to the bullion trade: spices (see SPICE TRADE), TEA, coffee, SUGAR, silk, calicoes, muslins and similar TEXTILES were increasingly dispatched to Europe, where they provided the basis for lucrative processing industries – calico-printing, sugar-refining and so on – and a re-export trade. And, from the late seventeenth century, Europe began exporting more manufactures to these markets, especially the Americas. The rise of the Atlantic traffic brought great prosperity to Bordeaux, Nantes, Glasgow, Bristol and Liverpool.

Thus the boom economies of the eighteenth century were the economies of the Atlantic seaboard (including the nations with ports on the North Sea and, to a lesser degree, the Baltic). The Netherlands formed the first model of the new transoceanic economies of north-west Europe. Amsterdam proved a prodigious entrepôt, pioneering sugar refineries and TOBACCO-processing, while textiles flourished around Leiden, the Dutch specializing in the bleaching of German, French and Flemish linen and Italian silk and, more generally, in handling cloth, dye-stuffs and chemicals. The Dutch case reveals the intimate interdependence between trade and manufactures, which was also seen from the late seventeenth century in London, Bristol and its environs, and Liverpool, with its twin textile towns developing in the Lancashire hinterland. This trade–manufacture axis proved more successful in the long run in Britain than in the United Provinces because of Britain's abundant supplies of minerals and fossil fuels. The Netherlands continued to lead the world in shipping, insurance, technological ingenuity, commercial acumen and international connections, especially in the EAST INDIES, into the early eighteenth century but eventually paid the price of being first and fell victim to its own success, as finance capital came to dominate policy to the detriment of mere trade and manufactures.

In an examination of shifting trade patterns and commercial supremacies, power politics and war must not be neglected. Seventeenth-century jurists disputed the principle of FREE TRADE on the oceans (*mare apertum* or *mare clausum*: was the sea open or closed?). The Navigation Act of 1651 staked the British claim to exclusive rights to its colonial carrying trade and to re-exports, and protectionism was pursued (*see* NAVIGATION ACTS). Around 1700 legislation was passed banning the import of Asian silks and calicoes, thus giving the home textile industries an important boost. As the British navy increasingly ruled the waves after the War of the Spanish Succession, and especially following the Seven Years War, trade became a key factor in foreign policy. In the writings of Adam Smith and others markets were seen as more valuable, cheaper and less trouble than colonies. Nevertheless, the steady spread of territories and outposts overseas continued to boost trade and create favourable preconditions for the British INDUSTRIAL REVOLUTION.

Maxine Berg, Pat Hudson and Michael Sonenscher (eds), *Manufacture in Town and Country before the Factory* (Cambridge: Cambridge University Press, 1983).

Ralph Davis, *The Rise of the English Shipping Industry in the Seventeenth and Eighteenth Centuries* (London: Macmillan, 1962).

Bernard Semmel, *The Rise of Free Trade Imperialism: Classical Political Economy, the Empire of Free Trade and Imperialism 1750–1850* (Cambridge: Cambridge University Press, 1970).

J. de Vries, *European Urbanization, 1500–1800* (Cambridge, Mass.: Harvard University Press; London: Methuen, 1984).

I. Wallerstein, *The Modern World-System*, vol. 2: *Mercantilism and the Consolidation of the European World-Economy* (New York: Academic Press, 1980); vol. 3: *The Second Era of Great Expansion of the Capitalist World-Economy* (San Diego, Calif.: Academic Press, 1989).

Judith Blow Williams, *British Commercial Policy and Trade Expansion, 1750–1850* (Oxford: Clarendon, 1972).

ROY PORTER

Trafalgar, Battle of (21 October 1805) The Battle of Trafalgar was fought between NELSON's British fleet of twenty-seven battleships and a combined fleet of eighteen French and fifteen Spanish under Villeneuve (1763–1806). Nelson was killed but thirteen French and ten Spanish ships were captured or sunk without British loss. This the biggest naval victory of the 1793–1815 wars had no impact on Napoleon BONAPARTE's victorious career on the Continent but it gave Britain five precious years of security from invasion until he built a new fleet at Antwerp. Spain, however, lacked the capacity to rebuild its fleet and Trafalgar was the death-blow to Spanish sea power.

MICHAEL DUFFY

transport *see* CANALS; ROADS.

transubstantiation   One of the fundamental tenets of Catholic ortho-doxy, promulgated at the Lateran Council of 1215, the doctrine of transubstantiation maintained that in the Eucharist the substance of the bread and wine were converted miraculously into the body and blood of Christ, with only the external 'accidents' (the part of the bread and wine that the senses could apprehend) remaining unchanged. During the sixteenth century Protestant reformers, although disagree-ing among themselves as to the precise nature of the relationship of the bread and wine to the body and blood of Christ, effectively denied the doctrine. Reforming Catholic clergy were concerned with the ways that the doctrine was bastardized by popular thought.

H. Jedin, *History of the Council of Trent*, trans. Ernest Graf (London: Nelson, 1957).

JEREMY GREGORY

Transylvania   When the Habsburgs conquered Transylvania in the 1690s, it was an autonomous principality under Ottoman protection. Prior to that, it had been an integral part of HUNGARY. The Habsburgs maintained its separate status, but the association with Hungary re-mained strong: Transylvania possessed the same kind of ancient con-stitution and was dominated by a landowning nobility which was Hungarian in speech and culture. Only the local German minority (known as 'Saxons'), a long-settled and comparatively prosperous urban community, could challenge that dominance; the largest element in the population, the mainly Romanian peasantry, enjoyed no rights at all.

From the 1740s the Viennese government sought reform in Transylvania, as elsewhere in the Habsburg lands. Employing authori-tarian methods, it achieved some success, notably in the areas of taxa-tion and military reorganization. But the obstacles proved too formidable: noble resistance was fortified by strong Protestant senti-ments and nascent Hungarian nationalism; the Saxons objected to the abolition of their organs of self-government; the Romanians indulged exaggerated expectations of change and broke out in a violent rebellion against their lords, which was equally brutally suppressed (1784–5). After 1790 Transylvania, like Hungary, reverted to conservative solutions, but an important legacy of influence from the Enlightenment remained.

B. Köpeczi (ed.), *Kurze Geschichte Siebenbürgens* (Budapest: Akadémia, 1990); English translation forthcoming.

R. J. W. EVANS

Triple Alliance (9 October 1716) Signed by Britain and France at The Hague, the Triple Alliance was at this time kept secret from the Dutch because of its furtherance of Austrian interests against the Dutch in the southern Netherlands and against Spain in Italy (which could only injure Dutch commerce in the Mediterranean). In fact, the alliance was but a continuation of the Anglo-French accord established at Utrecht (*see* TREATY OF UTRECHT); but it did include new emphases. These were essentially due to George I's electoral need of France's good offices in reaching an accommodation with Charles XII of Sweden over the Bremen and Verden duchies, and in persuading Peter I of Russia to abandon his design to annex the duchy of Mecklenburg. As regards the duc d'Orléans, regent of France, he was prepared to abandon French support for the Jacobite cause if he could have George I's support against the threat to his position in France from Philip V of Spain. The alliance was signed a second time, and more formally, though again without the Dutch, on 28 November. The Dutch actually acceded to the treaty on 4 January 1717, satisfied by French commercial concessions and out of concern to reinforce the Protestant succession in Britain. A heightening of Dutch jealousy over Anglo-Austrian understandings about the Dutch barrier fortresses was avoided, and the Dutch were kept in ignorance of any possibility of future hostilities with Spain.

E. Bourgeois, *La Diplomatie secrète au XVIII siècle: Ses debuts*, vol. 1 (Paris: Bélin Frères, 1909).
J. J. Murray, *An Honest Diplomat at the Hague: The Private Papers of Horatio Walpole 1715–16* (Bloomington, Ind.: Indiana University Press, 1953).

D. D. ALDRIDGE

Tronchin, Théodore (1709–1781) Genevan doctor. He attended many of the foremost figures of his day, including Voltaire, and is chiefly remembered for his acerbic, insightful and somewhat indiscreet opinions on Voltaire and Rousseau, and for contributing to their mutual antagonism.

DAVID HEMPTON

Tull, Jethro (1674–1741) English agriculturalist. He came from a family of minor gentry, and took up farming around the end of the seventeenth century in Oxfordshire and later in Berkshire. He believed that sowing seed thinly in widely spaced groups of drills, and keeping the soil in a fine tilth and free of weeds by hoeing, would produce good crops with a saving of both seed and manure. To this end he made, probably in 1701, the first known working seed-drill, although designs for such a machine had been produced earlier. He also advocated the use of a horse-drawn hoe and his own design of four-coultered plough. His books *The New Horse-Ploughing Husbandry* (1731) and *The Horse-Hoeing Husbandry* (1733) aroused much controversy. However, practical difficulties in the making and use of an effective drill restricted the impact of his ideas on contemporary farming, and it was only in the nineteenth century, when factory-made drills became available, that their use became commonplace. Horse-hoeing, in contrast to hand-hoeing, never became widespread because of the waste of land that it involved.

G. E. Fussell, *Jethro Tull: His Influence on Mechanized Agriculture* (Reading: Osprey, 1973).

G. E. MINGAY

Tunis *see* BARBARY STATES.

Turgot, Anne-Robert Jacques (1727–1781) French economist and statesman. Originally destined for the church, he became intendant of Limoges from 1761 to 1774. He contributed a number of influential articles to the *Encyclopédie* before its suppression, including 'Endowments', 'Etymology', 'Existence', 'Expansibility' and 'Fair' (*Foire*). His *Réflections sur la formation et la distribution des richesses* (Reflections on the Formation and Distribution of Riches, 1766) contributed to the refinement of QUESNAY's basic economic model and found a number of parallels in the writings of Adam Smith. Following the accession of Louis XVI in the summer of 1774, he was made controller-general of finance, to the great satisfaction of most of the *philosophes*. He embarked on a programme of sweeping but ill-fated reforms, including the restoration of free trade in grain and flour within France and the abolition of some artisanal corporations, which met with considerable resistance. In 1776 he fell from power and was soon succeeded by his rival Jacques Necker, who had attacked him in *Sur la législation et le commerce des grains*.

Michel C. Kiener, *Quand Turgot régnait en Limousin: un tremplin vers le pouvoir* (Paris: Fayard, 1979).

SYLVANA TOMASELLI

Tuscany   At the beginning of the eighteenth century Tuscany was ruled by the last of the Medicis, Cosimo III (*see* MEDICI) and Gian Gastone (1671–1737), after which it passed to the house of Lorraine, first under Francis II, husband of the Habsburg empress Maria Theresa, then his second son, Peter Leopold II, later Holy Roman Emperor, who was followed by Ferdinand III (1769–1824). It was, in effect, a satellite state of the Habsburg monarchy.

Tuscany was in a gradual state of decline under the Medicis, its political life still dominated by the ruling elite of Florence, which had become more landed than commercial, and by the church. Peter Leopold (*see* LEOPOLD II), especially, changed this with a series of enlightened, comprehensive reforms enacted with the help of his two great ministers, Neri and Gianni (1728–1801). A series of edicts from 1767 onwards freed the internal trade in grain; in 1786 a new criminal code was introduced which abolished capital punishment and judicial torture; between 1772 and 1782 a new court structure was created. In 1782 Peter Leopold and Gianni drew up a constitution for Tuscany, providing for a powerful elected assembly which involved Peter Leopold's renunciation of many of his powers; it was not enacted but proved very influential. Attempts to reform religious life, embodied in the work of the Synod of Pistoia (1786), and land tenure in favour of the indebted peasantry were less successful. The religious reforms and the freeing of the grain trade led to popular revolts in the 1780s and much of Peter Leopold's work was revoked by Ferdinand III.

M. S. Anderson, 'The Italian Reformers', in H. M. Scott (ed.), *Enlightened Absolutism* (London: Macmillan, 1990), pp. 55–74.
S. J. Woolf, *A History of Italy, 1700–1860* (London: Methuen, 1979).

MICHAEL BROERS

typhus   In the eighteenth century typhus was perceived as a new disease and a new public health problem. Previously, fevers had been characterized by inflammatory symptoms, for which the remedy was blood-letting and purging. But John Huxham (1692–1768) distinguished a new non-inflammatory 'putrid' type of fever. This distinction was subsequently clarified by William Cullen (1712–90), who referred to the new entity as 'typhus', from the Greek word for mist, because it was often accompanied by mental confusion or delirium.

Interest in typhus was not restricted to classification of the disease. Military reformers like John Pringle (1707–82) were concerned by outbreaks of the disease on board ships and in barracks. The prison reformer John Howard (1726–90) similarly traced the disease often referred to as 'gaol fever'. Physicians hypothesized that it was caused by an evil contagion that was bred in overcrowded spaces with stale air (twentieth-century medicine attributes its spread to lice), and recommended better sanitation and ventilation. Typhus was in many ways a representative illness of the eighteenth century, which Enlightenment medicine sought to address by dealing with problems of overcrowding and poverty as well as with the individual sickness.

G. B. Risse, '"Typhus" Fever in Eighteenth Century Hospitals: New Approaches to Medical Treatment', *Bulletin of the History of Medicine*, 59 (1985), 176–95.

MARY E. FISSELL

U

Ukraine   The Ukraine, or 'borderland', home to the Ukrainian Cossacks, or Zaporozhian Host, under their hetman, was also known as 'Little Russia' and 'Ruthenia'. In the late seventeenth century the region was divided and under dispute. The Left Bank (that is, east of the River Dnieper), with Kiev, was incorporated into Muscovy in 1654 (ratified by the 1686 Treaty of Moscow), while the Right Bank remained Polish. Local laws and customs prevailed, but in 1722 the Russian hetmanate was subordinated to the Little Russian department. Under Catherine II, Russian Ukraine was fully incorporated into the empire under the direction of Governor-General P. A. Rumiantsev (1725–96). The last hetman, Kirill Razumovskii (1728–1803), retired in 1764, and the Zaporozhian Host was disbanded in 1775. In the 1780s Russian provincial administration was extended there and in 1783 full serfdom and the poll tax were introduced. By the last two PARTITIONS OF POLAND, Russia gained the whole Ukraine – the Right Bank and Podolia in 1793, and Volhynia in 1795 – except for Galicia (with its capital, Lvov), Bukovina and Subcarpathia, which had been annexed by Austria in 1772. In 1796 the Left Bank was renamed Little Russia province and the Right Bank Kiev, Volhynia and Podolia provinces.

See also RUSSIA.

W. E. D. Allen, *The Ukraine: A History* (Cambridge: Cambridge University Press, 1940).

LINDSEY HUGHES

ultramontanism   Deriving from the Latin for 'beyond the mountains', the term 'ultramontanism' denoted support for the ultimate authority of the PAPACY above other loyalties, whether to secular or to ecclesiastical authorities. Such support was challenged by the growing 'nationalism' of Catholic states and churches in the eighteenth century. At Koblenz in 1769 and in the so-called Punctuation of Ems in 1786 the three German archbishop-electors challenged the authority of the papacy. Echoing traditional themes, they asserted that only a general council could wield supreme legislative and judicial power. Many clerics, while supporting the idea of a close church–state relationship, had no rigid view of its practical nature and, aware of the fluid nature of ecclesiastical life in the second half of the century, were prepared to accept significant changes. The revolutionary–Napoleonic period helped to lead to a conservative stress in which ultramontane views became more influential.

JEREMY BLACK

Uniate Church Uniates were also known as Eastern or Byzantine Rite Catholics and Greek Catholics. The Uniate Church was created in Poland under King Sigismund III (1566–1632) by the 1596 Union of Brest in order to weaken the influence of the Orthodox patriarchates of Moscow and Constantinople (the latter under Turkey) and associated political pressures. It represented a compromise between the ruling Catholic Church and nobles in the Ukraine and Belorussia: most Orthodox churchmen in Poland-Lithuania accepted the pope and Roman Catholic dogma but retained Orthodox rituals and customs, including icons and architectural conventions, married clergy, leavened bread and Church Slavonic as the liturgical language. The Treaty of Uzhgorod (1646) extended the arrangement to Orthodox communities in east Slovakia, Transcarpathia and Hungary. After the incorporation of Polish Ukraine and Belorussia into Russia by the Partitions of 1793 and 1795, many Uniates rejoined the ORTHODOX CHURCH under pressure. The church rallied in the reigns of Paul I (1796–1801) and Alexander I, but was reunited with the Orthodox Church under pressure from Nicholas I (reigned 1825–55) in 1839. Uniates survived in the Habsburg lands until the territorial redivisions of the Second World War and the church was resurrected under *glasnost* in the 1980s.

Mark Elliot, 'Uniates', *Modern Encyclopedia of Russian and Soviet History*, 40 (1985), 210–19.

LINDSEY HUGHES

Unigenitus Dei Filius (8 September 1713) The apostolic constitution or bull 'Unigenitus Dei Filius' (Only-Begotten Son of God) was issued by Pope CLEMENT XI. It condemned 101 propositions in a work by the Jansenist Oratorian priest Pasquier Quesnel (1634–1719), *Le Nouveau Testament en français, avec des réflexions morales sur chaque verset* which was published in 1671 as *Abrégé de la Morale de l'Évangile,* and in an expanded version under a new title in 1692, 1693 and 1694.

The bull condemned Jansenist views on predestination, irresistible grace, sin, Bible-reading and excommunication as 'false, captious, ill-sounding, offensive to pious ears, scandalous, pernicious, temerarious' and 'heretical' (see JANSENISM). Quesnel's book was approved in 1695 by the archbishop of Châlons, L. A. de Noailles (1651–1729), afterwards cardinal archbishop of Paris, but was condemned by Clement's brief 'Universi Dominici Gregis' of 13 July 1708. Louis XIV asked Rome to outlaw Quesnel's book by a bull according with French law, and in 1714 had 'Unigenitus' registered by the Paris *parlement*. Four French 'appellant' bishops in 1717 appealed from 'Unigenitus' to a future general council, invoking the church's 'Gallican liberties' against the Jesuits, monarchy and Rome. Cardinal FLEURY issued a royal declaration making the bull the law of France in 1730.

H. Denzinger, *Enchiridion Symbolorum* (Freiburg im Breisgau: Herder, 1932), pp. 391–8.

SHERIDAN GILLEY

Unitarianism The term 'Unitarianism' signifies belief in the absolute unity of God, and hence rejection of the doctrine of the Trinity and denial that the death of Christ was a sacrificial atonement for human sins. Unitarian doctrine varied considerably and was never centrally defined, but in the eighteenth century the Socinian emphasis predominated, differing from the older form of ARIANISM by its insistence on the humanity, and denial of the pre-existence, of Christ. Most European states disapproved of antitrinitarian ideas and at times persecuted those who held them. The emperor Joseph II was unusual in his toleration of Unitarians in Transylvania, although in England the laws against their worship (repealed in 1813) were rarely enforced and the Anglican seceder Theophilus Lindsey (1723–1808) inaugurated a Unitarian chapel in London in 1774. In the age of Joseph Priestley Unitarianism became associated with political RADICALISM, including pro-Americanism (a Unitarian chapel was opened in Boston in 1785) and sympathy with the French Revolution. Cut off from a popular following by their intellectualism, Unitarians were nevertheless well connected in politics and highly influential in the world of ideas.

E. M. Wilbur, *A History of Unitarianism*, 2 vols (Cambridge, Mass.: Harvard University Press, 1946–52).

G. M. DITCHFIELD

United Empire Loyalists At the close of the AMERICAN WAR OF INDEPENDENCE some 60,000 loyalists left the former thirteen colonies to settle in parts of CANADA, especially Nova Scotia, New Brunswick and Ontario. This reflected the strength of their loyalist convictions and laid the foundations for the expansion of English-speaking Canada. Although the American congress had called upon the states to pay compensation to loyalists who had lost homes or property during the war, only South Carolina responded to the appeal. By 1789 the British government had paid about £3 million in compensation to loyalists in Canada. A consequence of the increase in the English-speaking population of Canada was the Canada Act of 1791 which divided Canada into two provinces, Upper and Lower Canada, each with a representative assembly. As an indication of their devotion to the British empire, many of the loyalists who went to live in Canada added the initials 'UE' after their names, which is why they came to be known as 'United Empire Loyalists'.

J. H. Rose, A. P. Newton and E. A. Benians (eds), *The Cambridge History of the British Empire*, vol. 6 (Cambridge: Cambridge University Press, 1930).

JOHN W. DERRY

United Irishmen Originating as a debating society that pressed for constitutional reforms, the United Irishmen were influenced by the ideals of the French Revolution. Frustrated in their hopes of reform, under the leadership of Lord Edward Fitzgerald (1763–98) and Wolfe Tone (1763–98) they came to see a secular republic on the French model as the means of securing reconciliation between the Protestant and Catholic communities in Ireland and separation from Britain. By 1795 the United Irishmen was a secret organization planning a rebellion which would receive assistance from the French. But when the rising came in 1798 it was different from the national rising that had been envisaged: it turned out to be a large-scale rural disorder chiefly concentrated in Leinster, and French help, when it came, was too little and too late. Fitzgerald died of wounds received while resisting arrest and Wolfe Tone committed suicide in prison. The immediate legacy of the movement was heightened antagonism between Protestants and Catholics, and the parliamentary union of Britain and Ireland in 1801, but the United Irishmen proved a potent inspiration to later generations of Irish republicans.

M. Elliott, *Partners in Revolution: The United Irishmen and France* (New Haven, Conn.: Yale University Press, 1982).

JOHN W. DERRY

United Provinces (Dutch Republic) The United Provinces of the Netherlands, or the Dutch Republic, consisted of the seven northern provinces of the Low Countries – Holland, Zeeland, Utrecht, Gelderland, Overijssel, Friesland and Groningen – which in the late sixteenth century had established themselves as an independent republic following the revolt of the Netherlands against Spanish rule. Densely populated (with around 1,900,000 inhabitants in 1700 and 2,078,000 in 1795) and in its western regions highly urbanized, the republic was cosmopolitan in character, with substantial immigrant communities attracted by its general commercial prosperity and by the relative freedom of its religious and intellectual life. Political power was in the hands of a series of local, self-perpetuating oligarchies, whose members (known as regents) included wealthy businessmen, professional people and some landed nobility. The structure of government was federal and highly decentralized. Urban, noble and other local interests were represented in provincial assemblies (states of Holland and so on) which held ultimate sovereignty in the republic; while these assemblies in turn sent delegates to the States General at The Hague, a weaker body constitutionally more akin to a congress of ambassadors than to a national parliament like the British one.

Compared with the heroic achievements of the sixteenth and seventeenth centuries, the eighteenth century has usually been seen in Dutch historiography as a period of decline. Its public finances exhausted by forty years of almost continuous warfare against France (1672–1713), the republic gradually withdrew from international politics, seeking neutrality in wartime (1733–5, 1740–7, 1756–63, 1775–80) and finding itself reduced, by the 1780s, to the status of a pawn in the hands of the great powers. At the same time, its domestic politics became increasingly corrupt and inefficient, tarnished by nepotism, tax evasion and profit-making in public office. The French invasion of Dutch territory in 1747 precipitated a crisis which restored the house of Orange to power (*see* ORANGEISM). But neither the stadtholder, WILLIAM IV, nor those who succeeded him in office (*see* WILLIAM V) had the determination to make the fundamental reforms that the country needed. During the 1780s the middle-class Patriot movement succeeded in gaining control of town governments in Holland, Utrecht and elsewhere, bringing in a measure of democracy. But this initiative was crushed in 1787 by a combination of British diplomacy and Prussian armed force, and the Orangeists were briefly reinstated before the republic's final collapse in 1795 in the face of the armies of revolutionary France.

The picture of Dutch decline in the eighteenth century should not, however, be overdrawn. British and French commercial competition, combined with high wages in the Netherlands, undermined the republic's European trade and much of its manufacturing industry, but other sectors of the economy – the EAST INDIES trade, agriculture in Holland and Zeeland, AMSTERDAM's money market – continued to flourish. So too, in some respects, did the country's cultural life. Besides experiencing a modest Enlightenment of their own (evident, for example, in a lively periodical press and in the writings of liberal Protestant theologians), the Dutch contributed much to the wider Enlightenment of Europe and North America – through the influence of individual scholars like SPINOZA and Boerhaave, through the important international role of Dutch publishing-houses and through the potent image of the republic as the 'motherland of liberty'. If the leading Netherlands universities of Leiden and Utrecht no longer attracted large numbers of foreign students as in the seventeenth century, their teaching and curricula (notably in medicine) were widely imitated; while Dutch institutions of social welfare were singled out as models by reformers like John Howard (1726–90). Even the Dutch school of painting – once largely dismissed by connoisseurs outside the Netherlands – had become fashionable by the mid eighteenth century and helped to stimulate the growth of landscape and genre as significant themes in European art.

After the fall of the Dutch Republic to the French, a period of political and cultural transformation ensued during which the Netherlands was ruled successively as the BATAVIAN REPUBLIC (1795–1806), as a Bonapartist kingdom (1806–10), as a province of France (1810–13) and finally – from 1813 – as an independent constitutional monarchy, which until 1830 incorporated the Southern Netherlands as well as the former United Provinces.

See also AUSTRIAN NETHERLANDS, SPANISH NETHERLANDS.

E. H. Kossmann, The Low Countries 1780–1940 (Oxford: Clarendon, 1978).
Simon Schama, Patriots and Liberators: Revolution in the Netherlands 1780–1813 (London: Collins, 1977).

HUGH DUNTHORNE

United States of America   When representatives from the thirteen states meeting in Philadelphia as the continental congress issued a Declaration of Independence on 4 July 1776, the United States of America was born. At the time it consisted of the thirteen former British colonies along the Atlantic coastline of North America: New Hampshire, Massachusetts, Rhode Island, Connecticut, New York, New Jersey, Pennsylvania, Maryland, Delaware, Virginia, North Carolina, South Carolina and Georgia. The majority of the population of 2.5 million lived in a coastal belt 50 to 100 miles wide within easy reach of the guns of the Royal Navy. Settlement of the back country had been restricted by British policy and by the many Indians who were less than pleased by colonial incursions into their lands. Less than thirty years later, the land area of the new nation was to grow more than tenfold, extending from the Atlantic to the Rocky Mountains.

The Declaration of Independence was a model of Enlightenment ideals adapted to New World realities by practical colonists-cum-revolutionaries. In JEFFERSON's clear, classically influenced prose, the document carefully elaborated what was seen as the long train of abuses wrought by Britain's George III which abrogated the compact between king and colonies, ruler and ruled. The influence of Locke, Montesquieu, the post-Cromwellian English libertarians and others may be discerned in the declaration. It was a legal document designed for external consumption (international recognition being high on the American agenda), and at the same time an articulate summation of why Americans were fighting and what they were fighting for. It was a bold statement, for even as General Washington's troops around New York assembled to hear the declaration read, the top masts of a huge British invasion fleet were visible on the horizon.

Following the TREATY OF PARIS and the removal of the long-standing French threat from North America, many Americans found what they considered to be Britain's increasingly dictatorial policies unacceptable. Objections and demonstrations against these policies had widespread popular support, but protest was one thing and a complete break with the motherland another. Most Americans, including some in congress, found British colonial policy tyrannical and believed that taxation without representation was unconstitutional, but many drew the line at cutting all ties.

Thus, at the end of 1775, as Washington's army surrounded the British in Boston and another revolutionary force was at the gates of Quebec, colonial unity was so fragile that the word 'independence' could not be used. Moreover, while historians generally distinguish the states regionally as New England, the Middle Atlantic States and the South, this was very misleading; the people did not think of themselves in regional terms – instead, they were Massachusetts men or Marylanders. Well into the nineteenth century, when Thomas Jefferson wrote about his 'country', he was referring not to the United States but to Virginia. But as protest, dislike of British policies and the commencement of hostilities forced these reluctant bedfellows together, by July 1776 Americans who actively supported the revolutionaries and the independence movement were in the distinct minority. Probably half the population split themselves between the patriot (rebel or Whig) and loyal (Tory) camps. The others simply wanted to be left alone, and many sat out the war or moved westward away from the fighting.

The lack of unanimity became plain during the war when it took nearly five years for all the states to adopt the fundamental law of the compact between the states – the Articles of Confederation. Washington's already small army often shrank to pitiful dimensions when the states did not send supplies and reinforcements and there was no central authority to force them to do so. In the immediate post-bellum period the situation worsened. Disputations between states took so long to adjudicate that all but the most libertarian Americans recognized the need for some form of centralized government. The result was a convention in Philadelphia in the summer of 1787, which discussed and argued over what would become the Constitution, the basic law of the nation (*see* UNITED STATES CONSTITUTION).

The debate on constitutional ratification exacerbated the old animosities and created fresh ones (many of which were not to be resolved until the Civil War of 1861–5). Those who remembered the problems of weak government during the Revolution finally won the day. Delaware, Pennsylvania and New Jersey ratified in December 1787, but it was not until May 1790 when the last of the original thirteen states, Rhode Island, agreed to join the union. By then, factionalism and then regionalism – the banes of the founding fathers – reared their ugly heads, and a multiparty system quickly devolved.

Meanwhile, westward expansion continued unabated and new states were added to the union. Vermont, formerly the Hampshire Grants and long contested by New York and New Hampshire, became a state in 1791, followed by Kentucky (1792), Tennessee (1796) and Ohio (1803). Other territories waited for larger populations before applying to join. Jefferson's purchase of LOUISIANA from France in 1803 opened up the Mississippi River to trade and the rest of the continent to expansion and settlement.

See also AMERICAN WAR OF INDEPENDENCE.

Fame and the Founding Fathers: Essays by Douglass Adair, ed. Trevor Colbourn (New York: Norton, 1974).

John Morgan Dederer, *War in America to 1775* (New York: New York University Press, 1990).

Forrest McDonald, *E Pluribus Unum* (Boston: Houghton Mifflin, 1965).

James Kirby Martin, *Men in Rebellion* (New Brunswick, NJ: Rutgers University Press, 1973).

Henry F. May, *The Enlightenment in America* (New York: Oxford University Press, 1976).

JOHN MORGAN DEDERER

universities   As a creation of the Middle Ages, the institution of the university exhibited characteristics that were regarded with increasing hostility over the course of the eighteenth century. First, universities were often linked with church establishments which were themselves under attack in many parts of Europe; secondly, from their foundation they were, as corporate bodies, permitted privileges and exemptions which served as a bulwark between them and the state; and lastly, their curriculum which, since their foundation, had been largely based on an amalgam of Christian theology and Aristotelian philosophy, seemed remote from the achievements of the SCIENTIFIC REVOLUTION and the needs of the eighteenth century.

Of course, the force of such generalizations varied from country to country. In some parts of Europe, notably the Netherlands and Scotland, the universities' role in the education of the lay professions of medicine and law weakened their ecclesiastical connections and helped to make them major centres of activity in the development of secular disciplines both in the natural sciences and in the embryonic social sciences: in short, they were regarded as agents of ENLIGHTENMENT. By contrast, in places such as France, where anticlericalism was particularly rife, the universities were identified with an emphasis on tradition which was regarded as the antithesis of Enlightenment, even though the French universities were much less impervious to the major currents of eighteenth-century intellectual life than their critics claimed.

The extent of the universities' privileges and exemptions also varied considerably. Predictably, they tended to be least evident in the more recently founded universities, reflecting the growing power of the state towards the end of the seventeenth century. This was most obvious in the newly founded universities of Germany: HALLE (1694), GÖTTINGEN (1737) and Erlangen (1743) owed their existence to the desire of the local princes to enhance their prestige and the calibre of their servants in church and state. As one German official put it in 1770, the universities existed for the 'service of the state and the enlightenment of the nation'. In places like France and England, where universities with a long medieval past predominated, local privileges were more jealously guarded and the direct power of the state kept more firmly at bay – which accounts for their temporary abolition in France in 1793, along with other privileged corporations such as the guilds, after the Revolution gave birth to a more effectively centralized state than the old regime had ever known.

In late-eighteenth-century Spain, too, the universities were subject to unaccustomed attention from the state in the person of the would-be enlightened absolutist, Charles III who attempted to widen the power of the central government over privileged corporations such as the church and its institutional affiliate, the universities. The result was a movement for the reform of the curriculum and forms of Spanish academic life, the reverberations of which were felt from Salamanca to Guatemala. For in both the Spanish- and the English-speaking New World the universities naturally mirrored those of the metropolitan power although in British North America the number of available models – Oxford and Cambridge, the dissenting academies and the Scottish universities – helped to bring about a greater degree of colonial diversity than was evident in the more monolithic world of the Spanish university.

Among the changes wrought within the universities of both Old and New Spain under the stimulus of Charles III was a growth in the attention accorded to modern science and a consequent downplaying of systems of natural philosophy based on Aristotle. But, despite the universities' critics, such changes had become routine throughout much of the rest of Europe as the undergraduate curriculum in natural philosophy changed over the course of the late seventeenth and early eighteenth centuries from scholasticism to CARTESIANISM to Newtonianism (see NEWTON), sometimes combining elements of one or more systems. Such an intellectual metamorphosis did, however, mean unravelling the closely woven fabric of the traditional scholastic curriculum where a set of common philosophical assumptions had underlain and drawn together the different elements of university instruction. It also weakened the importance of the traditional method of examination by disputation, giving rise (especially in the English-speaking world) to new forms of examination based more on written than on verbal skills.

In many ways, then, the universities of the eighteenth century were institutions in the process of reshaping the forms of academic life and organization which they had inherited from the Middle Ages. Despite its critics, the eighteenth-century university showed its resilience by substantially modifying its curriculum (especially in natural philosophy), by accommodating a range of possible new associations with the state and, thanks particularly to the German universities, by laying the foundations for the research ideal that was to reshape the nature of the institution in the subsequent century.

L. W. B. Brockliss, *French Higher Education in the Seventeenth and Eighteenth Centuries: A Cultural History* (Oxford: Clarendon, 1987).

J. Gascoigne, *Cambridge in the Age of the Enlightenment: Science, Religion and Politics from the Restoration to the French Revolution* (Cambridge: Cambridge University Press, 1989).

J. T. Lanning, *The Eighteenth-Century Enlightenment in the University of San Carlos de Guatemala* (Ithaca, NY: Cornell University Press, 1956).

C. E. McClelland, *State, Society, and University in Germany 1700–1914* (Cambridge: Cambridge University Press, 1980).

L. S. Sutherland and L. G. Mitchell (eds), *The History of the University of Oxford: The Eighteenth Century* (Oxford: Oxford University Press, 1986).

JOHN GASCOIGNE

Utilitarianism   The moral and political doctrine advocating pursuit of the greatest happiness of the greatest number was known as utilitarianism. Deriving ultimately from the hedonic and atomistic individualism of Epicurus (*c*.341–270 BC), the doctrine was developed in the Enlightenment era by Hobbes, Hutcheson, Hume, Helvétius, Priestley and others, and given its most fully theoretical form by BENTHAM. For Bentham the principle of utility prescribed a naturalistic and scientific ethic that would render normally subjective judgements objective and normally qualitative ones quantitative, through a felicific calculus that would calibrate good or evil by the measurable tendency of actions to produce HAPPINESS. Utilitarians generally supported associationist theories of learning and sensationalist psychologies, and promoted the perfectibility of man through progress. Like his Italian counterpart, BECCARIA, Bentham particularly applied the utility principle to legal, penal and institutional reform, developing a blueprint of the utilitarian prison, the panopticon. Through such social theorists like Adam Smith and Malthus, utilitarianism's view of change produced by the pursuit of pleasure and the sanction of pain was to underpin progressive and evolutionary theories of man and society in the late Enlightenment and through the nineteenth century.

Elie Halévy, *The Growth of Philosophic Radicalism*, 2 vols (London: Faber, 1928).

ROY PORTER

utopianism The Enlightenment was more concerned with ideas of reform than with utopian schemes. Some of the ideal republics proposed in the eighteenth century were not particularly enticing. For example, MORELLY's model society, as described in his *Code de la nature*, was characterized by uniformity, regularity and sameness. Not only did its first law prohibit the possession of property except what a man 'used daily, for his needs, his pleasures, or his daily work', but everything was to be grouped and organized in multiples of ten, from the number of families in each tribe to the number of cities in each province; everyone was to live in identical houses; direct exchanges between citizens were forbidden; and all citizens were to marry on reaching puberty, celibacy being permitted only for those above 40. Curiously, Morelly's system included provisions for prisons and severe punishment, especially for adultery.

The work was persistently attributed to DIDEROT, who made every effort to distance himself from it. Like several other *philosophes*, Diderot was approached by Dom Léger-Marie Deschamps (1716–74), perhaps the most intriguing of the Enlightenment's utopians. Like them, he resisted Deschamps's attempt to convert him to his vision of a social state devoid of rulers, laws and property, and in which the very names of vices and virtues would be abolished. To the extent that he indulged in utopian fantasies at all, it is clear from such works as the *Supplément au voyage de Bougainville* that they were about worlds in which most sexual taboos would cease to matter and women would prove compliant. Nor did he place much trust in the power of education to end social ills. In contrast to such thinkers as Helvétius, who had high expectations of education, Diderot thought that while much could be achieved by ensuring adequate levels of education, nurture was only part of what made mankind as it was. Nature controlled the rest.

By and large the most important Enlightenment thinkers gave little thought to utopian ideas be they of their own making or those of others. In an essay entitled 'Idea of a Perfect Commonwealth' (1754) HUME argued that since people were governed by authority rather than reason, established governments had an infinite advantage over proposed ones: 'To tamper, therefore, in this affair, or try experiments merely upon the credit of supposed argument and philosophy, can never be the part of a wise magistrate, who will bear a reverence to what carries the marks of age; and though he may attempt some improvements for the public good, yet will he adjust his innovations, as much as possible, to the ancient fabric, and preserve entire the chief pillars and supports of the constitution.'

Franco Venturi, *Utopia and Reform in the Enlightenment* (Cambridge: Cambridge University Press, 1971).

SYLVANA TOMASELLI

Utrecht, Treaty of (1713) The Utrecht settlement ended the Grand Alliance against Louis XIV. Britain signed peace preliminaries on 27 September 1711. The peace conference began on 29 January 1712, France and Spain signing a treaty on 31 March 1713 with Britain, the United Provinces, Prussia, Portugal and Savoy-Piedmont. Louis XIV's grandson Philip V kept the throne of Spain, and concessions were given over territorial exchanges and barrier fortresses in the southern Netherlands (Belgium) against the French. Other agreements signed included the Anglo-Spanish peace treaty of 13 July, which conceded Gibraltar and Minorca to Britain, as well as the ASIENTO. Austria signed the Treaty of Rastadt on 6 March 1714, followed by the Treaty of Baden on 7 September, gaining the Spanish Netherlands and Spanish territories in Italy. In February 1715 Spain and Portugal signed the final Utrecht treaty, and the last (third) Barrier Treaty was signed on 4 November 1715.

J. M. Black, *The Rise of the European Powers, 1679–1793* (London: Arnold, 1990).

PHILIP WOODFINE

V

vaccination   The biggest medical success story of the Enlightenment was vaccination. Although INOCULATION had already provided a means of protection against SMALLPOX, vaccination was much safer. Inoculation meant giving a person a mild form of smallpox; vaccination utilized a milder disease, cowpox. The process was named 'vaccination' from the Latin for cow, *vacca*.

Edward Jenner (1749–1823), a Gloucestershire practitioner who had studied under John Hunter, discovered the process. Country-dwellers had long noted the lovely complexions of dairymaids, which were remarkable in an era when many people bore pitted smallpox scars on their faces. Folk wisdom hinted that cowpox, a disease of cattle transmissible to humans, could afford protection against smallpox. Jenner tested this hypothesis empirically, showing in his 1798 *Inquiry into the Causes and Effects of Variolae Vaccinae* that the mild disease provided immunity against the deadly one without harming the patient. His fame was immediate and world-wide. When in the early nineteenth century he petitioned for the release of prisoners of war, Napoleon said that he could refuse Jenner nothing, such was mankind's debt to him.

Donald Hopkins, *Princes and Peasants: Smallpox in History* (Chicago: University of Chicago Press, 1983).

MARY E. FISSELL

vampires   According to Horace Walpole, George II, who was 'not apt to believe more than his neighbours, had no doubt of the existence of vampires and their banquets on the dead'. Although such a view was not commonly held in Britain, on the Continent there had been rumours of vampire epidemics which had inspired Ossenfelder's 'The Vampire' (1748), Bürger's 'Lenore' (1773) and Goethe's 'The Bride of Corinth' (1797). These poems portray the revenant as a variation of the demon lover, who was primarily in pursuit of love and not blood. In English literature the vampire had been confined to folk ballads until 1818 when, for the ghost-story competition at Villa Diodati, John Polidori wrote 'The Vampyre', which was about the amorous Lord Ruthven, thought to be based on Byron. This short story paved the way for Bram Stoker's creation of the romantic Count Dracula in 1897. By the end of the nineteenth century, the deadly female of the undine and lamia legends which Robert Southey (1774–1843) had linked to vampirism in *Thalaba the Destroyer* (1797) had developed into an image of the female vampire as a sexual siren whose blood-lust had become synonymous with feminine evil.

James B. Twitchell, *The Living Dead: A Study of the Vampire in Romantic Literature* (Durham, NC: Duke University Press, 1981).

MARIE MULVEY ROBERTS

Vanbrugh, Sir John (1664–1726) English architect and playwright. A gentleman, like Wren, he was almost as much of a polymath. The first of his ten comedies, *The Relapse*, was produced in 1696, his best known, *The Provok'd Wife*, in 1697 and the last in 1705. In 1699, with some suddenness – 'Van's Genius without Thought or Lecture / Is hugely turned to Architecture', wrote Swift – he began a productive career as an architect at Castle Howard, Yorkshire (begun 1700), designed with the help of Nicholas Hawksmoor (1661–1736), with whom he also worked at Blenheim Palace, Oxfordshire (begun 1705). Vanbrugh seems to have brought to their partnership, which took English BAROQUE to its apogee, his gift for dynamic massing, while Hawksmoor had a genius for idiosyncratic detail, as well as the technical expertise. Vanbrugh's own house at Greenwich, London (*c.*1717) is a miniature fortress. The absence of pointed arches or other typical Gothic Revival details makes it all the more effective as a re-enactment not only of the medieval, but also of the Elizabethan (itself equally retrospective).

Kerry Downes, *Vanbrugh* (London: Zwemmer, 1977).

CHRISTINE STEVENSON

Vancouver, George (1757–1798) English navigator and explorer. Born at King's Lynn, he sailed as a midshipman on COOK's *Resolution* in 1772. Here he received training in navigation from the astronomer William Wales (?1734–98) and, thus equipped, became one of the most technically proficient surveyors of his age. Once again a midshipman on Cook's third voyage, he was introduced to the Pacific coast on which his later reputation was to be based. Following service in the West Indies during and after the American War of Independence, in 1791 he was appointed to command a voyage to the coast of America in pursuit of the legendary NORTH-WEST PASSAGE. This expedition was to last for more than four years. Using the Hawaiian islands as a winter base, his two ships, the *Discovery* and the *Chatham*, spent three summers exploring the North American coast between the Straits of Juan de Fuca and Cook Inlet. He failed to achieve his two principal objectives – the cession of Nootka Sound by Spain (*see* NOOTKA SOUND INCIDENT), and the discovery of a navigable passage – but his charting of the Canadian and Alaskan coasts were of a standard comparable to Cook's.

B. Anderson, *Surveyor of the Sea* (Seattle: University of Washington Press, 1960).

DAVID MACKAY

Vauban, Sébastien le Prestre de (1633–1707)   French military engineer. One of Louis XIV's most distinguished soldiers, he was born into a poor gentry family. He entered the king's service in 1653 and soon revealed his exceptional talent as a military engineer. He became the key figure in the policy of securing and defending France's vulnerable northern and north-eastern frontiers. He was a master of siege warfare but his outstanding contribution was to construct a complex set of fortifications based on the model of the duelling field, the *pré carré*, which provided linear defences by way of a series of linked fortresses. He became a marshal of France in 1703, the first engineer to attain the rank.

He also wrote critically about the social and financial inequities existing in his country. In 1707 he published *Dixième royale* (Project for a Royal Tithe), advocating a new income tax to be paid by all subjects, privileged and unprivileged alike (*see* DIXIÈME). His views were not well received by the king and the last days of this gifted, principled man were passed under a cloud of royal disfavour.

A. Rébelliau, *Vauban* (Paris: Fayard, 1962).

J. H. SHENNAN

Vaucanson, Jacques de (1709–1782)   French inventor. Born in Grenoble, he mastered the art of mechanics and constructed a precision clock using basic instruments while studying at a Jesuit college. His desire to study mechanical science took him to Paris where the statue of the flautist in the Tuileries gardens inspired him to make an automaton that played music. The music box took him several years to complete and won him the admiration of the Académie des Sciences in 1738.

He went on to make many more complex automata, but his talents were most in demand by industrialists. The cardinal Fleury invited him to survey the machinery employed by a silk factory and Vaucanson improved its efficiency by inventing a machine that produced a continuous chain of silk. His reputation for simplifying complex industrial machinery was such that on a trip to Lyon he was warmly welcomed by workers eager for an easier life. As a tribute to their laziness he built them a mechanical donkey that produced fabric flowers. On his death he bequeathed his cabinet of mechanics to the queen, who presented it to the Académie des Sciences. Men of commerce reclaimed machines relevant to their professions and the collection was dissipated.

M. L. BENJAMIN

Vendée The counter-revolutionary Vendée rising in western France from 1793 posed a severe test to the newly established republic, already at war with most of Europe. The revolt was triggered off when local authorities attempted to implement the conscription law of 23 February 1793. A massive peasant insurrection ensued, which was fought with unparalleled ferocity on both sides, and claimed up to 200,000 victims over the course of the 1790s. 'Church and king' was the rebel slogan: the CIVIL CONSTITUTION OF THE CLERGY of 1790 had already caused much discontent in this traditionally religious region; their royalism, however, was ill thought out. Rebel action was most successful where peasants used the natural advantages of the *bocage* environment, but less effective when they fought outside their area or in open battle – as was witnessed by defeats at Cholet (17 October 1793) and Savenay (23 December). The military threat posed by the Vendéans had ended by early 1794, but guerilla warfare continued. General Hoche's (1768–97) policy of repression and conciliation led to the Treaty of La Jaunaye (17 February 1795), which granted freedom of worship and an amnesty. Rebellion rumbled on sporadically throughout the late 1790s and was neutralized only during the Consulate.

COLIN JONES

Venezuela Although Spanish settlement dated from the sixteenth century, it was not until 1776 that the Spanish crown joined its extended coastal communities into a single province endowed with a captain-general and intendant, a high court of justice, a central treasury, a merchant guild and a regiment of soldiers, all resident in the new capital of Caracas. Between 1728 and 1784 the Royal Guipuzcoan Company had revitalized the economy by promoting the expansion of cacao exports to Spain, based on plantations operating with African slave labour. Thereafter, the creole landowners diversified production, adding coffee, cotton, sugar and indigo to their range. By 1800 Venezuela had a population of around 800,000, of which slaves comprised 15 per cent, most of whom dwelt in the fertile Aragua valley where Caracas was situated. The vast, burning plains (los Llanos) of the interior supported great herds of cattle and a vagrant race of cowhands and bandits. A beneficiary of the reforms introduced by Charles III, Venezuela was quick to learn of the Revolutions in the United States and France, and when the British naval blockade of 1796–1802 and 1802–8 sharply reduced exports the Caraqueño landowning elite seized their opportunity to end Spanish rule.

See SPANISH AMERICA.

M. P. McKinley, *Pre-revolutionary Caracas: Politics, Economy and Society 1777–1811* (Cambridge: Cambridge University Press, 1985).

D. A. BRADING

Venice The republic of Venice, one of the oldest states in Europe, conserved more of its origins as a city-state than the other Italian states in the eighteenth century. Its territories, comprising Venetia on the Italian mainland, the Dalmatian coast, Istria and the city of Venice itself, remained largely unchanged throughout the century. The republic remained neutral in all the wars of the early eighteenth century – to the envy of its contemporaries – due to the inherent weakness of the state as much as to desire. It was abolished by Napoleon in 1797, passing under Austrian rule thereafter, except for a brief period as part of the kingdom of ITALY from 1810 to 1814. Until the fall of the republic, Venice continued to be ruled by a narrow circle of wealthy patrician families whose names were inscribed in the famous 'Golden Book'. This oligarchy was not challenged in the course of the century, as no significant new bourgeois families emerged. The Venetian nobility had ceased to engage in commerce or banking, and now drew its wealth almost entirely from landed estates rented out to small peasant proprietors; no agricultural capitalism emerged here, in contrast to Lombardy. Venetian industry, too, remained largely artisanal in character, although a small textile industry developed in the city. Indeed, the most dynamic economic and intellectual forces in the republic were to be found not in Venice – despite its fierce retention of political and economic privileges – but in the smaller cities of the Veneto. The population of Venice actually declined in the course of the century, from 149,476 in 1760 to 137,240 in 1797, which was just below its level in 1696; throughout the period, Venice continued to lose trade to the Austrian port of Trieste.

See also MEDITERRANEAN.

S. J. Woolf, *A History of Italy, 1700–1860* (London: Methuen, 1979).

MICHAEL BROERS

Verri, Alessandro (1741–1814) Italian jurist. A younger brother of Pietro Verri, he was born in Milan where his father, who was a jurist, started him in the legal career that Pietro had rejected. Following college, a close and lasting relationship developed between the two brothers. Together, they were active in the Academia dei Pugni, which included Beccaria and others who were to become key figures in the reformist policy undertaken by the Habsburg administration. Alessandro was among the founders of the critical review *Il Caffè*, for which he wrote articles mainly concerned with the reform of traditional legal systems. However, he never completed his proposed new legal code, nor did he publish the *Storia d'Italia* (a work influenced by Muratori's historical writings), which, along with Beccaria's *Dei delitti e delle pene*, was expected to be the major event to emerge from the *école de Milan*. When, in 1766, quarrels (mainly provoked by Pietro's difficult temperament) tore the group apart, and brought to an end the publication of the journal, he moved to Rome and turned to literary interests and the pleasures of *salon* life. Despite his defection, he remained for thirty years his brother's confidante, and their intense relationship is reflected in a bulky correspondence which remains.

SANDRA CAVALLO

Verri, Pietro (1728–1797) Italian economist and writer. The eldest son of Count Gabriele, a member of the Milanese senate, he had a difficult youth, spent in futile rebellion against the conventions and conservatism of the local society and the narrow-mindedness of his father. He first encountered political economy and the works of the *philosophes* in Vienna, in 1760. On his return to Milan, he developed his new interests with the group that started to gather regularly at his house, the Academia dei Pugni. For two years the group published the periodical *Il Caffè*, where the major issues raised by European Enlightenment were discussed. In 1763 his *Considerazioni sul commercio*, on the factors hampering economic development in Lombardy, led to his employment in the Habsburg administration, which was already engaged in a programme of reforms. Two years later he sat in the Consiglio Supremo di Economia, a body newly created to superintend economic matters. However, his support of the interests of landowners, and his criticism of the policy of state control implemented in the 1770s prevented his promotion to higher positions and finally led to his removal from office. His writings include *Meditazioni sulla felicità* (1763), and *Meditazioni sull'economia politica* (1771), which advocates a free market economy.

F. Venturi, *The End of the Old Regime in Europe, 1768–1776*, trans. R. Burr Litchfield (Princeton, NJ: Princeton University Press, 1989).

SANDRA CAVALLO

Versailles   The royal palace of Versailles had as its nucleus a hunting-lodge built by Louis XIII (1601–43). His son Louis XIV employed the architects Le Vau (1612–70) and Mansart (1646–1708) to transform the building, and LE NÔTRE to reorganize the gardens. Much of the modern complex was completed by 1682, decorated, as it still is, with numerous images of Apollo, the sun king, which Louis had chosen as his emblem. By then, Versailles was becoming the focus of political and social life. It remained the home of successive kings of France (with the brief interlude of the Regency period, 1715–22), until the French Revolution.

The palace is marked by the genius of many painters, sculptors and decorative artists, including Lebrun (1619–90), Coysevox (1640–1720), Girardon (1628–1715) and Verbeckt (1704–71). Under Louis XV the architect Gabriel (1698–1782) designed new royal accommodation on a more human scale and, on the instructions of the king's mistress, Madame de Pompadour, planned the building in the palace grounds of the Petit Trianon.

Versailles had long been a social world apart, an island of extravagance perceived from the nearby capital as parasitic and self-indulgent. Its great days ended on 6 October 1789 when the royal family was forced to leave for Paris.

R. M. Hatton, 'Louis XIV: At the Court of the Sun King', in A. G. Dickens (ed.), *The Courts of Europe* (London: Thames & Hudson, 1977), pp. 233–62.

J. H. SHENNAN

Versailles, Treaty of (1783)   The Treaty of Versailles ended Franco-British hostilities associated with the AMERICAN WAR OF INDEPENDENCE. French gains, notably in the Caribbean and on the west African coast, were small, and did not compensate for losses suffered in the Seven Years War.

COLIN JONES

Vico, Giambattista (1668–1744)   Italian philosopher and historian. He studied law and was a tutor before becoming, in 1699, professor of rhetoric at the University of Naples and a member of the Palatine Academy. In 1710 he published *De antiquissima Italorum sapientia* (On the Ancient Wisdom of the Italians), then, turning to jurisprudence after reading Grotius's (1583–1645) *De Jura Belli et Pacis* (Law of War and Peace), he wrote *Diritto universale* (Universal Law, 1720–2). There followed his best-known work, *Scienza nuova* (The New Science, 1725), which he continued to revise for many years. In this many-faceted text he developed the ideas and themes of his earlier books, particularly on NATURAL LAW. He also sought to explain the relationship between the ideas and the social reality of previous ages, dividing the past into the superstitious, the heroic and the human periods. His *Autobiography* appeared in 1728.

He was influential during the second wave of the Neapolitan Enlightenment and his importance has gradually been more generally recognized. He is considered by some to have anticipated the work of many social scientists and to be the founder of the philosophy of history.

Peter Burke, *Vico* (Oxford: Oxford University Press, 1985).

SYLVANA TOMASELLI

Victor Amadeus II (1666–1732) Duke of Savoy (1682–1730). His father, Charles Emanuel II (1634–75), died in 1675, leaving his wife as regent, and it was only with the help of Louis XIV that Victor Amadeus was able to gain power in 1682. He reigned until his abdication in 1730. His reign was dominated by two wars (1690–6, 1703–13), and two periods of sweeping internal reforms (1696–1703, 1713–30). The first war saw him join the allies against Louis XIV and then change sides. In the second, the War of the Spanish Succession, his domains suffered greatly from French occupation and the fighting, but its outcome enabled his dynasty and territories to survive. In 1713 he gained Sicily only to lose it in 1718, for which he was compensated with Sardinia in 1720. He also gained territories in Lombardy. Internally, he transformed the state into an efficient, centralized absolutism on the French model, codified its laws and carried out a ruthless enquiry into noble titles and taxation, the *Perequazione*. In all this he laid the foundations of the Savoyard state, of which he was the most important ruler (*see* SAVOY-PIEDMONT).

G. Symcox, *Victor Amadeus II* (London: Thames & Hudson, 1983).

MICHAEL BROERS

Victor Amadeus III (1726–1796) Savoyard king of Sardinia (1773–96). The first years of his reign saw him replace his father's ministers, the bureaucratic establishment, with a group of young noble officers, many of them trained in Prussia. Although he was politically conservative, he carried out many administrative reforms until he declared war on revolutionary France in 1792. He was the only Italian ruler to do so.

S. J. Woolf, *A History of Italy, 1700–1860* (London: Mcthuen, 1979).

MICHAEL BROERS

Vienna Founded in the eleventh century, Vienna owed its growth to its position on major trade routes and as the residence of the rulers of Austria from the twelfth century, with brief interruptions. It grew substantially beyond its medieval centre after the TREATY OF CARLOWITZ finally removed the threat of Turkish attack. Under Leopold I, Joseph I and Charles VI, the city experienced a boom in new building, much of it in the imperial style (*Reichsstil*) designed to symbolize Habsburg power. Its population grew from 50,000 in 1680 to 175,000 in 1750. Berlin was the only other city to grow faster. In the eighteenth century Vienna was the largest German city and the administrative capital of the Habsburg lands and the HOLY ROMAN EMPIRE. It also became a major cultural and musical centre and in the later eighteenth century the site of major commercial and manufacturing enterprises. The city had always been a melting-pot, bringing together German, Italian, Magyar and Slav influences. Even in the eighteenth century people in other parts of Germany commented on the easy-going life-style of its inhabitants, characterized by dynastic loyalty and devotion to the Catholic faith.

E. Wangermann, *The Austrian Achievement 1700–1800* (London: Thames & Hudson, 1973).

MICHAEL HUGHES

Vienna, Treaties of (1719, 1731, 1735, 1738) (1) In January 1719 the emperor Charles VI, Hanover and Saxony allied to force a Russian evacuation of Mecklenburg and Poland. (2) In March 1731 Charles VI agreed to abandon the Ostend Company and allow Spain to occupy Parma and Piacenza, receiving in return British and Dutch guarantees of the PRAGMATIC SANCTION. (3) In October 1735 an agreement ended the WAR OF THE POLISH SUCCESSION. (4) In November 1738 this was confirmed by a treaty which gave Spain large gains in Italy, and established Francis, duke of Lorraine, as ruler of Tuscany.

J. O. Lindsay (ed.), *The New Cambridge Modern History*, vol. 7 (Cambridge: Cambridge University Press, 1957), ch. 9.

M. S. ANDERSON

Virginia Under a royal grant, the London Company established the first permanent English settlement in North America at Jamestown, Virginia in 1607. Rumours of gold attracted early adventurers, but it was TOBACCO that drew a steady stream of immigrants in spite of the high death rate from disease and Indian warfare. By the eighteenth century, however, Virginians were settling down to enjoy the fruits of the labours of earlier settlers.

Along its Tidewater Rivers, indentured servants and later imported African slaves worked on tobacco fields which gave the colony its wealth and allowed plantation-owners to assume the country-squire life-style of rural England. The elite lived opulently, unlike settlers anywhere else in the colonies, borrowing heavily on their tobacco crops to purchase luxury goods from England. A number of colonial and revolutionary leaders came from this class, including four of the first five American presidents. Tobacco, however, exhausted the soil, and except for a few, like WASHINGTON, who experimented with other crops, Tidewater Virginia fell on hard times after the Revolution. The Shenandoah Valley, populated by Irish, German, and Scots Irish herdsmen and small farmers, became the centre of grain production.

Edmund S. Morgan, *American Slavery, American Freedom: The Ordeal of Colonial Virginia* (New York: Norton, 1975).

JOHN MORGAN DEDERER

virtue Eighteenth-century reflections on the nature of virtue were set within the frame of reference provided by ancient Greek and Roman philosophers, and most examples of virtuous conduct were taken from ancient history. Brutus' condemnation of his children was, for instance, the first act to be mentioned in the *Encyclopédie* entry 'Vertu', and, as the author of the article noted, its merit was still very much a subject of contention. The neoclassical images produced during the latter part of the century, especially by the painter David, demonstrate the extent to which the ancients not only continued to set the terms and limits of ethical discourse in the eighteenth century, but also provided the principal models for men and women to emulate. Thus Diderot identified with Socrates and urged his friends and fellow *encyclopédists* to resemble the Athenian in all things.

In the *Kritik der reinen Vernunft* Kant explained how such ideals have practical power as regulative principles and how they provide the basis for the perfection of some actions. Virtue, he remarked, is like wisdom, an idea independent of the empirical world; similarly, the wise man of the Stoics served as an archetype in conformity with the idea of virture and wisdom, but existed in thought only. These ideals should not be dismissed as mere figments of the imagination, however, as they supply an internal standard for reason. Yet he considered the attempt to depict such ideals in fiction to be absurd: far from being edifying, it would belittle the idea of the good, as the world of appearances could never represent that of perfection.

The influence of Platonic and other ancient schools of moral philosophy was also marked on the other side of the Channel. In *The Theory of Moral Sentiments* Adam Smith examined what he regarded as the three main views on the nature of virtue, or 'of the temper of mind which constitutes the excellent and praise-worthy character', in Western history. First was that of Plato, Aristotle and Zeno which saw virtue as consisting 'in the propriety of conduct, or in the suitableness of the affection from which we act to the object which excites it'. Secondly, Epicurus believed that virtue consisted in prudence. The third view was that of those he called the Eclectics, the followers of Plato and Pythagoras, or Neoplatonists. Among them Smith included the Church Fathers, the Cambridge Platonists and his teacher Francis Hutcheson. Smith's own moral philosophy was greatly influenced by Stoicism, especially insofar as it made self-command the most essential virtue. However, the truly virtuous, in his view, were those who combined control over their passions with benevolence.

Wollstonecraft, who admired Smith as a moral philosopher, argued that virtue could not be expected of those who were kept in ignorance. She attributed the source of female folly and vice to women's lack of education. She also noted the importance of necessity, the mother of virtue as well as invention, for virtue was 'an acquirement to which pleasure must be sacrificed – and who sacrifices pleasure when it is within the grasp, whose mind has not been opened and strengthened by adversity, or the pursuit of knowledge goaded on by necessity?' Implacable in her judgement of the women of her time, and especially of those who led a life of leisure, Wollstonecraft argued that such women received their keep in exchange for 'health, liberty and virtue'. It was her aim 'to shew that elegance is inferior to virtue, that the first object of laudable ambition is to obtain a character as a human being, regardless of the distinction of sex'.

In contrast to ancient doctrines and civic humanism which regarded the aristocracy as the class most likely to exhibit virtue precisely because it was freer than any other rank in society from financial constraints and other forms of dependency, Wollstonecraft, like most Enlightenment political theorists, thought of the middle class as the virtuous one. Remarking that 'Abilities and virtues are absolutely necessary to raise men from the middle rank of life into notice', she concluded that 'the natural consequence is notorious, the middle rank contains most virtues and abilities'. What is more, equality was essential for excellence of character to prevail; 'virtue can only flourish amongst equals', she contended in her *Vindication of the Rights of Man*, 'and the man who submits to a fellow-creature, because it promotes his worldly interest, and he who relieves only because it is his duty to lay up a treasure in heaven, are much on a par, for both are radically degraded by their life'. Finally, Wollstonecraft also linked virtue with justice, courage and liberty. In the *Vindication of the Rights of Woman* she maintained that 'Liberty is the mother of virtue, and if women be, by their very constitution, slaves, and not allowed to breathe the sharp invigorating air of freedom, they must ever languish like exotics, and be reckoned beautiful flaws in nature.' Thus, true to the classical notion, Wollstonecraft believed the virtues to be one, and the rights she claimed for women were but the necessary means to the pursuit of virtue.

Edmund Burke, whose *Reflections on the French Revolution* prompted her to compose *Vindication of the Rights of Man*, was no less insistent on the crucial relation between LIBERTY and virtue. But liberty, in his view, withered with every infringement on property. 'It is better to cherish virtue and humanity', he argued, 'by leaving much to free will, even with some loss to the object, than to attempt to make men mere machine and instruments of a political benevolence. The world on the whole will gain by liberty, without which virtue cannot exist.'

In a period rich in deliberations on the true nature of virtue and the degree to which political virtue could be a meaningful notion in modern societies – characterized by a division of labour which relegated the defence of the nation to a professional army, rather than a militia, and its governance to politicians – Montesquieu's discussion of civic virtue in *L'Esprit des lois* is one of the most striking. Political virtue, in his typology of governments, was the exclusive principle of republics, be they democratic or aristocratic. It was incompatible with luxury and called for moderation in all things. The virtuous man who loved the laws of his state and acted for the love of his country was therefore a thing of the past. For Vico, on the other hand, religions could move people of whatever nation to perform virtuous deeds. He saw religion, whether pagan or Christian, as the only motivation to virtue. Many an Enlightenment man, most notably Diderot, was to endeavour to prove him wrong.

J. G. A. Pocock, *Virtue, Commerce and History: Essays on Political Thought and History, Chiefly in the Eighteenth Century* (Cambridge: Cambridge University Press, 1991).

SYLVANA TOMASELLI

vitalism The term 'vitalism' was rarely used in the eighteenth century, but there was much controversy as to whether some physically unidentifiable force, power, principle, substance, faculty or property was immanent in all living matter.

Vitalists opposed the belief that the human body was a machine whose functions and actions could be explained by the mechanical laws of physics. As experimental investigators began to study living systems (*see* BIOLOGY), it became essential to distinguish between living and non-living plants and animals. Among the doctrines proposed to account for the vital essence of life were STAHL's animism, HALLER's irritability and HUNTER's *materia vitae*. Although vitalist doctrines varied on many accounts, they agreed that life's vital essence was not reducible to basic mechanical properties. In particular, they argued that the mechanists had not accounted for the 'ultimate cause' responsible for the vital force that initiated life and maintained its activities. Many vitalist claims were spiritually related to NATURAL RELIGION. Vitalists contended that physical explanations of all living activities displaced God's central, intervening role in His natural world.

Although vitalism was overshadowed by the prevailing mechanical philosophy for a long time, it eventually gained much support from German *Naturphilosophie* chemists and nerve physiologists.

T. S. Hall, *Ideas of Life and Matter: Studies in the History of General Physiology, 600 B.C.–A.D. 1900* (Chicago: University of Chicago Press, 1969).

PHILIP K. WILSON

Vivaldi, Antonio (1678–1741)   Italian composer and violinist. Originally destined for the church, he was ordained in 1703. From 1703 to 1740 he was in charge of music at the Conservatorio della Pietà, an orphanage for girls, in Venice.

Vivaldi's op.3, *L'estro armonico*, printed by the Amsterdam publisher Estienne Roger (1711, republished in London and Paris) using an advanced engraving technique, contributed considerably to establishing his name quickly all over Europe. Even JOHANN SEBASTIAN BACH arranged some of his concertos. From that time Vivaldi toured Italy and Europe. Although he was quite successful, he died a poor man and was buried in a pauper's grave.

As a virtuoso, he developed the art and technique of violin-playing; as a composer he consolidated and developed the concerto, detaching it from the *concerto grosso* of Corelli. It is for his concertos, with their three-movement scheme, that he is most appreciated. Around 500 of them have survived, 220 for violin(s), including the popular *Four Seasons*. He also composed at least forty-five operas. His known compositions total around 770.

M. Collins and E. K. Kirk, *Opera and Vivaldi* (Austin: University of Texas Press, 1984).

M. Talbot, *Vivaldi* (London: Dent, 1978).

FRITZ WEBER

Volta, Alessandro Giuseppe Anastasio, count (1745–1827)   Italian physicist. He dominated Italian experimental physics during his forty years as professor of physics at Pavia from 1779. His talent for instrumentation led to the invention of the *elettroforo perpetuo*, the condensator (for detecting tiny amounts of electricity) and an improved and calibrated bottle electrometer, as well as his voltaic pile. ELECTRICITY was his chief interest and his *De vi attractiva* (1769) reduced standard electrical phenomena to a single attractive force and put forward the notions of electrical saturation and tension, but he also contributed to pneumatics, working out that the coefficient of the expansion of air is constant.

His opposition to GALVANI's theory of animal electricity led to his experiments with the electromotive force generated by circuits made of dissimilar metals and moist conductors in an attempt to prove his 'contact theory'. He presented his results in 1793 in an open letter addressed to Galvani's nephew and defender Giovanni Aldini (1762–1834), but it was not until 1800 that he announced his silver–zinc pile in a letter to Joseph Banks. His pile won him favours from Napoleon, including a state pension. After 1805 he virtually gave up his scientific work.

M. L. BENJAMIN

Voltaire, François Marie Arouet de (1694–1778) French writer. A polymathic genius, he is remembered today above all for his tales, especially *Candide* (1759) and for his campaigns on behalf of justice and religious tolerance. He bestrode the age of Enlightenment and was in many ways its epitome.

During his early career in Paris, he moved freely in the highest circles and achieved success in the leading genres of tragedy – *Oedipe* (Oedipus, 1718) – and epic – *La Ligue* (The League, 1723), later renamed *La Henriade* (The Epic of Henry (IV)) – but also incurred spells in the Bastille because of his satirical writings and importunate behaviour. After being exiled from Paris, he went to England where he stayed for over two years (1726–8). The greater freedom in English thinking and conduct was described in his *Lettres philosophiques* (Philosophical Letters, 1734), whose radical comments on philosophy and religion precipitated another scandal and a forced retreat to Cirey, in Champagne, where he lived off and on with Madame du Châtelet (*see* CHÂTELET-LOMONT) until her death in 1749. The following year he accepted Frederick II's invitation to the Prussian court; this ended in a quarrel and Voltaire's departure in 1753. He eventually settled in Geneva (1755) and later a few miles away at Ferney (1759) in France. There followed a more stable period of nearly twenty years, when his attack on *l'infâme* (the injustices arising from Catholic power) came fully into its own. He returned to Paris in February 1778, was rapturously received and died there in May.

The *Lettres philosophiques* have been described as the first bomb thrown at the *ancien régime*. They reveal Voltaire's polemical gifts in describing a civilization where things were better ordered than in France: an empirical approach to science (as shown by the great exemplars Locke and Newton), a secular approach to philosophy, politics and religious tolerance, the encouragement of commerce and of the arts. In his view, man, who was incapable of attaining to first truths, should work within his God-given limits of experimental enquiry. He continued to hold to these tenets firmly throughout his life.

His first published tale, *Zadig*, appeared in 1747, followed by many others, including *Candide* and *L'Ingénu* (1767). In them he generally sought to understand the enigma of evil, particularly in the form of human malice and social injustice, but none matches the trenchant ironies and the tragicomic tone of *Candide*, where a cruel world (with occasional flashes of goodwill) is laid bare, in an attempt to undermine the optimism of Leibniz and Pope. After *Candide*, he delivered an unremitting broadside against religious fanaticism, in an abundance of prose and poetry genres, and embarked on dynamic crusades on behalf of victims like Jean CALAS and the Sirven family. His enduring legacy lies in his fierce championing of intellectual freedom against every form of oppression.

H. Mason, *Voltaire* (London: Hutchinson, 1975).
H. Mason, *Voltaire: A Biography* (London: Granada, 1981).
R. Pomeau, *La Religion de Voltaire*, second edn (Paris: Nizet, 1969).

HAYDN MASON

W

Wales Before its spectacular growth as a chief coal, iron and steel centre in the nineteenth century, Wales was chiefly a rural backwater lacking even a capital. Its total population in 1700 was around 400,000. It was a pastoral economy, served by a number of market towns: Wrexham, the largest, had a mere 4,000 inhabitants around 1700, Cardiff just over a thousand. Mining, smelting and quarrying went on largely in isolated villages, off the beaten track. The province was governed from Westminster but mostly left to itself: no British monarch visited Wales, and some of its Anglican bishops never set foot within the principality. In social terms, Wales was dominated by a small-time squirarchy. In the relatively prosperous south-east, especially the Vale of Glamorgan, some agricultural improvement took place. Not until the 1770s did tourists swarm to the mountains. The London-based Society for the Propagation of Christian Knowledge inspired a circulating school movement from the 1730s, printing Welsh Bibles. The development of industry depended on English enterprise. From the 1770s, the pace of industrialization quickened, with the growth of the copper, iron and coal industries, which were centred on Swansea and Neath, and primed with capital mostly from Bristol and the West Midlands.

T. Herbert and G. E. Jones, *The Remaking of Wales in the Eighteenth Century* (Cardiff: University of Wales Press, 1988).

G. H. Jenkins, *The Foundations of Modern Wales 1642–1780* (Oxford: Clarendon, 1987).

ROY PORTER

Wallerius, Johan (1709–1785) Swedish scientist. He began his career in 1732 as a medical professor at Lund. From 1737 he also held the post of superintendent at a local spa where he analysed the spring water. While at Lund he began collecting minerals; eventually his collection was to comprise over 4,000 specimens. In 1741 he became a medical professor at Uppsala, lecturing on mineralogy and chemistry as well as *materia medica* and anatomy. He embarked on a programme of systematically categorizing the mineral world, which resulted in his acclaimed *Mineralogia eller Mineralriket* (1747); with *Hydrologia eller Wattu-Riket* (1748) he attempted similarly to classify different kinds of water. This début gained him an appointment as the first professor of chemistry in Sweden, at Uppsala in 1750.

He added agricultural chemistry to his repertoire: when illness forced him into early retirement in 1767, he put his commitment to the comparative study of plants and soils into practice and established a model farm. His 'Observations of Agriculture' (1779) won a prize from the Swedish Academy of Sciences. He was a taxonomist, not an experimentalist, and his science was conservative rather than innovative.

M. L. BENJAMIN

Walpole, Horace (1717–1797) English writer and wit. The third son of Sir Robert Walpole, he was educated at Eton and King's College, Cambridge. He served as member of parliament between 1741 and 1767, and wrote in a variety of subliterary genres. His most notable works were *Anecdotes of Painting in England* (1762–71); *The Castle of Otranto* (1764), the first Gothic novel; *Essay on Modern Gardening* (1785); and *Memoirs* of the reigns of George II and George III, published posthumously. In his own lifetime he was renowned as a wit and socialite, a connoisseur of art and collector of antiquities. Appropriately, therefore, his (voluminous) collected correspondence is his most important legacy. His letters, composed with an eye to posterity, constitute a sardonic, knowing and precise chronicle of the manners of the fashionable classes. He also left to posterity his whimsically designed Gothic house at Strawberry Hill, Twickenham – as much an antiquary's *jeu d'esprit* as *The Castle of Otranto*. It was here that he kept a printing-press, producing not only his own works, but also those of friends like Thomas Gray.

W. H. Smith (ed.), *Horace Walpole: Writer, Politician, and Connoisseur* (New Haven, Conn.: Yale University Press, 1967).

JOHN MULLAN

Walpole, Sir Robert (1676–1745) English statesman. Often called the first British prime minister, he shaped the office by his long hold on power. He first entered parliament in 1701, and from 1702 to 1742 was member for King's Lynn, Norfolk. He built his fortune on the profits of office, including a magnificent Palladian country house, Houghton Hall. But he was also a sincere Whig (see WHIGS), a believer in the post-1688 settlement, an established church and a Protestant monarch. He cultivated stability through compromise, peace abroad, prosperity and low land taxes. Joining the Whig ministry in April 1720, he was soon at the helm of finance and power, emerging by 1721 as the leading minister. Often charged with corruption, he did not create the materialism and patronage of eighteenth-century politics but certainly systematized them. Crucially, he had the favour and support of both George I and George II. He was a skilled manager of parliament and a sensible and effective speaker, although he could not overcome public protest campaigns, like the Excise Crisis of 1733 and the pro-war agitation of 1738–42. He resigned in February 1742 and was made earl of Orford.

J. M. Black, *Robert Walpole and the Nature of Politics in Early Eighteenth-Century Britain* (London: Macmillan, 1990).

PHILIP WOODFINE

warfare   Looking back after the era of Napoleon, Carl Maria von Clausewitz (1780–1831) saw Frederick the Great of Prussia as the originator of modern warfare, of the various modes of armed aggression used by societies in dispute. The key was an abrasive diplomacy based on the resources of a large, well-drilled army, and a bureaucratic machinery to recruit, supply and finance such armed forces.

Older modes of warfare were still current, however, notably under Nadir Quli Khan, shah of Persia from 1736. With massed forces, he manœuvred and marched at speed, throwing his troops into pitched battles. His armies established Persia as an independent great power, and showed the continuing strength of central Asiatic warfare, with its emphasis on leadership, ethnic savagery and looting. Having conquered territories from the Ottoman Empire, Nadir pushed eastward between 1738 and 1740 against Mughal India. He took the Khyber Pass in a dazzling outflanking march, surged through the Punjab and pillaged and massacred in Delhi. Warfare on this scale accelerated geopolitical change. The insurgence of Nadir's hordes was a crucial blow to Mughal dynasty prestige, after some 200 years of dominance.

As Nadir returned from Delhi carrying untold Mughal wealth, including the peacock throne of Shah Jahan, Frederick the Great was setting out with his forces to capture Silesia, a wealthy province of the ancient Habsburg dynasty. Instead of pillage, however, his aim was to annex a strategic and economically productive province. The Prussian administration existed to make possible the raising and deployment of sizeable armies. These armies in turn engaged in a warfare with significant modern features. Unlike the illiterate former shepherd Nadir, military leaders such as Frederick studied and wrote on the art of warfare. In Europe armies became more or less evenly matched in terms of their equipment, drill and organization. The states that could afford to do so maintained large armed forces. Various methods such as the cantonal system ensured that ARMIES could be raised without undue damage to the normal routines of society and the economy. Modes of warfare also changed. Disciplined and often rapid movement in the course of battles replaced older patterns of static mass encounters. Fighting became possible on difficult terrain, and increasingly in the later eighteenth century light infantry forces and skirmishing units were used. ARTILLERY became more important, armies in the field larger, and encounters more decisive.

It was for such reasons that eighteenth-century observers commonly held that theirs was an age of limited, almost professional, warfare. The most virulent features of war had been tamed, and states could engage in violent contest without the savagery and lasting damage of earlier times. A characteristic enterprise of the second half of the eighteenth century was the endeavour of writers like Emmerich de Vattell (1714–67) and Immanuel Kant to lay down rules for the conduct of war, as well as justifications for entering into the state of war. Most thinkers distinguished between just and unjust wars, and envisaged limited conflicts which would respect the common humanity of all, and the rights of civilians and neutrals. Linked to the idea of justified warfare was the tendency of rulers in the period to invoke popular support for their wars.

The idea of limited war, however, belies the hardship and deaths involved, and the major strains of warfare on states geared to it. The most successful of the competing states had centralized political and fiscal management, providing large-scale financing. Armies were most successful also where the noble elites were committed to their role as the officer class. In Britain an aristocratic government supported yet contained the armed forces, while the strains of warfare created a new administrative structure from the 1690s, upheld by buoyant financial institutions. In France, too, there was a new growth of administration and bureaucracy, but the burden of war proved ultimately destructive. Lesser countries were also affected by the more professionalized warfare of the age. Small German states often provided the mercenary forces that supplemented the armed designs of the great powers: HESSE-KASSEL in 1730 had around 14,000 men under arms from a population of only 250,000. The recruitment reforms introduced by the landgrave Frederick II after 1762 brought this strange economic specialization to its highest point. In the British subsidy treaty of 1776, Frederick provided 19,000 Hessians to fight in America. In turn, however, this led to a loss of respect for gentry administrators and a sharp increase in rural unrest.

Eighteenth-century European warfare became truly global, the mid-century conflict of the SEVEN YEARS WAR seeing fighting from Canada and the Caribbean to India. The foundations for imperial expansion were laid by the conflicts between the European powers. The clash of old and new modes of warfare can be seen in the meeting of Europe and the Muslim world in the late eighteenth century. The once-mighty Ottoman Empire had by then to concede diplomatic equality to European powers, and had lost the Crimea to Russia. Yet the decisive meeting of the 'military revolution' of the West and the old mass warfare of the Middle East came in 1798. The invasion of Egypt by Napoleon BONAPARTE was an unexpected and total defeat. Like the invasion of northern India by Nadir, it came as a shattering blow to the morale of an ancient dynasty. Ottoman power had existed for 500 years, and for nearly 300 years it had held sway over most of the Muslim world. Now the dynasty could survive only if it adapted to the new forms of warfare. The efforts of Sultan Selim III (1789–1807) to modernize the army were frustrated by vested interests, and so the expansion of the European powers was ensured. Armed valour was no substitute for the state organization geared to warfare which was the hallmark of eighteenth-century Europe.

See also NAVIES.

M. S. Anderson, *War and Society in Europe of the Old Régime 1618–1789* (Leicester: Leicester University Press, 1988).

G. Best, *Humanity in Warfare: The Modern History of the International Law of Armed Conflicts* (London: Weidenfeld & Nicolson, 1980).

J. M. Black, *A Military Revolution? Military Change and European Society 1550–1800* (London: Macmillan, 1990).

PHILIP WOODFINE

Warsaw Given the highly decentralized character of the Polish-Lithuanian Commonwealth, the status of Warsaw was less significant than that of the capitals of most European states. During the Great Northern War of 1700–21 it changed hands several times without conferring control of the country to its captors. Although it was the principal venue of the Polish parliament, the absence of a large permanent court was a major disadvantage; both Saxon kings, Augustus II and Augustus III, preferred to reside in Saxony. In 1700 its total population may have numbered some 20,000, reaching 25,000 by 1756. In 1756 AUGUSTUS III, who had been expelled from Saxony by Frederick the Great, took up permanent residence in Warsaw, and the city's population finally experienced sustained growth, to 30,000 by

1763. Under his successor, Stanislaw Augustus PONIATOWSKI, growth peaked at over 100,000 by 1791. Warsaw was the focus of national resistance during the KOŚCIUSZKO insurrection of 1794. The population declined to around 60,000 after the city was reduced to the status of a Prussian provincial town following the third partition of 1795. *See* POLAND.

J. T. Lukowski, *Liberty's Folly: The Polish-Lithuanian Commonwealth in the Eighteenth Century* (London: Routledge, 1991).

J. T. LUKOWSKI

Washington, George (1732–1799) Agriculturalist, soldier, statesman and first president of the United States. Born to a Virginia family of modest means, he worked hard from youth, invested shrewdly and married well. A hero of Braddock's (1695–1755) ill-fated march of 1755, he was in 1775 appointed to command the nascent American army in the War of Independence. Washington faced difficulties unimaginable to any other eighteenth-century general. While learning war through war, with few troops, few arms and almost no funds, he kept his army – and the revolution – alive and in the field for nine years, until final victory. Though not a great general, he was nevertheless a superb leader of men. (*See* AMERICAN WAR OF INDEPENDENCE.)

In 1787 he presided over the Constitutional Convention, legitimizing the proceedings by his very presence. Such was his prestige that agreement over a chief executive was reached only because he agreed to fill the position. He served for two terms (1789–97) before retiring to his beloved Mount Vernon estate. Not particularly well educated but an inquisitive, pragmatic man, he long sought economic self-sufficiency, corresponding with agriculturalists like Arthur Young for advice. He was much revered; as Henry Lee eulogized him, 'First in war, first in peace, and first in the hearts of his countrymen'.

James T. Flexner, *George Washington*, 4 vols (Boston: Little, Brown, 1965–9).

JOHN MORGAN DEDERER

Waterloo, Battle of (18 June 1815) Napoleon BONAPARTE's final desperate attempt to repair his fortunes was foiled at the Battle of Waterloo. Having defeated the Prussians at Ligny on 16 June and sent part of his force to chase them out of Flanders, he turned, with 72,000 men, on the allied forces of 67,000 men under the duke of WELLINGTON at Waterloo. Unaware that the Prussians had in fact eluded Marshal Grouchy (1766–1847), he waited until late morning before attacking. A heavy bombardment by artillery was followed by fierce infantry and cavalry attacks against Wellington's position throughout the afternoon.

The arrival of the Prussians on the French right wing drew off increasing numbers of Napoleon's troops. Even so, the crisis of the battle came as late as 6 p.m., when La Haie Sainte, one of the farms garrisoned by the allies, fell to Marshal Ney's (1769–1815) columns. However, no French reinforcements were forthcoming, and by the time Napoleon sent forward the Imperial Guard for the final assault the allied line had been restored and was prepared. The musketry of Wellington's troops destroyed the heads of the Guard's columns and the French began a disorderly retreat. On 22 June Napoleon abdicated.

D. Chandler, *Waterloo and the Hundred Days* (London: G. Philip, 1987).

TONY HAYTER

water power   The principal source of mechanical energy in Asia, Europe and North America was water power. An ancient technology, it was developed significantly in the eighteenth and nineteenth centuries, under the stimulus of increasing industrial demand. The systematic experimental investigations of John Smeaton (1724–92), Antoine de Parcieux (1703–68), and Christopher Polhem (1661–1751) began to inform the millwrights' empirical craft tradition from the mid eighteenth century. They quantified the superior efficiency of overshot to undershot wheels where the fall of water was high, and of the new breast (mid-height) wheels where it was low. Substituting iron parts for wood gave greater durability and power: an average output of 10 to 15 horsepower in 1800 was approximately double that achieved in 1700. These were the vertical water-wheels typical of north-western Europe, but from the horizontal wheels of Asia and the rest of Europe were to stem hydraulic and steam turbines; study of turbine principles in the eighteenth century was to come to fruition in the nineteenth. Water power long enjoyed crucial advantages over steam: lower maintenance and running costs, greater reliability and smoother action. Disadvantages related to the flow of water, which was often too low in summer, too high and fast or frozen in winter; these were sometimes met by a supplementary STEAM ENGINE, but locational limitations and shortage of sites were ultimately to tell in the latter's favour.

Terry S. Reynolds, *Stronger than a Hundred Men: A History of the Vertical Water Wheel* (Baltimore: Johns Hopkins University Press, 1983).

CHRISTINE MACLEOD

Watt, James (1736–1819)   Scottish engineer and inventor. He did not invent the STEAM ENGINE, but he greatly improved it. Born in Greenock and educated at its grammar school, he established a business manufacturing mathematical instruments in nearby Glasgow in 1756. In the process of repairing a model Newcomen engine for Glasgow University in 1763–4, he invented the separate condenser, which could be cooled to create a vacuum while the working cylinder remained hot; this trebled the engine's fuel efficiency. John Roebuck (1718–94) of the Carron Iron Foundry financed its initial development and patent (1769) but in 1773 Matthew BOULTON replaced him. Watt, glad to abandon his canal-surveying practice in Scotland, joined Boulton in Birmingham and their first engine was installed in 1776. Adaptation to rotative motion in 1782 to drive industrial machinery necessitated further inventions. However, Watt's tight control of his patents and his fear of above-atmospheric pressures subsequently retarded steam technology.

Active in the Lunar Society and elected to the Royal Society in 1785, he maintained wide intellectual interests and friendships, for which he had more time when the success of his business allowed him to retire comfortably to his estates in Radnorshire and Warwickshire in 1800.

H. W. Dickinson, *James Watt, Craftsman and Engineer* (Cambridge: Cambridge University Press, 1936).

CHRISTINE MACLEOD

Watteau, Jean Antoine (1684–1721) French ROCOCO painter of Flemish origin. Most of his work was produced within a remarkably short period. He was active from 1704, but his greatest works were painted after 1716, when the death of Louis XIV and the coming of the Regency triggered a shift in painting from artistic formalism to a more domestic and emotional style that drew on Rubens (1577–1640) and Veronese (1528–88). In contrast to the history pieces produced in the previous reign, Watteau produced *fêtes galantes*, pastoral scenes of men and women, such as *L'Embarquement pour l'Île de Cythère* (The Embarkation for the Island of Cythera, 1717). His pictures were more than sylvan idylls, however; he imbued his figures, even in the many theatrical paintings, with a profound sense of melancholy which marked a departure from the often unemotional classicism of his predecessors. An exceptional draughtsman, he left hundreds of sketches and studies. He died of tuberculosis following a trip to London in 1719 to seek medical advice. His career had been short but was enormously influential, not only on painters like Boucher and Fragonard, but also on the Impressionists.

D. Posner, *Antoine Watteau* (London: Weidenfeld & Nicolson, 1984).

IAIN PEARS

wealth The possession of material riches was almost exclusively the lot of the landed classes (*see* LANDOWNERSHIP). Land was acquired through inheritance, marriage, royal favour and, in new territories, conquest and settlement. It was maintained by active estate management and the legal device of entail, boosted by the spoils of office and fortunate speculations and dissipated by high living, large families and political miscalculation. COMMERCIAL SOCIETY, however, offered growing opportunities for wealth creation in industry, the PROFESSIONS and, above all, finance, shipping and trade (see BOURGEOISIE). Yet genuinely self-made men were rare: most successful businessmen built on an inheritance of wealth.

Great inequality of wealth distribution was universal in Western and Asian societies; the propertyless formed an increasing majority. The possession of wealth was challenging the hereditary nobility's hold on social status: old societies denied it the highest ranks but colonial America accorded it prestige and political power. Economists and moralists debated the proper use of wealth. Adam Smith's ridicule of fashionable moralizing against the evils of LUXURY stemmed from a conviction that antique society had been superseded and therefore neither the pursuit of material prosperity nor its enjoyment would enervate civilization or weaken the state.

W. D. Rubinstein (ed.), *Wealth and the Wealthy in the Modern World* (London: Croom Helm, 1980).

CHRISTINE MACLEOD

Wedgwood, Josiah (1730–1795) English master potter. He rose to become the most distinguished British ceramics manufacturer. Born in Burslem in the West Midlands, the son of a minor potter, he was apprenticed early to his brother and was soon managing his own kilns, as well as becoming active in the improvement of local canals and chapels. Having laid sound foundations, in the 1760s he turned to artistic pottery, drawing on archaeological finds from Pompeii and Greek designs from southern Italy, and helping to translate the neoclassical revival into artefacts (see NEOCLASSICISM). After going into partnership with Thomas Bentley (1731–80) of Liverpool, he opened his major works near Hanley, which he called 'Etruria'; it soon became one of the wonders of the new British industrial world.

He cultivated the highest aesthetic standards, using artists like John Flaxman (1755–1826) and at the same time pursuing scientific researches into improvements in ceramic technology (kilns, glazes, clays). He was a pioneer both of scientific management and of consumer psychology. He recognized the importance of snob appeal, and was astute in the naming of his products ('Queensware' and so forth) and in the pioneering of smart showrooms in London. With Erasmus Darwin, Matthew Boulton, Joseph Priestley and other friends, he was a founder member of the LUNAR SOCIETY of Birmingham. In politics he was of a liberal persuasion, in religion he tended towards Unitarianism.

B. and H. Wedgwood, *The Wedgwood Circle 1730–1897* (London: Studio Vista, 1980).

ROY PORTER

Wellington, Arthur Wellesley, first duke of (1769–1852)   British soldier and statesman. He gained a formidable military reputation during the Mahratta war in India (1803) and distinguished himself by defeating the French at Vimeiro in 1808 at the beginning of the PENINSULAR WAR. In 1809 he became commander of the British expeditionary force, having been cleared of responsibility for the controversial Convention of Cintra. Believing that it was possible to deny Portugal to the French, he secured his base near Lisbon and in a series of victories demonstrated that the British line could defeat the French column, especially when defensive positions were wisely chosen. At Salamanca (1812) he defeated his opponent by brilliantly aggressive tactics, and in 1813 during the Vittoria campaign his exploitation of British sea power was imaginative. In 1814 he invaded France, and the BATTLE OF WATERLOO confirmed his status as the greatest British general since Marlborough. He served the nation as a diplomat and politician, becoming prime minister in 1828. His latter years saw him as a respected public figure, his popularity restored after being blighted by involvement in political controversies.

E. Longford, *Wellington: The Years of the Sword* (London: Weidenfeld & Nicolson, 1969).
E. Longford, *Wellington: Pillar of State* (London: Weidenfeld & Nicolson, 1972).

JOHN W. DERRY

Wesley, Charles (1707–1788)   English hymn-writer and evangelist. Like his brother John WESLEY, he was a member of the Oxford 'Holy Club'. He also accompanied John on his missionary venture to Georgia in 1735, and experienced a Moravian-inspired conversion in 1738. Often regarded as the more humane of the brothers, he contributed to METHODISM a large body of hymns (over 7,000). Although most of them were unremarkable, some have become devotional classics, and many are still used in the different Christian denominations today. The Methodist hymn-book of 1780 – 'a little body of experimental divinity' – is a testimony to the religious power of his language and to the importance of hymn-singing in the Methodist revival.

F. Baker, *Charles Wesley as Revealed in his Letters* (London: Epworth, 1948).

DAVID HEMPTON

Wesley, John (1703–1791)   English evangelist and founder of METHODISM. The son of Samuel Wesley (1662–1735), the rector of Epworth, Lincolnshire, and his wife Susannah, he was educated at

Charterhouse and at Christ Church, Oxford. In 1726 he was elected fellow of Lincoln College, Oxford and gathered around him a 'Holy Club' of earnest seekers after holiness. After a disastrous missionary experience in Georgia (1735–7), he returned to England, where he came under the influence of the MORAVIANS and underwent a life-changing experience at a meeting in London on 24 May 1738. Variously interpreted as an evangelical conversion and as an emotional supercharge for older beliefs, this event, to Wesley's mind at least, unlocked the door to over half a century of relentless itinerant preaching throughout Britain and Ireland.

Wesley's achievements, especially as the organizer of the Methodist movement, are incontestable, but despite the large corpus of literature written by and about him, he remains an enigmatic figure. He loved an idealized Church of England, but led a movement that eventually separated from it. He was a formidable logician yet would believe almost any 'supernatural' occurrence on the empirical foundation of reliable witnesses. He was an autocrat with Tory sympathies, but despised the indulgent consumerism of the rich and urged his followers, for a time at least, to share their goods in common. He advocated religious toleration, but not for Catholics. He believed that 'perfection' was possible in this life, but never laid claim to it himself. He was, by any standards, one of the most remarkable men of the century.

H. Rack, *Reasonable Enthusiast: John Wesley and the Rise of Methodism* (London: Epworth, 1989).

DAVID HEMPTON

West Indies *see* CARIBBEAN.

Whigs The Whig party was forged in the struggle of 1679–81 to exclude from the British throne the duke of York, later James II (1633–1701). Then, and in the crisis of 1688–9, they favoured limited monarchy with guarantees for liberties and religious freedom, and opposed absolutism. Consistency and national organization were not, however, the hallmarks of eighteenth-century parties. The national party changed and so did the network of loyalties and local concerns in the counties. Broadly, the years 1689–1714 saw fierce conflicts between Whigs and TORIES, while from 1714 to 1760 the Whigs dominated successive ministries, opposed by a Tory minority which was organized, but excluded from place and power. The old language of court (executive) and country allowed some coalitions of country (opposition) Whigs and Tories against the ministry. From 1760 to 1790 Whigs of two kinds dominated politics. Some, who stood for ancient liberties and against 'secret influence' – Rockingham (1730–82), Portland (1738–1809), Fox and Grey (1764–1845) – were very party-political. They opposed successive ministries of government Whigs, who stood for executive authority and stability – North, Pitt and Liverpool (1770–1828). By the 1790s these pro-executive Whigs formed the basis of the new party grouping which in the 1800s bore the revived Tory name.

F. O'Gorman, *Voters, Patrons, and Parties: The Unreformed Electorate of Hanoverian England, 1734–1832* (Oxford: Clarendon, 1989).

PHILIP WOODFINE

Wieland, Christoph Martin (1733–1813)   German poet and writer of romances. Initially, he espoused a manner of 'seraphic Christianity'. After publishing the Lucretian poem *Die Natur der Dinge* (On the Nature of Things, 1752), he moved to Switzerland at the invitation of BODMER, where he produced sentimental works like the epic *Der geprüfte Abraham* (Abraham Tested, 1753) and the prose *Sympathiens* (Sympathies, 1756). In 1760 he returned to Germany, undergoing a 'great revolution', following which he produced erotica in a graceful, rococo style, as well as his Shakespeare translations (twenty-two plays in eight volumes, 1762–6), which was a key text for the STURM UND DRANG. He attained maturity with *Don Silvio von Rosalva* (1764) and his great philosophical novel *Geschichte des Agathon* (The History of Agathon, 1766), the first German *Bildungsroman*. His ideas had now crystallized into a classical humanism. After moving to Weimar in 1772, he launched his highly influential journal *Der Teutsche Merkur* (The German Mercury) in 1773, which for almost forty years campaigned tirelessly for these ideals, advocating a cosmopolitan philosophy of moral harmony and 'grace'. His urbanity paved the way for the more profound classicism of Goethe and Schiller.

Derek van Abbé, *Christoph Martin Wieland: A Literary Biography* (London: Harrap, 1961).

JEREMY ADLER

Wilberforce, William (1759–1833)   British politician and philanthropist. Born in Hull of an old Yorkshire family, and educated at Cambridge University, he became an outstanding figure in the movement for evangelical religious and spiritual reform in late-eighteenth-century and early-nineteenth-century Britain. Entering the House of Commons in 1780, he early became a supporter of William Pitt the younger. A man of great moral earnestness, his perception of the need for national moral improvement was spurred by his hatred of the French Revolution and his fears of the spread of radicalism to a morally lax Britain. His first major achievement lay in procuring in 1787 a royal proclamation against vice. In 1802 he founded the Society for the Suppression of Vice (the Proclamation Society) which denounced aristocratic vices like gambling but chiefly directed its attention to the sins of the poor, including drunkenness, debauchery and cruel sports. A key member of the evangelical 'Clapham Sect', Wilberforce translated his piety into a form of middle-class morality in his *Practical Christianity* (1797). Much of his political energy was devoted to campaigns for the abolition of slavery and the slave trade. Parliament abolished the trade in 1807; slavery was effectively abolished within the British Empire in the year of Wilberforce's death.

R. Furneaux, *William Wilberforce* (London: Hamish Hamilton, 1974).

ROY PORTER

wild men In his *Histoire naturelle* Buffon remarked of the orang-utan that 'As there is a greater similarity between this animal and man than between those creatures which resemble him most, as the Barbary ape . . . the Indians are to be excused for associating him with the human species, under the denomination of orang-outang, or wild man.' The naturalist Edward Bancroft (1744–1821) had also noted that this animal was called 'wild man' in the various languages of the countries where it was found. Eighteenth-century naturalists, however, differed as to whether primates were closest to man. Some, like Pieter Camper (1722–89), who dissected one in the 1770s, argued that the connection was very remote.

But 'wild man' was also applied to men like Peter (*fl* 1725–85), who was found living wild in the Harz forest in Hanover, and brought to England where he aroused much interest. Swift and Defoe were among those who wrote about him. In his *Origin and Progress of Language* (1773–92) Lord Monboddo (1714–99) mentioned Peter, whom he met in 1782, in the context of his evolutionary theory, which cast the orang-utan in a central role. Although both kinds of wild men were taken to constitute evidence in favour of or against the various eighteenth-century views about the true nature of man, it is as well to remember that Rousseau's depiction of man in the state of nature was, as he himself stressed, a purely theoretical construct (*see* CULT OF THE NOBLE SAVAGE).

See also ANTHROPOLOGY, PRIMITIVISM.

Robert Wokler, 'Tyson and Buffon on the Orang-Utan', *Studies on Voltaire and the Eighteenth Century*, 155 (1976), 2301–19.

SYLVANA TOMASELLI

Wilkes, John (1727–1797) English politician. A critic of the TREATY OF PARIS of 1763, he was arrested under a general warrant for his attacks on the king's ministers in no. 45 of *North Briton*. His struggle for the freedom of the press and defence of the traditional liberties of the subject gained widespread support. Expelled from the Commons, he fled to France. On his return in 1768 he was elected member of parliament for the county of Middlesex. The Commons refused to allow him to take his seat and he became the spokesman for the freeholders of Middlesex, arguing that the rights of electors took precedence over the privileges of parliament. He supported economic and parliamentary reform, defended the American colonists and denounced corruption in public life. Allowed to take his seat in 1774, he became lord mayor of the city of London. Always a traditionalist, he became more conservative as he grew older, helping to suppress the GORDON RIOTS and opposing the French Revolution. His denunciations of the executive and the abuse of privileges by the House of Commons invigorated popular radicalism at a crucial epoch.

A. Williamson, *Wilkes* (London: Allen & Unwin, 1974).

JOHN W. DERRY

William III (1650–1702) Dutch stadtholder (1672–1702), king of Great Britain and Ireland (1689–1702). He was the posthumous son of William II of Orange and Mary (1631–60), the daughter of Charles I (1600–49) of England. His youth was overshadowed by republican reaction in Holland (*see* ORANGEISM) until 1666, when the states assumed his guardianship and the grand Pensionary John de Witt (1625–72) his political education. In the crisis of 1672, precipitated by France and England's attack on the United Provinces, he was made captain-general of the Dutch army and stadtholder – first of Holland and Zeeland alone, and then, with increased powers, of Utrecht, Gelderland and Overijssel. He at once embarked on what became his life's work – the long series of wars (1672–8, 1689–97) and diplomatic negotiations to secure the Netherlands and Europe against French aggression. To involve Britain in this endeavour, he made peace with Charles II (1630–85) in 1674, married his English cousin Mary Stuart (1662–94) in 1677 and engineered the invitation from the parliamentary opposition which led to his successful invasion of England and acceptance of the crown in 1688–9 (*see* GLORIOUS REVOLUTION). Besides making Britain a major European power and conceding to parliament a part in the formulation of foreign policy, he played a crucial role in British domestic politics, notably in the passage of the Toleration Act (1689).

S. B. Baxter, *William III* (London: Longman, 1966).
K. H. D. Haley, *The British and the Dutch* (London: G. Philip, 1988).
J. I. Israel (ed.), *The Anglo-Dutch Moment: Essays on the Glorious Revolution* (Cambridge: Cambridge University Press, 1991).

HUGH DUNTHORNE

William IV [Friso, William Charles Henry] (1711–1751)   Dutch stadtholder (1747–51). Born into the Nassau-Dietz family of Friesland and married in 1734 to Anna (1709–59), daughter of George II of Britain, he remained in provincial obscurity until 1747, when France's invasion of Dutch territory triggered a crisis in the republic which led to his appointment as captain/admiral-general and hereditary stadtholder, with unprecedented powers (*see* ORANGEISM). Despite the ministerial advice of William Bentinck (1704–74) and widespread middle-class agitation for political reform, he was, however, too cautious and too much of a traditionalist to make any significant changes to the Dutch political system.

H. Dunthorne, 'Prince and Republic: The House of Orange in Dutch and Anglo-Dutch Politics', *Studies in History and Politics*, 4 (1985), 19–34.

HUGH DUNTHORNE

William V (1748–1806)   Dutch stadtholder (1751–95). Under-educated and overawed by his mother, Princess Anna of Hanover (1709–59), and Louis, duke of Brunswick, who ruled during his minority (1751–66), he was the last and least able prince of Orange to hold the office of stadtholder. Pro-British in the American War of Independence, when his compatriots were pro-American, he was forced unwillingly into the fourth Anglo-Dutch War (1780–4). The Patriot movement compelled him to give up some of his authority, but he was reinstated thanks to Anglo-Prussian intervention in 1787, only to be toppled by the invading armies of revolutionary France in 1795. He spent his last decade in English exile at Kew.

H. H. Rowen, *The Princes of Orange* (Cambridge: Cambridge University Press, 1988).

HUGH DUNTHORNE

Winckelmann, Johann Joachim (1717–1768)   German art historian and theorist of NEOCLASSICISM. He was the author of books on Greece (1755) and a much translated work on ancient art (1764). In 1755 he left his native Dresden and settled permanently in Rome as librarian to Cardinal Albani (1692–1779). One of the first historians to draw a distinction between Greek art and Roman copies, he advocated the Greek style as the more perfect and encouraged its imitation. He recommended that artists should not simply copy antique models, but rather attempt to re-create the spirit behind the making of them, so that what he considered its 'noble simplicity and calm grandeur' could be reproduced instead of what he considered to be the empty decorative effects of rococo. He also enlarged on the theories of Montesquieu to account for national styles. Through MENGS he had an enormous impact on painting, and his enthusiasm for Greek sculpture, which he knew primarily through Roman copies for he never travelled to Greece, influenced a school of sculptors from Canova (1757–1822) in Italy to Thorwaldsen (1770–1844) in Scandinavia. He was murdered in Trieste, apparently by robbers.

M. Praz, *On Neoclassicism* (London: Thames & Hudson, 1969).

IAIN PEARS

witch-hunting   In the eighteenth century women believed to be witches continued to arouse the hostility of their immediate neighbours throughout Europe, especially in rural areas. But the kind of witch-hunting that was sanctioned by the authorities, which led to trials and executions, had already disappeared in the western nations and by 1750 it had ended almost everywhere. The only countries that still experienced it were those where the conditions that had earlier encouraged it elsewhere continued to prevail or made a late appearance – belief in diabolism, inquisitorial legal methods and the use of torture, and religious and social intolerance.

Styria and the Tyrol were severely affected in the 1680s and 1690s, Hungary in the 1720s and Poland between 1675 and 1725. The celebrated cases at Salem in Massachusetts in 1692, where thirty witches were convicted, also conformed broadly to this pattern. Generally, the eighteenth century was marked by official prohibitions of witch-hunting, from Louis XIV's in 1682 to Maria Theresa's in 1768, and by the repeal of witchcraft legislation, for example that of England (1736) and Sweden (1779). The last hanging for the crime in England was in 1685, the last burning in Scotland in 1727. The final legal execution took place in Switzerland in 1782.

See also DEMONOLOGY.

B. Levack, *The Witch-Hunt in Early Modern Europe* (London: Longman, 1987).

STUART CLARK

Wittelsbachs   The Wittelsbachs were an ancient German noble family whose many branches ruled a large number of German states, the most important being BAVARIA and the PALATINATE. They had lavish ambitions, including the crown of the Holy Roman Empire and a re-created kingdom of Burgundy. They were also the main rivals of the Habsburgs and their clients for high office in the German Catholic Church. Rivalry between the various branches ended when they entered house unions in 1724 and 1733 to co-ordinate efforts to increase their standing in German and European affairs. In the eighteenth century the importance of the Palatinate declined and the Bavarian line became the main standard-bearers of dynastic ambition. Their campaign to increase their power by alliance with France culminated in the brief reign of the elector Charles Albert as emperor Charles VII. After that their influence waned: their pretensions were not matched by their resources. In the second half of the century the house suffered a decline in fertility as branch after branch died out, and after the French Revolution it lost much of its land to France and other German states. After 1806 only Bavaria remained in Wittelsbach hands.

H. Grundmann (ed.), *Gebhardt Handbuch der deutschen Geschichte*, vol. 2, ninth edn (Stuttgart: Union, 1970).

MICHAEL HUGHES

Wolfe, James (1727–1759) English soldier. He ranks alongside Marlborough and Wellington as one of the greatest British military commanders of the eighteenth century. After distinguished European service, he was instrumental in the capture of Louisbourg (1758), and his victory on the PLAINS OF ABRAHAM, where he was mortally wounded, ended French rule in North America.

Christopher Hibbert, *Wolfe at Quebec* (Cleveland: World Publishing, 1959).

JOHN MORGAN DEDERER

Wolff [Wolf], Christian von (1679–1754) German philosopher, mathematician and scientist. After studying at Breslau, Jena and Leipzig he became interested in E. W. von Tschirnhausen's (1651–1708) idea of mathematics as a philosophical method, and later came into contact with Leibniz. In 1707 he was appointed professor of mathematics at Halle and later to a chair in philosophy. He developed his ideas on mathematics and philosophy into what he called 'the mathematical method', which involved strictly logical thinking, based on two principles, the law of contradiction and the law of sufficient reason. Every philosophical reasoning could be as pure as mathematics following this deductive method. These ideas were published in *Vernüfftige Gedancken von Gott, der Welt and der Seele des Menchen, auch aller Dingen überhaupt* (1720), whose title reflects the grand ambition of its author.

In 1721 he gave a lecture on Confucius, which antagonized the Pietists, and he was expelled. He went to Marburg, where he began to publish his works in Latin and became well known as a philosopher. After publishing books on philosophy, cosmology and psychology, he produced the two volumes of *Theologia naturalis* (1736–7), in which he applied his mathematical method to theology and also showed how it could be used to reason with unbelievers. In the 1720s he was seen as a representative of the German Enlightenment, now he became a true apologetic and fought against enlightened philosophy.

One of Frederick the Great's first acts on his accession was to recall Wolff to Halle, where he became chancellor in 1743. He published books on law and ethics which were not as successful as his earlier works. His philosophy was criticized by scientists, especially by Maupertuis who was a devoted Newtonian. In 1762 Kant demonstrated that Wolff's moral philosophy was untenable, after which his reputation declined.

W. Schneider (ed.), *Christian Wolff 1679–1754: Interpretationen zu seiner Philosophie* (Hamburg: Felix Meiner, 1983).

TORE FRÄNGSMYR

Wollstonecraft, Mary (1759–1797)   Anglo-Irish polemical writer, educator and feminist. Her life was as dramatic as it was short. After a brief teaching career, she worked for the publisher Joseph Johnson (1738–1809) and became increasingly politicized. In 1792 after being romantically spurned by Fuseli, she left for Paris where she met and lived with the American Gilbert Imlay, by whom she had a daughter, Fanny. Again rejected, she attempted suicide, but found a new life in London when she returned to writing and reviewing. In 1797 she married GODWIN. She died of pueperal fever eleven days after the birth of their daughter, Mary (1797–1851), who was to marry the poet Percy Shelley.

Wollstonecraft played a major role alongside Paine, Richard Price and Godwin in shaping the Jacobin ideology of the day. Her defences, including *A Vindication of the Rights of Woman* (1792), and history of the French Revolution, written in reply to Burke, won her popular acclaim which, however, was withdrawn when her unconventional love-life became known through Godwin's *Memoirs* (1798). Less well known were her books on education and her two autobiographical fictions, *Mary: A Fiction* (1788) and *The Wrongs of Woman* (1798). *See also* FEMINISM, WOMEN.

Claire Tomalin, *The Life and Death of Mary Wollstonecraft* (New York: Harcourt, Brace, Jovanovich, 1974).

M. L. BENJAMIN

women   Much was said and written about women in the eighteenth century. They were denigrated and criticized, as well as praised and defended, by men as well as women. They were compared to men in intelligence, courage and virtue, as they had been in the seventeenth century. Their sexual appetite, their capacity to love and the extent of their desire for luxury continued to be subjects of interest as in earlier times. In many respects, the Enlightenment was a period like any other for women.

True, their education did seem to receive more attention than before. Following seventeenth-century discussions on the subject, education was increasingly used to explain sexual difference. Mary Astell (1668–1731) argued in *A Serious Proposal to the Ladies for the Advancement of their True and Greatest Interest* (1694) that 'The cause of the defects we labour under is, if not wholly, yet at least in the first place, to be ascribed to the mistakes of our Education, which like an Error in the first Concoction, spreads its ill influence through all our Lives.' 'Women', she added, 'are from their very infancy debar'd those Advantages, with the want of which they are afterwards reproached, and nursed up in those Vices which will hereafter be upbraided to them. So partial are Men as to expect Brick where they afford no Straw; and so abundantly civil as to take care we shou'd make good that obliging Epithet of *Ignorant*, which out of an excess of good Manners, they are pleas'd to bestow on us!'

Such sentiments were echoed throughout the century, and others published similar defences of the sex and pleaded for its education, including the historian Catherine Macaulay (1731–91), the philosopher Elizabeth Hamilton (1758–1816) and Mary Wollstonecraft. While the contents of an ideal curriculum were hotly debated, it was generally agreed that education was the key to reforming women. Reform was the perceived aim, for even the great champions of women's rights endorsed the view that women were wanting, indeed morally wanting, in some way or other. Among the aristocracy and upper middle classes in particular, women were deemed to be neglectful mothers, not only by the likes of Rousseau, who berated them for not breast-feeding their children, but also by those, like Wollstonecraft, who defended them from his accusations. They were thought to be vain and frivolous, their accomplishments were belittled, and they were regarded as having no skills apart from the art of seduction. It was thought that training their minds would keep them from straying from the path of VIRTUE, and make of them good mothers and better companions and wives. Far from being seen as the beginning of a challenge to the sexual division of labour, education was, generally speaking, presented as the means to ensure the stability of domestic and social arrangements, even by those who are now considered to be feminists.

Yet, what made the eighteenth century appear to be the century of women was the activities of the women that moralists were all too eager to criticize. The *salons*, narrow and exclusive as they were, demonstrated that women could lead a life independent of their roles as wives and mothers, and that they could play an important part in culture and civilization. It was seeing them in such contexts that led Diderot and Madame de Staël, among others, to reflect on the history of woman and her part in the progress of modern society. That the emancipation of some women from the confines of domestic life went hand in hand with the growing inequality among the sex as a whole was a fact which was not lost on those Enlightenment thinkers. Those women who lived almost like men could do so only because other women sold their labour as nannies, maids and domestic servants. *See also* FEMINISM.

Bridget Hill (ed.), *Eighteenth Century Women: An Anthology* (London: Allen & Unwin, 1987).

Paul Hoffmann, *La Femme dans la pensée des lumières* (Paris: Ophrys, 1977).

Joan B. Landes, *Women and the Public Sphere in the Age of the French Revolution* (Ithaca, NY: Cornell University Press, 1988).

Carolyn C. Lougee, *Le Paradis des Femmes: Women, Salons, and Social Stratification in Seventeenth-Century France* (Princeton, NJ: Princeton University Press, 1976).

Sylvana Tomaselli, 'The Enlightenment Debate on Women', *History Workshop Journal*, 20 (1985) 101–24.

SYLVANA TOMASELLI

Wordsworth, William (1770–1850) English romantic poet. Born in Cockermouth, he was educated at Hawkshead and at Cambridge, where he encountered revolutionary ideas. In 1790–1 he went on a walking tour of the Continent, and then spent a year in France. During this time he was inspired by the ideals of the French Revolution, and also fell in love with Annette Vallon, who bore him a daughter. When war broke out, he returned to England, and settled down to writing poetry and occasional defences of the Revolution. The Terror led to his disillusionment with the Revolution, which was reflected in *The Borderers* (1796–7).

In 1795 he set up house in Dorset with his sister Dorothy and met COLERIDGE, with whom he collaborated on the *Lyrical Ballads* (1798), which was a landmark in English ROMANTICISM. Wordsworth's preface to the volume is widely acknowledged to be a romantic manifesto. His highly autobiographical, subjective and reflective poetic style, which Keats (1795–1821) christened the 'egotistical sublime', was best exemplified in *The Prelude* (1805, 1850).

In 1799 he and Dorothy moved to Grasmere, and in 1802 he married Mary Hutchinson (b 1770), by whom he had five children. He became increasingly conservative in his later years, but continued to write poetry, and his popularity grew. In 1843 he succeeded Southey (1774–1843) as poet laureate. He died in Ambleside, where he had lived since 1813.

Stephen Gill, *William Wordsworth: A Life* (Oxford: Clarendon, 1989).

M. L. BENJAMIN

workhouse   The term 'workhouse' can, for the eighteenth century, be used to cover a wide variety of institutions. These had their origins in the sixteenth century: in the 1550s the London Bridewell formed the prototype English workhouse; later Dutch experiments were copied in the Southern Netherlands (where the famous Maison de Force of Ghent was completely rebuilt in 1773), Germany and Scandinavia; while, following experiments at Lyons in 1614, France adopted a system of *hôpitaux généraux*. From the start these institutions, like the wider projects for dealing with poverty of which they were a part, were bedevilled by problems which showed no sign of diminishing over the eighteenth century. An enduring belief in the Christian duty of charitable works (*see* CHARITY) jostled with a political desire to control the poor and an economic desire for a skilled workforce; thus workhouses accommodated members of the deserving poor, but also vagrants, petty criminals and prostitutes. Funding workhouses was always difficult, and likely to cause resentment among local taxpayers, and ultimately no plans for workhouses could, given the extent of eighteenth-century poverty, achieve major success.

In France the *hôpitaux généraux* survived into the eighteenth century, mainly as small institutions, often run by female religious orders, and often hampered by financial problems. They showed little sign of expansion, and their spasmodic attempts at industrial activity rarely created much profit or contributed much to labour discipline. The *hôpitaux généraux* could not be turned into effective workhouses, and in 1767 the French monarchy attempted to curb vagabonds and beggars by establishing *dépôts de mendicité* in all provinces: their success was negligible.

Other national experiences reinforce the conclusion that workhouses could, at best, offer little more than partial solutions for the problems they were meant to ameliorate. In Piedmont and Lombardy, as elsewhere, there was a special emphasis on disciplining the young. In England, where a decentralized and comparatively effective Poor Law system existed, the establishment of parish workhouses was encouraged by an Act of 1723. In Prussia and other German states *Arbeitshäuser* were founded from the 1740s, offering work for the poor and incarceration and labour discipline for vagrants. As befitted the traditional mercantilist orientation of many of the German states, these institutions tended to involve their inmates in the production of luxury goods. Even here, however, success was rare, and the workhouse, as so often, simply drifted into being a means of terrifying the poor. In Bavaria Count Rumford (1753–1814) tried to clear the streets of Munich of beggars by founding a workhouse in 1790. This institution, devoted mainly to the making of military clothing, made a profit for a few years but closed in 1799. Despite the ingenuity and good intentions of their founders, workhouses in most parts of Europe foundered on the economic realities of the period and on the sheer magnitude of the problem of poverty.

See also BEGGARS, POVERTY AND POOR RELIEF.

C. Lis and H. Soly, *Poverty and Capitalism in Pre-industrial Europe* (Brighton: Harvester, 1979).

J. A. SHARPE

Wren, Sir Christopher (1632–1723) English architect. An anatomist, mathematician and astronomer as well as an architect, he loved machines and models. John Evelyn (1620–1706) called him that 'Miracle of a Youth' in 1654; a decade later he had an Oxford chair in astronomy and had begun, with Pembroke College Chapel in Cambridge and the Sheldonian Theatre in Oxford, the architectural career that was to exercise most though not all of his intellectual vigour. Classicism had been almost exclusively a domestic style in England, but by the end of Wren's career London had a public architecture that was beginning to equal that of Paris, whose quays, domes and masonry technology he had admired in 1665. St Paul's Cathedral (completed 1711) was his 'monument'; others included the City churches, his work at Hampton Court Palace (begun 1670), Trinity College (Cambridge) Library (1676–84), the Chelsea Hospital (1682–92) and Greenwich Observatory (1675–6) and Hospital (begun 1696).

His dismissal, in 1718, as surveyor of works ended his fifty-year dominance of English architecture, and coincided with a call for a more austere and distinctively British style (*see* PALLADIANISM) in contrast to what was seen as his BAROQUE cosmopolitanism. The Georgians thought that he lacked taste.

K. Downes, *The Architecture of Wren*, second edn (Reading: Redhedge, 1988).

CHRISTINE STEVENSON

Württemberg An important medium-sized Protestant duchy in southwest Germany with a population in 1750 of 620,000, Württemberg was an active power in the Swabian Circle, one of the peace-keeping regions into which the Holy Roman Empire was divided. It was unusual in Germany in having no nobility – they were all direct subjects of the emperor – and powerful parliamentary estates, which were dominated by a Lutheran urban patriciate. In the sixteenth and seventeenth centuries the estates exploited the rivalry between their dukes and the Habsburgs, who had claims on the territory, to enhance their power. When in the later seventeenth century mutual fear of France pushed the dukes and Austria together, chronic and serious constitutional conflicts resumed, precipitated by the attempts of the dukes Eberhard

Louis (1676–1733), Charles Alexander (1684–1737) and CHARLES EUGENE (1728–93) to impose absolutism. These conflicts ended when a settlement was negotiated in 1770 by the emperor and a number of German Protestant states which had guaranteed the constitution. After that, Charles Eugene abandoned his absolutist ambitions and became a respected enlightened ruler. After 1803 Württemberg, as an ally of France, was enlarged and became a kingdom.

J. A. Vann, *The Making of a State: Württemberg 1593–1793* (Ithaca, NY: Cornell University Press, 1984).

MICHAEL HUGHES

Y

Yorktown, Battle of (1781) Yorktown, at the mouth of the York River in north-east Virginia, had no natural defences to landward and was thus an ill-chosen base for Cornwallis's (1738–1805) fine army of 7,000 men in August 1781, unless sustained from seaward. WASHINGTON seized his opportunity, and a forced march from New York by him and from Newport, Rhode Island by Rochambeau (1725–1807), from 21 August to 14 September, backed up by naval support from de Grasse's (1722–88) French forces, ensured Cornwallis's surrender on 19 October 1781, thereby ending the American War of Independence on land.

C. E. Hatch Jr, *Yorktown and the Siege of 1781* (Washington, DC: United States Government Printing Office, 1952).

D. D. ALDRIDGE

Young, Arthur (1741–1820) English agricultural writer. A prolific author, many of his writings arose from his travels and his own experience of farming. His best-known works are his three English *Tours* (1768–71), *Tour in Ireland* (1780) and *Travels in France* (1792). The last is particularly valuable for the light it throws on conditions in France on the eve of the Revolution. Also important are his specialized works on *Hiring and Stocking Farms* (1770) and *Political Arithmetic* (1774). From 1784 to 1815 he edited his periodical, *Annals of Agriculture*, an important collection of contemporary observations and discussions, and from 1793 he served as secretary to the first board of agriculture and wrote a number of its county reports. By his enthusiasm for progress and publicizing of innovations, together with the spreading of a scientific yet commercial attitude to experimentation, he made a major contribution to the advance of English agriculture. His reputation spread to the Continent and North America.

John G. Gazeley, *The Life of Arthur Young 1741–1820* (Philadelphia: American Philosophical Society, 1973).

G. E. Mingay (ed.), *Arthur Young and his Times* (London: Macmillan, 1975).

G. E. MINGAY

Young, Edward (1683–1765) English poet. He was the rector of Welwyn, Hertfordshire. His *Complaint, or Night Thoughts* (1742–6), a poem of Christian meditation in nine books of blank verse, was his most influential work. Earlier works included the satire *Love of Fame* (1725–8), several tragedies and miscellaneous verse. He was a friend and correspondent of the novelist Samuel Richardson.

JOHN MULLAN

Z

Zinzendorf, Nicolaus Ludwig, count von (1700–1760) German Pietist and founder of the Moravian Brethren. A North German nobleman, he was strongly religious from childhood. In 1722 he founded the Herrnhut religious community on his estate, from which grew the revived Moravian Brethren.

See also MORAVIANS, PIETISM.

A. J. Lewis, *Zinzendorf, the Ecumenical Pioneer* (London: SCM, 1962).

MICHAEL HUGHES

Zoffany, John (1733–1810) British painter of German birth. He studied in Rome and moved to London in 1760 where he developed a highly successful informal combination of the conversation piece and conventional portrait. Following his move to India in 1783, his popularity declined. He retired in 1800.

Mary Webster, *Zoffany* (London: National Portrait Gallery, 1976).

IAIN PEARS

Further Reading

The following is a list of reference books and broad interpretative works dealing with aspects of eighteenth-century history which may be used alongside the specific suggestions for further reading included with individual entries.

Works of Reference
Jack Babuscio and Richard Minta Dunn, *European Political Facts 1648–1789* (London: Macmillan, 1984).

Chris Cook and John Stevenson, *British Historical Facts 1760–1830* (London: Macmillan, 1980).

Chris Cook and John Stevenson, *The Longman Handbook of Modern European History 1763–1985* (London: Longman, 1987).

The Hamlyn Historical Atlas (London: Hamlyn, 1981).

The New Cambridge Modern History Atlas (Cambridge: Cambridge University Press, 1970).

Alan Palmer, *The Penguin Dictionary of Modern History* (Harmondsworth: Penguin, 1964).

The Penguin Atlas of World History, 2 vols (Harmondsworth: Penguin, 1974).

The Times Atlas of World History (London: The Times, 1978).

E. N. Williams, *The Penguin Dictionary of English and European History 1485–1789* (Harmondsworth: Penguin, 1980).

John Yolton, Roy Porter, Pat Rogers and Barbara Maria Stafford (eds), *The Blackwell Companion to the Enlightenment* (Oxford: Blackwell, 1991).

Bibliographies

The Eighteenth Century: A Current Bibliography (Philadelphia: American Society for Eighteenth Century Studies, 1978–   ).

Stanley Pargellis and D. J. Medley, *Bibliography of British History: The Eighteenth Century 1714–1789* (Oxford: Oxford University Press, 1951; repr. Hassocks, Harvester, 1977).

General Works

Matthew Anderson, *Historians and Eighteenth-Century Europe 1715–1789* (Oxford: Oxford University Press, 1979).

Matthew Anderson, *Europe in the Eighteenth Century 1713–1783*, third edn (London: Longman, 1987).

C. A. Bayley, *The New Cambridge History of India*, vol. 2.1: *Indian Society and the Making of the British Empire* (Cambridge: Cambridge University Press, 1988).

Leslie Bethell (ed.), *The Cambridge History of Latin America*, vols 1 and 2 (Cambridge: Cambridge University Press, 1984).

J. M. Black, *Eighteenth Century Europe 1700–1789* (London: Macmillan, 1990).

D. Carpanetto and G. Ricuperati, *Italy in the Age of Reason, 1685–1789* (London: Longman, 1987).

Alfred Cobban (ed.), *The Eighteenth Century: Europe in the Age of Enlightenment* (London: Thames & Hudson, 1969).

M. Cranston, *Philosophers and Pamphleteers: Political Theorists of the Enlightenment* (Oxford: Oxford University Press, 1986).

Lester G. Crocker, *An Age of Crisis: Man and World in Eighteenth Century France* (Baltimore: Johns Hopkins University Press, 1959).

Lester G. Crocker, *Nature and Culture: Ethical Thought in the French Enlightenment* (Baltimore: Johns Hopkins University Press, 1963).

Robert Darnton, *The Business of Enlightenment: A Publishing History of the Encyclopédie, 1775–1800* (Cambridge, Mass.: Harvard University Press, 1979).

Robert Darnton, *The Literary Underground of the Old Regime* (Cambridge, Mass.: Harvard University Press, 1982).

William Doyle, *The Old European Order 1660–1800* (Oxford: Oxford University Press, 1978).

Paul Dukes, *The Making of Russian Absolutism 1613–1801*, second edn (London: Longman, 1990).

Franklin L. Ford, *Europe 1780–1830* (London: Longman, 1970).

M. Foucault, *The Order of Things: An Archaeology of the Human Sciences* (London: Tavistock, 1970; repr. London: Routledge, 1989).

John Gagliardo, *Germany under the Old Regime 1600–1790* (London: Longman, 1991).

Peter Gay, *The Enlightenment: An Interpretation*, 2 vols (New York: Vintage, 1966–9).

Richard Gray (ed.), *The Cambridge History of Africa*, vol. 4: *From c.1600 to c.1790* (Cambridge: Cambridge University Press, 1975).

Elie Halévy, *The Growth of Philosophic Radicalism* (London: Faber, 1928).

Norman Hampson, *The Enlightenment* (Harmondsworth: Penguin, 1968).

Thomas L. Hankins, *Science and the Enlightenment* (Cambridge: Cambridge University Press, 1985).

Olwen Hufton, *Europe: Privilege and Protest, 1730–1789* (London: Fontana, 1980).

Peter Jackson and Laurence Lockhart (eds), *The Cambridge History of Iran*, vol. 6: *The Timurid and Safarid Periods* (Cambridge: Cambridge University Press, 1986).

B. Jelavich, *A History of the Balkans* (Cambridge: Cambridge University Press, 1983).

E. H. Kossmann, *The Low Countries 1780–1940* (Oxford: Oxford University Press, 1978).

J. T. Lukowski, *Liberty's Folly: The Polish–Lithuanian Commonwealth in the Eighteenth Century* (London: Routledge, 1991).

John Lynch, *Bourbon Spain 1700–1808* (Oxford: Blackwell, 1989).

Frank E. Manuel, *The Eighteenth Century Confronts the Gods* (New York: Atheneum, 1967).

Frank E. Manuel and Fritzie P. Manuel, *Utopian Thought in the Western World* (Cambridge, Mass.: Harvard University, 1979; Oxford: Blackwell, 1979).

P. J. Marshall, *The New Cambridge History of India*, vol. 2.2: *Bengal: The British Bridgehead* (Cambridge: Cambridge University Press, 1987).

The New Cambridge Modern History, 14 vols (Cambridge: Cambridge University Press, 1957–70).

J. H. Parry, *The Spanish Seaborne Empire* (Berkeley, Calif.: University of California Press, 1990).

Roy Porter and Mikuláš Teich (eds), *The Enlightenment in National Context* (Cambridge: Cambridge University Press, 1981).

Jacques Roger, *Les Sciences de la Vie dans la Pensée Française au XVIII Siècle* (Paris: Colin, 1963).

G. S. Rousseau and Roy Porter (eds), *The Ferment of Knowledge: Studies in the Historiography of Eighteenth Century Science* (Cambridge: Cambridge University Press, 1980).

George Rudé, *Europe in the Eighteenth Century: Aristocracy and the Bourgeois Challenge* (London: Weidenfeld & Nicolson, 1972).

R. V. Sampson, *Progress in the Age of Reason* (London: Heinemann, 1956).

Stanford J. Shaw, *History of the Ottoman Empire and Modern Turkey*, vol. 1: *Empire of the Gazis: The Rise and Decline of the Ottoman Empire, 1280–1808* (Cambridge: Cambridge University Press, 1976).

J. J. Sheehan, *German History 1770–1866* (Oxford: Oxford University Press, 1989).

Leslie Stephen, *History of English Thought in the Eighteenth Century*, 2 vols (New York: Brace & World, 1962).

Keith Thomas, *Man and the Natural World: Changing Attitudes in England, 1500–1800* (London: Allen Lane, 1983).

Ian Watt, *The Rise of the Novel* (London: Chatto & Windus, 1957).

Social and Economic Studies

M. Anderson, *Approaches to the History of the Western Family 1500–1914* (London: Macmillan, 1980).

Philippe Ariès, *Centuries of Childhood: A Social History of the Family* (New York: Knopf, 1962).

Philippe Ariès, *Western Attitudes towards Death: From the Middle Ages to the Present* (Baltimore: Johns Hopkins University Press, 1974; London: Marion Boyars, 1976).

Philippe Ariès and Georges Duby (gen. eds), *A History of Private Life* (Cambridge, Mass.: Harvard University Press), vol. 3: *Passions of the Renaissance*, trans. Arthur Goldhammer (1989); vol. 4: *From the Fires of Revolution to the Great War*, trans. Arthur Goldhammer (1990).

F. Braudel, *Civilization and Capitalism, 15th–18th Century* (New York: Harper & Row, 1985), vol. 1: *The Structures of Everyday Life*; vol. 2: *The Wheels of Commerce*; vol. 3: *The Perspective of the World*.

Peter Burke, *Popular Culture in Early Modern Europe* (London: Temple Smith, 1978).

The Cambridge Economic History of Europe, 8 vols (Cambridge: Cambridge University Press, 1941–89), vol. 4: *The Economy of Expanding Europe in the Sixteenth and Seventeenth Centuries*, ed. E. E. Rich and C. H. Wilson (1967); vol. 5: *The Economic Organisation of Early Modern Europe*, ed. E. E. Rich and C. H. Wilson (1977); vol. 6: *The Industrial Revolution and After*, 2 vols, ed. H. J. Habakkuk and M. Postan (1965).

Carlo Cipolla (ed.), *The Fontana Economic History of Europe*, 6 vols (London: Fontana, 1974), vol. 2: *The Sixteenth and Seventeenth Centuries*; vol. 3: *The Industrial Revolution*; vol. 4: *The Emergence of Industrial Societies*, 2 parts.

J. C. D. Clark, *English Society, 1688–1832: Ideology, Social Structure and Political Practice during the Ancien Régime* (Cambridge: Cambridge University Press, 1985).

Leslie Clarkson, *Proto-industrialization: The First Phase of Industrialization* (London: Economic History Society, 1985).

N. F. R. Crafts, 'Industrial Revolution in England and France: Some Thoughts on the Question, "Why was England First?"', *Economic History Review*, 30 (1977), 429–41.

N. F. R. Crafts, *British Economic Growth during the Industrial Revolution* (Oxford: Clarendon, 1985).

G. R. Cragg, *The Church in the Age of Reason, 1648–1789* (Harmondsworth: Penguin, 1960).

François Crouzet, *The First Industrialists: The Problem of Origins* (Cambridge: Cambridge University Press, 1985).

Phyllis Deane, *The First Industrial Revolution* (Cambridge: Cambridge University Press, 1965).

Phyllis Deane and W. A. Cole, *British Economic Growth, 1688–1959: Trends and Structure*, second edn (Cambridge: Cambridge University Press, 1967).

J. De Vries, *European Urbanization, 1500–1800* (Cambridge, Mass.: Harvard University Press, 1984).

Norbert Elias, *The Civilizing Process* (New York: Pantheon), vol. 1: *The History of Manners* (1978); vol. 2: *Power and Civility* (1982); vol. 3: *The Court Society* (1983).

Jean Louis Flandrin, *Families in Former Times: Kinship, Household, and Sexuality* (Cambridge: Cambridge University Press, 1979).

M. W. Flinn, *The European Demographic System, 1500–1820* (Hassocks: Harvester, 1981).

A. Goodwin (ed.), *The European Nobility in the Eighteenth Century* (London: A. & C. Black, 1953).

Jack Goody, *The Development of the Family and Marriage in Europe* (Cambridge: Cambridge University Press, 1983).

J. Hobsbawm, *Industry and Empire: From 1750 to the Present Day* (London: Weidenfeld & Nicolson, 1968; Harmondsworth: Penguin, 1969).

O. H. Hufton, *The Poor of Eighteenth Century France* (Oxford: Clarendon, 1974).

N. Jacobsen and H. J. Puhle (eds), *The Economies of Mexico and Peru during the Late Colonial Period, 1760–1810* (Berlin: Colloquium, 1986).

John Komlos, *Nutrition and Economic Development in the Eighteenth-Century Habsburg Monarchy: An Anthropometric History* (Princeton, NJ: Princeton University Press, 1989).

David S. Landes, *The Unbound Prometheus: Technological Change and Industrial Development in Western Europe from 1750 to the Present* (London: Cambridge University Press, 1960; repr. Cambridge: Cambridge University Press, 1969).

David Levine, *Family Formation in an Age of Nascent Capitalism* (New York: Academic Press, 1977).

C. Lis and H. Soly, *Poverty and Capitalism in Pre-Industrial Europe*, trans. J. Coonan (Hassocks: Harvester, 1979).

Bruce McGowan, *Economic Life in Ottoman Europe: Taxation, Trade and the Struggle for Land, 1600–1800* (Cambridge: Cambridge University Press, 1981).

Joseph C. Miller, *Way of Death: Merchant Capitalism and the Angolan Slave Trade, 1730–1830* (Madison Wisc: University of Wisconsin, 1988).

Susan Naquin and Evelyn S. Rawski, *Chinese Society in the Eighteenth Century* (New Haven, Conn.: Yale University Press, 1987).

Ronald Paulson, *Representations of Revolution 1789–1820* (New Haven, Conn.: Yale University Press, 1983).

Roy Porter, *English Society in the Eighteenth Century*, rev. edn (Harmondsworth: Penguin, 1990).

Jane Rendall, *The Origins of Modern Feminism: Women in Britain, France, and the United States, 1780–1860* (New York: Schocken, 1984).

G. Rozman, *Urban Networks in Russia, 1750–1800, and Premodern Periodization* (Princeton, NJ: Princeton University Press, 1976).

Peter Stearns, *European Society in Upheaval: Social History since 1750* (London: Collier Macmillan, 1975).

Lawrence Stone, *The Family, Sex and Marriage in England, 1500–1800* (London: Weidenfeld & Nicolson, 1977).

Lawrence Stone (ed.), *The University in Society*, 2 vols (Princeton, NJ: Princeton University Press, 1975).

James D. Tracy (ed.), *The Rise of Merchant Empires: Long-Distance Trade in the Early Modern World 1350–1750* (Cambridge: Cambridge University Press, 1990).

K. Verdery, *Transylvanian Villagers: Three Centuries of Political, Economic and Ethnic Change* (Berkeley, Calif.: University of California Press, 1983).

Peter Wagner, *Eros Revived: Erotica of the Enlightenment in England and America* (London: Secker & Warburg, 1988).

Immanuel M. Wallerstein, *The Modern World-System: Capitalist Agriculture and the Origins of the European World-Economy in the Sixteenth Century*, 3 vols, vol. 1 (New York: Academic Press, 1974).

Eugen Weber, *A Modern History of Europe: Men, Cultures, and Societies from the Renaissance to the Present* (London: Hale, 1973).

William Woodruff, *Impact of Western Man: A Study of Europe's Role in the World Economy, 1750–1960* (London: Macmillan, 1966).

Political History
J. M. Black, *The Rise of the European Powers, 1679–1793* (London: Arnold, 1990).

J. M. Black, *A Military Revolution? Military Change and European Society 1550–1800* (London: Macmillan, 1991).

W. Doyle, *The Ancien Regime* (London: Macmillan, 1986).

H. L. Kahn, *Monarchy in the Emperor's Eyes: Image and Reality in the Ch'ien-Lung Reign* (Cambridge, Mass.: Harvard University Press, 1971).

J. P. LeDonne, *Ruling Russia: Politics and Administration in the Age of Absolutism, 1762–1796* (Princeton, NJ: Princeton University Press, 1984).

R. R. Palmer, *The Age of the Democratic Revolution: A Political History of Europe and America, 1760–1800*, 2 vols (Princeton, NJ: Princeton University Press, 1959–64).

M. Raeff, *The Well-Ordered Police State: Social and Institutional Change through the Law in the Germanies and Russia, 1600–1800* (New Haven, Conn.: Yale University Press, 1983).

O. Subtelny, *Domination of Eastern Europe: Native Nobilities and Foreign Absolutism, 1500–1715* (Kingston: McGill University Press, 1986).

A. Walthall, *Social Protest and Popular Culture in Eighteenth-Century Japan* (Tucson, Ariz.: University of Arizona Press, 1986).

Religion
William J. Callahan and David Higgs (eds), *Church and Society in Catholic Europe of the Eighteenth Century* (Cambridge: Cambridge University Press, 1979).

James Cracraft, *The Church Reforms of Peter the Great* (London: Macmillan, 1971).

Gerald R. Cragg, *The Church and the Age of Reason, 1648–1789* (Harmondsworth: Penguin, 1960).

Jonathan Israel, *European Jewry in the Age of Mercantilism* (Oxford: Oxford University Press, 1985).

John McManners, *Death and the Enlightenment* (Oxford: Clarendon, 1981).

Exploration
Derek Howse (ed.), *Background to Discovery: Pacific Exploration from Dampier to Cook* (Berkeley, Calif.: University of California Press, 1990).

P. J. Marshall and G. Williams, *The Great Map of Mankind: British Perceptions of the World in the Age of Enlightenment* (London: Dent, 1982).

Ian K. Steele, *The English Atlantic 1675–1740: An Exploration of Communication and Community* (Oxford: Oxford University Press, 1986).

Cultural Studies
F. Blume, *Classic and Romantic Music: A Comprehensive Survey*, trans. M. D. Herker Norton (London: Faber, 1972).

P. Conisbee, *Painting in Eighteenth-Century France* (Oxford: Phaidon, 1981).

Hugh Honour, *Neo-classicism* (Harmondsworth: Penguin, 1968).

V. Lange, *The Classical Age of German Literature 1740–1815* (London: Arnold, 1982).

Journals
Many journals specialize in eighteenth-century studies, often devoting much space to reviews of new books and surveys of recent literature. Among the most useful are *Eighteenth-Century Studies, Eighteenth Century Life, The Eighteenth Century: Theory and Interpretation* (formerly known as *Studies in Burke and his Times*), *Journal of the History of Ideas, Enlightenment and Dissent, Studies in Eighteenth-Century Culture, The British Journal for Eighteenth-Century Studies, Dix-Huitième Siècle, Studies on Voltaire and the Eighteenth Century, Aufklärung.*

Chronology

INTERNAL EUROPEAN POLITICS		EUROPE-BASED INTERNATIONAL DEVELOPMENTS	
1700	Death of Charles II of Spain, leaving kingdom to duke of Anjou, grandson of Louis XIV (Nov.) Death of Innocent XII; succeeded by Clement XI (Nov.)	1700	Great Northern War begins Peace at Travendal between Charles XII of Sweden and Denmark (Aug.) Charles XII defeats Russians at Narra (Nov.)
1701	Coronation of elector of Brandenburg, Frederick I, king of Prussia (Jan.) Death of James II (Sept.) Rákóczi leads a revolt in Transylvania Act of Settlement in England	1701	Grand Alliance of The Hague Charles XII occupies Kurland Duke of Savoy and electors of Bavaria and Cologne side with France in War of the Spanish Succession
1702	Death of William III of England; succeeded by Queen Anne (Mar.)	1702	Charles XII enters Warsaw demanding deposition of king of Poland War declared against France and Spain at London, The Hague and Vienna
1703	Revolt in Hungary Camisards (Protestants) begin a rebellion in the Cévennes (France)	1703	Portugal joins Grand Alliance – Methuen Treaty (May) Treaty between Prussia and Sweden (July) Savoy joins Grand Alliance (Nov.) Charles XII defeats Augustus of Poland
1704	Villars suppresses revolt in the Cévennes Augustus II of Poland is deposed by Charles XII of Sweden (Feb.) Archduke Charles is proclaimed king of Spain Stanislas Leszczyński elected king of Poland (July)	1704	English under Rooke fail to take Barcelona but capture Gibraltar (Aug.) Battle of Blenheim – English victory (Aug.)

WORLD AFFAIRS	CULTURE
1700	1700 *The Way of the World* by William Congreve (1670–1729) Birth of Bartolomeo Rastrelli (*d* 1771)
1701	1701 *Ars Poetica* by Danish poet Reenberg (1656–1742) Peter the Great builds first public theatre *Louis XIV* painted by Hyacinthe Rigaud (1649–1743)
1702 French establish base at Mobile	1702 Moscow Religious Academy produces *Allegorical* in honour of Peter the Great Rebuilding of Melk Abbey (Austria) begins (finished in 1736) Death of Flemish sculptor Jean Delcour (*b* 1627)
1703	1703 First dictionary of music, written by French composer Sébastien de Brossard (1655–1730) Foundation of St Petersburg
1704	1704 Antonio Vivaldi established as a teacher at Conservatorio dell'Ospedale della Pietà, Venice Building of Abraham Ackerman House, Hackensack, New Jersey

INTERNAL EUROPEAN POLITICS		EUROPE-BASED INTERNATIONAL DEVELOPMENTS	
1705	Death of Emperor Leopold I; succeeded by Joseph I Rákóczi aided by France Whig majority in English parliament	1705	Tsar Peter the Great invades Kurland (Feb.) Capture of Barcelona by Peterborough (Oct.) Charles XII invades Silesia Denmark brought into Russo-Polish political alliance
1706	John V becomes king of Portugal Augustus II renounces Polish crown and Russian alliance	1706	Battle of Ramillies (May) Battle of Turin (Sept.) Charles XII invades Saxony Treaty of Altranstädt (Sept.)
1707	Union of England and Scotland (May) Joseph I is proclaimed king in Naples after Austrian conquest	1707	French troops leave Italy Convention of Milan (Mar.) secures north Italy for the allies Battle of Almanza (Apr.) assures throne of Spain to the house of Bourbon Alliance between Frederick of Prussia and Charles XII
1708	Ministry in Britain is wholly Whig (Feb.); joined by Walpole Attempt of the Stuart Pretender to land in Scotland fails (Mar.) Jesuits expelled from Holland Death of Prince George of Denmark, husband of Anne Rákóczi is defeated by the Imperialists	1708	Charles XII invades the Ukraine Italy is lost to the Spanish monarchy Battle of Oudenarde (July) Siege of Lille (Aug.) Capture of Sardinia and Minorca by Stanhope and Leake

WORLD AFFAIRS		CULTURE
1705	1705	Performance in Hamburg of the first opera, *Almira*, by G. F. Handel Building of Blenheim Palace begins (finished 1724) Death of Chinese Painter Chu Ta, forerunner of Individualist school of painters
1706	1706	Publication of the *Recueil de Contredanses* by Raoul Feuillet *Premier Livre de Pièces à Clavecin*, the first published work by Jean Philippe Rameau Birth of Giovanni Battista Martini (*d* 1784) Henry Mill invents carriage springs
1707	Death of Aurangzeb; decline of Mughal power in India	1707	First organ built in Frauenstein by Gottfried Silbermann (1683–1753) Death of German composer Dietrich Buxtehude (*b* 1637) Death of Dutch marine painter Willem Velde II Denis Papin invents the steamboat
1708	1708	*Le Légataire universel* by Jean-François Regnard (1655–1790) Handel's first oratorio, *La Resurrezione*, performed in Rome J. S. Bach goes to Weimar as court organist to Duke Wilhelm Ernst

	INTERNAL EUROPEAN POLITICS		EUROPE-BASED INTERNATIONAL DEVELOPMENTS
1709	Great Plague in Russia Peter the Great restores Augustus to the Polish throne	1709	Conference at The Hague for peace negotiations begins (Feb.) Negotiations break down (May) Charles XII is defeated at Poltava (July) Battle of Malplaquet (Aug.)
1710	Ragotsky is overthrown in Hungary Fall of Whig ministry and formation of a Tory government in Britain	1710	Alliance of The Hague formed Destruction of Port Royal Congress at Gertruydenberg to discuss peace (Feb.) The sultan, at the instigation of Charles XII, declares war on Russia British defeated at Brihuega and Starhemberg and Austrians at Villa Viciosa (Dec.); Philip V assured of throne
1711	Rákóczi rising in Hungary ended by Treaty of Szatmár Creation of the Senate in Russia Death of Emperor Joseph I (Apr.)	1711	Alliance between king of Denmark and elector of Hanover Treaty of the Pruth between Russia and Turkey (July)

WORLD AFFAIRS		CULTURE
1709	1709	*The Secret Diary of W. B. Westover* by William Byrd (1674–1744) *Turcaret* by Alain-René le Sage (1668–1747) First performance of *Agrippina* by Handel Bartolomeo Cristofori (1655–1731) constructs the first mechanism for a true pianoforte in Padua Discovery of the technique of manufacture of true Chinese porcelain by J. F. Böttger and E. W. von Tschirnhausen Discovery of prussic acid
1710 Mauritius is abandoned by the Dutch East India Company	1710	*Almanide* (anonymous), the first opera to be sung wholly in Italian in London Birth of Wilhelm Friedemann Bach (*d* 1784) Birth of Giovanni Battista Pergolesi Founding of the Meissen porcelain factory
1711	1711	Addison and Steele edit *The Spectator* Death of Chinese poet Wang Shih-chen Building of Mafra Palace, Portugal, one of the largest baroque palaces in Europe, begun by John V of Portugal

	Death of dauphin in France (Apr.); duke of Burgundy becomes heir-apparent Archduke Charles elected Emperor Charles VI (Dec.)		
1712	Emperor is crowned king of Hungary Death of duke and duchess of Burgundy (Feb.) and their son the duke of Britanny (Mar.); youngest son becomes dauphin, later Louis XV	1712	Congress of Utrecht opens (Jan.) English sign truce with France (May) Battle of Denain: Villars defeats the Dutch (July)
1713	Death of Frederick I of Prussia, succeeded by Frederick-William I (Feb.) Clement XI issues Bull 'Unigenitus', a controversial move in the dispute over Jansenism Victor Amadeus is crowned king of Sicily (Dec.) Pragmatic Sanction issued	1713	Treaty of Utrecht finally agreed (Apr.) ending War of the Spanish Succession for Britain and the Dutch The Pragmatic Sanction brought forward by Charles VI (Apr.) Sequestration Treaty between Russia, Poland and Prussia (Oct.)
1714	Death of Marie Louise of Savoy, queen of Spain (Feb.) Philip V marries Elizabeth Farnese Death of Queen Anne (Aug.); accession of George I Philip V's *Nueva Planta* begin in Spain	1714	Treaty of Rastadt between Austria and France (Mar.) Treaty of Baden between France and the Empire (Sept.) Secret treaty between France and Bavaria Peter the Great conquers Finland and the island of Åland

WORLD AFFAIRS	CULTURE
	Building of Schloss Weissenstein, Germany
1712	1712 Handel visits London and remains until his death Birth of French engraver Pierre Simon Fournier
1713 Under Treaty of Utrecht, France cedes Nova Scotia, Newfoundland, Hudson Bay and St Kitts to Britain	1713 *Cato* by English journalist and playwright Joseph Addison *Merope* by Italian playwright Scipione Maffei Birth of French neoclassical architect Jacques Soufflot
1714 Tripolitania establishes its independence from the Ottoman Empire Mughals defeat rebellion of the Sikhs under Banda Bahadur	1714 Birth of German composer Christoph Willibald Gluck Birth of Carl Philipp Emanuel Bach Birth of Italian composer Niccolò Jommelli Gabriel Daniel Fahrenheit constructs mercury thermometer Death of Chinese Individualist painter Tao Chi (*b* 1667) Cathedral of Saints Peter and Paul, St Petersburg, built by Trezzini

	INTERNAL EUROPEAN POLITICS		EUROPE-BASED INTERNATIONAL DEVELOPMENTS
1715	Death of Louis XIV (Sept.); Orléans becomes regent Jacobite rebellion in Britain (Sept.) Defeat of Jacobites at Preston and Sheriffmuir (Nov.)	1715	Peace signed between Spain and Portugal (Feb.) Prussia makes offensive alliance with Denmark, Hanover, Saxony and Poland (Apr.); later joined by Russia (Nov.) King of Denmark makes treaty with George I (May) George I declares war against Sweden The Barrier Treaty (Nov.) Treaty of Commerce between Britain and Spain (Dec.)
1716	Arrival of Pretender in Scotland (Jan.) followed by return to France on defeat of the Jacobites (Feb.) Septennial Act in Britain (Apr.) Death of Leopold, only son of Charles VI (Nov.) Birth of Don Carlos, son of Philip V	1716	Treaty of Westminster between Austria and Britain (Apr.) Convention between tsar and Frederick IV of Denmark to use forces against Charles XII (June) Battle of Peterwardein: imperialists defeat Turks (Aug.) Asiento Treaty between England and Spain is signed (Aug.) Convention of Hanover signed by Dubois and Stanhope (Oct.), the basis of the Triple Alliance
1717	Birth of Maria Theresa (May), daughter of Charles VI Whig schism; resignation of Walpole and Townshend (Apr.), Stanhope becomes prime minister	1717	Triple Alliance concluded between France, Britain and Holland (Jan.) Convention signed at Amsterdam between France, Russia and Prussia (Aug.)

WORLD AFFAIRS		CULTURE

1715

1715   First performance of
Amadigi di Gaula, by
Handel
Gil Blas de Santillane
by French novelist and
playwright Alain-René
Lesage (1668–1747)
Building of the German
abbey church of
Weingarten
Publication of first
volume of *Vitruvius
Britannicus*
Death of Japanese artist
Nishikawa Sukenobu (*b*
1671)

1716

1716   Karlskirche, Vienna,
built by Johann Fischer
von Erlach (1656–1723)
Petrovdorets, St
Petersburg, built by
Trezzini, Le Blond
(1679–1719) and
Rastrelli (1700–71)
Birth of American
architect Peter Harrison
(*d* 1775)
Death of Japanese artist
Ogata (*b* 1658)

1717

1717   J. S. Bach goes to
Cöthen, as conductor of
court orchestra
St Jakob's church,
Innsbruck, built by
Johann Herkommer
(1648–1717)

INTERNAL EUROPEAN POLITICS		EUROPE-BASED INTERNATIONAL DEVELOPMENTS
		Battle of Belgrade won by Eugene (Aug.) Island of Sardinia conquered by Spain.
1718	Peter the Great kills his son Alexis (July) Death of Charles XII (Dec.) Creation of administrative colleges (ministries) in Russia Revolution in Sweden; the aristocracy comes into power	1718	Åland Conference between Russia and Sweden opens (May) Spaniards conquer Sicily (July) but are defeated by British at the Battle of Cape Passaro (Aug.) Treaty of Passarowitz between Austria and Turkey (July) Charles VI joins Triple Alliance; signs Treaty of London, forming the Quadruple Alliance (Aug.) Britain declares war on Spain (Dec.)
1719	Ulrika Eleonora elected queen of Sweden; monarchy converted from an absolute into an elective one (Jan.)	1719	Renewal of war between Russia and Sweden Carteret negotiates peace between Sweden and the Northern League France declares war on Spain (Jan.) Austrians defeated in Sicily (June) Sweden makes treaty with Hanover (Nov.)

WORLD AFFAIRS		CULTURE
		Victor Amadeus II begins work on huge church at Superga (finished 1727): architect Filippo Juvarra
		L'Embarquement pour l'Île de Cythère painted by Watteau (1684–1721)
		Italian painter Giovanni Paolo Panini settles in Rome
1718	New Orleans founded by the French	1718	Independent movement of fixed stars discovered by Halley
		Performance of Leonardo Leo's opera *Sofonisba*
		Palazzo Madama, Turin, built by Filippo Juvarra
		Building of Aldersbach Abbey begins
1719		1719	*Peder Paars* by Ludvig, baron Holberg
		Foundation of music publishers Breitkopf & Härtel at Leipzig
		Building of the Würzburg Residence, Würzburg, begins
		Rebuilding of Einsiedeln Abbey near Lake Zürich, Switzerland, by Caspar Moosbrugger (1656–1723) begins
		Vienna produces first porcelain to rival Meissen

INTERNAL EUROPEAN POLITICS		EUROPE-BASED INTERNATIONAL DEVELOPMENTS	
1720	Collapse of John Law's financial schemes in France Ulrika Eleonora abdicates in favour of her husband who is elected King Frederick I Birth of Don Philip, son of Philip V Plague in Marseilles kills some 40,000 people South Sea Bubble brings about crisis in British politics (Dec.)	1720	Treaty of Stockholm between Sweden and Prussia (Feb.) Treaty between Sweden and Hanover (Feb.) War between France and Spain ends (Feb.) Treaty between Sweden and Denmark (July) Spain begins negotiations with Quadruple Alliance
1721	Death of Clement XI; succeeded by Innocent XIII Walpole becomes first lord of the treasury in Britain	1721	Treaty between Britain and Spain confirming commercial arrangements (June) Defensive alliance between France, Spain and Britain (June) Treaty of Nystad between Russia and Sweden (Aug.)
1722	Diet of Hungary agrees to the Pragmatic Sanction Charles VI founds the Dutch East India Company General Directory established in Prussia Table of Ranks issued in Russia	1722	Peter the Great takes Baku, opening a way to the Black Sea

WORLD AFFAIRS	CULTURE
1720	1720 First opera season of Royal Academy in London Development of English creamware pottery begins Development by J. G. Höroldt of a range of enamel colours for ceramic decorations at Meissen Death of Chinese artist Wang Hui (*b* 1632)
1721	1721 Ludvig Holberg becomes director of Danish Theatre in Copenhagen Belvedere Summer Palace, Vienna, built for Prince Eugene St Martin-in-the-Fields, London, built by James Gibbs (1682–1754) The Spanish Steps, Rome, built by Franscesco de Sanctis (1693–1740) and Alessandro Specchi (1668–1729)
1722 Isfahan sacked by the Afghans	1722 *Moll Flanders* by Daniel Defoe *The Conscious Lovers* by Richard Steele Earliest of all musical periodicals, *Musica Critica*, by Johann Mattheson (1681–1764) begins publication Building of Cadiz Cathedral by Vincente Acero begins

INTERNAL EUROPEAN POLITICS	EUROPE-BASED INTERNATIONAL DEVELOPMENTS
1723 A charter is given to the Dutch East India Company Louis XV attains majority; end of the regency (Feb.)	1723 Turkey attacks Persia
1724 Philip V abdicates the throne of Spain (Jan.) Death of Innocent XIII; election of Benedict XIII Death of Don Luis and reaccession of Philip V (Aug.)	1724 Congress of Cambrai meets Treaty of Constantinople between Russia and Turkey for the partition of Persia (June)
1725 Death of Peter the Great (Feb.); his wife, Catherine I, succeeds Marriage of Louis to Marie Leszczyński	1725 Congress of Cambrai breaks up Treaty of Vienna between Austria and Spain (Apr.) Treaty of Hanover between Britain, France and Prussia to oppose Treaty of Vienna (Sept.) Secret treaty between Austria and Spain (Nov.)

WORLD AFFAIRS		CULTURE
1723	1723	*Odes* by Jean-Baptiste Rousseau (1671–1741) *Histoire de la Danse sacrée et profane* published by Bonnet First opera by Jean Philippe Rameau, *L'Endriague* J. S. Bach goes to Leipzig as cantor at St Thomas's
1724	1724	Beginning of Three Choirs Festival – Gloucester, Worcester and Hereford First part of *50 Psalms* published by Italian composer Benedetto Marcello (1686–1739) *The Four Evangelists* – the last paintings by Bolivian painter Melchor Perez Holguin (*c*.1660–*c*.1725) French portraitist Maurice de la Tour (1704–88) sets up in Paris
1725	1725	Building of Chiswick House by Lord Burlington (1695–1753) and William Kent Chantilly porcelain factory starts to make wares in Japanese kakiemon style Death of Italian composer Alessandro Scarlatti First publication by Richard Cooper, Scottish music engraver (*d* 1764)

	INTERNAL EUROPEAN POLITICS		EUROPE-BASED INTERNATIONAL DEVELOPMENTS
1726	Fleury replaces Bourbon as leading minister of France until his death in 1743	1726	Treaty between Austria and Russia (Aug.) Treaty of Wusterhausen between Austria and Prussia (Oct.) Russia guarantees the Pragmatic Sanction
1727	Death of Catherine I (May); succeeded by Peter II Death of George I (July); George II crowned (Oct.)	1727	War between England and Spain; siege of Gibraltar (Feb.)
1728		1728	Convention of the Pardo ends short war between Spain and England (Mar.) Congress of Soissons opened; attempt to settle European problems (June) Secret Treaty of Berlin between Charles VI and Frederick-William (Dec.)

WORLD AFFAIRS	CULTURE
1726	1726 *Gulliver's Travels* by Jonathan Swift Spanish dictionary issued by the Academy (founded 1714) Stage début of French dancer Maria Camargo (1710–70) John Harrison invents a compensating balance for clocks Building of Westover, Charles City County, Virginia, begins
1727	1727 Building of La Cartuja, Granada, by Francisco Izquierdo (1669–1725) begins Building of Christ Church, Philadelphia, by John Kearsley (1684–1722) begins Stephen Hales isolates oxygen *Migdal Oz* by Hebrew poet Moses Hazim Luzzatto (1707–47) performed in the Netherlands
1728 Bering discovers strait separating north-east Asia from north-west America	1728 *Manon Lescaut* by Abbé Prévost *The Beggars' Opera* by John Gay Birth of German piano-maker Johann Andreas Stein (*d* 1792) Birth of Scottish architect Robert Adam (*d* 1792) Birth of French architect Étienne-Louis Boullée (*d* 1799)

INTERNAL EUROPEAN POLITICS		EUROPE-BASED INTERNATIONAL DEVELOPMENTS
1729	Double marriage between the houses of Spain and Portugal, Ferdinand of Spain marries Portuguese princess Methodist Society founded at Oxford by John Wesley	1729	Congress of Soissons dissolved (July) Treaty of Seville between France, Britain and Spain, later joined by Holland (Nov.) End of the Austro-Spanish alliance; Franco-Spanish alliance takes its place
1730	Frederick, prince-royal of Prussia, is imprisoned by his father, Frederick-William I Death of Peter II (Feb.); succeeded by Anna Ivanovna who overthrows oligarchy of nobles and restores absolutism Ahmed III deposed (Sept.); succeeded by Mahmud I	1730	

WORLD AFFAIRS		CULTURE
		Founding of the royal glass factory at La Granja, Spain
		Building of Steinhausen Church, Germany, by Dominikus Zimmerman (1685–1766) and Johann Baptiste Zimmerman (1680–1758)
1729	Baltimore founded by the British	1729	Satiric poems by Russian poet Antioch Dmitrievich, Prince Kantemir (1709–44)
		Publication of secular Turkish works begins in Constantinople
		First performance of *St Matthew Passion* by J. S. Bach
		Birth of Dutch violinist and composer Pierre van Maldere (*d* 1768)
		Discovery of aberration of light of fixed stars by James Bradley
		Building of Plaza Mayor, Salamanca, by Alberto de Churri-guera (1676–1750) and Andrea Garcia de Quiñones (*fl* 1750–55) begins
1730	Revival of ancient empire of Bornu (central Sudan) (*c.*1730)	1730	*Kritische Dichtkunst* by German critic Johann Christoph Gottsched
		Death of Turkish poet Ahmed Nedim (*b* 1681)
		Production of Johann Adolph Hasse's opera *Artaserse* in Venice
		Building of University Church, Pest, Hungary by Andreas Mayerhoffer (*fl* 1720–54) begins

	INTERNAL EUROPEAN POLITICS		EUROPE-BASED INTERNATIONAL DEVELOPMENTS
	Struggle between Jesuits and Jansenists over Bull 'Unigenitus' becomes acute in France		
	Abdication of Victor Amadeus II, king of Sardinia (Sept.); succeeded by Charles Emanuel III		
	Christian VI becomes king of Denmark (Oct.)		
	Death of Benedict XIII; succeeded by Clement XII		
1731	Death of duke of Parma (Jan.)	1731	Second Treaty of Vienna between Austria, Britain and the Dutch (Mar.); Spain joins (July), isolating France
	Grand duke of Tuscany recognizes Don Carlos as his heir		
	Don Carlos takes possession of Parma		Treaty proposed between Austria, Russia and Prussia, opposing Stanislas Leszczyński in Poland (Dec.)
1732	Protestants driven from Salzburg take refuge in Prussia	1732	Anne Ivanovna makes treaty with Nadir Shah of Persia
			Diet of Ratisbon accepts the Pragmatic Sanction but Bavaria, Saxony and the Palatinate refuse to guarantee it
			Final settlement of the dispute between Prussia and house of Orange

WORLD AFFAIRS	CULTURE
	William Hogarth begins his sequence of narrative pictures Replanning of Bath begins
1731	1731 *La Vie de Marianne* by French novelist and playwright Pierre Carlet de Chamblain de Marivaux *De Hollandische Spectator* by Justus Van Effen (1684–1735) First operas by Pergolesi performed in Naples Building of Independence Hall, Philadelphia, begins John Hadley invents navigational sextant
1732 English colony of Georgia founded Russians abandon their gains in Persia	1732 Birth of Franz Joseph Haydn Covent Garden Theatre opens in London Building of Trevi Fountain, Rome, by Niccolò Salvi (1697–1751) Building of the Transparante, Toledo Cathedral, by Narciso Tomé *Sonate da Cimbalo di Piano* by Lodovico Giustini, probably the earliest printed piano music

INTERNAL EUROPEAN POLITICS		EUROPE-BASED INTERNATIONAL DEVELOPMENTS	
1733	Excise Crisis in Britain Death of Augustus of Poland and Saxony (Feb.) Stanislas Leszczyński elected king of Poland (Sept.) Augustus III elected King of Poland (Oct.). Russians invade Poland	1733	War of the Polish Succession begins Treaty of Turin between France and Sardinia (Sept.) France declares war on Austria (Oct.) Siege of Danzig begins(Oct.) First Family Compact secretly arranged between France and Spain (Treaty of Escurial) (Nov.)
1734	Britain: Princess Royal marries Prince of Orange (Mar.)	1734	French victory over the Austrians at Parma (June) Turks at war with Nadir Shah Don Carlos, son of Philip V, conquers Naples and south Italy Danzig capitulates to Russians, Stanislas Leszczyński flees into Prussian territory (July)
1735	Walpole wins general election	1735	Spaniards besiege Mantua Preliminaries of the Treaty of Vienna signed by France and the Emperor (Oct.) Turkey makes peace with Nadir Shah (Oct.)
1736	Marriage of Maria Theresa to duke of Lorraine (Feb.) Death of Prince Eugene Porteous riots break out in Edinburgh (June)	1736	Beginning of war of Turkey with Austria and Russia (May)

WORLD AFFAIRS	CULTURE
1733	Savannah founded by British settlers	1733	*Essay on Man* by Alexander Pope
Death of François Couperin (*b* 1668)
Performance of the opera *Rosamund* by Thomas Augustine Arne (1710–78) in London
French painter Jean-Baptiste Oudry is made director and chief designer of the Gobelin tapestry works
1734	Rebellion in Ceylon against Dutch influence	1734	Death of Irish music publisher John Neale
Birth of Swedish topographer and music historian Abraham Abrahamsson Hülphers (*d* 1798)
Building of the Royal Library, The Hague, by Daniel Marot (1661–1752)
Founding of Mennecy porcelain factory in Paris
1735		1735	Birth of Johann Christian Bach
Building of the royal palace of La Granja near Segovia begins
1736	Safavid dynasty of Persia deposed by Nadir Shah	1736	Death of Pergolesi
Birth of French architect Claude Nicolas Ledoux (*d* 1806)

1737	Death of grand duke of Tuscany, the last of the Medicis (June) Death of Queen Caroline in Britain (Nov.) Orry establishes the *corvée* throughout France	1737	Formal end of War of the Polish Succession
1738	'Hats' in Sweden overthrow Count Horn and the 'Caps'; Count Gyllenborg becomes head of the government Wesley forms a society in London and Methodist revival begins	1738	France makes alliance with Sweden (Oct.) Third Treaty of Vienna is signed (Nov.)
1739		1739	Secret treaty between Austria and France (Jan.) Secret treaty between Prussia and France (Apr.) War of Jenkins' Ear breaks out between Britain and Spain Treaty of Belgrade between Austria and Turkey (Sept.)

	WORLD AFFAIRS		CULTURE
1737		1737	*Poetica* by Ignacio Luzán de Suelvas y Guerra (1702–54)
			Building of Ottobeuem Abbey by Johann Fischer von Erlach begins
			French astronomical expedition to Lapland
1738		1738	Founding of the Royal Society of Musicians of Great Britain
			Performance of full version of J. S. Bach's Mass in B minor
			Building of the cathedral of St George, L'vov, Russia, begins
			Building of Royal Palace, Madrid, by Filippo Juvarra and Giovanni Sacchetti begins
			Invention of fly-shuttle by John Kay
1739	Nadir Shah of Persia defeats Mughal emperor at Karnal and sacks Delhi	1739	Birth of Austrian violinist and composer Karl Ditters von Dittersdorf (*d* 1799)
			First performances in London of Handel's oratorios *Saul* and *Israel in Egypt*
			First performance of Francisco Antonio d'Almeida's comic opera *La Spinalba*
			First successful American glass company established in New Jersey by the German Caspar Wistar (1696–1752)

INTERNAL EUROPEAN POLITICS	EUROPE-BASED INTERNATIONAL DEVELOPMENTS
1740 Death of Frederick-William I of Prussia (May); accession of Frederick II, the Great Death of Charles VI (Oct.) Death of Anne of Russia; Anne, mother of Ivan VI, becomes regent (Nov.) Benedict XIV succeeds Clement XII as pope	1740 Treaty made by Sweden with Turkey (July) War of the Austrian Succession begins when Frederick II of Prussia invades Silesia (Dec.)
1741 Maria Theresa receives Hungarian crown Revolution in Russia; accession of Elizabeth	1741 Battle of Mollwitz (Apr.) Sweden declares war against Russia (Aug.) Secret treaty between George II and Maria Theresa of Austria
1742 Charles Albert of Bavaria elected Emperor (Jan.) and crowned as Charles VII (Feb.) Resignation of Walpole (Feb.); Wilmington becomes prime minister	1742 Treaty of Berlin (July); Prussia and Saxony withdraw from coalition against Maria Theresa; end of First Silesian War

	WORLD AFFAIRS		CULTURE
1740		1740	*Pamela, or Virtue Rewarded* by Samuel Richardson Birth of English organ-builder Samuel Green (*d* 1796) *A Musical Dictionary* by English musical lexicographer James Grassineau (*c.*1715–67) Death of Italian singer, harpsichordist and composer Domenico Alberti (*b* 1710) Birth of Scottish architect Charles Cameron Portrait of *Captain Coram* painted by William Hogarth Production of crucible steel by Benjamin Huntsman of Sheffield
1741	Unsuccessful British attacks on Spanish-ruled Carthagena and Cuba	1741	*Mélanide* by Pierre Claude Nivelle de la Chaussée (1692–1754) Founding of the Madrigal Society in London Birth of French composer André Ernest Grétry (*d* 1813) Death of Antonio Vivaldi First opera by Christoph Willibald von Gluck, *Artaserse*, produced in Milan
1742		1742	*Les Confessions du Comte de * * * * by Charles Pinot Duclos (1704–72) First Performance in Dublin of Handel's *Messiah*

1743		**1743**	George II wins Battle of Dettingen against the French (June). Treaty of Åbo ends war between Russia and Sweden (Aug.) Maria Theresa signs Treaty of Worms with Britain and Sardinia (Sept.) Treaty of Fontainebleau between France and Spain (Oct.) Treaty between Austria and Saxony (Dec.)
1744	Fall of Carteret (Nov.); reconstruction of the government	**1744**	France declares war on Britain (Mar.) Union of Frankfurt (May) Beginning of Second Silesian War between Prussia and Austria (Aug.)
1745	Death of Charles VII (Jan.) Grand Duke Francis elected Emperor Francis I (Sept.)	**1745**	Treaty of Füssen between Austria and Bavaria Austria makes Treaty of Warsaw with Saxony for the partition of Prussia (May) Treaty of Dresden ends Second Silesian War (Dec.)

WORLD AFFAIRS		CULTURE
		Foundation of the Kosta glassworks, Sweden
		Celsius proposes 100-division thermometer scale
1743	1743	*Mérope* by Voltaire
		Establishment of Capo-di-Monte factory in Naples
		Death of Japanese potter Ogata Kenzan
		Excavations at Herculaneum begin
1744	1744	Death of French composer for the ballet André Campra (*b* 1660)
In Canada, extensive preparations made for the struggle with the British		Establishment of porcelain factories at Chelsea, Bow, Derby and Lowestoft
		Book 2 of *The Well Tempered Clavier* by J. S. Bach
		Six Concertos for the Organ or Harpsichord with Instrumental Parts by William Felton (1715–69)
1745	1745	Building of the Palace of Sans Souci, Potsdam, by Georg von Knobelsdorff
		The Excise Act in Britain taxes glass by weight
		Carceri d'Invezione, a series of etchings by Giovanni Battista Piranesi

INTERNAL EUROPEAN POLITICS	EUROPE-BASED INTERNATIONAL DEVELOPMENTS
1746 Death of Philip V of Spain (July); succeeded by Ferdinand VI Victory of Culloden (Apr.); final defeat of Jacobites and escape of Charles Edward to France (Sept.)	1746 Austrian victory over Spain at the Battle of Piacenza (June) Treaty of St Petersburg between Austria and Russia (June) French Marshal Saxe wins victory at Roucoux (Oct.)
1747 Orange party takes over control in province of Holland	1747 Prusso-Swedish treaty signed at Stockholm (May) Alliance between Russia and Britain (June) Convention of St Petersburg between Holland, Britain and Russia (Nov.)
1748	1748 Turkey makes treaty of neutrality with Russia Treaty of Aix-la-Chapelle ends War of the Austrian Succession (Oct.)

	WORLD AFFAIRS		CULTURE
1746	French fleet takes Madras Major rising in western Szechwan (China)	1746	*A Treatise concerning Religious Affections* by American clergyman Jonathan Edwards (1703–58) *A New Book of Ornaments* by English designer Henry Copland, introducing rococo ornament for English furniture
1747	Nadir Shah assassinated Ahmad Khan Abdali founds kingdom of Afghanistan and invades India	1747	David Garrick joins management at Drury Lane Jean Le Rond d'Alembert researches into vibrating strings Birth of French violin-bow maker François Tourte (*d* 1835) Building of St Andrew's Cathedral, Kiev, by Bartolomeo Rastrelli Death of Neapolitan baroque painter Francesco Solimena (*b* 1657)
1748	Peace between Persia and Turkey	1748	*L'Esprit des Lois* by Montesquieu *The Adventures of Roderick Random* by novelist Tobias George Smollett *Sémiramis* by Voltaire In *L'Homme Machine* La Mettrie abandons distinction between mind and matter and denies existence of soul Abbé Nollet recognizes the phenomenon of osmosis English landscape designer and gardener 'Capability' Brown executes first independent design at Warwick Castle

	INTERNAL EUROPEAN POLITICS		EUROPE-BASED INTERNATIONAL DEVELOPMENTS
1749		1749	Ferdinand VI of Spain severs himself from the Family Compact with France
1750	Death of John V of Portugal; succeeded by Joseph I Pombal becomes chief minister in Portugal until 1777	1750	Britain makes treaty with Spain
1751	Death of Stadtholder William IV Death of Frederick, prince of Wales (Mar.) Death of Frederick, king of Sweden (Apr.); Adolf Fredrik of Holstein-Gottorp succeeds to Swedish throne	1751	Treaty between Spain and Portugal to settle dispute about their South American possessions Diplomatic relations between Prussia and Russia cease

	WORLD AFFAIRS		CULTURE
1749		1749	*Arcana Coelestica* by Swedish philosopher and scientist Emanuel Swedenborg
			The History of Tom Jones by Henry Fielding
			Count Buffon begins to publish *Histoire naturelle*
			Traité des systèmes by Condillac
			Formation of the Virginia Company of Comedians by Thomas Keen and Walter Murray
			Birth of Italian composer Domenico Cimarosa (*d* 1801)
			Rebuilding of Strawberry Hill, Twickenham, by Horace Walpole and his 'Committee of Taste' begins
1750	Charlotte, North Carolina, founded by the British	1750	Death of J. S. Bach
			Death of Tomaso Albinoni
			Replanning of Nancy by Emmanuel Héré (1705–63)
			Italian fresco artist Giovanni Battista Tiepolo commissioned to decorate palace of Würzburg
			Musschenbroek constructs the pyrometer
1751	The Chinese overrun Tibet	1751	First volume of *Encyclopédie* edited by Denis Diderot appears
			Elegy Written in a Country Churchyard by Thomas Gray
			Death of Japanese artist Gion Nanki (*b* 1677)
			Chaumette invents breech-loading gun

INTERNAL EUROPEAN POLITICS	EUROPE-BASED INTERNATIONAL DEVELOPMENTS
1752	1752 Treaty of Aranjuez between Austria and Spain settles Italian disputes
1753 Kaunitz becomes chancellor of Austria, holds post until 1793	1753
1754 Birth of Louis XVI	1754 Quarrels between Britain and France over Ohio River basin in North America

WORLD AFFAIRS	CULTURE
1752	**1752** Posthumous publication of the works of Chinese poet Chao Chih-hsin (1662–1744) Birth of English composer and amateur musician John Marsh (*d* 1828) Birth of Italian pianist and composer Muzio Clementi (*d* 1832) Benjamin Franklin demonstrates lightning to be electricity
1753	**1753** Battersea enamel factory develops printed decoration for porcelain *Essai sur l'architecture* by Marc-Antoine Laugier (1713–69) *Lettre sur la Musique français* by Jean Jacques Rousseau Swedish Academy of Letters founded First book published in Transylvania
1754 Virginian militia under Washington defeated by the French	**1754** Danish Royal Academy of Art founded by Frederik V Death of Dutch ceiling-painter Jacob de Wit (*b* 1695) Building of Winter Palace, St Petersburg, by Rastrelli begins *The Gentleman and Cabinet-Maker's Director* by Thomas Chippendale

INTERNAL EUROPEAN POLITICS	EUROPE-BASED INTERNATIONAL DEVELOPMENTS
1755 Earthquake at Lisbon (Nov.)	1755 Treaty of St Petersburg between Britain and Russia (Sept.) End of alliance between Austria and Britain (Aug.)
1756	1756 Convention of Westminster between Britain and Prussia (Jan.) Britain declares war on France (May) Treaty of Versailles between France and Austria (May) Frederick the Great attacks Saxony (Aug.) and begins the Seven Years War
1757 Formation of the Pitt–Newcastle ministry in Britain until 1761	1757 The Empire declares war against Frederick (Jan.) Treaty of alliance between Russia and Austria (Feb.) Second Treaty of Versailles between France and Austria (May) Frederick crushes the French at Battle of Rossbach

1755	Defeat of General Braddock in America by the French (July) Rangoon founded by Burmese leader Alaungpaya	1755	*Dictionary of the English Language* by Samuel Johnson *Cephalus and Prokris* by Francesco Araia, the first opera to be written in Russian *Thoughts on the Imitation of Greek Works* by Johann Winckelmann Term 'rococo' first used by Charles-Nicolas Cochin
1756	Many Englishmen die in the Black Hole of Calcutta Calcutta falls to the nawab of Bengal	1756	Birth of Wolfgang Amadeus Mozart Death of English painter John Wootton
1757	Clive defeats nawab of Bengal at Plassey (June)	1757	*Lettere Virgiliane* by Italian critic, historian and poet Saverio Bettinelli First scholarly Russian grammar published Building of the Panthéon, Paris, by Jacques Soufflot First public concert in Philadelphia Death of Giuseppe Domenico Scarlatti Founding of the first German acting academy by Konrad Ekhov

INTERNAL EUROPEAN POLITICS	EUROPE-BASED INTERNATIONAL DEVELOPMENTS
1758 Clement XIII succeeds Benedict XIV Duke of Choiseul becomes chief minister in France, holds post until 1770	**1758**
1759 Accession of Charles III to throne of Spain (Aug.) Jesuits expelled from Portugal (Sept.) Tanucci becomes chief minister in Naples until 1776	**1759** Battle of Minden; Ferdinand of Brunswick at head of Anglo-German army defeats the French (Aug.) Prussians defeated at Battle of Kunersdorf (Aug.)
1760 Death of George II; accession of George III (Oct.)	**1760** Prussians defeated at Battle of Landshut (June). Austrians defeated at Battle of Torgau (Nov).
1761 Confiscation of Jesuit property in Portugal (Sept.)	**1761** France and Spain make the Family Compact, guaranteeing the possessions of all Bourbon powers (Aug.)

1758	Abercrombie succeeds Loudoun as commander-in-chief in North America Revolt against Dutch influence in Ceylon	1758	*Fray Gerundio* by Spanish satirist José de Isla Threshing-machine invented
1759	Capture of Quebec by Britain (Sept.) British naval victories at Quiberon Bay and Lagos	1759	*Candide* by Voltaire Death of Handel First canal in England
1760	Amherst captures Montreal (Sept.); end of New France	1760	Ossian cult begins with *Fragments of Ancient Poetry* by James Macpherson *The Life and Opinions of Tristram Shandy* by Laurence Sterne First volume of a collection of cathedral music published by William Boyce
1761	Afghans defeat the Mahrattas in the Battle of Panipat (Jan.) Coote captures Pondicherry; collapse of French power in India	1761	*Contes moraux* by Jean François Marmontel *Fingal* by James Macpherson Society for purification of Hungarian language organized Noblemen and Gentlemen's Catch Club formed in London Metalware factory established by Matthew Boulton Opening of porcelain factory in Berlin by Johann Ernst Gotzkowsky

INTERNAL EUROPEAN POLITICS	EUROPE-BASED INTERNATIONAL DEVELOPMENTS
1762 Abolition of compulsory state service for the nobility in Russia Death of Tsarina Elizabeth (Jan.) and accession of Peter III Deposition of Peter and accession of Catherine II (July)	1762 Britain declares war against Spain (Jan.) Peace between Prussia and Russia, and Prussia and Sweden (May) Spain invades Portugal; the Portuguese, aided by the British, check the Spaniards
1763 Death of Augustus III of Poland	1763 Treaty of Paris between Spain, France and Britain (Feb.) Treaty of Hubertusburg between Prussia and Austria (Feb.) Peace is made between Spain and Portugal (Feb.)
1764 Death of Madame de Pompadour Stanislas Poniatowski elected king of Poland (Oct.) Expulsion of the Jesuits from France	1764 Defensive alliance between Prussia and Russia (Apr.)

WORLD AFFAIRS		CULTURE	
1762	The British capture Spanish-ruled Havana and Manila	1762	*Du contrat social, ou principes du droit politique* by Jean Jacques Rousseau *Gedanken* by Anton Mengs calls for uplifting art Paisij Xilendarski's Slavo-Bulgarian history marks beginning of the Bulgarian nationalist revival *Orfeo ed Euridice* by Gluck Royal Artillery Band formed
1763	Treaty of Paris, by which the British acquire Canada	1763	*La Frusta Letteraria*, a periodical, produced by Italian critic and prose writer Giuseppe Buretti (1719–89) The first part of *Il Giorno* by Giuseppe Parini (1729–99) Mozart, aged 7, plays before the court at Versailles American painter Benjamin West (1738–1820) settles in London
1764		1764	*Dictionnaire philosophique* by Voltaire *The Castle of Otranto* by Horace Walpole *The Shepherd's Artifice* by English composer Charles Dibdin (1745–1814) performed James Hargreaves produces final version of spinning-jenny

INTERNAL EUROPEAN POLITICS		EUROPE-BASED INTERNATIONAL DEVELOPMENTS	
1765	Death of Emperor Francis (Aug.); Joseph II becomes emperor Death of Don Philip of Parma Archduke Leopold begins his government of Tuscany	1765	
1766	Christian VII succeeds Fredrik V on the Danish throne William V of Holland begins to rule *Codex Theresianus* in Austria, a new legal code for all German Habsburg territories	1766	
1767	Jesuits expelled from Spain, Parma and the Two Sicilies Legislative Commission meets in Russia	1767	Treaty of alliance between Prussia and Russia is renewed (Apr.)
1768		1768	Turkey declares war on Russia (Oct.) French buy Corsica from Genoa

WORLD AFFAIRS		CULTURE	
1765	Under Treaty of Allahabad, the British East India Company gains financial administrative control of Bengal and Bihar	1765	The Teatr Narodowy, the first Polish public theatre, opens in Warsaw Josiah Wedgwood produces Queen's-ware pottery François Boucher is made king's painter James Watt invents the separate condenser for the steam engine
1766	English force occupies the Falkland Islands Dutch cedes seaboard of Ceylon	1766	*The Vicar of Wakefield* by Oliver Goldsmith Building of Hôtel Alexandre, Paris, by Étienne-Louis Boullée *The Anatomy of the Horse* by George Stubbs Henry Cavendish discovers hydrogen to be an element and analyses air
1767	Burmese invasion of Siam (Thailand)	1767	*Phädon* by Moses Mendelssohn Building of the John Street Theatre, New York, by Lewis Hallam The first National Theatre was opened in Hamburg by Konrad Ackermann (1710–71) First production in Vienna of *Alceste* by Gluck First performance of Mozart's first dramatic work, *Die Schuldigkeit des Ersten Gebotes*
1768	James Cook charts coasts of New Zealand and explores east coast of Australia (1768–71); confirms existence of Torres Strait	1768	The Birmingham Music Festivals established Debut by French violoncellist Jean Louis Duport

| 1769 | | 1769 | Russians defeat the Turks and occupy Moldavia (Sept.) and Bucharest (Nov.) Renewal of alliance between Russia and Prussia (Oct.) Treaty between Russia and Denmark to prevent the overthrow of the Swedish constitution of 1720 (Dec.) |
| 1770 | Struensee begins to govern Denmark Lord North becomes chief minister in Britain until 1782 | 1770 | |

WORLD AFFAIRS	CULTURE
	The building of the Adelphi, London, by Robert and James Adam
	The building of the Marble Palace, St Petersburg, by Antonio Rinaldi (*c.*1709–94)
	Discovery of kaolin in Cornwall by William Cookworthy
	Sir Joshua Reynolds elected president of the Royal Academy
	The Building of the Royal Crescent, Bath, by John Wood the younger, begins
1769 **1769**	*Hermannsschlacht*, glorification of ancient Germans, by Friedrich Klopstock
	Les Saisons by Jean-François de Saint-Lambert (1716–1803)
	Critical Forests by Johann Gottfried von Herder praises folk-songs
	Richard Arkwright invents the water-powered spinning-frame
1770 Spanish force seizes the **1770**	*The Monitor*, a literary periodical, published in Poland
Falkland Islands	In *Système de la Nature* baron d'Holbach argues that man is simply a machine forced to act in certain ways and without either free will or a soul
'Boston Massacre'	First performance of Handel's *Messiah* in New York
	Birth of Ludwig van Beethoven

INTERNAL EUROPEAN POLITICS	EUROPE-BASED INTERNATIONAL DEVELOPMENTS
1771 The 'Maupeou Revolution': reorganization of the French *parlements* Accession of Gustav III to Swedish throne (Aug.)	1771 Austria makes treaty with Turkey to force Russia to restore her conquests (July)
1772 Struensee executed (Apr.) Revolution in Sweden carried out by Gustav III (Aug.)	1772 First Partition of Poland Treaty of Kuchuk-Kainardji (July) ends war between Russia and Turkey with Russian gains Denmark and Russia make secret alliance (Aug.)
1773 Death of Charles Emanuel III of Sardinia; succeeded by Victor Amadeus III Clement XIV abolishes order of the Jesuits Revolt of the Cossacks of the Don under Pugachev	1773

1771 Burma becomes a tributary of China	**1771** Collection of poems by Danish poet Johannes Ewald (1743–81) *Oden* by Klopstock replaces classical with Germanic myths *The West Indian* by Richard Cumberland (1732–1811) Censorship abolished in Denmark Foundation of Royal Theatre Ballet Company in Copenhagen Founding of the oldest Vienna music society, Tonkünstler-Societät, by Florian Gassmann (1729–74) Giambattista Bodoni begins to cut typefaces; his style dominates printing for fifty years
1772 James Cook makes a circuit of the Southern oceans and charts the New Hebrides (1772–5)	**1772** *A Poem on the Rising Glory of America* by American poet Philip Morin Freneau (1752–1832) *Emilia Galotti* by Lessing produced by Friedrich Ludwig Schroder (1744–1816) *O Tempora*, a comedy by Catherine the Great First Chester Music Festival Daniel Rutherford discovers nitrogen
1773 Boston Tea Riots (Dec.)	**1773** *She Stoops to Conquer* by Oliver Goldsmith *Götz von Berlichingen* by Johann Wolfgang Goethe Foundation of an opera and ballet company in Stockholm

	INTERNAL EUROPEAN POLITICS		EUROPE-BASED INTERNATIONAL DEVELOPMENTS
1774	Accession of Sultan Abdülhamid (Jan.) who fails against the Russians Death of Louis XV (May); accession of Louis XVI; fall of Maupeou Louis XVI recalls the *parlements*	1774	
1775	Pius VI becomes pope Reform of provincial administration in Russia	1775	Treaty between Austria and Turkey (May)
1776	Abolition of the *corvée* in France	1776	

WORLD AFFAIRS		CULTURE
1774	Quebec Act Warren Hastings made first governor-general of Bengal	1774	*Werther* by Goethe *Caras Marruecas* by José de Cadalso y Vazquez (1741–82) First performance of the opera *La Finta Giardiniera* by Pasquale Anfossi (1727–97) in Rome Josiah Wedgwood produces jasper-ware Joseph Priestley isolates oxygen Karl Scheele discovers chlorine
1775	American War of Independence begins Unsuccessful Spanish attack on Algiers	1775	*Leonore* by German poet Gottfried August Burger (1747–94) *Le Barbier de Seville* by Beaumarchais Place Royale, Brussels, designed by Nicholas Barré (*fl* 1730–88) and Gilles Barnabé Guimard (*d* 1792) *The Hundred Poets and their Poems in Brocade*, polychrome colour prints by Katsukawa Shunsho (1726–92) James Watt perfects the steam engine
1776	The Americans are driven from Canada (Mar.) American Declaration of Independence proclaimed (July)	1776	*De Poesi Fennica* (1776–8) by Finnish- Swedish scholar Henrik Gabriel Porthan (1739– 1804) Joseph II actively backs German-level drama, establishing a German national theatre in Vienna The British open a theatre of their own in Calcutta

1777	Death of Joseph I of Portugal; accession of Maria I and her husband, Peter III (Feb.) Death of Maximilian Joseph, elector of Bavaria (Dec.); dominions fall to Charles Theodore	1777	Treaty of Ildefonso between Spain and Portugal settles dispute concerning south America
1778		1778	France signs treaty of alliance and commerce with the Americans (Feb.); begins maritime struggle with Britain (Mar.) Charles Theodore makes a convention with Joseph II, giving him most of Bavaria (Jan.) Frederick the Great declares war on Austria, beginning War of the Bavarian Succession (July)

WORLD AFFAIRS		CULTURE
		Rebuilding of Somerset House, London, by Sir William Chambers (1723–96) begins
		Founding of porcelain factory at Verbilki, Moscow (1776–80)
		First use of a submarine, David Bushnell's *Turtle*
1777	Howe defeats Washington and occupies Philadelphia	1777	*Della Tirannide* by Italian playwright and poet Vittorio Alfieri (1749–1803)
		A collection of love poems by Swedish critic and poet Johann Henric Kellgren (1751–95)
		The School for Scandal by Richard Brinsley Sheridan
		David Bushnell invents the torpedo
		Foundation of the Felix Meritis Society in Amsterdam
1778	Discovery of Nootka Sound by Cook (Jan.) St Lucia taken by the British admiral Barrington	1778	*Evelina* by Fanny Burney
		Death of Linnaeus
		The Fishers by Denmark's first tragic writer Johannes Ewald (1743–81)
		Joseph Wright (1734–97) has his first exhibition at the Royal Academy
		Friedrich Mesmer first practises 'mesmerism' in Paris
		Cagliostro establishes 'Egyptian Freemasonry'

INTERNAL EUROPEAN POLITICS	EUROPE-BASED INTERNATIONAL DEVELOPMENTS
1779	1779 Spain joins American colonists and declares war on Britain (Apr.) Treaty of Teschen ends War of the Bavarian Succession (May) Siege of Gibraltar begins
1780 Gordon 'no-popery' riots break out in England (May) Death of Maria Theresa (Nov.)	1780 Catherine II heads the armed neutrality against Britain Rodney defeats Spanish fleet and relieves Gibraltar (Jan.) Britain declares war against United Provinces (Nov.)
1781 Joseph II issues the Toleration Edict, granting religious liberty to non-Catholic Christians (Oct.)	1781 The French land in Jersey but are overthrown by Pierson and the militia (Jan.) An alliance is made between Austria and Russia (June)

WORLD AFFAIRS		CULTURE	
1779	D'Estaing takes St Vincent and Grenada First Kaffir War (between the Xhosa and the Boers) in South Africa (1779–81) James Cook killed on Hawaii	1779	*Satires* by Polish writer Ignacy, Count Krasicki (1735–1801) Samuel Crompton perfects the spinning-mule
1780	British capture Charleston and defeat Americans at Camden	1780	*Messias* by Klopstock Invention of the bolero in Spain by the dancer Sebastian Cerezo First appearance of the waltz in Germany and Austria (*c.*1780) Rebuilding of Vich Cathedral, Spain, by José Morato Development of underglaze printing on ceramics (1780–90) Caughley pottery, Shropshire, makes first willow-pattern plate (*c.*1780) William Withering discovers the use of digitalis in medicine
1781	Eyre Coote defeats Hyder Ali of Mysore at Porto Novo Cornwallis surrenders at Yorktown (Oct.)	1781	First Polish encyclopedia published *Nightmare* Fuseli's vision of the mysterious Mozart arrives in Vienna where he remains based for the rest of his life Henry Cavendish is the first to determine the composition of water William Herschel discovers the planet Uranus, the first planet to be discovered since antiquity

	INTERNAL EUROPEAN POLITICS		EUROPE-BASED INTERNATIONAL DEVELOPMENTS
1782	Irish given legislative independence; fall of Lord North's government in Britain Pius VI visits Vienna	1782	Capture of Minorca by the French and the Spaniards (Feb.)
1783		1783	Catherine II annexes the Crimea (Apr.) Treaty of Versailles ends war of France and Spain with Britain (Sept.)
1784	Crown Prince Frederick becomes regent of Denmark British elections (May) give William Pitt the younger a large majority	1784	Treaty of Constantinople between Turkey and Russia, by which the Turks accept Russian gain of Crimea (Jan.)

|

WORLD AFFAIRS	CULTURE
1782 Rodney destroys French fleet in the West Indies (Apr.) Death of Hyder Ali (Dec.); succeeded by Tippoo Sahib	**1782** *Les Liaisons dangereuses* by Pierre Ambroise Choderlos de Laclos (1741–1803) *Saul* by Vittorio Amedeo Alfieri (1749–1803) Birth of Italian composer Niccolò Paganini (*d* 1840) Building of Le Hameau, Versailles, by Richard Mique (1728–94)
1783 Definitive treaty between Britain and America is signed (Sept.) Treaty of Versailles extends the frontiers of the United States to the Great Lakes in the north and the Mississippi in the west	**1783** *Felitsa* by Russian poet Gavriil Romanovich Derzhavin (1743–1816) First performance in Salzburg of Mozart's Mass in C minor The Glee Club formed in London Building of the Academy of Sciences, St Petersburg, by Giacomo Quarenghi (1744–1817) First demonstration of hot-air and hydrogen balloons Jouffroy d'Abbans demonstrates the first workable steamboat
1784 Second Anglo-Mysore war ends	**1784** *William Leevend* (1784–5) by Dutch novelists Elisabeth Wolff-Bekker (1738–1804) and Agatha Deken (1741–1804) *Was ist Aufklärung?* by Immanuel Kant *Le mariage de Figaro* by Beaumarchais

INTERNAL EUROPEAN POLITICS		EUROPE-BASED INTERNATIONAL DEVELOPMENTS	
1785	Charters to the nobility and the towns issued in Russia	1785	Commercial treaty between Catherine II and Joseph II Treaty of Fontainebleau is made between Joseph II and the Dutch (Nov.) Alliance between the French and the Dutch (Nov.)
1786	Death of Frederick the Great (Aug.); accession of Frederick-William II	1786	Commercial treaty between France and Britain (Sept.)
1787	Movement for the abolition of the slave trade in Britain Assembly of Notables meets in France; Calonne replaced by Brienne	1787	Catherine II and Joseph II journey to the Crimea (Jan.) Prussian army invades Holland (Sept.); stadtholder restored (Oct.) Turkey declares war on Russia (Sept.)

	WORLD AFFAIRS		CULTURE
1785	Burmese invade Arakan	1785	*The Task* by William Cowper (1731–1800) *Poesie Campestrie* by Italian poet and letter-writer Ippolito Pindemonte (1753–1828) *The Bhagvat-Geeta, or Dialogues of Kreeshna and Arjoon* by Charles Wilkins, the first major translation of a Hindu Sanskrit text into a European language The Caecilian Society is formed in London Spanish botanical expedition sent to Spanish America Matthew Boulton applies engine to cotton-spinning
1786	Cornwallis becomes governor-general of Bengal (Feb.) Insurrection of the mamluks in Egypt suppressed by the grand vizier The British establish base at Penang	1786	*Poems chiefly in the Scottish Dialect* by Robert Burns Foundation of the Swedish Academy by Gustav III Death of English landscape artist Alexander Cozens (*b* 1717)
1787	The Tuareg extinguish the Pashalik of Timbuctoo	1787	*Paul et Virginie* by Jacques-Henri Bernardin de Saint-Pierre (1737–1814) *Don Carlos* by Schiller *The Contrast* by Royall Taylor (1757–1826) *Méthode de Nomenclature chimique* by Antoine Lavoisier First ascent of Mont Blanc, by Horace Saussure

	INTERNAL EUROPEAN POLITICS		EUROPE-BASED INTERNATIONAL DEVELOPMENTS
1788	Death of Charles Edward Stuart (Jan.) Death of Charles III of Spain (Dec.) Assembly of Notables in France fails; Estates General summoned; Brienne replaced by Necker	1788	Joseph II declares war on Turkey (Feb.) Triple Alliance formed between Britain, Prussia and Holland (Apr.–July) Gustav III of Sweden declares war on Russia (June) The Danes invade Sweden on behalf of Russia, but are persuaded to desist
1789	The French Revolution Estates General meets; fall of the Bastille (July 14); Estates General becomes National Assembly; Declaration of the Rights of Man and the Citizen Charles VI becomes king of Spain (Jan.) Revolution in Sweden by Gustav III makes the monarchy absolute (Feb.) Selim III succeeds Abdülhamid as sultan (Apr.) Revolution in Austrian Netherlands, against Austrian rule, breaks out in the autumn	1789	Renewed alliance between Austria and Russia Austrian and Russian forces defeat the Turks in Battle of Foksany (July)
1790	Death of Joseph II; succeeded by Leopold II	1790	Treaty of Reichenbach between Austria and Prussia (July) Treaty of Verela ends war between Sweden and Russia (Aug.)

WORLD AFFAIRS	CULTURE
1788 First British settlement established at Port Jackson (Sydney) Abortive Chinese invasion of Tongking Chinese expedition into Nepal	1788 *Etelka* by Hungarian playwright, novelist and mathematician András Dugonics (1740–1818) Building of the Botanicum, Uppsala, Sweden, by Jean Louis Desprez (1743–1804)
1789 The Spanish seize British merchantmen at Nootka Sound	1789 *Songs of Innocence* by William Blake *Egmont* by Goethe Antoine Lavoisier produces first table of elements
1790 Third Anglo-Mysore war begins	1790 *Letters of a Russian Traveller* by Nikolai Mikhaylovich Karamzin (1766–1826) *Journey from Petersburg to Moscow* by Alexander Niko-layevich Radishchev (1749–1802) Washington planned by Pierre L'Enfant (1754–1825) on the scheme of a French hunting-park

INTERNAL EUROPEAN POLITICS		EUROPE-BASED INTERNATIONAL DEVELOPMENTS	
1791	Louis XVI's flight to Varennes Revolution in Poland in favour of a new monarchical constitution (May)	1791	Treaty of Sistova ends war between Austria and Turkey (Aug.) Treaty between Prussia and Austria guarantees a 'free Consti-tution of Poland' Ochakov Crisis: Britain and Prussia threaten Russia with war, but Catherine refuses to return her conquests from Turks
1792	Death of Leopold II (Mar.); succeeded by his son Francis II Murder of Gustav III (Mar.) Fall of the monarchy in France; republic declared	1792	Russia and Turkey make Treaty of Jassy, with Russian gains (Jan.) Treaty of Berlin between Prussia and Austria (Feb.) Russia invades Poland France declares war on Austria (Apr.) and Prussia (July)
1793	Execution of Louis XVI (Jan.) Committee of General Defence formed in France (Jan.) Overthrow of the Girondins; the Reign of Terror begins Committee of Public Safety formed (July)	1793	France declares war on Britain and Holland (Feb.) France declares war on Spain (Mar.) The Empire declares war on France (Mar.) Portugal and Tuscany declare war on France Second Partition of Poland; Prussia and Russia make gains (Sept.)

WORLD AFFAIRS		CULTURE	
1791	Bangalore stormed by British	1791	*Justine, ou les malheurs de la vertu* by marquis de Sade *Idyllios Maritimos* by Manuel Maria Barbosa de Bocage (1776–1805) *The Life of Samuel Johnson* by James Boswell *The Magic Flute* by Mozart Death of Mozart Luigi Galvani advances the theory of animal electricity Ordnance Survey established in Britain
1792	Seringapatam besieged successfully. Mysore sues for peace.	1792	*Labyrinthen* by the Danish poet Jens Immanuel Baggesen (1764–1826) Building of the Capitol, Washington, by William Thornton (1759–1828) begins Invention of cable-making machine
1793	Second Kaffir War in South Africa between the Xhosa and the Boers	1793	*Bassvilliana* by Italian prose-writer and poet Vincenzo Monti (1754–1828) Establishment of the Louvre as a public art gallery

INTERNAL EUROPEAN POLITICS		EUROPE-BASED INTERNATIONAL DEVELOPMENTS	
1794	Rising of the Poles under Kosciusko (Mar.) Overthrow of Robespierre on 9 Thermidor Prussian *Allgemeines Landrecht* published: legal codification	1794	French fleet defeated by Howe (June) Austria abandons the Netherlands (July) Russians defeat Kosciusko and the Poles (Oct.–Nov.) and enter Warsaw (Nov.) Duke of York defeated by the French
1795	Insurrection of 12 Germinal fails Insurrection of 15 Vendémiaire is put down by Bonaparte (Oct.) The Directory is established in power in France (Nov.)	1795	The Treaty of Basle signed between France and Spain Tuscany and Naples make peace with France (Feb.) Spain declares war on Britain Poland is partitioned between Austria, Prussia and Russia (Oct.)
1796	Bonaparte assumes the command in Italy (Apr.) Death of Catherine II of Russia (Nov.); succeeded by Paul I Irish rebellion breaks out; revolutionary committee arrested	1796	Pitt negotiates for peace with France through the Swiss minister (Mar.) Prussia makes treaty with France (Aug.) Treaty of San Ildefonso is made between Spain and France French expedition under Hoche to Bantry Bay (Ireland) fails (Dec.)

WORLD AFFAIRS		CULTURE	
1794	Britain takes Guadaloupe, Martinique, St Lucia and other Caribbean islands The French retake Guadaloupe	1794	*The Mysteries of Udolpho* by Mrs Ann Radcliffe (1764–1823) *The Miracle* by Polish playwright Wojciech Boguslawski (1757–1829) Performance of the first opera by Simone Johann Simon Mayr (1763–1845) Invention of cotton gin by Eli Whitney
1795	Spain makes treaty with the United States defining contraband of war White Lotus rebellion breaks out in China The British take the Cape of Good Hope from the Dutch British expedition to Quiberon Bay fails The French retake St Lucia Mungo Park explores West Africa and the River Niger	1795	In *Philosophy in the Boudoir*, marquis de Sade argues that murder is natural First theatre for Bengali plays opens in Calcutta Conservatoire de Musique established in Paris *Theory of the Earth* by James Hutton outlines the new science of geology
1796	The British take St Lucia, St Vincent, Grenada and Ceylon Aga Mahomed Khan Qajar establishes a new regime in Shiraz and brings a measure of stability to Persia	1796	*The Monk* by Matthew Gregory Lewis (1775–1818) Building of Fonthill Abbey by James Wyatt (1746–1813) begins Joseph Mallord William Turner (1775–1851) exhibits his first work in oils, *Fishermen at Sea* Edward Jenner introduces smallpox vaccination

	INTERNAL EUROPEAN POLITICS		EUROPE-BASED INTERNATIONAL DEVELOPMENTS
1797	General Lake puts down rebellion in Ulster Revolution of 18 Fructidor in France Frederick-William III succeeds to the throne of Prussia (Nov.)	1797	Defeat of Austrians by Hoche; Austria signs the Treaty of Campo Formio (Oct.) Battle of Camperdown; defeat of Dutch by Duncan Venice occupied by France (May)
1798	Rebellion breaks out in Ireland Helvetic Republic proclaimed Roman Republic proclaimed (Feb.) Lake defeats Irish rebels at Vinegar Hill (June) Bonaparte lands in Egypt	1798	Napoleon lands in Egypt (July) Nelson wins Battle of the Nile (Aug.) Turkey declares war on France (Sept.) Ferdinand IV of Naples declares war against the French and makes treaties with Russia (Nov.) and Britain (Dec.)
1799	French take Naples (Jan.) Bonaparte leaves Egypt (July) Death of Pius VI (Aug.) Revolution of 18 Brumaire in France (Nov.), overthrowing the Directory, making Bonaparte practically ruler of France Government of the Consulate established in France (Dec.)	1799	The Turks and the Russians take the Ionian Islands (Mar.) Austria declares war (Mar.) War between France and Austria begins (Apr.) Pitt forms the Second Coalition against France of Britain, Russia, Austria, Turkey, Portugal and Naples (June)

	WORLD AFFAIRS		CULTURE
1797	Abercromby takes Trinidad (Feb.) Nelson and Jervis win Battle of St Vincent (Feb.) London Missionary Society sends missionaries to Tahiti	1797	Birth of Franz Peter Schubert (*d* 1828) Thomas Bewick (1755– 1828) publishes *A History of British Birds* (1797–1804)
1798	Lord Mornington becomes governor-general of India (May) French expedition to Egypt (May) Bonaparte wins Battle of the Pyramids (July) and conquers Egypt Nelson destroys French fleet at Battle of Aboukir Bay (Aug.)	1798	*Lyrical Ballads*, a collection of poems by William Wordsworth and Samuel Taylor Coleridge Building of the Bank of Pennsylvania, Philadelphia, by Benjamin Latrobe, the first marble Greek Revival building in the USA Death of Scottish painter and antiquarian Gavin Hamilton (*b* 1723) Herschel discovers infra-red band of the spectrum
1799	Capture of Seringapatam; death of Tippoo; conquest of Mysore (May) British influence over Tanjore is established (Oct.)	1799	First public performance in Vienna of *Haydn's Creation* *Los Caprichos*, a series of prints by Francisco Goya Alessandro Volta invents the battery of cells and the dry pile
1800			
1801			
1802			
1803	Louisiana purchase nearly doubles the size of the United States of America		
1804	The Fulanis conquer the Hausa		

Dynastic charts

Austria

Leopold I	1659–1705
Joseph I	1705–11
Charles VI	1711–40
Maria Theresa	1740–80
Joseph II	1780–90
Leopold II	1790–2
Francis II	1792–1835

China (Ch'ing (Qing) dynasty emperors)

Reign title	Personal name	Year of accession
T'ung-chih (Tongzhi)	Fu-lin (Fulin)	1644
K'ang-hsi (Kangxi)	Hsüan-yeh (Xuanye)	1662
Yung-cheng (Yongzheng)	Yin-chen (Yinzhen)	1723
Ch'ien-lung (Qianlong)	Hung-li (Hongli)	1736
Chia-ch'ing (Jiaqing)	Yung-yen (Yongyan)	1798
Tao-kuang (Daoguang)	Min-ning (Minning)	1821
Hsien-feng (Xianfeng)	I-chu (Yizhu)	1851

Note: Emperors are usually referred to by their reign title, for example the T'ung-chih Emperor. First spelling is in the Wade-Giles system; spelling in parentheses is the modern Hanyu Pinyin romanization.

Dutch Republic (stadtholders)

William III	1672–1702
Stadtholderless Republic	1702–47

William IV	1747–51
William V	1751–95
Batavian Republic	1795–1806
King Louis Bonaparte	1806–10
Annexed by France	1810–14
King William I	1818–40

France

Louis XIV	1643–1715
Louis XV	1715–74
(Regency 1715–23)	
Louis XVI	1774–92
(Executed 1793)	
Convention	1792–5
Directory	1795–9
Napoleon	1800–14
Louis XVIII	1814–24
Charles X	1824–30

Great Britain

Charles II	1660–85
James II	1685–8
William III	1689–1702
(and Mary II	1689–94)
Anne	1702–14
George I	1714–27
George II	1727–60
George III	1760–1820
George IV	1820–30

India (Mughal emperors)

Auragzeb	1658–1707
Azam Shah	1707
Kam Bakhsh (in the Deccan)	1707
Shah Alam I	1707–12
Azim ush Shan	1712
Muizz ud Din Jahandar	1712–13
Farrukhsiyar	1713–19
Shams ud Din Rafi ud Darajat	1719
Rafi ud Daula Shah Kahan II	1719
Nikusiyar	1719
Nasir ud Din Muhammad	1719–48
Ahmad Shah Bahadur	1748–54

Aziz ud Din Alamgir	1754–60
Shah Jahan III	1760
Jalal ud din Ali Jauhar Shah Alam II	
(first reign)	1760–88
Bidar Bakht	1788
Shah Alam II (second reign)	1788–1806
Muin ud Din Akbar II	1806–37
Siraj ud Din Bahadur Shah II	1837–58

Poland

John III Sobieski	1674–96
Augustus II of Saxony	1697–1704
Stanislas Leszcyński	1704–9
Augustus II	1709–33
Augustus III	1733–63
Stanislas Poniatowski	1764–95
Partitions of Poland	1772, 1793, 1795
Grand Duchy of Warsaw	1807–15

Popes

Innocent XI	1676–89
Alexander VIII	1689–91
Innocent XII	1691–1700
Clement XI	1700–21
Innocent XIII	1721–4
Benedict XIII	1724–30
Clement XII	1730–40
Benedict XIV	1740–58
Clement XIII	1758–69
Clement XIV	1769–74
Pius VI	1775–99
Pius VII	1800–23

Prussia

Frederick-William	
(the Great Elector)	1640–88
Frederick I	1688–1713
Frederick-William I	1713–40
Frederick II (the Great)	1740–86
Frederick-William II	1786–97
Frederick-William III	1797–1840

Russia

Alexis	1645–76
Fedor III	1676–82
Ivan V	1682–96
Peter I (the Great) (co-ruler 1682–96)	1682–1725
Catherine I	1725–7
Peter II	1727–30
Anna	1730–40
Elizabeth	1741–62
Peter III	1762
Catherine II (the Great)	1762–96
Paul	1796–1801
Alexander I	1801–25
Nicholas I	1825–55

Spain

Charles II	1665–1700
Philip V	1700–46
Ferdinand VI	1746–59
Charles III	1759–88
Charles IV	1788–1808
Joseph Bonaparte	1808–12
Ferdinand VII	1812–33

Sweden

Charles XI	1660–97
Charles XII	1697–1718
Ulrika Eleonora	1718–20
Fredrik I	1720–51
Adolf-Fredrik	1751–71
Gustav III	1771–92
Gustav IV	1792–1809
Charles XIII	1809–10
Charles XIV (Bernadotte)	1810–44

Turkish Empire (sultans)

Mehmed IV	1648–87
Süleyman II	1687–91
Ahmed II	1691–5
Mustafa II	1695–1703
Ahmed III	1703–30

Mahmud I   1730–54
Osman III   1754–7
Mustafa III   1757–74
Abdülhamid I   1774–89
Selim III   1789–1807
Mustafa IV   1807–8
Mahmud II   1808–39

United States

George Washington   1789–97
John Adams   1797–1801
Thomas Jefferson   1801–9
James Madison   1809–17
James Monroe   1817–25
John Quincy Adams   1825–9
Andrew Jackson   1829–37

Note: Date of transfer – 4 March in each case; popular election – year before taking office.

Maps

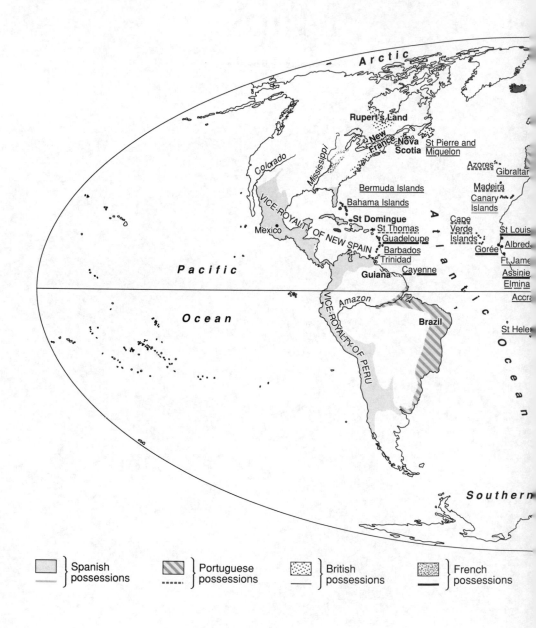

Arctic

Rupert's Land

New
France
Nova
Scotia

St Pierre and
Miquelon

Colorado

Mississippi

Azores
Gibraltar

Madeira

VICE-ROYALTY OF NEW SPAIN

Bermuda Islands

Bahama Islands

Canary
Islands

Cape
Verde
Islands

St Louis

Mexico

St Domingue

St Thomas

Guadeloupe

Gorée

Albred.

Pacific

Barbados

Trinidad

Cayenne

Ft Jame

Assinie

Elmina

Guiana

Accra

Ocean

Amazon

Atlantic Ocean

VICE-ROYALTY OF PERU

Brazil

St Hele

Southern

Spanish
possessions

Portuguese
possessions

British
possessions

French
possessions

Map 1: The World, 1714

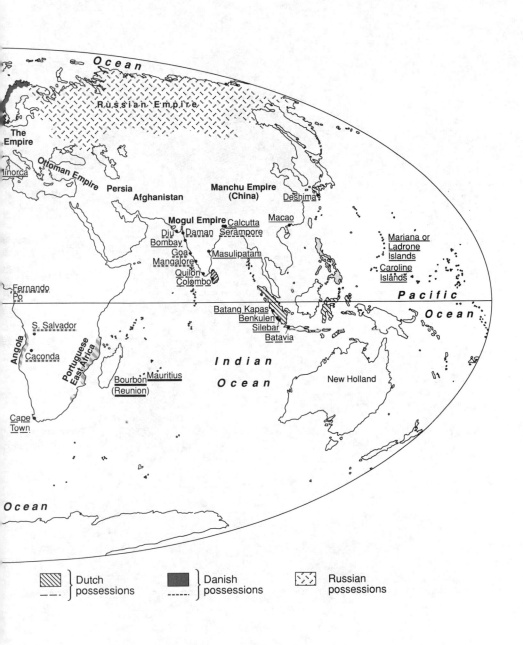

Ocean

Russian Empire

The
Empire

Ottoman Empire

Minorca

Persia

Afghanistan

Manchu Empire
(China)

Deshima

Mogul Empire

Macao

Diu Daman

Calcutta
Serampore

Mariana or
Ladrone
Islands

Bombay

Caroline
Islands

Goa
Mangalore

Masulipatam

Pacific

Quilon
Colombo

Fernando
Po

Ocean

S. Salvador

Batang Kapas
Benkulen
Silebar
Batavia

Angola

Caconda

Indian

Portuguese
East Africa

Ocean

New Holland

Bourbon
(Reunion)

Mauritius

Cape
Town

Ocean

	Dutch possessions			Danish possessions			Russian possessions

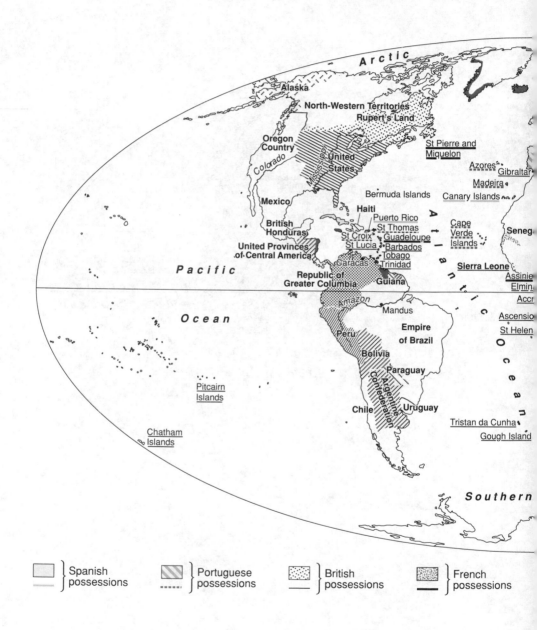

Map 2: The World, 1830

Spanish possessions

Portuguese possessions

British possessions

French possessions

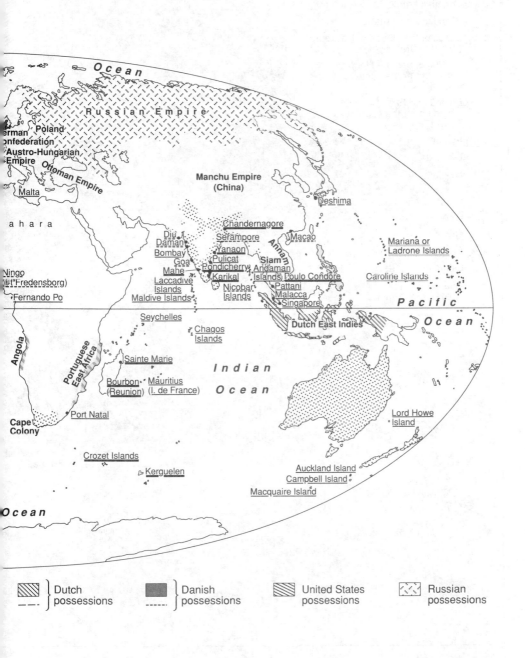

Ocean

Russian Empire

German
Confederation
Austro-Hungarian
Empire

Poland

Ottoman Empire

Malta

ahara

Manchu Empire
(China)

Deshima

Ningo
(Ft Fredensborg)

Fernando Po

Diu
Daman
Bombay
Goa
Mahe
Laccadive
Islands
Maldive Islands

Chandernagore

Serampore

Yanaon
Pulicat
Pondicherry
Karikal

Macao

Siam
Andaman
Islands Poulo Condore
Nicobar   Pattani
Islands   Malacca
Singapore

Annam

Mariana or
Ladrone Islands

Caroline Islands

Pacific

Dutch East Indies

Ocean

Seychelles

Chagos
Islands

Angola

Portuguese
East Africa

Sainte Marie

Bourbon   Mauritius
(Reunion) (I. de France)

Indian

Ocean

Lord Howe
Island

Cape
Colony

Port Natal

Crozet Islands

Kerguelen

Auckland Island
Campbell Island

Macquaire Island

Ocean

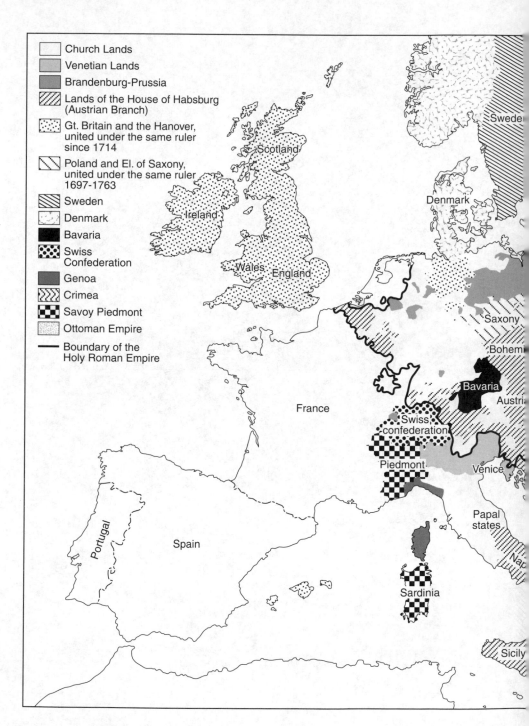

Map 3: Ancien régime Europe

Legend:

- Church Lands
- Venetian Lands
- Brandenburg-Prussia
- Lands of the House of Habsburg (Austrian Branch)
- Gt. Britain and the Hanover, united under the same ruler since 1714
- Poland and El. of Saxony, united under the same ruler 1697-1763
- Sweden
- Denmark
- Bavaria
- Swiss Confederation
- Genoa
- Crimea
- Savoy Piedmont
- Ottoman Empire
- Boundary of the Holy Roman Empire

Map labels: Swede[n], Denmark, Scotland, Ireland, Wales, England, Saxony, Bohem[ia], Bavaria, Austri[a], France, Swiss confederation, Piedmont, Venice, Portugal, Spain, Papal states, Nap[les], Sardinia, Sicily

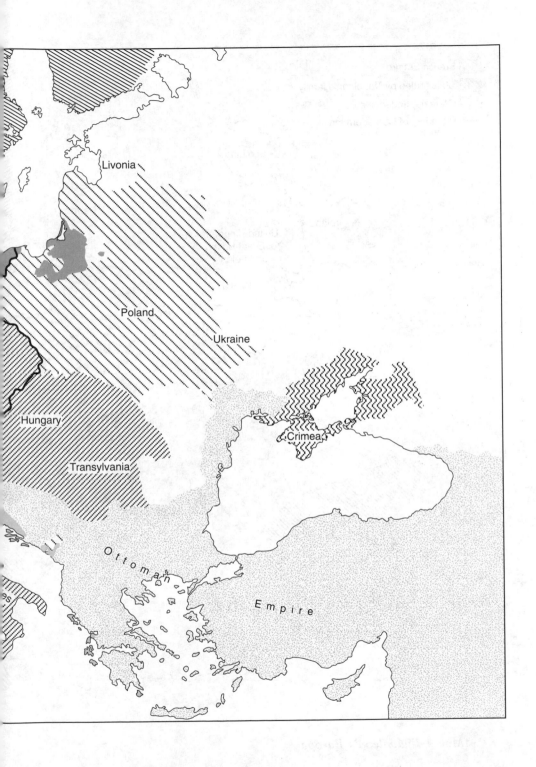

Livonia

Poland

Ukraine

Hungary

Crimea

Transylvania

O t t o m a n

E m p i r e

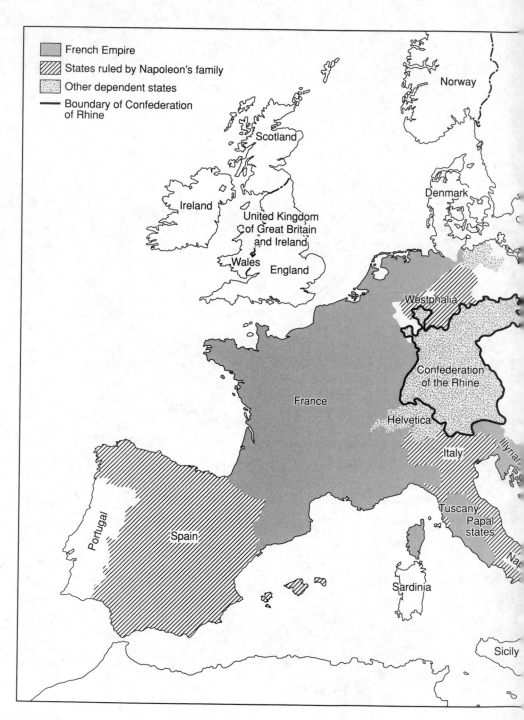

Map 4: Napoleon's Europe

Prussia

Gr. Duchy
of Warsaw

A u s t r i a
Hungary
Transylvania

Provinces

Ottoman

Empire

Map 5: *Europe after the Congress of Vienna*